HEALTH CARE STATE RANKINGS
2006

Health Care in the 50 United States

Kathleen O'Leary Morgan and Scott Morgan, Editors

Morgan Quitno Press
© Copyright 2006, All Rights Reserved

512 East 9th Street, P.O. Box 1656
Lawrence, KS 66044-8656
USA
800-457-0742 or 785-841-3534
www.statestats.com
Fourteenth Edition

ISBN: 0-7401-0745-3
ISSN: 1065-1403

Health Care State Rankings 2006 sells for $59.95 ($6 shipping) and is only available in paper binding. For those who prefer ranking information tailored to a particular state, we also offer *Health Care State Perspectives*, state-specific reports for each of the 50 states. These individual guides provide information on a state's data and rank for each of the categories featured in the national *Health Care State Rankings* volume. Perspectives sell for $19 or $9.50 if ordered with *Health Care State Rankings*. If crime statistics are your interest, please ask about our annual *Crime State Rankings* ($59.95 paper). If you are interested in city and metropolitan crime data, we offer *City Crime Rankings* ($49.95 paper). For a general view of the states, please ask about our annual *State Rankings* reference book ($59.95 paper) or our new annual *State Trends* ($59.95 paper). Also available is *Education State Rankings*. This view of preK-12 education at the state level is $49.95. All of our books are available on CD-ROM in PDF format (same price as printed book) or with both PDF format and data sets in various database formats ($99.95). Shipping and handling is $6 per order. For information, please visit our website at www.statestats.com.

Fourteenth Edition
Printed in the United States of America
March 2006

PREFACE

As the American system of health care continues to grow increasingly complicated and expensive, access to reliable, easy-to-understand health care information is more important than ever. This newly revised, 14th edition of *Health Care State Rankings* provides an extensive collection of state health care data. Births and reproductive health, deaths, disease, insurance and finance, health care providers, facilities and physical fitness are compared state-by-state. Find out how much workers in your state are paying in health insurance premiums, learn how your state's teen birth rate compares to others and discover what percentage of your state's citizens are obese. In all, more than 500 tables of state comparisons are provided, covering virtually every aspect of health care in the 50 United States.

Important Notes About *Health Care State Rankings 2006*

Health Care State Rankings 2006 presents information from government and private sector sources in one user-friendly volume. Our goal is to translate complicated and often convoluted health care data into easy-to-understand, meaningful state comparisons. As we revise this volume each year, we reexamine each table, update most, delete others and add new tables of interest to our readers.

We make every effort to present the data in *Health Care State Rankings 2006* as simply and straightforwardly as possible. Source information and other pertinent footnotes are clearly shown at the bottom of each page. National totals, rates and percentages are prominently displayed at the top of each table. Every other line is shaded in gray for easier reading. In addition, numerous information-finding tools are provided: a thorough table of contents, table listings at the beginning of each chapter, a roster of sources with addresses and phone numbers, a detailed index and a chapter thumb index.

For the ease of our readers, the numbers shown in *Health Care State Rankings* require no additional calculations to convert them from millions, thousands, etc. All states are ranked on a high to low basis, with any ties among the states listed alphabetically for a given ranking. Negative numbers are shown in parentheses "( )." For tables with national totals (as opposed to rates, per capitas, etc.) a separate column is included showing what percent of the national total each individual state's total represents. This column is headed by "% of USA." This percentage figure is particularly interesting when compared with a state's share of the nation's population for a particular year (provided in an appendix).

For those researchers needing information for just one state, our *Health Care State Perspective* series of publications fills the bill. These 21-page comb bound reports feature data and ranking information for an individual state, as reported in *Health Care State Rankings 2006.* (For example *California Health Care in Perspective* features information about the state of California only.) These serve as handy, quick reference guides for those who do not want to page through the entire *Health Care State Rankings* volume searching for information for their particular state. *Health Care State Perspectives* sell for $19. When purchased with a copy of *Health Care State Rankings 2006*, these handy quick reference guides are just $9.50. For additional information, please call us toll-free at 1-800-457-0742.

Other Books From Morgan Quitno Press

In addition to *Health Care State Rankings 2006*, our company offers five other rankings reference books. *State Rankings* is our original rankings reference book, providing a general view of the states. Now in its 17th edition, *State Ranking 2006* provides easy-to-understand state statistics for categories ranging from agriculture to transportation, government finance to social welfare and crime to housing. *Education State Rankings 2005-2006* compares states in teachers' salaries, class sizes, graduation rates and more than 400 other categories relating to preK-12 education. *Crime State Rankings 2006* provides a huge collection of user-friendly state statistics regarding law enforcement personnel and expenditures, corrections, juvenile crime and delinquency, arrests and offenses. For crime information in communities, *City Crime Rankings* compares crime in all metropolitan areas and cities of 75,000 or more population (approx. 380 cities). Numbers of crimes, crime rates and changes in crime rates over one and five years are presented for all major crime categories reported by the FBI. Final 2004 crime data are featured in the most recent 12th edition. *State Trends* is the newest reference book in Morgan Quitno's collection. Now in its second edition, this volume has earned rave reviews for providing a quick and easy way to track important quality of life changes in the 50 United States. One, five, 10 and 20-year trends are measured in health care, taxes, crime, education and more.

The information in all our books also is available on CD-ROM. These electronic editions provide a searchable PDF version of each book as well as the raw data in .dbf, Excel and ASCII formats. Additional information about all of our publications, including prices and ISBN numbers, is available online at www.statestats. com or by calling 1-800-457-0742.

Finally, many thanks to the librarians, government and health care industry officials who help us year after year. Thanks also to you, our readers. We always welcome your thoughts and suggestions. Please send your comments via email (information@morganquitno.com) or by phone at 1-800-457-0742. We look forward to hearing from you.

- THE EDITORS

WHICH STATE IS HEALTHIEST?

For the fifth time in six years, Vermont has earned the title of the nation's Healthiest State. Morgan Quitno's 14th annual Healthiest State Award honors the Green Mountain State for its healthy population and access to affordable and reliable health care. Following Vermont were New Hampshire, Minnesota, Maine and Iowa.

At the opposite end of the rankings, Mississippi, also for the fifth time in six years, moved back to last place. Mississippi was preceded by New Mexico, Louisiana, Nevada and Texas.

Methodology

The Healthiest State designation is awarded based on 21 factors chosen from the 2006 edition of our annual reference book, *Health Care State Rankings*. These factors reflect access to health care providers, affordability of health care and a generally healthy population (see box below.)

As in previous years, the 21 factors were divided into two groups: those that are "negative" for which a high ranking would be considered bad for a state, and those that are "positive" for which a high ranking would be considered good for a state.

2006 HEALTHIEST STATE AWARD

RANK	STATE	SUM	05	RANK	STATE	SUM	05
1	Vermont	21.99	1	26	Kentucky	1.56	32
2	New Hampshire	21.47	2	27	Montana	1.30	25
3	Minnesota	18.66	4	28	Indiana	0.64	24
4	Maine	16.47	5	29	Pennsylvania	0.53	21
5	Iowa	16.13	6	30	North Carolina	0.23	33
6	Massachusetts	16.06	3	31	New York	0.00	31
7	Nebraska	15.81	9	32	Colorado	(0.68)	27
8	Utah	14.74	7	33	Illinois	(2.87)	34
9	Connecticut	14.09	10	34	Missouri	(3.10)	36
10	Hawaii	12.34	8	35	Maryland	(4.59)	29
11	North Dakota	10.08	11	36	Arkansas	(4.69)	40
12	Kansas	9.48	15	37	Delaware	(5.34)	35
13	Rhode Island	9.19	12	38	Tennessee	(7.58)	38
14	Wisconsin	8.94	14	39	Alaska	(8.10)	37
15	Oregon	8.12	19	40	Arizona	(8.98)	39
16	New Jersey	7.79	16	41	Florida	(9.42)	44
17	South Dakota	7.26	22	42	Alabama	(10.05)	41
18	Idaho	7.25	20	42	South Carolina	(10.05)	43
19	California	6.84	18	44	Georgia	(11.11)	42
20	Washington	6.76	13	45	Oklahoma	(11.87)	46
21	Virginia	5.43	17	46	Texas	(12.98)	45
22	West Virginia	3.35	28	47	Nevada	(15.44)	47
23	Michigan	2.71	23	48	Louisiana	(17.44)	50
24	Ohio	2.60	26	49	New Mexico	(19.45)	48
25	Wyoming	2.11	30	50	Mississippi	(23.08)	49

"positive" for which a high ranking would be considered good for a state. Rates for each of the 21 factors were processed through a formula that measures how a state compares to the national average for a given category. The positive and negative nature of each factor was taken into account as part of the formula. Once these computations were made, the factors then were weighted equally. These weighted scores then were added together to get a state's final score ("SUM" on the table above). This way, states are assessed based on how they stack up against the national average. The end result is that the farther below the national average a state's health ranking is, the lower (and less healthy) it ranks. The farther above the national average, the higher (and healthier) a state ranks. For this year's award, only one factor was changed. Instead of using the percent of adults who exercise vigorously as a positive factor, we substituted the percent of adults who do not exercise as a negative factor.

The table above shows how each state fared in the 2006 Healthiest State Award as well as its placement in 2005. We acknowledge that the factors we choose have a lot to do with the placement of states. However, our point is to encourage meaningful debate about the health of states and challenge others to choose factors they think reflect the general health of states. The exact order may change but the general placement would likely be the same regardless of the factors used. There are many reasons why a Vermont has a healthier population than Mississippi, but that does not invalidate the findings.

Congratulations (again) to the citizens of Vermont!

- THE EDITORS

POSITIVE (+) AND NEGATIVE (-) FACTORS CONSIDERED:
1. Births of Low Birthweight as a Percent of All Births (Table 14) -
2. Teenage Birth Rate (Table 33) -
3. Percent of Mothers Receiving Late or No Prenatal Care (Table 62) -
4. Age-Adjusted Death Rate (Table 90) -
5. Infant Mortality Rate (Table 98) -
6. Age-Adjusted Death Rate by Malignant Neoplasms (Table 159) -
7. Age-Adjusted Death Rate by Suicide (Table 183) -
8. Average Annual Family Coverage Health Insurance Premium (Table 240) -
9. Percent of Population Not Covered by Health Insurance (Table 244) -
10. Percent of Children Not Covered by Health Insurance (Table 248) -
11. Estimated Rate of New Cancer Cases (Table 324) -

12. AIDS Rate (Table 352) -
13. Sexually Transmitted Disease Rate (Table 389) -
14. Percent of Population Lacking Access to Primary Care (Table 412) -
15. Percent of Adults Who Are Binge Drinkers (Table 495) -
16. Percent of Adults Who Smoke (Table 496) -
17. Percent of Adults Who Are Obese (Table 502) -
18. Percent of Adults Who Do Not Exercise (Table 505) -
19. Beds in Community Hospitals per 100,000 Population (Table 200) +
20. Percent of Children Aged 19-35 Months Immunized (Table 385) +
21. Safety Belt Usage Rate (Table 513) +

TABLE OF CONTENTS

I. Births and Reproductive Health

TABLE OF CONTENTS (continued)

Abortions

II. Deaths

TABLE OF CONTENTS (continued)

TABLE OF CONTENTS (continued)

III. Facilities

TABLE OF CONTENTS (continued)

IV. Finance

TABLE OF CONTENTS (continued)

V. Incidence of Disease

TABLE OF CONTENTS (continued)

VI. Providers

TABLE OF CONTENTS (continued)

TABLE OF CONTENTS (continued)

IX. Sources

X. Index

I. BIRTHS AND REPRODUCTIVE HEALTH

1   Births in 2004
2   Birth Rate in 2004
3   Percent Change in Birth Rate: 1995 to 2004
4   Births in 2003
5   Birth Rate in 2003
6   Fertility Rate in 2004
7   Births to White Women in 2004
8   White Births as a Percent of All Births in 2004
9   Births to Black Women in 2004
10 Black Births as a Percent of All Births in 2004
11 Births to Hispanic Women in 2004
12 Hispanic Births as a Percent of All Births in 2004
13 Births of Low Birthweight in 2004
14 Births of Low Birthweight as a Percent of All Births in 2004
15 Births of Low Birthweight to White Women in 2004
16 Births of Low Birthweight to White Women as a Percent of All Births to White Women in 2004
17 Births of Low Birthweight to Black Women in 2004
18 Births of Low Birthweight to Black Women as a Percent of All Births to Black Women in 2004
19 Births of Low Birthweight to Hispanic Women in 2004
20 Births of Low Birthweight to Hispanic Women as a Percent of All Births to Hispanic Women in 2004
21 Births to Unmarried Women in 2004
22 Births to Unmarried Women as a Percent of All Births in 2004
23 Births to Unmarried White Women in 2004
24 Births to Unmarried White Women as a Percent of All Births to White Women in 2004
25 Births to Unmarried Black Women in 2004
26 Births to Unmarried Black Women as a Percent of All Births to Black Women in 2004
27 Births to Unmarried Hispanic Women in 2004
28 Births to Unmarried Hispanic Women as a Percent of All Births to Hispanic Women in 2004
29 Pregnancy Rate in 2002
30 Pregnancy Rate for 15 to 19 Year Old Women in 2002
31 Percent Change in Pregnancy Rate for 15 to 19 Year Old Women: 1999 to 2002
32 Births to Teenage Mothers in 2004
33 Teenage Birth Rate in 2004
34 Births to Teenage Mothers as a Percent of Births in 2004
35 Percent Change in Teenage Birth Rate: 2000 to 2004
36 Teenage Birth Rate in 2003
37 Births to White Teenage Mothers in 2004
38 White Teenage Birth Rate in 2004
39 Births to White Teenage Mothers as a Percent of White Births in 2004
40 Births to Black Teenage Mothers in 2004
41 Black Teenage Birth Rate in 2004
42 Births to Black Teenage Mothers as a Percent of Black Births in 2004
43 Births to Young Teenagers: 2000 to 2002
44 Young Teen Birthrate: 2000 to 2002
45 Births to Women 35 to 54 Years Old in 2002
46 Births to Women 35 to 54 Years Old as a Percent of All Births in 2002
47 Births by Vaginal Delivery in 2004
48 Percent of Births by Vaginal Delivery in 2004
49 Births by Cesarean Delivery in 2004
50 Percent of Births by Cesarean Delivery in 2004
51 Percent Change in Rate of Cesarean Births: 2000 to 2004
52 Percent of Vaginal Births After a Cesarean (VBAC) in 2003
53 Assisted Reproductive Technology Procedures in 2002
54 Infants Born from Assisted Reproductive Technology Procedures in 2002
55 Percent of Assisted Reproductive Technology Procedures that Resulted in Live Births in 2002
56 Percent of Total Live Births Resulting from Assisted Reproductive Technology Procedures (ARTP) in 2002
57 Percent of Infants Born in Multiple-Birth Deliveries as a Percent of All Infants Born Through ARTP in 2002
58 Percent of Mothers Beginning Prenatal Care in First Trimester in 2003
59 Percent of White Mothers Beginning Prenatal Care in First Trimester in 2003
60 Percent of Black Mothers Beginning Prenatal Care in First Trimester in 2003
61 Percent of Hispanic Mothers Beginning Prenatal Care in First Trimester in 2003

I. BIRTHS AND REPRODUCTIVE HEALTH (CONTINUED)

Abortions

Births in 2004

National Total = 4,115,590 Live Births*

ALPHA ORDER

RANK	STATE	BIRTHS	% of USA
24	Alabama	59,549	1.4%
47	Alaska	10,338	0.3%
13	Arizona	93,672	2.3%
33	Arkansas	38,602	0.9%
1	California	545,071	13.2%
22	Colorado	68,520	1.7%
31	Connecticut	42,099	1.0%
46	Delaware	11,299	0.3%
4	Florida	218,034	5.3%
8	Georgia	138,851	3.4%
40	Hawaii	18,280	0.4%
38	Idaho	22,527	0.5%
5	Illinois	180,934	4.4%
14	Indiana	86,733	2.1%
34	Iowa	38,439	0.9%
32	Kansas	39,581	1.0%
26	Kentucky	54,451	1.3%
23	Louisiana	65,399	1.6%
42	Maine	13,945	0.3%
19	Maryland	74,605	1.8%
17	Massachusetts	78,566	1.9%
9	Michigan	129,768	3.2%
20	Minnesota	70,615	1.7%
30	Mississippi	42,810	1.0%
18	Missouri	77,780	1.9%
44	Montana	11,525	0.3%
37	Nebraska	26,331	0.6%
35	Nevada	35,188	0.9%
41	New Hampshire	14,566	0.4%
11	New Jersey	114,916	2.8%
36	New Mexico	28,386	0.7%
3	New York	250,894	6.1%
10	North Carolina	119,851	2.9%
48	North Dakota	8,189	0.2%
6	Ohio	149,154	3.6%
27	Oklahoma	51,283	1.2%
29	Oregon	45,693	1.1%
7	Pennsylvania	145,768	3.5%
43	Rhode Island	12,778	0.3%
25	South Carolina	56,592	1.4%
45	South Dakota	11,340	0.3%
16	Tennessee	79,641	1.9%
2	Texas	384,389	9.3%
28	Utah	50,669	1.2%
50	Vermont	6,565	0.2%
12	Virginia	103,915	2.5%
15	Washington	81,740	2.0%
39	West Virginia	20,855	0.5%
21	Wisconsin	70,154	1.7%
49	Wyoming	6,807	0.2%

RANK ORDER

RANK	STATE	BIRTHS	% of USA
1	California	545,071	13.2%
2	Texas	384,389	9.3%
3	New York	250,894	6.1%
4	Florida	218,034	5.3%
5	Illinois	180,934	4.4%
6	Ohio	149,154	3.6%
7	Pennsylvania	145,768	3.5%
8	Georgia	138,851	3.4%
9	Michigan	129,768	3.2%
10	North Carolina	119,851	2.9%
11	New Jersey	114,916	2.8%
12	Virginia	103,915	2.5%
13	Arizona	93,672	2.3%
14	Indiana	86,733	2.1%
15	Washington	81,740	2.0%
16	Tennessee	79,641	1.9%
17	Massachusetts	78,566	1.9%
18	Missouri	77,780	1.9%
19	Maryland	74,605	1.8%
20	Minnesota	70,615	1.7%
21	Wisconsin	70,154	1.7%
22	Colorado	68,520	1.7%
23	Louisiana	65,399	1.6%
24	Alabama	59,549	1.4%
25	South Carolina	56,592	1.4%
26	Kentucky	54,451	1.3%
27	Oklahoma	51,283	1.2%
28	Utah	50,669	1.2%
29	Oregon	45,693	1.1%
30	Mississippi	42,810	1.0%
31	Connecticut	42,099	1.0%
32	Kansas	39,581	1.0%
33	Arkansas	38,602	0.9%
34	Iowa	38,439	0.9%
35	Nevada	35,188	0.9%
36	New Mexico	28,386	0.7%
37	Nebraska	26,331	0.6%
38	Idaho	22,527	0.5%
39	West Virginia	20,855	0.5%
40	Hawaii	18,280	0.4%
41	New Hampshire	14,566	0.4%
42	Maine	13,945	0.3%
43	Rhode Island	12,778	0.3%
44	Montana	11,525	0.3%
45	South Dakota	11,340	0.3%
46	Delaware	11,299	0.3%
47	Alaska	10,338	0.3%
48	North Dakota	8,189	0.2%
49	Wyoming	6,807	0.2%
50	Vermont	6,565	0.2%
	District of Columbia	7,932	0.2%

Source: U.S. Department of Health and Human Services, National Center for Health Statistics
    "National Vital Statistics Reports" (Vol. 54, No. 8, December 29, 2005)
*Preliminary data by state of residence.

Birth Rate in 2004

National Rate = 14.0 Live Births per 1,000 Population*

ALPHA ORDER

RANK	STATE	RATE
32	Alabama	13.1
5	Alaska	15.8
3	Arizona	16.3
19	Arkansas	14.0
7	California	15.2
10	Colorado	14.9
44	Connecticut	12.0
24	Delaware	13.6
41	Florida	12.5
6	Georgia	15.7
15	Hawaii	14.5
4	Idaho	16.2
18	Illinois	14.2
21	Indiana	13.9
34	Iowa	13.0
15	Kansas	14.5
32	Kentucky	13.1
15	Louisiana	14.5
49	Maine	10.6
28	Maryland	13.4
43	Massachusetts	12.2
38	Michigan	12.8
23	Minnesota	13.8
12	Mississippi	14.7
25	Missouri	13.5
42	Montana	12.4
8	Nebraska	15.1
8	Nevada	15.1
48	New Hampshire	11.2
30	New Jersey	13.2
10	New Mexico	14.9
34	New York	13.0
19	North Carolina	14.0
37	North Dakota	12.9
34	Ohio	13.0
14	Oklahoma	14.6
39	Oregon	12.7
46	Pennsylvania	11.7
45	Rhode Island	11.8
25	South Carolina	13.5
12	South Dakota	14.7
25	Tennessee	13.5
2	Texas	17.1
1	Utah	21.2
49	Vermont	10.6
21	Virginia	13.9
30	Washington	13.2
47	West Virginia	11.5
39	Wisconsin	12.7
28	Wyoming	13.4

RANK ORDER

RANK	STATE	RATE
1	Utah	21.2
2	Texas	17.1
3	Arizona	16.3
4	Idaho	16.2
5	Alaska	15.8
6	Georgia	15.7
7	California	15.2
8	Nebraska	15.1
8	Nevada	15.1
10	Colorado	14.9
10	New Mexico	14.9
12	Mississippi	14.7
12	South Dakota	14.7
14	Oklahoma	14.6
15	Hawaii	14.5
15	Kansas	14.5
15	Louisiana	14.5
18	Illinois	14.2
19	Arkansas	14.0
19	North Carolina	14.0
21	Indiana	13.9
21	Virginia	13.9
23	Minnesota	13.8
24	Delaware	13.6
25	Missouri	13.5
25	South Carolina	13.5
25	Tennessee	13.5
28	Maryland	13.4
28	Wyoming	13.4
30	New Jersey	13.2
30	Washington	13.2
32	Alabama	13.1
32	Kentucky	13.1
34	Iowa	13.0
34	New York	13.0
34	Ohio	13.0
37	North Dakota	12.9
38	Michigan	12.8
39	Oregon	12.7
39	Wisconsin	12.7
41	Florida	12.5
42	Montana	12.4
43	Massachusetts	12.2
44	Connecticut	12.0
45	Rhode Island	11.8
46	Pennsylvania	11.7
47	West Virginia	11.5
48	New Hampshire	11.2
49	Maine	10.6
49	Vermont	10.6
	District of Columbia	14.3

Source: U.S. Department of Health and Human Services, National Center for Health Statistics
    "National Vital Statistics Reports" (Vol. 54, No. 8, December 29, 2005)
*Preliminary data by state of residence.

Percent Change in Birth Rate: 1995 to 2004

National Percent Change = 5.4% Decrease*

ALPHA ORDER

RANK	STATE	PERCENT CHANGE
39	Alabama	(7.7)
36	Alaska	(7.1)
28	Arizona	(5.2)
16	Arkansas	(1.4)
49	California	(13.1)
6	Colorado	2.8
47	Connecticut	(11.1)
27	Delaware	(4.9)
31	Florida	(6.0)
9	Georgia	0.6
38	Hawaii	(7.6)
3	Idaho	4.5
46	Illinois	(9.6)
19	Indiana	(2.8)
10	Iowa	0.0
10	Kansas	0.0
23	Kentucky	(3.7)
26	Louisiana	(4.0)
29	Maine	(5.4)
33	Maryland	(6.9)
43	Massachusetts	(9.0)
45	Michigan	(9.2)
8	Minnesota	0.7
25	Mississippi	(3.9)
17	Missouri	(1.5)
22	Montana	(3.1)
1	Nebraska	6.3
40	Nevada	(7.9)
48	New Hampshire	(12.5)
43	New Jersey	(9.0)
33	New Mexico	(6.9)
50	New York	(13.3)
13	North Carolina	(0.7)
18	North Dakota	(2.3)
30	Ohio	(5.8)
2	Oklahoma	5.0
32	Oregon	(6.6)
36	Pennsylvania	(7.1)
41	Rhode Island	(8.5)
20	South Carolina	(2.9)
7	South Dakota	2.1
20	Tennessee	(2.9)
12	Texas	(0.6)
4	Utah	4.4
42	Vermont	(8.6)
13	Virginia	(0.7)
35	Washington	(7.0)
15	West Virginia	(0.9)
24	Wisconsin	(3.8)
5	Wyoming	3.1

RANK ORDER

RANK	STATE	PERCENT CHANGE
1	Nebraska	6.3
2	Oklahoma	5.0
3	Idaho	4.5
4	Utah	4.4
5	Wyoming	3.1
6	Colorado	2.8
7	South Dakota	2.1
8	Minnesota	0.7
9	Georgia	0.6
10	Iowa	0.0
10	Kansas	0.0
12	Texas	(0.6)
13	North Carolina	(0.7)
13	Virginia	(0.7)
15	West Virginia	(0.9)
16	Arkansas	(1.4)
17	Missouri	(1.5)
18	North Dakota	(2.3)
19	Indiana	(2.8)
20	South Carolina	(2.9)
20	Tennessee	(2.9)
22	Montana	(3.1)
23	Kentucky	(3.7)
24	Wisconsin	(3.8)
25	Mississippi	(3.9)
26	Louisiana	(4.0)
27	Delaware	(4.9)
28	Arizona	(5.2)
29	Maine	(5.4)
30	Ohio	(5.8)
31	Florida	(6.0)
32	Oregon	(6.6)
33	Maryland	(6.9)
33	New Mexico	(6.9)
35	Washington	(7.0)
36	Alaska	(7.1)
36	Pennsylvania	(7.1)
38	Hawaii	(7.6)
39	Alabama	(7.7)
40	Nevada	(7.9)
41	Rhode Island	(8.5)
42	Vermont	(8.6)
43	Massachusetts	(9.0)
43	New Jersey	(9.0)
45	Michigan	(9.2)
46	Illinois	(9.6)
47	Connecticut	(11.1)
48	New Hampshire	(12.5)
49	California	(13.1)
50	New York	(13.3)

| | District of Columbia | (12.3) |

Source: Morgan Quitno Press using data from U.S. Department of Health and Human Services
  "National Vital Statistics Reports" (Vol. 54, No. 8, December 29, 2005)
  "Monthly Vital Statistics Report" (Vol. 45, No. 11s, Supplement, June 10, 1997)
*By state of residence.

Births in 2003

National Total = 4,089,950 Live Births*

ALPHA ORDER

RANK	STATE	BIRTHS	% of USA
24	Alabama	59,552	1.5%
47	Alaska	10,086	0.2%
13	Arizona	90,967	2.2%
34	Arkansas	37,784	0.9%
1	California	540,997	13.2%
22	Colorado	69,339	1.7%
30	Connecticut	42,873	1.0%
45	Delaware	11,329	0.3%
4	Florida	212,250	5.2%
8	Georgia	135,979	3.3%
40	Hawaii	18,100	0.4%
38	Idaho	21,800	0.5%
5	Illinois	182,495	4.5%
14	Indiana	86,434	2.1%
33	Iowa	38,174	0.9%
32	Kansas	39,476	1.0%
26	Kentucky	55,236	1.4%
23	Louisiana	65,040	1.6%
42	Maine	13,855	0.3%
19	Maryland	74,930	1.8%
16	Massachusetts	80,184	2.0%
9	Michigan	131,094	3.2%
20	Minnesota	70,050	1.7%
31	Mississippi	42,380	1.0%
18	Missouri	77,045	1.9%
44	Montana	11,422	0.3%
37	Nebraska	25,917	0.6%
35	Nevada	33,647	0.8%
41	New Hampshire	14,393	0.4%
11	New Jersey	116,983	2.9%
36	New Mexico	27,821	0.7%
3	New York	253,714	6.2%
10	North Carolina	118,323	2.9%
48	North Dakota	7,972	0.2%
6	Ohio	149,679	3.7%
27	Oklahoma	50,981	1.2%
29	Oregon	45,953	1.1%
7	Pennsylvania	145,959	3.6%
43	Rhode Island	13,209	0.3%
25	South Carolina	55,649	1.4%
46	South Dakota	11,027	0.3%
17	Tennessee	78,890	1.9%
2	Texas	377,476	9.2%
28	Utah	49,860	1.2%
50	Vermont	6,589	0.2%
12	Virginia	101,254	2.5%
15	Washington	80,489	2.0%
39	West Virginia	20,935	0.5%
21	Wisconsin	70,040	1.7%
49	Wyoming	6,700	0.2%

RANK ORDER

RANK	STATE	BIRTHS	% of USA
1	California	540,997	13.2%
2	Texas	377,476	9.2%
3	New York	253,714	6.2%
4	Florida	212,250	5.2%
5	Illinois	182,495	4.5%
6	Ohio	149,679	3.7%
7	Pennsylvania	145,959	3.6%
8	Georgia	135,979	3.3%
9	Michigan	131,094	3.2%
10	North Carolina	118,323	2.9%
11	New Jersey	116,983	2.9%
12	Virginia	101,254	2.5%
13	Arizona	90,967	2.2%
14	Indiana	86,434	2.1%
15	Washington	80,489	2.0%
16	Massachusetts	80,184	2.0%
17	Tennessee	78,890	1.9%
18	Missouri	77,045	1.9%
19	Maryland	74,930	1.8%
20	Minnesota	70,050	1.7%
21	Wisconsin	70,040	1.7%
22	Colorado	69,339	1.7%
23	Louisiana	65,040	1.6%
24	Alabama	59,552	1.5%
25	South Carolina	55,649	1.4%
26	Kentucky	55,236	1.4%
27	Oklahoma	50,981	1.2%
28	Utah	49,860	1.2%
29	Oregon	45,953	1.1%
30	Connecticut	42,873	1.0%
31	Mississippi	42,380	1.0%
32	Kansas	39,476	1.0%
33	Iowa	38,174	0.9%
34	Arkansas	37,784	0.9%
35	Nevada	33,647	0.8%
36	New Mexico	27,821	0.7%
37	Nebraska	25,917	0.6%
38	Idaho	21,800	0.5%
39	West Virginia	20,935	0.5%
40	Hawaii	18,100	0.4%
41	New Hampshire	14,393	0.4%
42	Maine	13,855	0.3%
43	Rhode Island	13,209	0.3%
44	Montana	11,422	0.3%
45	Delaware	11,329	0.3%
46	South Dakota	11,027	0.3%
47	Alaska	10,086	0.2%
48	North Dakota	7,972	0.2%
49	Wyoming	6,700	0.2%
50	Vermont	6,589	0.2%
	District of Columbia	7,619	0.2%

*Source: U.S. Department of Health and Human Services, National Center for Health Statistics
"National Vital Statistics Reports" (Vol. 54, No. 2, September 8, 2005)*
Final data by state of residence.

Birth Rate in 2003

National Rate = 14.1 Live Births per 1,000 Population*

ALPHA ORDER			RANK ORDER		
RANK	STATE	RATE	RANK	STATE	RATE
32	Alabama	13.2	1	Utah	21.2
6	Alaska	15.5	2	Texas	17.1
3	Arizona	16.3	3	Arizona	16.3
21	Arkansas	13.9	4	Idaho	16.0
7	California	15.2	5	Georgia	15.7
7	Colorado	15.2	6	Alaska	15.5
44	Connecticut	12.3	7	California	15.2
21	Delaware	13.9	7	Colorado	15.2
41	Florida	12.5	9	Nevada	15.0
5	Georgia	15.7	10	Nebraska	14.9
16	Hawaii	14.4	11	New Mexico	14.8
4	Idaho	16.0	12	Mississippi	14.7
16	Illinois	14.4	13	Kansas	14.5
20	Indiana	14.0	13	Louisiana	14.5
36	Iowa	13.0	13	Oklahoma	14.5
13	Kansas	14.5	16	Hawaii	14.4
29	Kentucky	13.4	16	Illinois	14.4
13	Louisiana	14.5	16	South Dakota	14.4
49	Maine	10.6	19	North Carolina	14.1
25	Maryland	13.6	20	Indiana	14.0
41	Massachusetts	12.5	21	Arkansas	13.9
36	Michigan	13.0	21	Delaware	13.9
23	Minnesota	13.8	23	Minnesota	13.8
12	Mississippi	14.7	24	Virginia	13.7
26	Missouri	13.5	25	Maryland	13.6
43	Montana	12.4	26	Missouri	13.5
10	Nebraska	14.9	26	New Jersey	13.5
9	Nevada	15.0	26	Tennessee	13.5
48	New Hampshire	11.2	29	Kentucky	13.4
26	New Jersey	13.5	29	South Carolina	13.4
11	New Mexico	14.8	29	Wyoming	13.4
32	New York	13.2	32	Alabama	13.2
19	North Carolina	14.1	32	New York	13.2
40	North Dakota	12.6	34	Ohio	13.1
34	Ohio	13.1	34	Washington	13.1
13	Oklahoma	14.5	36	Iowa	13.0
38	Oregon	12.9	36	Michigan	13.0
46	Pennsylvania	11.8	38	Oregon	12.9
44	Rhode Island	12.3	39	Wisconsin	12.8
29	South Carolina	13.4	40	North Dakota	12.6
16	South Dakota	14.4	41	Florida	12.5
26	Tennessee	13.5	41	Massachusetts	12.5
2	Texas	17.1	43	Montana	12.4
1	Utah	21.2	44	Connecticut	12.3
49	Vermont	10.6	44	Rhode Island	12.3
24	Virginia	13.7	46	Pennsylvania	11.8
34	Washington	13.1	47	West Virginia	11.6
47	West Virginia	11.6	48	New Hampshire	11.2
39	Wisconsin	12.8	49	Maine	10.6
29	Wyoming	13.4	49	Vermont	10.6
				District of Columbia	13.5

Source: U.S. Department of Health and Human Services, National Center for Health Statistics
"National Vital Statistics Reports" (Vol. 54, No. 2, September 8, 2005)
*Final data by state of residence.

Fertility Rate in 2004

National Rate = 66.3 Live Births per 1,000 Women 15 to 44 Years Old*

RANK	STATE	RATE	RANK	STATE	RATE
35	Alabama	62.5	1	Utah	92.3
5	Alaska	74.4	2	Arizona	79.5
2	Arizona	79.5	3	Texas	78.0
16	Arkansas	68.4	4	Idaho	77.2
11	California	70.4	5	Alaska	74.4
15	Colorado	68.8	6	Hawaii	74.0
43	Connecticut	58.8	7	Nebraska	72.6
30	Delaware	63.4	7	Nevada	72.6
26	Florida	64.1	9	South Dakota	72.4
13	Georgia	70.1	10	New Mexico	71.9
6	Hawaii	74.0	11	California	70.4
4	Idaho	77.2	12	Oklahoma	70.2
18	Illinois	66.7	13	Georgia	70.1
18	Indiana	66.7	14	Kansas	69.6
28	Iowa	63.8	15	Colorado	68.8
14	Kansas	69.6	16	Arkansas	68.4
37	Kentucky	62.2	17	Mississippi	68.3
18	Louisiana	66.7	18	Illinois	66.7
49	Maine	52.4	18	Indiana	66.7
36	Maryland	62.3	18	Louisiana	66.7
46	Massachusetts	56.5	21	Wyoming	66.5
40	Michigan	61.4	22	North Carolina	66.0
24	Minnesota	64.5	23	Virginia	65.0
17	Mississippi	68.3	24	Minnesota	64.5
25	Missouri	64.3	25	Missouri	64.3
33	Montana	62.8	26	Florida	64.1
7	Nebraska	72.6	27	New Jersey	64.0
7	Nevada	72.6	28	Iowa	63.8
48	New Hampshire	53.4	29	South Carolina	63.6
27	New Jersey	64.0	30	Delaware	63.4
10	New Mexico	71.9	30	Tennessee	63.4
41	New York	60.9	32	North Dakota	63.2
22	North Carolina	66.0	33	Montana	62.8
32	North Dakota	63.2	33	Ohio	62.8
33	Ohio	62.8	35	Alabama	62.5
12	Oklahoma	70.2	36	Maryland	62.3
38	Oregon	61.8	37	Kentucky	62.2
44	Pennsylvania	58.5	38	Oregon	61.8
47	Rhode Island	55.0	39	Washington	61.7
29	South Carolina	63.6	40	Michigan	61.4
9	South Dakota	72.4	41	New York	60.9
30	Tennessee	63.4	42	Wisconsin	60.7
3	Texas	78.0	43	Connecticut	58.8
1	Utah	92.3	44	Pennsylvania	58.5
50	Vermont	51.8	45	West Virginia	58.3
23	Virginia	65.0	46	Massachusetts	56.5
39	Washington	61.7	47	Rhode Island	55.0
45	West Virginia	58.3	48	New Hampshire	53.4
42	Wisconsin	60.7	49	Maine	52.4
21	Wyoming	66.5	50	Vermont	51.8
				District of Columbia	58.2

Source: U.S. Department of Health and Human Services, National Center for Health Statistics
"National Vital Statistics Reports" (Vol. 54, No. 8, December 29, 2005)
*Preliminary data by state of residence.

Births to White Women in 2004

National Total = 3,229,814 Live Births to White Women*

ALPHA ORDER

RANK	STATE	BIRTHS	% of USA
26	Alabama	40,550	1.3%
47	Alaska	6,588	0.2%
12	Arizona	81,171	2.5%
33	Arkansas	30,363	0.9%
1	California	441,315	13.7%
18	Colorado	62,514	1.9%
32	Connecticut	34,454	1.1%
45	Delaware	7,919	0.2%
4	Florida	157,701	4.9%
9	Georgia	89,771	2.8%
50	Hawaii	5,177	0.2%
38	Idaho	21,710	0.7%
5	Illinois	140,867	4.4%
13	Indiana	75,418	2.3%
30	Iowa	35,727	1.1%
31	Kansas	35,089	1.1%
22	Kentucky	48,665	1.5%
28	Louisiana	37,144	1.2%
41	Maine	13,382	0.4%
24	Maryland	43,909	1.4%
17	Massachusetts	64,031	2.0%
8	Michigan	102,802	3.2%
21	Minnesota	59,565	1.8%
37	Mississippi	23,558	0.7%
16	Missouri	64,152	2.0%
43	Montana	9,827	0.3%
36	Nebraska	23,703	0.7%
34	Nevada	29,032	0.9%
40	New Hampshire	13,767	0.4%
11	New Jersey	84,139	2.6%
35	New Mexico	23,856	0.7%
3	New York	178,771	5.5%
10	North Carolina	87,414	2.7%
46	North Dakota	7,017	0.2%
6	Ohio	121,516	3.8%
27	Oklahoma	40,042	1.2%
25	Oregon	41,251	1.3%
7	Pennsylvania	117,754	3.6%
42	Rhode Island	10,874	0.3%
29	South Carolina	35,789	1.1%
44	South Dakota	9,199	0.3%
19	Tennessee	60,406	1.9%
2	Texas	327,511	10.1%
23	Utah	48,256	1.5%
48	Vermont	6,383	0.2%
14	Virginia	73,953	2.3%
15	Washington	67,157	2.1%
39	West Virginia	19,992	0.6%
20	Wisconsin	59,998	1.9%
49	Wyoming	6,359	0.2%

RANK ORDER

RANK	STATE	BIRTHS	% of USA
1	California	441,315	13.7%
2	Texas	327,511	10.1%
3	New York	178,771	5.5%
4	Florida	157,701	4.9%
5	Illinois	140,867	4.4%
6	Ohio	121,516	3.8%
7	Pennsylvania	117,754	3.6%
8	Michigan	102,802	3.2%
9	Georgia	89,771	2.8%
10	North Carolina	87,414	2.7%
11	New Jersey	84,139	2.6%
12	Arizona	81,171	2.5%
13	Indiana	75,418	2.3%
14	Virginia	73,953	2.3%
15	Washington	67,157	2.1%
16	Missouri	64,152	2.0%
17	Massachusetts	64,031	2.0%
18	Colorado	62,514	1.9%
19	Tennessee	60,406	1.9%
20	Wisconsin	59,998	1.9%
21	Minnesota	59,565	1.8%
22	Kentucky	48,665	1.5%
23	Utah	48,256	1.5%
24	Maryland	43,909	1.4%
25	Oregon	41,251	1.3%
26	Alabama	40,550	1.3%
27	Oklahoma	40,042	1.2%
28	Louisiana	37,144	1.2%
29	South Carolina	35,789	1.1%
30	Iowa	35,727	1.1%
31	Kansas	35,089	1.1%
32	Connecticut	34,454	1.1%
33	Arkansas	30,363	0.9%
34	Nevada	29,032	0.9%
35	New Mexico	23,856	0.7%
36	Nebraska	23,703	0.7%
37	Mississippi	23,558	0.7%
38	Idaho	21,710	0.7%
39	West Virginia	19,992	0.6%
40	New Hampshire	13,767	0.4%
41	Maine	13,382	0.4%
42	Rhode Island	10,874	0.3%
43	Montana	9,827	0.3%
44	South Dakota	9,199	0.3%
45	Delaware	7,919	0.2%
46	North Dakota	7,017	0.2%
47	Alaska	6,588	0.2%
48	Vermont	6,383	0.2%
49	Wyoming	6,359	0.2%
50	Hawaii	5,177	0.2%
	District of Columbia	2,302	0.1%

Source: U.S. Department of Health and Human Services, National Center for Health Statistics
    "National Vital Statistics Reports" (Vol. 54, No. 8, December 29, 2005)
*Preliminary data by state of residence. By race of mother.

White Births as a Percent of All Births in 2004

National Percent = 78.5% of Live Births*

ALPHA ORDER

RANK	STATE	PERCENT
43	Alabama	68.1
45	Alaska	63.7
15	Arizona	86.7
33	Arkansas	78.7
30	California	81.0
9	Colorado	91.2
26	Connecticut	81.8
42	Delaware	70.1
39	Florida	72.3
44	Georgia	64.7
50	Hawaii	28.3
2	Idaho	96.4
35	Illinois	77.9
14	Indiana	87.0
8	Iowa	92.9
13	Kansas	88.7
12	Kentucky	89.4
48	Louisiana	56.8
3	Maine	96.0
47	Maryland	58.9
27	Massachusetts	81.5
32	Michigan	79.2
21	Minnesota	84.4
49	Mississippi	55.0
23	Missouri	82.5
18	Montana	85.3
11	Nebraska	90.0
23	Nevada	82.5
6	New Hampshire	94.5
37	New Jersey	73.2
22	New Mexico	84.0
40	New York	71.3
38	North Carolina	72.9
16	North Dakota	85.7
27	Ohio	81.5
34	Oklahoma	78.1
10	Oregon	90.3
31	Pennsylvania	80.8
20	Rhode Island	85.1
46	South Carolina	63.2
29	South Dakota	81.1
36	Tennessee	75.8
19	Texas	85.2
5	Utah	95.2
1	Vermont	97.2
41	Virginia	71.2
25	Washington	82.2
4	West Virginia	95.9
17	Wisconsin	85.5
7	Wyoming	93.4

RANK ORDER

RANK	STATE	PERCENT
1	Vermont	97.2
2	Idaho	96.4
3	Maine	96.0
4	West Virginia	95.9
5	Utah	95.2
6	New Hampshire	94.5
7	Wyoming	93.4
8	Iowa	92.9
9	Colorado	91.2
10	Oregon	90.3
11	Nebraska	90.0
12	Kentucky	89.4
13	Kansas	88.7
14	Indiana	87.0
15	Arizona	86.7
16	North Dakota	85.7
17	Wisconsin	85.5
18	Montana	85.3
19	Texas	85.2
20	Rhode Island	85.1
21	Minnesota	84.4
22	New Mexico	84.0
23	Missouri	82.5
23	Nevada	82.5
25	Washington	82.2
26	Connecticut	81.8
27	Massachusetts	81.5
27	Ohio	81.5
29	South Dakota	81.1
30	California	81.0
31	Pennsylvania	80.8
32	Michigan	79.2
33	Arkansas	78.7
34	Oklahoma	78.1
35	Illinois	77.9
36	Tennessee	75.8
37	New Jersey	73.2
38	North Carolina	72.9
39	Florida	72.3
40	New York	71.3
41	Virginia	71.2
42	Delaware	70.1
43	Alabama	68.1
44	Georgia	64.7
45	Alaska	63.7
46	South Carolina	63.2
47	Maryland	58.9
48	Louisiana	56.8
49	Mississippi	55.0
50	Hawaii	28.3

| | District of Columbia | 29.0 |

Source: Morgan Quitno Press using data from U.S. Dept. of Health and Human Services, Nat'l Center for Health Statistics
"National Vital Statistics Reports" (Vol. 54, No. 8, December 29, 2005)
*Preliminary data by state of residence. By race of mother.

Births to Black Women in 2004

National Total = 612,493 Live Births to Black Women*

<table>
<tr><td colspan="4">ALPHA ORDER</td><td colspan="4">RANK ORDER</td></tr>
<tr><th>RANK</th><th>STATE</th><th>BIRTHS</th><th>% of USA</th><th>RANK</th><th>STATE</th><th>BIRTHS</th><th>% of USA</th></tr>
<tr><td>17</td><td>Alabama</td><td>18,057</td><td>2.9%</td><td>1</td><td>Florida</td><td>52,758</td><td>8.6%</td></tr>
<tr><td>41</td><td>Alaska</td><td>397</td><td>0.1%</td><td>2</td><td>New York</td><td>49,765</td><td>8.1%</td></tr>
<tr><td>29</td><td>Arizona</td><td>3,426</td><td>0.6%</td><td>3</td><td>Georgia</td><td>44,001</td><td>7.2%</td></tr>
<tr><td>22</td><td>Arkansas</td><td>7,396</td><td>1.2%</td><td>4</td><td>Texas</td><td>42,422</td><td>6.9%</td></tr>
<tr><td>5</td><td>California</td><td>32,106</td><td>5.2%</td><td>5</td><td>California</td><td>32,106</td><td>5.2%</td></tr>
<tr><td>31</td><td>Colorado</td><td>2,929</td><td>0.5%</td><td>6</td><td>Illinois</td><td>30,874</td><td>5.0%</td></tr>
<tr><td>24</td><td>Connecticut</td><td>5,279</td><td>0.9%</td><td>7</td><td>North Carolina</td><td>27,623</td><td>4.5%</td></tr>
<tr><td>32</td><td>Delaware</td><td>2,895</td><td>0.5%</td><td>8</td><td>Louisiana</td><td>26,732</td><td>4.4%</td></tr>
<tr><td>1</td><td>Florida</td><td>52,758</td><td>8.6%</td><td>9</td><td>Maryland</td><td>25,721</td><td>4.2%</td></tr>
<tr><td>3</td><td>Georgia</td><td>44,001</td><td>7.2%</td><td>10</td><td>Ohio</td><td>23,910</td><td>3.9%</td></tr>
<tr><td>39</td><td>Hawaii</td><td>573</td><td>0.1%</td><td>11</td><td>Virginia</td><td>22,899</td><td>3.7%</td></tr>
<tr><td>46</td><td>Idaho</td><td>109</td><td>0.0%</td><td>12</td><td>Pennsylvania</td><td>22,081</td><td>3.6%</td></tr>
<tr><td>6</td><td>Illinois</td><td>30,874</td><td>5.0%</td><td>13</td><td>Michigan</td><td>21,705</td><td>3.5%</td></tr>
<tr><td>20</td><td>Indiana</td><td>9,655</td><td>1.6%</td><td>14</td><td>New Jersey</td><td>19,730</td><td>3.2%</td></tr>
<tr><td>35</td><td>Iowa</td><td>1,478</td><td>0.2%</td><td>15</td><td>South Carolina</td><td>19,613</td><td>3.2%</td></tr>
<tr><td>33</td><td>Kansas</td><td>2,837</td><td>0.5%</td><td>16</td><td>Mississippi</td><td>18,516</td><td>3.0%</td></tr>
<tr><td>25</td><td>Kentucky</td><td>4,878</td><td>0.8%</td><td>17</td><td>Alabama</td><td>18,057</td><td>2.9%</td></tr>
<tr><td>8</td><td>Louisiana</td><td>26,732</td><td>4.4%</td><td>18</td><td>Tennessee</td><td>17,401</td><td>2.8%</td></tr>
<tr><td>44</td><td>Maine</td><td>225</td><td>0.0%</td><td>19</td><td>Missouri</td><td>11,455</td><td>1.9%</td></tr>
<tr><td>9</td><td>Maryland</td><td>25,721</td><td>4.2%</td><td>20</td><td>Indiana</td><td>9,655</td><td>1.6%</td></tr>
<tr><td>21</td><td>Massachusetts</td><td>8,720</td><td>1.4%</td><td>21</td><td>Massachusetts</td><td>8,720</td><td>1.4%</td></tr>
<tr><td>13</td><td>Michigan</td><td>21,705</td><td>3.5%</td><td>22</td><td>Arkansas</td><td>7,396</td><td>1.2%</td></tr>
<tr><td>27</td><td>Minnesota</td><td>4,646</td><td>0.8%</td><td>23</td><td>Wisconsin</td><td>6,601</td><td>1.1%</td></tr>
<tr><td>16</td><td>Mississippi</td><td>18,516</td><td>3.0%</td><td>24</td><td>Connecticut</td><td>5,279</td><td>0.9%</td></tr>
<tr><td>19</td><td>Missouri</td><td>11,455</td><td>1.9%</td><td>25</td><td>Kentucky</td><td>4,878</td><td>0.8%</td></tr>
<tr><td>50</td><td>Montana</td><td>53</td><td>0.0%</td><td>26</td><td>Oklahoma</td><td>4,705</td><td>0.8%</td></tr>
<tr><td>34</td><td>Nebraska</td><td>1,573</td><td>0.3%</td><td>27</td><td>Minnesota</td><td>4,646</td><td>0.8%</td></tr>
<tr><td>30</td><td>Nevada</td><td>2,958</td><td>0.5%</td><td>28</td><td>Washington</td><td>4,059</td><td>0.7%</td></tr>
<tr><td>43</td><td>New Hampshire</td><td>256</td><td>0.0%</td><td>29</td><td>Arizona</td><td>3,426</td><td>0.6%</td></tr>
<tr><td>14</td><td>New Jersey</td><td>19,730</td><td>3.2%</td><td>30</td><td>Nevada</td><td>2,958</td><td>0.5%</td></tr>
<tr><td>40</td><td>New Mexico</td><td>502</td><td>0.1%</td><td>31</td><td>Colorado</td><td>2,929</td><td>0.5%</td></tr>
<tr><td>2</td><td>New York</td><td>49,765</td><td>8.1%</td><td>32</td><td>Delaware</td><td>2,895</td><td>0.5%</td></tr>
<tr><td>7</td><td>North Carolina</td><td>27,623</td><td>4.5%</td><td>33</td><td>Kansas</td><td>2,837</td><td>0.5%</td></tr>
<tr><td>47</td><td>North Dakota</td><td>96</td><td>0.0%</td><td>34</td><td>Nebraska</td><td>1,573</td><td>0.3%</td></tr>
<tr><td>10</td><td>Ohio</td><td>23,910</td><td>3.9%</td><td>35</td><td>Iowa</td><td>1,478</td><td>0.2%</td></tr>
<tr><td>26</td><td>Oklahoma</td><td>4,705</td><td>0.8%</td><td>36</td><td>Rhode Island</td><td>1,196</td><td>0.2%</td></tr>
<tr><td>37</td><td>Oregon</td><td>1,057</td><td>0.2%</td><td>37</td><td>Oregon</td><td>1,057</td><td>0.2%</td></tr>
<tr><td>12</td><td>Pennsylvania</td><td>22,081</td><td>3.6%</td><td>38</td><td>West Virginia</td><td>673</td><td>0.1%</td></tr>
<tr><td>36</td><td>Rhode Island</td><td>1,196</td><td>0.2%</td><td>39</td><td>Hawaii</td><td>573</td><td>0.1%</td></tr>
<tr><td>15</td><td>South Carolina</td><td>19,613</td><td>3.2%</td><td>40</td><td>New Mexico</td><td>502</td><td>0.1%</td></tr>
<tr><td>45</td><td>South Dakota</td><td>147</td><td>0.0%</td><td>41</td><td>Alaska</td><td>397</td><td>0.1%</td></tr>
<tr><td>18</td><td>Tennessee</td><td>17,401</td><td>2.8%</td><td>42</td><td>Utah</td><td>299</td><td>0.0%</td></tr>
<tr><td>4</td><td>Texas</td><td>42,422</td><td>6.9%</td><td>43</td><td>New Hampshire</td><td>256</td><td>0.0%</td></tr>
<tr><td>42</td><td>Utah</td><td>299</td><td>0.0%</td><td>44</td><td>Maine</td><td>225</td><td>0.0%</td></tr>
<tr><td>48</td><td>Vermont</td><td>58</td><td>0.0%</td><td>45</td><td>South Dakota</td><td>147</td><td>0.0%</td></tr>
<tr><td>11</td><td>Virginia</td><td>22,899</td><td>3.7%</td><td>46</td><td>Idaho</td><td>109</td><td>0.0%</td></tr>
<tr><td>28</td><td>Washington</td><td>4,059</td><td>0.7%</td><td>47</td><td>North Dakota</td><td>96</td><td>0.0%</td></tr>
<tr><td>38</td><td>West Virginia</td><td>673</td><td>0.1%</td><td>48</td><td>Vermont</td><td>58</td><td>0.0%</td></tr>
<tr><td>23</td><td>Wisconsin</td><td>6,601</td><td>1.1%</td><td>49</td><td>Wyoming</td><td>55</td><td>0.0%</td></tr>
<tr><td>49</td><td>Wyoming</td><td>55</td><td>0.0%</td><td>50</td><td>Montana</td><td>53</td><td>0.0%</td></tr>
<tr><td></td><td></td><td></td><td></td><td></td><td>District of Columbia</td><td>5,392</td><td>0.9%</td></tr>
</table>

Source: U.S. Department of Health and Human Services, National Center for Health Statistics
"National Vital Statistics Reports" (Vol. 54, No. 8, December 29, 2005)
*Preliminary data by state of residence. By race of mother.

Black Births as a Percent of All Births in 2004

National Percent = 14.9% of Live Births*

<table>
<tr><td colspan="3">ALPHA ORDER</td><td colspan="3">RANK ORDER</td></tr>
<tr><td>RANK</td><td>STATE</td><td>PERCENT</td><td>RANK</td><td>STATE</td><td>PERCENT</td></tr>
<tr><td>6</td><td>Alabama</td><td>30.3</td><td>1</td><td>Mississippi</td><td>43.3</td></tr>
<tr><td>35</td><td>Alaska</td><td>3.8</td><td>2</td><td>Louisiana</td><td>40.9</td></tr>
<tr><td>37</td><td>Arizona</td><td>3.7</td><td>3</td><td>South Carolina</td><td>34.7</td></tr>
<tr><td>13</td><td>Arkansas</td><td>19.2</td><td>4</td><td>Maryland</td><td>34.5</td></tr>
<tr><td>32</td><td>California</td><td>5.9</td><td>5</td><td>Georgia</td><td>31.7</td></tr>
<tr><td>34</td><td>Colorado</td><td>4.3</td><td>6</td><td>Alabama</td><td>30.3</td></tr>
<tr><td>20</td><td>Connecticut</td><td>12.5</td><td>7</td><td>Delaware</td><td>25.6</td></tr>
<tr><td>7</td><td>Delaware</td><td>25.6</td><td>8</td><td>Florida</td><td>24.2</td></tr>
<tr><td>8</td><td>Florida</td><td>24.2</td><td>9</td><td>North Carolina</td><td>23.0</td></tr>
<tr><td>5</td><td>Georgia</td><td>31.7</td><td>10</td><td>Virginia</td><td>22.0</td></tr>
<tr><td>39</td><td>Hawaii</td><td>3.1</td><td>11</td><td>Tennessee</td><td>21.8</td></tr>
<tr><td>49</td><td>Idaho</td><td>0.5</td><td>12</td><td>New York</td><td>19.8</td></tr>
<tr><td>15</td><td>Illinois</td><td>17.1</td><td>13</td><td>Arkansas</td><td>19.2</td></tr>
<tr><td>21</td><td>Indiana</td><td>11.1</td><td>14</td><td>New Jersey</td><td>17.2</td></tr>
<tr><td>35</td><td>Iowa</td><td>3.8</td><td>15</td><td>Illinois</td><td>17.1</td></tr>
<tr><td>29</td><td>Kansas</td><td>7.2</td><td>16</td><td>Michigan</td><td>16.7</td></tr>
<tr><td>27</td><td>Kentucky</td><td>9.0</td><td>17</td><td>Ohio</td><td>16.0</td></tr>
<tr><td>2</td><td>Louisiana</td><td>40.9</td><td>18</td><td>Pennsylvania</td><td>15.1</td></tr>
<tr><td>43</td><td>Maine</td><td>1.6</td><td>19</td><td>Missouri</td><td>14.7</td></tr>
<tr><td>4</td><td>Maryland</td><td>34.5</td><td>20</td><td>Connecticut</td><td>12.5</td></tr>
<tr><td>21</td><td>Massachusetts</td><td>11.1</td><td>21</td><td>Indiana</td><td>11.1</td></tr>
<tr><td>16</td><td>Michigan</td><td>16.7</td><td>21</td><td>Massachusetts</td><td>11.1</td></tr>
<tr><td>30</td><td>Minnesota</td><td>6.6</td><td>23</td><td>Texas</td><td>11.0</td></tr>
<tr><td>1</td><td>Mississippi</td><td>43.3</td><td>24</td><td>Rhode Island</td><td>9.4</td></tr>
<tr><td>19</td><td>Missouri</td><td>14.7</td><td>24</td><td>Wisconsin</td><td>9.4</td></tr>
<tr><td>49</td><td>Montana</td><td>0.5</td><td>26</td><td>Oklahoma</td><td>9.2</td></tr>
<tr><td>31</td><td>Nebraska</td><td>6.0</td><td>27</td><td>Kentucky</td><td>9.0</td></tr>
<tr><td>28</td><td>Nevada</td><td>8.4</td><td>28</td><td>Nevada</td><td>8.4</td></tr>
<tr><td>41</td><td>New Hampshire</td><td>1.8</td><td>29</td><td>Kansas</td><td>7.2</td></tr>
<tr><td>14</td><td>New Jersey</td><td>17.2</td><td>30</td><td>Minnesota</td><td>6.6</td></tr>
<tr><td>41</td><td>New Mexico</td><td>1.8</td><td>31</td><td>Nebraska</td><td>6.0</td></tr>
<tr><td>12</td><td>New York</td><td>19.8</td><td>32</td><td>California</td><td>5.9</td></tr>
<tr><td>9</td><td>North Carolina</td><td>23.0</td><td>33</td><td>Washington</td><td>5.0</td></tr>
<tr><td>45</td><td>North Dakota</td><td>1.2</td><td>34</td><td>Colorado</td><td>4.3</td></tr>
<tr><td>17</td><td>Ohio</td><td>16.0</td><td>35</td><td>Alaska</td><td>3.8</td></tr>
<tr><td>26</td><td>Oklahoma</td><td>9.2</td><td>35</td><td>Iowa</td><td>3.8</td></tr>
<tr><td>40</td><td>Oregon</td><td>2.3</td><td>37</td><td>Arizona</td><td>3.7</td></tr>
<tr><td>18</td><td>Pennsylvania</td><td>15.1</td><td>38</td><td>West Virginia</td><td>3.2</td></tr>
<tr><td>24</td><td>Rhode Island</td><td>9.4</td><td>39</td><td>Hawaii</td><td>3.1</td></tr>
<tr><td>3</td><td>South Carolina</td><td>34.7</td><td>40</td><td>Oregon</td><td>2.3</td></tr>
<tr><td>44</td><td>South Dakota</td><td>1.3</td><td>41</td><td>New Hampshire</td><td>1.8</td></tr>
<tr><td>11</td><td>Tennessee</td><td>21.8</td><td>41</td><td>New Mexico</td><td>1.8</td></tr>
<tr><td>23</td><td>Texas</td><td>11.0</td><td>43</td><td>Maine</td><td>1.6</td></tr>
<tr><td>48</td><td>Utah</td><td>0.6</td><td>44</td><td>South Dakota</td><td>1.3</td></tr>
<tr><td>46</td><td>Vermont</td><td>0.9</td><td>45</td><td>North Dakota</td><td>1.2</td></tr>
<tr><td>10</td><td>Virginia</td><td>22.0</td><td>46</td><td>Vermont</td><td>0.9</td></tr>
<tr><td>33</td><td>Washington</td><td>5.0</td><td>47</td><td>Wyoming</td><td>0.8</td></tr>
<tr><td>38</td><td>West Virginia</td><td>3.2</td><td>48</td><td>Utah</td><td>0.6</td></tr>
<tr><td>24</td><td>Wisconsin</td><td>9.4</td><td>49</td><td>Idaho</td><td>0.5</td></tr>
<tr><td>47</td><td>Wyoming</td><td>0.8</td><td>49</td><td>Montana</td><td>0.5</td></tr>
<tr><td></td><td></td><td></td><td></td><td>District of Columbia</td><td>68.0</td></tr>
</table>

Source: Morgan Quitno Press using data from U.S. Dept. of Health and Human Services, Nat'l Center for Health Statistics "National Vital Statistics Reports" (Vol. 54, No. 8, December 29, 2005)
Preliminary data by state of residence. By race of mother.

Births to Hispanic Women in 2004

National Total = 944,993 Live Births to Hispanic Women*

ALPHA ORDER					RANK ORDER			
RANK	STATE	BIRTHS	% of USA		RANK	STATE	BIRTHS	% of USA
33	Alabama	3,346	0.4%		1	California	275,365	29.1%
42	Alaska	877	0.1%		2	Texas	189,586	20.1%
6	Arizona	41,427	4.4%		3	New York	57,081	6.0%
31	Arkansas	3,510	0.4%		4	Florida	55,407	5.9%
1	California	275,365	29.1%		5	Illinois	42,608	4.5%
8	Colorado	21,746	2.3%		6	Arizona	41,427	4.4%
20	Connecticut	7,598	0.8%		7	New Jersey	27,312	2.9%
40	Delaware	1,519	0.2%		8	Colorado	21,746	2.3%
4	Florida	55,407	5.9%		9	Georgia	20,113	2.1%
9	Georgia	20,113	2.1%		10	North Carolina	17,295	1.8%
36	Hawaii	2,679	0.3%		11	New Mexico	15,163	1.6%
34	Idaho	3,241	0.3%		12	Washington	14,254	1.5%
5	Illinois	42,608	4.5%		13	Nevada	13,060	1.4%
21	Indiana	7,257	0.8%		14	Virginia	11,691	1.2%
35	Iowa	2,835	0.3%		15	Pennsylvania	11,686	1.2%
27	Kansas	5,472	0.6%		16	Massachusetts	9,847	1.0%
38	Kentucky	2,177	0.2%		17	Oregon	8,836	0.9%
39	Louisiana	1,954	0.2%		18	Michigan	7,826	0.8%
47	Maine	180	0.0%		19	Maryland	7,637	0.8%
19	Maryland	7,637	0.8%		20	Connecticut	7,598	0.8%
16	Massachusetts	9,847	1.0%		21	Indiana	7,257	0.8%
18	Michigan	7,826	0.8%		22	Utah	7,180	0.8%
28	Minnesota	5,330	0.6%		23	Oklahoma	6,007	0.6%
41	Mississippi	1,052	0.1%		24	Wisconsin	5,888	0.6%
30	Missouri	3,844	0.4%		25	Tennessee	5,838	0.6%
46	Montana	374	0.0%		26	Ohio	5,737	0.6%
32	Nebraska	3,446	0.4%		27	Kansas	5,472	0.6%
13	Nevada	13,060	1.4%		28	Minnesota	5,330	0.6%
44	New Hampshire	461	0.0%		29	South Carolina	4,334	0.5%
7	New Jersey	27,312	2.9%		30	Missouri	3,844	0.4%
11	New Mexico	15,163	1.6%		31	Arkansas	3,510	0.4%
3	New York	57,081	6.0%		32	Nebraska	3,446	0.4%
10	North Carolina	17,295	1.8%		33	Alabama	3,346	0.4%
48	North Dakota	167	0.0%		34	Idaho	3,241	0.3%
26	Ohio	5,737	0.6%		35	Iowa	2,835	0.3%
23	Oklahoma	6,007	0.6%		36	Hawaii	2,679	0.3%
17	Oregon	8,836	0.9%		37	Rhode Island	2,429	0.3%
15	Pennsylvania	11,686	1.2%		38	Kentucky	2,177	0.2%
37	Rhode Island	2,429	0.3%		39	Louisiana	1,954	0.2%
29	South Carolina	4,334	0.5%		40	Delaware	1,519	0.2%
45	South Dakota	395	0.0%		41	Mississippi	1,052	0.1%
25	Tennessee	5,838	0.6%		42	Alaska	877	0.1%
2	Texas	189,586	20.1%		43	Wyoming	699	0.1%
22	Utah	7,180	0.8%		44	New Hampshire	461	0.0%
50	Vermont	75	0.0%		45	South Dakota	395	0.0%
14	Virginia	11,691	1.2%		46	Montana	374	0.0%
12	Washington	14,254	1.5%		47	Maine	180	0.0%
49	West Virginia	151	0.0%		48	North Dakota	167	0.0%
24	Wisconsin	5,888	0.6%		49	West Virginia	151	0.0%
43	Wyoming	699	0.1%		50	Vermont	75	0.0%
						District of Columbia	998	0.1%

Source: U.S. Department of Health and Human Services, National Center for Health Statistics
   "National Vital Statistics Reports" (Vol. 54, No. 8, December 29, 2005)
*Preliminary data by state of residence. By race of mother. Persons of Hispanic origin may be of any race.

Hispanic Births as a Percent of All Births in 2004

National Percent = 23.0% of Live Births*

ALPHA ORDER

RANK ORDER

RANK	STATE	PERCENT	RANK	STATE	PERCENT
38	Alabama	5.6	1	New Mexico	53.4
29	Alaska	8.5	2	California	50.5
4	Arizona	44.2	3	Texas	49.3
28	Arkansas	9.1	4	Arizona	44.2
2	California	50.5	5	Nevada	37.1
6	Colorado	31.7	6	Colorado	31.7
13	Connecticut	18.0	7	Florida	25.4
21	Delaware	13.4	8	New Jersey	23.8
7	Florida	25.4	9	Illinois	23.5
16	Georgia	14.5	10	New York	22.8
15	Hawaii	14.7	11	Oregon	19.3
17	Idaho	14.4	12	Rhode Island	19.0
9	Illinois	23.5	13	Connecticut	18.0
30	Indiana	8.4	14	Washington	17.4
35	Iowa	7.4	15	Hawaii	14.7
20	Kansas	13.8	16	Georgia	14.5
40	Kentucky	4.0	17	Idaho	14.4
45	Louisiana	3.0	17	North Carolina	14.4
48	Maine	1.3	19	Utah	14.2
27	Maryland	10.2	20	Kansas	13.8
23	Massachusetts	12.5	21	Delaware	13.4
37	Michigan	6.0	22	Nebraska	13.1
34	Minnesota	7.5	23	Massachusetts	12.5
46	Mississippi	2.5	24	Oklahoma	11.7
39	Missouri	4.9	25	Virginia	11.3
43	Montana	3.2	26	Wyoming	10.3
22	Nebraska	13.1	27	Maryland	10.2
5	Nevada	37.1	28	Arkansas	9.1
43	New Hampshire	3.2	29	Alaska	8.5
8	New Jersey	23.8	30	Indiana	8.4
1	New Mexico	53.4	30	Wisconsin	8.4
10	New York	22.8	32	Pennsylvania	8.0
17	North Carolina	14.4	33	South Carolina	7.7
47	North Dakota	2.0	34	Minnesota	7.5
41	Ohio	3.8	35	Iowa	7.4
24	Oklahoma	11.7	36	Tennessee	7.3
11	Oregon	19.3	37	Michigan	6.0
32	Pennsylvania	8.0	38	Alabama	5.6
12	Rhode Island	19.0	39	Missouri	4.9
33	South Carolina	7.7	40	Kentucky	4.0
42	South Dakota	3.5	41	Ohio	3.8
36	Tennessee	7.3	42	South Dakota	3.5
3	Texas	49.3	43	Montana	3.2
19	Utah	14.2	43	New Hampshire	3.2
49	Vermont	1.1	45	Louisiana	3.0
25	Virginia	11.3	46	Mississippi	2.5
14	Washington	17.4	47	North Dakota	2.0
50	West Virginia	0.7	48	Maine	1.3
30	Wisconsin	8.4	49	Vermont	1.1
26	Wyoming	10.3	50	West Virginia	0.7

District of Columbia 12.6

Source: Morgan Quitno Press using data from U.S. Dept. of Health and Human Services, Nat'l Center for Health Statistics
"National Vital Statistics Reports" (Vol. 54, No. 8, December 29, 2005)
*Preliminary data by state of residence. By race of mother. Persons of Hispanic origin may be of any race.

Births of Low Birthweight in 2004

National Total = 333,363 Live Births*

RANK	STATE	BIRTHS	% of USA
19	Alabama	6,193	1.9%
47	Alaska	620	0.2%
17	Arizona	6,744	2.0%
29	Arkansas	3,590	1.1%
1	California	36,520	11.0%
20	Colorado	6,167	1.8%
31	Connecticut	3,284	1.0%
42	Delaware	1,017	0.3%
4	Florida	18,533	5.6%
6	Georgia	12,913	3.9%
40	Hawaii	1,444	0.4%
39	Idaho	1,532	0.5%
5	Illinois	15,198	4.6%
15	Indiana	7,025	2.1%
35	Iowa	2,691	0.8%
32	Kansas	2,889	0.9%
26	Kentucky	4,683	1.4%
14	Louisiana	7,128	2.1%
44	Maine	892	0.3%
16	Maryland	6,938	2.1%
21	Massachusetts	6,128	1.8%
10	Michigan	10,771	3.2%
27	Minnesota	4,590	1.4%
24	Mississippi	4,966	1.5%
18	Missouri	6,456	1.9%
45	Montana	876	0.3%
38	Nebraska	1,843	0.6%
33	Nevada	2,815	0.8%
43	New Hampshire	990	0.3%
11	New Jersey	9,423	2.8%
36	New Mexico	2,299	0.7%
3	New York	20,573	6.2%
9	North Carolina	10,787	3.2%
49	North Dakota	540	0.2%
7	Ohio	12,678	3.8%
28	Oklahoma	4,103	1.2%
34	Oregon	2,742	0.8%
8	Pennsylvania	11,661	3.5%
41	Rhode Island	1,022	0.3%
22	South Carolina	5,772	1.7%
46	South Dakota	782	0.2%
13	Tennessee	7,327	2.2%
2	Texas	30,751	9.2%
30	Utah	3,395	1.0%
50	Vermont	427	0.1%
12	Virginia	8,625	2.6%
23	Washington	5,068	1.5%
37	West Virginia	1,919	0.6%
25	Wisconsin	4,911	1.5%
48	Wyoming	585	0.2%

RANK	STATE	BIRTHS	% of USA
1	California	36,520	11.0%
2	Texas	30,751	9.2%
3	New York	20,573	6.2%
4	Florida	18,533	5.6%
5	Illinois	15,198	4.6%
6	Georgia	12,913	3.9%
7	Ohio	12,678	3.8%
8	Pennsylvania	11,661	3.5%
9	North Carolina	10,787	3.2%
10	Michigan	10,771	3.2%
11	New Jersey	9,423	2.8%
12	Virginia	8,625	2.6%
13	Tennessee	7,327	2.2%
14	Louisiana	7,128	2.1%
15	Indiana	7,025	2.1%
16	Maryland	6,938	2.1%
17	Arizona	6,744	2.0%
18	Missouri	6,456	1.9%
19	Alabama	6,193	1.9%
20	Colorado	6,167	1.8%
21	Massachusetts	6,128	1.8%
22	South Carolina	5,772	1.7%
23	Washington	5,068	1.5%
24	Mississippi	4,966	1.5%
25	Wisconsin	4,911	1.5%
26	Kentucky	4,683	1.4%
27	Minnesota	4,590	1.4%
28	Oklahoma	4,103	1.2%
29	Arkansas	3,590	1.1%
30	Utah	3,395	1.0%
31	Connecticut	3,284	1.0%
32	Kansas	2,889	0.9%
33	Nevada	2,815	0.8%
34	Oregon	2,742	0.8%
35	Iowa	2,691	0.8%
36	New Mexico	2,299	0.7%
37	West Virginia	1,919	0.6%
38	Nebraska	1,843	0.6%
39	Idaho	1,532	0.5%
40	Hawaii	1,444	0.4%
41	Rhode Island	1,022	0.3%
42	Delaware	1,017	0.3%
43	New Hampshire	990	0.3%
44	Maine	892	0.3%
45	Montana	876	0.3%
46	South Dakota	782	0.2%
47	Alaska	620	0.2%
48	Wyoming	585	0.2%
49	North Dakota	540	0.2%
50	Vermont	427	0.1%
	District of Columbia	880	0.3%

Source: Morgan Quitno Press using data from U.S. Dept. of Health and Human Services, Nat'l Center for Health Statistics "National Vital Statistics Reports" (Vol. 54, No. 8, December 29, 2005)

*Preliminary data by state of residence. Births of less than 2,500 grams (5 pounds 8 ounces).

Births of Low Birthweight as a Percent of All Births in 2004

National Percent = 8.1% of Live Births*

ALPHA ORDER

RANK	STATE	PERCENT		RANK	STATE	PERCENT
3	Alabama	10.4		1	Mississippi	11.6
49	Alaska	6.0		2	Louisiana	10.9
35	Arizona	7.2		3	Alabama	10.4
5	Arkansas	9.3		4	South Carolina	10.2
42	California	6.7		5	Arkansas	9.3
10	Colorado	9.0		5	Georgia	9.3
31	Connecticut	7.8		5	Maryland	9.3
10	Delaware	9.0		8	Tennessee	9.2
15	Florida	8.5		8	West Virginia	9.2
5	Georgia	9.3		10	Colorado	9.0
30	Hawaii	7.9		10	Delaware	9.0
40	Idaho	6.8		10	North Carolina	9.0
17	Illinois	8.4		13	Kentucky	8.6
23	Indiana	8.1		13	Wyoming	8.6
36	Iowa	7.0		15	Florida	8.5
34	Kansas	7.3		15	Ohio	8.5
13	Kentucky	8.6		17	Illinois	8.4
2	Louisiana	10.9		18	Michigan	8.3
47	Maine	6.4		18	Missouri	8.3
5	Maryland	9.3		18	Virginia	8.3
31	Massachusetts	7.8		21	New Jersey	8.2
18	Michigan	8.3		21	New York	8.2
45	Minnesota	6.5		23	Indiana	8.1
1	Mississippi	11.6		23	New Mexico	8.1
18	Missouri	8.3		25	Nevada	8.0
33	Montana	7.6		25	Oklahoma	8.0
36	Nebraska	7.0		25	Pennsylvania	8.0
25	Nevada	8.0		25	Rhode Island	8.0
40	New Hampshire	6.8		25	Texas	8.0
21	New Jersey	8.2		30	Hawaii	7.9
23	New Mexico	8.1		31	Connecticut	7.8
21	New York	8.2		31	Massachusetts	7.8
10	North Carolina	9.0		33	Montana	7.6
44	North Dakota	6.6		34	Kansas	7.3
15	Ohio	8.5		35	Arizona	7.2
25	Oklahoma	8.0		36	Iowa	7.0
49	Oregon	6.0		36	Nebraska	7.0
25	Pennsylvania	8.0		36	Wisconsin	7.0
25	Rhode Island	8.0		39	South Dakota	6.9
4	South Carolina	10.2		40	Idaho	6.8
39	South Dakota	6.9		40	New Hampshire	6.8
8	Tennessee	9.2		42	California	6.7
25	Texas	8.0		42	Utah	6.7
42	Utah	6.7		44	North Dakota	6.6
45	Vermont	6.5		45	Minnesota	6.5
18	Virginia	8.3		45	Vermont	6.5
48	Washington	6.2		47	Maine	6.4
8	West Virginia	9.2		48	Washington	6.2
36	Wisconsin	7.0		49	Alaska	6.0
13	Wyoming	8.6		49	Oregon	6.0
					District of Columbia	11.1

Source: U.S. Department of Health and Human Services, National Center for Health Statistics
"National Vital Statistics Reports" (Vol. 54, No. 8, December 29, 2005)
*Preliminary data by state of residence. Births of less than 2,500 grams (5 pounds 8 ounces).

Births of Low Birthweight to White Women in 2004

National Total = 229,317 Live Births*

<table>
<tr><td colspan="4">ALPHA ORDER</td><td colspan="4">RANK ORDER</td></tr>
<tr><td>RANK</td><td>STATE</td><td>BIRTHS</td><td>% of USA</td><td>RANK</td><td>STATE</td><td>BIRTHS</td><td>% of USA</td></tr>
<tr><td>23</td><td>Alabama</td><td>3,406</td><td>1.5%</td><td>1</td><td>California</td><td>27,362</td><td>11.9%</td></tr>
<tr><td>49</td><td>Alaska</td><td>369</td><td>0.2%</td><td>2</td><td>Texas</td><td>23,908</td><td>10.4%</td></tr>
<tr><td>12</td><td>Arizona</td><td>5,682</td><td>2.5%</td><td>3</td><td>New York</td><td>12,514</td><td>5.5%</td></tr>
<tr><td>31</td><td>Arkansas</td><td>2,399</td><td>1.0%</td><td>4</td><td>Florida</td><td>11,354</td><td>5.0%</td></tr>
<tr><td>1</td><td>California</td><td>27,362</td><td>11.9%</td><td>5</td><td>Illinois</td><td>10,002</td><td>4.4%</td></tr>
<tr><td>14</td><td>Colorado</td><td>5,439</td><td>2.4%</td><td>6</td><td>Ohio</td><td>8,992</td><td>3.9%</td></tr>
<tr><td>29</td><td>Connecticut</td><td>2,446</td><td>1.1%</td><td>7</td><td>Pennsylvania</td><td>8,243</td><td>3.6%</td></tr>
<tr><td>45</td><td>Delaware</td><td>570</td><td>0.2%</td><td>8</td><td>Michigan</td><td>7,299</td><td>3.2%</td></tr>
<tr><td>4</td><td>Florida</td><td>11,354</td><td>5.0%</td><td>9</td><td>North Carolina</td><td>6,469</td><td>2.8%</td></tr>
<tr><td>10</td><td>Georgia</td><td>6,374</td><td>2.8%</td><td>10</td><td>Georgia</td><td>6,374</td><td>2.8%</td></tr>
<tr><td>50</td><td>Hawaii</td><td>326</td><td>0.1%</td><td>11</td><td>New Jersey</td><td>6,058</td><td>2.6%</td></tr>
<tr><td>39</td><td>Idaho</td><td>1,455</td><td>0.6%</td><td>12</td><td>Arizona</td><td>5,682</td><td>2.5%</td></tr>
<tr><td>5</td><td>Illinois</td><td>10,002</td><td>4.4%</td><td>13</td><td>Indiana</td><td>5,581</td><td>2.4%</td></tr>
<tr><td>13</td><td>Indiana</td><td>5,581</td><td>2.4%</td><td>14</td><td>Colorado</td><td>5,439</td><td>2.4%</td></tr>
<tr><td>30</td><td>Iowa</td><td>2,429</td><td>1.1%</td><td>15</td><td>Virginia</td><td>5,103</td><td>2.2%</td></tr>
<tr><td>33</td><td>Kansas</td><td>2,386</td><td>1.0%</td><td>16</td><td>Tennessee</td><td>4,893</td><td>2.1%</td></tr>
<tr><td>19</td><td>Kentucky</td><td>3,991</td><td>1.7%</td><td>17</td><td>Massachusetts</td><td>4,802</td><td>2.1%</td></tr>
<tr><td>27</td><td>Louisiana</td><td>2,972</td><td>1.3%</td><td>18</td><td>Missouri</td><td>4,683</td><td>2.0%</td></tr>
<tr><td>41</td><td>Maine</td><td>843</td><td>0.4%</td><td>19</td><td>Kentucky</td><td>3,991</td><td>1.7%</td></tr>
<tr><td>24</td><td>Maryland</td><td>3,205</td><td>1.4%</td><td>20</td><td>Washington</td><td>3,895</td><td>1.7%</td></tr>
<tr><td>17</td><td>Massachusetts</td><td>4,802</td><td>2.1%</td><td>21</td><td>Wisconsin</td><td>3,780</td><td>1.6%</td></tr>
<tr><td>8</td><td>Michigan</td><td>7,299</td><td>3.2%</td><td>22</td><td>Minnesota</td><td>3,693</td><td>1.6%</td></tr>
<tr><td>22</td><td>Minnesota</td><td>3,693</td><td>1.6%</td><td>23</td><td>Alabama</td><td>3,406</td><td>1.5%</td></tr>
<tr><td>35</td><td>Mississippi</td><td>2,026</td><td>0.9%</td><td>24</td><td>Maryland</td><td>3,205</td><td>1.4%</td></tr>
<tr><td>18</td><td>Missouri</td><td>4,683</td><td>2.0%</td><td>25</td><td>Utah</td><td>3,137</td><td>1.4%</td></tr>
<tr><td>43</td><td>Montana</td><td>747</td><td>0.3%</td><td>26</td><td>Oklahoma</td><td>3,083</td><td>1.3%</td></tr>
<tr><td>38</td><td>Nebraska</td><td>1,612</td><td>0.7%</td><td>27</td><td>Louisiana</td><td>2,972</td><td>1.3%</td></tr>
<tr><td>34</td><td>Nevada</td><td>2,090</td><td>0.9%</td><td>28</td><td>South Carolina</td><td>2,792</td><td>1.2%</td></tr>
<tr><td>40</td><td>New Hampshire</td><td>936</td><td>0.4%</td><td>29</td><td>Connecticut</td><td>2,446</td><td>1.1%</td></tr>
<tr><td>11</td><td>New Jersey</td><td>6,058</td><td>2.6%</td><td>30</td><td>Iowa</td><td>2,429</td><td>1.1%</td></tr>
<tr><td>36</td><td>New Mexico</td><td>1,932</td><td>0.8%</td><td>31</td><td>Arkansas</td><td>2,399</td><td>1.0%</td></tr>
<tr><td>3</td><td>New York</td><td>12,514</td><td>5.5%</td><td>32</td><td>Oregon</td><td>2,393</td><td>1.0%</td></tr>
<tr><td>9</td><td>North Carolina</td><td>6,469</td><td>2.8%</td><td>33</td><td>Kansas</td><td>2,386</td><td>1.0%</td></tr>
<tr><td>47</td><td>North Dakota</td><td>456</td><td>0.2%</td><td>34</td><td>Nevada</td><td>2,090</td><td>0.9%</td></tr>
<tr><td>6</td><td>Ohio</td><td>8,992</td><td>3.9%</td><td>35</td><td>Mississippi</td><td>2,026</td><td>0.9%</td></tr>
<tr><td>26</td><td>Oklahoma</td><td>3,083</td><td>1.3%</td><td>36</td><td>New Mexico</td><td>1,932</td><td>0.8%</td></tr>
<tr><td>32</td><td>Oregon</td><td>2,393</td><td>1.0%</td><td>37</td><td>West Virginia</td><td>1,819</td><td>0.8%</td></tr>
<tr><td>7</td><td>Pennsylvania</td><td>8,243</td><td>3.6%</td><td>38</td><td>Nebraska</td><td>1,612</td><td>0.7%</td></tr>
<tr><td>42</td><td>Rhode Island</td><td>805</td><td>0.4%</td><td>39</td><td>Idaho</td><td>1,455</td><td>0.6%</td></tr>
<tr><td>28</td><td>South Carolina</td><td>2,792</td><td>1.2%</td><td>40</td><td>New Hampshire</td><td>936</td><td>0.4%</td></tr>
<tr><td>44</td><td>South Dakota</td><td>626</td><td>0.3%</td><td>41</td><td>Maine</td><td>843</td><td>0.4%</td></tr>
<tr><td>16</td><td>Tennessee</td><td>4,893</td><td>2.1%</td><td>42</td><td>Rhode Island</td><td>805</td><td>0.4%</td></tr>
<tr><td>2</td><td>Texas</td><td>23,908</td><td>10.4%</td><td>43</td><td>Montana</td><td>747</td><td>0.3%</td></tr>
<tr><td>25</td><td>Utah</td><td>3,137</td><td>1.4%</td><td>44</td><td>South Dakota</td><td>626</td><td>0.3%</td></tr>
<tr><td>48</td><td>Vermont</td><td>402</td><td>0.2%</td><td>45</td><td>Delaware</td><td>570</td><td>0.2%</td></tr>
<tr><td>15</td><td>Virginia</td><td>5,103</td><td>2.2%</td><td>46</td><td>Wyoming</td><td>541</td><td>0.2%</td></tr>
<tr><td>20</td><td>Washington</td><td>3,895</td><td>1.7%</td><td>47</td><td>North Dakota</td><td>456</td><td>0.2%</td></tr>
<tr><td>37</td><td>West Virginia</td><td>1,819</td><td>0.8%</td><td>48</td><td>Vermont</td><td>402</td><td>0.2%</td></tr>
<tr><td>21</td><td>Wisconsin</td><td>3,780</td><td>1.6%</td><td>49</td><td>Alaska</td><td>369</td><td>0.2%</td></tr>
<tr><td>46</td><td>Wyoming</td><td>541</td><td>0.2%</td><td>50</td><td>Hawaii</td><td>326</td><td>0.1%</td></tr>
<tr><td></td><td></td><td></td><td></td><td></td><td>District of Columbia</td><td>138</td><td>0.1%</td></tr>
</table>

Source: Morgan Quitno Press using data from U.S. Dept. of Health and Human Services, Nat'l Center for Health Statistics
"National Vital Statistics Reports" (Vol. 54, No. 8, December 29, 2005)
*Preliminary data by state of residence. Births of less than 2,500 grams (5 pounds 8 ounces).

Births of Low Birthweight to White Women
As a Percent of All Births to White Women in 2004
National Percent = 7.1% of Live Births to White Women*

<table>
<tr><td colspan="3">ALPHA ORDER</td><td colspan="3">RANK ORDER</td></tr>
<tr><td>RANK</td><td>STATE</td><td>PERCENT</td><td>RANK</td><td>STATE</td><td>PERCENT</td></tr>
<tr><td>5</td><td>Alabama</td><td>8.4</td><td>1</td><td>West Virginia</td><td>9.1</td></tr>
<tr><td>50</td><td>Alaska</td><td>5.6</td><td>2</td><td>Colorado</td><td>8.7</td></tr>
<tr><td>30</td><td>Arizona</td><td>7.0</td><td>3</td><td>Mississippi</td><td>8.6</td></tr>
<tr><td>10</td><td>Arkansas</td><td>7.9</td><td>4</td><td>Wyoming</td><td>8.5</td></tr>
<tr><td>46</td><td>California</td><td>6.2</td><td>5</td><td>Alabama</td><td>8.4</td></tr>
<tr><td>2</td><td>Colorado</td><td>8.7</td><td>6</td><td>Kentucky</td><td>8.2</td></tr>
<tr><td>26</td><td>Connecticut</td><td>7.1</td><td>7</td><td>New Mexico</td><td>8.1</td></tr>
<tr><td>22</td><td>Delaware</td><td>7.2</td><td>7</td><td>Tennessee</td><td>8.1</td></tr>
<tr><td>22</td><td>Florida</td><td>7.2</td><td>9</td><td>Louisiana</td><td>8.0</td></tr>
<tr><td>26</td><td>Georgia</td><td>7.1</td><td>10</td><td>Arkansas</td><td>7.9</td></tr>
<tr><td>42</td><td>Hawaii</td><td>6.3</td><td>11</td><td>South Carolina</td><td>7.8</td></tr>
<tr><td>39</td><td>Idaho</td><td>6.7</td><td>12</td><td>Oklahoma</td><td>7.7</td></tr>
<tr><td>26</td><td>Illinois</td><td>7.1</td><td>13</td><td>Montana</td><td>7.6</td></tr>
<tr><td>15</td><td>Indiana</td><td>7.4</td><td>14</td><td>Massachusetts</td><td>7.5</td></tr>
<tr><td>34</td><td>Iowa</td><td>6.8</td><td>15</td><td>Indiana</td><td>7.4</td></tr>
<tr><td>34</td><td>Kansas</td><td>6.8</td><td>15</td><td>North Carolina</td><td>7.4</td></tr>
<tr><td>6</td><td>Kentucky</td><td>8.2</td><td>15</td><td>Ohio</td><td>7.4</td></tr>
<tr><td>9</td><td>Louisiana</td><td>8.0</td><td>15</td><td>Rhode Island</td><td>7.4</td></tr>
<tr><td>42</td><td>Maine</td><td>6.3</td><td>19</td><td>Maryland</td><td>7.3</td></tr>
<tr><td>19</td><td>Maryland</td><td>7.3</td><td>19</td><td>Missouri</td><td>7.3</td></tr>
<tr><td>14</td><td>Massachusetts</td><td>7.5</td><td>19</td><td>Texas</td><td>7.3</td></tr>
<tr><td>26</td><td>Michigan</td><td>7.1</td><td>22</td><td>Delaware</td><td>7.2</td></tr>
<tr><td>46</td><td>Minnesota</td><td>6.2</td><td>22</td><td>Florida</td><td>7.2</td></tr>
<tr><td>3</td><td>Mississippi</td><td>8.6</td><td>22</td><td>Nevada</td><td>7.2</td></tr>
<tr><td>19</td><td>Missouri</td><td>7.3</td><td>22</td><td>New Jersey</td><td>7.2</td></tr>
<tr><td>13</td><td>Montana</td><td>7.6</td><td>26</td><td>Connecticut</td><td>7.1</td></tr>
<tr><td>34</td><td>Nebraska</td><td>6.8</td><td>26</td><td>Georgia</td><td>7.1</td></tr>
<tr><td>22</td><td>Nevada</td><td>7.2</td><td>26</td><td>Illinois</td><td>7.1</td></tr>
<tr><td>34</td><td>New Hampshire</td><td>6.8</td><td>26</td><td>Michigan</td><td>7.1</td></tr>
<tr><td>22</td><td>New Jersey</td><td>7.2</td><td>30</td><td>Arizona</td><td>7.0</td></tr>
<tr><td>7</td><td>New Mexico</td><td>8.1</td><td>30</td><td>New York</td><td>7.0</td></tr>
<tr><td>30</td><td>New York</td><td>7.0</td><td>30</td><td>Pennsylvania</td><td>7.0</td></tr>
<tr><td>15</td><td>North Carolina</td><td>7.4</td><td>33</td><td>Virginia</td><td>6.9</td></tr>
<tr><td>40</td><td>North Dakota</td><td>6.5</td><td>34</td><td>Iowa</td><td>6.8</td></tr>
<tr><td>15</td><td>Ohio</td><td>7.4</td><td>34</td><td>Kansas</td><td>6.8</td></tr>
<tr><td>12</td><td>Oklahoma</td><td>7.7</td><td>34</td><td>Nebraska</td><td>6.8</td></tr>
<tr><td>48</td><td>Oregon</td><td>5.8</td><td>34</td><td>New Hampshire</td><td>6.8</td></tr>
<tr><td>30</td><td>Pennsylvania</td><td>7.0</td><td>34</td><td>South Dakota</td><td>6.8</td></tr>
<tr><td>15</td><td>Rhode Island</td><td>7.4</td><td>39</td><td>Idaho</td><td>6.7</td></tr>
<tr><td>11</td><td>South Carolina</td><td>7.8</td><td>40</td><td>North Dakota</td><td>6.5</td></tr>
<tr><td>34</td><td>South Dakota</td><td>6.8</td><td>40</td><td>Utah</td><td>6.5</td></tr>
<tr><td>7</td><td>Tennessee</td><td>8.1</td><td>42</td><td>Hawaii</td><td>6.3</td></tr>
<tr><td>19</td><td>Texas</td><td>7.3</td><td>42</td><td>Maine</td><td>6.3</td></tr>
<tr><td>40</td><td>Utah</td><td>6.5</td><td>42</td><td>Vermont</td><td>6.3</td></tr>
<tr><td>42</td><td>Vermont</td><td>6.3</td><td>42</td><td>Wisconsin</td><td>6.3</td></tr>
<tr><td>33</td><td>Virginia</td><td>6.9</td><td>46</td><td>California</td><td>6.2</td></tr>
<tr><td>48</td><td>Washington</td><td>5.8</td><td>46</td><td>Minnesota</td><td>6.2</td></tr>
<tr><td>1</td><td>West Virginia</td><td>9.1</td><td>48</td><td>Oregon</td><td>5.8</td></tr>
<tr><td>42</td><td>Wisconsin</td><td>6.3</td><td>48</td><td>Washington</td><td>5.8</td></tr>
<tr><td>4</td><td>Wyoming</td><td>8.5</td><td>50</td><td>Alaska</td><td>5.6</td></tr>
<tr><td></td><td></td><td></td><td></td><td>District of Columbia</td><td>6.0</td></tr>
</table>

Source: U.S. Department of Health and Human Services, National Center for Health Statistics
    "National Vital Statistics Reports" (Vol. 54, No. 8, December 29, 2005)
*Preliminary data by state of residence. Births of less than 2,500 grams (5 pounds 8 ounces).

Births of Low Birthweight to Black Women in 2004

National Total = 82,074 Live Births*

ALPHA ORDER					RANK ORDER			
RANK	STATE	BIRTHS	% of USA		RANK	STATE	BIRTHS	% of USA
16	Alabama	2,727	3.3%		1	Florida	6,595	8.0%
41	Alaska	44	0.1%		2	New York	6,171	7.5%
31	Arizona	384	0.5%		3	Georgia	6,116	7.5%
21	Arkansas	1,146	1.4%		4	Texas	5,854	7.1%
8	California	3,917	4.8%		5	Illinois	4,477	5.5%
29	Colorado	422	0.5%		6	Louisiana	4,037	4.9%
24	Connecticut	649	0.8%		7	North Carolina	3,922	4.8%
33	Delaware	336	0.4%		8	California	3,917	4.8%
1	Florida	6,595	8.0%		9	Maryland	3,318	4.0%
3	Georgia	6,116	7.5%		10	Ohio	3,300	4.0%
40	Hawaii	54	0.1%		11	Michigan	3,082	3.8%
NA	Idaho**	NA	NA		12	Virginia	2,908	3.5%
5	Illinois	4,477	5.5%		13	South Carolina	2,883	3.5%
20	Indiana	1,313	1.6%		14	Mississippi	2,870	3.5%
35	Iowa	163	0.2%		15	Pennsylvania	2,848	3.5%
32	Kansas	383	0.5%		16	Alabama	2,727	3.3%
25	Kentucky	634	0.8%		17	New Jersey	2,545	3.1%
6	Louisiana	4,037	4.9%		18	Tennessee	2,280	2.8%
NA	Maine**	NA	NA		19	Missouri	1,581	1.9%
9	Maryland	3,318	4.0%		20	Indiana	1,313	1.6%
22	Massachusetts	950	1.2%		21	Arkansas	1,146	1.4%
11	Michigan	3,082	3.8%		22	Massachusetts	950	1.2%
27	Minnesota	455	0.6%		23	Wisconsin	891	1.1%
14	Mississippi	2,870	3.5%		24	Connecticut	649	0.8%
19	Missouri	1,581	1.9%		25	Kentucky	634	0.8%
NA	Montana**	NA	NA		26	Oklahoma	607	0.7%
34	Nebraska	184	0.2%		27	Minnesota	455	0.6%
30	Nevada	402	0.5%		28	Washington	426	0.5%
NA	New Hampshire**	NA	NA		29	Colorado	422	0.5%
17	New Jersey	2,545	3.1%		30	Nevada	402	0.5%
39	New Mexico	68	0.1%		31	Arizona	384	0.5%
2	New York	6,171	7.5%		32	Kansas	383	0.5%
7	North Carolina	3,922	4.8%		33	Delaware	336	0.4%
NA	North Dakota**	NA	NA		34	Nebraska	184	0.2%
10	Ohio	3,300	4.0%		35	Iowa	163	0.2%
26	Oklahoma	607	0.7%		36	Rhode Island	136	0.2%
37	Oregon	111	0.1%		37	Oregon	111	0.1%
15	Pennsylvania	2,848	3.5%		38	West Virginia	95	0.1%
36	Rhode Island	136	0.2%		39	New Mexico	68	0.1%
13	South Carolina	2,883	3.5%		40	Hawaii	54	0.1%
NA	South Dakota**	NA	NA		41	Alaska	44	0.1%
18	Tennessee	2,280	2.8%		42	Utah	29	0.0%
4	Texas	5,854	7.1%		NA	Idaho**	NA	NA
42	Utah	29	0.0%		NA	Maine**	NA	NA
NA	Vermont**	NA	NA		NA	Montana**	NA	NA
12	Virginia	2,908	3.5%		NA	New Hampshire**	NA	NA
28	Washington	426	0.5%		NA	North Dakota**	NA	NA
38	West Virginia	95	0.1%		NA	South Dakota**	NA	NA
23	Wisconsin	891	1.1%		NA	Vermont**	NA	NA
NA	Wyoming**	NA	NA		NA	Wyoming**	NA	NA
						District of Columbia	717	0.9%

Source: Morgan Quitno Press using data from U.S. Dept. of Health and Human Services, Nat'l Center for Health Statistics
"National Vital Statistics Reports" (Vol. 54, No. 8, December 29, 2005)
*Preliminary data by state of residence. Births of less than 2,500 grams (5 pounds 8 ounces).
**Not available. Fewer than 20 births of low birthweight to black women.

Births of Low Birthweight to Black Women
As a Percent of All Births to Black Women In 2004
National Percent = 13.4% of Live Births to Black Women*

ALPHA ORDER

RANK	STATE	PERCENT
3	Alabama	15.1
35	Alaska	11.1
34	Arizona	11.2
1	Arkansas	15.5
30	California	12.2
7	Colorado	14.4
29	Connecticut	12.3
32	Delaware	11.6
27	Florida	12.5
11	Georgia	13.9
42	Hawaii	9.5
NA	Idaho**	NA
6	Illinois	14.5
15	Indiana	13.6
36	Iowa	11.0
18	Kansas	13.5
21	Kentucky	13.0
3	Louisiana	15.1
NA	Maine**	NA
22	Maryland	12.9
37	Massachusetts	10.9
8	Michigan	14.2
40	Minnesota	9.8
1	Mississippi	15.5
12	Missouri	13.8
NA	Montana**	NA
31	Nebraska	11.7
15	Nevada	13.6
NA	New Hampshire**	NA
22	New Jersey	12.9
15	New Mexico	13.6
28	New York	12.4
8	North Carolina	14.2
NA	North Dakota**	NA
12	Ohio	13.8
22	Oklahoma	12.9
38	Oregon	10.5
22	Pennsylvania	12.9
33	Rhode Island	11.4
5	South Carolina	14.7
NA	South Dakota**	NA
20	Tennessee	13.1
12	Texas	13.8
40	Utah	9.8
NA	Vermont**	NA
26	Virginia	12.7
38	Washington	10.5
10	West Virginia	14.1
18	Wisconsin	13.5
NA	Wyoming**	NA

RANK ORDER

RANK	STATE	PERCENT
1	Arkansas	15.5
1	Mississippi	15.5
3	Alabama	15.1
3	Louisiana	15.1
5	South Carolina	14.7
6	Illinois	14.5
7	Colorado	14.4
8	Michigan	14.2
8	North Carolina	14.2
10	West Virginia	14.1
11	Georgia	13.9
12	Missouri	13.8
12	Ohio	13.8
12	Texas	13.8
15	Indiana	13.6
15	Nevada	13.6
15	New Mexico	13.6
18	Kansas	13.5
18	Wisconsin	13.5
20	Tennessee	13.1
21	Kentucky	13.0
22	Maryland	12.9
22	New Jersey	12.9
22	Oklahoma	12.9
22	Pennsylvania	12.9
26	Virginia	12.7
27	Florida	12.5
28	New York	12.4
29	Connecticut	12.3
30	California	12.2
31	Nebraska	11.7
32	Delaware	11.6
33	Rhode Island	11.4
34	Arizona	11.2
35	Alaska	11.1
36	Iowa	11.0
37	Massachusetts	10.9
38	Oregon	10.5
38	Washington	10.5
40	Minnesota	9.8
40	Utah	9.8
42	Hawaii	9.5
NA	Idaho**	NA
NA	Maine**	NA
NA	Montana**	NA
NA	New Hampshire**	NA
NA	North Dakota**	NA
NA	South Dakota**	NA
NA	Vermont**	NA
NA	Wyoming**	NA
	District of Columbia	13.3

Source: U.S. Department of Health and Human Services, National Center for Health Statistics
"National Vital Statistics Reports" (Vol. 54, No. 8, December 29, 2005)
Preliminary data by state of residence. Births of less than 2,500 grams (5 pounds 8 ounces).
**Not available. Fewer than 20 births of low birthweight to black women.*

Births of Low Birthweight to Hispanic Women in 2004

National Total = 64,260 Live Births*

ALPHA ORDER					RANK ORDER			
RANK	STATE	BIRTHS	% of USA		RANK	STATE	BIRTHS	% of USA
31	Alabama	228	0.4%		1	California	16,797	26.1%
43	Alaska	47	0.1%		2	Texas	13,650	21.2%
5	Arizona	2,817	4.4%		3	New York	4,281	6.7%
33	Arkansas	214	0.3%		4	Florida	3,878	6.0%
1	California	16,797	26.1%		5	Arizona	2,817	4.4%
8	Colorado	1,870	2.9%		6	Illinois	2,812	4.4%
17	Connecticut	646	1.0%		7	New Jersey	1,966	3.1%
40	Delaware	96	0.1%		8	Colorado	1,870	2.9%
4	Florida	3,878	6.0%		9	New Mexico	1,243	1.9%
10	Georgia	1,207	1.9%		10	Georgia	1,207	1.9%
34	Hawaii	212	0.3%		11	North Carolina	1,107	1.7%
32	Idaho	227	0.4%		12	Pennsylvania	1,040	1.6%
6	Illinois	2,812	4.4%		13	Washington	869	1.4%
22	Indiana	457	0.7%		14	Massachusetts	847	1.3%
37	Iowa	173	0.3%		15	Nevada	823	1.3%
27	Kansas	345	0.5%		16	Virginia	748	1.2%
38	Kentucky	155	0.2%		17	Connecticut	646	1.0%
39	Louisiana	150	0.2%		18	Maryland	558	0.9%
NA	Maine**	NA	NA		19	Utah	546	0.8%
18	Maryland	558	0.9%		20	Michigan	501	0.8%
14	Massachusetts	847	1.3%		21	Oregon	459	0.7%
20	Michigan	501	0.8%		22	Indiana	457	0.7%
28	Minnesota	336	0.5%		23	Ohio	402	0.6%
41	Mississippi	81	0.1%		24	Oklahoma	396	0.6%
30	Missouri	254	0.4%		25	Wisconsin	377	0.6%
44	Montana	32	0.0%		26	Tennessee	350	0.5%
35	Nebraska	203	0.3%		27	Kansas	345	0.5%
15	Nevada	823	1.3%		28	Minnesota	336	0.5%
45	New Hampshire	30	0.0%		29	South Carolina	273	0.4%
7	New Jersey	1,966	3.1%		30	Missouri	254	0.4%
9	New Mexico	1,243	1.9%		31	Alabama	228	0.4%
3	New York	4,281	6.7%		32	Idaho	227	0.4%
11	North Carolina	1,107	1.7%		33	Arkansas	214	0.3%
NA	North Dakota**	NA	NA		34	Hawaii	212	0.3%
23	Ohio	402	0.6%		35	Nebraska	203	0.3%
24	Oklahoma	396	0.6%		36	Rhode Island	202	0.3%
21	Oregon	459	0.7%		37	Iowa	173	0.3%
12	Pennsylvania	1,040	1.6%		38	Kentucky	155	0.2%
36	Rhode Island	202	0.3%		39	Louisiana	150	0.2%
29	South Carolina	273	0.4%		40	Delaware	96	0.1%
NA	South Dakota**	NA	NA		41	Mississippi	81	0.1%
26	Tennessee	350	0.5%		42	Wyoming	59	0.1%
2	Texas	13,650	21.2%		43	Alaska	47	0.1%
19	Utah	546	0.8%		44	Montana	32	0.0%
NA	Vermont**	NA	NA		45	New Hampshire	30	0.0%
16	Virginia	748	1.2%		NA	Maine**	NA	NA
13	Washington	869	1.4%		NA	North Dakota**	NA	NA
NA	West Virginia**	NA	NA		NA	South Dakota**	NA	NA
25	Wisconsin	377	0.6%		NA	Vermont**	NA	NA
42	Wyoming	59	0.1%		NA	West Virginia**	NA	NA
						District of Columbia	78	0.1%

Source: Morgan Quitno Press using data from U.S. Dept. of Health and Human Services, Nat'l Center for Health Statistics
"National Vital Statistics Reports" (Vol. 54, No. 8, December 29, 2005)
*Preliminary data by state of residence. Births of less than 2,500 grams (5 pounds 8 ounces). Hispanic can be of any race.
**Not available. Fewer than 20 births of low birthweight to Hispanic women.

Births of Low Birthweight to Hispanic Women
As a Percent of All Births to Hispanic Women in 2004
National Percent = 6.8% of Live Births to Hispanic Women*

RANK	STATE	PERCENT
21	Alabama	6.8
44	Alaska	5.4
21	Arizona	6.8
37	Arkansas	6.1
37	California	6.1
2	Colorado	8.6
5	Connecticut	8.5
31	Delaware	6.3
18	Florida	7.0
41	Georgia	6.0
9	Hawaii	7.9
18	Idaho	7.0
23	Illinois	6.6
31	Indiana	6.3
37	Iowa	6.1
31	Kansas	6.3
17	Kentucky	7.1
10	Louisiana	7.7
NA	Maine**	NA
14	Maryland	7.3
2	Massachusetts	8.6
27	Michigan	6.4
31	Minnesota	6.3
10	Mississippi	7.7
23	Missouri	6.6
2	Montana	8.6
43	Nebraska	5.9
31	Nevada	6.3
26	New Hampshire	6.5
15	New Jersey	7.2
8	New Mexico	8.2
13	New York	7.5
27	North Carolina	6.4
NA	North Dakota**	NA
18	Ohio	7.0
23	Oklahoma	6.6
45	Oregon	5.2
1	Pennsylvania	8.9
7	Rhode Island	8.3
31	South Carolina	6.3
NA	South Dakota**	NA
41	Tennessee	6.0
15	Texas	7.2
12	Utah	7.6
NA	Vermont**	NA
27	Virginia	6.4
37	Washington	6.1
NA	West Virginia**	NA
27	Wisconsin	6.4
6	Wyoming	8.4

RANK	STATE	PERCENT
1	Pennsylvania	8.9
2	Colorado	8.6
2	Massachusetts	8.6
2	Montana	8.6
5	Connecticut	8.5
6	Wyoming	8.4
7	Rhode Island	8.3
8	New Mexico	8.2
9	Hawaii	7.9
10	Louisiana	7.7
10	Mississippi	7.7
12	Utah	7.6
13	New York	7.5
14	Maryland	7.3
15	New Jersey	7.2
15	Texas	7.2
17	Kentucky	7.1
18	Florida	7.0
18	Idaho	7.0
18	Ohio	7.0
21	Alabama	6.8
21	Arizona	6.8
23	Illinois	6.6
23	Missouri	6.6
23	Oklahoma	6.6
26	New Hampshire	6.5
27	Michigan	6.4
27	North Carolina	6.4
27	Virginia	6.4
27	Wisconsin	6.4
31	Delaware	6.3
31	Indiana	6.3
31	Kansas	6.3
31	Minnesota	6.3
31	Nevada	6.3
31	South Carolina	6.3
37	Arkansas	6.1
37	California	6.1
37	Iowa	6.1
37	Washington	6.1
41	Georgia	6.0
41	Tennessee	6.0
43	Nebraska	5.9
44	Alaska	5.4
45	Oregon	5.2
NA	Maine**	NA
NA	North Dakota**	NA
NA	South Dakota**	NA
NA	Vermont**	NA
NA	West Virginia**	NA

	District of Columbia	7.8

Source: U.S. Department of Health and Human Services, National Center for Health Statistics
    "National Vital Statistics Reports" (Vol. 54, No. 8, December 29, 2005)
*Preliminary data by state of residence. Births of less than 2,500 grams (5 pounds 8 ounces). Hispanic can be of any race.
**Not available. Fewer than 20 births of low birthweight to Hispanic women.

Births to Unmarried Women in 2004

National Total = 1,469,266 Live Births*

ALPHA ORDER

RANK	STATE	BIRTHS	% of USA	RANK	STATE	BIRTHS	% of USA
23	Alabama	21,616	1.5%	1	California	187,504	12.8%
47	Alaska	3,577	0.2%	2	Texas	137,996	9.4%
11	Arizona	39,530	2.7%	3	New York	94,838	6.5%
29	Arkansas	14,978	1.0%	4	Florida	89,830	6.1%
1	California	187,504	12.8%	5	Illinois	65,498	4.5%
28	Colorado	18,843	1.3%	6	Ohio	55,784	3.8%
34	Connecticut	12,882	0.9%	7	Georgia	54,430	3.7%
41	Delaware	4,802	0.3%	8	Pennsylvania	50,727	3.5%
4	Florida	89,830	6.1%	9	Michigan	46,327	3.2%
7	Georgia	54,430	3.7%	10	North Carolina	44,225	3.0%
39	Hawaii	6,087	0.4%	11	Arizona	39,530	2.7%
40	Idaho	5,091	0.3%	12	New Jersey	34,590	2.4%
5	Illinois	65,498	4.5%	13	Indiana	33,826	2.3%
13	Indiana	33,826	2.3%	14	Virginia	32,214	2.2%
35	Iowa	11,916	0.8%	15	Louisiana	32,176	2.2%
33	Kansas	12,943	0.9%	16	Tennessee	30,423	2.1%
27	Kentucky	19,276	1.3%	17	Missouri	28,701	2.0%
15	Louisiana	32,176	2.2%	18	Maryland	26,634	1.8%
43	Maine	4,741	0.3%	19	Washington	24,849	1.7%
18	Maryland	26,634	1.8%	20	South Carolina	23,938	1.6%
21	Massachusetts	22,391	1.5%	21	Massachusetts	22,391	1.5%
9	Michigan	46,327	3.2%	22	Wisconsin	21,958	1.5%
25	Minnesota	20,478	1.4%	23	Alabama	21,616	1.5%
24	Mississippi	20,677	1.4%	24	Mississippi	20,677	1.4%
17	Missouri	28,701	2.0%	25	Minnesota	20,478	1.4%
45	Montana	3,953	0.3%	26	Oklahoma	19,693	1.3%
37	Nebraska	7,952	0.5%	27	Kentucky	19,276	1.3%
31	Nevada	13,934	0.9%	28	Colorado	18,843	1.3%
46	New Hampshire	3,860	0.3%	29	Arkansas	14,978	1.0%
12	New Jersey	34,590	2.4%	30	Oregon	14,850	1.0%
32	New Mexico	13,881	0.9%	31	Nevada	13,934	0.9%
3	New York	94,838	6.5%	32	New Mexico	13,881	0.9%
10	North Carolina	44,225	3.0%	33	Kansas	12,943	0.9%
48	North Dakota	2,449	0.2%	34	Connecticut	12,882	0.9%
6	Ohio	55,784	3.8%	35	Iowa	11,916	0.8%
26	Oklahoma	19,693	1.3%	36	Utah	8,867	0.6%
30	Oregon	14,850	1.0%	37	Nebraska	7,952	0.5%
8	Pennsylvania	50,727	3.5%	38	West Virginia	7,278	0.5%
42	Rhode Island	4,766	0.3%	39	Hawaii	6,087	0.4%
20	South Carolina	23,938	1.6%	40	Idaho	5,091	0.3%
44	South Dakota	3,980	0.3%	41	Delaware	4,802	0.3%
16	Tennessee	30,423	2.1%	42	Rhode Island	4,766	0.3%
2	Texas	137,996	9.4%	43	Maine	4,741	0.3%
36	Utah	8,867	0.6%	44	South Dakota	3,980	0.3%
50	Vermont	2,120	0.1%	45	Montana	3,953	0.3%
14	Virginia	32,214	2.2%	46	New Hampshire	3,860	0.3%
19	Washington	24,849	1.7%	47	Alaska	3,577	0.2%
38	West Virginia	7,278	0.5%	48	North Dakota	2,449	0.2%
22	Wisconsin	21,958	1.5%	49	Wyoming	2,158	0.1%
49	Wyoming	2,158	0.1%	50	Vermont	2,120	0.1%
					District of Columbia	4,402	0.3%

Source: Morgan Quitno Press using data from U.S. Dept. of Health and Human Services, Nat'l Center for Health Statistics "National Vital Statistics Reports" (Vol. 54, No. 8, December 29, 2005)
*Preliminary data by state of residence.

Births to Unmarried Women as a Percent of All Births in 2004

National Percent = 35.7% of Live Births*

ALPHA ORDER

RANK	STATE	PERCENT
19	Alabama	36.3
28	Alaska	34.6
6	Arizona	42.2
11	Arkansas	38.8
29	California	34.4
47	Colorado	27.5
40	Connecticut	30.6
4	Delaware	42.5
7	Florida	41.2
9	Georgia	39.2
32	Hawaii	33.3
49	Idaho	22.6
20	Illinois	36.2
10	Indiana	39.0
38	Iowa	31.0
33	Kansas	32.7
24	Kentucky	35.4
1	Louisiana	49.2
31	Maine	34.0
22	Maryland	35.7
46	Massachusetts	28.5
22	Michigan	35.7
45	Minnesota	29.0
3	Mississippi	48.3
17	Missouri	36.9
30	Montana	34.3
42	Nebraska	30.2
8	Nevada	39.6
48	New Hampshire	26.5
43	New Jersey	30.1
2	New Mexico	48.9
14	New York	37.8
17	North Carolina	36.9
44	North Dakota	29.9
15	Ohio	37.4
12	Oklahoma	38.4
34	Oregon	32.5
27	Pennsylvania	34.8
16	Rhode Island	37.3
5	South Carolina	42.3
25	South Dakota	35.1
13	Tennessee	38.2
21	Texas	35.9
50	Utah	17.5
35	Vermont	32.3
38	Virginia	31.0
41	Washington	30.4
26	West Virginia	34.9
37	Wisconsin	31.3
36	Wyoming	31.7

RANK ORDER

RANK	STATE	PERCENT
1	Louisiana	49.2
2	New Mexico	48.9
3	Mississippi	48.3
4	Delaware	42.5
5	South Carolina	42.3
6	Arizona	42.2
7	Florida	41.2
8	Nevada	39.6
9	Georgia	39.2
10	Indiana	39.0
11	Arkansas	38.8
12	Oklahoma	38.4
13	Tennessee	38.2
14	New York	37.8
15	Ohio	37.4
16	Rhode Island	37.3
17	Missouri	36.9
17	North Carolina	36.9
19	Alabama	36.3
20	Illinois	36.2
21	Texas	35.9
22	Maryland	35.7
22	Michigan	35.7
24	Kentucky	35.4
25	South Dakota	35.1
26	West Virginia	34.9
27	Pennsylvania	34.8
28	Alaska	34.6
29	California	34.4
30	Montana	34.3
31	Maine	34.0
32	Hawaii	33.3
33	Kansas	32.7
34	Oregon	32.5
35	Vermont	32.3
36	Wyoming	31.7
37	Wisconsin	31.3
38	Iowa	31.0
38	Virginia	31.0
40	Connecticut	30.6
41	Washington	30.4
42	Nebraska	30.2
43	New Jersey	30.1
44	North Dakota	29.9
45	Minnesota	29.0
46	Massachusetts	28.5
47	Colorado	27.5
48	New Hampshire	26.5
49	Idaho	22.6
50	Utah	17.5
	District of Columbia	55.5

Source: U.S. Department of Health and Human Services, National Center for Health Statistics
   "National Vital Statistics Reports" (Vol. 54, No. 8, December 29, 2005)
*Preliminary data by state of residence.

Births to Unmarried White Women in 2004

National Total = 985,093 Live Births*

ALPHA ORDER

RANK ORDER

RANK	STATE	BIRTHS	% of USA		RANK	STATE	BIRTHS	% of USA
34	Alabama	8,718	0.9%		1	California	156,226	15.9%
49	Alaska	1,535	0.2%		2	Texas	109,389	11.1%
8	Arizona	32,387	3.3%		3	New York	56,849	5.8%
32	Arkansas	9,109	0.9%		4	Florida	53,303	5.4%
1	California	156,226	15.9%		5	Illinois	40,851	4.1%
18	Colorado	16,629	1.7%		6	Ohio	37,184	3.8%
33	Connecticut	9,096	0.9%		7	Pennsylvania	33,207	3.4%
44	Delaware	2,685	0.3%		8	Arizona	32,387	3.3%
4	Florida	53,303	5.4%		9	Michigan	29,607	3.0%
11	Georgia	24,597	2.5%		10	Indiana	26,019	2.6%
50	Hawaii	1,351	0.1%		11	Georgia	24,597	2.5%
39	Idaho	4,754	0.5%		12	North Carolina	24,039	2.4%
5	Illinois	40,851	4.1%		13	New Jersey	21,371	2.2%
10	Indiana	26,019	2.6%		14	Missouri	19,502	2.0%
30	Iowa	10,468	1.1%		15	Washington	19,476	2.0%
29	Kansas	10,492	1.1%		16	Tennessee	17,397	1.8%
20	Kentucky	15,427	1.6%		17	Virginia	17,305	1.8%
25	Louisiana	11,255	1.1%		18	Colorado	16,629	1.7%
40	Maine	4,536	0.5%		19	Massachusetts	16,392	1.7%
28	Maryland	10,802	1.1%		20	Kentucky	15,427	1.6%
19	Massachusetts	16,392	1.7%		21	Wisconsin	15,419	1.6%
9	Michigan	29,607	3.0%		22	Minnesota	15,010	1.5%
22	Minnesota	15,010	1.5%		23	Oklahoma	13,374	1.4%
38	Mississippi	6,219	0.6%		24	Oregon	13,200	1.3%
14	Missouri	19,502	2.0%		25	Louisiana	11,255	1.1%
43	Montana	2,791	0.3%		26	Nevada	10,887	1.1%
37	Nebraska	6,447	0.7%		27	New Mexico	10,854	1.1%
26	Nevada	10,887	1.1%		28	Maryland	10,802	1.1%
42	New Hampshire	3,690	0.4%		29	Kansas	10,492	1.1%
13	New Jersey	21,371	2.2%		30	Iowa	10,468	1.1%
27	New Mexico	10,854	1.1%		31	South Carolina	9,591	1.0%
3	New York	56,849	5.8%		32	Arkansas	9,109	0.9%
12	North Carolina	24,039	2.4%		33	Connecticut	9,096	0.9%
48	North Dakota	1,656	0.2%		34	Alabama	8,718	0.9%
6	Ohio	37,184	3.8%		35	Utah	8,107	0.8%
23	Oklahoma	13,374	1.4%		36	West Virginia	6,717	0.7%
24	Oregon	13,200	1.3%		37	Nebraska	6,447	0.7%
7	Pennsylvania	33,207	3.4%		38	Mississippi	6,219	0.6%
41	Rhode Island	3,697	0.4%		39	Idaho	4,754	0.5%
31	South Carolina	9,591	1.0%		40	Maine	4,536	0.5%
45	South Dakota	2,392	0.2%		41	Rhode Island	3,697	0.4%
16	Tennessee	17,397	1.8%		42	New Hampshire	3,690	0.4%
2	Texas	109,389	11.1%		43	Montana	2,791	0.3%
35	Utah	8,107	0.8%		44	Delaware	2,685	0.3%
46	Vermont	2,074	0.2%		45	South Dakota	2,392	0.2%
17	Virginia	17,305	1.8%		46	Vermont	2,074	0.2%
15	Washington	19,476	2.0%		47	Wyoming	1,920	0.2%
36	West Virginia	6,717	0.7%		48	North Dakota	1,656	0.2%
21	Wisconsin	15,419	1.6%		49	Alaska	1,535	0.2%
47	Wyoming	1,920	0.2%		50	Hawaii	1,351	0.1%

	District of Columbia	260	0.0%

Source: Morgan Quitno Press using data from U.S. Dept. of Health and Human Services, Nat'l Center for Health Statistics
    "National Vital Statistics Reports" (Vol. 54, No. 8, December 29, 2005)
*Preliminary data by state of residence. By race of mother.

Births to Unmarried White Women
As a Percent of All Births to White Women in 2004
National Percent = 30.5% of Live Births*

ALPHA ORDER

RANK	STATE	PERCENT
49	Alabama	21.5
47	Alaska	23.3
2	Arizona	39.9
21	Arkansas	30.0
4	California	35.4
35	Colorado	26.6
36	Connecticut	26.4
7	Delaware	33.9
9	Florida	33.8
31	Georgia	27.4
38	Hawaii	26.1
48	Idaho	21.9
24	Illinois	29.0
5	Indiana	34.5
23	Iowa	29.3
22	Kansas	29.9
16	Kentucky	31.7
19	Louisiana	30.3
7	Maine	33.9
44	Maryland	24.6
41	Massachusetts	25.6
26	Michigan	28.8
43	Minnesota	25.2
36	Mississippi	26.4
18	Missouri	30.4
28	Montana	28.4
32	Nebraska	27.2
3	Nevada	37.5
33	New Hampshire	26.8
42	New Jersey	25.4
1	New Mexico	45.5
15	New York	31.8
30	North Carolina	27.5
45	North Dakota	23.6
17	Ohio	30.6
11	Oklahoma	33.4
14	Oregon	32.0
29	Pennsylvania	28.2
6	Rhode Island	34.0
33	South Carolina	26.8
39	South Dakota	26.0
26	Tennessee	28.8
11	Texas	33.4
50	Utah	16.8
13	Vermont	32.5
46	Virginia	23.4
24	Washington	29.0
10	West Virginia	33.6
40	Wisconsin	25.7
20	Wyoming	30.2

RANK ORDER

RANK	STATE	PERCENT
1	New Mexico	45.5
2	Arizona	39.9
3	Nevada	37.5
4	California	35.4
5	Indiana	34.5
6	Rhode Island	34.0
7	Delaware	33.9
7	Maine	33.9
9	Florida	33.8
10	West Virginia	33.6
11	Oklahoma	33.4
11	Texas	33.4
13	Vermont	32.5
14	Oregon	32.0
15	New York	31.8
16	Kentucky	31.7
17	Ohio	30.6
18	Missouri	30.4
19	Louisiana	30.3
20	Wyoming	30.2
21	Arkansas	30.0
22	Kansas	29.9
23	Iowa	29.3
24	Illinois	29.0
24	Washington	29.0
26	Michigan	28.8
26	Tennessee	28.8
28	Montana	28.4
29	Pennsylvania	28.2
30	North Carolina	27.5
31	Georgia	27.4
32	Nebraska	27.2
33	New Hampshire	26.8
33	South Carolina	26.8
35	Colorado	26.6
36	Connecticut	26.4
36	Mississippi	26.4
38	Hawaii	26.1
39	South Dakota	26.0
40	Wisconsin	25.7
41	Massachusetts	25.6
42	New Jersey	25.4
43	Minnesota	25.2
44	Maryland	24.6
45	North Dakota	23.6
46	Virginia	23.4
47	Alaska	23.3
48	Idaho	21.9
49	Alabama	21.5
50	Utah	16.8
	District of Columbia	11.3

Source: U.S. Department of Health and Human Services, National Center for Health Statistics
    "National Vital Statistics Reports" (Vol. 54, No. 8, December 29, 2005)
*Preliminary data by state of residence. By race of mother.

Births to Unmarried Black Women in 2004

National Total = 420,783 Live Births*

RANK	STATE	BIRTHS	% of USA
16	Alabama	12,730	3.0%
41	Alaska	161	0.0%
29	Arizona	2,114	0.5%
21	Arkansas	5,680	1.3%
7	California	20,227	4.8%
33	Colorado	1,561	0.4%
25	Connecticut	3,532	0.8%
30	Delaware	2,067	0.5%
1	Florida	34,873	8.3%
3	Georgia	29,129	6.9%
40	Hawaii	167	0.0%
46	Idaho	42	0.0%
5	Illinois	23,835	5.7%
20	Indiana	7,512	1.8%
35	Iowa	1,079	0.3%
32	Kansas	2,014	0.5%
24	Kentucky	3,659	0.9%
6	Louisiana	20,503	4.9%
44	Maine	78	0.0%
12	Maryland	15,278	3.6%
23	Massachusetts	5,101	1.2%
11	Michigan	15,693	3.7%
27	Minnesota	2,620	0.6%
14	Mississippi	14,165	3.4%
19	Missouri	8,797	2.1%
47	Montana	28	0.0%
34	Nebraska	1,089	0.3%
31	Nevada	2,023	0.5%
43	New Hampshire	115	0.0%
18	New Jersey	12,588	3.0%
39	New Mexico	285	0.1%
2	New York	33,542	8.0%
8	North Carolina	18,784	4.5%
49	North Dakota	25	0.0%
9	Ohio	17,956	4.3%
26	Oklahoma	3,364	0.8%
37	Oregon	688	0.2%
10	Pennsylvania	16,495	3.9%
36	Rhode Island	757	0.2%
15	South Carolina	14,082	3.3%
45	South Dakota	65	0.0%
17	Tennessee	12,616	3.0%
4	Texas	27,108	6.4%
42	Utah	134	0.0%
47	Vermont	28	0.0%
13	Virginia	14,243	3.4%
28	Washington	2,200	0.5%
38	West Virginia	515	0.1%
22	Wisconsin	5,406	1.3%
49	Wyoming	25	0.0%

RANK	STATE	BIRTHS	% of USA
1	Florida	34,873	8.3%
2	New York	33,542	8.0%
3	Georgia	29,129	6.9%
4	Texas	27,108	6.4%
5	Illinois	23,835	5.7%
6	Louisiana	20,503	4.9%
7	California	20,227	4.8%
8	North Carolina	18,784	4.5%
9	Ohio	17,956	4.3%
10	Pennsylvania	16,495	3.9%
11	Michigan	15,693	3.7%
12	Maryland	15,278	3.6%
13	Virginia	14,243	3.4%
14	Mississippi	14,165	3.4%
15	South Carolina	14,082	3.3%
16	Alabama	12,730	3.0%
17	Tennessee	12,616	3.0%
18	New Jersey	12,588	3.0%
19	Missouri	8,797	2.1%
20	Indiana	7,512	1.8%
21	Arkansas	5,680	1.3%
22	Wisconsin	5,406	1.3%
23	Massachusetts	5,101	1.2%
24	Kentucky	3,659	0.9%
25	Connecticut	3,532	0.8%
26	Oklahoma	3,364	0.8%
27	Minnesota	2,620	0.6%
28	Washington	2,200	0.5%
29	Arizona	2,114	0.5%
30	Delaware	2,067	0.5%
31	Nevada	2,023	0.5%
32	Kansas	2,014	0.5%
33	Colorado	1,561	0.4%
34	Nebraska	1,089	0.3%
35	Iowa	1,079	0.3%
36	Rhode Island	757	0.2%
37	Oregon	688	0.2%
38	West Virginia	515	0.1%
39	New Mexico	285	0.1%
40	Hawaii	167	0.0%
41	Alaska	161	0.0%
42	Utah	134	0.0%
43	New Hampshire	115	0.0%
44	Maine	78	0.0%
45	South Dakota	65	0.0%
46	Idaho	42	0.0%
47	Montana	28	0.0%
47	Vermont	28	0.0%
49	North Dakota	25	0.0%
49	Wyoming	25	0.0%
	District of Columbia	4,098	1.0%

Source: Morgan Quitno Press using data from U.S. Dept. of Health and Human Services, Nat'l Center for Health Statistics "National Vital Statistics Reports" (Vol. 54, No. 8, December 29, 2005)
*Preliminary data by state of residence. By race of mother.

Births to Unmarried Black Women
As a Percent of All Births to Black Women in 2004
National Percent = 68.7% of Live Births*

RANK	STATE	PERCENT
19	Alabama	70.5
46	Alaska	40.6
33	Arizona	61.7
4	Arkansas	76.8
31	California	63.0
39	Colorado	53.3
24	Connecticut	66.9
17	Delaware	71.4
26	Florida	66.1
25	Georgia	66.2
49	Hawaii	29.1
47	Idaho	38.5
3	Illinois	77.2
2	Indiana	77.8
12	Iowa	73.0
18	Kansas	71.0
10	Kentucky	75.0
6	Louisiana	76.7
48	Maine	34.7
34	Maryland	59.4
35	Massachusetts	58.5
14	Michigan	72.3
37	Minnesota	56.4
7	Mississippi	76.5
4	Missouri	76.8
40	Montana	52.8
20	Nebraska	69.2
21	Nevada	68.4
43	New Hampshire	44.9
29	New Jersey	63.8
36	New Mexico	56.8
23	New York	67.4
22	North Carolina	68.0
50	North Dakota	26.0
9	Ohio	75.1
16	Oklahoma	71.5
27	Oregon	65.1
11	Pennsylvania	74.7
30	Rhode Island	63.3
15	South Carolina	71.8
45	South Dakota	44.2
13	Tennessee	72.5
28	Texas	63.9
44	Utah	44.8
41	Vermont	48.3
32	Virginia	62.2
38	Washington	54.2
7	West Virginia	76.5
1	Wisconsin	81.9
42	Wyoming	45.5

RANK	STATE	PERCENT
1	Wisconsin	81.9
2	Indiana	77.8
3	Illinois	77.2
4	Arkansas	76.8
4	Missouri	76.8
6	Louisiana	76.7
7	Mississippi	76.5
7	West Virginia	76.5
9	Ohio	75.1
10	Kentucky	75.0
11	Pennsylvania	74.7
12	Iowa	73.0
13	Tennessee	72.5
14	Michigan	72.3
15	South Carolina	71.8
16	Oklahoma	71.5
17	Delaware	71.4
18	Kansas	71.0
19	Alabama	70.5
20	Nebraska	69.2
21	Nevada	68.4
22	North Carolina	68.0
23	New York	67.4
24	Connecticut	66.9
25	Georgia	66.2
26	Florida	66.1
27	Oregon	65.1
28	Texas	63.9
29	New Jersey	63.8
30	Rhode Island	63.3
31	California	63.0
32	Virginia	62.2
33	Arizona	61.7
34	Maryland	59.4
35	Massachusetts	58.5
36	New Mexico	56.8
37	Minnesota	56.4
38	Washington	54.2
39	Colorado	53.3
40	Montana	52.8
41	Vermont	48.3
42	Wyoming	45.5
43	New Hampshire	44.9
44	Utah	44.8
45	South Dakota	44.2
46	Alaska	40.6
47	Idaho	38.5
48	Maine	34.7
49	Hawaii	29.1
50	North Dakota	26.0
	District of Columbia	76.0

Source: U.S. Department of Health and Human Services, National Center for Health Statistics
"National Vital Statistics Reports" (Vol. 54, No. 8, December 29, 2005)
*Preliminary data by state of residence. By race of mother.

Births to Unmarried Hispanic Women in 2004

National Total = 438,477 Live Births*

ALPHA ORDER				RANK ORDER			
RANK	STATE	BIRTHS	% of USA	RANK	STATE	BIRTHS	% of USA
39	Alabama	840	0.2%	1	California	122,537	27.9%
43	Alaska	306	0.1%	2	Texas	76,972	17.6%
5	Arizona	22,412	5.1%	3	New York	35,162	8.0%
32	Arkansas	1,488	0.3%	4	Florida	23,936	5.5%
1	California	122,537	27.9%	5	Arizona	22,412	5.1%
9	Colorado	9,046	2.1%	6	Illinois	19,344	4.4%
17	Connecticut	4,726	1.1%	7	New Jersey	14,858	3.4%
38	Delaware	883	0.2%	8	Georgia	9,091	2.1%
4	Florida	23,936	5.5%	9	Colorado	9,046	2.1%
8	Georgia	9,091	2.1%	10	North Carolina	8,665	2.0%
36	Hawaii	1,198	0.3%	11	New Mexico	8,461	1.9%
35	Idaho	1,206	0.3%	12	Pennsylvania	7,117	1.6%
6	Illinois	19,344	4.4%	13	Washington	6,300	1.4%
19	Indiana	3,824	0.9%	14	Nevada	6,230	1.4%
34	Iowa	1,259	0.3%	15	Massachusetts	6,213	1.4%
28	Kansas	2,468	0.6%	16	Virginia	5,144	1.2%
37	Kentucky	1,069	0.2%	17	Connecticut	4,726	1.1%
40	Louisiana	793	0.2%	18	Oregon	3,932	0.9%
48	Maine	57	0.0%	19	Indiana	3,824	0.9%
20	Maryland	3,727	0.8%	20	Maryland	3,727	0.8%
15	Massachusetts	6,213	1.4%	21	Michigan	3,576	0.8%
21	Michigan	3,576	0.8%	22	Ohio	3,006	0.7%
27	Minnesota	2,745	0.6%	23	Utah	2,908	0.7%
41	Mississippi	500	0.1%	24	Tennessee	2,849	0.6%
30	Missouri	1,826	0.4%	25	Wisconsin	2,814	0.6%
46	Montana	152	0.0%	26	Oklahoma	2,769	0.6%
31	Nebraska	1,513	0.3%	27	Minnesota	2,745	0.6%
14	Nevada	6,230	1.4%	28	Kansas	2,468	0.6%
44	New Hampshire	187	0.0%	29	South Carolina	1,916	0.4%
7	New Jersey	14,858	3.4%	30	Missouri	1,826	0.4%
11	New Mexico	8,461	1.9%	31	Nebraska	1,513	0.3%
3	New York	35,162	8.0%	32	Arkansas	1,488	0.3%
10	North Carolina	8,665	2.0%	33	Rhode Island	1,474	0.3%
47	North Dakota	59	0.0%	34	Iowa	1,259	0.3%
22	Ohio	3,006	0.7%	35	Idaho	1,206	0.3%
26	Oklahoma	2,769	0.6%	36	Hawaii	1,198	0.3%
18	Oregon	3,932	0.9%	37	Kentucky	1,069	0.2%
12	Pennsylvania	7,117	1.6%	38	Delaware	883	0.2%
33	Rhode Island	1,474	0.3%	39	Alabama	840	0.2%
29	South Carolina	1,916	0.4%	40	Louisiana	793	0.2%
45	South Dakota	185	0.0%	41	Mississippi	500	0.1%
24	Tennessee	2,849	0.6%	42	Wyoming	342	0.1%
2	Texas	76,972	17.6%	43	Alaska	306	0.1%
23	Utah	2,908	0.7%	44	New Hampshire	187	0.0%
50	Vermont	26	0.0%	45	South Dakota	185	0.0%
16	Virginia	5,144	1.2%	46	Montana	152	0.0%
13	Washington	6,300	1.4%	47	North Dakota	59	0.0%
49	West Virginia	52	0.0%	48	Maine	57	0.0%
25	Wisconsin	2,814	0.6%	49	West Virginia	52	0.0%
42	Wyoming	342	0.1%	50	Vermont	26	0.0%
					District of Columbia	620	0.1%

Source: Morgan Quitno Press using data from U.S. Dept. of Health and Human Services, Nat'l Center for Health Statistics "National Vital Statistics Reports" (Vol. 54, No. 8, December 29, 2005)

*Preliminary data by state of residence. Hispanic can be of any race.

**Not available. Fewer than 20 births to unmarried Hispanic women.

Births to Unmarried Hispanic Women
As a Percent of All Births to Hispanic Women in 2004
National Percent = 46.4% of Live Births*

ALPHA ORDER

RANK	STATE	PERCENT
50	Alabama	25.1
46	Alaska	34.9
9	Arizona	54.1
37	Arkansas	42.4
29	California	44.5
38	Colorado	41.6
2	Connecticut	62.2
6	Delaware	58.1
36	Florida	43.2
26	Georgia	45.2
28	Hawaii	44.7
44	Idaho	37.2
25	Illinois	45.4
10	Indiana	52.7
31	Iowa	44.4
27	Kansas	45.1
14	Kentucky	49.1
39	Louisiana	40.6
49	Maine	31.7
16	Maryland	48.8
1	Massachusetts	63.1
24	Michigan	45.7
12	Minnesota	51.5
20	Mississippi	47.5
20	Missouri	47.5
39	Montana	40.6
35	Nebraska	43.9
19	Nevada	47.7
39	New Hampshire	40.6
8	New Jersey	54.4
7	New Mexico	55.8
3	New York	61.6
13	North Carolina	50.1
45	North Dakota	35.3
11	Ohio	52.4
23	Oklahoma	46.1
29	Oregon	44.5
4	Pennsylvania	60.9
5	Rhode Island	60.7
32	South Carolina	44.2
22	South Dakota	46.8
16	Tennessee	48.8
39	Texas	40.6
43	Utah	40.5
47	Vermont	34.7
34	Virginia	44.0
32	Washington	44.2
48	West Virginia	34.3
18	Wisconsin	47.8
15	Wyoming	48.9

RANK ORDER

RANK	STATE	PERCENT
1	Massachusetts	63.1
2	Connecticut	62.2
3	New York	61.6
4	Pennsylvania	60.9
5	Rhode Island	60.7
6	Delaware	58.1
7	New Mexico	55.8
8	New Jersey	54.4
9	Arizona	54.1
10	Indiana	52.7
11	Ohio	52.4
12	Minnesota	51.5
13	North Carolina	50.1
14	Kentucky	49.1
15	Wyoming	48.9
16	Maryland	48.8
16	Tennessee	48.8
18	Wisconsin	47.8
19	Nevada	47.7
20	Mississippi	47.5
20	Missouri	47.5
22	South Dakota	46.8
23	Oklahoma	46.1
24	Michigan	45.7
25	Illinois	45.4
26	Georgia	45.2
27	Kansas	45.1
28	Hawaii	44.7
29	California	44.5
29	Oregon	44.5
31	Iowa	44.4
32	South Carolina	44.2
32	Washington	44.2
34	Virginia	44.0
35	Nebraska	43.9
36	Florida	43.2
37	Arkansas	42.4
38	Colorado	41.6
39	Louisiana	40.6
39	Montana	40.6
39	New Hampshire	40.6
39	Texas	40.6
43	Utah	40.5
44	Idaho	37.2
45	North Dakota	35.3
46	Alaska	34.9
47	Vermont	34.7
48	West Virginia	34.3
49	Maine	31.7
50	Alabama	25.1
	District of Columbia	62.1

Source: U.S. Department of Health and Human Services, National Center for Health Statistics
"National Vital Statistics Reports" (Vol. 54, No. 8, December 29, 2005)
*Preliminary data by state of residence. Hispanic can be of any race.
**Not available. Fewer than 20 births to unmarried Hispanic women.

Pregnancy Rate in 2002

National Rate = 69.2 Births and Abortions per 1,000 Women 15-49 Years Old*

<table>
<tr><td colspan="3">ALPHA ORDER</td><td colspan="3">RANK ORDER</td></tr>
<tr><td>RANK</td><td>STATE</td><td>RATE</td><td>RANK</td><td>STATE</td><td>RATE</td></tr>
<tr><td>30</td><td>Alabama</td><td>63.7</td><td>1</td><td>Utah</td><td>88.1</td></tr>
<tr><td>NA</td><td>Alaska**</td><td>NA</td><td>2</td><td>Nevada</td><td>82.7</td></tr>
<tr><td>4</td><td>Arizona</td><td>77.8</td><td>3</td><td>Texas</td><td>82.4</td></tr>
<tr><td>22</td><td>Arkansas</td><td>66.1</td><td>4</td><td>Arizona</td><td>77.8</td></tr>
<tr><td>NA</td><td>California**</td><td>NA</td><td>4</td><td>New York</td><td>77.8</td></tr>
<tr><td>23</td><td>Colorado</td><td>65.8</td><td>6</td><td>Florida</td><td>76.9</td></tr>
<tr><td>27</td><td>Connecticut</td><td>65.5</td><td>7</td><td>Delaware</td><td>76.6</td></tr>
<tr><td>7</td><td>Delaware</td><td>76.6</td><td>8</td><td>Kansas</td><td>76.2</td></tr>
<tr><td>6</td><td>Florida</td><td>76.9</td><td>9</td><td>Georgia</td><td>75.4</td></tr>
<tr><td>9</td><td>Georgia</td><td>75.4</td><td>10</td><td>Hawaii</td><td>74.3</td></tr>
<tr><td>10</td><td>Hawaii</td><td>74.3</td><td>11</td><td>Illinois</td><td>71.7</td></tr>
<tr><td>16</td><td>Idaho</td><td>68.1</td><td>12</td><td>New Mexico</td><td>71.5</td></tr>
<tr><td>11</td><td>Illinois</td><td>71.7</td><td>13</td><td>North Carolina</td><td>70.1</td></tr>
<tr><td>31</td><td>Indiana</td><td>63.5</td><td>14</td><td>Nebraska</td><td>69.6</td></tr>
<tr><td>36</td><td>Iowa</td><td>62.0</td><td>15</td><td>New Jersey</td><td>69.5</td></tr>
<tr><td>8</td><td>Kansas</td><td>76.2</td><td>16</td><td>Idaho</td><td>68.1</td></tr>
<tr><td>43</td><td>Kentucky</td><td>56.8</td><td>17</td><td>Rhode Island</td><td>68.0</td></tr>
<tr><td>28</td><td>Louisiana</td><td>65.4</td><td>17</td><td>Washington</td><td>68.0</td></tr>
<tr><td>47</td><td>Maine</td><td>50.1</td><td>19</td><td>Oregon</td><td>67.8</td></tr>
<tr><td>35</td><td>Maryland</td><td>62.4</td><td>20</td><td>Virginia</td><td>67.3</td></tr>
<tr><td>32</td><td>Massachusetts</td><td>63.4</td><td>21</td><td>Oklahoma</td><td>66.4</td></tr>
<tr><td>33</td><td>Michigan</td><td>63.3</td><td>22</td><td>Arkansas</td><td>66.1</td></tr>
<tr><td>25</td><td>Minnesota</td><td>65.6</td><td>23</td><td>Colorado</td><td>65.8</td></tr>
<tr><td>34</td><td>Mississippi</td><td>62.7</td><td>23</td><td>Ohio</td><td>65.8</td></tr>
<tr><td>38</td><td>Missouri</td><td>59.9</td><td>25</td><td>Minnesota</td><td>65.6</td></tr>
<tr><td>37</td><td>Montana</td><td>61.6</td><td>25</td><td>Tennessee</td><td>65.6</td></tr>
<tr><td>14</td><td>Nebraska</td><td>69.6</td><td>27</td><td>Connecticut</td><td>65.5</td></tr>
<tr><td>2</td><td>Nevada</td><td>82.7</td><td>28</td><td>Louisiana</td><td>65.4</td></tr>
<tr><td>NA</td><td>New Hampshire**</td><td>NA</td><td>29</td><td>South Dakota</td><td>64.4</td></tr>
<tr><td>15</td><td>New Jersey</td><td>69.5</td><td>30</td><td>Alabama</td><td>63.7</td></tr>
<tr><td>12</td><td>New Mexico</td><td>71.5</td><td>31</td><td>Indiana</td><td>63.5</td></tr>
<tr><td>4</td><td>New York</td><td>77.8</td><td>32</td><td>Massachusetts</td><td>63.4</td></tr>
<tr><td>13</td><td>North Carolina</td><td>70.1</td><td>33</td><td>Michigan</td><td>63.3</td></tr>
<tr><td>40</td><td>North Dakota</td><td>59.1</td><td>34</td><td>Mississippi</td><td>62.7</td></tr>
<tr><td>23</td><td>Ohio</td><td>65.8</td><td>35</td><td>Maryland</td><td>62.4</td></tr>
<tr><td>21</td><td>Oklahoma</td><td>66.4</td><td>36</td><td>Iowa</td><td>62.0</td></tr>
<tr><td>19</td><td>Oregon</td><td>67.8</td><td>37</td><td>Montana</td><td>61.6</td></tr>
<tr><td>42</td><td>Pennsylvania</td><td>58.4</td><td>38</td><td>Missouri</td><td>59.9</td></tr>
<tr><td>17</td><td>Rhode Island</td><td>68.0</td><td>39</td><td>South Carolina</td><td>59.8</td></tr>
<tr><td>39</td><td>South Carolina</td><td>59.8</td><td>40</td><td>North Dakota</td><td>59.1</td></tr>
<tr><td>29</td><td>South Dakota</td><td>64.4</td><td>41</td><td>Wisconsin</td><td>58.9</td></tr>
<tr><td>25</td><td>Tennessee</td><td>65.6</td><td>42</td><td>Pennsylvania</td><td>58.4</td></tr>
<tr><td>3</td><td>Texas</td><td>82.4</td><td>43</td><td>Kentucky</td><td>56.8</td></tr>
<tr><td>1</td><td>Utah</td><td>88.1</td><td>44</td><td>Wyoming</td><td>54.0</td></tr>
<tr><td>46</td><td>Vermont</td><td>52.5</td><td>45</td><td>West Virginia</td><td>52.7</td></tr>
<tr><td>20</td><td>Virginia</td><td>67.3</td><td>46</td><td>Vermont</td><td>52.5</td></tr>
<tr><td>17</td><td>Washington</td><td>68.0</td><td>47</td><td>Maine</td><td>50.1</td></tr>
<tr><td>45</td><td>West Virginia</td><td>52.7</td><td>NA</td><td>Alaska**</td><td>NA</td></tr>
<tr><td>41</td><td>Wisconsin</td><td>58.9</td><td>NA</td><td>California**</td><td>NA</td></tr>
<tr><td>44</td><td>Wyoming</td><td>54.0</td><td>NA</td><td>New Hampshire**</td><td>NA</td></tr>
<tr><td></td><td></td><td></td><td></td><td>District of Columbia</td><td>81.5</td></tr>
</table>

Source: Morgan Quitno Press using data from US Dept of Health & Human Serv's, Centers for Disease Control-Prevention "Abortion Surveillance-United States, 2002" (Morbidity and Mortality Weekly Report, Vol. 54, No. SS-7, 11/25/05)
*The sum of live births and legal induced abortions per 1,000 women aged 15-49 years old. Births by state of residence, abortions by state of occurrence. Miscarriages are not included in these rates. National rate includes only states reporting abortions and births.
**Not available.

Pregnancy Rate for 15 to 19 Year Old Women in 2002

National Rate = 59.8 Births and Abortions per 1,000 Women 15-19 Years Old*

ALPHA ORDER

RANK ORDER

RANK	STATE	RATE		RANK	STATE	RATE
11	Alabama	68.9		1	Texas	78.7
NA	Alaska**	NA		2	Nevada	77.9
6	Arizona	72.7		3	New Mexico	77.6
9	Arkansas	70.3		4	Georgia	74.0
NA	California**	NA		5	Delaware	73.2
19	Colorado	57.8		6	Arizona	72.7
28	Connecticut	50.6		7	Mississippi	71.0
5	Delaware	73.2		8	North Carolina	70.5
NA	Florida**	NA		9	Arkansas	70.3
4	Georgia	74.0		10	Tennessee	69.9
18	Hawaii	59.2		11	Alabama	68.9
37	Idaho	42.5		11	Louisiana	68.9
NA	Illinois**	NA		13	Oklahoma	67.4
24	Indiana	53.4		14	New York	66.4
34	Iowa	44.0		15	Kansas	66.1
15	Kansas	66.1		16	Rhode Island	64.4
28	Kentucky	50.6		17	South Carolina	61.6
11	Louisiana	68.9		18	Hawaii	59.2
44	Maine	36.0		19	Colorado	57.8
NA	Maryland**	NA		20	Washington	56.2
36	Massachusetts	42.6		21	Oregon	56.1
30	Michigan	49.2		22	Ohio	55.7
41	Minnesota	39.8		23	Virginia	53.8
7	Mississippi	71.0		24	Indiana	53.4
26	Missouri	51.0		25	West Virginia	51.9
26	Montana	51.0		26	Missouri	51.0
32	Nebraska	48.0		26	Montana	51.0
2	Nevada	77.9		28	Connecticut	50.6
NA	New Hampshire**	NA		28	Kentucky	50.6
31	New Jersey	48.2		30	Michigan	49.2
3	New Mexico	77.6		31	New Jersey	48.2
14	New York	66.4		32	Nebraska	48.0
8	North Carolina	70.5		33	Pennsylvania	46.7
43	North Dakota	38.1		34	Iowa	44.0
22	Ohio	55.7		35	South Dakota	43.7
13	Oklahoma	67.4		36	Massachusetts	42.6
21	Oregon	56.1		37	Idaho	42.5
33	Pennsylvania	46.7		38	Utah	42.3
16	Rhode Island	64.4		39	Wisconsin	42.0
17	South Carolina	61.6		40	Wyoming	40.2
35	South Dakota	43.7		41	Minnesota	39.8
10	Tennessee	69.9		41	Vermont	39.8
1	Texas	78.7		43	North Dakota	38.1
38	Utah	42.3		44	Maine	36.0
41	Vermont	39.8		NA	Alaska**	NA
23	Virginia	53.8		NA	California**	NA
20	Washington	56.2		NA	Florida**	NA
25	West Virginia	51.9		NA	Illinois**	NA
39	Wisconsin	42.0		NA	Maryland**	NA
40	Wyoming	40.2		NA	New Hampshire**	NA

District of Columbia   153.6

Source: Morgan Quitno Press using data from US Dept of Health & Human Serv's, Centers for Disease Control-Prevention "Abortion Surveillance-United States, 2002" (Morbidity and Mortality Weekly Report, Vol. 54, No. SS-7, 11/25/05)
*The sum of live births and legal induced abortions per 1,000 women aged 15-19 years old. Births by state of residence, abortions by state of occurrence. Miscarriages are not included in these rates. National rate includes only states reporting abortions and births.
**Not available.

Percent Change in Pregnancy Rate for 15 to 19 Year Old Women: 1999 to 2002

National Percent Change = 12.2% Decrease*

ALPHA ORDER			RANK ORDER		
RANK	**STATE**	**PERCENT CHANGE**	**RANK**	**STATE**	**PERCENT CHANGE**
29	Alabama	(14.1)	1	Colorado	3.0
NA	Alaska**	NA	2	South Dakota	0.5
22	Arizona	(11.0)	3	Rhode Island	(3.2)
27	Arkansas	(12.9)	4	North Dakota	(3.5)
NA	California**	NA	5	Wyoming	(3.8)
1	Colorado	3.0	6	Montana	(4.3)
38	Connecticut	(16.4)	7	Nevada	(5.5)
32	Delaware	(14.4)	8	New Mexico	(6.1)
NA	Florida**	NA	9	West Virginia	(7.3)
36	Georgia	(15.3)	10	Iowa	(7.6)
28	Hawaii	(13.8)	11	Vermont	(7.7)
23	Idaho	(11.3)	12	Nebraska	(8.4)
NA	Illinois**	NA	13	Utah	(8.6)
33	Indiana	(14.7)	14	Louisiana	(8.9)
10	Iowa	(7.6)	14	Wisconsin	(8.9)
19	Kansas	(10.3)	16	Minnesota	(9.5)
42	Kentucky	(20.8)	17	Michigan	(9.6)
14	Louisiana	(8.9)	18	Missouri	(10.2)
37	Maine	(16.3)	19	Kansas	(10.3)
NA	Maryland**	NA	20	Texas	(10.7)
40	Massachusetts	(18.1)	21	Mississippi	(10.9)
17	Michigan	(9.6)	22	Arizona	(11.0)
16	Minnesota	(9.5)	23	Idaho	(11.3)
21	Mississippi	(10.9)	24	Pennsylvania	(11.6)
18	Missouri	(10.2)	25	Ohio	(12.7)
6	Montana	(4.3)	26	Tennessee	(12.8)
12	Nebraska	(8.4)	27	Arkansas	(12.9)
7	Nevada	(5.5)	28	Hawaii	(13.8)
NA	New Hampshire**	NA	29	Alabama	(14.1)
41	New Jersey	(18.9)	30	North Carolina	(14.2)
8	New Mexico	(6.1)	31	Washington	(14.3)
39	New York	(16.8)	32	Delaware	(14.4)
30	North Carolina	(14.2)	33	Indiana	(14.7)
4	North Dakota	(3.5)	33	Virginia	(14.7)
25	Ohio	(12.7)	35	South Carolina	(14.8)
NA	Oklahoma**	NA	36	Georgia	(15.3)
43	Oregon	(22.2)	37	Maine	(16.3)
24	Pennsylvania	(11.6)	38	Connecticut	(16.4)
3	Rhode Island	(3.2)	39	New York	(16.8)
35	South Carolina	(14.8)	40	Massachusetts	(18.1)
2	South Dakota	0.5	41	New Jersey	(18.9)
26	Tennessee	(12.8)	42	Kentucky	(20.8)
20	Texas	(10.7)	43	Oregon	(22.2)
13	Utah	(8.6)	NA	Alaska**	NA
11	Vermont	(7.7)	NA	California**	NA
33	Virginia	(14.7)	NA	Florida**	NA
31	Washington	(14.3)	NA	Illinois**	NA
9	West Virginia	(7.3)	NA	Maryland**	NA
14	Wisconsin	(8.9)	NA	New Hampshire**	NA
5	Wyoming	(3.8)	NA	Oklahoma**	NA
				District of Columbia	(20.3)

Source: Morgan Quitno Press using data from US Dept of Health & Human Serv's, Centers for Disease Control-Prevention "Abortion Surveillance-United States, 2002" (Morbidity and Mortality Weekly Report, Vol. 54, No. SS-7, 11/25/05)
*The sum of live births and legal induced abortions per 1,000 women aged 15-19 years old. Births by state of residence, abortions by state of occurrence. Miscarriages are not included in these rates. National rate includes only states reporting abortions and births.
**Not available.

Births to Teenage Mothers in 2004

National Total = 423,906 Live Births*

ALPHA ORDER

RANK ORDER

RANK	STATE	BIRTHS	% of USA		RANK	STATE	BIRTHS	% of USA
17	Alabama	8,277	2.0%		1	Texas	52,661	12.4%
46	Alaska	1,085	0.3%		2	California	50,692	12.0%
11	Arizona	11,896	2.8%		3	Florida	23,766	5.6%
27	Arkansas	5,829	1.4%		4	Illinois	17,732	4.2%
2	California	50,692	12.0%		5	New York	17,312	4.1%
21	Colorado	6,852	1.6%		6	Georgia	16,523	3.9%
36	Connecticut	2,905	0.7%		7	Ohio	15,512	3.7%
42	Delaware	1,198	0.3%		8	North Carolina	13,903	3.3%
3	Florida	23,766	5.6%		9	Pennsylvania	12,973	3.1%
6	Georgia	16,523	3.9%		10	Michigan	12,458	2.9%
40	Hawaii	1,462	0.3%		11	Arizona	11,896	2.8%
39	Idaho	2,072	0.5%		12	Tennessee	10,274	2.4%
4	Illinois	17,732	4.2%		13	Louisiana	9,679	2.3%
14	Indiana	9,541	2.3%		14	Indiana	9,541	2.3%
34	Iowa	3,267	0.8%		15	Virginia	8,937	2.1%
32	Kansas	3,998	0.9%		16	Missouri	8,867	2.1%
24	Kentucky	6,697	1.6%		17	Alabama	8,277	2.0%
13	Louisiana	9,679	2.3%		18	South Carolina	7,583	1.8%
45	Maine	1,116	0.3%		19	New Jersey	7,010	1.7%
25	Maryland	6,341	1.5%		20	Oklahoma	6,974	1.6%
29	Massachusetts	4,635	1.1%		21	Colorado	6,852	1.6%
10	Michigan	12,458	2.9%		22	Washington	6,784	1.6%
28	Minnesota	5,014	1.2%		23	Mississippi	6,721	1.6%
23	Mississippi	6,721	1.6%		24	Kentucky	6,697	1.6%
16	Missouri	8,867	2.1%		25	Maryland	6,341	1.5%
41	Montana	1,222	0.3%		26	Wisconsin	6,103	1.4%
38	Nebraska	2,291	0.5%		27	Arkansas	5,829	1.4%
33	Nevada	3,871	0.9%		28	Minnesota	5,014	1.2%
47	New Hampshire	845	0.2%		29	Massachusetts	4,635	1.1%
19	New Jersey	7,010	1.7%		30	New Mexico	4,457	1.1%
30	New Mexico	4,457	1.1%		31	Oregon	4,067	1.0%
5	New York	17,312	4.1%		32	Kansas	3,998	0.9%
8	North Carolina	13,903	3.3%		33	Nevada	3,871	0.9%
49	North Dakota	631	0.1%		34	Iowa	3,267	0.8%
7	Ohio	15,512	3.7%		35	Utah	3,243	0.8%
20	Oklahoma	6,974	1.6%		36	Connecticut	2,905	0.7%
31	Oregon	4,067	1.0%		37	West Virginia	2,503	0.6%
9	Pennsylvania	12,973	3.1%		38	Nebraska	2,291	0.5%
43	Rhode Island	1,176	0.3%		39	Idaho	2,072	0.5%
18	South Carolina	7,583	1.8%		40	Hawaii	1,462	0.3%
44	South Dakota	1,134	0.3%		41	Montana	1,222	0.3%
12	Tennessee	10,274	2.4%		42	Delaware	1,198	0.3%
1	Texas	52,661	12.4%		43	Rhode Island	1,176	0.3%
35	Utah	3,243	0.8%		44	South Dakota	1,134	0.3%
50	Vermont	466	0.1%		45	Maine	1,116	0.3%
15	Virginia	8,937	2.1%		46	Alaska	1,085	0.3%
22	Washington	6,784	1.6%		47	New Hampshire	845	0.2%
37	West Virginia	2,503	0.6%		48	Wyoming	817	0.2%
26	Wisconsin	6,103	1.4%		49	North Dakota	631	0.1%
48	Wyoming	817	0.2%		50	Vermont	466	0.1%
						District of Columbia	888	0.2%

Source: Morgan Quitno Press using data from U.S. Dept. of Health and Human Services, Nat'l Center for Health Statistics "National Vital Statistics Reports" (Vol. 54, No. 8, December 29, 2005)

*Preliminary estimates of live births to women 15 to 19 years old by state of residence.

Teenage Birth Rate in 2004

National Rate = 42.0 Live Births per 1,000 Women 15 to 19 Years Old*

ALPHA ORDER

RANK ORDER

RANK	STATE	RATE		RANK	STATE	RATE
9	Alabama	53.4		1	Texas	64.2
25	Alaska	39.4		2	Mississippi	63.6
5	Arizona	60.9		3	New Mexico	61.6
4	Arkansas	61.5		4	Arkansas	61.5
24	California	40.2		5	Arizona	60.9
15	Colorado	44.4		6	Louisiana	57.5
45	Connecticut	24.7		7	Oklahoma	56.5
17	Delaware	44.2		8	Georgia	54.5
21	Florida	43.0		9	Alabama	53.4
8	Georgia	54.5		10	Tennessee	53.1
29	Hawaii	36.5		11	South Carolina	52.9
26	Idaho	39.1		12	Nevada	52.1
22	Illinois	40.7		13	North Carolina	50.1
19	Indiana	43.8		14	Kentucky	49.2
38	Iowa	31.9		15	Colorado	44.4
23	Kansas	40.6		15	West Virginia	44.4
14	Kentucky	49.2		17	Delaware	44.2
6	Louisiana	57.5		18	Missouri	44.0
46	Maine	24.4		19	Indiana	43.8
37	Maryland	32.9		20	Wyoming	43.1
48	Massachusetts	22.6		21	Florida	43.0
33	Michigan	34.7		22	Illinois	40.7
44	Minnesota	27.2		23	Kansas	40.6
2	Mississippi	63.6		24	California	40.2
18	Missouri	44.0		25	Alaska	39.4
31	Montana	35.9		26	Idaho	39.1
30	Nebraska	36.3		26	Ohio	39.1
12	Nevada	52.1		28	South Dakota	38.9
50	New Hampshire	18.1		29	Hawaii	36.5
46	New Jersey	24.4		30	Nebraska	36.3
3	New Mexico	61.6		31	Montana	35.9
43	New York	27.3		32	Virginia	35.8
13	North Carolina	50.1		33	Michigan	34.7
42	North Dakota	27.6		34	Utah	34.4
26	Ohio	39.1		35	Oregon	33.9
7	Oklahoma	56.5		36	Rhode Island	33.6
35	Oregon	33.9		37	Maryland	32.9
40	Pennsylvania	30.9		38	Iowa	31.9
36	Rhode Island	33.6		39	Washington	31.5
11	South Carolina	52.9		40	Pennsylvania	30.9
28	South Dakota	38.9		41	Wisconsin	30.7
10	Tennessee	53.1		42	North Dakota	27.6
1	Texas	64.2		43	New York	27.3
34	Utah	34.4		44	Minnesota	27.2
49	Vermont	21.1		45	Connecticut	24.7
32	Virginia	35.8		46	Maine	24.4
39	Washington	31.5		46	New Jersey	24.4
15	West Virginia	44.4		48	Massachusetts	22.6
41	Wisconsin	30.7		49	Vermont	21.1
20	Wyoming	43.1		50	New Hampshire	18.1

District of Columbia 68.6

Source: Morgan Quitno Press using data from U.S. Dept. of Health and Human Services, Nat'l Center for Health Statistics
"National Vital Statistics Reports" (Vol. 54, No. 8, December 29, 2005)
*Preliminary data by state of residence.

Births to Teenage Mothers as a Percent of Births in 2004

National Percent = 10.3% of Live Births*

ALPHA ORDER			RANK ORDER		
RANK	STATE	PERCENT	RANK	STATE	PERCENT
5	Alabama	13.9	1	Mississippi	15.7
22	Alaska	10.5	1	New Mexico	15.7
10	Arizona	12.7	3	Arkansas	15.1
3	Arkansas	15.1	4	Louisiana	14.8
29	California	9.3	5	Alabama	13.9
25	Colorado	10.0	6	Texas	13.7
45	Connecticut	6.9	7	Oklahoma	13.6
20	Delaware	10.6	8	South Carolina	13.4
19	Florida	10.9	9	Tennessee	12.9
14	Georgia	11.9	10	Arizona	12.7
40	Hawaii	8.0	11	Kentucky	12.3
30	Idaho	9.2	12	West Virginia	12.0
27	Illinois	9.8	12	Wyoming	12.0
17	Indiana	11.0	14	Georgia	11.9
37	Iowa	8.5	15	North Carolina	11.6
24	Kansas	10.1	16	Missouri	11.4
11	Kentucky	12.3	17	Indiana	11.0
4	Louisiana	14.8	17	Nevada	11.0
40	Maine	8.0	19	Florida	10.9
37	Maryland	8.5	20	Delaware	10.6
49	Massachusetts	5.9	20	Montana	10.6
28	Michigan	9.6	22	Alaska	10.5
43	Minnesota	7.1	23	Ohio	10.4
1	Mississippi	15.7	24	Kansas	10.1
16	Missouri	11.4	25	Colorado	10.0
20	Montana	10.6	25	South Dakota	10.0
34	Nebraska	8.7	27	Illinois	9.8
17	Nevada	11.0	28	Michigan	9.6
50	New Hampshire	5.8	29	California	9.3
48	New Jersey	6.1	30	Idaho	9.2
1	New Mexico	15.7	30	Rhode Island	9.2
45	New York	6.9	32	Oregon	8.9
15	North Carolina	11.6	32	Pennsylvania	8.9
42	North Dakota	7.7	34	Nebraska	8.7
23	Ohio	10.4	34	Wisconsin	8.7
7	Oklahoma	13.6	36	Virginia	8.6
32	Oregon	8.9	37	Iowa	8.5
32	Pennsylvania	8.9	37	Maryland	8.5
30	Rhode Island	9.2	39	Washington	8.3
8	South Carolina	13.4	40	Hawaii	8.0
25	South Dakota	10.0	40	Maine	8.0
9	Tennessee	12.9	42	North Dakota	7.7
6	Texas	13.7	43	Minnesota	7.1
47	Utah	6.4	43	Vermont	7.1
43	Vermont	7.1	45	Connecticut	6.9
36	Virginia	8.6	45	New York	6.9
39	Washington	8.3	47	Utah	6.4
12	West Virginia	12.0	48	New Jersey	6.1
34	Wisconsin	8.7	49	Massachusetts	5.9
12	Wyoming	12.0	50	New Hampshire	5.8
				District of Columbia	11.2

Source: U.S. Department of Health and Human Services, National Center for Health Statistics
"National Vital Statistics Reports" (Vol. 54, No. 8, December 29, 2005)
*Preliminary data. Live births to women 15 to 19 years old by state of residence.

Percent Change in Teenage Birth Rate: 2000 to 2004

National Percent Change = 13.4% Decrease*

RANK	STATE (ALPHA ORDER)	PERCENT CHANGE		RANK	STATE (RANK ORDER)	PERCENT CHANGE
35	Alabama	(15.1)		1	Wyoming	5.6
9	Alaska	(7.1)		2	South Dakota	4.6
23	Arizona	(11.9)		3	Montana	0.3
17	Arkansas	(10.2)		4	North Dakota	(2.1)
40	California	(17.1)		5	Nebraska	(2.4)
15	Colorado	(9.8)		6	West Virginia	(4.3)
47	Connecticut	(22.6)		7	Oklahoma	(6.0)
32	Delaware	(14.3)		8	New Mexico	(6.9)
43	Florida	(18.3)		9	Alaska	(7.1)
35	Georgia	(15.1)		10	Texas	(7.2)
44	Hawaii	(19.1)		11	Louisiana	(7.4)
14	Idaho	(9.3)		12	Iowa	(8.1)
42	Illinois	(17.8)		12	Minnesota	(8.1)
29	Indiana	(12.9)		14	Idaho	(9.3)
12	Iowa	(8.1)		15	Colorado	(9.8)
18	Kansas	(10.4)		15	Missouri	(9.8)
19	Kentucky	(11.0)		17	Arkansas	(10.2)
11	Louisiana	(7.4)		18	Kansas	(10.4)
34	Maine	(15.0)		19	Kentucky	(11.0)
45	Maryland	(20.9)		19	Wisconsin	(11.0)
39	Massachusetts	(16.6)		21	Michigan	(11.5)
21	Michigan	(11.5)		22	Mississippi	(11.7)
12	Minnesota	(8.1)		23	Arizona	(11.9)
22	Mississippi	(11.7)		24	Pennsylvania	(12.2)
15	Missouri	(9.8)		25	Virginia	(12.3)
3	Montana	0.3		26	Vermont	(12.4)
5	Nebraska	(2.4)		27	Rhode Island	(12.5)
37	Nevada	(16.2)		28	South Carolina	(12.7)
47	New Hampshire	(22.6)		29	Indiana	(12.9)
49	New Jersey	(23.0)		30	Tennessee	(13.7)
8	New Mexico	(6.9)		31	Utah	(14.0)
50	New York	(23.3)		32	Delaware	(14.3)
38	North Carolina	(16.4)		32	Ohio	(14.3)
4	North Dakota	(2.1)		34	Maine	(15.0)
32	Ohio	(14.3)		35	Alabama	(15.1)
7	Oklahoma	(6.0)		35	Georgia	(15.1)
46	Oregon	(21.5)		37	Nevada	(16.2)
24	Pennsylvania	(12.2)		38	North Carolina	(16.4)
27	Rhode Island	(12.5)		39	Massachusetts	(16.6)
28	South Carolina	(12.7)		40	California	(17.1)
2	South Dakota	4.6		41	Washington	(17.5)
30	Tennessee	(13.7)		42	Illinois	(17.8)
10	Texas	(7.2)		43	Florida	(18.3)
31	Utah	(14.0)		44	Hawaii	(19.1)
26	Vermont	(12.4)		45	Maryland	(20.9)
25	Virginia	(12.3)		46	Oregon	(21.5)
41	Washington	(17.5)		47	Connecticut	(22.6)
6	West Virginia	(4.3)		47	New Hampshire	(22.6)
19	Wisconsin	(11.0)		49	New Jersey	(23.0)
1	Wyoming	5.6		50	New York	(23.3)
					District of Columbia	(15.0)

Source: Morgan Quitno Press using data from U.S. Dept. of Health and Human Services, Nat'l Center for Health Statistics "National Vital Statistics Reports" (Vol. 54, No. 8, December 29, 2005)
*Preliminary data by state of residence. Births to women aged 15 to 19 years old.

Teenage Birth Rate in 2003

National Rate = 41.6 Live Births per 1,000 Women 15 to 19 Years Old*

ALPHA ORDER

RANK	STATE	RATE
11	Alabama	52.4
27	Alaska	38.6
4	Arizona	61.1
5	Arkansas	59.0
24	California	40.1
17	Colorado	43.9
47	Connecticut	24.8
15	Delaware	44.9
20	Florida	42.5
8	Georgia	53.5
28	Hawaii	37.3
26	Idaho	39.3
23	Illinois	40.4
18	Indiana	43.5
37	Iowa	31.9
21	Kansas	41.2
13	Kentucky	49.6
6	Louisiana	56.0
46	Maine	24.9
36	Maryland	33.3
48	Massachusetts	23.0
34	Michigan	34.4
44	Minnesota	26.6
3	Mississippi	62.5
19	Missouri	43.2
31	Montana	35.0
30	Nebraska	36.0
10	Nevada	53.0
50	New Hampshire	18.2
45	New Jersey	25.5
2	New Mexico	62.7
42	New York	28.2
14	North Carolina	49.0
43	North Dakota	26.8
25	Ohio	39.4
7	Oklahoma	55.9
34	Oregon	34.4
41	Pennsylvania	31.2
39	Rhode Island	31.3
12	South Carolina	51.5
32	South Dakota	34.7
8	Tennessee	53.5
1	Texas	62.9
33	Utah	34.6
49	Vermont	18.9
29	Virginia	36.1
38	Washington	31.5
16	West Virginia	44.8
39	Wisconsin	31.3
22	Wyoming	40.8

RANK ORDER

RANK	STATE	RATE
1	Texas	62.9
2	New Mexico	62.7
3	Mississippi	62.5
4	Arizona	61.1
5	Arkansas	59.0
6	Louisiana	56.0
7	Oklahoma	55.9
8	Georgia	53.5
8	Tennessee	53.5
10	Nevada	53.0
11	Alabama	52.4
12	South Carolina	51.5
13	Kentucky	49.6
14	North Carolina	49.0
15	Delaware	44.9
16	West Virginia	44.8
17	Colorado	43.9
18	Indiana	43.5
19	Missouri	43.2
20	Florida	42.5
21	Kansas	41.2
22	Wyoming	40.8
23	Illinois	40.4
24	California	40.1
25	Ohio	39.4
26	Idaho	39.3
27	Alaska	38.6
28	Hawaii	37.3
29	Virginia	36.1
30	Nebraska	36.0
31	Montana	35.0
32	South Dakota	34.7
33	Utah	34.6
34	Michigan	34.4
34	Oregon	34.4
36	Maryland	33.3
37	Iowa	31.9
38	Washington	31.5
39	Rhode Island	31.3
39	Wisconsin	31.3
41	Pennsylvania	31.2
42	New York	28.2
43	North Dakota	26.8
44	Minnesota	26.6
45	New Jersey	25.5
46	Maine	24.9
47	Connecticut	24.8
48	Massachusetts	23.0
49	Vermont	18.9
50	New Hampshire	18.2

District of Columbia   60.3

Source: Morgan Quitno Press using data from U.S. Dept. of Health and Human Services, Nat'l Center for Health Statistics
"National Vital Statistics Reports" (Vol. 54, No. 2, September 8, 2005)
*Final data by state of residence.

Births to White Teenage Mothers in 2004

National Total = 300,373 Live Births*

ALPHA ORDER				RANK ORDER			
RANK	STATE	BIRTHS	% of USA	RANK	STATE	BIRTHS	% of USA
20	Alabama	4,663	1.6%	1	Texas	44,541	14.8%
47	Alaska	514	0.2%	2	California	43,690	14.5%
7	Arizona	10,065	3.4%	3	Florida	14,508	4.8%
23	Arkansas	4,069	1.4%	4	Illinois	11,269	3.8%
2	California	43,690	14.5%	5	New York	11,084	3.7%
15	Colorado	6,189	2.1%	6	Ohio	10,693	3.6%
37	Connecticut	2,136	0.7%	7	Arizona	10,065	3.4%
46	Delaware	665	0.2%	8	Georgia	9,157	3.0%
3	Florida	14,508	4.8%	9	North Carolina	8,392	2.8%
8	Georgia	9,157	3.0%	10	Pennsylvania	8,243	2.7%
50	Hawaii	321	0.1%	11	Michigan	8,224	2.7%
38	Idaho	1,976	0.7%	12	Indiana	7,617	2.5%
4	Illinois	11,269	3.8%	13	Tennessee	6,765	2.3%
12	Indiana	7,617	2.5%	14	Missouri	6,479	2.2%
33	Iowa	2,894	1.0%	15	Colorado	6,189	2.1%
30	Kansas	3,369	1.1%	16	Kentucky	5,791	1.9%
16	Kentucky	5,791	1.9%	17	Washington	5,507	1.8%
24	Louisiana	3,863	1.3%	18	Virginia	5,251	1.7%
40	Maine	1,071	0.4%	19	Oklahoma	4,965	1.7%
35	Maryland	2,722	0.9%	20	Alabama	4,663	1.6%
28	Massachusetts	3,522	1.2%	21	New Jersey	4,291	1.4%
11	Michigan	8,224	2.7%	22	Wisconsin	4,080	1.4%
29	Minnesota	3,514	1.2%	23	Arkansas	4,069	1.4%
34	Mississippi	2,827	0.9%	24	Louisiana	3,863	1.3%
14	Missouri	6,479	2.2%	25	New Mexico	3,745	1.2%
42	Montana	845	0.3%	26	South Carolina	3,722	1.2%
39	Nebraska	1,825	0.6%	27	Oregon	3,671	1.2%
31	Nevada	3,164	1.1%	28	Massachusetts	3,522	1.2%
43	New Hampshire	812	0.3%	29	Minnesota	3,514	1.2%
21	New Jersey	4,291	1.4%	30	Kansas	3,369	1.1%
25	New Mexico	3,745	1.2%	31	Nevada	3,164	1.1%
5	New York	11,084	3.7%	32	Utah	3,040	1.0%
9	North Carolina	8,392	2.8%	33	Iowa	2,894	1.0%
49	North Dakota	407	0.1%	34	Mississippi	2,827	0.9%
6	Ohio	10,693	3.6%	35	Maryland	2,722	0.9%
19	Oklahoma	4,965	1.7%	36	West Virginia	2,359	0.8%
27	Oregon	3,671	1.2%	37	Connecticut	2,136	0.7%
10	Pennsylvania	8,243	2.7%	38	Idaho	1,976	0.7%
41	Rhode Island	903	0.3%	39	Nebraska	1,825	0.6%
26	South Carolina	3,722	1.2%	40	Maine	1,071	0.4%
45	South Dakota	681	0.2%	41	Rhode Island	903	0.3%
13	Tennessee	6,765	2.3%	42	Montana	845	0.3%
1	Texas	44,541	14.8%	43	New Hampshire	812	0.3%
32	Utah	3,040	1.0%	44	Wyoming	744	0.2%
48	Vermont	460	0.2%	45	South Dakota	681	0.2%
18	Virginia	5,251	1.7%	46	Delaware	665	0.2%
17	Washington	5,507	1.8%	47	Alaska	514	0.2%
36	West Virginia	2,359	0.8%	48	Vermont	460	0.2%
22	Wisconsin	4,080	1.4%	49	North Dakota	407	0.1%
44	Wyoming	744	0.2%	50	Hawaii	321	0.1%
					District of Columbia	32	0.0%

Source: Morgan Quitno Press using data from U.S. Dept. of Health and Human Services, Nat'l Center for Health Statistics "National Vital Statistics Reports" (Vol. 54, No. 8, December 29, 2005)
*Preliminary estimates of live births to women 15 to 19 years old by state of residence.

White Teenage Birth Rate in 2004

National Rate = 37.7 Births per 1,000 White Teenage Women*

ALPHA ORDER			RANK ORDER		
RANK	STATE	RATE	RANK	STATE	RATE
10	Alabama	46.3	1	Texas	65.7
37	Alaska	26.7	2	New Mexico	62.8
3	Arizona	60.1	3	Arizona	60.1
4	Arkansas	55.5	4	Arkansas	55.5
12	California	44.1	5	Oklahoma	51.8
13	Colorado	44.0	6	Nevada	51.3
43	Connecticut	21.7	7	Mississippi	49.9
25	Delaware	33.9	8	Georgia	49.4
23	Florida	35.1	9	Kentucky	47.5
8	Georgia	49.4	10	Alabama	46.3
50	Hawaii	17.8	11	Tennessee	45.6
20	Idaho	38.6	12	California	44.1
26	Illinois	33.4	13	Colorado	44.0
19	Indiana	39.7	14	West Virginia	43.9
30	Iowa	29.7	15	North Carolina	43.8
22	Kansas	38.0	16	South Carolina	42.2
9	Kentucky	47.5	17	Wyoming	41.2
18	Louisiana	40.2	18	Louisiana	40.2
38	Maine	24.2	19	Indiana	39.7
42	Maryland	22.8	20	Idaho	38.6
46	Massachusetts	20.0	21	Missouri	38.3
34	Michigan	28.5	22	Kansas	38.0
44	Minnesota	21.5	23	Florida	35.1
7	Mississippi	49.9	24	Utah	34.2
21	Missouri	38.3	25	Delaware	33.9
35	Montana	27.7	26	Illinois	33.4
29	Nebraska	31.5	27	Oregon	33.2
6	Nevada	51.3	28	Ohio	31.9
49	New Hampshire	18.0	29	Nebraska	31.5
47	New Jersey	19.8	30	Iowa	29.7
2	New Mexico	62.8	30	Rhode Island	29.7
38	New York	24.2	32	Virginia	29.5
15	North Carolina	43.8	33	Washington	29.4
48	North Dakota	19.5	34	Michigan	28.5
28	Ohio	31.9	35	Montana	27.7
5	Oklahoma	51.8	36	South Dakota	27.2
27	Oregon	33.2	37	Alaska	26.7
40	Pennsylvania	23.3	38	Maine	24.2
30	Rhode Island	29.7	38	New York	24.2
16	South Carolina	42.2	40	Pennsylvania	23.3
36	South Dakota	27.2	40	Wisconsin	23.3
11	Tennessee	45.6	42	Maryland	22.8
1	Texas	65.7	43	Connecticut	21.7
24	Utah	34.2	44	Minnesota	21.5
45	Vermont	21.3	45	Vermont	21.3
32	Virginia	29.5	46	Massachusetts	20.0
33	Washington	29.4	47	New Jersey	19.8
14	West Virginia	43.9	48	North Dakota	19.5
40	Wisconsin	23.3	49	New Hampshire	18.0
17	Wyoming	41.2	50	Hawaii	17.8

	District of Columbia	6.3

Source: Morgan Quitno Press using data from U.S. Dept. of Health and Human Services, Nat'l Center for Health Statistics
   "National Vital Statistics Reports" (Vol. 54, No. 8, December 29, 2005)
*Preliminary data. Live births to women age 15 to 19 years old by state of residence. Rates calculated using
Census 2004 estimates for females ages 15 to 19 years old in the category of "White Alone or in Combination."

Births to White Teenage Mothers as a Percent of White Births in 2004

National Percent = 9.3% of White Live Births*

ALPHA ORDER

RANK	STATE	PERCENT
10	Alabama	11.5
34	Alaska	7.8
4	Arizona	12.4
3	Arkansas	13.4
18	California	9.9
18	Colorado	9.9
42	Connecticut	6.2
27	Delaware	8.4
22	Florida	9.2
15	Georgia	10.2
42	Hawaii	6.2
23	Idaho	9.1
31	Illinois	8.0
16	Indiana	10.1
30	Iowa	8.1
20	Kansas	9.6
7	Kentucky	11.9
13	Louisiana	10.4
31	Maine	8.0
42	Maryland	6.2
49	Massachusetts	5.5
31	Michigan	8.0
46	Minnesota	5.9
6	Mississippi	12.0
16	Missouri	10.1
26	Montana	8.6
35	Nebraska	7.7
12	Nevada	10.9
46	New Hampshire	5.9
50	New Jersey	5.1
1	New Mexico	15.7
42	New York	6.2
20	North Carolina	9.6
48	North Dakota	5.8
25	Ohio	8.8
4	Oklahoma	12.4
24	Oregon	8.9
39	Pennsylvania	7.0
28	Rhode Island	8.3
13	South Carolina	10.4
36	South Dakota	7.4
11	Tennessee	11.2
2	Texas	13.6
41	Utah	6.3
37	Vermont	7.2
38	Virginia	7.1
29	Washington	8.2
8	West Virginia	11.8
40	Wisconsin	6.8
9	Wyoming	11.7

RANK ORDER

RANK	STATE	PERCENT
1	New Mexico	15.7
2	Texas	13.6
3	Arkansas	13.4
4	Arizona	12.4
4	Oklahoma	12.4
6	Mississippi	12.0
7	Kentucky	11.9
8	West Virginia	11.8
9	Wyoming	11.7
10	Alabama	11.5
11	Tennessee	11.2
12	Nevada	10.9
13	Louisiana	10.4
13	South Carolina	10.4
15	Georgia	10.2
16	Indiana	10.1
16	Missouri	10.1
18	California	9.9
18	Colorado	9.9
20	Kansas	9.6
20	North Carolina	9.6
22	Florida	9.2
23	Idaho	9.1
24	Oregon	8.9
25	Ohio	8.8
26	Montana	8.6
27	Delaware	8.4
28	Rhode Island	8.3
29	Washington	8.2
30	Iowa	8.1
31	Illinois	8.0
31	Maine	8.0
31	Michigan	8.0
34	Alaska	7.8
35	Nebraska	7.7
36	South Dakota	7.4
37	Vermont	7.2
38	Virginia	7.1
39	Pennsylvania	7.0
40	Wisconsin	6.8
41	Utah	6.3
42	Connecticut	6.2
42	Hawaii	6.2
42	Maryland	6.2
42	New York	6.2
46	Minnesota	5.9
46	New Hampshire	5.9
48	North Dakota	5.8
49	Massachusetts	5.5
50	New Jersey	5.1

| | District of Columbia | 1.4 |

Source: U.S. Department of Health and Human Services, National Center for Health Statistics
    "National Vital Statistics Reports" (Vol. 54, No. 8, December 29, 2005)
*Preliminary data. Live births to women 15 to 19 years old by state of residence.

Births to Black Teenage Mothers in 2004

National Total = 104,736 Live Births*

ALPHA ORDER				RANK ORDER			
RANK	STATE	BIRTHS	% of USA	RANK	STATE	BIRTHS	% of USA
14	Alabama	3,593	3.4%	1	Florida	8,758	8.4%
42	Alaska	41	0.0%	2	Texas	7,636	7.3%
28	Arizona	569	0.5%	3	Georgia	7,172	6.8%
21	Arkansas	1,679	1.6%	4	Illinois	6,391	6.1%
9	California	4,495	4.3%	5	New York	5,823	5.6%
32	Colorado	483	0.5%	6	Louisiana	5,640	5.4%
26	Connecticut	729	0.7%	7	North Carolina	4,972	4.7%
30	Delaware	524	0.5%	8	Ohio	4,686	4.5%
1	Florida	8,758	8.4%	9	California	4,495	4.3%
3	Georgia	7,172	6.8%	10	Pennsylvania	4,416	4.2%
41	Hawaii	43	0.0%	11	Michigan	3,929	3.8%
NA	Idaho**	NA	NA	12	Mississippi	3,796	3.6%
4	Illinois	6,391	6.1%	13	South Carolina	3,785	3.6%
20	Indiana	1,902	1.8%	14	Alabama	3,593	3.4%
35	Iowa	288	0.3%	15	Maryland	3,549	3.4%
29	Kansas	525	0.5%	16	Virginia	3,526	3.4%
25	Kentucky	883	0.8%	17	Tennessee	3,393	3.2%
6	Louisiana	5,640	5.4%	18	New Jersey	2,585	2.5%
NA	Maine**	NA	NA	19	Missouri	2,302	2.2%
15	Maryland	3,549	3.4%	20	Indiana	1,902	1.8%
23	Massachusetts	907	0.9%	21	Arkansas	1,679	1.6%
11	Michigan	3,929	3.8%	22	Wisconsin	1,538	1.5%
27	Minnesota	571	0.5%	23	Massachusetts	907	0.9%
12	Mississippi	3,796	3.6%	24	Oklahoma	903	0.9%
19	Missouri	2,302	2.2%	25	Kentucky	883	0.8%
NA	Montana**	NA	NA	26	Connecticut	729	0.7%
34	Nebraska	319	0.3%	27	Minnesota	571	0.5%
33	Nevada	473	0.5%	28	Arizona	569	0.5%
43	New Hampshire	28	0.0%	29	Kansas	525	0.5%
18	New Jersey	2,585	2.5%	30	Delaware	524	0.5%
39	New Mexico	70	0.1%	31	Washington	520	0.5%
5	New York	5,823	5.6%	32	Colorado	483	0.5%
7	North Carolina	4,972	4.7%	33	Nevada	473	0.5%
NA	North Dakota**	NA	NA	34	Nebraska	319	0.3%
8	Ohio	4,686	4.5%	35	Iowa	288	0.3%
24	Oklahoma	903	0.9%	36	Rhode Island	170	0.2%
37	Oregon	162	0.2%	37	Oregon	162	0.2%
10	Pennsylvania	4,416	4.2%	38	West Virginia	126	0.1%
36	Rhode Island	170	0.2%	39	New Mexico	70	0.1%
13	South Carolina	3,785	3.6%	40	Utah	45	0.0%
44	South Dakota	27	0.0%	41	Hawaii	43	0.0%
17	Tennessee	3,393	3.2%	42	Alaska	41	0.0%
2	Texas	7,636	7.3%	43	New Hampshire	28	0.0%
40	Utah	45	0.0%	44	South Dakota	27	0.0%
NA	Vermont**	NA	NA	NA	Idaho**	NA	NA
16	Virginia	3,526	3.4%	NA	Maine**	NA	NA
31	Washington	520	0.5%	NA	Montana**	NA	NA
38	West Virginia	126	0.1%	NA	North Dakota**	NA	NA
22	Wisconsin	1,538	1.5%	NA	Vermont**	NA	NA
NA	Wyoming**	NA	NA	NA	Wyoming**	NA	NA
					District of Columbia	847	0.8%

Source: Morgan Quitno Press using data from U.S. Dept. of Health and Human Services, Nat'l Center for Health Statistics
"National Vital Statistics Reports" (Vol. 54, No. 8, December 29, 2005)
*Preliminary data. Estimated live births to women 15 to 19 years old by state of residence.
**Not available. Fewer than 20 births to black teenage women.

Black Teenage Birth Rate in 2004

National Rate = 63.3 Births per 1,000 Black Teenage Women*

ALPHA ORDER				RANK ORDER		
RANK	STATE	RATE		RANK	STATE	RATE
17	Alabama	68.3		1	Wisconsin	93.4
42	Alaska	29.5		2	Nebraska	84.4
26	Arizona	56.8		3	Arkansas	84.2
3	Arkansas	84.2		4	Iowa	82.9
40	California	38.7		5	Louisiana	81.5
28	Colorado	54.2		6	Mississippi	79.4
35	Connecticut	45.1		7	Tennessee	78.9
14	Delaware	74.0		8	Indiana	78.7
16	Florida	68.7		9	Ohio	78.2
22	Georgia	64.5		10	Missouri	76.8
44	Hawaii	25.6		11	Pennsylvania	76.3
NA	Idaho**	NA		12	Illinois	76.0
12	Illinois	76.0		13	South Dakota	75.6
8	Indiana	78.7		14	Delaware	74.0
4	Iowa	82.9		15	South Carolina	70.7
18	Kansas	67.4		16	Florida	68.7
21	Kentucky	65.7		17	Alabama	68.3
5	Louisiana	81.5		18	Kansas	67.4
NA	Maine**	NA		19	Oklahoma	67.3
29	Maryland	53.4		20	Texas	65.8
34	Massachusetts	45.9		21	Kentucky	65.7
24	Michigan	62.7		22	Georgia	64.5
31	Minnesota	52.0		23	North Carolina	63.6
6	Mississippi	79.4		24	Michigan	62.7
10	Missouri	76.8		25	Nevada	58.8
NA	Montana**	NA		26	Arizona	56.8
2	Nebraska	84.4		27	Virginia	56.0
25	Nevada	58.8		28	Colorado	54.2
39	New Hampshire	38.8		29	Maryland	53.4
33	New Jersey	48.0		30	Rhode Island	53.1
41	New Mexico	30.0		31	Minnesota	52.0
38	New York	41.7		32	West Virginia	49.4
23	North Carolina	63.6		33	New Jersey	48.0
NA	North Dakota**	NA		34	Massachusetts	45.9
9	Ohio	78.2		35	Connecticut	45.1
19	Oklahoma	67.3		36	Oregon	43.6
36	Oregon	43.6		36	Washington	43.6
11	Pennsylvania	76.3		38	New York	41.7
30	Rhode Island	53.1		39	New Hampshire	38.8
15	South Carolina	70.7		40	California	38.7
13	South Dakota	75.6		41	New Mexico	30.0
7	Tennessee	78.9		42	Alaska	29.5
20	Texas	65.8		43	Utah	28.9
43	Utah	28.9		44	Hawaii	25.6
NA	Vermont**	NA		NA	Idaho**	NA
27	Virginia	56.0		NA	Maine**	NA
36	Washington	43.6		NA	Montana**	NA
32	West Virginia	49.4		NA	North Dakota**	NA
1	Wisconsin	93.4		NA	Vermont**	NA
NA	Wyoming**	NA		NA	Wyoming**	NA

District of Columbia   113.1

Source: Morgan Quitno Press using data from U.S. Dept. of Health and Human Services, Nat'l Center for Health Statistics "National Vital Statistics Reports" (Vol. 54, No. 8, December 29, 2005)
Preliminary data. Live births to women age 15 to 19 years old by state of residence. Rates calculated using Census 2004 estimates for females ages 15 to 19 years old in the category of "Black Alone or in Combination."
***Insufficient number of births for a reliable figure.*

Births to Black Teenage Mothers as a Percent of Black Births in 2004

National Percent = 17.1% of Black Live Births*

ALPHA ORDER

RANK ORDER

RANK	STATE	PERCENT		RANK	STATE	PERCENT
9	Alabama	19.9		1	Wisconsin	23.3
43	Alaska	10.3		2	Arkansas	22.7
24	Arizona	16.6		3	Louisiana	21.1
2	Arkansas	22.7		4	Illinois	20.7
33	California	14.0		5	Mississippi	20.5
26	Colorado	16.5		6	Nebraska	20.3
35	Connecticut	13.8		7	Missouri	20.1
19	Delaware	18.1		8	Pennsylvania	20.0
24	Florida	16.6		9	Alabama	19.9
27	Georgia	16.3		10	Indiana	19.7
44	Hawaii	7.5		11	Ohio	19.6
NA	Idaho**	NA		12	Iowa	19.5
4	Illinois	20.7		12	Tennessee	19.5
10	Indiana	19.7		14	South Carolina	19.3
12	Iowa	19.5		15	Oklahoma	19.2
17	Kansas	18.5		16	West Virginia	18.7
19	Kentucky	18.1		17	Kansas	18.5
3	Louisiana	21.1		18	South Dakota	18.4
NA	Maine**	NA		19	Delaware	18.1
35	Maryland	13.8		19	Kentucky	18.1
42	Massachusetts	10.4		19	Michigan	18.1
19	Michigan	18.1		22	North Carolina	18.0
39	Minnesota	12.3		22	Texas	18.0
5	Mississippi	20.5		24	Arizona	16.6
7	Missouri	20.1		24	Florida	16.6
NA	Montana**	NA		26	Colorado	16.5
6	Nebraska	20.3		27	Georgia	16.3
28	Nevada	16.0		28	Nevada	16.0
41	New Hampshire	10.9		29	Virginia	15.4
37	New Jersey	13.1		30	Oregon	15.3
34	New Mexico	13.9		31	Utah	15.0
40	New York	11.7		32	Rhode Island	14.2
22	North Carolina	18.0		33	California	14.0
NA	North Dakota**	NA		34	New Mexico	13.9
11	Ohio	19.6		35	Connecticut	13.8
15	Oklahoma	19.2		35	Maryland	13.8
30	Oregon	15.3		37	New Jersey	13.1
8	Pennsylvania	20.0		38	Washington	12.8
32	Rhode Island	14.2		39	Minnesota	12.3
14	South Carolina	19.3		40	New York	11.7
18	South Dakota	18.4		41	New Hampshire	10.9
12	Tennessee	19.5		42	Massachusetts	10.4
22	Texas	18.0		43	Alaska	10.3
31	Utah	15.0		44	Hawaii	7.5
NA	Vermont**	NA		NA	Idaho**	NA
29	Virginia	15.4		NA	Maine**	NA
38	Washington	12.8		NA	Montana**	NA
16	West Virginia	18.7		NA	North Dakota**	NA
1	Wisconsin	23.3		NA	Vermont**	NA
NA	Wyoming**	NA		NA	Wyoming**	NA

District of Columbia 15.7

Source: U.S. Department of Health and Human Services, National Center for Health Statistics
   "National Vital Statistics Reports" (Vol. 54, No. 8, December 29, 2005)
*Preliminary data. Live births to women 15 to 19 years old by state of residence.
**Not available. Fewer than 20 births to black teenage women.

Births to Young Teenagers: 2000 to 2002

National Total = 23,615 Live Births*

ALPHA ORDER

RANK	STATE	BIRTHS	% of USA
15	Alabama	556	2.4%
43	Alaska	45	0.2%
13	Arizona	625	2.6%
22	Arkansas	346	1.5%
2	California	2,448	10.4%
24	Colorado	336	1.4%
32	Connecticut	178	0.8%
37	Delaware	85	0.4%
3	Florida	1,458	6.2%
4	Georgia	1,118	4.7%
41	Hawaii	59	0.2%
42	Idaho	53	0.2%
5	Illinois	1,050	4.4%
20	Indiana	391	1.7%
35	Iowa	111	0.5%
34	Kansas	157	0.7%
25	Kentucky	332	1.4%
10	Louisiana	743	3.1%
46	Maine	20	0.1%
18	Maryland	475	2.0%
29	Massachusetts	241	1.0%
11	Michigan	659	2.8%
30	Minnesota	230	1.0%
12	Mississippi	626	2.7%
21	Missouri	379	1.6%
45	Montana	26	0.1%
38	Nebraska	83	0.4%
33	Nevada	175	0.7%
49	New Hampshire	12	0.1%
19	New Jersey	421	1.8%
28	New Mexico	246	1.0%
6	New York	972	4.1%
7	North Carolina	906	3.8%
48	North Dakota	14	0.1%
8	Ohio	848	3.6%
23	Oklahoma	338	1.4%
31	Oregon	183	0.8%
9	Pennsylvania	792	3.4%
40	Rhode Island	68	0.3%
16	South Carolina	537	2.3%
44	South Dakota	44	0.2%
14	Tennessee	624	2.6%
1	Texas	3,204	13.6%
36	Utah	102	0.4%
50	Vermont	7	0.0%
17	Virginia	506	2.1%
26	Washington	308	1.3%
39	West Virginia	82	0.3%
27	Wisconsin	287	1.2%
46	Wyoming	20	0.1%

RANK ORDER

RANK	STATE	BIRTHS	% of USA
1	Texas	3,204	13.6%
2	California	2,448	10.4%
3	Florida	1,458	6.2%
4	Georgia	1,118	4.7%
5	Illinois	1,050	4.4%
6	New York	972	4.1%
7	North Carolina	906	3.8%
8	Ohio	848	3.6%
9	Pennsylvania	792	3.4%
10	Louisiana	743	3.1%
11	Michigan	659	2.8%
12	Mississippi	626	2.7%
13	Arizona	625	2.6%
14	Tennessee	624	2.6%
15	Alabama	556	2.4%
16	South Carolina	537	2.3%
17	Virginia	506	2.1%
18	Maryland	475	2.0%
19	New Jersey	421	1.8%
20	Indiana	391	1.7%
21	Missouri	379	1.6%
22	Arkansas	346	1.5%
23	Oklahoma	338	1.4%
24	Colorado	336	1.4%
25	Kentucky	332	1.4%
26	Washington	308	1.3%
27	Wisconsin	287	1.2%
28	New Mexico	246	1.0%
29	Massachusetts	241	1.0%
30	Minnesota	230	1.0%
31	Oregon	183	0.8%
32	Connecticut	178	0.8%
33	Nevada	175	0.7%
34	Kansas	157	0.7%
35	Iowa	111	0.5%
36	Utah	102	0.4%
37	Delaware	85	0.4%
38	Nebraska	83	0.4%
39	West Virginia	82	0.3%
40	Rhode Island	68	0.3%
41	Hawaii	59	0.2%
42	Idaho	53	0.2%
43	Alaska	45	0.2%
44	South Dakota	44	0.2%
45	Montana	26	0.1%
46	Maine	20	0.1%
46	Wyoming	20	0.1%
48	North Dakota	14	0.1%
49	New Hampshire	12	0.1%
50	Vermont	7	0.0%
	District of Columbia	89	0.4%

Source: U.S. Department of Health and Human Services, National Center for Health Statistics
"National Vital Statistics Reports" (Vol. 53, No. 7, November 15, 2004)
*Final data. Births to 10 to 14 years old during the three years of 2000 to 2002 by state of residence.

Young Teen Birthrate: 2000 to 2002

National Rate = 0.8 Live Births per 1,000 10 to 14 Year Old Females*

<table>
<tr><td colspan="3">ALPHA ORDER</td><td colspan="3">RANK ORDER</td></tr>
<tr><th>RANK</th><th>STATE</th><th>RATE</th><th>RANK</th><th>STATE</th><th>RATE</th></tr>
<tr><td>5</td><td>Alabama</td><td>1.2</td><td>1</td><td>Mississippi</td><td>2.0</td></tr>
<tr><td>28</td><td>Alaska</td><td>0.5</td><td>2</td><td>Louisiana</td><td>1.5</td></tr>
<tr><td>8</td><td>Arizona</td><td>1.1</td><td>3</td><td>South Carolina</td><td>1.3</td></tr>
<tr><td>5</td><td>Arkansas</td><td>1.2</td><td>3</td><td>Texas</td><td>1.3</td></tr>
<tr><td>23</td><td>California</td><td>0.6</td><td>5</td><td>Alabama</td><td>1.2</td></tr>
<tr><td>19</td><td>Colorado</td><td>0.7</td><td>5</td><td>Arkansas</td><td>1.2</td></tr>
<tr><td>28</td><td>Connecticut</td><td>0.5</td><td>5</td><td>Georgia</td><td>1.2</td></tr>
<tr><td>8</td><td>Delaware</td><td>1.1</td><td>8</td><td>Arizona</td><td>1.1</td></tr>
<tr><td>13</td><td>Florida</td><td>0.9</td><td>8</td><td>Delaware</td><td>1.1</td></tr>
<tr><td>5</td><td>Georgia</td><td>1.2</td><td>8</td><td>New Mexico</td><td>1.1</td></tr>
<tr><td>28</td><td>Hawaii</td><td>0.5</td><td>8</td><td>North Carolina</td><td>1.1</td></tr>
<tr><td>45</td><td>Idaho</td><td>0.3</td><td>8</td><td>Tennessee</td><td>1.1</td></tr>
<tr><td>15</td><td>Illinois</td><td>0.8</td><td>13</td><td>Florida</td><td>0.9</td></tr>
<tr><td>23</td><td>Indiana</td><td>0.6</td><td>13</td><td>Oklahoma</td><td>0.9</td></tr>
<tr><td>39</td><td>Iowa</td><td>0.4</td><td>15</td><td>Illinois</td><td>0.8</td></tr>
<tr><td>28</td><td>Kansas</td><td>0.5</td><td>15</td><td>Kentucky</td><td>0.8</td></tr>
<tr><td>15</td><td>Kentucky</td><td>0.8</td><td>15</td><td>Maryland</td><td>0.8</td></tr>
<tr><td>2</td><td>Louisiana</td><td>1.5</td><td>15</td><td>Nevada</td><td>0.8</td></tr>
<tr><td>47</td><td>Maine</td><td>0.2</td><td>19</td><td>Colorado</td><td>0.7</td></tr>
<tr><td>15</td><td>Maryland</td><td>0.8</td><td>19</td><td>Ohio</td><td>0.7</td></tr>
<tr><td>39</td><td>Massachusetts</td><td>0.4</td><td>19</td><td>Rhode Island</td><td>0.7</td></tr>
<tr><td>23</td><td>Michigan</td><td>0.6</td><td>19</td><td>Virginia</td><td>0.7</td></tr>
<tr><td>39</td><td>Minnesota</td><td>0.4</td><td>23</td><td>California</td><td>0.6</td></tr>
<tr><td>1</td><td>Mississippi</td><td>2.0</td><td>23</td><td>Indiana</td><td>0.6</td></tr>
<tr><td>23</td><td>Missouri</td><td>0.6</td><td>23</td><td>Michigan</td><td>0.6</td></tr>
<tr><td>45</td><td>Montana</td><td>0.3</td><td>23</td><td>Missouri</td><td>0.6</td></tr>
<tr><td>39</td><td>Nebraska</td><td>0.4</td><td>23</td><td>Pennsylvania</td><td>0.6</td></tr>
<tr><td>15</td><td>Nevada</td><td>0.8</td><td>28</td><td>Alaska</td><td>0.5</td></tr>
<tr><td>NA</td><td>New Hampshire**</td><td>NA</td><td>28</td><td>Connecticut</td><td>0.5</td></tr>
<tr><td>28</td><td>New Jersey</td><td>0.5</td><td>28</td><td>Hawaii</td><td>0.5</td></tr>
<tr><td>8</td><td>New Mexico</td><td>1.1</td><td>28</td><td>Kansas</td><td>0.5</td></tr>
<tr><td>28</td><td>New York</td><td>0.5</td><td>28</td><td>New Jersey</td><td>0.5</td></tr>
<tr><td>8</td><td>North Carolina</td><td>1.1</td><td>28</td><td>New York</td><td>0.5</td></tr>
<tr><td>NA</td><td>North Dakota**</td><td>NA</td><td>28</td><td>Oregon</td><td>0.5</td></tr>
<tr><td>19</td><td>Ohio</td><td>0.7</td><td>28</td><td>South Dakota</td><td>0.5</td></tr>
<tr><td>13</td><td>Oklahoma</td><td>0.9</td><td>28</td><td>Washington</td><td>0.5</td></tr>
<tr><td>28</td><td>Oregon</td><td>0.5</td><td>28</td><td>West Virginia</td><td>0.5</td></tr>
<tr><td>23</td><td>Pennsylvania</td><td>0.6</td><td>28</td><td>Wisconsin</td><td>0.5</td></tr>
<tr><td>19</td><td>Rhode Island</td><td>0.7</td><td>39</td><td>Iowa</td><td>0.4</td></tr>
<tr><td>3</td><td>South Carolina</td><td>1.3</td><td>39</td><td>Massachusetts</td><td>0.4</td></tr>
<tr><td>28</td><td>South Dakota</td><td>0.5</td><td>39</td><td>Minnesota</td><td>0.4</td></tr>
<tr><td>8</td><td>Tennessee</td><td>1.1</td><td>39</td><td>Nebraska</td><td>0.4</td></tr>
<tr><td>3</td><td>Texas</td><td>1.3</td><td>39</td><td>Utah</td><td>0.4</td></tr>
<tr><td>39</td><td>Utah</td><td>0.4</td><td>39</td><td>Wyoming</td><td>0.4</td></tr>
<tr><td>NA</td><td>Vermont**</td><td>NA</td><td>45</td><td>Idaho</td><td>0.3</td></tr>
<tr><td>19</td><td>Virginia</td><td>0.7</td><td>45</td><td>Montana</td><td>0.3</td></tr>
<tr><td>28</td><td>Washington</td><td>0.5</td><td>47</td><td>Maine</td><td>0.2</td></tr>
<tr><td>28</td><td>West Virginia</td><td>0.5</td><td>NA</td><td>New Hampshire**</td><td>NA</td></tr>
<tr><td>28</td><td>Wisconsin</td><td>0.5</td><td>NA</td><td>North Dakota**</td><td>NA</td></tr>
<tr><td>39</td><td>Wyoming</td><td>0.4</td><td>NA</td><td>Vermont**</td><td>NA</td></tr>
<tr><td></td><td></td><td></td><td></td><td>District of Columbia</td><td>2.0</td></tr>
</table>

Source: U.S. Department of Health and Human Services, National Center for Health Statistics
"National Vital Statistics Reports" (Vol. 53, No. 7, November 15, 2004)
Final data. Births to 10 to 14 years old during the three years of 2000 to 2002 by state of residence.
**Insufficient data for a reliable rate.*

Births to Women 35 to 54 Years Old in 2002

National Total = 555,202 Live Births*

ALPHA ORDER				RANK ORDER			
RANK	STATE	BIRTHS	% of USA	RANK	STATE	BIRTHS	% of USA
27	Alabama	5,052	0.9%	1	California	87,615	15.8%
45	Alaska	1,352	0.2%	2	New York	48,802	8.8%
18	Arizona	9,673	1.7%	3	Texas	39,097	7.0%
38	Arkansas	2,744	0.5%	4	Florida	29,372	5.3%
1	California	87,615	15.8%	5	Illinois	26,258	4.7%
17	Colorado	9,709	1.7%	6	New Jersey	24,261	4.4%
20	Connecticut	9,169	1.7%	7	Pennsylvania	22,143	4.0%
44	Delaware	1,499	0.3%	8	Massachusetts	18,383	3.3%
4	Florida	29,372	5.3%	9	Ohio	17,784	3.2%
12	Georgia	15,735	2.8%	10	Michigan	16,755	3.0%
36	Hawaii	2,880	0.5%	11	Virginia	15,747	2.8%
41	Idaho	2,034	0.4%	12	Georgia	15,735	2.8%
5	Illinois	26,258	4.7%	13	Maryland	13,539	2.4%
21	Indiana	8,712	1.6%	14	North Carolina	13,311	2.4%
31	Iowa	4,073	0.7%	15	Washington	11,650	2.1%
30	Kansas	4,293	0.8%	16	Minnesota	10,281	1.9%
28	Kentucky	4,841	0.9%	17	Colorado	9,709	1.7%
24	Louisiana	5,775	1.0%	18	Arizona	9,673	1.7%
42	Maine	1,887	0.3%	19	Wisconsin	9,297	1.7%
13	Maryland	13,539	2.4%	20	Connecticut	9,169	1.7%
8	Massachusetts	18,383	3.3%	21	Indiana	8,712	1.6%
10	Michigan	16,755	3.0%	22	Missouri	8,289	1.5%
16	Minnesota	10,281	1.9%	23	Tennessee	7,411	1.3%
34	Mississippi	3,024	0.5%	24	Louisiana	5,775	1.0%
22	Missouri	8,289	1.5%	25	Oregon	5,774	1.0%
46	Montana	1,264	0.2%	26	South Carolina	5,750	1.0%
35	Nebraska	2,949	0.5%	27	Alabama	5,052	0.9%
32	Nevada	4,058	0.7%	28	Kentucky	4,841	0.9%
39	New Hampshire	2,675	0.5%	29	Utah	4,304	0.8%
6	New Jersey	24,261	4.4%	30	Kansas	4,293	0.8%
37	New Mexico	2,858	0.5%	31	Iowa	4,073	0.7%
2	New York	48,802	8.8%	32	Nevada	4,058	0.7%
14	North Carolina	13,311	2.4%	33	Oklahoma	4,034	0.7%
49	North Dakota	878	0.2%	34	Mississippi	3,024	0.5%
9	Ohio	17,784	3.2%	35	Nebraska	2,949	0.5%
33	Oklahoma	4,034	0.7%	36	Hawaii	2,880	0.5%
25	Oregon	5,774	1.0%	37	New Mexico	2,858	0.5%
7	Pennsylvania	22,143	4.0%	38	Arkansas	2,744	0.5%
40	Rhode Island	2,264	0.4%	39	New Hampshire	2,675	0.5%
26	South Carolina	5,750	1.0%	40	Rhode Island	2,264	0.4%
48	South Dakota	1,107	0.2%	41	Idaho	2,034	0.4%
23	Tennessee	7,411	1.3%	42	Maine	1,887	0.3%
3	Texas	39,097	7.0%	43	West Virginia	1,712	0.3%
29	Utah	4,304	0.8%	44	Delaware	1,499	0.3%
47	Vermont	1,109	0.2%	45	Alaska	1,352	0.2%
11	Virginia	15,747	2.8%	46	Montana	1,264	0.2%
15	Washington	11,650	2.1%	47	Vermont	1,109	0.2%
43	West Virginia	1,712	0.3%	48	South Dakota	1,107	0.2%
19	Wisconsin	9,297	1.7%	49	North Dakota	878	0.2%
50	Wyoming	600	0.1%	50	Wyoming	600	0.1%
					District of Columbia	1,419	0.3%

Source: Morgan Quitno Press using data from U.S. Dept of Health & Human Services, National Center for Health Statistics (unpublished data)
*Final data by state of residence.

Births to Women 35 to 54 Years Old as a Percent of All Births in 2002

National Percent = 13.8% of Live Births*

ALPHA ORDER

RANK	STATE	PERCENT		RANK	STATE	PERCENT
46	Alabama	8.6		1	Massachusetts	22.8
19	Alaska	13.6		2	Connecticut	21.8
31	Arizona	11.0		3	New Jersey	21.1
49	Arkansas	7.3		4	New York	19.4
9	California	16.6		5	Maryland	18.5
17	Colorado	14.2		5	New Hampshire	18.5
2	Connecticut	21.8		7	Rhode Island	17.6
21	Delaware	13.5		8	Vermont	17.4
16	Florida	14.3		9	California	16.6
26	Georgia	11.8		10	Hawaii	16.5
10	Hawaii	16.5		11	Virginia	15.8
40	Idaho	9.7		12	Pennsylvania	15.5
15	Illinois	14.5		13	Minnesota	15.1
39	Indiana	10.2		14	Washington	14.7
34	Iowa	10.8		15	Illinois	14.5
33	Kansas	10.9		16	Florida	14.3
43	Kentucky	8.9		17	Colorado	14.2
43	Louisiana	8.9		18	Maine	13.9
18	Maine	13.9		19	Alaska	13.6
5	Maryland	18.5		19	Wisconsin	13.6
1	Massachusetts	22.8		21	Delaware	13.5
22	Michigan	12.9		22	Michigan	12.9
13	Minnesota	15.1		23	Oregon	12.8
49	Mississippi	7.3		24	Nevada	12.5
31	Missouri	11.0		25	Ohio	12.0
28	Montana	11.4		26	Georgia	11.8
27	Nebraska	11.6		27	Nebraska	11.6
24	Nevada	12.5		28	Montana	11.4
5	New Hampshire	18.5		29	North Carolina	11.3
3	New Jersey	21.1		29	North Dakota	11.3
37	New Mexico	10.3		31	Arizona	11.0
4	New York	19.4		31	Missouri	11.0
29	North Carolina	11.3		33	Kansas	10.9
29	North Dakota	11.3		34	Iowa	10.8
25	Ohio	12.0		35	South Carolina	10.5
48	Oklahoma	8.0		35	Texas	10.5
23	Oregon	12.8		37	New Mexico	10.3
12	Pennsylvania	15.5		37	South Dakota	10.3
7	Rhode Island	17.6		39	Indiana	10.2
35	South Carolina	10.5		40	Idaho	9.7
37	South Dakota	10.3		41	Tennessee	9.6
41	Tennessee	9.6		42	Wyoming	9.2
35	Texas	10.5		43	Kentucky	8.9
45	Utah	8.8		43	Louisiana	8.9
8	Vermont	17.4		45	Utah	8.8
11	Virginia	15.8		46	Alabama	8.6
14	Washington	14.7		47	West Virginia	8.3
47	West Virginia	8.3		48	Oklahoma	8.0
19	Wisconsin	13.6		49	Arkansas	7.3
42	Wyoming	9.2		49	Mississippi	7.3

District of Columbia 18.9

Source: Morgan Quitno Press using data from U.S. Dept of Health & Human Services, National Center for Health Statistics (unpublished data)
Final data by state of residence.

Births by Vaginal Delivery in 2004

National Total = 2,917,953 Live Births*

<table>
<tr><th colspan="4">ALPHA ORDER</th><th colspan="4">RANK ORDER</th></tr>
<tr><th>RANK</th><th>STATE</th><th>BIRTHS</th><th>% of USA</th><th>RANK</th><th>STATE</th><th>BIRTHS</th><th>% of USA</th></tr>
<tr><td>24</td><td>Alabama</td><td>40,910</td><td>1.4%</td><td>1</td><td>California</td><td>385,365</td><td>13.2%</td></tr>
<tr><td>46</td><td>Alaska</td><td>8,177</td><td>0.3%</td><td>2</td><td>Texas</td><td>263,306</td><td>9.0%</td></tr>
<tr><td>13</td><td>Arizona</td><td>71,846</td><td>2.5%</td><td>3</td><td>New York</td><td>174,120</td><td>6.0%</td></tr>
<tr><td>34</td><td>Arkansas</td><td>26,635</td><td>0.9%</td><td>4</td><td>Florida</td><td>145,647</td><td>5.0%</td></tr>
<tr><td>1</td><td>California</td><td>385,365</td><td>13.2%</td><td>5</td><td>Illinois</td><td>131,177</td><td>4.5%</td></tr>
<tr><td>21</td><td>Colorado</td><td>52,212</td><td>1.8%</td><td>6</td><td>Ohio</td><td>109,032</td><td>3.7%</td></tr>
<tr><td>30</td><td>Connecticut</td><td>29,427</td><td>1.0%</td><td>7</td><td>Pennsylvania</td><td>105,682</td><td>3.6%</td></tr>
<tr><td>47</td><td>Delaware</td><td>7,875</td><td>0.3%</td><td>8</td><td>Georgia</td><td>98,307</td><td>3.4%</td></tr>
<tr><td>4</td><td>Florida</td><td>145,647</td><td>5.0%</td><td>9</td><td>Michigan</td><td>93,563</td><td>3.2%</td></tr>
<tr><td>8</td><td>Georgia</td><td>98,307</td><td>3.4%</td><td>10</td><td>North Carolina</td><td>85,813</td><td>2.9%</td></tr>
<tr><td>40</td><td>Hawaii</td><td>13,856</td><td>0.5%</td><td>11</td><td>New Jersey</td><td>74,810</td><td>2.6%</td></tr>
<tr><td>38</td><td>Idaho</td><td>17,526</td><td>0.6%</td><td>12</td><td>Virginia</td><td>72,429</td><td>2.5%</td></tr>
<tr><td>5</td><td>Illinois</td><td>131,177</td><td>4.5%</td><td>13</td><td>Arizona</td><td>71,846</td><td>2.5%</td></tr>
<tr><td>14</td><td>Indiana</td><td>63,315</td><td>2.2%</td><td>14</td><td>Indiana</td><td>63,315</td><td>2.2%</td></tr>
<tr><td>33</td><td>Iowa</td><td>28,330</td><td>1.0%</td><td>15</td><td>Washington</td><td>59,425</td><td>2.0%</td></tr>
<tr><td>32</td><td>Kansas</td><td>28,459</td><td>1.0%</td><td>16</td><td>Tennessee</td><td>55,589</td><td>1.9%</td></tr>
<tr><td>27</td><td>Kentucky</td><td>37,027</td><td>1.3%</td><td>17</td><td>Missouri</td><td>55,302</td><td>1.9%</td></tr>
<tr><td>23</td><td>Louisiana</td><td>44,341</td><td>1.5%</td><td>18</td><td>Massachusetts</td><td>54,289</td><td>1.9%</td></tr>
<tr><td>42</td><td>Maine</td><td>10,082</td><td>0.3%</td><td>19</td><td>Wisconsin</td><td>54,229</td><td>1.9%</td></tr>
<tr><td>22</td><td>Maryland</td><td>51,925</td><td>1.8%</td><td>20</td><td>Minnesota</td><td>53,456</td><td>1.8%</td></tr>
<tr><td>18</td><td>Massachusetts</td><td>54,289</td><td>1.9%</td><td>21</td><td>Colorado</td><td>52,212</td><td>1.8%</td></tr>
<tr><td>9</td><td>Michigan</td><td>93,563</td><td>3.2%</td><td>22</td><td>Maryland</td><td>51,925</td><td>1.8%</td></tr>
<tr><td>20</td><td>Minnesota</td><td>53,456</td><td>1.8%</td><td>23</td><td>Louisiana</td><td>44,341</td><td>1.5%</td></tr>
<tr><td>31</td><td>Mississippi</td><td>28,640</td><td>1.0%</td><td>24</td><td>Alabama</td><td>40,910</td><td>1.4%</td></tr>
<tr><td>17</td><td>Missouri</td><td>55,302</td><td>1.9%</td><td>25</td><td>Utah</td><td>40,282</td><td>1.4%</td></tr>
<tr><td>44</td><td>Montana</td><td>8,575</td><td>0.3%</td><td>26</td><td>South Carolina</td><td>38,766</td><td>1.3%</td></tr>
<tr><td>37</td><td>Nebraska</td><td>18,642</td><td>0.6%</td><td>27</td><td>Kentucky</td><td>37,027</td><td>1.3%</td></tr>
<tr><td>35</td><td>Nevada</td><td>24,843</td><td>0.9%</td><td>28</td><td>Oklahoma</td><td>35,385</td><td>1.2%</td></tr>
<tr><td>41</td><td>New Hampshire</td><td>10,633</td><td>0.4%</td><td>29</td><td>Oregon</td><td>33,584</td><td>1.2%</td></tr>
<tr><td>11</td><td>New Jersey</td><td>74,810</td><td>2.6%</td><td>30</td><td>Connecticut</td><td>29,427</td><td>1.0%</td></tr>
<tr><td>36</td><td>New Mexico</td><td>22,340</td><td>0.8%</td><td>31</td><td>Mississippi</td><td>28,640</td><td>1.0%</td></tr>
<tr><td>3</td><td>New York</td><td>174,120</td><td>6.0%</td><td>32</td><td>Kansas</td><td>28,459</td><td>1.0%</td></tr>
<tr><td>10</td><td>North Carolina</td><td>85,813</td><td>2.9%</td><td>33</td><td>Iowa</td><td>28,330</td><td>1.0%</td></tr>
<tr><td>48</td><td>North Dakota</td><td>6,125</td><td>0.2%</td><td>34</td><td>Arkansas</td><td>26,635</td><td>0.9%</td></tr>
<tr><td>6</td><td>Ohio</td><td>109,032</td><td>3.7%</td><td>35</td><td>Nevada</td><td>24,843</td><td>0.9%</td></tr>
<tr><td>28</td><td>Oklahoma</td><td>35,385</td><td>1.2%</td><td>36</td><td>New Mexico</td><td>22,340</td><td>0.8%</td></tr>
<tr><td>29</td><td>Oregon</td><td>33,584</td><td>1.2%</td><td>37</td><td>Nebraska</td><td>18,642</td><td>0.6%</td></tr>
<tr><td>7</td><td>Pennsylvania</td><td>105,682</td><td>3.6%</td><td>38</td><td>Idaho</td><td>17,526</td><td>0.6%</td></tr>
<tr><td>43</td><td>Rhode Island</td><td>9,085</td><td>0.3%</td><td>39</td><td>West Virginia</td><td>13,910</td><td>0.5%</td></tr>
<tr><td>26</td><td>South Carolina</td><td>38,766</td><td>1.3%</td><td>40</td><td>Hawaii</td><td>13,856</td><td>0.5%</td></tr>
<tr><td>45</td><td>South Dakota</td><td>8,437</td><td>0.3%</td><td>41</td><td>New Hampshire</td><td>10,633</td><td>0.4%</td></tr>
<tr><td>16</td><td>Tennessee</td><td>55,589</td><td>1.9%</td><td>42</td><td>Maine</td><td>10,082</td><td>0.3%</td></tr>
<tr><td>2</td><td>Texas</td><td>263,306</td><td>9.0%</td><td>43</td><td>Rhode Island</td><td>9,085</td><td>0.3%</td></tr>
<tr><td>25</td><td>Utah</td><td>40,282</td><td>1.4%</td><td>44</td><td>Montana</td><td>8,575</td><td>0.3%</td></tr>
<tr><td>50</td><td>Vermont</td><td>4,983</td><td>0.2%</td><td>45</td><td>South Dakota</td><td>8,437</td><td>0.3%</td></tr>
<tr><td>12</td><td>Virginia</td><td>72,429</td><td>2.5%</td><td>46</td><td>Alaska</td><td>8,177</td><td>0.3%</td></tr>
<tr><td>15</td><td>Washington</td><td>59,425</td><td>2.0%</td><td>47</td><td>Delaware</td><td>7,875</td><td>0.3%</td></tr>
<tr><td>39</td><td>West Virginia</td><td>13,910</td><td>0.5%</td><td>48</td><td>North Dakota</td><td>6,125</td><td>0.2%</td></tr>
<tr><td>19</td><td>Wisconsin</td><td>54,229</td><td>1.9%</td><td>49</td><td>Wyoming</td><td>5,146</td><td>0.2%</td></tr>
<tr><td>49</td><td>Wyoming</td><td>5,146</td><td>0.2%</td><td>50</td><td>Vermont</td><td>4,983</td><td>0.2%</td></tr>
<tr><td></td><td></td><td></td><td></td><td></td><td>District of Columbia</td><td>5,537</td><td>0.2%</td></tr>
</table>

Source: Morgan Quitno Press using data from U.S. Dept. of Health and Human Services, Nat'l Center for Health Statistics
"National Vital Statistics Reports" (Vol. 54, No. 8, December 29, 2005)
*Preliminary estimates by state of residence.

Percent of Births by Vaginal Delivery in 2004

National Percent = 70.9% of Live Births*

ALPHA ORDER			RANK ORDER		
RANK	STATE	PERCENT	RANK	STATE	PERCENT
42	Alabama	68.7	1	Utah	79.5
2	Alaska	79.1	2	Alaska	79.1
6	Arizona	76.7	3	New Mexico	78.7
40	Arkansas	69.0	4	Idaho	77.8
31	California	70.7	5	Wisconsin	77.3
7	Colorado	76.2	6	Arizona	76.7
33	Connecticut	69.9	7	Colorado	76.2
35	Delaware	69.7	8	Vermont	75.9
48	Florida	66.8	9	Hawaii	75.8
29	Georgia	70.8	10	Minnesota	75.7
9	Hawaii	75.8	11	Wyoming	75.6
4	Idaho	77.8	12	North Dakota	74.8
21	Illinois	72.5	13	Montana	74.4
18	Indiana	73.0	13	South Dakota	74.4
15	Iowa	73.7	15	Iowa	73.7
25	Kansas	71.9	16	Oregon	73.5
45	Kentucky	68.0	17	Ohio	73.1
46	Louisiana	67.8	18	Indiana	73.0
23	Maine	72.3	18	New Hampshire	73.0
37	Maryland	69.6	20	Washington	72.7
39	Massachusetts	69.1	21	Illinois	72.5
24	Michigan	72.1	21	Pennsylvania	72.5
10	Minnesota	75.7	23	Maine	72.3
47	Mississippi	66.9	24	Michigan	72.1
27	Missouri	71.1	25	Kansas	71.9
13	Montana	74.4	26	North Carolina	71.6
29	Nebraska	70.8	27	Missouri	71.1
32	Nevada	70.6	27	Rhode Island	71.1
18	New Hampshire	73.0	29	Georgia	70.8
50	New Jersey	65.1	29	Nebraska	70.8
3	New Mexico	78.7	31	California	70.7
38	New York	69.4	32	Nevada	70.6
26	North Carolina	71.6	33	Connecticut	69.9
12	North Dakota	74.8	34	Tennessee	69.8
17	Ohio	73.1	35	Delaware	69.7
40	Oklahoma	69.0	35	Virginia	69.7
16	Oregon	73.5	37	Maryland	69.6
21	Pennsylvania	72.5	38	New York	69.4
27	Rhode Island	71.1	39	Massachusetts	69.1
43	South Carolina	68.5	40	Arkansas	69.0
13	South Dakota	74.4	40	Oklahoma	69.0
34	Tennessee	69.8	42	Alabama	68.7
43	Texas	68.5	43	South Carolina	68.5
1	Utah	79.5	43	Texas	68.5
8	Vermont	75.9	45	Kentucky	68.0
35	Virginia	69.7	46	Louisiana	67.8
20	Washington	72.7	47	Mississippi	66.9
49	West Virginia	66.7	48	Florida	66.8
5	Wisconsin	77.3	49	West Virginia	66.7
11	Wyoming	75.6	50	New Jersey	65.1
				District of Columbia	69.8

Source: Morgan Quitno Press using data from U.S. Dept. of Health and Human Services, Nat'l Center for Health Statistics "National Vital Statistics Reports" (Vol. 54, No. 8, December 29, 2005)
Preliminary data by state of residence.

Births by Cesarean Delivery in 2004

National Total = 1,197,637 Live Cesarean Births*

RANK	STATE	BIRTHS	% of USA
21	Alabama	18,639	1.6%
47	Alaska	2,161	0.2%
19	Arizona	21,826	1.8%
31	Arkansas	11,967	1.0%
1	California	159,706	13.3%
25	Colorado	16,308	1.4%
29	Connecticut	12,672	1.1%
44	Delaware	3,424	0.3%
4	Florida	72,387	6.0%
6	Georgia	40,544	3.4%
40	Hawaii	4,424	0.4%
39	Idaho	5,001	0.4%
5	Illinois	49,757	4.2%
15	Indiana	23,418	2.0%
35	Iowa	10,109	0.8%
32	Kansas	11,122	0.9%
23	Kentucky	17,424	1.5%
20	Louisiana	21,058	1.8%
42	Maine	3,863	0.3%
16	Maryland	22,680	1.9%
13	Massachusetts	24,277	2.0%
10	Michigan	36,205	3.0%
24	Minnesota	17,159	1.4%
28	Mississippi	14,170	1.2%
17	Missouri	22,478	1.9%
45	Montana	2,950	0.2%
36	Nebraska	7,689	0.6%
34	Nevada	10,345	0.9%
41	New Hampshire	3,933	0.3%
8	New Jersey	40,106	3.3%
38	New Mexico	6,046	0.5%
3	New York	76,774	6.4%
11	North Carolina	34,038	2.8%
48	North Dakota	2,064	0.2%
7	Ohio	40,122	3.4%
27	Oklahoma	15,898	1.3%
30	Oregon	12,109	1.0%
9	Pennsylvania	40,086	3.3%
43	Rhode Island	3,693	0.3%
22	South Carolina	17,826	1.5%
46	South Dakota	2,903	0.2%
14	Tennessee	24,052	2.0%
2	Texas	121,083	10.1%
33	Utah	10,387	0.9%
50	Vermont	1,582	0.1%
12	Virginia	31,486	2.6%
18	Washington	22,315	1.9%
37	West Virginia	6,945	0.6%
26	Wisconsin	15,925	1.3%
49	Wyoming	1,661	0.1%

RANK	STATE	BIRTHS	% of USA
1	California	159,706	13.3%
2	Texas	121,083	10.1%
3	New York	76,774	6.4%
4	Florida	72,387	6.0%
5	Illinois	49,757	4.2%
6	Georgia	40,544	3.4%
7	Ohio	40,122	3.4%
8	New Jersey	40,106	3.3%
9	Pennsylvania	40,086	3.3%
10	Michigan	36,205	3.0%
11	North Carolina	34,038	2.8%
12	Virginia	31,486	2.6%
13	Massachusetts	24,277	2.0%
14	Tennessee	24,052	2.0%
15	Indiana	23,418	2.0%
16	Maryland	22,680	1.9%
17	Missouri	22,478	1.9%
18	Washington	22,315	1.9%
19	Arizona	21,826	1.8%
20	Louisiana	21,058	1.8%
21	Alabama	18,639	1.6%
22	South Carolina	17,826	1.5%
23	Kentucky	17,424	1.5%
24	Minnesota	17,159	1.4%
25	Colorado	16,308	1.4%
26	Wisconsin	15,925	1.3%
27	Oklahoma	15,898	1.3%
28	Mississippi	14,170	1.2%
29	Connecticut	12,672	1.1%
30	Oregon	12,109	1.0%
31	Arkansas	11,967	1.0%
32	Kansas	11,122	0.9%
33	Utah	10,387	0.9%
34	Nevada	10,345	0.9%
35	Iowa	10,109	0.8%
36	Nebraska	7,689	0.6%
37	West Virginia	6,945	0.6%
38	New Mexico	6,046	0.5%
39	Idaho	5,001	0.4%
40	Hawaii	4,424	0.4%
41	New Hampshire	3,933	0.3%
42	Maine	3,863	0.3%
43	Rhode Island	3,693	0.3%
44	Delaware	3,424	0.3%
45	Montana	2,950	0.2%
46	South Dakota	2,903	0.2%
47	Alaska	2,161	0.2%
48	North Dakota	2,064	0.2%
49	Wyoming	1,661	0.1%
50	Vermont	1,582	0.1%
	District of Columbia	2,395	0.2%

Source: Morgan Quitno Press using data from U.S. Dept. of Health and Human Services, Nat'l Center for Health Statistics
   "National Vital Statistics Reports" (Vol. 54, No. 8, December 29, 2005)
*Preliminary estimates by state of residence.

Percent of Births by Cesarean Delivery in 2004

National Percent = 29.1% of Live Births*

RANK	STATE	PERCENT
9	Alabama	31.3
49	Alaska	20.9
45	Arizona	23.3
10	Arkansas	31.0
20	California	29.3
44	Colorado	23.8
18	Connecticut	30.1
15	Delaware	30.3
3	Florida	33.2
21	Georgia	29.2
42	Hawaii	24.2
47	Idaho	22.2
29	Illinois	27.5
32	Indiana	27.0
36	Iowa	26.3
26	Kansas	28.1
6	Kentucky	32.0
5	Louisiana	32.2
28	Maine	27.7
14	Maryland	30.4
12	Massachusetts	30.9
27	Michigan	27.9
41	Minnesota	24.3
4	Mississippi	33.1
23	Missouri	28.9
37	Montana	25.6
21	Nebraska	29.2
19	Nevada	29.4
32	New Hampshire	27.0
1	New Jersey	34.9
48	New Mexico	21.3
13	New York	30.6
25	North Carolina	28.4
39	North Dakota	25.2
34	Ohio	26.9
10	Oklahoma	31.0
35	Oregon	26.5
29	Pennsylvania	27.5
23	Rhode Island	28.9
7	South Carolina	31.5
37	South Dakota	25.6
17	Tennessee	30.2
7	Texas	31.5
50	Utah	20.5
43	Vermont	24.1
15	Virginia	30.3
31	Washington	27.3
2	West Virginia	33.3
46	Wisconsin	22.7
40	Wyoming	24.4

RANK	STATE	PERCENT
1	New Jersey	34.9
2	West Virginia	33.3
3	Florida	33.2
4	Mississippi	33.1
5	Louisiana	32.2
6	Kentucky	32.0
7	South Carolina	31.5
7	Texas	31.5
9	Alabama	31.3
10	Arkansas	31.0
10	Oklahoma	31.0
12	Massachusetts	30.9
13	New York	30.6
14	Maryland	30.4
15	Delaware	30.3
15	Virginia	30.3
17	Tennessee	30.2
18	Connecticut	30.1
19	Nevada	29.4
20	California	29.3
21	Georgia	29.2
21	Nebraska	29.2
23	Missouri	28.9
23	Rhode Island	28.9
25	North Carolina	28.4
26	Kansas	28.1
27	Michigan	27.9
28	Maine	27.7
29	Illinois	27.5
29	Pennsylvania	27.5
31	Washington	27.3
32	Indiana	27.0
32	New Hampshire	27.0
34	Ohio	26.9
35	Oregon	26.5
36	Iowa	26.3
37	Montana	25.6
37	South Dakota	25.6
39	North Dakota	25.2
40	Wyoming	24.4
41	Minnesota	24.3
42	Hawaii	24.2
43	Vermont	24.1
44	Colorado	23.8
45	Arizona	23.3
46	Wisconsin	22.7
47	Idaho	22.2
48	New Mexico	21.3
49	Alaska	20.9
50	Utah	20.5
	District of Columbia	30.2

Source: U.S. Department of Health and Human Services, National Center for Health Statistics
    "National Vital Statistics Reports" (Vol. 54, No. 8, December 29, 2005)
*Preliminary data by state of residence.

Percent Change in Rate of Cesarean Births: 2000 to 2004

National Percent Change = 27.1% Increase*

ALPHA ORDER			RANK ORDER		
RANK	STATE	PERCENT CHANGE	RANK	STATE	PERCENT CHANGE
47	Alabama	18.6	1	Hawaii	64.6
37	Alaska	22.9	2	Vermont	39.3
31	Arizona	25.3	3	Connecticut	38.1
48	Arkansas	17.4	4	Oregon	35.9
32	California	25.2	5	Montana	34.7
15	Colorado	30.1	6	Nevada	34.2
3	Connecticut	38.1	7	Ohio	33.8
39	Delaware	22.2	8	Florida	32.8
8	Florida	32.8	9	Washington	31.9
17	Georgia	29.2	10	Rhode Island	31.4
1	Hawaii	64.6	11	Illinois	31.0
42	Idaho	21.3	12	Virginia	30.6
11	Illinois	31.0	12	West Virginia	30.6
33	Indiana	25.0	14	Massachusetts	30.4
29	Iowa	25.8	15	Colorado	30.1
28	Kansas	26.0	16	Wisconsin	29.7
19	Kentucky	29.0	17	Georgia	29.2
44	Louisiana	21.1	17	Nebraska	29.2
45	Maine	21.0	19	Kentucky	29.0
27	Maryland	26.1	20	Missouri	28.4
14	Massachusetts	30.4	21	Oklahoma	28.1
24	Michigan	26.8	22	New Hampshire	28.0
40	Minnesota	22.1	23	New Jersey	26.9
49	Mississippi	17.0	24	Michigan	26.8
20	Missouri	28.4	25	Pennsylvania	26.7
5	Montana	34.7	26	Texas	26.5
17	Nebraska	29.2	27	Maryland	26.1
6	Nevada	34.2	28	Kansas	26.0
22	New Hampshire	28.0	29	Iowa	25.8
23	New Jersey	26.9	29	Wyoming	25.8
36	New Mexico	23.8	31	Arizona	25.3
35	New York	23.9	32	California	25.2
37	North Carolina	22.9	33	Indiana	25.0
46	North Dakota	20.6	34	South Carolina	24.5
7	Ohio	33.8	35	New York	23.9
21	Oklahoma	28.1	36	New Mexico	23.8
4	Oregon	35.9	37	Alaska	22.9
25	Pennsylvania	26.7	37	North Carolina	22.9
10	Rhode Island	31.4	39	Delaware	22.2
34	South Carolina	24.5	40	Minnesota	22.1
50	South Dakota	12.3	41	Utah	22.0
42	Tennessee	21.3	42	Idaho	21.3
26	Texas	26.5	42	Tennessee	21.3
41	Utah	22.0	44	Louisiana	21.1
2	Vermont	39.3	45	Maine	21.0
12	Virginia	30.6	46	North Dakota	20.6
9	Washington	31.9	47	Alabama	18.6
12	West Virginia	30.6	48	Arkansas	17.4
16	Wisconsin	29.7	49	Mississippi	17.0
29	Wyoming	25.8	50	South Dakota	12.3
				District of Columbia	33.6

Source: Morgan Quitno Press using data from U.S. Dept. of Health and Human Services, Nat'l Center for Health Statistics "National Vital Statistics Reports" (Vol. 54, No. 8, December 29, 2005 and Vol. 50, No. 5, February 12, 2002)
*Preliminary data by state of residence.

Percent of Vaginal Births After a Cesarean (VBAC) in 2003

National Percent = 10.6% of Live Births to Women Who Have Had a Cesarean*

ALPHA ORDER				RANK ORDER		
RANK	STATE	PERCENT		RANK	STATE	PERCENT
44	Alabama	6.9		1	Vermont	24.0
7	Alaska	16.5		2	Utah	21.8
42	Arizona	7.8		3	Pennsylvania	20.4
37	Arkansas	8.7		4	New Mexico	18.7
45	California	6.6		5	Washington	17.7
12	Colorado	14.9		6	Hawaii	16.7
24	Connecticut	11.2		7	Alaska	16.5
28	Delaware	10.9		8	New York	16.2
49	Florida	5.7		9	Montana	15.8
34	Georgia	9.2		10	Maryland	15.4
6	Hawaii	16.7		10	Wisconsin	15.4
16	Idaho	14.1		12	Colorado	14.9
20	Illinois	13.5		13	Ohio	14.6
32	Indiana	10.2		13	South Dakota	14.6
31	Iowa	10.4		15	New Jersey	14.3
35	Kansas	9.0		16	Idaho	14.1
45	Kentucky	6.6		17	Minnesota	13.9
50	Louisiana	5.1		18	North Dakota	13.7
40	Maine	8.2		19	Oregon	13.6
10	Maryland	15.4		20	Illinois	13.5
22	Massachusetts	12.6		21	Wyoming	13.4
23	Michigan	11.4		22	Massachusetts	12.6
17	Minnesota	13.9		23	Michigan	11.4
48	Mississippi	5.8		24	Connecticut	11.2
24	Missouri	11.2		24	Missouri	11.2
9	Montana	15.8		24	New Hampshire	11.2
38	Nebraska	8.6		24	Rhode Island	11.2
41	Nevada	8.0		28	Delaware	10.9
24	New Hampshire	11.2		29	North Carolina	10.7
15	New Jersey	14.3		29	Virginia	10.7
4	New Mexico	18.7		31	Iowa	10.4
8	New York	16.2		32	Indiana	10.2
29	North Carolina	10.7		33	Tennessee	9.6
18	North Dakota	13.7		34	Georgia	9.2
13	Ohio	14.6		35	Kansas	9.0
43	Oklahoma	7.6		36	West Virginia	8.8
19	Oregon	13.6		37	Arkansas	8.7
3	Pennsylvania	20.4		38	Nebraska	8.6
24	Rhode Island	11.2		39	South Carolina	8.3
39	South Carolina	8.3		40	Maine	8.2
13	South Dakota	14.6		41	Nevada	8.0
33	Tennessee	9.6		42	Arizona	7.8
45	Texas	6.6		43	Oklahoma	7.6
2	Utah	21.8		44	Alabama	6.9
1	Vermont	24.0		45	California	6.6
29	Virginia	10.7		45	Kentucky	6.6
5	Washington	17.7		45	Texas	6.6
36	West Virginia	8.8		48	Mississippi	5.8
10	Wisconsin	15.4		49	Florida	5.7
21	Wyoming	13.4		50	Louisiana	5.1
					District of Columbia	10.3

Source: U.S. Department of Health and Human Services, National Center for Health Statistics
    "National Vital Statistics Reports" (Vol. 54, No. 2, September 8, 2005)
*Final data. Vaginal births after a cesarean delivery as a percent of all births to women with a previous cesarean delivery giving birth in 2003.

Assisted Reproductive Technology Procedures in 2002

National Total = 113,637 Procedures*

ALPHA ORDER					RANK ORDER			
RANK	STATE	PROCEDURES	% of USA		RANK	STATE	PROCEDURES	% of USA
35	Alabama	549	0.5%		1	California	15,117	13.3%
49	Alaska	94	0.1%		2	New York	13,276	11.7%
18	Arizona	1,661	1.5%		3	Massachusetts	8,631	7.6%
39	Arkansas	407	0.4%		4	New Jersey	7,744	6.8%
1	California	15,117	13.3%		5	Illinois	7,492	6.6%
20	Colorado	1,624	1.4%		6	Texas	5,716	5.0%
19	Connecticut	1,656	1.5%		7	Florida	4,999	4.4%
38	Delaware	414	0.4%		8	Pennsylvania	4,329	3.8%
7	Florida	4,999	4.4%		9	Maryland	4,200	3.7%
13	Georgia	2,553	2.2%		10	Ohio	3,411	3.0%
27	Hawaii	775	0.7%		11	Virginia	3,364	3.0%
40	Idaho	371	0.3%		12	Michigan	3,288	2.9%
5	Illinois	7,492	6.6%		13	Georgia	2,553	2.2%
17	Indiana	1,871	1.6%		14	Minnesota	2,211	1.9%
23	Iowa	998	0.9%		15	Washington	2,101	1.8%
30	Kansas	706	0.6%		16	North Carolina	1,947	1.7%
24	Kentucky	868	0.8%		17	Indiana	1,871	1.6%
32	Louisiana	605	0.5%		18	Arizona	1,661	1.5%
44	Maine	176	0.2%		19	Connecticut	1,656	1.5%
9	Maryland	4,200	3.7%		20	Colorado	1,624	1.4%
3	Massachusetts	8,631	7.6%		21	Missouri	1,260	1.1%
12	Michigan	3,288	2.9%		22	Wisconsin	1,231	1.1%
14	Minnesota	2,211	1.9%		23	Iowa	998	0.9%
41	Mississippi	370	0.3%		24	Kentucky	868	0.8%
21	Missouri	1,260	1.1%		25	Oregon	815	0.7%
48	Montana	111	0.1%		26	Tennessee	787	0.7%
31	Nebraska	675	0.6%		27	Hawaii	775	0.7%
33	Nevada	603	0.5%		28	South Carolina	772	0.7%
37	New Hampshire	512	0.5%		29	Rhode Island	759	0.7%
4	New Jersey	7,744	6.8%		30	Kansas	706	0.6%
42	New Mexico	223	0.2%		31	Nebraska	675	0.6%
2	New York	13,276	11.7%		32	Louisiana	605	0.5%
16	North Carolina	1,947	1.7%		33	Nevada	603	0.5%
43	North Dakota	207	0.2%		34	Utah	574	0.5%
10	Ohio	3,411	3.0%		35	Alabama	549	0.5%
36	Oklahoma	535	0.5%		36	Oklahoma	535	0.5%
25	Oregon	815	0.7%		37	New Hampshire	512	0.5%
8	Pennsylvania	4,329	3.8%		38	Delaware	414	0.4%
29	Rhode Island	759	0.7%		39	Arkansas	407	0.4%
28	South Carolina	772	0.7%		40	Idaho	371	0.3%
47	South Dakota	146	0.1%		41	Mississippi	370	0.3%
26	Tennessee	787	0.7%		42	New Mexico	223	0.2%
6	Texas	5,716	5.0%		43	North Dakota	207	0.2%
34	Utah	574	0.5%		44	Maine	176	0.2%
45	Vermont	175	0.2%		45	Vermont	175	0.2%
11	Virginia	3,364	3.0%		46	West Virginia	172	0.2%
15	Washington	2,101	1.8%		47	South Dakota	146	0.1%
46	West Virginia	172	0.2%		48	Montana	111	0.1%
22	Wisconsin	1,231	1.1%		49	Alaska	94	0.1%
50	Wyoming	68	0.1%		50	Wyoming	68	0.1%
						District of Columbia	488	0.4%

Source: U.S. Department of Health and Human Services, Centers for Disease Control and Prevention
"Assisted Reproductive Technology, 2002" (Morbidity and Mortality Weekly Report, Vol. 54, No. SS-02, 06/03/05)
*By patient's residence. Does not include 1,732 procedures for patients with residences outside the U.S. Assisted reproductive technology (ART) includes treatments in which both eggs and sperm are handled in the laboratory. In 2002, 74% of ART treatments were freshly fertilized embryos using the patient's eggs, 14% were thawed embryos using the patient's eggs, 8% were freshly fertilized embryos from donor eggs and 3% were thawed embryos from donor eggs.

Infants Born from Assisted Reproductive Technology Procedures in 2002

National Total = 45,038 Live Births*

ALPHA ORDER

RANK	STATE	BIRTHS	% of USA
32	Alabama	258	0.6%
50	Alaska	41	0.1%
18	Arizona	668	1.5%
39	Arkansas	161	0.4%
1	California	6,001	13.3%
14	Colorado	973	2.2%
20	Connecticut	625	1.4%
40	Delaware	154	0.3%
7	Florida	2,020	4.5%
13	Georgia	1,082	2.4%
35	Hawaii	233	0.5%
37	Idaho	203	0.5%
5	Illinois	2,598	5.8%
18	Indiana	668	1.5%
25	Iowa	422	0.9%
28	Kansas	317	0.7%
23	Kentucky	450	1.0%
36	Louisiana	231	0.5%
45	Maine	84	0.2%
10	Maryland	1,423	3.2%
4	Massachusetts	3,086	6.9%
12	Michigan	1,282	2.8%
15	Minnesota	942	2.1%
42	Mississippi	145	0.3%
21	Missouri	608	1.3%
48	Montana	55	0.1%
31	Nebraska	260	0.6%
34	Nevada	251	0.6%
38	New Hampshire	191	0.4%
3	New Jersey	3,106	6.9%
41	New Mexico	149	0.3%
2	New York	4,742	10.5%
17	North Carolina	896	2.0%
44	North Dakota	85	0.2%
8	Ohio	1,457	3.2%
30	Oklahoma	280	0.6%
24	Oregon	425	0.9%
9	Pennsylvania	1,449	3.2%
29	Rhode Island	285	0.6%
27	South Carolina	362	0.8%
47	South Dakota	59	0.1%
26	Tennessee	366	0.8%
6	Texas	2,559	5.7%
32	Utah	258	0.6%
43	Vermont	95	0.2%
11	Virginia	1,324	2.9%
16	Washington	931	2.1%
46	West Virginia	75	0.2%
22	Wisconsin	478	1.1%
49	Wyoming	48	0.1%

RANK ORDER

RANK	STATE	BIRTHS	% of USA
1	California	6,001	13.3%
2	New York	4,742	10.5%
3	New Jersey	3,106	6.9%
4	Massachusetts	3,086	6.9%
5	Illinois	2,598	5.8%
6	Texas	2,559	5.7%
7	Florida	2,020	4.5%
8	Ohio	1,457	3.2%
9	Pennsylvania	1,449	3.2%
10	Maryland	1,423	3.2%
11	Virginia	1,324	2.9%
12	Michigan	1,282	2.8%
13	Georgia	1,082	2.4%
14	Colorado	973	2.2%
15	Minnesota	942	2.1%
16	Washington	931	2.1%
17	North Carolina	896	2.0%
18	Arizona	668	1.5%
18	Indiana	668	1.5%
20	Connecticut	625	1.4%
21	Missouri	608	1.3%
22	Wisconsin	478	1.1%
23	Kentucky	450	1.0%
24	Oregon	425	0.9%
25	Iowa	422	0.9%
26	Tennessee	366	0.8%
27	South Carolina	362	0.8%
28	Kansas	317	0.7%
29	Rhode Island	285	0.6%
30	Oklahoma	280	0.6%
31	Nebraska	260	0.6%
32	Alabama	258	0.6%
32	Utah	258	0.6%
34	Nevada	251	0.6%
35	Hawaii	233	0.5%
36	Louisiana	231	0.5%
37	Idaho	203	0.5%
38	New Hampshire	191	0.4%
39	Arkansas	161	0.4%
40	Delaware	154	0.3%
41	New Mexico	149	0.3%
42	Mississippi	145	0.3%
43	Vermont	95	0.2%
44	North Dakota	85	0.2%
45	Maine	84	0.2%
46	West Virginia	75	0.2%
47	South Dakota	59	0.1%
48	Montana	55	0.1%
49	Wyoming	48	0.1%
50	Alaska	41	0.1%
	District of Columbia	177	0.4%

Source: U.S. Department of Health and Human Services, Centers for Disease Control and Prevention
"Assisted Reproductive Technology, 2002" (Morbidity and Mortality Weekly Report, Vol. 54, No. SS-02, 06/03/05)
By patient's residence. Does not include 708 births to patients with residences outside the U.S. Assisted reproductive technology (ART) includes treatments in which both eggs and sperm are handled in the laboratory. In 2002, 74% of ART treatments were freshly fertilized embryos using the patient's eggs, 14% were thawed embryos using the patient's eggs, 8% were freshly fertilized embryos from donor eggs and 3% were thawed embryos from donor eggs.

Percent of Assisted Reproductive Technology Procedures that Resulted in Live Births in 2002
National Percent = 28.7%*

ALPHA ORDER

RANK	STATE	PERCENT
12	Alabama	33.0
23	Alaska	30.9
38	Arizona	27.9
31	Arkansas	29.0
33	California	28.7
3	Colorado	41.9
39	Connecticut	27.8
40	Delaware	27.5
29	Florida	29.4
26	Georgia	30.1
50	Hawaii	21.5
5	Idaho	37.7
47	Illinois	25.2
48	Indiana	25.1
22	Iowa	31.0
21	Kansas	31.3
8	Kentucky	35.3
34	Louisiana	28.6
17	Maine	31.8
46	Maryland	25.3
43	Massachusetts	26.9
36	Michigan	28.3
13	Minnesota	32.3
42	Mississippi	27.3
11	Missouri	33.6
9	Montana	35.1
37	Nebraska	28.1
31	Nevada	29.0
44	New Hampshire	26.8
30	New Jersey	29.3
2	New Mexico	44.4
45	New York	26.1
19	North Carolina	31.4
27	North Dakota	29.5
25	Ohio	30.3
4	Oklahoma	37.9
7	Oregon	36.8
49	Pennsylvania	24.1
35	Rhode Island	28.5
10	South Carolina	34.3
24	South Dakota	30.8
18	Tennessee	31.6
15	Texas	32.0
16	Utah	31.9
6	Vermont	37.1
27	Virginia	29.5
14	Washington	32.2
19	West Virginia	31.4
41	Wisconsin	27.4
1	Wyoming	48.5

RANK ORDER

RANK	STATE	PERCENT
1	Wyoming	48.5
2	New Mexico	44.4
3	Colorado	41.9
4	Oklahoma	37.9
5	Idaho	37.7
6	Vermont	37.1
7	Oregon	36.8
8	Kentucky	35.3
9	Montana	35.1
10	South Carolina	34.3
11	Missouri	33.6
12	Alabama	33.0
13	Minnesota	32.3
14	Washington	32.2
15	Texas	32.0
16	Utah	31.9
17	Maine	31.8
18	Tennessee	31.6
19	North Carolina	31.4
19	West Virginia	31.4
21	Kansas	31.3
22	Iowa	31.0
23	Alaska	30.9
24	South Dakota	30.8
25	Ohio	30.3
26	Georgia	30.1
27	North Dakota	29.5
27	Virginia	29.5
29	Florida	29.4
30	New Jersey	29.3
31	Arkansas	29.0
31	Nevada	29.0
33	California	28.7
34	Louisiana	28.6
35	Rhode Island	28.5
36	Michigan	28.3
37	Nebraska	28.1
38	Arizona	27.9
39	Connecticut	27.8
40	Delaware	27.5
41	Wisconsin	27.4
42	Mississippi	27.3
43	Massachusetts	26.9
44	New Hampshire	26.8
45	New York	26.1
46	Maryland	25.3
47	Illinois	25.2
48	Indiana	25.1
49	Pennsylvania	24.1
50	Hawaii	21.5

	District of Columbia	28.3

Source: U.S. Department of Health and Human Services, Centers for Disease Control and Prevention
   "Assisted Reproductive Technology, 2002" (Morbidity and Mortality Weekly Report, Vol. 54, No. SS-02, 06/03/05)
*By patient's residence. Assisted reproductive technology (ART) includes treatments in which both eggs and sperm are handled in the laboratory. In 2002, 74% of ART treatments were freshly fertilized embryos using the patient's eggs, 14% were thawed embryos using the patient's eggs, 8% were freshly fertilized embryos from donor eggs and 3% were thawed embryos from donor eggs.

Percent of Total Live Births Resulting from
Assisted Reproductive Technology Procedures in 2002
National Percent = 1.1% of Live Births*

ALPHA ORDER

RANK	STATE	PERCENT	RANK	STATE	PERCENT
45	Alabama	0.4	1	Massachusetts	3.8
45	Alaska	0.4	2	New Jersey	2.7
26	Arizona	0.8	3	Rhode Island	2.2
45	Arkansas	0.4	4	Maryland	1.9
16	California	1.1	4	New York	1.9
8	Colorado	1.4	6	Connecticut	1.5
6	Connecticut	1.5	6	Vermont	1.5
8	Delaware	1.4	8	Colorado	1.4
19	Florida	1.0	8	Delaware	1.4
26	Georgia	0.8	8	Illinois	1.4
12	Hawaii	1.3	8	Minnesota	1.4
19	Idaho	1.0	12	Hawaii	1.3
8	Illinois	1.4	12	New Hampshire	1.3
26	Indiana	0.8	12	Virginia	1.3
16	Iowa	1.1	15	Washington	1.2
26	Kansas	0.8	16	California	1.1
26	Kentucky	0.8	16	Iowa	1.1
45	Louisiana	0.4	16	North Dakota	1.1
38	Maine	0.6	19	Florida	1.0
4	Maryland	1.9	19	Idaho	1.0
1	Massachusetts	3.8	19	Michigan	1.0
19	Michigan	1.0	19	Nebraska	1.0
8	Minnesota	1.4	19	Ohio	1.0
50	Mississippi	0.3	19	Pennsylvania	1.0
26	Missouri	0.8	25	Oregon	0.9
41	Montana	0.5	26	Arizona	0.8
19	Nebraska	1.0	26	Georgia	0.8
26	Nevada	0.8	26	Indiana	0.8
12	New Hampshire	1.3	26	Kansas	0.8
2	New Jersey	2.7	26	Kentucky	0.8
41	New Mexico	0.5	26	Missouri	0.8
4	New York	1.9	26	Nevada	0.8
26	North Carolina	0.8	26	North Carolina	0.8
16	North Dakota	1.1	34	South Carolina	0.7
19	Ohio	1.0	34	Texas	0.7
38	Oklahoma	0.6	34	Wisconsin	0.7
25	Oregon	0.9	34	Wyoming	0.7
19	Pennsylvania	1.0	38	Maine	0.6
3	Rhode Island	2.2	38	Oklahoma	0.6
34	South Carolina	0.7	38	South Dakota	0.6
38	South Dakota	0.6	41	Montana	0.5
41	Tennessee	0.5	41	New Mexico	0.5
34	Texas	0.7	41	Tennessee	0.5
41	Utah	0.5	41	Utah	0.5
6	Vermont	1.5	45	Alabama	0.4
12	Virginia	1.3	45	Alaska	0.4
15	Washington	1.2	45	Arkansas	0.4
45	West Virginia	0.4	45	Louisiana	0.4
34	Wisconsin	0.7	45	West Virginia	0.4
34	Wyoming	0.7	50	Mississippi	0.3

District of Columbia   2.4

Source: Morgan Quitno Press using data from US Dept of Health & Human Serv's, Centers for Disease Control-Prevention
"Assisted Reproductive Technology, 2002" (Morbidity and Mortality Weekly Report, Vol. 54, No. SS-02, 06/03/05)
"National Vital Statistics Reports" (Vol. 52, No. 10, December 17, 2003)
*By patient's residence. Does not include births or procedures to patients with residences outside the U.S. Assisted reproductive technology (ART) includes treatments in which both eggs and sperm are handled in the laboratory (i.e. in vitro fertilization and related procedures).

Percent of Infants Born in Multiple-Birth Deliveries as a Percent of All Infants Born Through Assisted Reproductive Technology Procedures in 2002
National Percent = 52.8% of Births*

ALPHA ORDER				RANK ORDER		
RANK	STATE	PERCENT		RANK	STATE	PERCENT
17	Alabama	55.8		1	New Mexico	64.4
16	Alaska	56.1		2	Maine	64.3
13	Arizona	57.0		3	Wyoming	62.5
41	Arkansas	50.9		4	North Carolina	60.3
29	California	53.1		5	Vermont	60.0
12	Colorado	57.1		6	Idaho	59.6
40	Connecticut	51.0		6	Kentucky	59.6
45	Delaware	48.7		8	Kansas	59.0
34	Florida	52.2		8	Nevada	59.0
22	Georgia	54.5		10	Tennessee	58.2
28	Hawaii	53.2		11	Missouri	58.1
6	Idaho	59.6		12	Colorado	57.1
37	Illinois	52.0		13	Arizona	57.0
19	Indiana	55.1		14	Wisconsin	56.9
36	Iowa	52.1		15	Oregon	56.7
8	Kansas	59.0		16	Alaska	56.1
6	Kentucky	59.6		17	Alabama	55.8
47	Louisiana	47.6		18	Utah	55.4
2	Maine	64.3		19	Indiana	55.1
44	Maryland	49.3		19	Ohio	55.1
46	Massachusetts	48.3		21	Texas	55.0
31	Michigan	52.7		22	Georgia	54.5
49	Minnesota	46.7		22	Montana	54.5
26	Mississippi	53.8		22	New Hampshire	54.5
11	Missouri	58.1		25	North Dakota	54.1
22	Montana	54.5		26	Mississippi	53.8
42	Nebraska	50.8		27	West Virginia	53.3
8	Nevada	59.0		28	Hawaii	53.2
22	New Hampshire	54.5		29	California	53.1
37	New Jersey	52.0		30	Washington	52.8
1	New Mexico	64.4		31	Michigan	52.7
39	New York	51.6		31	Pennsylvania	52.7
4	North Carolina	60.3		33	Oklahoma	52.5
25	North Dakota	54.1		34	Florida	52.2
19	Ohio	55.1		34	South Carolina	52.2
33	Oklahoma	52.5		36	Iowa	52.1
15	Oregon	56.7		37	Illinois	52.0
31	Pennsylvania	52.7		37	New Jersey	52.0
43	Rhode Island	49.5		39	New York	51.6
34	South Carolina	52.2		40	Connecticut	51.0
50	South Dakota	44.1		41	Arkansas	50.9
10	Tennessee	58.2		42	Nebraska	50.8
21	Texas	55.0		43	Rhode Island	49.5
18	Utah	55.4		44	Maryland	49.3
5	Vermont	60.0		45	Delaware	48.7
48	Virginia	47.5		46	Massachusetts	48.3
30	Washington	52.8		47	Louisiana	47.6
27	West Virginia	53.3		48	Virginia	47.5
14	Wisconsin	56.9		49	Minnesota	46.7
3	Wyoming	62.5		50	South Dakota	44.1
					District of Columbia	42.4

Source: U.S. Department of Health and Human Services, Centers for Disease Control and Prevention
   "Assisted Reproductive Technology, 2002" (Morbidity and Mortality Weekly Report, Vol. 54, No. SS-02, 06/03/05)
*By patient's residence. Includes births and procedures to patients with residences outside the U.S. Assisted reproductive technology (ART) includes treatments in which both eggs and sperm are handled in the laboratory (i.e. in vitro fertilization and related procedures).

Percent of Mothers Beginning Prenatal Care in First Trimester in 2003

National Percent = 84.1% of Mothers*

ALPHA ORDER				RANK ORDER		
RANK	STATE	PERCENT		RANK	STATE	PERCENT
28	Alabama	83.8		1	New Hampshire	92.8
41	Alaska	79.8		2	Rhode Island	90.9
46	Arizona	76.6		3	Vermont	90.6
36	Arkansas	81.3		4	Massachusetts	90.0
11	California	87.3		5	Iowa	88.9
42	Colorado	79.3		6	Connecticut	88.7
6	Connecticut	88.7		7	Missouri	88.4
24	Delaware	84.4		8	Kansas	87.8
17	Florida	85.8		9	Ohio	87.7
27	Georgia	84.0		10	Maine	87.5
32	Hawaii	82.4		11	California	87.3
35	Idaho	81.4		11	North Dakota	87.3
19	Illinois	85.4		13	Kentucky	87.0
34	Indiana	81.5		14	Minnesota	86.5
5	Iowa	88.9		15	Wyoming	86.4
8	Kansas	87.8		16	Michigan	86.1
13	Kentucky	87.0		17	Florida	85.8
26	Louisiana	84.1		17	West Virginia	85.8
10	Maine	87.5		19	Illinois	85.4
29	Maryland	83.7		20	Virginia	85.3
4	Massachusetts	90.0		21	Mississippi	84.9
16	Michigan	86.1		21	Wisconsin	84.9
14	Minnesota	86.5		23	North Carolina	84.5
21	Mississippi	84.9		24	Delaware	84.4
7	Missouri	88.4		24	Montana	84.4
24	Montana	84.4		26	Louisiana	84.1
30	Nebraska	83.4		27	Georgia	84.0
48	Nevada	75.8		28	Alabama	83.8
1	New Hampshire	92.8		29	Maryland	83.7
40	New Jersey	80.2		30	Nebraska	83.4
50	New Mexico	68.9		30	Tennessee	83.4
32	New York	82.4		32	Hawaii	82.4
23	North Carolina	84.5		32	New York	82.4
11	North Dakota	87.3		34	Indiana	81.5
9	Ohio	87.7		35	Idaho	81.4
44	Oklahoma	77.8		36	Arkansas	81.3
37	Oregon	81.2		37	Oregon	81.2
47	Pennsylvania	76.0		38	Texas	80.9
2	Rhode Island	90.9		39	Utah	80.3
45	South Carolina	77.5		40	New Jersey	80.2
43	South Dakota	78.4		41	Alaska	79.8
30	Tennessee	83.4		42	Colorado	79.3
38	Texas	80.9		43	South Dakota	78.4
39	Utah	80.3		44	Oklahoma	77.8
3	Vermont	90.6		45	South Carolina	77.5
20	Virginia	85.3		46	Arizona	76.6
49	Washington	74.0		47	Pennsylvania	76.0
17	West Virginia	85.8		48	Nevada	75.8
21	Wisconsin	84.9		49	Washington	74.0
15	Wyoming	86.4		50	New Mexico	68.9
					District of Columbia	76.1

Source: U.S. Department of Health and Human Services, National Center for Health Statistics
    "National Vital Statistics Reports" (Vol. 54, No. 2, September 8, 2005)
*Final data by state of residence.

Percent of White Mothers Beginning Prenatal Care in First Trimester in 2003

National Percent = 85.7% of White Mothers*

<table>
<tr><td colspan="3">ALPHA ORDER</td><td colspan="3">RANK ORDER</td></tr>
<tr><th>RANK</th><th>STATE</th><th>PERCENT</th><th>RANK</th><th>STATE</th><th>PERCENT</th></tr>
<tr><td>22</td><td>Alabama</td><td>87.3</td><td>1</td><td>New Hampshire</td><td>93.0</td></tr>
<tr><td>34</td><td>Alaska</td><td>83.7</td><td>2</td><td>Rhode Island</td><td>92.2</td></tr>
<tr><td>47</td><td>Arizona</td><td>76.9</td><td>3</td><td>Massachusetts</td><td>91.4</td></tr>
<tr><td>36</td><td>Arkansas</td><td>83.2</td><td>4</td><td>Vermont</td><td>90.8</td></tr>
<tr><td>21</td><td>California</td><td>87.4</td><td>5</td><td>Mississippi</td><td>90.7</td></tr>
<tr><td>44</td><td>Colorado</td><td>79.8</td><td>6</td><td>Louisiana</td><td>90.0</td></tr>
<tr><td>7</td><td>Connecticut</td><td>89.8</td><td>7</td><td>Connecticut</td><td>89.8</td></tr>
<tr><td>27</td><td>Delaware</td><td>86.2</td><td>8</td><td>Missouri</td><td>89.7</td></tr>
<tr><td>16</td><td>Florida</td><td>88.1</td><td>8</td><td>North Dakota</td><td>89.7</td></tr>
<tr><td>27</td><td>Georgia</td><td>86.2</td><td>10</td><td>Iowa</td><td>89.5</td></tr>
<tr><td>31</td><td>Hawaii</td><td>85.5</td><td>11</td><td>Ohio</td><td>89.3</td></tr>
<tr><td>39</td><td>Idaho</td><td>81.6</td><td>12</td><td>Michigan</td><td>89.0</td></tr>
<tr><td>19</td><td>Illinois</td><td>87.7</td><td>13</td><td>Minnesota</td><td>88.8</td></tr>
<tr><td>37</td><td>Indiana</td><td>83.0</td><td>14</td><td>Maryland</td><td>88.7</td></tr>
<tr><td>10</td><td>Iowa</td><td>89.5</td><td>15</td><td>Kansas</td><td>88.5</td></tr>
<tr><td>15</td><td>Kansas</td><td>88.5</td><td>16</td><td>Florida</td><td>88.1</td></tr>
<tr><td>19</td><td>Kentucky</td><td>87.7</td><td>17</td><td>Maine</td><td>87.9</td></tr>
<tr><td>6</td><td>Louisiana</td><td>90.0</td><td>17</td><td>Virginia</td><td>87.9</td></tr>
<tr><td>17</td><td>Maine</td><td>87.9</td><td>19</td><td>Illinois</td><td>87.7</td></tr>
<tr><td>14</td><td>Maryland</td><td>88.7</td><td>19</td><td>Kentucky</td><td>87.7</td></tr>
<tr><td>3</td><td>Massachusetts</td><td>91.4</td><td>21</td><td>California</td><td>87.4</td></tr>
<tr><td>12</td><td>Michigan</td><td>89.0</td><td>22</td><td>Alabama</td><td>87.3</td></tr>
<tr><td>13</td><td>Minnesota</td><td>88.8</td><td>23</td><td>Wyoming</td><td>87.0</td></tr>
<tr><td>5</td><td>Mississippi</td><td>90.7</td><td>24</td><td>Montana</td><td>86.9</td></tr>
<tr><td>8</td><td>Missouri</td><td>89.7</td><td>24</td><td>North Carolina</td><td>86.9</td></tr>
<tr><td>24</td><td>Montana</td><td>86.9</td><td>24</td><td>Wisconsin</td><td>86.9</td></tr>
<tr><td>33</td><td>Nebraska</td><td>84.4</td><td>27</td><td>Delaware</td><td>86.2</td></tr>
<tr><td>48</td><td>Nevada</td><td>75.8</td><td>27</td><td>Georgia</td><td>86.2</td></tr>
<tr><td>1</td><td>New Hampshire</td><td>93.0</td><td>27</td><td>Tennessee</td><td>86.2</td></tr>
<tr><td>35</td><td>New Jersey</td><td>83.4</td><td>27</td><td>West Virginia</td><td>86.2</td></tr>
<tr><td>50</td><td>New Mexico</td><td>70.2</td><td>31</td><td>Hawaii</td><td>85.5</td></tr>
<tr><td>32</td><td>New York</td><td>85.2</td><td>32</td><td>New York</td><td>85.2</td></tr>
<tr><td>24</td><td>North Carolina</td><td>86.9</td><td>33</td><td>Nebraska</td><td>84.4</td></tr>
<tr><td>8</td><td>North Dakota</td><td>89.7</td><td>34</td><td>Alaska</td><td>83.7</td></tr>
<tr><td>11</td><td>Ohio</td><td>89.3</td><td>35</td><td>New Jersey</td><td>83.4</td></tr>
<tr><td>45</td><td>Oklahoma</td><td>79.6</td><td>36</td><td>Arkansas</td><td>83.2</td></tr>
<tr><td>40</td><td>Oregon</td><td>81.5</td><td>37</td><td>Indiana</td><td>83.0</td></tr>
<tr><td>46</td><td>Pennsylvania</td><td>79.2</td><td>38</td><td>South Dakota</td><td>82.8</td></tr>
<tr><td>2</td><td>Rhode Island</td><td>92.2</td><td>39</td><td>Idaho</td><td>81.6</td></tr>
<tr><td>43</td><td>South Carolina</td><td>81.0</td><td>40</td><td>Oregon</td><td>81.5</td></tr>
<tr><td>38</td><td>South Dakota</td><td>82.8</td><td>41</td><td>Utah</td><td>81.2</td></tr>
<tr><td>27</td><td>Tennessee</td><td>86.2</td><td>42</td><td>Texas</td><td>81.1</td></tr>
<tr><td>42</td><td>Texas</td><td>81.1</td><td>43</td><td>South Carolina</td><td>81.0</td></tr>
<tr><td>41</td><td>Utah</td><td>81.2</td><td>44</td><td>Colorado</td><td>79.8</td></tr>
<tr><td>4</td><td>Vermont</td><td>90.8</td><td>45</td><td>Oklahoma</td><td>79.6</td></tr>
<tr><td>17</td><td>Virginia</td><td>87.9</td><td>46</td><td>Pennsylvania</td><td>79.2</td></tr>
<tr><td>49</td><td>Washington</td><td>75.0</td><td>47</td><td>Arizona</td><td>76.9</td></tr>
<tr><td>27</td><td>West Virginia</td><td>86.2</td><td>48</td><td>Nevada</td><td>75.8</td></tr>
<tr><td>24</td><td>Wisconsin</td><td>86.9</td><td>49</td><td>Washington</td><td>75.0</td></tr>
<tr><td>23</td><td>Wyoming</td><td>87.0</td><td>50</td><td>New Mexico</td><td>70.2</td></tr>
<tr><td></td><td></td><td></td><td></td><td>District of Columbia</td><td>86.4</td></tr>
</table>

Source: U.S. Department of Health and Human Services, National Center for Health Statistics
    "National Vital Statistics Reports" (Vol. 54, No. 2, September 8, 2005)
*Final data by state of residence.

Percent of Black Mothers Beginning Prenatal Care in First Trimester in 2003

National Percent = 75.9% of Black Mothers*

RANK	STATE	PERCENT
26	Alabama	75.7
9	Alaska	81.8
25	Arizona	76.0
33	Arkansas	73.5
7	California	84.1
40	Colorado	70.9
11	Connecticut	81.0
16	Delaware	78.8
19	Florida	77.9
15	Georgia	79.1
2	Hawaii	89.3
3	Idaho	87.8
30	Illinois	74.2
44	Indiana	69.3
23	Iowa	76.8
14	Kansas	80.1
13	Kentucky	80.7
27	Louisiana	75.5
28	Maine	74.9
29	Maryland	74.6
10	Massachusetts	81.5
37	Michigan	72.8
39	Minnesota	72.3
20	Mississippi	77.8
11	Missouri	81.0
4	Montana	86.0
38	Nebraska	72.7
41	Nevada	70.7
6	New Hampshire	85.1
48	New Jersey	64.4
45	New Mexico	68.7
35	New York	73.1
23	North Carolina	76.8
5	North Dakota	85.2
16	Ohio	78.8
43	Oklahoma	69.8
18	Oregon	78.0
50	Pennsylvania	57.2
8	Rhode Island	82.8
42	South Carolina	70.5
47	South Dakota	64.8
36	Tennessee	73.0
21	Texas	77.0
49	Utah	63.2
31	Vermont	74.0
22	Virginia	76.9
46	Washington	67.9
33	West Virginia	73.5
32	Wisconsin	73.6
1	Wyoming	96.2

RANK	STATE	PERCENT
1	Wyoming	96.2
2	Hawaii	89.3
3	Idaho	87.8
4	Montana	86.0
5	North Dakota	85.2
6	New Hampshire	85.1
7	California	84.1
8	Rhode Island	82.8
9	Alaska	81.8
10	Massachusetts	81.5
11	Connecticut	81.0
11	Missouri	81.0
13	Kentucky	80.7
14	Kansas	80.1
15	Georgia	79.1
16	Delaware	78.8
16	Ohio	78.8
18	Oregon	78.0
19	Florida	77.9
20	Mississippi	77.8
21	Texas	77.0
22	Virginia	76.9
23	Iowa	76.8
23	North Carolina	76.8
25	Arizona	76.0
26	Alabama	75.7
27	Louisiana	75.5
28	Maine	74.9
29	Maryland	74.6
30	Illinois	74.2
31	Vermont	74.0
32	Wisconsin	73.6
33	Arkansas	73.5
33	West Virginia	73.5
35	New York	73.1
36	Tennessee	73.0
37	Michigan	72.8
38	Nebraska	72.7
39	Minnesota	72.3
40	Colorado	70.9
41	Nevada	70.7
42	South Carolina	70.5
43	Oklahoma	69.8
44	Indiana	69.3
45	New Mexico	68.7
46	Washington	67.9
47	South Dakota	64.8
48	New Jersey	64.4
49	Utah	63.2
50	Pennsylvania	57.2
	District of Columbia	71.1

Source: U.S. Department of Health and Human Services, National Center for Health Statistics
    "National Vital Statistics Reports" (Vol. 54, No. 2, September 8, 2005)
*Final data by state of residence.

Percent of Hispanic Mothers Beginning Prenatal Care in First Trimester in 2003

National Percent = 77.5% of Hispanic Mothers*

ALPHA ORDER				RANK ORDER		
RANK	STATE	PERCENT		RANK	STATE	PERCENT
50	Alabama	52.0		1	Rhode Island	86.9
14	Alaska	79.6		2	California	85.2
39	Arizona	66.7		3	New Hampshire	84.4
26	Arkansas	71.5		4	Florida	84.2
2	California	85.2		5	Massachusetts	83.9
38	Colorado	67.0		6	Louisiana	83.3
18	Connecticut	78.2		7	Vermont	81.5
25	Delaware	71.9		8	Missouri	81.0
4	Florida	84.2		9	Hawaii	80.8
35	Georgia	69.1		10	Maine	80.7
9	Hawaii	80.8		11	Montana	80.6
37	Idaho	68.3		12	Wyoming	80.1
13	Illinois	80.0		13	Illinois	80.0
41	Indiana	66.0		14	Alaska	79.6
23	Iowa	74.8		14	Mississippi	79.6
20	Kansas	77.2		16	North Dakota	79.5
24	Kentucky	74.0		17	Ohio	79.0
6	Louisiana	83.3		18	Connecticut	78.2
10	Maine	80.7		19	Michigan	77.6
30	Maryland	70.1		20	Kansas	77.2
5	Massachusetts	83.9		21	New York	76.2
19	Michigan	77.6		22	Texas	75.5
28	Minnesota	71.0		23	Iowa	74.8
14	Mississippi	79.6		24	Kentucky	74.0
8	Missouri	81.0		25	Delaware	71.9
11	Montana	80.6		26	Arkansas	71.5
32	Nebraska	69.8		27	Virginia	71.2
44	Nevada	64.1		28	Minnesota	71.0
3	New Hampshire	84.4		29	Wisconsin	70.7
36	New Jersey	68.6		30	Maryland	70.1
40	New Mexico	66.2		31	Oregon	70.0
21	New York	76.2		32	Nebraska	69.8
33	North Carolina	69.6		33	North Carolina	69.6
16	North Dakota	79.5		34	West Virginia	69.3
17	Ohio	79.0		35	Georgia	69.1
42	Oklahoma	65.5		36	New Jersey	68.6
31	Oregon	70.0		37	Idaho	68.3
48	Pennsylvania	61.2		38	Colorado	67.0
1	Rhode Island	86.9		39	Arizona	66.7
49	South Carolina	56.9		40	New Mexico	66.2
45	South Dakota	64.0		41	Indiana	66.0
46	Tennessee	63.7		42	Oklahoma	65.5
22	Texas	75.5		43	Utah	65.1
43	Utah	65.1		44	Nevada	64.1
7	Vermont	81.5		45	South Dakota	64.0
27	Virginia	71.2		46	Tennessee	63.7
47	Washington	63.1		47	Washington	63.1
34	West Virginia	69.3		48	Pennsylvania	61.2
29	Wisconsin	70.7		49	South Carolina	56.9
12	Wyoming	80.1		50	Alabama	52.0
					District of Columbia	69.6

Source: U.S. Department of Health and Human Services, National Center for Health Statistics
   "National Vital Statistics Reports" (Vol. 54, No. 2, September 8, 2005)
*Final data by state of residence. Persons of Hispanic origin may be of any race.

Percent of Mothers Receiving Late or No Prenatal Care in 2003

National Percent = 3.5% of Mothers*

ALPHA ORDER			RANK ORDER		
RANK	STATE	PERCENT	RANK	STATE	PERCENT
24	Alabama	3.5	1	New Mexico	8.1
6	Alaska	5.2	2	Arizona	7.3
2	Arizona	7.3	3	Nevada	6.4
15	Arkansas	4.3	4	Washington	5.8
38	California	2.5	5	Pennsylvania	5.6
12	Colorado	4.4	6	Alaska	5.2
48	Connecticut	1.5	7	South Carolina	4.9
12	Delaware	4.4	8	Oklahoma	4.8
32	Florida	2.8	9	New Jersey	4.7
19	Georgia	3.8	9	Texas	4.7
22	Hawaii	3.6	11	New York	4.5
25	Idaho	3.4	12	Colorado	4.4
32	Illinois	2.8	12	Delaware	4.4
19	Indiana	3.8	12	Utah	4.4
44	Iowa	2.0	15	Arkansas	4.3
40	Kansas	2.3	16	Oregon	4.0
37	Kentucky	2.6	17	Maryland	3.9
25	Louisiana	3.4	17	South Dakota	3.9
46	Maine	1.7	19	Georgia	3.8
17	Maryland	3.9	19	Indiana	3.8
44	Massachusetts	2.0	19	Tennessee	3.8
27	Michigan	3.1	22	Hawaii	3.6
42	Minnesota	2.2	22	Virginia	3.6
30	Mississippi	2.9	24	Alabama	3.5
42	Missouri	2.2	25	Idaho	3.4
35	Montana	2.7	25	Louisiana	3.4
32	Nebraska	2.8	27	Michigan	3.1
3	Nevada	6.4	27	Wisconsin	3.1
49	New Hampshire	1.1	29	Ohio	3.0
9	New Jersey	4.7	30	Mississippi	2.9
1	New Mexico	8.1	30	North Carolina	2.9
11	New York	4.5	32	Florida	2.8
30	North Carolina	2.9	32	Illinois	2.8
35	North Dakota	2.7	32	Nebraska	2.8
29	Ohio	3.0	35	Montana	2.7
8	Oklahoma	4.8	35	North Dakota	2.7
16	Oregon	4.0	37	Kentucky	2.6
5	Pennsylvania	5.6	38	California	2.5
49	Rhode Island	1.1	38	Wyoming	2.5
7	South Carolina	4.9	40	Kansas	2.3
17	South Dakota	3.9	40	West Virginia	2.3
19	Tennessee	3.8	42	Minnesota	2.2
9	Texas	4.7	42	Missouri	2.2
12	Utah	4.4	44	Iowa	2.0
47	Vermont	1.6	44	Massachusetts	2.0
22	Virginia	3.6	46	Maine	1.7
4	Washington	5.8	47	Vermont	1.6
40	West Virginia	2.3	48	Connecticut	1.5
27	Wisconsin	3.1	49	New Hampshire	1.1
38	Wyoming	2.5	49	Rhode Island	1.1
				District of Columbia	6.6

Source: U.S. Department of Health and Human Services, National Center for Health Statistics
"National Vital Statistics Reports" (Vol. 54, No. 2, September 8, 2005)
*Final data by state of residence. "Late" means care begun in third trimester.

Percent of White Mothers Receiving Late or No Prenatal Care in 2003

National Percent = 3.0% of White Mothers*

ALPHA ORDER				RANK ORDER		
RANK	STATE	PERCENT		RANK	STATE	PERCENT
20	Alabama	3.0		1	New Mexico	7.5
5	Alaska	4.7		2	Arizona	7.3
2	Arizona	7.3		3	Nevada	6.3
13	Arkansas	3.7		4	Washington	5.4
25	California	2.5		5	Alaska	4.7
8	Colorado	4.3		5	Texas	4.7
48	Connecticut	1.3		7	Pennsylvania	4.5
16	Delaware	3.4		8	Colorado	4.3
29	Florida	2.3		9	Oklahoma	4.2
18	Georgia	3.3		10	Utah	4.0
35	Hawaii	2.1		11	Oregon	3.9
16	Idaho	3.4		11	South Carolina	3.9
37	Illinois	2.0		13	Arkansas	3.7
18	Indiana	3.3		14	New Jersey	3.6
40	Iowa	1.8		15	New York	3.5
35	Kansas	2.1		16	Delaware	3.4
26	Kentucky	2.4		16	Idaho	3.4
42	Louisiana	1.7		18	Georgia	3.3
43	Maine	1.6		18	Indiana	3.3
29	Maryland	2.3		20	Alabama	3.0
43	Massachusetts	1.6		20	Tennessee	3.0
33	Michigan	2.2		22	Virginia	2.8
43	Minnesota	1.6		23	Nebraska	2.6
43	Mississippi	1.6		23	Wisconsin	2.6
40	Missouri	1.8		25	California	2.5
37	Montana	2.0		26	Kentucky	2.4
23	Nebraska	2.6		26	North Carolina	2.4
3	Nevada	6.3		26	Ohio	2.4
49	New Hampshire	1.0		29	Florida	2.3
14	New Jersey	3.6		29	Maryland	2.3
1	New Mexico	7.5		29	West Virginia	2.3
15	New York	3.5		29	Wyoming	2.3
26	North Carolina	2.4		33	Michigan	2.2
39	North Dakota	1.9		33	South Dakota	2.2
26	Ohio	2.4		35	Hawaii	2.1
9	Oklahoma	4.2		35	Kansas	2.1
11	Oregon	3.9		37	Illinois	2.0
7	Pennsylvania	4.5		37	Montana	2.0
49	Rhode Island	1.0		39	North Dakota	1.9
11	South Carolina	3.9		40	Iowa	1.8
33	South Dakota	2.2		40	Missouri	1.8
20	Tennessee	3.0		42	Louisiana	1.7
5	Texas	4.7		43	Maine	1.6
10	Utah	4.0		43	Massachusetts	1.6
43	Vermont	1.6		43	Minnesota	1.6
22	Virginia	2.8		43	Mississippi	1.6
4	Washington	5.4		43	Vermont	1.6
29	West Virginia	2.3		48	Connecticut	1.3
23	Wisconsin	2.6		49	New Hampshire	1.0
29	Wyoming	2.3		49	Rhode Island	1.0
					District of Columbia	2.5

Source: U.S. Department of Health and Human Services, National Center for Health Statistics
"National Vital Statistics Reports" (Vol. 54, No. 2, September 8, 2005)
*Final data by state of residence. "Late" means care begun in third trimester.

Percent of Black Mothers Receiving Late or No Prenatal Care in 2003

National Percent = 6.0% of Black Mothers*

ALPHA ORDER				RANK ORDER		
RANK	STATE	PERCENT		RANK	STATE	PERCENT
29	Alabama	4.8		1	Utah	13.6
NA	Alaska**	NA		2	Pennsylvania	12.6
6	Arizona	8.2		3	New Jersey	10.6
13	Arkansas	6.9		4	Nevada	8.6
38	California	3.2		5	New York	8.3
14	Colorado	6.8		6	Arizona	8.2
39	Connecticut	3.0		6	Washington	8.2
9	Delaware	7.3		8	Indiana	8.1
29	Florida	4.8		9	Delaware	7.3
29	Georgia	4.8		9	Michigan	7.3
NA	Hawaii**	NA		11	Tennessee	7.2
NA	Idaho**	NA		12	Oklahoma	7.1
15	Illinois	6.7		13	Arkansas	6.9
8	Indiana	8.1		14	Colorado	6.8
23	Iowa	5.5		15	Illinois	6.7
33	Kansas	4.4		15	Maryland	6.7
29	Kentucky	4.8		15	South Carolina	6.7
21	Louisiana	5.8		18	Wisconsin	6.4
NA	Maine**	NA		19	Ohio	6.1
15	Maryland	6.7		20	New Mexico	5.9
27	Massachusetts	5.2		21	Louisiana	5.8
9	Michigan	7.3		21	Virginia	5.8
26	Minnesota	5.4		23	Iowa	5.5
33	Mississippi	4.4		23	Oregon	5.5
33	Missouri	4.4		23	Texas	5.5
NA	Montana**	NA		26	Minnesota	5.4
36	Nebraska	3.8		27	Massachusetts	5.2
4	Nevada	8.6		28	North Carolina	4.9
NA	New Hampshire**	NA		29	Alabama	4.8
3	New Jersey	10.6		29	Florida	4.8
20	New Mexico	5.9		29	Georgia	4.8
5	New York	8.3		29	Kentucky	4.8
28	North Carolina	4.9		33	Kansas	4.4
NA	North Dakota**	NA		33	Mississippi	4.4
19	Ohio	6.1		33	Missouri	4.4
12	Oklahoma	7.1		36	Nebraska	3.8
23	Oregon	5.5		37	West Virginia	3.7
2	Pennsylvania	12.6		38	California	3.2
40	Rhode Island	2.3		39	Connecticut	3.0
15	South Carolina	6.7		40	Rhode Island	2.3
NA	South Dakota**	NA		NA	Alaska**	NA
11	Tennessee	7.2		NA	Hawaii**	NA
23	Texas	5.5		NA	Idaho**	NA
1	Utah	13.6		NA	Maine**	NA
NA	Vermont**	NA		NA	Montana**	NA
21	Virginia	5.8		NA	New Hampshire**	NA
6	Washington	8.2		NA	North Dakota**	NA
37	West Virginia	3.7		NA	South Dakota**	NA
18	Wisconsin	6.4		NA	Vermont**	NA
NA	Wyoming**	NA		NA	Wyoming**	NA
					District of Columbia	8.5

Source: U.S. Department of Health and Human Services, National Center for Health Statistics
"National Vital Statistics Reports" (Vol. 54, No. 2, September 8, 2005)
*Final data by state of residence. "Late" means care begun in third trimester.
**Insufficient data.

Percent of Hispanic Mothers Receiving Late or No Prenatal Care in 2003

National Percent = 5.3% of Hispanic Mothers*

ALPHA ORDER

RANK	STATE	PERCENT
1	Alabama	21.6
29	Alaska	5.2
3	Arizona	11.1
14	Arkansas	7.6
39	California	3.0
15	Colorado	7.4
41	Connecticut	2.8
18	Delaware	6.8
38	Florida	3.1
10	Georgia	8.3
39	Hawaii	3.0
16	Idaho	6.9
37	Illinois	3.2
12	Indiana	7.7
34	Iowa	4.1
31	Kansas	4.7
21	Kentucky	6.4
36	Louisiana	3.8
NA	Maine**	NA
21	Maryland	6.4
42	Massachusetts	2.6
31	Michigan	4.7
30	Minnesota	5.0
16	Mississippi	6.9
35	Missouri	3.9
NA	Montana**	NA
23	Nebraska	6.3
5	Nevada	9.9
NA	New Hampshire**	NA
18	New Jersey	6.8
7	New Mexico	9.1
28	New York	5.5
26	North Carolina	6.0
NA	North Dakota**	NA
33	Ohio	4.6
20	Oklahoma	6.7
25	Oregon	6.2
8	Pennsylvania	8.8
43	Rhode Island	1.4
4	South Carolina	11.0
6	South Dakota	9.4
2	Tennessee	12.4
23	Texas	6.3
9	Utah	8.6
NA	Vermont**	NA
12	Virginia	7.7
11	Washington	8.0
NA	West Virginia**	NA
27	Wisconsin	5.9
NA	Wyoming**	NA

RANK ORDER

RANK	STATE	PERCENT
1	Alabama	21.6
2	Tennessee	12.4
3	Arizona	11.1
4	South Carolina	11.0
5	Nevada	9.9
6	South Dakota	9.4
7	New Mexico	9.1
8	Pennsylvania	8.8
9	Utah	8.6
10	Georgia	8.3
11	Washington	8.0
12	Indiana	7.7
12	Virginia	7.7
14	Arkansas	7.6
15	Colorado	7.4
16	Idaho	6.9
16	Mississippi	6.9
18	Delaware	6.8
18	New Jersey	6.8
20	Oklahoma	6.7
21	Kentucky	6.4
21	Maryland	6.4
23	Nebraska	6.3
23	Texas	6.3
25	Oregon	6.2
26	North Carolina	6.0
27	Wisconsin	5.9
28	New York	5.5
29	Alaska	5.2
30	Minnesota	5.0
31	Kansas	4.7
31	Michigan	4.7
33	Ohio	4.6
34	Iowa	4.1
35	Missouri	3.9
36	Louisiana	3.8
37	Illinois	3.2
38	Florida	3.1
39	California	3.0
39	Hawaii	3.0
41	Connecticut	2.8
42	Massachusetts	2.6
43	Rhode Island	1.4
NA	Maine**	NA
NA	Montana**	NA
NA	New Hampshire**	NA
NA	North Dakota**	NA
NA	Vermont**	NA
NA	West Virginia**	NA
NA	Wyoming**	NA
	District of Columbia	4.7

Source: U.S. Department of Health and Human Services, National Center for Health Statistics
  "National Vital Statistics Reports" (Vol. 54, No. 2, September 8, 2005)
*Final data by state of residence. "Late" means care begun in third trimester.
**Insufficient data.

Reported Legal Abortions in 2002

Reporting States' Total = 854,122 Abortions*

ALPHA ORDER

RANK	STATE	ABORTIONS	% of USA
19	Alabama	12,249	1.4%
NA	Alaska**	NA	NA
22	Arizona	10,677	1.3%
32	Arkansas	5,316	0.6%
NA	California**	NA	NA
27	Colorado	7,757	0.9%
17	Connecticut	13,470	1.6%
34	Delaware	4,493	0.5%
2	Florida	87,964	10.3%
7	Georgia	34,091	4.0%
35	Hawaii	3,920	0.5%
45	Idaho	829	0.1%
4	Illinois	46,945	5.5%
21	Indiana	10,937	1.3%
30	Iowa	6,240	0.7%
20	Kansas	11,765	1.4%
39	Kentucky	3,502	0.4%
24	Louisiana	10,451	1.2%
40	Maine	2,315	0.3%
16	Maryland	13,595	1.6%
11	Massachusetts	25,249	3.0%
9	Michigan	29,231	3.4%
15	Minnesota	14,187	1.7%
37	Mississippi	3,605	0.4%
26	Missouri	8,201	1.0%
41	Montana	2,248	0.3%
36	Nebraska	3,775	0.4%
25	Nevada	9,960	1.2%
NA	New Hampshire**	NA	NA
8	New Jersey	32,854	3.8%
33	New Mexico	5,069	0.6%
1	New York	127,983	15.0%
10	North Carolina	29,229	3.4%
44	North Dakota	1,219	0.1%
5	Ohio	35,830	4.2%
29	Oklahoma	6,500	0.8%
18	Oregon	13,172	1.5%
6	Pennsylvania	35,167	4.1%
31	Rhode Island	5,550	0.6%
28	South Carolina	6,657	0.8%
46	South Dakota	826	0.1%
14	Tennessee	17,807	2.1%
3	Texas	79,929	9.4%
38	Utah	3,524	0.4%
43	Vermont	1,635	0.2%
13	Virginia	24,992	2.9%
12	Washington	25,148	2.9%
42	West Virginia	2,049	0.2%
23	Wisconsin	10,489	1.2%
47	Wyoming	10	0.0%

RANK ORDER

RANK	STATE	ABORTIONS	% of USA
1	New York	127,983	15.0%
2	Florida	87,964	10.3%
3	Texas	79,929	9.4%
4	Illinois	46,945	5.5%
5	Ohio	35,830	4.2%
6	Pennsylvania	35,167	4.1%
7	Georgia	34,091	4.0%
8	New Jersey	32,854	3.8%
9	Michigan	29,231	3.4%
10	North Carolina	29,229	3.4%
11	Massachusetts	25,249	3.0%
12	Washington	25,148	2.9%
13	Virginia	24,992	2.9%
14	Tennessee	17,807	2.1%
15	Minnesota	14,187	1.7%
16	Maryland	13,595	1.6%
17	Connecticut	13,470	1.6%
18	Oregon	13,172	1.5%
19	Alabama	12,249	1.4%
20	Kansas	11,765	1.4%
21	Indiana	10,937	1.3%
22	Arizona	10,677	1.3%
23	Wisconsin	10,489	1.2%
24	Louisiana	10,451	1.2%
25	Nevada	9,960	1.2%
26	Missouri	8,201	1.0%
27	Colorado	7,757	0.9%
28	South Carolina	6,657	0.8%
29	Oklahoma	6,500	0.8%
30	Iowa	6,240	0.7%
31	Rhode Island	5,550	0.6%
32	Arkansas	5,316	0.6%
33	New Mexico	5,069	0.6%
34	Delaware	4,493	0.5%
35	Hawaii	3,920	0.5%
36	Nebraska	3,775	0.4%
37	Mississippi	3,605	0.4%
38	Utah	3,524	0.4%
39	Kentucky	3,502	0.4%
40	Maine	2,315	0.3%
41	Montana	2,248	0.3%
42	West Virginia	2,049	0.2%
43	Vermont	1,635	0.2%
44	North Dakota	1,219	0.1%
45	Idaho	829	0.1%
46	South Dakota	826	0.1%
47	Wyoming	10	0.0%
NA	Alaska**	NA	NA
NA	California**	NA	NA
NA	New Hampshire**	NA	NA

	District of Columbia	5,511	0.6%

Source: U.S. Department of Health and Human Services, Centers for Disease Control and Prevention
    "Abortion Surveillance-United States, 2002" (Morbidity and Mortality Weekly Report, Vol. 54, No. SS-7, 11/25/05)
By state of occurrence. Total is for reporting states only.
**Not reported.*

Percent Change in Reported Legal Abortions: 1999 to 2002

National Percent Change = 1.6% Decrease*

ALPHA ORDER				RANK ORDER		
RANK	**STATE**	**PERCENT CHANGE**		**RANK**	**STATE**	**PERCENT CHANGE**
33	Alabama	(7.7)		1	Nevada	71.5
NA	Alaska**	NA		2	Colorado	54.6
17	Arizona	(0.8)		3	Maryland	21.8
32	Arkansas	(7.6)		4	South Dakota	11.6
NA	California**	NA		5	Michigan	11.5
2	Colorado	54.6		6	Rhode Island	10.9
10	Connecticut	4.0		7	Tennessee	5.2
40	Delaware	(12.9)		8	Florida	4.8
8	Florida	4.8		9	Utah	4.2
11	Georgia	3.0		10	Connecticut	4.0
39	Hawaii	(11.0)		11	Georgia	3.0
22	Idaho	(4.4)		12	Illinois	2.2
12	Illinois	2.2		12	Iowa	2.2
37	Indiana	(9.7)		14	Pennsylvania	2.0
12	Iowa	2.2		15	Missouri	1.1
25	Kansas	(5.1)		16	New Mexico	(0.6)
45	Kentucky	(36.0)		17	Arizona	(0.8)
41	Louisiana	(13.0)		18	Texas	(1.0)
23	Maine	(4.6)		19	Minnesota	(1.1)
3	Maryland	21.8		20	Washington	(1.5)
26	Massachusetts	(6.0)		21	Ohio	(3.3)
5	Michigan	11.5		22	Idaho	(4.4)
19	Minnesota	(1.1)		23	Maine	(4.6)
31	Mississippi	(7.0)		24	Wisconsin	(4.8)
15	Missouri	1.1		25	Kansas	(5.1)
38	Montana	(10.0)		26	Massachusetts	(6.0)
43	Nebraska	(17.3)		27	New Jersey	(6.5)
1	Nevada	71.5		27	Vermont	(6.5)
NA	New Hampshire**	NA		29	New York	(6.7)
27	New Jersey	(6.5)		30	Oregon	(6.9)
16	New Mexico	(0.6)		31	Mississippi	(7.0)
29	New York	(6.7)		32	Arkansas	(7.6)
35	North Carolina	(8.9)		33	Alabama	(7.7)
36	North Dakota	(9.4)		34	Virginia	(8.6)
21	Ohio	(3.3)		35	North Carolina	(8.9)
NA	Oklahoma**	NA		36	North Dakota	(9.4)
30	Oregon	(6.9)		37	Indiana	(9.7)
14	Pennsylvania	2.0		38	Montana	(10.0)
6	Rhode Island	10.9		39	Hawaii	(11.0)
42	South Carolina	(13.4)		40	Delaware	(12.9)
4	South Dakota	11.6		41	Louisiana	(13.0)
7	Tennessee	5.2		42	South Carolina	(13.4)
18	Texas	(1.0)		43	Nebraska	(17.3)
9	Utah	4.2		44	West Virginia	(18.0)
27	Vermont	(6.5)		45	Kentucky	(36.0)
34	Virginia	(8.6)		46	Wyoming	(90.9)
20	Washington	(1.5)		NA	Alaska**	NA
44	West Virginia	(18.0)		NA	California**	NA
24	Wisconsin	(4.8)		NA	New Hampshire**	NA
46	Wyoming	(90.9)		NA	Oklahoma**	NA
					District of Columbia	(25.3)

Source: Morgan Quitno Press using data from US Dept of Health & Human Serv's, Centers for Disease Control-Prevention
"Abortion Surveillance-United States, 2002" (Morbidity and Mortality Weekly Report, Vol. 54, No. SS-7, 11/25/05)
"Abortion Surveillance-United States, 1999" (Morbidity and Mortality Weekly Report, Vol. 51, No. SS-9, 11/29/02)
By state of occurrence. Percent change is only for states reporting in both years.
**Not reported.*

Reported Legal Abortions per 1,000 Live Births in 2002

Reporting States' Ratio = 246 Abortions per 1,000 Live Births*

ALPHA ORDER				RANK ORDER		
RANK	STATE	RATIO		RANK	STATE	RATIO
24	Alabama	208		1	New York	509
NA	Alaska**	NA		2	Rhode Island	430
37	Arizona	122		3	Florida	428
34	Arkansas	142		4	Delaware	405
NA	California**	NA		5	Connecticut	321
39	Colorado	113		6	Washington	318
5	Connecticut	321		7	Massachusetts	313
4	Delaware	405		8	Nevada	306
3	Florida	428		9	Kansas	299
13	Georgia	256		10	Oregon	291
21	Hawaii	224		11	New Jersey	286
46	Idaho	40		12	Illinois	260
12	Illinois	260		13	Georgia	256
35	Indiana	129		13	Vermont	256
29	Iowa	166		15	Virginia	251
9	Kansas	299		16	North Carolina	249
45	Kentucky	65		17	Pennsylvania	246
30	Louisiana	161		18	Ohio	241
28	Maine	171		19	Tennessee	230
26	Maryland	185		20	Michigan	225
7	Massachusetts	313		21	Hawaii	224
20	Michigan	225		22	Texas	215
23	Minnesota	209		23	Minnesota	209
42	Mississippi	87		24	Alabama	208
40	Missouri	109		25	Montana	203
25	Montana	203		26	Maryland	185
33	Nebraska	149		27	New Mexico	183
8	Nevada	306		28	Maine	171
NA	New Hampshire**	NA		29	Iowa	166
11	New Jersey	286		30	Louisiana	161
27	New Mexico	183		31	North Dakota	157
1	New York	509		32	Wisconsin	153
16	North Carolina	249		33	Nebraska	149
31	North Dakota	157		34	Arkansas	142
18	Ohio	241		35	Indiana	129
35	Oklahoma	129		35	Oklahoma	129
10	Oregon	291		37	Arizona	122
17	Pennsylvania	246		37	South Carolina	122
2	Rhode Island	430		39	Colorado	113
37	South Carolina	122		40	Missouri	109
43	South Dakota	77		41	West Virginia	99
19	Tennessee	230		42	Mississippi	87
22	Texas	215		43	South Dakota	77
44	Utah	72		44	Utah	72
13	Vermont	256		45	Kentucky	65
15	Virginia	251		46	Idaho	40
6	Washington	318		NA	Alaska**	NA
41	West Virginia	99		NA	California**	NA
32	Wisconsin	153		NA	New Hampshire**	NA
NA	Wyoming**	NA		NA	Wyoming**	NA

	District of Columbia	735

Source: U.S. Department of Health and Human Services, Centers for Disease Control and Prevention
"Abortion Surveillance-United States, 2002" (Morbidity and Mortality Weekly Report, Vol. 54, No. SS-7, 11/25/05)
*By state of occurrence. National figure is for reporting states only.
**Not reported.

Reported Legal Abortions per 1,000 Women Ages 15 to 44 in 2002

Reporting States' Rate = 16 Abortions per 1,000 Women Ages 15 to 44*

ALPHA ORDER

RANK	STATE	RATE
22	Alabama	13
NA	Alaska**	NA
31	Arizona	9
31	Arkansas	9
NA	California**	NA
37	Colorado	8
7	Connecticut	19
3	Delaware	26
2	Florida	27
9	Georgia	18
15	Hawaii	16
46	Idaho	3
13	Illinois	17
37	Indiana	8
29	Iowa	10
6	Kansas	21
45	Kentucky	4
27	Louisiana	11
31	Maine	9
27	Maryland	11
9	Massachusetts	18
19	Michigan	14
22	Minnesota	13
42	Mississippi	6
40	Missouri	7
26	Montana	12
29	Nebraska	10
5	Nevada	22
NA	New Hampshire**	NA
9	New Jersey	18
22	New Mexico	13
1	New York	31
15	North Carolina	16
31	North Dakota	9
18	Ohio	15
31	Oklahoma	9
9	Oregon	18
19	Pennsylvania	14
4	Rhode Island	24
37	South Carolina	8
44	South Dakota	5
19	Tennessee	14
13	Texas	17
40	Utah	7
22	Vermont	13
15	Virginia	16
7	Washington	19
42	West Virginia	6
31	Wisconsin	9
NA	Wyoming**	NA

RANK ORDER

RANK	STATE	RATE
1	New York	31
2	Florida	27
3	Delaware	26
4	Rhode Island	24
5	Nevada	22
6	Kansas	21
7	Connecticut	19
7	Washington	19
9	Georgia	18
9	Massachusetts	18
9	New Jersey	18
9	Oregon	18
13	Illinois	17
13	Texas	17
15	Hawaii	16
15	North Carolina	16
15	Virginia	16
18	Ohio	15
19	Michigan	14
19	Pennsylvania	14
19	Tennessee	14
22	Alabama	13
22	Minnesota	13
22	New Mexico	13
22	Vermont	13
26	Montana	12
27	Louisiana	11
27	Maryland	11
29	Iowa	10
29	Nebraska	10
31	Arizona	9
31	Arkansas	9
31	Maine	9
31	North Dakota	9
31	Oklahoma	9
31	Wisconsin	9
37	Colorado	8
37	Indiana	8
37	South Carolina	8
40	Missouri	7
40	Utah	7
42	Mississippi	6
42	West Virginia	6
44	South Dakota	5
45	Kentucky	4
46	Idaho	3
NA	Alaska**	NA
NA	California**	NA
NA	New Hampshire**	NA
NA	Wyoming**	NA
	District of Columbia	39

Source: U.S. Department of Health and Human Services, Centers for Disease Control and Prevention
    "Abortion Surveillance-United States, 2002" (Morbidity and Mortality Weekly Report, Vol. 54, No. SS-7, 11/25/05)
*By state of occurrence. National figure is for reporting states only.
**Not reported.

Percent of Legal Abortions Obtained by Out-Of-State Residents in 2002

Reporting States' Percent = 8.8% of Abortions*

RANK	STATE	PERCENT
6	Alabama	18.0
NA	Alaska**	NA
40	Arizona	2.6
9	Arkansas	15.1
NA	California**	NA
15	Colorado	11.5
32	Connecticut	4.2
3	Delaware	27.3
NA	Florida**	NA
16	Georgia	11.3
42	Hawaii	0.3
38	Idaho	3.5
21	Illinois	9.0
27	Indiana	4.9
NA	Iowa**	NA
1	Kansas	47.1
10	Kentucky	14.6
NA	Louisiana**	NA
37	Maine	3.6
11	Maryland	14.3
24	Massachusetts	6.6
39	Michigan	3.4
20	Minnesota	9.1
32	Mississippi	4.2
18	Missouri	9.5
19	Montana	9.4
8	Nebraska	15.8
23	Nevada	7.0
NA	New Hampshire**	NA
34	New Jersey	4.1
35	New Mexico	4.0
NA	New York**	NA
11	North Carolina	14.3
2	North Dakota	36.2
22	Ohio	8.8
30	Oklahoma	4.4
14	Oregon	12.4
28	Pennsylvania	4.7
4	Rhode Island	25.3
31	South Carolina	4.3
7	South Dakota	17.1
5	Tennessee	20.1
36	Texas	3.7
25	Utah	6.4
13	Vermont	13.7
26	Virginia	5.7
28	Washington	4.7
17	West Virginia	10.8
41	Wisconsin	1.8
43	Wyoming	0.0

RANK	STATE	PERCENT
1	Kansas	47.1
2	North Dakota	36.2
3	Delaware	27.3
4	Rhode Island	25.3
5	Tennessee	20.1
6	Alabama	18.0
7	South Dakota	17.1
8	Nebraska	15.8
9	Arkansas	15.1
10	Kentucky	14.6
11	Maryland	14.3
11	North Carolina	14.3
13	Vermont	13.7
14	Oregon	12.4
15	Colorado	11.5
16	Georgia	11.3
17	West Virginia	10.8
18	Missouri	9.5
19	Montana	9.4
20	Minnesota	9.1
21	Illinois	9.0
22	Ohio	8.8
23	Nevada	7.0
24	Massachusetts	6.6
25	Utah	6.4
26	Virginia	5.7
27	Indiana	4.9
28	Pennsylvania	4.7
28	Washington	4.7
30	Oklahoma	4.4
31	South Carolina	4.3
32	Connecticut	4.2
32	Mississippi	4.2
34	New Jersey	4.1
35	New Mexico	4.0
36	Texas	3.7
37	Maine	3.6
38	Idaho	3.5
39	Michigan	3.4
40	Arizona	2.6
41	Wisconsin	1.8
42	Hawaii	0.3
43	Wyoming	0.0
NA	Alaska**	NA
NA	California**	NA
NA	Florida**	NA
NA	Iowa**	NA
NA	Louisiana**	NA
NA	New Hampshire**	NA
NA	New York**	NA

	District of Columbia	56.1

Source: U.S. Department of Health and Human Services, Centers for Disease Control and Prevention
    "Abortion Surveillance-United States, 2002" (Morbidity and Mortality Weekly Report, Vol. 54, No. SS-7, 11/25/05)
By state of occurrence. National figure is for reporting states only.
**Not reported.*

Percent of Reported Legal Abortions that were First-Time Abortions: 2002

Reporting States' Percent = 54.4% of Abortions*

ALPHA ORDER

RANK	STATE	PERCENT
10	Alabama	64.5
NA	Alaska**	NA
NA	Arizona**	NA
15	Arkansas	61.4
NA	California**	NA
8	Colorado	65.0
NA	Connecticut**	NA
24	Delaware	56.8
NA	Florida**	NA
18	Georgia	60.4
25	Hawaii	56.0
2	Idaho	75.6
NA	Illinois**	NA
17	Indiana	60.5
12	Iowa	62.8
19	Kansas	59.7
29	Kentucky	54.7
NA	Louisiana**	NA
6	Maine	66.2
39	Maryland	28.5
36	Massachusetts	49.5
35	Michigan	50.8
21	Minnesota	59.3
7	Mississippi	65.5
23	Missouri	56.9
26	Montana	55.6
4	Nebraska	69.4
33	Nevada	52.0
NA	New Hampshire**	NA
5	New Jersey	67.0
14	New Mexico	61.7
37	New York	47.4
NA	North Carolina**	NA
3	North Dakota	71.9
38	Ohio	44.0
13	Oklahoma	61.9
27	Oregon	55.0
27	Pennsylvania	55.0
30	Rhode Island	54.1
16	South Carolina	61.2
1	South Dakota	90.7
34	Tennessee	51.7
22	Texas	58.5
9	Utah	64.7
19	Vermont	59.7
31	Virginia	53.9
32	Washington	52.9
11	West Virginia	64.1
NA	Wisconsin**	NA
NA	Wyoming**	NA

RANK ORDER

RANK	STATE	PERCENT
1	South Dakota	90.7
2	Idaho	75.6
3	North Dakota	71.9
4	Nebraska	69.4
5	New Jersey	67.0
6	Maine	66.2
7	Mississippi	65.5
8	Colorado	65.0
9	Utah	64.7
10	Alabama	64.5
11	West Virginia	64.1
12	Iowa	62.8
13	Oklahoma	61.9
14	New Mexico	61.7
15	Arkansas	61.4
16	South Carolina	61.2
17	Indiana	60.5
18	Georgia	60.4
19	Kansas	59.7
19	Vermont	59.7
21	Minnesota	59.3
22	Texas	58.5
23	Missouri	56.9
24	Delaware	56.8
25	Hawaii	56.0
26	Montana	55.6
27	Oregon	55.0
27	Pennsylvania	55.0
29	Kentucky	54.7
30	Rhode Island	54.1
31	Virginia	53.9
32	Washington	52.9
33	Nevada	52.0
34	Tennessee	51.7
35	Michigan	50.8
36	Massachusetts	49.5
37	New York	47.4
38	Ohio	44.0
39	Maryland	28.5
NA	Alaska**	NA
NA	Arizona**	NA
NA	California**	NA
NA	Connecticut**	NA
NA	Florida**	NA
NA	Illinois**	NA
NA	Louisiana**	NA
NA	New Hampshire**	NA
NA	North Carolina**	NA
NA	Wisconsin**	NA
NA	Wyoming**	NA
	District of Columbia**	NA

Source: U.S. Department of Health and Human Services, Centers for Disease Control and Prevention
"Abortion Surveillance-United States, 2002" (Morbidity and Mortality Weekly Report, Vol. 54, No. SS-7, 11/25/05)
*By state of occurrence. National figure is for reporting states only. Percent of abortions to women who had no previous abortions.
**Not reported.

Percent of Reported Legal Abortions Obtained by White Women in 2002

Reporting States' Percent = 54.0% of Abortions*

ALPHA ORDER

RANK	STATE	PERCENT
28	Alabama	45.4
NA	Alaska**	NA
NA	Arizona**	NA
19	Arkansas	58.7
NA	California**	NA
8	Colorado	80.5
NA	Connecticut**	NA
24	Delaware	54.7
NA	Florida**	NA
31	Georgia	40.5
36	Hawaii	24.7
2	Idaho	92.8
NA	Illinois**	NA
18	Indiana	63.7
7	Iowa	80.8
13	Kansas	70.8
14	Kentucky	70.5
32	Louisiana	39.8
4	Maine	85.6
34	Maryland	27.2
25	Massachusetts	52.9
NA	Michigan**	NA
17	Minnesota	65.0
35	Mississippi	26.9
21	Missouri	57.9
10	Montana	78.6
NA	Nebraska**	NA
NA	Nevada**	NA
NA	New Hampshire**	NA
33	New Jersey	31.0
9	New Mexico	79.9
30	New York**	42.4
29	North Carolina	44.2
6	North Dakota	83.1
20	Ohio	58.4
16	Oklahoma	67.6
5	Oregon	84.0
23	Pennsylvania	55.6
NA	Rhode Island**	NA
22	South Carolina	55.7
NA	South Dakota**	NA
26	Tennessee	52.6
12	Texas	71.8
11	Utah	74.6
1	Vermont	94.7
27	Virginia	47.7
NA	Washington**	NA
3	West Virginia	87.3
15	Wisconsin	68.4
NA	Wyoming**	NA

RANK ORDER

RANK	STATE	PERCENT
1	Vermont	94.7
2	Idaho	92.8
3	West Virginia	87.3
4	Maine	85.6
5	Oregon	84.0
6	North Dakota	83.1
7	Iowa	80.8
8	Colorado	80.5
9	New Mexico	79.9
10	Montana	78.6
11	Utah	74.6
12	Texas	71.8
13	Kansas	70.8
14	Kentucky	70.5
15	Wisconsin	68.4
16	Oklahoma	67.6
17	Minnesota	65.0
18	Indiana	63.7
19	Arkansas	58.7
20	Ohio	58.4
21	Missouri	57.9
22	South Carolina	55.7
23	Pennsylvania	55.6
24	Delaware	54.7
25	Massachusetts	52.9
26	Tennessee	52.6
27	Virginia	47.7
28	Alabama	45.4
29	North Carolina	44.2
30	New York**	42.4
31	Georgia	40.5
32	Louisiana	39.8
33	New Jersey	31.0
34	Maryland	27.2
35	Mississippi	26.9
36	Hawaii	24.7
NA	Alaska**	NA
NA	Arizona**	NA
NA	California**	NA
NA	Connecticut**	NA
NA	Florida**	NA
NA	Illinois**	NA
NA	Michigan**	NA
NA	Nebraska**	NA
NA	Nevada**	NA
NA	New Hampshire**	NA
NA	Rhode Island**	NA
NA	South Dakota**	NA
NA	Washington**	NA
NA	Wyoming**	NA

District of Columbia 11.5

Source: U.S. Department of Health and Human Services, Centers for Disease Control and Prevention
"Abortion Surveillance-United States, 2002" (Morbidity and Mortality Weekly Report, Vol. 54, No. SS-7, 11/25/05)
*By state of occurrence. Includes those of Hispanic ethnicity. National percent is for reporting states only.
**Not reported. New York's number is for New York City only.

Percent of Reported Legal Abortions Obtained by Black Women in 2002

Reporting States' Percent = 35.6% of Abortions*

ALPHA ORDER

RANK ORDER

RANK	STATE	PERCENT		RANK	STATE	PERCENT
4	Alabama	52.2		1	Mississippi	72.3
NA	Alaska**	NA		2	Georgia	55.3
NA	Arizona**	NA		3	Maryland	53.9
16	Arkansas	35.1		4	Alabama	52.2
NA	California**	NA		5	Louisiana	51.6
28	Colorado	4.9		6	New York**	48.8
NA	Connecticut**	NA		7	New Jersey	44.4
10	Delaware	41.4		8	Tennessee	44.3
NA	Florida**	NA		9	North Carolina	42.1
2	Georgia	55.3		10	Delaware	41.4
29	Hawaii	3.3		11	South Carolina	41.3
33	Idaho	1.8		12	Virginia	41.1
NA	Illinois**	NA		13	Pennsylvania	40.7
17	Indiana	27.0		14	Missouri	37.1
26	Iowa	7.4		15	Ohio	35.4
19	Kansas	23.6		16	Arkansas	35.1
23	Kentucky	20.1		17	Indiana	27.0
5	Louisiana	51.6		18	Wisconsin	24.5
31	Maine	2.3		19	Kansas	23.6
3	Maryland	53.9		20	Massachusetts	21.3
20	Massachusetts	21.3		21	Texas	21.1
NA	Michigan**	NA		22	Minnesota	20.5
22	Minnesota	20.5		23	Kentucky	20.1
1	Mississippi	72.3		24	Oklahoma	17.8
14	Missouri	37.1		25	West Virginia	10.4
36	Montana	0.8		26	Iowa	7.4
NA	Nebraska**	NA		27	Oregon	5.6
NA	Nevada**	NA		28	Colorado	4.9
NA	New Hampshire**	NA		29	Hawaii	3.3
7	New Jersey	44.4		29	New Mexico	3.3
29	New Mexico	3.3		31	Maine	2.3
6	New York**	48.8		32	North Dakota	2.1
9	North Carolina	42.1		33	Idaho	1.8
32	North Dakota	2.1		33	Utah	1.8
15	Ohio	35.4		33	Vermont	1.8
24	Oklahoma	17.8		36	Montana	0.8
27	Oregon	5.6		NA	Alaska**	NA
13	Pennsylvania	40.7		NA	Arizona**	NA
NA	Rhode Island**	NA		NA	California**	NA
11	South Carolina	41.3		NA	Connecticut**	NA
NA	South Dakota**	NA		NA	Florida**	NA
8	Tennessee	44.3		NA	Illinois**	NA
21	Texas	21.1		NA	Michigan**	NA
33	Utah	1.8		NA	Nebraska**	NA
33	Vermont	1.8		NA	Nevada**	NA
12	Virginia	41.1		NA	New Hampshire**	NA
NA	Washington**	NA		NA	Rhode Island**	NA
25	West Virginia	10.4		NA	South Dakota**	NA
18	Wisconsin	24.5		NA	Washington**	NA
NA	Wyoming**	NA		NA	Wyoming**	NA
					District of Columbia	72.1

Source: U.S. Department of Health and Human Services, Centers for Disease Control and Prevention
    "Abortion Surveillance-United States, 2002" (Morbidity and Mortality Weekly Report, Vol. 54, No. SS-7, 11/25/05)
*By state of occurrence. National percent is for reporting states only.
**Not reported. New York's number is for New York City only.

Percent of Reported Legal Abortions Obtained by Hispanic Women in 2002

Reporting States' Percent = 17.7%*

ALPHA ORDER				RANK ORDER		
RANK	STATE	PERCENT		RANK	STATE	PERCENT
21	Alabama	2.6		1	New Mexico	49.5
NA	Alaska**	NA		2	Texas	37.7
NA	Arizona**	NA		3	Wyoming	30.0
23	Arkansas	1.7		4	New York**	26.2
NA	California**	NA		5	New Jersey	24.3
6	Colorado	17.0		6	Colorado	17.0
NA	Connecticut**	NA		7	Utah	15.7
10	Delaware	8.0		8	Idaho	10.9
NA	Florida**	NA		9	Oregon	10.4
13	Georgia	6.2		10	Delaware	8.0
17	Hawaii	5.0		11	Wisconsin	7.2
8	Idaho	10.9		12	Kansas	6.9
NA	Illinois**	NA		13	Georgia	6.2
14	Indiana	6.0		14	Indiana	6.0
NA	Iowa**	NA		15	Minnesota	5.5
12	Kansas	6.9		16	Pennsylvania	5.2
26	Kentucky	0.6		17	Hawaii	5.0
NA	Louisiana**	NA		18	South Carolina	3.7
NA	Maine**	NA		19	Ohio	3.1
NA	Maryland**	NA		19	Tennessee	3.1
NA	Massachusetts**	NA		21	Alabama	2.6
NA	Michigan**	NA		22	Missouri	2.0
15	Minnesota	5.5		23	Arkansas	1.7
24	Mississippi	1.2		24	Mississippi	1.2
22	Missouri	2.0		24	Vermont	1.2
NA	Montana**	NA		26	Kentucky	0.6
NA	Nebraska**	NA		26	West Virginia	0.6
NA	Nevada**	NA		NA	Alaska**	NA
NA	New Hampshire**	NA		NA	Arizona**	NA
5	New Jersey	24.3		NA	California**	NA
1	New Mexico	49.5		NA	Connecticut**	NA
4	New York**	26.2		NA	Florida**	NA
NA	North Carolina**	NA		NA	Illinois**	NA
NA	North Dakota**	NA		NA	Iowa**	NA
19	Ohio	3.1		NA	Louisiana**	NA
NA	Oklahoma**	NA		NA	Maine**	NA
9	Oregon	10.4		NA	Maryland**	NA
16	Pennsylvania	5.2		NA	Massachusetts**	NA
NA	Rhode Island**	NA		NA	Michigan**	NA
18	South Carolina	3.7		NA	Montana**	NA
NA	South Dakota**	NA		NA	Nebraska**	NA
19	Tennessee	3.1		NA	Nevada**	NA
2	Texas	37.7		NA	New Hampshire**	NA
7	Utah	15.7		NA	North Carolina**	NA
24	Vermont	1.2		NA	North Dakota**	NA
NA	Virginia**	NA		NA	Oklahoma**	NA
NA	Washington**	NA		NA	Rhode Island**	NA
26	West Virginia	0.6		NA	South Dakota**	NA
11	Wisconsin	7.2		NA	Virginia**	NA
3	Wyoming	30.0		NA	Washington**	NA

District of Columbia   8.2

Source: U.S. Department of Health and Human Services, Centers for Disease Control and Prevention
"Abortion Surveillance-United States, 2002" (Morbidity and Mortality Weekly Report, Vol. 54, No. SS-7, 11/25/05)
*By state of occurrence. National percent is for reporting states only. Hispanic can be of any race.
**Not reported. New York's number is for New York City only.

Percent of Reported Legal Abortions Obtained by Married Women in 2002

Reporting States' Percent = 17.7% of Abortions*

ALPHA ORDER

RANK	STATE	PERCENT
36	Alabama	14.0
NA	Alaska**	NA
NA	Arizona**	NA
14	Arkansas	18.6
NA	California**	NA
11	Colorado	19.1
NA	Connecticut**	NA
33	Delaware	14.6
NA	Florida**	NA
17	Georgia	18.2
14	Hawaii	18.6
5	Idaho	21.5
29	Illinois	16.3
35	Indiana	14.1
7	Iowa	20.4
16	Kansas	18.3
20	Kentucky	17.7
NA	Louisiana**	NA
NA	Maine**	NA
NA	Maryland**	NA
13	Massachusetts	18.7
33	Michigan	14.6
9	Minnesota	19.4
37	Mississippi	12.6
8	Missouri	19.9
20	Montana	17.7
NA	Nebraska**	NA
1	Nevada	22.9
NA	New Hampshire**	NA
25	New Jersey	16.6
32	New Mexico	14.9
30	New York**	15.8
4	North Carolina	21.6
25	North Dakota	16.6
25	Ohio	16.6
10	Oklahoma	19.2
1	Oregon	22.9
30	Pennsylvania	15.8
NA	Rhode Island**	NA
24	South Carolina	17.1
18	South Dakota	18.0
19	Tennessee	17.8
6	Texas	20.6
1	Utah	22.9
25	Vermont	16.6
12	Virginia	18.9
NA	Washington**	NA
22	West Virginia	17.4
23	Wisconsin	17.2
38	Wyoming	10.0

RANK ORDER

RANK	STATE	PERCENT
1	Nevada	22.9
1	Oregon	22.9
1	Utah	22.9
4	North Carolina	21.6
5	Idaho	21.5
6	Texas	20.6
7	Iowa	20.4
8	Missouri	19.9
9	Minnesota	19.4
10	Oklahoma	19.2
11	Colorado	19.1
12	Virginia	18.9
13	Massachusetts	18.7
14	Arkansas	18.6
14	Hawaii	18.6
16	Kansas	18.3
17	Georgia	18.2
18	South Dakota	18.0
19	Tennessee	17.8
20	Kentucky	17.7
20	Montana	17.7
22	West Virginia	17.4
23	Wisconsin	17.2
24	South Carolina	17.1
25	New Jersey	16.6
25	North Dakota	16.6
25	Ohio	16.6
25	Vermont	16.6
29	Illinois	16.3
30	New York**	15.8
30	Pennsylvania	15.8
32	New Mexico	14.9
33	Delaware	14.6
33	Michigan	14.6
35	Indiana	14.1
36	Alabama	14.0
37	Mississippi	12.6
38	Wyoming	10.0
NA	Alaska**	NA
NA	Arizona**	NA
NA	California**	NA
NA	Connecticut**	NA
NA	Florida**	NA
NA	Louisiana**	NA
NA	Maine**	NA
NA	Maryland**	NA
NA	Nebraska**	NA
NA	New Hampshire**	NA
NA	Rhode Island**	NA
NA	Washington**	NA

	District of Columbia	13.1

Source: U.S. Department of Health and Human Services, Centers for Disease Control and Prevention
    "Abortion Surveillance-United States, 2002" (Morbidity and Mortality Weekly Report, Vol. 54, No. SS-7, 11/25/05)
By state of occurrence. National percent is for reporting states only.
**Not reported. New York's number is for New York City only.*

Percent of Reported Legal Abortions Obtained by Unmarried Women in 2002

Reporting States' Percent = 80.0% of Abortions*

ALPHA ORDER

RANK	STATE	PERCENT
6	Alabama	84.3
NA	Alaska**	NA
NA	Arizona**	NA
24	Arkansas	79.7
NA	California**	NA
22	Colorado	80.2
NA	Connecticut**	NA
3	Delaware	85.4
NA	Florida**	NA
21	Georgia	80.3
20	Hawaii	80.4
29	Idaho	78.4
16	Illinois	81.5
34	Indiana	73.7
25	Iowa	79.3
15	Kansas	81.6
12	Kentucky	82.3
NA	Louisiana**	NA
NA	Maine**	NA
NA	Maryland**	NA
27	Massachusetts	78.5
4	Michigan	84.6
26	Minnesota	79.1
2	Mississippi	86.9
27	Missouri	78.5
35	Montana	73.3
NA	Nebraska**	NA
36	Nevada	73.2
NA	New Hampshire**	NA
9	New Jersey	83.1
5	New Mexico	84.5
13	New York**	82.2
37	North Carolina	72.7
8	North Dakota	83.3
17	Ohio	81.3
18	Oklahoma	80.8
32	Oregon	75.8
7	Pennsylvania	84.2
NA	Rhode Island**	NA
10	South Carolina	82.9
14	South Dakota	82.0
19	Tennessee	80.6
30	Texas	77.4
38	Utah	68.5
31	Vermont	76.3
33	Virginia	73.8
NA	Washington**	NA
23	West Virginia	80.0
11	Wisconsin	82.4
1	Wyoming	90.0

RANK ORDER

RANK	STATE	PERCENT
1	Wyoming	90.0
2	Mississippi	86.9
3	Delaware	85.4
4	Michigan	84.6
5	New Mexico	84.5
6	Alabama	84.3
7	Pennsylvania	84.2
8	North Dakota	83.3
9	New Jersey	83.1
10	South Carolina	82.9
11	Wisconsin	82.4
12	Kentucky	82.3
13	New York**	82.2
14	South Dakota	82.0
15	Kansas	81.6
16	Illinois	81.5
17	Ohio	81.3
18	Oklahoma	80.8
19	Tennessee	80.6
20	Hawaii	80.4
21	Georgia	80.3
22	Colorado	80.2
23	West Virginia	80.0
24	Arkansas	79.7
25	Iowa	79.3
26	Minnesota	79.1
27	Massachusetts	78.5
27	Missouri	78.5
29	Idaho	78.4
30	Texas	77.4
31	Vermont	76.3
32	Oregon	75.8
33	Virginia	73.8
34	Indiana	73.7
35	Montana	73.3
36	Nevada	73.2
37	North Carolina	72.7
38	Utah	68.5
NA	Alaska**	NA
NA	Arizona**	NA
NA	California**	NA
NA	Connecticut**	NA
NA	Florida**	NA
NA	Louisiana**	NA
NA	Maine**	NA
NA	Maryland**	NA
NA	Nebraska**	NA
NA	New Hampshire**	NA
NA	Rhode Island**	NA
NA	Washington**	NA

	District of Columbia	77.3

Source: U.S. Department of Health and Human Services, Centers for Disease Control and Prevention
"Abortion Surveillance-United States, 2002" (Morbidity and Mortality Weekly Report, Vol. 54, No. SS-7, 11/25/05)

By state of occurrence. National percent is for reporting states only.
**Not reported. New York's number is for New York City only.*

Reported Legal Abortions Obtained by Teenagers in 2002

Reporting States' Total = 121,178 Abortions Obtained by Teenagers*

ALPHA ORDER

RANK	STATE	ABORTIONS	% of USA
17	Alabama	2,246	1.9%
NA	Alaska**	NA	NA
18	Arizona	2,032	1.7%
29	Arkansas	1,006	0.8%
NA	California**	NA	NA
23	Colorado	1,538	1.3%
13	Connecticut	2,751	2.3%
32	Delaware	711	0.6%
NA	Florida**	NA	NA
6	Georgia	5,312	4.4%
31	Hawaii	837	0.7%
41	Idaho	180	0.1%
NA	Illinois**	NA	NA
20	Indiana	1,895	1.6%
26	Iowa	1,212	1.0%
14	Kansas	2,324	1.9%
43	Kentucky	18	0.0%
21	Louisiana	1,862	1.5%
37	Maine	490	0.4%
NA	Maryland**	NA	NA
11	Massachusetts	3,840	3.2%
7	Michigan	5,073	4.2%
16	Minnesota	2,254	1.9%
34	Mississippi	680	0.6%
24	Missouri	1,421	1.2%
36	Montana	510	0.4%
32	Nebraska	711	0.6%
22	Nevada	1,609	1.3%
NA	New Hampshire**	NA	NA
5	New Jersey	5,875	4.8%
28	New Mexico	1,098	0.9%
1	New York	22,852	18.9%
9	North Carolina	4,785	3.9%
40	North Dakota	266	0.2%
3	Ohio	6,375	5.3%
27	Oklahoma	1,190	1.0%
15	Oregon	2,288	1.9%
4	Pennsylvania	6,188	5.1%
30	Rhode Island	975	0.8%
25	South Carolina	1,277	1.1%
42	South Dakota	171	0.1%
12	Tennessee	2,966	2.4%
2	Texas	11,247	9.3%
35	Utah	564	0.5%
39	Vermont	347	0.3%
10	Virginia	3,889	3.2%
8	Washington	4,936	4.1%
38	West Virginia	368	0.3%
19	Wisconsin	1,910	1.6%
44	Wyoming	3	0.0%

RANK ORDER

RANK	STATE	ABORTIONS	% of USA
1	New York	22,852	18.9%
2	Texas	11,247	9.3%
3	Ohio	6,375	5.3%
4	Pennsylvania	6,188	5.1%
5	New Jersey	5,875	4.8%
6	Georgia	5,312	4.4%
7	Michigan	5,073	4.2%
8	Washington	4,936	4.1%
9	North Carolina	4,785	3.9%
10	Virginia	3,889	3.2%
11	Massachusetts	3,840	3.2%
12	Tennessee	2,966	2.4%
13	Connecticut	2,751	2.3%
14	Kansas	2,324	1.9%
15	Oregon	2,288	1.9%
16	Minnesota	2,254	1.9%
17	Alabama	2,246	1.9%
18	Arizona	2,032	1.7%
19	Wisconsin	1,910	1.6%
20	Indiana	1,895	1.6%
21	Louisiana	1,862	1.5%
22	Nevada	1,609	1.3%
23	Colorado	1,538	1.3%
24	Missouri	1,421	1.2%
25	South Carolina	1,277	1.1%
26	Iowa	1,212	1.0%
27	Oklahoma	1,190	1.0%
28	New Mexico	1,098	0.9%
29	Arkansas	1,006	0.8%
30	Rhode Island	975	0.8%
31	Hawaii	837	0.7%
32	Delaware	711	0.6%
32	Nebraska	711	0.6%
34	Mississippi	680	0.6%
35	Utah	564	0.5%
36	Montana	510	0.4%
37	Maine	490	0.4%
38	West Virginia	368	0.3%
39	Vermont	347	0.3%
40	North Dakota	266	0.2%
41	Idaho	180	0.1%
42	South Dakota	171	0.1%
43	Kentucky	18	0.0%
44	Wyoming	3	0.0%
NA	Alaska**	NA	NA
NA	California**	NA	NA
NA	Florida**	NA	NA
NA	Illinois**	NA	NA
NA	Maryland**	NA	NA
NA	New Hampshire**	NA	NA
	District of Columbia	1,096	0.9%

Source: U.S. Department of Health and Human Services, Centers for Disease Control and Prevention
    "Abortion Surveillance-United States, 2002" (Morbidity and Mortality Weekly Report, Vol. 54, No. SS-7, 11/25/05)
*Nineteen years old and younger by state of occurrence. National total is for reporting states only.
**Not reported.

Percent of Reported Legal Abortions Obtained by Teenagers in 2002

Reporting States' Percent = 17.4% of Abortions*

ALPHA ORDER

RANK	STATE	PERCENT
23	Alabama	18.3
NA	Alaska**	NA
17	Arizona	19.0
18	Arkansas	18.9
NA	California**	NA
12	Colorado	19.8
11	Connecticut	20.4
3	Delaware	21.8
NA	Florida**	NA
42	Georgia	15.6
7	Hawaii	21.3
5	Idaho	21.7
21	Illinois	18.6
32	Indiana	17.3
15	Iowa	19.5
13	Kansas	19.7
42	Kentucky	15.6
28	Louisiana	17.8
8	Maine	21.2
37	Maryland	16.6
45	Massachusetts	15.2
32	Michigan	17.3
41	Minnesota	15.9
18	Mississippi	18.9
32	Missouri	17.3
2	Montana	22.7
20	Nebraska	18.8
39	Nevada	16.2
NA	New Hampshire**	NA
25	New Jersey	17.9
6	New Mexico	21.6
25	New York	17.9
38	North Carolina	16.4
3	North Dakota	21.8
28	Ohio	17.8
23	Oklahoma	18.3
32	Oregon	17.3
30	Pennsylvania	17.6
31	Rhode Island	17.5
16	South Carolina	19.2
10	South Dakota	20.7
36	Tennessee	16.7
46	Texas	14.1
40	Utah	16.0
8	Vermont	21.2
44	Virginia	15.5
14	Washington	19.6
25	West Virginia	17.9
21	Wisconsin	18.6
1	Wyoming	30.0

RANK ORDER

RANK	STATE	PERCENT
1	Wyoming	30.0
2	Montana	22.7
3	Delaware	21.8
3	North Dakota	21.8
5	Idaho	21.7
6	New Mexico	21.6
7	Hawaii	21.3
8	Maine	21.2
8	Vermont	21.2
10	South Dakota	20.7
11	Connecticut	20.4
12	Colorado	19.8
13	Kansas	19.7
14	Washington	19.6
15	Iowa	19.5
16	South Carolina	19.2
17	Arizona	19.0
18	Arkansas	18.9
18	Mississippi	18.9
20	Nebraska	18.8
21	Illinois	18.6
21	Wisconsin	18.6
23	Alabama	18.3
23	Oklahoma	18.3
25	New Jersey	17.9
25	New York	17.9
25	West Virginia	17.9
28	Louisiana	17.8
28	Ohio	17.8
30	Pennsylvania	17.6
31	Rhode Island	17.5
32	Indiana	17.3
32	Michigan	17.3
32	Missouri	17.3
32	Oregon	17.3
36	Tennessee	16.7
37	Maryland	16.6
38	North Carolina	16.4
39	Nevada	16.2
40	Utah	16.0
41	Minnesota	15.9
42	Georgia	15.6
42	Kentucky	15.6
44	Virginia	15.5
45	Massachusetts	15.2
46	Texas	14.1
NA	Alaska**	NA
NA	California**	NA
NA	Florida**	NA
NA	New Hampshire**	NA

District of Columbia   20.2

Source: U.S. Department of Health and Human Services, Centers for Disease Control and Prevention
   "Abortion Surveillance-United States, 2002" (Morbidity and Mortality Weekly Report, Vol. 54, No. SS-7, 11/25/05)
*Nineteen years old and younger by state of occurrence. National total is for reporting states only.
**Not reported.

Reported Legal Abortions Obtained by Teenagers 17 Years and Younger in 2002

Reporting States' Total = 46,631 Abortions*

ALPHA ORDER					RANK ORDER			
RANK	STATE	ABORTIONS	% of USA		RANK	STATE	ABORTIONS	% of USA
15	Alabama	876	1.9%		1	New York	9,716	20.8%
NA	Alaska**	NA	NA		2	Texas	3,654	7.8%
17	Arizona	766	1.6%		3	Ohio	2,511	5.4%
29	Arkansas	405	0.9%		4	New Jersey	2,447	5.2%
NA	California**	NA	NA		5	Pennsylvania	2,206	4.7%
23	Colorado	610	1.3%		6	Georgia	2,087	4.5%
12	Connecticut	1,205	2.6%		7	Michigan	1,937	4.2%
31	Delaware	302	0.6%		8	Washington	1,935	4.1%
NA	Florida**	NA	NA		9	North Carolina	1,836	3.9%
6	Georgia	2,087	4.5%		10	Virginia	1,346	2.9%
30	Hawaii	357	0.8%		11	Massachusetts	1,245	2.7%
42	Idaho	70	0.2%		12	Connecticut	1,205	2.6%
NA	Illinois**	NA	NA		13	Tennessee	1,114	2.4%
21	Indiana	706	1.5%		14	Kansas	885	1.9%
27	Iowa	448	1.0%		15	Alabama	876	1.9%
14	Kansas	885	1.9%		16	Oregon	847	1.8%
43	Kentucky	18	0.0%		17	Arizona	766	1.6%
19	Louisiana	742	1.6%		17	Minnesota	766	1.6%
36	Maine	198	0.4%		19	Louisiana	742	1.6%
NA	Maryland**	NA	NA		20	Wisconsin	710	1.5%
11	Massachusetts	1,245	2.7%		21	Indiana	706	1.5%
7	Michigan	1,937	4.2%		22	Nevada	660	1.4%
17	Minnesota	766	1.6%		23	Colorado	610	1.3%
34	Mississippi	253	0.5%		24	South Carolina	576	1.2%
25	Missouri	467	1.0%		25	Missouri	467	1.0%
35	Montana	216	0.5%		26	New Mexico	463	1.0%
33	Nebraska	275	0.6%		27	Iowa	448	1.0%
22	Nevada	660	1.4%		28	Oklahoma	415	0.9%
NA	New Hampshire**	NA	NA		29	Arkansas	405	0.9%
4	New Jersey	2,447	5.2%		30	Hawaii	357	0.8%
26	New Mexico	463	1.0%		31	Delaware	302	0.6%
1	New York	9,716	20.8%		32	Rhode Island	291	0.6%
9	North Carolina	1,836	3.9%		33	Nebraska	275	0.6%
40	North Dakota	79	0.2%		34	Mississippi	253	0.5%
3	Ohio	2,511	5.4%		35	Montana	216	0.5%
28	Oklahoma	415	0.9%		36	Maine	198	0.4%
16	Oregon	847	1.8%		37	Utah	183	0.4%
5	Pennsylvania	2,206	4.7%		38	Vermont	141	0.3%
32	Rhode Island	291	0.6%		39	West Virginia	122	0.3%
24	South Carolina	576	1.2%		40	North Dakota	79	0.2%
41	South Dakota	76	0.2%		41	South Dakota	76	0.2%
13	Tennessee	1,114	2.4%		42	Idaho	70	0.2%
2	Texas	3,654	7.8%		43	Kentucky	18	0.0%
37	Utah	183	0.4%		44	Wyoming	1	0.0%
38	Vermont	141	0.3%		NA	Alaska**	NA	NA
10	Virginia	1,346	2.9%		NA	California**	NA	NA
8	Washington	1,935	4.1%		NA	Florida**	NA	NA
39	West Virginia	122	0.3%		NA	Illinois**	NA	NA
20	Wisconsin	710	1.5%		NA	Maryland**	NA	NA
44	Wyoming	1	0.0%		NA	New Hampshire**	NA	NA
						District of Columbia	468	1.0%

Source: U.S. Department of Health and Human Services, Centers for Disease Control and Prevention
    "Abortion Surveillance-United States, 2002" (Morbidity and Mortality Weekly Report, Vol. 54, No. SS-7, 11/25/05)
*By state of occurrence. National total is for reporting states only.
**Not reported.

Percent of Reported Legal Abortions Obtained
By Teenagers 17 Years and Younger in 2002
Reporting States' Percent = 6.6% of Abortions*

ALPHA ORDER

RANK	STATE	PERCENT
18	Alabama	7.2
NA	Alaska**	NA
18	Arizona	7.2
13	Arkansas	7.6
NA	California**	NA
11	Colorado	7.9
6	Connecticut	8.9
25	Delaware	6.7
NA	Florida**	NA
35	Georgia	6.1
4	Hawaii	9.1
10	Idaho	8.4
NA	Illinois**	NA
28	Indiana	6.5
18	Iowa	7.2
15	Kansas	7.5
44	Kentucky	0.5
21	Louisiana	7.1
8	Maine	8.6
NA	Maryland**	NA
42	Massachusetts	4.9
26	Michigan	6.6
38	Minnesota	5.4
22	Mississippi	7.0
37	Missouri	5.7
2	Montana	9.6
17	Nebraska	7.3
26	Nevada	6.6
NA	New Hampshire**	NA
16	New Jersey	7.4
4	New Mexico	9.1
13	New York	7.6
32	North Carolina	6.3
28	North Dakota	6.5
22	Ohio	7.0
30	Oklahoma	6.4
30	Oregon	6.4
32	Pennsylvania	6.3
40	Rhode Island	5.2
7	South Carolina	8.7
3	South Dakota	9.2
32	Tennessee	6.3
43	Texas	4.6
40	Utah	5.2
8	Vermont	8.6
38	Virginia	5.4
12	Washington	7.7
36	West Virginia	6.0
24	Wisconsin	6.8
1	Wyoming	10.0

RANK ORDER

RANK	STATE	PERCENT
1	Wyoming	10.0
2	Montana	9.6
3	South Dakota	9.2
4	Hawaii	9.1
4	New Mexico	9.1
6	Connecticut	8.9
7	South Carolina	8.7
8	Maine	8.6
8	Vermont	8.6
10	Idaho	8.4
11	Colorado	7.9
12	Washington	7.7
13	Arkansas	7.6
13	New York	7.6
15	Kansas	7.5
16	New Jersey	7.4
17	Nebraska	7.3
18	Alabama	7.2
18	Arizona	7.2
18	Iowa	7.2
21	Louisiana	7.1
22	Mississippi	7.0
22	Ohio	7.0
24	Wisconsin	6.8
25	Delaware	6.7
26	Michigan	6.6
26	Nevada	6.6
28	Indiana	6.5
28	North Dakota	6.5
30	Oklahoma	6.4
30	Oregon	6.4
32	North Carolina	6.3
32	Pennsylvania	6.3
32	Tennessee	6.3
35	Georgia	6.1
36	West Virginia	6.0
37	Missouri	5.7
38	Minnesota	5.4
38	Virginia	5.4
40	Rhode Island	5.2
40	Utah	5.2
42	Massachusetts	4.9
43	Texas	4.6
44	Kentucky	0.5
NA	Alaska**	NA
NA	California**	NA
NA	Florida**	NA
NA	Illinois**	NA
NA	Maryland**	NA
NA	New Hampshire**	NA

District of Columbia   8.5

Source: Morgan Quitno Press using data from US Dept of Health & Human Serv's, Centers for Disease Control-Prevention
"Abortion Surveillance-United States, 2002" (Morbidity and Mortality Weekly Report, Vol. 54, No. SS-7, 11/25/05)
*By state of occurrence. National percent is for reporting states only.
**Not reported.

Percent of Teenage Abortions Obtained
By Teenagers 17 Years and Younger in 2002
Reporting States' Percent = 38.4% of Teenage Abortions*

ALPHA ORDER

RANK	STATE	PERCENT
20	Alabama	39.0
NA	Alaska**	NA
26	Arizona	37.7
14	Arkansas	40.3
NA	California**	NA
16	Colorado	39.7
4	Connecticut	43.9
7	Delaware	42.5
NA	Florida**	NA
17	Georgia	39.4
5	Hawaii	42.6
21	Idaho	38.9
NA	Illinois**	NA
28	Indiana	37.2
31	Iowa	37.0
25	Kansas	38.1
1	Kentucky	100.0
15	Louisiana	39.9
13	Maine	40.4
NA	Maryland**	NA
41	Massachusetts	32.4
24	Michigan	38.2
36	Minnesota	34.0
28	Mississippi	37.2
39	Missouri	32.8
8	Montana	42.4
22	Nebraska	38.7
11	Nevada	41.0
NA	New Hampshire**	NA
10	New Jersey	41.7
9	New Mexico	42.2
5	New York	42.6
23	North Carolina	38.5
44	North Dakota	29.7
17	Ohio	39.4
34	Oklahoma	34.9
31	Oregon	37.0
33	Pennsylvania	35.6
43	Rhode Island	29.8
2	South Carolina	45.1
3	South Dakota	44.4
27	Tennessee	37.6
40	Texas	32.5
41	Utah	32.4
12	Vermont	40.7
35	Virginia	34.6
19	Washington	39.2
38	West Virginia	33.1
30	Wisconsin	37.1
37	Wyoming	33.3

RANK ORDER

RANK	STATE	PERCENT
1	Kentucky	100.0
2	South Carolina	45.1
3	South Dakota	44.4
4	Connecticut	43.9
5	Hawaii	42.6
5	New York	42.6
7	Delaware	42.5
8	Montana	42.4
9	New Mexico	42.2
10	New Jersey	41.7
11	Nevada	41.0
12	Vermont	40.7
13	Maine	40.4
14	Arkansas	40.3
15	Louisiana	39.9
16	Colorado	39.7
17	Georgia	39.4
17	Ohio	39.4
19	Washington	39.2
20	Alabama	39.0
21	Idaho	38.9
22	Nebraska	38.7
23	North Carolina	38.5
24	Michigan	38.2
25	Kansas	38.1
26	Arizona	37.7
27	Tennessee	37.6
28	Indiana	37.2
28	Mississippi	37.2
30	Wisconsin	37.1
31	Iowa	37.0
31	Oregon	37.0
33	Pennsylvania	35.6
34	Oklahoma	34.9
35	Virginia	34.6
36	Minnesota	34.0
37	Wyoming	33.3
38	West Virginia	33.1
39	Missouri	32.8
40	Texas	32.5
41	Massachusetts	32.4
41	Utah	32.4
43	Rhode Island	29.8
44	North Dakota	29.7
NA	Alaska**	NA
NA	California**	NA
NA	Florida**	NA
NA	Illinois**	NA
NA	Maryland**	NA
NA	New Hampshire**	NA

District of Columbia   42.6

Source: U.S. Department of Health and Human Services, Centers for Disease Control and Prevention
"Abortion Surveillance-United States, 2002" (Morbidity and Mortality Weekly Report, Vol. 54, No. SS-7, 11/25/05)
*By state of occurrence. National percent is for reporting states only.
**Not reported.

Reported Legal Abortions Performed at 12 Weeks or Less of Gestation in 2002

Reporting States' Total = 585,810 Abortions*

ALPHA ORDER					RANK ORDER			
RANK	STATE	ABORTIONS	% of USA		RANK	STATE	ABORTIONS	% of USA
15	Alabama	10,796	1.8%		1	New York	106,687	18.2%
NA	Alaska**	NA	NA		2	Texas	70,053	12.0%
18	Arizona	9,439	1.6%		3	Pennsylvania	30,939	5.3%
28	Arkansas	4,418	0.8%		4	Ohio	30,575	5.2%
NA	California**	NA	NA		5	Georgia	29,332	5.0%
23	Colorado	6,832	1.2%		6	New Jersey	26,151	4.5%
13	Connecticut	11,760	2.0%		7	Michigan	25,795	4.4%
34	Delaware	2,856	0.5%		8	North Carolina	24,505	4.2%
NA	Florida**	NA	NA		9	Virginia	24,002	4.1%
5	Georgia	29,332	5.0%		10	Washington	22,113	3.8%
30	Hawaii	3,258	0.6%		11	Tennessee	16,961	2.9%
40	Idaho	799	0.1%		12	Minnesota	12,769	2.2%
NA	Illinois**	NA	NA		13	Connecticut	11,760	2.0%
16	Indiana	10,499	1.8%		14	Oregon	11,391	1.9%
26	Iowa	5,838	1.0%		15	Alabama	10,796	1.8%
17	Kansas	9,896	1.7%		16	Indiana	10,499	1.8%
33	Kentucky	2,923	0.5%		17	Kansas	9,896	1.7%
21	Louisiana	8,288	1.4%		18	Arizona	9,439	1.6%
35	Maine	2,250	0.4%		19	Wisconsin	8,957	1.5%
NA	Maryland**	NA	NA		20	Nevada	8,848	1.5%
NA	Massachusetts**	NA	NA		21	Louisiana	8,288	1.4%
7	Michigan	25,795	4.4%		22	Missouri	7,512	1.3%
12	Minnesota	12,769	2.2%		23	Colorado	6,832	1.2%
31	Mississippi	3,105	0.5%		24	South Carolina	6,423	1.1%
22	Missouri	7,512	1.3%		25	Oklahoma	5,943	1.0%
36	Montana	1,915	0.3%		26	Iowa	5,838	1.0%
NA	Nebraska**	NA	NA		27	Rhode Island	4,953	0.8%
20	Nevada	8,848	1.5%		28	Arkansas	4,418	0.8%
NA	New Hampshire**	NA	NA		29	New Mexico	4,363	0.7%
6	New Jersey	26,151	4.5%		30	Hawaii	3,258	0.6%
29	New Mexico	4,363	0.7%		31	Mississippi	3,105	0.5%
1	New York	106,687	18.2%		32	Utah	2,926	0.5%
8	North Carolina	24,505	4.2%		33	Kentucky	2,923	0.5%
39	North Dakota	1,089	0.2%		34	Delaware	2,856	0.5%
4	Ohio	30,575	5.2%		35	Maine	2,250	0.4%
25	Oklahoma	5,943	1.0%		36	Montana	1,915	0.3%
14	Oregon	11,391	1.9%		37	West Virginia	1,698	0.3%
3	Pennsylvania	30,939	5.3%		38	Vermont	1,539	0.3%
27	Rhode Island	4,953	0.8%		39	North Dakota	1,089	0.2%
24	South Carolina	6,423	1.1%		40	Idaho	799	0.1%
41	South Dakota	788	0.1%		41	South Dakota	788	0.1%
11	Tennessee	16,961	2.9%		42	Wyoming	10	0.0%
2	Texas	70,053	12.0%		NA	Alaska**	NA	NA
32	Utah	2,926	0.5%		NA	California**	NA	NA
38	Vermont	1,539	0.3%		NA	Florida**	NA	NA
9	Virginia	24,002	4.1%		NA	Illinois**	NA	NA
10	Washington	22,113	3.8%		NA	Maryland**	NA	NA
37	West Virginia	1,698	0.3%		NA	Massachusetts**	NA	NA
19	Wisconsin	8,957	1.5%		NA	Nebraska**	NA	NA
42	Wyoming	10	0.0%		NA	New Hampshire**	NA	NA
					District of Columbia		4,616	0.8%

Source: Morgan Quitno Press using data from US Dept of Health & Human Serv's, Centers for Disease Control-Prevention "Abortion Surveillance-United States, 2002" (Morbidity and Mortality Weekly Report, Vol. 54, No. SS-7, 11/25/05)
*By state of occurrence. National total is for reporting states only.
**Not reported.

Percent of Reported Legal Abortions Performed
At 12 Weeks or Less of Gestation in 2002
Reporting States' Percent = 86.7% of Abortions*

ALPHA ORDER

RANK	STATE	PERCENT
18	Alabama	88.2
NA	Alaska**	NA
17	Arizona	88.3
36	Arkansas	83.1
NA	California**	NA
42	Colorado	79.1
24	Connecticut	87.3
23	Delaware	87.4
NA	Florida**	NA
28	Georgia	86.1
36	Hawaii	83.1
4	Idaho	96.4
NA	Illinois**	NA
6	Indiana	96.0
10	Iowa	93.6
32	Kansas	84.1
34	Kentucky	83.5
41	Louisiana	79.3
2	Maine	97.2
NA	Maryland**	NA
NA	Massachusetts**	NA
18	Michigan	88.2
13	Minnesota	90.0
27	Mississippi	86.2
11	Missouri	91.7
31	Montana	85.2
NA	Nebraska**	NA
16	Nevada	88.9
NA	New Hampshire**	NA
40	New Jersey	79.5
28	New Mexico	86.1
35	New York	83.4
33	North Carolina	83.9
14	North Dakota	89.3
30	Ohio	85.3
12	Oklahoma	91.5
26	Oregon	86.4
20	Pennsylvania	88.0
14	Rhode Island	89.3
3	South Carolina	96.6
7	South Dakota	95.4
8	Tennessee	95.3
22	Texas	87.7
38	Utah	83.0
9	Vermont	94.2
5	Virginia	96.1
20	Washington	88.0
39	West Virginia	82.9
25	Wisconsin	87.0
1	Wyoming	100.0

RANK ORDER

RANK	STATE	PERCENT
1	Wyoming	100.0
2	Maine	97.2
3	South Carolina	96.6
4	Idaho	96.4
5	Virginia	96.1
6	Indiana	96.0
7	South Dakota	95.4
8	Tennessee	95.3
9	Vermont	94.2
10	Iowa	93.6
11	Missouri	91.7
12	Oklahoma	91.5
13	Minnesota	90.0
14	North Dakota	89.3
14	Rhode Island	89.3
16	Nevada	88.9
17	Arizona	88.3
18	Alabama	88.2
18	Michigan	88.2
20	Pennsylvania	88.0
20	Washington	88.0
22	Texas	87.7
23	Delaware	87.4
24	Connecticut	87.3
25	Wisconsin	87.0
26	Oregon	86.4
27	Mississippi	86.2
28	Georgia	86.1
28	New Mexico	86.1
30	Ohio	85.3
31	Montana	85.2
32	Kansas	84.1
33	North Carolina	83.9
34	Kentucky	83.5
35	New York	83.4
36	Arkansas	83.1
36	Hawaii	83.1
38	Utah	83.0
39	West Virginia	82.9
40	New Jersey	79.5
41	Louisiana	79.3
42	Colorado	79.1
NA	Alaska**	NA
NA	California**	NA
NA	Florida**	NA
NA	Illinois**	NA
NA	Maryland**	NA
NA	Massachusetts**	NA
NA	Nebraska**	NA
NA	New Hampshire**	NA

	District of Columbia	83.7

Source: Morgan Quitno Press using data from US Dept of Health & Human Serv's, Centers for Disease Control-Prevention "Abortion Surveillance-United States, 2002" (Morbidity and Mortality Weekly Report, Vol. 54, No. SS-7, 11/25/05)
By state of occurrence. National percent is for reporting states only.
**Not reported.

Reported Legal Abortions Performed At or After 21 Weeks of Gestation in 2002

Reporting States' Total = 9,312 Abortions*

RANK	STATE	ABORTIONS	% of USA
15	Alabama	80	0.9%
NA	Alaska**	NA	NA
26	Arizona	21	0.2%
22	Arkansas	37	0.4%
NA	California**	NA	NA
13	Colorado	184	2.0%
21	Connecticut	40	0.4%
27	Delaware	14	0.2%
NA	Florida**	NA	NA
3	Georgia	875	9.4%
22	Hawaii	37	0.4%
34	Idaho	3	0.0%
NA	Illinois**	NA	NA
39	Indiana	0	0.0%
36	Iowa	2	0.0%
6	Kansas	625	6.7%
16	Kentucky	64	0.7%
9	Louisiana	292	3.1%
34	Maine	3	0.0%
NA	Maryland**	NA	NA
NA	Massachusetts**	NA	NA
11	Michigan	199	2.1%
14	Minnesota	114	1.2%
36	Mississippi	2	0.0%
24	Missouri	29	0.3%
31	Montana	8	0.1%
NA	Nebraska**	NA	NA
19	Nevada	53	0.6%
NA	New Hampshire**	NA	NA
4	New Jersey	793	8.5%
17	New Mexico	59	0.6%
1	New York	2,669	28.7%
20	North Carolina	52	0.6%
39	North Dakota	0	0.0%
5	Ohio	706	7.6%
28	Oklahoma	12	0.1%
10	Oregon	282	3.0%
8	Pennsylvania	353	3.8%
31	Rhode Island	8	0.1%
25	South Carolina	28	0.3%
33	South Dakota	4	0.0%
29	Tennessee	10	0.1%
2	Texas	921	9.9%
39	Utah	0	0.0%
38	Vermont	1	0.0%
18	Virginia	57	0.6%
7	Washington	473	5.1%
29	West Virginia	10	0.1%
12	Wisconsin	192	2.1%
39	Wyoming	0	0.0%

RANK	STATE	ABORTIONS	% of USA
1	New York	2,669	28.7%
2	Texas	921	9.9%
3	Georgia	875	9.4%
4	New Jersey	793	8.5%
5	Ohio	706	7.6%
6	Kansas	625	6.7%
7	Washington	473	5.1%
8	Pennsylvania	353	3.8%
9	Louisiana	292	3.1%
10	Oregon	282	3.0%
11	Michigan	199	2.1%
12	Wisconsin	192	2.1%
13	Colorado	184	2.0%
14	Minnesota	114	1.2%
15	Alabama	80	0.9%
16	Kentucky	64	0.7%
17	New Mexico	59	0.6%
18	Virginia	57	0.6%
19	Nevada	53	0.6%
20	North Carolina	52	0.6%
21	Connecticut	40	0.4%
22	Arkansas	37	0.4%
22	Hawaii	37	0.4%
24	Missouri	29	0.3%
25	South Carolina	28	0.3%
26	Arizona	21	0.2%
27	Delaware	14	0.2%
28	Oklahoma	12	0.1%
29	Tennessee	10	0.1%
29	West Virginia	10	0.1%
31	Montana	8	0.1%
31	Rhode Island	8	0.1%
33	South Dakota	4	0.0%
34	Idaho	3	0.0%
34	Maine	3	0.0%
36	Iowa	2	0.0%
36	Mississippi	2	0.0%
38	Vermont	1	0.0%
39	Indiana	0	0.0%
39	North Dakota	0	0.0%
39	Utah	0	0.0%
39	Wyoming	0	0.0%
NA	Alaska**	NA	NA
NA	California**	NA	NA
NA	Florida**	NA	NA
NA	Illinois**	NA	NA
NA	Maryland**	NA	NA
NA	Massachusetts**	NA	NA
NA	Nebraska**	NA	NA
NA	New Hampshire**	NA	NA
	District of Columbia	0	0.0%

Source: U.S. Department of Health and Human Services, Centers for Disease Control and Prevention
"Abortion Surveillance-United States, 2002" (Morbidity and Mortality Weekly Report, Vol. 54, No. SS-7, 11/25/05)
*By state of occurrence. National total is for reporting states only.
**Not reported.

Percent of Reported Legal Abortions Performed At or After
21 Weeks of Gestation in 2002
Reporting States' Percent = 1.4% of Abortions*

ALPHA ORDER

RANK	STATE	PERCENT
17	Alabama	0.7
NA	Alaska**	NA
29	Arizona	0.2
17	Arkansas	0.7
NA	California**	NA
4	Colorado	2.4
28	Connecticut	0.3
23	Delaware	0.4
NA	Florida**	NA
3	Georgia	2.6
15	Hawaii	0.9
23	Idaho	0.4
NA	Illinois**	NA
38	Indiana	0.0
38	Iowa	0.0
1	Kansas	5.3
11	Kentucky	1.8
2	Louisiana	2.8
33	Maine	0.1
NA	Maryland**	NA
NA	Massachusetts**	NA
17	Michigan	0.7
16	Minnesota	0.8
33	Mississippi	0.1
23	Missouri	0.4
23	Montana	0.4
NA	Nebraska**	NA
20	Nevada	0.5
NA	New Hampshire**	NA
4	New Jersey	2.4
12	New Mexico	1.2
6	New York	2.1
29	North Carolina	0.2
38	North Dakota	0.0
8	Ohio	2.0
29	Oklahoma	0.2
6	Oregon	2.1
14	Pennsylvania	1.0
33	Rhode Island	0.1
23	South Carolina	0.4
20	South Dakota	0.5
33	Tennessee	0.1
12	Texas	1.2
38	Utah	0.0
33	Vermont	0.1
29	Virginia	0.2
9	Washington	1.9
20	West Virginia	0.5
9	Wisconsin	1.9
38	Wyoming	0.0

RANK ORDER

RANK	STATE	PERCENT
1	Kansas	5.3
2	Louisiana	2.8
3	Georgia	2.6
4	Colorado	2.4
4	New Jersey	2.4
6	New York	2.1
6	Oregon	2.1
8	Ohio	2.0
9	Washington	1.9
9	Wisconsin	1.9
11	Kentucky	1.8
12	New Mexico	1.2
12	Texas	1.2
14	Pennsylvania	1.0
15	Hawaii	0.9
16	Minnesota	0.8
17	Alabama	0.7
17	Arkansas	0.7
17	Michigan	0.7
20	Nevada	0.5
20	South Dakota	0.5
20	West Virginia	0.5
23	Delaware	0.4
23	Idaho	0.4
23	Missouri	0.4
23	Montana	0.4
23	South Carolina	0.4
28	Connecticut	0.3
29	Arizona	0.2
29	North Carolina	0.2
29	Oklahoma	0.2
29	Virginia	0.2
33	Maine	0.1
33	Mississippi	0.1
33	Rhode Island	0.1
33	Tennessee	0.1
33	Vermont	0.1
38	Indiana	0.0
38	Iowa	0.0
38	North Dakota	0.0
38	Utah	0.0
38	Wyoming	0.0
NA	Alaska**	NA
NA	California**	NA
NA	Florida**	NA
NA	Illinois**	NA
NA	Maryland**	NA
NA	Massachusetts**	NA
NA	Nebraska**	NA
NA	New Hampshire**	NA
	District of Columbia	0.0

Source: U.S. Department of Health and Human Services, Centers for Disease Control and Prevention
"Abortion Surveillance-United States, 2002" (Morbidity and Mortality Weekly Report, Vol. 54, No. SS-7, 11/25/05)
*By state of occurrence. National percent is for reporting states only.
**Not reported.

II. DEATHS

II. DEATHS (Continued)

Deaths in 2004

National Total = 2,392,547 Deaths*

ALPHA ORDER					RANK ORDER			
RANK	STATE	DEATHS	% of USA		RANK	STATE	DEATHS	% of USA
17	Alabama	45,986	1.9%		1	California	238,958	10.0%
50	Alaska	3,055	0.1%		2	Florida	168,939	7.1%
21	Arizona	43,054	1.8%		3	New York	151,656	6.3%
31	Arkansas	27,597	1.2%		4	Texas	151,123	6.3%
1	California	238,958	10.0%		5	Pennsylvania	125,654	5.3%
29	Colorado	28,296	1.2%		6	Ohio	105,776	4.4%
28	Connecticut	29,196	1.2%		7	Illinois	101,752	4.3%
45	Delaware	7,111	0.3%		8	Michigan	85,216	3.6%
2	Florida	168,939	7.1%		9	North Carolina	72,437	3.0%
11	Georgia	65,842	2.8%		10	New Jersey	71,496	3.0%
43	Hawaii	8,741	0.4%		11	Georgia	65,842	2.8%
40	Idaho	10,071	0.4%		12	Virginia	56,642	2.4%
7	Illinois	101,752	4.3%		13	Tennessee	55,555	2.3%
14	Indiana	54,288	2.3%		14	Indiana	54,288	2.3%
32	Iowa	26,940	1.1%		15	Missouri	53,904	2.3%
33	Kansas	23,935	1.0%		16	Massachusetts	52,611	2.2%
23	Kentucky	38,412	1.6%		17	Alabama	45,986	1.9%
22	Louisiana	42,048	1.8%		18	Wisconsin	45,613	1.9%
39	Maine	12,372	0.5%		19	Washington	44,540	1.9%
20	Maryland	43,300	1.8%		20	Maryland	43,300	1.8%
16	Massachusetts	52,611	2.2%		21	Arizona	43,054	1.8%
8	Michigan	85,216	3.6%		22	Louisiana	42,048	1.8%
24	Minnesota	36,930	1.5%		23	Kentucky	38,412	1.6%
30	Mississippi	27,626	1.2%		24	Minnesota	36,930	1.5%
15	Missouri	53,904	2.3%		25	South Carolina	36,055	1.5%
44	Montana	8,046	0.3%		26	Oklahoma	34,648	1.4%
36	Nebraska	14,673	0.6%		27	Oregon	30,306	1.3%
35	Nevada	17,735	0.7%		28	Connecticut	29,196	1.2%
41	New Hampshire	10,051	0.4%		29	Colorado	28,296	1.2%
10	New Jersey	71,496	3.0%		30	Mississippi	27,626	1.2%
37	New Mexico	14,061	0.6%		31	Arkansas	27,597	1.2%
3	New York	151,656	6.3%		32	Iowa	26,940	1.1%
9	North Carolina	72,437	3.0%		33	Kansas	23,935	1.0%
47	North Dakota	5,603	0.2%		34	West Virginia	20,584	0.9%
6	Ohio	105,776	4.4%		35	Nevada	17,735	0.7%
26	Oklahoma	34,648	1.4%		36	Nebraska	14,673	0.6%
27	Oregon	30,306	1.3%		37	New Mexico	14,061	0.6%
5	Pennsylvania	125,654	5.3%		38	Utah	13,331	0.6%
42	Rhode Island	9,804	0.4%		39	Maine	12,372	0.5%
25	South Carolina	36,055	1.5%		40	Idaho	10,071	0.4%
46	South Dakota	6,836	0.3%		41	New Hampshire	10,051	0.4%
13	Tennessee	55,555	2.3%		42	Rhode Island	9,804	0.4%
4	Texas	151,123	6.3%		43	Hawaii	8,741	0.4%
38	Utah	13,331	0.6%		44	Montana	8,046	0.3%
48	Vermont	4,949	0.2%		45	Delaware	7,111	0.3%
12	Virginia	56,642	2.4%		46	South Dakota	6,836	0.3%
19	Washington	44,540	1.9%		47	North Dakota	5,603	0.2%
34	West Virginia	20,584	0.9%		48	Vermont	4,949	0.2%
18	Wisconsin	45,613	1.9%		49	Wyoming	3,843	0.2%
49	Wyoming	3,843	0.2%		50	Alaska	3,055	0.1%
						District of Columbia	5,350	0.2%

Source: U.S. Department of Health and Human Services, National Center for Health Statistics
"National Vital Statistics Reports" (Vol. 53, No. 21, June 28, 2005)
*Provisional data for 12 months ending with December by state of residence.

Death Rate in 2004

National Rate = 814.7 Deaths per 100,000 Population*

ALPHA ORDER

RANK	STATE	RATE
2	Alabama	1,016.2
50	Alaska	464.5
39	Arizona	750.1
4	Arkansas	1,003.5
47	California	666.7
48	Colorado	614.9
27	Connecticut	834.4
22	Delaware	856.7
6	Florida	971.7
41	Georgia	738.3
45	Hawaii	692.6
43	Idaho	721.9
31	Illinois	800.4
19	Indiana	871.9
14	Iowa	912.3
18	Kansas	875.6
12	Kentucky	927.4
11	Louisiana	933.0
9	Maine	940.8
34	Maryland	778.6
30	Massachusetts	821.1
25	Michigan	843.4
42	Minnesota	724.6
7	Mississippi	952.4
10	Missouri	935.9
20	Montana	868.0
26	Nebraska	839.6
36	Nevada	760.2
35	New Hampshire	773.6
29	New Jersey	823.2
40	New Mexico	738.9
33	New York	786.6
23	North Carolina	848.2
17	North Dakota	880.5
13	Ohio	923.8
5	Oklahoma	983.3
24	Oregon	843.9
3	Pennsylvania	1,013.8
15	Rhode Island	907.8
21	South Carolina	858.9
16	South Dakota	887.1
8	Tennessee	942.7
46	Texas	672.5
49	Utah	550.7
32	Vermont	796.6
38	Virginia	757.1
44	Washington	717.6
1	West Virginia	1,135.6
28	Wisconsin	828.8
37	Wyoming	759.7

RANK ORDER

RANK	STATE	RATE
1	West Virginia	1,135.6
2	Alabama	1,016.2
3	Pennsylvania	1,013.8
4	Arkansas	1,003.5
5	Oklahoma	983.3
6	Florida	971.7
7	Mississippi	952.4
8	Tennessee	942.7
9	Maine	940.8
10	Missouri	935.9
11	Louisiana	933.0
12	Kentucky	927.4
13	Ohio	923.8
14	Iowa	912.3
15	Rhode Island	907.8
16	South Dakota	887.1
17	North Dakota	880.5
18	Kansas	875.6
19	Indiana	871.9
20	Montana	868.0
21	South Carolina	858.9
22	Delaware	856.7
23	North Carolina	848.2
24	Oregon	843.9
25	Michigan	843.4
26	Nebraska	839.6
27	Connecticut	834.4
28	Wisconsin	828.8
29	New Jersey	823.2
30	Massachusetts	821.1
31	Illinois	800.4
32	Vermont	796.6
33	New York	786.6
34	Maryland	778.6
35	New Hampshire	773.6
36	Nevada	760.2
37	Wyoming	759.7
38	Virginia	757.1
39	Arizona	750.1
40	New Mexico	738.9
41	Georgia	738.3
42	Minnesota	724.6
43	Idaho	721.9
44	Washington	717.6
45	Hawaii	692.6
46	Texas	672.5
47	California	666.7
48	Colorado	614.9
49	Utah	550.7
50	Alaska	464.5

District of Columbia — 965.3

Source: Morgan Quitno Press using data from US Dept of Health & Human Services, National Center for Health Statistics
"National Vital Statistics Reports" (Vol. 53, No. 15, February 28, 2005)
*Provisional data for 12 months ending with December by state of residence. Not age-adjusted.

Deaths in 2003

National Total = 2,443,908 Deaths*

ALPHA ORDER

RANK ORDER

RANK	STATE	DEATHS	% of USA		RANK	STATE	DEATHS	% of USA
15	Alabama	46,726	1.9%		1	Florida	168,607	6.9%
48	Alaska	3,185	0.1%		2	New York	155,852	6.4%
19	Arizona	43,496	1.8%		3	Texas	155,171	6.3%
30	Arkansas	27,924	1.1%		4	Pennsylvania	129,767	5.3%
NA	California**	NA	NA		5	Ohio	108,660	4.4%
26	Colorado	29,542	1.2%		6	Michigan	86,710	3.5%
27	Connecticut	29,432	1.2%		7	New Jersey	73,683	3.0%
44	Delaware	7,070	0.3%		8	North Carolina	73,548	3.0%
1	Florida	168,607	6.9%		9	Georgia	66,473	2.7%
9	Georgia	66,473	2.7%		10	Virginia	58,415	2.4%
41	Hawaii	8,987	0.4%		11	Tennessee	57,306	2.3%
38	Idaho	10,385	0.4%		12	Massachusetts	56,297	2.3%
NA	Illinois**	NA	NA		13	Indiana	56,193	2.3%
13	Indiana	56,193	2.3%		14	Missouri	55,569	2.3%
29	Iowa	28,080	1.1%		15	Alabama	46,726	1.9%
31	Kansas	24,596	1.0%		16	Wisconsin	46,174	1.9%
21	Kentucky	40,236	1.6%		17	Washington	45,964	1.9%
20	Louisiana	42,893	1.8%		18	Maryland	44,500	1.8%
37	Maine	12,534	0.5%		19	Arizona	43,496	1.8%
18	Maryland	44,500	1.8%		20	Louisiana	42,893	1.8%
12	Massachusetts	56,297	2.3%		21	Kentucky	40,236	1.6%
6	Michigan	86,710	3.5%		22	South Carolina	38,111	1.6%
23	Minnesota	37,636	1.5%		23	Minnesota	37,636	1.5%
28	Mississippi	28,535	1.2%		24	Oklahoma	35,733	1.5%
14	Missouri	55,569	2.3%		25	Oregon	30,934	1.3%
42	Montana	8,467	0.3%		26	Colorado	29,542	1.2%
34	Nebraska	15,466	0.6%		27	Connecticut	29,432	1.2%
33	Nevada	17,864	0.7%		28	Mississippi	28,535	1.2%
40	New Hampshire	9,691	0.4%		29	Iowa	28,080	1.1%
7	New Jersey	73,683	3.0%		30	Arkansas	27,924	1.1%
35	New Mexico	14,877	0.6%		31	Kansas	24,596	1.0%
2	New York	155,852	6.4%		32	West Virginia	21,299	0.9%
8	North Carolina	73,548	3.0%		33	Nevada	17,864	0.7%
45	North Dakota	6,095	0.2%		34	Nebraska	15,466	0.6%
5	Ohio	108,660	4.4%		35	New Mexico	14,877	0.6%
24	Oklahoma	35,733	1.5%		36	Utah	13,408	0.5%
25	Oregon	30,934	1.3%		37	Maine	12,534	0.5%
4	Pennsylvania	129,767	5.3%		38	Idaho	10,385	0.4%
39	Rhode Island	10,038	0.4%		39	Rhode Island	10,038	0.4%
22	South Carolina	38,111	1.6%		40	New Hampshire	9,691	0.4%
43	South Dakota	7,133	0.3%		41	Hawaii	8,987	0.4%
11	Tennessee	57,306	2.3%		42	Montana	8,467	0.3%
3	Texas	155,171	6.3%		43	South Dakota	7,133	0.3%
36	Utah	13,408	0.5%		44	Delaware	7,070	0.3%
46	Vermont	5,112	0.2%		45	North Dakota	6,095	0.2%
10	Virginia	58,415	2.4%		46	Vermont	5,112	0.2%
17	Washington	45,964	1.9%		47	Wyoming	4,173	0.2%
32	West Virginia	21,299	0.9%		48	Alaska	3,185	0.1%
16	Wisconsin	46,174	1.9%		NA	California**	NA	NA
47	Wyoming	4,173	0.2%		NA	Illinois**	NA	NA
						District of Columbia	5,513	0.2%

*Source: U.S. Department of Health and Human Services, National Center for Health Statistics
"National Vital Statistics Reports" (Vol. 53, No. 15, February 28, 2005)*
Preliminary data by state of residence.
***Not available by state but are included in national total.*

Death Rate in 2003

National Rate = 840.4 Deaths per 100,000 Population*

ALPHA ORDER

RANK	STATE	RATE
3	Alabama	1,038.2
48	Alaska	490.9
38	Arizona	779.4
4	Arkansas	1,024.5
NA	California**	NA
46	Colorado	649.2
29	Connecticut	844.9
26	Delaware	864.8
6	Florida	990.7
39	Georgia	765.4
44	Hawaii	714.6
40	Idaho	760.1
NA	Illinois**	NA
20	Indiana	907.0
14	Iowa	953.8
21	Kansas	903.1
9	Kentucky	977.1
13	Louisiana	954.0
12	Maine	959.9
34	Maryland	807.8
23	Massachusetts	875.1
27	Michigan	860.2
43	Minnesota	743.9
7	Mississippi	990.4
10	Missouri	974.1
18	Montana	922.7
22	Nebraska	889.2
35	Nevada	797.1
41	New Hampshire	752.6
28	New Jersey	853.0
36	New Mexico	793.6
33	New York	812.1
24	North Carolina	874.8
11	North Dakota	961.6
15	Ohio	950.2
5	Oklahoma	1,017.6
25	Oregon	869.0
2	Pennsylvania	1,049.4
17	Rhode Island	932.8
19	South Carolina	919.0
16	South Dakota	933.3
8	Tennessee	981.0
45	Texas	701.5
47	Utah	570.2
32	Vermont	825.7
37	Virginia	790.9
42	Washington	749.6
1	West Virginia	1,176.5
30	Wisconsin	843.8
31	Wyoming	832.5

RANK ORDER

RANK	STATE	RATE
1	West Virginia	1,176.5
2	Pennsylvania	1,049.4
3	Alabama	1,038.2
4	Arkansas	1,024.5
5	Oklahoma	1,017.6
6	Florida	990.7
7	Mississippi	990.4
8	Tennessee	981.0
9	Kentucky	977.1
10	Missouri	974.1
11	North Dakota	961.6
12	Maine	959.9
13	Louisiana	954.0
14	Iowa	953.8
15	Ohio	950.2
16	South Dakota	933.3
17	Rhode Island	932.8
18	Montana	922.7
19	South Carolina	919.0
20	Indiana	907.0
21	Kansas	903.1
22	Nebraska	889.2
23	Massachusetts	875.1
24	North Carolina	874.8
25	Oregon	869.0
26	Delaware	864.8
27	Michigan	860.2
28	New Jersey	853.0
29	Connecticut	844.9
30	Wisconsin	843.8
31	Wyoming	832.5
32	Vermont	825.7
33	New York	812.1
34	Maryland	807.8
35	Nevada	797.1
36	New Mexico	793.6
37	Virginia	790.9
38	Arizona	779.4
39	Georgia	765.4
40	Idaho	760.1
41	New Hampshire	752.6
42	Washington	749.6
43	Minnesota	743.9
44	Hawaii	714.6
45	Texas	701.5
46	Colorado	649.2
47	Utah	570.2
48	Alaska	490.9
NA	California**	NA
NA	Illinois**	NA

District of Columbia   976.9

Source: U.S. Department of Health and Human Services, National Center for Health Statistics
    "National Vital Statistics Reports" (Vol. 53, No. 15, February 28, 2005)

*Preliminary data by state of residence. Not age-adjusted.
**Not available by state but are included in national rate.

Age-Adjusted Death Rate in 2003

National Rate = 831.2 Deaths per 100,000 Population*

ALPHA ORDER				RANK ORDER		
RANK	STATE	RATE		RANK	STATE	RATE
3	Alabama	1,001.9		1	Mississippi	1,015.2
23	Alaska	831.3		2	Louisiana	1,007.4
33	Arizona	788.9		3	Alabama	1,001.9
9	Arkansas	937.6		4	West Virginia	994.5
NA	California**	NA		5	Tennessee	982.1
35	Colorado	785.3		6	Kentucky	976.9
46	Connecticut	729.5		7	Oklahoma	973.9
22	Delaware	844.3		8	Georgia	946.4
39	Florida	775.7		9	Arkansas	937.6
8	Georgia	946.4		10	South Carolina	934.8
48	Hawaii	650.1		11	Nevada	925.0
29	Idaho	797.5		12	North Carolina	906.8
NA	Illinois**	NA		13	Missouri	902.4
14	Indiana	898.1		14	Indiana	898.1
41	Iowa	769.0		15	Ohio	886.2
26	Kansas	824.0		16	Texas	857.2
6	Kentucky	976.9		17	Maryland	852.9
2	Louisiana	1,007.4		18	Virginia	852.8
27	Maine	821.9		19	Wyoming	850.6
17	Maryland	852.9		20	Michigan	850.3
37	Massachusetts	778.8		21	Pennsylvania	849.1
20	Michigan	850.3		22	Delaware	844.3
47	Minnesota	713.4		23	Alaska	831.3
1	Mississippi	1,015.2		24	Montana	828.3
13	Missouri	902.4		25	New Mexico	827.7
24	Montana	828.3		26	Kansas	824.0
31	Nebraska	790.6		27	Maine	821.9
11	Nevada	925.0		28	Oregon	808.9
45	New Hampshire	748.4		29	Idaho	797.5
30	New Jersey	794.7		30	New Jersey	794.7
25	New Mexico	827.7		31	Nebraska	790.6
44	New York	759.8		32	South Dakota	790.5
12	North Carolina	906.8		33	Arizona	788.9
42	North Dakota	767.5		34	Rhode Island	786.6
15	Ohio	886.2		35	Colorado	785.3
7	Oklahoma	973.9		36	Utah	782.1
28	Oregon	808.9		37	Massachusetts	778.8
21	Pennsylvania	849.1		38	Washington	776.6
34	Rhode Island	786.6		39	Florida	775.7
10	South Carolina	934.8		40	Wisconsin	772.3
32	South Dakota	790.5		41	Iowa	769.0
5	Tennessee	982.1		42	North Dakota	767.5
16	Texas	857.2		43	Vermont	764.1
36	Utah	782.1		44	New York	759.8
43	Vermont	764.1		45	New Hampshire	748.4
18	Virginia	852.8		46	Connecticut	729.5
38	Washington	776.6		47	Minnesota	713.4
4	West Virginia	994.5		48	Hawaii	650.1
40	Wisconsin	772.3		NA	California**	NA
19	Wyoming	850.6		NA	Illinois**	NA
					District of Columbia	968.2

Source: U.S. Department of Health and Human Services, National Center for Health Statistics
"National Vital Statistics Reports" (Vol. 53, No. 15, February 28, 2005)
*Preliminary data by state of residence. Age-adjusted rates eliminate the distorting effects of the aging of the population. Rates based on the year 2000 standard population.
**Not available by state but are included in national rate.

Percent Change in Death Rate: 1994 to 2003

National Percent Change = 4.0% Decrease*

ALPHA ORDER				RANK ORDER		
RANK	STATE	PERCENT CHANGE		RANK	STATE	PERCENT CHANGE
8	Alabama	5.0		1	Alaska	21.7
1	Alaska	21.7		2	Hawaii	14.8
47	Arizona	(7.4)		3	Wyoming	13.8
40	Arkansas	(4.5)		4	New Mexico	8.2
NA	California**	NA		5	Montana	7.3
29	Colorado	(2.1)		6	West Virginia	6.4
43	Connecticut	(5.5)		7	Louisiana	5.5
35	Delaware	(3.6)		8	Alabama	5.0
46	Florida	(7.1)		9	South Carolina	4.3
40	Georgia	(4.5)		10	North Dakota	4.1
2	Hawaii	14.8		11	Utah	3.9
14	Idaho	2.0		12	Oklahoma	2.6
NA	Illinois**	NA		13	Ohio	2.2
21	Indiana	(0.5)		14	Idaho	2.0
33	Iowa	(2.6)		14	Maine	2.0
23	Kansas	(1.2)		16	Kentucky	0.6
16	Kentucky	0.6		17	Tennessee	0.5
7	Louisiana	5.5		18	Washington	0.2
14	Maine	2.0		19	Vermont	0.1
27	Maryland	(1.5)		20	South Dakota	(0.2)
36	Massachusetts	(3.8)		21	Indiana	(0.5)
27	Michigan	(1.5)		22	Virginia	(0.7)
45	Minnesota	(7.0)		23	Kansas	(1.2)
26	Mississippi	(1.3)		23	Pennsylvania	(1.2)
39	Missouri	(4.4)		23	Rhode Island	(1.2)
5	Montana	7.3		26	Mississippi	(1.3)
37	Nebraska	(3.9)		27	Maryland	(1.5)
32	Nevada	(2.5)		27	Michigan	(1.5)
38	New Hampshire	(4.1)		29	Colorado	(2.1)
44	New Jersey	(6.8)		30	North Carolina	(2.2)
4	New Mexico	8.2		30	Oregon	(2.2)
48	New York	(12.6)		32	Nevada	(2.5)
30	North Carolina	(2.2)		33	Iowa	(2.6)
10	North Dakota	4.1		34	Wisconsin	(3.5)
13	Ohio	2.2		35	Delaware	(3.6)
12	Oklahoma	2.6		36	Massachusetts	(3.8)
30	Oregon	(2.2)		37	Nebraska	(3.9)
23	Pennsylvania	(1.2)		38	New Hampshire	(4.1)
23	Rhode Island	(1.2)		39	Missouri	(4.4)
9	South Carolina	4.3		40	Arkansas	(4.5)
20	South Dakota	(0.2)		40	Georgia	(4.5)
17	Tennessee	0.5		42	Texas	(5.3)
42	Texas	(5.3)		43	Connecticut	(5.5)
11	Utah	3.9		44	New Jersey	(6.8)
19	Vermont	0.1		45	Minnesota	(7.0)
22	Virginia	(0.7)		46	Florida	(7.1)
18	Washington	0.2		47	Arizona	(7.4)
6	West Virginia	6.4		48	New York	(12.6)
34	Wisconsin	(3.5)		NA	California**	NA
3	Wyoming	13.8		NA	Illinois**	NA
					District of Columbia	(22.7)

Source: Morgan Quitno Press using data from US Dept of Health & Human Services, National Center for Health Statistics
    "National Vital Statistics Reports" (Vol. 53, No. 21, June 28, 2005)
    "Monthly Vital Statistics Report" (Vol. 45, No. 3(S), September 30, 1996)
*By state of residence. Not age-adjusted.
**Not available.

Deaths in 2002

National Total = 2,443,387 Deaths*

ALPHA ORDER

RANK	STATE	DEATHS	% of USA
18	Alabama	46,069	1.9%
50	Alaska	3,030	0.1%
21	Arizona	42,816	1.8%
31	Arkansas	28,513	1.2%
1	California	234,565	9.6%
29	Colorado	29,210	1.2%
28	Connecticut	30,122	1.2%
46	Delaware	6,861	0.3%
2	Florida	167,814	6.9%
11	Georgia	65,449	2.7%
43	Hawaii	8,801	0.4%
41	Idaho	9,923	0.4%
7	Illinois	106,667	4.4%
16	Indiana	55,396	2.3%
32	Iowa	27,978	1.1%
33	Kansas	25,021	1.0%
23	Kentucky	40,697	1.7%
22	Louisiana	41,984	1.7%
39	Maine	12,694	0.5%
20	Maryland	43,970	1.8%
13	Massachusetts	56,928	2.3%
8	Michigan	87,795	3.6%
24	Minnesota	38,510	1.6%
30	Mississippi	28,853	1.2%
15	Missouri	55,940	2.3%
44	Montana	8,506	0.3%
36	Nebraska	15,738	0.6%
35	Nevada	16,927	0.7%
42	New Hampshire	9,853	0.4%
9	New Jersey	74,009	3.0%
37	New Mexico	14,344	0.6%
3	New York	158,118	6.5%
10	North Carolina	72,027	2.9%
47	North Dakota	5,892	0.2%
6	Ohio	109,766	4.5%
26	Oklahoma	35,502	1.5%
27	Oregon	31,119	1.3%
5	Pennsylvania	130,223	5.3%
40	Rhode Island	10,246	0.4%
25	South Carolina	37,736	1.5%
45	South Dakota	6,898	0.3%
14	Tennessee	56,606	2.3%
4	Texas	155,524	6.4%
38	Utah	13,116	0.5%
48	Vermont	5,075	0.2%
12	Virginia	57,196	2.3%
19	Washington	45,338	1.9%
34	West Virginia	21,016	0.9%
17	Wisconsin	46,981	1.9%
49	Wyoming	4,174	0.2%

RANK ORDER

RANK	STATE	DEATHS	% of USA
1	California	234,565	9.6%
2	Florida	167,814	6.9%
3	New York	158,118	6.5%
4	Texas	155,524	6.4%
5	Pennsylvania	130,223	5.3%
6	Ohio	109,766	4.5%
7	Illinois	106,667	4.4%
8	Michigan	87,795	3.6%
9	New Jersey	74,009	3.0%
10	North Carolina	72,027	2.9%
11	Georgia	65,449	2.7%
12	Virginia	57,196	2.3%
13	Massachusetts	56,928	2.3%
14	Tennessee	56,606	2.3%
15	Missouri	55,940	2.3%
16	Indiana	55,396	2.3%
17	Wisconsin	46,981	1.9%
18	Alabama	46,069	1.9%
19	Washington	45,338	1.9%
20	Maryland	43,970	1.8%
21	Arizona	42,816	1.8%
22	Louisiana	41,984	1.7%
23	Kentucky	40,697	1.7%
24	Minnesota	38,510	1.6%
25	South Carolina	37,736	1.5%
26	Oklahoma	35,502	1.5%
27	Oregon	31,119	1.3%
28	Connecticut	30,122	1.2%
29	Colorado	29,210	1.2%
30	Mississippi	28,853	1.2%
31	Arkansas	28,513	1.2%
32	Iowa	27,978	1.1%
33	Kansas	25,021	1.0%
34	West Virginia	21,016	0.9%
35	Nevada	16,927	0.7%
36	Nebraska	15,738	0.6%
37	New Mexico	14,344	0.6%
38	Utah	13,116	0.5%
39	Maine	12,694	0.5%
40	Rhode Island	10,246	0.4%
41	Idaho	9,923	0.4%
42	New Hampshire	9,853	0.4%
43	Hawaii	8,801	0.4%
44	Montana	8,506	0.3%
45	South Dakota	6,898	0.3%
46	Delaware	6,861	0.3%
47	North Dakota	5,892	0.2%
48	Vermont	5,075	0.2%
49	Wyoming	4,174	0.2%
50	Alaska	3,030	0.1%
	District of Columbia	5,851	0.2%

*Source: U.S. Department of Health and Human Services, National Center for Health Statistics
"National Vital Statistics Reports" (Vol. 53, No. 5, October 12, 2004)
Final data by state of residence.

Death Rate in 2002

National Rate = 847.3 Deaths per 100,000 Population*

RANK	STATE	RATE		RANK	STATE	RATE
ALPHA ORDER				RANK ORDER		
4	Alabama	1,026.8		1	West Virginia	1,166.3
50	Alaska	470.7		2	Pennsylvania	1,055.7
36	Arizona	784.7		3	Arkansas	1,052.1
3	Arkansas	1,052.1		4	Alabama	1,026.8
47	California	668.0		5	Oklahoma	1,016.2
48	Colorado	648.2		6	Mississippi	1,004.7
26	Connecticut	870.5		7	Florida	1,004.1
30	Delaware	849.8		8	Kentucky	994.3
7	Florida	1,004.1		9	Missouri	986.1
42	Georgia	764.6		10	Maine	980.6
46	Hawaii	707.0		11	Tennessee	976.4
44	Idaho	739.9		12	Ohio	961.1
31	Illinois	846.5		13	Rhode Island	957.8
22	Indiana	899.4		14	Iowa	952.7
14	Iowa	952.7		15	Louisiana	936.6
18	Kansas	921.3		16	Montana	935.3
8	Kentucky	994.3		17	North Dakota	929.2
15	Louisiana	936.6		18	Kansas	921.3
10	Maine	980.6		19	South Carolina	918.8
35	Maryland	805.6		20	Nebraska	910.1
23	Massachusetts	885.7		21	South Dakota	906.4
25	Michigan	873.5		22	Indiana	899.4
41	Minnesota	767.2		23	Massachusetts	885.7
6	Mississippi	1,004.7		24	Oregon	883.7
9	Missouri	986.1		25	Michigan	873.5
16	Montana	935.3		26	Connecticut	870.5
20	Nebraska	910.1		27	North Carolina	865.7
38	Nevada	778.8		28	Wisconsin	863.4
40	New Hampshire	772.8		29	New Jersey	861.5
29	New Jersey	861.5		30	Delaware	849.8
39	New Mexico	773.2		31	Illinois	846.5
33	New York	825.4		32	Wyoming	837.0
27	North Carolina	865.7		33	New York	825.4
17	North Dakota	929.2		34	Vermont	823.1
12	Ohio	961.1		35	Maryland	805.6
5	Oklahoma	1,016.2		36	Arizona	784.7
24	Oregon	883.7		37	Virginia	784.2
2	Pennsylvania	1,055.7		38	Nevada	778.8
13	Rhode Island	957.8		39	New Mexico	773.2
19	South Carolina	918.8		40	New Hampshire	772.8
21	South Dakota	906.4		41	Minnesota	767.2
11	Tennessee	976.4		42	Georgia	764.6
45	Texas	714.1		43	Washington	747.0
49	Utah	566.3		44	Idaho	739.9
34	Vermont	823.1		45	Texas	714.1
37	Virginia	784.2		46	Hawaii	707.0
43	Washington	747.0		47	California	668.0
1	West Virginia	1,166.3		48	Colorado	648.2
28	Wisconsin	863.4		49	Utah	566.3
32	Wyoming	837.0		50	Alaska	470.7
					District of Columbia	1,024.9

Source: U.S. Department of Health and Human Services, National Center for Health Statistics
"National Vital Statistics Reports" (Vol. 53, No. 5, October 12, 2004)
*Final data by state of residence. Not age-adjusted.

Age-Adjusted Death Rate in 2002

National Rate = 845.3 Deaths per 100,000 Population*

ALPHA ORDER				RANK ORDER		
RANK	STATE	RATE		RANK	STATE	RATE
3	Alabama	998.1		1	Mississippi	1,036.3
37	Alaska	789.1		2	Louisiana	1,000.5
33	Arizona	795.7		3	Alabama	998.1
8	Arkansas	964.4		4	Kentucky	993.9
47	California	757.8		5	West Virginia	991.7
36	Colorado	790.2		6	Tennessee	981.5
46	Connecticut	762.4		7	Oklahoma	973.2
26	Delaware	838.2		8	Arkansas	964.4
38	Florida	786.4		9	Georgia	949.1
9	Georgia	949.1		10	South Carolina	946.9
50	Hawaii	660.6		11	Missouri	916.7
34	Idaho	793.0		12	Nevada	916.5
22	Illinois	856.0		13	Ohio	908.2
15	Indiana	899.6		14	North Carolina	906.1
44	Iowa	774.5		15	Indiana	899.6
25	Kansas	843.5		16	Michigan	876.2
4	Kentucky	993.9		17	Texas	870.0
2	Louisiana	1,000.5		18	Wyoming	864.3
24	Maine	846.5		19	Maryland	864.1
19	Maryland	864.1		20	Pennsylvania	862.1
35	Massachusetts	791.9		21	Virginia	856.6
16	Michigan	876.2		22	Illinois	856.0
49	Minnesota	747.5		23	Montana	849.7
1	Mississippi	1,036.3		24	Maine	846.5
11	Missouri	916.7		25	Kansas	843.5
23	Montana	849.7		26	Delaware	838.2
29	Nebraska	814.8		27	Oregon	834.2
12	Nevada	916.5		28	New Mexico	815.0
42	New Hampshire	781.7		29	Nebraska	814.8
31	New Jersey	808.7		30	Rhode Island	809.5
28	New Mexico	815.0		31	New Jersey	808.7
40	New York	783.3		32	Wisconsin	799.8
14	North Carolina	906.1		33	Arizona	795.7
48	North Dakota	749.8		34	Idaho	793.0
13	Ohio	908.2		35	Massachusetts	791.9
7	Oklahoma	973.2		36	Colorado	790.2
27	Oregon	834.2		37	Alaska	789.1
20	Pennsylvania	862.1		38	Florida	786.4
30	Rhode Island	809.5		39	Washington	785.3
10	South Carolina	946.9		40	New York	783.3
45	South Dakota	771.2		41	Utah	782.0
6	Tennessee	981.5		42	New Hampshire	781.7
17	Texas	870.0		43	Vermont	775.0
41	Utah	782.0		44	Iowa	774.5
43	Vermont	775.0		45	South Dakota	771.2
21	Virginia	856.6		46	Connecticut	762.4
39	Washington	785.3		47	California	757.8
5	West Virginia	991.7		48	North Dakota	749.8
32	Wisconsin	799.8		49	Minnesota	747.5
18	Wyoming	864.3		50	Hawaii	660.6
					District of Columbia	1,021.4

*Source: U.S. Department of Health and Human Services, National Center for Health Statistics
"National Vital Statistics Reports" (Vol. 53, No. 5, October 12, 2004)*
*Final data by state of residence. Age-adjusted rates eliminate the distorting effects of the aging of the population.
Rates based on the year 2000 standard population.*

Infant Deaths in 2004

National Total = 27,337 Infant Deaths*

ALPHA ORDER

RANK	STATE	DEATHS	% of USA
19	Alabama	507	1.9%
45	Alaska	65	0.2%
16	Arizona	626	2.3%
29	Arkansas	334	1.2%
1	California	2,781	10.2%
22	Colorado	443	1.6%
33	Connecticut	234	0.9%
43	Delaware	87	0.3%
4	Florida	1,505	5.5%
6	Georgia	1,173	4.3%
40	Hawaii	95	0.3%
38	Idaho	152	0.6%
5	Illinois	1,253	4.6%
12	Indiana	726	2.7%
35	Iowa	198	0.7%
30	Kansas	290	1.1%
26	Kentucky	348	1.3%
15	Louisiana	653	2.4%
44	Maine	81	0.3%
14	Maryland	657	2.4%
28	Massachusetts	341	1.2%
10	Michigan	997	3.6%
26	Minnesota	348	1.3%
25	Mississippi	391	1.4%
18	Missouri	557	2.0%
48	Montana	50	0.2%
36	Nebraska	176	0.6%
34	Nevada	223	0.8%
41	New Hampshire	89	0.3%
17	New Jersey	573	2.1%
37	New Mexico	170	0.6%
3	New York	1,561	5.7%
8	North Carolina	1,022	3.7%
49	North Dakota	40	0.1%
7	Ohio	1,120	4.1%
23	Oklahoma	422	1.5%
32	Oregon	250	0.9%
9	Pennsylvania	1,002	3.7%
47	Rhode Island	59	0.2%
20	South Carolina	476	1.7%
41	South Dakota	89	0.3%
13	Tennessee	675	2.5%
2	Texas	2,334	8.5%
31	Utah	257	0.9%
50	Vermont	30	0.1%
11	Virginia	741	2.7%
21	Washington	444	1.6%
39	West Virginia	135	0.5%
24	Wisconsin	413	1.5%
46	Wyoming	62	0.2%

RANK ORDER

RANK	STATE	DEATHS	% of USA
1	California	2,781	10.2%
2	Texas	2,334	8.5%
3	New York	1,561	5.7%
4	Florida	1,505	5.5%
5	Illinois	1,253	4.6%
6	Georgia	1,173	4.3%
7	Ohio	1,120	4.1%
8	North Carolina	1,022	3.7%
9	Pennsylvania	1,002	3.7%
10	Michigan	997	3.6%
11	Virginia	741	2.7%
12	Indiana	726	2.7%
13	Tennessee	675	2.5%
14	Maryland	657	2.4%
15	Louisiana	653	2.4%
16	Arizona	626	2.3%
17	New Jersey	573	2.1%
18	Missouri	557	2.0%
19	Alabama	507	1.9%
20	South Carolina	476	1.7%
21	Washington	444	1.6%
22	Colorado	443	1.6%
23	Oklahoma	422	1.5%
24	Wisconsin	413	1.5%
25	Mississippi	391	1.4%
26	Kentucky	348	1.3%
26	Minnesota	348	1.3%
28	Massachusetts	341	1.2%
29	Arkansas	334	1.2%
30	Kansas	290	1.1%
31	Utah	257	0.9%
32	Oregon	250	0.9%
33	Connecticut	234	0.9%
34	Nevada	223	0.8%
35	Iowa	198	0.7%
36	Nebraska	176	0.6%
37	New Mexico	170	0.6%
38	Idaho	152	0.6%
39	West Virginia	135	0.5%
40	Hawaii	95	0.3%
41	New Hampshire	89	0.3%
41	South Dakota	89	0.3%
43	Delaware	87	0.3%
44	Maine	81	0.3%
45	Alaska	65	0.2%
46	Wyoming	62	0.2%
47	Rhode Island	59	0.2%
48	Montana	50	0.2%
49	North Dakota	40	0.1%
50	Vermont	30	0.1%
	District of Columbia	82	0.3%

Source: U.S. Department of Health and Human Services, National Center for Health Statistics
"National Vital Statistics Reports" (Vol. 53, No. 21, June 28, 2005)
*Provisional data for 12 months ending with December. Deaths under 1 year old by state of residence.

Infant Mortality Rate in 2004

National Rate = 6.6 Infant Deaths per 1,000 Live Births*

ALPHA ORDER

RANK ORDER

RANK	STATE	RATE
5	Alabama	8.6
28	Alaska	6.3
24	Arizona	6.7
5	Arkansas	8.6
42	California	5.1
26	Colorado	6.5
37	Connecticut	5.6
15	Delaware	7.6
21	Florida	6.9
9	Georgia	8.4
40	Hawaii	5.2
23	Idaho	6.8
20	Illinois	7.0
11	Indiana	8.3
40	Iowa	5.2
17	Kansas	7.2
28	Kentucky	6.3
1	Louisiana	10.0
36	Maine	5.8
4	Maryland	8.7
49	Massachusetts	4.3
13	Michigan	7.7
45	Minnesota	4.9
2	Mississippi	9.2
17	Missouri	7.2
49	Montana	4.3
24	Nebraska	6.7
28	Nevada	6.3
32	New Hampshire	6.0
44	New Jersey	5.0
32	New Mexico	6.0
32	New York	6.0
7	North Carolina	8.5
45	North Dakota	4.9
16	Ohio	7.5
12	Oklahoma	8.2
38	Oregon	5.5
21	Pennsylvania	6.9
47	Rhode Island	4.6
9	South Carolina	8.4
13	South Dakota	7.7
7	Tennessee	8.5
31	Texas	6.1
42	Utah	5.1
47	Vermont	4.6
19	Virginia	7.1
39	Washington	5.4
26	West Virginia	6.5
35	Wisconsin	5.9
2	Wyoming	9.2

RANK	STATE	RATE
1	Louisiana	10.0
2	Mississippi	9.2
2	Wyoming	9.2
4	Maryland	8.7
5	Alabama	8.6
5	Arkansas	8.6
7	North Carolina	8.5
7	Tennessee	8.5
9	Georgia	8.4
9	South Carolina	8.4
11	Indiana	8.3
12	Oklahoma	8.2
13	Michigan	7.7
13	South Dakota	7.7
15	Delaware	7.6
16	Ohio	7.5
17	Kansas	7.2
17	Missouri	7.2
19	Virginia	7.1
20	Illinois	7.0
21	Florida	6.9
21	Pennsylvania	6.9
23	Idaho	6.8
24	Arizona	6.7
24	Nebraska	6.7
26	Colorado	6.5
26	West Virginia	6.5
28	Alaska	6.3
28	Kentucky	6.3
28	Nevada	6.3
31	Texas	6.1
32	New Hampshire	6.0
32	New Mexico	6.0
32	New York	6.0
35	Wisconsin	5.9
36	Maine	5.8
37	Connecticut	5.6
38	Oregon	5.5
39	Washington	5.4
40	Hawaii	5.2
40	Iowa	5.2
42	California	5.1
42	Utah	5.1
44	New Jersey	5.0
45	Minnesota	4.9
45	North Dakota	4.9
47	Rhode Island	4.6
47	Vermont	4.6
49	Massachusetts	4.3
49	Montana	4.3

	District of Columbia	11.0

Source: U.S. Department of Health and Human Services, National Center for Health Statistics
     "National Vital Statistics Reports" (Vol. 53, No. 21, June 28, 2005)
Provisional data for 12 months ending with December. Deaths under 1 year old by state of residence.

Infant Deaths in 2003

National Total = 27,477 Infant Deaths*

ALPHA ORDER

RANK	STATE	DEATHS	% of USA
19	Alabama	502	1.8%
45	Alaska	67	0.2%
17	Arizona	591	2.2%
28	Arkansas	333	1.2%
1	California	2,560	9.3%
24	Colorado	416	1.5%
33	Connecticut	222	0.8%
41	Delaware	97	0.4%
4	Florida	1,576	5.7%
7	Georgia	1,158	4.2%
40	Hawaii	139	0.5%
36	Idaho	158	0.6%
5	Illinois	1,361	5.0%
13	Indiana	672	2.4%
34	Iowa	207	0.8%
31	Kansas	261	0.9%
27	Kentucky	341	1.2%
16	Louisiana	596	2.2%
46	Maine	64	0.2%
15	Maryland	645	2.3%
22	Massachusetts	425	1.5%
8	Michigan	1,130	4.1%
29	Minnesota	325	1.2%
22	Mississippi	425	1.5%
18	Missouri	587	2.1%
43	Montana	79	0.3%
39	Nebraska	145	0.5%
35	Nevada	203	0.7%
48	New Hampshire	52	0.2%
14	New Jersey	660	2.4%
37	New Mexico	157	0.6%
3	New York	1,642	6.0%
10	North Carolina	931	3.4%
47	North Dakota	57	0.2%
6	Ohio	1,162	4.2%
26	Oklahoma	378	1.4%
30	Oregon	270	1.0%
9	Pennsylvania	981	3.6%
44	Rhode Island	76	0.3%
20	South Carolina	451	1.6%
42	South Dakota	80	0.3%
12	Tennessee	717	2.6%
2	Texas	2,400	8.7%
32	Utah	252	0.9%
50	Vermont	32	0.1%
11	Virginia	758	2.8%
24	Washington	416	1.5%
38	West Virginia	153	0.6%
20	Wisconsin	451	1.6%
49	Wyoming	46	0.2%

RANK ORDER

RANK	STATE	DEATHS	% of USA
1	California	2,560	9.3%
2	Texas	2,400	8.7%
3	New York	1,642	6.0%
4	Florida	1,576	5.7%
5	Illinois	1,361	5.0%
6	Ohio	1,162	4.2%
7	Georgia	1,158	4.2%
8	Michigan	1,130	4.1%
9	Pennsylvania	981	3.6%
10	North Carolina	931	3.4%
11	Virginia	758	2.8%
12	Tennessee	717	2.6%
13	Indiana	672	2.4%
14	New Jersey	660	2.4%
15	Maryland	645	2.3%
16	Louisiana	596	2.2%
17	Arizona	591	2.2%
18	Missouri	587	2.1%
19	Alabama	502	1.8%
20	South Carolina	451	1.6%
20	Wisconsin	451	1.6%
22	Massachusetts	425	1.5%
22	Mississippi	425	1.5%
24	Colorado	416	1.5%
24	Washington	416	1.5%
26	Oklahoma	378	1.4%
27	Kentucky	341	1.2%
28	Arkansas	333	1.2%
29	Minnesota	325	1.2%
30	Oregon	270	1.0%
31	Kansas	261	0.9%
32	Utah	252	0.9%
33	Connecticut	222	0.8%
34	Iowa	207	0.8%
35	Nevada	203	0.7%
36	Idaho	158	0.6%
37	New Mexico	157	0.6%
38	West Virginia	153	0.6%
39	Nebraska	145	0.5%
40	Hawaii	139	0.5%
41	Delaware	97	0.4%
42	South Dakota	80	0.3%
43	Montana	79	0.3%
44	Rhode Island	76	0.3%
45	Alaska	67	0.2%
46	Maine	64	0.2%
47	North Dakota	57	0.2%
48	New Hampshire	52	0.2%
49	Wyoming	46	0.2%
50	Vermont	32	0.1%
	District of Columbia	70	0.3%

Source: U.S. Department of Health and Human Services, National Center for Health Statistics
"National Vital Statistics Reports" (Vol. 53, No. 21, June 28, 2005)
*Preliminary data. Deaths under 1 year old by state of residence.

Infant Mortality Rate in 2003

National Rate = 6.7 Infant Deaths per 1,000 Live Births*

RANK	STATE	RATE
6	Alabama	8.5
27	Alaska	6.7
28	Arizona	6.5
4	Arkansas	8.7
47	California	4.7
34	Colorado	6.0
44	Connecticut	5.1
6	Delaware	8.5
18	Florida	7.4
6	Georgia	8.5
13	Hawaii	7.7
21	Idaho	7.2
16	Illinois	7.5
13	Indiana	7.7
41	Iowa	5.4
29	Kansas	6.4
33	Kentucky	6.2
2	Louisiana	9.2
48	Maine	4.6
6	Maryland	8.5
42	Massachusetts	5.3
5	Michigan	8.6
48	Minnesota	4.6
1	Mississippi	10.1
13	Missouri	7.7
25	Montana	6.9
39	Nebraska	5.6
34	Nevada	6.0
50	New Hampshire	3.6
39	New Jersey	5.6
38	New Mexico	5.7
32	New York	6.3
11	North Carolina	7.9
21	North Dakota	7.2
12	Ohio	7.8
18	Oklahoma	7.4
36	Oregon	5.9
25	Pennsylvania	6.9
37	Rhode Island	5.8
10	South Carolina	8.1
23	South Dakota	7.1
3	Tennessee	9.1
29	Texas	6.4
45	Utah	5.0
46	Vermont	4.9
16	Virginia	7.5
43	Washington	5.2
20	West Virginia	7.3
29	Wisconsin	6.4
24	Wyoming	7.0

RANK	STATE	RATE
1	Mississippi	10.1
2	Louisiana	9.2
3	Tennessee	9.1
4	Arkansas	8.7
5	Michigan	8.6
6	Alabama	8.5
6	Delaware	8.5
6	Georgia	8.5
6	Maryland	8.5
10	South Carolina	8.1
11	North Carolina	7.9
12	Ohio	7.8
13	Hawaii	7.7
13	Indiana	7.7
13	Missouri	7.7
16	Illinois	7.5
16	Virginia	7.5
18	Florida	7.4
18	Oklahoma	7.4
20	West Virginia	7.3
21	Idaho	7.2
21	North Dakota	7.2
23	South Dakota	7.1
24	Wyoming	7.0
25	Montana	6.9
25	Pennsylvania	6.9
27	Alaska	6.7
28	Arizona	6.5
29	Kansas	6.4
29	Texas	6.4
29	Wisconsin	6.4
32	New York	6.3
33	Kentucky	6.2
34	Colorado	6.0
34	Nevada	6.0
36	Oregon	5.9
37	Rhode Island	5.8
38	New Mexico	5.7
39	Nebraska	5.6
39	New Jersey	5.6
41	Iowa	5.4
42	Massachusetts	5.3
43	Washington	5.2
44	Connecticut	5.1
45	Utah	5.0
46	Vermont	4.9
47	California	4.7
48	Maine	4.6
48	Minnesota	4.6
50	New Hampshire	3.6
	District of Columbia	9.4

Source: U.S. Department of Health and Human Services, National Center for Health Statistics
"National Vital Statistics Reports" (Vol. 53, No. 21, June 28, 2005)
*Preliminary data. Deaths under 1 year old by state of residence.

Percent Change in Infant Mortality Rate: 1994 to 2003

National Percent Change = 16.3% Decrease*

RANK	STATE	PERCENT CHANGE		RANK	STATE	PERCENT CHANGE
27	Alabama	(15.8)		1	Delaware	25.0
21	Alaska	(11.8)		2	Rhode Island	16.0
30	Arizona	(16.7)		3	Hawaii	14.9
11	Arkansas	(5.4)		4	West Virginia	9.0
46	California	(32.9)		5	Wyoming	4.5
26	Colorado	(14.3)		6	Idaho	4.3
49	Connecticut	(35.4)		7	Tennessee	2.2
1	Delaware	25.0		8	Michigan	0.0
16	Florida	(8.6)		8	North Dakota	0.0
30	Georgia	(16.7)		10	Missouri	(4.9)
3	Hawaii	14.9		11	Arkansas	(5.4)
6	Idaho	4.3		12	Maryland	(5.6)
36	Illinois	(19.4)		13	Montana	(6.8)
22	Indiana	(12.5)		14	Nevada	(7.7)
44	Iowa	(28.0)		15	Mississippi	(8.2)
32	Kansas	(16.9)		16	Florida	(8.6)
38	Kentucky	(20.5)		17	Virginia	(9.6)
25	Louisiana	(13.2)		18	Texas	(9.9)
40	Maine	(25.8)		19	Ohio	(10.3)
12	Maryland	(5.6)		20	Massachusetts	(11.7)
20	Massachusetts	(11.7)		21	Alaska	(11.8)
8	Michigan	0.0		22	Indiana	(12.5)
47	Minnesota	(34.3)		23	Oklahoma	(12.9)
15	Mississippi	(8.2)		23	South Carolina	(12.9)
10	Missouri	(4.9)		25	Louisiana	(13.2)
13	Montana	(6.8)		26	Colorado	(14.3)
42	Nebraska	(27.3)		27	Alabama	(15.8)
14	Nevada	(7.7)		28	Pennsylvania	(15.9)
50	New Hampshire	(41.9)		29	Washington	(16.1)
42	New Jersey	(27.3)		30	Arizona	(16.7)
45	New Mexico	(31.3)		30	Georgia	(16.7)
35	New York	(19.2)		32	Kansas	(16.9)
39	North Carolina	(21.0)		32	Oregon	(16.9)
8	North Dakota	0.0		34	Wisconsin	(19.0)
19	Ohio	(10.3)		35	New York	(19.2)
23	Oklahoma	(12.9)		36	Illinois	(19.4)
32	Oregon	(16.9)		36	Utah	(19.4)
28	Pennsylvania	(15.9)		38	Kentucky	(20.5)
2	Rhode Island	16.0		39	North Carolina	(21.0)
23	South Carolina	(12.9)		40	Maine	(25.8)
41	South Dakota	(26.0)		41	South Dakota	(26.0)
7	Tennessee	2.2		42	Nebraska	(27.3)
18	Texas	(9.9)		42	New Jersey	(27.3)
36	Utah	(19.4)		44	Iowa	(28.0)
48	Vermont	(34.7)		45	New Mexico	(31.3)
17	Virginia	(9.6)		46	California	(32.9)
29	Washington	(16.1)		47	Minnesota	(34.3)
4	West Virginia	9.0		48	Vermont	(34.7)
34	Wisconsin	(19.0)		49	Connecticut	(35.4)
5	Wyoming	4.5		50	New Hampshire	(41.9)
					District of Columbia	(48.4)

*Source: Morgan Quitno Press using data from US Dept of Health & Human Services, National Center for Health Statistics
"National Vital Statistics Reports" (Vol. 53, No. 21, June 28, 2005)
"Monthly Vital Statistics Report" (Vol. 45, No. 3(S), September 30, 1996)*
*By state of residence. Infant deaths are those occurring under 1 year, exclusive of fetal deaths.

Infant Deaths in 2002

National Total = 28,034 Infant Deaths*

ALPHA ORDER

RANK	STATE	DEATHS	% of USA
19	Alabama	539	1.9%
47	Alaska	55	0.2%
17	Arizona	559	2.0%
29	Arkansas	312	1.1%
1	California	2,889	10.3%
24	Colorado	415	1.5%
31	Connecticut	274	1.0%
41	Delaware	96	0.3%
3	Florida	1,548	5.5%
6	Georgia	1,192	4.3%
40	Hawaii	127	0.5%
39	Idaho	128	0.5%
5	Illinois	1,339	4.8%
14	Indiana	657	2.3%
34	Iowa	199	0.7%
30	Kansas	281	1.0%
27	Kentucky	392	1.4%
13	Louisiana	665	2.4%
46	Maine	59	0.2%
18	Maryland	551	2.0%
26	Massachusetts	395	1.4%
9	Michigan	1,057	3.8%
28	Minnesota	364	1.3%
23	Mississippi	428	1.5%
16	Missouri	637	2.3%
43	Montana	83	0.3%
37	Nebraska	178	0.6%
35	Nevada	197	0.7%
44	New Hampshire	72	0.3%
15	New Jersey	655	2.3%
38	New Mexico	174	0.6%
4	New York	1,519	5.4%
10	North Carolina	959	3.4%
48	North Dakota	49	0.2%
7	Ohio	1,180	4.2%
25	Oklahoma	410	1.5%
33	Oregon	260	0.9%
8	Pennsylvania	1,091	3.9%
42	Rhode Island	90	0.3%
20	South Carolina	507	1.8%
45	South Dakota	70	0.2%
12	Tennessee	727	2.6%
2	Texas	2,368	8.4%
32	Utah	273	1.0%
50	Vermont	28	0.1%
11	Virginia	741	2.6%
22	Washington	456	1.6%
36	West Virginia	188	0.7%
21	Wisconsin	472	1.7%
49	Wyoming	44	0.2%

RANK ORDER

RANK	STATE	DEATHS	% of USA
1	California	2,889	10.3%
2	Texas	2,368	8.4%
3	Florida	1,548	5.5%
4	New York	1,519	5.4%
5	Illinois	1,339	4.8%
6	Georgia	1,192	4.3%
7	Ohio	1,180	4.2%
8	Pennsylvania	1,091	3.9%
9	Michigan	1,057	3.8%
10	North Carolina	959	3.4%
11	Virginia	741	2.6%
12	Tennessee	727	2.6%
13	Louisiana	665	2.4%
14	Indiana	657	2.3%
15	New Jersey	655	2.3%
16	Missouri	637	2.3%
17	Arizona	559	2.0%
18	Maryland	551	2.0%
19	Alabama	539	1.9%
20	South Carolina	507	1.8%
21	Wisconsin	472	1.7%
22	Washington	456	1.6%
23	Mississippi	428	1.5%
24	Colorado	415	1.5%
25	Oklahoma	410	1.5%
26	Massachusetts	395	1.4%
27	Kentucky	392	1.4%
28	Minnesota	364	1.3%
29	Arkansas	312	1.1%
30	Kansas	281	1.0%
31	Connecticut	274	1.0%
32	Utah	273	1.0%
33	Oregon	260	0.9%
34	Iowa	199	0.7%
35	Nevada	197	0.7%
36	West Virginia	188	0.7%
37	Nebraska	178	0.6%
38	New Mexico	174	0.6%
39	Idaho	128	0.5%
40	Hawaii	127	0.5%
41	Delaware	96	0.3%
42	Rhode Island	90	0.3%
43	Montana	83	0.3%
44	New Hampshire	72	0.3%
45	South Dakota	70	0.2%
46	Maine	59	0.2%
47	Alaska	55	0.2%
48	North Dakota	49	0.2%
49	Wyoming	44	0.2%
50	Vermont	28	0.1%
	District of Columbia	85	0.3%

Source: U.S. Department of Health and Human Services, National Center for Health Statistics
   "National Vital Statistics Reports" (Vol. 53, No. 5, October 12, 2004)
*Final data. Deaths under 1 year old by state of residence.

Infant Mortality Rate in 2002

National Rate = 7.0 Infant Deaths per 1,000 Live Births*

ALPHA ORDER

RANK	STATE	RATE
5	Alabama	9.1
43	Alaska	5.5
31	Arizona	6.4
10	Arkansas	8.3
43	California	5.5
35	Colorado	6.1
29	Connecticut	6.5
8	Delaware	8.7
17	Florida	7.5
7	Georgia	8.9
22	Hawaii	7.3
35	Idaho	6.1
20	Illinois	7.4
15	Indiana	7.7
46	Iowa	5.3
24	Kansas	7.1
23	Kentucky	7.2
1	Louisiana	10.3
49	Maine	4.4
17	Maryland	7.5
48	Massachusetts	4.9
12	Michigan	8.1
45	Minnesota	5.4
1	Mississippi	10.3
9	Missouri	8.5
17	Montana	7.5
25	Nebraska	7.0
37	Nevada	6.0
47	New Hampshire	5.0
41	New Jersey	5.7
33	New Mexico	6.3
37	New York	6.0
11	North Carolina	8.2
33	North Dakota	6.3
14	Ohio	7.9
12	Oklahoma	8.1
39	Oregon	5.8
16	Pennsylvania	7.6
25	Rhode Island	7.0
4	South Carolina	9.3
29	South Dakota	6.5
3	Tennessee	9.4
31	Texas	6.4
42	Utah	5.6
49	Vermont	4.4
20	Virginia	7.4
39	Washington	5.8
5	West Virginia	9.1
27	Wisconsin	6.9
28	Wyoming	6.7

RANK ORDER

RANK	STATE	RATE
1	Louisiana	10.3
1	Mississippi	10.3
3	Tennessee	9.4
4	South Carolina	9.3
5	Alabama	9.1
5	West Virginia	9.1
7	Georgia	8.9
8	Delaware	8.7
9	Missouri	8.5
10	Arkansas	8.3
11	North Carolina	8.2
12	Michigan	8.1
12	Oklahoma	8.1
14	Ohio	7.9
15	Indiana	7.7
16	Pennsylvania	7.6
17	Florida	7.5
17	Maryland	7.5
17	Montana	7.5
20	Illinois	7.4
20	Virginia	7.4
22	Hawaii	7.3
23	Kentucky	7.2
24	Kansas	7.1
25	Nebraska	7.0
25	Rhode Island	7.0
27	Wisconsin	6.9
28	Wyoming	6.7
29	Connecticut	6.5
29	South Dakota	6.5
31	Arizona	6.4
31	Texas	6.4
33	New Mexico	6.3
33	North Dakota	6.3
35	Colorado	6.1
35	Idaho	6.1
37	Nevada	6.0
37	New York	6.0
39	Oregon	5.8
39	Washington	5.8
41	New Jersey	5.7
42	Utah	5.6
43	Alaska	5.5
43	California	5.5
45	Minnesota	5.4
46	Iowa	5.3
47	New Hampshire	5.0
48	Massachusetts	4.9
49	Maine	4.4
49	Vermont	4.4
	District of Columbia	11.3

Source: U.S. Department of Health and Human Services, National Center for Health Statistics
"National Vital Statistics Reports" (Vol. 53, No. 5, October 12, 2004)
*Final data. Deaths under 1 year old by state of residence.

White Infant Deaths in 2002

National Total = 18,369 Deaths*

ALPHA ORDER

ALPHA ORDER

RANK ORDER

RANK	STATE	DEATHS	% of USA
23	Alabama	283	1.5%
49	Alaska	27	0.1%
12	Arizona	475	2.6%
31	Arkansas	201	1.1%
1	California	2,212	12.0%
18	Colorado	342	1.9%
32	Connecticut	191	1.0%
43	Delaware	58	0.3%
4	Florida	893	4.9%
9	Georgia	569	3.1%
50	Hawaii	18	0.1%
39	Idaho	123	0.7%
5	Illinois	780	4.2%
11	Indiana	503	2.7%
33	Iowa	179	1.0%
29	Kansas	228	1.2%
20	Kentucky	318	1.7%
26	Louisiana	253	1.4%
44	Maine	56	0.3%
27	Maryland	240	1.3%
21	Massachusetts	302	1.6%
8	Michigan	619	3.4%
22	Minnesota	290	1.6%
35	Mississippi	155	0.8%
13	Missouri	443	2.4%
42	Montana	68	0.4%
36	Nebraska	141	0.8%
37	Nevada	138	0.8%
40	New Hampshire	72	0.4%
16	New Jersey	382	2.1%
38	New Mexico	132	0.7%
3	New York	977	5.3%
10	North Carolina	505	2.7%
47	North Dakota	38	0.2%
7	Ohio	761	4.1%
24	Oklahoma	279	1.5%
28	Oregon	229	1.2%
6	Pennsylvania	772	4.2%
41	Rhode Island	71	0.4%
30	South Carolina	213	1.2%
45	South Dakota	42	0.2%
14	Tennessee	419	2.3%
2	Texas	1,773	9.7%
25	Utah	255	1.4%
48	Vermont	28	0.2%
15	Virginia	394	2.1%
17	Washington	366	2.0%
34	West Virginia	169	0.9%
19	Wisconsin	329	1.8%
45	Wyoming	42	0.2%

RANK	STATE	DEATHS	% of USA
1	California	2,212	12.0%
2	Texas	1,773	9.7%
3	New York	977	5.3%
4	Florida	893	4.9%
5	Illinois	780	4.2%
6	Pennsylvania	772	4.2%
7	Ohio	761	4.1%
8	Michigan	619	3.4%
9	Georgia	569	3.1%
10	North Carolina	505	2.7%
11	Indiana	503	2.7%
12	Arizona	475	2.6%
13	Missouri	443	2.4%
14	Tennessee	419	2.3%
15	Virginia	394	2.1%
16	New Jersey	382	2.1%
17	Washington	366	2.0%
18	Colorado	342	1.9%
19	Wisconsin	329	1.8%
20	Kentucky	318	1.7%
21	Massachusetts	302	1.6%
22	Minnesota	290	1.6%
23	Alabama	283	1.5%
24	Oklahoma	279	1.5%
25	Utah	255	1.4%
26	Louisiana	253	1.4%
27	Maryland	240	1.3%
28	Oregon	229	1.2%
29	Kansas	228	1.2%
30	South Carolina	213	1.2%
31	Arkansas	201	1.1%
32	Connecticut	191	1.0%
33	Iowa	179	1.0%
34	West Virginia	169	0.9%
35	Mississippi	155	0.8%
36	Nebraska	141	0.8%
37	Nevada	138	0.8%
38	New Mexico	132	0.7%
39	Idaho	123	0.7%
40	New Hampshire	72	0.4%
41	Rhode Island	71	0.4%
42	Montana	68	0.4%
43	Delaware	58	0.3%
44	Maine	56	0.3%
45	South Dakota	42	0.2%
45	Wyoming	42	0.2%
47	North Dakota	38	0.2%
48	Vermont	28	0.2%
49	Alaska	27	0.1%
50	Hawaii	18	0.1%
	District of Columbia	16	0.1%

*Source: U.S. Department of Health and Human Services, National Center for Health Statistics
"National Vital Statistics Reports" (Vol. 53, No. 5, October 12, 2004)*
Final data. Deaths of infants under 1 year old, exclusive of fetal deaths. Based on race of the mother.

White Infant Mortality Rate in 2002

National Rate = 5.8 White Infant Deaths per 1,000 White Live Births*

ALPHA ORDER

RANK	STATE	RATE
3	Alabama	7.1
49	Alaska	4.2
18	Arizona	6.2
8	Arkansas	6.9
40	California	5.2
32	Colorado	5.5
32	Connecticut	5.5
2	Delaware	7.3
25	Florida	5.8
13	Georgia	6.6
NA	Hawaii**	NA
20	Idaho	6.1
27	Illinois	5.6
11	Indiana	6.8
41	Iowa	5.1
16	Kansas	6.5
13	Kentucky	6.6
8	Louisiana	6.9
48	Maine	4.3
38	Maryland	5.3
45	Massachusetts	4.5
22	Michigan	6.0
43	Minnesota	5.0
8	Mississippi	6.9
3	Missouri	7.1
3	Montana	7.1
20	Nebraska	6.1
41	Nevada	5.1
38	New Hampshire	5.3
45	New Jersey	4.5
26	New Mexico	5.7
37	New York	5.4
24	North Carolina	5.9
27	North Dakota	5.6
18	Ohio	6.2
3	Oklahoma	7.1
27	Oregon	5.6
13	Pennsylvania	6.6
17	Rhode Island	6.4
22	South Carolina	6.0
44	South Dakota	4.9
7	Tennessee	7.0
27	Texas	5.6
32	Utah	5.5
45	Vermont	4.5
32	Virginia	5.5
32	Washington	5.5
1	West Virginia	8.5
27	Wisconsin	5.6
11	Wyoming	6.8

RANK ORDER

RANK	STATE	RATE
1	West Virginia	8.5
2	Delaware	7.3
3	Alabama	7.1
3	Missouri	7.1
3	Montana	7.1
3	Oklahoma	7.1
7	Tennessee	7.0
8	Arkansas	6.9
8	Louisiana	6.9
8	Mississippi	6.9
11	Indiana	6.8
11	Wyoming	6.8
13	Georgia	6.6
13	Kentucky	6.6
13	Pennsylvania	6.6
16	Kansas	6.5
17	Rhode Island	6.4
18	Arizona	6.2
18	Ohio	6.2
20	Idaho	6.1
20	Nebraska	6.1
22	Michigan	6.0
22	South Carolina	6.0
24	North Carolina	5.9
25	Florida	5.8
26	New Mexico	5.7
27	Illinois	5.6
27	North Dakota	5.6
27	Oregon	5.6
27	Texas	5.6
27	Wisconsin	5.6
32	Colorado	5.5
32	Connecticut	5.5
32	Utah	5.5
32	Virginia	5.5
32	Washington	5.5
37	New York	5.4
38	Maryland	5.3
38	New Hampshire	5.3
40	California	5.2
41	Iowa	5.1
41	Nevada	5.1
43	Minnesota	5.0
44	South Dakota	4.9
45	Massachusetts	4.5
45	New Jersey	4.5
45	Vermont	4.5
48	Maine	4.3
49	Alaska	4.2
NA	Hawaii**	NA
	District of Columbia**	NA

Source: U.S. Department of Health and Human Services, National Center for Health Statistics
   "National Vital Statistics Reports" (Vol. 53, No. 5, October 12, 2004)
*Final data. Deaths of infants under 1 year old, exclusive of fetal deaths. Based on race of the mother.
**Not available, fewer than 20 white infant deaths.

Black Infant Deaths in 2002

National Total = 8,524 Deaths*

ALPHA ORDER

RANK	STATE	DEATHS	% of USA
17	Alabama	255	3.0%
41	Alaska	6	0.1%
32	Arizona	36	0.4%
22	Arkansas	103	1.2%
7	California	420	4.9%
27	Colorado	62	0.7%
25	Connecticut	74	0.9%
33	Delaware	35	0.4%
1	Florida	629	7.4%
2	Georgia	588	6.9%
40	Hawaii	7	0.1%
46	Idaho	1	0.0%
4	Illinois	519	6.1%
20	Indiana	143	1.7%
36	Iowa	17	0.2%
30	Kansas	44	0.5%
26	Kentucky	70	0.8%
9	Louisiana	401	4.7%
46	Maine	1	0.0%
14	Maryland	298	3.5%
24	Massachusetts	76	0.9%
8	Michigan	416	4.9%
28	Minnesota	50	0.6%
16	Mississippi	269	3.2%
19	Missouri	189	2.2%
43	Montana	3	0.0%
34	Nebraska	30	0.4%
29	Nevada	48	0.6%
48	New Hampshire	0	0.0%
17	New Jersey	255	3.0%
39	New Mexico	11	0.1%
5	New York	493	5.8%
6	North Carolina	430	5.0%
45	North Dakota	2	0.0%
10	Ohio	400	4.7%
23	Oklahoma	81	1.0%
38	Oregon	13	0.2%
12	Pennsylvania	305	3.6%
37	Rhode Island	15	0.2%
15	South Carolina	287	3.4%
43	South Dakota	3	0.0%
13	Tennessee	299	3.5%
3	Texas	561	6.6%
41	Utah	6	0.1%
48	Vermont	0	0.0%
11	Virginia	323	3.8%
31	Washington	43	0.5%
35	West Virginia	19	0.2%
21	Wisconsin	121	1.4%
48	Wyoming	0	0.0%

RANK ORDER

RANK	STATE	DEATHS	% of USA
1	Florida	629	7.4%
2	Georgia	588	6.9%
3	Texas	561	6.6%
4	Illinois	519	6.1%
5	New York	493	5.8%
6	North Carolina	430	5.0%
7	California	420	4.9%
8	Michigan	416	4.9%
9	Louisiana	401	4.7%
10	Ohio	400	4.7%
11	Virginia	323	3.8%
12	Pennsylvania	305	3.6%
13	Tennessee	299	3.5%
14	Maryland	298	3.5%
15	South Carolina	287	3.4%
16	Mississippi	269	3.2%
17	Alabama	255	3.0%
17	New Jersey	255	3.0%
19	Missouri	189	2.2%
20	Indiana	143	1.7%
21	Wisconsin	121	1.4%
22	Arkansas	103	1.2%
23	Oklahoma	81	1.0%
24	Massachusetts	76	0.9%
25	Connecticut	74	0.9%
26	Kentucky	70	0.8%
27	Colorado	62	0.7%
28	Minnesota	50	0.6%
29	Nevada	48	0.6%
30	Kansas	44	0.5%
31	Washington	43	0.5%
32	Arizona	36	0.4%
33	Delaware	35	0.4%
34	Nebraska	30	0.4%
35	West Virginia	19	0.2%
36	Iowa	17	0.2%
37	Rhode Island	15	0.2%
38	Oregon	13	0.2%
39	New Mexico	11	0.1%
40	Hawaii	7	0.1%
41	Alaska	6	0.1%
41	Utah	6	0.1%
43	Montana	3	0.0%
43	South Dakota	3	0.0%
45	North Dakota	2	0.0%
46	Idaho	1	0.0%
46	Maine	1	0.0%
48	New Hampshire	0	0.0%
48	Vermont	0	0.0%
48	Wyoming	0	0.0%
	District of Columbia	67	0.8%

Source: U.S. Department of Health and Human Services, National Center for Health Statistics
"National Vital Statistics Reports" (Vol. 53, No. 5, October 12, 2004)
Final data. Deaths of infants under 1 year old, exclusive of fetal deaths. Based on race of the mother.

Black Infant Mortality Rate in 2002

National Rate = 14.4 Black Infant Deaths per 1,000 Black Live Births*

ALPHA ORDER				RANK ORDER		
RANK	STATE	RATE		RANK	STATE	RATE
21	Alabama	13.9		1	Colorado	21.1
NA	Alaska**	NA		2	Nebraska	20.8
26	Arizona	13.0		3	Wisconsin	18.9
21	Arkansas	13.9		4	Michigan	18.5
27	California	12.9		5	Nevada	18.4
1	Colorado	21.1		6	Tennessee	18.3
19	Connecticut	14.2		7	Ohio	17.7
27	Delaware	12.9		8	Oklahoma	17.2
24	Florida	13.6		9	Missouri	17.1
23	Georgia	13.7		10	Illinois	16.3
NA	Hawaii**	NA		11	South Carolina	15.8
NA	Idaho**	NA		12	North Carolina	15.6
10	Illinois	16.3		13	Indiana	15.3
13	Indiana	15.3		14	Kansas	15.2
NA	Iowa**	NA		15	Pennsylvania	15.1
14	Kansas	15.2		16	Louisiana	15.0
19	Kentucky	14.2		17	Mississippi	14.8
16	Louisiana	15.0		18	Virginia	14.6
NA	Maine**	NA		19	Connecticut	14.2
31	Maryland	12.3		19	Kentucky	14.2
34	Massachusetts	9.1		21	Alabama	13.9
4	Michigan	18.5		21	Arkansas	13.9
32	Minnesota	10.3		23	Georgia	13.7
17	Mississippi	14.8		24	Florida	13.6
9	Missouri	17.1		25	Texas	13.5
NA	Montana**	NA		26	Arizona	13.0
2	Nebraska	20.8		27	California	12.9
5	Nevada	18.4		27	Delaware	12.9
NA	New Hampshire**	NA		29	New Jersey	12.8
29	New Jersey	12.8		30	Washington	12.7
NA	New Mexico**	NA		31	Maryland	12.3
33	New York	9.9		32	Minnesota	10.3
12	North Carolina	15.6		33	New York	9.9
NA	North Dakota**	NA		34	Massachusetts	9.1
7	Ohio	17.7		NA	Alaska**	NA
8	Oklahoma	17.2		NA	Hawaii**	NA
NA	Oregon**	NA		NA	Idaho**	NA
15	Pennsylvania	15.1		NA	Iowa**	NA
NA	Rhode Island**	NA		NA	Maine**	NA
11	South Carolina	15.8		NA	Montana**	NA
NA	South Dakota**	NA		NA	New Hampshire**	NA
6	Tennessee	18.3		NA	New Mexico**	NA
25	Texas	13.5		NA	North Dakota**	NA
NA	Utah**	NA		NA	Oregon**	NA
NA	Vermont**	NA		NA	Rhode Island**	NA
18	Virginia	14.6		NA	South Dakota**	NA
30	Washington	12.7		NA	Utah**	NA
NA	West Virginia**	NA		NA	Vermont**	NA
3	Wisconsin	18.9		NA	West Virginia**	NA
NA	Wyoming**	NA		NA	Wyoming**	NA
					District of Columbia	14.5

Source: U.S. Department of Health and Human Services, National Center for Health Statistics
   "National Vital Statistics Reports" (Vol. 53, No. 5, October 12, 2004)
*Final data. Deaths of infants under 1 year old, exclusive of fetal deaths. Based on race of the mother.
**Not available, fewer than 20 black infant deaths.

Neonatal Deaths in 2002

National Total = 18,747 Deaths*

ALPHA ORDER

RANK ORDER

RANK	STATE	DEATHS	% of USA
20	Alabama	345	1.8%
49	Alaska	20	0.1%
18	Arizona	361	1.9%
30	Arkansas	191	1.0%
1	California	1,934	10.3%
25	Colorado	275	1.5%
29	Connecticut	198	1.1%
41	Delaware	78	0.4%
4	Florida	1,032	5.5%
8	Georgia	792	4.2%
40	Hawaii	83	0.4%
39	Idaho	84	0.4%
5	Illinois	911	4.9%
14	Indiana	448	2.4%
34	Iowa	134	0.7%
30	Kansas	191	1.0%
28	Kentucky	228	1.2%
15	Louisiana	429	2.3%
45	Maine	43	0.2%
17	Maryland	394	2.1%
22	Massachusetts	298	1.6%
9	Michigan	720	3.8%
27	Minnesota	240	1.3%
24	Mississippi	281	1.5%
16	Missouri	417	2.2%
43	Montana	54	0.3%
36	Nebraska	121	0.6%
35	Nevada	126	0.7%
44	New Hampshire	51	0.3%
12	New Jersey	471	2.5%
37	New Mexico	120	0.6%
3	New York	1,074	5.7%
10	North Carolina	659	3.5%
47	North Dakota	32	0.2%
6	Ohio	800	4.3%
26	Oklahoma	257	1.4%
33	Oregon	172	0.9%
6	Pennsylvania	800	4.3%
42	Rhode Island	62	0.3%
19	South Carolina	346	1.8%
46	South Dakota	38	0.2%
13	Tennessee	456	2.4%
2	Texas	1,451	7.7%
32	Utah	186	1.0%
50	Vermont	19	0.1%
11	Virginia	513	2.7%
23	Washington	291	1.6%
38	West Virginia	109	0.6%
21	Wisconsin	330	1.8%
48	Wyoming	25	0.1%

RANK	STATE	DEATHS	% of USA
1	California	1,934	10.3%
2	Texas	1,451	7.7%
3	New York	1,074	5.7%
4	Florida	1,032	5.5%
5	Illinois	911	4.9%
6	Ohio	800	4.3%
6	Pennsylvania	800	4.3%
8	Georgia	792	4.2%
9	Michigan	720	3.8%
10	North Carolina	659	3.5%
11	Virginia	513	2.7%
12	New Jersey	471	2.5%
13	Tennessee	456	2.4%
14	Indiana	448	2.4%
15	Louisiana	429	2.3%
16	Missouri	417	2.2%
17	Maryland	394	2.1%
18	Arizona	361	1.9%
19	South Carolina	346	1.8%
20	Alabama	345	1.8%
21	Wisconsin	330	1.8%
22	Massachusetts	298	1.6%
23	Washington	291	1.6%
24	Mississippi	281	1.5%
25	Colorado	275	1.5%
26	Oklahoma	257	1.4%
27	Minnesota	240	1.3%
28	Kentucky	228	1.2%
29	Connecticut	198	1.1%
30	Arkansas	191	1.0%
30	Kansas	191	1.0%
32	Utah	186	1.0%
33	Oregon	172	0.9%
34	Iowa	134	0.7%
35	Nevada	126	0.7%
36	Nebraska	121	0.6%
37	New Mexico	120	0.6%
38	West Virginia	109	0.6%
39	Idaho	84	0.4%
40	Hawaii	83	0.4%
41	Delaware	78	0.4%
42	Rhode Island	62	0.3%
43	Montana	54	0.3%
44	New Hampshire	51	0.3%
45	Maine	43	0.2%
46	South Dakota	38	0.2%
47	North Dakota	32	0.2%
48	Wyoming	25	0.1%
49	Alaska	20	0.1%
50	Vermont	19	0.1%
	District of Columbia	57	0.3%

Source: U.S. Department of Health and Human Services, National Center for Health Statistics
"National Vital Statistics Reports" (Vol. 53, No. 5, October 12, 2004)
*Final data. Deaths of infants under 28 days, exclusive of fetal deaths.

Neonatal Death Rate in 2002

National Rate = 4.7 Deaths per 1,000 Live Births*

ALPHA ORDER

RANK	STATE	RATE
5	Alabama	5.9
49	Alaska	2.0
31	Arizona	4.1
16	Arkansas	5.1
41	California	3.7
34	Colorado	4.0
26	Connecticut	4.7
1	Delaware	7.0
19	Florida	5.0
5	Georgia	5.9
26	Hawaii	4.7
34	Idaho	4.0
19	Illinois	5.0
14	Indiana	5.3
44	Iowa	3.6
22	Kansas	4.8
30	Kentucky	4.2
3	Louisiana	6.6
48	Maine	3.2
12	Maryland	5.4
41	Massachusetts	3.7
10	Michigan	5.5
46	Minnesota	3.5
2	Mississippi	6.8
10	Missouri	5.5
21	Montana	4.9
22	Nebraska	4.8
36	Nevada	3.9
46	New Hampshire	3.5
31	New Jersey	4.1
28	New Mexico	4.3
28	New York	4.3
8	North Carolina	5.6
31	North Dakota	4.1
12	Ohio	5.4
16	Oklahoma	5.1
38	Oregon	3.8
8	Pennsylvania	5.6
22	Rhode Island	4.8
4	South Carolina	6.3
44	South Dakota	3.6
5	Tennessee	5.9
36	Texas	3.9
38	Utah	3.8
NA	Vermont**	NA
16	Virginia	5.1
41	Washington	3.7
14	West Virginia	5.3
22	Wisconsin	4.8
38	Wyoming	3.8

RANK ORDER

RANK	STATE	RATE
1	Delaware	7.0
2	Mississippi	6.8
3	Louisiana	6.6
4	South Carolina	6.3
5	Alabama	5.9
5	Georgia	5.9
5	Tennessee	5.9
8	North Carolina	5.6
8	Pennsylvania	5.6
10	Michigan	5.5
10	Missouri	5.5
12	Maryland	5.4
12	Ohio	5.4
14	Indiana	5.3
14	West Virginia	5.3
16	Arkansas	5.1
16	Oklahoma	5.1
16	Virginia	5.1
19	Florida	5.0
19	Illinois	5.0
21	Montana	4.9
22	Kansas	4.8
22	Nebraska	4.8
22	Rhode Island	4.8
22	Wisconsin	4.8
26	Connecticut	4.7
26	Hawaii	4.7
28	New Mexico	4.3
28	New York	4.3
30	Kentucky	4.2
31	Arizona	4.1
31	New Jersey	4.1
31	North Dakota	4.1
34	Colorado	4.0
34	Idaho	4.0
36	Nevada	3.9
36	Texas	3.9
38	Oregon	3.8
38	Utah	3.8
38	Wyoming	3.8
41	California	3.7
41	Massachusetts	3.7
41	Washington	3.7
44	Iowa	3.6
44	South Dakota	3.6
46	Minnesota	3.5
46	New Hampshire	3.5
48	Maine	3.2
49	Alaska	2.0
NA	Vermont**	NA

District of Columbia   7.6

Source: U.S. Department of Health and Human Services, National Center for Health Statistics
    "National Vital Statistics Reports" (Vol. 53, No. 5, October 12, 2004)
*Final data. Deaths of infants under 28 days, exclusive of fetal deaths.
**Not available. Fewer than 20 neonatal deaths.

White Neonatal Deaths in 2002

National Total = 12,354 Deaths*

ALPHA ORDER

RANK	STATE	DEATHS	% of USA
23	Alabama	182	1.5%
50	Alaska	11	0.1%
12	Arizona	318	2.6%
32	Arkansas	123	1.0%
1	California	1,505	12.2%
20	Colorado	227	1.8%
30	Connecticut	144	1.2%
41	Delaware	48	0.4%
4	Florida	596	4.8%
9	Georgia	360	2.9%
49	Hawaii	12	0.1%
39	Idaho	82	0.7%
6	Illinois	557	4.5%
10	Indiana	347	2.8%
32	Iowa	123	1.0%
29	Kansas	155	1.3%
22	Kentucky	193	1.6%
27	Louisiana	162	1.3%
44	Maine	41	0.3%
24	Maryland	178	1.4%
17	Massachusetts	234	1.9%
8	Michigan	430	3.5%
21	Minnesota	205	1.7%
35	Mississippi	99	0.8%
13	Missouri	292	2.4%
43	Montana	45	0.4%
36	Nebraska	96	0.8%
38	Nevada	90	0.7%
40	New Hampshire	51	0.4%
14	New Jersey	273	2.2%
37	New Mexico	92	0.7%
3	New York	709	5.7%
11	North Carolina	326	2.6%
45	North Dakota	25	0.2%
7	Ohio	512	4.1%
26	Oklahoma	172	1.4%
28	Oregon	158	1.3%
5	Pennsylvania	581	4.7%
41	Rhode Island	48	0.4%
31	South Carolina	138	1.1%
45	South Dakota	25	0.2%
16	Tennessee	250	2.0%
2	Texas	1,082	8.8%
25	Utah	176	1.4%
48	Vermont	19	0.2%
15	Virginia	260	2.1%
19	Washington	230	1.9%
34	West Virginia	100	0.8%
17	Wisconsin	234	1.9%
47	Wyoming	24	0.2%

RANK ORDER

RANK	STATE	DEATHS	% of USA
1	California	1,505	12.2%
2	Texas	1,082	8.8%
3	New York	709	5.7%
4	Florida	596	4.8%
5	Pennsylvania	581	4.7%
6	Illinois	557	4.5%
7	Ohio	512	4.1%
8	Michigan	430	3.5%
9	Georgia	360	2.9%
10	Indiana	347	2.8%
11	North Carolina	326	2.6%
12	Arizona	318	2.6%
13	Missouri	292	2.4%
14	New Jersey	273	2.2%
15	Virginia	260	2.1%
16	Tennessee	250	2.0%
17	Massachusetts	234	1.9%
17	Wisconsin	234	1.9%
19	Washington	230	1.9%
20	Colorado	227	1.8%
21	Minnesota	205	1.7%
22	Kentucky	193	1.6%
23	Alabama	182	1.5%
24	Maryland	178	1.4%
25	Utah	176	1.4%
26	Oklahoma	172	1.4%
27	Louisiana	162	1.3%
28	Oregon	158	1.3%
29	Kansas	155	1.3%
30	Connecticut	144	1.2%
31	South Carolina	138	1.1%
32	Arkansas	123	1.0%
32	Iowa	123	1.0%
34	West Virginia	100	0.8%
35	Mississippi	99	0.8%
36	Nebraska	96	0.8%
37	New Mexico	92	0.7%
38	Nevada	90	0.7%
39	Idaho	82	0.7%
40	New Hampshire	51	0.4%
41	Delaware	48	0.4%
41	Rhode Island	48	0.4%
43	Montana	45	0.4%
44	Maine	41	0.3%
45	North Dakota	25	0.2%
45	South Dakota	25	0.2%
47	Wyoming	24	0.2%
48	Vermont	19	0.2%
49	Hawaii	12	0.1%
50	Alaska	11	0.1%
	District of Columbia	14	0.1%

Source: U.S. Department of Health and Human Services, National Center for Health Statistics
"National Vital Statistics Reports" (Vol. 53, No. 5, October 12, 2004)
*Final data. Deaths of infants under 28 days, exclusive of fetal deaths. Based on race of the mother.

White Neonatal Death Rate in 2002

National Rate = 3.9 White Neonatal Deaths per 1,000 White Live Births*

RANK	STATE	RATE
7	Alabama	4.6
NA	Alaska**	NA
20	Arizona	4.1
13	Arkansas	4.2
38	California	3.5
36	Colorado	3.6
13	Connecticut	4.2
1	Delaware	6.1
26	Florida	3.9
13	Georgia	4.2
NA	Hawaii**	NA
20	Idaho	4.1
22	Illinois	4.0
4	Indiana	4.7
38	Iowa	3.5
8	Kansas	4.4
22	Kentucky	4.0
8	Louisiana	4.4
46	Maine	3.1
26	Maryland	3.9
38	Massachusetts	3.5
13	Michigan	4.2
38	Minnesota	3.5
8	Mississippi	4.4
4	Missouri	4.7
4	Montana	4.7
13	Nebraska	4.2
44	Nevada	3.3
34	New Hampshire	3.7
45	New Jersey	3.2
22	New Mexico	4.0
26	New York	3.9
31	North Carolina	3.8
34	North Dakota	3.7
13	Ohio	4.2
8	Oklahoma	4.4
31	Oregon	3.8
3	Pennsylvania	4.9
12	Rhode Island	4.3
26	South Carolina	3.9
47	South Dakota	2.9
13	Tennessee	4.2
43	Texas	3.4
31	Utah	3.8
NA	Vermont**	NA
36	Virginia	3.6
38	Washington	3.5
2	West Virginia	5.0
22	Wisconsin	4.0
26	Wyoming	3.9

RANK	STATE	RATE
1	Delaware	6.1
2	West Virginia	5.0
3	Pennsylvania	4.9
4	Indiana	4.7
4	Missouri	4.7
4	Montana	4.7
7	Alabama	4.6
8	Kansas	4.4
8	Louisiana	4.4
8	Mississippi	4.4
8	Oklahoma	4.4
12	Rhode Island	4.3
13	Arkansas	4.2
13	Connecticut	4.2
13	Georgia	4.2
13	Michigan	4.2
13	Nebraska	4.2
13	Ohio	4.2
13	Tennessee	4.2
20	Arizona	4.1
20	Idaho	4.1
22	Illinois	4.0
22	Kentucky	4.0
22	New Mexico	4.0
22	Wisconsin	4.0
26	Florida	3.9
26	Maryland	3.9
26	New York	3.9
26	South Carolina	3.9
26	Wyoming	3.9
31	North Carolina	3.8
31	Oregon	3.8
31	Utah	3.8
34	New Hampshire	3.7
34	North Dakota	3.7
36	Colorado	3.6
36	Virginia	3.6
38	California	3.5
38	Iowa	3.5
38	Massachusetts	3.5
38	Minnesota	3.5
38	Washington	3.5
43	Texas	3.4
44	Nevada	3.3
45	New Jersey	3.2
46	Maine	3.1
47	South Dakota	2.9
NA	Alaska**	NA
NA	Hawaii**	NA
NA	Vermont**	NA
	District of Columbia**	NA

Source: U.S. Department of Health and Human Services, National Center for Health Statistics
    "National Vital Statistics Reports" (Vol. 53, No. 5, October 12, 2004)
Final data. Deaths of infants under 28 days, exclusive of fetal deaths. Based on race of the mother.
**Not available. Fewer than 20 white neonatal deaths.*

Black Neonatal Deaths in 2002

National Total = 5,646 Deaths*

<table>
<tr><th colspan="4">ALPHA ORDER</th><th colspan="4">RANK ORDER</th></tr>
<tr><th>RANK</th><th>STATE</th><th>DEATHS</th><th>% of USA</th><th>RANK</th><th>STATE</th><th>DEATHS</th><th>% of USA</th></tr>
<tr><td>18</td><td>Alabama</td><td>163</td><td>2.9%</td><td>1</td><td>Florida</td><td>419</td><td>7.4%</td></tr>
<tr><td>45</td><td>Alaska</td><td>1</td><td>0.0%</td><td>2</td><td>Georgia</td><td>404</td><td>7.2%</td></tr>
<tr><td>34</td><td>Arizona</td><td>16</td><td>0.3%</td><td>3</td><td>Texas</td><td>347</td><td>6.1%</td></tr>
<tr><td>22</td><td>Arkansas</td><td>62</td><td>1.1%</td><td>4</td><td>New York</td><td>334</td><td>5.9%</td></tr>
<tr><td>9</td><td>California</td><td>260</td><td>4.6%</td><td>5</td><td>Illinois</td><td>324</td><td>5.7%</td></tr>
<tr><td>26</td><td>Colorado</td><td>40</td><td>0.7%</td><td>6</td><td>North Carolina</td><td>318</td><td>5.6%</td></tr>
<tr><td>25</td><td>Connecticut</td><td>47</td><td>0.8%</td><td>7</td><td>Michigan</td><td>272</td><td>4.8%</td></tr>
<tr><td>30</td><td>Delaware</td><td>28</td><td>0.5%</td><td>7</td><td>Ohio</td><td>272</td><td>4.8%</td></tr>
<tr><td>1</td><td>Florida</td><td>419</td><td>7.4%</td><td>9</td><td>California</td><td>260</td><td>4.6%</td></tr>
<tr><td>2</td><td>Georgia</td><td>404</td><td>7.2%</td><td>10</td><td>Louisiana</td><td>259</td><td>4.6%</td></tr>
<tr><td>39</td><td>Hawaii</td><td>5</td><td>0.1%</td><td>11</td><td>Virginia</td><td>239</td><td>4.2%</td></tr>
<tr><td>46</td><td>Idaho</td><td>0</td><td>0.0%</td><td>12</td><td>Maryland</td><td>206</td><td>3.6%</td></tr>
<tr><td>5</td><td>Illinois</td><td>324</td><td>5.7%</td><td>12</td><td>Pennsylvania</td><td>206</td><td>3.6%</td></tr>
<tr><td>20</td><td>Indiana</td><td>90</td><td>1.6%</td><td>14</td><td>South Carolina</td><td>203</td><td>3.6%</td></tr>
<tr><td>36</td><td>Iowa</td><td>9</td><td>0.2%</td><td>14</td><td>Tennessee</td><td>203</td><td>3.6%</td></tr>
<tr><td>29</td><td>Kansas</td><td>29</td><td>0.5%</td><td>16</td><td>New Jersey</td><td>184</td><td>3.3%</td></tr>
<tr><td>27</td><td>Kentucky</td><td>33</td><td>0.6%</td><td>17</td><td>Mississippi</td><td>178</td><td>3.2%</td></tr>
<tr><td>10</td><td>Louisiana</td><td>259</td><td>4.6%</td><td>18</td><td>Alabama</td><td>163</td><td>2.9%</td></tr>
<tr><td>46</td><td>Maine</td><td>0</td><td>0.0%</td><td>19</td><td>Missouri</td><td>121</td><td>2.1%</td></tr>
<tr><td>12</td><td>Maryland</td><td>206</td><td>3.6%</td><td>20</td><td>Indiana</td><td>90</td><td>1.6%</td></tr>
<tr><td>24</td><td>Massachusetts</td><td>51</td><td>0.9%</td><td>21</td><td>Wisconsin</td><td>83</td><td>1.5%</td></tr>
<tr><td>7</td><td>Michigan</td><td>272</td><td>4.8%</td><td>22</td><td>Arkansas</td><td>62</td><td>1.1%</td></tr>
<tr><td>32</td><td>Minnesota</td><td>24</td><td>0.4%</td><td>23</td><td>Oklahoma</td><td>52</td><td>0.9%</td></tr>
<tr><td>17</td><td>Mississippi</td><td>178</td><td>3.2%</td><td>24</td><td>Massachusetts</td><td>51</td><td>0.9%</td></tr>
<tr><td>19</td><td>Missouri</td><td>121</td><td>2.1%</td><td>25</td><td>Connecticut</td><td>47</td><td>0.8%</td></tr>
<tr><td>42</td><td>Montana</td><td>2</td><td>0.0%</td><td>26</td><td>Colorado</td><td>40</td><td>0.7%</td></tr>
<tr><td>33</td><td>Nebraska</td><td>22</td><td>0.4%</td><td>27</td><td>Kentucky</td><td>33</td><td>0.6%</td></tr>
<tr><td>30</td><td>Nevada</td><td>28</td><td>0.5%</td><td>28</td><td>Washington</td><td>30</td><td>0.5%</td></tr>
<tr><td>46</td><td>New Hampshire</td><td>0</td><td>0.0%</td><td>29</td><td>Kansas</td><td>29</td><td>0.5%</td></tr>
<tr><td>16</td><td>New Jersey</td><td>184</td><td>3.3%</td><td>30</td><td>Delaware</td><td>28</td><td>0.5%</td></tr>
<tr><td>38</td><td>New Mexico</td><td>7</td><td>0.1%</td><td>30</td><td>Nevada</td><td>28</td><td>0.5%</td></tr>
<tr><td>4</td><td>New York</td><td>334</td><td>5.9%</td><td>32</td><td>Minnesota</td><td>24</td><td>0.4%</td></tr>
<tr><td>6</td><td>North Carolina</td><td>318</td><td>5.6%</td><td>33</td><td>Nebraska</td><td>22</td><td>0.4%</td></tr>
<tr><td>42</td><td>North Dakota</td><td>2</td><td>0.0%</td><td>34</td><td>Arizona</td><td>16</td><td>0.3%</td></tr>
<tr><td>7</td><td>Ohio</td><td>272</td><td>4.8%</td><td>35</td><td>Rhode Island</td><td>11</td><td>0.2%</td></tr>
<tr><td>23</td><td>Oklahoma</td><td>52</td><td>0.9%</td><td>36</td><td>Iowa</td><td>9</td><td>0.2%</td></tr>
<tr><td>39</td><td>Oregon</td><td>5</td><td>0.1%</td><td>36</td><td>West Virginia</td><td>9</td><td>0.2%</td></tr>
<tr><td>12</td><td>Pennsylvania</td><td>206</td><td>3.6%</td><td>38</td><td>New Mexico</td><td>7</td><td>0.1%</td></tr>
<tr><td>35</td><td>Rhode Island</td><td>11</td><td>0.2%</td><td>39</td><td>Hawaii</td><td>5</td><td>0.1%</td></tr>
<tr><td>14</td><td>South Carolina</td><td>203</td><td>3.6%</td><td>39</td><td>Oregon</td><td>5</td><td>0.1%</td></tr>
<tr><td>42</td><td>South Dakota</td><td>2</td><td>0.0%</td><td>41</td><td>Utah</td><td>3</td><td>0.1%</td></tr>
<tr><td>14</td><td>Tennessee</td><td>203</td><td>3.6%</td><td>42</td><td>Montana</td><td>2</td><td>0.0%</td></tr>
<tr><td>3</td><td>Texas</td><td>347</td><td>6.1%</td><td>42</td><td>North Dakota</td><td>2</td><td>0.0%</td></tr>
<tr><td>41</td><td>Utah</td><td>3</td><td>0.1%</td><td>42</td><td>South Dakota</td><td>2</td><td>0.0%</td></tr>
<tr><td>46</td><td>Vermont</td><td>0</td><td>0.0%</td><td>45</td><td>Alaska</td><td>1</td><td>0.0%</td></tr>
<tr><td>11</td><td>Virginia</td><td>239</td><td>4.2%</td><td>46</td><td>Idaho</td><td>0</td><td>0.0%</td></tr>
<tr><td>28</td><td>Washington</td><td>30</td><td>0.5%</td><td>46</td><td>Maine</td><td>0</td><td>0.0%</td></tr>
<tr><td>36</td><td>West Virginia</td><td>9</td><td>0.2%</td><td>46</td><td>New Hampshire</td><td>0</td><td>0.0%</td></tr>
<tr><td>21</td><td>Wisconsin</td><td>83</td><td>1.5%</td><td>46</td><td>Vermont</td><td>0</td><td>0.0%</td></tr>
<tr><td>46</td><td>Wyoming</td><td>0</td><td>0.0%</td><td>46</td><td>Wyoming</td><td>0</td><td>0.0%</td></tr>
<tr><td></td><td></td><td></td><td></td><td></td><td>District of Columbia</td><td>43</td><td>0.8%</td></tr>
</table>

Source: U.S. Department of Health and Human Services, National Center for Health Statistics
   "National Vital Statistics Reports" (Vol. 53, No. 5, October 12, 2004)
*Final data. Deaths of infants under 28 days, exclusive of fetal deaths. Based on race of the mother.

Black Neonatal Death Rate in 2002

National Rate = 9.5 Black Neonatal Deaths per 1,000 Black Live Births*

ALPHA ORDER

RANK	STATE	RATE
24	Alabama	8.9
NA	Alaska**	NA
NA	Arizona**	NA
27	Arkansas	8.3
29	California	8.0
2	Colorado	13.6
23	Connecticut	9.0
13	Delaware	10.3
22	Florida	9.1
20	Georgia	9.4
NA	Hawaii**	NA
NA	Idaho**	NA
14	Illinois	10.2
19	Indiana	9.6
NA	Iowa**	NA
16	Kansas	10.0
30	Kentucky	6.7
18	Louisiana	9.7
NA	Maine**	NA
26	Maryland	8.5
32	Massachusetts	6.1
5	Michigan	12.1
33	Minnesota	4.9
17	Mississippi	9.8
10	Missouri	11.0
NA	Montana**	NA
1	Nebraska	15.3
12	Nevada	10.7
NA	New Hampshire**	NA
21	New Jersey	9.2
NA	New Mexico**	NA
30	New York	6.7
7	North Carolina	11.5
NA	North Dakota**	NA
5	Ohio	12.1
9	Oklahoma	11.1
NA	Oregon**	NA
14	Pennsylvania	10.2
NA	Rhode Island**	NA
8	South Carolina	11.2
NA	South Dakota**	NA
4	Tennessee	12.5
27	Texas	8.3
NA	Utah**	NA
NA	Vermont**	NA
11	Virginia	10.8
25	Washington	8.8
NA	West Virginia**	NA
3	Wisconsin	12.9
NA	Wyoming**	NA

RANK ORDER

RANK	STATE	RATE
1	Nebraska	15.3
2	Colorado	13.6
3	Wisconsin	12.9
4	Tennessee	12.5
5	Michigan	12.1
5	Ohio	12.1
7	North Carolina	11.5
8	South Carolina	11.2
9	Oklahoma	11.1
10	Missouri	11.0
11	Virginia	10.8
12	Nevada	10.7
13	Delaware	10.3
14	Illinois	10.2
14	Pennsylvania	10.2
16	Kansas	10.0
17	Mississippi	9.8
18	Louisiana	9.7
19	Indiana	9.6
20	Georgia	9.4
21	New Jersey	9.2
22	Florida	9.1
23	Connecticut	9.0
24	Alabama	8.9
25	Washington	8.8
26	Maryland	8.5
27	Arkansas	8.3
27	Texas	8.3
29	California	8.0
30	Kentucky	6.7
30	New York	6.7
32	Massachusetts	6.1
33	Minnesota	4.9
NA	Alaska**	NA
NA	Arizona**	NA
NA	Hawaii**	NA
NA	Idaho**	NA
NA	Iowa**	NA
NA	Maine**	NA
NA	Montana**	NA
NA	New Hampshire**	NA
NA	New Mexico**	NA
NA	North Dakota**	NA
NA	Oregon**	NA
NA	Rhode Island**	NA
NA	South Dakota**	NA
NA	Utah**	NA
NA	Vermont**	NA
NA	West Virginia**	NA
NA	Wyoming**	NA

District of Columbia	9.3

Source: U.S. Department of Health and Human Services, National Center for Health Statistics
"National Vital Statistics Reports" (Vol. 53, No. 5, October 12, 2004)
*Final data. Deaths of infants under 28 days, exclusive of fetal deaths. Based on race of the mother.
**Not available. Fewer than 20 black neonatal deaths.

Deaths by AIDS in 2002

National Total = 14,095 Deaths*

<table>
<tr><td colspan="4">ALPHA ORDER</td><td colspan="4">RANK ORDER</td></tr>
<tr><td>RANK</td><td>STATE</td><td>DEATHS</td><td>% of USA</td><td>RANK</td><td>STATE</td><td>DEATHS</td><td>% of USA</td></tr>
<tr><td>18</td><td>Alabama</td><td>190</td><td>1.3%</td><td>1</td><td>New York</td><td>1,980</td><td>14.0%</td></tr>
<tr><td>42</td><td>Alaska</td><td>16</td><td>0.1%</td><td>2</td><td>Florida</td><td>1,719</td><td>12.2%</td></tr>
<tr><td>21</td><td>Arizona</td><td>165</td><td>1.2%</td><td>3</td><td>California</td><td>1,435</td><td>10.2%</td></tr>
<tr><td>29</td><td>Arkansas</td><td>81</td><td>0.6%</td><td>4</td><td>Texas</td><td>1,075</td><td>7.6%</td></tr>
<tr><td>3</td><td>California</td><td>1,435</td><td>10.2%</td><td>5</td><td>New Jersey</td><td>762</td><td>5.4%</td></tr>
<tr><td>25</td><td>Colorado</td><td>105</td><td>0.7%</td><td>6</td><td>Georgia</td><td>708</td><td>5.0%</td></tr>
<tr><td>19</td><td>Connecticut</td><td>186</td><td>1.3%</td><td>7</td><td>Maryland</td><td>610</td><td>4.3%</td></tr>
<tr><td>32</td><td>Delaware</td><td>70</td><td>0.5%</td><td>8</td><td>Pennsylvania</td><td>497</td><td>3.5%</td></tr>
<tr><td>2</td><td>Florida</td><td>1,719</td><td>12.2%</td><td>9</td><td>Illinois</td><td>490</td><td>3.5%</td></tr>
<tr><td>6</td><td>Georgia</td><td>708</td><td>5.0%</td><td>10</td><td>North Carolina</td><td>486</td><td>3.4%</td></tr>
<tr><td>37</td><td>Hawaii</td><td>26</td><td>0.2%</td><td>11</td><td>Louisiana</td><td>364</td><td>2.6%</td></tr>
<tr><td>45</td><td>Idaho</td><td>11</td><td>0.1%</td><td>12</td><td>Tennessee</td><td>347</td><td>2.5%</td></tr>
<tr><td>9</td><td>Illinois</td><td>490</td><td>3.5%</td><td>13</td><td>South Carolina</td><td>301</td><td>2.1%</td></tr>
<tr><td>24</td><td>Indiana</td><td>118</td><td>0.8%</td><td>14</td><td>Virginia</td><td>261</td><td>1.9%</td></tr>
<tr><td>36</td><td>Iowa</td><td>29</td><td>0.2%</td><td>15</td><td>Ohio</td><td>241</td><td>1.7%</td></tr>
<tr><td>34</td><td>Kansas</td><td>37</td><td>0.3%</td><td>16</td><td>Michigan</td><td>240</td><td>1.7%</td></tr>
<tr><td>26</td><td>Kentucky</td><td>98</td><td>0.7%</td><td>17</td><td>Massachusetts</td><td>232</td><td>1.6%</td></tr>
<tr><td>11</td><td>Louisiana</td><td>364</td><td>2.6%</td><td>18</td><td>Alabama</td><td>190</td><td>1.3%</td></tr>
<tr><td>44</td><td>Maine</td><td>12</td><td>0.1%</td><td>19</td><td>Connecticut</td><td>186</td><td>1.3%</td></tr>
<tr><td>7</td><td>Maryland</td><td>610</td><td>4.3%</td><td>20</td><td>Mississippi</td><td>185</td><td>1.3%</td></tr>
<tr><td>17</td><td>Massachusetts</td><td>232</td><td>1.6%</td><td>21</td><td>Arizona</td><td>165</td><td>1.2%</td></tr>
<tr><td>16</td><td>Michigan</td><td>240</td><td>1.7%</td><td>22</td><td>Missouri</td><td>123</td><td>0.9%</td></tr>
<tr><td>33</td><td>Minnesota</td><td>53</td><td>0.4%</td><td>23</td><td>Washington</td><td>119</td><td>0.8%</td></tr>
<tr><td>20</td><td>Mississippi</td><td>185</td><td>1.3%</td><td>24</td><td>Indiana</td><td>118</td><td>0.8%</td></tr>
<tr><td>22</td><td>Missouri</td><td>123</td><td>0.9%</td><td>25</td><td>Colorado</td><td>105</td><td>0.7%</td></tr>
<tr><td>46</td><td>Montana</td><td>8</td><td>0.1%</td><td>26</td><td>Kentucky</td><td>98</td><td>0.7%</td></tr>
<tr><td>39</td><td>Nebraska</td><td>21</td><td>0.1%</td><td>27</td><td>Oklahoma</td><td>91</td><td>0.6%</td></tr>
<tr><td>31</td><td>Nevada</td><td>76</td><td>0.5%</td><td>27</td><td>Oregon</td><td>91</td><td>0.6%</td></tr>
<tr><td>43</td><td>New Hampshire</td><td>13</td><td>0.1%</td><td>29</td><td>Arkansas</td><td>81</td><td>0.6%</td></tr>
<tr><td>5</td><td>New Jersey</td><td>762</td><td>5.4%</td><td>30</td><td>Wisconsin</td><td>77</td><td>0.5%</td></tr>
<tr><td>35</td><td>New Mexico</td><td>35</td><td>0.2%</td><td>31</td><td>Nevada</td><td>76</td><td>0.5%</td></tr>
<tr><td>1</td><td>New York</td><td>1,980</td><td>14.0%</td><td>32</td><td>Delaware</td><td>70</td><td>0.5%</td></tr>
<tr><td>10</td><td>North Carolina</td><td>486</td><td>3.4%</td><td>33</td><td>Minnesota</td><td>53</td><td>0.4%</td></tr>
<tr><td>50</td><td>North Dakota</td><td>1</td><td>0.0%</td><td>34</td><td>Kansas</td><td>37</td><td>0.3%</td></tr>
<tr><td>15</td><td>Ohio</td><td>241</td><td>1.7%</td><td>35</td><td>New Mexico</td><td>35</td><td>0.2%</td></tr>
<tr><td>27</td><td>Oklahoma</td><td>91</td><td>0.6%</td><td>36</td><td>Iowa</td><td>29</td><td>0.2%</td></tr>
<tr><td>27</td><td>Oregon</td><td>91</td><td>0.6%</td><td>37</td><td>Hawaii</td><td>26</td><td>0.2%</td></tr>
<tr><td>8</td><td>Pennsylvania</td><td>497</td><td>3.5%</td><td>38</td><td>Rhode Island</td><td>23</td><td>0.2%</td></tr>
<tr><td>38</td><td>Rhode Island</td><td>23</td><td>0.2%</td><td>39</td><td>Nebraska</td><td>21</td><td>0.1%</td></tr>
<tr><td>13</td><td>South Carolina</td><td>301</td><td>2.1%</td><td>40</td><td>West Virginia</td><td>20</td><td>0.1%</td></tr>
<tr><td>48</td><td>South Dakota</td><td>5</td><td>0.0%</td><td>41</td><td>Utah</td><td>19</td><td>0.1%</td></tr>
<tr><td>12</td><td>Tennessee</td><td>347</td><td>2.5%</td><td>42</td><td>Alaska</td><td>16</td><td>0.1%</td></tr>
<tr><td>4</td><td>Texas</td><td>1,075</td><td>7.6%</td><td>43</td><td>New Hampshire</td><td>13</td><td>0.1%</td></tr>
<tr><td>41</td><td>Utah</td><td>19</td><td>0.1%</td><td>44</td><td>Maine</td><td>12</td><td>0.1%</td></tr>
<tr><td>46</td><td>Vermont</td><td>8</td><td>0.1%</td><td>45</td><td>Idaho</td><td>11</td><td>0.1%</td></tr>
<tr><td>14</td><td>Virginia</td><td>261</td><td>1.9%</td><td>46</td><td>Montana</td><td>8</td><td>0.1%</td></tr>
<tr><td>23</td><td>Washington</td><td>119</td><td>0.8%</td><td>46</td><td>Vermont</td><td>8</td><td>0.1%</td></tr>
<tr><td>40</td><td>West Virginia</td><td>20</td><td>0.1%</td><td>48</td><td>South Dakota</td><td>5</td><td>0.0%</td></tr>
<tr><td>30</td><td>Wisconsin</td><td>77</td><td>0.5%</td><td>49</td><td>Wyoming</td><td>2</td><td>0.0%</td></tr>
<tr><td>49</td><td>Wyoming</td><td>2</td><td>0.0%</td><td>50</td><td>North Dakota</td><td>1</td><td>0.0%</td></tr>
<tr><td></td><td></td><td></td><td></td><td></td><td>District of Columbia</td><td>233</td><td>1.7%</td></tr>
</table>

Source: U.S. Department of Health and Human Services, National Center for Health Statistics
   "National Vital Statistics Reports" (Vol. 53, No. 5, October 12, 2004)
*AIDS is Acquired Immunodeficiency Syndrome. It is a specific group of diseases or conditions which are indicative
of severe immunosuppression related to infection with the Human Immunodeficiency Virus (HIV).

Death Rate by AIDS in 2002

National Rate = 4.9 Deaths per 100,000 Population*

ALPHA ORDER

RANK	STATE	RATE
14	Alabama	4.2
NA	Alaska**	NA
21	Arizona	3.0
21	Arkansas	3.0
15	California	4.1
27	Colorado	2.3
12	Connecticut	5.4
5	Delaware	8.7
2	Florida	10.3
6	Georgia	8.3
30	Hawaii	2.1
NA	Idaho**	NA
17	Illinois	3.9
33	Indiana	1.9
40	Iowa	1.0
35	Kansas	1.4
25	Kentucky	2.4
7	Louisiana	8.1
NA	Maine**	NA
1	Maryland	11.2
18	Massachusetts	3.6
25	Michigan	2.4
38	Minnesota	1.1
9	Mississippi	6.4
28	Missouri	2.2
NA	Montana**	NA
37	Nebraska	1.2
20	Nevada	3.5
NA	New Hampshire**	NA
4	New Jersey	8.9
33	New Mexico	1.9
2	New York	10.3
11	North Carolina	5.8
NA	North Dakota**	NA
30	Ohio	2.1
23	Oklahoma	2.6
23	Oregon	2.6
16	Pennsylvania	4.0
28	Rhode Island	2.2
8	South Carolina	7.3
NA	South Dakota**	NA
10	Tennessee	6.0
13	Texas	4.9
NA	Utah**	NA
NA	Vermont**	NA
18	Virginia	3.6
32	Washington	2.0
38	West Virginia	1.1
35	Wisconsin	1.4
NA	Wyoming**	NA

RANK ORDER

RANK	STATE	RATE
1	Maryland	11.2
2	Florida	10.3
2	New York	10.3
4	New Jersey	8.9
5	Delaware	8.7
6	Georgia	8.3
7	Louisiana	8.1
8	South Carolina	7.3
9	Mississippi	6.4
10	Tennessee	6.0
11	North Carolina	5.8
12	Connecticut	5.4
13	Texas	4.9
14	Alabama	4.2
15	California	4.1
16	Pennsylvania	4.0
17	Illinois	3.9
18	Massachusetts	3.6
18	Virginia	3.6
20	Nevada	3.5
21	Arizona	3.0
21	Arkansas	3.0
23	Oklahoma	2.6
23	Oregon	2.6
25	Kentucky	2.4
25	Michigan	2.4
27	Colorado	2.3
28	Missouri	2.2
28	Rhode Island	2.2
30	Hawaii	2.1
30	Ohio	2.1
32	Washington	2.0
33	Indiana	1.9
33	New Mexico	1.9
35	Kansas	1.4
35	Wisconsin	1.4
37	Nebraska	1.2
38	Minnesota	1.1
38	West Virginia	1.1
40	Iowa	1.0
NA	Alaska**	NA
NA	Idaho**	NA
NA	Maine**	NA
NA	Montana**	NA
NA	New Hampshire**	NA
NA	North Dakota**	NA
NA	South Dakota**	NA
NA	Utah**	NA
NA	Vermont**	NA
NA	Wyoming**	NA

	District of Columbia	40.8

Source: U.S. Department of Health and Human Services, National Center for Health Statistics
   "National Vital Statistics Reports" (Vol. 53, No. 5, October 12, 2004)
*AIDS is Acquired Immunodeficiency Syndrome. It is a specific group of diseases or conditions which are indicative of severe immunosuppression related to infection with the Human Immunodeficiency Virus (HIV). Not age-adjusted.
**Insufficient data to determine a reliable rate.

Age-Adjusted Death Rate by AIDS in 2002

National Rate = 4.9 Deaths per 100,000 Population*

ALPHA ORDER				RANK ORDER		
RANK	STATE	RATE		RANK	STATE	RATE
14	Alabama	4.3		1	Maryland	10.7
NA	Alaska**	NA		2	Florida	10.4
21	Arizona	3.3		3	New York	10.2
22	Arkansas	3.2		4	Delaware	8.5
15	California	4.2		4	New Jersey	8.5
26	Colorado	2.3		6	Louisiana	8.4
12	Connecticut	5.2		7	Georgia	8.2
4	Delaware	8.5		8	South Carolina	7.4
2	Florida	10.4		9	Mississippi	6.8
7	Georgia	8.2		10	Tennessee	5.9
30	Hawaii	2.1		11	North Carolina	5.8
NA	Idaho**	NA		12	Connecticut	5.2
17	Illinois	3.9		13	Texas	5.1
32	Indiana	2.0		14	Alabama	4.3
39	Iowa	1.0		15	California	4.2
35	Kansas	1.4		16	Pennsylvania	4.0
26	Kentucky	2.3		17	Illinois	3.9
6	Louisiana	8.4		18	Massachusetts	3.5
NA	Maine**	NA		18	Nevada	3.5
1	Maryland	10.7		18	Virginia	3.5
18	Massachusetts	3.5		21	Arizona	3.3
25	Michigan	2.4		22	Arkansas	3.2
39	Minnesota	1.0		23	Oklahoma	2.7
9	Mississippi	6.8		24	Oregon	2.6
28	Missouri	2.2		25	Michigan	2.4
NA	Montana**	NA		26	Colorado	2.3
37	Nebraska	1.3		26	Kentucky	2.3
18	Nevada	3.5		28	Missouri	2.2
NA	New Hampshire**	NA		28	Ohio	2.2
4	New Jersey	8.5		30	Hawaii	2.1
32	New Mexico	2.0		30	Rhode Island	2.1
3	New York	10.2		32	Indiana	2.0
11	North Carolina	5.8		32	New Mexico	2.0
NA	North Dakota**	NA		34	Washington	1.9
28	Ohio	2.2		35	Kansas	1.4
23	Oklahoma	2.7		35	Wisconsin	1.4
24	Oregon	2.6		37	Nebraska	1.3
16	Pennsylvania	4.0		38	West Virginia	1.1
30	Rhode Island	2.1		39	Iowa	1.0
8	South Carolina	7.4		39	Minnesota	1.0
NA	South Dakota**	NA		NA	Alaska**	NA
10	Tennessee	5.9		NA	Idaho**	NA
13	Texas	5.1		NA	Maine**	NA
NA	Utah**	NA		NA	Montana**	NA
NA	Vermont**	NA		NA	New Hampshire**	NA
18	Virginia	3.5		NA	North Dakota**	NA
34	Washington	1.9		NA	South Dakota**	NA
38	West Virginia	1.1		NA	Utah**	NA
35	Wisconsin	1.4		NA	Vermont**	NA
NA	Wyoming**	NA		NA	Wyoming**	NA
					District of Columbia	40.8

Source: U.S. Department of Health and Human Services, National Center for Health Statistics
 "National Vital Statistics Reports" (Vol. 53, No. 5, October 12, 2004)
*AIDS is Acquired Immunodeficiency Syndrome. It is a specific group of diseases or conditions which are indicative of severe immunosuppression related to infection with the Human Immunodeficiency Virus (HIV). Age-adjusted rates based on the year 2000 standard population.
**Insufficient data to determine a reliable rate.

Estimated Deaths by Cancer in 2005

National Estimated Total = 570,280 Deaths

RANK	STATE	DEATHS	% of USA
20	Alabama	10,100	1.8%
50	Alaska	800	0.1%
21	Arizona	9,920	1.7%
32	Arkansas	6,210	1.1%
1	California	56,090	9.8%
29	Colorado	6,680	1.2%
28	Connecticut	7,030	1.2%
46	Delaware	1,580	0.3%
2	Florida	39,960	7.0%
11	Georgia	14,810	2.6%
44	Hawaii	1,990	0.3%
42	Idaho	2,280	0.4%
6	Illinois	24,810	4.4%
14	Indiana	13,250	2.3%
30	Iowa	6,610	1.2%
33	Kansas	5,370	0.9%
23	Kentucky	9,560	1.7%
22	Louisiana	9,670	1.7%
38	Maine	3,220	0.6%
19	Maryland	10,570	1.9%
13	Massachusetts	13,720	2.4%
8	Michigan	20,860	3.7%
24	Minnesota	9,510	1.7%
31	Mississippi	6,220	1.1%
16	Missouri	12,550	2.2%
43	Montana	2,040	0.4%
36	Nebraska	3,460	0.6%
35	Nevada	4,620	0.8%
40	New Hampshire	2,620	0.5%
9	New Jersey	17,860	3.1%
37	New Mexico	3,230	0.6%
3	New York	36,160	6.3%
10	North Carolina	16,830	3.0%
47	North Dakota	1,280	0.2%
7	Ohio	24,790	4.3%
26	Oklahoma	7,670	1.3%
27	Oregon	7,360	1.3%
5	Pennsylvania	29,840	5.2%
41	Rhode Island	2,440	0.4%
25	South Carolina	9,080	1.6%
45	South Dakota	1,620	0.3%
15	Tennessee	12,910	2.3%
4	Texas	36,090	6.3%
39	Utah	2,650	0.5%
48	Vermont	1,260	0.2%
12	Virginia	13,990	2.5%
17	Washington	11,360	2.0%
34	West Virginia	4,650	0.8%
18	Wisconsin	10,940	1.9%
49	Wyoming	990	0.2%

RANK	STATE	DEATHS	% of USA
1	California	56,090	9.8%
2	Florida	39,960	7.0%
3	New York	36,160	6.3%
4	Texas	36,090	6.3%
5	Pennsylvania	29,840	5.2%
6	Illinois	24,810	4.4%
7	Ohio	24,790	4.3%
8	Michigan	20,860	3.7%
9	New Jersey	17,860	3.1%
10	North Carolina	16,830	3.0%
11	Georgia	14,810	2.6%
12	Virginia	13,990	2.5%
13	Massachusetts	13,720	2.4%
14	Indiana	13,250	2.3%
15	Tennessee	12,910	2.3%
16	Missouri	12,550	2.2%
17	Washington	11,360	2.0%
18	Wisconsin	10,940	1.9%
19	Maryland	10,570	1.9%
20	Alabama	10,100	1.8%
21	Arizona	9,920	1.7%
22	Louisiana	9,670	1.7%
23	Kentucky	9,560	1.7%
24	Minnesota	9,510	1.7%
25	South Carolina	9,080	1.6%
26	Oklahoma	7,670	1.3%
27	Oregon	7,360	1.3%
28	Connecticut	7,030	1.2%
29	Colorado	6,680	1.2%
30	Iowa	6,610	1.2%
31	Mississippi	6,220	1.1%
32	Arkansas	6,210	1.1%
33	Kansas	5,370	0.9%
34	West Virginia	4,650	0.8%
35	Nevada	4,620	0.8%
36	Nebraska	3,460	0.6%
37	New Mexico	3,230	0.6%
38	Maine	3,220	0.6%
39	Utah	2,650	0.5%
40	New Hampshire	2,620	0.5%
41	Rhode Island	2,440	0.4%
42	Idaho	2,280	0.4%
43	Montana	2,040	0.4%
44	Hawaii	1,990	0.3%
45	South Dakota	1,620	0.3%
46	Delaware	1,580	0.3%
47	North Dakota	1,280	0.2%
48	Vermont	1,260	0.2%
49	Wyoming	990	0.2%
50	Alaska	800	0.1%
	District of Columbia	1,170	0.2%

Source: American Cancer Society
"Cancer Facts & Figures 2005" (Copyright 2005, American Cancer Society)

Estimated Death Rate by Cancer in 2005

National Estimated Rate = 194.2 Deaths per 100,000 Population*

ALPHA ORDER

RANK	STATE	RATE
9	Alabama	222.9
49	Alaska	122.1
41	Arizona	172.7
7	Arkansas	225.6
47	California	156.3
48	Colorado	145.2
27	Connecticut	200.7
35	Delaware	190.3
5	Florida	229.7
43	Georgia	167.7
46	Hawaii	157.6
44	Idaho	163.6
34	Illinois	195.1
19	Indiana	212.4
8	Iowa	223.7
32	Kansas	196.3
4	Kentucky	230.6
17	Louisiana	214.1
2	Maine	244.4
36	Maryland	190.2
18	Massachusetts	213.8
21	Michigan	206.3
39	Minnesota	186.4
16	Mississippi	214.3
12	Missouri	218.1
10	Montana	220.1
29	Nebraska	198.0
30	Nevada	197.9
26	New Hampshire	201.6
22	New Jersey	205.3
42	New Mexico	169.7
37	New York	188.1
31	North Carolina	197.0
25	North Dakota	201.8
14	Ohio	216.3
13	Oklahoma	217.7
23	Oregon	204.8
3	Pennsylvania	240.5
6	Rhode Island	225.8
14	South Carolina	216.3
20	South Dakota	210.1
11	Tennessee	218.8
45	Texas	160.5
50	Utah	110.9
24	Vermont	202.8
38	Virginia	187.5
40	Washington	183.1
1	West Virginia	256.1
28	Wisconsin	198.6
33	Wyoming	195.4

RANK ORDER

RANK	STATE	RATE
1	West Virginia	256.1
2	Maine	244.4
3	Pennsylvania	240.5
4	Kentucky	230.6
5	Florida	229.7
6	Rhode Island	225.8
7	Arkansas	225.6
8	Iowa	223.7
9	Alabama	222.9
10	Montana	220.1
11	Tennessee	218.8
12	Missouri	218.1
13	Oklahoma	217.7
14	Ohio	216.3
14	South Carolina	216.3
16	Mississippi	214.3
17	Louisiana	214.1
18	Massachusetts	213.8
19	Indiana	212.4
20	South Dakota	210.1
21	Michigan	206.3
22	New Jersey	205.3
23	Oregon	204.8
24	Vermont	202.8
25	North Dakota	201.8
26	New Hampshire	201.6
27	Connecticut	200.7
28	Wisconsin	198.6
29	Nebraska	198.0
30	Nevada	197.9
31	North Carolina	197.0
32	Kansas	196.3
33	Wyoming	195.4
34	Illinois	195.1
35	Delaware	190.3
36	Maryland	190.2
37	New York	188.1
38	Virginia	187.5
39	Minnesota	186.4
40	Washington	183.1
41	Arizona	172.7
42	New Mexico	169.7
43	Georgia	167.7
44	Idaho	163.6
45	Texas	160.5
46	Hawaii	157.6
47	California	156.3
48	Colorado	145.2
49	Alaska	122.1
50	Utah	110.9

District of Columbia 211.4

Source: Morgan Quitno Press using data from American Cancer Society
"Cancer Facts & Figures 2005" (Copyright 2005, American Cancer Society)
*Rates calculated using 2004 Census resident population estimates. Not age-adjusted.

Age-Adjusted Death Rate by Cancer for Males in 2001

National Rate = 251.1 Deaths per 100,000 Male Population*

ALPHA ORDER				RANK ORDER		
RANK	STATE	RATE		RANK	STATE	RATE
4	Alabama	290.4		1	Mississippi	306.7
38	Alaska	235.5		2	Louisiana	303.8
46	Arizona	212.3		3	Kentucky	298.9
8	Arkansas	277.3		4	Alabama	290.4
44	California	221.3		5	Tennessee	287.2
47	Colorado	210.9		6	West Virginia	282.9
39	Connecticut	234.7		7	South Carolina	281.0
14	Delaware	265.5		8	Arkansas	277.3
37	Florida	236.2		9	Indiana	274.2
11	Georgia	272.5		10	North Carolina	272.7
49	Hawaii	195.7		11	Georgia	272.5
45	Idaho	220.0		12	Ohio	269.3
19	Illinois	263.5		13	Virginia	265.8
9	Indiana	274.2		14	Delaware	265.5
32	Iowa	241.2		15	Maryland	265.3
34	Kansas	239.2		16	Oklahoma	265.2
3	Kentucky	298.9		17	Maine	264.7
2	Louisiana	303.8		18	Rhode Island	264.4
17	Maine	264.7		19	Illinois	263.5
15	Maryland	265.3		20	Missouri	262.4
22	Massachusetts	258.3		21	Pennsylvania	260.9
24	Michigan	255.7		22	Massachusetts	258.3
40	Minnesota	234.2		23	New Hampshire	256.7
1	Mississippi	306.7		24	Michigan	255.7
20	Missouri	262.4		25	New Jersey	255.2
30	Montana	244.4		26	Texas	252.1
43	Nebraska	231.6		27	Vermont	250.3
28	Nevada	249.5		28	Nevada	249.5
23	New Hampshire	256.7		29	Wisconsin	244.8
25	New Jersey	255.2		30	Montana	244.4
48	New Mexico	209.0		31	South Dakota	242.3
35	New York	238.3		32	Iowa	241.2
10	North Carolina	272.7		33	Oregon	240.9
41	North Dakota	234.0		34	Kansas	239.2
12	Ohio	269.3		35	New York	238.3
16	Oklahoma	265.2		36	Washington	236.5
33	Oregon	240.9		37	Florida	236.2
21	Pennsylvania	260.9		38	Alaska	235.5
18	Rhode Island	264.4		39	Connecticut	234.7
7	South Carolina	281.0		40	Minnesota	234.2
31	South Dakota	242.3		41	North Dakota	234.0
5	Tennessee	287.2		42	Wyoming	232.6
26	Texas	252.1		43	Nebraska	231.6
50	Utah	187.3		44	California	221.3
27	Vermont	250.3		45	Idaho	220.0
13	Virginia	265.8		46	Arizona	212.3
36	Washington	236.5		47	Colorado	210.9
6	West Virginia	282.9		48	New Mexico	209.0
29	Wisconsin	244.8		49	Hawaii	195.7
42	Wyoming	232.6		50	Utah	187.3
					District of Columbia	310.7

Source: American Cancer Society
    "Cancer Facts & Figures 2005" (Copyright 2005, American Cancer Society)
*For 1997 to 2001. Age-adjusted to the 2000 U.S. standard population.

117

Age-Adjusted Death Rate by Cancer for Females in 2001

National Rate = 166.7 Deaths per 100,000 Female Population*

ALPHA ORDER			RANK ORDER		
RANK	STATE	RATE	RANK	STATE	RATE
28	Alabama	167.1	1	Delaware	186.6
16	Alaska	172.4	2	West Virginia	186.0
46	Arizona	150.5	3	Louisiana	183.5
25	Arkansas	167.9	4	Kentucky	180.9
37	California	158.9	5	New Jersey	179.7
47	Colorado	148.0	6	Nevada	179.3
29	Connecticut	165.5	7	Maine	179.1
1	Delaware	186.6	8	Maryland	177.1
39	Florida	157.7	9	Ohio	176.9
31	Georgia	164.1	10	Indiana	176.8
49	Hawaii	127.7	11	Rhode Island	175.9
44	Idaho	151.6	12	Illinois	175.3
12	Illinois	175.3	13	Pennsylvania	174.1
10	Indiana	176.8	14	Massachusetts	173.9
41	Iowa	157.4	15	Missouri	173.2
40	Kansas	157.5	16	Alaska	172.4
4	Kentucky	180.9	17	New Hampshire	172.3
3	Louisiana	183.5	18	Tennessee	171.5
7	Maine	179.1	19	Michigan	171.4
8	Maryland	177.1	19	Oregon	171.4
14	Massachusetts	173.9	21	Virginia	171.3
19	Michigan	171.4	22	Vermont	169.4
38	Minnesota	157.9	23	Mississippi	169.2
23	Mississippi	169.2	24	Oklahoma	168.1
15	Missouri	173.2	25	Arkansas	167.9
35	Montana	161.4	26	Washington	167.7
43	Nebraska	154.1	27	New York	167.2
6	Nevada	179.3	28	Alabama	167.1
17	New Hampshire	172.3	29	Connecticut	165.5
5	New Jersey	179.7	30	South Carolina	164.8
48	New Mexico	145.7	31	Georgia	164.1
27	New York	167.2	32	North Carolina	163.4
32	North Carolina	163.4	33	Wyoming	163.0
45	North Dakota	151.5	34	Wisconsin	162.1
9	Ohio	176.9	35	Montana	161.4
24	Oklahoma	168.1	36	Texas	160.6
19	Oregon	171.4	37	California	158.9
13	Pennsylvania	174.1	38	Minnesota	157.9
11	Rhode Island	175.9	39	Florida	157.7
30	South Carolina	164.8	40	Kansas	157.5
42	South Dakota	155.6	41	Iowa	157.4
18	Tennessee	171.5	42	South Dakota	155.6
36	Texas	160.6	43	Nebraska	154.1
50	Utah	126.3	44	Idaho	151.6
22	Vermont	169.4	45	North Dakota	151.5
21	Virginia	171.3	46	Arizona	150.5
26	Washington	167.7	47	Colorado	148.0
2	West Virginia	186.0	48	New Mexico	145.7
34	Wisconsin	162.1	49	Hawaii	127.7
33	Wyoming	163.0	50	Utah	126.3
				District of Columbia	198.7

Source: American Cancer Society
   "Cancer Facts & Figures 2005" (Copyright 2005, American Cancer Society)
*For 1997 to 2001. Age-adjusted to the 2000 U.S. standard population.

Estimated Deaths by Brain Cancer in 2005

National Estimated Total = 12,760 Deaths

ALPHA ORDER

RANK	STATE	DEATHS	% of USA
21	Alabama	210	1.6%
NA	Alaska*	NA	NA
20	Arizona	240	1.9%
29	Arkansas	160	1.3%
1	California	1,460	11.4%
25	Colorado	180	1.4%
32	Connecticut	140	1.1%
NA	Delaware*	NA	NA
2	Florida	930	7.3%
14	Georgia	300	2.4%
NA	Hawaii*	NA	NA
39	Idaho	70	0.5%
7	Illinois	480	3.8%
11	Indiana	320	2.5%
29	Iowa	160	1.3%
33	Kansas	130	1.0%
29	Kentucky	160	1.3%
23	Louisiana	190	1.5%
38	Maine	80	0.6%
22	Maryland	200	1.6%
15	Massachusetts	280	2.2%
8	Michigan	450	3.5%
19	Minnesota	250	2.0%
27	Mississippi	170	1.3%
17	Missouri	260	2.0%
42	Montana	50	0.4%
34	Nebraska	90	0.7%
34	Nevada	90	0.7%
39	New Hampshire	70	0.5%
11	New Jersey	320	2.5%
39	New Mexico	70	0.5%
4	New York	720	5.6%
10	North Carolina	340	2.7%
NA	North Dakota*	NA	NA
5	Ohio	530	4.2%
27	Oklahoma	170	1.3%
23	Oregon	190	1.5%
6	Pennsylvania	520	4.1%
42	Rhode Island	50	0.4%
25	South Carolina	180	1.4%
42	South Dakota	50	0.4%
11	Tennessee	320	2.5%
3	Texas	910	7.1%
34	Utah	90	0.7%
NA	Vermont*	NA	NA
16	Virginia	270	2.1%
9	Washington	350	2.7%
34	West Virginia	90	0.7%
17	Wisconsin	260	2.0%
NA	Wyoming*	NA	NA

RANK ORDER

RANK	STATE	DEATHS	% of USA
1	California	1,460	11.4%
2	Florida	930	7.3%
3	Texas	910	7.1%
4	New York	720	5.6%
5	Ohio	530	4.2%
6	Pennsylvania	520	4.1%
7	Illinois	480	3.8%
8	Michigan	450	3.5%
9	Washington	350	2.7%
10	North Carolina	340	2.7%
11	Indiana	320	2.5%
11	New Jersey	320	2.5%
11	Tennessee	320	2.5%
14	Georgia	300	2.4%
15	Massachusetts	280	2.2%
16	Virginia	270	2.1%
17	Missouri	260	2.0%
17	Wisconsin	260	2.0%
19	Minnesota	250	2.0%
20	Arizona	240	1.9%
21	Alabama	210	1.6%
22	Maryland	200	1.6%
23	Louisiana	190	1.5%
23	Oregon	190	1.5%
25	Colorado	180	1.4%
25	South Carolina	180	1.4%
27	Mississippi	170	1.3%
27	Oklahoma	170	1.3%
29	Arkansas	160	1.3%
29	Iowa	160	1.3%
29	Kentucky	160	1.3%
32	Connecticut	140	1.1%
33	Kansas	130	1.0%
34	Nebraska	90	0.7%
34	Nevada	90	0.7%
34	Utah	90	0.7%
34	West Virginia	90	0.7%
38	Maine	80	0.6%
39	Idaho	70	0.5%
39	New Hampshire	70	0.5%
39	New Mexico	70	0.5%
42	Montana	50	0.4%
42	Rhode Island	50	0.4%
42	South Dakota	50	0.4%
NA	Alaska*	NA	NA
NA	Delaware*	NA	NA
NA	Hawaii*	NA	NA
NA	North Dakota*	NA	NA
NA	Vermont*	NA	NA
NA	Wyoming*	NA	NA
	District of Columbia*	NA	NA

Source: American Cancer Society
"Cancer Facts & Figures 2005" (Copyright 2005, American Cancer Society)
*Fewer than 50 deaths.

Estimated Death Rate by Brain Cancer in 2005

National Estimated Rate = 4.3 Deaths per 100,000 Population*

ALPHA ORDER

RANK ORDER

RANK	STATE	RATE		RANK	STATE	RATE
20	Alabama	4.6		1	South Dakota	6.5
NA	Alaska**	NA		2	Maine	6.1
27	Arizona	4.2		3	Mississippi	5.9
4	Arkansas	5.8		4	Arkansas	5.8
30	California	4.1		5	Washington	5.6
34	Colorado	3.9		6	Iowa	5.4
31	Connecticut	4.0		6	Montana	5.4
NA	Delaware**	NA		6	New Hampshire	5.4
10	Florida	5.3		6	Tennessee	5.4
44	Georgia	3.4		10	Florida	5.3
NA	Hawaii**	NA		10	Oregon	5.3
14	Idaho	5.0		12	Nebraska	5.2
37	Illinois	3.8		13	Indiana	5.1
13	Indiana	5.1		14	Idaho	5.0
6	Iowa	5.4		14	West Virginia	5.0
17	Kansas	4.8		16	Minnesota	4.9
34	Kentucky	3.9		17	Kansas	4.8
27	Louisiana	4.2		17	Oklahoma	4.8
2	Maine	6.1		19	Wisconsin	4.7
42	Maryland	3.6		20	Alabama	4.6
24	Massachusetts	4.4		20	Ohio	4.6
24	Michigan	4.4		20	Rhode Island	4.6
16	Minnesota	4.9		23	Missouri	4.5
3	Mississippi	5.9		24	Massachusetts	4.4
23	Missouri	4.5		24	Michigan	4.4
6	Montana	5.4		26	South Carolina	4.3
12	Nebraska	5.2		27	Arizona	4.2
34	Nevada	3.9		27	Louisiana	4.2
6	New Hampshire	5.4		27	Pennsylvania	4.2
39	New Jersey	3.7		30	California	4.1
39	New Mexico	3.7		31	Connecticut	4.0
39	New York	3.7		31	North Carolina	4.0
31	North Carolina	4.0		31	Texas	4.0
NA	North Dakota**	NA		34	Colorado	3.9
20	Ohio	4.6		34	Kentucky	3.9
17	Oklahoma	4.8		34	Nevada	3.9
10	Oregon	5.3		37	Illinois	3.8
27	Pennsylvania	4.2		37	Utah	3.8
20	Rhode Island	4.6		39	New Jersey	3.7
26	South Carolina	4.3		39	New Mexico	3.7
1	South Dakota	6.5		39	New York	3.7
6	Tennessee	5.4		42	Maryland	3.6
31	Texas	4.0		42	Virginia	3.6
37	Utah	3.8		44	Georgia	3.4
NA	Vermont**	NA		NA	Alaska**	NA
42	Virginia	3.6		NA	Delaware**	NA
5	Washington	5.6		NA	Hawaii**	NA
14	West Virginia	5.0		NA	North Dakota**	NA
19	Wisconsin	4.7		NA	Vermont**	NA
NA	Wyoming**	NA		NA	Wyoming**	NA
					District of Columbia**	NA

Source: Morgan Quitno Press using data from American Cancer Society
   "Cancer Facts & Figures 2005" (Copyright 2005, American Cancer Society)
*Rates calculated using 2004 Census resident population estimates. Not age-adjusted.
**Fewer than 50 deaths.

Estimated Deaths by Female Breast Cancer in 2005

National Estimated Total = 40,410 Deaths

ALPHA ORDER

RANK	STATE	DEATHS	% of USA
21	Alabama	730	1.8%
49	Alaska	50	0.1%
22	Arizona	720	1.8%
32	Arkansas	400	1.0%
1	California	4,050	10.0%
29	Colorado	490	1.2%
27	Connecticut	520	1.3%
45	Delaware	120	0.3%
3	Florida	2,570	6.4%
12	Georgia	1,120	2.8%
43	Hawaii	130	0.3%
39	Idaho	180	0.4%
7	Illinois	1,780	4.4%
14	Indiana	880	2.2%
31	Iowa	440	1.1%
33	Kansas	380	0.9%
23	Kentucky	630	1.6%
20	Louisiana	740	1.8%
40	Maine	170	0.4%
16	Maryland	840	2.1%
13	Massachusetts	940	2.3%
9	Michigan	1,380	3.4%
25	Minnesota	620	1.5%
30	Mississippi	450	1.1%
15	Missouri	870	2.2%
43	Montana	130	0.3%
36	Nebraska	230	0.6%
34	Nevada	310	0.8%
40	New Hampshire	170	0.4%
8	New Jersey	1,480	3.7%
38	New Mexico	190	0.5%
2	New York	2,760	6.8%
10	North Carolina	1,210	3.0%
46	North Dakota	100	0.2%
6	Ohio	1,850	4.6%
26	Oklahoma	540	1.3%
28	Oregon	500	1.2%
5	Pennsylvania	2,170	5.4%
42	Rhode Island	150	0.4%
23	South Carolina	630	1.6%
46	South Dakota	100	0.2%
17	Tennessee	810	2.0%
4	Texas	2,460	6.1%
37	Utah	220	0.5%
48	Vermont	90	0.2%
11	Virginia	1,150	2.8%
19	Washington	750	1.9%
35	West Virginia	270	0.7%
18	Wisconsin	790	2.0%
49	Wyoming	50	0.1%

RANK ORDER

RANK	STATE	DEATHS	% of USA
1	California	4,050	10.0%
2	New York	2,760	6.8%
3	Florida	2,570	6.4%
4	Texas	2,460	6.1%
5	Pennsylvania	2,170	5.4%
6	Ohio	1,850	4.6%
7	Illinois	1,780	4.4%
8	New Jersey	1,480	3.7%
9	Michigan	1,380	3.4%
10	North Carolina	1,210	3.0%
11	Virginia	1,150	2.8%
12	Georgia	1,120	2.8%
13	Massachusetts	940	2.3%
14	Indiana	880	2.2%
15	Missouri	870	2.2%
16	Maryland	840	2.1%
17	Tennessee	810	2.0%
18	Wisconsin	790	2.0%
19	Washington	750	1.9%
20	Louisiana	740	1.8%
21	Alabama	730	1.8%
22	Arizona	720	1.8%
23	Kentucky	630	1.6%
23	South Carolina	630	1.6%
25	Minnesota	620	1.5%
26	Oklahoma	540	1.3%
27	Connecticut	520	1.3%
28	Oregon	500	1.2%
29	Colorado	490	1.2%
30	Mississippi	450	1.1%
31	Iowa	440	1.1%
32	Arkansas	400	1.0%
33	Kansas	380	0.9%
34	Nevada	310	0.8%
35	West Virginia	270	0.7%
36	Nebraska	230	0.6%
37	Utah	220	0.5%
38	New Mexico	190	0.5%
39	Idaho	180	0.4%
40	Maine	170	0.4%
40	New Hampshire	170	0.4%
42	Rhode Island	150	0.4%
43	Hawaii	130	0.3%
43	Montana	130	0.3%
45	Delaware	120	0.3%
46	North Dakota	100	0.2%
46	South Dakota	100	0.2%
48	Vermont	90	0.2%
49	Alaska	50	0.1%
49	Wyoming	50	0.1%
	District of Columbia	100	0.2%

Source: American Cancer Society
"Cancer Facts & Figures 2005" (Copyright 2005, American Cancer Society)

Age-Adjusted Death Rate by Female Breast Cancer in 2001

National Rate = 27.0 Deaths per 100,000 Female Population*

ALPHA ORDER			RANK ORDER		
RANK	STATE	RATE	RANK	STATE	RATE
23	Alabama	26.6	1	New Jersey	30.5
44	Alaska	23.9	2	Delaware	30.0
37	Arizona	25.2	3	Louisiana	29.9
38	Arkansas	25.1	4	Illinois	29.2
32	California	25.7	5	Ohio	29.0
45	Colorado	23.6	6	New York	28.9
17	Connecticut	27.2	7	Maryland	28.8
2	Delaware	30.0	7	Pennsylvania	28.8
42	Florida	24.7	9	Virginia	28.4
24	Georgia	26.5	10	Mississippi	28.2
50	Hawaii	19.7	11	Massachusetts	27.8
34	Idaho	25.5	12	Michigan	27.5
4	Illinois	29.2	13	Indiana	27.4
13	Indiana	27.4	13	South Carolina	27.4
34	Iowa	25.5	13	Vermont	27.4
36	Kansas	25.3	16	West Virginia	27.3
19	Kentucky	27.1	17	Connecticut	27.2
3	Louisiana	29.9	17	Rhode Island	27.2
38	Maine	25.1	19	Kentucky	27.1
7	Maryland	28.8	19	New Hampshire	27.1
11	Massachusetts	27.8	21	Missouri	26.9
12	Michigan	27.5	22	Tennessee	26.8
30	Minnesota	25.9	23	Alabama	26.6
10	Mississippi	28.2	24	Georgia	26.5
21	Missouri	26.9	24	North Carolina	26.5
45	Montana	23.6	26	Nevada	26.4
43	Nebraska	24.4	26	Oklahoma	26.4
26	Nevada	26.4	28	Oregon	26.3
19	New Hampshire	27.1	29	Wisconsin	26.2
1	New Jersey	30.5	30	Minnesota	25.9
47	New Mexico	23.4	30	North Dakota	25.9
6	New York	28.9	32	California	25.7
24	North Carolina	26.5	33	Texas	25.6
30	North Dakota	25.9	34	Idaho	25.5
5	Ohio	29.0	34	Iowa	25.5
26	Oklahoma	26.4	36	Kansas	25.3
28	Oregon	26.3	37	Arizona	25.2
7	Pennsylvania	28.8	38	Arkansas	25.1
17	Rhode Island	27.2	38	Maine	25.1
13	South Carolina	27.4	38	Wyoming	25.1
48	South Dakota	23.3	41	Washington	25.0
22	Tennessee	26.8	42	Florida	24.7
33	Texas	25.6	43	Nebraska	24.4
48	Utah	23.3	44	Alaska	23.9
13	Vermont	27.4	45	Colorado	23.6
9	Virginia	28.4	45	Montana	23.6
41	Washington	25.0	47	New Mexico	23.4
16	West Virginia	27.3	48	South Dakota	23.3
29	Wisconsin	26.2	48	Utah	23.3
38	Wyoming	25.1	50	Hawaii	19.7
				District of Columbia	37.3

Source: American Cancer Society
"Cancer Facts & Figures 2005" (Copyright 2005, American Cancer Society)
*For 1997 to 2001. Age-adjusted to the 2000 U.S. standard population.

Estimated Deaths by Colon and Rectum Cancer in 2005

National Estimated Total = 56,290 Deaths

ALPHA ORDER

RANK	STATE	DEATHS	% of USA
23	Alabama	890	1.6%
50	Alaska	80	0.1%
21	Arizona	970	1.7%
31	Arkansas	630	1.1%
1	California	5,450	9.7%
30	Colorado	640	1.1%
29	Connecticut	650	1.2%
46	Delaware	160	0.3%
2	Florida	3,820	6.8%
13	Georgia	1,350	2.4%
42	Hawaii	210	0.4%
42	Idaho	210	0.4%
6	Illinois	2,560	4.5%
14	Indiana	1,320	2.3%
28	Iowa	660	1.2%
33	Kansas	610	1.1%
22	Kentucky	910	1.6%
20	Louisiana	1,000	1.8%
38	Maine	310	0.6%
17	Maryland	1,070	1.9%
11	Massachusetts	1,380	2.5%
8	Michigan	1,870	3.3%
25	Minnesota	860	1.5%
31	Mississippi	630	1.1%
15	Missouri	1,250	2.2%
44	Montana	180	0.3%
36	Nebraska	400	0.7%
35	Nevada	480	0.9%
41	New Hampshire	240	0.4%
9	New Jersey	1,810	3.2%
37	New Mexico	340	0.6%
3	New York	3,760	6.7%
10	North Carolina	1,590	2.8%
47	North Dakota	140	0.2%
7	Ohio	2,520	4.5%
26	Oklahoma	780	1.4%
27	Oregon	680	1.2%
5	Pennsylvania	3,150	5.6%
40	Rhode Island	250	0.4%
23	South Carolina	890	1.6%
44	South Dakota	180	0.3%
16	Tennessee	1,220	2.2%
4	Texas	3,590	6.4%
39	Utah	260	0.5%
48	Vermont	130	0.2%
11	Virginia	1,380	2.5%
19	Washington	1,030	1.8%
34	West Virginia	490	0.9%
17	Wisconsin	1,070	1.9%
49	Wyoming	110	0.2%

RANK ORDER

RANK	STATE	DEATHS	% of USA
1	California	5,450	9.7%
2	Florida	3,820	6.8%
3	New York	3,760	6.7%
4	Texas	3,590	6.4%
5	Pennsylvania	3,150	5.6%
6	Illinois	2,560	4.5%
7	Ohio	2,520	4.5%
8	Michigan	1,870	3.3%
9	New Jersey	1,810	3.2%
10	North Carolina	1,590	2.8%
11	Massachusetts	1,380	2.5%
11	Virginia	1,380	2.5%
13	Georgia	1,350	2.4%
14	Indiana	1,320	2.3%
15	Missouri	1,250	2.2%
16	Tennessee	1,220	2.2%
17	Maryland	1,070	1.9%
17	Wisconsin	1,070	1.9%
19	Washington	1,030	1.8%
20	Louisiana	1,000	1.8%
21	Arizona	970	1.7%
22	Kentucky	910	1.6%
23	Alabama	890	1.6%
23	South Carolina	890	1.6%
25	Minnesota	860	1.5%
26	Oklahoma	780	1.4%
27	Oregon	680	1.2%
28	Iowa	660	1.2%
29	Connecticut	650	1.2%
30	Colorado	640	1.1%
31	Arkansas	630	1.1%
31	Mississippi	630	1.1%
33	Kansas	610	1.1%
34	West Virginia	490	0.9%
35	Nevada	480	0.9%
36	Nebraska	400	0.7%
37	New Mexico	340	0.6%
38	Maine	310	0.6%
39	Utah	260	0.5%
40	Rhode Island	250	0.4%
41	New Hampshire	240	0.4%
42	Hawaii	210	0.4%
42	Idaho	210	0.4%
44	Montana	180	0.3%
44	South Dakota	180	0.3%
46	Delaware	160	0.3%
47	North Dakota	140	0.2%
48	Vermont	130	0.2%
49	Wyoming	110	0.2%
50	Alaska	80	0.1%
	District of Columbia	130	0.2%

Source: American Cancer Society
   "Cancer Facts & Figures 2005" (Copyright 2005, American Cancer Society)

Estimated Death Rate by Colon and Rectum Cancer in 2005

National Estimated Rate = 19.2 Deaths per 100,000 Population*

ALPHA ORDER

RANK	STATE	RATE
27	Alabama	19.6
49	Alaska	12.2
40	Arizona	16.9
6	Arkansas	22.9
46	California	15.2
48	Colorado	13.9
34	Connecticut	18.6
31	Delaware	19.3
13	Florida	22.0
45	Georgia	15.3
42	Hawaii	16.6
47	Idaho	15.1
26	Illinois	20.1
20	Indiana	21.2
8	Iowa	22.3
8	Kansas	22.3
15	Kentucky	21.9
10	Louisiana	22.1
3	Maine	23.5
31	Maryland	19.3
19	Massachusetts	21.5
36	Michigan	18.5
40	Minnesota	16.9
16	Mississippi	21.7
16	Missouri	21.7
29	Montana	19.4
6	Nebraska	22.9
25	Nevada	20.6
36	New Hampshire	18.5
23	New Jersey	20.8
39	New Mexico	17.9
27	New York	19.6
34	North Carolina	18.6
10	North Dakota	22.1
13	Ohio	22.0
10	Oklahoma	22.1
33	Oregon	18.9
2	Pennsylvania	25.4
5	Rhode Island	23.1
20	South Carolina	21.2
4	South Dakota	23.3
24	Tennessee	20.7
44	Texas	16.0
50	Utah	10.9
22	Vermont	20.9
36	Virginia	18.5
42	Washington	16.6
1	West Virginia	27.0
29	Wisconsin	19.4
16	Wyoming	21.7

RANK ORDER

RANK	STATE	RATE
1	West Virginia	27.0
2	Pennsylvania	25.4
3	Maine	23.5
4	South Dakota	23.3
5	Rhode Island	23.1
6	Arkansas	22.9
6	Nebraska	22.9
8	Iowa	22.3
8	Kansas	22.3
10	Louisiana	22.1
10	North Dakota	22.1
10	Oklahoma	22.1
13	Florida	22.0
13	Ohio	22.0
15	Kentucky	21.9
16	Mississippi	21.7
16	Missouri	21.7
16	Wyoming	21.7
19	Massachusetts	21.5
20	Indiana	21.2
20	South Carolina	21.2
22	Vermont	20.9
23	New Jersey	20.8
24	Tennessee	20.7
25	Nevada	20.6
26	Illinois	20.1
27	Alabama	19.6
27	New York	19.6
29	Montana	19.4
29	Wisconsin	19.4
31	Delaware	19.3
31	Maryland	19.3
33	Oregon	18.9
34	Connecticut	18.6
34	North Carolina	18.6
36	Michigan	18.5
36	New Hampshire	18.5
36	Virginia	18.5
39	New Mexico	17.9
40	Arizona	16.9
40	Minnesota	16.9
42	Hawaii	16.6
42	Washington	16.6
44	Texas	16.0
45	Georgia	15.3
46	California	15.2
47	Idaho	15.1
48	Colorado	13.9
49	Alaska	12.2
50	Utah	10.9

District of Columbia   23.5

Source: Morgan Quitno Press using data from American Cancer Society
    "Cancer Facts & Figures 2005" (Copyright 2005, American Cancer Society)
*Rates calculated using 2004 Census resident population estimates. Not age-adjusted.

Estimated Deaths by Leukemia in 2005

National Estimated Total = 22,570 Deaths

ALPHA ORDER					RANK ORDER			
RANK	STATE		DEATHS	% of USA	RANK	STATE	DEATHS	% of USA
22	Alabama		360	1.6%	1	California	2,190	9.7%
NA	Alaska*		NA	NA	2	Florida	1,700	7.5%
21	Arizona		400	1.8%	3	Texas	1,460	6.5%
30	Arkansas		260	1.2%	4	New York	1,410	6.2%
1	California		2,190	9.7%	5	Pennsylvania	1,060	4.7%
27	Colorado		300	1.3%	6	Illinois	1,050	4.7%
30	Connecticut		260	1.2%	7	Ohio	980	4.3%
43	Delaware		80	0.4%	8	Michigan	810	3.6%
2	Florida		1,700	7.5%	9	New Jersey	710	3.1%
13	Georgia		530	2.3%	10	North Carolina	640	2.8%
43	Hawaii		80	0.4%	11	Missouri	540	2.4%
40	Idaho		100	0.4%	11	Virginia	540	2.4%
6	Illinois		1,050	4.7%	13	Georgia	530	2.3%
13	Indiana		530	2.3%	13	Indiana	530	2.3%
26	Iowa		310	1.4%	15	Massachusetts	500	2.2%
33	Kansas		230	1.0%	15	Wisconsin	500	2.2%
25	Kentucky		320	1.4%	17	Tennessee	490	2.2%
23	Louisiana		350	1.6%	18	Washington	470	2.1%
40	Maine		100	0.4%	19	Maryland	440	1.9%
19	Maryland		440	1.9%	20	Minnesota	430	1.9%
15	Massachusetts		500	2.2%	21	Arizona	400	1.8%
8	Michigan		810	3.6%	22	Alabama	360	1.6%
20	Minnesota		430	1.9%	23	Louisiana	350	1.6%
32	Mississippi		240	1.1%	24	South Carolina	330	1.5%
11	Missouri		540	2.4%	25	Kentucky	320	1.4%
42	Montana		90	0.4%	26	Iowa	310	1.4%
35	Nebraska		160	0.7%	27	Colorado	300	1.3%
34	Nevada		170	0.8%	27	Oklahoma	300	1.3%
38	New Hampshire		110	0.5%	29	Oregon	270	1.2%
9	New Jersey		710	3.1%	30	Arkansas	260	1.2%
38	New Mexico		110	0.5%	30	Connecticut	260	1.2%
4	New York		1,410	6.2%	32	Mississippi	240	1.1%
10	North Carolina		640	2.8%	33	Kansas	230	1.0%
46	North Dakota		70	0.3%	34	Nevada	170	0.8%
7	Ohio		980	4.3%	35	Nebraska	160	0.7%
27	Oklahoma		300	1.3%	36	Utah	140	0.6%
29	Oregon		270	1.2%	36	West Virginia	140	0.6%
5	Pennsylvania		1,060	4.7%	38	New Hampshire	110	0.5%
43	Rhode Island		80	0.4%	38	New Mexico	110	0.5%
24	South Carolina		330	1.5%	40	Idaho	100	0.4%
46	South Dakota		70	0.3%	40	Maine	100	0.4%
17	Tennessee		490	2.2%	42	Montana	90	0.4%
3	Texas		1,460	6.5%	43	Delaware	80	0.4%
36	Utah		140	0.6%	43	Hawaii	80	0.4%
48	Vermont		60	0.3%	43	Rhode Island	80	0.4%
11	Virginia		540	2.4%	46	North Dakota	70	0.3%
18	Washington		470	2.1%	46	South Dakota	70	0.3%
36	West Virginia		140	0.6%	48	Vermont	60	0.3%
15	Wisconsin		500	2.2%	NA	Alaska*	NA	NA
NA	Wyoming*		NA	NA	NA	Wyoming*	NA	NA
						District of Columbia*	NA	NA

Source: American Cancer Society
    "Cancer Facts & Figures 2005" (Copyright 2005, American Cancer Society)
*Fewer than 50 deaths.

Estimated Death Rate by Leukemia in 2005

National Estimated Rate = 7.7 Deaths per 100,000 Population*

ALPHA ORDER

RANK	STATE	RATE
24	Alabama	7.9
NA	Alaska**	NA
41	Arizona	7.0
7	Arkansas	9.4
45	California	6.1
42	Colorado	6.5
35	Connecticut	7.4
6	Delaware	9.6
3	Florida	9.8
46	Georgia	6.0
44	Hawaii	6.3
39	Idaho	7.2
19	Illinois	8.3
13	Indiana	8.5
2	Iowa	10.5
17	Kansas	8.4
29	Kentucky	7.7
27	Louisiana	7.8
31	Maine	7.6
24	Maryland	7.9
27	Massachusetts	7.8
23	Michigan	8.0
17	Minnesota	8.4
19	Mississippi	8.3
7	Missouri	9.4
4	Montana	9.7
9	Nebraska	9.2
37	Nevada	7.3
13	New Hampshire	8.5
22	New Jersey	8.2
48	New Mexico	5.8
37	New York	7.3
33	North Carolina	7.5
1	North Dakota	11.0
12	Ohio	8.6
13	Oklahoma	8.5
33	Oregon	7.5
13	Pennsylvania	8.5
35	Rhode Island	7.4
24	South Carolina	7.9
10	South Dakota	9.1
19	Tennessee	8.3
42	Texas	6.5
47	Utah	5.9
4	Vermont	9.7
39	Virginia	7.2
31	Washington	7.6
29	West Virginia	7.7
10	Wisconsin	9.1
NA	Wyoming**	NA

RANK ORDER

RANK	STATE	RATE
1	North Dakota	11.0
2	Iowa	10.5
3	Florida	9.8
4	Montana	9.7
4	Vermont	9.7
6	Delaware	9.6
7	Arkansas	9.4
7	Missouri	9.4
9	Nebraska	9.2
10	South Dakota	9.1
10	Wisconsin	9.1
12	Ohio	8.6
13	Indiana	8.5
13	New Hampshire	8.5
13	Oklahoma	8.5
13	Pennsylvania	8.5
17	Kansas	8.4
17	Minnesota	8.4
19	Illinois	8.3
19	Mississippi	8.3
19	Tennessee	8.3
22	New Jersey	8.2
23	Michigan	8.0
24	Alabama	7.9
24	Maryland	7.9
24	South Carolina	7.9
27	Louisiana	7.8
27	Massachusetts	7.8
29	Kentucky	7.7
29	West Virginia	7.7
31	Maine	7.6
31	Washington	7.6
33	North Carolina	7.5
33	Oregon	7.5
35	Connecticut	7.4
35	Rhode Island	7.4
37	Nevada	7.3
37	New York	7.3
39	Idaho	7.2
39	Virginia	7.2
41	Arizona	7.0
42	Colorado	6.5
42	Texas	6.5
44	Hawaii	6.3
45	California	6.1
46	Georgia	6.0
47	Utah	5.9
48	New Mexico	5.8
NA	Alaska**	NA
NA	Wyoming**	NA
	District of Columbia**	NA

Source: Morgan Quitno Press using data from American Cancer Society
"Cancer Facts & Figures 2005" (Copyright 2005, American Cancer Society)
*Rates calculated using 2004 Census resident population estimates. Not age-adjusted.
**Fewer than 50 deaths.

Estimated Deaths by Liver Cancer in 2005

National Estimated Total = 15,420 Deaths

ALPHA ORDER					RANK ORDER			
RANK	STATE		DEATHS	% of USA	RANK	STATE	DEATHS	% of USA
17	Alabama		290	1.9%	1	California	2,070	13.4%
NA	Alaska*		NA	NA	2	Texas	1,280	8.3%
17	Arizona		290	1.9%	3	Florida	1,110	7.2%
25	Arkansas		200	1.3%	4	New York	1,010	6.5%
1	California		2,070	13.4%	5	Pennsylvania	730	4.7%
27	Colorado		170	1.1%	6	Illinois	680	4.4%
27	Connecticut		170	1.1%	7	Ohio	570	3.7%
NA	Delaware*		NA	NA	8	Michigan	530	3.4%
3	Florida		1,110	7.2%	9	New Jersey	410	2.7%
12	Georgia		340	2.2%	10	North Carolina	380	2.5%
37	Hawaii		100	0.6%	11	Massachusetts	370	2.4%
43	Idaho		50	0.3%	12	Georgia	340	2.2%
6	Illinois		680	4.4%	12	Virginia	340	2.2%
22	Indiana		250	1.6%	12	Washington	340	2.2%
33	Iowa		120	0.8%	15	Louisiana	310	2.0%
33	Kansas		120	0.8%	16	Tennessee	300	1.9%
25	Kentucky		200	1.3%	17	Alabama	290	1.9%
15	Louisiana		310	2.0%	17	Arizona	290	1.9%
38	Maine		70	0.5%	17	Missouri	290	1.9%
21	Maryland		260	1.7%	17	Wisconsin	290	1.9%
11	Massachusetts		370	2.4%	21	Maryland	260	1.7%
8	Michigan		530	3.4%	22	Indiana	250	1.6%
24	Minnesota		210	1.4%	23	South Carolina	220	1.4%
31	Mississippi		150	1.0%	24	Minnesota	210	1.4%
17	Missouri		290	1.9%	25	Arkansas	200	1.3%
43	Montana		50	0.3%	25	Kentucky	200	1.3%
40	Nebraska		60	0.4%	27	Colorado	170	1.1%
33	Nevada		120	0.8%	27	Connecticut	170	1.1%
38	New Hampshire		70	0.5%	27	Oklahoma	170	1.1%
9	New Jersey		410	2.7%	30	Oregon	160	1.0%
32	New Mexico		130	0.8%	31	Mississippi	150	1.0%
4	New York		1,010	6.5%	32	New Mexico	130	0.8%
10	North Carolina		380	2.5%	33	Iowa	120	0.8%
NA	North Dakota*		NA	NA	33	Kansas	120	0.8%
7	Ohio		570	3.7%	33	Nevada	120	0.8%
27	Oklahoma		170	1.1%	36	West Virginia	110	0.7%
30	Oregon		160	1.0%	37	Hawaii	100	0.6%
5	Pennsylvania		730	4.7%	38	Maine	70	0.5%
40	Rhode Island		60	0.4%	38	New Hampshire	70	0.5%
23	South Carolina		220	1.4%	40	Nebraska	60	0.4%
NA	South Dakota*		NA	NA	40	Rhode Island	60	0.4%
16	Tennessee		300	1.9%	40	Utah	60	0.4%
2	Texas		1,280	8.3%	43	Idaho	50	0.3%
40	Utah		60	0.4%	43	Montana	50	0.3%
NA	Vermont*		NA	NA	NA	Alaska*	NA	NA
12	Virginia		340	2.2%	NA	Delaware*	NA	NA
12	Washington		340	2.2%	NA	North Dakota*	NA	NA
36	West Virginia		110	0.7%	NA	South Dakota*	NA	NA
17	Wisconsin		290	1.9%	NA	Vermont*	NA	NA
NA	Wyoming*		NA	NA	NA	Wyoming*	NA	NA
						District of Columbia*	NA	NA

Source: American Cancer Society
   "Cancer Facts & Figures 2005" (Copyright 2005, American Cancer Society)
*Fewer than 50 deaths.

Estimated Death Rate by Liver Cancer in 2005

National Estimated Rate = 5.3 Deaths per 100,000 Population*

ALPHA ORDER				RANK ORDER		
RANK	STATE	RATE		RANK	STATE	RATE
5	Alabama	6.4		1	Hawaii	7.9
NA	Alaska**	NA		2	Arkansas	7.3
25	Arizona	5.0		3	Louisiana	6.9
2	Arkansas	7.3		4	New Mexico	6.8
9	California	5.8		5	Alabama	6.4
41	Colorado	3.7		5	Florida	6.4
28	Connecticut	4.9		7	West Virginia	6.1
NA	Delaware**	NA		8	Pennsylvania	5.9
5	Florida	6.4		9	California	5.8
40	Georgia	3.9		9	Massachusetts	5.8
1	Hawaii	7.9		11	Texas	5.7
42	Idaho	3.6		12	Rhode Island	5.6
16	Illinois	5.3		13	Washington	5.5
39	Indiana	4.0		14	Montana	5.4
37	Iowa	4.1		14	New Hampshire	5.4
35	Kansas	4.4		16	Illinois	5.3
29	Kentucky	4.8		16	Maine	5.3
3	Louisiana	6.9		16	New York	5.3
16	Maine	5.3		16	Wisconsin	5.3
31	Maryland	4.7		20	Michigan	5.2
9	Massachusetts	5.8		20	Mississippi	5.2
20	Michigan	5.2		20	South Carolina	5.2
37	Minnesota	4.1		23	Nevada	5.1
20	Mississippi	5.2		23	Tennessee	5.1
25	Missouri	5.0		25	Arizona	5.0
14	Montana	5.4		25	Missouri	5.0
43	Nebraska	3.4		25	Ohio	5.0
23	Nevada	5.1		28	Connecticut	4.9
14	New Hampshire	5.4		29	Kentucky	4.8
31	New Jersey	4.7		29	Oklahoma	4.8
4	New Mexico	6.8		31	Maryland	4.7
16	New York	5.3		31	New Jersey	4.7
35	North Carolina	4.4		33	Virginia	4.6
NA	North Dakota**	NA		34	Oregon	4.5
25	Ohio	5.0		35	Kansas	4.4
29	Oklahoma	4.8		35	North Carolina	4.4
34	Oregon	4.5		37	Iowa	4.1
8	Pennsylvania	5.9		37	Minnesota	4.1
12	Rhode Island	5.6		39	Indiana	4.0
20	South Carolina	5.2		40	Georgia	3.9
NA	South Dakota**	NA		41	Colorado	3.7
23	Tennessee	5.1		42	Idaho	3.6
11	Texas	5.7		43	Nebraska	3.4
44	Utah	2.5		44	Utah	2.5
NA	Vermont**	NA		NA	Alaska**	NA
33	Virginia	4.6		NA	Delaware**	NA
13	Washington	5.5		NA	North Dakota**	NA
7	West Virginia	6.1		NA	South Dakota**	NA
16	Wisconsin	5.3		NA	Vermont**	NA
NA	Wyoming**	NA		NA	Wyoming**	NA
				NA	District of Columbia**	NA

Source: Morgan Quitno Press using data from American Cancer Society
"Cancer Facts & Figures 2005" (Copyright 2005, American Cancer Society)
*Rates calculated using 2004 Census resident population estimates. Not age-adjusted.
**Fewer than 50 deaths.

Estimated Deaths by Lung Cancer in 2005

National Estimated Total = 163,510 Deaths

ALPHA ORDER

RANK	STATE	DEATHS	% of USA
19	Alabama	3,160	1.9%
50	Alaska	210	0.1%
24	Arizona	2,720	1.7%
27	Arkansas	2,400	1.5%
1	California	14,350	8.8%
32	Colorado	1,660	1.0%
30	Connecticut	1,850	1.1%
44	Delaware	460	0.3%
2	Florida	12,440	7.6%
11	Georgia	4,550	2.8%
43	Hawaii	480	0.3%
41	Idaho	600	0.4%
7	Illinois	6,840	4.2%
13	Indiana	4,180	2.6%
31	Iowa	1,700	1.0%
34	Kansas	1,540	0.9%
17	Kentucky	3,490	2.1%
21	Louisiana	2,930	1.8%
37	Maine	940	0.6%
20	Maryland	3,040	1.9%
16	Massachusetts	3,800	2.3%
8	Michigan	5,790	3.5%
25	Minnesota	2,480	1.5%
28	Mississippi	2,070	1.3%
15	Missouri	3,860	2.4%
42	Montana	590	0.4%
36	Nebraska	950	0.6%
35	Nevada	1,450	0.9%
38	New Hampshire	750	0.5%
10	New Jersey	4,580	2.8%
39	New Mexico	720	0.4%
4	New York	9,350	5.7%
9	North Carolina	5,230	3.2%
48	North Dakota	310	0.2%
6	Ohio	7,380	4.5%
26	Oklahoma	2,440	1.5%
29	Oregon	2,050	1.3%
5	Pennsylvania	8,030	4.9%
40	Rhode Island	680	0.4%
23	South Carolina	2,730	1.7%
46	South Dakota	410	0.3%
12	Tennessee	4,390	2.7%
3	Texas	10,620	6.5%
45	Utah	440	0.3%
47	Vermont	370	0.2%
14	Virginia	4,170	2.6%
18	Washington	3,260	2.0%
33	West Virginia	1,610	1.0%
22	Wisconsin	2,900	1.8%
49	Wyoming	270	0.2%

RANK ORDER

RANK	STATE	DEATHS	% of USA
1	California	14,350	8.8%
2	Florida	12,440	7.6%
3	Texas	10,620	6.5%
4	New York	9,350	5.7%
5	Pennsylvania	8,030	4.9%
6	Ohio	7,380	4.5%
7	Illinois	6,840	4.2%
8	Michigan	5,790	3.5%
9	North Carolina	5,230	3.2%
10	New Jersey	4,580	2.8%
11	Georgia	4,550	2.8%
12	Tennessee	4,390	2.7%
13	Indiana	4,180	2.6%
14	Virginia	4,170	2.6%
15	Missouri	3,860	2.4%
16	Massachusetts	3,800	2.3%
17	Kentucky	3,490	2.1%
18	Washington	3,260	2.0%
19	Alabama	3,160	1.9%
20	Maryland	3,040	1.9%
21	Louisiana	2,930	1.8%
22	Wisconsin	2,900	1.8%
23	South Carolina	2,730	1.7%
24	Arizona	2,720	1.7%
25	Minnesota	2,480	1.5%
26	Oklahoma	2,440	1.5%
27	Arkansas	2,400	1.5%
28	Mississippi	2,070	1.3%
29	Oregon	2,050	1.3%
30	Connecticut	1,850	1.1%
31	Iowa	1,700	1.0%
32	Colorado	1,660	1.0%
33	West Virginia	1,610	1.0%
34	Kansas	1,540	0.9%
35	Nevada	1,450	0.9%
36	Nebraska	950	0.6%
37	Maine	940	0.6%
38	New Hampshire	750	0.5%
39	New Mexico	720	0.4%
40	Rhode Island	680	0.4%
41	Idaho	600	0.4%
42	Montana	590	0.4%
43	Hawaii	480	0.3%
44	Delaware	460	0.3%
45	Utah	440	0.3%
46	South Dakota	410	0.3%
47	Vermont	370	0.2%
48	North Dakota	310	0.2%
49	Wyoming	270	0.2%
50	Alaska	210	0.1%
	District of Columbia	290	0.2%

Source: American Cancer Society
"Cancer Facts & Figures 2005" (Copyright 2005, American Cancer Society)

Estimated Death Rate by Lung Cancer in 2005

National Estimated Rate = 55.7 Deaths per 100,000 Population*

ALPHA ORDER			RANK ORDER		
RANK	STATE	RATE	RANK	STATE	RATE
8	Alabama	69.8	1	West Virginia	88.7
49	Alaska	32.0	2	Arkansas	87.2
42	Arizona	47.4	3	Kentucky	84.2
2	Arkansas	87.2	4	Tennessee	74.4
45	California	40.0	5	Florida	71.5
48	Colorado	36.1	6	Maine	71.4
34	Connecticut	52.8	7	Mississippi	71.3
28	Delaware	55.4	8	Alabama	69.8
5	Florida	71.5	9	Oklahoma	69.2
38	Georgia	51.5	10	Missouri	67.1
46	Hawaii	38.0	11	Indiana	67.0
44	Idaho	43.1	12	South Carolina	65.0
31	Illinois	53.8	13	Louisiana	64.9
11	Indiana	67.0	14	Pennsylvania	64.7
23	Iowa	57.5	15	Ohio	64.4
26	Kansas	56.3	16	Montana	63.7
3	Kentucky	84.2	17	Rhode Island	62.9
13	Louisiana	64.9	18	Nevada	62.1
6	Maine	71.4	19	North Carolina	61.2
29	Maryland	54.7	20	Vermont	59.5
21	Massachusetts	59.2	21	Massachusetts	59.2
24	Michigan	57.3	22	New Hampshire	57.7
40	Minnesota	48.6	23	Iowa	57.5
7	Mississippi	71.3	24	Michigan	57.3
10	Missouri	67.1	25	Oregon	57.0
16	Montana	63.7	26	Kansas	56.3
30	Nebraska	54.4	27	Virginia	55.9
18	Nevada	62.1	28	Delaware	55.4
22	New Hampshire	57.7	29	Maryland	54.7
35	New Jersey	52.7	30	Nebraska	54.4
47	New Mexico	37.8	31	Illinois	53.8
40	New York	48.6	32	Wyoming	53.3
19	North Carolina	61.2	33	South Dakota	53.2
39	North Dakota	48.9	34	Connecticut	52.8
15	Ohio	64.4	35	New Jersey	52.7
9	Oklahoma	69.2	36	Wisconsin	52.6
25	Oregon	57.0	37	Washington	52.5
14	Pennsylvania	64.7	38	Georgia	51.5
17	Rhode Island	62.9	39	North Dakota	48.9
12	South Carolina	65.0	40	Minnesota	48.6
33	South Dakota	53.2	40	New York	48.6
4	Tennessee	74.4	42	Arizona	47.4
43	Texas	47.2	43	Texas	47.2
50	Utah	18.4	44	Idaho	43.1
20	Vermont	59.5	45	California	40.0
27	Virginia	55.9	46	Hawaii	38.0
37	Washington	52.5	47	New Mexico	37.8
1	West Virginia	88.7	48	Colorado	36.1
36	Wisconsin	52.6	49	Alaska	32.0
32	Wyoming	53.3	50	Utah	18.4
				District of Columbia	52.4

Source: Morgan Quitno Press using data from American Cancer Society
  "Cancer Facts & Figures 2005" (Copyright 2005, American Cancer Society)
*Rates calculated using 2004 Census resident population estimates. Not age-adjusted.

Estimated Deaths by Non-Hodgkin's Lymphoma in 2005

National Estimated Total = 19,200 Deaths

ALPHA ORDER

RANK	STATE	DEATHS	% of USA
25	Alabama	320	1.7%
NA	Alaska*	NA	NA
20	Arizona	360	1.9%
31	Arkansas	220	1.1%
1	California	1,940	10.1%
27	Colorado	300	1.6%
29	Connecticut	250	1.3%
44	Delaware	70	0.4%
2	Florida	1,180	6.1%
14	Georgia	470	2.4%
41	Hawaii	90	0.5%
44	Idaho	70	0.4%
6	Illinois	750	3.9%
12	Indiana	480	2.5%
28	Iowa	260	1.4%
31	Kansas	220	1.1%
24	Kentucky	330	1.7%
20	Louisiana	360	1.9%
41	Maine	90	0.5%
22	Maryland	350	1.8%
17	Massachusetts	430	2.2%
7	Michigan	730	3.8%
14	Minnesota	470	2.4%
33	Mississippi	180	0.9%
11	Missouri	520	2.7%
44	Montana	70	0.4%
36	Nebraska	130	0.7%
35	Nevada	150	0.8%
38	New Hampshire	110	0.6%
9	New Jersey	600	3.1%
38	New Mexico	110	0.6%
4	New York	1,000	5.2%
9	North Carolina	600	3.1%
47	North Dakota	60	0.3%
8	Ohio	670	3.5%
30	Oklahoma	230	1.2%
23	Oregon	340	1.8%
5	Pennsylvania	980	5.1%
40	Rhode Island	100	0.5%
25	South Carolina	320	1.7%
43	South Dakota	80	0.4%
16	Tennessee	460	2.4%
3	Texas	1,040	5.4%
36	Utah	130	0.7%
47	Vermont	60	0.3%
18	Virginia	400	2.1%
12	Washington	480	2.5%
34	West Virginia	170	0.9%
19	Wisconsin	380	2.0%
NA	Wyoming*	NA	NA

RANK ORDER

RANK	STATE	DEATHS	% of USA
1	California	1,940	10.1%
2	Florida	1,180	6.1%
3	Texas	1,040	5.4%
4	New York	1,000	5.2%
5	Pennsylvania	980	5.1%
6	Illinois	750	3.9%
7	Michigan	730	3.8%
8	Ohio	670	3.5%
9	New Jersey	600	3.1%
9	North Carolina	600	3.1%
11	Missouri	520	2.7%
12	Indiana	480	2.5%
12	Washington	480	2.5%
14	Georgia	470	2.4%
14	Minnesota	470	2.4%
16	Tennessee	460	2.4%
17	Massachusetts	430	2.2%
18	Virginia	400	2.1%
19	Wisconsin	380	2.0%
20	Arizona	360	1.9%
20	Louisiana	360	1.9%
22	Maryland	350	1.8%
23	Oregon	340	1.8%
24	Kentucky	330	1.7%
25	Alabama	320	1.7%
25	South Carolina	320	1.7%
27	Colorado	300	1.6%
28	Iowa	260	1.4%
29	Connecticut	250	1.3%
30	Oklahoma	230	1.2%
31	Arkansas	220	1.1%
31	Kansas	220	1.1%
33	Mississippi	180	0.9%
34	West Virginia	170	0.9%
35	Nevada	150	0.8%
36	Nebraska	130	0.7%
36	Utah	130	0.7%
38	New Hampshire	110	0.6%
38	New Mexico	110	0.6%
40	Rhode Island	100	0.5%
41	Hawaii	90	0.5%
41	Maine	90	0.5%
43	South Dakota	80	0.4%
44	Delaware	70	0.4%
44	Idaho	70	0.4%
44	Montana	70	0.4%
47	North Dakota	60	0.3%
47	Vermont	60	0.3%
NA	Alaska*	NA	NA
NA	Wyoming*	NA	NA
	District of Columbia*	NA	NA

Source: American Cancer Society
"Cancer Facts & Figures 2005" (Copyright 2005, American Cancer Society)
*Fewer than 50 deaths.

Estimated Death Rate by Non-Hodgkin's Lymphoma in 2005

National Estimated Rate = 6.5 Deaths per 100,000 Population*

ALPHA ORDER				RANK ORDER		
RANK	STATE	RATE		RANK	STATE	RATE
24	Alabama	7.1		1	South Dakota	10.4
NA	Alaska**	NA		2	Vermont	9.7
36	Arizona	6.3		3	North Dakota	9.5
12	Arkansas	8.0		3	Oregon	9.5
42	California	5.4		5	West Virginia	9.4
33	Colorado	6.5		6	Rhode Island	9.3
24	Connecticut	7.1		7	Minnesota	9.2
11	Delaware	8.4		8	Missouri	9.0
30	Florida	6.8		9	Iowa	8.8
45	Georgia	5.3		10	New Hampshire	8.5
24	Hawaii	7.1		11	Delaware	8.4
47	Idaho	5.0		12	Arkansas	8.0
39	Illinois	5.9		12	Kansas	8.0
18	Indiana	7.7		12	Kentucky	8.0
9	Iowa	8.8		12	Louisiana	8.0
12	Kansas	8.0		16	Pennsylvania	7.9
12	Kentucky	8.0		17	Tennessee	7.8
12	Louisiana	8.0		18	Indiana	7.7
30	Maine	6.8		18	Washington	7.7
36	Maryland	6.3		20	Montana	7.6
32	Massachusetts	6.7		20	South Carolina	7.6
23	Michigan	7.2		22	Nebraska	7.4
7	Minnesota	9.2		23	Michigan	7.2
38	Mississippi	6.2		24	Alabama	7.1
8	Missouri	9.0		24	Connecticut	7.1
20	Montana	7.6		24	Hawaii	7.1
22	Nebraska	7.4		27	North Carolina	7.0
35	Nevada	6.4		28	New Jersey	6.9
10	New Hampshire	8.5		28	Wisconsin	6.9
28	New Jersey	6.9		30	Florida	6.8
40	New Mexico	5.8		30	Maine	6.8
46	New York	5.2		32	Massachusetts	6.7
27	North Carolina	7.0		33	Colorado	6.5
3	North Dakota	9.5		33	Oklahoma	6.5
40	Ohio	5.8		35	Nevada	6.4
33	Oklahoma	6.5		36	Arizona	6.3
3	Oregon	9.5		36	Maryland	6.3
16	Pennsylvania	7.9		38	Mississippi	6.2
6	Rhode Island	9.3		39	Illinois	5.9
20	South Carolina	7.6		40	New Mexico	5.8
1	South Dakota	10.4		40	Ohio	5.8
17	Tennessee	7.8		42	California	5.4
48	Texas	4.6		42	Utah	5.4
42	Utah	5.4		42	Virginia	5.4
2	Vermont	9.7		45	Georgia	5.3
42	Virginia	5.4		46	New York	5.2
18	Washington	7.7		47	Idaho	5.0
5	West Virginia	9.4		48	Texas	4.6
28	Wisconsin	6.9		NA	Alaska**	NA
NA	Wyoming**	NA		NA	Wyoming**	NA
					District of Columbia**	NA

Source: Morgan Quitno Press using data from American Cancer Society
"Cancer Facts & Figures 2005" (Copyright 2005, American Cancer Society)
*Rates calculated using 2004 Census resident population estimates. Not age-adjusted.
**Fewer than 50 deaths.

Estimated Deaths by Pancreatic Cancer in 2005

National Estimated Total = 31,800 Deaths

ALPHA ORDER

RANK	STATE	DEATHS	% of USA
22	Alabama	530	1.7%
49	Alaska	50	0.2%
20	Arizona	550	1.7%
32	Arkansas	310	1.0%
1	California	3,150	9.9%
28	Colorado	400	1.3%
25	Connecticut	430	1.4%
44	Delaware	100	0.3%
3	Florida	2,250	7.1%
12	Georgia	770	2.4%
40	Hawaii	150	0.5%
43	Idaho	130	0.4%
6	Illinois	1,470	4.6%
14	Indiana	690	2.2%
29	Iowa	390	1.2%
33	Kansas	290	0.9%
26	Kentucky	420	1.3%
23	Louisiana	520	1.6%
36	Maine	180	0.6%
19	Maryland	590	1.9%
11	Massachusetts	850	2.7%
8	Michigan	1,140	3.6%
20	Minnesota	550	1.7%
31	Mississippi	330	1.0%
17	Missouri	670	2.1%
44	Montana	100	0.3%
36	Nebraska	180	0.6%
34	Nevada	230	0.7%
41	New Hampshire	140	0.4%
9	New Jersey	1,050	3.3%
36	New Mexico	180	0.6%
2	New York	2,270	7.1%
10	North Carolina	910	2.9%
47	North Dakota	80	0.3%
7	Ohio	1,300	4.1%
30	Oklahoma	360	1.1%
27	Oregon	410	1.3%
5	Pennsylvania	1,670	5.3%
41	Rhode Island	140	0.4%
24	South Carolina	510	1.6%
46	South Dakota	90	0.3%
16	Tennessee	680	2.1%
4	Texas	1,950	6.1%
39	Utah	170	0.5%
48	Vermont	70	0.2%
13	Virginia	750	2.4%
14	Washington	690	2.2%
35	West Virginia	200	0.6%
18	Wisconsin	650	2.0%
49	Wyoming	50	0.2%

RANK ORDER

RANK	STATE	DEATHS	% of USA
1	California	3,150	9.9%
2	New York	2,270	7.1%
3	Florida	2,250	7.1%
4	Texas	1,950	6.1%
5	Pennsylvania	1,670	5.3%
6	Illinois	1,470	4.6%
7	Ohio	1,300	4.1%
8	Michigan	1,140	3.6%
9	New Jersey	1,050	3.3%
10	North Carolina	910	2.9%
11	Massachusetts	850	2.7%
12	Georgia	770	2.4%
13	Virginia	750	2.4%
14	Indiana	690	2.2%
14	Washington	690	2.2%
16	Tennessee	680	2.1%
17	Missouri	670	2.1%
18	Wisconsin	650	2.0%
19	Maryland	590	1.9%
20	Arizona	550	1.7%
20	Minnesota	550	1.7%
22	Alabama	530	1.7%
23	Louisiana	520	1.6%
24	South Carolina	510	1.6%
25	Connecticut	430	1.4%
26	Kentucky	420	1.3%
27	Oregon	410	1.3%
28	Colorado	400	1.3%
29	Iowa	390	1.2%
30	Oklahoma	360	1.1%
31	Mississippi	330	1.0%
32	Arkansas	310	1.0%
33	Kansas	290	0.9%
34	Nevada	230	0.7%
35	West Virginia	200	0.6%
36	Maine	180	0.6%
36	Nebraska	180	0.6%
36	New Mexico	180	0.6%
39	Utah	170	0.5%
40	Hawaii	150	0.5%
41	New Hampshire	140	0.4%
41	Rhode Island	140	0.4%
43	Idaho	130	0.4%
44	Delaware	100	0.3%
44	Montana	100	0.3%
46	South Dakota	90	0.3%
47	North Dakota	80	0.3%
48	Vermont	70	0.2%
49	Alaska	50	0.2%
49	Wyoming	50	0.2%
	District of Columbia	60	0.2%

Source: American Cancer Society
"Cancer Facts & Figures 2005" (Copyright 2005, American Cancer Society)

Estimated Death Rate by Pancreatic Cancer in 2005

National Estimated Rate = 10.8 Deaths per 100,000 Population*

ALPHA ORDER

RANK	STATE	RATE
15	Alabama	11.7
49	Alaska	7.6
42	Arizona	9.6
23	Arkansas	11.3
45	California	8.8
46	Colorado	8.7
8	Connecticut	12.3
11	Delaware	12.0
6	Florida	12.9
46	Georgia	8.7
12	Hawaii	11.9
44	Idaho	9.3
17	Illinois	11.6
27	Indiana	11.1
3	Iowa	13.2
34	Kansas	10.6
38	Kentucky	10.1
19	Louisiana	11.5
1	Maine	13.7
34	Maryland	10.6
3	Massachusetts	13.2
23	Michigan	11.3
30	Minnesota	10.8
21	Mississippi	11.4
17	Missouri	11.6
30	Montana	10.8
36	Nebraska	10.3
40	Nevada	9.9
30	New Hampshire	10.8
9	New Jersey	12.1
43	New Mexico	9.5
13	New York	11.8
33	North Carolina	10.7
7	North Dakota	12.6
23	Ohio	11.3
37	Oklahoma	10.2
21	Oregon	11.4
2	Pennsylvania	13.5
5	Rhode Island	13.0
9	South Carolina	12.1
15	South Dakota	11.7
19	Tennessee	11.5
46	Texas	8.7
50	Utah	7.1
23	Vermont	11.3
38	Virginia	10.1
27	Washington	11.1
29	West Virginia	11.0
13	Wisconsin	11.8
40	Wyoming	9.9

RANK ORDER

RANK	STATE	RATE
1	Maine	13.7
2	Pennsylvania	13.5
3	Iowa	13.2
3	Massachusetts	13.2
5	Rhode Island	13.0
6	Florida	12.9
7	North Dakota	12.6
8	Connecticut	12.3
9	New Jersey	12.1
9	South Carolina	12.1
11	Delaware	12.0
12	Hawaii	11.9
13	New York	11.8
13	Wisconsin	11.8
15	Alabama	11.7
15	South Dakota	11.7
17	Illinois	11.6
17	Missouri	11.6
19	Louisiana	11.5
19	Tennessee	11.5
21	Mississippi	11.4
21	Oregon	11.4
23	Arkansas	11.3
23	Michigan	11.3
23	Ohio	11.3
23	Vermont	11.3
27	Indiana	11.1
27	Washington	11.1
29	West Virginia	11.0
30	Minnesota	10.8
30	Montana	10.8
30	New Hampshire	10.8
33	North Carolina	10.7
34	Kansas	10.6
34	Maryland	10.6
36	Nebraska	10.3
37	Oklahoma	10.2
38	Kentucky	10.1
38	Virginia	10.1
40	Nevada	9.9
40	Wyoming	9.9
42	Arizona	9.6
43	New Mexico	9.5
44	Idaho	9.3
45	California	8.8
46	Colorado	8.7
46	Georgia	8.7
46	Texas	8.7
49	Alaska	7.6
50	Utah	7.1

District of Columbia   10.8

*Source: Morgan Quitno Press using data from American Cancer Society
"Cancer Facts & Figures 2005" (Copyright 2005, American Cancer Society)
Rates calculated using 2004 Census resident population estimates. Not age-adjusted.

Estimated Deaths by Prostate Cancer in 2005

National Estimated Total = 30,350 Deaths

ALPHA ORDER

RANK	STATE	DEATHS	% of USA
16	Alabama	570	1.9%
NA	Alaska*	NA	NA
22	Arizona	510	1.7%
32	Arkansas	270	0.9%
1	California	3,270	10.8%
29	Colorado	350	1.2%
24	Connecticut	440	1.4%
46	Delaware	80	0.3%
2	Florida	2,570	8.5%
12	Georgia	740	2.4%
43	Hawaii	120	0.4%
39	Idaho	150	0.5%
7	Illinois	1,230	4.1%
15	Indiana	640	2.1%
26	Iowa	400	1.3%
32	Kansas	270	0.9%
30	Kentucky	330	1.1%
23	Louisiana	450	1.5%
38	Maine	170	0.6%
19	Maryland	550	1.8%
14	Massachusetts	700	2.3%
8	Michigan	1,000	3.3%
16	Minnesota	570	1.9%
25	Mississippi	420	1.4%
26	Missouri	400	1.3%
42	Montana	130	0.4%
37	Nebraska	180	0.6%
34	Nevada	260	0.9%
39	New Hampshire	150	0.5%
10	New Jersey	840	2.8%
35	New Mexico	220	0.7%
3	New York	1,860	6.1%
9	North Carolina	890	2.9%
46	North Dakota	80	0.3%
6	Ohio	1,420	4.7%
31	Oklahoma	320	1.1%
28	Oregon	390	1.3%
5	Pennsylvania	1,720	5.7%
45	Rhode Island	110	0.4%
19	South Carolina	550	1.8%
43	South Dakota	120	0.4%
18	Tennessee	560	1.8%
4	Texas	1,750	5.8%
39	Utah	150	0.5%
49	Vermont	60	0.2%
11	Virginia	750	2.5%
13	Washington	720	2.4%
36	West Virginia	190	0.6%
21	Wisconsin	530	1.7%
46	Wyoming	80	0.3%

RANK ORDER

RANK	STATE	DEATHS	% of USA
1	California	3,270	10.8%
2	Florida	2,570	8.5%
3	New York	1,860	6.1%
4	Texas	1,750	5.8%
5	Pennsylvania	1,720	5.7%
6	Ohio	1,420	4.7%
7	Illinois	1,230	4.1%
8	Michigan	1,000	3.3%
9	North Carolina	890	2.9%
10	New Jersey	840	2.8%
11	Virginia	750	2.5%
12	Georgia	740	2.4%
13	Washington	720	2.4%
14	Massachusetts	700	2.3%
15	Indiana	640	2.1%
16	Alabama	570	1.9%
16	Minnesota	570	1.9%
18	Tennessee	560	1.8%
19	Maryland	550	1.8%
19	South Carolina	550	1.8%
21	Wisconsin	530	1.7%
22	Arizona	510	1.7%
23	Louisiana	450	1.5%
24	Connecticut	440	1.4%
25	Mississippi	420	1.4%
26	Iowa	400	1.3%
26	Missouri	400	1.3%
28	Oregon	390	1.3%
29	Colorado	350	1.2%
30	Kentucky	330	1.1%
31	Oklahoma	320	1.1%
32	Arkansas	270	0.9%
32	Kansas	270	0.9%
34	Nevada	260	0.9%
35	New Mexico	220	0.7%
36	West Virginia	190	0.6%
37	Nebraska	180	0.6%
38	Maine	170	0.6%
39	Idaho	150	0.5%
39	New Hampshire	150	0.5%
39	Utah	150	0.5%
42	Montana	130	0.4%
43	Hawaii	120	0.4%
43	South Dakota	120	0.4%
45	Rhode Island	110	0.4%
46	Delaware	80	0.3%
46	North Dakota	80	0.3%
46	Wyoming	80	0.3%
49	Vermont	60	0.2%
NA	Alaska*	NA	NA
	District of Columbia	80	0.3%

Source: American Cancer Society
   "Cancer Facts & Figures 2005" (Copyright 2005, American Cancer Society)
*Fewer than 50 deaths.

Age-Adjusted Death Rate by Prostate Cancer in 2001

National Rate = 31.5 Deaths per 100,000 Male Population*

ALPHA ORDER RANK	STATE	RATE		RANK ORDER RANK	STATE	RATE
2	Alabama	40.1		1	Mississippi	43.2
49	Alaska	25.1		2	Alabama	40.1
48	Arizona	26.7		2	South Carolina	40.1
12	Arkansas	33.6		4	Louisiana	38.1
46	California	28.0		5	Georgia	38.0
39	Colorado	29.6		6	North Carolina	36.9
45	Connecticut	28.6		7	Wyoming	36.3
19	Delaware	32.4		8	Virginia	36.1
47	Florida	26.9		9	Maryland	34.6
5	Georgia	38.0		10	Tennessee	34.3
50	Hawaii	21.2		11	Montana	34.2
22	Idaho	32.3		12	Arkansas	33.6
12	Illinois	33.6		12	Illinois	33.6
14	Indiana	33.5		14	Indiana	33.5
30	Iowa	31.2		15	Utah	33.1
42	Kansas	28.8		16	Michigan	33.0
22	Kentucky	32.3		17	Minnesota	32.9
4	Louisiana	38.1		18	Wisconsin	32.6
33	Maine	30.3		19	Delaware	32.4
9	Maryland	34.6		19	North Dakota	32.4
27	Massachusetts	31.7		19	Oregon	32.4
16	Michigan	33.0		22	Idaho	32.3
17	Minnesota	32.9		22	Kentucky	32.3
1	Mississippi	43.2		24	Ohio	32.2
41	Missouri	29.4		25	Rhode Island	32.0
11	Montana	34.2		26	Pennsylvania	31.8
43	Nebraska	28.7		27	Massachusetts	31.7
37	Nevada	29.8		28	South Dakota	31.6
35	New Hampshire	30.0		29	New Jersey	31.5
29	New Jersey	31.5		30	Iowa	31.2
38	New Mexico	29.7		31	Texas	31.1
32	New York	30.4		32	New York	30.4
6	North Carolina	36.9		33	Maine	30.3
19	North Dakota	32.4		34	West Virginia	30.1
24	Ohio	32.2		35	New Hampshire	30.0
39	Oklahoma	29.6		36	Vermont	29.9
19	Oregon	32.4		37	Nevada	29.8
26	Pennsylvania	31.8		38	New Mexico	29.7
25	Rhode Island	32.0		39	Colorado	29.6
2	South Carolina	40.1		39	Oklahoma	29.6
28	South Dakota	31.6		41	Missouri	29.4
10	Tennessee	34.3		42	Kansas	28.8
31	Texas	31.1		43	Nebraska	28.7
15	Utah	33.1		43	Washington	28.7
36	Vermont	29.9		45	Connecticut	28.6
8	Virginia	36.1		46	California	28.0
43	Washington	28.7		47	Florida	26.9
34	West Virginia	30.1		48	Arizona	26.7
18	Wisconsin	32.6		49	Alaska	25.1
7	Wyoming	36.3		50	Hawaii	21.2
					District of Columbia	49.9

Source: American Cancer Society
"Cancer Facts & Figures 2005" (Copyright 2005, American Cancer Society)
*For 1997 to 2001. Age-adjusted to the 2000 U.S. standard population.

Estimated Deaths by Ovarian Cancer in 2005

National Estimated Total = 16,210 Deaths

ALPHA ORDER

RANK ORDER

RANK	STATE	DEATHS	% of USA	RANK	STATE	DEATHS	% of USA
20	Alabama	300	1.9%	1	California	1,720	10.6%
NA	Alaska*	NA	NA	2	Florida	1,120	6.9%
21	Arizona	290	1.8%	3	New York	1,080	6.7%
31	Arkansas	160	1.0%	4	Texas	960	5.9%
1	California	1,720	10.6%	5	Pennsylvania	880	5.4%
25	Colorado	220	1.4%	6	Ohio	660	4.1%
28	Connecticut	200	1.2%	7	Illinois	650	4.0%
45	Delaware	50	0.3%	8	Michigan	590	3.6%
2	Florida	1,120	6.9%	9	New Jersey	540	3.3%
11	Georgia	420	2.6%	10	North Carolina	470	2.9%
45	Hawaii	50	0.3%	11	Georgia	420	2.6%
40	Idaho	80	0.5%	12	Virginia	400	2.5%
7	Illinois	650	4.0%	13	Washington	390	2.4%
14	Indiana	380	2.3%	14	Indiana	380	2.3%
27	Iowa	210	1.3%	14	Massachusetts	380	2.3%
31	Kansas	160	1.0%	16	Tennessee	350	2.2%
24	Kentucky	230	1.4%	17	Missouri	340	2.1%
25	Louisiana	220	1.4%	18	Wisconsin	320	2.0%
36	Maine	100	0.6%	19	Maryland	310	1.9%
19	Maryland	310	1.9%	20	Alabama	300	1.9%
14	Massachusetts	380	2.3%	21	Arizona	290	1.8%
8	Michigan	590	3.6%	22	Minnesota	270	1.7%
22	Minnesota	270	1.7%	23	Oregon	240	1.5%
31	Mississippi	160	1.0%	24	Kentucky	230	1.4%
17	Missouri	340	2.1%	25	Colorado	220	1.4%
41	Montana	70	0.4%	25	Louisiana	220	1.4%
36	Nebraska	100	0.6%	27	Iowa	210	1.3%
35	Nevada	120	0.7%	28	Connecticut	200	1.2%
42	New Hampshire	60	0.4%	29	South Carolina	190	1.2%
9	New Jersey	540	3.3%	30	Oklahoma	180	1.1%
38	New Mexico	90	0.6%	31	Arkansas	160	1.0%
3	New York	1,080	6.7%	31	Kansas	160	1.0%
10	North Carolina	470	2.9%	31	Mississippi	160	1.0%
NA	North Dakota*	NA	NA	34	West Virginia	140	0.9%
6	Ohio	660	4.1%	35	Nevada	120	0.7%
30	Oklahoma	180	1.1%	36	Maine	100	0.6%
23	Oregon	240	1.5%	36	Nebraska	100	0.6%
5	Pennsylvania	880	5.4%	38	New Mexico	90	0.6%
42	Rhode Island	60	0.4%	38	Utah	90	0.6%
29	South Carolina	190	1.2%	40	Idaho	80	0.5%
42	South Dakota	60	0.4%	41	Montana	70	0.4%
16	Tennessee	350	2.2%	42	New Hampshire	60	0.4%
4	Texas	960	5.9%	42	Rhode Island	60	0.4%
38	Utah	90	0.6%	42	South Dakota	60	0.4%
NA	Vermont*	NA	NA	45	Delaware	50	0.3%
12	Virginia	400	2.5%	45	Hawaii	50	0.3%
13	Washington	390	2.4%	NA	Alaska*	NA	NA
34	West Virginia	140	0.9%	NA	North Dakota*	NA	NA
18	Wisconsin	320	2.0%	NA	Vermont*	NA	NA
NA	Wyoming*	NA	NA	NA	Wyoming*	NA	NA
					District of Columbia*	NA	NA

Source: American Cancer Society
   "Cancer Facts & Figures 2005" (Copyright 2005, American Cancer Society)
*Fewer than 50 deaths.

Estimated Death Rate by Ovarian Cancer in 2005

National Estimated Rate = 11.3 Deaths per 100,000 Female Population*

ALPHA ORDER

RANK	STATE	RATE
7	Alabama	13.8
NA	Alaska**	NA
35	Arizona	10.4
17	Arkansas	12.0
40	California	9.7
41	Colorado	9.6
20	Connecticut	11.8
12	Delaware	12.6
9	Florida	13.4
38	Georgia	9.8
45	Hawaii	7.9
23	Idaho	11.7
33	Illinois	10.5
13	Indiana	12.5
6	Iowa	14.5
20	Kansas	11.8
29	Kentucky	11.4
37	Louisiana	10.1
3	Maine	15.7
24	Maryland	11.6
15	Massachusetts	12.2
18	Michigan	11.9
32	Minnesota	10.8
28	Mississippi	11.5
15	Missouri	12.2
4	Montana	15.3
24	Nebraska	11.6
33	Nevada	10.5
42	New Hampshire	9.5
10	New Jersey	12.8
38	New Mexico	9.8
24	New York	11.6
29	North Carolina	11.4
NA	North Dakota**	NA
18	Ohio	11.9
35	Oklahoma	10.4
8	Oregon	13.6
5	Pennsylvania	14.7
24	Rhode Island	11.6
43	South Carolina	9.4
2	South Dakota	15.8
14	Tennessee	12.3
44	Texas	8.7
46	Utah	7.6
NA	Vermont**	NA
31	Virginia	11.0
10	Washington	12.8
1	West Virginia	15.9
20	Wisconsin	11.8
NA	Wyoming**	NA

RANK ORDER

RANK	STATE	RATE
1	West Virginia	15.9
2	South Dakota	15.8
3	Maine	15.7
4	Montana	15.3
5	Pennsylvania	14.7
6	Iowa	14.5
7	Alabama	13.8
8	Oregon	13.6
9	Florida	13.4
10	New Jersey	12.8
10	Washington	12.8
12	Delaware	12.6
13	Indiana	12.5
14	Tennessee	12.3
15	Massachusetts	12.2
15	Missouri	12.2
17	Arkansas	12.0
18	Michigan	11.9
18	Ohio	11.9
20	Connecticut	11.8
20	Kansas	11.8
20	Wisconsin	11.8
23	Idaho	11.7
24	Maryland	11.6
24	Nebraska	11.6
24	New York	11.6
24	Rhode Island	11.6
28	Mississippi	11.5
29	Kentucky	11.4
29	North Carolina	11.4
31	Virginia	11.0
32	Minnesota	10.8
33	Illinois	10.5
33	Nevada	10.5
35	Arizona	10.4
35	Oklahoma	10.4
37	Louisiana	10.1
38	Georgia	9.8
38	New Mexico	9.8
40	California	9.7
41	Colorado	9.6
42	New Hampshire	9.5
43	South Carolina	9.4
44	Texas	8.7
45	Hawaii	7.9
46	Utah	7.6
NA	Alaska**	NA
NA	North Dakota**	NA
NA	Vermont**	NA
NA	Wyoming**	NA
	District of Columbia**	NA

Source: Morgan Quitno Press using data from American Cancer Society
"Cancer Facts & Figures 2005" (Copyright 2005, American Cancer Society)
*Rates calculated using 2003 Census female population estimates. Not age-adjusted.
**Fewer than 50 deaths.

Deaths by Alzheimer's Disease in 2002

National Total = 58,866 Deaths*

RANK	STATE	DEATHS	% of USA
20	Alabama	1,189	2.0%
50	Alaska	61	0.1%
15	Arizona	1,433	2.4%
33	Arkansas	551	0.9%
1	California	5,421	9.2%
26	Colorado	954	1.6%
32	Connecticut	570	1.0%
48	Delaware	128	0.2%
2	Florida	4,052	6.9%
12	Georgia	1,525	2.6%
47	Hawaii	141	0.2%
38	Idaho	318	0.5%
6	Illinois	2,398	4.1%
14	Indiana	1,475	2.5%
27	Iowa	899	1.5%
29	Kansas	755	1.3%
24	Kentucky	1,013	1.7%
23	Louisiana	1,111	1.9%
34	Maine	513	0.9%
28	Maryland	866	1.5%
11	Massachusetts	1,570	2.7%
9	Michigan	1,958	3.3%
19	Minnesota	1,192	2.0%
31	Mississippi	574	1.0%
21	Missouri	1,187	2.0%
42	Montana	285	0.5%
35	Nebraska	460	0.8%
44	Nevada	253	0.4%
39	New Hampshire	311	0.5%
13	New Jersey	1,522	2.6%
37	New Mexico	325	0.6%
10	New York	1,803	3.1%
8	North Carolina	1,962	3.3%
41	North Dakota	294	0.5%
5	Ohio	2,599	4.4%
30	Oklahoma	754	1.3%
22	Oregon	1,124	1.9%
4	Pennsylvania	2,823	4.8%
43	Rhode Island	264	0.4%
25	South Carolina	967	1.6%
45	South Dakota	167	0.3%
18	Tennessee	1,299	2.2%
3	Texas	3,793	6.4%
40	Utah	303	0.5%
46	Vermont	163	0.3%
16	Virginia	1,368	2.3%
7	Washington	2,195	3.7%
36	West Virginia	405	0.7%
17	Wisconsin	1,344	2.3%
49	Wyoming	122	0.2%

RANK	STATE	DEATHS	% of USA
1	California	5,421	9.2%
2	Florida	4,052	6.9%
3	Texas	3,793	6.4%
4	Pennsylvania	2,823	4.8%
5	Ohio	2,599	4.4%
6	Illinois	2,398	4.1%
7	Washington	2,195	3.7%
8	North Carolina	1,962	3.3%
9	Michigan	1,958	3.3%
10	New York	1,803	3.1%
11	Massachusetts	1,570	2.7%
12	Georgia	1,525	2.6%
13	New Jersey	1,522	2.6%
14	Indiana	1,475	2.5%
15	Arizona	1,433	2.4%
16	Virginia	1,368	2.3%
17	Wisconsin	1,344	2.3%
18	Tennessee	1,299	2.2%
19	Minnesota	1,192	2.0%
20	Alabama	1,189	2.0%
21	Missouri	1,187	2.0%
22	Oregon	1,124	1.9%
23	Louisiana	1,111	1.9%
24	Kentucky	1,013	1.7%
25	South Carolina	967	1.6%
26	Colorado	954	1.6%
27	Iowa	899	1.5%
28	Maryland	866	1.5%
29	Kansas	755	1.3%
30	Oklahoma	754	1.3%
31	Mississippi	574	1.0%
32	Connecticut	570	1.0%
33	Arkansas	551	0.9%
34	Maine	513	0.9%
35	Nebraska	460	0.8%
36	West Virginia	405	0.7%
37	New Mexico	325	0.6%
38	Idaho	318	0.5%
39	New Hampshire	311	0.5%
40	Utah	303	0.5%
41	North Dakota	294	0.5%
42	Montana	285	0.5%
43	Rhode Island	264	0.4%
44	Nevada	253	0.4%
45	South Dakota	167	0.3%
46	Vermont	163	0.3%
47	Hawaii	141	0.2%
48	Delaware	128	0.2%
49	Wyoming	122	0.2%
50	Alaska	61	0.1%
	District of Columbia	107	0.2%

Source: U.S. Department of Health and Human Services, National Center for Health Statistics
"National Vital Statistics Reports" (Vol. 53, No. 5, October 12, 2004)

*Final data by state of residence. A degenerative disease of the brain cells producing loss of memory and general intellectual impairment. It usually affects people over age 65. As the disease progresses, a variety of symptoms may become apparent, including confusion, irritability, and restlessness, as well as disorientation and impaired judgment and concentration.

Death Rate by Alzheimer's Disease in 2002

National Rate = 20.4 Deaths per 100,000 Population*

ALPHA ORDER

RANK	STATE	RATE
9	Alabama	26.5
49	Alaska	9.5
11	Arizona	26.3
33	Arkansas	20.3
45	California	15.4
31	Colorado	21.2
42	Connecticut	16.5
43	Delaware	15.9
19	Florida	24.2
38	Georgia	17.8
48	Hawaii	11.3
21	Idaho	23.7
36	Illinois	19.0
20	Indiana	23.9
6	Iowa	30.6
7	Kansas	27.8
12	Kentucky	24.8
12	Louisiana	24.8
2	Maine	39.6
43	Maryland	15.9
17	Massachusetts	24.4
35	Michigan	19.5
21	Minnesota	23.7
34	Mississippi	20.0
32	Missouri	20.9
5	Montana	31.3
8	Nebraska	26.6
47	Nevada	11.6
17	New Hampshire	24.4
39	New Jersey	17.7
40	New Mexico	17.5
50	New York	9.4
23	North Carolina	23.6
1	North Dakota	46.4
26	Ohio	22.8
30	Oklahoma	21.6
4	Oregon	31.9
25	Pennsylvania	22.9
14	Rhode Island	24.7
24	South Carolina	23.5
29	South Dakota	21.9
28	Tennessee	22.4
41	Texas	17.4
46	Utah	13.1
10	Vermont	26.4
37	Virginia	18.8
3	Washington	36.2
27	West Virginia	22.5
14	Wisconsin	24.7
16	Wyoming	24.5

RANK ORDER

RANK	STATE	RATE
1	North Dakota	46.4
2	Maine	39.6
3	Washington	36.2
4	Oregon	31.9
5	Montana	31.3
6	Iowa	30.6
7	Kansas	27.8
8	Nebraska	26.6
9	Alabama	26.5
10	Vermont	26.4
11	Arizona	26.3
12	Kentucky	24.8
12	Louisiana	24.8
14	Rhode Island	24.7
14	Wisconsin	24.7
16	Wyoming	24.5
17	Massachusetts	24.4
17	New Hampshire	24.4
19	Florida	24.2
20	Indiana	23.9
21	Idaho	23.7
21	Minnesota	23.7
23	North Carolina	23.6
24	South Carolina	23.5
25	Pennsylvania	22.9
26	Ohio	22.8
27	West Virginia	22.5
28	Tennessee	22.4
29	South Dakota	21.9
30	Oklahoma	21.6
31	Colorado	21.2
32	Missouri	20.9
33	Arkansas	20.3
34	Mississippi	20.0
35	Michigan	19.5
36	Illinois	19.0
37	Virginia	18.8
38	Georgia	17.8
39	New Jersey	17.7
40	New Mexico	17.5
41	Texas	17.4
42	Connecticut	16.5
43	Delaware	15.9
43	Maryland	15.9
45	California	15.4
46	Utah	13.1
47	Nevada	11.6
48	Hawaii	11.3
49	Alaska	9.5
50	New York	9.4

District of Columbia	18.7

Source: U.S. Department of Health and Human Services, National Center for Health Statistics
    "National Vital Statistics Reports" (Vol. 53, No. 5, October 12, 2004)
*Final data by state of residence. A degenerative disease of the brain cells producing loss of memory and general intellectual impairment. It usually affects people over age 65. As the disease progresses, a variety of symptoms may become apparent, including confusion, irritability, and restlessness, as well as disorientation and impaired judgment and concentration. Not age-adjusted.

Age-Adjusted Death Rate by Alzheimer's Disease in 2002

National Rate = 20.2 Deaths per 100,000 Population*

ALPHA ORDER RANK	STATE	RATE	RANK ORDER RANK	STATE	RATE
10	Alabama	26.1	1	Washington	37.9
15	Alaska	25.4	2	North Dakota	33.2
8	Arizona	27.5	3	Maine	33.0
39	Arkansas	18.2	4	Oregon	29.0
40	California	18.0	5	Colorado	28.0
5	Colorado	28.0	6	Louisiana	27.8
48	Connecticut	13.4	7	Montana	27.6
46	Delaware	16.2	8	Arizona	27.5
42	Florida	17.5	9	Wyoming	26.3
16	Georgia	24.7	10	Alabama	26.1
49	Hawaii	10.6	10	South Carolina	26.1
13	Idaho	25.6	12	North Carolina	25.9
36	Illinois	18.8	13	Idaho	25.6
19	Indiana	23.7	13	Kentucky	25.6
23	Iowa	22.2	15	Alaska	25.4
20	Kansas	23.6	16	Georgia	24.7
13	Kentucky	25.6	16	New Hampshire	24.7
6	Louisiana	27.8	18	Vermont	24.6
3	Maine	33.0	19	Indiana	23.7
40	Maryland	18.0	20	Kansas	23.6
30	Massachusetts	20.6	21	Tennessee	23.3
32	Michigan	19.6	22	Texas	23.0
24	Minnesota	22.0	23	Iowa	22.2
29	Mississippi	21.0	24	Minnesota	22.0
37	Missouri	18.7	25	Nebraska	21.9
7	Montana	27.6	26	Virginia	21.7
25	Nebraska	21.9	27	Wisconsin	21.6
44	Nevada	16.7	28	Ohio	21.2
16	New Hampshire	24.7	29	Mississippi	21.0
46	New Jersey	16.2	30	Massachusetts	20.6
33	New Mexico	19.4	31	Oklahoma	20.5
50	New York	8.6	32	Michigan	19.6
12	North Carolina	25.9	33	New Mexico	19.4
2	North Dakota	33.2	33	Utah	19.4
28	Ohio	21.2	35	Rhode Island	19.0
31	Oklahoma	20.5	36	Illinois	18.8
4	Oregon	29.0	37	Missouri	18.7
43	Pennsylvania	17.3	37	West Virginia	18.7
35	Rhode Island	19.0	39	Arkansas	18.2
10	South Carolina	26.1	40	California	18.0
45	South Dakota	16.6	40	Maryland	18.0
21	Tennessee	23.3	42	Florida	17.5
22	Texas	23.0	43	Pennsylvania	17.3
33	Utah	19.4	44	Nevada	16.7
18	Vermont	24.6	45	South Dakota	16.6
26	Virginia	21.7	46	Delaware	16.2
1	Washington	37.9	46	New Jersey	16.2
37	West Virginia	18.7	48	Connecticut	13.4
27	Wisconsin	21.6	49	Hawaii	10.6
9	Wyoming	26.3	50	New York	8.6

	District of Columbia	18.3

Source: U.S. Department of Health and Human Services, National Center for Health Statistics
"National Vital Statistics Reports" (Vol. 53, No. 5, October 12, 2004)

*Final data by state of residence. A degenerative disease of the brain cells producing loss of memory and general intellectual impairment. It usually affects people over age 65. As the disease progresses, a variety of symptoms may become apparent, including confusion, irritability, and restlessness, as well as disorientation and impaired judgment and concentration. Age-adjusted rates based on the year 2000 standard population.

Deaths by Cerebrovascular Diseases in 2002

National Total = 162,672 Deaths*

RANK	STATE	DEATHS	% of USA
19	Alabama	3,201	2.0%
50	Alaska	158	0.1%
26	Arizona	2,535	1.6%
28	Arkansas	2,232	1.4%
1	California	17,626	10.8%
31	Colorado	1,915	1.2%
32	Connecticut	1,861	1.1%
47	Delaware	405	0.2%
3	Florida	10,269	6.3%
10	Georgia	4,261	2.6%
39	Hawaii	812	0.5%
40	Idaho	736	0.5%
7	Illinois	7,183	4.4%
16	Indiana	3,717	2.3%
29	Iowa	2,226	1.4%
33	Kansas	1,845	1.1%
25	Kentucky	2,554	1.6%
24	Louisiana	2,595	1.6%
38	Maine	823	0.5%
21	Maryland	2,811	1.7%
17	Massachusetts	3,559	2.2%
8	Michigan	5,814	3.6%
22	Minnesota	2,706	1.7%
30	Mississippi	1,926	1.2%
14	Missouri	3,885	2.4%
42	Montana	639	0.4%
35	Nebraska	1,103	0.7%
36	Nevada	976	0.6%
43	New Hampshire	627	0.4%
11	New Jersey	4,016	2.5%
41	New Mexico	715	0.4%
5	New York	7,625	4.7%
9	North Carolina	5,259	3.2%
46	North Dakota	469	0.3%
6	Ohio	7,252	4.5%
27	Oklahoma	2,427	1.5%
23	Oregon	2,645	1.6%
4	Pennsylvania	8,579	5.3%
44	Rhode Island	605	0.4%
20	South Carolina	2,822	1.7%
45	South Dakota	518	0.3%
12	Tennessee	3,980	2.4%
2	Texas	10,548	6.5%
37	Utah	903	0.6%
48	Vermont	335	0.2%
13	Virginia	3,960	2.4%
15	Washington	3,753	2.3%
34	West Virginia	1,260	0.8%
18	Wisconsin	3,479	2.1%
49	Wyoming	243	0.1%

RANK	STATE	DEATHS	% of USA
1	California	17,626	10.8%
2	Texas	10,548	6.5%
3	Florida	10,269	6.3%
4	Pennsylvania	8,579	5.3%
5	New York	7,625	4.7%
6	Ohio	7,252	4.5%
7	Illinois	7,183	4.4%
8	Michigan	5,814	3.6%
9	North Carolina	5,259	3.2%
10	Georgia	4,261	2.6%
11	New Jersey	4,016	2.5%
12	Tennessee	3,980	2.4%
13	Virginia	3,960	2.4%
14	Missouri	3,885	2.4%
15	Washington	3,753	2.3%
16	Indiana	3,717	2.3%
17	Massachusetts	3,559	2.2%
18	Wisconsin	3,479	2.1%
19	Alabama	3,201	2.0%
20	South Carolina	2,822	1.7%
21	Maryland	2,811	1.7%
22	Minnesota	2,706	1.7%
23	Oregon	2,645	1.6%
24	Louisiana	2,595	1.6%
25	Kentucky	2,554	1.6%
26	Arizona	2,535	1.6%
27	Oklahoma	2,427	1.5%
28	Arkansas	2,232	1.4%
29	Iowa	2,226	1.4%
30	Mississippi	1,926	1.2%
31	Colorado	1,915	1.2%
32	Connecticut	1,861	1.1%
33	Kansas	1,845	1.1%
34	West Virginia	1,260	0.8%
35	Nebraska	1,103	0.7%
36	Nevada	976	0.6%
37	Utah	903	0.6%
38	Maine	823	0.5%
39	Hawaii	812	0.5%
40	Idaho	736	0.5%
41	New Mexico	715	0.4%
42	Montana	639	0.4%
43	New Hampshire	627	0.4%
44	Rhode Island	605	0.4%
45	South Dakota	518	0.3%
46	North Dakota	469	0.3%
47	Delaware	405	0.2%
48	Vermont	335	0.2%
49	Wyoming	243	0.1%
50	Alaska	158	0.1%
	District of Columbia	279	0.2%

Source: U.S. Department of Health and Human Services, National Center for Health Statistics
"National Vital Statistics Reports" (Vol. 53, No. 5, October 12, 2004)
Final data by state of residence. Cerebrovascular diseases include stroke and other disorders of the blood vessels of the brain.

Death Rate by Cerebrovascular Diseases in 2002

National Rate = 56.4 Deaths per 100,000 Population*

ALPHA ORDER

RANK	STATE	RATE
5	Alabama	71.3
50	Alaska	24.5
44	Arizona	46.5
1	Arkansas	82.4
37	California	50.2
46	Colorado	42.5
35	Connecticut	53.8
37	Delaware	50.2
24	Florida	61.4
39	Georgia	49.8
16	Hawaii	65.2
31	Idaho	54.9
28	Illinois	57.0
25	Indiana	60.4
2	Iowa	75.8
14	Kansas	67.9
22	Kentucky	62.4
26	Louisiana	57.9
19	Maine	63.6
36	Maryland	51.5
30	Massachusetts	55.4
27	Michigan	57.8
34	Minnesota	53.9
15	Mississippi	67.1
12	Missouri	68.5
6	Montana	70.3
18	Nebraska	63.8
45	Nevada	44.9
40	New Hampshire	49.2
43	New Jersey	46.8
49	New Mexico	38.5
47	New York	39.8
21	North Carolina	63.2
4	North Dakota	74.0
20	Ohio	63.5
8	Oklahoma	69.5
3	Oregon	75.1
8	Pennsylvania	69.5
29	Rhode Island	56.6
10	South Carolina	68.7
13	South Dakota	68.1
10	Tennessee	68.7
42	Texas	48.4
48	Utah	39.0
32	Vermont	54.3
32	Virginia	54.3
23	Washington	61.8
7	West Virginia	69.9
17	Wisconsin	63.9
41	Wyoming	48.7

RANK ORDER

RANK	STATE	RATE
1	Arkansas	82.4
2	Iowa	75.8
3	Oregon	75.1
4	North Dakota	74.0
5	Alabama	71.3
6	Montana	70.3
7	West Virginia	69.9
8	Oklahoma	69.5
8	Pennsylvania	69.5
10	South Carolina	68.7
10	Tennessee	68.7
12	Missouri	68.5
13	South Dakota	68.1
14	Kansas	67.9
15	Mississippi	67.1
16	Hawaii	65.2
17	Wisconsin	63.9
18	Nebraska	63.8
19	Maine	63.6
20	Ohio	63.5
21	North Carolina	63.2
22	Kentucky	62.4
23	Washington	61.8
24	Florida	61.4
25	Indiana	60.4
26	Louisiana	57.9
27	Michigan	57.8
28	Illinois	57.0
29	Rhode Island	56.6
30	Massachusetts	55.4
31	Idaho	54.9
32	Vermont	54.3
32	Virginia	54.3
34	Minnesota	53.9
35	Connecticut	53.8
36	Maryland	51.5
37	California	50.2
37	Delaware	50.2
39	Georgia	49.8
40	New Hampshire	49.2
41	Wyoming	48.7
42	Texas	48.4
43	New Jersey	46.8
44	Arizona	46.5
45	Nevada	44.9
46	Colorado	42.5
47	New York	39.8
48	Utah	39.0
49	New Mexico	38.5
50	Alaska	24.5
	District of Columbia	48.9

Source: U.S. Department of Health and Human Services, National Center for Health Statistics
   "National Vital Statistics Reports" (Vol. 53, No. 5, October 12, 2004)
*Final data by state of residence. Cerebrovascular diseases include stroke and other disorders of the blood vessels of the brain. Not age-adjusted.

Age-Adjusted Death Rate by Cerebrovascular Diseases in 2002

National Rate = 56.2 Deaths per 100,000 Population*

ALPHA ORDER

RANK	STATE	RATE
4	Alabama	69.6
31	Alaska	55.1
44	Arizona	47.7
1	Arkansas	74.3
24	California	58.0
34	Colorado	54.4
47	Connecticut	45.6
41	Delaware	50.4
45	Florida	46.0
9	Georgia	65.3
17	Hawaii	60.6
20	Idaho	59.4
27	Illinois	57.2
18	Indiana	60.1
25	Iowa	57.9
19	Kansas	59.5
11	Kentucky	63.5
12	Louisiana	63.0
37	Maine	53.7
30	Maryland	56.7
43	Massachusetts	48.1
23	Michigan	58.1
39	Minnesota	51.3
5	Mississippi	69.5
13	Missouri	62.5
14	Montana	62.4
32	Nebraska	54.7
28	Nevada	56.8
42	New Hampshire	50.1
48	New Jersey	43.4
49	New Mexico	41.5
50	New York	37.4
7	North Carolina	67.8
33	North Dakota	54.6
20	Ohio	59.4
8	Oklahoma	66.2
5	Oregon	69.5
34	Pennsylvania	54.4
46	Rhode Island	45.8
2	South Carolina	72.7
36	South Dakota	54.2
3	Tennessee	70.1
15	Texas	61.8
28	Utah	56.8
40	Vermont	50.9
16	Virginia	61.2
10	Washington	65.2
22	West Virginia	58.3
26	Wisconsin	57.7
38	Wyoming	51.5

RANK ORDER

RANK	STATE	RATE
1	Arkansas	74.3
2	South Carolina	72.7
3	Tennessee	70.1
4	Alabama	69.6
5	Mississippi	69.5
5	Oregon	69.5
7	North Carolina	67.8
8	Oklahoma	66.2
9	Georgia	65.3
10	Washington	65.2
11	Kentucky	63.5
12	Louisiana	63.0
13	Missouri	62.5
14	Montana	62.4
15	Texas	61.8
16	Virginia	61.2
17	Hawaii	60.6
18	Indiana	60.1
19	Kansas	59.5
20	Idaho	59.4
20	Ohio	59.4
22	West Virginia	58.3
23	Michigan	58.1
24	California	58.0
25	Iowa	57.9
26	Wisconsin	57.7
27	Illinois	57.2
28	Nevada	56.8
28	Utah	56.8
30	Maryland	56.7
31	Alaska	55.1
32	Nebraska	54.7
33	North Dakota	54.6
34	Colorado	54.4
34	Pennsylvania	54.4
36	South Dakota	54.2
37	Maine	53.7
38	Wyoming	51.5
39	Minnesota	51.3
40	Vermont	50.9
41	Delaware	50.4
42	New Hampshire	50.1
43	Massachusetts	48.1
44	Arizona	47.7
45	Florida	46.0
46	Rhode Island	45.8
47	Connecticut	45.6
48	New Jersey	43.4
49	New Mexico	41.5
50	New York	37.4
	District of Columbia	48.7

*Source: U.S. Department of Health and Human Services, National Center for Health Statistics
"National Vital Statistics Reports" (Vol. 53, No. 5, October 12, 2004)*
Final data by state of residence. Cerebrovascular diseases include stroke and other disorders of the blood vessels of the brain. Age-adjusted rates based on the year 2000 standard population.

Deaths by Chronic Liver Disease and Cirrhosis in 2002

National Total = 27,257 Deaths*

ALPHA ORDER

RANK	STATE	DEATHS	% of USA
22	Alabama	425	1.6%
50	Alaska	55	0.2%
12	Arizona	671	2.5%
33	Arkansas	222	0.8%
1	California	3,747	13.7%
23	Colorado	415	1.5%
29	Connecticut	318	1.2%
44	Delaware	88	0.3%
3	Florida	2,151	7.9%
11	Georgia	696	2.6%
45	Hawaii	79	0.3%
42	Idaho	105	0.4%
6	Illinois	1,068	3.9%
17	Indiana	514	1.9%
34	Iowa	220	0.8%
36	Kansas	187	0.7%
25	Kentucky	377	1.4%
27	Louisiana	365	1.3%
41	Maine	116	0.4%
18	Maryland	443	1.6%
14	Massachusetts	602	2.2%
8	Michigan	993	3.6%
28	Minnesota	320	1.2%
32	Mississippi	229	0.8%
20	Missouri	433	1.6%
39	Montana	127	0.5%
39	Nebraska	127	0.5%
31	Nevada	268	1.0%
42	New Hampshire	105	0.4%
10	New Jersey	730	2.7%
30	New Mexico	317	1.2%
4	New York	1,338	4.9%
9	North Carolina	735	2.7%
49	North Dakota	63	0.2%
7	Ohio	1,047	3.8%
21	Oklahoma	428	1.6%
26	Oregon	367	1.3%
5	Pennsylvania	1,156	4.2%
38	Rhode Island	128	0.5%
24	South Carolina	386	1.4%
46	South Dakota	75	0.3%
13	Tennessee	611	2.2%
2	Texas	2,284	8.4%
37	Utah	133	0.5%
48	Vermont	66	0.2%
15	Virginia	598	2.2%
16	Washington	525	1.9%
35	West Virginia	209	0.8%
19	Wisconsin	437	1.6%
47	Wyoming	70	0.3%

RANK ORDER

RANK	STATE	DEATHS	% of USA
1	California	3,747	13.7%
2	Texas	2,284	8.4%
3	Florida	2,151	7.9%
4	New York	1,338	4.9%
5	Pennsylvania	1,156	4.2%
6	Illinois	1,068	3.9%
7	Ohio	1,047	3.8%
8	Michigan	993	3.6%
9	North Carolina	735	2.7%
10	New Jersey	730	2.7%
11	Georgia	696	2.6%
12	Arizona	671	2.5%
13	Tennessee	611	2.2%
14	Massachusetts	602	2.2%
15	Virginia	598	2.2%
16	Washington	525	1.9%
17	Indiana	514	1.9%
18	Maryland	443	1.6%
19	Wisconsin	437	1.6%
20	Missouri	433	1.6%
21	Oklahoma	428	1.6%
22	Alabama	425	1.6%
23	Colorado	415	1.5%
24	South Carolina	386	1.4%
25	Kentucky	377	1.4%
26	Oregon	367	1.3%
27	Louisiana	365	1.3%
28	Minnesota	320	1.2%
29	Connecticut	318	1.2%
30	New Mexico	317	1.2%
31	Nevada	268	1.0%
32	Mississippi	229	0.8%
33	Arkansas	222	0.8%
34	Iowa	220	0.8%
35	West Virginia	209	0.8%
36	Kansas	187	0.7%
37	Utah	133	0.5%
38	Rhode Island	128	0.5%
39	Montana	127	0.5%
39	Nebraska	127	0.5%
41	Maine	116	0.4%
42	Idaho	105	0.4%
42	New Hampshire	105	0.4%
44	Delaware	88	0.3%
45	Hawaii	79	0.3%
46	South Dakota	75	0.3%
47	Wyoming	70	0.3%
48	Vermont	66	0.2%
49	North Dakota	63	0.2%
50	Alaska	55	0.2%
	District of Columbia	88	0.3%

*Source: U.S. Department of Health and Human Services, National Center for Health Statistics
"National Vital Statistics Reports" (Vol. 53, No. 5, October 12, 2004)*
Final data by state of residence. Cirrhosis of the liver is characterized by the replacement of normal tissue with fibrous tissue and the loss of functional liver cells. It can result from alcohol abuse, nutritional deprivation, or infection especially by the hepatitis virus.

Death Rate by Chronic Liver Disease and Cirrhosis in 2002

National Rate = 9.5 Deaths per 100,000 Population*

ALPHA ORDER

RANK ORDER

RANK	STATE	RATE		RANK	STATE	RATE
19	Alabama	9.5		1	New Mexico	17.1
30	Alaska	8.5		2	Montana	14.0
5	Arizona	12.3		2	Wyoming	14.0
34	Arkansas	8.2		4	Florida	12.9
11	California	10.7		5	Arizona	12.3
23	Colorado	9.2		5	Nevada	12.3
23	Connecticut	9.2		5	Oklahoma	12.3
10	Delaware	10.9		8	Rhode Island	12.0
4	Florida	12.9		9	West Virginia	11.6
37	Georgia	8.1		10	Delaware	10.9
49	Hawaii	6.3		11	California	10.7
42	Idaho	7.8		11	Vermont	10.7
30	Illinois	8.5		13	Tennessee	10.5
33	Indiana	8.3		13	Texas	10.5
44	Iowa	7.5		15	Oregon	10.4
47	Kansas	6.9		16	Michigan	9.9
23	Kentucky	9.2		16	North Dakota	9.9
37	Louisiana	8.1		16	South Dakota	9.9
27	Maine	9.0		19	Alabama	9.5
37	Maryland	8.1		20	Massachusetts	9.4
20	Massachusetts	9.4		20	Pennsylvania	9.4
16	Michigan	9.9		20	South Carolina	9.4
48	Minnesota	6.4		23	Colorado	9.2
40	Mississippi	8.0		23	Connecticut	9.2
43	Missouri	7.6		23	Kentucky	9.2
2	Montana	14.0		23	Ohio	9.2
45	Nebraska	7.3		27	Maine	9.0
5	Nevada	12.3		28	North Carolina	8.8
34	New Hampshire	8.2		29	Washington	8.7
30	New Jersey	8.5		30	Alaska	8.5
1	New Mexico	17.1		30	Illinois	8.5
46	New York	7.0		30	New Jersey	8.5
28	North Carolina	8.8		33	Indiana	8.3
16	North Dakota	9.9		34	Arkansas	8.2
23	Ohio	9.2		34	New Hampshire	8.2
5	Oklahoma	12.3		34	Virginia	8.2
15	Oregon	10.4		37	Georgia	8.1
20	Pennsylvania	9.4		37	Louisiana	8.1
8	Rhode Island	12.0		37	Maryland	8.1
20	South Carolina	9.4		40	Mississippi	8.0
16	South Dakota	9.9		40	Wisconsin	8.0
13	Tennessee	10.5		42	Idaho	7.8
13	Texas	10.5		43	Missouri	7.6
50	Utah	5.7		44	Iowa	7.5
11	Vermont	10.7		45	Nebraska	7.3
34	Virginia	8.2		46	New York	7.0
29	Washington	8.7		47	Kansas	6.9
9	West Virginia	11.6		48	Minnesota	6.4
40	Wisconsin	8.0		49	Hawaii	6.3
2	Wyoming	14.0		50	Utah	5.7

District of Columbia 15.4

Source: U.S. Department of Health and Human Services, National Center for Health Statistics
"National Vital Statistics Reports" (Vol. 53, No. 5, October 12, 2004)
*Final data by state of residence. Cirrhosis of the liver is characterized by the replacement of normal tissue with fibrous tissue and the loss of functional liver cells. It can result from alcohol abuse, nutritional deprivation, or infection especially by the hepatitis virus. Not age-adjusted.

Age-Adjusted Death Rate by Chronic Liver Disease and Cirrhosis in 2002

National Rate = 9.4 Deaths per 100,000 Population*

ALPHA ORDER

RANK	STATE	RATE
21	Alabama	9.1
19	Alaska	9.3
4	Arizona	12.6
42	Arkansas	7.7
8	California	11.6
15	Colorado	9.9
30	Connecticut	8.5
11	Delaware	10.4
9	Florida	11.2
23	Georgia	9.0
50	Hawaii	6.0
34	Idaho	8.2
29	Illinois	8.7
31	Indiana	8.4
46	Iowa	6.8
46	Kansas	6.8
24	Kentucky	8.8
31	Louisiana	8.4
40	Maine	7.9
37	Maryland	8.1
24	Massachusetts	8.8
17	Michigan	9.7
49	Minnesota	6.5
34	Mississippi	8.2
44	Missouri	7.3
3	Montana	12.8
44	Nebraska	7.3
5	Nevada	12.4
37	New Hampshire	8.1
39	New Jersey	8.0
1	New Mexico	17.1
48	New York	6.7
24	North Carolina	8.8
19	North Dakota	9.3
24	Ohio	8.8
6	Oklahoma	11.9
14	Oregon	10.0
34	Pennsylvania	8.2
10	Rhode Island	11.1
21	South Carolina	9.1
17	South Dakota	9.7
12	Tennessee	10.2
7	Texas	11.7
42	Utah	7.7
15	Vermont	9.9
31	Virginia	8.4
24	Washington	8.8
13	West Virginia	10.1
41	Wisconsin	7.8
2	Wyoming	13.4

RANK ORDER

RANK	STATE	RATE
1	New Mexico	17.1
2	Wyoming	13.4
3	Montana	12.8
4	Arizona	12.6
5	Nevada	12.4
6	Oklahoma	11.9
7	Texas	11.7
8	California	11.6
9	Florida	11.2
10	Rhode Island	11.1
11	Delaware	10.4
12	Tennessee	10.2
13	West Virginia	10.1
14	Oregon	10.0
15	Colorado	9.9
15	Vermont	9.9
17	Michigan	9.7
17	South Dakota	9.7
19	Alaska	9.3
19	North Dakota	9.3
21	Alabama	9.1
21	South Carolina	9.1
23	Georgia	9.0
24	Kentucky	8.8
24	Massachusetts	8.8
24	North Carolina	8.8
24	Ohio	8.8
24	Washington	8.8
29	Illinois	8.7
30	Connecticut	8.5
31	Indiana	8.4
31	Louisiana	8.4
31	Virginia	8.4
34	Idaho	8.2
34	Mississippi	8.2
34	Pennsylvania	8.2
37	Maryland	8.1
37	New Hampshire	8.1
39	New Jersey	8.0
40	Maine	7.9
41	Wisconsin	7.8
42	Arkansas	7.7
42	Utah	7.7
44	Missouri	7.3
44	Nebraska	7.3
46	Iowa	6.8
46	Kansas	6.8
48	New York	6.7
49	Minnesota	6.5
50	Hawaii	6.0

District of Columbia   15.5

Source: U.S. Department of Health and Human Services, National Center for Health Statistics
   "National Vital Statistics Reports" (Vol. 53, No. 5, October 12, 2004)
*Final data by state of residence. Cirrhosis of the liver is characterized by the replacement of normal tissue with fibrous tissue and the loss of functional liver cells. It can result from alcohol abuse, nutritional deprivation, or infection especially by the hepatitis virus. Age-adjusted rates based on the year 2000 standard population.

Deaths by Chronic Lower Respiratory Diseases in 2002

National Total = 124,816 Deaths*

ALPHA ORDER

RANK	STATE	DEATHS	% of USA
21	Alabama	2,328	1.9%
50	Alaska	142	0.1%
18	Arizona	2,575	2.1%
31	Arkansas	1,441	1.2%
1	California	12,684	10.2%
26	Colorado	1,848	1.5%
30	Connecticut	1,453	1.2%
45	Delaware	350	0.3%
2	Florida	9,062	7.3%
10	Georgia	3,163	2.5%
49	Hawaii	265	0.2%
40	Idaho	595	0.5%
7	Illinois	4,827	3.9%
11	Indiana	3,138	2.5%
29	Iowa	1,580	1.3%
33	Kansas	1,367	1.1%
19	Kentucky	2,401	1.9%
28	Louisiana	1,696	1.4%
38	Maine	791	0.6%
24	Maryland	1,944	1.6%
16	Massachusetts	2,745	2.2%
8	Michigan	4,431	3.6%
23	Minnesota	1,971	1.6%
32	Mississippi	1,378	1.1%
14	Missouri	2,867	2.3%
42	Montana	576	0.5%
36	Nebraska	934	0.7%
35	Nevada	1,174	0.9%
41	New Hampshire	577	0.5%
13	New Jersey	2,885	2.3%
37	New Mexico	857	0.7%
4	New York	6,966	5.6%
9	North Carolina	3,674	2.9%
47	North Dakota	322	0.3%
5	Ohio	6,063	4.9%
22	Oklahoma	1,988	1.6%
27	Oregon	1,845	1.5%
6	Pennsylvania	6,017	4.8%
43	Rhode Island	521	0.4%
25	South Carolina	1,889	1.5%
44	South Dakota	383	0.3%
12	Tennessee	3,011	2.4%
3	Texas	7,720	6.2%
39	Utah	603	0.5%
48	Vermont	276	0.2%
15	Virginia	2,752	2.2%
17	Washington	2,721	2.2%
34	West Virginia	1,228	1.0%
20	Wisconsin	2,335	1.9%
46	Wyoming	324	0.3%

RANK ORDER

RANK	STATE	DEATHS	% of USA
1	California	12,684	10.2%
2	Florida	9,062	7.3%
3	Texas	7,720	6.2%
4	New York	6,966	5.6%
5	Ohio	6,063	4.9%
6	Pennsylvania	6,017	4.8%
7	Illinois	4,827	3.9%
8	Michigan	4,431	3.6%
9	North Carolina	3,674	2.9%
10	Georgia	3,163	2.5%
11	Indiana	3,138	2.5%
12	Tennessee	3,011	2.4%
13	New Jersey	2,885	2.3%
14	Missouri	2,867	2.3%
15	Virginia	2,752	2.2%
16	Massachusetts	2,745	2.2%
17	Washington	2,721	2.2%
18	Arizona	2,575	2.1%
19	Kentucky	2,401	1.9%
20	Wisconsin	2,335	1.9%
21	Alabama	2,328	1.9%
22	Oklahoma	1,988	1.6%
23	Minnesota	1,971	1.6%
24	Maryland	1,944	1.6%
25	South Carolina	1,889	1.5%
26	Colorado	1,848	1.5%
27	Oregon	1,845	1.5%
28	Louisiana	1,696	1.4%
29	Iowa	1,580	1.3%
30	Connecticut	1,453	1.2%
31	Arkansas	1,441	1.2%
32	Mississippi	1,378	1.1%
33	Kansas	1,367	1.1%
34	West Virginia	1,228	1.0%
35	Nevada	1,174	0.9%
36	Nebraska	934	0.7%
37	New Mexico	857	0.7%
38	Maine	791	0.6%
39	Utah	603	0.5%
40	Idaho	595	0.5%
41	New Hampshire	577	0.5%
42	Montana	576	0.5%
43	Rhode Island	521	0.4%
44	South Dakota	383	0.3%
45	Delaware	350	0.3%
46	Wyoming	324	0.3%
47	North Dakota	322	0.3%
48	Vermont	276	0.2%
49	Hawaii	265	0.2%
50	Alaska	142	0.1%
	District of Columbia	133	0.1%

Source: U.S. Department of Health and Human Services, National Center for Health Statistics "National Vital Statistics Reports" (Vol. 53, No. 5, October 12, 2004)
*Final data by state of residence. Chronic lower respiratory diseases are diseases of the lungs including bronchitis, emphysema and asthma. Includes allied conditions.

Death Rate by Chronic Lower Respiratory Diseases in 2002

National Rate = 43.3 Deaths per 100,000 Population*

ALPHA ORDER

RANK	STATE	RATE
14	Alabama	51.9
49	Alaska	22.1
24	Arizona	47.2
11	Arkansas	53.2
44	California	36.1
37	Colorado	41.0
36	Connecticut	42.0
33	Delaware	43.3
7	Florida	54.2
42	Georgia	36.9
50	Hawaii	21.3
30	Idaho	44.4
39	Illinois	38.3
16	Indiana	50.9
10	Iowa	53.8
19	Kansas	50.3
5	Kentucky	58.7
40	Louisiana	37.8
4	Maine	61.1
45	Maryland	35.6
35	Massachusetts	42.7
32	Michigan	44.1
38	Minnesota	39.3
23	Mississippi	48.0
18	Missouri	50.5
3	Montana	63.3
8	Nebraska	54.0
8	Nevada	54.0
27	New Hampshire	45.3
47	New Jersey	33.6
25	New Mexico	46.2
43	New York	36.4
31	North Carolina	44.2
17	North Dakota	50.8
12	Ohio	53.1
6	Oklahoma	56.9
13	Oregon	52.4
21	Pennsylvania	48.8
22	Rhode Island	48.7
26	South Carolina	46.0
19	South Dakota	50.3
14	Tennessee	51.9
46	Texas	35.4
48	Utah	26.0
28	Vermont	44.8
41	Virginia	37.7
28	Washington	44.8
1	West Virginia	68.2
34	Wisconsin	42.9
2	Wyoming	65.0

RANK ORDER

RANK	STATE	RATE
1	West Virginia	68.2
2	Wyoming	65.0
3	Montana	63.3
4	Maine	61.1
5	Kentucky	58.7
6	Oklahoma	56.9
7	Florida	54.2
8	Nebraska	54.0
8	Nevada	54.0
10	Iowa	53.8
11	Arkansas	53.2
12	Ohio	53.1
13	Oregon	52.4
14	Alabama	51.9
14	Tennessee	51.9
16	Indiana	50.9
17	North Dakota	50.8
18	Missouri	50.5
19	Kansas	50.3
19	South Dakota	50.3
21	Pennsylvania	48.8
22	Rhode Island	48.7
23	Mississippi	48.0
24	Arizona	47.2
25	New Mexico	46.2
26	South Carolina	46.0
27	New Hampshire	45.3
28	Vermont	44.8
28	Washington	44.8
30	Idaho	44.4
31	North Carolina	44.2
32	Michigan	44.1
33	Delaware	43.3
34	Wisconsin	42.9
35	Massachusetts	42.7
36	Connecticut	42.0
37	Colorado	41.0
38	Minnesota	39.3
39	Illinois	38.3
40	Louisiana	37.8
41	Virginia	37.7
42	Georgia	36.9
43	New York	36.4
44	California	36.1
45	Maryland	35.6
46	Texas	35.4
47	New Jersey	33.6
48	Utah	26.0
49	Alaska	22.1
50	Hawaii	21.3
	District of Columbia	23.3

Source: U.S. Department of Health and Human Services, National Center for Health Statistics
"National Vital Statistics Reports" (Vol. 53, No. 5, October 12, 2004)
Final data by state of residence. Chronic lower respiratory diseases are diseases of the lungs including bronchitis, emphysema and asthma. Includes allied conditions. Not age-adjusted.

Age-Adjusted Death Rate by Chronic Lower Respiratory Diseases in 2002

National Rate = 43.5 Deaths per 100,000 Population*

ALPHA ORDER

RANK	STATE	RATE
11	Alabama	50.3
24	Alaska	46.9
21	Arizona	47.4
19	Arkansas	48.2
34	California	42.0
8	Colorado	52.2
47	Connecticut	36.7
32	Delaware	42.7
39	Florida	40.5
20	Georgia	47.8
50	Hawaii	19.7
17	Idaho	48.6
41	Illinois	39.3
10	Indiana	51.3
30	Iowa	44.3
24	Kansas	46.9
3	Kentucky	58.7
37	Louisiana	41.0
7	Maine	52.7
42	Maryland	39.1
45	Massachusetts	38.3
29	Michigan	44.5
42	Minnesota	39.1
13	Mississippi	50.0
23	Missouri	47.1
4	Montana	57.7
16	Nebraska	48.8
2	Nevada	65.5
26	New Hampshire	46.6
49	New Jersey	31.5
15	New Mexico	49.3
48	New York	34.6
27	North Carolina	46.5
36	North Dakota	41.6
14	Ohio	49.9
6	Oklahoma	54.3
12	Oregon	50.2
44	Pennsylvania	38.9
38	Rhode Island	40.9
21	South Carolina	47.4
31	South Dakota	43.0
8	Tennessee	52.2
28	Texas	44.9
46	Utah	37.7
33	Vermont	42.5
35	Virginia	41.9
18	Washington	48.3
5	West Virginia	56.4
40	Wisconsin	40.1
1	Wyoming	67.7

RANK ORDER

RANK	STATE	RATE
1	Wyoming	67.7
2	Nevada	65.5
3	Kentucky	58.7
4	Montana	57.7
5	West Virginia	56.4
6	Oklahoma	54.3
7	Maine	52.7
8	Colorado	52.2
8	Tennessee	52.2
10	Indiana	51.3
11	Alabama	50.3
12	Oregon	50.2
13	Mississippi	50.0
14	Ohio	49.9
15	New Mexico	49.3
16	Nebraska	48.8
17	Idaho	48.6
18	Washington	48.3
19	Arkansas	48.2
20	Georgia	47.8
21	Arizona	47.4
21	South Carolina	47.4
23	Missouri	47.1
24	Alaska	46.9
24	Kansas	46.9
26	New Hampshire	46.6
27	North Carolina	46.5
28	Texas	44.9
29	Michigan	44.5
30	Iowa	44.3
31	South Dakota	43.0
32	Delaware	42.7
33	Vermont	42.5
34	California	42.0
35	Virginia	41.9
36	North Dakota	41.6
37	Louisiana	41.0
38	Rhode Island	40.9
39	Florida	40.5
40	Wisconsin	40.1
41	Illinois	39.3
42	Maryland	39.1
42	Minnesota	39.1
44	Pennsylvania	38.9
45	Massachusetts	38.3
46	Utah	37.7
47	Connecticut	36.7
48	New York	34.6
49	New Jersey	31.5
50	Hawaii	19.7

	District of Columbia	23.5

Source: U.S. Department of Health and Human Services, National Center for Health Statistics
    "National Vital Statistics Reports" (Vol. 53, No. 5, October 12, 2004)
*Final data by state of residence. Chronic lower respiratory diseases are diseases of the lungs including bronchitis, emphysema and asthma. Includes allied conditions. Age-adjusted rates based on the year 2000 standard population.

Deaths by Diabetes Mellitus in 2002

National Total = 73,249 Deaths*

ALPHA ORDER

RANK	STATE	DEATHS	% of USA
19	Alabama	1,486	2.0%
50	Alaska	86	0.1%
24	Arizona	1,231	1.7%
29	Arkansas	793	1.1%
1	California	6,807	9.3%
34	Colorado	659	0.9%
32	Connecticut	675	0.9%
43	Delaware	215	0.3%
3	Florida	4,583	6.3%
15	Georgia	1,576	2.2%
46	Hawaii	204	0.3%
40	Idaho	322	0.4%
7	Illinois	3,011	4.1%
13	Indiana	1,688	2.3%
31	Iowa	734	1.0%
30	Kansas	765	1.0%
23	Kentucky	1,265	1.7%
11	Louisiana	1,774	2.4%
37	Maine	404	0.6%
17	Maryland	1,519	2.1%
20	Massachusetts	1,423	1.9%
8	Michigan	2,785	3.8%
22	Minnesota	1,317	1.8%
33	Mississippi	671	0.9%
14	Missouri	1,625	2.2%
45	Montana	210	0.3%
38	Nebraska	393	0.5%
39	Nevada	343	0.5%
41	New Hampshire	311	0.4%
9	New Jersey	2,532	3.5%
35	New Mexico	582	0.8%
4	New York	3,934	5.4%
10	North Carolina	2,205	3.0%
44	North Dakota	214	0.3%
5	Ohio	3,846	5.3%
26	Oklahoma	1,064	1.5%
27	Oregon	1,041	1.4%
6	Pennsylvania	3,708	5.1%
42	Rhode Island	263	0.4%
25	South Carolina	1,112	1.5%
47	South Dakota	195	0.3%
12	Tennessee	1,749	2.4%
2	Texas	5,654	7.7%
36	Utah	514	0.7%
48	Vermont	174	0.2%
16	Virginia	1,558	2.1%
18	Washington	1,494	2.0%
28	West Virginia	846	1.2%
21	Wisconsin	1,353	1.8%
49	Wyoming	145	0.2%

RANK ORDER

RANK	STATE	DEATHS	% of USA
1	California	6,807	9.3%
2	Texas	5,654	7.7%
3	Florida	4,583	6.3%
4	New York	3,934	5.4%
5	Ohio	3,846	5.3%
6	Pennsylvania	3,708	5.1%
7	Illinois	3,011	4.1%
8	Michigan	2,785	3.8%
9	New Jersey	2,532	3.5%
10	North Carolina	2,205	3.0%
11	Louisiana	1,774	2.4%
12	Tennessee	1,749	2.4%
13	Indiana	1,688	2.3%
14	Missouri	1,625	2.2%
15	Georgia	1,576	2.2%
16	Virginia	1,558	2.1%
17	Maryland	1,519	2.1%
18	Washington	1,494	2.0%
19	Alabama	1,486	2.0%
20	Massachusetts	1,423	1.9%
21	Wisconsin	1,353	1.8%
22	Minnesota	1,317	1.8%
23	Kentucky	1,265	1.7%
24	Arizona	1,231	1.7%
25	South Carolina	1,112	1.5%
26	Oklahoma	1,064	1.5%
27	Oregon	1,041	1.4%
28	West Virginia	846	1.2%
29	Arkansas	793	1.1%
30	Kansas	765	1.0%
31	Iowa	734	1.0%
32	Connecticut	675	0.9%
33	Mississippi	671	0.9%
34	Colorado	659	0.9%
35	New Mexico	582	0.8%
36	Utah	514	0.7%
37	Maine	404	0.6%
38	Nebraska	393	0.5%
39	Nevada	343	0.5%
40	Idaho	322	0.4%
41	New Hampshire	311	0.4%
42	Rhode Island	263	0.4%
43	Delaware	215	0.3%
44	North Dakota	214	0.3%
45	Montana	210	0.3%
46	Hawaii	204	0.3%
47	South Dakota	195	0.3%
48	Vermont	174	0.2%
49	Wyoming	145	0.2%
50	Alaska	86	0.1%
	District of Columbia	191	0.3%

Source: U.S. Department of Health and Human Services, National Center for Health Statistics
    "National Vital Statistics Reports" (Vol. 53, No. 5, October 12, 2004)
*Final data by state of residence. A severe, chronic form of diabetes caused by insufficient production of insulin and resulting in abnormal metabolism of carbohydrates, fats, and proteins. The disease, which typically appears in childhood or adolescence, is characterized by increased sugar levels Mell the blood and urine, excessive thirst and frequent urination.

Death Rate by Diabetes Mellitus in 2002

National Rate = 25.4 Deaths per 100,000 Population*

ALPHA ORDER

RANK	STATE	RATE
5	Alabama	33.1
50	Alaska	13.4
39	Arizona	22.6
14	Arkansas	29.3
45	California	19.4
49	Colorado	14.6
44	Connecticut	19.5
24	Delaware	26.6
21	Florida	27.4
46	Georgia	18.4
47	Hawaii	16.4
34	Idaho	24.0
35	Illinois	23.9
21	Indiana	27.4
29	Iowa	25.0
17	Kansas	28.2
8	Kentucky	30.9
2	Louisiana	39.6
7	Maine	31.2
19	Maryland	27.8
41	Massachusetts	22.1
20	Michigan	27.7
26	Minnesota	26.2
36	Mississippi	23.4
16	Missouri	28.6
37	Montana	23.1
38	Nebraska	22.7
48	Nevada	15.8
33	New Hampshire	24.4
13	New Jersey	29.5
6	New Mexico	31.4
43	New York	20.5
25	North Carolina	26.5
3	North Dakota	33.7
3	Ohio	33.7
9	Oklahoma	30.5
12	Oregon	29.6
11	Pennsylvania	30.1
31	Rhode Island	24.6
23	South Carolina	27.1
28	South Dakota	25.6
10	Tennessee	30.2
27	Texas	26.0
40	Utah	22.2
17	Vermont	28.2
42	Virginia	21.4
31	Washington	24.6
1	West Virginia	47.0
30	Wisconsin	24.9
15	Wyoming	29.1

RANK ORDER

RANK	STATE	RATE
1	West Virginia	47.0
2	Louisiana	39.6
3	North Dakota	33.7
3	Ohio	33.7
5	Alabama	33.1
6	New Mexico	31.4
7	Maine	31.2
8	Kentucky	30.9
9	Oklahoma	30.5
10	Tennessee	30.2
11	Pennsylvania	30.1
12	Oregon	29.6
13	New Jersey	29.5
14	Arkansas	29.3
15	Wyoming	29.1
16	Missouri	28.6
17	Kansas	28.2
17	Vermont	28.2
19	Maryland	27.8
20	Michigan	27.7
21	Florida	27.4
21	Indiana	27.4
23	South Carolina	27.1
24	Delaware	26.6
25	North Carolina	26.5
26	Minnesota	26.2
27	Texas	26.0
28	South Dakota	25.6
29	Iowa	25.0
30	Wisconsin	24.9
31	Rhode Island	24.6
31	Washington	24.6
33	New Hampshire	24.4
34	Idaho	24.0
35	Illinois	23.9
36	Mississippi	23.4
37	Montana	23.1
38	Nebraska	22.7
39	Arizona	22.6
40	Utah	22.2
41	Massachusetts	22.1
42	Virginia	21.4
43	New York	20.5
44	Connecticut	19.5
45	California	19.4
46	Georgia	18.4
47	Hawaii	16.4
48	Nevada	15.8
49	Colorado	14.6
50	Alaska	13.4
	District of Columbia	33.5

Source: U.S. Department of Health and Human Services, National Center for Health Statistics
  "National Vital Statistics Reports" (Vol. 53, No. 5, October 12, 2004)

*Final data by state of residence. A severe, chronic form of diabetes caused by insufficient production of insulin and resulting in abnormal metabolism of carbohydrates, fats, and proteins. The disease, which typically appears in childhood or adolescence, is characterized by increased sugar levels in the blood and urine, excessive thirst and frequent urination. Not age-adjusted.

Age-Adjusted Death Rate by Diabetes Mellitus in 2002

National Rate = 25.4 Deaths per 100,000 Population*

ALPHA ORDER

RANK	STATE	RATE
4	Alabama	31.9
39	Alaska	21.7
36	Arizona	22.7
21	Arkansas	26.8
38	California	22.2
47	Colorado	17.7
49	Connecticut	17.2
27	Delaware	25.9
40	Florida	21.4
35	Georgia	22.9
50	Hawaii	15.2
26	Idaho	26.0
31	Illinois	24.4
16	Indiana	27.5
43	Iowa	20.7
24	Kansas	26.3
8	Kentucky	30.7
1	Louisiana	42.1
19	Maine	27.0
11	Maryland	29.9
45	Massachusetts	20.1
14	Michigan	27.8
27	Minnesota	25.9
32	Mississippi	24.2
22	Missouri	26.7
42	Montana	21.0
44	Nebraska	20.6
48	Nevada	17.5
29	New Hampshire	24.6
14	New Jersey	27.8
3	New Mexico	32.9
46	New York	19.6
16	North Carolina	27.5
20	North Dakota	26.9
5	Ohio	31.8
12	Oklahoma	29.2
13	Oregon	28.2
29	Pennsylvania	24.6
41	Rhode Island	21.2
18	South Carolina	27.4
37	South Dakota	22.6
9	Tennessee	30.1
6	Texas	31.7
7	Utah	31.4
23	Vermont	26.6
34	Virginia	23.1
25	Washington	26.2
2	West Virginia	39.3
33	Wisconsin	23.3
10	Wyoming	30.0

RANK ORDER

RANK	STATE	RATE
1	Louisiana	42.1
2	West Virginia	39.3
3	New Mexico	32.9
4	Alabama	31.9
5	Ohio	31.8
6	Texas	31.7
7	Utah	31.4
8	Kentucky	30.7
9	Tennessee	30.1
10	Wyoming	30.0
11	Maryland	29.9
12	Oklahoma	29.2
13	Oregon	28.2
14	Michigan	27.8
14	New Jersey	27.8
16	Indiana	27.5
16	North Carolina	27.5
18	South Carolina	27.4
19	Maine	27.0
20	North Dakota	26.9
21	Arkansas	26.8
22	Missouri	26.7
23	Vermont	26.6
24	Kansas	26.3
25	Washington	26.2
26	Idaho	26.0
27	Delaware	25.9
27	Minnesota	25.9
29	New Hampshire	24.6
29	Pennsylvania	24.6
31	Illinois	24.4
32	Mississippi	24.2
33	Wisconsin	23.3
34	Virginia	23.1
35	Georgia	22.9
36	Arizona	22.7
37	South Dakota	22.6
38	California	22.2
39	Alaska	21.7
40	Florida	21.4
41	Rhode Island	21.2
42	Montana	21.0
43	Iowa	20.7
44	Nebraska	20.6
45	Massachusetts	20.1
46	New York	19.6
47	Colorado	17.7
48	Nevada	17.5
49	Connecticut	17.2
50	Hawaii	15.2
	District of Columbia	33.7

Source: U.S. Department of Health and Human Services, National Center for Health Statistics
"National Vital Statistics Reports" (Vol. 53, No. 5, October 12, 2004)
*Final data by state of residence. A severe, chronic form of diabetes caused by insufficient production of insulin and resulting in abnormal metabolism of carbohydrates, fats, and proteins. The disease, which typically appears in childhood or adolescence, is characterized by increased sugar levels in the blood and urine, excessive thirst and frequent urination. Age-adjusted rates based on the year 2000 standard population.

153

Deaths by Diseases of the Heart in 2002

National Total = 696,947 Deaths*

ALPHA ORDER

RANK	STATE	DEATHS	% of USA
17	Alabama	13,197	1.9%
50	Alaska	567	0.1%
24	Arizona	10,852	1.6%
29	Arkansas	8,330	1.2%
1	California	68,797	9.9%
33	Colorado	6,425	0.9%
27	Connecticut	8,815	1.3%
46	Delaware	1,918	0.3%
3	Florida	49,235	7.1%
11	Georgia	17,529	2.5%
43	Hawaii	2,512	0.4%
42	Idaho	2,532	0.4%
7	Illinois	30,821	4.4%
14	Indiana	15,321	2.2%
30	Iowa	8,181	1.2%
32	Kansas	6,680	1.0%
20	Kentucky	11,696	1.7%
22	Louisiana	11,185	1.6%
38	Maine	3,170	0.5%
19	Maryland	12,008	1.7%
16	Massachusetts	14,736	2.1%
8	Michigan	26,659	3.8%
28	Minnesota	8,602	1.2%
26	Mississippi	9,061	1.3%
12	Missouri	16,708	2.4%
44	Montana	1,944	0.3%
36	Nebraska	4,242	0.6%
35	Nevada	4,421	0.6%
41	New Hampshire	2,776	0.4%
9	New Jersey	22,510	3.2%
37	New Mexico	3,360	0.5%
2	New York	56,672	8.1%
10	North Carolina	18,524	2.7%
47	North Dakota	1,623	0.2%
6	Ohio	31,388	4.5%
21	Oklahoma	11,230	1.6%
31	Oregon	7,262	1.0%
5	Pennsylvania	38,852	5.6%
39	Rhode Island	3,109	0.4%
25	South Carolina	9,659	1.4%
45	South Dakota	1,937	0.3%
13	Tennessee	16,226	2.3%
4	Texas	43,452	6.2%
40	Utah	2,977	0.4%
48	Vermont	1,370	0.2%
15	Virginia	14,952	2.1%
23	Washington	11,141	1.6%
34	West Virginia	6,189	0.9%
18	Wisconsin	12,923	1.9%
49	Wyoming	1,005	0.1%

RANK ORDER

RANK	STATE	DEATHS	% of USA
1	California	68,797	9.9%
2	New York	56,672	8.1%
3	Florida	49,235	7.1%
4	Texas	43,452	6.2%
5	Pennsylvania	38,852	5.6%
6	Ohio	31,388	4.5%
7	Illinois	30,821	4.4%
8	Michigan	26,659	3.8%
9	New Jersey	22,510	3.2%
10	North Carolina	18,524	2.7%
11	Georgia	17,529	2.5%
12	Missouri	16,708	2.4%
13	Tennessee	16,226	2.3%
14	Indiana	15,321	2.2%
15	Virginia	14,952	2.1%
16	Massachusetts	14,736	2.1%
17	Alabama	13,197	1.9%
18	Wisconsin	12,923	1.9%
19	Maryland	12,008	1.7%
20	Kentucky	11,696	1.7%
21	Oklahoma	11,230	1.6%
22	Louisiana	11,185	1.6%
23	Washington	11,141	1.6%
24	Arizona	10,852	1.6%
25	South Carolina	9,659	1.4%
26	Mississippi	9,061	1.3%
27	Connecticut	8,815	1.3%
28	Minnesota	8,602	1.2%
29	Arkansas	8,330	1.2%
30	Iowa	8,181	1.2%
31	Oregon	7,262	1.0%
32	Kansas	6,680	1.0%
33	Colorado	6,425	0.9%
34	West Virginia	6,189	0.9%
35	Nevada	4,421	0.6%
36	Nebraska	4,242	0.6%
37	New Mexico	3,360	0.5%
38	Maine	3,170	0.5%
39	Rhode Island	3,109	0.4%
40	Utah	2,977	0.4%
41	New Hampshire	2,776	0.4%
42	Idaho	2,532	0.4%
43	Hawaii	2,512	0.4%
44	Montana	1,944	0.3%
45	South Dakota	1,937	0.3%
46	Delaware	1,918	0.3%
47	North Dakota	1,623	0.2%
48	Vermont	1,370	0.2%
49	Wyoming	1,005	0.1%
50	Alaska	567	0.1%
	District of Columbia	1,666	0.2%

Source: U.S. Department of Health and Human Services, National Center for Health Statistics "National Vital Statistics Reports" (Vol. 53, No. 5, October 12, 2004)
*Final data by state of residence.

Death Rate by Diseases of the Heart in 2002

National Rate = 241.7 Deaths per 100,000 Population*

ALPHA ORDER

RANK	STATE	RATE
9	Alabama	294.1
50	Alaska	88.1
42	Arizona	198.9
5	Arkansas	307.4
43	California	195.9
48	Colorado	142.6
18	Connecticut	254.7
26	Delaware	237.6
7	Florida	294.6
37	Georgia	204.8
39	Hawaii	201.8
44	Idaho	188.8
25	Illinois	244.6
21	Indiana	248.8
13	Iowa	278.6
22	Kansas	246.0
11	Kentucky	285.8
20	Louisiana	249.5
24	Maine	244.9
32	Maryland	220.0
29	Massachusetts	229.3
15	Michigan	265.3
47	Minnesota	171.4
3	Mississippi	315.5
8	Missouri	294.5
34	Montana	213.8
23	Nebraska	245.3
38	Nevada	203.4
33	New Hampshire	217.7
16	New Jersey	262.0
46	New Mexico	181.1
6	New York	295.8
30	North Carolina	222.6
17	North Dakota	255.9
14	Ohio	274.8
2	Oklahoma	321.4
35	Oregon	206.2
4	Pennsylvania	315.0
10	Rhode Island	290.6
28	South Carolina	235.2
19	South Dakota	254.5
12	Tennessee	279.9
41	Texas	199.5
49	Utah	128.5
31	Vermont	222.2
36	Virginia	205.0
45	Washington	183.6
1	West Virginia	343.5
27	Wisconsin	237.5
40	Wyoming	201.5

RANK ORDER

RANK	STATE	RATE
1	West Virginia	343.5
2	Oklahoma	321.4
3	Mississippi	315.5
4	Pennsylvania	315.0
5	Arkansas	307.4
6	New York	295.8
7	Florida	294.6
8	Missouri	294.5
9	Alabama	294.1
10	Rhode Island	290.6
11	Kentucky	285.8
12	Tennessee	279.9
13	Iowa	278.6
14	Ohio	274.8
15	Michigan	265.3
16	New Jersey	262.0
17	North Dakota	255.9
18	Connecticut	254.7
19	South Dakota	254.5
20	Louisiana	249.5
21	Indiana	248.8
22	Kansas	246.0
23	Nebraska	245.3
24	Maine	244.9
25	Illinois	244.6
26	Delaware	237.6
27	Wisconsin	237.5
28	South Carolina	235.2
29	Massachusetts	229.3
30	North Carolina	222.6
31	Vermont	222.2
32	Maryland	220.0
33	New Hampshire	217.7
34	Montana	213.8
35	Oregon	206.2
36	Virginia	205.0
37	Georgia	204.8
38	Nevada	203.4
39	Hawaii	201.8
40	Wyoming	201.5
41	Texas	199.5
42	Arizona	198.9
43	California	195.9
44	Idaho	188.8
45	Washington	183.6
46	New Mexico	181.1
47	Minnesota	171.4
48	Colorado	142.6
49	Utah	128.5
50	Alaska	88.1

	District of Columbia	291.8

Source: U.S. Department of Health and Human Services, National Center for Health Statistics
"National Vital Statistics Reports" (Vol. 53, No. 5, October 12, 2004)
*Final data by state of residence. Not age-adjusted.

Age-Adjusted Death Rate by Diseases of the Heart in 2002

National Rate = 240.8 Deaths per 100,000 Population*

ALPHA ORDER

RANK	STATE	RATE
5	Alabama	285.8
49	Alaska	166.0
39	Arizona	202.9
7	Arkansas	278.7
26	California	225.7
48	Colorado	178.9
31	Connecticut	217.6
23	Delaware	236.0
27	Florida	222.0
12	Georgia	261.8
46	Hawaii	188.3
38	Idaho	203.0
17	Illinois	246.4
16	Indiana	248.4
30	Iowa	219.5
28	Kansas	220.6
4	Kentucky	287.0
10	Louisiana	269.6
36	Maine	208.5
21	Maryland	239.6
40	Massachusetts	201.3
11	Michigan	266.0
50	Minnesota	164.7
1	Mississippi	326.6
9	Missouri	270.3
45	Montana	191.6
33	Nebraska	213.5
18	Nevada	245.1
29	New Hampshire	220.2
20	New Jersey	243.5
42	New Mexico	193.3
8	New York	277.4
24	North Carolina	235.2
40	North Dakota	201.3
13	Ohio	258.2
2	Oklahoma	306.0
44	Oregon	192.3
14	Pennsylvania	250.1
22	Rhode Island	239.1
19	South Carolina	244.4
35	South Dakota	209.7
6	Tennessee	282.4
15	Texas	249.8
47	Utah	185.1
37	Vermont	208.3
25	Virginia	226.8
42	Washington	193.3
3	West Virginia	287.3
32	Wisconsin	216.5
34	Wyoming	210.0

RANK ORDER

RANK	STATE	RATE
1	Mississippi	326.6
2	Oklahoma	306.0
3	West Virginia	287.3
4	Kentucky	287.0
5	Alabama	285.8
6	Tennessee	282.4
7	Arkansas	278.7
8	New York	277.4
9	Missouri	270.3
10	Louisiana	269.6
11	Michigan	266.0
12	Georgia	261.8
13	Ohio	258.2
14	Pennsylvania	250.1
15	Texas	249.8
16	Indiana	248.4
17	Illinois	246.4
18	Nevada	245.1
19	South Carolina	244.4
20	New Jersey	243.5
21	Maryland	239.6
22	Rhode Island	239.1
23	Delaware	236.0
24	North Carolina	235.2
25	Virginia	226.8
26	California	225.7
27	Florida	222.0
28	Kansas	220.6
29	New Hampshire	220.2
30	Iowa	219.5
31	Connecticut	217.6
32	Wisconsin	216.5
33	Nebraska	213.5
34	Wyoming	210.0
35	South Dakota	209.7
36	Maine	208.5
37	Vermont	208.3
38	Idaho	203.0
39	Arizona	202.9
40	Massachusetts	201.3
40	North Dakota	201.3
42	New Mexico	193.3
42	Washington	193.3
44	Oregon	192.3
45	Montana	191.6
46	Hawaii	188.3
47	Utah	185.1
48	Colorado	178.9
49	Alaska	166.0
50	Minnesota	164.7
	District of Columbia	291.7

Source: U.S. Department of Health and Human Services, National Center for Health Statistics
"National Vital Statistics Reports" (Vol. 53, No. 5, October 12, 2004)
Final data by state of residence. Age-adjusted rates based on the year 2000 standard population.

Deaths by Malignant Neoplasms in 2002

National Total = 557,271 Deaths*

ALPHA ORDER					RANK ORDER			
RANK	STATE	DEATHS	% of USA		RANK	STATE	DEATHS	% of USA
20	Alabama	9,698	1.7%		1	California	54,143	9.7%
50	Alaska	715	0.1%		2	Florida	39,140	7.0%
23	Arizona	9,359	1.7%		3	New York	36,661	6.6%
31	Arkansas	6,282	1.1%		4	Texas	34,164	6.1%
1	California	54,143	9.7%		5	Pennsylvania	29,849	5.4%
30	Colorado	6,384	1.1%		6	Ohio	25,173	4.5%
28	Connecticut	7,163	1.3%		7	Illinois	24,737	4.4%
45	Delaware	1,621	0.3%		8	Michigan	19,985	3.6%
2	Florida	39,140	7.0%		9	New Jersey	17,827	3.2%
11	Georgia	13,975	2.5%		10	North Carolina	16,210	2.9%
43	Hawaii	1,945	0.3%		11	Georgia	13,975	2.5%
42	Idaho	2,138	0.4%		12	Massachusetts	13,914	2.5%
7	Illinois	24,737	4.4%		13	Virginia	13,602	2.4%
14	Indiana	12,865	2.3%		14	Indiana	12,865	2.3%
29	Iowa	6,473	1.2%		15	Tennessee	12,518	2.2%
33	Kansas	5,362	1.0%		16	Missouri	12,322	2.2%
22	Kentucky	9,438	1.7%		17	Washington	10,858	1.9%
21	Louisiana	9,441	1.7%		18	Wisconsin	10,828	1.9%
37	Maine	3,206	0.6%		19	Maryland	10,395	1.9%
19	Maryland	10,395	1.9%		20	Alabama	9,698	1.7%
12	Massachusetts	13,914	2.5%		21	Louisiana	9,441	1.7%
8	Michigan	19,985	3.6%		22	Kentucky	9,438	1.7%
24	Minnesota	9,210	1.7%		23	Arizona	9,359	1.7%
32	Mississippi	6,069	1.1%		24	Minnesota	9,210	1.7%
16	Missouri	12,322	2.2%		25	South Carolina	8,333	1.5%
44	Montana	1,911	0.3%		26	Oklahoma	7,474	1.3%
36	Nebraska	3,433	0.6%		27	Oregon	7,249	1.3%
35	Nevada	3,937	0.7%		28	Connecticut	7,163	1.3%
39	New Hampshire	2,529	0.5%		29	Iowa	6,473	1.2%
9	New Jersey	17,827	3.2%		30	Colorado	6,384	1.1%
38	New Mexico	3,067	0.6%		31	Arkansas	6,282	1.1%
3	New York	36,661	6.6%		32	Mississippi	6,069	1.1%
10	North Carolina	16,210	2.9%		33	Kansas	5,362	1.0%
47	North Dakota	1,293	0.2%		34	West Virginia	4,652	0.8%
6	Ohio	25,173	4.5%		35	Nevada	3,937	0.7%
26	Oklahoma	7,474	1.3%		36	Nebraska	3,433	0.6%
27	Oregon	7,249	1.3%		37	Maine	3,206	0.6%
5	Pennsylvania	29,849	5.4%		38	New Mexico	3,067	0.6%
40	Rhode Island	2,404	0.4%		39	New Hampshire	2,529	0.5%
25	South Carolina	8,333	1.5%		40	Rhode Island	2,404	0.4%
46	South Dakota	1,562	0.3%		41	Utah	2,376	0.4%
15	Tennessee	12,518	2.2%		42	Idaho	2,138	0.4%
4	Texas	34,164	6.1%		43	Hawaii	1,945	0.3%
41	Utah	2,376	0.4%		44	Montana	1,911	0.3%
48	Vermont	1,224	0.2%		45	Delaware	1,621	0.3%
13	Virginia	13,602	2.4%		46	South Dakota	1,562	0.3%
17	Washington	10,858	1.9%		47	North Dakota	1,293	0.2%
34	West Virginia	4,652	0.8%		48	Vermont	1,224	0.2%
18	Wisconsin	10,828	1.9%		49	Wyoming	859	0.2%
49	Wyoming	859	0.2%		50	Alaska	715	0.1%
						District of Columbia	1,298	0.2%

Source: U.S. Department of Health and Human Services, National Center for Health Statistics
"National Vital Statistics Reports" (Vol. 53, No. 5, October 12, 2004)
*Final data by state of residence. Neoplasms are abnormal tissue, tumors. Includes many cancers.

157

Death Rate by Malignant Neoplasms in 2002

National Rate = 193.2 Deaths per 100,000 Population*

ALPHA ORDER			RANK ORDER		
RANK	STATE	RATE	RANK	STATE	RATE
12	Alabama	216.2	1	West Virginia	258.2
49	Alaska	111.1	2	Maine	247.7
41	Arizona	171.5	3	Pennsylvania	242.0
5	Arkansas	231.8	4	Florida	234.2
47	California	154.2	5	Arkansas	231.8
48	Colorado	141.7	6	Kentucky	230.6
20	Connecticut	207.0	7	Rhode Island	224.7
25	Delaware	200.8	8	Iowa	220.4
4	Florida	234.2	8	Ohio	220.4
43	Georgia	163.3	10	Missouri	217.2
46	Hawaii	156.2	11	Massachusetts	216.5
44	Idaho	159.4	12	Alabama	216.2
32	Illinois	196.3	13	Tennessee	215.9
18	Indiana	208.9	14	Oklahoma	213.9
8	Iowa	220.4	15	Mississippi	211.3
31	Kansas	197.4	16	Louisiana	210.6
6	Kentucky	230.6	17	Montana	210.1
16	Louisiana	210.6	18	Indiana	208.9
2	Maine	247.7	19	New Jersey	207.5
35	Maryland	190.4	20	Connecticut	207.0
11	Massachusetts	216.5	21	Oregon	205.8
27	Michigan	198.8	22	South Dakota	205.2
37	Minnesota	183.5	23	North Dakota	203.9
15	Mississippi	211.3	24	South Carolina	202.9
10	Missouri	217.2	25	Delaware	200.8
17	Montana	210.1	26	Wisconsin	199.0
28	Nebraska	198.5	27	Michigan	198.8
38	Nevada	181.1	28	Nebraska	198.5
30	New Hampshire	198.3	28	Vermont	198.5
19	New Jersey	207.5	30	New Hampshire	198.3
42	New Mexico	165.3	31	Kansas	197.4
34	New York	191.4	32	Illinois	196.3
33	North Carolina	194.8	33	North Carolina	194.8
23	North Dakota	203.9	34	New York	191.4
8	Ohio	220.4	35	Maryland	190.4
14	Oklahoma	213.9	36	Virginia	186.5
21	Oregon	205.8	37	Minnesota	183.5
3	Pennsylvania	242.0	38	Nevada	181.1
7	Rhode Island	224.7	39	Washington	178.9
24	South Carolina	202.9	40	Wyoming	172.2
22	South Dakota	205.2	41	Arizona	171.5
13	Tennessee	215.9	42	New Mexico	165.3
45	Texas	156.9	43	Georgia	163.3
50	Utah	102.6	44	Idaho	159.4
28	Vermont	198.5	45	Texas	156.9
36	Virginia	186.5	46	Hawaii	156.2
39	Washington	178.9	47	California	154.2
1	West Virginia	258.2	48	Colorado	141.7
26	Wisconsin	199.0	49	Alaska	111.1
40	Wyoming	172.2	50	Utah	102.6
				District of Columbia	227.4

Source: U.S. Department of Health and Human Services, National Center for Health Statistics
   "National Vital Statistics Reports" (Vol. 53, No. 5, October 12, 2004)
*Final data by state of residence. Neoplasms are abnormal tissue, tumors. Includes many cancers. Not age-adjusted.

Age-Adjusted Death Rate by Malignant Neoplasms in 2002

National Rate = 193.5 Deaths per 100,000 Population*

RANK	STATE	RATE
10	Alabama	207.5
36	Alaska	185.9
48	Arizona	171.6
7	Arkansas	212.1
42	California	176.0
47	Colorado	171.8
35	Connecticut	186.4
27	Delaware	193.8
40	Florida	183.4
20	Georgia	199.6
49	Hawaii	145.4
46	Idaho	172.2
15	Illinois	201.9
8	Indiana	209.8
32	Iowa	189.0
33	Kansas	188.1
1	Kentucky	226.3
2	Louisiana	222.9
5	Maine	214.2
16	Maryland	201.6
22	Massachusetts	199.2
22	Michigan	199.2
38	Minnesota	185.0
3	Mississippi	218.3
11	Missouri	204.3
28	Montana	190.7
36	Nebraska	185.9
14	Nevada	202.0
21	New Hampshire	199.5
26	New Jersey	196.3
45	New Mexico	172.5
39	New York	184.0
18	North Carolina	200.4
44	North Dakota	175.0
9	Ohio	208.8
12	Oklahoma	204.2
24	Oregon	197.8
17	Pennsylvania	200.8
25	Rhode Island	196.9
13	South Carolina	203.7
41	South Dakota	182.4
6	Tennessee	213.6
30	Texas	189.6
50	Utah	143.3
34	Vermont	186.7
19	Virginia	199.8
29	Washington	189.9
4	West Virginia	215.3
31	Wisconsin	189.5
43	Wyoming	175.1

RANK	STATE	RATE
1	Kentucky	226.3
2	Louisiana	222.9
3	Mississippi	218.3
4	West Virginia	215.3
5	Maine	214.2
6	Tennessee	213.6
7	Arkansas	212.1
8	Indiana	209.8
9	Ohio	208.8
10	Alabama	207.5
11	Missouri	204.3
12	Oklahoma	204.2
13	South Carolina	203.7
14	Nevada	202.0
15	Illinois	201.9
16	Maryland	201.6
17	Pennsylvania	200.8
18	North Carolina	200.4
19	Virginia	199.8
20	Georgia	199.6
21	New Hampshire	199.5
22	Massachusetts	199.2
22	Michigan	199.2
24	Oregon	197.8
25	Rhode Island	196.9
26	New Jersey	196.3
27	Delaware	193.8
28	Montana	190.7
29	Washington	189.9
30	Texas	189.6
31	Wisconsin	189.5
32	Iowa	189.0
33	Kansas	188.1
34	Vermont	186.7
35	Connecticut	186.4
36	Alaska	185.9
36	Nebraska	185.9
38	Minnesota	185.0
39	New York	184.0
40	Florida	183.4
41	South Dakota	182.4
42	California	176.0
43	Wyoming	175.1
44	North Dakota	175.0
45	New Mexico	172.5
46	Idaho	172.2
47	Colorado	171.8
48	Arizona	171.6
49	Hawaii	145.4
50	Utah	143.3

	District of Columbia	230.0

*Source: U.S. Department of Health and Human Services, National Center for Health Statistics
    "National Vital Statistics Reports" (Vol. 53, No. 5, October 12, 2004)*
Final data by state of residence. Neoplasms are abnormal tissue, tumors. Includes many cancers. Age-adjusted rates based on the year 2000 standard population.

Deaths by Nephritis and Other Kidney Diseases in 2002

National Total = 40,974 Deaths*

ALPHA ORDER

RANK	STATE	DEATHS	% of USA
16	Alabama	1,032	2.5%
50	Alaska	21	0.1%
23	Arizona	622	1.5%
24	Arkansas	601	1.5%
6	California	2,164	5.3%
31	Colorado	417	1.0%
27	Connecticut	554	1.4%
44	Delaware	117	0.3%
4	Florida	2,201	5.4%
11	Georgia	1,335	3.3%
42	Hawaii	136	0.3%
46	Idaho	86	0.2%
3	Illinois	2,328	5.7%
14	Indiana	1,222	3.0%
36	Iowa	261	0.6%
28	Kansas	517	1.3%
19	Kentucky	813	2.0%
17	Louisiana	983	2.4%
37	Maine	232	0.6%
22	Maryland	630	1.5%
12	Massachusetts	1,297	3.2%
9	Michigan	1,618	3.9%
21	Minnesota	649	1.6%
26	Mississippi	580	1.4%
15	Missouri	1,076	2.6%
45	Montana	105	0.3%
34	Nebraska	277	0.7%
32	Nevada	372	0.9%
41	New Hampshire	141	0.3%
8	New Jersey	1,662	4.1%
38	New Mexico	220	0.5%
2	New York	2,465	6.0%
10	North Carolina	1,437	3.5%
47	North Dakota	57	0.1%
7	Ohio	2,027	4.9%
29	Oklahoma	500	1.2%
35	Oregon	266	0.6%
1	Pennsylvania	2,944	7.2%
40	Rhode Island	142	0.3%
20	South Carolina	781	1.9%
43	South Dakota	128	0.3%
25	Tennessee	586	1.4%
5	Texas	2,166	5.3%
39	Utah	184	0.4%
48	Vermont	53	0.1%
13	Virginia	1,236	3.0%
33	Washington	306	0.7%
30	West Virginia	462	1.1%
18	Wisconsin	852	2.1%
49	Wyoming	43	0.1%

RANK ORDER

RANK	STATE	DEATHS	% of USA
1	Pennsylvania	2,944	7.2%
2	New York	2,465	6.0%
3	Illinois	2,328	5.7%
4	Florida	2,201	5.4%
5	Texas	2,166	5.3%
6	California	2,164	5.3%
7	Ohio	2,027	4.9%
8	New Jersey	1,662	4.1%
9	Michigan	1,618	3.9%
10	North Carolina	1,437	3.5%
11	Georgia	1,335	3.3%
12	Massachusetts	1,297	3.2%
13	Virginia	1,236	3.0%
14	Indiana	1,222	3.0%
15	Missouri	1,076	2.6%
16	Alabama	1,032	2.5%
17	Louisiana	983	2.4%
18	Wisconsin	852	2.1%
19	Kentucky	813	2.0%
20	South Carolina	781	1.9%
21	Minnesota	649	1.6%
22	Maryland	630	1.5%
23	Arizona	622	1.5%
24	Arkansas	601	1.5%
25	Tennessee	586	1.4%
26	Mississippi	580	1.4%
27	Connecticut	554	1.4%
28	Kansas	517	1.3%
29	Oklahoma	500	1.2%
30	West Virginia	462	1.1%
31	Colorado	417	1.0%
32	Nevada	372	0.9%
33	Washington	306	0.7%
34	Nebraska	277	0.7%
35	Oregon	266	0.6%
36	Iowa	261	0.6%
37	Maine	232	0.6%
38	New Mexico	220	0.5%
39	Utah	184	0.4%
40	Rhode Island	142	0.3%
41	New Hampshire	141	0.3%
42	Hawaii	136	0.3%
43	South Dakota	128	0.3%
44	Delaware	117	0.3%
45	Montana	105	0.3%
46	Idaho	86	0.2%
47	North Dakota	57	0.1%
48	Vermont	53	0.1%
49	Wyoming	43	0.1%
50	Alaska	21	0.1%
	District of Columbia	70	0.2%

Source: U.S. Department of Health and Human Services, National Center for Health Statistics
"National Vital Statistics Reports" (Vol. 53, No. 5, October 12, 2004)
Final data by state of residence. Includes nephrotic syndrome and nephrosis.

Death Rate by Nephritis and Other Kidney Diseases in 2002

National Rate = 14.2 Deaths per 100,000 Population*

ALPHA ORDER				RANK ORDER		
RANK	STATE	RATE		RANK	STATE	RATE
3	Alabama	23.0		1	West Virginia	25.6
50	Alaska	3.3		2	Pennsylvania	23.9
35	Arizona	11.4		3	Alabama	23.0
4	Arkansas	22.2		4	Arkansas	22.2
48	California	6.2		5	Louisiana	21.9
40	Colorado	9.3		6	Massachusetts	20.2
22	Connecticut	16.0		6	Mississippi	20.2
26	Delaware	14.5		8	Kentucky	19.9
29	Florida	13.2		9	Indiana	19.8
25	Georgia	15.6		10	New Jersey	19.3
37	Hawaii	10.9		11	Kansas	19.0
47	Idaho	6.4		11	Missouri	19.0
14	Illinois	18.5		11	South Carolina	19.0
9	Indiana	19.8		14	Illinois	18.5
42	Iowa	8.9		15	Maine	17.9
11	Kansas	19.0		16	Ohio	17.7
8	Kentucky	19.9		17	North Carolina	17.3
5	Louisiana	21.9		18	Nevada	17.1
15	Maine	17.9		19	Virginia	16.9
33	Maryland	11.5		20	South Dakota	16.8
6	Massachusetts	20.2		21	Michigan	16.1
21	Michigan	16.1		22	Connecticut	16.0
30	Minnesota	12.9		22	Nebraska	16.0
6	Mississippi	20.2		24	Wisconsin	15.7
11	Missouri	19.0		25	Georgia	15.6
33	Montana	11.5		26	Delaware	14.5
22	Nebraska	16.0		27	Oklahoma	14.3
18	Nevada	17.1		28	Rhode Island	13.3
36	New Hampshire	11.1		29	Florida	13.2
10	New Jersey	19.3		30	Minnesota	12.9
32	New Mexico	11.9		30	New York	12.9
30	New York	12.9		32	New Mexico	11.9
17	North Carolina	17.3		33	Maryland	11.5
41	North Dakota	9.0		33	Montana	11.5
16	Ohio	17.7		35	Arizona	11.4
27	Oklahoma	14.3		36	New Hampshire	11.1
46	Oregon	7.6		37	Hawaii	10.9
2	Pennsylvania	23.9		38	Tennessee	10.1
28	Rhode Island	13.3		39	Texas	9.9
11	South Carolina	19.0		40	Colorado	9.3
20	South Dakota	16.8		41	North Dakota	9.0
38	Tennessee	10.1		42	Iowa	8.9
39	Texas	9.9		43	Vermont	8.6
45	Utah	7.9		43	Wyoming	8.6
43	Vermont	8.6		45	Utah	7.9
19	Virginia	16.9		46	Oregon	7.6
49	Washington	5.0		47	Idaho	6.4
1	West Virginia	25.6		48	California	6.2
24	Wisconsin	15.7		49	Washington	5.0
43	Wyoming	8.6		50	Alaska	3.3
					District of Columbia	12.3

Source: U.S. Department of Health and Human Services, National Center for Health Statistics
   "National Vital Statistics Reports" (Vol. 53, No. 5, October 12, 2004)
*Final data by state of residence. Includes nephrotic syndrome and nephrosis.
Not age-adjusted.

Age-Adjusted Death Rate by Nephritis and Other Kidney Diseases in 2002

National Rate = 14.2 Deaths per 100,000 Population*

ALPHA ORDER

RANK	STATE	RATE
2	Alabama	22.4
49	Alaska	6.7
34	Arizona	11.6
6	Arkansas	20.2
44	California	7.1
33	Colorado	11.7
25	Connecticut	13.9
22	Delaware	14.3
41	Florida	10.0
7	Georgia	20.1
40	Hawaii	10.1
47	Idaho	6.9
13	Illinois	18.7
9	Indiana	19.8
46	Iowa	7.0
18	Kansas	17.1
7	Kentucky	20.1
1	Louisiana	23.7
21	Maine	15.3
29	Maryland	12.5
16	Massachusetts	17.8
20	Michigan	16.2
29	Minnesota	12.5
4	Mississippi	20.9
17	Missouri	17.4
38	Montana	10.4
24	Nebraska	14.1
5	Nevada	20.6
36	New Hampshire	11.3
15	New Jersey	18.1
28	New Mexico	12.7
32	New York	12.2
14	North Carolina	18.3
48	North Dakota	6.8
19	Ohio	16.7
26	Oklahoma	13.7
44	Oregon	7.1
11	Pennsylvania	19.0
37	Rhode Island	11.1
9	South Carolina	19.8
26	South Dakota	13.7
39	Tennessee	10.2
31	Texas	12.4
35	Utah	11.5
43	Vermont	8.2
12	Virginia	18.8
50	Washington	5.3
3	West Virginia	21.4
22	Wisconsin	14.3
42	Wyoming	9.0

RANK ORDER

RANK	STATE	RATE
1	Louisiana	23.7
2	Alabama	22.4
3	West Virginia	21.4
4	Mississippi	20.9
5	Nevada	20.6
6	Arkansas	20.2
7	Georgia	20.1
7	Kentucky	20.1
9	Indiana	19.8
9	South Carolina	19.8
11	Pennsylvania	19.0
12	Virginia	18.8
13	Illinois	18.7
14	North Carolina	18.3
15	New Jersey	18.1
16	Massachusetts	17.8
17	Missouri	17.4
18	Kansas	17.1
19	Ohio	16.7
20	Michigan	16.2
21	Maine	15.3
22	Delaware	14.3
22	Wisconsin	14.3
24	Nebraska	14.1
25	Connecticut	13.9
26	Oklahoma	13.7
26	South Dakota	13.7
28	New Mexico	12.7
29	Maryland	12.5
29	Minnesota	12.5
31	Texas	12.4
32	New York	12.2
33	Colorado	11.7
34	Arizona	11.6
35	Utah	11.5
36	New Hampshire	11.3
37	Rhode Island	11.1
38	Montana	10.4
39	Tennessee	10.2
40	Hawaii	10.1
41	Florida	10.0
42	Wyoming	9.0
43	Vermont	8.2
44	California	7.1
44	Oregon	7.1
46	Iowa	7.0
47	Idaho	6.9
48	North Dakota	6.8
49	Alaska	6.7
50	Washington	5.3
	District of Columbia	12.4

Source: U.S. Department of Health and Human Services, National Center for Health Statistics
    "National Vital Statistics Reports" (Vol. 53, No. 5, October 12, 2004)
*Final data by state of residence. Includes nephrotic syndrome and nephrosis.
Age-adjusted rates based on the year 2000 standard population.

Deaths by Pneumonia and Influenza in 2002

National Total = 65,681 Deaths*

ALPHA ORDER

RANK	STATE	DEATHS	% of USA
20	Alabama	1,218	1.9%
50	Alaska	51	0.1%
17	Arizona	1,319	2.0%
30	Arkansas	776	1.2%
1	California	8,128	12.4%
31	Colorado	752	1.1%
28	Connecticut	888	1.4%
46	Delaware	168	0.3%
4	Florida	3,290	5.0%
12	Georgia	1,791	2.7%
43	Hawaii	246	0.4%
41	Idaho	265	0.4%
6	Illinois	2,940	4.5%
16	Indiana	1,360	2.1%
23	Iowa	942	1.4%
32	Kansas	698	1.1%
19	Kentucky	1,236	1.9%
22	Louisiana	956	1.5%
40	Maine	317	0.5%
21	Maryland	1,121	1.7%
8	Massachusetts	2,087	3.2%
9	Michigan	2,029	3.1%
27	Minnesota	900	1.4%
29	Mississippi	801	1.2%
14	Missouri	1,619	2.5%
42	Montana	255	0.4%
36	Nebraska	418	0.6%
38	Nevada	368	0.6%
45	New Hampshire	237	0.4%
10	New Jersey	1,973	3.0%
37	New Mexico	372	0.6%
2	New York	5,368	8.2%
11	North Carolina	1,898	2.9%
47	North Dakota	162	0.2%
7	Ohio	2,487	3.8%
24	Oklahoma	914	1.4%
33	Oregon	666	1.0%
5	Pennsylvania	2,957	4.5%
39	Rhode Island	319	0.5%
25	South Carolina	910	1.4%
44	South Dakota	240	0.4%
13	Tennessee	1,710	2.6%
3	Texas	3,673	5.6%
35	Utah	424	0.6%
49	Vermont	111	0.2%
15	Virginia	1,480	2.3%
26	Washington	907	1.4%
34	West Virginia	427	0.7%
18	Wisconsin	1,291	2.0%
48	Wyoming	135	0.2%

RANK ORDER

RANK	STATE	DEATHS	% of USA
1	California	8,128	12.4%
2	New York	5,368	8.2%
3	Texas	3,673	5.6%
4	Florida	3,290	5.0%
5	Pennsylvania	2,957	4.5%
6	Illinois	2,940	4.5%
7	Ohio	2,487	3.8%
8	Massachusetts	2,087	3.2%
9	Michigan	2,029	3.1%
10	New Jersey	1,973	3.0%
11	North Carolina	1,898	2.9%
12	Georgia	1,791	2.7%
13	Tennessee	1,710	2.6%
14	Missouri	1,619	2.5%
15	Virginia	1,480	2.3%
16	Indiana	1,360	2.1%
17	Arizona	1,319	2.0%
18	Wisconsin	1,291	2.0%
19	Kentucky	1,236	1.9%
20	Alabama	1,218	1.9%
21	Maryland	1,121	1.7%
22	Louisiana	956	1.5%
23	Iowa	942	1.4%
24	Oklahoma	914	1.4%
25	South Carolina	910	1.4%
26	Washington	907	1.4%
27	Minnesota	900	1.4%
28	Connecticut	888	1.4%
29	Mississippi	801	1.2%
30	Arkansas	776	1.2%
31	Colorado	752	1.1%
32	Kansas	698	1.1%
33	Oregon	666	1.0%
34	West Virginia	427	0.7%
35	Utah	424	0.6%
36	Nebraska	418	0.6%
37	New Mexico	372	0.6%
38	Nevada	368	0.6%
39	Rhode Island	319	0.5%
40	Maine	317	0.5%
41	Idaho	265	0.4%
42	Montana	255	0.4%
43	Hawaii	246	0.4%
44	South Dakota	240	0.4%
45	New Hampshire	237	0.4%
46	Delaware	168	0.3%
47	North Dakota	162	0.2%
48	Wyoming	135	0.2%
49	Vermont	111	0.2%
50	Alaska	51	0.1%
	District of Columbia	81	0.1%

Source: U.S. Department of Health and Human Services, National Center for Health Statistics
   "National Vital Statistics Reports" (Vol. 53, No. 5, October 12, 2004)
*Final data by state of residence.

Death Rate by Pneumonia and Influenza in 2002

National Rate = 22.8 Deaths per 100,000 Population*

ALPHA ORDER			RANK ORDER		
RANK	STATE	RATE	RANK	STATE	RATE
12	Alabama	27.1	1	Massachusetts	32.5
50	Alaska	7.9	2	Iowa	32.1
19	Arizona	24.2	3	South Dakota	31.5
7	Arkansas	28.6	4	Kentucky	30.2
25	California	23.1	5	Rhode Island	29.8
48	Colorado	16.7	6	Tennessee	29.5
15	Connecticut	25.7	7	Arkansas	28.6
33	Delaware	20.8	8	Missouri	28.5
40	Florida	19.7	9	Montana	28.0
32	Georgia	20.9	9	New York	28.0
38	Hawaii	19.8	11	Mississippi	27.9
38	Idaho	19.8	12	Alabama	27.1
24	Illinois	23.3	12	Wyoming	27.1
29	Indiana	22.1	14	Oklahoma	26.2
2	Iowa	32.1	15	Connecticut	25.7
15	Kansas	25.7	15	Kansas	25.7
4	Kentucky	30.2	17	North Dakota	25.5
31	Louisiana	21.3	18	Maine	24.5
18	Maine	24.5	19	Arizona	24.2
34	Maryland	20.5	19	Nebraska	24.2
1	Massachusetts	32.5	21	Pennsylvania	24.0
36	Michigan	20.2	22	West Virginia	23.7
45	Minnesota	17.9	22	Wisconsin	23.7
11	Mississippi	27.9	24	Illinois	23.3
8	Missouri	28.5	25	California	23.1
9	Montana	28.0	26	New Jersey	23.0
19	Nebraska	24.2	27	North Carolina	22.8
46	Nevada	16.9	28	South Carolina	22.2
42	New Hampshire	18.6	29	Indiana	22.1
26	New Jersey	23.0	30	Ohio	21.8
37	New Mexico	20.1	31	Louisiana	21.3
9	New York	28.0	32	Georgia	20.9
27	North Carolina	22.8	33	Delaware	20.8
17	North Dakota	25.5	34	Maryland	20.5
30	Ohio	21.8	35	Virginia	20.3
14	Oklahoma	26.2	36	Michigan	20.2
41	Oregon	18.9	37	New Mexico	20.1
21	Pennsylvania	24.0	38	Hawaii	19.8
5	Rhode Island	29.8	38	Idaho	19.8
28	South Carolina	22.2	40	Florida	19.7
3	South Dakota	31.5	41	Oregon	18.9
6	Tennessee	29.5	42	New Hampshire	18.6
46	Texas	16.9	43	Utah	18.3
43	Utah	18.3	44	Vermont	18.0
44	Vermont	18.0	45	Minnesota	17.9
35	Virginia	20.3	46	Nevada	16.9
49	Washington	14.9	46	Texas	16.9
22	West Virginia	23.7	48	Colorado	16.7
22	Wisconsin	23.7	49	Washington	14.9
12	Wyoming	27.1	50	Alaska	7.9
				District of Columbia	14.2

Source: U.S. Department of Health and Human Services, National Center for Health Statistics
    "National Vital Statistics Reports" (Vol. 53, No. 5, October 12, 2004)
*Final data by state of residence. Not age-adjusted.

Age-Adjusted Death Rate by Pneumonia and Influenza in 2002

National Rate = 22.6 Deaths per 100,000 Population*

ALPHA ORDER

RANK	STATE	RATE
8	Alabama	26.6
41	Alaska	19.2
15	Arizona	24.9
12	Arkansas	25.7
7	California	26.8
30	Colorado	21.3
33	Connecticut	21.2
35	Delaware	20.9
50	Florida	14.8
5	Georgia	27.8
44	Hawaii	18.4
30	Idaho	21.3
22	Illinois	23.2
27	Indiana	21.9
18	Iowa	24.0
25	Kansas	22.3
1	Kentucky	30.8
21	Louisiana	23.5
36	Maine	20.5
24	Maryland	22.7
5	Massachusetts	27.8
39	Michigan	20.3
47	Minnesota	16.7
3	Mississippi	28.9
11	Missouri	25.9
13	Montana	25.0
37	Nebraska	20.4
26	Nevada	22.1
42	New Hampshire	18.9
30	New Jersey	21.3
28	New Mexico	21.7
10	New York	26.1
17	North Carolina	24.6
44	North Dakota	18.4
37	Ohio	20.4
15	Oklahoma	24.9
46	Oregon	17.3
43	Pennsylvania	18.6
19	Rhode Island	23.9
20	South Carolina	23.8
13	South Dakota	25.0
2	Tennessee	30.2
29	Texas	21.6
8	Utah	26.6
47	Vermont	16.7
23	Virginia	23.1
49	Washington	15.6
40	West Virginia	19.8
34	Wisconsin	21.0
4	Wyoming	28.5

RANK ORDER

RANK	STATE	RATE
1	Kentucky	30.8
2	Tennessee	30.2
3	Mississippi	28.9
4	Wyoming	28.5
5	Georgia	27.8
5	Massachusetts	27.8
7	California	26.8
8	Alabama	26.6
8	Utah	26.6
10	New York	26.1
11	Missouri	25.9
12	Arkansas	25.7
13	Montana	25.0
13	South Dakota	25.0
15	Arizona	24.9
15	Oklahoma	24.9
17	North Carolina	24.6
18	Iowa	24.0
19	Rhode Island	23.9
20	South Carolina	23.8
21	Louisiana	23.5
22	Illinois	23.2
23	Virginia	23.1
24	Maryland	22.7
25	Kansas	22.3
26	Nevada	22.1
27	Indiana	21.9
28	New Mexico	21.7
29	Texas	21.6
30	Colorado	21.3
30	Idaho	21.3
30	New Jersey	21.3
33	Connecticut	21.2
34	Wisconsin	21.0
35	Delaware	20.9
36	Maine	20.5
37	Nebraska	20.4
37	Ohio	20.4
39	Michigan	20.3
40	West Virginia	19.8
41	Alaska	19.2
42	New Hampshire	18.9
43	Pennsylvania	18.6
44	Hawaii	18.4
44	North Dakota	18.4
46	Oregon	17.3
47	Minnesota	16.7
47	Vermont	16.7
49	Washington	15.6
50	Florida	14.8
	District of Columbia	14.1

Source: U.S. Department of Health and Human Services, National Center for Health Statistics
  "National Vital Statistics Reports" (Vol. 53, No. 5, October 12, 2004)
Final data by state of residence. Age-adjusted rates based on the year 2000 standard population.

165

Deaths by Injury in 2002

National Total = 159,231 Deaths*

ALPHA ORDER

RANK	STATE	DEATHS	% of USA
19	Alabama	3,169	2.0%
43	Alaska	533	0.3%
12	Arizona	4,031	2.5%
30	Arkansas	1,992	1.3%
1	California	15,930	10.0%
23	Colorado	2,784	1.7%
33	Connecticut	1,563	1.0%
48	Delaware	411	0.3%
3	Florida	10,780	6.8%
10	Georgia	4,864	3.1%
42	Hawaii	577	0.4%
39	Idaho	868	0.5%
6	Illinois	6,462	4.1%
16	Indiana	3,371	2.1%
35	Iowa	1,453	0.9%
31	Kansas	1,622	1.0%
22	Kentucky	2,846	1.8%
18	Louisiana	3,271	2.1%
41	Maine	689	0.4%
21	Maryland	3,006	1.9%
25	Massachusetts	2,630	1.7%
9	Michigan	5,316	3.3%
26	Minnesota	2,562	1.6%
27	Mississippi	2,314	1.5%
13	Missouri	3,742	2.4%
40	Montana	750	0.5%
38	Nebraska	1,039	0.7%
34	Nevada	1,513	1.0%
44	New Hampshire	515	0.3%
15	New Jersey	3,545	2.2%
32	New Mexico	1,598	1.0%
4	New York	6,918	4.3%
8	North Carolina	5,321	3.3%
49	North Dakota	346	0.2%
7	Ohio	6,004	3.8%
28	Oklahoma	2,281	1.4%
29	Oregon	2,085	1.3%
5	Pennsylvania	6,747	4.2%
45	Rhode Island	494	0.3%
24	South Carolina	2,743	1.7%
46	South Dakota	470	0.3%
11	Tennessee	4,041	2.5%
2	Texas	12,039	7.6%
37	Utah	1,266	0.8%
50	Vermont	345	0.2%
14	Virginia	3,701	2.3%
17	Washington	3,290	2.1%
36	West Virginia	1,386	0.9%
20	Wisconsin	3,112	2.0%
47	Wyoming	424	0.3%

RANK ORDER

RANK	STATE	DEATHS	% of USA
1	California	15,930	10.0%
2	Texas	12,039	7.6%
3	Florida	10,780	6.8%
4	New York	6,918	4.3%
5	Pennsylvania	6,747	4.2%
6	Illinois	6,462	4.1%
7	Ohio	6,004	3.8%
8	North Carolina	5,321	3.3%
9	Michigan	5,316	3.3%
10	Georgia	4,864	3.1%
11	Tennessee	4,041	2.5%
12	Arizona	4,031	2.5%
13	Missouri	3,742	2.4%
14	Virginia	3,701	2.3%
15	New Jersey	3,545	2.2%
16	Indiana	3,371	2.1%
17	Washington	3,290	2.1%
18	Louisiana	3,271	2.1%
19	Alabama	3,169	2.0%
20	Wisconsin	3,112	2.0%
21	Maryland	3,006	1.9%
22	Kentucky	2,846	1.8%
23	Colorado	2,784	1.7%
24	South Carolina	2,743	1.7%
25	Massachusetts	2,630	1.7%
26	Minnesota	2,562	1.6%
27	Mississippi	2,314	1.5%
28	Oklahoma	2,281	1.4%
29	Oregon	2,085	1.3%
30	Arkansas	1,992	1.3%
31	Kansas	1,622	1.0%
32	New Mexico	1,598	1.0%
33	Connecticut	1,563	1.0%
34	Nevada	1,513	1.0%
35	Iowa	1,453	0.9%
36	West Virginia	1,386	0.9%
37	Utah	1,266	0.8%
38	Nebraska	1,039	0.7%
39	Idaho	868	0.5%
40	Montana	750	0.5%
41	Maine	689	0.4%
42	Hawaii	577	0.4%
43	Alaska	533	0.3%
44	New Hampshire	515	0.3%
45	Rhode Island	494	0.3%
46	South Dakota	470	0.3%
47	Wyoming	424	0.3%
48	Delaware	411	0.3%
49	North Dakota	346	0.2%
50	Vermont	345	0.2%
	District of Columbia	472	0.3%

*Source: U.S. Department of Health and Human Services, National Center for Health Statistics
(http://wonder.cdc.gov)*
**By state of residence. Injury as used here includes Accidents (including motor vehicle), Suicides, Homicides and
"Other" undetermined.*

Death Rate by Injury in 2002

National Rate = 55.2 Deaths per 100,000 Population*

ALPHA ORDER

RANK	STATE	RATE
10	Alabama	70.8
3	Alaska	83.1
7	Arizona	74.1
8	Arkansas	73.6
45	California	45.5
20	Colorado	61.8
46	Connecticut	45.2
39	Delaware	51.0
17	Florida	64.6
26	Georgia	56.9
43	Hawaii	46.5
17	Idaho	64.6
38	Illinois	51.3
30	Indiana	54.7
42	Iowa	49.5
23	Kansas	59.8
13	Kentucky	69.6
9	Louisiana	73.1
35	Maine	53.2
29	Maryland	55.2
48	Massachusetts	41.0
36	Michigan	52.9
39	Minnesota	51.0
5	Mississippi	80.8
15	Missouri	66.0
4	Montana	82.4
22	Nebraska	60.1
11	Nevada	69.8
49	New Hampshire	40.4
47	New Jersey	41.3
1	New Mexico	86.2
50	New York	36.2
19	North Carolina	64.1
32	North Dakota	54.6
37	Ohio	52.6
16	Oklahoma	65.4
24	Oregon	59.2
30	Pennsylvania	54.7
44	Rhode Island	46.2
14	South Carolina	66.9
20	South Dakota	61.8
11	Tennessee	69.8
28	Texas	55.4
32	Utah	54.6
27	Vermont	55.9
41	Virginia	50.8
34	Washington	54.2
6	West Virginia	76.8
25	Wisconsin	57.2
2	Wyoming	85.0

RANK ORDER

RANK	STATE	RATE
1	New Mexico	86.2
2	Wyoming	85.0
3	Alaska	83.1
4	Montana	82.4
5	Mississippi	80.8
6	West Virginia	76.8
7	Arizona	74.1
8	Arkansas	73.6
9	Louisiana	73.1
10	Alabama	70.8
11	Nevada	69.8
11	Tennessee	69.8
13	Kentucky	69.6
14	South Carolina	66.9
15	Missouri	66.0
16	Oklahoma	65.4
17	Florida	64.6
17	Idaho	64.6
19	North Carolina	64.1
20	Colorado	61.8
20	South Dakota	61.8
22	Nebraska	60.1
23	Kansas	59.8
24	Oregon	59.2
25	Wisconsin	57.2
26	Georgia	56.9
27	Vermont	55.9
28	Texas	55.4
29	Maryland	55.2
30	Indiana	54.7
30	Pennsylvania	54.7
32	North Dakota	54.6
32	Utah	54.6
34	Washington	54.2
35	Maine	53.2
36	Michigan	52.9
37	Ohio	52.6
38	Illinois	51.3
39	Delaware	51.0
39	Minnesota	51.0
41	Virginia	50.8
42	Iowa	49.5
43	Hawaii	46.5
44	Rhode Island	46.2
45	California	45.5
46	Connecticut	45.2
47	New Jersey	41.3
48	Massachusetts	41.0
49	New Hampshire	40.4
50	New York	36.2
	District of Columbia	83.0

Source: U.S. Department of Health and Human Services, National Center for Health Statistics
   (http://wonder.cdc.gov)
*By state of residence. Injury as used here includes Accidents (including motor vehicle), Suicides, Homicides and
"Other" undetermined. Not age-adjusted.

Age-Adjusted Death Rate by Injury in 2002

National Rate = 55.0 Deaths per 100,000 Population*

ALPHA ORDER

RANK	STATE	RATE
11	Alabama	70.3
2	Alaska	88.0
6	Arizona	75.3
9	Arkansas	73.0
42	California	46.6
19	Colorado	64.4
46	Connecticut	43.3
39	Delaware	50.9
20	Florida	62.0
22	Georgia	59.6
44	Hawaii	45.2
15	Idaho	66.2
37	Illinois	51.2
30	Indiana	54.7
43	Iowa	45.6
24	Kansas	58.4
13	Kentucky	69.3
8	Louisiana	73.9
37	Maine	51.2
28	Maryland	55.5
49	Massachusetts	39.1
33	Michigan	52.9
41	Minnesota	49.7
4	Mississippi	81.7
16	Missouri	64.8
5	Montana	79.7
26	Nebraska	57.7
10	Nevada	72.4
48	New Hampshire	40.3
47	New Jersey	40.5
1	New Mexico	88.4
50	New York	35.4
18	North Carolina	64.6
39	North Dakota	50.9
35	Ohio	51.8
16	Oklahoma	64.8
27	Oregon	57.4
34	Pennsylvania	52.1
45	Rhode Island	43.4
14	South Carolina	67.3
23	South Dakota	59.4
12	Tennessee	69.6
25	Texas	58.1
21	Utah	61.9
32	Vermont	53.7
36	Virginia	51.7
31	Washington	54.2
7	West Virginia	74.4
29	Wisconsin	54.9
3	Wyoming	84.8

RANK ORDER

RANK	STATE	RATE
1	New Mexico	88.4
2	Alaska	88.0
3	Wyoming	84.8
4	Mississippi	81.7
5	Montana	79.7
6	Arizona	75.3
7	West Virginia	74.4
8	Louisiana	73.9
9	Arkansas	73.0
10	Nevada	72.4
11	Alabama	70.3
12	Tennessee	69.6
13	Kentucky	69.3
14	South Carolina	67.3
15	Idaho	66.2
16	Missouri	64.8
16	Oklahoma	64.8
18	North Carolina	64.6
19	Colorado	64.4
20	Florida	62.0
21	Utah	61.9
22	Georgia	59.6
23	South Dakota	59.4
24	Kansas	58.4
25	Texas	58.1
26	Nebraska	57.7
27	Oregon	57.4
28	Maryland	55.5
29	Wisconsin	54.9
30	Indiana	54.7
31	Washington	54.2
32	Vermont	53.7
33	Michigan	52.9
34	Pennsylvania	52.1
35	Ohio	51.8
36	Virginia	51.7
37	Illinois	51.2
37	Maine	51.2
39	Delaware	50.9
39	North Dakota	50.9
41	Minnesota	49.7
42	California	46.6
43	Iowa	45.6
44	Hawaii	45.2
45	Rhode Island	43.4
46	Connecticut	43.3
47	New Jersey	40.5
48	New Hampshire	40.3
49	Massachusetts	39.1
50	New York	35.4

District of Columbia   78.9

Source: U.S. Department of Health and Human Services, National Center for Health Statistics (http://wonder.cdc.gov)

*By state of residence. Injury as used here includes Accidents (including motor vehicle), Suicides, Homicides and "Other" undetermined. Age-adjusted rates based on the year 2000 standard population.

Deaths by Accidents in 2002

National Total = 106,742 Deaths*

ALPHA ORDER

RANK	STATE	DEATHS	% of USA
17	Alabama	2,228	2.1%
45	Alaska	346	0.3%
14	Arizona	2,577	2.4%
30	Arkansas	1,311	1.2%
1	California	10,107	9.5%
24	Colorado	1,812	1.7%
31	Connecticut	1,182	1.1%
46	Delaware	292	0.3%
3	Florida	7,396	6.9%
9	Georgia	3,333	3.1%
42	Hawaii	393	0.4%
39	Idaho	611	0.6%
6	Illinois	4,222	4.0%
19	Indiana	2,148	2.0%
34	Iowa	1,093	1.0%
32	Kansas	1,139	1.1%
21	Kentucky	2,090	2.0%
20	Louisiana	2,115	2.0%
41	Maine	511	0.5%
29	Maryland	1,332	1.2%
27	Massachusetts	1,413	1.3%
10	Michigan	3,285	3.1%
23	Minnesota	1,928	1.8%
25	Mississippi	1,642	1.5%
12	Missouri	2,641	2.5%
40	Montana	524	0.5%
37	Nebraska	762	0.7%
36	Nevada	860	0.8%
43	New Hampshire	357	0.3%
13	New Jersey	2,599	2.4%
33	New Mexico	1,105	1.0%
5	New York	4,663	4.4%
8	North Carolina	3,700	3.5%
49	North Dakota	246	0.2%
7	Ohio	4,146	3.9%
26	Oklahoma	1,580	1.5%
28	Oregon	1,397	1.3%
4	Pennsylvania	4,728	4.4%
48	Rhode Island	277	0.3%
22	South Carolina	1,972	1.8%
44	South Dakota	348	0.3%
11	Tennessee	2,744	2.6%
2	Texas	8,232	7.7%
38	Utah	714	0.7%
50	Vermont	240	0.2%
15	Virginia	2,479	2.3%
18	Washington	2,203	2.1%
35	West Virginia	956	0.9%
16	Wisconsin	2,274	2.1%
47	Wyoming	289	0.3%

RANK ORDER

RANK	STATE	DEATHS	% of USA
1	California	10,107	9.5%
2	Texas	8,232	7.7%
3	Florida	7,396	6.9%
4	Pennsylvania	4,728	4.4%
5	New York	4,663	4.4%
6	Illinois	4,222	4.0%
7	Ohio	4,146	3.9%
8	North Carolina	3,700	3.5%
9	Georgia	3,333	3.1%
10	Michigan	3,285	3.1%
11	Tennessee	2,744	2.6%
12	Missouri	2,641	2.5%
13	New Jersey	2,599	2.4%
14	Arizona	2,577	2.4%
15	Virginia	2,479	2.3%
16	Wisconsin	2,274	2.1%
17	Alabama	2,228	2.1%
18	Washington	2,203	2.1%
19	Indiana	2,148	2.0%
20	Louisiana	2,115	2.0%
21	Kentucky	2,090	2.0%
22	South Carolina	1,972	1.8%
23	Minnesota	1,928	1.8%
24	Colorado	1,812	1.7%
25	Mississippi	1,642	1.5%
26	Oklahoma	1,580	1.5%
27	Massachusetts	1,413	1.3%
28	Oregon	1,397	1.3%
29	Maryland	1,332	1.2%
30	Arkansas	1,311	1.2%
31	Connecticut	1,182	1.1%
32	Kansas	1,139	1.1%
33	New Mexico	1,105	1.0%
34	Iowa	1,093	1.0%
35	West Virginia	956	0.9%
36	Nevada	860	0.8%
37	Nebraska	762	0.7%
38	Utah	714	0.7%
39	Idaho	611	0.6%
40	Montana	524	0.5%
41	Maine	511	0.5%
42	Hawaii	393	0.4%
43	New Hampshire	357	0.3%
44	South Dakota	348	0.3%
45	Alaska	346	0.3%
46	Delaware	292	0.3%
47	Wyoming	289	0.3%
48	Rhode Island	277	0.3%
49	North Dakota	246	0.2%
50	Vermont	240	0.2%
	District of Columbia	200	0.2%

Source: U.S. Department of Health and Human Services, National Center for Health Statistics
 "National Vital Statistics Reports" (Vol. 53, No. 5, October 12, 2004)
Final data by state of residence. Includes motor vehicle deaths, poisoning, falls, drowning and other accidents.

Death Rate by Accidents in 2002

National Rate = 37.0 Deaths per 100,000 Population*

RANK	STATE	RATE
8	Alabama	49.7
5	Alaska	53.7
12	Arizona	47.2
9	Arkansas	48.4
45	California	28.8
23	Colorado	40.2
38	Connecticut	34.2
36	Delaware	36.2
19	Florida	44.3
27	Georgia	38.9
42	Hawaii	31.6
16	Idaho	45.6
40	Illinois	33.5
37	Indiana	34.9
33	Iowa	37.2
21	Kansas	41.9
7	Kentucky	51.1
12	Louisiana	47.2
26	Maine	39.5
48	Maryland	24.4
50	Massachusetts	22.0
41	Michigan	32.7
30	Minnesota	38.4
4	Mississippi	57.2
14	Missouri	46.6
3	Montana	57.6
20	Nebraska	44.1
25	Nevada	39.6
46	New Hampshire	28.0
44	New Jersey	30.3
1	New Mexico	59.6
49	New York	24.3
18	North Carolina	44.5
29	North Dakota	38.8
34	Ohio	36.3
17	Oklahoma	45.2
24	Oregon	39.7
31	Pennsylvania	38.3
47	Rhode Island	25.9
10	South Carolina	48.0
15	South Dakota	45.7
11	Tennessee	47.3
32	Texas	37.8
43	Utah	30.8
27	Vermont	38.9
39	Virginia	34.0
34	Washington	36.3
6	West Virginia	53.1
22	Wisconsin	41.8
2	Wyoming	58.0

RANK	STATE	RATE
1	New Mexico	59.6
2	Wyoming	58.0
3	Montana	57.6
4	Mississippi	57.2
5	Alaska	53.7
6	West Virginia	53.1
7	Kentucky	51.1
8	Alabama	49.7
9	Arkansas	48.4
10	South Carolina	48.0
11	Tennessee	47.3
12	Arizona	47.2
12	Louisiana	47.2
14	Missouri	46.6
15	South Dakota	45.7
16	Idaho	45.6
17	Oklahoma	45.2
18	North Carolina	44.5
19	Florida	44.3
20	Nebraska	44.1
21	Kansas	41.9
22	Wisconsin	41.8
23	Colorado	40.2
24	Oregon	39.7
25	Nevada	39.6
26	Maine	39.5
27	Georgia	38.9
27	Vermont	38.9
29	North Dakota	38.8
30	Minnesota	38.4
31	Pennsylvania	38.3
32	Texas	37.8
33	Iowa	37.2
34	Ohio	36.3
34	Washington	36.3
36	Delaware	36.2
37	Indiana	34.9
38	Connecticut	34.2
39	Virginia	34.0
40	Illinois	33.5
41	Michigan	32.7
42	Hawaii	31.6
43	Utah	30.8
44	New Jersey	30.3
45	California	28.8
46	New Hampshire	28.0
47	Rhode Island	25.9
48	Maryland	24.4
49	New York	24.3
50	Massachusetts	22.0
	District of Columbia	35.0

Source: U.S. Department of Health and Human Services, National Center for Health Statistics
"National Vital Statistics Reports" (Vol. 53, No. 5, October 12, 2004)
*Final data by state of residence. Includes motor vehicle deaths, poisoning, falls, drowning and other accidents. Not age-adjusted.

Age-Adjusted Death Rate by Accidents in 2002

National Rate = 36.9 Deaths per 100,000 Population*

ALPHA ORDER

RANK	STATE	RATE
8	Alabama	49.2
2	Alaska	59.0
10	Arizona	48.1
13	Arkansas	47.3
44	California	29.9
19	Colorado	42.8
42	Connecticut	32.5
32	Delaware	35.9
20	Florida	41.9
22	Georgia	41.8
43	Hawaii	30.4
14	Idaho	46.8
39	Illinois	33.5
38	Indiana	34.8
40	Iowa	33.3
24	Kansas	40.6
7	Kentucky	50.5
11	Louisiana	48.0
28	Maine	37.6
47	Maryland	25.1
50	Massachusetts	20.5
41	Michigan	32.7
29	Minnesota	37.3
3	Mississippi	57.9
15	Missouri	45.3
5	Montana	55.2
23	Nebraska	41.4
20	Nevada	41.9
46	New Hampshire	28.1
45	New Jersey	29.5
1	New Mexico	61.1
48	New York	23.7
16	North Carolina	45.2
36	North Dakota	35.0
33	Ohio	35.6
17	Oklahoma	44.6
27	Oregon	38.1
33	Pennsylvania	35.6
49	Rhode Island	23.1
9	South Carolina	48.2
18	South Dakota	43.3
12	Tennessee	47.4
25	Texas	40.1
33	Utah	35.6
30	Vermont	37.2
36	Virginia	35.0
31	Washington	36.5
6	West Virginia	50.7
26	Wisconsin	39.7
3	Wyoming	57.9

RANK ORDER

RANK	STATE	RATE
1	New Mexico	61.1
2	Alaska	59.0
3	Mississippi	57.9
3	Wyoming	57.9
5	Montana	55.2
6	West Virginia	50.7
7	Kentucky	50.5
8	Alabama	49.2
9	South Carolina	48.2
10	Arizona	48.1
11	Louisiana	48.0
12	Tennessee	47.4
13	Arkansas	47.3
14	Idaho	46.8
15	Missouri	45.3
16	North Carolina	45.2
17	Oklahoma	44.6
18	South Dakota	43.3
19	Colorado	42.8
20	Florida	41.9
20	Nevada	41.9
22	Georgia	41.8
23	Nebraska	41.4
24	Kansas	40.6
25	Texas	40.1
26	Wisconsin	39.7
27	Oregon	38.1
28	Maine	37.6
29	Minnesota	37.3
30	Vermont	37.2
31	Washington	36.5
32	Delaware	35.9
33	Ohio	35.6
33	Pennsylvania	35.6
33	Utah	35.6
36	North Dakota	35.0
36	Virginia	35.0
38	Indiana	34.8
39	Illinois	33.5
40	Iowa	33.3
41	Michigan	32.7
42	Connecticut	32.5
43	Hawaii	30.4
44	California	29.9
45	New Jersey	29.5
46	New Hampshire	28.1
47	Maryland	25.1
48	New York	23.7
49	Rhode Island	23.1
50	Massachusetts	20.5

	District of Columbia	34.5

Source: U.S. Department of Health and Human Services, National Center for Health Statistics
     "National Vital Statistics Reports" (Vol. 53, No. 5, October 12, 2004)
*Final data by state of residence. Includes motor vehicle deaths, poisoning, falls, drowning and other accidents.
Age-adjusted rates based on the year 2000 standard population.

Deaths by Motor Vehicle Accidents in 2002

National Total = 45,380 Deaths*

ALPHA ORDER

RANK	STATE	DEATHS	% of USA
13	Alabama	1,115	2.5%
47	Alaska	112	0.2%
14	Arizona	1,105	2.4%
28	Arkansas	693	1.5%
1	California	4,248	9.4%
23	Colorado	781	1.7%
36	Connecticut	348	0.8%
45	Delaware	121	0.3%
3	Florida	3,196	7.0%
9	Georgia	1,526	3.4%
45	Hawaii	121	0.3%
39	Idaho	296	0.7%
8	Illinois	1,579	3.5%
16	Indiana	963	2.1%
32	Iowa	426	0.9%
30	Kansas	563	1.2%
19	Kentucky	923	2.0%
18	Louisiana	959	2.1%
41	Maine	215	0.5%
27	Maryland	718	1.6%
29	Massachusetts	565	1.2%
10	Michigan	1,386	3.1%
26	Minnesota	744	1.6%
20	Mississippi	879	1.9%
12	Missouri	1,213	2.7%
40	Montana	255	0.6%
37	Nebraska	337	0.7%
35	Nevada	386	0.9%
44	New Hampshire	125	0.3%
22	New Jersey	786	1.7%
33	New Mexico	423	0.9%
5	New York	1,695	3.7%
6	North Carolina	1,690	3.7%
48	North Dakota	111	0.2%
7	Ohio	1,602	3.5%
24	Oklahoma	766	1.7%
31	Oregon	462	1.0%
4	Pennsylvania	1,739	3.8%
49	Rhode Island	95	0.2%
15	South Carolina	1,024	2.3%
42	South Dakota	186	0.4%
11	Tennessee	1,250	2.8%
2	Texas	4,024	8.9%
38	Utah	329	0.7%
50	Vermont	78	0.2%
16	Virginia	963	2.1%
25	Washington	760	1.7%
34	West Virginia	414	0.9%
21	Wisconsin	870	1.9%
43	Wyoming	157	0.3%

RANK ORDER

RANK	STATE	DEATHS	% of USA
1	California	4,248	9.4%
2	Texas	4,024	8.9%
3	Florida	3,196	7.0%
4	Pennsylvania	1,739	3.8%
5	New York	1,695	3.7%
6	North Carolina	1,690	3.7%
7	Ohio	1,602	3.5%
8	Illinois	1,579	3.5%
9	Georgia	1,526	3.4%
10	Michigan	1,386	3.1%
11	Tennessee	1,250	2.8%
12	Missouri	1,213	2.7%
13	Alabama	1,115	2.5%
14	Arizona	1,105	2.4%
15	South Carolina	1,024	2.3%
16	Indiana	963	2.1%
16	Virginia	963	2.1%
18	Louisiana	959	2.1%
19	Kentucky	923	2.0%
20	Mississippi	879	1.9%
21	Wisconsin	870	1.9%
22	New Jersey	786	1.7%
23	Colorado	781	1.7%
24	Oklahoma	766	1.7%
25	Washington	760	1.7%
26	Minnesota	744	1.6%
27	Maryland	718	1.6%
28	Arkansas	693	1.5%
29	Massachusetts	565	1.2%
30	Kansas	563	1.2%
31	Oregon	462	1.0%
32	Iowa	426	0.9%
33	New Mexico	423	0.9%
34	West Virginia	414	0.9%
35	Nevada	386	0.9%
36	Connecticut	348	0.8%
37	Nebraska	337	0.7%
38	Utah	329	0.7%
39	Idaho	296	0.7%
40	Montana	255	0.6%
41	Maine	215	0.5%
42	South Dakota	186	0.4%
43	Wyoming	157	0.3%
44	New Hampshire	125	0.3%
45	Delaware	121	0.3%
45	Hawaii	121	0.3%
47	Alaska	112	0.2%
48	North Dakota	111	0.2%
49	Rhode Island	95	0.2%
50	Vermont	78	0.2%
	District of Columbia	58	0.1%

*Source: U.S. Department of Health and Human Services, National Center for Health Statistics
"National Vital Statistics Reports" (Vol. 53, No. 5, October 12, 2004)*

*Final data by state of residence. These numbers are compiled from death certificates by the Centers for Disease Control and Prevention. They may differ from motor vehicle deaths collected by the U.S. Department of Transportation from other sources.

Death Rate by Motor Vehicle Accidents in 2002

National Rate = 15.7 Deaths per 100,000 Population*

ALPHA ORDER

RANK	STATE	RATE
5	Alabama	24.9
25	Alaska	17.4
17	Arizona	20.3
4	Arkansas	25.6
43	California	12.1
26	Colorado	17.3
44	Connecticut	10.1
30	Delaware	15.0
20	Florida	19.1
22	Georgia	17.8
46	Hawaii	9.7
11	Idaho	22.1
41	Illinois	12.5
29	Indiana	15.6
32	Iowa	14.5
16	Kansas	20.7
10	Kentucky	22.6
14	Louisiana	21.4
27	Maine	16.6
37	Maryland	13.2
49	Massachusetts	8.8
36	Michigan	13.8
31	Minnesota	14.8
2	Mississippi	30.6
14	Missouri	21.4
3	Montana	28.0
19	Nebraska	19.5
22	Nevada	17.8
45	New Hampshire	9.8
47	New Jersey	9.1
9	New Mexico	22.8
49	New York	8.8
17	North Carolina	20.3
24	North Dakota	17.5
35	Ohio	14.0
12	Oklahoma	21.9
39	Oregon	13.1
34	Pennsylvania	14.1
48	Rhode Island	8.9
5	South Carolina	24.9
7	South Dakota	24.4
13	Tennessee	21.6
21	Texas	18.5
33	Utah	14.2
40	Vermont	12.7
37	Virginia	13.2
41	Washington	12.5
8	West Virginia	23.0
28	Wisconsin	16.0
1	Wyoming	31.5

RANK ORDER

RANK	STATE	RATE
1	Wyoming	31.5
2	Mississippi	30.6
3	Montana	28.0
4	Arkansas	25.6
5	Alabama	24.9
5	South Carolina	24.9
7	South Dakota	24.4
8	West Virginia	23.0
9	New Mexico	22.8
10	Kentucky	22.6
11	Idaho	22.1
12	Oklahoma	21.9
13	Tennessee	21.6
14	Louisiana	21.4
14	Missouri	21.4
16	Kansas	20.7
17	Arizona	20.3
17	North Carolina	20.3
19	Nebraska	19.5
20	Florida	19.1
21	Texas	18.5
22	Georgia	17.8
22	Nevada	17.8
24	North Dakota	17.5
25	Alaska	17.4
26	Colorado	17.3
27	Maine	16.6
28	Wisconsin	16.0
29	Indiana	15.6
30	Delaware	15.0
31	Minnesota	14.8
32	Iowa	14.5
33	Utah	14.2
34	Pennsylvania	14.1
35	Ohio	14.0
36	Michigan	13.8
37	Maryland	13.2
37	Virginia	13.2
39	Oregon	13.1
40	Vermont	12.7
41	Illinois	12.5
41	Washington	12.5
43	California	12.1
44	Connecticut	10.1
45	New Hampshire	9.8
46	Hawaii	9.7
47	New Jersey	9.1
48	Rhode Island	8.9
49	Massachusetts	8.8
49	New York	8.8
	District of Columbia	10.2

Source: U.S. Department of Health and Human Services, National Center for Health Statistics
     "National Vital Statistics Reports" (Vol. 53, No. 5, October 12, 2004)
*Final data by state of residence. These numbers are compiled from death certificates by the Centers for Disease
Control and Prevention. They may differ from motor vehicle deaths collected by the U.S. Department of
Transportation from other sources. Not age-adjusted.

Age-Adjusted Death Rate by Motor Vehicle Accidents in 2002

National Rate = 15.7 Deaths per 100,000 Population*

ALPHA ORDER

RANK	STATE	RATE		RANK	STATE	RATE
5	Alabama	24.7		1	Wyoming	31.2
19	Alaska	19.1		2	Mississippi	30.6
16	Arizona	20.5		3	Montana	27.4
4	Arkansas	25.4		4	Arkansas	25.4
43	California	12.2		5	Alabama	24.7
25	Colorado	17.4		6	South Carolina	24.6
44	Connecticut	10.2		7	South Dakota	23.9
30	Delaware	14.8		8	New Mexico	22.7
20	Florida	18.9		9	West Virginia	22.4
24	Georgia	18.1		10	Idaho	22.2
46	Hawaii	9.5		11	Kentucky	22.1
10	Idaho	22.2		12	Oklahoma	21.6
40	Illinois	12.5		13	Tennessee	21.5
29	Indiana	15.5		14	Louisiana	21.3
33	Iowa	13.9		15	Missouri	21.1
17	Kansas	20.3		16	Arizona	20.5
11	Kentucky	22.1		17	Kansas	20.3
14	Louisiana	21.3		17	North Carolina	20.3
27	Maine	16.1		19	Alaska	19.1
37	Maryland	13.3		20	Florida	18.9
49	Massachusetts	8.6		20	Nebraska	18.9
35	Michigan	13.8		22	Texas	18.7
32	Minnesota	14.6		23	Nevada	18.3
2	Mississippi	30.6		24	Georgia	18.1
15	Missouri	21.1		25	Colorado	17.4
3	Montana	27.4		26	North Dakota	16.6
20	Nebraska	18.9		27	Maine	16.1
23	Nevada	18.3		28	Wisconsin	15.6
45	New Hampshire	9.8		29	Indiana	15.5
47	New Jersey	9.2		30	Delaware	14.8
8	New Mexico	22.7		31	Utah	14.7
48	New York	8.7		32	Minnesota	14.6
17	North Carolina	20.3		33	Iowa	13.9
26	North Dakota	16.6		33	Ohio	13.9
33	Ohio	13.9		35	Michigan	13.8
12	Oklahoma	21.6		35	Pennsylvania	13.8
39	Oregon	12.8		37	Maryland	13.3
35	Pennsylvania	13.8		38	Virginia	13.2
50	Rhode Island	8.5		39	Oregon	12.8
6	South Carolina	24.6		40	Illinois	12.5
7	South Dakota	23.9		40	Vermont	12.5
13	Tennessee	21.5		40	Washington	12.5
22	Texas	18.7		43	California	12.2
31	Utah	14.7		44	Connecticut	10.2
40	Vermont	12.5		45	New Hampshire	9.8
38	Virginia	13.2		46	Hawaii	9.5
40	Washington	12.5		47	New Jersey	9.2
9	West Virginia	22.4		48	New York	8.7
28	Wisconsin	15.6		49	Massachusetts	8.6
1	Wyoming	31.2		50	Rhode Island	8.5
					District of Columbia	9.4

RANK ORDER

Source: U.S. Department of Health and Human Services, National Center for Health Statistics
   "National Vital Statistics Reports" (Vol. 52, No. 3, September 18, 2003)
*Final data by state of residence. These numbers are compiled from death certificates by the Centers for Disease Control and Prevention. They may differ from motor vehicle deaths collected by the U.S. Department of Transportation from other sources. Age-adjusted rates based on the year 2000 standard population.

Deaths by Firearm Injury in 2002

National Total = 30,242 Deaths*

ALPHA ORDER

RANK	STATE	DEATHS	% of USA
15	Alabama	724	2.4%
41	Alaska	127	0.4%
11	Arizona	968	3.2%
26	Arkansas	441	1.5%
1	California	3,410	11.3%
22	Colorado	517	1.7%
38	Connecticut	147	0.5%
45	Delaware	74	0.2%
3	Florida	1,886	6.2%
7	Georgia	1,133	3.7%
50	Hawaii	36	0.1%
37	Idaho	163	0.5%
4	Illinois	1,231	4.1%
16	Indiana	723	2.4%
36	Iowa	201	0.7%
33	Kansas	268	0.9%
21	Kentucky	544	1.8%
13	Louisiana	876	2.9%
43	Maine	88	0.3%
18	Maryland	615	2.0%
35	Massachusetts	204	0.7%
8	Michigan	1,092	3.6%
30	Minnesota	306	1.0%
23	Mississippi	492	1.6%
17	Missouri	696	2.3%
40	Montana	134	0.4%
39	Nebraska	140	0.5%
29	Nevada	370	1.2%
44	New Hampshire	76	0.3%
27	New Jersey	415	1.4%
31	New Mexico	304	1.0%
10	New York	994	3.3%
6	North Carolina	1,136	3.8%
48	North Dakota	58	0.2%
9	Ohio	1,069	3.5%
24	Oklahoma	452	1.5%
28	Oregon	374	1.2%
5	Pennsylvania	1,220	4.0%
49	Rhode Island	55	0.2%
20	South Carolina	566	1.9%
47	South Dakota	61	0.2%
12	Tennessee	905	3.0%
2	Texas	2,301	7.6%
34	Utah	207	0.7%
46	Vermont	62	0.2%
14	Virginia	806	2.7%
19	Washington	568	1.9%
32	West Virginia	271	0.9%
25	Wisconsin	446	1.5%
42	Wyoming	95	0.3%

RANK ORDER

RANK	STATE	DEATHS	% of USA
1	California	3,410	11.3%
2	Texas	2,301	7.6%
3	Florida	1,886	6.2%
4	Illinois	1,231	4.1%
5	Pennsylvania	1,220	4.0%
6	North Carolina	1,136	3.8%
7	Georgia	1,133	3.7%
8	Michigan	1,092	3.6%
9	Ohio	1,069	3.5%
10	New York	994	3.3%
11	Arizona	968	3.2%
12	Tennessee	905	3.0%
13	Louisiana	876	2.9%
14	Virginia	806	2.7%
15	Alabama	724	2.4%
16	Indiana	723	2.4%
17	Missouri	696	2.3%
18	Maryland	615	2.0%
19	Washington	568	1.9%
20	South Carolina	566	1.9%
21	Kentucky	544	1.8%
22	Colorado	517	1.7%
23	Mississippi	492	1.6%
24	Oklahoma	452	1.5%
25	Wisconsin	446	1.5%
26	Arkansas	441	1.5%
27	New Jersey	415	1.4%
28	Oregon	374	1.2%
29	Nevada	370	1.2%
30	Minnesota	306	1.0%
31	New Mexico	304	1.0%
32	West Virginia	271	0.9%
33	Kansas	268	0.9%
34	Utah	207	0.7%
35	Massachusetts	204	0.7%
36	Iowa	201	0.7%
37	Idaho	163	0.5%
38	Connecticut	147	0.5%
39	Nebraska	140	0.5%
40	Montana	134	0.4%
41	Alaska	127	0.4%
42	Wyoming	95	0.3%
43	Maine	88	0.3%
44	New Hampshire	76	0.3%
45	Delaware	74	0.2%
46	Vermont	62	0.2%
47	South Dakota	61	0.2%
48	North Dakota	58	0.2%
49	Rhode Island	55	0.2%
50	Hawaii	36	0.1%
	District of Columbia	195	0.6%

Source: U.S. Department of Health and Human Services, National Center for Health Statistics
  "National Vital Statistics Reports" (Vol. 53, No. 5, October 12, 2004)
*Final data by state of residence.

Death Rate by Firearm Injury in 2002

National Rate = 10.5 Deaths per 100,000 Population*

ALPHA ORDER

RANK	STATE	RATE
9	Alabama	16.1
1	Alaska	19.7
4	Arizona	17.7
8	Arkansas	16.3
32	California	9.7
21	Colorado	11.5
48	Connecticut	4.2
35	Delaware	9.2
22	Florida	11.3
16	Georgia	13.2
50	Hawaii	2.9
19	Idaho	12.2
31	Illinois	9.8
20	Indiana	11.7
41	Iowa	6.8
29	Kansas	9.9
15	Kentucky	13.3
2	Louisiana	19.5
41	Maine	6.8
22	Maryland	11.3
49	Massachusetts	3.2
25	Michigan	10.9
43	Minnesota	6.1
5	Mississippi	17.1
18	Missouri	12.3
12	Montana	14.7
39	Nebraska	8.1
6	Nevada	17.0
44	New Hampshire	6.0
47	New Jersey	4.8
7	New Mexico	16.4
45	New York	5.2
14	North Carolina	13.7
36	North Dakota	9.1
33	Ohio	9.4
17	Oklahoma	12.9
26	Oregon	10.6
29	Pennsylvania	9.9
46	Rhode Island	5.1
13	South Carolina	13.8
40	South Dakota	8.0
10	Tennessee	15.6
26	Texas	10.6
37	Utah	8.9
28	Vermont	10.1
24	Virginia	11.1
33	Washington	9.4
11	West Virginia	15.0
38	Wisconsin	8.2
3	Wyoming	19.0

RANK ORDER

RANK	STATE	RATE
1	Alaska	19.7
2	Louisiana	19.5
3	Wyoming	19.0
4	Arizona	17.7
5	Mississippi	17.1
6	Nevada	17.0
7	New Mexico	16.4
8	Arkansas	16.3
9	Alabama	16.1
10	Tennessee	15.6
11	West Virginia	15.0
12	Montana	14.7
13	South Carolina	13.8
14	North Carolina	13.7
15	Kentucky	13.3
16	Georgia	13.2
17	Oklahoma	12.9
18	Missouri	12.3
19	Idaho	12.2
20	Indiana	11.7
21	Colorado	11.5
22	Florida	11.3
22	Maryland	11.3
24	Virginia	11.1
25	Michigan	10.9
26	Oregon	10.6
26	Texas	10.6
28	Vermont	10.1
29	Kansas	9.9
29	Pennsylvania	9.9
31	Illinois	9.8
32	California	9.7
33	Ohio	9.4
33	Washington	9.4
35	Delaware	9.2
36	North Dakota	9.1
37	Utah	8.9
38	Wisconsin	8.2
39	Nebraska	8.1
40	South Dakota	8.0
41	Iowa	6.8
41	Maine	6.8
43	Minnesota	6.1
44	New Hampshire	6.0
45	New York	5.2
46	Rhode Island	5.1
47	New Jersey	4.8
48	Connecticut	4.2
49	Massachusetts	3.2
50	Hawaii	2.9
	District of Columbia	34.2

Source: U.S. Department of Health and Human Services, National Center for Health Statistics
"National Vital Statistics Reports" (Vol. 53, No. 5, October 12, 2004)
*Final data by state of residence. Not age-adjusted.

Age-Adjusted Death Rate by Firearm Injury in 2002

National Rate = 10.4 Deaths per 100,000 Population*

ALPHA ORDER

RANK	STATE	RATE
9	Alabama	16.0
1	Alaska	20.0
4	Arizona	17.9
8	Arkansas	16.3
29	California	9.7
21	Colorado	11.5
48	Connecticut	4.3
36	Delaware	9.0
23	Florida	11.1
15	Georgia	13.4
50	Hawaii	2.8
18	Idaho	12.4
29	Illinois	9.7
20	Indiana	11.7
41	Iowa	6.7
29	Kansas	9.7
16	Kentucky	12.9
2	Louisiana	19.4
42	Maine	6.5
22	Maryland	11.4
49	Massachusetts	3.1
25	Michigan	10.9
43	Minnesota	6.0
6	Mississippi	17.2
19	Missouri	12.2
12	Montana	14.5
38	Nebraska	8.1
5	Nevada	17.3
44	New Hampshire	5.8
47	New Jersey	4.9
7	New Mexico	16.6
45	New York	5.1
13	North Carolina	13.6
36	North Dakota	9.0
35	Ohio	9.3
17	Oklahoma	12.8
27	Oregon	10.5
28	Pennsylvania	9.9
46	Rhode Island	5.0
13	South Carolina	13.6
40	South Dakota	7.9
10	Tennessee	15.4
26	Texas	10.8
32	Utah	9.6
32	Vermont	9.6
24	Virginia	11.0
34	Washington	9.4
11	West Virginia	14.7
39	Wisconsin	8.0
3	Wyoming	18.8

RANK ORDER

RANK	STATE	RATE
1	Alaska	20.0
2	Louisiana	19.4
3	Wyoming	18.8
4	Arizona	17.9
5	Nevada	17.3
6	Mississippi	17.2
7	New Mexico	16.6
8	Arkansas	16.3
9	Alabama	16.0
10	Tennessee	15.4
11	West Virginia	14.7
12	Montana	14.5
13	North Carolina	13.6
13	South Carolina	13.6
15	Georgia	13.4
16	Kentucky	12.9
17	Oklahoma	12.8
18	Idaho	12.4
19	Missouri	12.2
20	Indiana	11.7
21	Colorado	11.5
22	Maryland	11.4
23	Florida	11.1
24	Virginia	11.0
25	Michigan	10.9
26	Texas	10.8
27	Oregon	10.5
28	Pennsylvania	9.9
29	California	9.7
29	Illinois	9.7
29	Kansas	9.7
32	Utah	9.6
32	Vermont	9.6
34	Washington	9.4
35	Ohio	9.3
36	Delaware	9.0
36	North Dakota	9.0
38	Nebraska	8.1
39	Wisconsin	8.0
40	South Dakota	7.9
41	Iowa	6.7
42	Maine	6.5
43	Minnesota	6.0
44	New Hampshire	5.8
45	New York	5.1
46	Rhode Island	5.0
47	New Jersey	4.9
48	Connecticut	4.3
49	Massachusetts	3.1
50	Hawaii	2.8

	District of Columbia	31.3

Source: U.S. Department of Health and Human Services, National Center for Health Statistics
"National Vital Statistics Reports" (Vol. 53, No. 5, October 12, 2004)
*Final data by state of residence. Age-adjusted rates based on the year 2000 standard population.

Deaths by Homicide in 2002

National Total = 17,638 Homicides*

RANK	STATE	HOMICIDES	% of USA
15	Alabama	416	2.4%
40	Alaska	40	0.2%
13	Arizona	504	2.9%
25	Arkansas	194	1.1%
1	California	2,485	14.1%
28	Colorado	184	1.0%
34	Connecticut	98	0.6%
41	Delaware	38	0.2%
4	Florida	1,008	5.7%
7	Georgia	672	3.8%
41	Hawaii	38	0.2%
43	Idaho	32	0.2%
3	Illinois	1,016	5.8%
17	Indiana	385	2.2%
36	Iowa	56	0.3%
31	Kansas	129	0.7%
24	Kentucky	195	1.1%
10	Louisiana	607	3.4%
47	Maine	11	0.1%
12	Maryland	540	3.1%
27	Massachusetts	185	1.0%
6	Michigan	696	3.9%
32	Minnesota	127	0.7%
21	Mississippi	305	1.7%
18	Missouri	366	2.1%
44	Montana	23	0.1%
38	Nebraska	50	0.3%
29	Nevada	175	1.0%
48	New Hampshire	9	0.1%
19	New Jersey	333	1.9%
30	New Mexico	161	0.9%
5	New York	929	5.3%
8	North Carolina	644	3.7%
50	North Dakota	7	0.0%
11	Ohio	549	3.1%
23	Oklahoma	196	1.1%
33	Oregon	106	0.6%
9	Pennsylvania	640	3.6%
39	Rhode Island	43	0.2%
20	South Carolina	326	1.8%
46	South Dakota	22	0.1%
14	Tennessee	467	2.6%
2	Texas	1,421	8.1%
37	Utah	54	0.3%
49	Vermont	8	0.0%
16	Virginia	397	2.3%
22	Washington	213	1.2%
35	West Virginia	95	0.5%
26	Wisconsin	191	1.1%
44	Wyoming	23	0.1%

RANK	STATE	HOMICIDES	% of USA
1	California	2,485	14.1%
2	Texas	1,421	8.1%
3	Illinois	1,016	5.8%
4	Florida	1,008	5.7%
5	New York	929	5.3%
6	Michigan	696	3.9%
7	Georgia	672	3.8%
8	North Carolina	644	3.7%
9	Pennsylvania	640	3.6%
10	Louisiana	607	3.4%
11	Ohio	549	3.1%
12	Maryland	540	3.1%
13	Arizona	504	2.9%
14	Tennessee	467	2.6%
15	Alabama	416	2.4%
16	Virginia	397	2.3%
17	Indiana	385	2.2%
18	Missouri	366	2.1%
19	New Jersey	333	1.9%
20	South Carolina	326	1.8%
21	Mississippi	305	1.7%
22	Washington	213	1.2%
23	Oklahoma	196	1.1%
24	Kentucky	195	1.1%
25	Arkansas	194	1.1%
26	Wisconsin	191	1.1%
27	Massachusetts	185	1.0%
28	Colorado	184	1.0%
29	Nevada	175	1.0%
30	New Mexico	161	0.9%
31	Kansas	129	0.7%
32	Minnesota	127	0.7%
33	Oregon	106	0.6%
34	Connecticut	98	0.6%
35	West Virginia	95	0.5%
36	Iowa	56	0.3%
37	Utah	54	0.3%
38	Nebraska	50	0.3%
39	Rhode Island	43	0.2%
40	Alaska	40	0.2%
41	Delaware	38	0.2%
41	Hawaii	38	0.2%
43	Idaho	32	0.2%
44	Montana	23	0.1%
44	Wyoming	23	0.1%
46	South Dakota	22	0.1%
47	Maine	11	0.1%
48	New Hampshire	9	0.1%
49	Vermont	8	0.0%
50	North Dakota	7	0.0%
	District of Columbia	229	1.3%

*Source: U.S. Department of Health and Human Services, National Center for Health Statistics
"National Vital Statistics Reports" (Vol. 53, No. 5, October 12, 2004)*
By state of residence. Includes legal intervention. Homicide data shown here are collected by the Centers for Disease Control and Prevention based on death certificates and differ from murder data collected by the F.B.I. from other sources.

Death Rate by Homicide in 2002

National Rate = 6.1 Deaths per 100,000 Population*

ALPHA ORDER			RANK ORDER		
RANK	STATE	RATE	RANK	STATE	RATE
4	Alabama	9.3	1	Louisiana	13.5
19	Alaska	6.2	2	Mississippi	10.6
5	Arizona	9.2	3	Maryland	9.9
13	Arkansas	7.2	4	Alabama	9.3
14	California	7.1	5	Arizona	9.2
31	Colorado	4.1	6	New Mexico	8.7
41	Connecticut	2.8	7	Illinois	8.1
28	Delaware	4.7	7	Nevada	8.1
20	Florida	6.0	7	Tennessee	8.1
10	Georgia	7.9	10	Georgia	7.9
36	Hawaii	3.1	10	South Carolina	7.9
44	Idaho	2.4	12	North Carolina	7.7
7	Illinois	8.1	13	Arkansas	7.2
18	Indiana	6.3	14	California	7.1
46	Iowa	1.9	15	Michigan	6.9
28	Kansas	4.7	16	Missouri	6.5
25	Kentucky	4.8	16	Texas	6.5
1	Louisiana	13.5	18	Indiana	6.3
NA	Maine**	NA	19	Alaska	6.2
3	Maryland	9.9	20	Florida	6.0
38	Massachusetts	2.9	21	Oklahoma	5.6
15	Michigan	6.9	22	Virginia	5.4
42	Minnesota	2.5	23	West Virginia	5.3
2	Mississippi	10.6	24	Pennsylvania	5.2
16	Missouri	6.5	25	Kentucky	4.8
42	Montana	2.5	25	New York	4.8
38	Nebraska	2.9	25	Ohio	4.8
7	Nevada	8.1	28	Delaware	4.7
NA	New Hampshire**	NA	28	Kansas	4.7
33	New Jersey	3.9	30	Wyoming	4.6
6	New Mexico	8.7	31	Colorado	4.1
25	New York	4.8	32	Rhode Island	4.0
12	North Carolina	7.7	33	New Jersey	3.9
NA	North Dakota**	NA	34	Washington	3.5
25	Ohio	4.8	34	Wisconsin	3.5
21	Oklahoma	5.6	36	Hawaii	3.1
37	Oregon	3.0	37	Oregon	3.0
24	Pennsylvania	5.2	38	Massachusetts	2.9
32	Rhode Island	4.0	38	Nebraska	2.9
10	South Carolina	7.9	38	South Dakota	2.9
38	South Dakota	2.9	41	Connecticut	2.8
7	Tennessee	8.1	42	Minnesota	2.5
16	Texas	6.5	42	Montana	2.5
45	Utah	2.3	44	Idaho	2.4
NA	Vermont**	NA	45	Utah	2.3
22	Virginia	5.4	46	Iowa	1.9
34	Washington	3.5	NA	Maine**	NA
23	West Virginia	5.3	NA	New Hampshire**	NA
34	Wisconsin	3.5	NA	North Dakota**	NA
30	Wyoming	4.6	NA	Vermont**	NA
				District of Columbia	40.1

Source: U.S. Department of Health and Human Services, National Center for Health Statistics
    "National Vital Statistics Reports" (Vol. 53, No. 5, October 12, 2004)

*By state of residence. Includes legal intervention. Homicide data shown here are collected by the Centers for Disease Control and Prevention based on death certificates and differ from murder data collected by the F.B.I. from other sources. Not age-adjusted.

**Insufficient data to determine a reliable rate.

Age-Adjusted Death Rate by Homicide in 2002

National Rate = 6.1 Deaths per 100,000 Population*

<table>
<tr><td colspan="3">ALPHA ORDER</td><td colspan="3">RANK ORDER</td></tr>
<tr><th>RANK</th><th>STATE</th><th>RATE</th><th>RANK</th><th>STATE</th><th>RATE</th></tr>
<tr><td>4</td><td>Alabama</td><td>9.2</td><td>1</td><td>Louisiana</td><td>13.3</td></tr>
<tr><td>20</td><td>Alaska</td><td>6.0</td><td>2</td><td>Mississippi</td><td>10.7</td></tr>
<tr><td>4</td><td>Arizona</td><td>9.2</td><td>3</td><td>Maryland</td><td>10.0</td></tr>
<tr><td>13</td><td>Arkansas</td><td>7.2</td><td>4</td><td>Alabama</td><td>9.2</td></tr>
<tr><td>15</td><td>California</td><td>6.8</td><td>4</td><td>Arizona</td><td>9.2</td></tr>
<tr><td>31</td><td>Colorado</td><td>4.0</td><td>6</td><td>New Mexico</td><td>8.7</td></tr>
<tr><td>38</td><td>Connecticut</td><td>3.0</td><td>7</td><td>Nevada</td><td>8.1</td></tr>
<tr><td>27</td><td>Delaware</td><td>4.7</td><td>8</td><td>Tennessee</td><td>8.0</td></tr>
<tr><td>18</td><td>Florida</td><td>6.3</td><td>9</td><td>Illinois</td><td>7.9</td></tr>
<tr><td>12</td><td>Georgia</td><td>7.5</td><td>10</td><td>South Carolina</td><td>7.8</td></tr>
<tr><td>36</td><td>Hawaii</td><td>3.1</td><td>11</td><td>North Carolina</td><td>7.6</td></tr>
<tr><td>44</td><td>Idaho</td><td>2.4</td><td>12</td><td>Georgia</td><td>7.5</td></tr>
<tr><td>9</td><td>Illinois</td><td>7.9</td><td>13</td><td>Arkansas</td><td>7.2</td></tr>
<tr><td>19</td><td>Indiana</td><td>6.2</td><td>14</td><td>Michigan</td><td>7.0</td></tr>
<tr><td>46</td><td>Iowa</td><td>1.9</td><td>15</td><td>California</td><td>6.8</td></tr>
<tr><td>27</td><td>Kansas</td><td>4.7</td><td>16</td><td>Missouri</td><td>6.5</td></tr>
<tr><td>27</td><td>Kentucky</td><td>4.7</td><td>17</td><td>Texas</td><td>6.4</td></tr>
<tr><td>1</td><td>Louisiana</td><td>13.3</td><td>18</td><td>Florida</td><td>6.3</td></tr>
<tr><td>NA</td><td>Maine**</td><td>NA</td><td>19</td><td>Indiana</td><td>6.2</td></tr>
<tr><td>3</td><td>Maryland</td><td>10.0</td><td>20</td><td>Alaska</td><td>6.0</td></tr>
<tr><td>40</td><td>Massachusetts</td><td>2.9</td><td>21</td><td>Oklahoma</td><td>5.6</td></tr>
<tr><td>14</td><td>Michigan</td><td>7.0</td><td>22</td><td>West Virginia</td><td>5.5</td></tr>
<tr><td>42</td><td>Minnesota</td><td>2.5</td><td>23</td><td>Pennsylvania</td><td>5.4</td></tr>
<tr><td>2</td><td>Mississippi</td><td>10.7</td><td>23</td><td>Virginia</td><td>5.4</td></tr>
<tr><td>16</td><td>Missouri</td><td>6.5</td><td>25</td><td>Ohio</td><td>4.9</td></tr>
<tr><td>42</td><td>Montana</td><td>2.5</td><td>26</td><td>New York</td><td>4.8</td></tr>
<tr><td>40</td><td>Nebraska</td><td>2.9</td><td>27</td><td>Delaware</td><td>4.7</td></tr>
<tr><td>7</td><td>Nevada</td><td>8.1</td><td>27</td><td>Kansas</td><td>4.7</td></tr>
<tr><td>NA</td><td>New Hampshire**</td><td>NA</td><td>27</td><td>Kentucky</td><td>4.7</td></tr>
<tr><td>31</td><td>New Jersey</td><td>4.0</td><td>27</td><td>Wyoming</td><td>4.7</td></tr>
<tr><td>6</td><td>New Mexico</td><td>8.7</td><td>31</td><td>Colorado</td><td>4.0</td></tr>
<tr><td>26</td><td>New York</td><td>4.8</td><td>31</td><td>New Jersey</td><td>4.0</td></tr>
<tr><td>11</td><td>North Carolina</td><td>7.6</td><td>31</td><td>Rhode Island</td><td>4.0</td></tr>
<tr><td>NA</td><td>North Dakota**</td><td>NA</td><td>34</td><td>Washington</td><td>3.5</td></tr>
<tr><td>25</td><td>Ohio</td><td>4.9</td><td>34</td><td>Wisconsin</td><td>3.5</td></tr>
<tr><td>21</td><td>Oklahoma</td><td>5.6</td><td>36</td><td>Hawaii</td><td>3.1</td></tr>
<tr><td>36</td><td>Oregon</td><td>3.1</td><td>36</td><td>Oregon</td><td>3.1</td></tr>
<tr><td>23</td><td>Pennsylvania</td><td>5.4</td><td>38</td><td>Connecticut</td><td>3.0</td></tr>
<tr><td>31</td><td>Rhode Island</td><td>4.0</td><td>38</td><td>South Dakota</td><td>3.0</td></tr>
<tr><td>10</td><td>South Carolina</td><td>7.8</td><td>40</td><td>Massachusetts</td><td>2.9</td></tr>
<tr><td>38</td><td>South Dakota</td><td>3.0</td><td>40</td><td>Nebraska</td><td>2.9</td></tr>
<tr><td>8</td><td>Tennessee</td><td>8.0</td><td>42</td><td>Minnesota</td><td>2.5</td></tr>
<tr><td>17</td><td>Texas</td><td>6.4</td><td>42</td><td>Montana</td><td>2.5</td></tr>
<tr><td>45</td><td>Utah</td><td>2.3</td><td>44</td><td>Idaho</td><td>2.4</td></tr>
<tr><td>NA</td><td>Vermont**</td><td>NA</td><td>45</td><td>Utah</td><td>2.3</td></tr>
<tr><td>23</td><td>Virginia</td><td>5.4</td><td>46</td><td>Iowa</td><td>1.9</td></tr>
<tr><td>34</td><td>Washington</td><td>3.5</td><td>NA</td><td>Maine**</td><td>NA</td></tr>
<tr><td>22</td><td>West Virginia</td><td>5.5</td><td>NA</td><td>New Hampshire**</td><td>NA</td></tr>
<tr><td>34</td><td>Wisconsin</td><td>3.5</td><td>NA</td><td>North Dakota**</td><td>NA</td></tr>
<tr><td>27</td><td>Wyoming</td><td>4.7</td><td>NA</td><td>Vermont**</td><td>NA</td></tr>
<tr><td></td><td></td><td></td><td></td><td>District of Columbia</td><td>37.2</td></tr>
</table>

Source: U.S. Department of Health and Human Services, National Center for Health Statistics
 "National Vital Statistics Reports" (Vol. 52, No. 3, September 18, 2003)
*By state of residence. Includes legal intervention. Homicide data shown here are collected by the Centers for Disease Control and Prevention based on death certificates and differ from murder data collected by the F.B.I. from other sources. Age-adjusted rates based on the year 2000 standard population.
**Insufficient data to determine a reliable rate.

Deaths by Suicide in 2002

National Total = 31,655 Suicides*

ALPHA ORDER					RANK ORDER			
RANK	STATE	SUICIDES	% of USA		RANK	STATE	SUICIDES	% of USA
22	Alabama	514	1.6%		1	California	3,228	10.2%
42	Alaska	132	0.4%		2	Florida	2,338	7.4%
11	Arizona	886	2.8%		3	Texas	2,311	7.3%
30	Arkansas	377	1.2%		4	Pennsylvania	1,341	4.2%
1	California	3,228	10.2%		5	Ohio	1,287	4.1%
16	Colorado	727	2.3%		6	New York	1,228	3.9%
37	Connecticut	260	0.8%		7	Illinois	1,145	3.6%
50	Delaware	74	0.2%		8	Michigan	1,106	3.5%
2	Florida	2,338	7.4%		9	North Carolina	986	3.1%
10	Georgia	909	2.9%		10	Georgia	909	2.9%
44	Hawaii	120	0.4%		11	Arizona	886	2.8%
38	Idaho	202	0.6%		12	Washington	811	2.6%
7	Illinois	1,145	3.6%		13	Virginia	799	2.5%
15	Indiana	743	2.3%		14	Tennessee	778	2.5%
35	Iowa	314	1.0%		15	Indiana	743	2.3%
32	Kansas	345	1.1%		16	Colorado	727	2.3%
20	Kentucky	540	1.7%		17	Missouri	693	2.2%
24	Louisiana	499	1.6%		18	Wisconsin	627	2.0%
41	Maine	166	0.5%		19	New Jersey	553	1.7%
26	Maryland	477	1.5%		20	Kentucky	540	1.7%
28	Massachusetts	436	1.4%		21	Oregon	518	1.6%
8	Michigan	1,106	3.5%		22	Alabama	514	1.6%
25	Minnesota	497	1.6%		23	Oklahoma	501	1.6%
33	Mississippi	343	1.1%		24	Louisiana	499	1.6%
17	Missouri	693	2.2%		25	Minnesota	497	1.6%
40	Montana	184	0.6%		26	Maryland	477	1.5%
39	Nebraska	201	0.6%		27	South Carolina	440	1.4%
29	Nevada	423	1.3%		28	Massachusetts	436	1.4%
42	New Hampshire	132	0.4%		29	Nevada	423	1.3%
19	New Jersey	553	1.7%		30	Arkansas	377	1.2%
31	New Mexico	349	1.1%		31	New Mexico	349	1.1%
6	New York	1,228	3.9%		32	Kansas	345	1.1%
9	North Carolina	986	3.1%		33	Mississippi	343	1.1%
48	North Dakota	91	0.3%		34	Utah	340	1.1%
5	Ohio	1,287	4.1%		35	Iowa	314	1.0%
23	Oklahoma	501	1.6%		36	West Virginia	276	0.9%
21	Oregon	518	1.6%		37	Connecticut	260	0.8%
4	Pennsylvania	1,341	4.2%		38	Idaho	202	0.6%
49	Rhode Island	86	0.3%		39	Nebraska	201	0.6%
27	South Carolina	440	1.4%		40	Montana	184	0.6%
46	South Dakota	94	0.3%		41	Maine	166	0.5%
14	Tennessee	778	2.5%		42	Alaska	132	0.4%
3	Texas	2,311	7.3%		42	New Hampshire	132	0.4%
34	Utah	340	1.1%		44	Hawaii	120	0.4%
47	Vermont	92	0.3%		45	Wyoming	105	0.3%
13	Virginia	799	2.5%		46	South Dakota	94	0.3%
12	Washington	811	2.6%		47	Vermont	92	0.3%
36	West Virginia	276	0.9%		48	North Dakota	91	0.3%
18	Wisconsin	627	2.0%		49	Rhode Island	86	0.3%
45	Wyoming	105	0.3%		50	Delaware	74	0.2%
						District of Columbia	31	0.1%

*Source: U.S. Department of Health and Human Services, National Center for Health Statistics
"National Vital Statistics Reports" (Vol. 53, No. 5, October 12, 2004)*
Final data by state of residence.

Death Rate by Suicide in 2002

National Rate = 11.0 Deaths per 100,000 Population*

ALPHA ORDER

RANK	STATE	RATE
28	Alabama	11.5
2	Alaska	20.5
6	Arizona	16.2
16	Arkansas	13.9
42	California	9.2
7	Colorado	16.1
47	Connecticut	7.5
42	Delaware	9.2
15	Florida	14.0
37	Georgia	10.6
41	Hawaii	9.6
9	Idaho	15.1
44	Illinois	9.1
24	Indiana	12.1
35	Iowa	10.7
21	Kansas	12.7
19	Kentucky	13.2
31	Louisiana	11.1
20	Maine	12.8
45	Maryland	8.7
48	Massachusetts	6.8
32	Michigan	11.0
40	Minnesota	9.9
25	Mississippi	11.9
23	Missouri	12.2
3	Montana	20.2
27	Nebraska	11.6
4	Nevada	19.5
39	New Hampshire	10.4
49	New Jersey	6.4
5	New Mexico	18.8
49	New York	6.4
25	North Carolina	11.9
13	North Dakota	14.4
30	Ohio	11.3
14	Oklahoma	14.3
11	Oregon	14.7
34	Pennsylvania	10.9
46	Rhode Island	8.0
35	South Carolina	10.7
22	South Dakota	12.4
17	Tennessee	13.4
37	Texas	10.6
11	Utah	14.7
10	Vermont	14.9
32	Virginia	11.0
17	Washington	13.4
8	West Virginia	15.3
28	Wisconsin	11.5
1	Wyoming	21.1

RANK ORDER

RANK	STATE	RATE
1	Wyoming	21.1
2	Alaska	20.5
3	Montana	20.2
4	Nevada	19.5
5	New Mexico	18.8
6	Arizona	16.2
7	Colorado	16.1
8	West Virginia	15.3
9	Idaho	15.1
10	Vermont	14.9
11	Oregon	14.7
11	Utah	14.7
13	North Dakota	14.4
14	Oklahoma	14.3
15	Florida	14.0
16	Arkansas	13.9
17	Tennessee	13.4
17	Washington	13.4
19	Kentucky	13.2
20	Maine	12.8
21	Kansas	12.7
22	South Dakota	12.4
23	Missouri	12.2
24	Indiana	12.1
25	Mississippi	11.9
25	North Carolina	11.9
27	Nebraska	11.6
28	Alabama	11.5
28	Wisconsin	11.5
30	Ohio	11.3
31	Louisiana	11.1
32	Michigan	11.0
32	Virginia	11.0
34	Pennsylvania	10.9
35	Iowa	10.7
35	South Carolina	10.7
37	Georgia	10.6
37	Texas	10.6
39	New Hampshire	10.4
40	Minnesota	9.9
41	Hawaii	9.6
42	California	9.2
42	Delaware	9.2
44	Illinois	9.1
45	Maryland	8.7
46	Rhode Island	8.0
47	Connecticut	7.5
48	Massachusetts	6.8
49	New Jersey	6.4
49	New York	6.4
	District of Columbia	5.4

Source: U.S. Department of Health and Human Services, National Center for Health Statistics
"National Vital Statistics Reports" (Vol. 53, No. 5, October 12, 2004)
*Final data by state of residence. Not age-adjusted.

Age-Adjusted Death Rate by Suicide in 2002

National Rate = 10.9 Deaths per 100,000 Population*

ALPHA ORDER

RANK	STATE	RATE
28	Alabama	11.4
1	Alaska	21.0
6	Arizona	16.5
15	Arkansas	14.0
41	California	9.6
7	Colorado	16.2
47	Connecticut	7.4
44	Delaware	9.0
16	Florida	13.4
32	Georgia	11.0
42	Hawaii	9.5
9	Idaho	15.5
43	Illinois	9.1
23	Indiana	12.1
38	Iowa	10.5
20	Kansas	12.6
19	Kentucky	12.8
30	Louisiana	11.2
21	Maine	12.3
45	Maryland	8.7
48	Massachusetts	6.5
32	Michigan	11.0
40	Minnesota	9.7
23	Mississippi	12.1
23	Missouri	12.1
3	Montana	19.9
27	Nebraska	11.7
4	Nevada	19.8
39	New Hampshire	10.2
49	New Jersey	6.3
5	New Mexico	19.1
49	New York	6.3
26	North Carolina	11.8
13	North Dakota	14.2
30	Ohio	11.2
12	Oklahoma	14.3
11	Oregon	14.4
36	Pennsylvania	10.7
46	Rhode Island	7.9
37	South Carolina	10.6
22	South Dakota	12.2
18	Tennessee	13.2
32	Texas	11.0
8	Utah	16.1
14	Vermont	14.1
35	Virginia	10.9
17	Washington	13.3
10	West Virginia	14.8
29	Wisconsin	11.3
2	Wyoming	20.7

RANK ORDER

RANK	STATE	RATE
1	Alaska	21.0
2	Wyoming	20.7
3	Montana	19.9
4	Nevada	19.8
5	New Mexico	19.1
6	Arizona	16.5
7	Colorado	16.2
8	Utah	16.1
9	Idaho	15.5
10	West Virginia	14.8
11	Oregon	14.4
12	Oklahoma	14.3
13	North Dakota	14.2
14	Vermont	14.1
15	Arkansas	14.0
16	Florida	13.4
17	Washington	13.3
18	Tennessee	13.2
19	Kentucky	12.8
20	Kansas	12.6
21	Maine	12.3
22	South Dakota	12.2
23	Indiana	12.1
23	Mississippi	12.1
23	Missouri	12.1
26	North Carolina	11.8
27	Nebraska	11.7
28	Alabama	11.4
29	Wisconsin	11.3
30	Louisiana	11.2
30	Ohio	11.2
32	Georgia	11.0
32	Michigan	11.0
32	Texas	11.0
35	Virginia	10.9
36	Pennsylvania	10.7
37	South Carolina	10.6
38	Iowa	10.5
39	New Hampshire	10.2
40	Minnesota	9.7
41	California	9.6
42	Hawaii	9.5
43	Illinois	9.1
44	Delaware	9.0
45	Maryland	8.7
46	Rhode Island	7.9
47	Connecticut	7.4
48	Massachusetts	6.5
49	New Jersey	6.3
49	New York	6.3
	District of Columbia	5.1

Source: U.S. Department of Health and Human Services, National Center for Health Statistics
   "National Vital Statistics Reports" (Vol. 53, No. 5, October 12, 2004)
*Final data by state of residence. Age-adjusted rates based on the year 2000 standard population.

Alcohol-Induced Deaths in 2002

National Total = 19,928 Deaths*

ALPHA ORDER

ALPHA ORDER

RANK	STATE	DEATHS	% of USA
29	Alabama	208	1.0%
37	Alaska	124	0.6%
11	Arizona	510	2.6%
35	Arkansas	133	0.7%
1	California	3,511	17.6%
10	Colorado	511	2.6%
31	Connecticut	191	1.0%
44	Delaware	75	0.4%
2	Florida	1,402	7.0%
12	Georgia	506	2.5%
50	Hawaii	43	0.2%
38	Idaho	120	0.6%
8	Illinois	573	2.9%
21	Indiana	321	1.6%
33	Iowa	160	0.8%
32	Kansas	167	0.8%
27	Kentucky	231	1.2%
28	Louisiana	223	1.1%
42	Maine	101	0.5%
24	Maryland	289	1.5%
17	Massachusetts	380	1.9%
5	Michigan	668	3.4%
20	Minnesota	322	1.6%
34	Mississippi	152	0.8%
21	Missouri	321	1.6%
41	Montana	107	0.5%
40	Nebraska	108	0.5%
30	Nevada	207	1.0%
43	New Hampshire	77	0.4%
14	New Jersey	482	2.4%
23	New Mexico	310	1.6%
4	New York	1,078	5.4%
6	North Carolina	642	3.2%
47	North Dakota	69	0.3%
7	Ohio	584	2.9%
26	Oklahoma	283	1.4%
15	Oregon	432	2.2%
13	Pennsylvania	497	2.5%
46	Rhode Island	73	0.4%
25	South Carolina	286	1.4%
49	South Dakota	55	0.3%
16	Tennessee	387	1.9%
3	Texas	1,237	6.2%
39	Utah	118	0.6%
48	Vermont	67	0.3%
19	Virginia	326	1.6%
9	Washington	571	2.9%
36	West Virginia	125	0.6%
18	Wisconsin	375	1.9%
45	Wyoming	74	0.4%

RANK ORDER

RANK	STATE	DEATHS	% of USA
1	California	3,511	17.6%
2	Florida	1,402	7.0%
3	Texas	1,237	6.2%
4	New York	1,078	5.4%
5	Michigan	668	3.4%
6	North Carolina	642	3.2%
7	Ohio	584	2.9%
8	Illinois	573	2.9%
9	Washington	571	2.9%
10	Colorado	511	2.6%
11	Arizona	510	2.6%
12	Georgia	506	2.5%
13	Pennsylvania	497	2.5%
14	New Jersey	482	2.4%
15	Oregon	432	2.2%
16	Tennessee	387	1.9%
17	Massachusetts	380	1.9%
18	Wisconsin	375	1.9%
19	Virginia	326	1.6%
20	Minnesota	322	1.6%
21	Indiana	321	1.6%
21	Missouri	321	1.6%
23	New Mexico	310	1.6%
24	Maryland	289	1.5%
25	South Carolina	286	1.4%
26	Oklahoma	283	1.4%
27	Kentucky	231	1.2%
28	Louisiana	223	1.1%
29	Alabama	208	1.0%
30	Nevada	207	1.0%
31	Connecticut	191	1.0%
32	Kansas	167	0.8%
33	Iowa	160	0.8%
34	Mississippi	152	0.8%
35	Arkansas	133	0.7%
36	West Virginia	125	0.6%
37	Alaska	124	0.6%
38	Idaho	120	0.6%
39	Utah	118	0.6%
40	Nebraska	108	0.5%
41	Montana	107	0.5%
42	Maine	101	0.5%
43	New Hampshire	77	0.4%
44	Delaware	75	0.4%
45	Wyoming	74	0.4%
46	Rhode Island	73	0.4%
47	North Dakota	69	0.3%
48	Vermont	67	0.3%
49	South Dakota	55	0.3%
50	Hawaii	43	0.2%
	District of Columbia	116	0.6%

Source: U.S. Department of Health and Human Services, National Center for Health Statistics (http://wonder.cdc.gov)

*By state of residence. Includes excessive blood level of alcohol, accidental poisoning by alcohol and the following alcohol-related causes: psychoses, dependence syndrome, polyneuropathy, cardiomyopathy, gastritis, chronic liver disease and cirrhosis. Excludes accidents, homicides and other causes indirectly related to alcohol use.

Death Rate by Alcohol-Induced Deaths in 2002

National Rate = 6.9 Deaths per 100,000 Population*

ALPHA ORDER

RANK	STATE	RATE
46	Alabama	4.6
1	Alaska	19.3
11	Arizona	9.4
45	Arkansas	4.9
9	California	10.0
6	Colorado	11.3
37	Connecticut	5.5
13	Delaware	9.3
15	Florida	8.4
30	Georgia	5.9
50	Hawaii	3.5
14	Idaho	8.9
46	Illinois	4.6
41	Indiana	5.2
38	Iowa	5.4
27	Kansas	6.2
34	Kentucky	5.6
44	Louisiana	5.0
17	Maine	7.8
39	Maryland	5.3
30	Massachusetts	5.9
24	Michigan	6.7
26	Minnesota	6.4
39	Mississippi	5.3
32	Missouri	5.7
5	Montana	11.8
27	Nebraska	6.2
10	Nevada	9.5
29	New Hampshire	6.0
34	New Jersey	5.6
2	New Mexico	16.7
34	New York	5.6
18	North Carolina	7.7
7	North Dakota	10.9
42	Ohio	5.1
16	Oklahoma	8.1
4	Oregon	12.3
49	Pennsylvania	4.0
23	Rhode Island	6.8
20	South Carolina	7.0
19	South Dakota	7.2
24	Tennessee	6.7
32	Texas	5.7
42	Utah	5.1
7	Vermont	10.9
48	Virginia	4.5
11	Washington	9.4
21	West Virginia	6.9
21	Wisconsin	6.9
3	Wyoming	14.8

RANK ORDER

RANK	STATE	RATE
1	Alaska	19.3
2	New Mexico	16.7
3	Wyoming	14.8
4	Oregon	12.3
5	Montana	11.8
6	Colorado	11.3
7	North Dakota	10.9
7	Vermont	10.9
9	California	10.0
10	Nevada	9.5
11	Arizona	9.4
11	Washington	9.4
13	Delaware	9.3
14	Idaho	8.9
15	Florida	8.4
16	Oklahoma	8.1
17	Maine	7.8
18	North Carolina	7.7
19	South Dakota	7.2
20	South Carolina	7.0
21	West Virginia	6.9
21	Wisconsin	6.9
23	Rhode Island	6.8
24	Michigan	6.7
24	Tennessee	6.7
26	Minnesota	6.4
27	Kansas	6.2
27	Nebraska	6.2
29	New Hampshire	6.0
30	Georgia	5.9
30	Massachusetts	5.9
32	Missouri	5.7
32	Texas	5.7
34	Kentucky	5.6
34	New Jersey	5.6
34	New York	5.6
37	Connecticut	5.5
38	Iowa	5.4
39	Maryland	5.3
39	Mississippi	5.3
41	Indiana	5.2
42	Ohio	5.1
42	Utah	5.1
44	Louisiana	5.0
45	Arkansas	4.9
46	Alabama	4.6
46	Illinois	4.6
48	Virginia	4.5
49	Pennsylvania	4.0
50	Hawaii	3.5

| | District of Columbia | 20.4 |

Source: U.S. Department of Health and Human Services, National Center for Health Statistics (http://wonder.cdc.gov)

By state of residence. Includes excessive blood level of alcohol, accidental poisoning by alcohol and the following alcohol-related causes: psychoses, dependence syndrome, polyneuropathy, cardiomyopathy, gastritis, chronic liver disease and cirrhosis. Excludes accidents, homicides and other causes indirectly related to alcohol use. Not age-adjusted.

185

Age-Adjusted Death Rate by Alcohol-Induced Deaths in 2002

National Rate = 6.8 Deaths per 100,000 Population*

<table>
<tr><td colspan="3">ALPHA ORDER</td><td colspan="3">RANK ORDER</td></tr>
<tr><td>RANK</td><td>STATE</td><td>RATE</td><td>RANK</td><td>STATE</td><td>RATE</td></tr>
<tr><td>47</td><td>Alabama</td><td>4.5</td><td>1</td><td>Alaska</td><td>19.9</td></tr>
<tr><td>1</td><td>Alaska</td><td>19.9</td><td>2</td><td>New Mexico</td><td>16.8</td></tr>
<tr><td>10</td><td>Arizona</td><td>9.8</td><td>3</td><td>Wyoming</td><td>14.0</td></tr>
<tr><td>45</td><td>Arkansas</td><td>4.7</td><td>4</td><td>Oregon</td><td>11.8</td></tr>
<tr><td>7</td><td>California</td><td>10.6</td><td>5</td><td>Colorado</td><td>11.7</td></tr>
<tr><td>5</td><td>Colorado</td><td>11.7</td><td>6</td><td>Montana</td><td>10.9</td></tr>
<tr><td>41</td><td>Connecticut</td><td>5.1</td><td>7</td><td>California</td><td>10.6</td></tr>
<tr><td>14</td><td>Delaware</td><td>8.9</td><td>8</td><td>North Dakota</td><td>10.5</td></tr>
<tr><td>16</td><td>Florida</td><td>7.8</td><td>9</td><td>Vermont</td><td>9.9</td></tr>
<tr><td>29</td><td>Georgia</td><td>6.2</td><td>10</td><td>Arizona</td><td>9.8</td></tr>
<tr><td>50</td><td>Hawaii</td><td>3.3</td><td>11</td><td>Nevada</td><td>9.5</td></tr>
<tr><td>13</td><td>Idaho</td><td>9.3</td><td>12</td><td>Washington</td><td>9.4</td></tr>
<tr><td>46</td><td>Illinois</td><td>4.6</td><td>13</td><td>Idaho</td><td>9.3</td></tr>
<tr><td>39</td><td>Indiana</td><td>5.2</td><td>14</td><td>Delaware</td><td>8.9</td></tr>
<tr><td>39</td><td>Iowa</td><td>5.2</td><td>15</td><td>Oklahoma</td><td>7.9</td></tr>
<tr><td>29</td><td>Kansas</td><td>6.2</td><td>16</td><td>Florida</td><td>7.8</td></tr>
<tr><td>35</td><td>Kentucky</td><td>5.4</td><td>17</td><td>North Carolina</td><td>7.6</td></tr>
<tr><td>41</td><td>Louisiana</td><td>5.1</td><td>18</td><td>South Dakota</td><td>7.4</td></tr>
<tr><td>19</td><td>Maine</td><td>7.0</td><td>19</td><td>Maine</td><td>7.0</td></tr>
<tr><td>41</td><td>Maryland</td><td>5.1</td><td>20</td><td>South Carolina</td><td>6.8</td></tr>
<tr><td>32</td><td>Massachusetts</td><td>5.6</td><td>21</td><td>Wisconsin</td><td>6.7</td></tr>
<tr><td>22</td><td>Michigan</td><td>6.5</td><td>22</td><td>Michigan</td><td>6.5</td></tr>
<tr><td>25</td><td>Minnesota</td><td>6.4</td><td>22</td><td>Rhode Island</td><td>6.5</td></tr>
<tr><td>35</td><td>Mississippi</td><td>5.4</td><td>22</td><td>Utah</td><td>6.5</td></tr>
<tr><td>34</td><td>Missouri</td><td>5.5</td><td>25</td><td>Minnesota</td><td>6.4</td></tr>
<tr><td>6</td><td>Montana</td><td>10.9</td><td>25</td><td>Tennessee</td><td>6.4</td></tr>
<tr><td>27</td><td>Nebraska</td><td>6.3</td><td>27</td><td>Nebraska</td><td>6.3</td></tr>
<tr><td>11</td><td>Nevada</td><td>9.5</td><td>27</td><td>West Virginia</td><td>6.3</td></tr>
<tr><td>32</td><td>New Hampshire</td><td>5.6</td><td>29</td><td>Georgia</td><td>6.2</td></tr>
<tr><td>38</td><td>New Jersey</td><td>5.3</td><td>29</td><td>Kansas</td><td>6.2</td></tr>
<tr><td>2</td><td>New Mexico</td><td>16.8</td><td>29</td><td>Texas</td><td>6.2</td></tr>
<tr><td>35</td><td>New York</td><td>5.4</td><td>32</td><td>Massachusetts</td><td>5.6</td></tr>
<tr><td>17</td><td>North Carolina</td><td>7.6</td><td>32</td><td>New Hampshire</td><td>5.6</td></tr>
<tr><td>8</td><td>North Dakota</td><td>10.5</td><td>34</td><td>Missouri</td><td>5.5</td></tr>
<tr><td>44</td><td>Ohio</td><td>4.9</td><td>35</td><td>Kentucky</td><td>5.4</td></tr>
<tr><td>15</td><td>Oklahoma</td><td>7.9</td><td>35</td><td>Mississippi</td><td>5.4</td></tr>
<tr><td>4</td><td>Oregon</td><td>11.8</td><td>35</td><td>New York</td><td>5.4</td></tr>
<tr><td>49</td><td>Pennsylvania</td><td>3.7</td><td>38</td><td>New Jersey</td><td>5.3</td></tr>
<tr><td>22</td><td>Rhode Island</td><td>6.5</td><td>39</td><td>Indiana</td><td>5.2</td></tr>
<tr><td>20</td><td>South Carolina</td><td>6.8</td><td>39</td><td>Iowa</td><td>5.2</td></tr>
<tr><td>18</td><td>South Dakota</td><td>7.4</td><td>41</td><td>Connecticut</td><td>5.1</td></tr>
<tr><td>25</td><td>Tennessee</td><td>6.4</td><td>41</td><td>Louisiana</td><td>5.1</td></tr>
<tr><td>29</td><td>Texas</td><td>6.2</td><td>41</td><td>Maryland</td><td>5.1</td></tr>
<tr><td>22</td><td>Utah</td><td>6.5</td><td>44</td><td>Ohio</td><td>4.9</td></tr>
<tr><td>9</td><td>Vermont</td><td>9.9</td><td>45</td><td>Arkansas</td><td>4.7</td></tr>
<tr><td>48</td><td>Virginia</td><td>4.4</td><td>46</td><td>Illinois</td><td>4.6</td></tr>
<tr><td>12</td><td>Washington</td><td>9.4</td><td>47</td><td>Alabama</td><td>4.5</td></tr>
<tr><td>27</td><td>West Virginia</td><td>6.3</td><td>48</td><td>Virginia</td><td>4.4</td></tr>
<tr><td>21</td><td>Wisconsin</td><td>6.7</td><td>49</td><td>Pennsylvania</td><td>3.7</td></tr>
<tr><td>3</td><td>Wyoming</td><td>14.0</td><td>50</td><td>Hawaii</td><td>3.3</td></tr>
<tr><td></td><td></td><td></td><td></td><td>District of Columbia</td><td>20.2</td></tr>
</table>

Source: U.S. Department of Health and Human Services, National Center for Health Statistics (http://wonder.cdc.gov)

By state of residence. Includes excessive blood level of alcohol, accidental poisoning by alcohol and the following alcohol-related causes: psychoses, dependence syndrome, polyneuropathy, cardiomyopathy, gastritis, chronic liver disease and cirrhosis. Excludes accidents, homicides and other causes indirectly related to alcohol use. Age-adjusted rates based on the year 2000 standard population.

Occupational Fatalities in 2004

National Total = 5,703 Deaths*

ALPHA ORDER

RANK ORDER

RANK	STATE	DEATHS	% of USA	RANK	STATE	DEATHS	% of USA
15	Alabama	133	2.3%	1	Texas	440	7.7%
40	Alaska	40	0.7%	2	Florida	422	7.4%
25	Arizona	84	1.5%	3	California	416	7.3%
30	Arkansas	70	1.2%	4	New York	254	4.5%
3	California	416	7.3%	5	Georgia	231	4.1%
19	Colorado	117	2.1%	6	Pennsylvania	230	4.0%
36	Connecticut	54	0.9%	7	Illinois	208	3.6%
48	Delaware	10	0.2%	8	Ohio	202	3.5%
2	Florida	422	7.4%	9	North Carolina	183	3.2%
5	Georgia	231	4.1%	10	Virginia	171	3.0%
43	Hawaii	25	0.4%	11	Missouri	165	2.9%
42	Idaho	38	0.7%	12	Indiana	153	2.7%
7	Illinois	208	3.6%	13	Tennessee	144	2.5%
12	Indiana	153	2.7%	14	Kentucky	143	2.5%
26	Iowa	82	1.4%	15	Alabama	133	2.3%
28	Kansas	80	1.4%	16	New Jersey	129	2.3%
14	Kentucky	143	2.5%	17	Michigan	126	2.2%
18	Louisiana	121	2.1%	18	Louisiana	121	2.1%
46	Maine	16	0.3%	19	Colorado	117	2.1%
27	Maryland	81	1.4%	20	South Carolina	110	1.9%
30	Massachusetts	70	1.2%	21	Washington	98	1.7%
17	Michigan	126	2.2%	22	Wisconsin	94	1.6%
28	Minnesota	80	1.4%	23	Oklahoma	91	1.6%
24	Mississippi	88	1.5%	24	Mississippi	88	1.5%
11	Missouri	165	2.9%	25	Arizona	84	1.5%
41	Montana	39	0.7%	26	Iowa	82	1.4%
38	Nebraska	46	0.8%	27	Maryland	81	1.4%
32	Nevada	61	1.1%	28	Kansas	80	1.4%
47	New Hampshire	15	0.3%	28	Minnesota	80	1.4%
16	New Jersey	129	2.3%	30	Arkansas	70	1.2%
35	New Mexico	57	1.0%	30	Massachusetts	70	1.2%
4	New York	254	4.5%	32	Nevada	61	1.1%
9	North Carolina	183	3.2%	33	Oregon	60	1.1%
44	North Dakota	24	0.4%	34	West Virginia	58	1.0%
8	Ohio	202	3.5%	35	New Mexico	57	1.0%
23	Oklahoma	91	1.6%	36	Connecticut	54	0.9%
33	Oregon	60	1.1%	37	Utah	50	0.9%
6	Pennsylvania	230	4.0%	38	Nebraska	46	0.8%
49	Rhode Island	7	0.1%	39	Wyoming	43	0.8%
20	South Carolina	110	1.9%	40	Alaska	40	0.7%
44	South Dakota	24	0.4%	41	Montana	39	0.7%
13	Tennessee	144	2.5%	42	Idaho	38	0.7%
1	Texas	440	7.7%	43	Hawaii	25	0.4%
37	Utah	50	0.9%	44	North Dakota	24	0.4%
49	Vermont	7	0.1%	44	South Dakota	24	0.4%
10	Virginia	171	3.0%	46	Maine	16	0.3%
21	Washington	98	1.7%	47	New Hampshire	15	0.3%
34	West Virginia	58	1.0%	48	Delaware	10	0.2%
22	Wisconsin	94	1.6%	49	Rhode Island	7	0.1%
39	Wyoming	43	0.8%	49	Vermont	7	0.1%
					District of Columbia	11	0.2%

Source: U.S. Department of Labor, Bureau of Labor Statistics
"National Census of Fatal Occupational Injuries, 2004" (press release, August 25, 2005)
*Includes two fatalities that occurred within the territorial boundaries of the United States but for which a state of incident could not be determined.

Occupational Fatality Rate in 2004

National Rate = 4.1 Deaths per 100,000 Workers*

ALPHA ORDER				RANK ORDER		
RANK	STATE	RATE		RANK	STATE	RATE
8	Alabama	6.6		1	Wyoming	15.9
2	Alaska	13.0		2	Alaska	13.0
35	Arizona	3.2		3	Montana	8.4
15	Arkansas	5.7		4	West Virginia	7.8
44	California	2.5		5	Kentucky	7.6
24	Colorado	4.9		6	Mississippi	7.1
35	Connecticut	3.2		7	North Dakota	7.0
44	Delaware	2.5		8	Alabama	6.6
20	Florida	5.3		8	New Mexico	6.6
18	Georgia	5.5		10	Louisiana	6.2
29	Hawaii	4.2		11	Kansas	5.8
15	Idaho	5.7		11	Missouri	5.8
33	Illinois	3.5		11	South Carolina	5.8
23	Indiana	5.1		11	South Dakota	5.8
20	Iowa	5.3		15	Arkansas	5.7
11	Kansas	5.8		15	Idaho	5.7
5	Kentucky	7.6		17	Oklahoma	5.6
10	Louisiana	6.2		18	Georgia	5.5
46	Maine	2.4		19	Nevada	5.4
40	Maryland	2.9		20	Florida	5.3
47	Massachusetts	2.2		20	Iowa	5.3
43	Michigan	2.7		22	Tennessee	5.2
42	Minnesota	2.8		23	Indiana	5.1
6	Mississippi	7.1		24	Colorado	4.9
11	Missouri	5.8		24	Nebraska	4.9
3	Montana	8.4		26	Virginia	4.7
24	Nebraska	4.9		27	North Carolina	4.6
19	Nevada	5.4		28	Utah	4.4
47	New Hampshire	2.2		29	Hawaii	4.2
39	New Jersey	3.1		29	Texas	4.2
8	New Mexico	6.6		31	Pennsylvania	3.9
40	New York	2.9		32	Ohio	3.7
27	North Carolina	4.6		33	Illinois	3.5
7	North Dakota	7.0		33	Oregon	3.5
32	Ohio	3.7		35	Arizona	3.2
17	Oklahoma	5.6		35	Connecticut	3.2
33	Oregon	3.5		35	Washington	3.2
31	Pennsylvania	3.9		35	Wisconsin	3.2
50	Rhode Island	1.3		39	New Jersey	3.1
11	South Carolina	5.8		40	Maryland	2.9
11	South Dakota	5.8		40	New York	2.9
22	Tennessee	5.2		42	Minnesota	2.8
29	Texas	4.2		43	Michigan	2.7
28	Utah	4.4		44	California	2.5
49	Vermont	2.1		44	Delaware	2.5
26	Virginia	4.7		46	Maine	2.4
35	Washington	3.2		47	Massachusetts	2.2
4	West Virginia	7.8		47	New Hampshire	2.2
35	Wisconsin	3.2		49	Vermont	2.1
1	Wyoming	15.9		50	Rhode Island	1.3
					District of Columbia	4.0

Source: Morgan Quitno Press using data from U.S. Department of Labor, Bureau of Labor Statistics
 "National Census of Fatal Occupational Injuries, 2004" (press release, August 25, 2005)
Based on employed civilian labor force.

III. FACILITIES

Community Hospitals in 2004

National Total = 4,919 Hospitals*

ALPHA ORDER

RANK	STATE	HOSPITALS	% of USA		RANK	STATE	HOSPITALS	% of USA
20	Alabama	108	2.2%		1	Texas	418	8.5%
47	Alaska	19	0.4%		2	California	361	7.3%
30	Arizona	62	1.3%		3	New York	206	4.2%
24	Arkansas	87	1.8%		4	Florida	203	4.1%
2	California	361	7.3%		5	Pennsylvania	197	4.0%
29	Colorado	70	1.4%		6	Illinois	191	3.9%
42	Connecticut	35	0.7%		7	Ohio	166	3.4%
50	Delaware	6	0.1%		8	Georgia	146	3.0%
4	Florida	203	4.1%		9	Michigan	144	2.9%
8	Georgia	146	3.0%		10	Kansas	134	2.7%
45	Hawaii	24	0.5%		11	Minnesota	132	2.7%
39	Idaho	39	0.8%		12	Louisiana	131	2.7%
6	Illinois	191	3.9%		13	Tennessee	127	2.6%
18	Indiana	113	2.3%		14	Wisconsin	121	2.5%
16	Iowa	115	2.3%		15	Missouri	119	2.4%
10	Kansas	134	2.7%		16	Iowa	115	2.3%
21	Kentucky	105	2.1%		16	North Carolina	115	2.3%
12	Louisiana	131	2.7%		18	Indiana	113	2.3%
40	Maine	37	0.8%		19	Oklahoma	109	2.2%
36	Maryland	50	1.0%		20	Alabama	108	2.2%
28	Massachusetts	78	1.6%		21	Kentucky	105	2.1%
9	Michigan	144	2.9%		22	Mississippi	93	1.9%
11	Minnesota	132	2.7%		23	Virginia	88	1.8%
22	Mississippi	93	1.9%		24	Arkansas	87	1.8%
15	Missouri	119	2.4%		25	Nebraska	85	1.7%
34	Montana	54	1.1%		25	Washington	85	1.7%
25	Nebraska	85	1.7%		27	New Jersey	80	1.6%
43	Nevada	30	0.6%		28	Massachusetts	78	1.6%
44	New Hampshire	28	0.6%		29	Colorado	70	1.4%
27	New Jersey	80	1.6%		30	Arizona	62	1.3%
40	New Mexico	37	0.8%		30	South Carolina	62	1.3%
3	New York	206	4.2%		32	Oregon	58	1.2%
16	North Carolina	115	2.3%		33	West Virginia	57	1.2%
38	North Dakota	40	0.8%		34	Montana	54	1.1%
7	Ohio	166	3.4%		35	South Dakota	51	1.0%
19	Oklahoma	109	2.2%		36	Maryland	50	1.0%
32	Oregon	58	1.2%		37	Utah	43	0.9%
5	Pennsylvania	197	4.0%		38	North Dakota	40	0.8%
49	Rhode Island	11	0.2%		39	Idaho	39	0.8%
30	South Carolina	62	1.3%		40	Maine	37	0.8%
35	South Dakota	51	1.0%		40	New Mexico	37	0.8%
13	Tennessee	127	2.6%		42	Connecticut	35	0.7%
1	Texas	418	8.5%		43	Nevada	30	0.6%
37	Utah	43	0.9%		44	New Hampshire	28	0.6%
48	Vermont	14	0.3%		45	Hawaii	24	0.5%
23	Virginia	88	1.8%		45	Wyoming	24	0.5%
25	Washington	85	1.7%		47	Alaska	19	0.4%
33	West Virginia	57	1.2%		48	Vermont	14	0.3%
14	Wisconsin	121	2.5%		49	Rhode Island	11	0.2%
45	Wyoming	24	0.5%		50	Delaware	6	0.1%
						District of Columbia	11	0.2%

Source: American Hospital Association (Chicago, IL)
"Hospital Statistics" (2006 edition)

*Community hospitals are all nonfederal, short-term, general and special hospitals whose facilities and services are available to the public.

Rate of Community Hospitals in 2004

National Rate = 1.7 Community Hospitals per 100,000 Population*

ALPHA ORDER

RANK	STATE	RATE
18	Alabama	2.4
12	Alaska	2.9
43	Arizona	1.1
8	Arkansas	3.2
45	California	1.0
32	Colorado	1.5
45	Connecticut	1.0
50	Delaware	0.7
40	Florida	1.2
29	Georgia	1.6
24	Hawaii	1.9
14	Idaho	2.8
32	Illinois	1.5
27	Indiana	1.8
7	Iowa	3.9
4	Kansas	4.9
17	Kentucky	2.5
12	Louisiana	2.9
14	Maine	2.8
48	Maryland	0.9
40	Massachusetts	1.2
35	Michigan	1.4
16	Minnesota	2.6
8	Mississippi	3.2
23	Missouri	2.1
3	Montana	5.8
4	Nebraska	4.9
38	Nevada	1.3
20	New Hampshire	2.2
48	New Jersey	0.9
24	New Mexico	1.9
43	New York	1.1
38	North Carolina	1.3
2	North Dakota	6.3
35	Ohio	1.4
10	Oklahoma	3.1
29	Oregon	1.6
29	Pennsylvania	1.6
45	Rhode Island	1.0
32	South Carolina	1.5
1	South Dakota	6.6
20	Tennessee	2.2
24	Texas	1.9
27	Utah	1.8
19	Vermont	2.3
40	Virginia	1.2
35	Washington	1.4
10	West Virginia	3.1
20	Wisconsin	2.2
6	Wyoming	4.7

RANK ORDER

RANK	STATE	RATE
1	South Dakota	6.6
2	North Dakota	6.3
3	Montana	5.8
4	Kansas	4.9
4	Nebraska	4.9
6	Wyoming	4.7
7	Iowa	3.9
8	Arkansas	3.2
8	Mississippi	3.2
10	Oklahoma	3.1
10	West Virginia	3.1
12	Alaska	2.9
12	Louisiana	2.9
14	Idaho	2.8
14	Maine	2.8
16	Minnesota	2.6
17	Kentucky	2.5
18	Alabama	2.4
19	Vermont	2.3
20	New Hampshire	2.2
20	Tennessee	2.2
20	Wisconsin	2.2
23	Missouri	2.1
24	Hawaii	1.9
24	New Mexico	1.9
24	Texas	1.9
27	Indiana	1.8
27	Utah	1.8
29	Georgia	1.6
29	Oregon	1.6
29	Pennsylvania	1.6
32	Colorado	1.5
32	Illinois	1.5
32	South Carolina	1.5
35	Michigan	1.4
35	Ohio	1.4
35	Washington	1.4
38	Nevada	1.3
38	North Carolina	1.3
40	Florida	1.2
40	Massachusetts	1.2
40	Virginia	1.2
43	Arizona	1.1
43	New York	1.1
45	California	1.0
45	Connecticut	1.0
45	Rhode Island	1.0
48	Maryland	0.9
48	New Jersey	0.9
50	Delaware	0.7
	District of Columbia	2.0

Source: Morgan Quitno Press using data from American Hospital Association (Chicago, IL)
    "Hospital Statistics" (2006 edition)
*Community hospitals are all nonfederal, short-term, general and special hospitals whose facilities and services are available to the public.

Community Hospitals per 1,000 Square Miles in 2004

National Rate = 1.3 Community Hospitals*

ALPHA ORDER RANK ORDER

RANK	STATE	RATE		RANK	STATE	RATE
21	Alabama	2.1		1	New Jersey	9.2
50	Alaska**	0.0		2	Massachusetts	7.4
43	Arizona	0.5		3	Rhode Island	7.1
29	Arkansas	1.6		4	Connecticut	6.3
19	California	2.2		5	Pennsylvania	4.3
39	Colorado	0.7		6	Maryland	4.0
4	Connecticut	6.3		7	New York	3.8
17	Delaware	2.4		8	Ohio	3.7
10	Florida	3.1		9	Illinois	3.3
15	Georgia	2.5		10	Florida	3.1
19	Hawaii	2.2		10	Indiana	3.1
43	Idaho	0.5		12	New Hampshire	3.0
9	Illinois	3.3		12	Tennessee	3.0
10	Indiana	3.1		14	Kentucky	2.6
24	Iowa	2.0		15	Georgia	2.5
29	Kansas	1.6		15	Louisiana	2.5
14	Kentucky	2.6		17	Delaware	2.4
15	Louisiana	2.5		17	West Virginia	2.4
38	Maine	1.0		19	California	2.2
6	Maryland	4.0		19	Hawaii	2.2
2	Massachusetts	7.4		21	Alabama	2.1
33	Michigan	1.5		21	North Carolina	2.1
33	Minnesota	1.5		21	Virginia	2.1
25	Mississippi	1.9		24	Iowa	2.0
28	Missouri	1.7		25	Mississippi	1.9
46	Montana	0.4		25	South Carolina	1.9
37	Nebraska	1.1		27	Wisconsin	1.8
47	Nevada	0.3		28	Missouri	1.7
12	New Hampshire	3.0		29	Arkansas	1.6
1	New Jersey	9.2		29	Kansas	1.6
47	New Mexico	0.3		29	Oklahoma	1.6
7	New York	3.8		29	Texas	1.6
21	North Carolina	2.1		33	Michigan	1.5
41	North Dakota	0.6		33	Minnesota	1.5
8	Ohio	3.7		33	Vermont	1.5
29	Oklahoma	1.6		36	Washington	1.2
41	Oregon	0.6		37	Nebraska	1.1
5	Pennsylvania	4.3		38	Maine	1.0
3	Rhode Island	7.1		39	Colorado	0.7
25	South Carolina	1.9		39	South Dakota	0.7
39	South Dakota	0.7		41	North Dakota	0.6
12	Tennessee	3.0		41	Oregon	0.6
29	Texas	1.6		43	Arizona	0.5
43	Utah	0.5		43	Idaho	0.5
33	Vermont	1.5		43	Utah	0.5
21	Virginia	2.1		46	Montana	0.4
36	Washington	1.2		47	Nevada	0.3
17	West Virginia	2.4		47	New Mexico	0.3
27	Wisconsin	1.8		49	Wyoming	0.2
49	Wyoming	0.2		50	Alaska**	0.0
					District of Columbia***	NA

Source: Morgan Quitno Press using data from American Hospital Association (Chicago, IL)
    "Hospital Statistics" (2006 edition)
*Based on land and water area figures. Community hospitals are nonfederal short-term general and other special hospitals, whose facilities and services are available to the public.
**Alaska has 19 community hospitals for its 663,267 square miles.
***The District of Columbia has 11 community hospitals for its 68 square miles.

Community Hospitals in Urban Areas in 2004

National Total = 2,916 Hospitals*

<table>
<tr><td colspan="4">ALPHA ORDER</td><td colspan="4">RANK ORDER</td></tr>
<tr><td>RANK</td><td>STATE</td><td>HOSPITALS</td><td>% of USA</td><td>RANK</td><td>STATE</td><td>HOSPITALS</td><td>% of USA</td></tr>
<tr><td>17</td><td>Alabama</td><td>59</td><td>2.0%</td><td>1</td><td>California</td><td>327</td><td>11.2%</td></tr>
<tr><td>47</td><td>Alaska</td><td>5</td><td>0.2%</td><td>2</td><td>Texas</td><td>268</td><td>9.2%</td></tr>
<tr><td>22</td><td>Arizona</td><td>46</td><td>1.6%</td><td>3</td><td>Florida</td><td>172</td><td>5.9%</td></tr>
<tr><td>27</td><td>Arkansas</td><td>36</td><td>1.2%</td><td>4</td><td>New York</td><td>166</td><td>5.7%</td></tr>
<tr><td>1</td><td>California</td><td>327</td><td>11.2%</td><td>5</td><td>Pennsylvania</td><td>149</td><td>5.1%</td></tr>
<tr><td>28</td><td>Colorado</td><td>34</td><td>1.2%</td><td>6</td><td>Illinois</td><td>126</td><td>4.3%</td></tr>
<tr><td>31</td><td>Connecticut</td><td>30</td><td>1.0%</td><td>7</td><td>Ohio</td><td>113</td><td>3.9%</td></tr>
<tr><td>48</td><td>Delaware</td><td>4</td><td>0.1%</td><td>8</td><td>Michigan</td><td>85</td><td>2.9%</td></tr>
<tr><td>3</td><td>Florida</td><td>172</td><td>5.9%</td><td>9</td><td>Georgia</td><td>81</td><td>2.8%</td></tr>
<tr><td>9</td><td>Georgia</td><td>81</td><td>2.8%</td><td>9</td><td>Louisiana</td><td>81</td><td>2.8%</td></tr>
<tr><td>40</td><td>Hawaii</td><td>13</td><td>0.4%</td><td>11</td><td>New Jersey</td><td>80</td><td>2.7%</td></tr>
<tr><td>40</td><td>Idaho</td><td>13</td><td>0.4%</td><td>12</td><td>Massachusetts</td><td>76</td><td>2.6%</td></tr>
<tr><td>6</td><td>Illinois</td><td>126</td><td>4.3%</td><td>13</td><td>Tennessee</td><td>73</td><td>2.5%</td></tr>
<tr><td>14</td><td>Indiana</td><td>72</td><td>2.5%</td><td>14</td><td>Indiana</td><td>72</td><td>2.5%</td></tr>
<tr><td>30</td><td>Iowa</td><td>31</td><td>1.1%</td><td>15</td><td>Missouri</td><td>67</td><td>2.3%</td></tr>
<tr><td>29</td><td>Kansas</td><td>32</td><td>1.1%</td><td>16</td><td>Wisconsin</td><td>64</td><td>2.2%</td></tr>
<tr><td>25</td><td>Kentucky</td><td>41</td><td>1.4%</td><td>17</td><td>Alabama</td><td>59</td><td>2.0%</td></tr>
<tr><td>9</td><td>Louisiana</td><td>81</td><td>2.8%</td><td>18</td><td>Virginia</td><td>58</td><td>2.0%</td></tr>
<tr><td>37</td><td>Maine</td><td>15</td><td>0.5%</td><td>19</td><td>North Carolina</td><td>57</td><td>2.0%</td></tr>
<tr><td>24</td><td>Maryland</td><td>44</td><td>1.5%</td><td>20</td><td>Washington</td><td>52</td><td>1.8%</td></tr>
<tr><td>12</td><td>Massachusetts</td><td>76</td><td>2.6%</td><td>21</td><td>Minnesota</td><td>49</td><td>1.7%</td></tr>
<tr><td>8</td><td>Michigan</td><td>85</td><td>2.9%</td><td>22</td><td>Arizona</td><td>46</td><td>1.6%</td></tr>
<tr><td>21</td><td>Minnesota</td><td>49</td><td>1.7%</td><td>22</td><td>Oklahoma</td><td>46</td><td>1.6%</td></tr>
<tr><td>33</td><td>Mississippi</td><td>26</td><td>0.9%</td><td>24</td><td>Maryland</td><td>44</td><td>1.5%</td></tr>
<tr><td>15</td><td>Missouri</td><td>67</td><td>2.3%</td><td>25</td><td>Kentucky</td><td>41</td><td>1.4%</td></tr>
<tr><td>45</td><td>Montana</td><td>6</td><td>0.2%</td><td>26</td><td>South Carolina</td><td>38</td><td>1.3%</td></tr>
<tr><td>37</td><td>Nebraska</td><td>15</td><td>0.5%</td><td>27</td><td>Arkansas</td><td>36</td><td>1.2%</td></tr>
<tr><td>36</td><td>Nevada</td><td>21</td><td>0.7%</td><td>28</td><td>Colorado</td><td>34</td><td>1.2%</td></tr>
<tr><td>42</td><td>New Hampshire</td><td>11</td><td>0.4%</td><td>29</td><td>Kansas</td><td>32</td><td>1.1%</td></tr>
<tr><td>11</td><td>New Jersey</td><td>80</td><td>2.7%</td><td>30</td><td>Iowa</td><td>31</td><td>1.1%</td></tr>
<tr><td>37</td><td>New Mexico</td><td>15</td><td>0.5%</td><td>31</td><td>Connecticut</td><td>30</td><td>1.0%</td></tr>
<tr><td>4</td><td>New York</td><td>166</td><td>5.7%</td><td>32</td><td>Oregon</td><td>29</td><td>1.0%</td></tr>
<tr><td>19</td><td>North Carolina</td><td>57</td><td>2.0%</td><td>33</td><td>Mississippi</td><td>26</td><td>0.9%</td></tr>
<tr><td>45</td><td>North Dakota</td><td>6</td><td>0.2%</td><td>34</td><td>Utah</td><td>25</td><td>0.9%</td></tr>
<tr><td>7</td><td>Ohio</td><td>113</td><td>3.9%</td><td>34</td><td>West Virginia</td><td>25</td><td>0.9%</td></tr>
<tr><td>22</td><td>Oklahoma</td><td>46</td><td>1.6%</td><td>36</td><td>Nevada</td><td>21</td><td>0.7%</td></tr>
<tr><td>32</td><td>Oregon</td><td>29</td><td>1.0%</td><td>37</td><td>Maine</td><td>15</td><td>0.5%</td></tr>
<tr><td>5</td><td>Pennsylvania</td><td>149</td><td>5.1%</td><td>37</td><td>Nebraska</td><td>15</td><td>0.5%</td></tr>
<tr><td>42</td><td>Rhode Island</td><td>11</td><td>0.4%</td><td>37</td><td>New Mexico</td><td>15</td><td>0.5%</td></tr>
<tr><td>26</td><td>South Carolina</td><td>38</td><td>1.3%</td><td>40</td><td>Hawaii</td><td>13</td><td>0.4%</td></tr>
<tr><td>44</td><td>South Dakota</td><td>8</td><td>0.3%</td><td>40</td><td>Idaho</td><td>13</td><td>0.4%</td></tr>
<tr><td>13</td><td>Tennessee</td><td>73</td><td>2.5%</td><td>42</td><td>New Hampshire</td><td>11</td><td>0.4%</td></tr>
<tr><td>2</td><td>Texas</td><td>268</td><td>9.2%</td><td>42</td><td>Rhode Island</td><td>11</td><td>0.4%</td></tr>
<tr><td>34</td><td>Utah</td><td>25</td><td>0.9%</td><td>44</td><td>South Dakota</td><td>8</td><td>0.3%</td></tr>
<tr><td>49</td><td>Vermont</td><td>2</td><td>0.1%</td><td>45</td><td>Montana</td><td>6</td><td>0.2%</td></tr>
<tr><td>18</td><td>Virginia</td><td>58</td><td>2.0%</td><td>45</td><td>North Dakota</td><td>6</td><td>0.2%</td></tr>
<tr><td>20</td><td>Washington</td><td>52</td><td>1.8%</td><td>47</td><td>Alaska</td><td>5</td><td>0.2%</td></tr>
<tr><td>34</td><td>West Virginia</td><td>25</td><td>0.9%</td><td>48</td><td>Delaware</td><td>4</td><td>0.1%</td></tr>
<tr><td>16</td><td>Wisconsin</td><td>64</td><td>2.2%</td><td>49</td><td>Vermont</td><td>2</td><td>0.1%</td></tr>
<tr><td>49</td><td>Wyoming</td><td>2</td><td>0.1%</td><td>49</td><td>Wyoming</td><td>2</td><td>0.1%</td></tr>
<tr><td></td><td></td><td></td><td></td><td></td><td>District of Columbia</td><td>11</td><td>0.4%</td></tr>
</table>

Source: American Hospital Association (Chicago, IL)
    "Hospital Statistics" (2006 edition)
Community hospitals are all nonfederal, short-term, general and special hospitals whose facilities and services are available to the public. Urban is defined as any area inside a metropolitan statistical area as defined by the U.S. Office of Management and Budget.

Percent of Community Hospitals in Urban Areas in 2004

National Percent = 59.3% of Community Hospitals*

ALPHA ORDER

RANK ORDER

RANK	STATE	PERCENT		RANK	STATE	PERCENT
26	Alabama	54.6		1	New Jersey	100.0
43	Alaska	26.3		1	Rhode Island	100.0
10	Arizona	74.2		3	Massachusetts	97.4
34	Arkansas	41.4		4	California	90.6
4	California	90.6		5	Maryland	88.0
31	Colorado	48.6		6	Connecticut	85.7
6	Connecticut	85.7		7	Florida	84.7
13	Delaware	66.7		8	New York	80.6
7	Florida	84.7		9	Pennsylvania	75.6
25	Georgia	55.5		10	Arizona	74.2
27	Hawaii	54.2		11	Nevada	70.0
40	Idaho	33.3		12	Ohio	68.1
14	Illinois	66.0		13	Delaware	66.7
17	Indiana	63.7		14	Illinois	66.0
42	Iowa	27.0		15	Virginia	65.9
44	Kansas	23.9		16	Texas	64.1
38	Kentucky	39.0		17	Indiana	63.7
18	Louisiana	61.8		18	Louisiana	61.8
35	Maine	40.5		19	South Carolina	61.3
5	Maryland	88.0		20	Washington	61.2
3	Massachusetts	97.4		21	Michigan	59.0
21	Michigan	59.0		22	Utah	58.1
39	Minnesota	37.1		23	Tennessee	57.5
41	Mississippi	28.0		24	Missouri	56.3
24	Missouri	56.3		25	Georgia	55.5
49	Montana	11.1		26	Alabama	54.6
45	Nebraska	17.6		27	Hawaii	54.2
11	Nevada	70.0		28	Wisconsin	52.9
37	New Hampshire	39.3		29	Oregon	50.0
1	New Jersey	100.0		30	North Carolina	49.6
35	New Mexico	40.5		31	Colorado	48.6
8	New York	80.6		32	West Virginia	43.9
30	North Carolina	49.6		33	Oklahoma	42.2
47	North Dakota	15.0		34	Arkansas	41.4
12	Ohio	68.1		35	Maine	40.5
33	Oklahoma	42.2		35	New Mexico	40.5
29	Oregon	50.0		37	New Hampshire	39.3
9	Pennsylvania	75.6		38	Kentucky	39.0
1	Rhode Island	100.0		39	Minnesota	37.1
19	South Carolina	61.3		40	Idaho	33.3
46	South Dakota	15.7		41	Mississippi	28.0
23	Tennessee	57.5		42	Iowa	27.0
16	Texas	64.1		43	Alaska	26.3
22	Utah	58.1		44	Kansas	23.9
48	Vermont	14.3		45	Nebraska	17.6
15	Virginia	65.9		46	South Dakota	15.7
20	Washington	61.2		47	North Dakota	15.0
32	West Virginia	43.9		48	Vermont	14.3
28	Wisconsin	52.9		49	Montana	11.1
50	Wyoming	8.3		50	Wyoming	8.3

District of Columbia 100.0

Source: Morgan Quitno Press using data from American Hospital Association (Chicago, IL)
     "Hospital Statistics" (2006 edition)
*Community hospitals are all nonfederal, short-term, general and special hospitals whose facilities and services are available to the public. Urban is defined as any area inside a metropolitan statistical area as defined by the U.S. Office of Management and Budget.

Community Hospitals in Rural Areas in 2004

National Total = 2,003 Hospitals*

ALPHA ORDER

RANK	STATE	HOSPITALS	% of USA
19	Alabama	49	2.4%
41	Alaska	14	0.7%
40	Arizona	16	0.8%
17	Arkansas	51	2.5%
26	California	34	1.7%
25	Colorado	36	1.8%
46	Connecticut	5	0.2%
47	Delaware	2	0.1%
30	Florida	31	1.5%
7	Georgia	65	3.2%
43	Hawaii	11	0.5%
33	Idaho	26	1.3%
7	Illinois	65	3.2%
23	Indiana	41	2.0%
3	Iowa	84	4.2%
2	Kansas	102	5.1%
9	Kentucky	64	3.2%
18	Louisiana	50	2.5%
35	Maine	22	1.1%
45	Maryland	6	0.3%
47	Massachusetts	2	0.1%
11	Michigan	59	2.9%
4	Minnesota	83	4.1%
6	Mississippi	67	3.3%
16	Missouri	52	2.6%
20	Montana	48	2.4%
5	Nebraska	70	3.5%
44	Nevada	9	0.4%
39	New Hampshire	17	0.8%
49	New Jersey	0	0.0%
35	New Mexico	22	1.1%
24	New York	40	2.0%
12	North Carolina	58	2.9%
26	North Dakota	34	1.7%
15	Ohio	53	2.6%
10	Oklahoma	63	3.1%
32	Oregon	29	1.4%
20	Pennsylvania	48	2.4%
49	Rhode Island	0	0.0%
34	South Carolina	24	1.2%
22	South Dakota	43	2.1%
14	Tennessee	54	2.7%
1	Texas	150	7.5%
38	Utah	18	0.9%
42	Vermont	12	0.6%
31	Virginia	30	1.5%
28	Washington	33	1.6%
29	West Virginia	32	1.6%
13	Wisconsin	57	2.8%
35	Wyoming	22	1.1%

RANK ORDER

RANK	STATE	HOSPITALS	% of USA
1	Texas	150	7.5%
2	Kansas	102	5.1%
3	Iowa	84	4.2%
4	Minnesota	83	4.1%
5	Nebraska	70	3.5%
6	Mississippi	67	3.3%
7	Georgia	65	3.2%
7	Illinois	65	3.2%
9	Kentucky	64	3.2%
10	Oklahoma	63	3.1%
11	Michigan	59	2.9%
12	North Carolina	58	2.9%
13	Wisconsin	57	2.8%
14	Tennessee	54	2.7%
15	Ohio	53	2.6%
16	Missouri	52	2.6%
17	Arkansas	51	2.5%
18	Louisiana	50	2.5%
19	Alabama	49	2.4%
20	Montana	48	2.4%
20	Pennsylvania	48	2.4%
22	South Dakota	43	2.1%
23	Indiana	41	2.0%
24	New York	40	2.0%
25	Colorado	36	1.8%
26	California	34	1.7%
26	North Dakota	34	1.7%
28	Washington	33	1.6%
29	West Virginia	32	1.6%
30	Florida	31	1.5%
31	Virginia	30	1.5%
32	Oregon	29	1.4%
33	Idaho	26	1.3%
34	South Carolina	24	1.2%
35	Maine	22	1.1%
35	New Mexico	22	1.1%
35	Wyoming	22	1.1%
38	Utah	18	0.9%
39	New Hampshire	17	0.8%
40	Arizona	16	0.8%
41	Alaska	14	0.7%
42	Vermont	12	0.6%
43	Hawaii	11	0.5%
44	Nevada	9	0.4%
45	Maryland	6	0.3%
46	Connecticut	5	0.2%
47	Delaware	2	0.1%
47	Massachusetts	2	0.1%
49	New Jersey	0	0.0%
49	Rhode Island	0	0.0%
	District of Columbia	0	0.0%

Source: American Hospital Association (Chicago, IL)
"Hospital Statistics" (2006 edition)
*Community hospitals are all nonfederal, short-term, general and special hospitals whose facilities and services are available to the public. Rural is defined as any area outside a metropolitan statistical area as defined by the U.S. Office of Management and Budget.

Percent of Community Hospitals in Rural Areas in 2004

National Percent = 40.7% of Community Hospitals*

ALPHA ORDER			RANK ORDER		
RANK	STATE	PERCENT	RANK	STATE	PERCENT
25	Alabama	45.4	1	Wyoming	91.7
8	Alaska	73.7	2	Montana	88.9
41	Arizona	25.8	3	Vermont	85.7
17	Arkansas	58.6	4	North Dakota	85.0
47	California	9.4	5	South Dakota	84.3
20	Colorado	51.4	6	Nebraska	82.4
45	Connecticut	14.3	7	Kansas	76.1
38	Delaware	33.3	8	Alaska	73.7
44	Florida	15.3	9	Iowa	73.0
26	Georgia	44.5	10	Mississippi	72.0
24	Hawaii	45.8	11	Idaho	66.7
11	Idaho	66.7	12	Minnesota	62.9
37	Illinois	34.0	13	Kentucky	61.0
34	Indiana	36.3	14	New Hampshire	60.7
9	Iowa	73.0	15	Maine	59.5
7	Kansas	76.1	15	New Mexico	59.5
13	Kentucky	61.0	17	Arkansas	58.6
33	Louisiana	38.2	18	Oklahoma	57.8
15	Maine	59.5	19	West Virginia	56.1
46	Maryland	12.0	20	Colorado	51.4
48	Massachusetts	2.6	21	North Carolina	50.4
30	Michigan	41.0	22	Oregon	50.0
12	Minnesota	62.9	23	Wisconsin	47.1
10	Mississippi	72.0	24	Hawaii	45.8
27	Missouri	43.7	25	Alabama	45.4
2	Montana	88.9	26	Georgia	44.5
6	Nebraska	82.4	27	Missouri	43.7
40	Nevada	30.0	28	Tennessee	42.5
14	New Hampshire	60.7	29	Utah	41.9
49	New Jersey	0.0	30	Michigan	41.0
15	New Mexico	59.5	31	Washington	38.8
43	New York	19.4	32	South Carolina	38.7
21	North Carolina	50.4	33	Louisiana	38.2
4	North Dakota	85.0	34	Indiana	36.3
39	Ohio	31.9	35	Texas	35.9
18	Oklahoma	57.8	36	Virginia	34.1
22	Oregon	50.0	37	Illinois	34.0
42	Pennsylvania	24.4	38	Delaware	33.3
49	Rhode Island	0.0	39	Ohio	31.9
32	South Carolina	38.7	40	Nevada	30.0
5	South Dakota	84.3	41	Arizona	25.8
28	Tennessee	42.5	42	Pennsylvania	24.4
35	Texas	35.9	43	New York	19.4
29	Utah	41.9	44	Florida	15.3
3	Vermont	85.7	45	Connecticut	14.3
36	Virginia	34.1	46	Maryland	12.0
31	Washington	38.8	47	California	9.4
19	West Virginia	56.1	48	Massachusetts	2.6
23	Wisconsin	47.1	49	New Jersey	0.0
1	Wyoming	91.7	49	Rhode Island	0.0
				District of Columbia	0.0

Source: Morgan Quitno Press using data from American Hospital Association (Chicago, IL)
    "Hospital Statistics" (2006 edition)
*Community hospitals are all nonfederal, short-term, general and special hospitals whose facilities and services are available to the public. Rural is defined as any area outside a metropolitan statistical area as defined by the U.S. Office of Management and Budget.

Nongovernment Not-For-Profit Hospitals in 2004

National Total = 2,967 Hospitals*

ALPHA ORDER

RANK	STATE	HOSPITALS	% of USA
32	Alabama	35	1.2%
47	Alaska	10	0.3%
31	Arizona	38	1.3%
22	Arkansas	50	1.7%
1	California	200	6.7%
36	Colorado	32	1.1%
35	Connecticut	33	1.1%
49	Delaware	6	0.2%
10	Florida	89	3.0%
18	Georgia	62	2.1%
43	Hawaii	17	0.6%
45	Idaho	13	0.4%
5	Illinois	152	5.1%
19	Indiana	60	2.0%
21	Iowa	56	1.9%
19	Kansas	60	2.0%
13	Kentucky	72	2.4%
33	Louisiana	34	1.1%
33	Maine	34	1.1%
23	Maryland	48	1.6%
14	Massachusetts	66	2.2%
7	Michigan	122	4.1%
9	Minnesota	91	3.1%
38	Mississippi	25	0.8%
15	Missouri	64	2.2%
24	Montana	44	1.5%
24	Nebraska	44	1.5%
47	Nevada	10	0.3%
39	New Hampshire	24	0.8%
11	New Jersey	75	2.5%
42	New Mexico	18	0.6%
2	New York	180	6.1%
12	North Carolina	74	2.5%
30	North Dakota	40	1.3%
6	Ohio	138	4.7%
28	Oklahoma	42	1.4%
27	Oregon	43	1.4%
3	Pennsylvania	172	5.8%
46	Rhode Island	11	0.4%
39	South Carolina	24	0.8%
24	South Dakota	44	1.5%
15	Tennessee	64	2.2%
4	Texas	153	5.2%
41	Utah	22	0.7%
44	Vermont	14	0.5%
15	Virginia	64	2.2%
29	Washington	41	1.4%
37	West Virginia	31	1.0%
8	Wisconsin	115	3.9%
50	Wyoming	4	0.1%

RANK ORDER

RANK	STATE	HOSPITALS	% of USA
1	California	200	6.7%
2	New York	180	6.1%
3	Pennsylvania	172	5.8%
4	Texas	153	5.2%
5	Illinois	152	5.1%
6	Ohio	138	4.7%
7	Michigan	122	4.1%
8	Wisconsin	115	3.9%
9	Minnesota	91	3.1%
10	Florida	89	3.0%
11	New Jersey	75	2.5%
12	North Carolina	74	2.5%
13	Kentucky	72	2.4%
14	Massachusetts	66	2.2%
15	Missouri	64	2.2%
15	Tennessee	64	2.2%
15	Virginia	64	2.2%
18	Georgia	62	2.1%
19	Indiana	60	2.0%
19	Kansas	60	2.0%
21	Iowa	56	1.9%
22	Arkansas	50	1.7%
23	Maryland	48	1.6%
24	Montana	44	1.5%
24	Nebraska	44	1.5%
24	South Dakota	44	1.5%
27	Oregon	43	1.4%
28	Oklahoma	42	1.4%
29	Washington	41	1.4%
30	North Dakota	40	1.3%
31	Arizona	38	1.3%
32	Alabama	35	1.2%
33	Louisiana	34	1.1%
33	Maine	34	1.1%
35	Connecticut	33	1.1%
36	Colorado	32	1.1%
37	West Virginia	31	1.0%
38	Mississippi	25	0.8%
39	New Hampshire	24	0.8%
39	South Carolina	24	0.8%
41	Utah	22	0.7%
42	New Mexico	18	0.6%
43	Hawaii	17	0.6%
44	Vermont	14	0.5%
45	Idaho	13	0.4%
46	Rhode Island	11	0.4%
47	Alaska	10	0.3%
47	Nevada	10	0.3%
49	Delaware	6	0.2%
50	Wyoming	4	0.1%
	District of Columbia	7	0.2%

Source: American Hospital Association (Chicago, IL)
  "Hospital Statistics" (2006 edition)
*Nongovernment not-for-profit hospitals are a subset of community hospitals.

Investor-Owned (For-Profit) Hospitals in 2004

National Total = 835 Hospitals*

ALPHA ORDER

RANK	STATE	HOSPITALS	% of USA
6	Alabama	36	4.3%
36	Alaska	2	0.2%
14	Arizona	19	2.3%
10	Arkansas	22	2.6%
3	California	89	10.7%
22	Colorado	11	1.3%
40	Connecticut	1	0.1%
43	Delaware	0	0.0%
2	Florida	94	11.3%
7	Georgia	30	3.6%
43	Hawaii	0	0.0%
36	Idaho	2	0.2%
23	Illinois	10	1.2%
17	Indiana	16	1.9%
43	Iowa	0	0.0%
21	Kansas	13	1.6%
12	Kentucky	20	2.4%
4	Louisiana	44	5.3%
40	Maine	1	0.1%
36	Maryland	2	0.2%
25	Massachusetts	9	1.1%
29	Michigan	4	0.5%
43	Minnesota	0	0.0%
8	Mississippi	26	3.1%
14	Missouri	19	2.3%
43	Montana	0	0.0%
36	Nebraska	2	0.2%
20	Nevada	14	1.7%
29	New Hampshire	4	0.5%
29	New Jersey	4	0.5%
23	New Mexico	10	1.2%
33	New York	3	0.4%
25	North Carolina	9	1.1%
43	North Dakota	0	0.0%
27	Ohio	5	0.6%
10	Oklahoma	22	2.6%
33	Oregon	3	0.4%
9	Pennsylvania	24	2.9%
43	Rhode Island	0	0.0%
14	South Carolina	19	2.3%
40	South Dakota	1	0.1%
5	Tennessee	39	4.7%
1	Texas	139	16.6%
19	Utah	15	1.8%
43	Vermont	0	0.0%
12	Virginia	20	2.4%
27	Washington	5	0.6%
17	West Virginia	16	1.9%
29	Wisconsin	4	0.5%
33	Wyoming	3	0.4%

RANK ORDER

RANK	STATE	HOSPITALS	% of USA
1	Texas	139	16.6%
2	Florida	94	11.3%
3	California	89	10.7%
4	Louisiana	44	5.3%
5	Tennessee	39	4.7%
6	Alabama	36	4.3%
7	Georgia	30	3.6%
8	Mississippi	26	3.1%
9	Pennsylvania	24	2.9%
10	Arkansas	22	2.6%
10	Oklahoma	22	2.6%
12	Kentucky	20	2.4%
12	Virginia	20	2.4%
14	Arizona	19	2.3%
14	Missouri	19	2.3%
14	South Carolina	19	2.3%
17	Indiana	16	1.9%
17	West Virginia	16	1.9%
19	Utah	15	1.8%
20	Nevada	14	1.7%
21	Kansas	13	1.6%
22	Colorado	11	1.3%
23	Illinois	10	1.2%
23	New Mexico	10	1.2%
25	Massachusetts	9	1.1%
25	North Carolina	9	1.1%
27	Ohio	5	0.6%
27	Washington	5	0.6%
29	Michigan	4	0.5%
29	New Hampshire	4	0.5%
29	New Jersey	4	0.5%
29	Wisconsin	4	0.5%
33	New York	3	0.4%
33	Oregon	3	0.4%
33	Wyoming	3	0.4%
36	Alaska	2	0.2%
36	Idaho	2	0.2%
36	Maryland	2	0.2%
36	Nebraska	2	0.2%
40	Connecticut	1	0.1%
40	Maine	1	0.1%
40	South Dakota	1	0.1%
43	Delaware	0	0.0%
43	Hawaii	0	0.0%
43	Iowa	0	0.0%
43	Minnesota	0	0.0%
43	Montana	0	0.0%
43	North Dakota	0	0.0%
43	Rhode Island	0	0.0%
43	Vermont	0	0.0%
	District of Columbia	4	0.5%

Source: American Hospital Association (Chicago, IL)
"Hospital Statistics" (2006 edition)
Investor-owned (for-profit) hospitals are a subset of community hospitals.

State and Local Government-Owned Hospitals in 2004

National Total = 1,117 Hospitals*

ALPHA ORDER

RANK	STATE	HOSPITALS	% of USA	RANK	STATE	HOSPITALS	% of USA
12	Alabama	37	3.3%	1	Texas	126	11.3%
32	Alaska	7	0.6%	2	California	72	6.4%
37	Arizona	5	0.4%	3	Kansas	61	5.5%
26	Arkansas	15	1.3%	4	Iowa	59	5.3%
2	California	72	6.4%	5	Georgia	54	4.8%
17	Colorado	27	2.4%	6	Louisiana	53	4.7%
42	Connecticut	1	0.1%	7	Oklahoma	45	4.0%
45	Delaware	0	0.0%	8	Mississippi	42	3.8%
22	Florida	20	1.8%	9	Minnesota	41	3.7%
5	Georgia	54	4.8%	10	Nebraska	39	3.5%
32	Hawaii	7	0.6%	10	Washington	39	3.5%
18	Idaho	24	2.1%	12	Alabama	37	3.3%
16	Illinois	29	2.6%	12	Indiana	37	3.3%
12	Indiana	37	3.3%	14	Missouri	36	3.2%
4	Iowa	59	5.3%	15	North Carolina	32	2.9%
3	Kansas	61	5.5%	16	Illinois	29	2.6%
27	Kentucky	13	1.2%	17	Colorado	27	2.4%
6	Louisiana	53	4.7%	18	Idaho	24	2.1%
40	Maine	2	0.2%	18	Tennessee	24	2.1%
45	Maryland	0	0.0%	20	New York	23	2.1%
39	Massachusetts	3	0.3%	20	Ohio	23	2.1%
24	Michigan	18	1.6%	22	Florida	20	1.8%
9	Minnesota	41	3.7%	23	South Carolina	19	1.7%
8	Mississippi	42	3.8%	24	Michigan	18	1.6%
14	Missouri	36	3.2%	25	Wyoming	17	1.5%
29	Montana	10	0.9%	26	Arkansas	15	1.3%
10	Nebraska	39	3.5%	27	Kentucky	13	1.2%
34	Nevada	6	0.5%	28	Oregon	12	1.1%
45	New Hampshire	0	0.0%	29	Montana	10	0.9%
42	New Jersey	1	0.1%	29	West Virginia	10	0.9%
31	New Mexico	9	0.8%	31	New Mexico	9	0.8%
20	New York	23	2.1%	32	Alaska	7	0.6%
15	North Carolina	32	2.9%	32	Hawaii	7	0.6%
45	North Dakota	0	0.0%	34	Nevada	6	0.5%
20	Ohio	23	2.1%	34	South Dakota	6	0.5%
7	Oklahoma	45	4.0%	34	Utah	6	0.5%
28	Oregon	12	1.1%	37	Arizona	5	0.4%
42	Pennsylvania	1	0.1%	38	Virginia	4	0.4%
45	Rhode Island	0	0.0%	39	Massachusetts	3	0.3%
23	South Carolina	19	1.7%	40	Maine	2	0.2%
34	South Dakota	6	0.5%	40	Wisconsin	2	0.2%
18	Tennessee	24	2.1%	42	Connecticut	1	0.1%
1	Texas	126	11.3%	42	New Jersey	1	0.1%
34	Utah	6	0.5%	42	Pennsylvania	1	0.1%
45	Vermont	0	0.0%	45	Delaware	0	0.0%
38	Virginia	4	0.4%	45	Maryland	0	0.0%
10	Washington	39	3.5%	45	New Hampshire	0	0.0%
29	West Virginia	10	0.9%	45	North Dakota	0	0.0%
40	Wisconsin	2	0.2%	45	Rhode Island	0	0.0%
25	Wyoming	17	1.5%	45	Vermont	0	0.0%
					District of Columbia	0	0.0%

Source: American Hospital Association (Chicago, IL)
    "Hospital Statistics" (2006 edition)
State and local government-owned hospitals are a subset of community hospitals.

Beds in Community Hospitals in 2004

National Total = 808,127 Beds*

ALPHA ORDER				RANK ORDER			
RANK	STATE	BEDS	% of USA	RANK	STATE	BEDS	% of USA
19	Alabama	15,328	1.9%	1	California	71,910	8.9%
50	Alaska	1,427	0.2%	2	New York	64,205	7.9%
25	Arizona	11,166	1.4%	3	Texas	58,116	7.2%
30	Arkansas	9,580	1.2%	4	Florida	49,962	6.2%
1	California	71,910	8.9%	5	Pennsylvania	40,079	5.0%
31	Colorado	9,250	1.1%	6	Illinois	34,844	4.3%
32	Connecticut	7,826	1.0%	7	Ohio	33,398	4.1%
48	Delaware	1,955	0.2%	8	Michigan	25,953	3.2%
4	Florida	49,962	6.2%	9	Georgia	24,709	3.1%
9	Georgia	24,709	3.1%	10	North Carolina	23,498	2.9%
44	Hawaii	3,149	0.4%	11	New Jersey	21,952	2.7%
43	Idaho	3,434	0.4%	12	Tennessee	20,363	2.5%
6	Illinois	34,844	4.3%	13	Missouri	19,131	2.4%
14	Indiana	18,796	2.3%	14	Indiana	18,796	2.3%
27	Iowa	10,943	1.4%	15	Virginia	17,339	2.1%
29	Kansas	10,362	1.3%	16	Louisiana	17,199	2.1%
20	Kentucky	15,276	1.9%	17	Massachusetts	16,215	2.0%
16	Louisiana	17,199	2.1%	18	Minnesota	16,101	2.0%
42	Maine	3,549	0.4%	19	Alabama	15,328	1.9%
23	Maryland	11,489	1.4%	20	Kentucky	15,276	1.9%
17	Massachusetts	16,215	2.0%	21	Wisconsin	14,577	1.8%
8	Michigan	25,953	3.2%	22	Mississippi	13,143	1.6%
18	Minnesota	16,101	2.0%	23	Maryland	11,489	1.4%
22	Mississippi	13,143	1.6%	24	South Carolina	11,222	1.4%
13	Missouri	19,131	2.4%	25	Arizona	11,166	1.4%
39	Montana	4,337	0.5%	26	Washington	10,984	1.4%
34	Nebraska	7,336	0.9%	27	Iowa	10,943	1.4%
36	Nevada	4,752	0.6%	28	Oklahoma	10,804	1.3%
45	New Hampshire	2,807	0.3%	29	Kansas	10,362	1.3%
11	New Jersey	21,952	2.7%	30	Arkansas	9,580	1.2%
40	New Mexico	3,678	0.5%	31	Colorado	9,250	1.1%
2	New York	64,205	7.9%	32	Connecticut	7,826	1.0%
10	North Carolina	23,498	2.9%	33	West Virginia	7,412	0.9%
41	North Dakota	3,567	0.4%	34	Nebraska	7,336	0.9%
7	Ohio	33,398	4.1%	35	Oregon	6,505	0.8%
28	Oklahoma	10,804	1.3%	36	Nevada	4,752	0.6%
35	Oregon	6,505	0.8%	37	South Dakota	4,611	0.6%
5	Pennsylvania	40,079	5.0%	38	Utah	4,517	0.6%
46	Rhode Island	2,397	0.3%	39	Montana	4,337	0.5%
24	South Carolina	11,222	1.4%	40	New Mexico	3,678	0.5%
37	South Dakota	4,611	0.6%	41	North Dakota	3,567	0.4%
12	Tennessee	20,363	2.5%	42	Maine	3,549	0.4%
3	Texas	58,116	7.2%	43	Idaho	3,434	0.4%
38	Utah	4,517	0.6%	44	Hawaii	3,149	0.4%
49	Vermont	1,473	0.2%	45	New Hampshire	2,807	0.3%
15	Virginia	17,339	2.1%	46	Rhode Island	2,397	0.3%
26	Washington	10,984	1.4%	47	Wyoming	2,048	0.3%
33	West Virginia	7,412	0.9%	48	Delaware	1,955	0.2%
21	Wisconsin	14,577	1.8%	49	Vermont	1,473	0.2%
47	Wyoming	2,048	0.3%	50	Alaska	1,427	0.2%
					District of Columbia	3,453	0.4%

Source: American Hospital Association (Chicago, IL)
  "Hospital Statistics" (2006 edition)
*All nonfederal short-term general and other special hospitals, whose facilities and services are available to the public. Includes beds in hospital and nursing home units.

Rate of Beds in Community Hospitals in 2004

National Rate = 275 Beds per 100,000 Population*

ALPHA ORDER				RANK ORDER		
RANK	STATE	RATE		RANK	STATE	RATE
14	Alabama	339		1	South Dakota	598
40	Alaska	217		2	North Dakota	561
46	Arizona	195		3	Montana	468
12	Arkansas	348		4	Mississippi	453
44	California	201		5	Nebraska	420
44	Colorado	201		6	West Virginia	409
38	Connecticut	224		7	Wyoming	405
36	Delaware	236		8	Louisiana	382
22	Florida	287		9	Kansas	379
23	Georgia	277		10	Iowa	371
33	Hawaii	250		11	Kentucky	369
34	Idaho	246		12	Arkansas	348
25	Illinois	274		13	Tennessee	346
20	Indiana	302		14	Alabama	339
10	Iowa	371		15	New York	333
9	Kansas	379		16	Missouri	332
11	Kentucky	369		17	Pennsylvania	323
8	Louisiana	382		18	Minnesota	316
26	Maine	270		19	Oklahoma	307
42	Maryland	207		20	Indiana	302
31	Massachusetts	253		21	Ohio	292
30	Michigan	257		22	Florida	287
18	Minnesota	316		23	Georgia	277
4	Mississippi	453		24	North Carolina	275
16	Missouri	332		25	Illinois	274
3	Montana	468		26	Maine	270
5	Nebraska	420		27	South Carolina	267
43	Nevada	204		28	Wisconsin	265
41	New Hampshire	216		29	Texas	259
31	New Jersey	253		30	Michigan	257
47	New Mexico	193		31	Massachusetts	253
15	New York	333		31	New Jersey	253
24	North Carolina	275		33	Hawaii	250
2	North Dakota	561		34	Idaho	246
21	Ohio	292		35	Vermont	237
19	Oklahoma	307		36	Delaware	236
49	Oregon	181		37	Virginia	232
17	Pennsylvania	323		38	Connecticut	224
39	Rhode Island	222		39	Rhode Island	222
27	South Carolina	267		40	Alaska	217
1	South Dakota	598		41	New Hampshire	216
13	Tennessee	346		42	Maryland	207
29	Texas	259		43	Nevada	204
48	Utah	187		44	California	201
35	Vermont	237		44	Colorado	201
37	Virginia	232		46	Arizona	195
50	Washington	177		47	New Mexico	193
6	West Virginia	409		48	Utah	187
28	Wisconsin	265		49	Oregon	181
7	Wyoming	405		50	Washington	177
					District of Columbia	623

Source: Morgan Quitno Press using data from American Hospital Association (Chicago, IL)
  "Hospital Statistics" (2006 edition)
All nonfederal short-term general and other special hospitals, whose facilities and services are available to the public. Includes beds in hospital and nursing home units.

Average Number of Beds per Community Hospital in 2004

National Average = 164 Beds per Community Hospital*

ALPHA ORDER				RANK ORDER		
RANK	**STATE**	**BEDS**		**RANK**	**STATE**	**BEDS**
24	Alabama	142		1	Delaware	326
50	Alaska	75		2	New York	312
16	Arizona	180		3	New Jersey	274
35	Arkansas	110		4	Florida	246
12	California	199		5	Maryland	230
27	Colorado	132		6	Connecticut	224
6	Connecticut	224		7	Rhode Island	218
1	Delaware	326		8	Massachusetts	208
4	Florida	246		9	North Carolina	204
18	Georgia	169		10	Pennsylvania	203
28	Hawaii	131		11	Ohio	201
45	Idaho	88		12	California	199
14	Illinois	182		13	Virginia	197
19	Indiana	166		14	Illinois	182
42	Iowa	95		15	South Carolina	181
49	Kansas	77		16	Arizona	180
23	Kentucky	145		16	Michigan	180
28	Louisiana	131		18	Georgia	169
41	Maine	96		19	Indiana	166
5	Maryland	230		20	Missouri	161
8	Massachusetts	208		21	Tennessee	160
16	Michigan	180		22	Nevada	158
32	Minnesota	122		23	Kentucky	145
25	Mississippi	141		24	Alabama	142
20	Missouri	161		25	Mississippi	141
48	Montana	80		26	Texas	139
46	Nebraska	86		27	Colorado	132
22	Nevada	158		28	Hawaii	131
38	New Hampshire	100		28	Louisiana	131
3	New Jersey	274		30	West Virginia	130
39	New Mexico	99		31	Washington	129
2	New York	312		32	Minnesota	122
9	North Carolina	204		33	Wisconsin	120
44	North Dakota	89		34	Oregon	112
11	Ohio	201		35	Arkansas	110
39	Oklahoma	99		36	Utah	105
34	Oregon	112		36	Vermont	105
10	Pennsylvania	203		38	New Hampshire	100
7	Rhode Island	218		39	New Mexico	99
15	South Carolina	181		39	Oklahoma	99
43	South Dakota	90		41	Maine	96
21	Tennessee	160		42	Iowa	95
26	Texas	139		43	South Dakota	90
36	Utah	105		44	North Dakota	89
36	Vermont	105		45	Idaho	88
13	Virginia	197		46	Nebraska	86
31	Washington	129		47	Wyoming	85
30	West Virginia	130		48	Montana	80
33	Wisconsin	120		49	Kansas	77
47	Wyoming	85		50	Alaska	75
					District of Columbia	314

Source: Morgan Quitno Press using data from American Hospital Association (Chicago, IL)
   "Hospital Statistics" (2006 edition)
*All nonfederal short-term general and other special hospitals, whose facilities and services are available to the public. Includes beds in hospital and nursing home units.

Admissions to Community Hospitals in 2004

National Total = 35,086,061 Admissions*

ALPHA ORDER					RANK ORDER			
RANK	STATE	ADMISSIONS	% of USA		RANK	STATE	ADMISSIONS	% of USA
17	Alabama	715,709	2.0%		1	California	3,468,538	9.9%
50	Alaska	45,359	0.1%		2	New York	2,525,777	7.2%
21	Arizona	624,583	1.8%		3	Texas	2,516,718	7.2%
30	Arkansas	382,836	1.1%		4	Florida	2,322,370	6.6%
1	California	3,468,538	9.9%		5	Pennsylvania	1,846,702	5.3%
27	Colorado	435,001	1.2%		6	Illinois	1,586,401	4.5%
29	Connecticut	389,728	1.1%		7	Ohio	1,474,876	4.2%
46	Delaware	103,169	0.3%		8	Michigan	1,190,293	3.4%
4	Florida	2,322,370	6.6%		9	New Jersey	1,103,743	3.1%
11	Georgia	943,837	2.7%		10	North Carolina	1,005,965	2.9%
43	Hawaii	114,341	0.3%		11	Georgia	943,837	2.7%
40	Idaho	127,381	0.4%		12	Missouri	831,892	2.4%
6	Illinois	1,586,401	4.5%		13	Tennessee	825,269	2.4%
16	Indiana	730,610	2.1%		14	Massachusetts	801,137	2.3%
31	Iowa	359,611	1.0%		15	Virginia	770,482	2.2%
33	Kansas	330,712	0.9%		16	Indiana	730,610	2.1%
22	Kentucky	605,707	1.7%		17	Alabama	715,709	2.0%
18	Louisiana	696,154	2.0%		18	Louisiana	696,154	2.0%
39	Maine	151,135	0.4%		19	Maryland	661,449	1.9%
19	Maryland	661,449	1.9%		20	Minnesota	626,693	1.8%
14	Massachusetts	801,137	2.3%		21	Arizona	624,583	1.8%
8	Michigan	1,190,293	3.4%		22	Kentucky	605,707	1.7%
20	Minnesota	626,693	1.8%		23	Wisconsin	598,542	1.7%
28	Mississippi	427,401	1.2%		24	Washington	528,145	1.5%
12	Missouri	831,892	2.4%		25	South Carolina	512,908	1.5%
44	Montana	106,619	0.3%		26	Oklahoma	454,875	1.3%
37	Nebraska	211,025	0.6%		27	Colorado	435,001	1.2%
35	Nevada	232,603	0.7%		28	Mississippi	427,401	1.2%
42	New Hampshire	117,130	0.3%		29	Connecticut	389,728	1.1%
9	New Jersey	1,103,743	3.1%		30	Arkansas	382,836	1.1%
38	New Mexico	163,416	0.5%		31	Iowa	359,611	1.0%
2	New York	2,525,777	7.2%		32	Oregon	341,307	1.0%
10	North Carolina	1,005,965	2.9%		33	Kansas	330,712	0.9%
47	North Dakota	88,004	0.3%		34	West Virginia	297,957	0.8%
7	Ohio	1,474,876	4.2%		35	Nevada	232,603	0.7%
26	Oklahoma	454,875	1.3%		36	Utah	219,021	0.6%
32	Oregon	341,307	1.0%		37	Nebraska	211,025	0.6%
5	Pennsylvania	1,846,702	5.3%		38	New Mexico	163,416	0.5%
41	Rhode Island	125,308	0.4%		39	Maine	151,135	0.4%
25	South Carolina	512,908	1.5%		40	Idaho	127,381	0.4%
45	South Dakota	103,495	0.3%		41	Rhode Island	125,308	0.4%
13	Tennessee	825,269	2.4%		42	New Hampshire	117,130	0.3%
3	Texas	2,516,718	7.2%		43	Hawaii	114,341	0.3%
36	Utah	219,021	0.6%		44	Montana	106,619	0.3%
48	Vermont	52,853	0.2%		45	South Dakota	103,495	0.3%
15	Virginia	770,482	2.2%		46	Delaware	103,169	0.3%
24	Washington	528,145	1.5%		47	North Dakota	88,004	0.3%
34	West Virginia	297,957	0.8%		48	Vermont	52,853	0.2%
23	Wisconsin	598,542	1.7%		49	Wyoming	50,509	0.1%
49	Wyoming	50,509	0.1%		50	Alaska	45,359	0.1%
						District of Columbia	140,765	0.4%

Source: American Hospital Association (Chicago, IL)
   "Hospital Statistics" (2006 edition)
*Admissions to all nonfederal short-term general and other special hospitals, whose facilities and services are available to the public. Includes admissions to hospital and nursing home units.

Inpatient Days in Community Hospitals in 2004

National Total = 197,654,172 Inpatient Days*

ALPHA ORDER

RANK ORDER

RANK	STATE	DAYS	% of USA	RANK	STATE	DAYS	% of USA
19	Alabama	3,664,493	1.9%	1	New York	18,482,900	9.4%
50	Alaska	285,999	0.1%	2	California	18,351,443	9.3%
24	Arizona	2,781,888	1.4%	3	Texas	13,200,657	6.7%
32	Arkansas	2,050,766	1.0%	4	Florida	12,099,072	6.1%
2	California	18,351,443	9.3%	5	Pennsylvania	10,259,088	5.2%
30	Colorado	2,147,534	1.1%	6	Illinois	8,405,800	4.3%
29	Connecticut	2,249,861	1.1%	7	Ohio	7,718,229	3.9%
47	Delaware	642,401	0.3%	8	Michigan	6,279,987	3.2%
4	Florida	12,099,072	6.1%	9	North Carolina	6,115,774	3.1%
10	Georgia	6,093,697	3.1%	10	Georgia	6,093,697	3.1%
40	Hawaii	875,714	0.4%	11	New Jersey	5,911,631	3.0%
44	Idaho	667,687	0.3%	12	Tennessee	4,673,861	2.4%
6	Illinois	8,405,800	4.3%	13	Virginia	4,468,361	2.3%
16	Indiana	4,059,031	2.1%	14	Massachusetts	4,428,800	2.2%
28	Iowa	2,358,165	1.2%	15	Missouri	4,407,818	2.2%
31	Kansas	2,115,015	1.1%	16	Indiana	4,059,031	2.1%
20	Kentucky	3,384,932	1.7%	17	Minnesota	4,004,183	2.0%
18	Louisiana	3,856,768	2.0%	18	Louisiana	3,856,768	2.0%
41	Maine	820,114	0.4%	19	Alabama	3,664,493	1.9%
22	Maryland	3,189,302	1.6%	20	Kentucky	3,384,932	1.7%
14	Massachusetts	4,428,800	2.2%	21	Wisconsin	3,335,415	1.7%
8	Michigan	6,279,987	3.2%	22	Maryland	3,189,302	1.6%
17	Minnesota	4,004,183	2.0%	23	South Carolina	2,921,052	1.5%
25	Mississippi	2,771,304	1.4%	24	Arizona	2,781,888	1.4%
15	Missouri	4,407,818	2.2%	25	Mississippi	2,771,304	1.4%
37	Montana	1,042,530	0.5%	26	Washington	2,464,033	1.2%
34	Nebraska	1,612,857	0.8%	27	Oklahoma	2,370,273	1.2%
36	Nevada	1,246,727	0.6%	28	Iowa	2,358,165	1.2%
46	New Hampshire	648,454	0.3%	29	Connecticut	2,249,861	1.1%
11	New Jersey	5,911,631	3.0%	30	Colorado	2,147,534	1.1%
42	New Mexico	781,150	0.4%	31	Kansas	2,115,015	1.1%
1	New York	18,482,900	9.4%	32	Arkansas	2,050,766	1.0%
9	North Carolina	6,115,774	3.1%	33	West Virginia	1,707,211	0.9%
43	North Dakota	769,880	0.4%	34	Nebraska	1,612,857	0.8%
7	Ohio	7,718,229	3.9%	35	Oregon	1,461,923	0.7%
27	Oklahoma	2,370,273	1.2%	36	Nevada	1,246,727	0.6%
35	Oregon	1,461,923	0.7%	37	Montana	1,042,530	0.5%
5	Pennsylvania	10,259,088	5.2%	38	South Dakota	1,039,983	0.5%
45	Rhode Island	663,734	0.3%	39	Utah	953,754	0.5%
23	South Carolina	2,921,052	1.5%	40	Hawaii	875,714	0.4%
38	South Dakota	1,039,983	0.5%	41	Maine	820,114	0.4%
12	Tennessee	4,673,861	2.4%	42	New Mexico	781,150	0.4%
3	Texas	13,200,657	6.7%	43	North Dakota	769,880	0.4%
39	Utah	953,754	0.5%	44	Idaho	667,687	0.3%
49	Vermont	347,087	0.2%	45	Rhode Island	663,734	0.3%
13	Virginia	4,468,361	2.3%	46	New Hampshire	648,454	0.3%
26	Washington	2,464,033	1.2%	47	Delaware	642,401	0.3%
33	West Virginia	1,707,211	0.9%	48	Wyoming	394,422	0.2%
21	Wisconsin	3,335,415	1.7%	49	Vermont	347,087	0.2%
48	Wyoming	394,422	0.2%	50	Alaska	285,999	0.1%
					District of Columbia	981,412	0.5%

Source: American Hospital Association (Chicago, IL)
"Hospital Statistics" (2006 edition)
*Inpatient days in all nonfederal short-term general and other special hospitals, whose facilities and services are available to the public. Includes days in hospital and nursing home units.

Average Daily Census in Community Hospitals in 2004

National Average = 541,272 Inpatients*

ALPHA ORDER

RANK	STATE	INPATIENTS	RANK	STATE	INPATIENTS
19	Alabama	10,040	1	New York	50,638
50	Alaska	784	2	California	50,278
24	Arizona	7,622	3	Texas	36,166
32	Arkansas	5,619	4	Florida	33,148
2	California	50,278	5	Pennsylvania	28,107
30	Colorado	5,884	6	Illinois	23,030
29	Connecticut	6,164	7	Ohio	21,146
47	Delaware	1,760	8	Michigan	17,205
4	Florida	33,148	9	North Carolina	16,756
10	Georgia	16,695	10	Georgia	16,695
40	Hawaii	2,399	11	New Jersey	16,196
44	Idaho	1,829	12	Tennessee	12,805
6	Illinois	23,030	13	Virginia	12,242
16	Indiana	11,121	14	Massachusetts	12,134
28	Iowa	6,461	15	Missouri	12,076
31	Kansas	5,795	16	Indiana	11,121
20	Kentucky	9,274	17	Minnesota	10,970
18	Louisiana	10,566	18	Louisiana	10,566
41	Maine	2,247	19	Alabama	10,040
22	Maryland	8,738	20	Kentucky	9,274
14	Massachusetts	12,134	21	Wisconsin	9,138
8	Michigan	17,205	22	Maryland	8,738
17	Minnesota	10,970	23	South Carolina	8,003
25	Mississippi	7,593	24	Arizona	7,622
15	Missouri	12,076	25	Mississippi	7,593
37	Montana	2,856	26	Washington	6,751
34	Nebraska	4,419	27	Oklahoma	6,494
36	Nevada	3,416	28	Iowa	6,461
46	New Hampshire	1,777	29	Connecticut	6,164
11	New Jersey	16,196	30	Colorado	5,884
42	New Mexico	2,140	31	Kansas	5,795
1	New York	50,638	32	Arkansas	5,619
9	North Carolina	16,756	33	West Virginia	4,677
43	North Dakota	2,109	34	Nebraska	4,419
7	Ohio	21,146	35	Oregon	4,005
27	Oklahoma	6,494	36	Nevada	3,416
35	Oregon	4,005	37	Montana	2,856
5	Pennsylvania	28,107	38	South Dakota	2,849
45	Rhode Island	1,818	39	Utah	2,613
23	South Carolina	8,003	40	Hawaii	2,399
38	South Dakota	2,849	41	Maine	2,247
12	Tennessee	12,805	42	New Mexico	2,140
3	Texas	36,166	43	North Dakota	2,109
39	Utah	2,613	44	Idaho	1,829
49	Vermont	951	45	Rhode Island	1,818
13	Virginia	12,242	46	New Hampshire	1,777
26	Washington	6,751	47	Delaware	1,760
33	West Virginia	4,677	48	Wyoming	1,081
21	Wisconsin	9,138	49	Vermont	951
48	Wyoming	1,081	50	Alaska	784

District of Columbia 2,689

Source: Morgan Quitno Press using data from American Hospital Association (Chicago, IL)
   "Hospital Statistics" (2006 edition)
*Average total of inpatients receiving care in all nonfederal short-term general and other special hospitals, whose facilities and services are available to the public. Excludes newborns.

Average Stay in Community Hospitals in 2004

National Average = 5.6 Days*

ALPHA ORDER

RANK	STATE	DAYS
43	Alabama	5.1
14	Alaska	6.3
48	Arizona	4.5
29	Arkansas	5.4
33	California	5.3
44	Colorado	4.9
17	Connecticut	5.8
15	Delaware	6.2
38	Florida	5.2
10	Georgia	6.5
5	Hawaii	7.7
38	Idaho	5.2
33	Illinois	5.3
22	Indiana	5.6
8	Iowa	6.6
12	Kansas	6.4
22	Kentucky	5.6
26	Louisiana	5.5
29	Maine	5.4
45	Maryland	4.8
26	Massachusetts	5.5
33	Michigan	5.3
12	Minnesota	6.4
10	Mississippi	6.5
33	Missouri	5.3
2	Montana	9.8
6	Nebraska	7.6
29	Nevada	5.4
26	New Hampshire	5.5
29	New Jersey	5.4
45	New Mexico	4.8
7	New York	7.3
16	North Carolina	6.1
3	North Dakota	8.7
38	Ohio	5.2
38	Oklahoma	5.2
50	Oregon	4.3
22	Pennsylvania	5.6
33	Rhode Island	5.3
19	South Carolina	5.7
1	South Dakota	10.0
19	Tennessee	5.7
38	Texas	5.2
49	Utah	4.4
8	Vermont	6.6
17	Virginia	5.8
47	Washington	4.7
19	West Virginia	5.7
22	Wisconsin	5.6
4	Wyoming	7.8

RANK ORDER

RANK	STATE	DAYS
1	South Dakota	10.0
2	Montana	9.8
3	North Dakota	8.7
4	Wyoming	7.8
5	Hawaii	7.7
6	Nebraska	7.6
7	New York	7.3
8	Iowa	6.6
8	Vermont	6.6
10	Georgia	6.5
10	Mississippi	6.5
12	Kansas	6.4
12	Minnesota	6.4
14	Alaska	6.3
15	Delaware	6.2
16	North Carolina	6.1
17	Connecticut	5.8
17	Virginia	5.8
19	South Carolina	5.7
19	Tennessee	5.7
19	West Virginia	5.7
22	Indiana	5.6
22	Kentucky	5.6
22	Pennsylvania	5.6
22	Wisconsin	5.6
26	Louisiana	5.5
26	Massachusetts	5.5
26	New Hampshire	5.5
29	Arkansas	5.4
29	Maine	5.4
29	Nevada	5.4
29	New Jersey	5.4
33	California	5.3
33	Illinois	5.3
33	Michigan	5.3
33	Missouri	5.3
33	Rhode Island	5.3
38	Florida	5.2
38	Idaho	5.2
38	Ohio	5.2
38	Oklahoma	5.2
38	Texas	5.2
43	Alabama	5.1
44	Colorado	4.9
45	Maryland	4.8
45	New Mexico	4.8
47	Washington	4.7
48	Arizona	4.5
49	Utah	4.4
50	Oregon	4.3

	District of Columbia	7.0

Source: American Hospital Association (Chicago, IL)
    "Hospital Statistics" (2006 edition)
*All nonfederal short-term general and other special hospitals, whose facilities and services are available to the public.

Occupancy Rate in Community Hospitals in 2004

National Rate = 67.0% of Community Hospital Beds Occupied*

ALPHA ORDER

RANK ORDER

RANK	STATE	PERCENT
22	Alabama	65.5
48	Alaska	54.9
15	Arizona	68.3
43	Arkansas	58.7
14	California	69.9
24	Colorado	63.6
3	Connecticut	78.8
1	Delaware	90.0
18	Florida	66.3
17	Georgia	67.6
4	Hawaii	76.2
49	Idaho	53.3
20	Illinois	66.1
40	Indiana	59.2
42	Iowa	59.0
47	Kansas	55.9
37	Kentucky	60.7
36	Louisiana	61.4
25	Maine	63.3
5	Maryland	76.1
7	Massachusetts	74.8
18	Michigan	66.3
16	Minnesota	68.1
45	Mississippi	57.8
28	Missouri	63.1
21	Montana	65.9
38	Nebraska	60.2
9	Nevada	71.9
25	New Hampshire	63.3
8	New Jersey	73.8
44	New Mexico	58.2
2	New York	78.9
10	North Carolina	71.3
41	North Dakota	59.1
25	Ohio	63.3
39	Oklahoma	60.1
34	Oregon	61.6
13	Pennsylvania	70.1
6	Rhode Island	75.8
10	South Carolina	71.3
33	South Dakota	61.8
30	Tennessee	62.9
32	Texas	62.2
45	Utah	57.8
23	Vermont	64.6
12	Virginia	70.6
35	Washington	61.5
28	West Virginia	63.1
31	Wisconsin	62.7
50	Wyoming	52.8

RANK	STATE	PERCENT
1	Delaware	90.0
2	New York	78.9
3	Connecticut	78.8
4	Hawaii	76.2
5	Maryland	76.1
6	Rhode Island	75.8
7	Massachusetts	74.8
8	New Jersey	73.8
9	Nevada	71.9
10	North Carolina	71.3
10	South Carolina	71.3
12	Virginia	70.6
13	Pennsylvania	70.1
14	California	69.9
15	Arizona	68.3
16	Minnesota	68.1
17	Georgia	67.6
18	Florida	66.3
18	Michigan	66.3
20	Illinois	66.1
21	Montana	65.9
22	Alabama	65.5
23	Vermont	64.6
24	Colorado	63.6
25	Maine	63.3
25	New Hampshire	63.3
25	Ohio	63.3
28	Missouri	63.1
28	West Virginia	63.1
30	Tennessee	62.9
31	Wisconsin	62.7
32	Texas	62.2
33	South Dakota	61.8
34	Oregon	61.6
35	Washington	61.5
36	Louisiana	61.4
37	Kentucky	60.7
38	Nebraska	60.2
39	Oklahoma	60.1
40	Indiana	59.2
41	North Dakota	59.1
42	Iowa	59.0
43	Arkansas	58.7
44	New Mexico	58.2
45	Mississippi	57.8
45	Utah	57.8
47	Kansas	55.9
48	Alaska	54.9
49	Idaho	53.3
50	Wyoming	52.8
	District of Columbia	77.9

Source: Morgan Quitno Press using data from American Hospital Association (Chicago, IL) "Hospital Statistics" (2006 edition)

Average daily census compared to number of community hospital beds.

Outpatient Visits to Community Hospitals in 2004

National Total = 571,569,334 Visits*

ALPHA ORDER

RANK ORDER

RANK	STATE	VISITS	% of USA
23	Alabama	8,262,310	1.4%
49	Alaska	1,330,732	0.2%
31	Arizona	5,409,604	0.9%
34	Arkansas	4,842,303	0.8%
2	California	47,465,564	8.3%
27	Colorado	6,954,105	1.2%
26	Connecticut	7,005,863	1.2%
45	Delaware	1,865,949	0.3%
8	Florida	22,366,781	3.9%
14	Georgia	13,397,951	2.3%
46	Hawaii	1,855,956	0.3%
42	Idaho	2,429,887	0.4%
6	Illinois	28,334,842	5.0%
12	Indiana	15,512,685	2.7%
20	Iowa	9,684,866	1.7%
30	Kansas	5,860,647	1.0%
22	Kentucky	8,880,146	1.6%
17	Louisiana	10,380,097	1.8%
37	Maine	4,117,796	0.7%
28	Maryland	6,931,741	1.2%
9	Massachusetts	19,036,685	3.3%
7	Michigan	27,736,009	4.9%
21	Minnesota	9,530,685	1.7%
36	Mississippi	4,215,042	0.7%
11	Missouri	16,186,432	2.8%
40	Montana	2,895,310	0.5%
38	Nebraska	3,949,477	0.7%
41	Nevada	2,445,480	0.4%
39	New Hampshire	2,967,272	0.5%
10	New Jersey	17,722,403	3.1%
33	New Mexico	5,041,166	0.9%
1	New York	49,730,066	8.7%
13	North Carolina	15,314,534	2.7%
47	North Dakota	1,849,173	0.3%
5	Ohio	30,547,203	5.3%
32	Oklahoma	5,330,361	0.9%
24	Oregon	7,859,237	1.4%
3	Pennsylvania	33,412,844	5.8%
44	Rhode Island	2,143,664	0.4%
25	South Carolina	7,045,171	1.2%
48	South Dakota	1,570,990	0.3%
18	Tennessee	10,262,350	1.8%
4	Texas	32,441,860	5.7%
35	Utah	4,719,118	0.8%
43	Vermont	2,274,633	0.4%
15	Virginia	11,948,658	2.1%
19	Washington	10,093,842	1.8%
29	West Virginia	6,045,351	1.1%
16	Wisconsin	11,819,012	2.1%
50	Wyoming	920,058	0.2%

RANK	STATE	VISITS	% of USA
1	New York	49,730,066	8.7%
2	California	47,465,564	8.3%
3	Pennsylvania	33,412,844	5.8%
4	Texas	32,441,860	5.7%
5	Ohio	30,547,203	5.3%
6	Illinois	28,334,842	5.0%
7	Michigan	27,736,009	4.9%
8	Florida	22,366,781	3.9%
9	Massachusetts	19,036,685	3.3%
10	New Jersey	17,722,403	3.1%
11	Missouri	16,186,432	2.8%
12	Indiana	15,512,685	2.7%
13	North Carolina	15,314,534	2.7%
14	Georgia	13,397,951	2.3%
15	Virginia	11,948,658	2.1%
16	Wisconsin	11,819,012	2.1%
17	Louisiana	10,380,097	1.8%
18	Tennessee	10,262,350	1.8%
19	Washington	10,093,842	1.8%
20	Iowa	9,684,866	1.7%
21	Minnesota	9,530,685	1.7%
22	Kentucky	8,880,146	1.6%
23	Alabama	8,262,310	1.4%
24	Oregon	7,859,237	1.4%
25	South Carolina	7,045,171	1.2%
26	Connecticut	7,005,863	1.2%
27	Colorado	6,954,105	1.2%
28	Maryland	6,931,741	1.2%
29	West Virginia	6,045,351	1.1%
30	Kansas	5,860,647	1.0%
31	Arizona	5,409,604	0.9%
32	Oklahoma	5,330,361	0.9%
33	New Mexico	5,041,166	0.9%
34	Arkansas	4,842,303	0.8%
35	Utah	4,719,118	0.8%
36	Mississippi	4,215,042	0.7%
37	Maine	4,117,796	0.7%
38	Nebraska	3,949,477	0.7%
39	New Hampshire	2,967,272	0.5%
40	Montana	2,895,310	0.5%
41	Nevada	2,445,480	0.4%
42	Idaho	2,429,887	0.4%
43	Vermont	2,274,633	0.4%
44	Rhode Island	2,143,664	0.4%
45	Delaware	1,865,949	0.3%
46	Hawaii	1,855,956	0.3%
47	North Dakota	1,849,173	0.3%
48	South Dakota	1,570,990	0.3%
49	Alaska	1,330,732	0.2%
50	Wyoming	920,058	0.2%
	District of Columbia	1,625,423	0.3%

Source: American Hospital Association (Chicago, IL)
"Hospital Statistics" (2006 edition)

*All nonfederal short-term general and other special hospitals, whose facilities and services are available to the public. Includes emergency and other visits.

Emergency Outpatient Visits to Community Hospitals in 2004

National Total = 112,603,969 Visits*

ALPHA ORDER

RANK	STATE	VISITS	% of USA
21	Alabama	2,026,709	1.8%
48	Alaska	253,405	0.2%
23	Arizona	1,747,614	1.6%
30	Arkansas	1,220,658	1.1%
1	California	10,035,153	8.9%
29	Colorado	1,345,618	1.2%
27	Connecticut	1,419,179	1.3%
44	Delaware	325,692	0.3%
4	Florida	6,782,103	6.0%
9	Georgia	3,492,747	3.1%
43	Hawaii	325,843	0.3%
41	Idaho	479,734	0.4%
7	Illinois	4,947,646	4.4%
15	Indiana	2,624,977	2.3%
33	Iowa	1,065,819	0.9%
34	Kansas	933,816	0.8%
18	Kentucky	2,257,276	2.0%
17	Louisiana	2,468,882	2.2%
37	Maine	711,570	0.6%
19	Maryland	2,162,198	1.9%
14	Massachusetts	2,874,936	2.6%
8	Michigan	4,155,147	3.7%
26	Minnesota	1,558,720	1.4%
25	Mississippi	1,602,016	1.4%
16	Missouri	2,561,625	2.3%
45	Montana	294,359	0.3%
40	Nebraska	551,836	0.5%
38	Nevada	606,094	0.5%
39	New Hampshire	563,318	0.5%
11	New Jersey	3,027,063	2.7%
36	New Mexico	725,603	0.6%
3	New York	7,612,589	6.8%
10	North Carolina	3,483,332	3.1%
47	North Dakota	254,409	0.2%
5	Ohio	5,401,226	4.8%
28	Oklahoma	1,358,288	1.2%
31	Oregon	1,147,196	1.0%
6	Pennsylvania	5,277,055	4.7%
42	Rhode Island	431,433	0.4%
24	South Carolina	1,694,314	1.5%
50	South Dakota	215,168	0.2%
12	Tennessee	2,957,496	2.6%
2	Texas	7,966,137	7.1%
35	Utah	829,030	0.7%
46	Vermont	261,642	0.2%
13	Virginia	2,915,593	2.6%
20	Washington	2,070,588	1.8%
32	West Virginia	1,130,236	1.0%
22	Wisconsin	1,861,206	1.7%
49	Wyoming	215,438	0.2%

RANK ORDER

RANK	STATE	VISITS	% of USA
1	California	10,035,153	8.9%
2	Texas	7,966,137	7.1%
3	New York	7,612,589	6.8%
4	Florida	6,782,103	6.0%
5	Ohio	5,401,226	4.8%
6	Pennsylvania	5,277,055	4.7%
7	Illinois	4,947,646	4.4%
8	Michigan	4,155,147	3.7%
9	Georgia	3,492,747	3.1%
10	North Carolina	3,483,332	3.1%
11	New Jersey	3,027,063	2.7%
12	Tennessee	2,957,496	2.6%
13	Virginia	2,915,593	2.6%
14	Massachusetts	2,874,936	2.6%
15	Indiana	2,624,977	2.3%
16	Missouri	2,561,625	2.3%
17	Louisiana	2,468,882	2.2%
18	Kentucky	2,257,276	2.0%
19	Maryland	2,162,198	1.9%
20	Washington	2,070,588	1.8%
21	Alabama	2,026,709	1.8%
22	Wisconsin	1,861,206	1.7%
23	Arizona	1,747,614	1.6%
24	South Carolina	1,694,314	1.5%
25	Mississippi	1,602,016	1.4%
26	Minnesota	1,558,720	1.4%
27	Connecticut	1,419,179	1.3%
28	Oklahoma	1,358,288	1.2%
29	Colorado	1,345,618	1.2%
30	Arkansas	1,220,658	1.1%
31	Oregon	1,147,196	1.0%
32	West Virginia	1,130,236	1.0%
33	Iowa	1,065,819	0.9%
34	Kansas	933,816	0.8%
35	Utah	829,030	0.7%
36	New Mexico	725,603	0.6%
37	Maine	711,570	0.6%
38	Nevada	606,094	0.5%
39	New Hampshire	563,318	0.5%
40	Nebraska	551,836	0.5%
41	Idaho	479,734	0.4%
42	Rhode Island	431,433	0.4%
43	Hawaii	325,843	0.3%
44	Delaware	325,692	0.3%
45	Montana	294,359	0.3%
46	Vermont	261,642	0.2%
47	North Dakota	254,409	0.2%
48	Alaska	253,405	0.2%
49	Wyoming	215,438	0.2%
50	South Dakota	215,168	0.2%
	District of Columbia	374,237	0.3%

Source: American Hospital Association (Chicago, IL)
    "Hospital Statistics" (2006 edition)
*All nonfederal short-term general and other special hospitals, whose facilities and services are available to the public.

Surgical Operations in Community Hospitals in 2004

National Total = 27,401,836 Surgical Operations*

Source: American Hospital Association (Chicago, IL)
   "Hospital Statistics" (2006 edition)
*Includes inpatient and outpatient surgeries.

ALPHA ORDER

RANK	STATE	OPERATIONS	% of USA
19	Alabama	545,404	2.0%
48	Alaska	71,544	0.3%
26	Arizona	397,122	1.4%
34	Arkansas	261,586	1.0%
1	California	2,213,817	8.1%
27	Colorado	330,144	1.2%
29	Connecticut	311,690	1.1%
43	Delaware	94,014	0.3%
5	Florida	1,458,734	5.3%
10	Georgia	799,571	2.9%
46	Hawaii	75,444	0.3%
42	Idaho	101,175	0.4%
8	Illinois	1,133,839	4.1%
14	Indiana	640,554	2.3%
23	Iowa	442,694	1.6%
33	Kansas	264,932	1.0%
20	Kentucky	535,546	2.0%
24	Louisiana	440,059	1.6%
38	Maine	161,892	0.6%
18	Maryland	551,702	2.0%
11	Massachusetts	752,668	2.7%
7	Michigan	1,135,368	4.1%
21	Minnesota	489,114	1.8%
32	Mississippi	272,640	1.0%
15	Missouri	613,710	2.2%
49	Montana	70,978	0.3%
36	Nebraska	196,165	0.7%
37	Nevada	178,915	0.7%
39	New Hampshire	131,947	0.5%
13	New Jersey	708,155	2.6%
40	New Mexico	129,775	0.5%
2	New York	1,956,718	7.1%
9	North Carolina	913,409	3.3%
45	North Dakota	75,757	0.3%
6	Ohio	1,206,848	4.4%
28	Oklahoma	317,175	1.2%
30	Oregon	303,249	1.1%
4	Pennsylvania	1,540,473	5.6%
41	Rhode Island	127,974	0.5%
22	South Carolina	451,133	1.6%
44	South Dakota	82,201	0.3%
16	Tennessee	612,247	2.2%
3	Texas	1,807,876	6.6%
35	Utah	221,194	0.8%
47	Vermont	73,250	0.3%
12	Virginia	721,680	2.6%
25	Washington	437,713	1.6%
31	West Virginia	290,716	1.1%
17	Wisconsin	601,794	2.2%
50	Wyoming	43,030	0.2%

RANK ORDER

RANK	STATE	OPERATIONS	% of USA
1	California	2,213,817	8.1%
2	New York	1,956,718	7.1%
3	Texas	1,807,876	6.6%
4	Pennsylvania	1,540,473	5.6%
5	Florida	1,458,734	5.3%
6	Ohio	1,206,848	4.4%
7	Michigan	1,135,368	4.1%
8	Illinois	1,133,839	4.1%
9	North Carolina	913,409	3.3%
10	Georgia	799,571	2.9%
11	Massachusetts	752,668	2.7%
12	Virginia	721,680	2.6%
13	New Jersey	708,155	2.6%
14	Indiana	640,554	2.3%
15	Missouri	613,710	2.2%
16	Tennessee	612,247	2.2%
17	Wisconsin	601,794	2.2%
18	Maryland	551,702	2.0%
19	Alabama	545,404	2.0%
20	Kentucky	535,546	2.0%
21	Minnesota	489,114	1.8%
22	South Carolina	451,133	1.6%
23	Iowa	442,694	1.6%
24	Louisiana	440,059	1.6%
25	Washington	437,713	1.6%
26	Arizona	397,122	1.4%
27	Colorado	330,144	1.2%
28	Oklahoma	317,175	1.2%
29	Connecticut	311,690	1.1%
30	Oregon	303,249	1.1%
31	West Virginia	290,716	1.1%
32	Mississippi	272,640	1.0%
33	Kansas	264,932	1.0%
34	Arkansas	261,586	1.0%
35	Utah	221,194	0.8%
36	Nebraska	196,165	0.7%
37	Nevada	178,915	0.7%
38	Maine	161,892	0.6%
39	New Hampshire	131,947	0.5%
40	New Mexico	129,775	0.5%
41	Rhode Island	127,974	0.5%
42	Idaho	101,175	0.4%
43	Delaware	94,014	0.3%
44	South Dakota	82,201	0.3%
45	North Dakota	75,757	0.3%
46	Hawaii	75,444	0.3%
47	Vermont	73,250	0.3%
48	Alaska	71,544	0.3%
49	Montana	70,978	0.3%
50	Wyoming	43,030	0.2%
	District of Columbia	106,401	0.4%

Medicare and Medicaid Certified Facilities in 2006

National Total = 254,270 Facilities*

ALPHA ORDER

ALPHA ORDER

RANK	STATE	FACILITIES	% of USA
19	Alabama	4,393	1.7%
48	Alaska	583	0.2%
25	Arizona	3,934	1.5%
32	Arkansas	2,786	1.1%
1	California	24,457	9.6%
28	Colorado	3,370	1.3%
30	Connecticut	3,235	1.3%
47	Delaware	824	0.3%
3	Florida	16,907	6.6%
9	Georgia	7,804	3.1%
44	Hawaii	969	0.4%
40	Idaho	1,268	0.5%
6	Illinois	10,929	4.3%
11	Indiana	6,606	2.6%
27	Iowa	3,769	1.5%
29	Kansas	3,350	1.3%
23	Kentucky	4,117	1.6%
15	Louisiana	5,598	2.2%
39	Maine	1,326	0.5%
18	Maryland	4,449	1.7%
17	Massachusetts	4,638	1.8%
8	Michigan	8,277	3.3%
26	Minnesota	3,930	1.5%
31	Mississippi	3,040	1.2%
13	Missouri	6,179	2.4%
43	Montana	1,009	0.4%
35	Nebraska	2,169	0.9%
38	Nevada	1,478	0.6%
41	New Hampshire	1,172	0.5%
12	New Jersey	6,420	2.5%
36	New Mexico	1,679	0.7%
4	New York	12,592	5.0%
10	North Carolina	7,486	2.9%
46	North Dakota	876	0.3%
5	Ohio	11,832	4.7%
22	Oklahoma	4,120	1.6%
33	Oregon	2,697	1.1%
7	Pennsylvania	9,934	3.9%
45	Rhode Island	968	0.4%
24	South Carolina	4,065	1.6%
42	South Dakota	1,051	0.4%
14	Tennessee	5,706	2.2%
2	Texas	22,957	9.0%
37	Utah	1,613	0.6%
49	Vermont	566	0.2%
16	Virginia	5,477	2.2%
21	Washington	4,122	1.6%
34	West Virginia	2,214	0.9%
20	Wisconsin	4,142	1.6%
50	Wyoming	540	0.2%

RANK ORDER

RANK	STATE	FACILITIES	% of USA
1	California	24,457	9.6%
2	Texas	22,957	9.0%
3	Florida	16,907	6.6%
4	New York	12,592	5.0%
5	Ohio	11,832	4.7%
6	Illinois	10,929	4.3%
7	Pennsylvania	9,934	3.9%
8	Michigan	8,277	3.3%
9	Georgia	7,804	3.1%
10	North Carolina	7,486	2.9%
11	Indiana	6,606	2.6%
12	New Jersey	6,420	2.5%
13	Missouri	6,179	2.4%
14	Tennessee	5,706	2.2%
15	Louisiana	5,598	2.2%
16	Virginia	5,477	2.2%
17	Massachusetts	4,638	1.8%
18	Maryland	4,449	1.7%
19	Alabama	4,393	1.7%
20	Wisconsin	4,142	1.6%
21	Washington	4,122	1.6%
22	Oklahoma	4,120	1.6%
23	Kentucky	4,117	1.6%
24	South Carolina	4,065	1.6%
25	Arizona	3,934	1.5%
26	Minnesota	3,930	1.5%
27	Iowa	3,769	1.5%
28	Colorado	3,370	1.3%
29	Kansas	3,350	1.3%
30	Connecticut	3,235	1.3%
31	Mississippi	3,040	1.2%
32	Arkansas	2,786	1.1%
33	Oregon	2,697	1.1%
34	West Virginia	2,214	0.9%
35	Nebraska	2,169	0.9%
36	New Mexico	1,679	0.7%
37	Utah	1,613	0.6%
38	Nevada	1,478	0.6%
39	Maine	1,326	0.5%
40	Idaho	1,268	0.5%
41	New Hampshire	1,172	0.5%
42	South Dakota	1,051	0.4%
43	Montana	1,009	0.4%
44	Hawaii	969	0.4%
45	Rhode Island	968	0.4%
46	North Dakota	876	0.3%
47	Delaware	824	0.3%
48	Alaska	583	0.2%
49	Vermont	566	0.2%
50	Wyoming	540	0.2%
	District of Columbia	647	0.3%

*Source: U.S. Department of Health and Human Services, Centers for Medicare and Medicaid Services
OSCAR Report 10 (January 9, 2006)*

*Certified by CMS to participate in the Medicare/Medicaid programs. All provider groups including hospitals, home health agencies, rural health centers, community mental health centers, nursing facilities, outpatient physical therapy facilities, hospices and laboratories. National total does not include 1,379 certified facilities in U.S. territories.

Medicare and Medicaid Certified Hospitals in 2006

National Total = 6,115 Hospitals*

ALPHA ORDER				RANK ORDER			
RANK	STATE	HOSPITALS	% of USA	RANK	STATE	HOSPITALS	% of USA
20	Alabama	128	2.1%	1	Texas	527	8.6%
47	Alaska	24	0.4%	2	California	421	6.9%
29	Arizona	95	1.6%	3	New York	244	4.0%
26	Arkansas	107	1.7%	4	Pennsylvania	241	3.9%
2	California	421	6.9%	5	Florida	239	3.9%
30	Colorado	88	1.4%	6	Louisiana	236	3.9%
41	Connecticut	45	0.7%	7	Ohio	219	3.6%
50	Delaware	10	0.2%	8	Illinois	216	3.5%
5	Florida	239	3.9%	9	Georgia	177	2.9%
9	Georgia	177	2.9%	10	Michigan	176	2.9%
46	Hawaii	28	0.5%	11	Kansas	160	2.6%
39	Idaho	48	0.8%	12	Indiana	158	2.6%
8	Illinois	216	3.5%	13	Tennessee	155	2.5%
12	Indiana	158	2.6%	14	Oklahoma	154	2.5%
19	Iowa	129	2.1%	15	Missouri	150	2.5%
11	Kansas	160	2.6%	16	Minnesota	147	2.4%
21	Kentucky	121	2.0%	17	Wisconsin	144	2.4%
6	Louisiana	236	3.9%	18	North Carolina	136	2.2%
42	Maine	44	0.7%	19	Iowa	129	2.1%
34	Maryland	64	1.0%	20	Alabama	128	2.1%
23	Massachusetts	113	1.8%	21	Kentucky	121	2.0%
10	Michigan	176	2.9%	22	Mississippi	114	1.9%
16	Minnesota	147	2.4%	23	Massachusetts	113	1.8%
22	Mississippi	114	1.9%	24	Virginia	112	1.8%
15	Missouri	150	2.5%	25	New Jersey	110	1.8%
34	Montana	64	1.0%	26	Arkansas	107	1.7%
28	Nebraska	100	1.6%	27	Washington	102	1.7%
43	Nevada	43	0.7%	28	Nebraska	100	1.6%
44	New Hampshire	30	0.5%	29	Arizona	95	1.6%
25	New Jersey	110	1.8%	30	Colorado	88	1.4%
37	New Mexico	52	0.9%	31	South Carolina	78	1.3%
3	New York	244	4.0%	32	West Virginia	69	1.1%
18	North Carolina	136	2.2%	33	South Dakota	66	1.1%
38	North Dakota	50	0.8%	34	Maryland	64	1.0%
7	Ohio	219	3.6%	34	Montana	64	1.0%
14	Oklahoma	154	2.5%	36	Oregon	60	1.0%
36	Oregon	60	1.0%	37	New Mexico	52	0.9%
4	Pennsylvania	241	3.9%	38	North Dakota	50	0.8%
48	Rhode Island	15	0.2%	39	Idaho	48	0.8%
31	South Carolina	78	1.3%	39	Utah	48	0.8%
33	South Dakota	66	1.1%	41	Connecticut	45	0.7%
13	Tennessee	155	2.5%	42	Maine	44	0.7%
1	Texas	527	8.6%	43	Nevada	43	0.7%
39	Utah	48	0.8%	44	New Hampshire	30	0.5%
48	Vermont	15	0.2%	45	Wyoming	29	0.5%
24	Virginia	112	1.8%	46	Hawaii	28	0.5%
27	Washington	102	1.7%	47	Alaska	24	0.4%
32	West Virginia	69	1.1%	48	Rhode Island	15	0.2%
17	Wisconsin	144	2.4%	48	Vermont	15	0.2%
45	Wyoming	29	0.5%	50	Delaware	10	0.2%
					District of Columbia	14	0.2%

Source: U.S. Department of Health and Human Services, Centers for Medicare and Medicaid Services OSCAR Database (January 12, 2006)

*Certified by CMS to participate in the Medicare/Medicaid programs. Excludes licensed facilities that do not accept federal funding and facilities managed by the Department of Veterans Affairs. National total does not include 64 certified hospitals in U.S. territories.

Beds in Medicare and Medicaid Certified Hospitals in 2006

National Total = 935,691 Beds*

ALPHA ORDER

RANK	STATE	BEDS	% of USA	RANK	STATE	BEDS	% of USA
16	Alabama	19,679	2.1%	1	California	80,785	8.6%
49	Alaska	1,523	0.2%	2	New York	71,454	7.6%
25	Arizona	13,779	1.5%	3	Texas	65,449	7.0%
31	Arkansas	11,059	1.2%	4	Florida	56,534	6.0%
1	California	80,785	8.6%	5	Illinois	45,526	4.9%
28	Colorado	12,041	1.3%	6	Ohio	45,264	4.8%
32	Connecticut	10,243	1.1%	7	Pennsylvania	39,707	4.2%
47	Delaware	2,261	0.2%	8	New Jersey	30,658	3.3%
4	Florida	56,534	6.0%	9	Michigan	28,529	3.0%
11	Georgia	24,889	2.7%	10	North Carolina	25,671	2.7%
46	Hawaii	2,740	0.3%	11	Georgia	24,889	2.7%
44	Idaho	3,250	0.3%	12	Tennessee	24,669	2.6%
5	Illinois	45,526	4.9%	13	Missouri	24,217	2.6%
17	Indiana	19,676	2.1%	14	Louisiana	22,387	2.4%
29	Iowa	11,901	1.3%	15	Virginia	20,904	2.2%
30	Kansas	11,317	1.2%	16	Alabama	19,679	2.1%
20	Kentucky	17,405	1.9%	17	Indiana	19,676	2.1%
14	Louisiana	22,387	2.4%	18	Massachusetts	19,590	2.1%
39	Maine	4,173	0.4%	19	Wisconsin	18,354	2.0%
22	Maryland	15,868	1.7%	20	Kentucky	17,405	1.9%
18	Massachusetts	19,590	2.1%	21	Minnesota	16,300	1.7%
9	Michigan	28,529	3.0%	22	Maryland	15,868	1.7%
21	Minnesota	16,300	1.7%	23	Oklahoma	14,812	1.6%
26	Mississippi	13,060	1.4%	24	Washington	13,824	1.5%
13	Missouri	24,217	2.6%	25	Arizona	13,779	1.5%
45	Montana	2,931	0.3%	26	Mississippi	13,060	1.4%
35	Nebraska	6,678	0.7%	27	South Carolina	12,580	1.3%
36	Nevada	5,613	0.6%	28	Colorado	12,041	1.3%
41	New Hampshire	3,541	0.4%	29	Iowa	11,901	1.3%
8	New Jersey	30,658	3.3%	30	Kansas	11,317	1.2%
38	New Mexico	4,911	0.5%	31	Arkansas	11,059	1.2%
2	New York	71,454	7.6%	32	Connecticut	10,243	1.1%
10	North Carolina	25,671	2.7%	33	West Virginia	9,483	1.0%
43	North Dakota	3,259	0.3%	34	Oregon	7,456	0.8%
6	Ohio	45,264	4.8%	35	Nebraska	6,678	0.7%
23	Oklahoma	14,812	1.6%	36	Nevada	5,613	0.6%
34	Oregon	7,456	0.8%	37	Utah	5,113	0.5%
7	Pennsylvania	39,707	4.2%	38	New Mexico	4,911	0.5%
40	Rhode Island	3,664	0.4%	39	Maine	4,173	0.4%
27	South Carolina	12,580	1.3%	40	Rhode Island	3,664	0.4%
42	South Dakota	3,379	0.4%	41	New Hampshire	3,541	0.4%
12	Tennessee	24,669	2.6%	42	South Dakota	3,379	0.4%
3	Texas	65,449	7.0%	43	North Dakota	3,259	0.3%
37	Utah	5,113	0.5%	44	Idaho	3,250	0.3%
48	Vermont	1,828	0.2%	45	Montana	2,931	0.3%
15	Virginia	20,904	2.2%	46	Hawaii	2,740	0.3%
24	Washington	13,824	1.5%	47	Delaware	2,261	0.2%
33	West Virginia	9,483	1.0%	48	Vermont	1,828	0.2%
19	Wisconsin	18,354	2.0%	49	Alaska	1,523	0.2%
50	Wyoming	1,451	0.2%	50	Wyoming	1,451	0.2%
					District of Columbia	4,306	0.5%

Source: U.S. Department of Health and Human Services, Centers for Medicare and Medicaid Services OSCAR Database (January 12, 2006)

*Beds in hospitals certified by CMS to participate in the Medicare/Medicaid programs. Excludes licensed facilities that do not accept federal funding and facilities managed by the Department of Veterans Affairs. National total does not include 11,386 beds in U.S. territories.

Medicare and Medicaid Certified Children's Hospitals in 2006

National Total = 80 Hospitals*

ALPHA ORDER					RANK ORDER			
RANK	STATE	HOSPITALS	% of USA		RANK	STATE	HOSPITALS	% of USA
9	Alabama	2	2.5%		1	California	10	12.5%
34	Alaska	0	0.0%		2	Texas	8	10.0%
9	Arizona	2	2.5%		3	Ohio	7	8.8%
20	Arkansas	1	1.3%		4	Pennsylvania	6	7.5%
1	California	10	12.5%		5	Minnesota	3	3.8%
20	Colorado	1	1.3%		5	Missouri	3	3.8%
20	Connecticut	1	1.3%		5	Virginia	3	3.8%
20	Delaware	1	1.3%		5	Wisconsin	3	3.8%
9	Florida	2	2.5%		9	Alabama	2	2.5%
9	Georgia	2	2.5%		9	Arizona	2	2.5%
20	Hawaii	1	1.3%		9	Florida	2	2.5%
34	Idaho	0	0.0%		9	Georgia	2	2.5%
9	Illinois	2	2.5%		9	Illinois	2	2.5%
20	Indiana	1	1.3%		9	Maryland	2	2.5%
34	Iowa	0	0.0%		9	Massachusetts	2	2.5%
20	Kansas	1	1.3%		9	Nebraska	2	2.5%
34	Kentucky	0	0.0%		9	Oklahoma	2	2.5%
20	Louisiana	1	1.3%		9	Tennessee	2	2.5%
34	Maine	0	0.0%		9	Washington	2	2.5%
9	Maryland	2	2.5%		20	Arkansas	1	1.3%
9	Massachusetts	2	2.5%		20	Colorado	1	1.3%
20	Michigan	1	1.3%		20	Connecticut	1	1.3%
5	Minnesota	3	3.8%		20	Delaware	1	1.3%
34	Mississippi	0	0.0%		20	Hawaii	1	1.3%
5	Missouri	3	3.8%		20	Indiana	1	1.3%
34	Montana	0	0.0%		20	Kansas	1	1.3%
9	Nebraska	2	2.5%		20	Louisiana	1	1.3%
34	Nevada	0	0.0%		20	Michigan	1	1.3%
34	New Hampshire	0	0.0%		20	New Jersey	1	1.3%
20	New Jersey	1	1.3%		20	New Mexico	1	1.3%
20	New Mexico	1	1.3%		20	New York	1	1.3%
20	New York	1	1.3%		20	South Dakota	1	1.3%
34	North Carolina	0	0.0%		20	Utah	1	1.3%
34	North Dakota	0	0.0%		34	Alaska	0	0.0%
3	Ohio	7	8.8%		34	Idaho	0	0.0%
9	Oklahoma	2	2.5%		34	Iowa	0	0.0%
34	Oregon	0	0.0%		34	Kentucky	0	0.0%
4	Pennsylvania	6	7.5%		34	Maine	0	0.0%
34	Rhode Island	0	0.0%		34	Mississippi	0	0.0%
34	South Carolina	0	0.0%		34	Montana	0	0.0%
20	South Dakota	1	1.3%		34	Nevada	0	0.0%
9	Tennessee	2	2.5%		34	New Hampshire	0	0.0%
2	Texas	8	10.0%		34	North Carolina	0	0.0%
20	Utah	1	1.3%		34	North Dakota	0	0.0%
34	Vermont	0	0.0%		34	Oregon	0	0.0%
5	Virginia	3	3.8%		34	Rhode Island	0	0.0%
9	Washington	2	2.5%		34	South Carolina	0	0.0%
34	West Virginia	0	0.0%		34	Vermont	0	0.0%
5	Wisconsin	3	3.8%		34	West Virginia	0	0.0%
34	Wyoming	0	0.0%		34	Wyoming	0	0.0%
						District of Columbia	1	1.3%

Source: U.S. Department of Health and Human Services, Centers for Medicare and Medicaid Services
OSCAR Database (January 10, 2006)
*Certified by CMS to participate in the Medicare/Medicaid programs. National total does not include one facility in
U.S. territories. Excludes licensed facilities that do not accept federal funding and facilities managed by the
Department of Veterans Affairs.

Beds in Medicare and Medicaid Certified Children's Hospitals in 2006

National Total = 11,948 Beds*

RANK	STATE	BEDS	% of USA
7	Alabama	424	3.5%
34	Alaska	0	0.0%
17	Arizona	235	2.0%
13	Arkansas	280	2.3%
1	California	1,665	13.9%
16	Colorado	253	2.1%
26	Connecticut	97	0.8%
26	Delaware	97	0.8%
7	Florida	424	3.5%
5	Georgia	441	3.7%
20	Hawaii	201	1.7%
34	Idaho	0	0.0%
10	Illinois	339	2.8%
33	Indiana	20	0.2%
34	Iowa	0	0.0%
31	Kansas	34	0.3%
34	Kentucky	0	0.0%
21	Louisiana	188	1.6%
34	Maine	0	0.0%
24	Maryland	150	1.3%
9	Massachusetts	421	3.5%
19	Michigan	228	1.9%
10	Minnesota	339	2.8%
34	Mississippi	0	0.0%
6	Missouri	432	3.6%
34	Montana	0	0.0%
24	Nebraska	150	1.3%
34	Nevada	0	0.0%
34	New Hampshire	0	0.0%
30	New Jersey	74	0.6%
32	New Mexico	28	0.2%
29	New York	92	0.8%
34	North Carolina	0	0.0%
34	North Dakota	0	0.0%
3	Ohio	1,419	11.9%
23	Oklahoma	160	1.3%
34	Oregon	0	0.0%
4	Pennsylvania	679	5.7%
34	Rhode Island	0	0.0%
34	South Carolina	0	0.0%
28	South Dakota	96	0.8%
22	Tennessee	175	1.5%
2	Texas	1,494	12.5%
18	Utah	232	1.9%
34	Vermont	0	0.0%
12	Virginia	286	2.4%
14	Washington	276	2.3%
34	West Virginia	0	0.0%
14	Wisconsin	276	2.3%
34	Wyoming	0	0.0%

RANK	STATE	BEDS	% of USA
1	California	1,665	13.9%
2	Texas	1,494	12.5%
3	Ohio	1,419	11.9%
4	Pennsylvania	679	5.7%
5	Georgia	441	3.7%
6	Missouri	432	3.6%
7	Alabama	424	3.5%
7	Florida	424	3.5%
9	Massachusetts	421	3.5%
10	Illinois	339	2.8%
10	Minnesota	339	2.8%
12	Virginia	286	2.4%
13	Arkansas	280	2.3%
14	Washington	276	2.3%
14	Wisconsin	276	2.3%
16	Colorado	253	2.1%
17	Arizona	235	2.0%
18	Utah	232	1.9%
19	Michigan	228	1.9%
20	Hawaii	201	1.7%
21	Louisiana	188	1.6%
22	Tennessee	175	1.5%
23	Oklahoma	160	1.3%
24	Maryland	150	1.3%
24	Nebraska	150	1.3%
26	Connecticut	97	0.8%
26	Delaware	97	0.8%
28	South Dakota	96	0.8%
29	New York	92	0.8%
30	New Jersey	74	0.6%
31	Kansas	34	0.3%
32	New Mexico	28	0.2%
33	Indiana	20	0.2%
34	Alaska	0	0.0%
34	Idaho	0	0.0%
34	Iowa	0	0.0%
34	Kentucky	0	0.0%
34	Maine	0	0.0%
34	Mississippi	0	0.0%
34	Montana	0	0.0%
34	Nevada	0	0.0%
34	New Hampshire	0	0.0%
34	North Carolina	0	0.0%
34	North Dakota	0	0.0%
34	Oregon	0	0.0%
34	Rhode Island	0	0.0%
34	South Carolina	0	0.0%
34	Vermont	0	0.0%
34	West Virginia	0	0.0%
34	Wyoming	0	0.0%
	District of Columbia	243	2.0%

Source: U.S. Department of Health and Human Services, Centers for Medicare and Medicaid Services
    OSCAR Database (January 10, 2006)

*Certified by CMS to participate in the Medicare/Medicaid programs. National total does not include 215 beds in one facility in U.S. territories. Excludes licensed facilities that do not accept federal funding and facilities managed by the Department of Veterans Affairs.

Medicare and Medicaid Certified Rehabilitation Hospitals in 2006

National Total = 216 Hospitals*

ALPHA ORDER					RANK ORDER			
RANK	STATE	HOSPITALS	% of USA		RANK	STATE	HOSPITALS	% of USA
6	Alabama	7	3.2%		1	Texas	31	14.4%
41	Alaska	0	0.0%		2	Louisiana	26	12.0%
9	Arizona	6	2.8%		3	Pennsylvania	17	7.9%
6	Arkansas	7	3.2%		4	Florida	14	6.5%
9	California	6	2.8%		5	New Jersey	9	4.2%
21	Colorado	3	1.4%		6	Alabama	7	3.2%
30	Connecticut	1	0.5%		6	Arkansas	7	3.2%
41	Delaware	0	0.0%		6	Massachusetts	7	3.2%
4	Florida	14	6.5%		9	Arizona	6	2.8%
25	Georgia	2	0.9%		9	California	6	2.8%
30	Hawaii	1	0.5%		9	Indiana	6	2.8%
30	Idaho	1	0.5%		9	Kentucky	6	2.8%
19	Illinois	4	1.9%		9	Tennessee	6	2.8%
9	Indiana	6	2.8%		9	West Virginia	6	2.8%
41	Iowa	0	0.0%		15	Michigan	5	2.3%
19	Kansas	4	1.9%		15	New Mexico	5	2.3%
9	Kentucky	6	2.8%		15	South Carolina	5	2.3%
2	Louisiana	26	12.0%		15	Virginia	5	2.3%
30	Maine	1	0.5%		19	Illinois	4	1.9%
25	Maryland	2	0.9%		19	Kansas	4	1.9%
6	Massachusetts	7	3.2%		21	Colorado	3	1.4%
15	Michigan	5	2.3%		21	Missouri	3	1.4%
30	Minnesota	1	0.5%		21	Nevada	3	1.4%
41	Mississippi	0	0.0%		21	Ohio	3	1.4%
21	Missouri	3	1.4%		25	Georgia	2	0.9%
41	Montana	0	0.0%		25	Maryland	2	0.9%
30	Nebraska	1	0.5%		25	New Hampshire	2	0.9%
21	Nevada	3	1.4%		25	North Carolina	2	0.9%
25	New Hampshire	2	0.9%		25	Oklahoma	2	0.9%
5	New Jersey	9	4.2%		30	Connecticut	1	0.5%
15	New Mexico	5	2.3%		30	Hawaii	1	0.5%
30	New York	1	0.5%		30	Idaho	1	0.5%
25	North Carolina	2	0.9%		30	Maine	1	0.5%
41	North Dakota	0	0.0%		30	Minnesota	1	0.5%
21	Ohio	3	1.4%		30	Nebraska	1	0.5%
25	Oklahoma	2	0.9%		30	New York	1	0.5%
41	Oregon	0	0.0%		30	Rhode Island	1	0.5%
3	Pennsylvania	17	7.9%		30	Utah	1	0.5%
30	Rhode Island	1	0.5%		30	Washington	1	0.5%
15	South Carolina	5	2.3%		30	Wisconsin	1	0.5%
41	South Dakota	0	0.0%		41	Alaska	0	0.0%
9	Tennessee	6	2.8%		41	Delaware	0	0.0%
1	Texas	31	14.4%		41	Iowa	0	0.0%
30	Utah	1	0.5%		41	Mississippi	0	0.0%
41	Vermont	0	0.0%		41	Montana	0	0.0%
15	Virginia	5	2.3%		41	North Dakota	0	0.0%
30	Washington	1	0.5%		41	Oregon	0	0.0%
9	West Virginia	6	2.8%		41	South Dakota	0	0.0%
30	Wisconsin	1	0.5%		41	Vermont	0	0.0%
41	Wyoming	0	0.0%		41	Wyoming	0	0.0%
						District of Columbia	1	0.5%

Source: U.S. Department of Health and Human Services, Centers for Medicare and Medicaid Services
   OSCAR Database (January 10, 2006)
*Certified by CMS to participate in the Medicare/Medicaid programs. Excludes licensed facilities that do not accept federal funding and facilities managed by the Department of Veterans Affairs. National total does not include one certified hospital in U.S. territories.

Beds in Medicare and Medicaid Certified Rehabilitation Hospitals in 2006

National Total = 13,750 Beds*

ALPHA ORDER

RANK	STATE	BEDS	% of USA
12	Alabama	364	2.6%
41	Alaska	0	0.0%
15	Arizona	319	2.3%
7	Arkansas	485	3.5%
10	California	375	2.7%
22	Colorado	226	1.6%
37	Connecticut	60	0.4%
41	Delaware	0	0.0%
3	Florida	1,102	8.0%
27	Georgia	116	0.8%
31	Hawaii	100	0.7%
38	Idaho	56	0.4%
9	Illinois	448	3.3%
13	Indiana	340	2.5%
41	Iowa	0	0.0%
18	Kansas	257	1.9%
14	Kentucky	328	2.4%
6	Louisiana	685	5.0%
31	Maine	100	0.7%
28	Maryland	109	0.8%
5	Massachusetts	754	5.5%
17	Michigan	285	2.1%
40	Minnesota	15	0.1%
41	Mississippi	0	0.0%
21	Missouri	232	1.7%
41	Montana	0	0.0%
36	Nebraska	66	0.5%
25	Nevada	169	1.2%
26	New Hampshire	130	0.9%
4	New Jersey	756	5.5%
24	New Mexico	196	1.4%
39	New York	22	0.2%
19	North Carolina	233	1.7%
41	North Dakota	0	0.0%
23	Ohio	199	1.4%
29	Oklahoma	107	0.8%
41	Oregon	0	0.0%
2	Pennsylvania	1,464	10.6%
34	Rhode Island	82	0.6%
16	South Carolina	294	2.1%
41	South Dakota	0	0.0%
11	Tennessee	370	2.7%
1	Texas	1,796	13.1%
33	Utah	84	0.6%
41	Vermont	0	0.0%
19	Virginia	233	1.7%
30	Washington	102	0.7%
8	West Virginia	450	3.3%
35	Wisconsin	81	0.6%
41	Wyoming	0	0.0%

RANK ORDER

RANK	STATE	BEDS	% of USA
1	Texas	1,796	13.1%
2	Pennsylvania	1,464	10.6%
3	Florida	1,102	8.0%
4	New Jersey	756	5.5%
5	Massachusetts	754	5.5%
6	Louisiana	685	5.0%
7	Arkansas	485	3.5%
8	West Virginia	450	3.3%
9	Illinois	448	3.3%
10	California	375	2.7%
11	Tennessee	370	2.7%
12	Alabama	364	2.6%
13	Indiana	340	2.5%
14	Kentucky	328	2.4%
15	Arizona	319	2.3%
16	South Carolina	294	2.1%
17	Michigan	285	2.1%
18	Kansas	257	1.9%
19	North Carolina	233	1.7%
19	Virginia	233	1.7%
21	Missouri	232	1.7%
22	Colorado	226	1.6%
23	Ohio	199	1.4%
24	New Mexico	196	1.4%
25	Nevada	169	1.2%
26	New Hampshire	130	0.9%
27	Georgia	116	0.8%
28	Maryland	109	0.8%
29	Oklahoma	107	0.8%
30	Washington	102	0.7%
31	Hawaii	100	0.7%
31	Maine	100	0.7%
33	Utah	84	0.6%
34	Rhode Island	82	0.6%
35	Wisconsin	81	0.6%
36	Nebraska	66	0.5%
37	Connecticut	60	0.4%
38	Idaho	56	0.4%
39	New York	22	0.2%
40	Minnesota	15	0.1%
41	Alaska	0	0.0%
41	Delaware	0	0.0%
41	Iowa	0	0.0%
41	Mississippi	0	0.0%
41	Montana	0	0.0%
41	North Dakota	0	0.0%
41	Oregon	0	0.0%
41	South Dakota	0	0.0%
41	Vermont	0	0.0%
41	Wyoming	0	0.0%
	District of Columbia	160	1.2%

Source: U.S. Department of Health and Human Services, Centers for Medicare and Medicaid Services
    OSCAR Database (January 10, 2006)
*Beds in hospitals certified by CMS to participate in the Medicare/Medicaid programs. Excludes licensed facilities
that do not accept federal funding and facilities managed by the Department of Veterans Affairs. National total
does not include 32 beds in U.S. territories.

Medicare and Medicaid Certified Psychiatric Hospitals in 2006

National Total = 471 Psychiatric Hospitals*

ALPHA ORDER

RANK ORDER

RANK	STATE	HOSPITALS	% of USA	RANK	STATE	HOSPITALS	% of USA
18	Alabama	10	2.1%	1	Texas	35	7.4%
41	Alaska	2	0.4%	2	California	30	6.4%
27	Arizona	6	1.3%	3	New York	29	6.2%
14	Arkansas	11	2.3%	4	Louisiana	26	5.5%
2	California	30	6.4%	5	Pennsylvania	23	4.9%
29	Colorado	5	1.1%	6	Florida	20	4.2%
25	Connecticut	7	1.5%	6	Indiana	20	4.2%
37	Delaware	3	0.6%	8	Massachusetts	16	3.4%
6	Florida	20	4.2%	8	New Jersey	16	3.4%
11	Georgia	14	3.0%	10	Illinois	15	3.2%
48	Hawaii	1	0.2%	11	Georgia	14	3.0%
29	Idaho	5	1.1%	11	Ohio	14	3.0%
10	Illinois	15	3.2%	13	Missouri	13	2.8%
6	Indiana	20	4.2%	14	Arkansas	11	2.3%
31	Iowa	4	0.8%	14	Kentucky	11	2.3%
31	Kansas	4	0.8%	14	Tennessee	11	2.3%
14	Kentucky	11	2.3%	14	Wisconsin	11	2.3%
4	Louisiana	26	5.5%	18	Alabama	10	2.1%
31	Maine	4	0.8%	18	Virginia	10	2.1%
20	Maryland	9	1.9%	20	Maryland	9	1.9%
8	Massachusetts	16	3.4%	20	Michigan	9	1.9%
20	Michigan	9	1.9%	20	North Carolina	9	1.9%
25	Minnesota	7	1.5%	20	Oklahoma	9	1.9%
31	Mississippi	4	0.8%	24	South Carolina	8	1.7%
13	Missouri	13	2.8%	25	Connecticut	7	1.5%
41	Montana	2	0.4%	25	Minnesota	7	1.5%
31	Nebraska	4	0.8%	27	Arizona	6	1.3%
37	Nevada	3	0.6%	27	Washington	6	1.3%
41	New Hampshire	2	0.4%	29	Colorado	5	1.1%
8	New Jersey	16	3.4%	29	Idaho	5	1.1%
41	New Mexico	2	0.4%	31	Iowa	4	0.8%
3	New York	29	6.2%	31	Kansas	4	0.8%
20	North Carolina	9	1.9%	31	Maine	4	0.8%
37	North Dakota	3	0.6%	31	Mississippi	4	0.8%
11	Ohio	14	3.0%	31	Nebraska	4	0.8%
20	Oklahoma	9	1.9%	31	West Virginia	4	0.8%
41	Oregon	2	0.4%	37	Delaware	3	0.6%
5	Pennsylvania	23	4.9%	37	Nevada	3	0.6%
41	Rhode Island	2	0.4%	37	North Dakota	3	0.6%
24	South Carolina	8	1.7%	37	Utah	3	0.6%
48	South Dakota	1	0.2%	41	Alaska	2	0.4%
14	Tennessee	11	2.3%	41	Montana	2	0.4%
1	Texas	35	7.4%	41	New Hampshire	2	0.4%
37	Utah	3	0.6%	41	New Mexico	2	0.4%
48	Vermont	1	0.2%	41	Oregon	2	0.4%
18	Virginia	10	2.1%	41	Rhode Island	2	0.4%
27	Washington	6	1.3%	41	Wyoming	2	0.4%
31	West Virginia	4	0.8%	48	Hawaii	1	0.2%
14	Wisconsin	11	2.3%	48	South Dakota	1	0.2%
41	Wyoming	2	0.4%	48	Vermont	1	0.2%
					District of Columbia	3	0.6%

Source: U.S. Department of Health and Human Services, Centers for Medicare and Medicaid Services
   OSCAR Database (January 9, 2006)
*Certified by CMS to participate in the Medicare/Medicaid programs. Excludes licensed facilities that do not accept federal funding and facilities managed by the Department of Veterans Affairs. National total does not include four certified psychiatric hospitals in U.S. territories.

Beds in Medicare and Medicaid Certified Psychiatric Hospitals in 2006

National Total = 54,285 Beds*

ALPHA ORDER

RANK	STATE	BEDS	% of USA
26	Alabama	655	1.2%
45	Alaska	169	0.3%
31	Arizona	408	0.8%
23	Arkansas	939	1.7%
7	California	2,188	4.0%
27	Colorado	569	1.0%
19	Connecticut	1,091	2.0%
40	Delaware	237	0.4%
5	Florida	2,654	4.9%
10	Georgia	1,639	3.0%
49	Hawaii	88	0.2%
42	Idaho	221	0.4%
9	Illinois	1,694	3.1%
15	Indiana	1,333	2.5%
35	Iowa	350	0.6%
28	Kansas	561	1.0%
16	Kentucky	1,291	2.4%
11	Louisiana	1,463	2.7%
32	Maine	403	0.7%
8	Maryland	2,059	3.8%
12	Massachusetts	1,457	2.7%
18	Michigan	1,140	2.1%
20	Minnesota	1,069	2.0%
37	Mississippi	296	0.5%
22	Missouri	954	1.8%
43	Montana	182	0.3%
36	Nebraska	347	0.6%
39	Nevada	268	0.5%
34	New Hampshire	356	0.7%
3	New Jersey	3,103	5.7%
46	New Mexico	151	0.3%
1	New York	6,425	11.8%
6	North Carolina	2,340	4.3%
41	North Dakota	229	0.4%
17	Ohio	1,237	2.3%
29	Oklahoma	500	0.9%
38	Oregon	281	0.5%
2	Pennsylvania	3,869	7.1%
44	Rhode Island	177	0.3%
25	South Carolina	822	1.5%
48	South Dakota	133	0.2%
21	Tennessee	1,025	1.9%
4	Texas	2,840	5.2%
33	Utah	391	0.7%
47	Vermont	149	0.3%
24	Virginia	885	1.6%
13	Washington	1,415	2.6%
30	West Virginia	463	0.9%
14	Wisconsin	1,407	2.6%
50	Wyoming	70	0.1%

RANK ORDER

RANK	STATE	BEDS	% of USA
1	New York	6,425	11.8%
2	Pennsylvania	3,869	7.1%
3	New Jersey	3,103	5.7%
4	Texas	2,840	5.2%
5	Florida	2,654	4.9%
6	North Carolina	2,340	4.3%
7	California	2,188	4.0%
8	Maryland	2,059	3.8%
9	Illinois	1,694	3.1%
10	Georgia	1,639	3.0%
11	Louisiana	1,463	2.7%
12	Massachusetts	1,457	2.7%
13	Washington	1,415	2.6%
14	Wisconsin	1,407	2.6%
15	Indiana	1,333	2.5%
16	Kentucky	1,291	2.4%
17	Ohio	1,237	2.3%
18	Michigan	1,140	2.1%
19	Connecticut	1,091	2.0%
20	Minnesota	1,069	2.0%
21	Tennessee	1,025	1.9%
22	Missouri	954	1.8%
23	Arkansas	939	1.7%
24	Virginia	885	1.6%
25	South Carolina	822	1.5%
26	Alabama	655	1.2%
27	Colorado	569	1.0%
28	Kansas	561	1.0%
29	Oklahoma	500	0.9%
30	West Virginia	463	0.9%
31	Arizona	408	0.8%
32	Maine	403	0.7%
33	Utah	391	0.7%
34	New Hampshire	356	0.7%
35	Iowa	350	0.6%
36	Nebraska	347	0.6%
37	Mississippi	296	0.5%
38	Oregon	281	0.5%
39	Nevada	268	0.5%
40	Delaware	237	0.4%
41	North Dakota	229	0.4%
42	Idaho	221	0.4%
43	Montana	182	0.3%
44	Rhode Island	177	0.3%
45	Alaska	169	0.3%
46	New Mexico	151	0.3%
47	Vermont	149	0.3%
48	South Dakota	133	0.2%
49	Hawaii	88	0.2%
50	Wyoming	70	0.1%
	District of Columbia	292	0.5%

Source: U.S. Department of Health and Human Services, Centers for Medicare and Medicaid Services
OSCAR Database (January 9, 2006)
*Beds in hospitals certified by CMS to participate in the Medicare/Medicaid programs. Excludes licensed facilities that do not accept federal funding and facilities managed by the Department of Veterans Affairs. National total does not include 903 beds in U.S. territories.

Medicare and Medicaid Certified Outpatient Surgery Centers in 2006

National Total = 4,424 Centers*

ALPHA ORDER

RANK	STATE	CENTERS	% of USA
36	Alabama	30	0.7%
48	Alaska	8	0.2%
11	Arizona	135	3.1%
21	Arkansas	55	1.2%
1	California	604	13.7%
14	Colorado	87	2.0%
30	Connecticut	39	0.9%
37	Delaware	21	0.5%
3	Florida	326	7.4%
5	Georgia	218	4.9%
46	Hawaii	10	0.2%
25	Idaho	50	1.1%
13	Illinois	106	2.4%
12	Indiana	121	2.7%
41	Iowa	17	0.4%
22	Kansas	51	1.2%
35	Kentucky	34	0.8%
17	Louisiana	74	1.7%
41	Maine	17	0.4%
2	Maryland	353	8.0%
31	Massachusetts	38	0.9%
22	Michigan	51	1.2%
31	Minnesota	38	0.9%
19	Mississippi	60	1.4%
15	Missouri	81	1.8%
44	Montana	14	0.3%
34	Nebraska	36	0.8%
25	Nevada	50	1.1%
38	New Hampshire	20	0.5%
7	New Jersey	177	4.0%
39	New Mexico	19	0.4%
15	New York	81	1.8%
22	North Carolina	51	1.2%
39	North Dakota	19	0.4%
9	Ohio	173	3.9%
27	Oklahoma	48	1.1%
18	Oregon	66	1.5%
8	Pennsylvania	174	3.9%
49	Rhode Island	6	0.1%
20	South Carolina	57	1.3%
45	South Dakota	13	0.3%
10	Tennessee	139	3.1%
4	Texas	299	6.8%
29	Utah	40	0.9%
50	Vermont	1	0.0%
31	Virginia	38	0.9%
6	Washington	207	4.7%
46	West Virginia	10	0.2%
28	Wisconsin	41	0.9%
41	Wyoming	17	0.4%

RANK ORDER

RANK	STATE	CENTERS	% of USA
1	California	604	13.7%
2	Maryland	353	8.0%
3	Florida	326	7.4%
4	Texas	299	6.8%
5	Georgia	218	4.9%
6	Washington	207	4.7%
7	New Jersey	177	4.0%
8	Pennsylvania	174	3.9%
9	Ohio	173	3.9%
10	Tennessee	139	3.1%
11	Arizona	135	3.1%
12	Indiana	121	2.7%
13	Illinois	106	2.4%
14	Colorado	87	2.0%
15	Missouri	81	1.8%
15	New York	81	1.8%
17	Louisiana	74	1.7%
18	Oregon	66	1.5%
19	Mississippi	60	1.4%
20	South Carolina	57	1.3%
21	Arkansas	55	1.2%
22	Kansas	51	1.2%
22	Michigan	51	1.2%
22	North Carolina	51	1.2%
25	Idaho	50	1.1%
25	Nevada	50	1.1%
27	Oklahoma	48	1.1%
28	Wisconsin	41	0.9%
29	Utah	40	0.9%
30	Connecticut	39	0.9%
31	Massachusetts	38	0.9%
31	Minnesota	38	0.9%
31	Virginia	38	0.9%
34	Nebraska	36	0.8%
35	Kentucky	34	0.8%
36	Alabama	30	0.7%
37	Delaware	21	0.5%
38	New Hampshire	20	0.5%
39	New Mexico	19	0.4%
39	North Dakota	19	0.4%
41	Iowa	17	0.4%
41	Maine	17	0.4%
41	Wyoming	17	0.4%
44	Montana	14	0.3%
45	South Dakota	13	0.3%
46	Hawaii	10	0.2%
46	West Virginia	10	0.2%
48	Alaska	8	0.2%
49	Rhode Island	6	0.1%
50	Vermont	1	0.0%
	District of Columbia	4	0.1%

Source: U.S. Department of Health and Human Services, Centers for Medicare and Medicaid Services
   OSCAR Report 10 (January 9, 2006)
*Certified by CMS to participate in the Medicare/Medicaid programs. Excludes licensed facilities that do not accept federal funding and facilities managed by the Department of Veterans Affairs. National total does not include 24 certified outpatient surgery centers in U.S. territories. Also known as Ambulatory Surgical Centers.

Medicare and Medicaid Certified Community Mental Health Centers in 2006

National Total = 610 Centers*

ALPHA ORDER					RANK ORDER			
RANK	STATE		CENTERS	% of USA	RANK	STATE	CENTERS	% of USA
2	Alabama		65	10.7%	1	Florida	123	20.2%
41	Alaska		0	0.0%	2	Alabama	65	10.7%
30	Arizona		3	0.5%	3	Louisiana	37	6.1%
13	Arkansas		14	2.3%	4	Texas	35	5.7%
8	California		20	3.3%	5	New Jersey	33	5.4%
13	Colorado		14	2.3%	6	Washington	25	4.1%
28	Connecticut		5	0.8%	7	Tennessee	21	3.4%
41	Delaware		0	0.0%	8	California	20	3.3%
1	Florida		123	20.2%	8	North Carolina	20	3.3%
21	Georgia		9	1.5%	10	Kansas	15	2.5%
41	Hawaii		0	0.0%	10	New Mexico	15	2.5%
41	Idaho		0	0.0%	10	Pennsylvania	15	2.5%
19	Illinois		11	1.8%	13	Arkansas	14	2.3%
22	Indiana		8	1.3%	13	Colorado	14	2.3%
26	Iowa		6	1.0%	13	Minnesota	14	2.3%
10	Kansas		15	2.5%	16	Massachusetts	13	2.1%
19	Kentucky		11	1.8%	16	Ohio	13	2.1%
3	Louisiana		37	6.1%	18	Oregon	12	2.0%
41	Maine		0	0.0%	19	Illinois	11	1.8%
34	Maryland		2	0.3%	19	Kentucky	11	1.8%
16	Massachusetts		13	2.1%	21	Georgia	9	1.5%
24	Michigan		7	1.1%	22	Indiana	8	1.3%
13	Minnesota		14	2.3%	22	Oklahoma	8	1.3%
26	Mississippi		6	1.0%	24	Michigan	7	1.1%
24	Missouri		7	1.1%	24	Missouri	7	1.1%
41	Montana		0	0.0%	26	Iowa	6	1.0%
39	Nebraska		1	0.2%	26	Mississippi	6	1.0%
34	Nevada		2	0.3%	28	Connecticut	5	0.8%
39	New Hampshire		1	0.2%	29	New York	4	0.7%
5	New Jersey		33	5.4%	30	Arizona	3	0.5%
10	New Mexico		15	2.5%	30	South Carolina	3	0.5%
29	New York		4	0.7%	30	Virginia	3	0.5%
8	North Carolina		20	3.3%	30	Wyoming	3	0.5%
41	North Dakota		0	0.0%	34	Maryland	2	0.3%
16	Ohio		13	2.1%	34	Nevada	2	0.3%
22	Oklahoma		8	1.3%	34	South Dakota	2	0.3%
18	Oregon		12	2.0%	34	Utah	2	0.3%
10	Pennsylvania		15	2.5%	34	West Virginia	2	0.3%
41	Rhode Island		0	0.0%	39	Nebraska	1	0.2%
30	South Carolina		3	0.5%	39	New Hampshire	1	0.2%
34	South Dakota		2	0.3%	41	Alaska	0	0.0%
7	Tennessee		21	3.4%	41	Delaware	0	0.0%
4	Texas		35	5.7%	41	Hawaii	0	0.0%
34	Utah		2	0.3%	41	Idaho	0	0.0%
41	Vermont		0	0.0%	41	Maine	0	0.0%
30	Virginia		3	0.5%	41	Montana	0	0.0%
6	Washington		25	4.1%	41	North Dakota	0	0.0%
34	West Virginia		2	0.3%	41	Rhode Island	0	0.0%
41	Wisconsin		0	0.0%	41	Vermont	0	0.0%
30	Wyoming		3	0.5%	41	Wisconsin	0	0.0%
						District of Columbia	0	0.0%

Source: U.S. Department of Health and Human Services, Centers for Medicare and Medicaid Services
OSCAR Report 10 (January 9, 2006)

Certified by CMS to participate in the Medicare/Medicaid programs. Excludes licensed facilities that do not accept federal funding and facilities managed by the Department of Veterans Affairs. National total does not include 12 certified mental health centers in U.S. territories.

Medicare and Medicaid Certified Outpatient Physical Therapy Facilities in 2006

National Total = 2,961 Facilities*

ALPHA ORDER

RANK ORDER

RANK	STATE	FACILITIES	% of USA		RANK	STATE	FACILITIES	% of USA
24	Alabama	38	1.3%		1	Florida	333	11.2%
36	Alaska	15	0.5%		2	Michigan	251	8.5%
31	Arizona	27	0.9%		3	Texas	229	7.7%
27	Arkansas	30	1.0%		4	California	181	6.1%
4	California	181	6.1%		5	Ohio	140	4.7%
21	Colorado	51	1.7%		6	Pennsylvania	137	4.6%
26	Connecticut	33	1.1%		7	Virginia	118	4.0%
36	Delaware	15	0.5%		8	New Jersey	116	3.9%
1	Florida	333	11.2%		9	Georgia	112	3.8%
9	Georgia	112	3.8%		10	Maryland	94	3.2%
43	Hawaii	8	0.3%		11	Illinois	90	3.0%
38	Idaho	13	0.4%		12	Kentucky	87	2.9%
11	Illinois	90	3.0%		12	Tennessee	87	2.9%
18	Indiana	53	1.8%		14	Missouri	64	2.2%
25	Iowa	37	1.2%		15	Mississippi	57	1.9%
33	Kansas	21	0.7%		16	North Carolina	56	1.9%
12	Kentucky	87	2.9%		16	South Carolina	56	1.9%
19	Louisiana	52	1.8%		18	Indiana	53	1.8%
34	Maine	17	0.6%		19	Louisiana	52	1.8%
10	Maryland	94	3.2%		19	Oklahoma	52	1.8%
39	Massachusetts	12	0.4%		21	Colorado	51	1.7%
2	Michigan	251	8.5%		22	Wisconsin	49	1.7%
23	Minnesota	45	1.5%		23	Minnesota	45	1.5%
15	Mississippi	57	1.9%		24	Alabama	38	1.3%
14	Missouri	64	2.2%		25	Iowa	37	1.2%
44	Montana	6	0.2%		26	Connecticut	33	1.1%
41	Nebraska	10	0.3%		27	Arkansas	30	1.0%
32	Nevada	22	0.7%		27	Washington	30	1.0%
40	New Hampshire	11	0.4%		29	New York	29	1.0%
8	New Jersey	116	3.9%		30	New Mexico	28	0.9%
30	New Mexico	28	0.9%		31	Arizona	27	0.9%
29	New York	29	1.0%		32	Nevada	22	0.7%
16	North Carolina	56	1.9%		33	Kansas	21	0.7%
49	North Dakota	2	0.1%		34	Maine	17	0.6%
5	Ohio	140	4.7%		34	Oregon	17	0.6%
19	Oklahoma	52	1.8%		36	Alaska	15	0.5%
34	Oregon	17	0.6%		36	Delaware	15	0.5%
6	Pennsylvania	137	4.6%		38	Idaho	13	0.4%
47	Rhode Island	3	0.1%		39	Massachusetts	12	0.4%
16	South Carolina	56	1.9%		40	New Hampshire	11	0.4%
46	South Dakota	4	0.1%		41	Nebraska	10	0.3%
12	Tennessee	87	2.9%		42	West Virginia	9	0.3%
3	Texas	229	7.7%		43	Hawaii	8	0.3%
44	Utah	6	0.2%		44	Montana	6	0.2%
49	Vermont	2	0.1%		44	Utah	6	0.2%
7	Virginia	118	4.0%		46	South Dakota	4	0.1%
27	Washington	30	1.0%		47	Rhode Island	3	0.1%
42	West Virginia	9	0.3%		47	Wyoming	3	0.1%
22	Wisconsin	49	1.7%		49	North Dakota	2	0.1%
47	Wyoming	3	0.1%		49	Vermont	2	0.1%
						District of Columbia	3	0.1%

Source: U.S. Department of Health and Human Services, Centers for Medicare and Medicaid Services OSCAR Report 10 (January 9, 2006)

*Certified by CMS to participate in the Medicare/Medicaid programs. Excludes licensed facilities that do not accept federal funding and facilities managed by the Department of Veterans Affairs. National total does not include two certified outpatient physical therapy facilities in U.S. territories.

Medicare and Medicaid Certified Rural Health Clinics in 2006

National Total = 3,664 Rural Health Clinics*

ALPHA ORDER

RANK	STATE	CLINICS	% of USA
18	Alabama	66	1.8%
43	Alaska	5	0.1%
39	Arizona	13	0.4%
18	Arkansas	66	1.8%
3	California	253	6.9%
29	Colorado	45	1.2%
47	Connecticut	0	0.0%
47	Delaware	0	0.0%
7	Florida	160	4.4%
15	Georgia	97	2.6%
44	Hawaii	2	0.1%
28	Idaho	48	1.3%
4	Illinois	213	5.8%
23	Indiana	55	1.5%
9	Iowa	132	3.6%
5	Kansas	177	4.8%
10	Kentucky	122	3.3%
17	Louisiana	74	2.0%
32	Maine	41	1.1%
47	Maryland	0	0.0%
45	Massachusetts	1	0.0%
6	Michigan	162	4.4%
16	Minnesota	82	2.2%
8	Mississippi	151	4.1%
2	Missouri	294	8.0%
30	Montana	43	1.2%
12	Nebraska	112	3.1%
42	Nevada	6	0.2%
36	New Hampshire	17	0.5%
47	New Jersey	0	0.0%
39	New Mexico	13	0.4%
41	New York	9	0.2%
13	North Carolina	104	2.8%
20	North Dakota	64	1.7%
36	Ohio	17	0.5%
33	Oklahoma	40	1.1%
23	Oregon	55	1.5%
30	Pennsylvania	43	1.2%
45	Rhode Island	1	0.0%
14	South Carolina	98	2.7%
22	South Dakota	58	1.6%
26	Tennessee	52	1.4%
1	Texas	336	9.2%
38	Utah	15	0.4%
34	Vermont	20	0.5%
25	Virginia	53	1.4%
11	Washington	115	3.1%
20	West Virginia	64	1.7%
27	Wisconsin	51	1.4%
35	Wyoming	19	0.5%

RANK ORDER

RANK	STATE	CLINICS	% of USA
1	Texas	336	9.2%
2	Missouri	294	8.0%
3	California	253	6.9%
4	Illinois	213	5.8%
5	Kansas	177	4.8%
6	Michigan	162	4.4%
7	Florida	160	4.4%
8	Mississippi	151	4.1%
9	Iowa	132	3.6%
10	Kentucky	122	3.3%
11	Washington	115	3.1%
12	Nebraska	112	3.1%
13	North Carolina	104	2.8%
14	South Carolina	98	2.7%
15	Georgia	97	2.6%
16	Minnesota	82	2.2%
17	Louisiana	74	2.0%
18	Alabama	66	1.8%
18	Arkansas	66	1.8%
20	North Dakota	64	1.7%
20	West Virginia	64	1.7%
22	South Dakota	58	1.6%
23	Indiana	55	1.5%
23	Oregon	55	1.5%
25	Virginia	53	1.4%
26	Tennessee	52	1.4%
27	Wisconsin	51	1.4%
28	Idaho	48	1.3%
29	Colorado	45	1.2%
30	Montana	43	1.2%
30	Pennsylvania	43	1.2%
32	Maine	41	1.1%
33	Oklahoma	40	1.1%
34	Vermont	20	0.5%
35	Wyoming	19	0.5%
36	New Hampshire	17	0.5%
36	Ohio	17	0.5%
38	Utah	15	0.4%
39	Arizona	13	0.4%
39	New Mexico	13	0.4%
41	New York	9	0.2%
42	Nevada	6	0.2%
43	Alaska	5	0.1%
44	Hawaii	2	0.1%
45	Massachusetts	1	0.0%
45	Rhode Island	1	0.0%
47	Connecticut	0	0.0%
47	Delaware	0	0.0%
47	Maryland	0	0.0%
47	New Jersey	0	0.0%
	District of Columbia	0	0.0%

Source: U.S. Department of Health and Human Services, Centers for Medicare and Medicaid Services
OSCAR Report 10 (January 9, 2006)
*Certified by CMS to participate in the Medicare/Medicaid programs. Excludes licensed facilities that do not accept federal funding and facilities managed by the Department of Veterans Affairs. There are no certified rural health centers in U.S. territories.

Medicare and Medicaid Certified Home Health Agencies in 2006

National Total = 8,164 Home Health Agencies*

ALPHA ORDER

RANK	STATE	AGENCIES	% of USA
18	Alabama	142	1.7%
47	Alaska	16	0.2%
27	Arizona	75	0.9%
14	Arkansas	173	2.1%
2	California	660	8.1%
20	Colorado	137	1.7%
26	Connecticut	83	1.0%
47	Delaware	16	0.2%
3	Florida	632	7.7%
25	Georgia	100	1.2%
49	Hawaii	14	0.2%
38	Idaho	49	0.6%
5	Illinois	371	4.5%
12	Indiana	188	2.3%
13	Iowa	180	2.2%
21	Kansas	135	1.7%
24	Kentucky	104	1.3%
8	Louisiana	225	2.8%
43	Maine	29	0.4%
39	Maryland	48	0.6%
23	Massachusetts	117	1.4%
7	Michigan	292	3.6%
9	Minnesota	217	2.7%
35	Mississippi	57	0.7%
17	Missouri	164	2.0%
41	Montana	38	0.5%
28	Nebraska	70	0.9%
34	Nevada	58	0.7%
42	New Hampshire	36	0.4%
37	New Jersey	50	0.6%
30	New Mexico	68	0.8%
11	New York	193	2.4%
16	North Carolina	167	2.0%
45	North Dakota	26	0.3%
4	Ohio	421	5.2%
10	Oklahoma	202	2.5%
32	Oregon	60	0.7%
6	Pennsylvania	302	3.7%
46	Rhode Island	22	0.3%
28	South Carolina	70	0.9%
40	South Dakota	43	0.5%
19	Tennessee	139	1.7%
1	Texas	1,445	17.7%
36	Utah	56	0.7%
50	Vermont	12	0.1%
15	Virginia	169	2.1%
32	Washington	60	0.7%
31	West Virginia	62	0.8%
22	Wisconsin	123	1.5%
44	Wyoming	27	0.3%

RANK ORDER

RANK	STATE	AGENCIES	% of USA
1	Texas	1,445	17.7%
2	California	660	8.1%
3	Florida	632	7.7%
4	Ohio	421	5.2%
5	Illinois	371	4.5%
6	Pennsylvania	302	3.7%
7	Michigan	292	3.6%
8	Louisiana	225	2.8%
9	Minnesota	217	2.7%
10	Oklahoma	202	2.5%
11	New York	193	2.4%
12	Indiana	188	2.3%
13	Iowa	180	2.2%
14	Arkansas	173	2.1%
15	Virginia	169	2.1%
16	North Carolina	167	2.0%
17	Missouri	164	2.0%
18	Alabama	142	1.7%
19	Tennessee	139	1.7%
20	Colorado	137	1.7%
21	Kansas	135	1.7%
22	Wisconsin	123	1.5%
23	Massachusetts	117	1.4%
24	Kentucky	104	1.3%
25	Georgia	100	1.2%
26	Connecticut	83	1.0%
27	Arizona	75	0.9%
28	Nebraska	70	0.9%
28	South Carolina	70	0.9%
30	New Mexico	68	0.8%
31	West Virginia	62	0.8%
32	Oregon	60	0.7%
32	Washington	60	0.7%
34	Nevada	58	0.7%
35	Mississippi	57	0.7%
36	Utah	56	0.7%
37	New Jersey	50	0.6%
38	Idaho	49	0.6%
39	Maryland	48	0.6%
40	South Dakota	43	0.5%
41	Montana	38	0.5%
42	New Hampshire	36	0.4%
43	Maine	29	0.4%
44	Wyoming	27	0.3%
45	North Dakota	26	0.3%
46	Rhode Island	22	0.3%
47	Alaska	16	0.2%
47	Delaware	16	0.2%
49	Hawaii	14	0.2%
50	Vermont	12	0.1%
	District of Columbia	21	0.3%

Source: U.S. Department of Health and Human Services, Centers for Medicare and Medicaid Services
OSCAR Report 10 (January 9, 2006)

*Certified by CMS to participate in the Medicare/Medicaid programs. Excludes agencies that do not accept federal funding. National total does not include 55 certified home health agencies in U.S. territories. A home health agency provides health services to individuals in their homes for the purpose of promoting, maintaining or restoring health or maximizing the level of independence, while minimizing the effects of disability and illness.

Medicare and Medicaid Certified Hospices in 2006

National Total = 2,841 Hospices*

ALPHA ORDER

RANK	STATE	HOSPICES	% of USA
5	Alabama	108	3.8%
50	Alaska	3	0.1%
24	Arizona	50	1.8%
18	Arkansas	53	1.9%
2	California	189	6.7%
29	Colorado	43	1.5%
36	Connecticut	27	1.0%
48	Delaware	7	0.2%
31	Florida	41	1.4%
8	Georgia	94	3.3%
48	Hawaii	7	0.2%
34	Idaho	31	1.1%
6	Illinois	102	3.6%
14	Indiana	77	2.7%
15	Iowa	67	2.4%
26	Kansas	48	1.7%
36	Kentucky	27	1.0%
11	Louisiana	88	3.1%
40	Maine	19	0.7%
35	Maryland	28	1.0%
26	Massachusetts	48	1.7%
10	Michigan	89	3.1%
17	Minnesota	63	2.2%
9	Mississippi	92	3.2%
12	Missouri	86	3.0%
38	Montana	26	0.9%
32	Nebraska	32	1.1%
45	Nevada	12	0.4%
39	New Hampshire	21	0.7%
25	New Jersey	49	1.7%
29	New Mexico	43	1.5%
23	New York	51	1.8%
13	North Carolina	80	2.8%
44	North Dakota	14	0.5%
7	Ohio	98	3.4%
3	Oklahoma	139	4.9%
26	Oregon	48	1.7%
4	Pennsylvania	135	4.8%
47	Rhode Island	8	0.3%
21	South Carolina	52	1.8%
43	South Dakota	15	0.5%
18	Tennessee	53	1.9%
1	Texas	227	8.0%
21	Utah	52	1.8%
46	Vermont	10	0.4%
16	Virginia	65	2.3%
32	Washington	32	1.1%
40	West Virginia	19	0.7%
18	Wisconsin	53	1.9%
42	Wyoming	18	0.6%

RANK ORDER

RANK	STATE	HOSPICES	% of USA
1	Texas	227	8.0%
2	California	189	6.7%
3	Oklahoma	139	4.9%
4	Pennsylvania	135	4.8%
5	Alabama	108	3.8%
6	Illinois	102	3.6%
7	Ohio	98	3.4%
8	Georgia	94	3.3%
9	Mississippi	92	3.2%
10	Michigan	89	3.1%
11	Louisiana	88	3.1%
12	Missouri	86	3.0%
13	North Carolina	80	2.8%
14	Indiana	77	2.7%
15	Iowa	67	2.4%
16	Virginia	65	2.3%
17	Minnesota	63	2.2%
18	Arkansas	53	1.9%
18	Tennessee	53	1.9%
18	Wisconsin	53	1.9%
21	South Carolina	52	1.8%
21	Utah	52	1.8%
23	New York	51	1.8%
24	Arizona	50	1.8%
25	New Jersey	49	1.7%
26	Kansas	48	1.7%
26	Massachusetts	48	1.7%
26	Oregon	48	1.7%
29	Colorado	43	1.5%
29	New Mexico	43	1.5%
31	Florida	41	1.4%
32	Nebraska	32	1.1%
32	Washington	32	1.1%
34	Idaho	31	1.1%
35	Maryland	28	1.0%
36	Connecticut	27	1.0%
36	Kentucky	27	1.0%
38	Montana	26	0.9%
39	New Hampshire	21	0.7%
40	Maine	19	0.7%
40	West Virginia	19	0.7%
42	Wyoming	18	0.6%
43	South Dakota	15	0.5%
44	North Dakota	14	0.5%
45	Nevada	12	0.4%
46	Vermont	10	0.4%
47	Rhode Island	8	0.3%
48	Delaware	7	0.2%
48	Hawaii	7	0.2%
50	Alaska	3	0.1%
	District of Columbia	2	0.1%

Source: U.S. Department of Health and Human Services, Centers for Medicare and Medicaid Services
   OSCAR Report 10 (January 9, 2006)

*Certified by CMS to participate in the Medicare/Medicaid programs. Excludes licensed facilities that do not accept federal funding and facilities managed by the Department of Veterans Affairs. National total does not include 36 certified hospices in U.S. territories. An hospice provides specialized services for terminally ill people and their families.

Hospice Patients in Residential Facilities in 2006

National Total = 44,405 Patients*

ALPHA ORDER

RANK ORDER

RANK	STATE	PATIENTS	% of USA
25	Alabama	506	1.1%
50	Alaska	3	0.0%
21	Arizona	593	1.3%
32	Arkansas	316	0.7%
5	California	2,454	5.5%
15	Colorado	727	1.6%
35	Connecticut	232	0.5%
41	Delaware	70	0.2%
1	Florida	8,339	18.8%
7	Georgia	1,533	3.5%
43	Hawaii	53	0.1%
38	Idaho	108	0.2%
9	Illinois	1,214	2.7%
11	Indiana	1,130	2.5%
16	Iowa	685	1.5%
27	Kansas	377	0.8%
23	Kentucky	569	1.3%
28	Louisiana	363	0.8%
44	Maine	48	0.1%
30	Maryland	359	0.8%
18	Massachusetts	659	1.5%
24	Michigan	549	1.2%
22	Minnesota	591	1.3%
33	Mississippi	254	0.6%
8	Missouri	1,517	3.4%
34	Montana	249	0.6%
14	Nebraska	843	1.9%
36	Nevada	140	0.3%
45	New Hampshire	44	0.1%
16	New Jersey	685	1.5%
37	New Mexico	130	0.3%
10	New York	1,175	2.6%
12	North Carolina	1,100	2.5%
42	North Dakota	66	0.1%
4	Ohio	2,834	6.4%
6	Oklahoma	1,866	4.2%
13	Oregon	867	2.0%
3	Pennsylvania	3,783	8.5%
49	Rhode Island	8	0.0%
26	South Carolina	409	0.9%
47	South Dakota	22	0.0%
31	Tennessee	352	0.8%
2	Texas	4,766	10.7%
29	Utah	362	0.8%
46	Vermont	33	0.1%
39	Virginia	88	0.2%
19	Washington	615	1.4%
40	West Virginia	72	0.2%
20	Wisconsin	614	1.4%
48	Wyoming	18	0.0%

RANK	STATE	PATIENTS	% of USA
1	Florida	8,339	18.8%
2	Texas	4,766	10.7%
3	Pennsylvania	3,783	8.5%
4	Ohio	2,834	6.4%
5	California	2,454	5.5%
6	Oklahoma	1,866	4.2%
7	Georgia	1,533	3.5%
8	Missouri	1,517	3.4%
9	Illinois	1,214	2.7%
10	New York	1,175	2.6%
11	Indiana	1,130	2.5%
12	North Carolina	1,100	2.5%
13	Oregon	867	2.0%
14	Nebraska	843	1.9%
15	Colorado	727	1.6%
16	Iowa	685	1.5%
16	New Jersey	685	1.5%
18	Massachusetts	659	1.5%
19	Washington	615	1.4%
20	Wisconsin	614	1.4%
21	Arizona	593	1.3%
22	Minnesota	591	1.3%
23	Kentucky	569	1.3%
24	Michigan	549	1.2%
25	Alabama	506	1.1%
26	South Carolina	409	0.9%
27	Kansas	377	0.8%
28	Louisiana	363	0.8%
29	Utah	362	0.8%
30	Maryland	359	0.8%
31	Tennessee	352	0.8%
32	Arkansas	316	0.7%
33	Mississippi	254	0.6%
34	Montana	249	0.6%
35	Connecticut	232	0.5%
36	Nevada	140	0.3%
37	New Mexico	130	0.3%
38	Idaho	108	0.2%
39	Virginia	88	0.2%
40	West Virginia	72	0.2%
41	Delaware	70	0.2%
42	North Dakota	66	0.1%
43	Hawaii	53	0.1%
44	Maine	48	0.1%
45	New Hampshire	44	0.1%
46	Vermont	33	0.1%
47	South Dakota	22	0.0%
48	Wyoming	18	0.0%
49	Rhode Island	8	0.0%
50	Alaska	3	0.0%
	District of Columbia	15	0.0%

Source: U.S. Department of Health and Human Services, Centers for Medicare and Medicaid Services
OSCAR Database (January 9, 2006)

*Patients in facilities certified by CMS to participate in the Medicare/Medicaid programs. Excludes licensed facilities that do not accept federal funding and facilities managed by the Department of Veterans Affairs. National total does not include 50 patients in U.S. territories. A hospice provides specialized services for terminally ill people and their families.

Medicare and Medicaid Certified Nursing Care Facilities in 2006

National Total = 15,982 Nursing Care Facilities*

ALPHA ORDER

RANK ORDER

RANK	STATE	FACILITIES	% of USA	RANK	STATE	FACILITIES	% of USA
28	Alabama	229	1.4%	1	California	1,296	8.1%
50	Alaska	14	0.1%	2	Texas	1,131	7.1%
34	Arizona	133	0.8%	3	Ohio	970	6.1%
26	Arkansas	236	1.5%	4	Illinois	801	5.0%
1	California	1,296	8.1%	5	Pennsylvania	719	4.5%
30	Colorado	213	1.3%	6	Florida	686	4.3%
25	Connecticut	246	1.5%	7	New York	658	4.1%
47	Delaware	42	0.3%	8	Missouri	518	3.2%
6	Florida	686	4.3%	9	Indiana	509	3.2%
17	Georgia	362	2.3%	10	Iowa	456	2.9%
46	Hawaii	46	0.3%	10	Massachusetts	456	2.9%
43	Idaho	80	0.5%	12	Michigan	430	2.7%
4	Illinois	801	5.0%	13	North Carolina	422	2.6%
9	Indiana	509	3.2%	14	Minnesota	400	2.5%
10	Iowa	456	2.9%	14	Wisconsin	400	2.5%
18	Kansas	359	2.2%	16	New Jersey	363	2.3%
22	Kentucky	295	1.8%	17	Georgia	362	2.3%
21	Louisiana	303	1.9%	18	Kansas	359	2.2%
36	Maine	114	0.7%	19	Oklahoma	349	2.2%
26	Maryland	236	1.5%	20	Tennessee	329	2.1%
10	Massachusetts	456	2.9%	21	Louisiana	303	1.9%
12	Michigan	430	2.7%	22	Kentucky	295	1.8%
14	Minnesota	400	2.5%	23	Virginia	277	1.7%
31	Mississippi	205	1.3%	24	Washington	247	1.5%
8	Missouri	518	3.2%	25	Connecticut	246	1.5%
38	Montana	98	0.6%	26	Arkansas	236	1.5%
29	Nebraska	225	1.4%	26	Maryland	236	1.5%
45	Nevada	47	0.3%	28	Alabama	229	1.4%
42	New Hampshire	82	0.5%	29	Nebraska	225	1.4%
16	New Jersey	363	2.3%	30	Colorado	213	1.3%
44	New Mexico	76	0.5%	31	Mississippi	205	1.3%
7	New York	658	4.1%	32	South Carolina	176	1.1%
13	North Carolina	422	2.6%	33	Oregon	138	0.9%
41	North Dakota	83	0.5%	34	Arizona	133	0.8%
3	Ohio	970	6.1%	35	West Virginia	132	0.8%
19	Oklahoma	349	2.2%	36	Maine	114	0.7%
33	Oregon	138	0.9%	37	South Dakota	111	0.7%
5	Pennsylvania	719	4.5%	38	Montana	98	0.6%
40	Rhode Island	91	0.6%	39	Utah	93	0.6%
32	South Carolina	176	1.1%	40	Rhode Island	91	0.6%
37	South Dakota	111	0.7%	41	North Dakota	83	0.5%
20	Tennessee	329	2.1%	42	New Hampshire	82	0.5%
2	Texas	1,131	7.1%	43	Idaho	80	0.5%
39	Utah	93	0.6%	44	New Mexico	76	0.5%
48	Vermont	41	0.3%	45	Nevada	47	0.3%
23	Virginia	277	1.7%	46	Hawaii	46	0.3%
24	Washington	247	1.5%	47	Delaware	42	0.3%
35	West Virginia	132	0.8%	48	Vermont	41	0.3%
14	Wisconsin	400	2.5%	49	Wyoming	39	0.2%
49	Wyoming	39	0.2%	50	Alaska	14	0.1%
					District of Columbia	20	0.1%

Source: U.S. Department of Health and Human Services, Centers for Medicare and Medicaid Services
OSCAR Database (January 9, 2006)

Certified by CMS to participate in the Medicare/Medicaid programs. Excludes licensed facilities that do not accept federal funding and facilities managed by the Department of Veterans Affairs. National total does not include eight certified nursing facilities in U.S. territories.

Beds in Medicare and Medicaid Certified Nursing Care Facilities in 2006

National Total = 1,678,729 Beds*

RANK	STATE	BEDS	% of USA
24	Alabama	26,368	1.6%
50	Alaska	695	0.0%
32	Arizona	16,143	1.0%
26	Arkansas	24,190	1.4%
1	California	123,490	7.4%
29	Colorado	19,885	1.2%
22	Connecticut	30,074	1.8%
46	Delaware	4,200	0.3%
7	Florida	81,657	4.9%
14	Georgia	40,052	2.4%
47	Hawaii	4,039	0.2%
44	Idaho	6,170	0.4%
4	Illinois	97,046	5.8%
11	Indiana	47,862	2.9%
19	Iowa	33,471	2.0%
27	Kansas	23,721	1.4%
25	Kentucky	25,894	1.5%
16	Louisiana	37,496	2.2%
39	Maine	7,409	0.4%
23	Maryland	29,196	1.7%
10	Massachusetts	49,985	3.0%
12	Michigan	47,305	2.8%
18	Minnesota	36,122	2.2%
30	Mississippi	18,493	1.1%
9	Missouri	50,198	3.0%
40	Montana	7,364	0.4%
33	Nebraska	15,805	0.9%
45	Nevada	5,360	0.3%
37	New Hampshire	7,817	0.5%
8	New Jersey	51,221	3.1%
42	New Mexico	7,077	0.4%
2	New York	120,809	7.2%
13	North Carolina	43,150	2.6%
43	North Dakota	6,512	0.4%
5	Ohio	91,644	5.5%
21	Oklahoma	31,092	1.9%
34	Oregon	12,602	0.8%
6	Pennsylvania	88,819	5.3%
36	Rhode Island	9,186	0.5%
31	South Carolina	17,779	1.1%
41	South Dakota	7,078	0.4%
17	Tennessee	37,221	2.2%
3	Texas	116,306	6.9%
38	Utah	7,801	0.5%
48	Vermont	3,449	0.2%
20	Virginia	31,143	1.9%
28	Washington	22,521	1.3%
35	West Virginia	10,924	0.7%
15	Wisconsin	38,801	2.3%
49	Wyoming	3,051	0.2%

RANK	STATE	BEDS	% of USA
1	California	123,490	7.4%
2	New York	120,809	7.2%
3	Texas	116,306	6.9%
4	Illinois	97,046	5.8%
5	Ohio	91,644	5.5%
6	Pennsylvania	88,819	5.3%
7	Florida	81,657	4.9%
8	New Jersey	51,221	3.1%
9	Missouri	50,198	3.0%
10	Massachusetts	49,985	3.0%
11	Indiana	47,862	2.9%
12	Michigan	47,305	2.8%
13	North Carolina	43,150	2.6%
14	Georgia	40,052	2.4%
15	Wisconsin	38,801	2.3%
16	Louisiana	37,496	2.2%
17	Tennessee	37,221	2.2%
18	Minnesota	36,122	2.2%
19	Iowa	33,471	2.0%
20	Virginia	31,143	1.9%
21	Oklahoma	31,092	1.9%
22	Connecticut	30,074	1.8%
23	Maryland	29,196	1.7%
24	Alabama	26,368	1.6%
25	Kentucky	25,894	1.5%
26	Arkansas	24,190	1.4%
27	Kansas	23,721	1.4%
28	Washington	22,521	1.3%
29	Colorado	19,885	1.2%
30	Mississippi	18,493	1.1%
31	South Carolina	17,779	1.1%
32	Arizona	16,143	1.0%
33	Nebraska	15,805	0.9%
34	Oregon	12,602	0.8%
35	West Virginia	10,924	0.7%
36	Rhode Island	9,186	0.5%
37	New Hampshire	7,817	0.5%
38	Utah	7,801	0.5%
39	Maine	7,409	0.4%
40	Montana	7,364	0.4%
41	South Dakota	7,078	0.4%
42	New Mexico	7,077	0.4%
43	North Dakota	6,512	0.4%
44	Idaho	6,170	0.4%
45	Nevada	5,360	0.3%
46	Delaware	4,200	0.3%
47	Hawaii	4,039	0.2%
48	Vermont	3,449	0.2%
49	Wyoming	3,051	0.2%
50	Alaska	695	0.0%
	District of Columbia	3,036	0.2%

Source: U.S. Department of Health and Human Services, Centers for Medicare and Medicaid Services
OSCAR Database (January 9, 2006)
*Beds in nursing care facilities certified by CMS to participate in the Medicare/Medicaid programs. National total does not include 340 beds in U.S. territories.

Rate of Beds in Medicare and Medicaid Certified Nursing Care Facilities in 2006

National Rate = 345 Beds per 1,000 Population 85 Years and Older*

ALPHA ORDER

RANK	STATE	RATE
19	Alabama	398
47	Alaska	198
48	Arizona	188
3	Arkansas	506
43	California	240
26	Colorado	357
23	Connecticut	366
32	Delaware	317
46	Florida	215
15	Georgia	420
50	Hawaii	159
40	Idaho	274
10	Illinois	442
8	Indiana	456
7	Iowa	462
14	Kansas	431
13	Kentucky	439
1	Louisiana	622
39	Maine	295
27	Maryland	353
22	Massachusetts	367
41	Michigan	270
21	Minnesota	368
6	Mississippi	467
4	Missouri	500
17	Montana	404
11	Nebraska	440
44	Nevada	223
24	New Hampshire	360
33	New Jersey	315
42	New Mexico	264
30	New York	341
25	North Carolina	358
20	North Dakota	397
11	Ohio	440
2	Oklahoma	573
49	Oregon	180
34	Pennsylvania	305
28	Rhode Island	349
38	South Carolina	299
18	South Dakota	401
9	Tennessee	445
5	Texas	473
35	Utah	304
37	Vermont	300
35	Virginia	304
45	Washington	218
31	West Virginia	336
28	Wisconsin	349
16	Wyoming	414

RANK ORDER

RANK	STATE	RATE
1	Louisiana	622
2	Oklahoma	573
3	Arkansas	506
4	Missouri	500
5	Texas	473
6	Mississippi	467
7	Iowa	462
8	Indiana	456
9	Tennessee	445
10	Illinois	442
11	Nebraska	440
11	Ohio	440
13	Kentucky	439
14	Kansas	431
15	Georgia	420
16	Wyoming	414
17	Montana	404
18	South Dakota	401
19	Alabama	398
20	North Dakota	397
21	Minnesota	368
22	Massachusetts	367
23	Connecticut	366
24	New Hampshire	360
25	North Carolina	358
26	Colorado	357
27	Maryland	353
28	Rhode Island	349
28	Wisconsin	349
30	New York	341
31	West Virginia	336
32	Delaware	317
33	New Jersey	315
34	Pennsylvania	305
35	Utah	304
35	Virginia	304
37	Vermont	300
38	South Carolina	299
39	Maine	295
40	Idaho	274
41	Michigan	270
42	New Mexico	264
43	California	240
44	Nevada	223
45	Washington	218
46	Florida	215
47	Alaska	198
48	Arizona	188
49	Oregon	180
50	Hawaii	159

District of Columbia 327

Source: MQ Press using data from U.S. Dept of Health & Human Services, Centers for Medicare and Medicaid Services
OSCAR Database (January 9, 2006)

*Beds in nursing care facilities certified by CMS to participate in the Medicare/Medicaid programs. National rate does not include beds or population in U.S. territories. Calculated using 2004 Census population estimate.

Nursing Home Occupancy Rate in 2003

National Rate = 82.6% of Beds in Nursing Homes Occupied

ALPHA ORDER

RANK	STATE	RATE
14	Alabama	89.4
38	Alaska	76.8
35	Arizona	80.5
45	Arkansas	72.6
30	California	83.0
33	Colorado	81.2
8	Connecticut	91.6
26	Delaware	84.7
23	Florida	87.2
11	Georgia	90.9
1	Hawaii	93.8
40	Idaho	76.0
43	Illinois	74.8
44	Indiana	73.2
36	Iowa	78.5
37	Kansas	78.0
16	Kentucky	89.0
41	Louisiana	75.9
6	Maine	92.1
24	Maryland	86.1
12	Massachusetts	89.8
27	Michigan	84.4
6	Minnesota	92.1
18	Mississippi	88.5
48	Missouri	68.6
39	Montana	76.6
30	Nebraska	83.0
32	Nevada	82.9
9	New Hampshire	91.5
21	New Jersey	87.7
27	New Mexico	84.4
4	New York	92.5
20	North Carolina	88.2
2	North Dakota	93.2
42	Ohio	75.0
50	Oklahoma	66.2
49	Oregon	67.6
13	Pennsylvania	89.7
10	Rhode Island	91.0
17	South Carolina	88.6
5	South Dakota	92.4
19	Tennessee	88.3
46	Texas	72.0
47	Utah	71.3
3	Vermont	92.7
21	Virginia	87.7
29	Washington	84.2
15	West Virginia	89.3
25	Wisconsin	85.6
34	Wyoming	80.9

RANK ORDER

RANK	STATE	RATE
1	Hawaii	93.8
2	North Dakota	93.2
3	Vermont	92.7
4	New York	92.5
5	South Dakota	92.4
6	Maine	92.1
6	Minnesota	92.1
8	Connecticut	91.6
9	New Hampshire	91.5
10	Rhode Island	91.0
11	Georgia	90.9
12	Massachusetts	89.8
13	Pennsylvania	89.7
14	Alabama	89.4
15	West Virginia	89.3
16	Kentucky	89.0
17	South Carolina	88.6
18	Mississippi	88.5
19	Tennessee	88.3
20	North Carolina	88.2
21	New Jersey	87.7
21	Virginia	87.7
23	Florida	87.2
24	Maryland	86.1
25	Wisconsin	85.6
26	Delaware	84.7
27	Michigan	84.4
27	New Mexico	84.4
29	Washington	84.2
30	California	83.0
30	Nebraska	83.0
32	Nevada	82.9
33	Colorado	81.2
34	Wyoming	80.9
35	Arizona	80.5
36	Iowa	78.5
37	Kansas	78.0
38	Alaska	76.8
39	Montana	76.6
40	Idaho	76.0
41	Louisiana	75.9
42	Ohio	75.0
43	Illinois	74.8
44	Indiana	73.2
45	Arkansas	72.6
46	Texas	72.0
47	Utah	71.3
48	Missouri	68.6
49	Oregon	67.6
50	Oklahoma	66.2

| | District of Columbia | 91.9 |

Source: U.S. Department of Health and Human Services, Centers for Medicare and Medicaid Services
"Health, United States, 2005" (www.cdc.gov/nchs/data/hus/hus05.pdf)

Nursing Home Resident Rate in 2003

National Rate = 308.0 Residents per 1,000 Population Age 85 and Older*

ALPHA ORDER

RANK	STATE	RATE
26	Alabama	329.6
47	Alaska	185.2
49	Arizona	163.7
18	Arkansas	365.9
42	California	220.2
32	Colorado	300.7
6	Connecticut	386.8
30	Delaware	318.6
46	Florida	193.7
13	Georgia	375.4
48	Hawaii	172.4
41	Idaho	224.2
11	Illinois	377.4
3	Indiana	401.9
4	Iowa	394.8
7	Kansas	384.5
15	Kentucky	370.5
1	Louisiana	470.0
38	Maine	274.9
28	Maryland	326.1
16	Massachusetts	366.8
39	Michigan	256.5
10	Minnesota	380.0
16	Mississippi	366.8
20	Missouri	361.1
27	Montana	328.1
12	Nebraska	376.0
45	Nevada	195.3
21	New Hampshire	346.7
35	New Jersey	290.3
40	New Mexico	236.9
25	New York	330.5
29	North Carolina	320.1
9	North Dakota	380.8
2	Ohio	406.5
14	Oklahoma	372.6
50	Oregon	131.0
31	Pennsylvania	305.9
19	Rhode Island	363.1
36	South Carolina	278.1
5	South Dakota	391.4
8	Tennessee	383.6
22	Texas	343.7
43	Utah	213.3
34	Vermont	296.7
37	Virginia	277.9
44	Washington	205.9
33	West Virginia	298.4
23	Wisconsin	343.2
24	Wyoming	334.2

RANK ORDER

RANK	STATE	RATE
1	Louisiana	470.0
2	Ohio	406.5
3	Indiana	401.9
4	Iowa	394.8
5	South Dakota	391.4
6	Connecticut	386.8
7	Kansas	384.5
8	Tennessee	383.6
9	North Dakota	380.8
10	Minnesota	380.0
11	Illinois	377.4
12	Nebraska	376.0
13	Georgia	375.4
14	Oklahoma	372.6
15	Kentucky	370.5
16	Massachusetts	366.8
16	Mississippi	366.8
18	Arkansas	365.9
19	Rhode Island	363.1
20	Missouri	361.1
21	New Hampshire	346.7
22	Texas	343.7
23	Wisconsin	343.2
24	Wyoming	334.2
25	New York	330.5
26	Alabama	329.6
27	Montana	328.1
28	Maryland	326.1
29	North Carolina	320.1
30	Delaware	318.6
31	Pennsylvania	305.9
32	Colorado	300.7
33	West Virginia	298.4
34	Vermont	296.7
35	New Jersey	290.3
36	South Carolina	278.1
37	Virginia	277.9
38	Maine	274.9
39	Michigan	256.5
40	New Mexico	236.9
41	Idaho	224.2
42	California	220.2
43	Utah	213.3
44	Washington	205.9
45	Nevada	195.3
46	Florida	193.7
47	Alaska	185.2
48	Hawaii	172.4
49	Arizona	163.7
50	Oregon	131.0

District of Columbia	306.0

Source: U.S. Department of Health and Human Services, Centers for Medicare and Medicaid Services "Health, United States, 2005" (www.cdc.gov/nchs/data/hus/hus05.pdf)
Number of nursing home residents (all ages) per 1,000 resident population 85 years of age and over.

Nursing Home Population in 2003

National Total = 1,451,672

RANK	STATE	POPULATION	% of USA
23	Alabama	23,564	1.6%
50	Alaska	619	0.0%
33	Arizona	13,245	0.9%
28	Arkansas	17,997	1.2%
2	California	107,578	7.4%
29	Colorado	16,344	1.1%
19	Connecticut	28,622	2.0%
46	Delaware	3,962	0.3%
7	Florida	71,987	5.0%
15	Georgia	36,372	2.5%
47	Hawaii	3,806	0.3%
44	Idaho	4,754	0.3%
6	Illinois	79,833	5.5%
11	Indiana	40,623	2.8%
20	Iowa	27,805	1.9%
26	Kansas	21,085	1.5%
24	Kentucky	22,814	1.6%
18	Louisiana	29,151	2.0%
38	Maine	6,954	0.5%
22	Maryland	25,270	1.7%
8	Massachusetts	46,993	3.2%
10	Michigan	41,547	2.9%
16	Minnesota	36,231	2.5%
31	Mississippi	16,057	1.1%
13	Missouri	37,345	2.6%
42	Montana	5,739	0.4%
32	Nebraska	13,598	0.9%
45	Nevada	4,308	0.3%
37	New Hampshire	7,145	0.5%
9	New Jersey	44,356	3.1%
40	New Mexico	6,280	0.4%
1	New York	113,456	7.8%
12	North Carolina	37,936	2.6%
41	North Dakota	6,137	0.4%
5	Ohio	79,839	5.5%
25	Oklahoma	21,679	1.5%
35	Oregon	8,640	0.6%
4	Pennsylvania	81,474	5.6%
36	Rhode Island	8,528	0.6%
30	South Carolina	16,220	1.1%
39	South Dakota	6,803	0.5%
17	Tennessee	33,503	2.3%
3	Texas	87,470	6.0%
43	Utah	5,306	0.4%
48	Vermont	3,319	0.2%
21	Virginia	27,614	1.9%
27	Washington	19,968	1.4%
34	West Virginia	9,963	0.7%
14	Wisconsin	36,497	2.5%
49	Wyoming	2,475	0.2%

RANK	STATE	POPULATION	% of USA
1	New York	113,456	7.8%
2	California	107,578	7.4%
3	Texas	87,470	6.0%
4	Pennsylvania	81,474	5.6%
5	Ohio	79,839	5.5%
6	Illinois	79,833	5.5%
7	Florida	71,987	5.0%
8	Massachusetts	46,993	3.2%
9	New Jersey	44,356	3.1%
10	Michigan	41,547	2.9%
11	Indiana	40,623	2.8%
12	North Carolina	37,936	2.6%
13	Missouri	37,345	2.6%
14	Wisconsin	36,497	2.5%
15	Georgia	36,372	2.5%
16	Minnesota	36,231	2.5%
17	Tennessee	33,503	2.3%
18	Louisiana	29,151	2.0%
19	Connecticut	28,622	2.0%
20	Iowa	27,805	1.9%
21	Virginia	27,614	1.9%
22	Maryland	25,270	1.7%
23	Alabama	23,564	1.6%
24	Kentucky	22,814	1.6%
25	Oklahoma	21,679	1.5%
26	Kansas	21,085	1.5%
27	Washington	19,968	1.4%
28	Arkansas	17,997	1.2%
29	Colorado	16,344	1.1%
30	South Carolina	16,220	1.1%
31	Mississippi	16,057	1.1%
32	Nebraska	13,598	0.9%
33	Arizona	13,245	0.9%
34	West Virginia	9,963	0.7%
35	Oregon	8,640	0.6%
36	Rhode Island	8,528	0.6%
37	New Hampshire	7,145	0.5%
38	Maine	6,954	0.5%
39	South Dakota	6,803	0.5%
40	New Mexico	6,280	0.4%
41	North Dakota	6,137	0.4%
42	Montana	5,739	0.4%
43	Utah	5,306	0.4%
44	Idaho	4,754	0.3%
45	Nevada	4,308	0.3%
46	Delaware	3,962	0.3%
47	Hawaii	3,806	0.3%
48	Vermont	3,319	0.2%
49	Wyoming	2,475	0.2%
50	Alaska	619	0.0%
	District of Columbia	2,861	0.2%

Source: U.S. Department of Health and Human Services, Centers for Medicare and Medicaid Services "Health, United States, 2005" (www.cdc.gov/nchs/data/hus/hus05.pdf)

Health Care Establishments in 2003

National Total = 574,424 Establishments*

ALPHA ORDER

RANK	STATE	ESTABLISH'S	% of USA	RANK	STATE	ESTABLISH'S	% of USA
27	Alabama	7,423	1.3%	1	California	74,127	12.9%
47	Alaska	1,426	0.2%	2	New York	41,548	7.2%
18	Arizona	10,599	1.8%	3	Texas	39,631	6.9%
32	Arkansas	5,129	0.9%	4	Florida	38,745	6.7%
1	California	74,127	12.9%	5	Pennsylvania	26,492	4.6%
21	Colorado	9,715	1.7%	6	Illinois	23,050	4.0%
26	Connecticut	7,511	1.3%	7	Ohio	21,732	3.8%
45	Delaware	1,572	0.3%	8	Michigan	20,157	3.5%
4	Florida	38,745	6.7%	9	New Jersey	20,054	3.5%
10	Georgia	14,670	2.6%	10	Georgia	14,670	2.6%
41	Hawaii	2,729	0.5%	11	North Carolina	13,991	2.4%
40	Idaho	2,932	0.5%	12	Massachusetts	13,458	2.3%
6	Illinois	23,050	4.0%	13	Washington	12,537	2.2%
17	Indiana	10,833	1.9%	14	Virginia	12,450	2.2%
30	Iowa	5,480	1.0%	15	Maryland	11,558	2.0%
31	Kansas	5,435	0.9%	16	Missouri	11,026	1.9%
25	Kentucky	7,728	1.3%	17	Indiana	10,833	1.9%
23	Louisiana	8,612	1.5%	18	Arizona	10,599	1.8%
39	Maine	3,224	0.6%	19	Tennessee	10,457	1.8%
15	Maryland	11,558	2.0%	20	Wisconsin	10,029	1.7%
12	Massachusetts	13,458	2.3%	21	Colorado	9,715	1.7%
8	Michigan	20,157	3.5%	22	Minnesota	9,545	1.7%
22	Minnesota	9,545	1.7%	23	Louisiana	8,612	1.5%
34	Mississippi	4,144	0.7%	24	Oregon	8,160	1.4%
16	Missouri	11,026	1.9%	25	Kentucky	7,728	1.3%
44	Montana	2,190	0.4%	26	Connecticut	7,511	1.3%
37	Nebraska	3,286	0.6%	27	Alabama	7,423	1.3%
35	Nevada	4,139	0.7%	28	Oklahoma	7,071	1.2%
43	New Hampshire	2,304	0.4%	29	South Carolina	6,729	1.2%
9	New Jersey	20,054	3.5%	30	Iowa	5,480	1.0%
38	New Mexico	3,253	0.6%	31	Kansas	5,435	0.9%
2	New York	41,548	7.2%	32	Arkansas	5,129	0.9%
11	North Carolina	13,991	2.4%	33	Utah	4,737	0.8%
49	North Dakota	1,167	0.2%	34	Mississippi	4,144	0.7%
7	Ohio	21,732	3.8%	35	Nevada	4,139	0.7%
28	Oklahoma	7,071	1.2%	36	West Virginia	3,674	0.6%
24	Oregon	8,160	1.4%	37	Nebraska	3,286	0.6%
5	Pennsylvania	26,492	4.6%	38	New Mexico	3,253	0.6%
42	Rhode Island	2,428	0.4%	39	Maine	3,224	0.6%
29	South Carolina	6,729	1.2%	40	Idaho	2,932	0.5%
46	South Dakota	1,515	0.3%	41	Hawaii	2,729	0.5%
19	Tennessee	10,457	1.8%	42	Rhode Island	2,428	0.4%
3	Texas	39,631	6.9%	43	New Hampshire	2,304	0.4%
33	Utah	4,737	0.8%	44	Montana	2,190	0.4%
48	Vermont	1,418	0.2%	45	Delaware	1,572	0.3%
14	Virginia	12,450	2.2%	46	South Dakota	1,515	0.3%
13	Washington	12,537	2.2%	47	Alaska	1,426	0.2%
36	West Virginia	3,674	0.6%	48	Vermont	1,418	0.2%
20	Wisconsin	10,029	1.7%	49	North Dakota	1,167	0.2%
50	Wyoming	1,148	0.2%	50	Wyoming	1,148	0.2%
					District of Columbia	1,456	0.3%

Source: U.S. Bureau of the Census
"County Business Patterns 2003 (NAICS)" (http://censtats.census.gov/cbpnaic/cbpnaic.shtml)
*Includes establishments exempt from as well as subject to the federal income tax. Includes those establishments within the North American Industry Classification System (NAICS) classifications 621 (ambulatory health care services), 622 (hospitals) and 623 (nursing and residential care facilities). Does not include classification 624 (social assistance facilities).

IV. FINANCE

IV. FINANCE (Continued)

Average Medical Malpractice Payment in 2004

National Average = $298,460*

ALPHA ORDER

RANK	STATE	AVERAGE PAYMENT
15	Alabama	$346,279
48	Alaska	151,524
18	Arizona	324,558
27	Arkansas	295,465
45	California	185,746
21	Colorado	314,268
4	Connecticut	449,296
5	Delaware	430,490
35	Florida**	241,204
22	Georgia	312,392
3	Hawaii	457,755
17	Idaho	332,220
1	Illinois	516,529
31	Indiana**	274,316
2	Iowa	481,776
46	Kansas**	175,247
42	Kentucky	219,604
49	Louisiana**	139,746
9	Maine	385,403
14	Maryland	349,697
8	Massachusetts	401,886
50	Michigan	137,484
25	Minnesota	305,483
19	Mississippi	323,567
23	Missouri	311,882
32	Montana	272,637
43	Nebraska**	206,885
28	Nevada	291,095
20	New Hampshire	317,647
11	New Jersey	368,672
44	New Mexico**	200,046
7	New York	404,762
12	North Carolina	366,447
6	North Dakota	416,080
26	Ohio	304,287
38	Oklahoma	235,197
24	Oregon	310,527
16	Pennsylvania**	337,579
10	Rhode Island	370,834
36	South Carolina**	239,055
41	South Dakota	223,723
34	Tennessee	244,408
37	Texas	237,989
47	Utah	154,452
40	Vermont	225,570
30	Virginia	283,567
29	Washington	288,207
33	West Virginia	255,506
13	Wisconsin**	365,662
39	Wyoming	225,865

RANK ORDER

RANK	STATE	AVERAGE PAYMENT
1	Illinois	$516,529
2	Iowa	481,776
3	Hawaii	457,755
4	Connecticut	449,296
5	Delaware	430,490
6	North Dakota	416,080
7	New York	404,762
8	Massachusetts	401,886
9	Maine	385,403
10	Rhode Island	370,834
11	New Jersey	368,672
12	North Carolina	366,447
13	Wisconsin**	365,662
14	Maryland	349,697
15	Alabama	346,279
16	Pennsylvania**	337,579
17	Idaho	332,220
18	Arizona	324,558
19	Mississippi	323,567
20	New Hampshire	317,647
21	Colorado	314,268
22	Georgia	312,392
23	Missouri	311,882
24	Oregon	310,527
25	Minnesota	305,483
26	Ohio	304,287
27	Arkansas	295,465
28	Nevada	291,095
29	Washington	288,207
30	Virginia	283,567
31	Indiana**	274,316
32	Montana	272,637
33	West Virginia	255,506
34	Tennessee	244,408
35	Florida**	241,204
36	South Carolina**	239,055
37	Texas	237,989
38	Oklahoma	235,197
39	Wyoming	225,865
40	Vermont	225,570
41	South Dakota	223,723
42	Kentucky	219,604
43	Nebraska**	206,885
44	New Mexico**	200,046
45	California	185,746
46	Kansas**	175,247
47	Utah	154,452
48	Alaska	151,524
49	Louisiana**	139,746
50	Michigan	137,484
	District of Columbia	408,865

Source: U.S. Department of Health and Human Services, Bureau of Health Professions
    "National Practitioner Data Bank, 2004 Annual Report" (http://www.npdb-hipdb.com/annualrpt.html)
*National figure includes U.S. territories and U.S. Armed Forces locations overseas.
**The figures for these states have not been adjusted for payments by state compensation funds and other similar
funds. Average payments for these states understate the actual average amounts received by claimants.

Percent of Private-Sector Establishments That Offer Health Insurance: 2003

National Percent = 56.2%

ALPHA ORDER				RANK ORDER		
RANK	STATE	PERCENT		RANK	STATE	PERCENT
15	Alabama	58.3		1	Hawaii	86.2
42	Alaska	47.0		2	New Hampshire	68.8
35	Arizona	52.4		3	Massachusetts	65.6
50	Arkansas	42.2		4	Pennsylvania	65.4
20	California	55.9		5	Connecticut	65.3
34	Colorado	52.6		6	Rhode Island	63.6
5	Connecticut	65.3		7	Delaware	61.1
7	Delaware	61.1		7	Michigan	61.1
23	Florida	55.3		9	New Jersey	60.8
26	Georgia	54.6		10	Maryland	59.9
1	Hawaii	86.2		11	New York	59.7
36	Idaho	51.0		12	Ohio	59.6
24	Illinois	55.0		13	Virginia	59.4
30	Indiana	53.4		14	Nevada	58.7
37	Iowa	50.8		15	Alabama	58.3
28	Kansas	54.5		15	Oregon	58.3
17	Kentucky	57.5		17	Kentucky	57.5
39	Louisiana	50.0		18	Washington	57.1
29	Maine	53.5		19	North Carolina	56.5
10	Maryland	59.9		20	California	55.9
3	Massachusetts	65.6		20	Minnesota	55.9
7	Michigan	61.1		22	Wisconsin	55.7
20	Minnesota	55.9		23	Florida	55.3
44	Mississippi	45.9		24	Illinois	55.0
31	Missouri	53.3		25	Vermont	54.9
45	Montana	45.1		26	Georgia	54.6
46	Nebraska	44.7		26	South Carolina	54.6
14	Nevada	58.7		28	Kansas	54.5
2	New Hampshire	68.8		29	Maine	53.5
9	New Jersey	60.8		30	Indiana	53.4
38	New Mexico	50.5		31	Missouri	53.3
11	New York	59.7		32	Tennessee	53.0
19	North Carolina	56.5		33	West Virginia	52.8
46	North Dakota	44.7		34	Colorado	52.6
12	Ohio	59.6		35	Arizona	52.4
43	Oklahoma	46.4		36	Idaho	51.0
15	Oregon	58.3		37	Iowa	50.8
4	Pennsylvania	65.4		38	New Mexico	50.5
6	Rhode Island	63.6		39	Louisiana	50.0
26	South Carolina	54.6		40	Texas	48.7
48	South Dakota	44.2		41	Utah	48.6
32	Tennessee	53.0		42	Alaska	47.0
40	Texas	48.7		43	Oklahoma	46.4
41	Utah	48.6		44	Mississippi	45.9
25	Vermont	54.9		45	Montana	45.1
13	Virginia	59.4		46	Nebraska	44.7
18	Washington	57.1		46	North Dakota	44.7
33	West Virginia	52.8		48	South Dakota	44.2
22	Wisconsin	55.7		49	Wyoming	42.5
49	Wyoming	42.5		50	Arkansas	42.2

District of Columbia 79.3

Source: U.S. Department of Health and Human Services, Agency for Healthcare Research and Quality
"Private-Sector Data by Firm Size and State" (Table II Series, Medical Expenditures Panel Survey, July 2005)
(http://www.meps.ahrq.gov/MEPSDATA/ic/2003/Index203.htm)

Percent of Private-Sector Establishments with Fewer Than 50 Employees That Offer Health Insurance: 2003
National Percent = 43.2%

<table>
<tr><td colspan="3">ALPHA ORDER</td><td colspan="3">RANK ORDER</td></tr>
<tr><td>RANK</td><td>STATE</td><td>PERCENT</td><td>RANK</td><td>STATE</td><td>PERCENT</td></tr>
<tr><td>16</td><td>Alabama</td><td>44.8</td><td>1</td><td>Hawaii</td><td>81.5</td></tr>
<tr><td>41</td><td>Alaska</td><td>34.8</td><td>2</td><td>New Hampshire</td><td>60.1</td></tr>
<tr><td>32</td><td>Arizona</td><td>38.5</td><td>3</td><td>Massachusetts</td><td>56.2</td></tr>
<tr><td>50</td><td>Arkansas</td><td>25.7</td><td>4</td><td>Rhode Island</td><td>55.4</td></tr>
<tr><td>21</td><td>California</td><td>43.8</td><td>5</td><td>Connecticut</td><td>54.6</td></tr>
<tr><td>29</td><td>Colorado</td><td>40.8</td><td>6</td><td>Pennsylvania</td><td>54.4</td></tr>
<tr><td>5</td><td>Connecticut</td><td>54.6</td><td>7</td><td>New Jersey</td><td>51.6</td></tr>
<tr><td>10</td><td>Delaware</td><td>49.1</td><td>8</td><td>New York</td><td>50.5</td></tr>
<tr><td>25</td><td>Florida</td><td>41.4</td><td>9</td><td>Michigan</td><td>50.3</td></tr>
<tr><td>35</td><td>Georgia</td><td>36.9</td><td>10</td><td>Delaware</td><td>49.1</td></tr>
<tr><td>1</td><td>Hawaii</td><td>81.5</td><td>11</td><td>Virginia</td><td>47.7</td></tr>
<tr><td>28</td><td>Idaho</td><td>41.1</td><td>12</td><td>Maryland</td><td>47.3</td></tr>
<tr><td>30</td><td>Illinois</td><td>40.2</td><td>13</td><td>Oregon</td><td>47.2</td></tr>
<tr><td>37</td><td>Indiana</td><td>35.5</td><td>14</td><td>Vermont</td><td>46.1</td></tr>
<tr><td>34</td><td>Iowa</td><td>37.3</td><td>15</td><td>Washington</td><td>45.9</td></tr>
<tr><td>25</td><td>Kansas</td><td>41.4</td><td>16</td><td>Alabama</td><td>44.8</td></tr>
<tr><td>18</td><td>Kentucky</td><td>44.0</td><td>16</td><td>Nevada</td><td>44.8</td></tr>
<tr><td>39</td><td>Louisiana</td><td>34.9</td><td>18</td><td>Kentucky</td><td>44.0</td></tr>
<tr><td>24</td><td>Maine</td><td>42.7</td><td>18</td><td>Ohio</td><td>44.0</td></tr>
<tr><td>12</td><td>Maryland</td><td>47.3</td><td>18</td><td>Wisconsin</td><td>44.0</td></tr>
<tr><td>3</td><td>Massachusetts</td><td>56.2</td><td>21</td><td>California</td><td>43.8</td></tr>
<tr><td>9</td><td>Michigan</td><td>50.3</td><td>22</td><td>North Carolina</td><td>43.1</td></tr>
<tr><td>23</td><td>Minnesota</td><td>42.9</td><td>23</td><td>Minnesota</td><td>42.9</td></tr>
<tr><td>49</td><td>Mississippi</td><td>28.4</td><td>24</td><td>Maine</td><td>42.7</td></tr>
<tr><td>27</td><td>Missouri</td><td>41.2</td><td>25</td><td>Florida</td><td>41.4</td></tr>
<tr><td>36</td><td>Montana</td><td>36.3</td><td>25</td><td>Kansas</td><td>41.4</td></tr>
<tr><td>47</td><td>Nebraska</td><td>31.5</td><td>27</td><td>Missouri</td><td>41.2</td></tr>
<tr><td>16</td><td>Nevada</td><td>44.8</td><td>28</td><td>Idaho</td><td>41.1</td></tr>
<tr><td>2</td><td>New Hampshire</td><td>60.1</td><td>29</td><td>Colorado</td><td>40.8</td></tr>
<tr><td>7</td><td>New Jersey</td><td>51.6</td><td>30</td><td>Illinois</td><td>40.2</td></tr>
<tr><td>33</td><td>New Mexico</td><td>37.6</td><td>31</td><td>South Carolina</td><td>39.9</td></tr>
<tr><td>8</td><td>New York</td><td>50.5</td><td>32</td><td>Arizona</td><td>38.5</td></tr>
<tr><td>22</td><td>North Carolina</td><td>43.1</td><td>33</td><td>New Mexico</td><td>37.6</td></tr>
<tr><td>39</td><td>North Dakota</td><td>34.9</td><td>34</td><td>Iowa</td><td>37.3</td></tr>
<tr><td>18</td><td>Ohio</td><td>44.0</td><td>35</td><td>Georgia</td><td>36.9</td></tr>
<tr><td>45</td><td>Oklahoma</td><td>32.0</td><td>36</td><td>Montana</td><td>36.3</td></tr>
<tr><td>13</td><td>Oregon</td><td>47.2</td><td>37</td><td>Indiana</td><td>35.5</td></tr>
<tr><td>6</td><td>Pennsylvania</td><td>54.4</td><td>38</td><td>West Virginia</td><td>35.4</td></tr>
<tr><td>4</td><td>Rhode Island</td><td>55.4</td><td>39</td><td>Louisiana</td><td>34.9</td></tr>
<tr><td>31</td><td>South Carolina</td><td>39.9</td><td>39</td><td>North Dakota</td><td>34.9</td></tr>
<tr><td>41</td><td>South Dakota</td><td>34.8</td><td>41</td><td>Alaska</td><td>34.8</td></tr>
<tr><td>43</td><td>Tennessee</td><td>33.9</td><td>41</td><td>South Dakota</td><td>34.8</td></tr>
<tr><td>48</td><td>Texas</td><td>31.4</td><td>43</td><td>Tennessee</td><td>33.9</td></tr>
<tr><td>43</td><td>Utah</td><td>33.9</td><td>43</td><td>Utah</td><td>33.9</td></tr>
<tr><td>14</td><td>Vermont</td><td>46.1</td><td>45</td><td>Oklahoma</td><td>32.0</td></tr>
<tr><td>11</td><td>Virginia</td><td>47.7</td><td>46</td><td>Wyoming</td><td>31.9</td></tr>
<tr><td>15</td><td>Washington</td><td>45.9</td><td>47</td><td>Nebraska</td><td>31.5</td></tr>
<tr><td>38</td><td>West Virginia</td><td>35.4</td><td>48</td><td>Texas</td><td>31.4</td></tr>
<tr><td>18</td><td>Wisconsin</td><td>44.0</td><td>49</td><td>Mississippi</td><td>28.4</td></tr>
<tr><td>46</td><td>Wyoming</td><td>31.9</td><td>50</td><td>Arkansas</td><td>25.7</td></tr>
<tr><td></td><td></td><td></td><td></td><td>District of Columbia</td><td>69.1</td></tr>
</table>

Source: U.S. Department of Health and Human Services, Agency for Healthcare Research and Quality
"Private-Sector Data by Firm Size and State" (Table II Series, Medical Expenditures Panel Survey, July 2005)
(http://www.meps.ahrq.gov/MEPSDATA/ic/2003/Index203.htm)

Percent of Private-Sector Establishments with More Than 50 Employees That Offer Health Insurance: 2003
National Percent = 95.4%

ALPHA ORDER

RANK	STATE	PERCENT
11	Alabama	97.4
26	Alaska	95.4
48	Arizona	91.9
42	Arkansas	92.9
41	California	93.1
43	Colorado	92.8
19	Connecticut	96.2
26	Delaware	95.4
13	Florida	97.3
40	Georgia	93.3
2	Hawaii	99.9
17	Idaho	96.3
24	Illinois	95.7
25	Indiana	95.5
11	Iowa	97.4
13	Kansas	97.3
45	Kentucky	92.4
33	Louisiana	94.8
16	Maine	96.6
15	Maryland	96.7
31	Massachusetts	95.1
50	Michigan	91.4
7	Minnesota	98.0
23	Mississippi	95.8
47	Missouri	92.3
35	Montana	94.7
33	Nebraska	94.8
21	Nevada	96.0
3	New Hampshire	99.6
37	New Jersey	94.4
45	New Mexico	92.4
5	New York	98.6
32	North Carolina	95.0
17	North Dakota	96.3
6	Ohio	98.5
38	Oklahoma	94.3
7	Oregon	98.0
35	Pennsylvania	94.7
1	Rhode Island	100.0
29	South Carolina	95.2
48	South Dakota	91.9
29	Tennessee	95.2
20	Texas	96.1
21	Utah	96.0
4	Vermont	98.9
26	Virginia	95.4
9	Washington	97.9
10	West Virginia	97.5
38	Wisconsin	94.3
44	Wyoming	92.5

RANK ORDER

RANK	STATE	PERCENT
1	Rhode Island	100.0
2	Hawaii	99.9
3	New Hampshire	99.6
4	Vermont	98.9
5	New York	98.6
6	Ohio	98.5
7	Minnesota	98.0
7	Oregon	98.0
9	Washington	97.9
10	West Virginia	97.5
11	Alabama	97.4
11	Iowa	97.4
13	Florida	97.3
13	Kansas	97.3
15	Maryland	96.7
16	Maine	96.6
17	Idaho	96.3
17	North Dakota	96.3
19	Connecticut	96.2
20	Texas	96.1
21	Nevada	96.0
21	Utah	96.0
23	Mississippi	95.8
24	Illinois	95.7
25	Indiana	95.5
26	Alaska	95.4
26	Delaware	95.4
26	Virginia	95.4
29	South Carolina	95.2
29	Tennessee	95.2
31	Massachusetts	95.1
32	North Carolina	95.0
33	Louisiana	94.8
33	Nebraska	94.8
35	Montana	94.7
35	Pennsylvania	94.7
37	New Jersey	94.4
38	Oklahoma	94.3
38	Wisconsin	94.3
40	Georgia	93.3
41	California	93.1
42	Arkansas	92.9
43	Colorado	92.8
44	Wyoming	92.5
45	Kentucky	92.4
45	New Mexico	92.4
47	Missouri	92.3
48	Arizona	91.9
48	South Dakota	91.9
50	Michigan	91.4

	District of Columbia	99.2

Source: U.S. Department of Health and Human Services, Agency for Healthcare Research and Quality
  "Private-Sector Data by Firm Size and State" (Table II Series, Medical Expenditures Panel Survey, July 2005)
  (http://www.meps.ahrq.gov/MEPSDATA/ic/2003/Index203.htm)

Average Annual Single Coverage Health Insurance Premium per Enrolled Employee in 2003
National Average = $3,481*

<table>
<tr><td colspan="3">ALPHA ORDER</td><td colspan="3">RANK ORDER</td></tr>
<tr><td>RANK</td><td>STATE</td><td>PREMIUM</td><td>RANK</td><td>STATE</td><td>PREMIUM</td></tr>
<tr><td>47</td><td>Alabama</td><td>$3,156</td><td>1</td><td>Alaska</td><td>$4,011</td></tr>
<tr><td>1</td><td>Alaska</td><td>4,011</td><td>2</td><td>Delaware</td><td>3,854</td></tr>
<tr><td>46</td><td>Arizona</td><td>3,209</td><td>3</td><td>Maine</td><td>3,852</td></tr>
<tr><td>48</td><td>Arkansas</td><td>3,127</td><td>4</td><td>New Jersey</td><td>3,814</td></tr>
<tr><td>43</td><td>California</td><td>3,293</td><td>5</td><td>West Virginia</td><td>3,809</td></tr>
<tr><td>13</td><td>Colorado</td><td>3,645</td><td>6</td><td>Wisconsin</td><td>3,749</td></tr>
<tr><td>11</td><td>Connecticut</td><td>3,676</td><td>7</td><td>Rhode Island</td><td>3,725</td></tr>
<tr><td>2</td><td>Delaware</td><td>3,854</td><td>8</td><td>Wyoming</td><td>3,706</td></tr>
<tr><td>17</td><td>Florida</td><td>3,592</td><td>9</td><td>Illinois</td><td>3,692</td></tr>
<tr><td>14</td><td>Georgia</td><td>3,624</td><td>10</td><td>Minnesota</td><td>3,679</td></tr>
<tr><td>49</td><td>Hawaii</td><td>3,020</td><td>11</td><td>Connecticut</td><td>3,676</td></tr>
<tr><td>38</td><td>Idaho</td><td>3,331</td><td>12</td><td>Michigan</td><td>3,671</td></tr>
<tr><td>9</td><td>Illinois</td><td>3,692</td><td>13</td><td>Colorado</td><td>3,645</td></tr>
<tr><td>25</td><td>Indiana</td><td>3,493</td><td>14</td><td>Georgia</td><td>3,624</td></tr>
<tr><td>45</td><td>Iowa</td><td>3,270</td><td>15</td><td>Tennessee</td><td>3,597</td></tr>
<tr><td>31</td><td>Kansas</td><td>3,401</td><td>16</td><td>Vermont</td><td>3,596</td></tr>
<tr><td>27</td><td>Kentucky</td><td>3,437</td><td>17</td><td>Florida</td><td>3,592</td></tr>
<tr><td>40</td><td>Louisiana</td><td>3,317</td><td>17</td><td>New York</td><td>3,592</td></tr>
<tr><td>3</td><td>Maine</td><td>3,852</td><td>19</td><td>Nevada</td><td>3,578</td></tr>
<tr><td>28</td><td>Maryland</td><td>3,427</td><td>20</td><td>New Hampshire</td><td>3,563</td></tr>
<tr><td>24</td><td>Massachusetts</td><td>3,496</td><td>21</td><td>Washington</td><td>3,520</td></tr>
<tr><td>12</td><td>Michigan</td><td>3,671</td><td>22</td><td>Montana</td><td>3,506</td></tr>
<tr><td>10</td><td>Minnesota</td><td>3,679</td><td>22</td><td>Nebraska</td><td>3,506</td></tr>
<tr><td>41</td><td>Mississippi</td><td>3,305</td><td>24</td><td>Massachusetts</td><td>3,496</td></tr>
<tr><td>41</td><td>Missouri</td><td>3,305</td><td>25</td><td>Indiana</td><td>3,493</td></tr>
<tr><td>22</td><td>Montana</td><td>3,506</td><td>26</td><td>Pennsylvania</td><td>3,449</td></tr>
<tr><td>22</td><td>Nebraska</td><td>3,506</td><td>27</td><td>Kentucky</td><td>3,437</td></tr>
<tr><td>19</td><td>Nevada</td><td>3,578</td><td>28</td><td>Maryland</td><td>3,427</td></tr>
<tr><td>20</td><td>New Hampshire</td><td>3,563</td><td>29</td><td>Ohio</td><td>3,416</td></tr>
<tr><td>4</td><td>New Jersey</td><td>3,814</td><td>30</td><td>North Carolina</td><td>3,411</td></tr>
<tr><td>35</td><td>New Mexico</td><td>3,361</td><td>31</td><td>Kansas</td><td>3,401</td></tr>
<tr><td>17</td><td>New York</td><td>3,592</td><td>32</td><td>Texas</td><td>3,400</td></tr>
<tr><td>30</td><td>North Carolina</td><td>3,411</td><td>33</td><td>South Carolina</td><td>3,371</td></tr>
<tr><td>50</td><td>North Dakota</td><td>2,999</td><td>34</td><td>Oregon</td><td>3,362</td></tr>
<tr><td>29</td><td>Ohio</td><td>3,416</td><td>35</td><td>New Mexico</td><td>3,361</td></tr>
<tr><td>44</td><td>Oklahoma</td><td>3,285</td><td>35</td><td>South Dakota</td><td>3,361</td></tr>
<tr><td>34</td><td>Oregon</td><td>3,362</td><td>37</td><td>Utah</td><td>3,352</td></tr>
<tr><td>26</td><td>Pennsylvania</td><td>3,449</td><td>38</td><td>Idaho</td><td>3,331</td></tr>
<tr><td>7</td><td>Rhode Island</td><td>3,725</td><td>39</td><td>Virginia</td><td>3,322</td></tr>
<tr><td>33</td><td>South Carolina</td><td>3,371</td><td>40</td><td>Louisiana</td><td>3,317</td></tr>
<tr><td>35</td><td>South Dakota</td><td>3,361</td><td>41</td><td>Mississippi</td><td>3,305</td></tr>
<tr><td>15</td><td>Tennessee</td><td>3,597</td><td>41</td><td>Missouri</td><td>3,305</td></tr>
<tr><td>32</td><td>Texas</td><td>3,400</td><td>43</td><td>California</td><td>3,293</td></tr>
<tr><td>37</td><td>Utah</td><td>3,352</td><td>44</td><td>Oklahoma</td><td>3,285</td></tr>
<tr><td>16</td><td>Vermont</td><td>3,596</td><td>45</td><td>Iowa</td><td>3,270</td></tr>
<tr><td>39</td><td>Virginia</td><td>3,322</td><td>46</td><td>Arizona</td><td>3,209</td></tr>
<tr><td>21</td><td>Washington</td><td>3,520</td><td>47</td><td>Alabama</td><td>3,156</td></tr>
<tr><td>5</td><td>West Virginia</td><td>3,809</td><td>48</td><td>Arkansas</td><td>3,127</td></tr>
<tr><td>6</td><td>Wisconsin</td><td>3,749</td><td>49</td><td>Hawaii</td><td>3,020</td></tr>
<tr><td>8</td><td>Wyoming</td><td>3,706</td><td>50</td><td>North Dakota</td><td>2,999</td></tr>
<tr><td></td><td></td><td></td><td></td><td>District of Columbia</td><td>3,740</td></tr>
</table>

Source: U.S. Department of Health and Human Services, Agency for Healthcare Research and Quality
   "Private-Sector Data by Firm Size and State" (Table II Series, Medical Expenditures Panel Survey, July 2005)
   (http://www.meps.ahrq.gov/MEPSDATA/ic/2003/Index203.htm)
*Enrolled employees at private-sector establishments that offer health insurance coverage.

Average Annual Employee Contribution for
Single Coverage Health Insurance in 2003
National Average = $606*

ALPHA ORDER

RANK ORDER

RANK	STATE	PREMIUM
22	Alabama	$636
48	Alaska	433
36	Arizona	560
20	Arkansas	644
44	California	475
31	Colorado	581
5	Connecticut	789
13	Delaware	711
10	Florida	750
14	Georgia	699
50	Hawaii	251
39	Idaho	540
25	Illinois	625
11	Indiana	732
17	Iowa	682
6	Kansas	786
16	Kentucky	688
24	Louisiana	633
15	Maine	698
4	Maryland	791
12	Massachusetts	713
40	Michigan	538
29	Minnesota	604
43	Mississippi	503
34	Missouri	572
44	Montana	475
1	Nebraska	875
46	Nevada	474
9	New Hampshire	753
28	New Jersey	611
30	New Mexico	593
25	New York	625
38	North Carolina	541
35	North Dakota	571
32	Ohio	579
25	Oklahoma	625
47	Oregon	438
42	Pennsylvania	533
3	Rhode Island	820
18	South Carolina	668
7	South Dakota	771
8	Tennessee	760
37	Texas	548
21	Utah	638
19	Vermont	653
23	Virginia	634
49	Washington	385
40	West Virginia	538
2	Wisconsin	830
33	Wyoming	574

RANK	STATE	PREMIUM
1	Nebraska	$875
2	Wisconsin	830
3	Rhode Island	820
4	Maryland	791
5	Connecticut	789
6	Kansas	786
7	South Dakota	771
8	Tennessee	760
9	New Hampshire	753
10	Florida	750
11	Indiana	732
12	Massachusetts	713
13	Delaware	711
14	Georgia	699
15	Maine	698
16	Kentucky	688
17	Iowa	682
18	South Carolina	668
19	Vermont	653
20	Arkansas	644
21	Utah	638
22	Alabama	636
23	Virginia	634
24	Louisiana	633
25	Illinois	625
25	New York	625
25	Oklahoma	625
28	New Jersey	611
29	Minnesota	604
30	New Mexico	593
31	Colorado	581
32	Ohio	579
33	Wyoming	574
34	Missouri	572
35	North Dakota	571
36	Arizona	560
37	Texas	548
38	North Carolina	541
39	Idaho	540
40	Michigan	538
40	West Virginia	538
42	Pennsylvania	533
43	Mississippi	503
44	California	475
44	Montana	475
46	Nevada	474
47	Oregon	438
48	Alaska	433
49	Washington	385
50	Hawaii	251

District of Columbia   710

*Source: U.S. Department of Health and Human Services, Agency for Healthcare Research and Quality
"Private-Sector Data by Firm Size and State" (Table II Series, Medical Expenditures Panel Survey, July 2005)
(http://www.meps.ahrq.gov/MEPSDATA/ic/2003/Index203.htm)*
Enrolled employees at private-sector establishments that offer health insurance coverage.

Percent of Total Premiums for Single Coverage
Health Insurance Paid by Employees in 2003
National Average = 17.4%*

ALPHA ORDER

RANK	STATE	PERCENT
15	Alabama	20.2
49	Alaska	10.8
28	Arizona	17.5
13	Arkansas	20.6
43	California	14.4
37	Colorado	15.9
7	Connecticut	21.5
24	Delaware	18.4
11	Florida	20.9
18	Georgia	19.3
50	Hawaii	8.3
34	Idaho	16.2
31	Illinois	16.9
10	Indiana	21.0
12	Iowa	20.8
2	Kansas	23.1
16	Kentucky	20.0
19	Louisiana	19.1
26	Maine	18.1
2	Maryland	23.1
14	Massachusetts	20.4
42	Michigan	14.7
33	Minnesota	16.4
41	Mississippi	15.2
30	Missouri	17.3
45	Montana	13.5
1	Nebraska	25.0
46	Nevada	13.3
8	New Hampshire	21.1
36	New Jersey	16.0
27	New Mexico	17.6
29	New York	17.4
38	North Carolina	15.8
21	North Dakota	19.0
31	Ohio	16.9
21	Oklahoma	19.0
47	Oregon	13.0
40	Pennsylvania	15.4
6	Rhode Island	22.0
17	South Carolina	19.8
4	South Dakota	22.9
8	Tennessee	21.1
35	Texas	16.1
21	Utah	19.0
25	Vermont	18.2
19	Virginia	19.1
48	Washington	10.9
44	West Virginia	14.1
5	Wisconsin	22.1
39	Wyoming	15.5

RANK ORDER

RANK	STATE	PERCENT
1	Nebraska	25.0
2	Kansas	23.1
2	Maryland	23.1
4	South Dakota	22.9
5	Wisconsin	22.1
6	Rhode Island	22.0
7	Connecticut	21.5
8	New Hampshire	21.1
8	Tennessee	21.1
10	Indiana	21.0
11	Florida	20.9
12	Iowa	20.8
13	Arkansas	20.6
14	Massachusetts	20.4
15	Alabama	20.2
16	Kentucky	20.0
17	South Carolina	19.8
18	Georgia	19.3
19	Louisiana	19.1
19	Virginia	19.1
21	North Dakota	19.0
21	Oklahoma	19.0
21	Utah	19.0
24	Delaware	18.4
25	Vermont	18.2
26	Maine	18.1
27	New Mexico	17.6
28	Arizona	17.5
29	New York	17.4
30	Missouri	17.3
31	Illinois	16.9
31	Ohio	16.9
33	Minnesota	16.4
34	Idaho	16.2
35	Texas	16.1
36	New Jersey	16.0
37	Colorado	15.9
38	North Carolina	15.8
39	Wyoming	15.5
40	Pennsylvania	15.4
41	Mississippi	15.2
42	Michigan	14.7
43	California	14.4
44	West Virginia	14.1
45	Montana	13.5
46	Nevada	13.3
47	Oregon	13.0
48	Washington	10.9
49	Alaska	10.8
50	Hawaii	8.3

	District of Columbia	19.0

Source: U.S. Department of Health and Human Services, Agency for Healthcare Research and Quality
  "Private-Sector Data by Firm Size and State" (Table II Series, Medical Expenditures Panel Survey, July 2005)
  (http://www.meps.ahrq.gov/MEPSDATA/ic/2003/Index203.htm)
*Enrolled employees at private-sector establishments that offer health insurance coverage.

Average Annual Family Coverage Health Insurance Premium per Enrolled Employee in 2003
National Average = $9,249*

ALPHA ORDER

RANK	STATE	PREMIUM
47	Alabama	$8,045
1	Alaska	10,564
32	Arizona	8,972
48	Arkansas	7,977
30	California	9,091
13	Colorado	9,522
5	Connecticut	10,119
2	Delaware	10,499
18	Florida	9,331
39	Georgia	8,641
49	Hawaii	7,887
40	Idaho	8,563
9	Illinois	9,693
19	Indiana	9,315
44	Iowa	8,436
34	Kansas	8,907
29	Kentucky	9,118
38	Louisiana	8,735
3	Maine	10,308
22	Maryland	9,217
7	Massachusetts	9,867
16	Michigan	9,449
6	Minnesota	10,066
46	Mississippi	8,075
31	Missouri	8,984
41	Montana	8,542
26	Nebraska	9,139
36	Nevada	8,831
8	New Hampshire	9,776
4	New Jersey	10,168
20	New Mexico	9,299
17	New York	9,439
43	North Carolina	8,463
50	North Dakota	7,866
27	Ohio	9,136
37	Oklahoma	8,739
35	Oregon	8,861
28	Pennsylvania	9,133
15	Rhode Island	9,460
33	South Carolina	8,918
42	South Dakota	8,499
21	Tennessee	9,261
11	Texas	9,575
45	Utah	8,349
14	Vermont	9,483
24	Virginia	9,176
23	Washington	9,212
25	West Virginia	9,164
12	Wisconsin	9,562
10	Wyoming	9,612

RANK ORDER

RANK	STATE	PREMIUM
1	Alaska	$10,564
2	Delaware	10,499
3	Maine	10,308
4	New Jersey	10,168
5	Connecticut	10,119
6	Minnesota	10,066
7	Massachusetts	9,867
8	New Hampshire	9,776
9	Illinois	9,693
10	Wyoming	9,612
11	Texas	9,575
12	Wisconsin	9,562
13	Colorado	9,522
14	Vermont	9,483
15	Rhode Island	9,460
16	Michigan	9,449
17	New York	9,439
18	Florida	9,331
19	Indiana	9,315
20	New Mexico	9,299
21	Tennessee	9,261
22	Maryland	9,217
23	Washington	9,212
24	Virginia	9,176
25	West Virginia	9,164
26	Nebraska	9,139
27	Ohio	9,136
28	Pennsylvania	9,133
29	Kentucky	9,118
30	California	9,091
31	Missouri	8,984
32	Arizona	8,972
33	South Carolina	8,918
34	Kansas	8,907
35	Oregon	8,861
36	Nevada	8,831
37	Oklahoma	8,739
38	Louisiana	8,735
39	Georgia	8,641
40	Idaho	8,563
41	Montana	8,542
42	South Dakota	8,499
43	North Carolina	8,463
44	Iowa	8,436
45	Utah	8,349
46	Mississippi	8,075
47	Alabama	8,045
48	Arkansas	7,977
49	Hawaii	7,887
50	North Dakota	7,866

| | District of Columbia | 10,748 |

Source: U.S. Department of Health and Human Services, Agency for Healthcare Research and Quality
   "Private-Sector Data by Firm Size and State" (Table II Series, Medical Expenditures Panel Survey, July 2005)
   (http://www.meps.ahrq.gov/MEPSDATA/ic/2003/Index203.htm)
*Enrolled employees at private-sector establishments that offer health insurance coverage.

Average Annual Employee Contribution for Family Coverage Health Insurance in 2003
National Average = $2,283*

ALPHA ORDER

RANK	STATE	PREMIUM
29	Alabama	$2,290
48	Alaska	1,759
5	Arizona	2,697
22	Arkansas	2,347
31	California	2,282
16	Colorado	2,430
31	Connecticut	2,282
34	Delaware	2,233
2	Florida	2,810
24	Georgia	2,327
42	Hawaii	2,048
18	Idaho	2,395
35	Illinois	2,212
28	Indiana	2,301
36	Iowa	2,188
11	Kansas	2,566
27	Kentucky	2,303
8	Louisiana	2,587
1	Maine	2,872
4	Maryland	2,714
20	Massachusetts	2,385
49	Michigan	1,661
14	Minnesota	2,488
23	Mississippi	2,328
30	Missouri	2,286
19	Montana	2,388
6	Nebraska	2,646
39	Nevada	2,100
15	New Hampshire	2,435
44	New Jersey	2,007
13	New Mexico	2,506
47	New York	1,812
21	North Carolina	2,359
38	North Dakota	2,136
45	Ohio	1,946
17	Oklahoma	2,426
37	Oregon	2,159
41	Pennsylvania	2,055
12	Rhode Island	2,533
7	South Carolina	2,596
25	South Dakota	2,326
9	Tennessee	2,569
10	Texas	2,568
26	Utah	2,309
43	Vermont	2,020
3	Virginia	2,728
40	Washington	2,058
50	West Virginia	1,554
33	Wisconsin	2,258
46	Wyoming	1,941

RANK ORDER

RANK	STATE	PREMIUM
1	Maine	$2,872
2	Florida	2,810
3	Virginia	2,728
4	Maryland	2,714
5	Arizona	2,697
6	Nebraska	2,646
7	South Carolina	2,596
8	Louisiana	2,587
9	Tennessee	2,569
10	Texas	2,568
11	Kansas	2,566
12	Rhode Island	2,533
13	New Mexico	2,506
14	Minnesota	2,488
15	New Hampshire	2,435
16	Colorado	2,430
17	Oklahoma	2,426
18	Idaho	2,395
19	Montana	2,388
20	Massachusetts	2,385
21	North Carolina	2,359
22	Arkansas	2,347
23	Mississippi	2,328
24	Georgia	2,327
25	South Dakota	2,326
26	Utah	2,309
27	Kentucky	2,303
28	Indiana	2,301
29	Alabama	2,290
30	Missouri	2,286
31	California	2,282
31	Connecticut	2,282
33	Wisconsin	2,258
34	Delaware	2,233
35	Illinois	2,212
36	Iowa	2,188
37	Oregon	2,159
38	North Dakota	2,136
39	Nevada	2,100
40	Washington	2,058
41	Pennsylvania	2,055
42	Hawaii	2,048
43	Vermont	2,020
44	New Jersey	2,007
45	Ohio	1,946
46	Wyoming	1,941
47	New York	1,812
48	Alaska	1,759
49	Michigan	1,661
50	West Virginia	1,554

District of Columbia   2,474

Source: U.S. Department of Health and Human Services, Agency for Healthcare Research and Quality
"Private-Sector Data by Firm Size and State" (Table II Series, Medical Expenditures Panel Survey, July 2005)
(http://www.meps.ahrq.gov/MEPSDATA/ic/2003/Index203.htm)
*Enrolled employees at private-sector establishments that offer health insurance coverage.

Percent of Total Premiums for Family Coverage
Health Insurance Paid by Employees in 2003
National Average = 24.7%*

ALPHA ORDER

RANK	STATE	PERCENT
11	Alabama	28.5
50	Alaska	16.6
1	Arizona	30.1
6	Arkansas	29.4
30	California	25.1
27	Colorado	25.5
39	Connecticut	22.5
42	Delaware	21.3
1	Florida	30.1
21	Georgia	26.9
25	Hawaii	26.0
12	Idaho	28.0
38	Illinois	22.8
32	Indiana	24.7
26	Iowa	25.9
9	Kansas	28.8
29	Kentucky	25.3
4	Louisiana	29.6
14	Maine	27.9
5	Maryland	29.5
35	Massachusetts	24.2
48	Michigan	17.6
32	Minnesota	24.7
9	Mississippi	28.8
28	Missouri	25.4
12	Montana	28.0
8	Nebraska	29.0
36	Nevada	23.8
31	New Hampshire	24.9
46	New Jersey	19.7
21	New Mexico	26.9
47	New York	19.2
14	North Carolina	27.9
20	North Dakota	27.2
42	Ohio	21.3
16	Oklahoma	27.8
34	Oregon	24.4
39	Pennsylvania	22.5
23	Rhode Island	26.8
7	South Carolina	29.1
19	South Dakota	27.4
17	Tennessee	27.7
23	Texas	26.8
17	Utah	27.7
42	Vermont	21.3
3	Virginia	29.7
41	Washington	22.3
49	West Virginia	17.0
37	Wisconsin	23.6
45	Wyoming	20.2

RANK ORDER

RANK	STATE	PERCENT
1	Arizona	30.1
1	Florida	30.1
3	Virginia	29.7
4	Louisiana	29.6
5	Maryland	29.5
6	Arkansas	29.4
7	South Carolina	29.1
8	Nebraska	29.0
9	Kansas	28.8
9	Mississippi	28.8
11	Alabama	28.5
12	Idaho	28.0
12	Montana	28.0
14	Maine	27.9
14	North Carolina	27.9
16	Oklahoma	27.8
17	Tennessee	27.7
17	Utah	27.7
19	South Dakota	27.4
20	North Dakota	27.2
21	Georgia	26.9
21	New Mexico	26.9
23	Rhode Island	26.8
23	Texas	26.8
25	Hawaii	26.0
26	Iowa	25.9
27	Colorado	25.5
28	Missouri	25.4
29	Kentucky	25.3
30	California	25.1
31	New Hampshire	24.9
32	Indiana	24.7
32	Minnesota	24.7
34	Oregon	24.4
35	Massachusetts	24.2
36	Nevada	23.8
37	Wisconsin	23.6
38	Illinois	22.8
39	Connecticut	22.5
39	Pennsylvania	22.5
41	Washington	22.3
42	Delaware	21.3
42	Ohio	21.3
42	Vermont	21.3
45	Wyoming	20.2
46	New Jersey	19.7
47	New York	19.2
48	Michigan	17.6
49	West Virginia	17.0
50	Alaska	16.6

	District of Columbia	23.0

Source: U.S. Department of Health and Human Services, Agency for Healthcare Research and Quality
    "Private-Sector Data by Firm Size and State" (Table II Series, Medical Expenditures Panel Survey, July 2005)
    (http://www.meps.ahrq.gov/MEPSDATA/ic/2003/Index203.htm)
*Enrolled employees at private-sector establishments that offer health insurance coverage.

Persons Not Covered by Health Insurance in 2004

National Total = 45,820,000 Uninsured

ALPHA ORDER

RANK	STATE	UNINSURED	% of USA
23	Alabama	609,000	1.3%
46	Alaska	110,000	0.2%
13	Arizona	989,000	2.2%
30	Arkansas	448,000	1.0%
1	California	6,710,000	14.6%
18	Colorado	767,000	1.7%
32	Connecticut	407,000	0.9%
43	Delaware	120,000	0.3%
3	Florida	3,479,000	7.6%
6	Georgia	1,513,000	3.3%
43	Hawaii	120,000	0.3%
38	Idaho	212,000	0.5%
5	Illinois	1,764,000	3.8%
14	Indiana	872,000	1.9%
37	Iowa	277,000	0.6%
35	Kansas	297,000	0.6%
26	Kentucky	582,000	1.3%
19	Louisiana	761,000	1.7%
42	Maine	130,000	0.3%
16	Maryland	810,000	1.8%
20	Massachusetts	748,000	1.6%
11	Michigan	1,156,000	2.5%
29	Minnesota	458,000	1.0%
28	Mississippi	489,000	1.1%
21	Missouri	707,000	1.5%
40	Montana	174,000	0.4%
39	Nebraska	197,000	0.4%
31	Nevada	443,000	1.0%
41	New Hampshire	152,000	0.3%
8	New Jersey	1,322,000	2.9%
33	New Mexico	399,000	0.9%
4	New York	2,705,000	5.9%
8	North Carolina	1,322,000	2.9%
48	North Dakota	70,000	0.2%
10	Ohio	1,282,000	2.8%
22	Oklahoma	685,000	1.5%
25	Oregon	591,000	1.3%
7	Pennsylvania	1,454,000	3.2%
43	Rhode Island	120,000	0.3%
24	South Carolina	605,000	1.3%
47	South Dakota	90,000	0.2%
15	Tennessee	828,000	1.8%
2	Texas	5,583,000	12.2%
34	Utah	337,000	0.7%
50	Vermont	69,000	0.2%
12	Virginia	1,061,000	2.3%
17	Washington	793,000	1.7%
36	West Virginia	294,000	0.6%
27	Wisconsin	566,000	1.2%
48	Wyoming	70,000	0.2%

RANK ORDER

RANK	STATE	UNINSURED	% of USA
1	California	6,710,000	14.6%
2	Texas	5,583,000	12.2%
3	Florida	3,479,000	7.6%
4	New York	2,705,000	5.9%
5	Illinois	1,764,000	3.8%
6	Georgia	1,513,000	3.3%
7	Pennsylvania	1,454,000	3.2%
8	New Jersey	1,322,000	2.9%
8	North Carolina	1,322,000	2.9%
10	Ohio	1,282,000	2.8%
11	Michigan	1,156,000	2.5%
12	Virginia	1,061,000	2.3%
13	Arizona	989,000	2.2%
14	Indiana	872,000	1.9%
15	Tennessee	828,000	1.8%
16	Maryland	810,000	1.8%
17	Washington	793,000	1.7%
18	Colorado	767,000	1.7%
19	Louisiana	761,000	1.7%
20	Massachusetts	748,000	1.6%
21	Missouri	707,000	1.5%
22	Oklahoma	685,000	1.5%
23	Alabama	609,000	1.3%
24	South Carolina	605,000	1.3%
25	Oregon	591,000	1.3%
26	Kentucky	582,000	1.3%
27	Wisconsin	566,000	1.2%
28	Mississippi	489,000	1.1%
29	Minnesota	458,000	1.0%
30	Arkansas	448,000	1.0%
31	Nevada	443,000	1.0%
32	Connecticut	407,000	0.9%
33	New Mexico	399,000	0.9%
34	Utah	337,000	0.7%
35	Kansas	297,000	0.6%
36	West Virginia	294,000	0.6%
37	Iowa	277,000	0.6%
38	Idaho	212,000	0.5%
39	Nebraska	197,000	0.4%
40	Montana	174,000	0.4%
41	New Hampshire	152,000	0.3%
42	Maine	130,000	0.3%
43	Delaware	120,000	0.3%
43	Hawaii	120,000	0.3%
43	Rhode Island	120,000	0.3%
46	Alaska	110,000	0.2%
47	South Dakota	90,000	0.2%
48	North Dakota	70,000	0.2%
48	Wyoming	70,000	0.2%
50	Vermont	69,000	0.2%
	District of Columbia	73,000	0.2%

Source: U.S. Bureau of the Census
  "Health Insurance Coverage Status by State for All People: 2004"
   (http://ferret.bls.census.gov/macro/032005/health/h06_000.htm)

Percent of Population Not Covered by Health Insurance in 2004

National Percent = 15.5% of Population*

RANK	STATE	PERCENT
29	Alabama	13.5
8	Alaska	18.2
12	Arizona	17.0
14	Arkansas	16.7
7	California	18.4
13	Colorado	16.8
40	Connecticut	10.9
33	Delaware	11.8
6	Florida	18.5
15	Georgia	16.6
49	Hawaii	9.9
10	Idaho	17.3
22	Illinois	14.2
27	Indiana	13.7
48	Iowa	10.1
41	Kansas	10.8
25	Kentucky	13.9
5	Louisiana	18.8
43	Maine	10.6
24	Maryland	14.0
41	Massachusetts	10.8
37	Michigan	11.4
50	Minnesota	8.5
11	Mississippi	17.2
35	Missouri	11.7
9	Montana	17.9
38	Nebraska	11.0
4	Nevada	19.1
43	New Hampshire	10.6
21	New Jersey	14.4
2	New Mexico	21.4
20	New York	15.0
15	North Carolina	16.6
38	North Dakota	11.0
33	Ohio	11.8
3	Oklahoma	19.2
17	Oregon	16.1
36	Pennsylvania	11.5
45	Rhode Island	10.5
26	South Carolina	13.8
32	South Dakota	11.9
31	Tennessee	12.7
1	Texas	25.1
30	Utah	13.4
45	Vermont	10.5
28	Virginia	13.6
22	Washington	14.2
18	West Virginia	15.9
47	Wisconsin	10.4
18	Wyoming	15.9

RANK	STATE	PERCENT
1	Texas	25.1
2	New Mexico	21.4
3	Oklahoma	19.2
4	Nevada	19.1
5	Louisiana	18.8
6	Florida	18.5
7	California	18.4
8	Alaska	18.2
9	Montana	17.9
10	Idaho	17.3
11	Mississippi	17.2
12	Arizona	17.0
13	Colorado	16.8
14	Arkansas	16.7
15	Georgia	16.6
15	North Carolina	16.6
17	Oregon	16.1
18	West Virginia	15.9
18	Wyoming	15.9
20	New York	15.0
21	New Jersey	14.4
22	Illinois	14.2
22	Washington	14.2
24	Maryland	14.0
25	Kentucky	13.9
26	South Carolina	13.8
27	Indiana	13.7
28	Virginia	13.6
29	Alabama	13.5
30	Utah	13.4
31	Tennessee	12.7
32	South Dakota	11.9
33	Delaware	11.8
33	Ohio	11.8
35	Missouri	11.7
36	Pennsylvania	11.5
37	Michigan	11.4
38	Nebraska	11.0
38	North Dakota	11.0
40	Connecticut	10.9
41	Kansas	10.8
41	Massachusetts	10.8
43	Maine	10.6
43	New Hampshire	10.6
45	Rhode Island	10.5
45	Vermont	10.5
47	Wisconsin	10.4
48	Iowa	10.1
49	Hawaii	9.9
50	Minnesota	8.5
	District of Columbia	13.5

Source: U.S. Bureau of the Census
"Income, Poverty and Health Insurance Covered in the United States: 2004"
(http://www.census.gov/hhes/www/hlthins/hlthin04/hi04t11.pdf)
*Three-year average for 2002 through 2004.

Numerical Change in Persons Uninsured: 2000 to 2004

National Change = 7,137,000 Increase

ALPHA ORDER

RANK	STATE	CHANGE
39	Alabama	9,000
46	Alaska	(15,000)
11	Arizona	196,000
24	Arkansas	84,000
4	California	429,000
10	Colorado	204,000
18	Connecticut	144,000
31	Delaware	38,000
2	Florida	859,000
5	Georgia	378,000
41	Hawaii	3,000
36	Idaho	16,000
23	Illinois	105,000
15	Indiana	171,000
33	Iowa	29,000
45	Kansas	(4,000)
25	Kentucky	69,000
49	Louisiana	(49,000)
46	Maine	(15,000)
7	Maryland	309,000
17	Massachusetts	153,000
14	Michigan	174,000
34	Minnesota	28,000
21	Mississippi	125,000
22	Missouri	121,000
38	Montana	12,000
32	Nebraska	33,000
19	Nevada	132,000
26	New Hampshire	67,000
8	New Jersey	273,000
48	New Mexico	(28,000)
50	New York	(97,000)
6	North Carolina	342,000
43	North Dakota	1,000
35	Ohio	27,000
28	Oklahoma	49,000
20	Oregon	126,000
3	Pennsylvania	549,000
27	Rhode Island	65,000
16	South Carolina	157,000
40	South Dakota	8,000
9	Tennessee	251,000
1	Texas	1,158,000
29	Utah	41,000
42	Vermont	2,000
13	Virginia	175,000
37	Washington	13,000
30	West Virginia	40,000
12	Wisconsin	180,000
44	Wyoming	0

RANK ORDER

RANK	STATE	CHANGE
1	Texas	1,158,000
2	Florida	859,000
3	Pennsylvania	549,000
4	California	429,000
5	Georgia	378,000
6	North Carolina	342,000
7	Maryland	309,000
8	New Jersey	273,000
9	Tennessee	251,000
10	Colorado	204,000
11	Arizona	196,000
12	Wisconsin	180,000
13	Virginia	175,000
14	Michigan	174,000
15	Indiana	171,000
16	South Carolina	157,000
17	Massachusetts	153,000
18	Connecticut	144,000
19	Nevada	132,000
20	Oregon	126,000
21	Mississippi	125,000
22	Missouri	121,000
23	Illinois	105,000
24	Arkansas	84,000
25	Kentucky	69,000
26	New Hampshire	67,000
27	Rhode Island	65,000
28	Oklahoma	49,000
29	Utah	41,000
30	West Virginia	40,000
31	Delaware	38,000
32	Nebraska	33,000
33	Iowa	29,000
34	Minnesota	28,000
35	Ohio	27,000
36	Idaho	16,000
37	Washington	13,000
38	Montana	12,000
39	Alabama	9,000
40	South Dakota	8,000
41	Hawaii	3,000
42	Vermont	2,000
43	North Dakota	1,000
44	Wyoming	0
45	Kansas	(4,000)
46	Alaska	(15,000)
46	Maine	(15,000)
48	New Mexico	(28,000)
49	Louisiana	(49,000)
50	New York	(97,000)

District of Columbia   0

Source: Morgan Quitno Press using data from U.S. Bureau of the Census
"Health Insurance Coverage Status by State for All People: 2000" and
"Health Insurance Coverage Status by State for All People: 2004"
(http://ferret.bls.census.gov/macro/032005/health/h06_000.htm)

245

Percent Change in Persons Uninsured: 2000 to 2004

National Percent Change = 18.4% Increase

ALPHA ORDER				RANK ORDER		
RANK	STATE	PERCENT CHANGE		RANK	STATE	PERCENT CHANGE
42	Alabama	1.5		1	Rhode Island	118.2
50	Alaska	(12.0)		2	New Hampshire	78.8
20	Arizona	24.7		3	Maryland	61.7
22	Arkansas	23.1		4	Pennsylvania	60.7
35	California	6.8		5	Connecticut	54.8
10	Colorado	36.2		6	Wisconsin	46.6
5	Connecticut	54.8		7	Delaware	46.3
7	Delaware	46.3		8	Tennessee	43.5
15	Florida	32.8		9	Nevada	42.4
14	Georgia	33.3		10	Colorado	36.2
39	Hawaii	2.6		11	South Carolina	35.0
32	Idaho	8.2		12	North Carolina	34.9
37	Illinois	6.3		13	Mississippi	34.3
21	Indiana	24.4		14	Georgia	33.3
30	Iowa	11.7		15	Florida	32.8
45	Kansas	(1.3)		16	Oregon	27.1
29	Kentucky	13.5		17	Texas	26.2
47	Louisiana	(6.0)		18	New Jersey	26.0
49	Maine	(10.3)		19	Massachusetts	25.7
3	Maryland	61.7		20	Arizona	24.7
19	Massachusetts	25.7		21	Indiana	24.4
26	Michigan	17.7		22	Arkansas	23.1
36	Minnesota	6.5		23	Missouri	20.6
13	Mississippi	34.3		24	Nebraska	20.1
23	Missouri	20.6		25	Virginia	19.8
34	Montana	7.4		26	Michigan	17.7
24	Nebraska	20.1		27	West Virginia	15.7
9	Nevada	42.4		28	Utah	13.9
2	New Hampshire	78.8		29	Kentucky	13.5
18	New Jersey	26.0		30	Iowa	11.7
48	New Mexico	(6.6)		31	South Dakota	9.8
46	New York	(3.5)		32	Idaho	8.2
12	North Carolina	34.9		33	Oklahoma	7.7
43	North Dakota	1.4		34	Montana	7.4
40	Ohio	2.2		35	California	6.8
33	Oklahoma	7.7		36	Minnesota	6.5
16	Oregon	27.1		37	Illinois	6.3
4	Pennsylvania	60.7		38	Vermont	3.0
1	Rhode Island	118.2		39	Hawaii	2.6
11	South Carolina	35.0		40	Ohio	2.2
31	South Dakota	9.8		41	Washington	1.7
8	Tennessee	43.5		42	Alabama	1.5
17	Texas	26.2		43	North Dakota	1.4
28	Utah	13.9		44	Wyoming	0.0
38	Vermont	3.0		45	Kansas	(1.3)
25	Virginia	19.8		46	New York	(3.5)
41	Washington	1.7		47	Louisiana	(6.0)
27	West Virginia	15.7		48	New Mexico	(6.6)
6	Wisconsin	46.6		49	Maine	(10.3)
44	Wyoming	0.0		50	Alaska	(12.0)
					District of Columbia	0.0

Source: Morgan Quitno Press using data from U.S. Bureau of the Census
"Health Insurance Coverage Status by State for All People: 2000" and
"Health Insurance Coverage Status by State for All People: 2004"
(http://ferret.bls.census.gov/macro/032005/health/h06_000.htm)
*Based on three-year averages for 2002 through 2004 and 1998 through 2000.

Change in Percent of Population Uninsured: 2000 to 2004

National Percent Change = 7.6% Increase*

<table>
<tr><td colspan="3">ALPHA ORDER</td><td colspan="3">RANK ORDER</td></tr>
<tr><td>RANK</td><td>STATE</td><td>PERCENT CHANGE</td><td>RANK</td><td>STATE</td><td>PERCENT CHANGE</td></tr>
<tr><td>46</td><td>Alabama</td><td>(4.9)</td><td>1</td><td>Rhode Island</td><td>54.4</td></tr>
<tr><td>39</td><td>Alaska</td><td>0.6</td><td>2</td><td>Pennsylvania</td><td>38.6</td></tr>
<tr><td>50</td><td>Arizona</td><td>(13.3)</td><td>3</td><td>Missouri</td><td>31.5</td></tr>
<tr><td>21</td><td>Arkansas</td><td>9.2</td><td>4</td><td>Iowa</td><td>24.7</td></tr>
<tr><td>45</td><td>California</td><td>(4.2)</td><td>5</td><td>New Hampshire</td><td>21.8</td></tr>
<tr><td>8</td><td>Colorado</td><td>19.1</td><td>6</td><td>North Carolina</td><td>21.2</td></tr>
<tr><td>13</td><td>Connecticut</td><td>17.2</td><td>7</td><td>Indiana</td><td>20.2</td></tr>
<tr><td>29</td><td>Delaware</td><td>5.4</td><td>8</td><td>Colorado</td><td>19.1</td></tr>
<tr><td>25</td><td>Florida</td><td>7.6</td><td>9</td><td>Maryland</td><td>18.6</td></tr>
<tr><td>23</td><td>Georgia</td><td>8.5</td><td>10</td><td>Tennessee</td><td>17.6</td></tr>
<tr><td>37</td><td>Hawaii</td><td>1.0</td><td>11</td><td>Oregon</td><td>17.5</td></tr>
<tr><td>33</td><td>Idaho</td><td>4.2</td><td>12</td><td>Massachusetts</td><td>17.4</td></tr>
<tr><td>28</td><td>Illinois</td><td>6.0</td><td>13</td><td>Connecticut</td><td>17.2</td></tr>
<tr><td>7</td><td>Indiana</td><td>20.2</td><td>14</td><td>Nebraska</td><td>17.0</td></tr>
<tr><td>4</td><td>Iowa</td><td>24.7</td><td>15</td><td>Ohio</td><td>15.7</td></tr>
<tr><td>41</td><td>Kansas</td><td>(1.8)</td><td>16</td><td>Texas</td><td>13.1</td></tr>
<tr><td>27</td><td>Kentucky</td><td>6.1</td><td>17</td><td>Wisconsin</td><td>13.0</td></tr>
<tr><td>44</td><td>Louisiana</td><td>(4.1)</td><td>18</td><td>Washington</td><td>11.8</td></tr>
<tr><td>48</td><td>Maine</td><td>(7.0)</td><td>19</td><td>New Jersey</td><td>10.8</td></tr>
<tr><td>9</td><td>Maryland</td><td>18.6</td><td>20</td><td>Mississippi</td><td>9.6</td></tr>
<tr><td>12</td><td>Massachusetts</td><td>17.4</td><td>21</td><td>Arkansas</td><td>9.2</td></tr>
<tr><td>26</td><td>Michigan</td><td>6.5</td><td>22</td><td>Nevada</td><td>9.1</td></tr>
<tr><td>34</td><td>Minnesota</td><td>3.7</td><td>23</td><td>Georgia</td><td>8.5</td></tr>
<tr><td>20</td><td>Mississippi</td><td>9.6</td><td>23</td><td>Oklahoma</td><td>8.5</td></tr>
<tr><td>3</td><td>Missouri</td><td>31.5</td><td>25</td><td>Florida</td><td>7.6</td></tr>
<tr><td>43</td><td>Montana</td><td>(2.2)</td><td>26</td><td>Michigan</td><td>6.5</td></tr>
<tr><td>14</td><td>Nebraska</td><td>17.0</td><td>27</td><td>Kentucky</td><td>6.1</td></tr>
<tr><td>22</td><td>Nevada</td><td>9.1</td><td>28</td><td>Illinois</td><td>6.0</td></tr>
<tr><td>5</td><td>New Hampshire</td><td>21.8</td><td>29</td><td>Delaware</td><td>5.4</td></tr>
<tr><td>19</td><td>New Jersey</td><td>10.8</td><td>29</td><td>Virginia</td><td>5.4</td></tr>
<tr><td>47</td><td>New Mexico</td><td>(5.3)</td><td>31</td><td>Wyoming</td><td>5.3</td></tr>
<tr><td>42</td><td>New York</td><td>(2.0)</td><td>32</td><td>West Virginia</td><td>4.6</td></tr>
<tr><td>6</td><td>North Carolina</td><td>21.2</td><td>33</td><td>Idaho</td><td>4.2</td></tr>
<tr><td>49</td><td>North Dakota</td><td>(8.3)</td><td>34</td><td>Minnesota</td><td>3.7</td></tr>
<tr><td>15</td><td>Ohio</td><td>15.7</td><td>35</td><td>Vermont</td><td>2.9</td></tr>
<tr><td>23</td><td>Oklahoma</td><td>8.5</td><td>36</td><td>Utah</td><td>1.5</td></tr>
<tr><td>11</td><td>Oregon</td><td>17.5</td><td>37</td><td>Hawaii</td><td>1.0</td></tr>
<tr><td>2</td><td>Pennsylvania</td><td>38.6</td><td>38</td><td>South Carolina</td><td>0.7</td></tr>
<tr><td>1</td><td>Rhode Island</td><td>54.4</td><td>39</td><td>Alaska</td><td>0.6</td></tr>
<tr><td>38</td><td>South Carolina</td><td>0.7</td><td>40</td><td>South Dakota</td><td>(0.8)</td></tr>
<tr><td>40</td><td>South Dakota</td><td>(0.8)</td><td>41</td><td>Kansas</td><td>(1.8)</td></tr>
<tr><td>10</td><td>Tennessee</td><td>17.6</td><td>42</td><td>New York</td><td>(2.0)</td></tr>
<tr><td>16</td><td>Texas</td><td>13.1</td><td>43</td><td>Montana</td><td>(2.2)</td></tr>
<tr><td>36</td><td>Utah</td><td>1.5</td><td>44</td><td>Louisiana</td><td>(4.1)</td></tr>
<tr><td>35</td><td>Vermont</td><td>2.9</td><td>45</td><td>California</td><td>(4.2)</td></tr>
<tr><td>29</td><td>Virginia</td><td>5.4</td><td>46</td><td>Alabama</td><td>(4.9)</td></tr>
<tr><td>18</td><td>Washington</td><td>11.8</td><td>47</td><td>New Mexico</td><td>(5.3)</td></tr>
<tr><td>32</td><td>West Virginia</td><td>4.6</td><td>48</td><td>Maine</td><td>(7.0)</td></tr>
<tr><td>17</td><td>Wisconsin</td><td>13.0</td><td>49</td><td>North Dakota</td><td>(8.3)</td></tr>
<tr><td>31</td><td>Wyoming</td><td>5.3</td><td>50</td><td>Arizona</td><td>(13.3)</td></tr>
<tr><td></td><td></td><td></td><td></td><td>District of Columbia</td><td>(6.9)</td></tr>
</table>

Source: Morgan Quitno Press using data from U.S. Bureau of the Census
"Health Insurance Coverage Status by State for All People: 2000" and
"Health Insurance Coverage Status by State for All People: 2004"
(http://ferret.bls.census.gov/macro/032005/health/h06_000.htm)
*Based on three-year averages for 2002 through 2004 and 1998 through 2000.

Percent of Children Not Covered by Health Insurance in 2004

National Percent = 11.2% of Children*

ALPHA ORDER

RANK	STATE	PERCENT
37	Alabama	7.4
16	Alaska	10.9
8	Arizona	14.7
40	Arkansas	6.8
11	California	12.4
7	Colorado	15.0
28	Connecticut	8.5
10	Delaware	12.6
6	Florida	15.1
12	Georgia	11.7
48	Hawaii	5.4
26	Idaho	8.6
14	Illinois	11.4
24	Indiana	8.9
45	Iowa	6.0
43	Kansas	6.5
30	Kentucky	8.4
33	Louisiana	8.0
47	Maine	5.8
22	Maryland	9.6
43	Massachusetts	6.5
40	Michigan	6.8
40	Minnesota	6.8
9	Mississippi	14.2
28	Missouri	8.5
4	Montana	15.4
45	Nebraska	6.0
3	Nevada	16.1
34	New Hampshire	7.8
12	New Jersey	11.7
5	New Mexico	15.3
26	New York	8.6
15	North Carolina	11.2
22	North Dakota	9.6
36	Ohio	7.5
2	Oklahoma	16.9
20	Oregon	10.0
17	Pennsylvania	10.7
37	Rhode Island	7.4
35	South Carolina	7.7
31	South Dakota	8.3
19	Tennessee	10.1
1	Texas	21.4
18	Utah	10.4
50	Vermont	4.8
32	Virginia	8.1
39	Washington	7.0
25	West Virginia	8.8
49	Wisconsin	5.1
21	Wyoming	9.7

RANK ORDER

RANK	STATE	PERCENT
1	Texas	21.4
2	Oklahoma	16.9
3	Nevada	16.1
4	Montana	15.4
5	New Mexico	15.3
6	Florida	15.1
7	Colorado	15.0
8	Arizona	14.7
9	Mississippi	14.2
10	Delaware	12.6
11	California	12.4
12	Georgia	11.7
12	New Jersey	11.7
14	Illinois	11.4
15	North Carolina	11.2
16	Alaska	10.9
17	Pennsylvania	10.7
18	Utah	10.4
19	Tennessee	10.1
20	Oregon	10.0
21	Wyoming	9.7
22	Maryland	9.6
22	North Dakota	9.6
24	Indiana	8.9
25	West Virginia	8.8
26	Idaho	8.6
26	New York	8.6
28	Connecticut	8.5
28	Missouri	8.5
30	Kentucky	8.4
31	South Dakota	8.3
32	Virginia	8.1
33	Louisiana	8.0
34	New Hampshire	7.8
35	South Carolina	7.7
36	Ohio	7.5
37	Alabama	7.4
37	Rhode Island	7.4
39	Washington	7.0
40	Arkansas	6.8
40	Michigan	6.8
40	Minnesota	6.8
43	Kansas	6.5
43	Massachusetts	6.5
45	Iowa	6.0
45	Nebraska	6.0
47	Maine	5.8
48	Hawaii	5.4
49	Wisconsin	5.1
50	Vermont	4.8

District of Columbia	7.6

Source: U.S. Bureau of the Census
    "Health Insurance Coverage Status" (http://www.census.gov/hhes/www/hlthins/historic/hihistt5.html)
*Children under 18 years old.

Persons Covered by Health Insurance in 2004

National Total = 245,335,000 Insured

<table>
<tr><td colspan="4">ALPHA ORDER</td><td colspan="4">RANK ORDER</td></tr>
<tr><th>RANK</th><th>STATE</th><th>INSURED</th><th>% of USA</th><th>RANK</th><th>STATE</th><th>INSURED</th><th>% of USA</th></tr>
<tr><td>22</td><td>Alabama</td><td>3,902,000</td><td>1.6%</td><td>1</td><td>California</td><td>29,140,000</td><td>11.9%</td></tr>
<tr><td>49</td><td>Alaska</td><td>538,000</td><td>0.2%</td><td>2</td><td>Texas</td><td>16,741,000</td><td>6.8%</td></tr>
<tr><td>19</td><td>Arizona</td><td>4,778,000</td><td>1.9%</td><td>3</td><td>New York</td><td>16,345,000</td><td>6.7%</td></tr>
<tr><td>33</td><td>Arkansas</td><td>2,282,000</td><td>0.9%</td><td>4</td><td>Florida</td><td>13,987,000</td><td>5.7%</td></tr>
<tr><td>1</td><td>California</td><td>29,140,000</td><td>11.9%</td><td>5</td><td>Illinois</td><td>10,832,000</td><td>4.4%</td></tr>
<tr><td>23</td><td>Colorado</td><td>3,756,000</td><td>1.5%</td><td>6</td><td>Pennsylvania</td><td>10,724,000</td><td>4.4%</td></tr>
<tr><td>27</td><td>Connecticut</td><td>3,086,000</td><td>1.3%</td><td>7</td><td>Ohio</td><td>9,987,000</td><td>4.1%</td></tr>
<tr><td>45</td><td>Delaware</td><td>707,000</td><td>0.3%</td><td>8</td><td>Michigan</td><td>8,816,000</td><td>3.6%</td></tr>
<tr><td>4</td><td>Florida</td><td>13,987,000</td><td>5.7%</td><td>9</td><td>New Jersey</td><td>7,343,000</td><td>3.0%</td></tr>
<tr><td>10</td><td>Georgia</td><td>7,193,000</td><td>2.9%</td><td>10</td><td>Georgia</td><td>7,193,000</td><td>2.9%</td></tr>
<tr><td>42</td><td>Hawaii</td><td>1,130,000</td><td>0.5%</td><td>11</td><td>North Carolina</td><td>7,110,000</td><td>2.9%</td></tr>
<tr><td>39</td><td>Idaho</td><td>1,164,000</td><td>0.5%</td><td>12</td><td>Virginia</td><td>6,326,000</td><td>2.6%</td></tr>
<tr><td>5</td><td>Illinois</td><td>10,832,000</td><td>4.4%</td><td>13</td><td>Massachusetts</td><td>5,625,000</td><td>2.3%</td></tr>
<tr><td>15</td><td>Indiana</td><td>5,264,000</td><td>2.1%</td><td>14</td><td>Washington</td><td>5,323,000</td><td>2.2%</td></tr>
<tr><td>30</td><td>Iowa</td><td>2,629,000</td><td>1.1%</td><td>15</td><td>Indiana</td><td>5,264,000</td><td>2.1%</td></tr>
<tr><td>32</td><td>Kansas</td><td>2,377,000</td><td>1.0%</td><td>16</td><td>Tennessee</td><td>5,030,000</td><td>2.1%</td></tr>
<tr><td>26</td><td>Kentucky</td><td>3,492,000</td><td>1.4%</td><td>17</td><td>Missouri</td><td>4,908,000</td><td>2.0%</td></tr>
<tr><td>24</td><td>Louisiana</td><td>3,661,000</td><td>1.5%</td><td>18</td><td>Wisconsin</td><td>4,898,000</td><td>2.0%</td></tr>
<tr><td>39</td><td>Maine</td><td>1,164,000</td><td>0.5%</td><td>19</td><td>Arizona</td><td>4,778,000</td><td>1.9%</td></tr>
<tr><td>20</td><td>Maryland</td><td>4,739,000</td><td>1.9%</td><td>20</td><td>Maryland</td><td>4,739,000</td><td>1.9%</td></tr>
<tr><td>13</td><td>Massachusetts</td><td>5,625,000</td><td>2.3%</td><td>21</td><td>Minnesota</td><td>4,667,000</td><td>1.9%</td></tr>
<tr><td>8</td><td>Michigan</td><td>8,816,000</td><td>3.6%</td><td>22</td><td>Alabama</td><td>3,902,000</td><td>1.6%</td></tr>
<tr><td>21</td><td>Minnesota</td><td>4,667,000</td><td>1.9%</td><td>23</td><td>Colorado</td><td>3,756,000</td><td>1.5%</td></tr>
<tr><td>31</td><td>Mississippi</td><td>2,379,000</td><td>1.0%</td><td>24</td><td>Louisiana</td><td>3,661,000</td><td>1.5%</td></tr>
<tr><td>17</td><td>Missouri</td><td>4,908,000</td><td>2.0%</td><td>25</td><td>South Carolina</td><td>3,518,000</td><td>1.4%</td></tr>
<tr><td>44</td><td>Montana</td><td>737,000</td><td>0.3%</td><td>26</td><td>Kentucky</td><td>3,492,000</td><td>1.4%</td></tr>
<tr><td>36</td><td>Nebraska</td><td>1,531,000</td><td>0.6%</td><td>27</td><td>Connecticut</td><td>3,086,000</td><td>1.3%</td></tr>
<tr><td>35</td><td>Nevada</td><td>1,947,000</td><td>0.8%</td><td>28</td><td>Oregon</td><td>2,991,000</td><td>1.2%</td></tr>
<tr><td>41</td><td>New Hampshire</td><td>1,142,000</td><td>0.5%</td><td>29</td><td>Oklahoma</td><td>2,760,000</td><td>1.1%</td></tr>
<tr><td>9</td><td>New Jersey</td><td>7,343,000</td><td>3.0%</td><td>30</td><td>Iowa</td><td>2,629,000</td><td>1.1%</td></tr>
<tr><td>37</td><td>New Mexico</td><td>1,504,000</td><td>0.6%</td><td>31</td><td>Mississippi</td><td>2,379,000</td><td>1.0%</td></tr>
<tr><td>3</td><td>New York</td><td>16,345,000</td><td>6.7%</td><td>32</td><td>Kansas</td><td>2,377,000</td><td>1.0%</td></tr>
<tr><td>11</td><td>North Carolina</td><td>7,110,000</td><td>2.9%</td><td>33</td><td>Arkansas</td><td>2,282,000</td><td>0.9%</td></tr>
<tr><td>47</td><td>North Dakota</td><td>557,000</td><td>0.2%</td><td>34</td><td>Utah</td><td>2,056,000</td><td>0.8%</td></tr>
<tr><td>7</td><td>Ohio</td><td>9,987,000</td><td>4.1%</td><td>35</td><td>Nevada</td><td>1,947,000</td><td>0.8%</td></tr>
<tr><td>29</td><td>Oklahoma</td><td>2,760,000</td><td>1.1%</td><td>36</td><td>Nebraska</td><td>1,531,000</td><td>0.6%</td></tr>
<tr><td>28</td><td>Oregon</td><td>2,991,000</td><td>1.2%</td><td>37</td><td>New Mexico</td><td>1,504,000</td><td>0.6%</td></tr>
<tr><td>6</td><td>Pennsylvania</td><td>10,724,000</td><td>4.4%</td><td>38</td><td>West Virginia</td><td>1,499,000</td><td>0.6%</td></tr>
<tr><td>43</td><td>Rhode Island</td><td>937,000</td><td>0.4%</td><td>39</td><td>Idaho</td><td>1,164,000</td><td>0.5%</td></tr>
<tr><td>25</td><td>South Carolina</td><td>3,518,000</td><td>1.4%</td><td>39</td><td>Maine</td><td>1,164,000</td><td>0.5%</td></tr>
<tr><td>46</td><td>South Dakota</td><td>663,000</td><td>0.3%</td><td>41</td><td>New Hampshire</td><td>1,142,000</td><td>0.5%</td></tr>
<tr><td>16</td><td>Tennessee</td><td>5,030,000</td><td>2.1%</td><td>42</td><td>Hawaii</td><td>1,130,000</td><td>0.5%</td></tr>
<tr><td>2</td><td>Texas</td><td>16,741,000</td><td>6.8%</td><td>43</td><td>Rhode Island</td><td>937,000</td><td>0.4%</td></tr>
<tr><td>34</td><td>Utah</td><td>2,056,000</td><td>0.8%</td><td>44</td><td>Montana</td><td>737,000</td><td>0.3%</td></tr>
<tr><td>48</td><td>Vermont</td><td>548,000</td><td>0.2%</td><td>45</td><td>Delaware</td><td>707,000</td><td>0.3%</td></tr>
<tr><td>12</td><td>Virginia</td><td>6,326,000</td><td>2.6%</td><td>46</td><td>South Dakota</td><td>663,000</td><td>0.3%</td></tr>
<tr><td>14</td><td>Washington</td><td>5,323,000</td><td>2.2%</td><td>47</td><td>North Dakota</td><td>557,000</td><td>0.2%</td></tr>
<tr><td>38</td><td>West Virginia</td><td>1,499,000</td><td>0.6%</td><td>48</td><td>Vermont</td><td>548,000</td><td>0.2%</td></tr>
<tr><td>18</td><td>Wisconsin</td><td>4,898,000</td><td>2.0%</td><td>49</td><td>Alaska</td><td>538,000</td><td>0.2%</td></tr>
<tr><td>50</td><td>Wyoming</td><td>428,000</td><td>0.2%</td><td>50</td><td>Wyoming</td><td>428,000</td><td>0.2%</td></tr>
<tr><td></td><td></td><td></td><td></td><td></td><td>District of Columbia</td><td>474,000</td><td>0.2%</td></tr>
</table>

Source: U.S. Bureau of the Census
 "Health Insurance Coverage Status by State for All People: 2004"
  (http://ferret.bls.census.gov/macro/032005/health/h06_000.htm)

Percent of Population Covered by Health Insurance in 2004

National Percent = 84.5% of Population

ALPHA ORDER

RANK	STATE	PERCENT
22	Alabama	86.5
43	Alaska	81.8
39	Arizona	83.0
37	Arkansas	83.3
44	California	81.6
38	Colorado	83.2
11	Connecticut	89.1
17	Delaware	88.2
45	Florida	81.5
35	Georgia	83.4
2	Hawaii	90.1
41	Idaho	82.7
28	Illinois	85.8
24	Indiana	86.3
3	Iowa	89.9
9	Kansas	89.2
26	Kentucky	86.1
46	Louisiana	81.2
7	Maine	89.4
27	Maryland	86.0
9	Massachusetts	89.2
14	Michigan	88.6
1	Minnesota	91.5
40	Mississippi	82.8
16	Missouri	88.3
42	Montana	82.1
12	Nebraska	89.0
47	Nevada	80.9
7	New Hampshire	89.4
30	New Jersey	85.6
49	New Mexico	78.6
31	New York	85.0
35	North Carolina	83.4
12	North Dakota	89.0
17	Ohio	88.2
48	Oklahoma	80.8
34	Oregon	83.9
15	Pennsylvania	88.5
5	Rhode Island	89.5
25	South Carolina	86.2
19	South Dakota	88.1
20	Tennessee	87.3
50	Texas	74.9
21	Utah	86.6
5	Vermont	89.5
23	Virginia	86.4
28	Washington	85.8
32	West Virginia	84.1
4	Wisconsin	89.6
32	Wyoming	84.1

RANK ORDER

RANK	STATE	PERCENT
1	Minnesota	91.5
2	Hawaii	90.1
3	Iowa	89.9
4	Wisconsin	89.6
5	Rhode Island	89.5
5	Vermont	89.5
7	Maine	89.4
7	New Hampshire	89.4
9	Kansas	89.2
9	Massachusetts	89.2
11	Connecticut	89.1
12	Nebraska	89.0
12	North Dakota	89.0
14	Michigan	88.6
15	Pennsylvania	88.5
16	Missouri	88.3
17	Delaware	88.2
17	Ohio	88.2
19	South Dakota	88.1
20	Tennessee	87.3
21	Utah	86.6
22	Alabama	86.5
23	Virginia	86.4
24	Indiana	86.3
25	South Carolina	86.2
26	Kentucky	86.1
27	Maryland	86.0
28	Illinois	85.8
28	Washington	85.8
30	New Jersey	85.6
31	New York	85.0
32	West Virginia	84.1
32	Wyoming	84.1
34	Oregon	83.9
35	Georgia	83.4
35	North Carolina	83.4
37	Arkansas	83.3
38	Colorado	83.2
39	Arizona	83.0
40	Mississippi	82.8
41	Idaho	82.7
42	Montana	82.1
43	Alaska	81.8
44	California	81.6
45	Florida	81.5
46	Louisiana	81.2
47	Nevada	80.9
48	Oklahoma	80.8
49	New Mexico	78.6
50	Texas	74.9
	District of Columbia	86.5

Source: Morgan Quitno Press using data from U.S. Bureau of the Census
  "Income, Poverty and Health Insurance Covered in the United States: 2004"
  (http://www.census.gov/hhes/www/hlthins/hlthin04/hi04t11.pdf)
*Three-year average for 2002 through 2004.

Percent of Population Covered by Private Health Insurance in 2004

National Percent = 68.1% of Population*

ALPHA ORDER

RANK	STATE	PERCENT
34	Alabama	66.9
40	Alaska	63.5
43	Arizona	62.7
46	Arkansas	61.6
45	California	62.0
20	Colorado	72.0
12	Connecticut	74.3
23	Delaware	71.1
44	Florida	62.2
37	Georgia	65.6
16	Hawaii	72.9
25	Idaho	70.7
13	Illinois	73.9
22	Indiana	71.3
2	Iowa	79.6
6	Kansas	75.9
35	Kentucky	66.3
46	Louisiana	61.6
31	Maine	67.2
18	Maryland	72.7
14	Massachusetts	73.4
9	Michigan	74.7
1	Minnesota	81.7
48	Mississippi	59.2
27	Missouri	70.3
38	Montana	65.5
8	Nebraska	75.7
29	Nevada	68.6
3	New Hampshire	78.3
14	New Jersey	73.4
50	New Mexico	57.9
33	New York	67.0
31	North Carolina	67.2
4	North Dakota	76.8
9	Ohio	74.7
42	Oklahoma	62.8
24	Oregon	70.8
9	Pennsylvania	74.7
27	Rhode Island	70.3
36	South Carolina	65.7
21	South Dakota	71.8
39	Tennessee	64.6
48	Texas	59.2
6	Utah	75.9
30	Vermont	67.8
17	Virginia	72.8
26	Washington	70.4
41	West Virginia	63.4
5	Wisconsin	76.4
19	Wyoming	72.1

RANK ORDER

RANK	STATE	PERCENT
1	Minnesota	81.7
2	Iowa	79.6
3	New Hampshire	78.3
4	North Dakota	76.8
5	Wisconsin	76.4
6	Kansas	75.9
6	Utah	75.9
8	Nebraska	75.7
9	Michigan	74.7
9	Ohio	74.7
9	Pennsylvania	74.7
12	Connecticut	74.3
13	Illinois	73.9
14	Massachusetts	73.4
14	New Jersey	73.4
16	Hawaii	72.9
17	Virginia	72.8
18	Maryland	72.7
19	Wyoming	72.1
20	Colorado	72.0
21	South Dakota	71.8
22	Indiana	71.3
23	Delaware	71.1
24	Oregon	70.8
25	Idaho	70.7
26	Washington	70.4
27	Missouri	70.3
27	Rhode Island	70.3
29	Nevada	68.6
30	Vermont	67.8
31	Maine	67.2
31	North Carolina	67.2
33	New York	67.0
34	Alabama	66.9
35	Kentucky	66.3
36	South Carolina	65.7
37	Georgia	65.6
38	Montana	65.5
39	Tennessee	64.6
40	Alaska	63.5
41	West Virginia	63.4
42	Oklahoma	62.8
43	Arizona	62.7
44	Florida	62.2
45	California	62.0
46	Arkansas	61.6
46	Louisiana	61.6
48	Mississippi	59.2
48	Texas	59.2
50	New Mexico	57.9

District of Columbia 65.9

Source: U.S. Bureau of the Census
   "Health Insurance Coverage Status" (http://www.census.gov/hhes/www/hlthins/historic/hihistt4.html)
Private health insurance is coverage by a health plan provided through an employer or union or purchased by an individual from a private health insurance company.

Percent of Population Covered by Employment-Based Health Insurance in 2004
National Percent = 59.8% of Population*

ALPHA ORDER

RANK	STATE	PERCENT
26	Alabama	60.0
36	Alaska	58.2
46	Arizona	52.7
49	Arkansas	51.2
45	California	52.9
20	Colorado	62.7
7	Connecticut	67.2
8	Delaware	66.3
44	Florida	53.1
29	Georgia	59.4
4	Hawaii	68.0
29	Idaho	59.4
13	Illinois	65.2
17	Indiana	64.1
15	Iowa	64.9
18	Kansas	63.4
36	Kentucky	58.2
42	Louisiana	54.1
35	Maine	58.3
9	Maryland	66.1
10	Massachusetts	65.8
6	Michigan	67.5
2	Minnesota	69.2
47	Mississippi	51.8
24	Missouri	61.0
48	Montana	51.5
22	Nebraska	61.6
19	Nevada	63.1
1	New Hampshire	72.2
3	New Jersey	68.1
50	New Mexico	50.3
25	New York	60.8
33	North Carolina	58.6
28	North Dakota	59.5
5	Ohio	67.8
41	Oklahoma	54.4
32	Oregon	59.1
15	Pennsylvania	64.9
21	Rhode Island	62.2
38	South Carolina	57.7
39	South Dakota	55.5
40	Tennessee	55.0
43	Texas	53.2
12	Utah	65.3
29	Vermont	59.4
11	Virginia	65.5
23	Washington	61.1
34	West Virginia	58.4
14	Wisconsin	65.1
27	Wyoming	59.8

RANK ORDER

RANK	STATE	PERCENT
1	New Hampshire	72.2
2	Minnesota	69.2
3	New Jersey	68.1
4	Hawaii	68.0
5	Ohio	67.8
6	Michigan	67.5
7	Connecticut	67.2
8	Delaware	66.3
9	Maryland	66.1
10	Massachusetts	65.8
11	Virginia	65.5
12	Utah	65.3
13	Illinois	65.2
14	Wisconsin	65.1
15	Iowa	64.9
15	Pennsylvania	64.9
17	Indiana	64.1
18	Kansas	63.4
19	Nevada	63.1
20	Colorado	62.7
21	Rhode Island	62.2
22	Nebraska	61.6
23	Washington	61.1
24	Missouri	61.0
25	New York	60.8
26	Alabama	60.0
27	Wyoming	59.8
28	North Dakota	59.5
29	Georgia	59.4
29	Idaho	59.4
29	Vermont	59.4
32	Oregon	59.1
33	North Carolina	58.6
34	West Virginia	58.4
35	Maine	58.3
36	Alaska	58.2
36	Kentucky	58.2
38	South Carolina	57.7
39	South Dakota	55.5
40	Tennessee	55.0
41	Oklahoma	54.4
42	Louisiana	54.1
43	Texas	53.2
44	Florida	53.1
45	California	52.9
46	Arizona	52.7
47	Mississippi	51.8
48	Montana	51.5
49	Arkansas	51.2
50	New Mexico	50.3

	District of Columbia	58.7

Source: U.S. Bureau of the Census
"Health Insurance Coverage Status" (http://www.census.gov/hhes/www/hlthins/historic/hihistt4.html)
*Employment-based health insurance is private insurance coverage offered through one's own employment or a relative's. It may be offered by an employer or by a union.

Percent of Population Covered by Direct Purchase Health Insurance in 2004

National Percent = 9.3% of Population*

ALPHA ORDER				RANK ORDER		
RANK	**STATE**	**PERCENT**		**RANK**	**STATE**	**PERCENT**
35	Alabama	8.2		1	North Dakota	18.9
49	Alaska	5.6		2	South Dakota	17.3
16	Arizona	10.8		3	Iowa	15.6
15	Arkansas	10.9		4	Nebraska	15.4
22	California	10.0		5	Montana	14.8
14	Colorado	11.0		6	Kansas	14.0
29	Connecticut	8.9		7	Minnesota	13.4
50	Delaware	4.6		8	Oregon	12.5
18	Florida	10.6		9	Idaho	12.1
38	Georgia	7.6		10	Wisconsin	12.0
45	Hawaii	6.7		11	Tennessee	11.8
9	Idaho	12.1		12	Wyoming	11.5
21	Illinois	10.1		13	Missouri	11.3
35	Indiana	8.2		14	Colorado	11.0
3	Iowa	15.6		15	Arkansas	10.9
6	Kansas	14.0		16	Arizona	10.8
28	Kentucky	9.0		16	Utah	10.8
31	Louisiana	8.7		18	Florida	10.6
23	Maine	9.6		19	Washington	10.3
38	Maryland	7.6		20	Pennsylvania	10.2
40	Massachusetts	7.2		21	Illinois	10.1
43	Michigan	6.8		22	California	10.0
7	Minnesota	13.4		23	Maine	9.6
26	Mississippi	9.3		23	Virginia	9.6
13	Missouri	11.3		25	Vermont	9.5
5	Montana	14.8		26	Mississippi	9.3
4	Nebraska	15.4		27	Oklahoma	9.2
48	Nevada	6.0		28	Kentucky	9.0
46	New Hampshire	6.5		29	Connecticut	8.9
43	New Jersey	6.8		30	North Carolina	8.8
33	New Mexico	8.5		31	Louisiana	8.7
41	New York	7.1		31	South Carolina	8.7
30	North Carolina	8.8		33	New Mexico	8.5
1	North Dakota	18.9		34	Rhode Island	8.3
37	Ohio	7.7		35	Alabama	8.2
27	Oklahoma	9.2		35	Indiana	8.2
8	Oregon	12.5		37	Ohio	7.7
20	Pennsylvania	10.2		38	Georgia	7.6
34	Rhode Island	8.3		38	Maryland	7.6
31	South Carolina	8.7		40	Massachusetts	7.2
2	South Dakota	17.3		41	New York	7.1
11	Tennessee	11.8		42	Texas	6.9
42	Texas	6.9		43	Michigan	6.8
16	Utah	10.8		43	New Jersey	6.8
25	Vermont	9.5		45	Hawaii	6.7
23	Virginia	9.6		46	New Hampshire	6.5
19	Washington	10.3		47	West Virginia	6.4
47	West Virginia	6.4		48	Nevada	6.0
10	Wisconsin	12.0		49	Alaska	5.6
12	Wyoming	11.5		50	Delaware	4.6
					District of Columbia	6.7

Source: U.S. Bureau of the Census
   "Health Insurance Coverage Status" (http://www.census.gov/hhes/www/hlthins/historic/hihistt4.html)
*Direct-purchase health insurance is private insurance coverage though a plan purchased by an individual from a private company.

Percent of Population Covered by Government Health Insurance in 2004

National Percent = 27.2% of Population*

ALPHA ORDER				RANK ORDER		
RANK	STATE	PERCENT		RANK	STATE	PERCENT
14	Alabama	30.6		1	Maine	37.1
12	Alaska	30.7		2	Vermont	34.5
11	Arizona	31.6		3	Tennessee	33.9
6	Arkansas	33.2		4	Mississippi	33.5
24	California	28.1		4	New Mexico	33.5
49	Colorado	19.6		6	Arkansas	33.2
38	Connecticut	25.6		6	South Carolina	33.2
32	Delaware	26.0		8	West Virginia	33.1
16	Florida	30.3		9	Hawaii	33.0
29	Georgia	26.2		10	Kentucky	32.4
9	Hawaii	33.0		11	Arizona	31.6
42	Idaho	23.6		12	Alaska	30.7
41	Illinois	23.7		12	Oklahoma	30.7
31	Indiana	26.1		14	Alabama	30.6
32	Iowa	26.0		15	Louisiana	30.4
28	Kansas	26.3		16	Florida	30.3
10	Kentucky	32.4		17	Rhode Island	30.2
15	Louisiana	30.4		18	New York	29.9
1	Maine	37.1		19	Montana	29.6
44	Maryland	23.1		19	South Dakota	29.6
36	Massachusetts	25.8		21	Washington	29.2
26	Michigan	27.1		22	Missouri	28.7
47	Minnesota	20.3		23	North Carolina	28.3
4	Mississippi	33.5		24	California	28.1
22	Missouri	28.7		25	Oregon	27.4
19	Montana	29.6		26	Michigan	27.1
29	Nebraska	26.2		27	Pennsylvania	26.6
45	Nevada	21.1		28	Kansas	26.3
48	New Hampshire	19.7		29	Georgia	26.2
46	New Jersey	20.9		29	Nebraska	26.2
4	New Mexico	33.5		31	Indiana	26.1
18	New York	29.9		32	Delaware	26.0
23	North Carolina	28.3		32	Iowa	26.0
35	North Dakota	25.9		32	Wyoming	26.0
40	Ohio	25.1		35	North Dakota	25.9
12	Oklahoma	30.7		36	Massachusetts	25.8
25	Oregon	27.4		36	Wisconsin	25.8
27	Pennsylvania	26.6		38	Connecticut	25.6
17	Rhode Island	30.2		39	Virginia	25.5
6	South Carolina	33.2		40	Ohio	25.1
19	South Dakota	29.6		41	Illinois	23.7
3	Tennessee	33.9		42	Idaho	23.6
43	Texas	23.5		43	Texas	23.5
50	Utah	19.0		44	Maryland	23.1
2	Vermont	34.5		45	Nevada	21.1
39	Virginia	25.5		46	New Jersey	20.9
21	Washington	29.2		47	Minnesota	20.3
8	West Virginia	33.1		48	New Hampshire	19.7
36	Wisconsin	25.8		49	Colorado	19.6
32	Wyoming	26.0		50	Utah	19.0
					District of Columbia	31.3

Source: U.S. Bureau of the Census
   "Health Insurance Coverage Status" (http://www.census.gov/hhes/www/hlthins/historic/hihistt4.html)
*Includes Medicaid, Medicare, State Children's Health Insurance Program (SCHIP) and military health care.

Percent of Population Covered by Military Health Care in 2004

National Percent = 3.7% of Population*

ALPHA ORDER

RANK	STATE	PERCENT
16	Alabama	5.2
1	Alaska	11.6
27	Arizona	3.9
19	Arkansas	5.1
35	California	2.9
19	Colorado	5.1
41	Connecticut	2.5
29	Delaware	3.5
15	Florida	5.3
26	Georgia	4.0
2	Hawaii	11.2
34	Idaho	3.1
42	Illinois	2.3
38	Indiana	2.7
31	Iowa	3.3
19	Kansas	5.1
9	Kentucky	6.3
35	Louisiana	2.9
19	Maine	5.1
14	Maryland	5.4
49	Massachusetts	1.4
44	Michigan	2.2
44	Minnesota	2.2
25	Mississippi	4.4
33	Missouri	3.2
16	Montana	5.2
24	Nebraska	4.7
16	Nevada	5.2
31	New Hampshire	3.3
48	New Jersey	1.5
12	New Mexico	5.6
50	New York	1.3
6	North Carolina	6.6
13	North Dakota	5.5
46	Ohio	2.0
5	Oklahoma	6.7
35	Oregon	2.9
42	Pennsylvania	2.3
38	Rhode Island	2.7
4	South Carolina	6.8
8	South Dakota	6.5
11	Tennessee	6.0
30	Texas	3.4
38	Utah	2.7
23	Vermont	5.0
3	Virginia	8.2
6	Washington	6.6
28	West Virginia	3.6
47	Wisconsin	1.9
10	Wyoming	6.1

RANK ORDER

RANK	STATE	PERCENT
1	Alaska	11.6
2	Hawaii	11.2
3	Virginia	8.2
4	South Carolina	6.8
5	Oklahoma	6.7
6	North Carolina	6.6
6	Washington	6.6
8	South Dakota	6.5
9	Kentucky	6.3
10	Wyoming	6.1
11	Tennessee	6.0
12	New Mexico	5.6
13	North Dakota	5.5
14	Maryland	5.4
15	Florida	5.3
16	Alabama	5.2
16	Montana	5.2
16	Nevada	5.2
19	Arkansas	5.1
19	Colorado	5.1
19	Kansas	5.1
19	Maine	5.1
23	Vermont	5.0
24	Nebraska	4.7
25	Mississippi	4.4
26	Georgia	4.0
27	Arizona	3.9
28	West Virginia	3.6
29	Delaware	3.5
30	Texas	3.4
31	Iowa	3.3
31	New Hampshire	3.3
33	Missouri	3.2
34	Idaho	3.1
35	California	2.9
35	Louisiana	2.9
35	Oregon	2.9
38	Indiana	2.7
38	Rhode Island	2.7
38	Utah	2.7
41	Connecticut	2.5
42	Illinois	2.3
42	Pennsylvania	2.3
44	Michigan	2.2
44	Minnesota	2.2
46	Ohio	2.0
47	Wisconsin	1.9
48	New Jersey	1.5
49	Massachusetts	1.4
50	New York	1.3

District of Columbia   2.0

Source: U.S. Bureau of the Census
   "Health Insurance Coverage Status" (http://www.census.gov/hhes/www/hlthins/historic/hihistt4.html)
*Includes CHAMPUS (Comprehensive Health and Medical Plan for Uniformed Services)/Tricare, Veterans
and military health care.

Percent of Children Covered by Health Insurance in 2004

National Percent = 88.8% of Children*

ALPHA ORDER

RANK ORDER

RANK	STATE	PERCENT	RANK	STATE	PERCENT
13	Alabama	92.6	1	Vermont	95.2
35	Alaska	89.1	2	Wisconsin	94.9
43	Arizona	85.3	3	Hawaii	94.6
9	Arkansas	93.2	4	Maine	94.2
40	California	87.6	5	Iowa	94.0
44	Colorado	85.0	5	Nebraska	94.0
22	Connecticut	91.5	7	Kansas	93.5
41	Delaware	87.4	7	Massachusetts	93.5
45	Florida	84.9	9	Arkansas	93.2
38	Georgia	88.3	9	Michigan	93.2
3	Hawaii	94.6	9	Minnesota	93.2
24	Idaho	91.4	12	Washington	93.0
37	Illinois	88.6	13	Alabama	92.6
27	Indiana	91.1	13	Rhode Island	92.6
5	Iowa	94.0	15	Ohio	92.5
7	Kansas	93.5	16	South Carolina	92.3
21	Kentucky	91.6	17	New Hampshire	92.2
18	Louisiana	92.0	18	Louisiana	92.0
4	Maine	94.2	19	Virginia	91.9
28	Maryland	90.4	20	South Dakota	91.7
7	Massachusetts	93.5	21	Kentucky	91.6
9	Michigan	93.2	22	Connecticut	91.5
9	Minnesota	93.2	22	Missouri	91.5
42	Mississippi	85.8	24	Idaho	91.4
22	Missouri	91.5	24	New York	91.4
47	Montana	84.6	26	West Virginia	91.2
5	Nebraska	94.0	27	Indiana	91.1
48	Nevada	83.9	28	Maryland	90.4
17	New Hampshire	92.2	28	North Dakota	90.4
38	New Jersey	88.3	30	Wyoming	90.3
46	New Mexico	84.7	31	Oregon	90.0
24	New York	91.4	32	Tennessee	89.9
36	North Carolina	88.8	33	Utah	89.6
28	North Dakota	90.4	34	Pennsylvania	89.3
15	Ohio	92.5	35	Alaska	89.1
49	Oklahoma	83.1	36	North Carolina	88.8
31	Oregon	90.0	37	Illinois	88.6
34	Pennsylvania	89.3	38	Georgia	88.3
13	Rhode Island	92.6	38	New Jersey	88.3
16	South Carolina	92.3	40	California	87.6
20	South Dakota	91.7	41	Delaware	87.4
32	Tennessee	89.9	42	Mississippi	85.8
50	Texas	78.6	43	Arizona	85.3
33	Utah	89.6	44	Colorado	85.0
1	Vermont	95.2	45	Florida	84.9
19	Virginia	91.9	46	New Mexico	84.7
12	Washington	93.0	47	Montana	84.6
26	West Virginia	91.2	48	Nevada	83.9
2	Wisconsin	94.9	49	Oklahoma	83.1
30	Wyoming	90.3	50	Texas	78.6
				District of Columbia	92.4

Source: U.S. Bureau of the Census

"Health Insurance Coverage Status" (http://www.census.gov/hhes/www/hlthins/historic/hihistt5.html)

*Children under 18 covered by either private or government health insurance.

Percent of Children Covered by Private Health Insurance in 2004

National Percent = 65.6% of Children*

ALPHA ORDER

RANK ORDER

RANK	STATE	PERCENT		RANK	STATE	PERCENT
38	Alabama	62.2		1	New Hampshire	81.5
40	Alaska	60.3		2	Minnesota	80.3
45	Arizona	58.3		3	Massachusetts	76.9
42	Arkansas	59.4		4	Utah	76.3
44	California	59.0		5	Iowa	76.0
19	Colorado	71.6		6	New Jersey	75.6
7	Connecticut	75.0		7	Connecticut	75.0
22	Delaware	70.5		8	Virginia	74.5
37	Florida	62.3		9	Kansas	74.0
41	Georgia	59.5		10	Michigan	73.6
14	Hawaii	72.1		11	North Dakota	73.2
27	Idaho	67.5		12	Ohio	73.1
21	Illinois	71.2		12	Wisconsin	73.1
24	Indiana	68.9		14	Hawaii	72.1
5	Iowa	76.0		14	Nebraska	72.1
9	Kansas	74.0		16	Nevada	71.8
36	Kentucky	62.6		17	Oregon	71.7
46	Louisiana	58.1		17	Pennsylvania	71.7
29	Maine	67.0		19	Colorado	71.6
19	Maryland	71.6		19	Maryland	71.6
3	Massachusetts	76.9		21	Illinois	71.2
10	Michigan	73.6		22	Delaware	70.5
2	Minnesota	80.3		23	Wyoming	69.3
49	Mississippi	50.8		24	Indiana	68.9
26	Missouri	67.9		25	Rhode Island	68.3
43	Montana	59.3		26	Missouri	67.9
14	Nebraska	72.1		27	Idaho	67.5
16	Nevada	71.8		28	Washington	67.1
1	New Hampshire	81.5		29	Maine	67.0
6	New Jersey	75.6		30	South Dakota	66.1
50	New Mexico	50.6		31	Vermont	66.0
33	New York	64.6		32	Tennessee	65.0
34	North Carolina	64.4		33	New York	64.6
11	North Dakota	73.2		34	North Carolina	64.4
12	Ohio	73.1		35	South Carolina	63.3
47	Oklahoma	56.4		36	Kentucky	62.6
17	Oregon	71.7		37	Florida	62.3
17	Pennsylvania	71.7		38	Alabama	62.2
25	Rhode Island	68.3		38	West Virginia	62.2
35	South Carolina	63.3		40	Alaska	60.3
30	South Dakota	66.1		41	Georgia	59.5
32	Tennessee	65.0		42	Arkansas	59.4
48	Texas	54.4		43	Montana	59.3
4	Utah	76.3		44	California	59.0
31	Vermont	66.0		45	Arizona	58.3
8	Virginia	74.5		46	Louisiana	58.1
28	Washington	67.1		47	Oklahoma	56.4
38	West Virginia	62.2		48	Texas	54.4
12	Wisconsin	73.1		49	Mississippi	50.8
23	Wyoming	69.3		50	New Mexico	50.6

District of Columbia   54.7

Source: U.S. Bureau of the Census
"Health Insurance Coverage Status" (http://www.census.gov/hhes/www/hlthins/historic/hihistt5.html)
*Children under 18. Private health insurance is coverage by a health plan provided through an employer or union or purchased by an individual from a private health insurance company.

Percent of Children Covered by Employment-Based Health Insurance in 2004

National Percent = 60.8% of Children*

ALPHA ORDER

RANK ORDER

RANK	STATE	PERCENT		RANK	STATE	PERCENT
33	Alabama	59.4		1	New Hampshire	78.8
40	Alaska	56.2		2	Minnesota	73.9
47	Arizona	51.5		3	Massachusetts	73.2
43	Arkansas	53.8		3	New Jersey	73.2
46	California	52.0		5	Connecticut	71.8
20	Colorado	65.0		6	Hawaii	70.4
5	Connecticut	71.8		7	Virginia	70.1
14	Delaware	67.4		8	Michigan	69.6
37	Florida	57.1		8	Ohio	69.6
41	Georgia	55.5		10	Wisconsin	69.2
6	Hawaii	70.4		11	Utah	68.3
37	Idaho	57.1		12	Iowa	68.1
19	Illinois	65.3		13	Kansas	67.6
20	Indiana	65.0		14	Delaware	67.4
12	Iowa	68.1		15	Nevada	67.3
13	Kansas	67.6		16	Maryland	67.0
36	Kentucky	58.7		17	Pennsylvania	66.2
44	Louisiana	53.0		18	Nebraska	65.4
28	Maine	62.0		19	Illinois	65.3
16	Maryland	67.0		20	Colorado	65.0
3	Massachusetts	73.2		20	Indiana	65.0
8	Michigan	69.6		22	Wyoming	64.2
2	Minnesota	73.9		23	Oregon	64.0
50	Mississippi	46.5		24	Rhode Island	63.2
25	Missouri	62.9		25	Missouri	62.9
42	Montana	55.1		25	North Dakota	62.9
18	Nebraska	65.4		27	Vermont	62.1
15	Nevada	67.3		28	Maine	62.0
1	New Hampshire	78.8		28	Washington	62.0
3	New Jersey	73.2		30	New York	61.2
49	New Mexico	48.2		31	Tennessee	60.5
30	New York	61.2		32	North Carolina	59.8
32	North Carolina	59.8		33	Alabama	59.4
25	North Dakota	62.9		34	South Carolina	59.1
8	Ohio	69.6		35	West Virginia	58.9
45	Oklahoma	52.1		36	Kentucky	58.7
23	Oregon	64.0		37	Florida	57.1
17	Pennsylvania	66.2		37	Idaho	57.1
24	Rhode Island	63.2		39	South Dakota	56.5
34	South Carolina	59.1		40	Alaska	56.2
39	South Dakota	56.5		41	Georgia	55.5
31	Tennessee	60.5		42	Montana	55.1
47	Texas	51.5		43	Arkansas	53.8
11	Utah	68.3		44	Louisiana	53.0
27	Vermont	62.1		45	Oklahoma	52.1
7	Virginia	70.1		46	California	52.0
28	Washington	62.0		47	Arizona	51.5
35	West Virginia	58.9		47	Texas	51.5
10	Wisconsin	69.2		49	New Mexico	48.2
22	Wyoming	64.2		50	Mississippi	46.5

District of Columbia 49.9

Source: U.S. Bureau of the Census
   "Health Insurance Coverage Status" (http://www.census.gov/hhes/www/hlthins/historic/hihistt5.html)
*Children under 18. Employment-based health insurance is private insurance coverage offered through one's own employment or a relative's. It may be offered by an employer or by a union.

Percent of Children Covered by Direct Purchase Health Insurance in 2004

National Percent = 5.6% of Children*

ALPHA ORDER

RANK ORDER

RANK	STATE	PERCENT		RANK	STATE	PERCENT
38	Alabama	3.8		1	North Dakota	13.8
41	Alaska	3.7		2	Utah	11.0
12	Arizona	7.2		3	South Dakota	10.7
24	Arkansas	5.4		4	Idaho	9.8
6	California	8.2		5	Oregon	8.3
13	Colorado	7.1		6	California	8.2
22	Connecticut	5.6		7	Nebraska	7.9
50	Delaware	2.4		8	Iowa	7.7
18	Florida	6.4		8	Minnesota	7.7
16	Georgia	6.5		10	Kansas	7.6
37	Hawaii	3.9		10	Missouri	7.6
4	Idaho	9.8		12	Arizona	7.2
21	Illinois	6.1		13	Colorado	7.1
34	Indiana	4.0		14	Virginia	6.8
8	Iowa	7.7		15	Tennessee	6.6
10	Kansas	7.6		16	Georgia	6.5
29	Kentucky	4.6		16	Louisiana	6.5
16	Louisiana	6.5		18	Florida	6.4
34	Maine	4.0		19	Washington	6.3
28	Maryland	4.8		20	Mississippi	6.2
42	Massachusetts	3.6		21	Illinois	6.1
45	Michigan	3.1		22	Connecticut	5.6
8	Minnesota	7.7		22	Wisconsin	5.6
20	Mississippi	6.2		24	Arkansas	5.4
10	Missouri	7.6		24	Rhode Island	5.4
42	Montana	3.6		26	North Carolina	5.2
7	Nebraska	7.9		27	Pennsylvania	5.0
29	Nevada	4.6		28	Maryland	4.8
48	New Hampshire	2.8		29	Kentucky	4.6
47	New Jersey	2.9		29	Nevada	4.6
48	New Mexico	2.8		31	Vermont	4.5
34	New York	4.0		32	South Carolina	4.3
26	North Carolina	5.2		33	Wyoming	4.1
1	North Dakota	13.8		34	Indiana	4.0
38	Ohio	3.8		34	Maine	4.0
44	Oklahoma	3.3		34	New York	4.0
5	Oregon	8.3		37	Hawaii	3.9
27	Pennsylvania	5.0		38	Alabama	3.8
24	Rhode Island	5.4		38	Ohio	3.8
32	South Carolina	4.3		38	Texas	3.8
3	South Dakota	10.7		41	Alaska	3.7
15	Tennessee	6.6		42	Massachusetts	3.6
38	Texas	3.8		42	Montana	3.6
2	Utah	11.0		44	Oklahoma	3.3
31	Vermont	4.5		45	Michigan	3.1
14	Virginia	6.8		45	West Virginia	3.1
19	Washington	6.3		47	New Jersey	2.9
45	West Virginia	3.1		48	New Hampshire	2.8
22	Wisconsin	5.6		48	New Mexico	2.8
33	Wyoming	4.1		50	Delaware	2.4

District of Columbia   3.8

Source: U.S. Bureau of the Census
   "Health Insurance Coverage Status" (http://www.census.gov/hhes/www/hlthins/historic/hihistt5.html)
*Children under 18. Direct-purchase health insurance is private insurance coverage though a plan purchased by an individual from a private company.

Percent of Children Covered by Government Health Insurance in 2004

National Percent = 29.7% of Children*

ALPHA ORDER

RANK	STATE	PERCENT
11	Alabama	35.9
3	Alaska	43.1
19	Arizona	33.2
5	Arkansas	42.4
15	California	34.5
46	Colorado	18.9
43	Connecticut	22.3
44	Delaware	21.7
28	Florida	29.3
9	Georgia	36.8
13	Hawaii	35.0
27	Idaho	29.8
42	Illinois	22.7
26	Indiana	30.5
35	Iowa	26.4
33	Kansas	26.6
12	Kentucky	35.5
6	Louisiana	41.0
8	Maine	37.5
38	Maryland	23.7
41	Massachusetts	23.0
31	Michigan	28.3
48	Minnesota	17.3
2	Mississippi	43.5
25	Missouri	30.6
22	Montana	31.5
23	Nebraska	31.0
50	Nevada	16.4
47	New Hampshire	17.6
49	New Jersey	16.6
1	New Mexico	44.0
20	New York	33.1
23	North Carolina	31.0
40	North Dakota	23.1
36	Ohio	25.6
17	Oklahoma	33.6
39	Oregon	23.4
37	Pennsylvania	23.8
20	Rhode Island	33.1
7	South Carolina	38.3
17	South Dakota	33.6
16	Tennessee	34.3
29	Texas	28.7
45	Utah	20.4
4	Vermont	42.7
34	Virginia	26.5
10	Washington	36.2
14	West Virginia	34.7
32	Wisconsin	27.4
30	Wyoming	28.5

RANK ORDER

RANK	STATE	PERCENT
1	New Mexico	44.0
2	Mississippi	43.5
3	Alaska	43.1
4	Vermont	42.7
5	Arkansas	42.4
6	Louisiana	41.0
7	South Carolina	38.3
8	Maine	37.5
9	Georgia	36.8
10	Washington	36.2
11	Alabama	35.9
12	Kentucky	35.5
13	Hawaii	35.0
14	West Virginia	34.7
15	California	34.5
16	Tennessee	34.3
17	Oklahoma	33.6
17	South Dakota	33.6
19	Arizona	33.2
20	New York	33.1
20	Rhode Island	33.1
22	Montana	31.5
23	Nebraska	31.0
23	North Carolina	31.0
25	Missouri	30.6
26	Indiana	30.5
27	Idaho	29.8
28	Florida	29.3
29	Texas	28.7
30	Wyoming	28.5
31	Michigan	28.3
32	Wisconsin	27.4
33	Kansas	26.6
34	Virginia	26.5
35	Iowa	26.4
36	Ohio	25.6
37	Pennsylvania	23.8
38	Maryland	23.7
39	Oregon	23.4
40	North Dakota	23.1
41	Massachusetts	23.0
42	Illinois	22.7
43	Connecticut	22.3
44	Delaware	21.7
45	Utah	20.4
46	Colorado	18.9
47	New Hampshire	17.6
48	Minnesota	17.3
49	New Jersey	16.6
50	Nevada	16.4

| | District of Columbia | 44.3 |

Source: U.S. Bureau of the Census
    "Health Insurance Coverage Status" (http://www.census.gov/hhes/www/hlthins/historic/hihistt5.html)
*Children under 18. Includes Medicaid, Medicare, State Children's Health Insurance Program (SCHIP) and military health care.

Percent of Children Covered by Military Health Care in 2004

National Percent = 2.8% of Children*

ALPHA ORDER

RANK	STATE	PERCENT
17	Alabama	4.0
2	Alaska	12.6
38	Arizona	1.9
25	Arkansas	2.8
33	California	2.3
8	Colorado	4.9
35	Connecticut	2.1
25	Delaware	2.8
23	Florida	3.1
25	Georgia	2.8
1	Hawaii	13.6
29	Idaho	2.5
38	Illinois	1.9
33	Indiana	2.3
38	Iowa	1.9
8	Kansas	4.9
6	Kentucky	6.0
32	Louisiana	2.4
20	Maine	3.8
13	Maryland	4.7
48	Massachusetts	0.9
45	Michigan	1.3
47	Minnesota	1.1
21	Mississippi	3.7
41	Missouri	1.8
15	Montana	4.5
8	Nebraska	4.9
24	Nevada	3.0
29	New Hampshire	2.5
50	New Jersey	0.4
25	New Mexico	2.8
49	New York	0.7
4	North Carolina	6.9
12	North Dakota	4.8
42	Ohio	1.6
14	Oklahoma	4.6
46	Oregon	1.2
43	Pennsylvania	1.5
29	Rhode Island	2.5
15	South Carolina	4.5
7	South Dakota	5.7
17	Tennessee	4.0
35	Texas	2.1
35	Utah	2.1
8	Vermont	4.9
3	Virginia	8.3
5	Washington	6.7
19	West Virginia	3.9
43	Wisconsin	1.5
22	Wyoming	3.6

RANK ORDER

RANK	STATE	PERCENT
1	Hawaii	13.6
2	Alaska	12.6
3	Virginia	8.3
4	North Carolina	6.9
5	Washington	6.7
6	Kentucky	6.0
7	South Dakota	5.7
8	Colorado	4.9
8	Kansas	4.9
8	Nebraska	4.9
8	Vermont	4.9
12	North Dakota	4.8
13	Maryland	4.7
14	Oklahoma	4.6
15	Montana	4.5
15	South Carolina	4.5
17	Alabama	4.0
17	Tennessee	4.0
19	West Virginia	3.9
20	Maine	3.8
21	Mississippi	3.7
22	Wyoming	3.6
23	Florida	3.1
24	Nevada	3.0
25	Arkansas	2.8
25	Delaware	2.8
25	Georgia	2.8
25	New Mexico	2.8
29	Idaho	2.5
29	New Hampshire	2.5
29	Rhode Island	2.5
32	Louisiana	2.4
33	California	2.3
33	Indiana	2.3
35	Connecticut	2.1
35	Texas	2.1
35	Utah	2.1
38	Arizona	1.9
38	Illinois	1.9
38	Iowa	1.9
41	Missouri	1.8
42	Ohio	1.6
43	Pennsylvania	1.5
43	Wisconsin	1.5
45	Michigan	1.3
46	Oregon	1.2
47	Minnesota	1.1
48	Massachusetts	0.9
49	New York	0.7
50	New Jersey	0.4

District of Columbia   0.9

Source: U.S. Bureau of the Census
    "Health Insurance Coverage Status" (http://www.census.gov/hhes/www/hlthins/historic/hihistt5.html)
*Children under 18. Includes CHAMPUS (Comprehensive Health and Medical Plan for Uniformed Services)/Tricare, Veterans and military health care.

Percent of Children Covered by Medicaid in 2004

National Percent = 26.9% of Children*

ALPHA ORDER

RANK	STATE	PERCENT
9	Alabama	32.4
12	Alaska	31.7
14	Arizona	31.2
2	Arkansas	40.6
11	California	32.1
49	Colorado	14.0
40	Connecticut	20.2
45	Delaware	17.9
29	Florida	25.9
6	Georgia	34.1
37	Hawaii	21.6
25	Idaho	27.1
39	Illinois	20.4
23	Indiana	27.8
31	Iowa	24.7
36	Kansas	22.1
15	Kentucky	30.4
4	Louisiana	39.1
8	Maine	33.9
41	Maryland	19.1
35	Massachusetts	22.4
24	Michigan	27.5
47	Minnesota	16.2
3	Mississippi	39.5
21	Missouri	28.8
18	Montana	29.4
27	Nebraska	26.2
50	Nevada	13.3
48	New Hampshire	15.6
46	New Jersey	16.3
1	New Mexico	41.1
10	New York	32.2
32	North Carolina	24.0
42	North Dakota	18.2
33	Ohio	23.9
20	Oklahoma	29.1
34	Oregon	23.0
38	Pennsylvania	21.5
17	Rhode Island	29.9
7	South Carolina	34.0
22	South Dakota	28.6
19	Tennessee	29.3
26	Texas	26.5
43	Utah	18.1
5	Vermont	38.9
43	Virginia	18.1
16	Washington	30.2
13	West Virginia	31.4
28	Wisconsin	26.0
30	Wyoming	24.8

RANK ORDER

RANK	STATE	PERCENT
1	New Mexico	41.1
2	Arkansas	40.6
3	Mississippi	39.5
4	Louisiana	39.1
5	Vermont	38.9
6	Georgia	34.1
7	South Carolina	34.0
8	Maine	33.9
9	Alabama	32.4
10	New York	32.2
11	California	32.1
12	Alaska	31.7
13	West Virginia	31.4
14	Arizona	31.2
15	Kentucky	30.4
16	Washington	30.2
17	Rhode Island	29.9
18	Montana	29.4
19	Tennessee	29.3
20	Oklahoma	29.1
21	Missouri	28.8
22	South Dakota	28.6
23	Indiana	27.8
24	Michigan	27.5
25	Idaho	27.1
26	Texas	26.5
27	Nebraska	26.2
28	Wisconsin	26.0
29	Florida	25.9
30	Wyoming	24.8
31	Iowa	24.7
32	North Carolina	24.0
33	Ohio	23.9
34	Oregon	23.0
35	Massachusetts	22.4
36	Kansas	22.1
37	Hawaii	21.6
38	Pennsylvania	21.5
39	Illinois	20.4
40	Connecticut	20.2
41	Maryland	19.1
42	North Dakota	18.2
43	Utah	18.1
43	Virginia	18.1
45	Delaware	17.9
46	New Jersey	16.3
47	Minnesota	16.2
48	New Hampshire	15.6
49	Colorado	14.0
50	Nevada	13.3

	District of Columbia	43.1

Source: U.S. Bureau of the Census
   "Health Insurance Coverage Status" (http://www.census.gov/hhes/www/hlthins/historic/hihistt5.html)
*Children under 18 years old. Medicaid is a form of government insurance.

State Children's Health Insurance Program (SCHIP) Enrollment in 2004

National Total = 6,058,900 Children*

ALPHA ORDER

RANK	STATE	CHILDREN	% of USA
21	Alabama	79,400	1.3%
37	Alaska	18,900	0.3%
18	Arizona	87,700	1.4%
NA	Arkansas**	NA	NA
1	California	1,035,800	17.1%
24	Colorado	57,200	0.9%
34	Connecticut	21,400	0.4%
43	Delaware	10,300	0.2%
4	Florida	419,700	6.9%
5	Georgia	280,100	4.6%
36	Hawaii	19,200	0.3%
38	Idaho	17,400	0.3%
6	Illinois	234,000	3.9%
20	Indiana	80,700	1.3%
27	Iowa	40,800	0.7%
26	Kansas	44,400	0.7%
17	Kentucky	94,500	1.6%
14	Louisiana	105,600	1.7%
32	Maine	29,200	0.5%
13	Maryland	111,500	1.8%
11	Massachusetts	166,500	2.7%
NA	Michigan**	NA	NA
47	Minnesota	4,800	0.1%
19	Mississippi	82,900	1.4%
9	Missouri	176,000	2.9%
40	Montana	15,300	0.3%
31	Nebraska	33,300	0.5%
29	Nevada	38,500	0.6%
42	New Hampshire	11,000	0.2%
12	New Jersey	127,200	2.1%
35	New Mexico	20,800	0.3%
2	New York	826,600	13.6%
10	North Carolina	174,300	2.9%
46	North Dakota	5,100	0.1%
7	Ohio	220,200	3.6%
15	Oklahoma	100,800	1.7%
25	Oregon	46,700	0.8%
8	Pennsylvania	177,400	2.9%
33	Rhode Island	25,600	0.4%
22	South Carolina	75,600	1.2%
41	South Dakota	13,400	0.2%
NA	Tennessee**	NA	NA
3	Texas	650,900	10.7%
28	Utah	38,700	0.6%
44	Vermont	6,700	0.1%
16	Virginia	99,600	1.6%
39	Washington	17,000	0.3%
30	West Virginia	36,900	0.6%
23	Wisconsin	67,900	1.1%
45	Wyoming	5,500	0.1%

RANK ORDER

RANK	STATE	CHILDREN	% of USA
1	California	1,035,800	17.1%
2	New York	826,600	13.6%
3	Texas	650,900	10.7%
4	Florida	419,700	6.9%
5	Georgia	280,100	4.6%
6	Illinois	234,000	3.9%
7	Ohio	220,200	3.6%
8	Pennsylvania	177,400	2.9%
9	Missouri	176,000	2.9%
10	North Carolina	174,300	2.9%
11	Massachusetts	166,500	2.7%
12	New Jersey	127,200	2.1%
13	Maryland	111,500	1.8%
14	Louisiana	105,600	1.7%
15	Oklahoma	100,800	1.7%
16	Virginia	99,600	1.6%
17	Kentucky	94,500	1.6%
18	Arizona	87,700	1.4%
19	Mississippi	82,900	1.4%
20	Indiana	80,700	1.3%
21	Alabama	79,400	1.3%
22	South Carolina	75,600	1.2%
23	Wisconsin	67,900	1.1%
24	Colorado	57,200	0.9%
25	Oregon	46,700	0.8%
26	Kansas	44,400	0.7%
27	Iowa	40,800	0.7%
28	Utah	38,700	0.6%
29	Nevada	38,500	0.6%
30	West Virginia	36,900	0.6%
31	Nebraska	33,300	0.5%
32	Maine	29,200	0.5%
33	Rhode Island	25,600	0.4%
34	Connecticut	21,400	0.4%
35	New Mexico	20,800	0.3%
36	Hawaii	19,200	0.3%
37	Alaska	18,900	0.3%
38	Idaho	17,400	0.3%
39	Washington	17,000	0.3%
40	Montana	15,300	0.3%
41	South Dakota	13,400	0.2%
42	New Hampshire	11,000	0.2%
43	Delaware	10,300	0.2%
44	Vermont	6,700	0.1%
45	Wyoming	5,500	0.1%
46	North Dakota	5,100	0.1%
47	Minnesota	4,800	0.1%
NA	Arkansas**	NA	NA
NA	Michigan**	NA	NA
NA	Tennessee**	NA	NA
	District of Columbia	6,100	0.1%

Source: U.S. Department of Health and Human Services, Centers for Medicare and Medicaid Services
"Children's Health Insurance Program Annual Enrollment Report"
*Figures for fiscal year 2004. The State Children's Health Insurance Program (SCHIP) was created in 1997 to help states expand health insurance to children whose families earn too much to qualify for Medicaid, yet not enough to afford private health insurance.
**Not reported.

Percent Change in State Children's Health Insurance Program (SCHIP) Enrollment: 2003 to 2004
National Percent Change = 3.1% Increase*

ALPHA ORDER

RANK	STATE	PERCENT CHANGE
32	Alabama	1.1
43	Alaska	(17.6)
38	Arizona	(3.1)
NA	Arkansas**	NA
18	California	8.4
45	Colorado	(22.9)
31	Connecticut	2.0
25	Delaware	4.0
39	Florida	(5.3)
9	Georgia	11.3
3	Hawaii	59.7
28	Idaho	3.1
2	Illinois	72.6
16	Indiana	9.4
14	Iowa	10.1
37	Kansas	(2.8)
34	Kentucky	0.5
33	Louisiana	0.7
35	Maine	(0.9)
41	Maryland	(14.3)
4	Massachusetts	29.3
NA	Michigan**	NA
NA	Minnesota**	NA
12	Mississippi	10.5
7	Missouri	16.6
6	Montana	16.9
46	Nebraska	(26.8)
44	Nevada	(18.4)
10	New Hampshire	11.2
19	New Jersey	6.6
13	New Mexico	10.4
25	New York	4.0
8	North Carolina	15.9
29	North Dakota	3.0
20	Ohio	5.9
15	Oklahoma	9.7
24	Oregon	4.4
11	Pennsylvania	10.9
22	Rhode Island	4.5
42	South Carolina	(16.7)
17	South Dakota	9.0
NA	Tennessee**	NA
40	Texas	(10.4)
30	Utah	2.5
27	Vermont	3.6
5	Virginia	19.0
1	Washington	77.6
22	West Virginia	4.5
36	Wisconsin	(1.1)
21	Wyoming	4.9

RANK ORDER

RANK	STATE	PERCENT CHANGE
1	Washington	77.6
2	Illinois	72.6
3	Hawaii	59.7
4	Massachusetts	29.3
5	Virginia	19.0
6	Montana	16.9
7	Missouri	16.6
8	North Carolina	15.9
9	Georgia	11.3
10	New Hampshire	11.2
11	Pennsylvania	10.9
12	Mississippi	10.5
13	New Mexico	10.4
14	Iowa	10.1
15	Oklahoma	9.7
16	Indiana	9.4
17	South Dakota	9.0
18	California	8.4
19	New Jersey	6.6
20	Ohio	5.9
21	Wyoming	4.9
22	Rhode Island	4.5
22	West Virginia	4.5
24	Oregon	4.4
25	Delaware	4.0
25	New York	4.0
27	Vermont	3.6
28	Idaho	3.1
29	North Dakota	3.0
30	Utah	2.5
31	Connecticut	2.0
32	Alabama	1.1
33	Louisiana	0.7
34	Kentucky	0.5
35	Maine	(0.9)
36	Wisconsin	(1.1)
37	Kansas	(2.8)
38	Arizona	(3.1)
39	Florida	(5.3)
40	Texas	(10.4)
41	Maryland	(14.3)
42	South Carolina	(16.7)
43	Alaska	(17.6)
44	Nevada	(18.4)
45	Colorado	(22.9)
46	Nebraska	(26.8)
NA	Arkansas**	NA
NA	Michigan**	NA
NA	Minnesota**	NA
NA	Tennessee**	NA

	District of Columbia	3.8

Source: MQ Press using data from U.S. Dept of Health & Human Services, Centers for Medicare and Medicaid Services "Children's Health Insurance Program Annual Enrollment Report"

*Figures for fiscal year 2004. The State Children's Health Insurance Program (SCHIP) was created in 1997 to help states expand health insurance to children whose families earn too much to qualify for Medicaid, yet not enough to afford private health insurance.

**Not available.

Percent of Children Enrolled in State Children's Health Insurance Program (SCHIP) in 2004
National Percent = 8.8% of Children 17 Years and Younger*

ALPHA ORDER

RANK	STATE	PERCENT
22	Alabama	7.3
12	Alaska	10.0
31	Arizona	5.7
NA	Arkansas**	NA
7	California	10.8
39	Colorado	4.9
45	Connecticut	2.6
34	Delaware	5.3
8	Florida	10.5
3	Georgia	12.0
26	Hawaii	6.4
40	Idaho	4.7
23	Illinois	7.2
37	Indiana	5.0
29	Iowa	6.0
25	Kansas	6.5
13	Kentucky	9.6
15	Louisiana	9.1
11	Maine	10.3
17	Maryland	8.0
5	Massachusetts	11.4
NA	Michigan**	NA
47	Minnesota	0.4
6	Mississippi	11.1
2	Missouri	12.7
20	Montana	7.4
19	Nebraska	7.7
26	Nevada	6.4
44	New Hampshire	3.6
30	New Jersey	5.9
42	New Mexico	4.2
1	New York	18.1
16	North Carolina	8.2
43	North Dakota	3.7
18	Ohio	7.9
4	Oklahoma	11.7
32	Oregon	5.5
28	Pennsylvania	6.3
8	Rhode Island	10.5
20	South Carolina	7.4
24	South Dakota	7.0
NA	Tennessee**	NA
10	Texas	10.4
35	Utah	5.2
37	Vermont	5.0
32	Virginia	5.5
46	Washington	1.1
13	West Virginia	9.6
35	Wisconsin	5.2
40	Wyoming	4.7

RANK ORDER

RANK	STATE	PERCENT
1	New York	18.1
2	Missouri	12.7
3	Georgia	12.0
4	Oklahoma	11.7
5	Massachusetts	11.4
6	Mississippi	11.1
7	California	10.8
8	Florida	10.5
8	Rhode Island	10.5
10	Texas	10.4
11	Maine	10.3
12	Alaska	10.0
13	Kentucky	9.6
13	West Virginia	9.6
15	Louisiana	9.1
16	North Carolina	8.2
17	Maryland	8.0
18	Ohio	7.9
19	Nebraska	7.7
20	Montana	7.4
20	South Carolina	7.4
22	Alabama	7.3
23	Illinois	7.2
24	South Dakota	7.0
25	Kansas	6.5
26	Hawaii	6.4
26	Nevada	6.4
28	Pennsylvania	6.3
29	Iowa	6.0
30	New Jersey	5.9
31	Arizona	5.7
32	Oregon	5.5
32	Virginia	5.5
34	Delaware	5.3
35	Utah	5.2
35	Wisconsin	5.2
37	Indiana	5.0
37	Vermont	5.0
39	Colorado	4.9
40	Idaho	4.7
40	Wyoming	4.7
42	New Mexico	4.2
43	North Dakota	3.7
44	New Hampshire	3.6
45	Connecticut	2.6
46	Washington	1.1
47	Minnesota	0.4
NA	Arkansas**	NA
NA	Michigan**	NA
NA	Tennessee**	NA

District of Columbia   5.6

Source: MQ Press using data from U.S. Dept of Health & Human Services, Centers for Medicare and Medicaid Services
    "Children's Health Insurance Program Annual Enrollment Report"
*Figures for fiscal year 2004. The State Children's Health Insurance Program (SCHIP) was created in 1997 to help states expand health insurance to children whose families earn too much to qualify for Medicaid, yet not enough to afford private health insurance. Calculated using 2004 Census estimates for 17 and younger for reporting states.
**Not available.

Expenditures for State Children's Health Insurance Program (SCHIP) in 2004

National Total = $4,600,700,000*

ALPHA ORDER

RANK	STATE	EXPENDITURES	% of USA
39	Alabama	$19,400,000	0.4%
19	Alaska	72,800,000	1.6%
5	Arizona	258,900,000	5.6%
32	Arkansas	28,500,000	0.6%
1	California	661,600,000	14.4%
28	Colorado	37,600,000	0.8%
40	Connecticut	17,200,000	0.4%
47	Delaware	5,300,000	0.1%
8	Florida	176,500,000	3.8%
7	Georgia	215,000,000	4.7%
44	Hawaii	10,500,000	0.2%
41	Idaho	14,400,000	0.3%
2	Illinois	309,800,000	6.7%
22	Indiana	65,400,000	1.4%
29	Iowa	37,300,000	0.8%
27	Kansas	39,600,000	0.9%
21	Kentucky	71,500,000	1.6%
16	Louisiana	94,400,000	2.1%
35	Maine	25,200,000	0.5%
14	Maryland	106,400,000	2.3%
13	Massachusetts	119,100,000	2.6%
11	Michigan	159,500,000	3.5%
20	Minnesota	72,700,000	1.6%
15	Mississippi	101,900,000	2.2%
18	Missouri	80,200,000	1.7%
42	Montana	14,300,000	0.3%
30	Nebraska	35,300,000	0.8%
38	Nevada	20,600,000	0.4%
45	New Hampshire	7,300,000	0.2%
6	New Jersey	221,900,000	4.8%
37	New Mexico	21,400,000	0.5%
3	New York	296,900,000	6.5%
10	North Carolina	166,200,000	3.6%
46	North Dakota	6,900,000	0.1%
9	Ohio	167,100,000	3.6%
25	Oklahoma	46,100,000	1.0%
34	Oregon	25,300,000	0.5%
12	Pennsylvania	126,600,000	2.8%
35	Rhode Island	25,200,000	0.5%
24	South Carolina	50,800,000	1.1%
43	South Dakota	10,900,000	0.2%
49	Tennessee	4,500,000	0.1%
4	Texas	282,500,000	6.1%
33	Utah	28,000,000	0.6%
50	Vermont	3,200,000	0.1%
23	Virginia	63,000,000	1.4%
26	Washington	39,700,000	0.9%
31	West Virginia	30,800,000	0.7%
17	Wisconsin	93,700,000	2.0%
48	Wyoming	5,200,000	0.1%

RANK ORDER

RANK	STATE	EXPENDITURES	% of USA
1	California	$661,600,000	14.4%
2	Illinois	309,800,000	6.7%
3	New York	296,900,000	6.5%
4	Texas	282,500,000	6.1%
5	Arizona	258,900,000	5.6%
6	New Jersey	221,900,000	4.8%
7	Georgia	215,000,000	4.7%
8	Florida	176,500,000	3.8%
9	Ohio	167,100,000	3.6%
10	North Carolina	166,200,000	3.6%
11	Michigan	159,500,000	3.5%
12	Pennsylvania	126,600,000	2.8%
13	Massachusetts	119,100,000	2.6%
14	Maryland	106,400,000	2.3%
15	Mississippi	101,900,000	2.2%
16	Louisiana	94,400,000	2.1%
17	Wisconsin	93,700,000	2.0%
18	Missouri	80,200,000	1.7%
19	Alaska	72,800,000	1.6%
20	Minnesota	72,700,000	1.6%
21	Kentucky	71,500,000	1.6%
22	Indiana	65,400,000	1.4%
23	Virginia	63,000,000	1.4%
24	South Carolina	50,800,000	1.1%
25	Oklahoma	46,100,000	1.0%
26	Washington	39,700,000	0.9%
27	Kansas	39,600,000	0.9%
28	Colorado	37,600,000	0.8%
29	Iowa	37,300,000	0.8%
30	Nebraska	35,300,000	0.8%
31	West Virginia	30,800,000	0.7%
32	Arkansas	28,500,000	0.6%
33	Utah	28,000,000	0.6%
34	Oregon	25,300,000	0.5%
35	Maine	25,200,000	0.5%
35	Rhode Island	25,200,000	0.5%
37	New Mexico	21,400,000	0.5%
38	Nevada	20,600,000	0.4%
39	Alabama	19,400,000	0.4%
40	Connecticut	17,200,000	0.4%
41	Idaho	14,400,000	0.3%
42	Montana	14,300,000	0.3%
43	South Dakota	10,900,000	0.2%
44	Hawaii	10,500,000	0.2%
45	New Hampshire	7,300,000	0.2%
46	North Dakota	6,900,000	0.1%
47	Delaware	5,300,000	0.1%
48	Wyoming	5,200,000	0.1%
49	Tennessee	4,500,000	0.1%
50	Vermont	3,200,000	0.1%
	District of Columbia	7,200,000	0.2%

*Source: U.S. Department of Health and Human Services, Centers for Medicare and Medicaid Services
"Statement of Expenditures for the SCHIP Program" (CMS-21 Report)*

*Federal and state expenditures for fiscal year 2004. National total does not include funds spent in U.S. territories. The State Children's Health Insurance Program (SCHIP) was created in 1997 to help states expand health insurance to children whose families earn too much to qualify for Medicaid, yet not enough to afford private health insurance.

Per Capita Expenditures for State Children's
Health Insurance Program (SCHIP) in 2004
National Per Capita = $15.67*

ALPHA ORDER

RANK	STATE	PER CAPITA
49	Alabama	$4.29
1	Alaska	110.68
2	Arizona	45.11
34	Arkansas	10.36
14	California	18.46
42	Colorado	8.17
48	Connecticut	4.92
45	Delaware	6.39
38	Florida	10.15
6	Georgia	24.11
41	Hawaii	8.32
35	Idaho	10.32
5	Illinois	24.37
33	Indiana	10.50
27	Iowa	12.63
22	Kansas	14.49
15	Kentucky	17.26
8	Louisiana	20.95
11	Maine	19.16
12	Maryland	19.13
13	Massachusetts	18.59
18	Michigan	15.79
23	Minnesota	14.26
3	Mississippi	35.13
25	Missouri	13.92
19	Montana	15.43
9	Nebraska	20.20
39	Nevada	8.83
46	New Hampshire	5.62
4	New Jersey	25.55
31	New Mexico	11.25
20	New York	15.40
10	North Carolina	19.46
32	North Dakota	10.84
21	Ohio	14.59
26	Oklahoma	13.08
43	Oregon	7.04
37	Pennsylvania	10.21
7	Rhode Island	23.34
29	South Carolina	12.10
24	South Dakota	14.14
50	Tennessee	0.76
28	Texas	12.57
30	Utah	11.57
47	Vermont	5.15
40	Virginia	8.42
44	Washington	6.40
17	West Virginia	16.99
16	Wisconsin	17.03
36	Wyoming	10.28

RANK ORDER

RANK	STATE	PER CAPITA
1	Alaska	$110.68
2	Arizona	45.11
3	Mississippi	35.13
4	New Jersey	25.55
5	Illinois	24.37
6	Georgia	24.11
7	Rhode Island	23.34
8	Louisiana	20.95
9	Nebraska	20.20
10	North Carolina	19.46
11	Maine	19.16
12	Maryland	19.13
13	Massachusetts	18.59
14	California	18.46
15	Kentucky	17.26
16	Wisconsin	17.03
17	West Virginia	16.99
18	Michigan	15.79
19	Montana	15.43
20	New York	15.40
21	Ohio	14.59
22	Kansas	14.49
23	Minnesota	14.26
24	South Dakota	14.14
25	Missouri	13.92
26	Oklahoma	13.08
27	Iowa	12.63
28	Texas	12.57
29	South Carolina	12.10
30	Utah	11.57
31	New Mexico	11.25
32	North Dakota	10.84
33	Indiana	10.50
34	Arkansas	10.36
35	Idaho	10.32
36	Wyoming	10.28
37	Pennsylvania	10.21
38	Florida	10.15
39	Nevada	8.83
40	Virginia	8.42
41	Hawaii	8.32
42	Colorado	8.17
43	Oregon	7.04
44	Washington	6.40
45	Delaware	6.39
46	New Hampshire	5.62
47	Vermont	5.15
48	Connecticut	4.92
49	Alabama	4.29
50	Tennessee	0.76

| | District of Columbia | 12.99 |

Source: MQ Press using data from U.S. Dept of Health & Human Services, Centers for Medicare and Medicaid Services
    "Statement of Expenditures for the SCHIP Program" (CMS-21 Report)
*Federal and state expenditures for fiscal year 2004. National figure does not include funds spent in U.S.
territories. The State Children's Health Insurance Program (SCHIP) was created in 1997 to help states expand
health insurance to children whose families earn too much to qualify for Medicaid, yet not enough to afford private
health insurance.

Expenditures per State Children's Health Insurance Program (SCHIP) Participant in 2004
National Per Participant = $759*

ALPHA ORDER

RANK	STATE	PER PARTICIPANT
46	Alabama	$244
1	Alaska	3,852
2	Arizona	2,952
NA	Arkansas**	NA
34	California	639
33	Colorado	657
24	Connecticut	804
39	Delaware	515
44	Florida	421
25	Georgia	768
36	Hawaii	547
21	Idaho	828
7	Illinois	1,324
23	Indiana	810
16	Iowa	914
18	Kansas	892
27	Kentucky	757
17	Louisiana	894
19	Maine	863
12	Maryland	954
29	Massachusetts	715
NA	Michigan**	NA
NA	Minnesota**	NA
8	Mississippi	1,229
42	Missouri	456
15	Montana	935
9	Nebraska	1,060
38	Nevada	535
32	New Hampshire	664
4	New Jersey	1,744
10	New Mexico	1,029
45	New York	359
12	North Carolina	954
6	North Dakota	1,353
26	Ohio	759
41	Oklahoma	457
37	Oregon	542
30	Pennsylvania	714
11	Rhode Island	984
31	South Carolina	672
22	South Dakota	813
NA	Tennessee**	NA
43	Texas	434
28	Utah	724
40	Vermont	478
35	Virginia	633
3	Washington	2,335
20	West Virginia	835
5	Wisconsin	1,380
14	Wyoming	945

RANK ORDER

RANK	STATE	PER PARTICIPANT
1	Alaska	$3,852
2	Arizona	2,952
3	Washington	2,335
4	New Jersey	1,744
5	Wisconsin	1,380
6	North Dakota	1,353
7	Illinois	1,324
8	Mississippi	1,229
9	Nebraska	1,060
10	New Mexico	1,029
11	Rhode Island	984
12	Maryland	954
12	North Carolina	954
14	Wyoming	945
15	Montana	935
16	Iowa	914
17	Louisiana	894
18	Kansas	892
19	Maine	863
20	West Virginia	835
21	Idaho	828
22	South Dakota	813
23	Indiana	810
24	Connecticut	804
25	Georgia	768
26	Ohio	759
27	Kentucky	757
28	Utah	724
29	Massachusetts	715
30	Pennsylvania	714
31	South Carolina	672
32	New Hampshire	664
33	Colorado	657
34	California	639
35	Virginia	633
36	Hawaii	547
37	Oregon	542
38	Nevada	535
39	Delaware	515
40	Vermont	478
41	Oklahoma	457
42	Missouri	456
43	Texas	434
44	Florida	421
45	New York	359
46	Alabama	244
NA	Arkansas**	NA
NA	Michigan**	NA
NA	Minnesota**	NA
NA	Tennessee**	NA

	District of Columbia	1,180

Source: MQ Press using data from U.S. Dept of Health & Human Services, Centers for Medicare and Medicaid Services "Statement of Expenditures for the SCHIP Program" (CMS-21 Report)

For fiscal year 2004. National figure does not include expenditures in U.S. territories. The State Children's Health Insurance Program (SCHIP) was created in 1997 to help states expand health insurance to children whose families earn too much to qualify for Medicaid, yet not enough to afford private health insurance.
**Not available.*

Health Maintenance Organizations (HMOs) in 2005

National Total = 631 HMOs*

ALPHA ORDER

RANK	STATE	HMOs	% of USA
41	Alabama	5	0.8%
50	Alaska	0	0.0%
27	Arizona	10	1.6%
34	Arkansas	7	1.1%
1	California	33	5.2%
20	Colorado	12	1.9%
28	Connecticut	9	1.4%
37	Delaware	6	1.0%
2	Florida	30	4.8%
15	Georgia	15	2.4%
47	Hawaii	3	0.5%
41	Idaho	5	0.8%
6	Illinois	24	3.8%
12	Indiana	19	3.0%
20	Iowa	12	1.9%
29	Kansas	8	1.3%
20	Kentucky	12	1.9%
29	Louisiana	8	1.3%
37	Maine	6	1.0%
17	Maryland	13	2.1%
17	Massachusetts	13	2.1%
4	Michigan	27	4.3%
20	Minnesota	12	1.9%
47	Mississippi	3	0.5%
10	Missouri	20	3.2%
47	Montana	3	0.5%
34	Nebraska	7	1.1%
20	Nevada	12	1.9%
34	New Hampshire	7	1.1%
15	New Jersey	15	2.4%
41	New Mexico	5	0.8%
3	New York	28	4.4%
17	North Carolina	13	2.1%
37	North Dakota	6	1.0%
8	Ohio	21	3.3%
29	Oklahoma	8	1.3%
14	Oregon	18	2.9%
6	Pennsylvania	24	3.8%
29	Rhode Island	8	1.3%
20	South Carolina	12	1.9%
41	South Dakota	5	0.8%
26	Tennessee	11	1.7%
4	Texas	27	4.3%
29	Utah	8	1.3%
37	Vermont	6	1.0%
10	Virginia	20	3.2%
12	Washington	19	3.0%
46	West Virginia	4	0.6%
8	Wisconsin	21	3.3%
41	Wyoming	5	0.8%

RANK ORDER

RANK	STATE	HMOs	% of USA
1	California	33	5.2%
2	Florida	30	4.8%
3	New York	28	4.4%
4	Michigan	27	4.3%
4	Texas	27	4.3%
6	Illinois	24	3.8%
6	Pennsylvania	24	3.8%
8	Ohio	21	3.3%
8	Wisconsin	21	3.3%
10	Missouri	20	3.2%
10	Virginia	20	3.2%
12	Indiana	19	3.0%
12	Washington	19	3.0%
14	Oregon	18	2.9%
15	Georgia	15	2.4%
15	New Jersey	15	2.4%
17	Maryland	13	2.1%
17	Massachusetts	13	2.1%
17	North Carolina	13	2.1%
20	Colorado	12	1.9%
20	Iowa	12	1.9%
20	Kentucky	12	1.9%
20	Minnesota	12	1.9%
20	Nevada	12	1.9%
20	South Carolina	12	1.9%
26	Tennessee	11	1.7%
27	Arizona	10	1.6%
28	Connecticut	9	1.4%
29	Kansas	8	1.3%
29	Louisiana	8	1.3%
29	Oklahoma	8	1.3%
29	Rhode Island	8	1.3%
29	Utah	8	1.3%
34	Arkansas	7	1.1%
34	Nebraska	7	1.1%
34	New Hampshire	7	1.1%
37	Delaware	6	1.0%
37	Maine	6	1.0%
37	North Dakota	6	1.0%
37	Vermont	6	1.0%
41	Alabama	5	0.8%
41	Idaho	5	0.8%
41	New Mexico	5	0.8%
41	South Dakota	5	0.8%
41	Wyoming	5	0.8%
46	West Virginia	4	0.6%
47	Hawaii	3	0.5%
47	Mississippi	3	0.5%
47	Montana	3	0.5%
50	Alaska	0	0.0%
	District of Columbia	6	1.0%

Source: Lance Wolkenbrod, Data Analyst
   HealthLeaders - InterStudy (Nashville, TN)
*As of January 2005. This total is based on HMO's operating in each state. As a result, many HMOs are counted more than once. Total does not include HMOs in U.S. territories.

Enrollees in Health Maintenance Organizations (HMOs) in 2005

National Total = 69,835,829 Enrollees*

RANK	STATE	ENROLLEES	% of USA
38	Alabama	146,487	0.2%
50	Alaska	0	0.0%
21	Arizona	1,041,235	1.5%
40	Arkansas	122,629	0.2%
1	California	17,921,791	25.7%
17	Colorado	1,266,550	1.8%
18	Connecticut	1,216,242	1.7%
39	Delaware	145,914	0.2%
2	Florida	4,738,946	6.8%
13	Georgia	1,617,423	2.3%
26	Hawaii	554,664	0.8%
46	Idaho	41,360	0.1%
9	Illinois	2,052,363	2.9%
16	Indiana	1,295,177	1.9%
35	Iowa	304,885	0.4%
33	Kansas	332,744	0.5%
30	Kentucky	416,307	0.6%
29	Louisiana	435,870	0.6%
32	Maine	341,857	0.5%
8	Maryland	2,241,389	3.2%
7	Massachusetts	2,341,850	3.4%
6	Michigan	2,648,941	3.8%
20	Minnesota	1,094,957	1.6%
45	Mississippi	45,460	0.1%
19	Missouri	1,204,256	1.7%
47	Montana	35,173	0.1%
41	Nebraska	113,197	0.2%
25	Nevada	571,132	0.8%
36	New Hampshire	291,957	0.4%
10	New Jersey	2,034,299	2.9%
28	New Mexico	458,721	0.7%
3	New York	4,719,692	6.8%
24	North Carolina	806,425	1.2%
49	North Dakota	3,194	0.0%
11	Ohio	1,984,036	2.8%
37	Oklahoma	243,742	0.3%
22	Oregon	932,517	1.3%
4	Pennsylvania	4,085,578	5.9%
31	Rhode Island	354,938	0.5%
34	South Carolina	332,356	0.5%
44	South Dakota	61,322	0.1%
23	Tennessee	836,207	1.2%
5	Texas	2,917,637	4.2%
27	Utah	505,669	0.7%
42	Vermont	99,125	0.1%
15	Virginia	1,303,135	1.9%
12	Washington	1,679,005	2.4%
43	West Virginia	97,643	0.1%
14	Wisconsin	1,565,140	2.2%
48	Wyoming	10,786	0.0%

RANK	STATE	ENROLLEES	% of USA
1	California	17,921,791	25.7%
2	Florida	4,738,946	6.8%
3	New York	4,719,692	6.8%
4	Pennsylvania	4,085,578	5.9%
5	Texas	2,917,637	4.2%
6	Michigan	2,648,941	3.8%
7	Massachusetts	2,341,850	3.4%
8	Maryland	2,241,389	3.2%
9	Illinois	2,052,363	2.9%
10	New Jersey	2,034,299	2.9%
11	Ohio	1,984,036	2.8%
12	Washington	1,679,005	2.4%
13	Georgia	1,617,423	2.3%
14	Wisconsin	1,565,140	2.2%
15	Virginia	1,303,135	1.9%
16	Indiana	1,295,177	1.9%
17	Colorado	1,266,550	1.8%
18	Connecticut	1,216,242	1.7%
19	Missouri	1,204,256	1.7%
20	Minnesota	1,094,957	1.6%
21	Arizona	1,041,235	1.5%
22	Oregon	932,517	1.3%
23	Tennessee	836,207	1.2%
24	North Carolina	806,425	1.2%
25	Nevada	571,132	0.8%
26	Hawaii	554,664	0.8%
27	Utah	505,669	0.7%
28	New Mexico	458,721	0.7%
29	Louisiana	435,870	0.6%
30	Kentucky	416,307	0.6%
31	Rhode Island	354,938	0.5%
32	Maine	341,857	0.5%
33	Kansas	332,744	0.5%
34	South Carolina	332,356	0.5%
35	Iowa	304,885	0.4%
36	New Hampshire	291,957	0.4%
37	Oklahoma	243,742	0.3%
38	Alabama	146,487	0.2%
39	Delaware	145,914	0.2%
40	Arkansas	122,629	0.2%
41	Nebraska	113,197	0.2%
42	Vermont	99,125	0.1%
43	West Virginia	97,643	0.1%
44	South Dakota	61,322	0.1%
45	Mississippi	45,460	0.1%
46	Idaho	41,360	0.1%
47	Montana	35,173	0.1%
48	Wyoming	10,786	0.0%
49	North Dakota	3,194	0.0%
50	Alaska	0	0.0%
	District of Columbia	223,906	0.3%

Source: Lance Wolkenbrod, Data Analyst
HealthLeaders - InterStudy (Nashville, TN)
As of January 2005. Total does not include enrollees in U.S. territories.

Percent Change in Enrollees in Health Maintenance Organizations (HMOs): 2004 to 2005
National Percent Change = 3.9% Increase*

RANK	STATE	PERCENT CHANGE
16	Alabama	14.3
NA	Alaska**	NA
35	Arizona	(6.4)
40	Arkansas	(15.5)
21	California	5.3
26	Colorado	1.8
36	Connecticut	(10.7)
14	Delaware	21.5
17	Florida	12.2
8	Georgia	35.6
7	Hawaii	48.5
22	Idaho	5.1
12	Illinois	26.3
4	Indiana	84.4
24	Iowa	3.4
3	Kansas	89.9
49	Kentucky	(64.2)
41	Louisiana	(16.8)
9	Maine	32.0
9	Maryland	32.0
29	Massachusetts	(2.6)
31	Michigan	(3.5)
43	Minnesota	(18.0)
1	Mississippi	284.8
45	Missouri	(23.0)
48	Montana	(58.9)
38	Nebraska	(13.0)
19	Nevada	6.2
25	New Hampshire	2.6
34	New Jersey	(4.7)
44	New Mexico	(20.4)
42	New York	(17.8)
31	North Carolina	(3.5)
6	North Dakota	52.0
33	Ohio	(3.7)
37	Oklahoma	(12.2)
15	Oregon	19.9
20	Pennsylvania	5.9
23	Rhode Island	4.3
11	South Carolina	31.1
46	South Dakota	(25.3)
18	Tennessee	11.6
13	Texas	24.0
39	Utah	(15.4)
5	Vermont	66.6
30	Virginia	(3.0)
2	Washington	113.7
47	West Virginia	(45.6)
27	Wisconsin	0.6
28	Wyoming	(1.9)

RANK	STATE	PERCENT CHANGE
1	Mississippi	284.8
2	Washington	113.7
3	Kansas	89.9
4	Indiana	84.4
5	Vermont	66.6
6	North Dakota	52.0
7	Hawaii	48.5
8	Georgia	35.6
9	Maine	32.0
9	Maryland	32.0
11	South Carolina	31.1
12	Illinois	26.3
13	Texas	24.0
14	Delaware	21.5
15	Oregon	19.9
16	Alabama	14.3
17	Florida	12.2
18	Tennessee	11.6
19	Nevada	6.2
20	Pennsylvania	5.9
21	California	5.3
22	Idaho	5.1
23	Rhode Island	4.3
24	Iowa	3.4
25	New Hampshire	2.6
26	Colorado	1.8
27	Wisconsin	0.6
28	Wyoming	(1.9)
29	Massachusetts	(2.6)
30	Virginia	(3.0)
31	Michigan	(3.5)
31	North Carolina	(3.5)
33	Ohio	(3.7)
34	New Jersey	(4.7)
35	Arizona	(6.4)
36	Connecticut	(10.7)
37	Oklahoma	(12.2)
38	Nebraska	(13.0)
39	Utah	(15.4)
40	Arkansas	(15.5)
41	Louisiana	(16.8)
42	New York	(17.8)
43	Minnesota	(18.0)
44	New Mexico	(20.4)
45	Missouri	(23.0)
46	South Dakota	(25.3)
47	West Virginia	(45.6)
48	Montana	(58.9)
49	Kentucky	(64.2)
NA	Alaska**	NA

	District of Columbia	38.0

Source: Morgan Quitno Press using data from Lance Wolkenbrod, Data Analyst
    HealthLeaders - InterStudy (Nashville, TN)
*As of January 2005. Total does not include enrollees in U.S. territories.

Percent of Population Enrolled in Health Maintenance Organizations (HMOs) in 2005
National Percent = 23.8% Enrolled in HMOs*

ALPHA ORDER

RANK	STATE	PERCENT
45	Alabama	3.2
50	Alaska	0.0
25	Arizona	18.1
43	Arkansas	4.5
1	California	49.9
9	Colorado	27.5
5	Connecticut	34.7
26	Delaware	17.6
10	Florida	27.2
24	Georgia	18.3
2	Hawaii	43.9
46	Idaho	3.0
29	Illinois	16.1
23	Indiana	20.7
34	Iowa	10.3
33	Kansas	12.2
35	Kentucky	10.0
36	Louisiana	9.7
13	Maine	26.0
3	Maryland	40.3
4	Massachusetts	36.5
12	Michigan	26.1
20	Minnesota	21.5
48	Mississippi	1.6
22	Missouri	20.8
44	Montana	3.8
41	Nebraska	6.5
16	Nevada	24.4
19	New Hampshire	22.5
18	New Jersey	23.4
17	New Mexico	24.0
15	New York	24.5
37	North Carolina	9.4
49	North Dakota	0.5
28	Ohio	17.3
40	Oklahoma	6.9
14	Oregon	25.9
6	Pennsylvania	32.9
7	Rhode Island	32.8
39	South Carolina	7.9
38	South Dakota	8.0
31	Tennessee	14.2
32	Texas	13.0
21	Utah	21.2
30	Vermont	16.0
27	Virginia	17.4
11	Washington	27.1
42	West Virginia	5.4
8	Wisconsin	28.4
47	Wyoming	2.1

RANK ORDER

RANK	STATE	PERCENT
1	California	49.9
2	Hawaii	43.9
3	Maryland	40.3
4	Massachusetts	36.5
5	Connecticut	34.7
6	Pennsylvania	32.9
7	Rhode Island	32.8
8	Wisconsin	28.4
9	Colorado	27.5
10	Florida	27.2
11	Washington	27.1
12	Michigan	26.1
13	Maine	26.0
14	Oregon	25.9
15	New York	24.5
16	Nevada	24.4
17	New Mexico	24.0
18	New Jersey	23.4
19	New Hampshire	22.5
20	Minnesota	21.5
21	Utah	21.2
22	Missouri	20.8
23	Indiana	20.7
24	Georgia	18.3
25	Arizona	18.1
26	Delaware	17.6
27	Virginia	17.4
28	Ohio	17.3
29	Illinois	16.1
30	Vermont	16.0
31	Tennessee	14.2
32	Texas	13.0
33	Kansas	12.2
34	Iowa	10.3
35	Kentucky	10.0
36	Louisiana	9.7
37	North Carolina	9.4
38	South Dakota	8.0
39	South Carolina	7.9
40	Oklahoma	6.9
41	Nebraska	6.5
42	West Virginia	5.4
43	Arkansas	4.5
44	Montana	3.8
45	Alabama	3.2
46	Idaho	3.0
47	Wyoming	2.1
48	Mississippi	1.6
49	North Dakota	0.5
50	Alaska	0.0

District of Columbia 40.5

Source: Morgan Quitno Press using data from Lance Wolkenbrod, Data Analyst
    HealthLeaders - InterStudy (Nashville, TN)

*As of January 2005. Calculated using Census 2005 population estimates. National percent does not include enrollees or population in U.S. territories.

Percent of Insured Population Enrolled in
Health Maintenance Organizations (HMOs) in 2005
National Percent = 28.5% of Insured are Enrolled in HMOs*

ALPHA ORDER

RANK ORDER

RANK	STATE	PERCENT		RANK	STATE	PERCENT
45	Alabama	3.8		1	California	61.5
50	Alaska	0.0		2	Hawaii	49.1
25	Arizona	21.8		3	Maryland	47.3
43	Arkansas	5.4		4	Massachusetts	41.6
1	California	61.5		5	Connecticut	39.4
9	Colorado	33.7		6	Pennsylvania	38.1
5	Connecticut	39.4		7	Rhode Island	37.9
26	Delaware	20.6		8	Florida	33.9
8	Florida	33.9		9	Colorado	33.7
24	Georgia	22.5		10	Wisconsin	32.0
2	Hawaii	49.1		11	Washington	31.5
46	Idaho	3.6		12	Oregon	31.2
29	Illinois	18.9		13	New Mexico	30.5
20	Indiana	24.6		14	Michigan	30.0
36	Iowa	11.6		15	Maine	29.4
33	Kansas	14.0		16	Nevada	29.3
34	Kentucky	11.9		17	New York	28.9
34	Louisiana	11.9		18	New Jersey	27.7
15	Maine	29.4		19	New Hampshire	25.6
3	Maryland	47.3		20	Indiana	24.6
4	Massachusetts	41.6		20	Utah	24.6
14	Michigan	30.0		22	Missouri	24.5
23	Minnesota	23.5		23	Minnesota	23.5
48	Mississippi	1.9		24	Georgia	22.5
22	Missouri	24.5		25	Arizona	21.8
44	Montana	4.8		26	Delaware	20.6
41	Nebraska	7.4		26	Virginia	20.6
16	Nevada	29.3		28	Ohio	19.9
19	New Hampshire	25.6		29	Illinois	18.9
18	New Jersey	27.7		30	Vermont	18.1
13	New Mexico	30.5		31	Texas	17.4
17	New York	28.9		32	Tennessee	16.6
37	North Carolina	11.3		33	Kansas	14.0
49	North Dakota	0.6		34	Kentucky	11.9
28	Ohio	19.9		34	Louisiana	11.9
40	Oklahoma	8.8		36	Iowa	11.6
12	Oregon	31.2		37	North Carolina	11.3
6	Pennsylvania	38.1		38	South Carolina	9.4
7	Rhode Island	37.9		39	South Dakota	9.2
38	South Carolina	9.4		40	Oklahoma	8.8
39	South Dakota	9.2		41	Nebraska	7.4
32	Tennessee	16.6		42	West Virginia	6.5
31	Texas	17.4		43	Arkansas	5.4
20	Utah	24.6		44	Montana	4.8
30	Vermont	18.1		45	Alabama	3.8
26	Virginia	20.6		46	Idaho	3.6
11	Washington	31.5		47	Wyoming	2.5
42	West Virginia	6.5		48	Mississippi	1.9
10	Wisconsin	32.0		49	North Dakota	0.6
47	Wyoming	2.5		50	Alaska	0.0

District of Columbia   47.2

Source: Morgan Quitno Press using data from Lance Wolkenbrod, Data Analyst
    HealthLeaders - InterStudy (Nashville, TN)
*As of January 2005. Calculated using estimated number of insured as of 2004 from the U.S. Census Bureau.

Medicare Enrollees in 2004

National Total = 41,729,000 Enrollees*

ALPHA ORDER

RANK	STATE	ENROLLEES	% of USA
20	Alabama	733,000	1.8%
50	Alaska	50,000	0.1%
19	Arizona	754,000	1.8%
31	Arkansas	461,000	1.1%
1	California	4,142,000	9.9%
29	Colorado	506,000	1.2%
27	Connecticut	525,000	1.3%
45	Delaware	123,000	0.3%
2	Florida	2,980,000	7.1%
11	Georgia	995,000	2.4%
42	Hawaii	178,000	0.4%
41	Idaho	184,000	0.4%
7	Illinois	1,678,000	4.0%
16	Indiana	889,000	2.1%
30	Iowa	485,000	1.2%
33	Kansas	397,000	1.0%
23	Kentucky	660,000	1.6%
24	Louisiana	629,000	1.5%
38	Maine	231,000	0.6%
22	Maryland	685,000	1.6%
12	Massachusetts	969,000	2.3%
8	Michigan	1,466,000	3.5%
21	Minnesota	687,000	1.6%
32	Mississippi	446,000	1.1%
14	Missouri	896,000	2.1%
44	Montana	145,000	0.3%
36	Nebraska	259,000	0.6%
35	Nevada	287,000	0.7%
40	New Hampshire	186,000	0.4%
10	New Jersey	1,226,000	2.9%
37	New Mexico	256,000	0.6%
3	New York	2,779,000	6.7%
9	North Carolina	1,234,000	3.0%
47	North Dakota	103,000	0.2%
6	Ohio	1,740,000	4.2%
26	Oklahoma	529,000	1.3%
27	Oregon	525,000	1.3%
5	Pennsylvania	2,120,000	5.1%
43	Rhode Island	173,000	0.4%
25	South Carolina	623,000	1.5%
45	South Dakota	123,000	0.3%
15	Tennessee	891,000	2.1%
4	Texas	2,450,000	5.9%
39	Utah	227,000	0.5%
48	Vermont	94,000	0.2%
13	Virginia	966,000	2.3%
18	Washington	795,000	1.9%
34	West Virginia	351,000	0.8%
17	Wisconsin	814,000	2.0%
49	Wyoming	69,000	0.2%

RANK ORDER

RANK	STATE	ENROLLEES	% of USA
1	California	4,142,000	9.9%
2	Florida	2,980,000	7.1%
3	New York	2,779,000	6.7%
4	Texas	2,450,000	5.9%
5	Pennsylvania	2,120,000	5.1%
6	Ohio	1,740,000	4.2%
7	Illinois	1,678,000	4.0%
8	Michigan	1,466,000	3.5%
9	North Carolina	1,234,000	3.0%
10	New Jersey	1,226,000	2.9%
11	Georgia	995,000	2.4%
12	Massachusetts	969,000	2.3%
13	Virginia	966,000	2.3%
14	Missouri	896,000	2.1%
15	Tennessee	891,000	2.1%
16	Indiana	889,000	2.1%
17	Wisconsin	814,000	2.0%
18	Washington	795,000	1.9%
19	Arizona	754,000	1.8%
20	Alabama	733,000	1.8%
21	Minnesota	687,000	1.6%
22	Maryland	685,000	1.6%
23	Kentucky	660,000	1.6%
24	Louisiana	629,000	1.5%
25	South Carolina	623,000	1.5%
26	Oklahoma	529,000	1.3%
27	Connecticut	525,000	1.3%
27	Oregon	525,000	1.3%
29	Colorado	506,000	1.2%
30	Iowa	485,000	1.2%
31	Arkansas	461,000	1.1%
32	Mississippi	446,000	1.1%
33	Kansas	397,000	1.0%
34	West Virginia	351,000	0.8%
35	Nevada	287,000	0.7%
36	Nebraska	259,000	0.6%
37	New Mexico	256,000	0.6%
38	Maine	231,000	0.6%
39	Utah	227,000	0.5%
40	New Hampshire	186,000	0.4%
41	Idaho	184,000	0.4%
42	Hawaii	178,000	0.4%
43	Rhode Island	173,000	0.4%
44	Montana	145,000	0.3%
45	Delaware	123,000	0.3%
45	South Dakota	123,000	0.3%
47	North Dakota	103,000	0.2%
48	Vermont	94,000	0.2%
49	Wyoming	69,000	0.2%
50	Alaska	50,000	0.1%
	District of Columbia	74,000	0.2%

Source: U.S. Department of Health and Human Services, Centers for Medicare and Medicaid Services
"Annual Statistical Supplement 2005" (http://www.ssa.gov/policy/docs/statcomps/supplement/2005/)
*Includes aged and disabled enrollees. Total includes 933,000 enrollees in Puerto Rico and other outlying areas, foreign countries or whose address is unknown.

Percent Change in Medicare Enrollees: 2003 to 2004

National Percent Change = 1.6% Increase

ALPHA ORDER				RANK ORDER		
RANK	**STATE**	**PERCENT CHANGE**		**RANK**	**STATE**	**PERCENT CHANGE**
20	Alabama	1.9		1	Nevada	4.9
2	Alaska	4.7		2	Alaska	4.7
5	Arizona	3.4		3	New Hampshire	3.6
23	Arkansas	1.8		4	Idaho	3.5
26	California	1.6		5	Arizona	3.4
9	Colorado	2.5		6	Delaware	3.1
45	Connecticut	0.5		6	Utah	3.1
6	Delaware	3.1		8	South Carolina	2.8
19	Florida	2.0		9	Colorado	2.5
15	Georgia	2.2		9	Texas	2.5
20	Hawaii	1.9		9	Washington	2.5
4	Idaho	3.5		12	New Mexico	2.4
36	Illinois	1.0		12	North Carolina	2.4
33	Indiana	1.3		14	Oregon	2.3
42	Iowa	0.6		15	Georgia	2.2
39	Kansas	0.7		15	Tennessee	2.2
23	Kentucky	1.8		17	Mississippi	2.1
31	Louisiana	1.4		17	Virginia	2.1
20	Maine	1.9		19	Florida	2.0
26	Maryland	1.6		20	Alabama	1.9
48	Massachusetts	0.3		20	Hawaii	1.9
29	Michigan	1.5		20	Maine	1.9
26	Minnesota	1.6		23	Arkansas	1.8
17	Mississippi	2.1		23	Kentucky	1.8
33	Missouri	1.3		23	Montana	1.8
23	Montana	1.8		26	California	1.6
39	Nebraska	0.7		26	Maryland	1.6
1	Nevada	4.9		26	Minnesota	1.6
3	New Hampshire	3.6		29	Michigan	1.5
45	New Jersey	0.5		29	Oklahoma	1.5
12	New Mexico	2.4		31	Louisiana	1.4
42	New York	0.6		31	Vermont	1.4
12	North Carolina	2.4		33	Indiana	1.3
50	North Dakota	(0.2)		33	Missouri	1.3
39	Ohio	0.7		33	Wisconsin	1.3
29	Oklahoma	1.5		36	Illinois	1.0
14	Oregon	2.3		36	South Dakota	1.0
45	Pennsylvania	0.5		36	West Virginia	1.0
48	Rhode Island	0.3		39	Kansas	0.7
8	South Carolina	2.8		39	Nebraska	0.7
36	South Dakota	1.0		39	Ohio	0.7
15	Tennessee	2.2		42	Iowa	0.6
9	Texas	2.5		42	New York	0.6
6	Utah	3.1		42	Wyoming	0.6
31	Vermont	1.4		45	Connecticut	0.5
17	Virginia	2.1		45	New Jersey	0.5
9	Washington	2.5		45	Pennsylvania	0.5
36	West Virginia	1.0		48	Massachusetts	0.3
33	Wisconsin	1.3		48	Rhode Island	0.3
42	Wyoming	0.6		50	North Dakota	(0.2)
					District of Columbia	0.3

Source: MQ Press using data from U.S. Dept of Health & Human Services, Centers for Medicare and Medicaid Services "Annual Statistical Supplement 2005" (http://www.ssa.gov/policy/docs/statcomps/supplement/2005/)
*Includes aged and disabled enrollees. National rate includes enrollees in Puerto Rico and other outlying areas, foreign countries or whose address is unknown.

Percent of Population Enrolled in Medicare in 2004

National Percent = 13.9% of Population*

ALPHA ORDER

RANK	STATE	PERCENT	RANK	STATE	PERCENT
7	Alabama	16.2	1	West Virginia	19.4
50	Alaska	7.6	2	Maine	17.6
40	Arizona	13.1	3	Florida	17.1
5	Arkansas	16.8	3	Pennsylvania	17.1
45	California	11.6	5	Arkansas	16.8
47	Colorado	11.0	6	Iowa	16.4
19	Connecticut	15.0	7	Alabama	16.2
21	Delaware	14.8	7	North Dakota	16.2
3	Florida	17.1	9	Rhode Island	16.0
46	Georgia	11.2	9	South Dakota	16.0
32	Hawaii	14.1	11	Kentucky	15.9
38	Idaho	13.2	12	Missouri	15.6
38	Illinois	13.2	12	Montana	15.6
30	Indiana	14.3	14	Mississippi	15.4
6	Iowa	16.4	15	Ohio	15.2
26	Kansas	14.5	16	Massachusetts	15.1
11	Kentucky	15.9	16	Tennessee	15.1
34	Louisiana	14.0	16	Vermont	15.1
2	Maine	17.6	19	Connecticut	15.0
43	Maryland	12.3	19	Oklahoma	15.0
16	Massachusetts	15.1	21	Delaware	14.8
26	Michigan	14.5	21	Nebraska	14.8
36	Minnesota	13.5	21	South Carolina	14.8
14	Mississippi	15.4	21	Wisconsin	14.8
12	Missouri	15.6	25	Oregon	14.6
12	Montana	15.6	26	Kansas	14.5
21	Nebraska	14.8	26	Michigan	14.5
43	Nevada	12.3	28	New York	14.4
30	New Hampshire	14.3	28	North Carolina	14.4
32	New Jersey	14.1	30	Indiana	14.3
36	New Mexico	13.5	30	New Hampshire	14.3
28	New York	14.4	32	Hawaii	14.1
28	North Carolina	14.4	32	New Jersey	14.1
7	North Dakota	16.2	34	Louisiana	14.0
15	Ohio	15.2	35	Wyoming	13.6
19	Oklahoma	15.0	36	Minnesota	13.5
25	Oregon	14.6	36	New Mexico	13.5
3	Pennsylvania	17.1	38	Idaho	13.2
9	Rhode Island	16.0	38	Illinois	13.2
21	South Carolina	14.8	40	Arizona	13.1
9	South Dakota	16.0	41	Virginia	12.9
16	Tennessee	15.1	42	Washington	12.8
48	Texas	10.9	43	Maryland	12.3
49	Utah	9.4	43	Nevada	12.3
16	Vermont	15.1	45	California	11.6
41	Virginia	12.9	46	Georgia	11.2
42	Washington	12.8	47	Colorado	11.0
1	West Virginia	19.4	48	Texas	10.9
21	Wisconsin	14.8	49	Utah	9.4
35	Wyoming	13.6	50	Alaska	7.6

District of Columbia 13.4

Source: MQ Press using data from U.S. Dept of Health & Human Services, Centers for Medicare and Medicaid Services "Annual Statistical Supplement 2005" (http://www.ssa.gov/policy/docs/statcomps/supplement/2005/)
Includes aged and disabled enrollees. National rate includes only residents of the 50 states and the District of Columbia.

Enrollment in Medicare Prescription Drug Plans as of January 13, 2006

National Total = 23,750,661 Enrollees*

ALPHA ORDER					RANK ORDER			
RANK	STATE	ENROLLEES	% of USA		RANK	STATE	ENROLLEES	% of USA
20	Alabama	414,447	1.7%		1	California	2,988,048	12.6%
47	Alaska	41,672	0.2%		2	Florida	1,821,446	7.7%
16	Arizona	478,718	2.0%		3	New York	1,494,830	6.3%
31	Arkansas	246,218	1.0%		4	Texas	1,411,470	5.9%
1	California	2,988,048	12.6%		5	Pennsylvania	1,141,114	4.8%
25	Colorado	338,317	1.4%		6	Ohio	1,067,476	4.5%
29	Connecticut	269,524	1.1%		7	Illinois	951,888	4.0%
44	Delaware	76,771	0.3%		8	Michigan	861,203	3.6%
2	Florida	1,821,446	7.7%		9	North Carolina	778,838	3.3%
14	Georgia	543,280	2.3%		10	New Jersey	685,260	2.9%
37	Hawaii	153,481	0.6%		11	Massachusetts	583,733	2.5%
43	Idaho	83,794	0.4%		12	Virginia	572,184	2.4%
7	Illinois	951,888	4.0%		13	Tennessee	559,114	2.4%
18	Indiana	425,075	1.8%		14	Georgia	543,280	2.3%
34	Iowa	167,802	0.7%		15	Missouri	499,351	2.1%
36	Kansas	158,170	0.7%		16	Arizona	478,718	2.0%
24	Kentucky	350,979	1.5%		17	Washington	432,183	1.8%
22	Louisiana	373,127	1.6%		18	Indiana	425,075	1.8%
38	Maine	125,401	0.5%		19	Maryland	414,608	1.7%
19	Maryland	414,608	1.7%		20	Alabama	414,447	1.7%
11	Massachusetts	583,733	2.5%		21	Wisconsin	373,467	1.6%
8	Michigan	861,203	3.6%		22	Louisiana	373,127	1.6%
27	Minnesota	286,900	1.2%		23	South Carolina	372,920	1.6%
30	Mississippi	246,594	1.0%		24	Kentucky	350,979	1.5%
15	Missouri	499,351	2.1%		25	Colorado	338,317	1.4%
45	Montana	53,030	0.2%		26	Oklahoma	288,828	1.2%
41	Nebraska	107,943	0.5%		27	Minnesota	286,900	1.2%
32	Nevada	187,044	0.8%		28	Oregon	272,885	1.1%
42	New Hampshire	84,113	0.4%		29	Connecticut	269,524	1.1%
10	New Jersey	685,260	2.9%		30	Mississippi	246,594	1.0%
35	New Mexico	163,973	0.7%		31	Arkansas	246,218	1.0%
3	New York	1,494,830	6.3%		32	Nevada	187,044	0.8%
9	North Carolina	778,838	3.3%		33	West Virginia	184,556	0.8%
49	North Dakota	34,227	0.1%		34	Iowa	167,802	0.7%
6	Ohio	1,067,476	4.5%		35	New Mexico	163,973	0.7%
26	Oklahoma	288,828	1.2%		36	Kansas	158,170	0.7%
28	Oregon	272,885	1.1%		37	Hawaii	153,481	0.6%
5	Pennsylvania	1,141,114	4.8%		38	Maine	125,401	0.5%
40	Rhode Island	108,269	0.5%		39	Utah	116,163	0.5%
23	South Carolina	372,920	1.6%		40	Rhode Island	108,269	0.5%
48	South Dakota	41,588	0.2%		41	Nebraska	107,943	0.5%
13	Tennessee	559,114	2.4%		42	New Hampshire	84,113	0.4%
4	Texas	1,411,470	5.9%		43	Idaho	83,794	0.4%
39	Utah	116,163	0.5%		44	Delaware	76,771	0.3%
46	Vermont	48,793	0.2%		45	Montana	53,030	0.2%
12	Virginia	572,184	2.4%		46	Vermont	48,793	0.2%
17	Washington	432,183	1.8%		47	Alaska	41,672	0.2%
33	West Virginia	184,556	0.8%		48	South Dakota	41,588	0.2%
21	Wisconsin	373,467	1.6%		49	North Dakota	34,227	0.1%
50	Wyoming	28,410	0.1%		50	Wyoming	28,410	0.1%
						District of Columbia	49,451	0.2%

Source: U.S. Department of Health and Human Services, Centers for Medicare and Medicaid Services
"State-by-State Prescription Drug Enrollment" (http://new.cms.hhs.gov/apps/media/?media=pressr)
Press release dated January 19, 2006. National total includes 191,985 enrollees in U.S. territories.

Percent of Population Age 65 and Older Enrolled in
Medicare Prescription Drug Plans in 2006
National Percent = 64.9%*

RANK	STATE	PERCENT
15	Alabama	69.3
1	Alaska	99.5
22	Arizona	65.4
25	Arkansas	64.6
3	California	78.2
6	Colorado	75.0
37	Connecticut	56.9
12	Delaware	70.5
29	Florida	62.2
26	Georgia	64.1
2	Hawaii	89.2
41	Idaho	52.8
28	Illinois	62.6
39	Indiana	55.1
48	Iowa	38.7
46	Kansas	44.6
18	Kentucky	67.6
11	Louisiana	70.7
21	Maine	66.1
23	Maryland	65.3
17	Massachusetts	68.3
16	Michigan	69.1
43	Minnesota	46.6
14	Mississippi	69.9
24	Missouri	65.2
47	Montana	41.9
43	Nebraska	46.6
10	Nevada	71.4
40	New Hampshire	53.7
32	New Jersey	60.9
9	New Mexico	71.5
35	New York	60.0
5	North Carolina	75.5
50	North Dakota	36.7
13	Ohio	70.0
29	Oklahoma	62.2
36	Oregon	59.3
34	Pennsylvania	60.2
7	Rhode Island	71.9
8	South Carolina	71.7
49	South Dakota	38.0
4	Tennessee	75.8
27	Texas	63.7
38	Utah	55.9
33	Vermont	60.4
18	Virginia	67.6
31	Washington	61.5
20	West Virginia	66.3
42	Wisconsin	52.2
45	Wyoming	46.5

RANK	STATE	PERCENT
1	Alaska	99.5
2	Hawaii	89.2
3	California	78.2
4	Tennessee	75.8
5	North Carolina	75.5
6	Colorado	75.0
7	Rhode Island	71.9
8	South Carolina	71.7
9	New Mexico	71.5
10	Nevada	71.4
11	Louisiana	70.7
12	Delaware	70.5
13	Ohio	70.0
14	Mississippi	69.9
15	Alabama	69.3
16	Michigan	69.1
17	Massachusetts	68.3
18	Kentucky	67.6
18	Virginia	67.6
20	West Virginia	66.3
21	Maine	66.1
22	Arizona	65.4
23	Maryland	65.3
24	Missouri	65.2
25	Arkansas	64.6
26	Georgia	64.1
27	Texas	63.7
28	Illinois	62.6
29	Florida	62.2
29	Oklahoma	62.2
31	Washington	61.5
32	New Jersey	60.9
33	Vermont	60.4
34	Pennsylvania	60.2
35	New York	60.0
36	Oregon	59.3
37	Connecticut	56.9
38	Utah	55.9
39	Indiana	55.1
40	New Hampshire	53.7
41	Idaho	52.8
42	Wisconsin	52.2
43	Minnesota	46.6
43	Nebraska	46.6
45	Wyoming	46.5
46	Kansas	44.6
47	Montana	41.9
48	Iowa	38.7
49	South Dakota	38.0
50	North Dakota	36.7

| | District of Columbia | 73.6 |

Source: MQ Press using data from U.S. Dept of Health and Human Services, Centers for Medicare and Medicaid Services "State-by-State Prescription Drug Enrollment" (http://new.cms.hhs.gov/apps/media/?media=pressr)

*Press release dated January 19, 2006. National percent does not include enrollees in U.S. territories. Calculated with 2004 population data.

Average Medicare Covered Charge per Day in Short Stay Hospitals: 2004

National Average = $4,603*

ALPHA ORDER

RANK ORDER

RANK	STATE	CHARGE	RANK	STATE	CHARGE
12	Alabama	$4,609	1	New Jersey	$8,142
10	Alaska	4,951	2	California	7,976
4	Arizona	5,800	3	Nevada	6,889
38	Arkansas	3,491	4	Arizona	5,800
2	California	7,976	5	Colorado	5,539
5	Colorado	5,539	6	Florida	5,477
30	Connecticut	3,746	7	Pennsylvania	5,287
47	Delaware	2,954	8	Texas	5,049
6	Florida	5,477	9	Nebraska	4,968
24	Georgia	3,947	10	Alaska	4,951
19	Hawaii	4,170	11	Minnesota	4,683
33	Idaho	3,700	12	Alabama	4,609
14	Illinois	4,566	13	Washington	4,570
40	Indiana	3,477	14	Illinois	4,566
42	Iowa	3,391	15	Kansas	4,321
15	Kansas	4,321	16	South Carolina	4,240
37	Kentucky	3,497	17	Oregon	4,223
22	Louisiana	4,063	18	Utah	4,206
44	Maine	3,306	19	Hawaii	4,170
50	Maryland	2,141	20	New Mexico	4,112
41	Massachusetts	3,415	21	Missouri	4,107
31	Michigan	3,715	22	Louisiana	4,063
11	Minnesota	4,683	23	Wisconsin	3,984
46	Mississippi	3,278	24	Georgia	3,947
21	Missouri	4,107	25	Virginia	3,862
38	Montana	3,491	26	Ohio	3,861
9	Nebraska	4,968	27	Tennessee	3,798
3	Nevada	6,889	28	South Dakota	3,762
35	New Hampshire	3,676	29	New York	3,752
1	New Jersey	8,142	30	Connecticut	3,746
20	New Mexico	4,112	31	Michigan	3,715
29	New York	3,752	32	Rhode Island	3,703
45	North Carolina	3,303	33	Idaho	3,700
43	North Dakota	3,318	34	Oklahoma	3,696
26	Ohio	3,861	35	New Hampshire	3,676
34	Oklahoma	3,696	36	Wyoming	3,623
17	Oregon	4,223	37	Kentucky	3,497
7	Pennsylvania	5,287	38	Arkansas	3,491
32	Rhode Island	3,703	38	Montana	3,491
16	South Carolina	4,240	40	Indiana	3,477
28	South Dakota	3,762	41	Massachusetts	3,415
27	Tennessee	3,798	42	Iowa	3,391
8	Texas	5,049	43	North Dakota	3,318
18	Utah	4,206	44	Maine	3,306
48	Vermont	2,889	45	North Carolina	3,303
25	Virginia	3,862	46	Mississippi	3,278
13	Washington	4,570	47	Delaware	2,954
49	West Virginia	2,641	48	Vermont	2,889
23	Wisconsin	3,984	49	West Virginia	2,641
36	Wyoming	3,623	50	Maryland	2,141

District of Columbia   4,892

Source: U.S. Department of Health and Human Services, Centers for Medicare and Medicaid Services
    "Annual Statistical Supplement 2005" (http://www.ssa.gov/policy/docs/statcomps/supplement/2005/)
*National average is only for the 50 states and the District of Columbia.

Average Medicare Covered Charge per Day in Nursing Homes: 2004

National Average = $493*

ALPHA ORDER				RANK ORDER		
RANK	**STATE**	**CHARGE**		**RANK**	**STATE**	**CHARGE**
45	Alabama	$423		1	Alaska	$735
1	Alaska	735		2	California	702
44	Arizona	425		3	Louisiana	648
6	Arkansas	570		4	Hawaii	580
2	California	702		5	Oklahoma	575
23	Colorado	478		6	Arkansas	570
27	Connecticut	464		6	Iowa	570
36	Delaware	432		8	Illinois	550
31	Florida	447		9	New Mexico	549
48	Georgia	407		10	New Jersey	546
4	Hawaii	580		11	Missouri	542
29	Idaho	458		12	Mississippi	537
8	Illinois	550		13	Massachusetts	536
32	Indiana	446		14	Pennsylvania	528
6	Iowa	570		15	Nebraska	523
18	Kansas	497		16	Maine	510
26	Kentucky	469		17	New Hampshire	506
3	Louisiana	648		18	Kansas	497
16	Maine	510		19	Texas	496
39	Maryland	428		20	Utah	494
13	Massachusetts	536		21	South Dakota	485
37	Michigan	429		22	Ohio	484
41	Minnesota	427		23	Colorado	478
12	Mississippi	537		23	West Virginia	478
11	Missouri	542		25	Wyoming	473
46	Montana	415		26	Kentucky	469
15	Nebraska	523		27	Connecticut	464
39	Nevada	428		27	North Dakota	464
17	New Hampshire	506		29	Idaho	458
10	New Jersey	546		30	Vermont	452
9	New Mexico	549		31	Florida	447
32	New York	446		32	Indiana	446
50	North Carolina	397		32	New York	446
27	North Dakota	464		34	Washington	443
22	Ohio	484		35	Rhode Island	439
5	Oklahoma	575		36	Delaware	432
42	Oregon	426		37	Michigan	429
14	Pennsylvania	528		37	Wisconsin	429
35	Rhode Island	439		39	Maryland	428
49	South Carolina	404		39	Nevada	428
21	South Dakota	485		41	Minnesota	427
47	Tennessee	412		42	Oregon	426
19	Texas	496		42	Virginia	426
20	Utah	494		44	Arizona	425
30	Vermont	452		45	Alabama	423
42	Virginia	426		46	Montana	415
34	Washington	443		47	Tennessee	412
23	West Virginia	478		48	Georgia	407
37	Wisconsin	429		49	South Carolina	404
25	Wyoming	473		50	North Carolina	397
					District of Columbia	513

Source: U.S. Department of Health and Human Services, Centers for Medicare and Medicaid Services
"Annual Statistical Supplement 2005" (http://www.ssa.gov/policy/docs/statcomps/supplement/2005/)
National average is only for the 50 states and the District of Columbia.

Medicare Managed Care Enrollees in 2005

National Total = 5,438,359 Enrollees*

ALPHA ORDER

RANK	STATE	ENROLLEES	% of USA
22	Alabama	57,837	1.1%
42	Alaska	0	0.0%
6	Arizona	203,321	3.7%
42	Arkansas	0	0.0%
1	California	1,363,771	25.1%
10	Colorado	136,540	2.5%
27	Connecticut	28,241	0.5%
42	Delaware	0	0.0%
2	Florida	570,074	10.5%
31	Georgia	16,941	0.3%
20	Hawaii	59,495	1.1%
33	Idaho	16,483	0.3%
16	Illinois	81,505	1.5%
30	Indiana	17,377	0.3%
35	Iowa	6,876	0.1%
41	Kansas	300	0.0%
29	Kentucky	18,159	0.3%
18	Louisiana	68,685	1.3%
42	Maine	0	0.0%
23	Maryland	41,668	0.8%
9	Massachusetts	161,400	3.0%
28	Michigan	20,166	0.4%
13	Minnesota	100,835	1.9%
42	Mississippi	0	0.0%
11	Missouri	134,613	2.5%
42	Montana	0	0.0%
34	Nebraska	10,348	0.2%
15	Nevada	84,131	1.5%
38	New Hampshire	1,088	0.0%
14	New Jersey	90,775	1.7%
24	New Mexico	41,321	0.8%
3	New York	517,389	9.5%
19	North Carolina	60,075	1.1%
39	North Dakota	611	0.0%
5	Ohio	231,659	4.3%
25	Oklahoma	40,492	0.7%
8	Oregon	186,326	3.4%
4	Pennsylvania	510,708	9.4%
21	Rhode Island	58,077	1.1%
40	South Carolina	312	0.0%
42	South Dakota	0	0.0%
17	Tennessee	75,263	1.4%
7	Texas	189,511	3.5%
32	Utah	16,545	0.3%
42	Vermont	0	0.0%
37	Virginia	2,742	0.1%
12	Washington	124,922	2.3%
36	West Virginia	6,183	0.1%
26	Wisconsin	37,389	0.7%
42	Wyoming	0	0.0%

RANK ORDER

RANK	STATE	ENROLLEES	% of USA
1	California	1,363,771	25.1%
2	Florida	570,074	10.5%
3	New York	517,389	9.5%
4	Pennsylvania	510,708	9.4%
5	Ohio	231,659	4.3%
6	Arizona	203,321	3.7%
7	Texas	189,511	3.5%
8	Oregon	186,326	3.4%
9	Massachusetts	161,400	3.0%
10	Colorado	136,540	2.5%
11	Missouri	134,613	2.5%
12	Washington	124,922	2.3%
13	Minnesota	100,835	1.9%
14	New Jersey	90,775	1.7%
15	Nevada	84,131	1.5%
16	Illinois	81,505	1.5%
17	Tennessee	75,263	1.4%
18	Louisiana	68,685	1.3%
19	North Carolina	60,075	1.1%
20	Hawaii	59,495	1.1%
21	Rhode Island	58,077	1.1%
22	Alabama	57,837	1.1%
23	Maryland	41,668	0.8%
24	New Mexico	41,321	0.8%
25	Oklahoma	40,492	0.7%
26	Wisconsin	37,389	0.7%
27	Connecticut	28,241	0.5%
28	Michigan	20,166	0.4%
29	Kentucky	18,159	0.3%
30	Indiana	17,377	0.3%
31	Georgia	16,941	0.3%
32	Utah	16,545	0.3%
33	Idaho	16,483	0.3%
34	Nebraska	10,348	0.2%
35	Iowa	6,876	0.1%
36	West Virginia	6,183	0.1%
37	Virginia	2,742	0.1%
38	New Hampshire	1,088	0.0%
39	North Dakota	611	0.0%
40	South Carolina	312	0.0%
41	Kansas	300	0.0%
42	Alaska	0	0.0%
42	Arkansas	0	0.0%
42	Delaware	0	0.0%
42	Maine	0	0.0%
42	Mississippi	0	0.0%
42	Montana	0	0.0%
42	South Dakota	0	0.0%
42	Vermont	0	0.0%
42	Wyoming	0	0.0%
	District of Columbia	0	0.0%

Source: U.S. Department of Health and Human Services, Centers for Medicare and Medicaid Services
"Medicare Managed Care Report"
As of January 2005. Includes M + C, Cost, Health Care Prepayment Plans (HCPP) and other demo plans. National total includes 48,205 enrollees in the United Mine Workers' plan not shown separately by state.

Percent of Medicare Enrollees in Managed Care Programs in 2005

National Percent = 14% of Medicare Enrollees*

ALPHA ORDER

RANK	STATE	PERCENT
20	Alabama	8
39	Alaska	0
6	Arizona	29
39	Arkansas	0
3	California	34
6	Colorado	29
26	Connecticut	5
39	Delaware	0
9	Florida	19
32	Georgia	2
2	Hawaii	35
18	Idaho	9
26	Illinois	5
32	Indiana	2
35	Iowa	1
39	Kansas	0
31	Kentucky	3
17	Louisiana	11
39	Maine	0
25	Maryland	7
11	Massachusetts	17
35	Michigan	1
14	Minnesota	15
39	Mississippi	0
14	Missouri	15
39	Montana	0
29	Nebraska	4
4	Nevada	33
35	New Hampshire	1
20	New Jersey	8
11	New Mexico	17
9	New York	19
26	North Carolina	5
35	North Dakota	1
16	Ohio	13
20	Oklahoma	8
1	Oregon	38
8	Pennsylvania	24
4	Rhode Island	33
39	South Carolina	0
39	South Dakota	0
18	Tennessee	9
20	Texas	8
20	Utah	8
39	Vermont	0
39	Virginia	0
11	Washington	17
32	West Virginia	2
29	Wisconsin	4
39	Wyoming	0

RANK ORDER

RANK	STATE	PERCENT
1	Oregon	38
2	Hawaii	35
3	California	34
4	Nevada	33
4	Rhode Island	33
6	Arizona	29
6	Colorado	29
8	Pennsylvania	24
9	Florida	19
9	New York	19
11	Massachusetts	17
11	New Mexico	17
11	Washington	17
14	Minnesota	15
14	Missouri	15
16	Ohio	13
17	Louisiana	11
18	Idaho	9
18	Tennessee	9
20	Alabama	8
20	New Jersey	8
20	Oklahoma	8
20	Texas	8
20	Utah	8
25	Maryland	7
26	Connecticut	5
26	Illinois	5
26	North Carolina	5
29	Nebraska	4
29	Wisconsin	4
31	Kentucky	3
32	Georgia	2
32	Indiana	2
32	West Virginia	2
35	Iowa	1
35	Michigan	1
35	New Hampshire	1
35	North Dakota	1
39	Alaska	0
39	Arkansas	0
39	Delaware	0
39	Kansas	0
39	Maine	0
39	Mississippi	0
39	Montana	0
39	South Carolina	0
39	South Dakota	0
39	Vermont	0
39	Virginia	0
39	Wyoming	0
	District of Columbia	0

Source: U.S. Department of Health and Human Services, Centers for Medicare and Medicaid Services
"Medicare Managed Care Report"
*As of January 2005. Includes M + C, Cost, Health Care Prepayment Plans (HCPP) and other demo plans. National figure includes enrollees in the United Mine Workers' plan not shown separately by state.

Medicare Physicians in 2003

National Total = 914,303 Physicians*

ALPHA ORDER

RANK	STATE	PHYSICIANS	% of USA
28	Alabama	10,389	1.1%
49	Alaska	2,161	0.2%
23	Arizona	14,289	1.6%
31	Arkansas	8,762	1.0%
1	California	90,222	9.9%
22	Colorado	14,835	1.6%
29	Connecticut	10,064	1.1%
48	Delaware	2,689	0.3%
4	Florida	51,245	5.6%
12	Georgia	22,944	2.5%
41	Hawaii**	4,540	0.5%
27	Idaho	10,402	1.1%
42	Illinois	3,687	0.4%
8	Indiana	35,555	3.9%
18	Iowa	17,543	1.9%
30	Kansas	8,971	1.0%
24	Kentucky	12,473	1.4%
21	Louisiana	15,668	1.7%
6	Maine	37,314	4.1%
14	Maryland	21,154	2.3%
34	Massachusetts	6,350	0.7%
9	Michigan	32,264	3.5%
20	Minnesota	15,872	1.7%
15	Mississippi	19,600	2.1%
35	Missouri	6,289	0.7%
44	Montana	3,367	0.4%
11	Nebraska	25,715	2.8%
46	Nevada	2,875	0.3%
38	New Hampshire	5,809	0.6%
37	New Jersey	5,853	0.6%
10	New Mexico	32,038	3.5%
39	New York	4,951	0.5%
40	North Carolina	4,925	0.5%
2	North Dakota	74,194	8.1%
7	Ohio	37,111	4.1%
32	Oklahoma	8,445	0.9%
25	Oregon	11,834	1.3%
5	Pennsylvania	45,990	5.0%
43	Rhode Island	3,430	0.4%
26	South Carolina	11,577	1.3%
47	South Dakota	2,709	0.3%
16	Tennessee	19,309	2.1%
3	Texas	52,595	5.8%
33	Utah	6,566	0.7%
19	Vermont	17,204	1.9%
45	Virginia	3,029	0.3%
13	Washington	21,302	2.3%
17	West Virginia	19,198	2.1%
36	Wisconsin	5,914	0.6%
50	Wyoming	1,635	0.2%

RANK ORDER

RANK	STATE	PHYSICIANS	% of USA
1	California	90,222	9.9%
2	North Dakota	74,194	8.1%
3	Texas	52,595	5.8%
4	Florida	51,245	5.6%
5	Pennsylvania	45,990	5.0%
6	Maine	37,314	4.1%
7	Ohio	37,111	4.1%
8	Indiana	35,555	3.9%
9	Michigan	32,264	3.5%
10	New Mexico	32,038	3.5%
11	Nebraska	25,715	2.8%
12	Georgia	22,944	2.5%
13	Washington	21,302	2.3%
14	Maryland	21,154	2.3%
15	Mississippi	19,600	2.1%
16	Tennessee	19,309	2.1%
17	West Virginia	19,198	2.1%
18	Iowa	17,543	1.9%
19	Vermont	17,204	1.9%
20	Minnesota	15,872	1.7%
21	Louisiana	15,668	1.7%
22	Colorado	14,835	1.6%
23	Arizona	14,289	1.6%
24	Kentucky	12,473	1.4%
25	Oregon	11,834	1.3%
26	South Carolina	11,577	1.3%
27	Idaho	10,402	1.1%
28	Alabama	10,389	1.1%
29	Connecticut	10,064	1.1%
30	Kansas	8,971	1.0%
31	Arkansas	8,762	1.0%
32	Oklahoma	8,445	0.9%
33	Utah	6,566	0.7%
34	Massachusetts	6,350	0.7%
35	Missouri	6,289	0.7%
36	Wisconsin	5,914	0.6%
37	New Jersey	5,853	0.6%
38	New Hampshire	5,809	0.6%
39	New York	4,951	0.5%
40	North Carolina	4,925	0.5%
41	Hawaii**	4,540	0.5%
42	Illinois	3,687	0.4%
43	Rhode Island	3,430	0.4%
44	Montana	3,367	0.4%
45	Virginia	3,029	0.3%
46	Nevada	2,875	0.3%
47	South Dakota	2,709	0.3%
48	Delaware	2,689	0.3%
49	Alaska	2,161	0.2%
50	Wyoming	1,635	0.2%
	District of Columbia	4,546	0.5%

Source: U.S. Department of Health and Human Services, Centers for Medicare and Medicaid Services
   "2003 Data Compendium" (http://new.cms.hhs.gov/DataCompendium/)
Medicare Part B. "Physicians" include MD, DO, DDM, DDS, DPM, OD and CH. National total includes 6,891 physicians in Puerto Rico and the Virgin Islands.
Physicians for Guam are included in Hawaii's total.

Percent of Physicians Participating in Medicare in 2003

National Percent = 91.5% of Physicians Participate in Medicare*

ALPHA ORDER

RANK	STATE	PERCENT
4	Alabama	96.4
45	Alaska	87.2
35	Arizona	91.1
7	Arkansas	95.9
40	California	89.5
39	Colorado	90.0
25	Connecticut	93.4
32	Delaware	92.4
31	Florida	92.5
38	Georgia	90.4
15	Hawaii	94.7
47	Idaho	84.0
25	Illinois	93.4
44	Indiana	87.4
16	Iowa	94.6
11	Kansas	95.4
20	Kentucky	94.0
32	Louisiana	92.4
13	Maine	94.8
19	Maryland	94.3
6	Massachusetts	96.0
1	Michigan	97.3
49	Minnesota	80.6
46	Mississippi	86.1
20	Missouri	94.0
36	Montana	90.9
16	Nebraska	94.6
10	Nevada	95.6
20	New Hampshire	94.0
42	New Jersey	88.9
28	New Mexico	93.3
48	New York	82.3
34	North Carolina	91.9
1	North Dakota	97.3
9	Ohio	95.7
18	Oklahoma	94.4
25	Oregon	93.4
4	Pennsylvania	96.4
50	Rhode Island	77.2
29	South Carolina	92.8
37	South Dakota	90.6
30	Tennessee	92.6
41	Texas	89.4
3	Utah	97.0
23	Vermont	93.8
24	Virginia	93.7
8	Washington	95.8
13	West Virginia	94.8
12	Wisconsin	95.0
43	Wyoming	88.0

RANK ORDER

RANK	STATE	PERCENT
1	Michigan	97.3
1	North Dakota	97.3
3	Utah	97.0
4	Alabama	96.4
4	Pennsylvania	96.4
6	Massachusetts	96.0
7	Arkansas	95.9
8	Washington	95.8
9	Ohio	95.7
10	Nevada	95.6
11	Kansas	95.4
12	Wisconsin	95.0
13	Maine	94.8
13	West Virginia	94.8
15	Hawaii	94.7
16	Iowa	94.6
16	Nebraska	94.6
18	Oklahoma	94.4
19	Maryland	94.3
20	Kentucky	94.0
20	Missouri	94.0
20	New Hampshire	94.0
23	Vermont	93.8
24	Virginia	93.7
25	Connecticut	93.4
25	Illinois	93.4
25	Oregon	93.4
28	New Mexico	93.3
29	South Carolina	92.8
30	Tennessee	92.6
31	Florida	92.5
32	Delaware	92.4
32	Louisiana	92.4
34	North Carolina	91.9
35	Arizona	91.1
36	Montana	90.9
37	South Dakota	90.6
38	Georgia	90.4
39	Colorado	90.0
40	California	89.5
41	Texas	89.4
42	New Jersey	88.9
43	Wyoming	88.0
44	Indiana	87.4
45	Alaska	87.2
46	Mississippi	86.1
47	Idaho	84.0
48	New York	82.3
49	Minnesota	80.6
50	Rhode Island	77.2

	District of Columbia	91.3

Source: U.S. Department of Health and Human Services, Centers for Medicare and Medicaid Services
   "2003 Data Compendium" (http://new.cms.hhs.gov/DataCompendium/)
*As of January 1, 2003. Refers to Medicare Part B. Physicians include MDs, DOs, limited license practitioners and non-physician practitioners.

Medicare Benefit Payments in 2001

National Total = $245,186,000,000*

ALPHA ORDER					RANK ORDER			
RANK	STATE	BENEFITS	% of USA		RANK	STATE	BENEFITS	% of USA
19	Alabama	$4,058,221,000	1.7%		1	California	$26,919,858,000	11.0%
50	Alaska	254,145,000	0.1%		2	Florida	19,935,116,000	8.1%
22	Arizona	3,777,161,000	1.5%		3	New York	19,402,963,000	7.9%
32	Arkansas	2,354,085,000	1.0%		4	Texas	15,104,941,000	6.2%
1	California	26,919,858,000	11.0%		5	Pennsylvania	13,731,756,000	5.6%
30	Colorado	2,526,949,000	1.0%		6	Ohio	10,139,407,000	4.1%
24	Connecticut	3,463,305,000	1.4%		7	Illinois	10,072,716,000	4.1%
44	Delaware	753,991,000	0.3%		8	New Jersey	9,305,846,000	3.8%
2	Florida	19,935,116,000	8.1%		9	Michigan	9,227,281,000	3.8%
12	Georgia	5,486,318,000	2.2%		10	Massachusetts	6,651,188,000	2.7%
43	Hawaii	798,513,000	0.3%		11	North Carolina	6,299,915,000	2.6%
42	Idaho	834,950,000	0.3%		12	Georgia	5,486,318,000	2.2%
7	Illinois	10,072,716,000	4.1%		13	Missouri	5,009,583,000	2.0%
16	Indiana	4,773,470,000	1.9%		14	Tennessee	4,847,107,000	2.0%
31	Iowa	2,368,591,000	1.0%		15	Virginia	4,797,871,000	2.0%
33	Kansas	2,071,216,000	0.8%		16	Indiana	4,773,470,000	1.9%
23	Kentucky	3,600,612,000	1.5%		17	Maryland	4,674,796,000	1.9%
18	Louisiana	4,454,101,000	1.8%		18	Louisiana	4,454,101,000	1.8%
37	Maine	1,118,964,000	0.5%		19	Alabama	4,058,221,000	1.7%
17	Maryland	4,674,796,000	1.9%		20	Wisconsin	3,948,015,000	1.6%
10	Massachusetts	6,651,188,000	2.7%		21	Washington	3,862,966,000	1.6%
9	Michigan	9,227,281,000	3.8%		22	Arizona	3,777,161,000	1.5%
26	Minnesota	3,373,029,000	1.4%		23	Kentucky	3,600,612,000	1.5%
28	Mississippi	2,604,168,000	1.1%		24	Connecticut	3,463,305,000	1.4%
13	Missouri	5,009,583,000	2.0%		25	South Carolina	3,429,335,000	1.4%
45	Montana	658,649,000	0.3%		26	Minnesota	3,373,029,000	1.4%
36	Nebraska	1,325,208,000	0.5%		27	Oklahoma	3,043,503,000	1.2%
35	Nevada	1,495,977,000	0.6%		28	Mississippi	2,604,168,000	1.1%
41	New Hampshire	878,715,000	0.4%		29	Oregon	2,595,888,000	1.1%
8	New Jersey	9,305,846,000	3.8%		30	Colorado	2,526,949,000	1.0%
38	New Mexico	1,106,938,000	0.5%		31	Iowa	2,368,591,000	1.0%
3	New York	19,402,963,000	7.9%		32	Arkansas	2,354,085,000	1.0%
11	North Carolina	6,299,915,000	2.6%		33	Kansas	2,071,216,000	0.8%
48	North Dakota	479,025,000	0.2%		34	West Virginia	1,906,516,000	0.8%
6	Ohio	10,139,407,000	4.1%		35	Nevada	1,495,977,000	0.6%
27	Oklahoma	3,043,503,000	1.2%		36	Nebraska	1,325,208,000	0.5%
29	Oregon	2,595,888,000	1.1%		37	Maine	1,118,964,000	0.5%
5	Pennsylvania	13,731,756,000	5.6%		38	New Mexico	1,106,938,000	0.5%
39	Rhode Island	1,070,422,000	0.4%		39	Rhode Island	1,070,422,000	0.4%
25	South Carolina	3,429,335,000	1.4%		40	Utah	1,004,074,000	0.4%
46	South Dakota	540,327,000	0.2%		41	New Hampshire	878,715,000	0.4%
14	Tennessee	4,847,107,000	2.0%		42	Idaho	834,950,000	0.3%
4	Texas	15,104,941,000	6.2%		43	Hawaii	798,513,000	0.3%
40	Utah	1,004,074,000	0.4%		44	Delaware	753,991,000	0.3%
47	Vermont	480,466,000	0.2%		45	Montana	658,649,000	0.3%
15	Virginia	4,797,871,000	2.0%		46	South Dakota	540,327,000	0.2%
21	Washington	3,862,966,000	1.6%		47	Vermont	480,466,000	0.2%
34	West Virginia	1,906,516,000	0.8%		48	North Dakota	479,025,000	0.2%
20	Wisconsin	3,948,015,000	1.6%		49	Wyoming	338,211,000	0.1%
49	Wyoming	338,211,000	0.1%		50	Alaska	254,145,000	0.1%
						District of Columbia	568,988,000	0.2%

Source: U.S. Department of Health and Human Services, Centers for Medicare and Medicaid Services
"2004 Medicare and Medicaid Statistical Supplement" (http://new.cms.hhs.gov/MedicareMedicaidStatSupp)
*Revised figures for fiscal year 2001. Includes payments to aged and disabled enrollees. Total includes
$1,661,000,000 in payments to enrollees in Puerto Rico and other outlying areas.

Per Capita Medicare Benefit Payments in 2001

National Per Capita = $854*

ALPHA ORDER

RANK	STATE	PER CAPITA
13	Alabama	$908
50	Alaska	402
36	Arizona	713
18	Arkansas	875
26	California	780
48	Colorado	571
8	Connecticut	1,009
10	Delaware	948
1	Florida	1,219
44	Georgia	652
43	Hawaii	654
46	Idaho	632
24	Illinois	805
27	Indiana	779
23	Iowa	808
30	Kansas	767
16	Kentucky	885
9	Louisiana	998
19	Maine	870
20	Maryland	869
5	Massachusetts	1,040
11	Michigan	922
41	Minnesota	677
12	Mississippi	911
15	Missouri	888
34	Montana	727
28	Nebraska	771
35	Nevada	714
39	New Hampshire	698
3	New Jersey	1,094
47	New Mexico	604
6	New York	1,016
29	North Carolina	768
31	North Dakota	753
14	Ohio	891
17	Oklahoma	878
32	Oregon	747
2	Pennsylvania	1,117
7	Rhode Island	1,011
21	South Carolina	845
36	South Dakota	713
22	Tennessee	843
38	Texas	708
49	Utah	439
25	Vermont	784
42	Virginia	667
45	Washington	645
4	West Virginia	1,058
33	Wisconsin	731
40	Wyoming	685

RANK ORDER

RANK	STATE	PER CAPITA
1	Florida	$1,219
2	Pennsylvania	1,117
3	New Jersey	1,094
4	West Virginia	1,058
5	Massachusetts	1,040
6	New York	1,016
7	Rhode Island	1,011
8	Connecticut	1,009
9	Louisiana	998
10	Delaware	948
11	Michigan	922
12	Mississippi	911
13	Alabama	908
14	Ohio	891
15	Missouri	888
16	Kentucky	885
17	Oklahoma	878
18	Arkansas	875
19	Maine	870
20	Maryland	869
21	South Carolina	845
22	Tennessee	843
23	Iowa	808
24	Illinois	805
25	Vermont	784
26	California	780
27	Indiana	779
28	Nebraska	771
29	North Carolina	768
30	Kansas	767
31	North Dakota	753
32	Oregon	747
33	Wisconsin	731
34	Montana	727
35	Nevada	714
36	Arizona	713
36	South Dakota	713
38	Texas	708
39	New Hampshire	698
40	Wyoming	685
41	Minnesota	677
42	Virginia	667
43	Hawaii	654
44	Georgia	652
45	Washington	645
46	Idaho	632
47	New Mexico	604
48	Colorado	571
49	Utah	439
50	Alaska	402

District of Columbia 999

Source: MQ Press using data from U.S. Dept of Health & Human Services, Centers for Medicare and Medicaid Services "2004 Medicare and Medicaid Statistical Supplement" (http://new.cms.hhs.gov/MedicareMedicaidStatSupp)
*Revised figures for fiscal year 2001. Includes payments to aged and disabled enrollees. National rate does not include payments or enrollees in Puerto Rico and other outlying areas.

Medicare Payments per Enrollee in 2001

National Rate = $6,223*

ALPHA ORDER

RANK	STATE	PER ENROLLEE
21	Alabama	$5,833
22	Alaska	5,831
29	Arizona	5,418
31	Arkansas	5,328
7	California	6,828
32	Colorado	5,316
8	Connecticut	6,722
9	Delaware	6,592
5	Florida	6,972
20	Georgia	5,866
47	Hawaii	4,742
44	Idaho	4,934
14	Illinois	6,164
27	Indiana	5,567
43	Iowa	4,963
33	Kansas	5,300
25	Kentucky	5,714
2	Louisiana	7,354
39	Maine	5,100
4	Maryland	7,147
6	Massachusetts	6,941
12	Michigan	6,543
38	Minnesota	5,117
15	Mississippi	6,143
23	Missouri	5,776
46	Montana	4,758
36	Nebraska	5,207
18	Nevada	5,901
41	New Hampshire	5,085
1	New Jersey	7,730
49	New Mexico	4,641
3	New York	7,158
28	North Carolina	5,442
48	North Dakota	4,652
17	Ohio	5,952
16	Oklahoma	5,955
35	Oregon	5,216
10	Pennsylvania	6,558
13	Rhode Island	6,238
19	South Carolina	5,895
50	South Dakota	4,503
24	Tennessee	5,743
11	Texas	6,557
45	Utah	4,764
30	Vermont	5,343
34	Virginia	5,268
37	Washington	5,173
26	West Virginia	5,616
42	Wisconsin	5,016
40	Wyoming	5,095

RANK ORDER

RANK	STATE	PER ENROLLEE
1	New Jersey	$7,730
2	Louisiana	7,354
3	New York	7,158
4	Maryland	7,147
5	Florida	6,972
6	Massachusetts	6,941
7	California	6,828
8	Connecticut	6,722
9	Delaware	6,592
10	Pennsylvania	6,558
11	Texas	6,557
12	Michigan	6,543
13	Rhode Island	6,238
14	Illinois	6,164
15	Mississippi	6,143
16	Oklahoma	5,955
17	Ohio	5,952
18	Nevada	5,901
19	South Carolina	5,895
20	Georgia	5,866
21	Alabama	5,833
22	Alaska	5,831
23	Missouri	5,776
24	Tennessee	5,743
25	Kentucky	5,714
26	West Virginia	5,616
27	Indiana	5,567
28	North Carolina	5,442
29	Arizona	5,418
30	Vermont	5,343
31	Arkansas	5,328
32	Colorado	5,316
33	Kansas	5,300
34	Virginia	5,268
35	Oregon	5,216
36	Nebraska	5,207
37	Washington	5,173
38	Minnesota	5,117
39	Maine	5,100
40	Wyoming	5,095
41	New Hampshire	5,085
42	Wisconsin	5,016
43	Iowa	4,963
44	Idaho	4,934
45	Utah	4,764
46	Montana	4,758
47	Hawaii	4,742
48	North Dakota	4,652
49	New Mexico	4,641
50	South Dakota	4,503
	District of Columbia	7,683

Source: MQ Press using data from U.S. Dept of Health & Human Services, Centers for Medicare and Medicaid Services "2004 Medicare and Medicaid Statistical Supplement" (http://new.cms.hhs.gov/MedicareMedicaidStatSupp)
Revised figures for fiscal year 2001. Includes payments to aged and disabled enrollees. National rate does not include payments or enrollees in Puerto Rico and other outlying areas.

Medicaid Enrollment in 2004

National Total = 44,596,338 Enrollees*

ALPHA ORDER

ALPHA ORDER

RANK	STATE	ENROLLEES	% of USA
20	Alabama	800,177	1.8%
45	Alaska	99,439	0.2%
13	Arizona	992,055	2.2%
26	Arkansas	612,953	1.4%
1	California	6,454,112	14.5%
31	Colorado	407,565	0.9%
32	Connecticut	405,311	0.9%
43	Delaware	137,017	0.3%
4	Florida	2,237,376	5.0%
9	Georgia	1,340,174	3.0%
38	Hawaii	198,010	0.4%
41	Idaho	171,483	0.4%
5	Illinois	1,770,800	4.0%
18	Indiana	827,034	1.9%
34	Iowa	294,470	0.7%
35	Kansas	268,065	0.6%
23	Kentucky	686,813	1.5%
15	Louisiana	944,438	2.1%
36	Maine	266,098	0.6%
22	Maryland	705,914	1.6%
14	Massachusetts	973,233	2.2%
8	Michigan	1,350,343	3.0%
27	Minnesota	561,892	1.3%
24	Mississippi	644,210	1.4%
12	Missouri	1,001,999	2.2%
48	Montana	85,175	0.2%
37	Nebraska	200,512	0.4%
42	Nevada	170,109	0.4%
47	New Hampshire	97,178	0.2%
21	New Jersey	774,217	1.7%
30	New Mexico	416,092	0.9%
2	New York	3,952,005	8.9%
11	North Carolina	1,125,624	2.5%
50	North Dakota	53,104	0.1%
6	Ohio	1,661,388	3.7%
28	Oklahoma	530,480	1.2%
29	Oregon	423,275	0.9%
7	Pennsylvania	1,656,762	3.7%
40	Rhode Island	181,215	0.4%
17	South Carolina	849,049	1.9%
46	South Dakota	99,151	0.2%
10	Tennessee	1,336,691	3.0%
3	Texas	2,756,776	6.2%
39	Utah	192,163	0.4%
44	Vermont	130,372	0.3%
25	Virginia	641,359	1.4%
16	Washington	940,693	2.1%
33	West Virginia	299,788	0.7%
19	Wisconsin	804,769	1.8%
49	Wyoming	59,657	0.1%

RANK ORDER

RANK	STATE	ENROLLEES	% of USA
1	California	6,454,112	14.5%
2	New York	3,952,005	8.9%
3	Texas	2,756,776	6.2%
4	Florida	2,237,376	5.0%
5	Illinois	1,770,800	4.0%
6	Ohio	1,661,388	3.7%
7	Pennsylvania	1,656,762	3.7%
8	Michigan	1,350,343	3.0%
9	Georgia	1,340,174	3.0%
10	Tennessee	1,336,691	3.0%
11	North Carolina	1,125,624	2.5%
12	Missouri	1,001,999	2.2%
13	Arizona	992,055	2.2%
14	Massachusetts	973,233	2.2%
15	Louisiana	944,438	2.1%
16	Washington	940,693	2.1%
17	South Carolina	849,049	1.9%
18	Indiana	827,034	1.9%
19	Wisconsin	804,769	1.8%
20	Alabama	800,177	1.8%
21	New Jersey	774,217	1.7%
22	Maryland	705,914	1.6%
23	Kentucky	686,813	1.5%
24	Mississippi	644,210	1.4%
25	Virginia	641,359	1.4%
26	Arkansas	612,953	1.4%
27	Minnesota	561,892	1.3%
28	Oklahoma	530,480	1.2%
29	Oregon	423,275	0.9%
30	New Mexico	416,092	0.9%
31	Colorado	407,565	0.9%
32	Connecticut	405,311	0.9%
33	West Virginia	299,788	0.7%
34	Iowa	294,470	0.7%
35	Kansas	268,065	0.6%
36	Maine	266,098	0.6%
37	Nebraska	200,512	0.4%
38	Hawaii	198,010	0.4%
39	Utah	192,163	0.4%
40	Rhode Island	181,215	0.4%
41	Idaho	171,483	0.4%
42	Nevada	170,109	0.4%
43	Delaware	137,017	0.3%
44	Vermont	130,372	0.3%
45	Alaska	99,439	0.2%
46	South Dakota	99,151	0.2%
47	New Hampshire	97,178	0.2%
48	Montana	85,175	0.2%
49	Wyoming	59,657	0.1%
50	North Dakota	53,104	0.1%
	District of Columbia	139,595	0.3%

Source: U.S. Department of Health and Human Services, Centers for Medicare and Medicaid Services
"Medicaid Managed Care State Enrollment" (http://new.cms.hhs.gov/MedicaidDataSourcesGenInfo/)
*Unduplicated enrollment as of December 31, 2004.   National total includes 868,158 Medicaid enrollees in Puerto Rico and the Virgin Islands.

Percent of Population Enrolled in Medicaid in 2004

National Percent = 14.9% of Population*

ALPHA ORDER

RANK	STATE	PERCENT
11	Alabama	17.7
21	Alaska	15.1
13	Arizona	17.3
2	Arkansas	22.3
10	California	18.0
44	Colorado	8.9
38	Connecticut	11.6
16	Delaware	16.5
31	Florida	12.9
23	Georgia	15.0
18	Hawaii	15.7
34	Idaho	12.3
26	Illinois	13.9
29	Indiana	13.3
41	Iowa	10.0
42	Kansas	9.8
15	Kentucky	16.6
5	Louisiana	21.0
8	Maine	20.2
33	Maryland	12.7
19	Massachusetts	15.2
27	Michigan	13.4
40	Minnesota	11.0
3	Mississippi	22.2
12	Missouri	17.4
43	Montana	9.2
39	Nebraska	11.5
50	Nevada	7.3
49	New Hampshire	7.5
44	New Jersey	8.9
4	New Mexico	21.9
7	New York	20.5
30	North Carolina	13.2
47	North Dakota	8.3
25	Ohio	14.5
21	Oklahoma	15.1
36	Oregon	11.8
27	Pennsylvania	13.4
14	Rhode Island	16.8
8	South Carolina	20.2
31	South Dakota	12.9
1	Tennessee	22.7
34	Texas	12.3
48	Utah	7.9
5	Vermont	21.0
46	Virginia	8.6
19	Washington	15.2
16	West Virginia	16.5
24	Wisconsin	14.6
36	Wyoming	11.8

RANK ORDER

RANK	STATE	PERCENT
1	Tennessee	22.7
2	Arkansas	22.3
3	Mississippi	22.2
4	New Mexico	21.9
5	Louisiana	21.0
5	Vermont	21.0
7	New York	20.5
8	Maine	20.2
8	South Carolina	20.2
10	California	18.0
11	Alabama	17.7
12	Missouri	17.4
13	Arizona	17.3
14	Rhode Island	16.8
15	Kentucky	16.6
16	Delaware	16.5
16	West Virginia	16.5
18	Hawaii	15.7
19	Massachusetts	15.2
19	Washington	15.2
21	Alaska	15.1
21	Oklahoma	15.1
23	Georgia	15.0
24	Wisconsin	14.6
25	Ohio	14.5
26	Illinois	13.9
27	Michigan	13.4
27	Pennsylvania	13.4
29	Indiana	13.3
30	North Carolina	13.2
31	Florida	12.9
31	South Dakota	12.9
33	Maryland	12.7
34	Idaho	12.3
34	Texas	12.3
36	Oregon	11.8
36	Wyoming	11.8
38	Connecticut	11.6
39	Nebraska	11.5
40	Minnesota	11.0
41	Iowa	10.0
42	Kansas	9.8
43	Montana	9.2
44	Colorado	8.9
44	New Jersey	8.9
46	Virginia	8.6
47	North Dakota	8.3
48	Utah	7.9
49	New Hampshire	7.5
50	Nevada	7.3

District of Columbia		25.2

Source: MQ Press using data from U.S. Dept of Health & Human Services, Centers for Medicare and Medicaid Services
"Medicaid Managed Care State Enrollment" (http://new.cms.hhs.gov/MedicaidDataSourcesGenInfo/)
*Unduplicated enrollment as of December 31, 2004.   National percent does not include recipients or population in U.S. territories.

Medicaid Managed Care Enrollment in 2004

National Total = 27,337,457 Enrollees*

ALPHA ORDER

RANK ORDER

RANK	STATE	ENROLLEES	% of USA		RANK	STATE	ENROLLEES	% of USA
18	Alabama	490,833	1.8%		1	California	3,258,778	11.9%
48	Alaska	0	0.0%		2	New York	2,443,355	8.9%
9	Arizona	876,755	3.2%		3	Florida	1,510,004	5.5%
23	Arkansas	367,747	1.3%		4	Tennessee	1,336,691	4.9%
1	California	3,258,778	11.9%		5	Michigan	1,265,027	4.6%
22	Colorado	395,659	1.4%		6	Georgia	1,257,013	4.6%
28	Connecticut	305,689	1.1%		7	Pennsylvania	1,248,390	4.6%
40	Delaware	105,646	0.4%		8	Texas	1,194,058	4.4%
3	Florida	1,510,004	5.5%		9	Arizona	876,755	3.2%
6	Georgia	1,257,013	4.6%		10	Washington	823,479	3.0%
34	Hawaii	157,810	0.6%		11	North Carolina	782,437	2.9%
37	Idaho	138,586	0.5%		12	Louisiana	743,698	2.7%
32	Illinois	169,300	0.6%		13	Kentucky	637,890	2.3%
16	Indiana	525,900	1.9%		14	Massachusetts	604,665	2.2%
30	Iowa	265,229	1.0%		15	New Jersey	539,021	2.0%
35	Kansas	152,427	0.6%		16	Indiana	525,900	1.9%
13	Kentucky	637,890	2.3%		17	Ohio	518,327	1.9%
12	Louisiana	743,698	2.7%		18	Alabama	490,833	1.8%
33	Maine	162,318	0.6%		19	Maryland	479,134	1.8%
19	Maryland	479,134	1.8%		20	Missouri	442,622	1.6%
14	Massachusetts	604,665	2.2%		21	Virginia	415,687	1.5%
5	Michigan	1,265,027	4.6%		22	Colorado	395,659	1.4%
26	Minnesota	360,082	1.3%		23	Arkansas	367,747	1.3%
42	Mississippi	93,207	0.3%		24	Wisconsin	365,236	1.3%
20	Missouri	442,622	1.6%		25	Oklahoma	361,036	1.3%
46	Montana	57,169	0.2%		26	Minnesota	360,082	1.3%
36	Nebraska	146,854	0.5%		27	Oregon	339,208	1.2%
43	Nevada	85,090	0.3%		28	Connecticut	305,689	1.1%
48	New Hampshire	0	0.0%		29	New Mexico	267,057	1.0%
15	New Jersey	539,021	2.0%		30	Iowa	265,229	1.0%
29	New Mexico	267,057	1.0%		31	Utah	171,337	0.6%
2	New York	2,443,355	8.9%		32	Illinois	169,300	0.6%
11	North Carolina	782,437	2.9%		33	Maine	162,318	0.6%
47	North Dakota	32,767	0.1%		34	Hawaii	157,810	0.6%
17	Ohio	518,327	1.9%		35	Kansas	152,427	0.6%
25	Oklahoma	361,036	1.3%		36	Nebraska	146,854	0.5%
27	Oregon	339,208	1.2%		37	Idaho	138,586	0.5%
7	Pennsylvania	1,248,390	4.6%		38	West Virginia	132,967	0.5%
39	Rhode Island	126,028	0.5%		39	Rhode Island	126,028	0.5%
45	South Carolina	71,049	0.3%		40	Delaware	105,646	0.4%
41	South Dakota	96,777	0.4%		41	South Dakota	96,777	0.4%
4	Tennessee	1,336,691	4.9%		42	Mississippi	93,207	0.3%
8	Texas	1,194,058	4.4%		43	Nevada	85,090	0.3%
31	Utah	171,337	0.6%		44	Vermont	84,594	0.3%
44	Vermont	84,594	0.3%		45	South Carolina	71,049	0.3%
21	Virginia	415,687	1.5%		46	Montana	57,169	0.2%
10	Washington	823,479	3.0%		47	North Dakota	32,767	0.1%
38	West Virginia	132,967	0.5%		48	Alaska	0	0.0%
24	Wisconsin	365,236	1.3%		48	New Hampshire	0	0.0%
48	Wyoming	0	0.0%		48	Wyoming	0	0.0%
						District of Columbia	89,577	0.3%

Source: U.S. Department of Health and Human Services, Centers for Medicare and Medicaid Services
"Medicaid Managed Care State Enrollment" (http://new.cms.hhs.gov/MedicaidDataSourcesGenInfo/)
*Unduplicated enrollment as of December 31, 2004. Enrollment in state health care reform programs that expand eligibility beyond traditional Medicaid standards. National total includes 843,247 Medicaid managed care enrollees in Puerto Rico.

Percent of Medicaid Enrollees in Managed Care in 2004

National Percent = 61.3% of Medicaid Enrollees*

ALPHA ORDER

RANK ORDER

RANK	STATE	PERCENT		RANK	STATE	PERCENT
34	Alabama	61.3		1	Tennessee	100.0
48	Alaska	0.0		2	South Dakota	97.6
9	Arizona	88.4		3	Colorado	97.1
36	Arkansas	60.0		4	Georgia	93.8
38	California	50.5		5	Michigan	93.7
3	Colorado	97.1		6	Kentucky	92.9
16	Connecticut	75.4		7	Iowa	90.1
15	Delaware	77.1		8	Utah	89.2
24	Florida	67.5		9	Arizona	88.4
4	Georgia	93.8		10	Washington	87.5
13	Hawaii	79.7		11	Idaho	80.8
11	Idaho	80.8		12	Oregon	80.1
46	Illinois	9.6		13	Hawaii	79.7
30	Indiana	63.6		14	Louisiana	78.8
7	Iowa	90.1		15	Delaware	77.1
37	Kansas	56.9		16	Connecticut	75.4
6	Kentucky	92.9		16	Pennsylvania	75.4
14	Louisiana	78.8		18	Nebraska	73.2
35	Maine	61.0		19	New Jersey	69.6
23	Maryland	67.9		19	Rhode Island	69.6
31	Massachusetts	62.1		21	North Carolina	69.5
5	Michigan	93.7		22	Oklahoma	68.1
29	Minnesota	64.1		23	Maryland	67.9
45	Mississippi	14.5		24	Florida	67.5
42	Missouri	44.2		25	Montana	67.1
25	Montana	67.1		26	Vermont	64.9
18	Nebraska	73.2		27	Virginia	64.8
39	Nevada	50.0		28	New Mexico	64.2
48	New Hampshire	0.0		29	Minnesota	64.1
19	New Jersey	69.6		30	Indiana	63.6
28	New Mexico	64.2		31	Massachusetts	62.1
32	New York	61.8		32	New York	61.8
21	North Carolina	69.5		33	North Dakota	61.7
33	North Dakota	61.7		34	Alabama	61.3
44	Ohio	31.2		35	Maine	61.0
22	Oklahoma	68.1		36	Arkansas	60.0
12	Oregon	80.1		37	Kansas	56.9
16	Pennsylvania	75.4		38	California	50.5
19	Rhode Island	69.6		39	Nevada	50.0
47	South Carolina	8.4		40	Wisconsin	45.4
2	South Dakota	97.6		41	West Virginia	44.4
1	Tennessee	100.0		42	Missouri	44.2
43	Texas	43.3		43	Texas	43.3
8	Utah	89.2		44	Ohio	31.2
26	Vermont	64.9		45	Mississippi	14.5
27	Virginia	64.8		46	Illinois	9.6
10	Washington	87.5		47	South Carolina	8.4
41	West Virginia	44.4		48	Alaska	0.0
40	Wisconsin	45.4		48	New Hampshire	0.0
48	Wyoming	0.0		48	Wyoming	0.0
					District of Columbia	64.2

Source: MQ Press using data from U.S. Dept of Health & Human Services, Centers for Medicare and Medicaid Services "Medicaid Managed Care State Enrollment" (http://new.cms.hhs.gov/MedicaidDataSourcesGenInfo/)
*Unduplicated enrollment as of December 31, 2004. Enrollment in state health care reform programs that expand eligibility beyond traditional Medicaid standards. National percent includes Medicaid enrollees in Puerto Rico and the Virgin Islands.

Estimated Medicaid Expenditures in 2004

National Total = $259,736,000,000*

RANK	STATE	EXPENDITURES	% of USA
26	Alabama	$3,634,000,000	1.4%
46	Alaska	638,000,000	0.2%
17	Arizona	5,007,000,000	1.9%
28	Arkansas	2,760,000,000	1.1%
1	California	29,129,000,000	11.2%
30	Colorado	2,700,000,000	1.0%
16	Connecticut	5,444,000,000	2.1%
45	Delaware	728,000,000	0.3%
5	Florida	12,159,000,000	4.7%
15	Georgia	5,500,000,000	2.1%
43	Hawaii	911,000,000	0.4%
42	Idaho	928,000,000	0.4%
7	Illinois	11,590,000,000	4.5%
21	Indiana	4,378,000,000	1.7%
33	Iowa	2,124,000,000	0.8%
36	Kansas	1,727,000,000	0.7%
23	Kentucky	4,009,000,000	1.5%
19	Louisiana	4,772,000,000	1.8%
35	Maine	1,772,000,000	0.7%
20	Maryland	4,713,000,000	1.8%
12	Massachusetts	5,856,000,000	2.3%
8	Michigan	8,458,000,000	3.3%
18	Minnesota	4,983,000,000	1.9%
27	Mississippi	3,175,000,000	1.2%
14	Missouri	5,725,000,000	2.2%
47	Montana	634,000,000	0.2%
38	Nebraska	1,317,000,000	0.5%
40	Nevada	1,172,000,000	0.5%
41	New Hampshire	1,080,000,000	0.4%
9	New Jersey	7,538,000,000	2.9%
32	New Mexico	2,287,000,000	0.9%
2	New York	27,562,000,000	10.6%
11	North Carolina	7,011,000,000	2.7%
49	North Dakota	508,000,000	0.2%
6	Ohio	12,073,000,000	4.6%
31	Oklahoma	2,395,000,000	0.9%
29	Oregon	2,704,000,000	1.0%
4	Pennsylvania	14,375,000,000	5.5%
37	Rhode Island	1,568,000,000	0.6%
25	South Carolina	3,808,000,000	1.5%
48	South Dakota	557,000,000	0.2%
10	Tennessee	7,246,000,000	2.8%
3	Texas	14,903,000,000	5.7%
39	Utah	1,265,000,000	0.5%
44	Vermont	795,000,000	0.3%
24	Virginia	3,896,000,000	1.5%
13	Washington	5,783,000,000	2.2%
34	West Virginia	1,923,000,000	0.7%
22	Wisconsin	4,148,000,000	1.6%
50	Wyoming	368,000,000	0.1%

RANK	STATE	EXPENDITURES	% of USA
1	California	$29,129,000,000	11.2%
2	New York	27,562,000,000	10.6%
3	Texas	14,903,000,000	5.7%
4	Pennsylvania	14,375,000,000	5.5%
5	Florida	12,159,000,000	4.7%
6	Ohio	12,073,000,000	4.6%
7	Illinois	11,590,000,000	4.5%
8	Michigan	8,458,000,000	3.3%
9	New Jersey	7,538,000,000	2.9%
10	Tennessee	7,246,000,000	2.8%
11	North Carolina	7,011,000,000	2.7%
12	Massachusetts	5,856,000,000	2.3%
13	Washington	5,783,000,000	2.2%
14	Missouri	5,725,000,000	2.2%
15	Georgia	5,500,000,000	2.1%
16	Connecticut	5,444,000,000	2.1%
17	Arizona	5,007,000,000	1.9%
18	Minnesota	4,983,000,000	1.9%
19	Louisiana	4,772,000,000	1.8%
20	Maryland	4,713,000,000	1.8%
21	Indiana	4,378,000,000	1.7%
22	Wisconsin	4,148,000,000	1.6%
23	Kentucky	4,009,000,000	1.5%
24	Virginia	3,896,000,000	1.5%
25	South Carolina	3,808,000,000	1.5%
26	Alabama	3,634,000,000	1.4%
27	Mississippi	3,175,000,000	1.2%
28	Arkansas	2,760,000,000	1.1%
29	Oregon	2,704,000,000	1.0%
30	Colorado	2,700,000,000	1.0%
31	Oklahoma	2,395,000,000	0.9%
32	New Mexico	2,287,000,000	0.9%
33	Iowa	2,124,000,000	0.8%
34	West Virginia	1,923,000,000	0.7%
35	Maine	1,772,000,000	0.7%
36	Kansas	1,727,000,000	0.7%
37	Rhode Island	1,568,000,000	0.6%
38	Nebraska	1,317,000,000	0.5%
39	Utah	1,265,000,000	0.5%
40	Nevada	1,172,000,000	0.5%
41	New Hampshire	1,080,000,000	0.4%
42	Idaho	928,000,000	0.4%
43	Hawaii	911,000,000	0.4%
44	Vermont	795,000,000	0.3%
45	Delaware	728,000,000	0.3%
46	Alaska	638,000,000	0.2%
47	Montana	634,000,000	0.2%
48	South Dakota	557,000,000	0.2%
49	North Dakota	508,000,000	0.2%
50	Wyoming	368,000,000	0.1%
	District of Columbia**	NA	NA

Source: National Association of State Budget Officers
    "2003 State Expenditure Report" (http://www.nasbo.org/publications/PDFs/2003ExpendReport.pdf)
Estimates for fiscal year 2004.
**Not available.*

Estimated Per Capita Medicaid Expenditures in 2004

National Per Capita = $886*

ALPHA ORDER

RANK ORDER

RANK	STATE	PER CAPITA		RANK	STATE	PER CAPITA
30	Alabama	$803		1	Connecticut	$1,556
16	Alaska	970		2	Rhode Island	1,452
23	Arizona	872		3	New York	1,430
13	Arkansas	1,004		4	Maine	1,348
29	California	813		5	Vermont	1,280
47	Colorado	587		6	Tennessee	1,230
1	Connecticut	1,556		7	New Mexico	1,202
22	Delaware	877		8	Pennsylvania	1,160
40	Florida	699		9	Mississippi	1,095
46	Georgia	617		10	West Virginia	1,061
37	Hawaii	722		11	Louisiana	1,059
43	Idaho	665		12	Ohio	1,054
20	Illinois	912		13	Arkansas	1,004
39	Indiana	703		14	Missouri	994
38	Iowa	719		15	Minnesota	978
45	Kansas	632		16	Alaska	970
17	Kentucky	968		17	Kentucky	968
11	Louisiana	1,059		18	Washington	932
4	Maine	1,348		19	Massachusetts	914
25	Maryland	847		20	Illinois	912
19	Massachusetts	914		21	South Carolina	907
26	Michigan	837		22	Delaware	877
15	Minnesota	978		23	Arizona	872
9	Mississippi	1,095		24	New Jersey	868
14	Missouri	994		25	Maryland	847
41	Montana	684		26	Michigan	837
32	Nebraska	754		27	New Hampshire	831
50	Nevada	502		28	North Carolina	821
27	New Hampshire	831		29	California	813
24	New Jersey	868		30	Alabama	803
7	New Mexico	1,202		31	North Dakota	798
3	New York	1,430		32	Nebraska	754
28	North Carolina	821		32	Wisconsin	754
31	North Dakota	798		34	Oregon	753
12	Ohio	1,054		35	Wyoming	727
42	Oklahoma	680		36	South Dakota	723
34	Oregon	753		37	Hawaii	722
8	Pennsylvania	1,160		38	Iowa	719
2	Rhode Island	1,452		39	Indiana	703
21	South Carolina	907		40	Florida	699
36	South Dakota	723		41	Montana	684
6	Tennessee	1,230		42	Oklahoma	680
44	Texas	663		43	Idaho	665
48	Utah	523		44	Texas	663
5	Vermont	1,280		45	Kansas	632
49	Virginia	521		46	Georgia	617
18	Washington	932		47	Colorado	587
10	West Virginia	1,061		48	Utah	523
32	Wisconsin	754		49	Virginia	521
35	Wyoming	727		50	Nevada	502

District of Columbia**   NA

Source: Morgan Quitno Press using data from National Association of State Budget Officers
    "2003 State Expenditure Report" (http://www.nasbo.org/publications/PDFs/2003ExpendReport.pdf)
*Estimates for fiscal year 2004.
**Not available.

Estimated Medicaid Expenditures as a Percent of Total Expenditures in 2004

National Percent = 21.9%*

ALPHA ORDER				RANK ORDER		
RANK	STATE	PERCENT		RANK	STATE	PERCENT
35	Alabama	18.2		1	Tennessee	33.3
49	Alaska	8.4		2	Missouri	30.7
16	Arizona	24.1		3	Pennsylvania	29.5
32	Arkansas	18.9		4	Maine	29.0
36	California	17.6		5	New York	28.3
25	Colorado	20.2		6	Illinois	28.1
12	Connecticut	24.8		7	Vermont	27.5
48	Delaware	11.8		8	New Hampshire	26.4
18	Florida	22.5		9	Mississippi	26.3
30	Georgia	19.2		10	Rhode Island	25.5
46	Hawaii	12.0		11	Texas	25.1
32	Idaho	18.9		12	Connecticut	24.8
6	Illinois	28.1		12	Ohio	24.8
20	Indiana	21.6		14	South Carolina	24.7
43	Iowa	15.6		15	Louisiana	24.5
40	Kansas	16.9		16	Arizona	24.1
24	Kentucky	20.5		17	North Carolina	23.9
15	Louisiana	24.5		18	Florida	22.5
4	Maine	29.0		19	Washington	22.2
28	Maryland	19.6		20	Indiana	21.6
22	Massachusetts	21.4		21	Michigan	21.5
21	Michigan	21.5		22	Massachusetts	21.4
23	Minnesota	21.2		23	Minnesota	21.2
9	Mississippi	26.3		24	Kentucky	20.5
2	Missouri	30.7		25	Colorado	20.2
42	Montana	15.9		26	New Jersey	20.1
38	Nebraska	17.2		27	South Dakota	19.8
34	Nevada	18.7		28	Maryland	19.6
8	New Hampshire	26.4		29	New Mexico	19.4
26	New Jersey	20.1		30	Georgia	19.2
29	New Mexico	19.4		30	North Dakota	19.2
5	New York	28.3		32	Arkansas	18.9
17	North Carolina	23.9		32	Idaho	18.9
30	North Dakota	19.2		34	Nevada	18.7
12	Ohio	24.8		35	Alabama	18.2
39	Oklahoma	17.1		36	California	17.6
45	Oregon	13.7		37	Wisconsin	17.4
3	Pennsylvania	29.5		38	Nebraska	17.2
10	Rhode Island	25.5		39	Oklahoma	17.1
14	South Carolina	24.7		40	Kansas	16.9
27	South Dakota	19.8		41	Utah	16.0
1	Tennessee	33.3		42	Montana	15.9
11	Texas	25.1		43	Iowa	15.6
41	Utah	16.0		44	Virginia	13.9
7	Vermont	27.5		45	Oregon	13.7
44	Virginia	13.9		46	Hawaii	12.0
19	Washington	22.2		47	West Virginia	11.9
47	West Virginia	11.9		48	Delaware	11.8
37	Wisconsin	17.4		49	Alaska	8.4
50	Wyoming	8.3		50	Wyoming	8.3
					District of Columbia**	NA

Source: National Association of State Budget Officers
   "2003 State Expenditure Report" (http://www.nasbo.org/publications/PDFs/2003ExpendReport.pdf)
*Estimates for fiscal year 2004.
**Not available.

Percent Change in Medicaid Expenditures: 2003 to 2004

National Percent Change = 6.6% Increase*

ALPHA ORDER				RANK ORDER		
RANK	STATE	PERCENT CHANGE		RANK	STATE	PERCENT CHANGE
41	Alabama	1.8		1	South Dakota	30.4
50	Alaska	(18.8)		2	Arizona	23.7
2	Arizona	23.7		3	Illinois	21.1
10	Arkansas	11.9		4	Hawaii	17.1
47	California	(2.3)		5	Maryland	15.8
8	Colorado	14.6		6	Utah	15.4
33	Connecticut	5.0		7	Vermont	15.1
21	Delaware	8.7		8	Colorado	14.6
9	Florida	12.4		9	Florida	12.4
13	Georgia	11.5		10	Arkansas	11.9
4	Hawaii	17.1		11	New Mexico	11.8
20	Idaho	8.8		12	Ohio	11.6
3	Illinois	21.1		13	Georgia	11.5
16	Indiana	10.6		14	Montana	11.2
49	Iowa	(12.8)		15	Wyoming	10.8
25	Kansas	6.9		16	Indiana	10.6
32	Kentucky	5.1		16	West Virginia	10.6
24	Louisiana	7.2		18	Texas	9.9
39	Maine	3.5		19	New York	8.9
5	Maryland	15.8		20	Idaho	8.8
23	Massachusetts	8.0		21	Delaware	8.7
27	Michigan	6.3		22	Rhode Island	8.1
36	Minnesota	3.8		23	Massachusetts	8.0
31	Mississippi	5.3		24	Louisiana	7.2
45	Missouri	0.6		25	Kansas	6.9
14	Montana	11.2		25	Virginia	6.9
40	Nebraska	2.2		27	Michigan	6.3
43	Nevada	1.0		27	North Dakota	6.3
45	New Hampshire	0.6		29	Tennessee	5.6
42	New Jersey	1.1		30	Pennsylvania	5.5
11	New Mexico	11.8		31	Mississippi	5.3
19	New York	8.9		32	Kentucky	5.1
34	North Carolina	4.0		33	Connecticut	5.0
27	North Dakota	6.3		34	North Carolina	4.0
12	Ohio	11.6		35	Wisconsin	3.9
44	Oklahoma	0.8		36	Minnesota	3.8
48	Oregon	(4.3)		37	South Carolina	3.7
30	Pennsylvania	5.5		38	Washington	3.6
22	Rhode Island	8.1		39	Maine	3.5
37	South Carolina	3.7		40	Nebraska	2.2
1	South Dakota	30.4		41	Alabama	1.8
29	Tennessee	5.6		42	New Jersey	1.1
18	Texas	9.9		43	Nevada	1.0
6	Utah	15.4		44	Oklahoma	0.8
7	Vermont	15.1		45	Missouri	0.6
25	Virginia	6.9		45	New Hampshire	0.6
38	Washington	3.6		47	California	(2.3)
16	West Virginia	10.6		48	Oregon	(4.3)
35	Wisconsin	3.9		49	Iowa	(12.8)
15	Wyoming	10.8		50	Alaska	(18.8)
					District of Columbia**	NA

Source: National Association of State Budget Officers
"2003 State Expenditure Report" (http://www.nasbo.org/publications/PDFs/2003ExpendReport.pdf)
*Estimates for fiscal year 2004.
**Not available.

Medicaid Expenditures in 2002

National Total = $258,215,703,947*

ALPHA ORDER

RANK	STATE	EXPENDITURES	% of USA
26	Alabama	$3,194,533,347	1.2%
44	Alaska	739,298,984	0.3%
23	Arizona	3,756,081,872	1.5%
32	Arkansas	2,341,289,559	0.9%
2	California	29,055,962,876	11.3%
31	Colorado	2,412,662,030	0.9%
24	Connecticut	3,601,447,243	1.4%
46	Delaware	688,223,482	0.3%
5	Florida	10,399,890,023	4.0%
12	Georgia	6,543,869,834	2.5%
43	Hawaii	804,479,518	0.3%
42	Idaho	836,197,766	0.3%
7	Illinois	9,509,760,372	3.7%
18	Indiana	4,629,595,331	1.8%
29	Iowa	2,654,955,251	1.0%
33	Kansas	1,956,485,547	0.8%
22	Kentucky	3,863,644,180	1.5%
16	Louisiana	5,022,402,591	1.9%
36	Maine	1,489,946,220	0.6%
21	Maryland	3,887,964,555	1.5%
8	Massachusetts	8,380,230,124	3.2%
10	Michigan	7,398,430,918	2.9%
17	Minnesota	4,662,225,494	1.8%
27	Mississippi	2,964,678,399	1.1%
15	Missouri	5,576,240,323	2.2%
47	Montana	598,343,100	0.2%
38	Nebraska	1,421,120,229	0.6%
41	Nevada	864,326,670	0.3%
39	New Hampshire	1,074,659,079	0.4%
9	New Jersey	7,986,725,420	3.1%
34	New Mexico	1,840,381,319	0.7%
1	New York	37,476,829,499	14.5%
11	North Carolina	7,025,724,163	2.7%
49	North Dakota	483,927,418	0.2%
6	Ohio	9,977,722,136	3.9%
30	Oklahoma	2,427,516,069	0.9%
28	Oregon	2,797,752,585	1.1%
4	Pennsylvania	12,687,816,278	4.9%
37	Rhode Island	1,421,377,818	0.6%
25	South Carolina	3,426,386,192	1.3%
48	South Dakota	565,559,484	0.2%
13	Tennessee	6,032,137,360	2.3%
3	Texas	14,230,245,988	5.5%
40	Utah	1,062,248,510	0.4%
45	Vermont	715,911,686	0.3%
20	Virginia	3,999,512,661	1.5%
14	Washington	5,659,384,993	2.2%
35	West Virginia	1,657,175,989	0.6%
19	Wisconsin	4,379,588,928	1.7%
50	Wyoming	298,469,532	0.1%

RANK ORDER

RANK	STATE	EXPENDITURES	% of USA
1	New York	$37,476,829,499	14.5%
2	California	29,055,962,876	11.3%
3	Texas	14,230,245,988	5.5%
4	Pennsylvania	12,687,816,278	4.9%
5	Florida	10,399,890,023	4.0%
6	Ohio	9,977,722,136	3.9%
7	Illinois	9,509,760,372	3.7%
8	Massachusetts	8,380,230,124	3.2%
9	New Jersey	7,986,725,420	3.1%
10	Michigan	7,398,430,918	2.9%
11	North Carolina	7,025,724,163	2.7%
12	Georgia	6,543,869,834	2.5%
13	Tennessee	6,032,137,360	2.3%
14	Washington	5,659,384,993	2.2%
15	Missouri	5,576,240,323	2.2%
16	Louisiana	5,022,402,591	1.9%
17	Minnesota	4,662,225,494	1.8%
18	Indiana	4,629,595,331	1.8%
19	Wisconsin	4,379,588,928	1.7%
20	Virginia	3,999,512,661	1.5%
21	Maryland	3,887,964,555	1.5%
22	Kentucky	3,863,644,180	1.5%
23	Arizona	3,756,081,872	1.5%
24	Connecticut	3,601,447,243	1.4%
25	South Carolina	3,426,386,192	1.3%
26	Alabama	3,194,533,347	1.2%
27	Mississippi	2,964,678,399	1.1%
28	Oregon	2,797,752,585	1.1%
29	Iowa	2,654,955,251	1.0%
30	Oklahoma	2,427,516,069	0.9%
31	Colorado	2,412,662,030	0.9%
32	Arkansas	2,341,289,559	0.9%
33	Kansas	1,956,485,547	0.8%
34	New Mexico	1,840,381,319	0.7%
35	West Virginia	1,657,175,989	0.6%
36	Maine	1,489,946,220	0.6%
37	Rhode Island	1,421,377,818	0.6%
38	Nebraska	1,421,120,229	0.6%
39	New Hampshire	1,074,659,079	0.4%
40	Utah	1,062,248,510	0.4%
41	Nevada	864,326,670	0.3%
42	Idaho	836,197,766	0.3%
43	Hawaii	804,479,518	0.3%
44	Alaska	739,298,984	0.3%
45	Vermont	715,911,686	0.3%
46	Delaware	688,223,482	0.3%
47	Montana	598,343,100	0.2%
48	South Dakota	565,559,484	0.2%
49	North Dakota	483,927,418	0.2%
50	Wyoming	298,469,532	0.1%
	District of Columbia	1,081,784,750	0.4%

Source: U.S. Department of Health and Human Services, Centers for Medicare and Medicaid Services
"Medicaid Financial Statistics Tables (CMS-64 Report)"
*Revised figures for fiscal year 2002. National total includes $652,580,252 in expenditures in U.S. territories.
Includes Medical Assistance Payments and Administrative Costs.

Per Capita Medicaid Expenditures in 2002

National Per Capita = $894*

ALPHA ORDER

RANK	STATE	PER CAPITA
38	Alabama	$713
5	Alaska	1,154
40	Arizona	691
21	Arkansas	865
26	California	830
48	Colorado	536
9	Connecticut	1,041
22	Delaware	854
44	Florida	624
31	Georgia	763
43	Hawaii	652
45	Idaho	622
32	Illinois	756
33	Indiana	752
19	Iowa	905
36	Kansas	721
14	Kentucky	945
7	Louisiana	1,122
6	Maine	1,149
37	Maryland	714
3	Massachusetts	1,307
35	Michigan	737
17	Minnesota	928
10	Mississippi	1,034
13	Missouri	982
41	Montana	657
27	Nebraska	823
50	Nevada	399
24	New Hampshire	843
16	New Jersey	931
12	New Mexico	992
1	New York	1,956
23	North Carolina	845
30	North Dakota	764
20	Ohio	875
39	Oklahoma	696
29	Oregon	794
11	Pennsylvania	1,029
2	Rhode Island	1,330
25	South Carolina	835
34	South Dakota	744
8	Tennessee	1,042
42	Texas	655
49	Utah	455
4	Vermont	1,162
47	Virginia	549
15	Washington	933
18	West Virginia	918
28	Wisconsin	805
46	Wyoming	598

RANK ORDER

RANK	STATE	PER CAPITA
1	New York	$1,956
2	Rhode Island	1,330
3	Massachusetts	1,307
4	Vermont	1,162
5	Alaska	1,154
6	Maine	1,149
7	Louisiana	1,122
8	Tennessee	1,042
9	Connecticut	1,041
10	Mississippi	1,034
11	Pennsylvania	1,029
12	New Mexico	992
13	Missouri	982
14	Kentucky	945
15	Washington	933
16	New Jersey	931
17	Minnesota	928
18	West Virginia	918
19	Iowa	905
20	Ohio	875
21	Arkansas	865
22	Delaware	854
23	North Carolina	845
24	New Hampshire	843
25	South Carolina	835
26	California	830
27	Nebraska	823
28	Wisconsin	805
29	Oregon	794
30	North Dakota	764
31	Georgia	763
32	Illinois	756
33	Indiana	752
34	South Dakota	744
35	Michigan	737
36	Kansas	721
37	Maryland	714
38	Alabama	713
39	Oklahoma	696
40	Arizona	691
41	Montana	657
42	Texas	655
43	Hawaii	652
44	Florida	624
45	Idaho	622
46	Wyoming	598
47	Virginia	549
48	Colorado	536
49	Utah	455
50	Nevada	399

District of Columbia 1,916

Source: MQ Press using data from U.S. Dept of Health & Human Services, Centers for Medicare and Medicaid Services "Medicaid Financial Statistics Tables (CMS-64 Report)"
*Revised figures for fiscal year 2002. National figure does not include expenditures or enrollees in U.S. territories.
Includes Medical Assistance Payments and Administrative Costs.

Medicaid Expenditures per Beneficiary in 2002

National Rate = $5,235 per Beneficiary*

ALPHA ORDER

RANK	STATE	PER BENEFICIARY
40	Alabama	$4,174
12	Alaska	6,743
37	Arizona	4,276
43	Arkansas	4,042
50	California	3,124
17	Colorado	5,665
7	Connecticut	7,518
42	Delaware	4,117
46	Florida	3,886
45	Georgia	3,997
44	Hawaii	4,023
32	Idaho	4,738
21	Illinois	5,493
22	Indiana	5,450
6	Iowa	7,529
11	Kansas	6,762
31	Kentucky	4,780
19	Louisiana	5,588
24	Maine	5,402
18	Maryland	5,614
4	Massachusetts	7,864
27	Michigan	5,103
8	Minnesota	7,512
41	Mississippi	4,161
25	Missouri	5,382
16	Montana	5,775
20	Nebraska	5,556
38	Nevada	4,272
1	New Hampshire	10,320
3	New Jersey	8,368
36	New Mexico	4,362
2	New York	9,559
26	North Carolina	5,184
10	North Dakota	6,900
14	Ohio	6,025
48	Oklahoma	3,844
35	Oregon	4,502
5	Pennsylvania	7,797
9	Rhode Island	7,142
39	South Carolina	4,235
30	South Dakota	4,808
49	Tennessee	3,482
29	Texas	4,820
47	Utah	3,867
33	Vermont	4,657
15	Virginia	6,012
23	Washington	5,447
34	West Virginia	4,577
13	Wisconsin	6,114
28	Wyoming	5,053

RANK ORDER

RANK	STATE	PER BENEFICIARY
1	New Hampshire	$10,320
2	New York	9,559
3	New Jersey	8,368
4	Massachusetts	7,864
5	Pennsylvania	7,797
6	Iowa	7,529
7	Connecticut	7,518
8	Minnesota	7,512
9	Rhode Island	7,142
10	North Dakota	6,900
11	Kansas	6,762
12	Alaska	6,743
13	Wisconsin	6,114
14	Ohio	6,025
15	Virginia	6,012
16	Montana	5,775
17	Colorado	5,665
18	Maryland	5,614
19	Louisiana	5,588
20	Nebraska	5,556
21	Illinois	5,493
22	Indiana	5,450
23	Washington	5,447
24	Maine	5,402
25	Missouri	5,382
26	North Carolina	5,184
27	Michigan	5,103
28	Wyoming	5,053
29	Texas	4,820
30	South Dakota	4,808
31	Kentucky	4,780
32	Idaho	4,738
33	Vermont	4,657
34	West Virginia	4,577
35	Oregon	4,502
36	New Mexico	4,362
37	Arizona	4,276
38	Nevada	4,272
39	South Carolina	4,235
40	Alabama	4,174
41	Mississippi	4,161
42	Delaware	4,117
43	Arkansas	4,042
44	Hawaii	4,023
45	Georgia	3,997
46	Florida	3,886
47	Utah	3,867
48	Oklahoma	3,844
49	Tennessee	3,482
50	California	3,124

| | District of Columbia | 7,498 |

Source: MQ Press using data from U.S. Dept of Health & Human Services, Centers for Medicare and Medicaid Services
"Medicaid Financial Statistics Tables (CMS-64 Report)"
*Revised figures for fiscal year 2002. National figure includes expenditures and enrollees in U.S. territories.
Includes Medical Assistance Payments and Administrative Costs.

Federal Medicaid Matching Fund Rate for 2006

National Average = 72.13% of States' Funds Matched by Federal Government*

ALPHA ORDER				RANK ORDER		
RANK	STATE	RATE		RANK	STATE	RATE
9	Alabama	78.66		1	Mississippi	83.20
37	Alaska	65.11		2	Arkansas	81.64
13	Arizona	76.89		3	West Virginia	81.09
2	Arkansas	81.64		4	New Mexico	79.81
39	California	65.00		5	Utah	79.53
39	Colorado	65.00		6	Montana	79.38
39	Connecticut	65.00		7	Idaho	78.94
38	Delaware	65.06		8	Louisiana	78.85
28	Florida	71.22		9	Alabama	78.66
24	Georgia	72.42		10	South Carolina	78.52
29	Hawaii	71.17		11	Kentucky	78.48
7	Idaho	78.94		12	Oklahoma	77.54
39	Illinois	65.00		13	Arizona	76.89
19	Indiana	74.09		14	North Dakota	76.10
17	Iowa	74.53		15	South Dakota	75.55
25	Kansas	72.29		16	Tennessee	74.79
11	Kentucky	78.48		17	Iowa	74.53
8	Louisiana	78.85		18	North Carolina	74.44
20	Maine	74.03		19	Indiana	74.09
39	Maryland	65.00		20	Maine	74.03
39	Massachusetts	65.00		21	Missouri	73.35
32	Michigan	69.61		22	Oregon	73.10
39	Minnesota	65.00		23	Texas	72.46
1	Mississippi	83.20		24	Georgia	72.42
21	Missouri	73.35		25	Kansas	72.29
6	Montana	79.38		26	Ohio	71.92
27	Nebraska	71.78		27	Nebraska	71.78
34	Nevada	68.33		28	Florida	71.22
39	New Hampshire	65.00		29	Hawaii	71.17
39	New Jersey	65.00		30	Vermont	70.94
4	New Mexico	79.81		31	Wisconsin	70.36
39	New York	65.00		32	Michigan	69.61
18	North Carolina	74.44		33	Pennsylvania	68.54
14	North Dakota	76.10		34	Nevada	68.33
26	Ohio	71.92		35	Rhode Island	68.12
12	Oklahoma	77.54		36	Wyoming	67.96
22	Oregon	73.10		37	Alaska	65.11
33	Pennsylvania	68.54		38	Delaware	65.06
35	Rhode Island	68.12		39	California	65.00
10	South Carolina	78.52		39	Colorado	65.00
15	South Dakota	75.55		39	Connecticut	65.00
16	Tennessee	74.79		39	Illinois	65.00
23	Texas	72.46		39	Maryland	65.00
5	Utah	79.53		39	Massachusetts	65.00
30	Vermont	70.94		39	Minnesota	65.00
39	Virginia	65.00		39	New Hampshire	65.00
39	Washington	65.00		39	New Jersey	65.00
3	West Virginia	81.09		39	New York	65.00
31	Wisconsin	70.36		39	Virginia	65.00
36	Wyoming	67.96		39	Washington	65.00
					District of Columbia	79.00

*Source: U.S. Department of Health and Human Services, Centers for Medicare and Medicaid Services
"Enhanced Federal Medical Assistance Percentages" (http://aspe.os.dhhs.gov/health/fmap06.htm)
*For fiscal year 2006. These are "enhanced" matching rates established by the Children's Health Insurance
Program, signed into law in August 1997. Sixty-five percent is the minimum. National average is a simple average of
the 51 individual rates and is not weighted for population or funds.*

State and Local Government Expenditures for Hospitals in 2002

National Total = $87,247,337,000*

ALPHA ORDER

RANK	STATE	EXPENDITURES	% of USA
7	Alabama	$3,099,637,000	3.6%
44	Alaska	96,212,000	0.1%
34	Arizona	469,395,000	0.5%
31	Arkansas	626,078,000	0.7%
1	California	11,147,510,000	12.8%
26	Colorado	1,080,688,000	1.2%
23	Connecticut	1,379,290,000	1.6%
47	Delaware	68,578,000	0.1%
4	Florida	4,306,698,000	4.9%
6	Georgia	3,498,875,000	4.0%
41	Hawaii	184,789,000	0.2%
37	Idaho	445,773,000	0.5%
12	Illinois	2,209,318,000	2.5%
13	Indiana	2,201,067,000	2.5%
21	Iowa	1,452,361,000	1.7%
32	Kansas	624,755,000	0.7%
29	Kentucky	717,087,000	0.8%
8	Louisiana	3,066,062,000	3.5%
42	Maine	116,256,000	0.1%
39	Maryland	400,821,000	0.5%
25	Massachusetts	1,178,524,000	1.4%
16	Michigan	2,069,991,000	2.4%
24	Minnesota	1,180,564,000	1.4%
18	Mississippi	1,865,839,000	2.1%
19	Missouri	1,730,692,000	2.0%
45	Montana	87,915,000	0.1%
35	Nebraska	468,136,000	0.5%
30	Nevada	665,836,000	0.8%
48	New Hampshire	45,807,000	0.1%
20	New Jersey	1,496,652,000	1.7%
36	New Mexico	460,797,000	0.5%
2	New York	9,189,139,000	10.5%
5	North Carolina	4,088,445,000	4.7%
49	North Dakota	44,424,000	0.1%
9	Ohio	2,373,885,000	2.7%
28	Oklahoma	834,967,000	1.0%
22	Oregon	1,424,243,000	1.6%
15	Pennsylvania	2,148,955,000	2.5%
43	Rhode Island	114,204,000	0.1%
10	South Carolina	2,364,115,000	2.7%
46	South Dakota	75,162,000	0.1%
11	Tennessee	2,261,897,000	2.6%
3	Texas	7,418,558,000	8.5%
33	Utah	529,725,000	0.6%
50	Vermont	9,485,000	0.0%
17	Virginia	2,048,955,000	2.3%
14	Washington	2,161,826,000	2.5%
40	West Virginia	285,092,000	0.3%
27	Wisconsin	851,907,000	1.0%
38	Wyoming	403,430,000	0.5%

RANK ORDER

RANK	STATE	EXPENDITURES	% of USA
1	California	$11,147,510,000	12.8%
2	New York	9,189,139,000	10.5%
3	Texas	7,418,558,000	8.5%
4	Florida	4,306,698,000	4.9%
5	North Carolina	4,088,445,000	4.7%
6	Georgia	3,498,875,000	4.0%
7	Alabama	3,099,637,000	3.6%
8	Louisiana	3,066,062,000	3.5%
9	Ohio	2,373,885,000	2.7%
10	South Carolina	2,364,115,000	2.7%
11	Tennessee	2,261,897,000	2.6%
12	Illinois	2,209,318,000	2.5%
13	Indiana	2,201,067,000	2.5%
14	Washington	2,161,826,000	2.5%
15	Pennsylvania	2,148,955,000	2.5%
16	Michigan	2,069,991,000	2.4%
17	Virginia	2,048,955,000	2.3%
18	Mississippi	1,865,839,000	2.1%
19	Missouri	1,730,692,000	2.0%
20	New Jersey	1,496,652,000	1.7%
21	Iowa	1,452,361,000	1.7%
22	Oregon	1,424,243,000	1.6%
23	Connecticut	1,379,290,000	1.6%
24	Minnesota	1,180,564,000	1.4%
25	Massachusetts	1,178,524,000	1.4%
26	Colorado	1,080,688,000	1.2%
27	Wisconsin	851,907,000	1.0%
28	Oklahoma	834,967,000	1.0%
29	Kentucky	717,087,000	0.8%
30	Nevada	665,836,000	0.8%
31	Arkansas	626,078,000	0.7%
32	Kansas	624,755,000	0.7%
33	Utah	529,725,000	0.6%
34	Arizona	469,395,000	0.5%
35	Nebraska	468,136,000	0.5%
36	New Mexico	460,797,000	0.5%
37	Idaho	445,773,000	0.5%
38	Wyoming	403,430,000	0.5%
39	Maryland	400,821,000	0.5%
40	West Virginia	285,092,000	0.3%
41	Hawaii	184,789,000	0.2%
42	Maine	116,256,000	0.1%
43	Rhode Island	114,204,000	0.1%
44	Alaska	96,212,000	0.1%
45	Montana	87,915,000	0.1%
46	South Dakota	75,162,000	0.1%
47	Delaware	68,578,000	0.1%
48	New Hampshire	45,807,000	0.1%
49	North Dakota	44,424,000	0.1%
50	Vermont	9,485,000	0.0%

District of Columbia 176,920,000 0.2%

Source: U.S. Bureau of the Census, Governments Division
"State and Local Government Finances: 2002 Census" (http://www.census.gov/govs/www/estimate02.html)
*Financing, construction, acquisition, maintenance or operation of hospital facilities, provision of hospital care and support of public or private hospitals.

Per Capita State and Local Government Expenditures for Hospitals in 2002

National Per Capita = $303*

ALPHA ORDER

ALPHA ORDER

RANK	STATE	PER CAPITA		RANK	STATE	PER CAPITA
2	Alabama	$692		1	Wyoming	$808
39	Alaska	150		2	Alabama	692
45	Arizona	86		3	Louisiana	685
27	Arkansas	231		4	Mississippi	651
17	California	319		5	South Carolina	576
24	Colorado	240		6	Iowa	495
11	Connecticut	399		7	North Carolina	492
46	Delaware	85		8	New York	480
22	Florida	258		9	Georgia	410
9	Georgia	410		10	Oregon	404
39	Hawaii	150		11	Connecticut	399
16	Idaho	332		12	Tennessee	391
33	Illinois	176		13	Indiana	357
13	Indiana	357		14	Washington	356
6	Iowa	495		15	Texas	342
28	Kansas	230		16	Idaho	332
34	Kentucky	175		17	California	319
3	Louisiana	685		18	Nevada	307
44	Maine	90		19	Missouri	305
47	Maryland	74		20	Virginia	282
32	Massachusetts	184		21	Nebraska	271
31	Michigan	206		22	Florida	258
26	Minnesota	235		23	New Mexico	248
4	Mississippi	651		24	Colorado	240
19	Missouri	305		25	Oklahoma	239
43	Montana	97		26	Minnesota	235
21	Nebraska	271		27	Arkansas	231
18	Nevada	307		28	Kansas	230
49	New Hampshire	36		29	Utah	228
35	New Jersey	174		30	Ohio	208
23	New Mexico	248		31	Michigan	206
8	New York	480		32	Massachusetts	184
7	North Carolina	492		33	Illinois	176
48	North Dakota	70		34	Kentucky	175
30	Ohio	208		35	New Jersey	174
25	Oklahoma	239		35	Pennsylvania	174
10	Oregon	404		37	West Virginia	158
35	Pennsylvania	174		38	Wisconsin	157
41	Rhode Island	107		39	Alaska	150
5	South Carolina	576		39	Hawaii	150
42	South Dakota	99		41	Rhode Island	107
12	Tennessee	391		42	South Dakota	99
15	Texas	342		43	Montana	97
29	Utah	228		44	Maine	90
50	Vermont	15		45	Arizona	86
20	Virginia	282		46	Delaware	85
14	Washington	356		47	Maryland	74
37	West Virginia	158		48	North Dakota	70
38	Wisconsin	157		49	New Hampshire	36
1	Wyoming	808		50	Vermont	15
					District of Columbia	313

Source: Morgan Quitno Press using data from U.S. Bureau of the Census, Governments Division
    "State and Local Government Finances: 2002 Census" (http://www.census.gov/govs/www/estimate02.html)
*Financing, construction, acquisition, maintenance or operation of hospital facilities, provision of hospital care and support of public or private hospitals.

Percent of State and Local Government Expenditures
Used for Hospitals in 2002
National Percent = 5.0%*

	ALPHA ORDER				RANK ORDER	
RANK	**STATE**	**PERCENT**		**RANK**	**STATE**	**PERCENT**
1	Alabama	12.6		1	Alabama	12.6
47	Alaska	1.1		1	Louisiana	12.6
40	Arizona	1.9		3	Mississippi	12.1
21	Arkansas	4.8		4	Wyoming	10.5
23	California	4.7		5	South Carolina	9.9
27	Colorado	4.0		6	North Carolina	9.2
15	Connecticut	5.7		7	Iowa	8.5
45	Delaware	1.3		8	Georgia	7.8
20	Florida	4.9		8	Tennessee	7.8
8	Georgia	7.8		10	Indiana	6.7
39	Hawaii	2.2		11	Idaho	6.6
11	Idaho	6.6		11	Texas	6.6
33	Illinois	3.0		13	Oregon	6.2
10	Indiana	6.7		14	Missouri	6.0
7	Iowa	8.5		15	Connecticut	5.7
25	Kansas	4.2		15	Nevada	5.7
32	Kentucky	3.3		15	New York	5.7
1	Louisiana	12.6		18	Washington	5.6
44	Maine	1.5		19	Virginia	5.2
45	Maryland	1.3		20	Florida	4.9
36	Massachusetts	2.8		21	Arkansas	4.8
30	Michigan	3.4		21	Nebraska	4.8
30	Minnesota	3.4		23	California	4.7
3	Mississippi	12.1		24	Oklahoma	4.6
14	Missouri	6.0		25	Kansas	4.2
42	Montana	1.7		26	Utah	4.1
21	Nebraska	4.8		27	Colorado	4.0
15	Nevada	5.7		27	New Mexico	4.0
49	New Hampshire	0.7		29	Ohio	3.5
36	New Jersey	2.8		30	Michigan	3.4
27	New Mexico	4.0		30	Minnesota	3.4
15	New York	5.7		32	Kentucky	3.3
6	North Carolina	9.2		33	Illinois	3.0
47	North Dakota	1.1		34	Pennsylvania	2.9
29	Ohio	3.5		34	West Virginia	2.9
24	Oklahoma	4.6		36	Massachusetts	2.8
13	Oregon	6.2		36	New Jersey	2.8
34	Pennsylvania	2.9		38	Wisconsin	2.5
42	Rhode Island	1.7		39	Hawaii	2.2
5	South Carolina	9.9		40	Arizona	1.9
40	South Dakota	1.9		40	South Dakota	1.9
8	Tennessee	7.8		42	Montana	1.7
11	Texas	6.6		42	Rhode Island	1.7
26	Utah	4.1		44	Maine	1.5
50	Vermont	0.2		45	Delaware	1.3
19	Virginia	5.2		45	Maryland	1.3
18	Washington	5.6		47	Alaska	1.1
34	West Virginia	2.9		47	North Dakota	1.1
38	Wisconsin	2.5		49	New Hampshire	0.7
4	Wyoming	10.5		50	Vermont	0.2

District of Columbia		2.9

Source: Morgan Quitno Press using data from U.S. Bureau of the Census, Governments Division
"State and Local Government Finances: 2002 Census" (http://www.census.gov/govs/www/estimate02.html)
*As a percent of direct general expenditures. Financing, construction, acquisition, maintenance or operation of hospital facilities, provision of hospital care and support of public or private hospitals.

State and Local Government Expenditures for Health Programs in 2002

National Total = $59,132,241,000*

ALPHA ORDER

RANK	STATE	EXPENDITURES	% of USA
18	Alabama	$982,547,000	1.7%
43	Alaska	166,727,000	0.3%
23	Arizona	739,853,000	1.3%
37	Arkansas	289,169,000	0.5%
1	California	9,813,693,000	16.6%
19	Colorado	959,754,000	1.6%
29	Connecticut	523,784,000	0.9%
39	Delaware	258,062,000	0.4%
4	Florida	3,184,348,000	5.4%
12	Georgia	1,333,214,000	2.3%
31	Hawaii	466,935,000	0.8%
44	Idaho	159,685,000	0.3%
7	Illinois	2,989,614,000	5.1%
26	Indiana	675,081,000	1.1%
32	Iowa	433,367,000	0.7%
27	Kansas	606,145,000	1.0%
24	Kentucky	728,385,000	1.2%
28	Louisiana	555,215,000	0.9%
33	Maine	383,724,000	0.6%
16	Maryland	1,089,312,000	1.8%
10	Massachusetts	1,995,701,000	3.4%
3	Michigan	3,276,613,000	5.5%
20	Minnesota	784,524,000	1.3%
38	Mississippi	274,402,000	0.5%
25	Missouri	702,516,000	1.2%
36	Montana	290,174,000	0.5%
45	Nebraska	138,569,000	0.2%
40	Nevada	256,822,000	0.4%
46	New Hampshire	137,748,000	0.2%
13	New Jersey	1,239,632,000	2.1%
34	New Mexico	368,268,000	0.6%
2	New York	3,819,062,000	6.5%
9	North Carolina	1,998,981,000	3.4%
50	North Dakota	59,264,000	0.1%
5	Ohio	3,079,714,000	5.2%
30	Oklahoma	470,344,000	0.8%
22	Oregon	769,376,000	1.3%
6	Pennsylvania	3,003,948,000	5.1%
42	Rhode Island	184,603,000	0.3%
21	South Carolina	779,193,000	1.3%
48	South Dakota	95,543,000	0.2%
17	Tennessee	1,038,348,000	1.8%
8	Texas	2,685,724,000	4.5%
35	Utah	328,753,000	0.6%
49	Vermont	78,036,000	0.1%
15	Virginia	1,134,990,000	1.9%
11	Washington	1,851,162,000	3.1%
41	West Virginia	231,148,000	0.4%
14	Wisconsin	1,229,637,000	2.1%
47	Wyoming	112,886,000	0.2%

RANK ORDER

RANK	STATE	EXPENDITURES	% of USA
1	California	$9,813,693,000	16.6%
2	New York	3,819,062,000	6.5%
3	Michigan	3,276,613,000	5.5%
4	Florida	3,184,348,000	5.4%
5	Ohio	3,079,714,000	5.2%
6	Pennsylvania	3,003,948,000	5.1%
7	Illinois	2,989,614,000	5.1%
8	Texas	2,685,724,000	4.5%
9	North Carolina	1,998,981,000	3.4%
10	Massachusetts	1,995,701,000	3.4%
11	Washington	1,851,162,000	3.1%
12	Georgia	1,333,214,000	2.3%
13	New Jersey	1,239,632,000	2.1%
14	Wisconsin	1,229,637,000	2.1%
15	Virginia	1,134,990,000	1.9%
16	Maryland	1,089,312,000	1.8%
17	Tennessee	1,038,348,000	1.8%
18	Alabama	982,547,000	1.7%
19	Colorado	959,754,000	1.6%
20	Minnesota	784,524,000	1.3%
21	South Carolina	779,193,000	1.3%
22	Oregon	769,376,000	1.3%
23	Arizona	739,853,000	1.3%
24	Kentucky	728,385,000	1.2%
25	Missouri	702,516,000	1.2%
26	Indiana	675,081,000	1.1%
27	Kansas	606,145,000	1.0%
28	Louisiana	555,215,000	0.9%
29	Connecticut	523,784,000	0.9%
30	Oklahoma	470,344,000	0.8%
31	Hawaii	466,935,000	0.8%
32	Iowa	433,367,000	0.7%
33	Maine	383,724,000	0.6%
34	New Mexico	368,268,000	0.6%
35	Utah	328,753,000	0.6%
36	Montana	290,174,000	0.5%
37	Arkansas	289,169,000	0.5%
38	Mississippi	274,402,000	0.5%
39	Delaware	258,062,000	0.4%
40	Nevada	256,822,000	0.4%
41	West Virginia	231,148,000	0.4%
42	Rhode Island	184,603,000	0.3%
43	Alaska	166,727,000	0.3%
44	Idaho	159,685,000	0.3%
45	Nebraska	138,569,000	0.2%
46	New Hampshire	137,748,000	0.2%
47	Wyoming	112,886,000	0.2%
48	South Dakota	95,543,000	0.2%
49	Vermont	78,036,000	0.1%
50	North Dakota	59,264,000	0.1%
	District of Columbia	377,946,000	0.6%

Source: U.S. Bureau of the Census, Governments Division
"State and Local Government Finances: 2002 Census" (http://www.census.gov/govs/www/estimate02.html)
*Includes outpatient health services other than hospital care, research and education, categorical health programs, treatment and immunization clinics, nursing and environmental health activities. Includes capital expenditures.

Per Capita State and Local Government Expenditures for Health Programs in 2002
National Per Capita = $205*

ALPHA ORDER

RANK ORDER

RANK	STATE	PER CAPITA		RANK	STATE	PER CAPITA
17	Alabama	$219		1	Hawaii	$378
10	Alaska	260		2	Michigan	326
35	Arizona	136		3	Delaware	320
47	Arkansas	107		4	Montana	319
8	California	280		5	Massachusetts	311
19	Colorado	213		6	Washington	305
31	Connecticut	151		7	Maine	296
3	Delaware	320		8	California	280
23	Florida	191		9	Ohio	270
28	Georgia	156		10	Alaska	260
1	Hawaii	378		11	Pennsylvania	244
43	Idaho	119		12	North Carolina	240
13	Illinois	238		13	Illinois	238
45	Indiana	110		14	Wisconsin	226
32	Iowa	148		14	Wyoming	226
16	Kansas	223		16	Kansas	223
26	Kentucky	178		17	Alabama	219
40	Louisiana	124		18	Oregon	218
7	Maine	296		19	Colorado	213
20	Maryland	200		20	Maryland	200
5	Massachusetts	311		21	New Mexico	199
2	Michigan	326		21	New York	199
28	Minnesota	156		23	Florida	191
48	Mississippi	96		24	South Carolina	190
40	Missouri	124		25	Tennessee	179
4	Montana	319		26	Kentucky	178
50	Nebraska	80		27	Rhode Island	173
44	Nevada	118		28	Georgia	156
46	New Hampshire	108		28	Minnesota	156
33	New Jersey	145		28	Virginia	156
21	New Mexico	199		31	Connecticut	151
21	New York	199		32	Iowa	148
12	North Carolina	240		33	New Jersey	145
49	North Dakota	94		34	Utah	142
9	Ohio	270		35	Arizona	136
36	Oklahoma	135		36	Oklahoma	135
18	Oregon	218		37	West Virginia	128
11	Pennsylvania	244		38	Vermont	127
27	Rhode Island	173		39	South Dakota	126
24	South Carolina	190		40	Louisiana	124
39	South Dakota	126		40	Missouri	124
25	Tennessee	179		40	Texas	124
40	Texas	124		43	Idaho	119
34	Utah	142		44	Nevada	118
38	Vermont	127		45	Indiana	110
28	Virginia	156		46	New Hampshire	108
6	Washington	305		47	Arkansas	107
37	West Virginia	128		48	Mississippi	96
14	Wisconsin	226		49	North Dakota	94
14	Wyoming	226		50	Nebraska	80

District of Columbia		669

Source: Morgan Quitno Press using data from U.S. Bureau of the Census, Governments Division
"State and Local Government Finances: 2002 Census" (http://www.census.gov/govs/www/estimate02.html)
*Includes outpatient health services other than hospital care, research and education, categorical health programs, treatment and immunization clinics, nursing and environmental health activities. Includes capital expenditures.

Percent of State and Local Government Expenditures
Used for Health Programs in 2002
National Percent = 3.4%*

RANK	STATE	PERCENT
13	Alabama	4.0
47	Alaska	2.0
25	Arizona	2.9
40	Arkansas	2.2
10	California	4.2
18	Colorado	3.5
40	Connecticut	2.2
4	Delaware	4.8
15	Florida	3.7
24	Georgia	3.0
2	Hawaii	5.6
36	Idaho	2.3
13	Illinois	4.0
45	Indiana	2.1
31	Iowa	2.5
11	Kansas	4.1
19	Kentucky	3.4
36	Louisiana	2.3
4	Maine	4.8
19	Maryland	3.4
7	Massachusetts	4.7
3	Michigan	5.4
40	Minnesota	2.2
48	Mississippi	1.8
33	Missouri	2.4
1	Montana	5.7
50	Nebraska	1.4
40	Nevada	2.2
40	New Hampshire	2.2
36	New Jersey	2.3
23	New Mexico	3.2
33	New York	2.4
9	North Carolina	4.5
49	North Dakota	1.5
8	Ohio	4.6
29	Oklahoma	2.6
21	Oregon	3.3
11	Pennsylvania	4.1
28	Rhode Island	2.7
21	South Carolina	3.3
31	South Dakota	2.5
16	Tennessee	3.6
33	Texas	2.4
29	Utah	2.6
45	Vermont	2.1
25	Virginia	2.9
4	Washington	4.8
36	West Virginia	2.3
16	Wisconsin	3.6
25	Wyoming	2.9

RANK	STATE	PERCENT
1	Montana	5.7
2	Hawaii	5.6
3	Michigan	5.4
4	Delaware	4.8
4	Maine	4.8
4	Washington	4.8
7	Massachusetts	4.7
8	Ohio	4.6
9	North Carolina	4.5
10	California	4.2
11	Kansas	4.1
11	Pennsylvania	4.1
13	Alabama	4.0
13	Illinois	4.0
15	Florida	3.7
16	Tennessee	3.6
16	Wisconsin	3.6
18	Colorado	3.5
19	Kentucky	3.4
19	Maryland	3.4
21	Oregon	3.3
21	South Carolina	3.3
23	New Mexico	3.2
24	Georgia	3.0
25	Arizona	2.9
25	Virginia	2.9
25	Wyoming	2.9
28	Rhode Island	2.7
29	Oklahoma	2.6
29	Utah	2.6
31	Iowa	2.5
31	South Dakota	2.5
33	Missouri	2.4
33	New York	2.4
33	Texas	2.4
36	Idaho	2.3
36	Louisiana	2.3
36	New Jersey	2.3
36	West Virginia	2.3
40	Arkansas	2.2
40	Connecticut	2.2
40	Minnesota	2.2
40	Nevada	2.2
40	New Hampshire	2.2
45	Indiana	2.1
45	Vermont	2.1
47	Alaska	2.0
48	Mississippi	1.8
49	North Dakota	1.5
50	Nebraska	1.4

| | District of Columbia | 6.1 |

Source: Morgan Quitno Press using data from U.S. Bureau of the Census, Governments Division
   "State and Local Government Finances: 2002 Census" (http://www.census.gov/govs/www/estimate02.html)
*As a percent of direct general expenditures. Includes outpatient health services other than hospital care, research and education, categorical health programs, treatment and immunization clinics, nursing and environmental health activities. Includes capital expenditures.

Estimated Tobacco Settlement Revenues in FY 2006

National Total = $7,179,000,000*

ALPHA ORDER					RANK ORDER			
RANK	STATE	REVENUE	% of USA		RANK	STATE	REVENUE	% of USA
25	Alabama	$97,800,000	1.4%		1	California	$772,500,000	10.8%
49	Alaska	20,700,000	0.3%		2	New York	772,400,000	10.8%
26	Arizona	89,200,000	1.2%		3	Texas	501,200,000	7.0%
34	Arkansas	50,100,000	0.7%		4	Florida	391,600,000	5.5%
1	California	772,500,000	10.8%		5	Pennsylvania	347,800,000	4.8%
27	Colorado	83,000,000	1.2%		6	Ohio	304,900,000	4.2%
23	Connecticut	112,400,000	1.6%		7	Illinois	281,700,000	3.9%
45	Delaware	23,900,000	0.3%		8	Michigan	263,400,000	3.7%
4	Florida	391,600,000	5.5%		9	Massachusetts	244,400,000	3.4%
12	Georgia	148,500,000	2.1%		10	New Jersey	234,000,000	3.3%
39	Hawaii	36,400,000	0.5%		11	Minnesota	184,900,000	2.6%
47	Idaho	22,000,000	0.3%		12	Georgia	148,500,000	2.1%
7	Illinois	281,700,000	3.9%		13	Tennessee	147,700,000	2.1%
21	Indiana	123,500,000	1.7%		14	North Carolina	141,200,000	2.0%
32	Iowa	52,600,000	0.7%		15	Missouri	137,700,000	1.9%
33	Kansas	50,500,000	0.7%		16	Maryland	136,800,000	1.9%
24	Kentucky	106,600,000	1.5%		17	Louisiana	136,500,000	1.9%
17	Louisiana	136,500,000	1.9%		18	Wisconsin	125,400,000	1.7%
35	Maine	46,600,000	0.6%		19	Washington	124,300,000	1.7%
16	Maryland	136,800,000	1.9%		20	Virginia	123,800,000	1.7%
9	Massachusetts	244,400,000	3.4%		21	Indiana	123,500,000	1.7%
8	Michigan	263,400,000	3.7%		22	Mississippi	121,000,000	1.7%
11	Minnesota	184,900,000	2.6%		23	Connecticut	112,400,000	1.6%
22	Mississippi	121,000,000	1.7%		24	Kentucky	106,600,000	1.5%
15	Missouri	137,700,000	1.9%		25	Alabama	97,800,000	1.4%
43	Montana	25,700,000	0.4%		26	Arizona	89,200,000	1.2%
41	Nebraska	36,000,000	0.5%		27	Colorado	83,000,000	1.2%
38	Nevada	36,900,000	0.5%		28	South Carolina	71,200,000	1.0%
37	New Hampshire	40,300,000	0.6%		29	Oregon	69,500,000	1.0%
10	New Jersey	234,000,000	3.3%		30	Oklahoma	62,700,000	0.9%
40	New Mexico	36,100,000	0.5%		31	West Virginia	53,600,000	0.7%
2	New York	772,400,000	10.8%		32	Iowa	52,600,000	0.7%
14	North Carolina	141,200,000	2.0%		33	Kansas	50,500,000	0.7%
46	North Dakota	22,200,000	0.3%		34	Arkansas	50,100,000	0.7%
6	Ohio	304,900,000	4.2%		35	Maine	46,600,000	0.6%
30	Oklahoma	62,700,000	0.9%		36	Rhode Island	43,500,000	0.6%
29	Oregon	69,500,000	1.0%		37	New Hampshire	40,300,000	0.6%
5	Pennsylvania	347,800,000	4.8%		38	Nevada	36,900,000	0.5%
36	Rhode Island	43,500,000	0.6%		39	Hawaii	36,400,000	0.5%
28	South Carolina	71,200,000	1.0%		40	New Mexico	36,100,000	0.5%
48	South Dakota	21,100,000	0.3%		41	Nebraska	36,000,000	0.5%
13	Tennessee	147,700,000	2.1%		42	Utah	26,900,000	0.4%
3	Texas	501,200,000	7.0%		43	Montana	25,700,000	0.4%
42	Utah	26,900,000	0.4%		44	Vermont	24,900,000	0.3%
44	Vermont	24,900,000	0.3%		45	Delaware	23,900,000	0.3%
20	Virginia	123,800,000	1.7%		46	North Dakota	22,200,000	0.3%
19	Washington	124,300,000	1.7%		47	Idaho	22,000,000	0.3%
31	West Virginia	53,600,000	0.7%		48	South Dakota	21,100,000	0.3%
18	Wisconsin	125,400,000	1.7%		49	Alaska	20,700,000	0.3%
50	Wyoming	15,000,000	0.2%		50	Wyoming	15,000,000	0.2%
						District of Columbia	36,700,000	0.5%

Source: Campaign for Tobacco-Free Kids
"A Broken Promise to Our Children" (http://tobaccofreekids.org/reports/settlements/)
*For fiscal year 2006. Settlement originally reached in November 1998 and called for an estimated 25 years of payments.

Personal Health Care Expenditures in 2000

National Total = $1,136,115,000,000*

ALPHA ORDER

RANK	STATE	EXPENDITURES	% of USA
22	Alabama	$17,045,000,000	1.5%
48	Alaska	2,624,000,000	0.2%
23	Arizona	17,037,000,000	1.5%
33	Arkansas	9,402,000,000	0.8%
1	California	125,782,000,000	11.1%
26	Colorado	15,927,000,000	1.4%
24	Connecticut	16,970,000,000	1.5%
44	Delaware	3,472,000,000	0.3%
4	Florida	69,876,000,000	6.2%
12	Georgia	30,806,000,000	2.7%
42	Hawaii	4,827,000,000	0.4%
43	Idaho	3,914,000,000	0.3%
6	Illinois	49,273,000,000	4.3%
15	Indiana	23,524,000,000	2.1%
30	Iowa	11,135,000,000	1.0%
31	Kansas	10,473,000,000	0.9%
25	Kentucky	16,027,000,000	1.4%
21	Louisiana	17,402,000,000	1.5%
39	Maine	5,520,000,000	0.5%
20	Maryland	21,493,000,000	1.9%
10	Massachusetts	32,503,000,000	2.9%
8	Michigan	37,919,000,000	3.3%
18	Minnesota	22,258,000,000	2.0%
32	Mississippi	9,975,000,000	0.9%
16	Missouri	23,292,000,000	2.1%
45	Montana	3,240,000,000	0.3%
35	Nebraska	6,973,000,000	0.6%
36	Nevada	6,841,000,000	0.6%
40	New Hampshire	5,160,000,000	0.5%
9	New Jersey	37,260,000,000	3.3%
38	New Mexico	5,734,000,000	0.5%
2	New York	94,769,000,000	8.3%
11	North Carolina	31,284,000,000	2.8%
47	North Dakota	2,898,000,000	0.3%
7	Ohio	46,981,000,000	4.1%
29	Oklahoma	12,038,000,000	1.1%
28	Oregon	12,452,000,000	1.1%
5	Pennsylvania	55,236,000,000	4.9%
41	Rhode Island	4,855,000,000	0.4%
27	South Carolina	14,937,000,000	1.3%
46	South Dakota	3,047,000,000	0.3%
14	Tennessee	24,557,000,000	2.2%
3	Texas	76,697,000,000	6.8%
37	Utah	6,620,000,000	0.6%
49	Vermont	2,360,000,000	0.2%
13	Virginia	25,578,000,000	2.3%
19	Washington	22,050,000,000	1.9%
34	West Virginia	7,526,000,000	0.7%
17	Wisconsin	22,370,000,000	2.0%
50	Wyoming	1,560,000,000	0.1%

RANK ORDER

RANK	STATE	EXPENDITURES	% of USA
1	California	$125,782,000,000	11.1%
2	New York	94,769,000,000	8.3%
3	Texas	76,697,000,000	6.8%
4	Florida	69,876,000,000	6.2%
5	Pennsylvania	55,236,000,000	4.9%
6	Illinois	49,273,000,000	4.3%
7	Ohio	46,981,000,000	4.1%
8	Michigan	37,919,000,000	3.3%
9	New Jersey	37,260,000,000	3.3%
10	Massachusetts	32,503,000,000	2.9%
11	North Carolina	31,284,000,000	2.8%
12	Georgia	30,806,000,000	2.7%
13	Virginia	25,578,000,000	2.3%
14	Tennessee	24,557,000,000	2.2%
15	Indiana	23,524,000,000	2.1%
16	Missouri	23,292,000,000	2.1%
17	Wisconsin	22,370,000,000	2.0%
18	Minnesota	22,258,000,000	2.0%
19	Washington	22,050,000,000	1.9%
20	Maryland	21,493,000,000	1.9%
21	Louisiana	17,402,000,000	1.5%
22	Alabama	17,045,000,000	1.5%
23	Arizona	17,037,000,000	1.5%
24	Connecticut	16,970,000,000	1.5%
25	Kentucky	16,027,000,000	1.4%
26	Colorado	15,927,000,000	1.4%
27	South Carolina	14,937,000,000	1.3%
28	Oregon	12,452,000,000	1.1%
29	Oklahoma	12,038,000,000	1.1%
30	Iowa	11,135,000,000	1.0%
31	Kansas	10,473,000,000	0.9%
32	Mississippi	9,975,000,000	0.9%
33	Arkansas	9,402,000,000	0.8%
34	West Virginia	7,526,000,000	0.7%
35	Nebraska	6,973,000,000	0.6%
36	Nevada	6,841,000,000	0.6%
37	Utah	6,620,000,000	0.6%
38	New Mexico	5,734,000,000	0.5%
39	Maine	5,520,000,000	0.5%
40	New Hampshire	5,160,000,000	0.5%
41	Rhode Island	4,855,000,000	0.4%
42	Hawaii	4,827,000,000	0.4%
43	Idaho	3,914,000,000	0.3%
44	Delaware	3,472,000,000	0.3%
45	Montana	3,240,000,000	0.3%
46	South Dakota	3,047,000,000	0.3%
47	North Dakota	2,898,000,000	0.3%
48	Alaska	2,624,000,000	0.2%
49	Vermont	2,360,000,000	0.2%
50	Wyoming	1,560,000,000	0.1%
	District of Columbia	4,618,000,000	0.4%

Source: U.S. Department of Health and Human Services, Centers for Medicare and Medicaid Services
"State Health Care Expenditures" (http://www.cms.hhs.gov/NationalHealthExpendData/)
*By state of provider. Includes hospital care, physician services, dental services, home health care, drugs, vision products, nursing home care and other personal health care services and products.

Health Care Expenditures as a Percent of Gross State Product in 2000

National Percent = 11.7% of Total Gross State Product*

ALPHA ORDER

RANK	STATE	PERCENT
7	Alabama	14.7
46	Alaska	9.5
36	Arizona	10.8
9	Arkansas	14.1
44	California	9.7
47	Colorado	9.3
38	Connecticut	10.7
50	Delaware	8.2
6	Florida	14.9
38	Georgia	10.7
25	Hawaii	12.1
34	Idaho	11.1
40	Illinois	10.6
27	Indiana	12.0
24	Iowa	12.2
21	Kansas	12.5
9	Kentucky	14.1
15	Louisiana	13.2
3	Maine	15.6
29	Maryland	11.9
30	Massachusetts	11.7
33	Michigan	11.2
27	Minnesota	12.0
4	Mississippi	15.4
15	Missouri	13.2
5	Montana	15.0
21	Nebraska	12.5
47	Nevada	9.3
25	New Hampshire	12.1
36	New Jersey	10.8
31	New Mexico	11.4
23	New York	12.4
31	North Carolina	11.4
2	North Dakota	16.2
19	Ohio	12.6
13	Oklahoma	13.3
34	Oregon	11.1
11	Pennsylvania	14.0
8	Rhode Island	14.5
15	South Carolina	13.2
15	South Dakota	13.2
11	Tennessee	14.0
40	Texas	10.6
44	Utah	9.7
13	Vermont	13.3
43	Virginia	9.9
42	Washington	10.0
1	West Virginia	17.8
19	Wisconsin	12.6
49	Wyoming	8.8

RANK ORDER

RANK	STATE	PERCENT
1	West Virginia	17.8
2	North Dakota	16.2
3	Maine	15.6
4	Mississippi	15.4
5	Montana	15.0
6	Florida	14.9
7	Alabama	14.7
8	Rhode Island	14.5
9	Arkansas	14.1
9	Kentucky	14.1
11	Pennsylvania	14.0
11	Tennessee	14.0
13	Oklahoma	13.3
13	Vermont	13.3
15	Louisiana	13.2
15	Missouri	13.2
15	South Carolina	13.2
15	South Dakota	13.2
19	Ohio	12.6
19	Wisconsin	12.6
21	Kansas	12.5
21	Nebraska	12.5
23	New York	12.4
24	Iowa	12.2
25	Hawaii	12.1
25	New Hampshire	12.1
27	Indiana	12.0
27	Minnesota	12.0
29	Maryland	11.9
30	Massachusetts	11.7
31	New Mexico	11.4
31	North Carolina	11.4
33	Michigan	11.2
34	Idaho	11.1
34	Oregon	11.1
36	Arizona	10.8
36	New Jersey	10.8
38	Connecticut	10.7
38	Georgia	10.7
40	Illinois	10.6
40	Texas	10.6
42	Washington	10.0
43	Virginia	9.9
44	California	9.7
44	Utah	9.7
46	Alaska	9.5
47	Colorado	9.3
47	Nevada	9.3
49	Wyoming	8.8
50	Delaware	8.2
	District of Columbia	8.0

Source: U.S. Department of Health and Human Services, Centers for Medicare and Medicaid Services
"State Health Care Expenditures" (http://www.cms.hhs.gov/NationalHealthExpendData/)
*By state of provider. Includes hospital care, physician services, dental services, home health care, drugs, vision products, nursing home care and other personal health care services and products.

Per Capita Personal Health Care Expenditures in 2000

National Per Capita = $4,026*

ALPHA ORDER

RANK	STATE	PER CAPITA
30	Alabama	$3,828
13	Alaska	4,182
46	Arizona	3,298
42	Arkansas	3,510
36	California	3,699
37	Colorado	3,681
3	Connecticut	4,973
9	Delaware	4,415
10	Florida	4,354
33	Georgia	3,743
22	Hawaii	3,982
49	Idaho	3,012
23	Illinois	3,961
29	Indiana	3,861
32	Iowa	3,802
26	Kansas	3,889
24	Kentucky	3,958
25	Louisiana	3,894
11	Maine	4,321
20	Maryland	4,046
1	Massachusetts	5,109
31	Michigan	3,809
6	Minnesota	4,511
43	Mississippi	3,502
17	Missouri	4,155
41	Montana	3,586
19	Nebraska	4,070
45	Nevada	3,390
16	New Hampshire	4,159
8	New Jersey	4,418
48	New Mexico	3,148
2	New York	4,988
27	North Carolina	3,873
5	North Dakota	4,520
18	Ohio	4,134
44	Oklahoma	3,485
39	Oregon	3,629
7	Pennsylvania	4,496
4	Rhode Island	4,621
35	South Carolina	3,712
21	South Dakota	4,032
12	Tennessee	4,306
38	Texas	3,661
50	Utah	2,951
28	Vermont	3,869
40	Virginia	3,600
34	Washington	3,730
14	West Virginia	4,164
15	Wisconsin	4,162
47	Wyoming	3,157

RANK ORDER

RANK	STATE	PER CAPITA
1	Massachusetts	$5,109
2	New York	4,988
3	Connecticut	4,973
4	Rhode Island	4,621
5	North Dakota	4,520
6	Minnesota	4,511
7	Pennsylvania	4,496
8	New Jersey	4,418
9	Delaware	4,415
10	Florida	4,354
11	Maine	4,321
12	Tennessee	4,306
13	Alaska	4,182
14	West Virginia	4,164
15	Wisconsin	4,162
16	New Hampshire	4,159
17	Missouri	4,155
18	Ohio	4,134
19	Nebraska	4,070
20	Maryland	4,046
21	South Dakota	4,032
22	Hawaii	3,982
23	Illinois	3,961
24	Kentucky	3,958
25	Louisiana	3,894
26	Kansas	3,889
27	North Carolina	3,873
28	Vermont	3,869
29	Indiana	3,861
30	Alabama	3,828
31	Michigan	3,809
32	Iowa	3,802
33	Georgia	3,743
34	Washington	3,730
35	South Carolina	3,712
36	California	3,699
37	Colorado	3,681
38	Texas	3,661
39	Oregon	3,629
40	Virginia	3,600
41	Montana	3,586
42	Arkansas	3,510
43	Mississippi	3,502
44	Oklahoma	3,485
45	Nevada	3,390
46	Arizona	3,298
47	Wyoming	3,157
48	New Mexico	3,148
49	Idaho	3,012
50	Utah	2,951

District of Columbia 8,087

Source: MQ Press using data from U.S. Dept of Health & Human Services, Centers for Medicare and Medicaid Services
"State Health Care Expenditures" (http://www.cms.hhs.gov/NationalHealthExpendData/)
*By state of provider. Per capita calculated using resident population. These figures may be skewed due to residents crossing state borders for care. Includes hospital care, physician services, dental services, home health care, drugs, vision products, nursing home care and other personal health care services and products.

Expenditures for Hospital Care in 2000

National Total = $413,131,000,000*

RANK	STATE	EXPENDITURES	% of USA
22	Alabama	$6,316,000,000	1.5%
48	Alaska	1,151,000,000	0.3%
25	Arizona	5,764,000,000	1.4%
33	Arkansas	3,651,000,000	0.9%
1	California	41,672,000,000	10.1%
26	Colorado	5,548,000,000	1.3%
27	Connecticut	4,983,000,000	1.2%
47	Delaware	1,195,000,000	0.3%
4	Florida	22,694,000,000	5.5%
12	Georgia	11,166,000,000	2.7%
40	Hawaii	1,759,000,000	0.4%
43	Idaho	1,403,000,000	0.3%
6	Illinois	19,310,000,000	4.7%
15	Indiana	9,259,000,000	2.2%
28	Iowa	4,464,000,000	1.1%
32	Kansas	3,704,000,000	0.9%
23	Kentucky	6,208,000,000	1.5%
21	Louisiana	7,110,000,000	1.7%
39	Maine	2,040,000,000	0.5%
18	Maryland	7,631,000,000	1.8%
10	Massachusetts	12,181,000,000	2.9%
8	Michigan	14,872,000,000	3.6%
20	Minnesota	7,327,000,000	1.8%
30	Mississippi	4,262,000,000	1.0%
13	Missouri	9,728,000,000	2.4%
44	Montana	1,353,000,000	0.3%
35	Nebraska	2,963,000,000	0.7%
38	Nevada	2,184,000,000	0.5%
42	New Hampshire	1,729,000,000	0.4%
9	New Jersey	12,212,000,000	3.0%
37	New Mexico	2,382,000,000	0.6%
2	New York	34,256,000,000	8.3%
11	North Carolina	12,060,000,000	2.9%
46	North Dakota	1,267,000,000	0.3%
7	Ohio	17,291,000,000	4.2%
29	Oklahoma	4,444,000,000	1.1%
31	Oregon	4,169,000,000	1.0%
5	Pennsylvania	20,915,000,000	5.1%
40	Rhode Island	1,759,000,000	0.4%
24	South Carolina	5,914,000,000	1.4%
45	South Dakota	1,300,000,000	0.3%
16	Tennessee	8,801,000,000	2.1%
3	Texas	28,339,000,000	6.9%
36	Utah	2,467,000,000	0.6%
49	Vermont	824,000,000	0.2%
14	Virginia	9,316,000,000	2.3%
19	Washington	7,455,000,000	1.8%
34	West Virginia	3,067,000,000	0.7%
17	Wisconsin	7,965,000,000	1.9%
50	Wyoming	664,000,000	0.2%

RANK	STATE	EXPENDITURES	% of USA
1	California	$41,672,000,000	10.1%
2	New York	34,256,000,000	8.3%
3	Texas	28,339,000,000	6.9%
4	Florida	22,694,000,000	5.5%
5	Pennsylvania	20,915,000,000	5.1%
6	Illinois	19,310,000,000	4.7%
7	Ohio	17,291,000,000	4.2%
8	Michigan	14,872,000,000	3.6%
9	New Jersey	12,212,000,000	3.0%
10	Massachusetts	12,181,000,000	2.9%
11	North Carolina	12,060,000,000	2.9%
12	Georgia	11,166,000,000	2.7%
13	Missouri	9,728,000,000	2.4%
14	Virginia	9,316,000,000	2.3%
15	Indiana	9,259,000,000	2.2%
16	Tennessee	8,801,000,000	2.1%
17	Wisconsin	7,965,000,000	1.9%
18	Maryland	7,631,000,000	1.8%
19	Washington	7,455,000,000	1.8%
20	Minnesota	7,327,000,000	1.8%
21	Louisiana	7,110,000,000	1.7%
22	Alabama	6,316,000,000	1.5%
23	Kentucky	6,208,000,000	1.5%
24	South Carolina	5,914,000,000	1.4%
25	Arizona	5,764,000,000	1.4%
26	Colorado	5,548,000,000	1.3%
27	Connecticut	4,983,000,000	1.2%
28	Iowa	4,464,000,000	1.1%
29	Oklahoma	4,444,000,000	1.1%
30	Mississippi	4,262,000,000	1.0%
31	Oregon	4,169,000,000	1.0%
32	Kansas	3,704,000,000	0.9%
33	Arkansas	3,651,000,000	0.9%
34	West Virginia	3,067,000,000	0.7%
35	Nebraska	2,963,000,000	0.7%
36	Utah	2,467,000,000	0.6%
37	New Mexico	2,382,000,000	0.6%
38	Nevada	2,184,000,000	0.5%
39	Maine	2,040,000,000	0.5%
40	Hawaii	1,759,000,000	0.4%
40	Rhode Island	1,759,000,000	0.4%
42	New Hampshire	1,729,000,000	0.4%
43	Idaho	1,403,000,000	0.3%
44	Montana	1,353,000,000	0.3%
45	South Dakota	1,300,000,000	0.3%
46	North Dakota	1,267,000,000	0.3%
47	Delaware	1,195,000,000	0.3%
48	Alaska	1,151,000,000	0.3%
49	Vermont	824,000,000	0.2%
50	Wyoming	664,000,000	0.2%
	District of Columbia	2,637,000,000	0.6%

Source: U.S. Department of Health and Human Services, Centers for Medicare and Medicaid Services "State Health Care Expenditures" (http://www.cms.hhs.gov/NationalHealthExpendData/)
*By state of provider.

Percent of Total Personal Health Care Expenditures
Spent on Hospital Care in 2000
National Percent = 36.4%*

ALPHA ORDER

RANK	STATE	PERCENT
23	Alabama	37.1
1	Alaska	43.9
41	Arizona	33.8
17	Arkansas	38.8
45	California	33.1
39	Colorado	34.8
50	Connecticut	29.4
40	Delaware	34.4
48	Florida	32.5
30	Georgia	36.2
28	Hawaii	36.4
33	Idaho	35.8
15	Illinois	39.2
14	Indiana	39.4
12	Iowa	40.1
37	Kansas	35.4
18	Kentucky	38.7
10	Louisiana	40.9
24	Maine	37.0
36	Maryland	35.5
21	Massachusetts	37.5
15	Michigan	39.2
46	Minnesota	32.9
3	Mississippi	42.7
7	Missouri	41.8
7	Montana	41.8
6	Nebraska	42.5
49	Nevada	31.9
43	New Hampshire	33.5
47	New Jersey	32.8
9	New Mexico	41.5
32	New York	36.1
19	North Carolina	38.6
2	North Dakota	43.7
27	Ohio	36.8
25	Oklahoma	36.9
43	Oregon	33.5
20	Pennsylvania	37.9
30	Rhode Island	36.2
13	South Carolina	39.6
3	South Dakota	42.7
33	Tennessee	35.8
25	Texas	36.9
22	Utah	37.3
38	Vermont	34.9
28	Virginia	36.4
41	Washington	33.8
11	West Virginia	40.8
35	Wisconsin	35.6
5	Wyoming	42.6

RANK ORDER

RANK	STATE	PERCENT
1	Alaska	43.9
2	North Dakota	43.7
3	Mississippi	42.7
3	South Dakota	42.7
5	Wyoming	42.6
6	Nebraska	42.5
7	Missouri	41.8
7	Montana	41.8
9	New Mexico	41.5
10	Louisiana	40.9
11	West Virginia	40.8
12	Iowa	40.1
13	South Carolina	39.6
14	Indiana	39.4
15	Illinois	39.2
15	Michigan	39.2
17	Arkansas	38.8
18	Kentucky	38.7
19	North Carolina	38.6
20	Pennsylvania	37.9
21	Massachusetts	37.5
22	Utah	37.3
23	Alabama	37.1
24	Maine	37.0
25	Oklahoma	36.9
25	Texas	36.9
27	Ohio	36.8
28	Hawaii	36.4
28	Virginia	36.4
30	Georgia	36.2
30	Rhode Island	36.2
32	New York	36.1
33	Idaho	35.8
33	Tennessee	35.8
35	Wisconsin	35.6
36	Maryland	35.5
37	Kansas	35.4
38	Vermont	34.9
39	Colorado	34.8
40	Delaware	34.4
41	Arizona	33.8
41	Washington	33.8
43	New Hampshire	33.5
43	Oregon	33.5
45	California	33.1
46	Minnesota	32.9
47	New Jersey	32.8
48	Florida	32.5
49	Nevada	31.9
50	Connecticut	29.4

District of Columbia	57.1

Source: MQ Press using data from U.S. Dept of Health & Human Services, Centers for Medicare and Medicaid Services
"State Health Care Expenditures" (http://www.cms.hhs.gov/NationalHealthExpendData/)
*By state of provider.

Per Capita Expenditures for Hospital Care in 2000

National Per Capita = $1,464*

ALPHA ORDER

RANK	STATE	PER CAPITA
31	Alabama	$1,419
3	Alaska	1,834
47	Arizona	1,116
35	Arkansas	1,363
45	California	1,226
43	Colorado	1,282
27	Connecticut	1,460
18	Delaware	1,520
32	Florida	1,414
36	Georgia	1,357
28	Hawaii	1,451
50	Idaho	1,079
13	Illinois	1,552
18	Indiana	1,520
16	Iowa	1,524
34	Kansas	1,376
15	Kentucky	1,533
12	Louisiana	1,591
11	Maine	1,597
30	Maryland	1,437
2	Massachusetts	1,915
22	Michigan	1,494
24	Minnesota	1,485
21	Mississippi	1,496
5	Missouri	1,735
20	Montana	1,497
6	Nebraska	1,729
49	Nevada	1,082
33	New Hampshire	1,394
29	New Jersey	1,448
41	New Mexico	1,308
4	New York	1,803
23	North Carolina	1,493
1	North Dakota	1,976
17	Ohio	1,522
42	Oklahoma	1,287
46	Oregon	1,215
8	Pennsylvania	1,702
10	Rhode Island	1,674
26	South Carolina	1,470
7	South Dakota	1,720
14	Tennessee	1,543
37	Texas	1,353
48	Utah	1,100
38	Vermont	1,351
40	Virginia	1,311
44	Washington	1,261
9	West Virginia	1,697
25	Wisconsin	1,482
39	Wyoming	1,344

RANK ORDER

RANK	STATE	PER CAPITA
1	North Dakota	$1,976
2	Massachusetts	1,915
3	Alaska	1,834
4	New York	1,803
5	Missouri	1,735
6	Nebraska	1,729
7	South Dakota	1,720
8	Pennsylvania	1,702
9	West Virginia	1,697
10	Rhode Island	1,674
11	Maine	1,597
12	Louisiana	1,591
13	Illinois	1,552
14	Tennessee	1,543
15	Kentucky	1,533
16	Iowa	1,524
17	Ohio	1,522
18	Delaware	1,520
18	Indiana	1,520
20	Montana	1,497
21	Mississippi	1,496
22	Michigan	1,494
23	North Carolina	1,493
24	Minnesota	1,485
25	Wisconsin	1,482
26	South Carolina	1,470
27	Connecticut	1,460
28	Hawaii	1,451
29	New Jersey	1,448
30	Maryland	1,437
31	Alabama	1,419
32	Florida	1,414
33	New Hampshire	1,394
34	Kansas	1,376
35	Arkansas	1,363
36	Georgia	1,357
37	Texas	1,353
38	Vermont	1,351
39	Wyoming	1,344
40	Virginia	1,311
41	New Mexico	1,308
42	Oklahoma	1,287
43	Colorado	1,282
44	Washington	1,261
45	California	1,226
46	Oregon	1,215
47	Arizona	1,116
48	Utah	1,100
49	Nevada	1,082
50	Idaho	1,079

| | District of Columbia | 4,618 |

Source: MQ Press using data from U.S. Dept of Health & Human Services, Centers for Medicare and Medicaid Services "State Health Care Expenditures" (http://www.cms.hhs.gov/NationalHealthExpendData/)
*By state of provider. Per capita calculated using resident population. These figures may be skewed due to residents crossing state borders for care.

Expenditures for Physician and Other Professional Services in 2000

National Total = $328,983,000,000*

ALPHA ORDER

RANK	STATE	EXPENDITURES	% of USA
22	Alabama	$5,084,000,000	1.5%
47	Alaska	713,000,000	0.2%
20	Arizona	5,877,000,000	1.8%
32	Arkansas	2,524,000,000	0.8%
1	California	49,041,000,000	14.9%
23	Colorado	4,933,000,000	1.5%
24	Connecticut	4,866,000,000	1.5%
44	Delaware	922,000,000	0.3%
3	Florida	22,281,000,000	6.8%
10	Georgia	9,785,000,000	3.0%
37	Hawaii	1,648,000,000	0.5%
43	Idaho	1,093,000,000	0.3%
6	Illinois	13,304,000,000	4.0%
19	Indiana	6,143,000,000	1.9%
31	Iowa	2,640,000,000	0.8%
30	Kansas	2,829,000,000	0.9%
26	Kentucky	4,207,000,000	1.3%
25	Louisiana	4,678,000,000	1.4%
41	Maine	1,283,000,000	0.4%
16	Maryland	6,721,000,000	2.0%
11	Massachusetts	8,701,000,000	2.6%
9	Michigan	10,180,000,000	3.1%
14	Minnesota	7,175,000,000	2.2%
33	Mississippi	2,441,000,000	0.7%
21	Missouri	5,700,000,000	1.7%
46	Montana	802,000,000	0.2%
39	Nebraska	1,483,000,000	0.5%
34	Nevada	2,397,000,000	0.7%
40	New Hampshire	1,478,000,000	0.4%
8	New Jersey	10,913,000,000	3.3%
38	New Mexico	1,637,000,000	0.5%
4	New York	21,705,000,000	6.6%
12	North Carolina	8,025,000,000	2.4%
48	North Dakota	684,000,000	0.2%
7	Ohio	12,091,000,000	3.7%
29	Oklahoma	3,323,000,000	1.0%
27	Oregon	3,701,000,000	1.1%
5	Pennsylvania	14,405,000,000	4.4%
42	Rhode Island	1,115,000,000	0.3%
28	South Carolina	3,650,000,000	1.1%
45	South Dakota	819,000,000	0.2%
13	Tennessee	7,619,000,000	2.3%
2	Texas	22,865,000,000	7.0%
36	Utah	1,886,000,000	0.6%
49	Vermont	589,000,000	0.2%
15	Virginia	7,129,000,000	2.2%
17	Washington	6,477,000,000	2.0%
35	West Virginia	1,921,000,000	0.6%
18	Wisconsin	6,231,000,000	1.9%
50	Wyoming	361,000,000	0.1%

RANK ORDER

RANK	STATE	EXPENDITURES	% of USA
1	California	$49,041,000,000	14.9%
2	Texas	22,865,000,000	7.0%
3	Florida	22,281,000,000	6.8%
4	New York	21,705,000,000	6.6%
5	Pennsylvania	14,405,000,000	4.4%
6	Illinois	13,304,000,000	4.0%
7	Ohio	12,091,000,000	3.7%
8	New Jersey	10,913,000,000	3.3%
9	Michigan	10,180,000,000	3.1%
10	Georgia	9,785,000,000	3.0%
11	Massachusetts	8,701,000,000	2.6%
12	North Carolina	8,025,000,000	2.4%
13	Tennessee	7,619,000,000	2.3%
14	Minnesota	7,175,000,000	2.2%
15	Virginia	7,129,000,000	2.2%
16	Maryland	6,721,000,000	2.0%
17	Washington	6,477,000,000	2.0%
18	Wisconsin	6,231,000,000	1.9%
19	Indiana	6,143,000,000	1.9%
20	Arizona	5,877,000,000	1.8%
21	Missouri	5,700,000,000	1.7%
22	Alabama	5,084,000,000	1.5%
23	Colorado	4,933,000,000	1.5%
24	Connecticut	4,866,000,000	1.5%
25	Louisiana	4,678,000,000	1.4%
26	Kentucky	4,207,000,000	1.3%
27	Oregon	3,701,000,000	1.1%
28	South Carolina	3,650,000,000	1.1%
29	Oklahoma	3,323,000,000	1.0%
30	Kansas	2,829,000,000	0.9%
31	Iowa	2,640,000,000	0.8%
32	Arkansas	2,524,000,000	0.8%
33	Mississippi	2,441,000,000	0.7%
34	Nevada	2,397,000,000	0.7%
35	West Virginia	1,921,000,000	0.6%
36	Utah	1,886,000,000	0.6%
37	Hawaii	1,648,000,000	0.5%
38	New Mexico	1,637,000,000	0.5%
39	Nebraska	1,483,000,000	0.5%
40	New Hampshire	1,478,000,000	0.4%
41	Maine	1,283,000,000	0.4%
42	Rhode Island	1,115,000,000	0.3%
43	Idaho	1,093,000,000	0.3%
44	Delaware	922,000,000	0.3%
45	South Dakota	819,000,000	0.2%
46	Montana	802,000,000	0.2%
47	Alaska	713,000,000	0.2%
48	North Dakota	684,000,000	0.2%
49	Vermont	589,000,000	0.2%
50	Wyoming	361,000,000	0.1%
	District of Columbia	909,000,000	0.3%

Source: U.S. Department of Health and Human Services, Centers for Medicare and Medicaid Services
   "State Health Care Expenditures" (http://www.cms.hhs.gov/NationalHealthExpendData/)
*By state of provider. Includes "other professional services" previously listed as a separate category. These include services of licensed professionals such as chiropractors, optometrists, podiatrists and independently practicing nurses. Also includes specialty clinics, independently billing laboratories and Medicare ambulance services.

313

Percent of Total Personal Health Care Expenditures
Spent on Physician and Other Professional Services in 2000
National Percent = 29.0%*

ALPHA ORDER

RANK ORDER

RANK	STATE	PERCENT		RANK	STATE	PERCENT
11	Alabama	29.8		1	California	39.0
24	Alaska	27.2		2	Nevada	35.0
3	Arizona	34.5		3	Arizona	34.5
29	Arkansas	26.8		4	Hawaii	34.1
1	California	39.0		5	Minnesota	32.2
9	Colorado	31.0		6	Florida	31.9
16	Connecticut	28.7		7	Georgia	31.8
32	Delaware	26.6		8	Maryland	31.3
6	Florida	31.9		9	Colorado	31.0
7	Georgia	31.8		9	Tennessee	31.0
4	Hawaii	34.1		11	Alabama	29.8
20	Idaho	27.9		11	Texas	29.8
25	Illinois	27.0		13	Oregon	29.7
34	Indiana	26.1		14	Washington	29.4
44	Iowa	23.7		15	New Jersey	29.3
25	Kansas	27.0		16	Connecticut	28.7
33	Kentucky	26.2		17	New Hampshire	28.6
27	Louisiana	26.9		18	New Mexico	28.5
46	Maine	23.2		18	Utah	28.5
8	Maryland	31.3		20	Idaho	27.9
29	Massachusetts	26.8		20	Virginia	27.9
29	Michigan	26.8		20	Wisconsin	27.9
5	Minnesota	32.2		23	Oklahoma	27.6
41	Mississippi	24.5		24	Alaska	27.2
41	Missouri	24.5		25	Illinois	27.0
40	Montana	24.8		25	Kansas	27.0
50	Nebraska	21.3		27	Louisiana	26.9
2	Nevada	35.0		27	South Dakota	26.9
17	New Hampshire	28.6		29	Arkansas	26.8
15	New Jersey	29.3		29	Massachusetts	26.8
18	New Mexico	28.5		29	Michigan	26.8
49	New York	22.9		32	Delaware	26.6
36	North Carolina	25.7		33	Kentucky	26.2
45	North Dakota	23.6		34	Indiana	26.1
36	Ohio	25.7		34	Pennsylvania	26.1
23	Oklahoma	27.6		36	North Carolina	25.7
13	Oregon	29.7		36	Ohio	25.7
34	Pennsylvania	26.1		38	West Virginia	25.5
48	Rhode Island	23.0		39	Vermont	25.0
43	South Carolina	24.4		40	Montana	24.8
27	South Dakota	26.9		41	Mississippi	24.5
9	Tennessee	31.0		41	Missouri	24.5
11	Texas	29.8		43	South Carolina	24.4
18	Utah	28.5		44	Iowa	23.7
39	Vermont	25.0		45	North Dakota	23.6
20	Virginia	27.9		46	Maine	23.2
14	Washington	29.4		47	Wyoming	23.1
38	West Virginia	25.5		48	Rhode Island	23.0
20	Wisconsin	27.9		49	New York	22.9
47	Wyoming	23.1		50	Nebraska	21.3

District of Columbia   19.7

Source: MQ Press using data from U.S. Dept of Health & Human Services, Centers for Medicare and Medicaid Services "State Health Care Expenditures" (http://www.cms.hhs.gov/NationalHealthExpendData/)

*By state of provider. Includes "other professional services" previously listed as a separate category. These include services of licensed professionals such as chiropractors, optometrists, podiatrists and independently practicing nurses. Also includes specialty clinics, independently billing laboratories and Medicare ambulance services.

Per Capita Expenditures for Physician and Other Professional Services in 2000

National Per Capita = $1,166*

<table>
<thead>
<tr><th colspan="3">ALPHA ORDER</th><th colspan="3">RANK ORDER</th></tr>
<tr><th>RANK</th><th>STATE</th><th>PER CAPITA</th><th>RANK</th><th>STATE</th><th>PER CAPITA</th></tr>
</thead>
<tbody>
<tr><td>16</td><td>Alabama</td><td>$1,142</td><td>1</td><td>Minnesota</td><td>$1,454</td></tr>
<tr><td>20</td><td>Alaska</td><td>1,136</td><td>2</td><td>California</td><td>1,442</td></tr>
<tr><td>19</td><td>Arizona</td><td>1,138</td><td>3</td><td>Connecticut</td><td>1,426</td></tr>
<tr><td>41</td><td>Arkansas</td><td>942</td><td>4</td><td>Florida</td><td>1,388</td></tr>
<tr><td>2</td><td>California</td><td>1,442</td><td>5</td><td>Massachusetts</td><td>1,368</td></tr>
<tr><td>18</td><td>Colorado</td><td>1,140</td><td>6</td><td>Hawaii</td><td>1,360</td></tr>
<tr><td>3</td><td>Connecticut</td><td>1,426</td><td>7</td><td>Tennessee</td><td>1,336</td></tr>
<tr><td>13</td><td>Delaware</td><td>1,172</td><td>8</td><td>New Jersey</td><td>1,294</td></tr>
<tr><td>4</td><td>Florida</td><td>1,388</td><td>9</td><td>Maryland</td><td>1,265</td></tr>
<tr><td>11</td><td>Georgia</td><td>1,189</td><td>10</td><td>New Hampshire</td><td>1,191</td></tr>
<tr><td>6</td><td>Hawaii</td><td>1,360</td><td>11</td><td>Georgia</td><td>1,189</td></tr>
<tr><td>48</td><td>Idaho</td><td>841</td><td>12</td><td>Nevada</td><td>1,188</td></tr>
<tr><td>25</td><td>Illinois</td><td>1,069</td><td>13</td><td>Delaware</td><td>1,172</td></tr>
<tr><td>35</td><td>Indiana</td><td>1,008</td><td>13</td><td>Pennsylvania</td><td>1,172</td></tr>
<tr><td>43</td><td>Iowa</td><td>901</td><td>15</td><td>Wisconsin</td><td>1,159</td></tr>
<tr><td>30</td><td>Kansas</td><td>1,051</td><td>16</td><td>Alabama</td><td>1,142</td></tr>
<tr><td>32</td><td>Kentucky</td><td>1,039</td><td>16</td><td>New York</td><td>1,142</td></tr>
<tr><td>31</td><td>Louisiana</td><td>1,047</td><td>18</td><td>Colorado</td><td>1,140</td></tr>
<tr><td>36</td><td>Maine</td><td>1,004</td><td>19</td><td>Arizona</td><td>1,138</td></tr>
<tr><td>9</td><td>Maryland</td><td>1,265</td><td>20</td><td>Alaska</td><td>1,136</td></tr>
<tr><td>5</td><td>Massachusetts</td><td>1,368</td><td>21</td><td>Washington</td><td>1,096</td></tr>
<tr><td>33</td><td>Michigan</td><td>1,022</td><td>22</td><td>Texas</td><td>1,091</td></tr>
<tr><td>1</td><td>Minnesota</td><td>1,454</td><td>23</td><td>South Dakota</td><td>1,084</td></tr>
<tr><td>47</td><td>Mississippi</td><td>857</td><td>24</td><td>Oregon</td><td>1,079</td></tr>
<tr><td>34</td><td>Missouri</td><td>1,017</td><td>25</td><td>Illinois</td><td>1,069</td></tr>
<tr><td>45</td><td>Montana</td><td>888</td><td>26</td><td>North Dakota</td><td>1,067</td></tr>
<tr><td>46</td><td>Nebraska</td><td>866</td><td>27</td><td>Ohio</td><td>1,064</td></tr>
<tr><td>12</td><td>Nevada</td><td>1,188</td><td>28</td><td>West Virginia</td><td>1,063</td></tr>
<tr><td>10</td><td>New Hampshire</td><td>1,191</td><td>29</td><td>Rhode Island</td><td>1,061</td></tr>
<tr><td>8</td><td>New Jersey</td><td>1,294</td><td>30</td><td>Kansas</td><td>1,051</td></tr>
<tr><td>44</td><td>New Mexico</td><td>899</td><td>31</td><td>Louisiana</td><td>1,047</td></tr>
<tr><td>16</td><td>New York</td><td>1,142</td><td>32</td><td>Kentucky</td><td>1,039</td></tr>
<tr><td>38</td><td>North Carolina</td><td>993</td><td>33</td><td>Michigan</td><td>1,022</td></tr>
<tr><td>26</td><td>North Dakota</td><td>1,067</td><td>34</td><td>Missouri</td><td>1,017</td></tr>
<tr><td>27</td><td>Ohio</td><td>1,064</td><td>35</td><td>Indiana</td><td>1,008</td></tr>
<tr><td>40</td><td>Oklahoma</td><td>962</td><td>36</td><td>Maine</td><td>1,004</td></tr>
<tr><td>24</td><td>Oregon</td><td>1,079</td><td>36</td><td>Virginia</td><td>1,004</td></tr>
<tr><td>13</td><td>Pennsylvania</td><td>1,172</td><td>38</td><td>North Carolina</td><td>993</td></tr>
<tr><td>29</td><td>Rhode Island</td><td>1,061</td><td>39</td><td>Vermont</td><td>966</td></tr>
<tr><td>42</td><td>South Carolina</td><td>907</td><td>40</td><td>Oklahoma</td><td>962</td></tr>
<tr><td>23</td><td>South Dakota</td><td>1,084</td><td>41</td><td>Arkansas</td><td>942</td></tr>
<tr><td>7</td><td>Tennessee</td><td>1,336</td><td>42</td><td>South Carolina</td><td>907</td></tr>
<tr><td>22</td><td>Texas</td><td>1,091</td><td>43</td><td>Iowa</td><td>901</td></tr>
<tr><td>48</td><td>Utah</td><td>841</td><td>44</td><td>New Mexico</td><td>899</td></tr>
<tr><td>39</td><td>Vermont</td><td>966</td><td>45</td><td>Montana</td><td>888</td></tr>
<tr><td>36</td><td>Virginia</td><td>1,004</td><td>46</td><td>Nebraska</td><td>866</td></tr>
<tr><td>21</td><td>Washington</td><td>1,096</td><td>47</td><td>Mississippi</td><td>857</td></tr>
<tr><td>28</td><td>West Virginia</td><td>1,063</td><td>48</td><td>Idaho</td><td>841</td></tr>
<tr><td>15</td><td>Wisconsin</td><td>1,159</td><td>48</td><td>Utah</td><td>841</td></tr>
<tr><td>50</td><td>Wyoming</td><td>731</td><td>50</td><td>Wyoming</td><td>731</td></tr>
<tr><td></td><td></td><td></td><td></td><td>District of Columbia</td><td>1,592</td></tr>
</tbody>
</table>

Source: MQ Press using data from U.S. Dept of Health & Human Services, Centers for Medicare and Medicaid Services "State Health Care Expenditures" (http://www.cms.hhs.gov/NationalHealthExpendData/)
*By state of provider. Per capita calculated using resident population. These figures may be skewed due to residents crossing state borders for care. Includes "other professional services" previously listed as a separate category. Services include licensed professionals such as chiropractors, optometrists, podiatrists and independently practicing nurses.

Expenditures for Prescription Drugs in 2000

National Total = $121,539,000,000*

ALPHA ORDER

RANK	STATE	EXPENDITURES	% of USA
20	Alabama	$2,199,000,000	1.8%
49	Alaska	243,000,000	0.2%
26	Arizona	1,721,000,000	1.4%
33	Arkansas	1,096,000,000	0.9%
1	California	9,918,000,000	8.2%
27	Colorado	1,584,000,000	1.3%
24	Connecticut	1,784,000,000	1.5%
42	Delaware	437,000,000	0.4%
3	Florida	8,295,000,000	6.8%
11	Georgia	3,662,000,000	3.0%
43	Hawaii	420,000,000	0.3%
44	Idaho	414,000,000	0.3%
6	Illinois	5,201,000,000	4.3%
15	Indiana	2,825,000,000	2.3%
31	Iowa	1,190,000,000	1.0%
30	Kansas	1,249,000,000	1.0%
23	Kentucky	2,068,000,000	1.7%
22	Louisiana	2,164,000,000	1.8%
38	Maine	566,000,000	0.5%
18	Maryland	2,255,000,000	1.9%
13	Massachusetts	3,009,000,000	2.5%
8	Michigan	4,450,000,000	3.7%
21	Minnesota	2,178,000,000	1.8%
29	Mississippi	1,300,000,000	1.1%
17	Missouri	2,471,000,000	2.0%
45	Montana	346,000,000	0.3%
35	Nebraska	819,000,000	0.7%
36	Nevada	703,000,000	0.6%
40	New Hampshire	516,000,000	0.4%
9	New Jersey	4,446,000,000	3.7%
41	New Mexico	510,000,000	0.4%
2	New York	9,833,000,000	8.1%
10	North Carolina	3,882,000,000	3.2%
48	North Dakota	256,000,000	0.2%
7	Ohio	4,980,000,000	4.1%
28	Oklahoma	1,457,000,000	1.2%
32	Oregon	1,181,000,000	1.0%
5	Pennsylvania	6,204,000,000	5.1%
39	Rhode Island	550,000,000	0.5%
25	South Carolina	1,769,000,000	1.5%
46	South Dakota	260,000,000	0.2%
12	Tennessee	3,129,000,000	2.6%
4	Texas	8,021,000,000	6.6%
37	Utah	685,000,000	0.6%
47	Vermont	259,000,000	0.2%
14	Virginia	2,929,000,000	2.4%
18	Washington	2,255,000,000	1.9%
34	West Virginia	953,000,000	0.8%
16	Wisconsin	2,519,000,000	2.1%
50	Wyoming	173,000,000	0.1%

RANK ORDER

RANK	STATE	EXPENDITURES	% of USA
1	California	$9,918,000,000	8.2%
2	New York	9,833,000,000	8.1%
3	Florida	8,295,000,000	6.8%
4	Texas	8,021,000,000	6.6%
5	Pennsylvania	6,204,000,000	5.1%
6	Illinois	5,201,000,000	4.3%
7	Ohio	4,980,000,000	4.1%
8	Michigan	4,450,000,000	3.7%
9	New Jersey	4,446,000,000	3.7%
10	North Carolina	3,882,000,000	3.2%
11	Georgia	3,662,000,000	3.0%
12	Tennessee	3,129,000,000	2.6%
13	Massachusetts	3,009,000,000	2.5%
14	Virginia	2,929,000,000	2.4%
15	Indiana	2,825,000,000	2.3%
16	Wisconsin	2,519,000,000	2.1%
17	Missouri	2,471,000,000	2.0%
18	Maryland	2,255,000,000	1.9%
18	Washington	2,255,000,000	1.9%
20	Alabama	2,199,000,000	1.8%
21	Minnesota	2,178,000,000	1.8%
22	Louisiana	2,164,000,000	1.8%
23	Kentucky	2,068,000,000	1.7%
24	Connecticut	1,784,000,000	1.5%
25	South Carolina	1,769,000,000	1.5%
26	Arizona	1,721,000,000	1.4%
27	Colorado	1,584,000,000	1.3%
28	Oklahoma	1,457,000,000	1.2%
29	Mississippi	1,300,000,000	1.1%
30	Kansas	1,249,000,000	1.0%
31	Iowa	1,190,000,000	1.0%
32	Oregon	1,181,000,000	1.0%
33	Arkansas	1,096,000,000	0.9%
34	West Virginia	953,000,000	0.8%
35	Nebraska	819,000,000	0.7%
36	Nevada	703,000,000	0.6%
37	Utah	685,000,000	0.6%
38	Maine	566,000,000	0.5%
39	Rhode Island	550,000,000	0.5%
40	New Hampshire	516,000,000	0.4%
41	New Mexico	510,000,000	0.4%
42	Delaware	437,000,000	0.4%
43	Hawaii	420,000,000	0.3%
44	Idaho	414,000,000	0.3%
45	Montana	346,000,000	0.3%
46	South Dakota	260,000,000	0.2%
47	Vermont	259,000,000	0.2%
48	North Dakota	256,000,000	0.2%
49	Alaska	243,000,000	0.2%
50	Wyoming	173,000,000	0.1%
	District of Columbia	205,000,000	0.2%

Source: U.S. Department of Health and Human Services, Centers for Medicare and Medicaid Services
"State Health Care Expenditures" (http://www.cms.hhs.gov/NationalHealthExpendData/)
*Purchases in retail outlets. By state of outlet.

Percent of Total Personal Health Care Expenditures
Spent on Prescription Drugs in 2000
National Percent = 10.7%*

RANK	STATE	PERCENT
2	Alabama	12.9
44	Alaska	9.3
39	Arizona	10.1
16	Arkansas	11.7
50	California	7.9
41	Colorado	9.9
31	Connecticut	10.5
6	Delaware	12.6
11	Florida	11.9
11	Georgia	11.9
48	Hawaii	8.7
27	Idaho	10.6
27	Illinois	10.6
10	Indiana	12.0
25	Iowa	10.7
11	Kansas	11.9
2	Kentucky	12.9
7	Louisiana	12.4
35	Maine	10.3
31	Maryland	10.5
44	Massachusetts	9.3
16	Michigan	11.7
42	Minnesota	9.8
1	Mississippi	13.0
27	Missouri	10.6
25	Montana	10.7
16	Nebraska	11.7
35	Nevada	10.3
40	New Hampshire	10.0
11	New Jersey	11.9
46	New Mexico	8.9
34	New York	10.4
7	North Carolina	12.4
47	North Dakota	8.8
27	Ohio	10.6
9	Oklahoma	12.1
43	Oregon	9.5
22	Pennsylvania	11.2
20	Rhode Island	11.3
15	South Carolina	11.8
49	South Dakota	8.5
4	Tennessee	12.7
31	Texas	10.5
35	Utah	10.3
24	Vermont	11.0
19	Virginia	11.5
38	Washington	10.2
4	West Virginia	12.7
20	Wisconsin	11.3
23	Wyoming	11.1

RANK	STATE	PERCENT
1	Mississippi	13.0
2	Alabama	12.9
2	Kentucky	12.9
4	Tennessee	12.7
4	West Virginia	12.7
6	Delaware	12.6
7	Louisiana	12.4
7	North Carolina	12.4
9	Oklahoma	12.1
10	Indiana	12.0
11	Florida	11.9
11	Georgia	11.9
11	Kansas	11.9
11	New Jersey	11.9
15	South Carolina	11.8
16	Arkansas	11.7
16	Michigan	11.7
16	Nebraska	11.7
19	Virginia	11.5
20	Rhode Island	11.3
20	Wisconsin	11.3
22	Pennsylvania	11.2
23	Wyoming	11.1
24	Vermont	11.0
25	Iowa	10.7
25	Montana	10.7
27	Idaho	10.6
27	Illinois	10.6
27	Missouri	10.6
27	Ohio	10.6
31	Connecticut	10.5
31	Maryland	10.5
31	Texas	10.5
34	New York	10.4
35	Maine	10.3
35	Nevada	10.3
35	Utah	10.3
38	Washington	10.2
39	Arizona	10.1
40	New Hampshire	10.0
41	Colorado	9.9
42	Minnesota	9.8
43	Oregon	9.5
44	Alaska	9.3
44	Massachusetts	9.3
46	New Mexico	8.9
47	North Dakota	8.8
48	Hawaii	8.7
49	South Dakota	8.5
50	California	7.9

District of Columbia		4.4

Source: MQ Press using data from U.S. Dept of Health & Human Services, Centers for Medicare and Medicaid Services
   "State Health Care Expenditures" (http://www.cms.hhs.gov/NationalHealthExpendData/)
*Purchases in retail outlets. By state of outlet.

Per Capita Expenditures for Prescription Drugs in 2000

National Per Capita = $431*

ALPHA ORDER

RANK	STATE	PER CAPITA
11	Alabama	$494
36	Alaska	387
46	Arizona	333
33	Arkansas	409
49	California	292
40	Colorado	366
5	Connecticut	523
1	Delaware	556
8	Florida	517
21	Georgia	445
43	Hawaii	346
47	Idaho	319
30	Illinois	418
17	Indiana	464
34	Iowa	406
17	Kansas	464
9	Kentucky	511
12	Louisiana	484
22	Maine	443
27	Maryland	425
15	Massachusetts	473
20	Michigan	447
23	Minnesota	441
19	Mississippi	456
23	Missouri	441
37	Montana	383
14	Nebraska	478
42	Nevada	348
31	New Hampshire	416
3	New Jersey	527
50	New Mexico	280
7	New York	518
13	North Carolina	481
35	North Dakota	399
26	Ohio	438
29	Oklahoma	422
44	Oregon	344
10	Pennsylvania	505
5	Rhode Island	523
25	South Carolina	440
44	South Dakota	344
2	Tennessee	549
37	Texas	383
48	Utah	305
27	Vermont	425
32	Virginia	412
39	Washington	381
3	West Virginia	527
16	Wisconsin	469
41	Wyoming	350

RANK ORDER

RANK	STATE	PER CAPITA
1	Delaware	$556
2	Tennessee	549
3	New Jersey	527
3	West Virginia	527
5	Connecticut	523
5	Rhode Island	523
7	New York	518
8	Florida	517
9	Kentucky	511
10	Pennsylvania	505
11	Alabama	494
12	Louisiana	484
13	North Carolina	481
14	Nebraska	478
15	Massachusetts	473
16	Wisconsin	469
17	Indiana	464
17	Kansas	464
19	Mississippi	456
20	Michigan	447
21	Georgia	445
22	Maine	443
23	Minnesota	441
23	Missouri	441
25	South Carolina	440
26	Ohio	438
27	Maryland	425
27	Vermont	425
29	Oklahoma	422
30	Illinois	418
31	New Hampshire	416
32	Virginia	412
33	Arkansas	409
34	Iowa	406
35	North Dakota	399
36	Alaska	387
37	Montana	383
37	Texas	383
39	Washington	381
40	Colorado	366
41	Wyoming	350
42	Nevada	348
43	Hawaii	346
44	Oregon	344
44	South Dakota	344
46	Arizona	333
47	Idaho	319
48	Utah	305
49	California	292
50	New Mexico	280

District of Columbia	359

Source: MQ Press using data from U.S. Dept of Health & Human Services, Centers for Medicare and Medicaid Services "State Health Care Expenditures" (http://www.cms.hhs.gov/NationalHealthExpendData/)
*Purchases in retail outlets. By state of outlet. Per capita calculated using resident population. These figures may be skewed due to residents crossing state borders to make purchases.

Expenditures for Dental Services in 2000

National Total = $60,726,000,000*

ALPHA ORDER

RANK	STATE	EXPENDITURES	% of USA
27	Alabama	$708,000,000	1.2%
44	Alaska	184,000,000	0.3%
19	Arizona	1,058,000,000	1.7%
34	Arkansas	441,000,000	0.7%
1	California	9,022,000,000	14.9%
17	Colorado	1,146,000,000	1.9%
24	Connecticut	950,000,000	1.6%
44	Delaware	184,000,000	0.3%
4	Florida	3,345,000,000	5.5%
12	Georgia	1,646,000,000	2.7%
37	Hawaii	300,000,000	0.5%
38	Idaho	298,000,000	0.5%
5	Illinois	2,541,000,000	4.2%
18	Indiana	1,143,000,000	1.9%
32	Iowa	484,000,000	0.8%
30	Kansas	541,000,000	0.9%
28	Kentucky	587,000,000	1.0%
25	Louisiana	764,000,000	1.3%
39	Maine	279,000,000	0.5%
20	Maryland	1,049,000,000	1.7%
11	Massachusetts	1,776,000,000	2.9%
6	Michigan	2,356,000,000	3.9%
16	Minnesota	1,218,000,000	2.0%
35	Mississippi	353,000,000	0.6%
23	Missouri	979,000,000	1.6%
46	Montana	174,000,000	0.3%
36	Nebraska	324,000,000	0.5%
33	Nevada	468,000,000	0.8%
40	New Hampshire	274,000,000	0.5%
9	New Jersey	2,085,000,000	3.4%
43	New Mexico	225,000,000	0.4%
2	New York	4,043,000,000	6.7%
14	North Carolina	1,508,000,000	2.5%
49	North Dakota	122,000,000	0.2%
8	Ohio	2,233,000,000	3.7%
29	Oklahoma	586,000,000	1.0%
22	Oregon	983,000,000	1.6%
7	Pennsylvania	2,298,000,000	3.8%
41	Rhode Island	246,000,000	0.4%
26	South Carolina	729,000,000	1.2%
48	South Dakota	140,000,000	0.2%
21	Tennessee	990,000,000	1.6%
3	Texas	3,984,000,000	6.6%
31	Utah	527,000,000	0.9%
47	Vermont	148,000,000	0.2%
13	Virginia	1,560,000,000	2.6%
10	Washington	1,870,000,000	3.1%
42	West Virginia	234,000,000	0.4%
15	Wisconsin	1,376,000,000	2.3%
50	Wyoming	82,000,000	0.1%

RANK ORDER

RANK	STATE	EXPENDITURES	% of USA
1	California	$9,022,000,000	14.9%
2	New York	4,043,000,000	6.7%
3	Texas	3,984,000,000	6.6%
4	Florida	3,345,000,000	5.5%
5	Illinois	2,541,000,000	4.2%
6	Michigan	2,356,000,000	3.9%
7	Pennsylvania	2,298,000,000	3.8%
8	Ohio	2,233,000,000	3.7%
9	New Jersey	2,085,000,000	3.4%
10	Washington	1,870,000,000	3.1%
11	Massachusetts	1,776,000,000	2.9%
12	Georgia	1,646,000,000	2.7%
13	Virginia	1,560,000,000	2.6%
14	North Carolina	1,508,000,000	2.5%
15	Wisconsin	1,376,000,000	2.3%
16	Minnesota	1,218,000,000	2.0%
17	Colorado	1,146,000,000	1.9%
18	Indiana	1,143,000,000	1.9%
19	Arizona	1,058,000,000	1.7%
20	Maryland	1,049,000,000	1.7%
21	Tennessee	990,000,000	1.6%
22	Oregon	983,000,000	1.6%
23	Missouri	979,000,000	1.6%
24	Connecticut	950,000,000	1.6%
25	Louisiana	764,000,000	1.3%
26	South Carolina	729,000,000	1.2%
27	Alabama	708,000,000	1.2%
28	Kentucky	587,000,000	1.0%
29	Oklahoma	586,000,000	1.0%
30	Kansas	541,000,000	0.9%
31	Utah	527,000,000	0.9%
32	Iowa	484,000,000	0.8%
33	Nevada	468,000,000	0.8%
34	Arkansas	441,000,000	0.7%
35	Mississippi	353,000,000	0.6%
36	Nebraska	324,000,000	0.5%
37	Hawaii	300,000,000	0.5%
38	Idaho	298,000,000	0.5%
39	Maine	279,000,000	0.5%
40	New Hampshire	274,000,000	0.5%
41	Rhode Island	246,000,000	0.4%
42	West Virginia	234,000,000	0.4%
43	New Mexico	225,000,000	0.4%
44	Alaska	184,000,000	0.3%
44	Delaware	184,000,000	0.3%
46	Montana	174,000,000	0.3%
47	Vermont	148,000,000	0.2%
48	South Dakota	140,000,000	0.2%
49	North Dakota	122,000,000	0.2%
50	Wyoming	82,000,000	0.1%
	District of Columbia	163,000,000	0.3%

Source: U.S. Department of Health and Human Services, Centers for Medicare and Medicaid Services
    "State Health Care Expenditures" (http://www.cms.hhs.gov/NationalHealthExpendData/)
*By state of provider.

Percent of Total Personal Health Care Expenditures
Spent on Dental Services in 2000
National Percent = 5.3%*

<table>
<tr><th colspan="3">ALPHA ORDER</th><th colspan="3">RANK ORDER</th></tr>
<tr><th>RANK</th><th>STATE</th><th>PERCENT</th><th>RANK</th><th>STATE</th><th>PERCENT</th></tr>
<tr><td>42</td><td>Alabama</td><td>4.2</td><td>1</td><td>Washington</td><td>8.5</td></tr>
<tr><td>7</td><td>Alaska</td><td>7.0</td><td>2</td><td>Utah</td><td>8.0</td></tr>
<tr><td>10</td><td>Arizona</td><td>6.2</td><td>3</td><td>Oregon</td><td>7.9</td></tr>
<tr><td>36</td><td>Arkansas</td><td>4.7</td><td>4</td><td>Idaho</td><td>7.6</td></tr>
<tr><td>5</td><td>California</td><td>7.2</td><td>5</td><td>California</td><td>7.2</td></tr>
<tr><td>5</td><td>Colorado</td><td>7.2</td><td>5</td><td>Colorado</td><td>7.2</td></tr>
<tr><td>15</td><td>Connecticut</td><td>5.6</td><td>7</td><td>Alaska</td><td>7.0</td></tr>
<tr><td>20</td><td>Delaware</td><td>5.3</td><td>8</td><td>Nevada</td><td>6.8</td></tr>
<tr><td>33</td><td>Florida</td><td>4.8</td><td>9</td><td>Vermont</td><td>6.3</td></tr>
<tr><td>20</td><td>Georgia</td><td>5.3</td><td>10</td><td>Arizona</td><td>6.2</td></tr>
<tr><td>10</td><td>Hawaii</td><td>6.2</td><td>10</td><td>Hawaii</td><td>6.2</td></tr>
<tr><td>4</td><td>Idaho</td><td>7.6</td><td>10</td><td>Michigan</td><td>6.2</td></tr>
<tr><td>24</td><td>Illinois</td><td>5.2</td><td>10</td><td>Wisconsin</td><td>6.2</td></tr>
<tr><td>29</td><td>Indiana</td><td>4.9</td><td>14</td><td>Virginia</td><td>6.1</td></tr>
<tr><td>40</td><td>Iowa</td><td>4.3</td><td>15</td><td>Connecticut</td><td>5.6</td></tr>
<tr><td>24</td><td>Kansas</td><td>5.2</td><td>15</td><td>New Jersey</td><td>5.6</td></tr>
<tr><td>48</td><td>Kentucky</td><td>3.7</td><td>17</td><td>Massachusetts</td><td>5.5</td></tr>
<tr><td>39</td><td>Louisiana</td><td>4.4</td><td>17</td><td>Minnesota</td><td>5.5</td></tr>
<tr><td>27</td><td>Maine</td><td>5.1</td><td>19</td><td>Montana</td><td>5.4</td></tr>
<tr><td>29</td><td>Maryland</td><td>4.9</td><td>20</td><td>Delaware</td><td>5.3</td></tr>
<tr><td>17</td><td>Massachusetts</td><td>5.5</td><td>20</td><td>Georgia</td><td>5.3</td></tr>
<tr><td>10</td><td>Michigan</td><td>6.2</td><td>20</td><td>New Hampshire</td><td>5.3</td></tr>
<tr><td>17</td><td>Minnesota</td><td>5.5</td><td>20</td><td>Wyoming</td><td>5.3</td></tr>
<tr><td>49</td><td>Mississippi</td><td>3.5</td><td>24</td><td>Illinois</td><td>5.2</td></tr>
<tr><td>42</td><td>Missouri</td><td>4.2</td><td>24</td><td>Kansas</td><td>5.2</td></tr>
<tr><td>19</td><td>Montana</td><td>5.4</td><td>24</td><td>Texas</td><td>5.2</td></tr>
<tr><td>37</td><td>Nebraska</td><td>4.6</td><td>27</td><td>Maine</td><td>5.1</td></tr>
<tr><td>8</td><td>Nevada</td><td>6.8</td><td>27</td><td>Rhode Island</td><td>5.1</td></tr>
<tr><td>20</td><td>New Hampshire</td><td>5.3</td><td>29</td><td>Indiana</td><td>4.9</td></tr>
<tr><td>15</td><td>New Jersey</td><td>5.6</td><td>29</td><td>Maryland</td><td>4.9</td></tr>
<tr><td>47</td><td>New Mexico</td><td>3.9</td><td>29</td><td>Oklahoma</td><td>4.9</td></tr>
<tr><td>40</td><td>New York</td><td>4.3</td><td>29</td><td>South Carolina</td><td>4.9</td></tr>
<tr><td>33</td><td>North Carolina</td><td>4.8</td><td>33</td><td>Florida</td><td>4.8</td></tr>
<tr><td>42</td><td>North Dakota</td><td>4.2</td><td>33</td><td>North Carolina</td><td>4.8</td></tr>
<tr><td>33</td><td>Ohio</td><td>4.8</td><td>33</td><td>Ohio</td><td>4.8</td></tr>
<tr><td>29</td><td>Oklahoma</td><td>4.9</td><td>36</td><td>Arkansas</td><td>4.7</td></tr>
<tr><td>3</td><td>Oregon</td><td>7.9</td><td>37</td><td>Nebraska</td><td>4.6</td></tr>
<tr><td>42</td><td>Pennsylvania</td><td>4.2</td><td>37</td><td>South Dakota</td><td>4.6</td></tr>
<tr><td>27</td><td>Rhode Island</td><td>5.1</td><td>39</td><td>Louisiana</td><td>4.4</td></tr>
<tr><td>29</td><td>South Carolina</td><td>4.9</td><td>40</td><td>Iowa</td><td>4.3</td></tr>
<tr><td>37</td><td>South Dakota</td><td>4.6</td><td>40</td><td>New York</td><td>4.3</td></tr>
<tr><td>46</td><td>Tennessee</td><td>4.0</td><td>42</td><td>Alabama</td><td>4.2</td></tr>
<tr><td>24</td><td>Texas</td><td>5.2</td><td>42</td><td>Missouri</td><td>4.2</td></tr>
<tr><td>2</td><td>Utah</td><td>8.0</td><td>42</td><td>North Dakota</td><td>4.2</td></tr>
<tr><td>9</td><td>Vermont</td><td>6.3</td><td>42</td><td>Pennsylvania</td><td>4.2</td></tr>
<tr><td>14</td><td>Virginia</td><td>6.1</td><td>46</td><td>Tennessee</td><td>4.0</td></tr>
<tr><td>1</td><td>Washington</td><td>8.5</td><td>47</td><td>New Mexico</td><td>3.9</td></tr>
<tr><td>50</td><td>West Virginia</td><td>3.1</td><td>48</td><td>Kentucky</td><td>3.7</td></tr>
<tr><td>10</td><td>Wisconsin</td><td>6.2</td><td>49</td><td>Mississippi</td><td>3.5</td></tr>
<tr><td>20</td><td>Wyoming</td><td>5.3</td><td>50</td><td>West Virginia</td><td>3.1</td></tr>
<tr><td></td><td></td><td></td><td></td><td>District of Columbia</td><td>3.5</td></tr>
</table>

Source: MQ Press using data from U.S. Dept of Health & Human Services, Centers for Medicare and Medicaid Services "State Health Care Expenditures" (http://www.cms.hhs.gov/NationalHealthExpendData/)
*By state of provider.

Per Capita Expenditures for Dental Services in 2000

National Per Capita = $215*

<table>
<tr><td colspan="3">ALPHA ORDER</td><td colspan="3">RANK ORDER</td></tr>
<tr><th>RANK</th><th>STATE</th><th>PER CAPITA</th><th>RANK</th><th>STATE</th><th>PER CAPITA</th></tr>
<tr><td>46</td><td>Alabama</td><td>$159</td><td>1</td><td>Washington</td><td>$316</td></tr>
<tr><td>2</td><td>Alaska</td><td>293</td><td>2</td><td>Alaska</td><td>293</td></tr>
<tr><td>24</td><td>Arizona</td><td>205</td><td>3</td><td>Oregon</td><td>286</td></tr>
<tr><td>44</td><td>Arkansas</td><td>165</td><td>4</td><td>Massachusetts</td><td>279</td></tr>
<tr><td>6</td><td>California</td><td>265</td><td>5</td><td>Connecticut</td><td>278</td></tr>
<tr><td>6</td><td>Colorado</td><td>265</td><td>6</td><td>California</td><td>265</td></tr>
<tr><td>5</td><td>Connecticut</td><td>278</td><td>6</td><td>Colorado</td><td>265</td></tr>
<tr><td>15</td><td>Delaware</td><td>234</td><td>8</td><td>Wisconsin</td><td>256</td></tr>
<tr><td>23</td><td>Florida</td><td>208</td><td>9</td><td>Hawaii</td><td>247</td></tr>
<tr><td>27</td><td>Georgia</td><td>200</td><td>9</td><td>Minnesota</td><td>247</td></tr>
<tr><td>9</td><td>Hawaii</td><td>247</td><td>9</td><td>New Jersey</td><td>247</td></tr>
<tr><td>18</td><td>Idaho</td><td>229</td><td>12</td><td>Vermont</td><td>243</td></tr>
<tr><td>25</td><td>Illinois</td><td>204</td><td>13</td><td>Michigan</td><td>237</td></tr>
<tr><td>34</td><td>Indiana</td><td>188</td><td>14</td><td>Utah</td><td>235</td></tr>
<tr><td>44</td><td>Iowa</td><td>165</td><td>15</td><td>Delaware</td><td>234</td></tr>
<tr><td>26</td><td>Kansas</td><td>201</td><td>15</td><td>Rhode Island</td><td>234</td></tr>
<tr><td>47</td><td>Kentucky</td><td>145</td><td>17</td><td>Nevada</td><td>232</td></tr>
<tr><td>41</td><td>Louisiana</td><td>171</td><td>18</td><td>Idaho</td><td>229</td></tr>
<tr><td>21</td><td>Maine</td><td>218</td><td>19</td><td>New Hampshire</td><td>221</td></tr>
<tr><td>28</td><td>Maryland</td><td>197</td><td>20</td><td>Virginia</td><td>220</td></tr>
<tr><td>4</td><td>Massachusetts</td><td>279</td><td>21</td><td>Maine</td><td>218</td></tr>
<tr><td>13</td><td>Michigan</td><td>237</td><td>22</td><td>New York</td><td>213</td></tr>
<tr><td>9</td><td>Minnesota</td><td>247</td><td>23</td><td>Florida</td><td>208</td></tr>
<tr><td>49</td><td>Mississippi</td><td>124</td><td>24</td><td>Arizona</td><td>205</td></tr>
<tr><td>39</td><td>Missouri</td><td>175</td><td>25</td><td>Illinois</td><td>204</td></tr>
<tr><td>30</td><td>Montana</td><td>193</td><td>26</td><td>Kansas</td><td>201</td></tr>
<tr><td>33</td><td>Nebraska</td><td>189</td><td>27</td><td>Georgia</td><td>200</td></tr>
<tr><td>17</td><td>Nevada</td><td>232</td><td>28</td><td>Maryland</td><td>197</td></tr>
<tr><td>19</td><td>New Hampshire</td><td>221</td><td>28</td><td>Ohio</td><td>197</td></tr>
<tr><td>9</td><td>New Jersey</td><td>247</td><td>30</td><td>Montana</td><td>193</td></tr>
<tr><td>49</td><td>New Mexico</td><td>124</td><td>31</td><td>North Dakota</td><td>190</td></tr>
<tr><td>22</td><td>New York</td><td>213</td><td>31</td><td>Texas</td><td>190</td></tr>
<tr><td>35</td><td>North Carolina</td><td>187</td><td>33</td><td>Nebraska</td><td>189</td></tr>
<tr><td>31</td><td>North Dakota</td><td>190</td><td>34</td><td>Indiana</td><td>188</td></tr>
<tr><td>28</td><td>Ohio</td><td>197</td><td>35</td><td>North Carolina</td><td>187</td></tr>
<tr><td>42</td><td>Oklahoma</td><td>170</td><td>35</td><td>Pennsylvania</td><td>187</td></tr>
<tr><td>3</td><td>Oregon</td><td>286</td><td>37</td><td>South Dakota</td><td>185</td></tr>
<tr><td>35</td><td>Pennsylvania</td><td>187</td><td>38</td><td>South Carolina</td><td>181</td></tr>
<tr><td>15</td><td>Rhode Island</td><td>234</td><td>39</td><td>Missouri</td><td>175</td></tr>
<tr><td>38</td><td>South Carolina</td><td>181</td><td>40</td><td>Tennessee</td><td>174</td></tr>
<tr><td>37</td><td>South Dakota</td><td>185</td><td>41</td><td>Louisiana</td><td>171</td></tr>
<tr><td>40</td><td>Tennessee</td><td>174</td><td>42</td><td>Oklahoma</td><td>170</td></tr>
<tr><td>31</td><td>Texas</td><td>190</td><td>43</td><td>Wyoming</td><td>166</td></tr>
<tr><td>14</td><td>Utah</td><td>235</td><td>44</td><td>Arkansas</td><td>165</td></tr>
<tr><td>12</td><td>Vermont</td><td>243</td><td>44</td><td>Iowa</td><td>165</td></tr>
<tr><td>20</td><td>Virginia</td><td>220</td><td>46</td><td>Alabama</td><td>159</td></tr>
<tr><td>1</td><td>Washington</td><td>316</td><td>47</td><td>Kentucky</td><td>145</td></tr>
<tr><td>48</td><td>West Virginia</td><td>129</td><td>48</td><td>West Virginia</td><td>129</td></tr>
<tr><td>8</td><td>Wisconsin</td><td>256</td><td>49</td><td>Mississippi</td><td>124</td></tr>
<tr><td>43</td><td>Wyoming</td><td>166</td><td>49</td><td>New Mexico</td><td>124</td></tr>
<tr><td></td><td></td><td></td><td></td><td>District of Columbia</td><td>285</td></tr>
</table>

Source: MQ Press using data from U.S. Dept of Health & Human Services, Centers for Medicare and Medicaid Services
   "State Health Care Expenditures" (http://www.cms.hhs.gov/NationalHealthExpendData/)
*By state of provider. Per capita calculated using resident population. These figures may be skewed due to residents crossing state borders for care.

Projected National Health Care Expenditures in 2006

Total Health Care Expenditures = $2,077,500,000,000*

The 2000 health care expenditures broken down to the state level and shown on pages 307 to 321 were released in March of 2005 and are the most recent state health expenditure data available from the Centers for Medicare and Medicaid Services (CMS). The CMS plan to update these numbers but no updates were available as we went to press.

Given the high level of interest in health care finance data, we have assembled a table showing the most recent national level health care expenditure projections. We will continue to monitor CMS data releases and will include state expenditure updates in forthcoming editions.

	PROJECTED EXPENDITURES IN 2006	PROJECTED PERCENT CHANGE: 2005 TO 2006
Total Health Care Expenditures	$2,077,500,000,000	7.3
Per Capita Total Health Care Expenditures	$7,009	
Personal Health Care Expenditures	$1,781,300,000,000	7.1
Per Capita Personal Health Care Expenditures	$6,010	
Hospital Care Expenditures	$623,500,000,000	5.9
Per Capita Hospital Care Expenditures	$2,104	
Physician Services Expenditures	$453,800,000,000	6.6
Per Capita Physician Services Expenditures	$1,531	
Dental Services Expenditures	$90,000,000,000	7.0
Per Capita Dental Services Expenditures	$304	
Other Professional Services	$59,600,000,000	7.2
Per Capita Other Professional Services	$201	
Home Health Care Expenditures	$54,800,000,000	9.6
Per Capita Home Health Care Expenditures	$185	
Prescription Drugs	$249,300,000,000	11.5
Per Capita Prescription Drugs	$841	
Nursing Home Care	$127,100,000,000	5.0
Per Capita Nursing Home Care	$429	
Other Personal Care Expenditures	$63,900,000,000	9.8
Per Capita Other Personal Care Expenditures	$216	

Source: U.S. Department of Health and Human Services, Centers for Medicare and Medicaid Services
"National Health Expenditure Amounts and Average Annual Percent Change, by Type of Expenditure"
http://www.cms.hhs.gov/NationalHealthExpendData/downloads/nheprojections2004-2014.pdf
*Per Capita and percent change figures calculated by Morgan Quitno Press using 2005 Census population
estimates. For definitions see the corresponding 2000 state tables in this chapter.

V. INCIDENCE OF DISEASE

V. INCIDENCE OF DISEASE (Continued)

Estimated New Cancer Cases in 2005

National Estimated Total = 1,372,910 New Cases*

ALPHA ORDER

RANK	STATE	CASES	% of USA
20	Alabama	24,320	1.8%
50	Alaska	1,930	0.1%
21	Arizona	23,880	1.7%
32	Arkansas	14,950	1.1%
1	California	135,030	9.8%
29	Colorado	16,080	1.2%
28	Connecticut	16,920	1.2%
46	Delaware	3,800	0.3%
2	Florida	96,200	7.0%
11	Georgia	35,650	2.6%
44	Hawaii	4,790	0.3%
42	Idaho	5,490	0.4%
6	Illinois	59,730	4.4%
14	Indiana	31,900	2.3%
30	Iowa	15,910	1.2%
33	Kansas	12,930	0.9%
23	Kentucky	23,020	1.7%
22	Louisiana	23,280	1.7%
38	Maine	7,750	0.6%
19	Maryland	25,450	1.9%
13	Massachusetts	33,030	2.4%
8	Michigan	50,220	3.7%
24	Minnesota	22,890	1.7%
31	Mississippi	14,970	1.1%
16	Missouri	30,210	2.2%
43	Montana	4,910	0.4%
36	Nebraska	8,330	0.6%
35	Nevada	11,120	0.8%
40	New Hampshire	6,310	0.5%
9	New Jersey	43,000	3.1%
37	New Mexico	7,780	0.6%
3	New York	87,050	6.3%
10	North Carolina	40,520	3.0%
47	North Dakota	3,080	0.2%
7	Ohio	59,680	4.3%
26	Oklahoma	18,460	1.3%
27	Oregon	17,720	1.3%
5	Pennsylvania	71,840	5.2%
41	Rhode Island	5,870	0.4%
25	South Carolina	21,860	1.6%
45	South Dakota	3,900	0.3%
15	Tennessee	31,080	2.3%
4	Texas	86,880	6.3%
39	Utah	6,380	0.5%
48	Vermont	3,030	0.2%
12	Virginia	33,680	2.5%
17	Washington	27,350	2.0%
34	West Virginia	11,190	0.8%
18	Wisconsin	26,340	1.9%
49	Wyoming	2,380	0.2%

RANK ORDER

RANK	STATE	CASES	% of USA
1	California	135,030	9.8%
2	Florida	96,200	7.0%
3	New York	87,050	6.3%
4	Texas	86,880	6.3%
5	Pennsylvania	71,840	5.2%
6	Illinois	59,730	4.4%
7	Ohio	59,680	4.3%
8	Michigan	50,220	3.7%
9	New Jersey	43,000	3.1%
10	North Carolina	40,520	3.0%
11	Georgia	35,650	2.6%
12	Virginia	33,680	2.5%
13	Massachusetts	33,030	2.4%
14	Indiana	31,900	2.3%
15	Tennessee	31,080	2.3%
16	Missouri	30,210	2.2%
17	Washington	27,350	2.0%
18	Wisconsin	26,340	1.9%
19	Maryland	25,450	1.9%
20	Alabama	24,320	1.8%
21	Arizona	23,880	1.7%
22	Louisiana	23,280	1.7%
23	Kentucky	23,020	1.7%
24	Minnesota	22,890	1.7%
25	South Carolina	21,860	1.6%
26	Oklahoma	18,460	1.3%
27	Oregon	17,720	1.3%
28	Connecticut	16,920	1.2%
29	Colorado	16,080	1.2%
30	Iowa	15,910	1.2%
31	Mississippi	14,970	1.1%
32	Arkansas	14,950	1.1%
33	Kansas	12,930	0.9%
34	West Virginia	11,190	0.8%
35	Nevada	11,120	0.8%
36	Nebraska	8,330	0.6%
37	New Mexico	7,780	0.6%
38	Maine	7,750	0.6%
39	Utah	6,380	0.5%
40	New Hampshire	6,310	0.5%
41	Rhode Island	5,870	0.4%
42	Idaho	5,490	0.4%
43	Montana	4,910	0.4%
44	Hawaii	4,790	0.3%
45	South Dakota	3,900	0.3%
46	Delaware	3,800	0.3%
47	North Dakota	3,080	0.2%
48	Vermont	3,030	0.2%
49	Wyoming	2,380	0.2%
50	Alaska	1,930	0.1%

District of Columbia 2,820 0.2%

Source: American Cancer Society
   "Cancer Facts & Figures 2005" (Copyright 2005, American Cancer Society)
*These estimates are offered as a rough guide and should not be regarded as definitive. They are calculated according to the distribution of estimated 2005 cancer deaths by state. Totals do not include basal and squamous cell skin cancers or in situ carcinomas except urinary bladder.

Estimated Rate of New Cancer Cases in 2005

National Estimated Rate = 467.5 New Cases per 100,000 Population*

ALPHA ORDER				RANK ORDER		
RANK	STATE	RATE		RANK	STATE	RATE
9	Alabama	536.8		1	West Virginia	616.4
49	Alaska	294.5		2	Maine	588.3
41	Arizona	415.8		3	Pennsylvania	579.1
7	Arkansas	543.1		4	Kentucky	555.2
47	California	376.2		5	Florida	553.0
48	Colorado	349.5		6	Rhode Island	543.2
27	Connecticut	482.9		7	Arkansas	543.1
36	Delaware	457.6		8	Iowa	538.5
5	Florida	553.0		9	Alabama	536.8
43	Georgia	403.8		10	Montana	529.7
46	Hawaii	379.3		11	Tennessee	526.7
44	Idaho	394.0		12	Missouri	525.0
34	Illinois	469.8		13	Oklahoma	523.9
19	Indiana	511.4		14	Ohio	520.8
8	Iowa	538.5		15	South Carolina	520.7
32	Kansas	472.7		16	Mississippi	515.7
4	Kentucky	555.2		17	Louisiana	515.5
17	Louisiana	515.5		18	Massachusetts	514.8
2	Maine	588.3		19	Indiana	511.4
35	Maryland	457.9		20	South Dakota	505.9
18	Massachusetts	514.8		21	Michigan	496.6
21	Michigan	496.6		22	New Jersey	494.3
39	Minnesota	448.7		23	Oregon	493.0
16	Mississippi	515.7		24	Vermont	487.6
12	Missouri	525.0		25	New Hampshire	485.6
10	Montana	529.7		26	North Dakota	485.5
29	Nebraska	476.8		27	Connecticut	482.9
30	Nevada	476.3		28	Wisconsin	478.1
25	New Hampshire	485.6		29	Nebraska	476.8
22	New Jersey	494.3		30	Nevada	476.3
42	New Mexico	408.8		31	North Carolina	474.4
37	New York	452.7		32	Kansas	472.7
31	North Carolina	474.4		33	Wyoming	469.9
26	North Dakota	485.5		34	Illinois	469.8
14	Ohio	520.8		35	Maryland	457.9
13	Oklahoma	523.9		36	Delaware	457.6
23	Oregon	493.0		37	New York	452.7
3	Pennsylvania	579.1		38	Virginia	451.5
6	Rhode Island	543.2		39	Minnesota	448.7
15	South Carolina	520.7		40	Washington	440.9
20	South Dakota	505.9		41	Arizona	415.8
11	Tennessee	526.7		42	New Mexico	408.8
45	Texas	386.3		43	Georgia	403.8
50	Utah	267.1		44	Idaho	394.0
24	Vermont	487.6		45	Texas	386.3
38	Virginia	451.5		46	Hawaii	379.3
40	Washington	440.9		47	California	376.2
1	West Virginia	616.4		48	Colorado	349.5
28	Wisconsin	478.1		49	Alaska	294.5
33	Wyoming	469.9		50	Utah	267.1
					District of Columbia	509.5

Source: Morgan Quitno Press using data from American Cancer Society
    "Cancer Facts & Figures 2005" (Copyright 2005, American Cancer Society)
*These estimates are offered as a rough guide and should not be regarded as definitive. They are calculated according to the distribution of estimated 2005 cancer deaths by state. Totals do not include basal and squamous cell skin cancers or in situ carcinomas except urinary bladder. Rates calculated using 2004 Census resident population estimates.

Age-Adjusted Cancer Incidence Rates for Males in 2001

National Rate = 566.1 New Cases per 100,000 Male Population*

ALPHA ORDER

RANK	STATE	RATE
37	Alabama	505.5
18	Alaska	560.5
45	Arizona	466.3
30	Arkansas	533.7
33	California	525.4
36	Colorado	518.2
8	Connecticut	594.0
16	Delaware	566.2
14	Florida	569.1
26	Georgia	540.7
42	Hawaii	483.7
35	Idaho	520.0
12	Illinois	573.5
31	Indiana	532.0
19	Iowa	557.2
NA	Kansas**	NA
4	Kentucky	615.3
5	Louisiana	606.1
7	Maine	602.5
17	Maryland	565.0
6	Massachusetts	605.2
3	Michigan	615.4
21	Minnesota	554.3
NA	Mississippi**	NA
27	Missouri	539.3
23	Montana	552.7
25	Nebraska	545.9
40	Nevada	486.9
20	New Hampshire	555.0
2	New Jersey	628.7
44	New Mexico	470.7
15	New York	568.1
34	North Carolina	525.3
41	North Dakota	486.4
22	Ohio	553.6
29	Oklahoma	534.8
24	Oregon	546.3
NA	Pennsylvania**	NA
1	Rhode Island	634.9
11	South Carolina	576.7
39	South Dakota	492.5
NA	Tennessee**	NA
32	Texas	528.2
43	Utah	478.1
NA	Vermont**	NA
38	Virginia	498.7
10	Washington	579.1
9	West Virginia	583.9
13	Wisconsin	573.3
28	Wyoming	536.2

RANK ORDER

RANK	STATE	RATE
1	Rhode Island	634.9
2	New Jersey	628.7
3	Michigan	615.4
4	Kentucky	615.3
5	Louisiana	606.1
6	Massachusetts	605.2
7	Maine	602.5
8	Connecticut	594.0
9	West Virginia	583.9
10	Washington	579.1
11	South Carolina	576.7
12	Illinois	573.5
13	Wisconsin	573.3
14	Florida	569.1
15	New York	568.1
16	Delaware	566.2
17	Maryland	565.0
18	Alaska	560.5
19	Iowa	557.2
20	New Hampshire	555.0
21	Minnesota	554.3
22	Ohio	553.6
23	Montana	552.7
24	Oregon	546.3
25	Nebraska	545.9
26	Georgia	540.7
27	Missouri	539.3
28	Wyoming	536.2
29	Oklahoma	534.8
30	Arkansas	533.7
31	Indiana	532.0
32	Texas	528.2
33	California	525.4
34	North Carolina	525.3
35	Idaho	520.0
36	Colorado	518.2
37	Alabama	505.5
38	Virginia	498.7
39	South Dakota	492.5
40	Nevada	486.9
41	North Dakota	486.4
42	Hawaii	483.7
43	Utah	478.1
44	New Mexico	470.7
45	Arizona	466.3
NA	Kansas**	NA
NA	Mississippi**	NA
NA	Pennsylvania**	NA
NA	Tennessee**	NA
NA	Vermont**	NA

District of Columbia   667.7

Source: American Cancer Society
 "Cancer Facts & Figures 2005" (Copyright 2005, American Cancer Society)
*For 1997 to 2001. Age-adjusted to the 2000 U.S. standard population.
**Not available.

Age-Adjusted Cancer Incidence Rates for Females in 2001

National Rate = 420.0 New Cases per 100,000 Female Population*

ALPHA ORDER

RANK	STATE	RATE
41	Alabama	353.6
7	Alaska	441.9
38	Arizona	370.3
35	Arkansas	380.4
30	California	394.8
26	Colorado	400.2
4	Connecticut	449.3
11	Delaware	433.0
19	Florida	419.8
37	Georgia	373.5
33	Hawaii	384.4
28	Idaho	396.9
15	Illinois	425.4
25	Indiana	408.3
17	Iowa	421.9
NA	Kansas**	NA
8	Kentucky	440.3
27	Louisiana	397.7
6	Maine	442.1
21	Maryland	411.9
5	Massachusetts	448.1
9	Michigan	435.3
22	Minnesota	410.3
NA	Mississippi**	NA
23	Missouri	409.7
20	Montana	416.1
24	Nebraska	408.6
29	Nevada	395.8
16	New Hampshire	422.1
2	New Jersey	452.3
42	New Mexico	352.9
12	New York	432.7
38	North Carolina	370.3
45	North Dakota	341.3
18	Ohio	420.5
31	Oklahoma	393.5
10	Oregon	435.2
NA	Pennsylvania**	NA
1	Rhode Island	453.3
34	South Carolina	381.0
43	South Dakota	350.0
NA	Tennessee**	NA
36	Texas	377.3
44	Utah	346.1
NA	Vermont**	NA
40	Virginia	362.5
3	Washington	449.8
13	West Virginia	430.3
14	Wisconsin	425.5
32	Wyoming	386.6

RANK ORDER

RANK	STATE	RATE
1	Rhode Island	453.3
2	New Jersey	452.3
3	Washington	449.8
4	Connecticut	449.3
5	Massachusetts	448.1
6	Maine	442.1
7	Alaska	441.9
8	Kentucky	440.3
9	Michigan	435.3
10	Oregon	435.2
11	Delaware	433.0
12	New York	432.7
13	West Virginia	430.3
14	Wisconsin	425.5
15	Illinois	425.4
16	New Hampshire	422.1
17	Iowa	421.9
18	Ohio	420.5
19	Florida	419.8
20	Montana	416.1
21	Maryland	411.9
22	Minnesota	410.3
23	Missouri	409.7
24	Nebraska	408.6
25	Indiana	408.3
26	Colorado	400.2
27	Louisiana	397.7
28	Idaho	396.9
29	Nevada	395.8
30	California	394.8
31	Oklahoma	393.5
32	Wyoming	386.6
33	Hawaii	384.4
34	South Carolina	381.0
35	Arkansas	380.4
36	Texas	377.3
37	Georgia	373.5
38	Arizona	370.3
38	North Carolina	370.3
40	Virginia	362.5
41	Alabama	353.6
42	New Mexico	352.9
43	South Dakota	350.0
44	Utah	346.1
45	North Dakota	341.3
NA	Kansas**	NA
NA	Mississippi**	NA
NA	Pennsylvania**	NA
NA	Tennessee**	NA
NA	Vermont**	NA

District of Columbia — 437.8

Source: American Cancer Society
"Cancer Facts & Figures 2005" (Copyright 2005, American Cancer Society)
*For 1997 to 2001. Age-adjusted to the 2000 U.S. standard population.
**Not available.

Estimated New Cases of Bladder Cancer in 2005

National Estimated Total = 63,210 New Cases*

ALPHA ORDER

RANK	STATE	CASES	% of USA
24	Alabama	860	1.4%
49	Alaska	100	0.2%
17	Arizona	1,200	1.9%
32	Arkansas	620	1.0%
1	California	6,380	10.1%
29	Colorado	720	1.1%
24	Connecticut	860	1.4%
44	Delaware	190	0.3%
2	Florida	4,890	7.7%
12	Georgia	1,530	2.4%
44	Hawaii	190	0.3%
38	Idaho	340	0.5%
7	Illinois	2,640	4.2%
13	Indiana	1,390	2.2%
31	Iowa	670	1.1%
29	Kansas	720	1.1%
23	Kentucky	910	1.4%
28	Louisiana	770	1.2%
36	Maine	430	0.7%
18	Maryland	1,150	1.8%
10	Massachusetts	1,870	3.0%
8	Michigan	2,350	3.7%
18	Minnesota	1,150	1.8%
35	Mississippi	480	0.8%
18	Missouri	1,150	1.8%
43	Montana	240	0.4%
38	Nebraska	340	0.5%
34	Nevada	530	0.8%
37	New Hampshire	380	0.6%
9	New Jersey	2,060	3.3%
38	New Mexico	340	0.5%
3	New York	4,320	6.8%
11	North Carolina	1,580	2.5%
48	North Dakota	140	0.2%
6	Ohio	3,070	4.9%
27	Oklahoma	820	1.3%
22	Oregon	1,010	1.6%
4	Pennsylvania	3,600	5.7%
38	Rhode Island	340	0.5%
24	South Carolina	860	1.4%
44	South Dakota	190	0.3%
18	Tennessee	1,150	1.8%
5	Texas	3,410	5.4%
42	Utah	290	0.5%
44	Vermont	190	0.3%
13	Virginia	1,390	2.2%
16	Washington	1,250	2.0%
33	West Virginia	580	0.9%
15	Wisconsin	1,340	2.1%
49	Wyoming	100	0.2%

RANK ORDER

RANK	STATE	CASES	% of USA
1	California	6,380	10.1%
2	Florida	4,890	7.7%
3	New York	4,320	6.8%
4	Pennsylvania	3,600	5.7%
5	Texas	3,410	5.4%
6	Ohio	3,070	4.9%
7	Illinois	2,640	4.2%
8	Michigan	2,350	3.7%
9	New Jersey	2,060	3.3%
10	Massachusetts	1,870	3.0%
11	North Carolina	1,580	2.5%
12	Georgia	1,530	2.4%
13	Indiana	1,390	2.2%
13	Virginia	1,390	2.2%
15	Wisconsin	1,340	2.1%
16	Washington	1,250	2.0%
17	Arizona	1,200	1.9%
18	Maryland	1,150	1.8%
18	Minnesota	1,150	1.8%
18	Missouri	1,150	1.8%
18	Tennessee	1,150	1.8%
22	Oregon	1,010	1.6%
23	Kentucky	910	1.4%
24	Alabama	860	1.4%
24	Connecticut	860	1.4%
24	South Carolina	860	1.4%
27	Oklahoma	820	1.3%
28	Louisiana	770	1.2%
29	Colorado	720	1.1%
29	Kansas	720	1.1%
31	Iowa	670	1.1%
32	Arkansas	620	1.0%
33	West Virginia	580	0.9%
34	Nevada	530	0.8%
35	Mississippi	480	0.8%
36	Maine	430	0.7%
37	New Hampshire	380	0.6%
38	Idaho	340	0.5%
38	Nebraska	340	0.5%
38	New Mexico	340	0.5%
38	Rhode Island	340	0.5%
42	Utah	290	0.5%
43	Montana	240	0.4%
44	Delaware	190	0.3%
44	Hawaii	190	0.3%
44	South Dakota	190	0.3%
44	Vermont	190	0.3%
48	North Dakota	140	0.2%
49	Alaska	100	0.2%
49	Wyoming	100	0.2%
	District of Columbia	140	0.2%

Source: American Cancer Society
   "Cancer Facts & Figures 2005" (Copyright 2005, American Cancer Society)
*These estimates are offered as a rough guide and should be interpreted with caution. They are calculated according to the distribution of estimated 2005 cancer deaths by state.

Estimated Rate of New Bladder Cancer Cases in 2005

National Estimated Rate = 21.5 New Cases per 100,000 Population*

ALPHA ORDER

RANK	STATE	RATE
38	Alabama	19.0
47	Alaska	15.3
29	Arizona	20.9
23	Arkansas	22.5
42	California	17.8
46	Colorado	15.6
14	Connecticut	24.5
20	Delaware	22.9
8	Florida	28.1
43	Georgia	17.3
49	Hawaii	15.0
15	Idaho	24.4
30	Illinois	20.8
26	Indiana	22.3
21	Iowa	22.7
11	Kansas	26.3
28	Kentucky	21.9
44	Louisiana	17.1
1	Maine	32.6
31	Maryland	20.7
6	Massachusetts	29.1
19	Michigan	23.2
23	Minnesota	22.5
45	Mississippi	16.5
34	Missouri	20.0
12	Montana	25.9
36	Nebraska	19.5
21	Nevada	22.7
5	New Hampshire	29.2
17	New Jersey	23.7
41	New Mexico	17.9
23	New York	22.5
40	North Carolina	18.5
27	North Dakota	22.1
10	Ohio	26.8
18	Oklahoma	23.3
8	Oregon	28.1
7	Pennsylvania	29.0
3	Rhode Island	31.5
32	South Carolina	20.5
13	South Dakota	24.6
36	Tennessee	19.5
48	Texas	15.2
50	Utah	12.1
4	Vermont	30.6
39	Virginia	18.6
33	Washington	20.1
2	West Virginia	31.9
16	Wisconsin	24.3
35	Wyoming	19.7

RANK ORDER

RANK	STATE	RATE
1	Maine	32.6
2	West Virginia	31.9
3	Rhode Island	31.5
4	Vermont	30.6
5	New Hampshire	29.2
6	Massachusetts	29.1
7	Pennsylvania	29.0
8	Florida	28.1
8	Oregon	28.1
10	Ohio	26.8
11	Kansas	26.3
12	Montana	25.9
13	South Dakota	24.6
14	Connecticut	24.5
15	Idaho	24.4
16	Wisconsin	24.3
17	New Jersey	23.7
18	Oklahoma	23.3
19	Michigan	23.2
20	Delaware	22.9
21	Iowa	22.7
21	Nevada	22.7
23	Arkansas	22.5
23	Minnesota	22.5
23	New York	22.5
26	Indiana	22.3
27	North Dakota	22.1
28	Kentucky	21.9
29	Arizona	20.9
30	Illinois	20.8
31	Maryland	20.7
32	South Carolina	20.5
33	Washington	20.1
34	Missouri	20.0
35	Wyoming	19.7
36	Nebraska	19.5
36	Tennessee	19.5
38	Alabama	19.0
39	Virginia	18.6
40	North Carolina	18.5
41	New Mexico	17.9
42	California	17.8
43	Georgia	17.3
44	Louisiana	17.1
45	Mississippi	16.5
46	Colorado	15.6
47	Alaska	15.3
48	Texas	15.2
49	Hawaii	15.0
50	Utah	12.1

District of Columbia 25.3

Source: Morgan Quitno Press using data from American Cancer Society
    "Cancer Facts & Figures 2005" (Copyright 2005, American Cancer Society)
*These estimates are offered as a rough guide and should be interpreted with caution. They are calculated according to the distribution of estimated 2005 cancer deaths by state. Rates calculated using 2004 Census resident population estimates.

Estimated New Female Breast Cancer Cases in 2005

National Estimated Total = 211,240 New Cases*

ALPHA ORDER

RANK	STATE	CASES	% of USA
21	Alabama	3,820	1.8%
49	Alaska	260	0.1%
22	Arizona	3,760	1.8%
32	Arkansas	2,090	1.0%
1	California	21,170	10.0%
29	Colorado	2,560	1.2%
27	Connecticut	2,720	1.3%
45	Delaware	630	0.3%
3	Florida	13,430	6.4%
12	Georgia	5,850	2.8%
43	Hawaii	680	0.3%
39	Idaho	940	0.4%
7	Illinois	9,300	4.4%
14	Indiana	4,600	2.2%
31	Iowa	2,300	1.1%
33	Kansas	1,990	0.9%
23	Kentucky	3,290	1.6%
20	Louisiana	3,870	1.8%
40	Maine	890	0.4%
16	Maryland	4,390	2.1%
13	Massachusetts	4,910	2.3%
9	Michigan	7,210	3.4%
25	Minnesota	3,240	1.5%
30	Mississippi	2,350	1.1%
15	Missouri	4,550	2.2%
43	Montana	680	0.3%
36	Nebraska	1,200	0.6%
34	Nevada	1,620	0.8%
40	New Hampshire	890	0.4%
8	New Jersey	7,740	3.7%
38	New Mexico	990	0.5%
2	New York	14,430	6.8%
10	North Carolina	6,330	3.0%
46	North Dakota	520	0.2%
6	Ohio	9,670	4.6%
26	Oklahoma	2,820	1.3%
28	Oregon	2,610	1.2%
5	Pennsylvania	11,340	5.4%
42	Rhode Island	780	0.4%
23	South Carolina	3,290	1.6%
46	South Dakota	520	0.2%
17	Tennessee	4,230	2.0%
4	Texas	12,860	6.1%
37	Utah	1,150	0.5%
48	Vermont	470	0.2%
11	Virginia	6,010	2.8%
19	Washington	3,920	1.9%
35	West Virginia	1,410	0.7%
18	Wisconsin	4,130	2.0%
49	Wyoming	260	0.1%

RANK ORDER

RANK	STATE	CASES	% of USA
1	California	21,170	10.0%
2	New York	14,430	6.8%
3	Florida	13,430	6.4%
4	Texas	12,860	6.1%
5	Pennsylvania	11,340	5.4%
6	Ohio	9,670	4.6%
7	Illinois	9,300	4.4%
8	New Jersey	7,740	3.7%
9	Michigan	7,210	3.4%
10	North Carolina	6,330	3.0%
11	Virginia	6,010	2.8%
12	Georgia	5,850	2.8%
13	Massachusetts	4,910	2.3%
14	Indiana	4,600	2.2%
15	Missouri	4,550	2.2%
16	Maryland	4,390	2.1%
17	Tennessee	4,230	2.0%
18	Wisconsin	4,130	2.0%
19	Washington	3,920	1.9%
20	Louisiana	3,870	1.8%
21	Alabama	3,820	1.8%
22	Arizona	3,760	1.8%
23	Kentucky	3,290	1.6%
23	South Carolina	3,290	1.6%
25	Minnesota	3,240	1.5%
26	Oklahoma	2,820	1.3%
27	Connecticut	2,720	1.3%
28	Oregon	2,610	1.2%
29	Colorado	2,560	1.2%
30	Mississippi	2,350	1.1%
31	Iowa	2,300	1.1%
32	Arkansas	2,090	1.0%
33	Kansas	1,990	0.9%
34	Nevada	1,620	0.8%
35	West Virginia	1,410	0.7%
36	Nebraska	1,200	0.6%
37	Utah	1,150	0.5%
38	New Mexico	990	0.5%
39	Idaho	940	0.4%
40	Maine	890	0.4%
40	New Hampshire	890	0.4%
42	Rhode Island	780	0.4%
43	Hawaii	680	0.3%
43	Montana	680	0.3%
45	Delaware	630	0.3%
46	North Dakota	520	0.2%
46	South Dakota	520	0.2%
48	Vermont	470	0.2%
49	Alaska	260	0.1%
49	Wyoming	260	0.1%
	District of Columbia	520	0.2%

Source: American Cancer Society
"Cancer Facts & Figures 2005" (Copyright 2005, American Cancer Society)
*These estimates are offered as a rough guide and should be interpreted with caution. They are calculated according to the distribution of estimated 2005 cancer deaths by state.

Age-Adjusted Incidence Rate of Female Breast Cancer Cases in 2001

National Rate = 132.2 New Cases per 100,000 Female Population*

ALPHA ORDER

RANK	STATE	RATE
44	Alabama	114.4
5	Alaska	139.0
36	Arizona	121.9
35	Arkansas	122.5
16	California	133.1
8	Colorado	135.8
3	Connecticut	143.8
12	Delaware	134.0
29	Florida	126.5
37	Georgia	121.7
11	Hawaii	134.2
24	Idaho	130.0
14	Illinois	133.4
26	Indiana	127.4
20	Iowa	131.5
NA	Kansas**	NA
27	Kentucky	127.2
34	Louisiana	122.9
22	Maine	131.4
17	Maryland	132.9
4	Massachusetts	143.4
13	Michigan	133.5
6	Minnesota	138.5
NA	Mississippi**	NA
28	Missouri	126.7
14	Montana	133.4
18	Nebraska	132.1
45	Nevada	113.8
10	New Hampshire	135.4
7	New Jersey	138.2
43	New Mexico	116.2
23	New York	130.9
32	North Carolina	123.2
42	North Dakota	117.4
20	Ohio	131.5
25	Oklahoma	128.5
2	Oregon	145.8
NA	Pennsylvania**	NA
19	Rhode Island	131.7
32	South Carolina	123.2
30	South Dakota	125.5
NA	Tennessee**	NA
41	Texas	118.9
39	Utah	119.4
NA	Vermont**	NA
31	Virginia	123.7
1	Washington	148.8
40	West Virginia	119.2
9	Wisconsin	135.6
38	Wyoming	121.5

RANK ORDER

RANK	STATE	RATE
1	Washington	148.8
2	Oregon	145.8
3	Connecticut	143.8
4	Massachusetts	143.4
5	Alaska	139.0
6	Minnesota	138.5
7	New Jersey	138.2
8	Colorado	135.8
9	Wisconsin	135.6
10	New Hampshire	135.4
11	Hawaii	134.2
12	Delaware	134.0
13	Michigan	133.5
14	Illinois	133.4
14	Montana	133.4
16	California	133.1
17	Maryland	132.9
18	Nebraska	132.1
19	Rhode Island	131.7
20	Iowa	131.5
20	Ohio	131.5
22	Maine	131.4
23	New York	130.9
24	Idaho	130.0
25	Oklahoma	128.5
26	Indiana	127.4
27	Kentucky	127.2
28	Missouri	126.7
29	Florida	126.5
30	South Dakota	125.5
31	Virginia	123.7
32	North Carolina	123.2
32	South Carolina	123.2
34	Louisiana	122.9
35	Arkansas	122.5
36	Arizona	121.9
37	Georgia	121.7
38	Wyoming	121.5
39	Utah	119.4
40	West Virginia	119.2
41	Texas	118.9
42	North Dakota	117.4
43	New Mexico	116.2
44	Alabama	114.4
45	Nevada	113.8
NA	Kansas**	NA
NA	Mississippi**	NA
NA	Pennsylvania**	NA
NA	Tennessee**	NA
NA	Vermont**	NA
	District of Columbia	143.3

Source: American Cancer Society
    "Cancer Facts & Figures 2005" (Copyright 2005, American Cancer Society)
For 1997 to 2001. Age-adjusted to the 2000 U.S. standard population.
**Not available.*

Percent of Women 40 and Older Who Have Had a Mammogram in the Past Two Years: 2004
National Median = 74.6% of Women*

<table>
<tr><td colspan="3">ALPHA ORDER</td><td colspan="3">RANK ORDER</td></tr>
<tr><td>RANK</td><td>STATE</td><td>PERCENT</td><td>RANK</td><td>STATE</td><td>PERCENT</td></tr>
<tr><td>18</td><td>Alabama</td><td>75.5</td><td>1</td><td>Delaware</td><td>82.4</td></tr>
<tr><td>45</td><td>Alaska</td><td>67.0</td><td>1</td><td>Massachusetts</td><td>82.4</td></tr>
<tr><td>18</td><td>Arizona</td><td>75.5</td><td>1</td><td>Rhode Island</td><td>82.4</td></tr>
<tr><td>46</td><td>Arkansas</td><td>66.9</td><td>4</td><td>Maine</td><td>81.8</td></tr>
<tr><td>12</td><td>California</td><td>76.5</td><td>5</td><td>Connecticut</td><td>81.1</td></tr>
<tr><td>37</td><td>Colorado</td><td>71.2</td><td>6</td><td>Minnesota</td><td>80.4</td></tr>
<tr><td>5</td><td>Connecticut</td><td>81.1</td><td>7</td><td>New Hampshire</td><td>80.1</td></tr>
<tr><td>1</td><td>Delaware</td><td>82.4</td><td>8</td><td>Maryland</td><td>78.9</td></tr>
<tr><td>12</td><td>Florida</td><td>76.5</td><td>8</td><td>Michigan</td><td>78.9</td></tr>
<tr><td>26</td><td>Georgia</td><td>74.5</td><td>10</td><td>Tennessee</td><td>78.0</td></tr>
<tr><td>NA</td><td>Hawaii**</td><td>NA</td><td>11</td><td>North Carolina</td><td>77.4</td></tr>
<tr><td>49</td><td>Idaho</td><td>63.8</td><td>12</td><td>California</td><td>76.5</td></tr>
<tr><td>14</td><td>Illinois</td><td>76.0</td><td>12</td><td>Florida</td><td>76.5</td></tr>
<tr><td>38</td><td>Indiana</td><td>69.2</td><td>14</td><td>Illinois</td><td>76.0</td></tr>
<tr><td>23</td><td>Iowa</td><td>75.2</td><td>14</td><td>Kansas</td><td>76.0</td></tr>
<tr><td>14</td><td>Kansas</td><td>76.0</td><td>16</td><td>Nebraska</td><td>75.9</td></tr>
<tr><td>18</td><td>Kentucky</td><td>75.5</td><td>16</td><td>South Dakota</td><td>75.9</td></tr>
<tr><td>27</td><td>Louisiana</td><td>74.2</td><td>18</td><td>Alabama</td><td>75.5</td></tr>
<tr><td>4</td><td>Maine</td><td>81.8</td><td>18</td><td>Arizona</td><td>75.5</td></tr>
<tr><td>8</td><td>Maryland</td><td>78.9</td><td>18</td><td>Kentucky</td><td>75.5</td></tr>
<tr><td>1</td><td>Massachusetts</td><td>82.4</td><td>18</td><td>New York</td><td>75.5</td></tr>
<tr><td>8</td><td>Michigan</td><td>78.9</td><td>22</td><td>Wisconsin</td><td>75.4</td></tr>
<tr><td>6</td><td>Minnesota</td><td>80.4</td><td>23</td><td>Iowa</td><td>75.2</td></tr>
<tr><td>48</td><td>Mississippi</td><td>66.4</td><td>24</td><td>New Jersey</td><td>74.9</td></tr>
<tr><td>41</td><td>Missouri</td><td>68.9</td><td>25</td><td>Vermont</td><td>74.7</td></tr>
<tr><td>35</td><td>Montana</td><td>71.8</td><td>26</td><td>Georgia</td><td>74.5</td></tr>
<tr><td>16</td><td>Nebraska</td><td>75.9</td><td>27</td><td>Louisiana</td><td>74.2</td></tr>
<tr><td>38</td><td>Nevada</td><td>69.2</td><td>28</td><td>Virginia</td><td>73.6</td></tr>
<tr><td>7</td><td>New Hampshire</td><td>80.1</td><td>29</td><td>Ohio</td><td>73.5</td></tr>
<tr><td>24</td><td>New Jersey</td><td>74.9</td><td>30</td><td>Pennsylvania</td><td>73.4</td></tr>
<tr><td>40</td><td>New Mexico</td><td>69.0</td><td>31</td><td>Washington</td><td>72.7</td></tr>
<tr><td>18</td><td>New York</td><td>75.5</td><td>32</td><td>West Virginia</td><td>72.4</td></tr>
<tr><td>11</td><td>North Carolina</td><td>77.4</td><td>33</td><td>North Dakota</td><td>72.2</td></tr>
<tr><td>33</td><td>North Dakota</td><td>72.2</td><td>34</td><td>South Carolina</td><td>72.1</td></tr>
<tr><td>29</td><td>Ohio</td><td>73.5</td><td>35</td><td>Montana</td><td>71.8</td></tr>
<tr><td>44</td><td>Oklahoma</td><td>67.6</td><td>35</td><td>Oregon</td><td>71.8</td></tr>
<tr><td>35</td><td>Oregon</td><td>71.8</td><td>37</td><td>Colorado</td><td>71.2</td></tr>
<tr><td>30</td><td>Pennsylvania</td><td>73.4</td><td>38</td><td>Indiana</td><td>69.2</td></tr>
<tr><td>1</td><td>Rhode Island</td><td>82.4</td><td>38</td><td>Nevada</td><td>69.2</td></tr>
<tr><td>34</td><td>South Carolina</td><td>72.1</td><td>40</td><td>New Mexico</td><td>69.0</td></tr>
<tr><td>16</td><td>South Dakota</td><td>75.9</td><td>41</td><td>Missouri</td><td>68.9</td></tr>
<tr><td>10</td><td>Tennessee</td><td>78.0</td><td>42</td><td>Wyoming</td><td>68.1</td></tr>
<tr><td>43</td><td>Texas</td><td>67.7</td><td>43</td><td>Texas</td><td>67.7</td></tr>
<tr><td>47</td><td>Utah</td><td>66.6</td><td>44</td><td>Oklahoma</td><td>67.6</td></tr>
<tr><td>25</td><td>Vermont</td><td>74.7</td><td>45</td><td>Alaska</td><td>67.0</td></tr>
<tr><td>28</td><td>Virginia</td><td>73.6</td><td>46</td><td>Arkansas</td><td>66.9</td></tr>
<tr><td>31</td><td>Washington</td><td>72.7</td><td>47</td><td>Utah</td><td>66.6</td></tr>
<tr><td>32</td><td>West Virginia</td><td>72.4</td><td>48</td><td>Mississippi</td><td>66.4</td></tr>
<tr><td>22</td><td>Wisconsin</td><td>75.4</td><td>49</td><td>Idaho</td><td>63.8</td></tr>
<tr><td>42</td><td>Wyoming</td><td>68.1</td><td>NA</td><td>Hawaii**</td><td>NA</td></tr>
</table>

District of Columbia   80.8

Source: U.S. Department of Health and Human Services, Centers for Disease Control and Prevention
    "2004 Behavioral Risk Factor Surveillance Summary Prevalence Data" (http://apps.nccd.cdc.gov/brfss/)
Percent of women 40 years and older.
**Not available.*

Estimated New Colon and Rectum Cancer Cases in 2005

National Estimated Total = 145,290 New Cases*

ALPHA ORDER

RANK	STATE	CASES	% of USA
23	Alabama	2,300	1.6%
50	Alaska	210	0.1%
21	Arizona	2,500	1.7%
31	Arkansas	1,630	1.1%
1	California	14,070	9.7%
30	Colorado	1,650	1.1%
29	Connecticut	1,680	1.2%
46	Delaware	410	0.3%
2	Florida	9,860	6.8%
13	Georgia	3,480	2.4%
42	Hawaii	540	0.4%
42	Idaho	540	0.4%
6	Illinois	6,610	4.5%
14	Indiana	3,410	2.3%
28	Iowa	1,700	1.2%
33	Kansas	1,570	1.1%
22	Kentucky	2,350	1.6%
20	Louisiana	2,580	1.8%
38	Maine	800	0.6%
17	Maryland	2,760	1.9%
11	Massachusetts	3,560	2.5%
8	Michigan	4,830	3.3%
25	Minnesota	2,220	1.5%
31	Mississippi	1,630	1.1%
15	Missouri	3,230	2.2%
44	Montana	460	0.3%
36	Nebraska	1,030	0.7%
35	Nevada	1,240	0.9%
41	New Hampshire	620	0.4%
9	New Jersey	4,670	3.2%
37	New Mexico	880	0.6%
3	New York	9,700	6.7%
10	North Carolina	4,100	2.8%
47	North Dakota	360	0.2%
7	Ohio	6,500	4.5%
26	Oklahoma	2,010	1.4%
27	Oregon	1,760	1.2%
5	Pennsylvania	8,130	5.6%
40	Rhode Island	650	0.4%
23	South Carolina	2,300	1.6%
44	South Dakota	460	0.3%
16	Tennessee	3,150	2.2%
4	Texas	9,270	6.4%
39	Utah	670	0.5%
48	Vermont	340	0.2%
11	Virginia	3,560	2.5%
19	Washington	2,660	1.8%
34	West Virginia	1,260	0.9%
17	Wisconsin	2,760	1.9%
49	Wyoming	280	0.2%

RANK ORDER

RANK	STATE	CASES	% of USA
1	California	14,070	9.7%
2	Florida	9,860	6.8%
3	New York	9,700	6.7%
4	Texas	9,270	6.4%
5	Pennsylvania	8,130	5.6%
6	Illinois	6,610	4.5%
7	Ohio	6,500	4.5%
8	Michigan	4,830	3.3%
9	New Jersey	4,670	3.2%
10	North Carolina	4,100	2.8%
11	Massachusetts	3,560	2.5%
11	Virginia	3,560	2.5%
13	Georgia	3,480	2.4%
14	Indiana	3,410	2.3%
15	Missouri	3,230	2.2%
16	Tennessee	3,150	2.2%
17	Maryland	2,760	1.9%
17	Wisconsin	2,760	1.9%
19	Washington	2,660	1.8%
20	Louisiana	2,580	1.8%
21	Arizona	2,500	1.7%
22	Kentucky	2,350	1.6%
23	Alabama	2,300	1.6%
23	South Carolina	2,300	1.6%
25	Minnesota	2,220	1.5%
26	Oklahoma	2,010	1.4%
27	Oregon	1,760	1.2%
28	Iowa	1,700	1.2%
29	Connecticut	1,680	1.2%
30	Colorado	1,650	1.1%
31	Arkansas	1,630	1.1%
31	Mississippi	1,630	1.1%
33	Kansas	1,570	1.1%
34	West Virginia	1,260	0.9%
35	Nevada	1,240	0.9%
36	Nebraska	1,030	0.7%
37	New Mexico	880	0.6%
38	Maine	800	0.6%
39	Utah	670	0.5%
40	Rhode Island	650	0.4%
41	New Hampshire	620	0.4%
42	Hawaii	540	0.4%
42	Idaho	540	0.4%
44	Montana	460	0.3%
44	South Dakota	460	0.3%
46	Delaware	410	0.3%
47	North Dakota	360	0.2%
48	Vermont	340	0.2%
49	Wyoming	280	0.2%
50	Alaska	210	0.1%
	District of Columbia	340	0.2%

Source: American Cancer Society
"Cancer Facts & Figures 2005" (Copyright 2005, American Cancer Society)
*These estimates are offered as a rough guide and should be interpreted with caution. They are calculated according to the distribution of estimated 2005 cancer deaths by state.

Estimated Rate of New Colon and Rectum Cancer Cases in 2005

National Estimated Rate = 49.5 New Cases per 100,000 Population*

ALPHA ORDER

RANK	STATE	RATE
27	Alabama	50.8
49	Alaska	32.0
40	Arizona	43.5
6	Arkansas	59.2
46	California	39.2
48	Colorado	35.9
34	Connecticut	48.0
32	Delaware	49.4
12	Florida	56.7
45	Georgia	39.4
43	Hawaii	42.8
47	Idaho	38.8
26	Illinois	52.0
21	Indiana	54.7
8	Iowa	57.5
9	Kansas	57.4
12	Kentucky	56.7
10	Louisiana	57.1
3	Maine	60.7
30	Maryland	49.7
18	Massachusetts	55.5
36	Michigan	47.8
40	Minnesota	43.5
16	Mississippi	56.1
16	Missouri	56.1
31	Montana	49.6
7	Nebraska	59.0
25	Nevada	53.1
37	New Hampshire	47.7
23	New Jersey	53.7
39	New Mexico	46.2
28	New York	50.4
34	North Carolina	48.0
12	North Dakota	56.7
12	Ohio	56.7
11	Oklahoma	57.0
33	Oregon	49.0
2	Pennsylvania	65.5
4	Rhode Island	60.1
20	South Carolina	54.8
5	South Dakota	59.7
24	Tennessee	53.4
44	Texas	41.2
50	Utah	28.0
21	Vermont	54.7
37	Virginia	47.7
42	Washington	42.9
1	West Virginia	69.4
29	Wisconsin	50.1
19	Wyoming	55.3

RANK ORDER

RANK	STATE	RATE
1	West Virginia	69.4
2	Pennsylvania	65.5
3	Maine	60.7
4	Rhode Island	60.1
5	South Dakota	59.7
6	Arkansas	59.2
7	Nebraska	59.0
8	Iowa	57.5
9	Kansas	57.4
10	Louisiana	57.1
11	Oklahoma	57.0
12	Florida	56.7
12	Kentucky	56.7
12	North Dakota	56.7
12	Ohio	56.7
16	Mississippi	56.1
16	Missouri	56.1
18	Massachusetts	55.5
19	Wyoming	55.3
20	South Carolina	54.8
21	Indiana	54.7
21	Vermont	54.7
23	New Jersey	53.7
24	Tennessee	53.4
25	Nevada	53.1
26	Illinois	52.0
27	Alabama	50.8
28	New York	50.4
29	Wisconsin	50.1
30	Maryland	49.7
31	Montana	49.6
32	Delaware	49.4
33	Oregon	49.0
34	Connecticut	48.0
34	North Carolina	48.0
36	Michigan	47.8
37	New Hampshire	47.7
37	Virginia	47.7
39	New Mexico	46.2
40	Arizona	43.5
40	Minnesota	43.5
42	Washington	42.9
43	Hawaii	42.8
44	Texas	41.2
45	Georgia	39.4
46	California	39.2
47	Idaho	38.8
48	Colorado	35.9
49	Alaska	32.0
50	Utah	28.0

	District of Columbia	61.4

Source: Morgan Quitno Press using data from American Cancer Society
"Cancer Facts & Figures 2005" (Copyright 2005, American Cancer Society)
*These estimates are offered as a rough guide and should be interpreted with caution. They are calculated according to the distribution of estimated 2005 cancer deaths by state. Rates calculated using 2004 Census resident population estimates.

Percent of Adults Receiving Recent Sigmoidoscopy or Colonoscopy Exam: 2004
National Median = 52.9% of Adults*

ALPHA ORDER

ALPHA ORDER

RANK	STATE	PERCENT
30	Alabama	50.9
31	Alaska	50.6
28	Arizona	52.0
41	Arkansas	47.3
23	California	53.8
36	Colorado	50.0
2	Connecticut	63.6
5	Delaware	61.9
16	Florida	56.1
24	Georgia	53.7
NA	Hawaii**	NA
41	Idaho	47.3
38	Illinois	48.9
34	Indiana	50.5
29	Iowa	51.6
37	Kansas	49.8
43	Kentucky	47.1
49	Louisiana	44.8
11	Maine	59.1
3	Maryland	62.2
7	Massachusetts	61.2
8	Michigan	60.4
1	Minnesota	66.2
44	Mississippi	46.8
26	Missouri	52.7
27	Montana	52.5
47	Nebraska	46.2
45	Nevada	46.7
3	New Hampshire	62.2
15	New Jersey	56.6
31	New Mexico	50.6
14	New York	56.7
20	North Carolina	54.5
21	North Dakota	53.9
25	Ohio	53.1
46	Oklahoma	46.6
19	Oregon	54.8
21	Pennsylvania	53.9
6	Rhode Island	61.6
18	South Carolina	55.9
35	South Dakota	50.2
31	Tennessee	50.6
40	Texas	48.3
17	Utah	56.0
12	Vermont	58.8
9	Virginia	59.9
13	Washington	57.3
47	West Virginia	46.2
10	Wisconsin	59.4
39	Wyoming	48.4

RANK ORDER

RANK	STATE	PERCENT
1	Minnesota	66.2
2	Connecticut	63.6
3	Maryland	62.2
3	New Hampshire	62.2
5	Delaware	61.9
6	Rhode Island	61.6
7	Massachusetts	61.2
8	Michigan	60.4
9	Virginia	59.9
10	Wisconsin	59.4
11	Maine	59.1
12	Vermont	58.8
13	Washington	57.3
14	New York	56.7
15	New Jersey	56.6
16	Florida	56.1
17	Utah	56.0
18	South Carolina	55.9
19	Oregon	54.8
20	North Carolina	54.5
21	North Dakota	53.9
21	Pennsylvania	53.9
23	California	53.8
24	Georgia	53.7
25	Ohio	53.1
26	Missouri	52.7
27	Montana	52.5
28	Arizona	52.0
29	Iowa	51.6
30	Alabama	50.9
31	Alaska	50.6
31	New Mexico	50.6
31	Tennessee	50.6
34	Indiana	50.5
35	South Dakota	50.2
36	Colorado	50.0
37	Kansas	49.8
38	Illinois	48.9
39	Wyoming	48.4
40	Texas	48.3
41	Arkansas	47.3
41	Idaho	47.3
43	Kentucky	47.1
44	Mississippi	46.8
45	Nevada	46.7
46	Oklahoma	46.6
47	Nebraska	46.2
47	West Virginia	46.2
49	Louisiana	44.8
NA	Hawaii**	NA

District of Columbia 63.1

Source: U.S. Department of Health and Human Services, Centers for Disease Control and Prevention
"2004 Behavioral Risk Factor Surveillance Summary Prevalence Data" (http://apps.nccd.cdc.gov/brfss/)
Persons 50 and older.
**Not available.*

Estimated New Leukemia Cases in 2005

National Estimated Total = 34,810 New Cases*

ALPHA ORDER					RANK ORDER			
RANK	STATE	CASES	% of USA		RANK	STATE	CASES	% of USA
22	Alabama	560	1.6%		1	California	3,380	9.7%
50	Alaska	50	0.1%		2	Florida	2,620	7.5%
21	Arizona	620	1.8%		3	Texas	2,250	6.5%
30	Arkansas	400	1.1%		4	New York	2,170	6.2%
1	California	3,380	9.7%		5	Pennsylvania	1,630	4.7%
27	Colorado	460	1.3%		6	Illinois	1,620	4.7%
30	Connecticut	400	1.1%		7	Ohio	1,510	4.3%
43	Delaware	120	0.3%		8	Michigan	1,250	3.6%
2	Florida	2,620	7.5%		9	New Jersey	1,100	3.2%
13	Georgia	820	2.4%		10	North Carolina	990	2.8%
43	Hawaii	120	0.3%		11	Missouri	830	2.4%
40	Idaho	150	0.4%		11	Virginia	830	2.4%
6	Illinois	1,620	4.7%		13	Georgia	820	2.4%
13	Indiana	820	2.4%		13	Indiana	820	2.4%
26	Iowa	480	1.4%		15	Massachusetts	770	2.2%
33	Kansas	350	1.0%		15	Wisconsin	770	2.2%
25	Kentucky	490	1.4%		17	Tennessee	760	2.2%
23	Louisiana	540	1.6%		18	Washington	720	2.1%
40	Maine	150	0.4%		19	Maryland	680	2.0%
19	Maryland	680	2.0%		20	Minnesota	660	1.9%
15	Massachusetts	770	2.2%		21	Arizona	620	1.8%
8	Michigan	1,250	3.6%		22	Alabama	560	1.6%
20	Minnesota	660	1.9%		23	Louisiana	540	1.6%
32	Mississippi	370	1.1%		24	South Carolina	510	1.5%
11	Missouri	830	2.4%		25	Kentucky	490	1.4%
42	Montana	140	0.4%		26	Iowa	480	1.4%
35	Nebraska	250	0.7%		27	Colorado	460	1.3%
34	Nevada	260	0.7%		27	Oklahoma	460	1.3%
38	New Hampshire	170	0.5%		29	Oregon	420	1.2%
9	New Jersey	1,100	3.2%		30	Arkansas	400	1.1%
38	New Mexico	170	0.5%		30	Connecticut	400	1.1%
4	New York	2,170	6.2%		32	Mississippi	370	1.1%
10	North Carolina	990	2.8%		33	Kansas	350	1.0%
46	North Dakota	110	0.3%		34	Nevada	260	0.7%
7	Ohio	1,510	4.3%		35	Nebraska	250	0.7%
27	Oklahoma	460	1.3%		36	Utah	220	0.6%
29	Oregon	420	1.2%		36	West Virginia	220	0.6%
5	Pennsylvania	1,630	4.7%		38	New Hampshire	170	0.5%
43	Rhode Island	120	0.3%		38	New Mexico	170	0.5%
24	South Carolina	510	1.5%		40	Idaho	150	0.4%
46	South Dakota	110	0.3%		40	Maine	150	0.4%
17	Tennessee	760	2.2%		42	Montana	140	0.4%
3	Texas	2,250	6.5%		43	Delaware	120	0.3%
36	Utah	220	0.6%		43	Hawaii	120	0.3%
48	Vermont	90	0.3%		43	Rhode Island	120	0.3%
11	Virginia	830	2.4%		46	North Dakota	110	0.3%
18	Washington	720	2.1%		46	South Dakota	110	0.3%
36	West Virginia	220	0.6%		48	Vermont	90	0.3%
15	Wisconsin	770	2.2%		49	Wyoming	60	0.2%
49	Wyoming	60	0.2%		50	Alaska	50	0.1%
						District of Columbia	50	0.1%

Source: American Cancer Society
   "Cancer Facts & Figures 2005" (Copyright 2005, American Cancer Society)
*These estimates are offered as a rough guide and should be interpreted with caution. They are calculated
according to the distribution of estimated 2005 cancer deaths by state.
**Not available.

Estimated Rate of New Leukemia Cases in 2005

National Estimated Rate = 11.9 New Cases per 100,000 Population*

ALPHA ORDER				RANK ORDER		
RANK	STATE	RATE		RANK	STATE	RATE
23	Alabama	12.4		1	North Dakota	17.3
50	Alaska	7.6		2	Iowa	16.2
41	Arizona	10.8		3	Florida	15.1
5	Arkansas	14.5		3	Montana	15.1
46	California	9.4		5	Arkansas	14.5
43	Colorado	10.0		5	Delaware	14.5
35	Connecticut	11.4		5	Vermont	14.5
5	Delaware	14.5		8	Missouri	14.4
3	Florida	15.1		9	Nebraska	14.3
47	Georgia	9.3		9	South Dakota	14.3
45	Hawaii	9.5		11	Wisconsin	14.0
41	Idaho	10.8		12	Ohio	13.2
20	Illinois	12.7		13	Indiana	13.1
13	Indiana	13.1		13	New Hampshire	13.1
2	Iowa	16.2		13	Oklahoma	13.1
19	Kansas	12.8		13	Pennsylvania	13.1
30	Kentucky	11.8		17	Minnesota	12.9
28	Louisiana	12.0		17	Tennessee	12.9
35	Maine	11.4		19	Kansas	12.8
25	Maryland	12.2		20	Illinois	12.7
28	Massachusetts	12.0		20	Mississippi	12.7
23	Michigan	12.4		22	New Jersey	12.6
17	Minnesota	12.9		23	Alabama	12.4
20	Mississippi	12.7		23	Michigan	12.4
8	Missouri	14.4		25	Maryland	12.2
3	Montana	15.1		26	South Carolina	12.1
9	Nebraska	14.3		26	West Virginia	12.1
38	Nevada	11.1		28	Louisiana	12.0
13	New Hampshire	13.1		28	Massachusetts	12.0
22	New Jersey	12.6		30	Kentucky	11.8
49	New Mexico	8.9		30	Wyoming	11.8
37	New York	11.3		32	Oregon	11.7
33	North Carolina	11.6		33	North Carolina	11.6
1	North Dakota	17.3		33	Washington	11.6
12	Ohio	13.2		35	Connecticut	11.4
13	Oklahoma	13.1		35	Maine	11.4
32	Oregon	11.7		37	New York	11.3
13	Pennsylvania	13.1		38	Nevada	11.1
38	Rhode Island	11.1		38	Rhode Island	11.1
26	South Carolina	12.1		38	Virginia	11.1
9	South Dakota	14.3		41	Arizona	10.8
17	Tennessee	12.9		41	Idaho	10.8
43	Texas	10.0		43	Colorado	10.0
48	Utah	9.2		43	Texas	10.0
5	Vermont	14.5		45	Hawaii	9.5
38	Virginia	11.1		46	California	9.4
33	Washington	11.6		47	Georgia	9.3
26	West Virginia	12.1		48	Utah	9.2
11	Wisconsin	14.0		49	New Mexico	8.9
30	Wyoming	11.8		50	Alaska	7.6
					District of Columbia	9.0

*Source: Morgan Quitno Press using data from American Cancer Society
"Cancer Facts & Figures 2005" (Copyright 2005, American Cancer Society)*
These estimates are offered as a rough guide and should be interpreted with caution. They are calculated according to the distribution of estimated 2005 cancer deaths by state. Rates calculated using 2004 Census resident population estimates.

Estimated New Lung Cancer Cases in 2005

National Estimated Total = 172,570 New Cases*

ALPHA ORDER

RANK	STATE	CASES	% of USA
19	Alabama	3,340	1.9%
50	Alaska	220	0.1%
24	Arizona	2,870	1.7%
27	Arkansas	2,530	1.5%
1	California	15,150	8.8%
32	Colorado	1,750	1.0%
30	Connecticut	1,950	1.1%
44	Delaware	490	0.3%
2	Florida	13,130	7.6%
11	Georgia	4,800	2.8%
43	Hawaii	510	0.3%
41	Idaho	630	0.4%
7	Illinois	7,220	4.2%
13	Indiana	4,410	2.6%
31	Iowa	1,790	1.0%
34	Kansas	1,630	0.9%
17	Kentucky	3,680	2.1%
21	Louisiana	3,090	1.8%
37	Maine	990	0.6%
20	Maryland	3,210	1.9%
16	Massachusetts	4,010	2.3%
8	Michigan	6,110	3.5%
25	Minnesota	2,620	1.5%
28	Mississippi	2,180	1.3%
15	Missouri	4,070	2.4%
42	Montana	620	0.4%
36	Nebraska	1,000	0.6%
35	Nevada	1,530	0.9%
38	New Hampshire	790	0.5%
10	New Jersey	4,830	2.8%
39	New Mexico	760	0.4%
4	New York	9,870	5.7%
9	North Carolina	5,520	3.2%
48	North Dakota	330	0.2%
6	Ohio	7,790	4.5%
26	Oklahoma	2,580	1.5%
29	Oregon	2,160	1.3%
5	Pennsylvania	8,470	4.9%
40	Rhode Island	720	0.4%
23	South Carolina	2,880	1.7%
46	South Dakota	430	0.2%
12	Tennessee	4,630	2.7%
3	Texas	11,210	6.5%
45	Utah	460	0.3%
47	Vermont	390	0.2%
14	Virginia	4,400	2.5%
18	Washington	3,440	2.0%
33	West Virginia	1,700	1.0%
22	Wisconsin	3,060	1.8%
49	Wyoming	280	0.2%

RANK ORDER

RANK	STATE	CASES	% of USA
1	California	15,150	8.8%
2	Florida	13,130	7.6%
3	Texas	11,210	6.5%
4	New York	9,870	5.7%
5	Pennsylvania	8,470	4.9%
6	Ohio	7,790	4.5%
7	Illinois	7,220	4.2%
8	Michigan	6,110	3.5%
9	North Carolina	5,520	3.2%
10	New Jersey	4,830	2.8%
11	Georgia	4,800	2.8%
12	Tennessee	4,630	2.7%
13	Indiana	4,410	2.6%
14	Virginia	4,400	2.5%
15	Missouri	4,070	2.4%
16	Massachusetts	4,010	2.3%
17	Kentucky	3,680	2.1%
18	Washington	3,440	2.0%
19	Alabama	3,340	1.9%
20	Maryland	3,210	1.9%
21	Louisiana	3,090	1.8%
22	Wisconsin	3,060	1.8%
23	South Carolina	2,880	1.7%
24	Arizona	2,870	1.7%
25	Minnesota	2,620	1.5%
26	Oklahoma	2,580	1.5%
27	Arkansas	2,530	1.5%
28	Mississippi	2,180	1.3%
29	Oregon	2,160	1.3%
30	Connecticut	1,950	1.1%
31	Iowa	1,790	1.0%
32	Colorado	1,750	1.0%
33	West Virginia	1,700	1.0%
34	Kansas	1,630	0.9%
35	Nevada	1,530	0.9%
36	Nebraska	1,000	0.6%
37	Maine	990	0.6%
38	New Hampshire	790	0.5%
39	New Mexico	760	0.4%
40	Rhode Island	720	0.4%
41	Idaho	630	0.4%
42	Montana	620	0.4%
43	Hawaii	510	0.3%
44	Delaware	490	0.3%
45	Utah	460	0.3%
46	South Dakota	430	0.2%
47	Vermont	390	0.2%
48	North Dakota	330	0.2%
49	Wyoming	280	0.2%
50	Alaska	220	0.1%
	District of Columbia	310	0.2%

Source: American Cancer Society
   "Cancer Facts & Figures 2005" (Copyright 2005, American Cancer Society)
*These estimates are offered as a rough guide and should be interpreted with caution. They are calculated according to the distribution of estimated 2005 cancer deaths by state.

Estimated Rate of New Lung Cancer Cases in 2005

National Estimated Rate = 58.8 New Cases per 100,000 Population*

ALPHA ORDER			RANK ORDER		
RANK	STATE	RATE	RANK	STATE	RATE
8	Alabama	73.7	1	West Virginia	93.6
49	Alaska	33.6	2	Arkansas	91.9
42	Arizona	50.0	3	Kentucky	88.8
2	Arkansas	91.9	4	Tennessee	78.5
45	California	42.2	5	Florida	75.5
48	Colorado	38.0	6	Maine	75.2
33	Connecticut	55.7	7	Mississippi	75.1
27	Delaware	59.0	8	Alabama	73.7
5	Florida	75.5	9	Oklahoma	73.2
38	Georgia	54.4	10	Indiana	70.7
46	Hawaii	40.4	10	Missouri	70.7
44	Idaho	45.2	12	South Carolina	68.6
31	Illinois	56.8	13	Louisiana	68.4
10	Indiana	70.7	14	Pennsylvania	68.3
23	Iowa	60.6	15	Ohio	68.0
26	Kansas	59.6	16	Montana	66.9
3	Kentucky	88.8	17	Rhode Island	66.6
13	Louisiana	68.4	18	Nevada	65.5
6	Maine	75.2	19	North Carolina	64.6
29	Maryland	57.8	20	Vermont	62.8
21	Massachusetts	62.5	21	Massachusetts	62.5
24	Michigan	60.4	22	New Hampshire	60.8
40	Minnesota	51.4	23	Iowa	60.6
7	Mississippi	75.1	24	Michigan	60.4
10	Missouri	70.7	25	Oregon	60.1
16	Montana	66.9	26	Kansas	59.6
30	Nebraska	57.2	27	Delaware	59.0
18	Nevada	65.5	27	Virginia	59.0
22	New Hampshire	60.8	29	Maryland	57.8
34	New Jersey	55.5	30	Nebraska	57.2
47	New Mexico	39.9	31	Illinois	56.8
41	New York	51.3	32	South Dakota	55.8
19	North Carolina	64.6	33	Connecticut	55.7
39	North Dakota	52.0	34	New Jersey	55.5
15	Ohio	68.0	34	Wisconsin	55.5
9	Oklahoma	73.2	36	Washington	55.4
25	Oregon	60.1	37	Wyoming	55.3
14	Pennsylvania	68.3	38	Georgia	54.4
17	Rhode Island	66.6	39	North Dakota	52.0
12	South Carolina	68.6	40	Minnesota	51.4
32	South Dakota	55.8	41	New York	51.3
4	Tennessee	78.5	42	Arizona	50.0
43	Texas	49.8	43	Texas	49.8
50	Utah	19.3	44	Idaho	45.2
20	Vermont	62.8	45	California	42.2
27	Virginia	59.0	46	Hawaii	40.4
36	Washington	55.4	47	New Mexico	39.9
1	West Virginia	93.6	48	Colorado	38.0
34	Wisconsin	55.5	49	Alaska	33.6
37	Wyoming	55.3	50	Utah	19.3
				District of Columbia	56.0

Source: Morgan Quitno Press using data from American Cancer Society
"Cancer Facts & Figures 2005" (Copyright 2005, American Cancer Society)
*These estimates are offered as a rough guide and should be interpreted with caution. They are calculated according to the distribution of estimated 2005 cancer deaths by state. Rates calculated using 2004 Census resident population estimates.

Estimated New Non-Hodgkin's Lymphoma Cases in 2005

National Estimated Total = 56,390 New Cases*

ALPHA ORDER

RANK	STATE	CASES	% of USA
25	Alabama	940	1.7%
49	Alaska	90	0.2%
20	Arizona	1,060	1.9%
31	Arkansas	650	1.2%
1	California	5,700	10.1%
27	Colorado	880	1.6%
29	Connecticut	730	1.3%
44	Delaware	210	0.4%
2	Florida	3,470	6.2%
14	Georgia	1,380	2.4%
41	Hawaii	260	0.5%
44	Idaho	210	0.4%
6	Illinois	2,200	3.9%
12	Indiana	1,410	2.5%
28	Iowa	760	1.3%
31	Kansas	650	1.2%
24	Kentucky	970	1.7%
20	Louisiana	1,060	1.9%
41	Maine	260	0.5%
22	Maryland	1,030	1.8%
17	Massachusetts	1,260	2.2%
7	Michigan	2,140	3.8%
14	Minnesota	1,380	2.4%
33	Mississippi	530	0.9%
11	Missouri	1,530	2.7%
44	Montana	210	0.4%
36	Nebraska	380	0.7%
35	Nevada	440	0.8%
38	New Hampshire	320	0.6%
9	New Jersey	1,760	3.1%
38	New Mexico	320	0.6%
4	New York	2,940	5.2%
9	North Carolina	1,760	3.1%
47	North Dakota	180	0.3%
8	Ohio	1,970	3.5%
30	Oklahoma	680	1.2%
23	Oregon	1,000	1.8%
5	Pennsylvania	2,880	5.1%
40	Rhode Island	290	0.5%
25	South Carolina	940	1.7%
43	South Dakota	230	0.4%
16	Tennessee	1,350	2.4%
3	Texas	3,050	5.4%
36	Utah	380	0.7%
47	Vermont	180	0.3%
18	Virginia	1,170	2.1%
12	Washington	1,410	2.5%
34	West Virginia	500	0.9%
19	Wisconsin	1,120	2.0%
49	Wyoming	90	0.2%

RANK ORDER

RANK	STATE	CASES	% of USA
1	California	5,700	10.1%
2	Florida	3,470	6.2%
3	Texas	3,050	5.4%
4	New York	2,940	5.2%
5	Pennsylvania	2,880	5.1%
6	Illinois	2,200	3.9%
7	Michigan	2,140	3.8%
8	Ohio	1,970	3.5%
9	New Jersey	1,760	3.1%
9	North Carolina	1,760	3.1%
11	Missouri	1,530	2.7%
12	Indiana	1,410	2.5%
12	Washington	1,410	2.5%
14	Georgia	1,380	2.4%
14	Minnesota	1,380	2.4%
16	Tennessee	1,350	2.4%
17	Massachusetts	1,260	2.2%
18	Virginia	1,170	2.1%
19	Wisconsin	1,120	2.0%
20	Arizona	1,060	1.9%
20	Louisiana	1,060	1.9%
22	Maryland	1,030	1.8%
23	Oregon	1,000	1.8%
24	Kentucky	970	1.7%
25	Alabama	940	1.7%
25	South Carolina	940	1.7%
27	Colorado	880	1.6%
28	Iowa	760	1.3%
29	Connecticut	730	1.3%
30	Oklahoma	680	1.2%
31	Arkansas	650	1.2%
31	Kansas	650	1.2%
33	Mississippi	530	0.9%
34	West Virginia	500	0.9%
35	Nevada	440	0.8%
36	Nebraska	380	0.7%
36	Utah	380	0.7%
38	New Hampshire	320	0.6%
38	New Mexico	320	0.6%
40	Rhode Island	290	0.5%
41	Hawaii	260	0.5%
41	Maine	260	0.5%
43	South Dakota	230	0.4%
44	Delaware	210	0.4%
44	Idaho	210	0.4%
44	Montana	210	0.4%
47	North Dakota	180	0.3%
47	Vermont	180	0.3%
49	Alaska	90	0.2%
49	Wyoming	90	0.2%
	District of Columbia	90	0.2%

Source: American Cancer Society
"Cancer Facts & Figures 2005" (Copyright 2005, American Cancer Society)
*These estimates are offered as a rough guide and should be interpreted with caution. They are calculated according to the distribution of estimated 2005 cancer deaths by state.

Estimated Rate of New Non-Hodgkin's Lymphoma Cases in 2005

National Estimated Rate = 19.2 New Cases per 100,000 Population*

ALPHA ORDER				RANK ORDER		
RANK	STATE	RATE		RANK	STATE	RATE
25	Alabama	20.7		1	South Dakota	29.8
49	Alaska	13.7		2	Vermont	29.0
36	Arizona	18.5		3	North Dakota	28.4
13	Arkansas	23.6		4	Oregon	27.8
43	California	15.9		5	West Virginia	27.5
34	Colorado	19.1		6	Minnesota	27.1
24	Connecticut	20.8		7	Rhode Island	26.8
10	Delaware	25.3		8	Missouri	26.6
30	Florida	19.9		9	Iowa	25.7
46	Georgia	15.6		10	Delaware	25.3
26	Hawaii	20.6		11	New Hampshire	24.6
48	Idaho	15.1		12	Kansas	23.8
40	Illinois	17.3		13	Arkansas	23.6
20	Indiana	22.6		14	Louisiana	23.5
9	Iowa	25.7		15	Kentucky	23.4
12	Kansas	23.8		16	Pennsylvania	23.2
15	Kentucky	23.4		17	Tennessee	22.9
14	Louisiana	23.5		18	Montana	22.7
31	Maine	19.7		18	Washington	22.7
36	Maryland	18.5		20	Indiana	22.6
32	Massachusetts	19.6		21	South Carolina	22.4
23	Michigan	21.2		22	Nebraska	21.7
6	Minnesota	27.1		23	Michigan	21.2
38	Mississippi	18.3		24	Connecticut	20.8
8	Missouri	26.6		25	Alabama	20.7
18	Montana	22.7		26	Hawaii	20.6
22	Nebraska	21.7		26	North Carolina	20.6
35	Nevada	18.8		28	Wisconsin	20.3
11	New Hampshire	24.6		29	New Jersey	20.2
29	New Jersey	20.2		30	Florida	19.9
42	New Mexico	16.8		31	Maine	19.7
47	New York	15.3		32	Massachusetts	19.6
26	North Carolina	20.6		33	Oklahoma	19.3
3	North Dakota	28.4		34	Colorado	19.1
41	Ohio	17.2		35	Nevada	18.8
33	Oklahoma	19.3		36	Arizona	18.5
4	Oregon	27.8		36	Maryland	18.5
16	Pennsylvania	23.2		38	Mississippi	18.3
7	Rhode Island	26.8		39	Wyoming	17.8
21	South Carolina	22.4		40	Illinois	17.3
1	South Dakota	29.8		41	Ohio	17.2
17	Tennessee	22.9		42	New Mexico	16.8
50	Texas	13.6		43	California	15.9
43	Utah	15.9		43	Utah	15.9
2	Vermont	29.0		45	Virginia	15.7
45	Virginia	15.7		46	Georgia	15.6
18	Washington	22.7		47	New York	15.3
5	West Virginia	27.5		48	Idaho	15.1
28	Wisconsin	20.3		49	Alaska	13.7
39	Wyoming	17.8		50	Texas	13.6

District of Columbia   16.3

Source: Morgan Quitno Press using data from American Cancer Society
"Cancer Facts & Figures 2005" (Copyright 2005, American Cancer Society)
*These estimates are offered as a rough guide and should be interpreted with caution. They are calculated according to the distribution of estimated 2005 cancer deaths by state. Rates calculated using 2004 Census resident population estimates.

Estimated New Prostate Cancer Cases in 2005

National Estimated Total = 232,090 New Cases*

ALPHA ORDER				RANK ORDER			
RANK	STATE	CASES	% of USA	RANK	STATE	CASES	% of USA
16	Alabama	4,360	1.9%	1	California	25,010	10.8%
50	Alaska	310	0.1%	2	Florida	19,650	8.5%
22	Arizona	3,900	1.7%	3	New York	14,220	6.1%
32	Arkansas	2,060	0.9%	4	Texas	13,380	5.8%
1	California	25,010	10.8%	5	Pennsylvania	13,150	5.7%
29	Colorado	2,680	1.2%	6	Ohio	10,860	4.7%
24	Connecticut	3,360	1.4%	7	Illinois	9,410	4.1%
46	Delaware	610	0.3%	8	Michigan	7,650	3.3%
2	Florida	19,650	8.5%	9	North Carolina	6,810	2.9%
12	Georgia	5,660	2.4%	10	New Jersey	6,420	2.8%
43	Hawaii	920	0.4%	11	Virginia	5,740	2.5%
39	Idaho	1,150	0.5%	12	Georgia	5,660	2.4%
7	Illinois	9,410	4.1%	13	Washington	5,510	2.4%
15	Indiana	4,890	2.1%	14	Massachusetts	5,350	2.3%
26	Iowa	3,060	1.3%	15	Indiana	4,890	2.1%
32	Kansas	2,060	0.9%	16	Alabama	4,360	1.9%
30	Kentucky	2,520	1.1%	16	Minnesota	4,360	1.9%
23	Louisiana	3,440	1.5%	18	Tennessee	4,280	1.8%
38	Maine	1,300	0.6%	19	Maryland	4,210	1.8%
19	Maryland	4,210	1.8%	19	South Carolina	4,210	1.8%
14	Massachusetts	5,350	2.3%	21	Wisconsin	4,050	1.7%
8	Michigan	7,650	3.3%	22	Arizona	3,900	1.7%
16	Minnesota	4,360	1.9%	23	Louisiana	3,440	1.5%
25	Mississippi	3,210	1.4%	24	Connecticut	3,360	1.4%
26	Missouri	3,060	1.3%	25	Mississippi	3,210	1.4%
42	Montana	990	0.4%	26	Iowa	3,060	1.3%
37	Nebraska	1,380	0.6%	26	Missouri	3,060	1.3%
34	Nevada	1,990	0.9%	28	Oregon	2,980	1.3%
39	New Hampshire	1,150	0.5%	29	Colorado	2,680	1.2%
10	New Jersey	6,420	2.8%	30	Kentucky	2,520	1.1%
35	New Mexico	1,680	0.7%	31	Oklahoma	2,450	1.1%
3	New York	14,220	6.1%	32	Arkansas	2,060	0.9%
9	North Carolina	6,810	2.9%	32	Kansas	2,060	0.9%
46	North Dakota	610	0.3%	34	Nevada	1,990	0.9%
6	Ohio	10,860	4.7%	35	New Mexico	1,680	0.7%
31	Oklahoma	2,450	1.1%	36	West Virginia	1,450	0.6%
28	Oregon	2,980	1.3%	37	Nebraska	1,380	0.6%
5	Pennsylvania	13,150	5.7%	38	Maine	1,300	0.6%
45	Rhode Island	840	0.4%	39	Idaho	1,150	0.5%
19	South Carolina	4,210	1.8%	39	New Hampshire	1,150	0.5%
43	South Dakota	920	0.4%	39	Utah	1,150	0.5%
18	Tennessee	4,280	1.8%	42	Montana	990	0.4%
4	Texas	13,380	5.8%	43	Hawaii	920	0.4%
39	Utah	1,150	0.5%	43	South Dakota	920	0.4%
49	Vermont	460	0.2%	45	Rhode Island	840	0.4%
11	Virginia	5,740	2.5%	46	Delaware	610	0.3%
13	Washington	5,510	2.4%	46	North Dakota	610	0.3%
36	West Virginia	1,450	0.6%	46	Wyoming	610	0.3%
21	Wisconsin	4,050	1.7%	49	Vermont	460	0.2%
46	Wyoming	610	0.3%	50	Alaska	310	0.1%
					District of Columbia	610	0.3%

Source: American Cancer Society
"Cancer Facts & Figures 2005" (Copyright 2005, American Cancer Society)
*These estimates are offered as a rough guide and should be interpreted with caution. They are calculated according to the distribution of estimated 2005 cancer deaths by state.

Age-Adjusted Incidence Rate of Prostate Cancer Cases in 2001

National Rate = 166.7 New Cases per 100,000 Male Population*

ALPHA ORDER				RANK ORDER		
RANK	STATE	RATE		RANK	STATE	RATE
43	Alabama	128.7		1	Michigan	198.2
20	Alaska	164.5		2	New Jersey	198.0
44	Arizona	128.0		3	Minnesota	184.5
38	Arkansas	144.0		4	Massachusetts	183.0
27	California	157.6		5	South Dakota	180.2
22	Colorado	163.1		6	Utah	180.0
12	Connecticut	174.0		7	Rhode Island	177.9
19	Delaware	165.1		7	Wyoming	177.9
30	Florida	154.8		9	Maryland	177.6
26	Georgia	159.6		10	Washington	175.6
42	Hawaii	131.6		11	South Carolina	174.2
17	Idaho	167.9		12	Connecticut	174.0
25	Illinois	160.5		13	Louisiana	173.8
41	Indiana	132.9		14	Montana	172.7
32	Iowa	153.2		15	North Dakota	171.0
NA	Kansas**	NA		16	Maine	169.5
31	Kentucky	154.6		17	Idaho	167.9
13	Louisiana	173.8		18	Wisconsin	166.3
16	Maine	169.5		19	Delaware	165.1
9	Maryland	177.6		20	Alaska	164.5
4	Massachusetts	183.0		20	Oregon	164.5
1	Michigan	198.2		22	Colorado	163.1
3	Minnesota	184.5		23	New York	162.9
NA	Mississippi**	NA		24	Nebraska	162.4
40	Missouri	137.0		25	Illinois	160.5
14	Montana	172.7		26	Georgia	159.6
24	Nebraska	162.4		27	California	157.6
45	Nevada	121.6		28	New Hampshire	155.1
28	New Hampshire	155.1		29	Virginia	155.0
2	New Jersey	198.0		30	Florida	154.8
37	New Mexico	146.5		31	Kentucky	154.6
23	New York	162.9		32	Iowa	153.2
33	North Carolina	152.5		33	North Carolina	152.5
15	North Dakota	171.0		34	Ohio	150.0
34	Ohio	150.0		35	West Virginia	149.3
39	Oklahoma	141.7		36	Texas	148.4
20	Oregon	164.5		37	New Mexico	146.5
NA	Pennsylvania**	NA		38	Arkansas	144.0
7	Rhode Island	177.9		39	Oklahoma	141.7
11	South Carolina	174.2		40	Missouri	137.0
5	South Dakota	180.2		41	Indiana	132.9
NA	Tennessee**	NA		42	Hawaii	131.6
36	Texas	148.4		43	Alabama	128.7
6	Utah	180.0		44	Arizona	128.0
NA	Vermont**	NA		45	Nevada	121.6
29	Virginia	155.0		NA	Kansas**	NA
10	Washington	175.6		NA	Mississippi**	NA
35	West Virginia	149.3		NA	Pennsylvania**	NA
18	Wisconsin	166.3		NA	Tennessee**	NA
7	Wyoming	177.9		NA	Vermont**	NA
					District of Columbia	239.4

Source: American Cancer Society
    "Cancer Facts & Figures 2005" (Copyright 2005, American Cancer Society)
*For 1997 to 2001. Age-adjusted to the 2000 U.S. standard population.
**Not available.

Percent of Males Receiving Recent PSA Test for Prostate Cancer: 2004

National Median = 52.0% of Men*

ALPHA ORDER

RANK	STATE	PERCENT
20	Alabama	52.6
44	Alaska	45.5
8	Arizona	54.3
36	Arkansas	48.1
25	California	51.5
29	Colorado	49.9
21	Connecticut	52.5
7	Delaware	54.4
3	Florida	57.5
2	Georgia	57.8
NA	Hawaii**	NA
38	Idaho	47.8
30	Illinois	49.7
34	Indiana	48.9
23	Iowa	52.2
14	Kansas	53.4
37	Kentucky	48.0
15	Louisiana	53.1
48	Maine	44.5
10	Maryland	53.8
26	Massachusetts	50.9
12	Michigan	53.7
47	Minnesota	44.8
18	Mississippi	53.0
35	Missouri	48.5
10	Montana	53.8
27	Nebraska	50.7
39	Nevada	47.7
40	New Hampshire	47.5
9	New Jersey	54.2
33	New Mexico	49.0
13	New York	53.5
4	North Carolina	55.3
45	North Dakota	45.4
15	Ohio	53.1
28	Oklahoma	50.2
41	Oregon	47.0
31	Pennsylvania	49.4
5	Rhode Island	54.9
6	South Carolina	54.5
15	South Dakota	53.1
24	Tennessee	51.9
31	Texas	49.4
42	Utah	46.1
48	Vermont	44.5
19	Virginia	52.9
46	Washington	45.2
22	West Virginia	52.3
43	Wisconsin	45.9
1	Wyoming	59.8

RANK ORDER

RANK	STATE	PERCENT
1	Wyoming	59.8
2	Georgia	57.8
3	Florida	57.5
4	North Carolina	55.3
5	Rhode Island	54.9
6	South Carolina	54.5
7	Delaware	54.4
8	Arizona	54.3
9	New Jersey	54.2
10	Maryland	53.8
10	Montana	53.8
12	Michigan	53.7
13	New York	53.5
14	Kansas	53.4
15	Louisiana	53.1
15	Ohio	53.1
15	South Dakota	53.1
18	Mississippi	53.0
19	Virginia	52.9
20	Alabama	52.6
21	Connecticut	52.5
22	West Virginia	52.3
23	Iowa	52.2
24	Tennessee	51.9
25	California	51.5
26	Massachusetts	50.9
27	Nebraska	50.7
28	Oklahoma	50.2
29	Colorado	49.9
30	Illinois	49.7
31	Pennsylvania	49.4
31	Texas	49.4
33	New Mexico	49.0
34	Indiana	48.9
35	Missouri	48.5
36	Arkansas	48.1
37	Kentucky	48.0
38	Idaho	47.8
39	Nevada	47.7
40	New Hampshire	47.5
41	Oregon	47.0
42	Utah	46.1
43	Wisconsin	45.9
44	Alaska	45.5
45	North Dakota	45.4
46	Washington	45.2
47	Minnesota	44.8
48	Maine	44.5
48	Vermont	44.5
NA	Hawaii**	NA
	District of Columbia	57.8

Source: U.S. Department of Health and Human Services, Centers for Disease Control and Prevention
   "2004 Behavioral Risk Factor Surveillance Summary Prevalence Data" (http://apps.nccd.cdc.gov/brfss/)
*Men 40 and older receiving prostate-specific antigen (PSA) test within the past year.
**Not available.

Estimated New Skin Melanoma Cases in 2005

National Estimated Total = 59,580 New Cases*

ALPHA ORDER

RANK	STATE	CASES	% of USA
25	Alabama	920	1.5%
49	Alaska	80	0.1%
17	Arizona	1,300	2.2%
30	Arkansas	540	0.9%
1	California	5,440	9.1%
25	Colorado	920	1.5%
29	Connecticut	690	1.2%
43	Delaware	230	0.4%
2	Florida	4,600	7.7%
11	Georgia	1,610	2.7%
45	Hawaii	150	0.3%
37	Idaho	380	0.6%
7	Illinois	2,300	3.9%
14	Indiana	1,460	2.5%
30	Iowa	540	0.9%
30	Kansas	540	0.9%
20	Kentucky	1,150	1.9%
27	Louisiana	770	1.3%
37	Maine	380	0.6%
21	Maryland	1,070	1.8%
13	Massachusetts	1,530	2.6%
10	Michigan	1,840	3.1%
22	Minnesota	1,000	1.7%
34	Mississippi	460	0.8%
14	Missouri	1,460	2.5%
43	Montana	230	0.4%
37	Nebraska	380	0.6%
30	Nevada	540	0.9%
40	New Hampshire	310	0.5%
8	New Jersey	1,920	3.2%
40	New Mexico	310	0.5%
4	New York	3,220	5.4%
8	North Carolina	1,920	3.2%
49	North Dakota	80	0.1%
6	Ohio	2,450	4.1%
22	Oklahoma	1,000	1.7%
22	Oregon	1,000	1.7%
5	Pennsylvania	2,990	5.0%
40	Rhode Island	310	0.5%
27	South Carolina	770	1.3%
45	South Dakota	150	0.3%
17	Tennessee	1,300	2.2%
3	Texas	3,830	6.4%
34	Utah	460	0.8%
45	Vermont	150	0.3%
11	Virginia	1,610	2.7%
16	Washington	1,380	2.3%
34	West Virginia	460	0.8%
19	Wisconsin	1,230	2.1%
45	Wyoming	150	0.3%

RANK ORDER

RANK	STATE	CASES	% of USA
1	California	5,440	9.1%
2	Florida	4,600	7.7%
3	Texas	3,830	6.4%
4	New York	3,220	5.4%
5	Pennsylvania	2,990	5.0%
6	Ohio	2,450	4.1%
7	Illinois	2,300	3.9%
8	New Jersey	1,920	3.2%
8	North Carolina	1,920	3.2%
10	Michigan	1,840	3.1%
11	Georgia	1,610	2.7%
11	Virginia	1,610	2.7%
13	Massachusetts	1,530	2.6%
14	Indiana	1,460	2.5%
14	Missouri	1,460	2.5%
16	Washington	1,380	2.3%
17	Arizona	1,300	2.2%
17	Tennessee	1,300	2.2%
19	Wisconsin	1,230	2.1%
20	Kentucky	1,150	1.9%
21	Maryland	1,070	1.8%
22	Minnesota	1,000	1.7%
22	Oklahoma	1,000	1.7%
22	Oregon	1,000	1.7%
25	Alabama	920	1.5%
25	Colorado	920	1.5%
27	Louisiana	770	1.3%
27	South Carolina	770	1.3%
29	Connecticut	690	1.2%
30	Arkansas	540	0.9%
30	Iowa	540	0.9%
30	Kansas	540	0.9%
30	Nevada	540	0.9%
34	Mississippi	460	0.8%
34	Utah	460	0.8%
34	West Virginia	460	0.8%
37	Idaho	380	0.6%
37	Maine	380	0.6%
37	Nebraska	380	0.6%
40	New Hampshire	310	0.5%
40	New Mexico	310	0.5%
40	Rhode Island	310	0.5%
43	Delaware	230	0.4%
43	Montana	230	0.4%
45	Hawaii	150	0.3%
45	South Dakota	150	0.3%
45	Vermont	150	0.3%
45	Wyoming	150	0.3%
49	Alaska	80	0.1%
49	North Dakota	80	0.1%
	District of Columbia	80	0.1%

Source: American Cancer Society
   "Cancer Facts & Figures 2005" (Copyright 2005, American Cancer Society)
*These estimates are offered as a rough guide and should be interpreted with caution. They are calculated according to the distribution of estimated 2005 cancer deaths by state.

Estimated Rate of New Skin Melanoma Cases in 2005

National Estimated Rate = 20.3 New Cases per 100,000 Population*

ALPHA ORDER

RANK ORDER

RANK	STATE	RATE		RANK	STATE	RATE
28	Alabama	20.3		1	Wyoming	29.6
49	Alaska	12.2		2	Maine	28.8
19	Arizona	22.6		3	Rhode Island	28.7
32	Arkansas	19.6		4	Oklahoma	28.4
47	California	15.2		5	Oregon	27.8
29	Colorado	20.0		6	Delaware	27.7
30	Connecticut	19.7		6	Kentucky	27.7
6	Delaware	27.7		8	Idaho	27.3
9	Florida	26.4		9	Florida	26.4
39	Georgia	18.2		10	Missouri	25.4
50	Hawaii	11.9		11	West Virginia	25.3
8	Idaho	27.3		12	Montana	24.8
41	Illinois	18.1		13	Pennsylvania	24.1
17	Indiana	23.4		13	Vermont	24.1
37	Iowa	18.3		15	New Hampshire	23.9
30	Kansas	19.7		16	Massachusetts	23.8
6	Kentucky	27.7		17	Indiana	23.4
42	Louisiana	17.1		18	Nevada	23.1
2	Maine	28.8		19	Arizona	22.6
35	Maryland	19.3		20	North Carolina	22.5
16	Massachusetts	23.8		21	Wisconsin	22.3
39	Michigan	18.2		22	Washington	22.2
32	Minnesota	19.6		23	New Jersey	22.1
46	Mississippi	15.8		24	Tennessee	22.0
10	Missouri	25.4		25	Nebraska	21.7
12	Montana	24.8		26	Virginia	21.6
25	Nebraska	21.7		27	Ohio	21.4
18	Nevada	23.1		28	Alabama	20.3
15	New Hampshire	23.9		29	Colorado	20.0
23	New Jersey	22.1		30	Connecticut	19.7
45	New Mexico	16.3		30	Kansas	19.7
44	New York	16.7		32	Arkansas	19.6
20	North Carolina	22.5		32	Minnesota	19.6
48	North Dakota	12.6		34	South Dakota	19.5
27	Ohio	21.4		35	Maryland	19.3
4	Oklahoma	28.4		35	Utah	19.3
5	Oregon	27.8		37	Iowa	18.3
13	Pennsylvania	24.1		37	South Carolina	18.3
3	Rhode Island	28.7		39	Georgia	18.2
37	South Carolina	18.3		39	Michigan	18.2
34	South Dakota	19.5		41	Illinois	18.1
24	Tennessee	22.0		42	Louisiana	17.1
43	Texas	17.0		43	Texas	17.0
35	Utah	19.3		44	New York	16.7
13	Vermont	24.1		45	New Mexico	16.3
26	Virginia	21.6		46	Mississippi	15.8
22	Washington	22.2		47	California	15.2
11	West Virginia	25.3		48	North Dakota	12.6
21	Wisconsin	22.3		49	Alaska	12.2
1	Wyoming	29.6		50	Hawaii	11.9

District of Columbia 14.5

Source: Morgan Quitno Press using data from American Cancer Society
   "Cancer Facts & Figures 2005" (Copyright 2005, American Cancer Society)
*These estimates are offered as a rough guide and should be interpreted with caution. They are calculated according to the distribution of estimated 2005 cancer deaths by state. Rates calculated using 2004 Census resident population estimates.

Estimated New Cervical Cancer Cases in 2005

National Estimated Total = 10,370 New Cases[^]

ALPHA ORDER					RANK ORDER			
RANK	STATE		CASES	% of USA	RANK	STATE	CASES	% of USA
17	Alabama		200	1.9%	1	California	1,090	10.5%
NA	Alaska**		NA	NA	2	Texas	1,030	9.9%
17	Arizona		200	1.9%	3	New York	840	8.1%
20	Arkansas		170	1.6%	4	Florida	730	7.0%
1	California		1,090	10.5%	5	Illinois	500	4.8%
32	Colorado		80	0.8%	6	Ohio	390	3.8%
13	Connecticut		220	2.1%	6	Pennsylvania	390	3.8%
NA	Delaware**		NA	NA	8	Georgia	360	3.5%
4	Florida		730	7.0%	9	Michigan	340	3.3%
8	Georgia		360	3.5%	9	New Jersey	340	3.3%
36	Hawaii		60	0.6%	11	North Carolina	310	3.0%
36	Idaho		60	0.6%	12	Tennessee	280	2.7%
5	Illinois		500	4.8%	13	Connecticut	220	2.1%
20	Indiana		170	1.6%	13	Kentucky	220	2.1%
27	Iowa		110	1.1%	13	Louisiana	220	2.1%
32	Kansas		80	0.8%	13	Maryland	220	2.1%
13	Kentucky		220	2.1%	17	Alabama	200	1.9%
13	Louisiana		220	2.1%	17	Arizona	200	1.9%
NA	Maine**		NA	NA	17	Virginia	200	1.9%
13	Maryland		220	2.1%	20	Arkansas	170	1.6%
27	Massachusetts		110	1.1%	20	Indiana	170	1.6%
9	Michigan		340	3.3%	20	Missouri	170	1.6%
27	Minnesota		110	1.1%	20	South Carolina	170	1.6%
24	Mississippi		140	1.4%	24	Mississippi	140	1.4%
20	Missouri		170	1.6%	24	Oklahoma	140	1.4%
NA	Montana**		NA	NA	24	Oregon	140	1.4%
36	Nebraska		60	0.6%	27	Iowa	110	1.1%
32	Nevada		80	0.8%	27	Massachusetts	110	1.1%
NA	New Hampshire**		NA	NA	27	Minnesota	110	1.1%
9	New Jersey		340	3.3%	27	Washington	110	1.1%
36	New Mexico		60	0.6%	27	West Virginia	110	1.1%
3	New York		840	8.1%	32	Colorado	80	0.8%
11	North Carolina		310	3.0%	32	Kansas	80	0.8%
NA	North Dakota**		NA	NA	32	Nevada	80	0.8%
6	Ohio		390	3.8%	32	Wisconsin	80	0.8%
24	Oklahoma		140	1.4%	36	Hawaii	60	0.6%
24	Oregon		140	1.4%	36	Idaho	60	0.6%
6	Pennsylvania		390	3.8%	36	Nebraska	60	0.6%
36	Rhode Island		60	0.6%	36	New Mexico	60	0.6%
20	South Carolina		170	1.6%	36	Rhode Island	60	0.6%
NA	South Dakota**		NA	NA	NA	Alaska**	NA	NA
12	Tennessee		280	2.7%	NA	Delaware**	NA	NA
2	Texas		1,030	9.9%	NA	Maine**	NA	NA
NA	Utah**		NA	NA	NA	Montana**	NA	NA
NA	Vermont**		NA	NA	NA	New Hampshire**	NA	NA
17	Virginia		200	1.9%	NA	North Dakota**	NA	NA
27	Washington		110	1.1%	NA	South Dakota**	NA	NA
27	West Virginia		110	1.1%	NA	Utah**	NA	NA
32	Wisconsin		80	0.8%	NA	Vermont**	NA	NA
NA	Wyoming**		NA	NA	NA	Wyoming**	NA	NA
						District of Columbia**	NA	NA

Source: American Cancer Society
    "Cancer Facts & Figures 2005" (Copyright 2005, American Cancer Society)
*These estimates are offered as a rough guide and should be interpreted with caution. They are calculated according to the distribution of estimated 2004 cancer deaths by state.
**Not available.

Estimated Rate of New Cervical Cancer Cases in 2005

National Estimated Rate = 7.2 New Cases per 100,000 Female Population*

ALPHA ORDER

RANK	STATE	RATE
11	Alabama	9.2
NA	Alaska**	NA
24	Arizona	7.2
2	Arkansas	12.7
31	California	6.2
38	Colorado	3.5
1	Connecticut	13.0
NA	Delaware**	NA
13	Florida	8.8
15	Georgia	8.4
9	Hawaii	9.5
13	Idaho	8.8
18	Illinois	8.1
34	Indiana	5.6
22	Iowa	7.6
33	Kansas	5.9
5	Kentucky	10.9
6	Louisiana	10.1
NA	Maine**	NA
17	Maryland	8.3
38	Massachusetts	3.5
28	Michigan	6.9
36	Minnesota	4.4
7	Mississippi	10.0
32	Missouri	6.1
NA	Montana**	NA
25	Nebraska	7.0
25	Nevada	7.0
NA	New Hampshire**	NA
18	New Jersey	8.1
29	New Mexico	6.5
12	New York	9.1
23	North Carolina	7.5
NA	North Dakota**	NA
25	Ohio	7.0
18	Oklahoma	8.1
21	Oregon	7.9
29	Pennsylvania	6.5
4	Rhode Island	11.6
15	South Carolina	8.4
NA	South Dakota**	NA
8	Tennessee	9.8
10	Texas	9.4
NA	Utah**	NA
NA	Vermont**	NA
35	Virginia	5.5
37	Washington	3.6
3	West Virginia	12.5
40	Wisconsin	3.0
NA	Wyoming**	NA

RANK ORDER

RANK	STATE	RATE
1	Connecticut	13.0
2	Arkansas	12.7
3	West Virginia	12.5
4	Rhode Island	11.6
5	Kentucky	10.9
6	Louisiana	10.1
7	Mississippi	10.0
8	Tennessee	9.8
9	Hawaii	9.5
10	Texas	9.4
11	Alabama	9.2
12	New York	9.1
13	Florida	8.8
13	Idaho	8.8
15	Georgia	8.4
15	South Carolina	8.4
17	Maryland	8.3
18	Illinois	8.1
18	New Jersey	8.1
18	Oklahoma	8.1
21	Oregon	7.9
22	Iowa	7.6
23	North Carolina	7.5
24	Arizona	7.2
25	Nebraska	7.0
25	Nevada	7.0
25	Ohio	7.0
28	Michigan	6.9
29	New Mexico	6.5
29	Pennsylvania	6.5
31	California	6.2
32	Missouri	6.1
33	Kansas	5.9
34	Indiana	5.6
35	Virginia	5.5
36	Minnesota	4.4
37	Washington	3.6
38	Colorado	3.5
38	Massachusetts	3.5
40	Wisconsin	3.0
NA	Alaska**	NA
NA	Delaware**	NA
NA	Maine**	NA
NA	Montana**	NA
NA	New Hampshire**	NA
NA	North Dakota**	NA
NA	South Dakota**	NA
NA	Utah**	NA
NA	Vermont**	NA
NA	Wyoming**	NA

District of Columbia**   NA

Source: Morgan Quitno Press using data from American Cancer Society
    "Cancer Facts & Figures 2005" (Copyright 2005, American Cancer Society)
*These estimates are offered as a rough guide and should be interpreted with caution. They are calculated according to the distribution of estimated 2005 cancer deaths by state. Rates calculated using 2003 Census female population estimates.
**Not available.

Percent of Women 18 Years Old and Older
Who Had a Pap Smear Within the Past Three Years: 2004
National Median = 85.9% of Women 18 Years and Older[*]

ALPHA ORDER

RANK	STATE	PERCENT
14	Alabama	87.4
5	Alaska	88.8
31	Arizona	85.1
47	Arkansas	81.7
34	California	84.7
8	Colorado	88.2
11	Connecticut	87.7
12	Delaware	87.6
40	Florida	84.0
9	Georgia	87.9
NA	Hawaii**	NA
48	Idaho	78.8
14	Illinois	87.4
45	Indiana	82.4
24	Iowa	86.0
22	Kansas	86.1
32	Kentucky	84.9
30	Louisiana	85.2
6	Maine	88.7
3	Maryland	88.9
2	Massachusetts	89.3
20	Michigan	86.5
10	Minnesota	87.8
37	Mississippi	84.5
33	Missouri	84.8
22	Montana	86.1
26	Nebraska	85.8
34	Nevada	84.7
1	New Hampshire	89.7
38	New Jersey	84.3
34	New Mexico	84.7
28	New York	85.4
7	North Carolina	88.3
42	North Dakota	83.2
21	Ohio	86.4
43	Oklahoma	82.9
41	Oregon	83.5
38	Pennsylvania	84.3
3	Rhode Island	88.9
19	South Carolina	87.1
18	South Dakota	87.2
16	Tennessee	87.3
46	Texas	82.1
49	Utah	78.2
12	Vermont	87.6
16	Virginia	87.3
28	Washington	85.4
44	West Virginia	82.5
27	Wisconsin	85.7
25	Wyoming	85.9

RANK ORDER

RANK	STATE	PERCENT
1	New Hampshire	89.7
2	Massachusetts	89.3
3	Maryland	88.9
3	Rhode Island	88.9
5	Alaska	88.8
6	Maine	88.7
7	North Carolina	88.3
8	Colorado	88.2
9	Georgia	87.9
10	Minnesota	87.8
11	Connecticut	87.7
12	Delaware	87.6
12	Vermont	87.6
14	Alabama	87.4
14	Illinois	87.4
16	Tennessee	87.3
16	Virginia	87.3
18	South Dakota	87.2
19	South Carolina	87.1
20	Michigan	86.5
21	Ohio	86.4
22	Kansas	86.1
22	Montana	86.1
24	Iowa	86.0
25	Wyoming	85.9
26	Nebraska	85.8
27	Wisconsin	85.7
28	New York	85.4
28	Washington	85.4
30	Louisiana	85.2
31	Arizona	85.1
32	Kentucky	84.9
33	Missouri	84.8
34	California	84.7
34	Nevada	84.7
34	New Mexico	84.7
37	Mississippi	84.5
38	New Jersey	84.3
38	Pennsylvania	84.3
40	Florida	84.0
41	Oregon	83.5
42	North Dakota	83.2
43	Oklahoma	82.9
44	West Virginia	82.5
45	Indiana	82.4
46	Texas	82.1
47	Arkansas	81.7
48	Idaho	78.8
49	Utah	78.2
NA	Hawaii**	NA
	District of Columbia	88.4

Source: U.S. Department of Health and Human Services, Centers for Disease Control and Prevention
"2004 Behavioral Risk Factor Surveillance Summary Prevalence Data" (http://apps.nccd.cdc.gov/brfss/)
[*]A Pap test is a test for cancer, especially of the female genital tract such as cancer of the cervix. Named after George Papanicolaou (1883-1962), American anatomist.
***Not available.*

Estimated New Uterine Cancer Cases in 2005

National Estimated Total = 40,880 New Cases*

ALPHA ORDER

RANK	STATE	CASES	% of USA
20	Alabama	670	1.6%
49	Alaska	60	0.1%
22	Arizona	500	1.2%
32	Arkansas	340	0.8%
1	California	4,250	10.4%
28	Colorado	450	1.1%
22	Connecticut	500	1.2%
44	Delaware	110	0.3%
4	Florida	2,520	6.2%
14	Georgia	890	2.2%
40	Hawaii	170	0.4%
40	Idaho	170	0.4%
6	Illinois	2,010	4.9%
11	Indiana	1,010	2.5%
22	Iowa	500	1.2%
31	Kansas	390	1.0%
22	Kentucky	500	1.2%
22	Louisiana	500	1.2%
37	Maine	220	0.5%
18	Maryland	780	1.9%
11	Massachusetts	1,010	2.5%
9	Michigan	1,450	3.5%
20	Minnesota	670	1.6%
32	Mississippi	340	0.8%
16	Missouri	840	2.1%
40	Montana	170	0.4%
34	Nebraska	280	0.7%
37	Nevada	220	0.5%
40	New Hampshire	170	0.4%
8	New Jersey	1,790	4.4%
34	New Mexico	280	0.7%
2	New York	3,240	7.9%
10	North Carolina	1,170	2.9%
44	North Dakota	110	0.3%
7	Ohio	1,850	4.5%
28	Oklahoma	450	1.1%
28	Oregon	450	1.1%
3	Pennsylvania	2,570	6.3%
44	Rhode Island	110	0.3%
22	South Carolina	500	1.2%
44	South Dakota	110	0.3%
19	Tennessee	730	1.8%
5	Texas	2,400	5.9%
37	Utah	220	0.5%
44	Vermont	110	0.3%
11	Virginia	1,010	2.5%
14	Washington	890	2.2%
34	West Virginia	280	0.7%
16	Wisconsin	840	2.1%
49	Wyoming	60	0.1%

RANK ORDER

RANK	STATE	CASES	% of USA
1	California	4,250	10.4%
2	New York	3,240	7.9%
3	Pennsylvania	2,570	6.3%
4	Florida	2,520	6.2%
5	Texas	2,400	5.9%
6	Illinois	2,010	4.9%
7	Ohio	1,850	4.5%
8	New Jersey	1,790	4.4%
9	Michigan	1,450	3.5%
10	North Carolina	1,170	2.9%
11	Indiana	1,010	2.5%
11	Massachusetts	1,010	2.5%
11	Virginia	1,010	2.5%
14	Georgia	890	2.2%
14	Washington	890	2.2%
16	Missouri	840	2.1%
16	Wisconsin	840	2.1%
18	Maryland	780	1.9%
19	Tennessee	730	1.8%
20	Alabama	670	1.6%
20	Minnesota	670	1.6%
22	Arizona	500	1.2%
22	Connecticut	500	1.2%
22	Iowa	500	1.2%
22	Kentucky	500	1.2%
22	Louisiana	500	1.2%
22	South Carolina	500	1.2%
28	Colorado	450	1.1%
28	Oklahoma	450	1.1%
28	Oregon	450	1.1%
31	Kansas	390	1.0%
32	Arkansas	340	0.8%
32	Mississippi	340	0.8%
34	Nebraska	280	0.7%
34	New Mexico	280	0.7%
34	West Virginia	280	0.7%
37	Maine	220	0.5%
37	Nevada	220	0.5%
37	Utah	220	0.5%
40	Hawaii	170	0.4%
40	Idaho	170	0.4%
40	Montana	170	0.4%
40	New Hampshire	170	0.4%
44	Delaware	110	0.3%
44	North Dakota	110	0.3%
44	Rhode Island	110	0.3%
44	South Dakota	110	0.3%
44	Vermont	110	0.3%
49	Alaska	60	0.1%
49	Wyoming	60	0.1%
	District of Columbia	170	0.4%

Source: American Cancer Society
    "Cancer Facts & Figures 2005" (Copyright 2005, American Cancer Society)
*These estimates are offered as a rough guide and should be interpreted with caution. They are calculated according to the distribution of estimated 2005 cancer deaths by state.

Estimated Rate of New Uterine Cancer Cases in 2005

National Estimated Rate = 28.6 New Cases per 100,000 Female Population*

ALPHA ORDER

RANK	STATE	RATE
16	Alabama	30.7
49	Alaska	17.9
49	Arizona	17.9
34	Arkansas	25.5
40	California	24.0
46	Colorado	19.6
20	Connecticut	29.6
28	Delaware	27.6
18	Florida	30.2
45	Georgia	20.8
29	Hawaii	27.0
36	Idaho	24.8
13	Illinois	32.4
9	Indiana	33.2
8	Iowa	34.5
25	Kansas	28.9
36	Kentucky	24.8
42	Louisiana	22.9
7	Maine	34.6
21	Maryland	29.3
12	Massachusetts	32.5
21	Michigan	29.3
31	Minnesota	26.7
39	Mississippi	24.4
18	Missouri	30.2
3	Montana	37.2
11	Nebraska	32.6
47	Nevada	19.3
30	New Hampshire	26.8
2	New Jersey	42.6
17	New Mexico	30.4
5	New York	34.9
26	North Carolina	28.3
6	North Dakota	34.7
9	Ohio	33.2
32	Oklahoma	26.0
35	Oregon	25.4
1	Pennsylvania	42.9
44	Rhode Island	21.2
36	South Carolina	24.8
24	South Dakota	29.0
33	Tennessee	25.6
43	Texas	21.8
48	Utah	18.6
4	Vermont	36.2
27	Virginia	27.8
23	Washington	29.1
14	West Virginia	31.7
15	Wisconsin	31.0
41	Wyoming	23.8

RANK ORDER

RANK	STATE	RATE
1	Pennsylvania	42.9
2	New Jersey	42.6
3	Montana	37.2
4	Vermont	36.2
5	New York	34.9
6	North Dakota	34.7
7	Maine	34.6
8	Iowa	34.5
9	Indiana	33.2
9	Ohio	33.2
11	Nebraska	32.6
12	Massachusetts	32.5
13	Illinois	32.4
14	West Virginia	31.7
15	Wisconsin	31.0
16	Alabama	30.7
17	New Mexico	30.4
18	Florida	30.2
18	Missouri	30.2
20	Connecticut	29.6
21	Maryland	29.3
21	Michigan	29.3
23	Washington	29.1
24	South Dakota	29.0
25	Kansas	28.9
26	North Carolina	28.3
27	Virginia	27.8
28	Delaware	27.6
29	Hawaii	27.0
30	New Hampshire	26.8
31	Minnesota	26.7
32	Oklahoma	26.0
33	Tennessee	25.6
34	Arkansas	25.5
35	Oregon	25.4
36	Idaho	24.8
36	Kentucky	24.8
36	South Carolina	24.8
39	Mississippi	24.4
40	California	24.0
41	Wyoming	23.8
42	Louisiana	22.9
43	Texas	21.8
44	Rhode Island	21.2
45	Georgia	20.8
46	Colorado	19.6
47	Nevada	19.3
48	Utah	18.6
49	Alaska	17.9
49	Arizona	17.9

District of Columbia 63.9

Source: Morgan Quitno Press using data from American Cancer Society
   "Cancer Facts & Figures 2005" (Copyright 2005, American Cancer Society)
*These estimates are offered as a rough guide and should be interpreted with caution. They are calculated
according to the distribution of estimated 2005 cancer deaths by state. Rates calculated using 2003 Census
female population estimates.

AIDS Cases Reported in 2005

National Total = 30,568 New AIDS Cases*

ALPHA ORDER

RANK	STATE	CASES	% of USA
20	Alabama	385	1.3%
43	Alaska	25	0.1%
15	Arizona	473	1.5%
31	Arkansas	173	0.6%
3	California	3,105	10.2%
25	Colorado	260	0.9%
18	Connecticut	423	1.4%
32	Delaware	134	0.4%
2	Florida	3,963	13.0%
5	Georgia	1,701	5.6%
37	Hawaii	92	0.3%
45	Idaho	15	0.0%
6	Illinois	1,504	4.9%
22	Indiana	348	1.1%
38	Iowa	72	0.2%
36	Kansas	94	0.3%
28	Kentucky	198	0.6%
11	Louisiana	650	2.1%
44	Maine	19	0.1%
7	Maryland	1,370	4.5%
13	Massachusetts	561	1.8%
17	Michigan	439	1.4%
30	Minnesota	176	0.6%
24	Mississippi	288	0.9%
23	Missouri	299	1.0%
45	Montana	15	0.0%
41	Nebraska	27	0.1%
26	Nevada	236	0.8%
42	New Hampshire	26	0.1%
9	New Jersey	956	3.1%
34	New Mexico	115	0.4%
1	New York	4,413	14.4%
12	North Carolina	636	2.1%
48	North Dakota	9	0.0%
14	Ohio	518	1.7%
27	Oklahoma	229	0.7%
29	Oregon	193	0.6%
8	Pennsylvania	1,228	4.0%
35	Rhode Island	105	0.3%
19	South Carolina	413	1.4%
47	South Dakota	13	0.0%
10	Tennessee	675	2.2%
4	Texas	2,491	8.1%
39	Utah	55	0.2%
49	Vermont	7	0.0%
16	Virginia	441	1.4%
21	Washington	352	1.2%
40	West Virginia	51	0.2%
33	Wisconsin	120	0.4%
50	Wyoming	3	0.0%

RANK ORDER

RANK	STATE	CASES	% of USA
1	New York	4,413	14.4%
2	Florida	3,963	13.0%
3	California	3,105	10.2%
4	Texas	2,491	8.1%
5	Georgia	1,701	5.6%
6	Illinois	1,504	4.9%
7	Maryland	1,370	4.5%
8	Pennsylvania	1,228	4.0%
9	New Jersey	956	3.1%
10	Tennessee	675	2.2%
11	Louisiana	650	2.1%
12	North Carolina	636	2.1%
13	Massachusetts	561	1.8%
14	Ohio	518	1.7%
15	Arizona	473	1.5%
16	Virginia	441	1.4%
17	Michigan	439	1.4%
18	Connecticut	423	1.4%
19	South Carolina	413	1.4%
20	Alabama	385	1.3%
21	Washington	352	1.2%
22	Indiana	348	1.1%
23	Missouri	299	1.0%
24	Mississippi	288	0.9%
25	Colorado	260	0.9%
26	Nevada	236	0.8%
27	Oklahoma	229	0.7%
28	Kentucky	198	0.6%
29	Oregon	193	0.6%
30	Minnesota	176	0.6%
31	Arkansas	173	0.6%
32	Delaware	134	0.4%
33	Wisconsin	120	0.4%
34	New Mexico	115	0.4%
35	Rhode Island	105	0.3%
36	Kansas	94	0.3%
37	Hawaii	92	0.3%
38	Iowa	72	0.2%
39	Utah	55	0.2%
40	West Virginia	51	0.2%
41	Nebraska	27	0.1%
42	New Hampshire	26	0.1%
43	Alaska	25	0.1%
44	Maine	19	0.1%
45	Idaho	15	0.0%
45	Montana	15	0.0%
47	South Dakota	13	0.0%
48	North Dakota	9	0.0%
49	Vermont	7	0.0%
50	Wyoming	3	0.0%
	District of Columbia	474	1.6%

Source: U.S. Department of Health and Human Services, National Center for Health Statistics
    "Morbidity and Mortality Weekly Report" (January 6, 2006, Vol. 54, Nos. 51 & 52)
*Provisional data. AIDS is Acquired Immunodeficiency Syndrome. It is a specific group of diseases or conditions which are indicative of severe immunosuppression related to infection with the Human Immunodeficiency Virus (HIV). National total does not include 814 new cases in Puerto Rico.

AIDS Rate in 2005

National Rate = 10.3 New AIDS Cases Reported per 100,000 Population*

ALPHA ORDER

RANK ORDER

RANK	STATE	RATE
19	Alabama	8.4
35	Alaska	3.8
20	Arizona	8.0
24	Arkansas	6.2
18	California	8.6
27	Colorado	5.6
7	Connecticut	12.1
5	Delaware	15.9
3	Florida	22.3
4	Georgia	18.7
22	Hawaii	7.2
49	Idaho	1.0
8	Illinois	11.8
29	Indiana	5.5
39	Iowa	2.4
36	Kansas	3.4
32	Kentucky	4.7
6	Louisiana	14.4
46	Maine	1.4
1	Maryland	24.5
17	Massachusetts	8.8
34	Michigan	4.3
36	Minnesota	3.4
12	Mississippi	9.9
31	Missouri	5.2
44	Montana	1.6
45	Nebraska	1.5
14	Nevada	9.8
42	New Hampshire	2.0
10	New Jersey	11.0
25	New Mexico	6.0
2	New York	22.9
21	North Carolina	7.3
46	North Dakota	1.4
33	Ohio	4.5
23	Oklahoma	6.5
30	Oregon	5.3
12	Pennsylvania	9.9
14	Rhode Island	9.8
16	South Carolina	9.7
43	South Dakota	1.7
9	Tennessee	11.3
11	Texas	10.9
40	Utah	2.2
48	Vermont	1.1
26	Virginia	5.8
27	Washington	5.6
38	West Virginia	2.8
40	Wisconsin	2.2
50	Wyoming	0.6

RANK	STATE	RATE
1	Maryland	24.5
2	New York	22.9
3	Florida	22.3
4	Georgia	18.7
5	Delaware	15.9
6	Louisiana	14.4
7	Connecticut	12.1
8	Illinois	11.8
9	Tennessee	11.3
10	New Jersey	11.0
11	Texas	10.9
12	Mississippi	9.9
12	Pennsylvania	9.9
14	Nevada	9.8
14	Rhode Island	9.8
16	South Carolina	9.7
17	Massachusetts	8.8
18	California	8.6
19	Alabama	8.4
20	Arizona	8.0
21	North Carolina	7.3
22	Hawaii	7.2
23	Oklahoma	6.5
24	Arkansas	6.2
25	New Mexico	6.0
26	Virginia	5.8
27	Colorado	5.6
27	Washington	5.6
29	Indiana	5.5
30	Oregon	5.3
31	Missouri	5.2
32	Kentucky	4.7
33	Ohio	4.5
34	Michigan	4.3
35	Alaska	3.8
36	Kansas	3.4
36	Minnesota	3.4
38	West Virginia	2.8
39	Iowa	2.4
40	Utah	2.2
40	Wisconsin	2.2
42	New Hampshire	2.0
43	South Dakota	1.7
44	Montana	1.6
45	Nebraska	1.5
46	Maine	1.4
46	North Dakota	1.4
48	Vermont	1.1
49	Idaho	1.0
50	Wyoming	0.6

District of Columbia   86.1

*Source: Morgan Quitno Press using data from U.S. Dept. of Health & Human Serv's, National Center for Health Statistics
    "Morbidity and Mortality Weekly Report" (January 6, 2006, Vol. 54, Nos. 51 & 52)*
*Provisional data. AIDS is Acquired Immunodeficiency Syndrome. It is a specific group of diseases or conditions
which are indicative of severe immunosuppression related to infection with the Human Immunodeficiency Virus
(HIV). National rate does not include cases or population in U.S. territories.*

AIDS Cases Reported Through December 2004

National Total = 888,795 Reported AIDS Cases*

<table>
<tr><td colspan="4">ALPHA ORDER</td><td colspan="4">RANK ORDER</td></tr>
<tr><th>RANK</th><th>STATE</th><th>CASES</th><th>% of USA</th><th>RANK</th><th>STATE</th><th>CASES</th><th>% of USA</th></tr>
<tr><td>23</td><td>Alabama</td><td>7,744</td><td>0.9%</td><td>1</td><td>New York</td><td>166,814</td><td>18.8%</td></tr>
<tr><td>44</td><td>Alaska</td><td>597</td><td>0.1%</td><td>2</td><td>California</td><td>135,221</td><td>15.2%</td></tr>
<tr><td>21</td><td>Arizona</td><td>9,320</td><td>1.0%</td><td>3</td><td>Florida</td><td>96,712</td><td>10.9%</td></tr>
<tr><td>32</td><td>Arkansas</td><td>3,487</td><td>0.4%</td><td>4</td><td>Texas</td><td>64,479</td><td>7.3%</td></tr>
<tr><td>2</td><td>California</td><td>135,221</td><td>15.2%</td><td>5</td><td>New Jersey</td><td>47,224</td><td>5.3%</td></tr>
<tr><td>22</td><td>Colorado</td><td>8,141</td><td>0.9%</td><td>6</td><td>Illinois</td><td>31,020</td><td>3.5%</td></tr>
<tr><td>14</td><td>Connecticut</td><td>13,890</td><td>1.6%</td><td>7</td><td>Pennsylvania</td><td>30,526</td><td>3.4%</td></tr>
<tr><td>33</td><td>Delaware</td><td>3,302</td><td>0.4%</td><td>8</td><td>Georgia</td><td>28,248</td><td>3.2%</td></tr>
<tr><td>3</td><td>Florida</td><td>96,712</td><td>10.9%</td><td>9</td><td>Maryland</td><td>27,550</td><td>3.1%</td></tr>
<tr><td>8</td><td>Georgia</td><td>28,248</td><td>3.2%</td><td>10</td><td>Massachusetts</td><td>18,339</td><td>2.1%</td></tr>
<tr><td>34</td><td>Hawaii</td><td>2,770</td><td>0.3%</td><td>11</td><td>Louisiana</td><td>16,066</td><td>1.8%</td></tr>
<tr><td>45</td><td>Idaho</td><td>560</td><td>0.1%</td><td>12</td><td>Virginia</td><td>15,740</td><td>1.8%</td></tr>
<tr><td>6</td><td>Illinois</td><td>31,020</td><td>3.5%</td><td>13</td><td>North Carolina</td><td>14,078</td><td>1.6%</td></tr>
<tr><td>24</td><td>Indiana</td><td>7,569</td><td>0.9%</td><td>14</td><td>Connecticut</td><td>13,890</td><td>1.6%</td></tr>
<tr><td>39</td><td>Iowa</td><td>1,565</td><td>0.2%</td><td>15</td><td>Ohio</td><td>13,655</td><td>1.5%</td></tr>
<tr><td>35</td><td>Kansas</td><td>2,579</td><td>0.3%</td><td>16</td><td>Michigan</td><td>13,631</td><td>1.5%</td></tr>
<tr><td>30</td><td>Kentucky</td><td>4,241</td><td>0.5%</td><td>17</td><td>South Carolina</td><td>12,089</td><td>1.4%</td></tr>
<tr><td>11</td><td>Louisiana</td><td>16,066</td><td>1.8%</td><td>18</td><td>Tennessee</td><td>11,126</td><td>1.3%</td></tr>
<tr><td>42</td><td>Maine</td><td>1,056</td><td>0.1%</td><td>19</td><td>Washington</td><td>11,046</td><td>1.2%</td></tr>
<tr><td>9</td><td>Maryland</td><td>27,550</td><td>3.1%</td><td>20</td><td>Missouri</td><td>10,265</td><td>1.2%</td></tr>
<tr><td>10</td><td>Massachusetts</td><td>18,339</td><td>2.1%</td><td>21</td><td>Arizona</td><td>9,320</td><td>1.0%</td></tr>
<tr><td>16</td><td>Michigan</td><td>13,631</td><td>1.5%</td><td>22</td><td>Colorado</td><td>8,141</td><td>0.9%</td></tr>
<tr><td>28</td><td>Minnesota</td><td>4,415</td><td>0.5%</td><td>23</td><td>Alabama</td><td>7,744</td><td>0.9%</td></tr>
<tr><td>25</td><td>Mississippi</td><td>6,032</td><td>0.7%</td><td>24</td><td>Indiana</td><td>7,569</td><td>0.9%</td></tr>
<tr><td>20</td><td>Missouri</td><td>10,265</td><td>1.2%</td><td>25</td><td>Mississippi</td><td>6,032</td><td>0.7%</td></tr>
<tr><td>47</td><td>Montana</td><td>353</td><td>0.0%</td><td>26</td><td>Oregon</td><td>5,557</td><td>0.6%</td></tr>
<tr><td>41</td><td>Nebraska</td><td>1,329</td><td>0.1%</td><td>27</td><td>Nevada</td><td>5,190</td><td>0.6%</td></tr>
<tr><td>27</td><td>Nevada</td><td>5,190</td><td>0.6%</td><td>28</td><td>Minnesota</td><td>4,415</td><td>0.5%</td></tr>
<tr><td>43</td><td>New Hampshire</td><td>997</td><td>0.1%</td><td>29</td><td>Oklahoma</td><td>4,381</td><td>0.5%</td></tr>
<tr><td>5</td><td>New Jersey</td><td>47,224</td><td>5.3%</td><td>30</td><td>Kentucky</td><td>4,241</td><td>0.5%</td></tr>
<tr><td>37</td><td>New Mexico</td><td>2,396</td><td>0.3%</td><td>31</td><td>Wisconsin</td><td>4,217</td><td>0.5%</td></tr>
<tr><td>1</td><td>New York</td><td>166,814</td><td>18.8%</td><td>32</td><td>Arkansas</td><td>3,487</td><td>0.4%</td></tr>
<tr><td>13</td><td>North Carolina</td><td>14,078</td><td>1.6%</td><td>33</td><td>Delaware</td><td>3,302</td><td>0.4%</td></tr>
<tr><td>50</td><td>North Dakota</td><td>131</td><td>0.0%</td><td>34</td><td>Hawaii</td><td>2,770</td><td>0.3%</td></tr>
<tr><td>15</td><td>Ohio</td><td>13,655</td><td>1.5%</td><td>35</td><td>Kansas</td><td>2,579</td><td>0.3%</td></tr>
<tr><td>29</td><td>Oklahoma</td><td>4,381</td><td>0.5%</td><td>36</td><td>Rhode Island</td><td>2,413</td><td>0.3%</td></tr>
<tr><td>26</td><td>Oregon</td><td>5,557</td><td>0.6%</td><td>37</td><td>New Mexico</td><td>2,396</td><td>0.3%</td></tr>
<tr><td>7</td><td>Pennsylvania</td><td>30,526</td><td>3.4%</td><td>38</td><td>Utah</td><td>2,209</td><td>0.2%</td></tr>
<tr><td>36</td><td>Rhode Island</td><td>2,413</td><td>0.3%</td><td>39</td><td>Iowa</td><td>1,565</td><td>0.2%</td></tr>
<tr><td>17</td><td>South Carolina</td><td>12,089</td><td>1.4%</td><td>40</td><td>West Virginia</td><td>1,375</td><td>0.2%</td></tr>
<tr><td>48</td><td>South Dakota</td><td>226</td><td>0.0%</td><td>41</td><td>Nebraska</td><td>1,329</td><td>0.1%</td></tr>
<tr><td>18</td><td>Tennessee</td><td>11,126</td><td>1.3%</td><td>42</td><td>Maine</td><td>1,056</td><td>0.1%</td></tr>
<tr><td>4</td><td>Texas</td><td>64,479</td><td>7.3%</td><td>43</td><td>New Hampshire</td><td>997</td><td>0.1%</td></tr>
<tr><td>38</td><td>Utah</td><td>2,209</td><td>0.2%</td><td>44</td><td>Alaska</td><td>597</td><td>0.1%</td></tr>
<tr><td>46</td><td>Vermont</td><td>445</td><td>0.1%</td><td>45</td><td>Idaho</td><td>560</td><td>0.1%</td></tr>
<tr><td>12</td><td>Virginia</td><td>15,740</td><td>1.8%</td><td>46</td><td>Vermont</td><td>445</td><td>0.1%</td></tr>
<tr><td>19</td><td>Washington</td><td>11,046</td><td>1.2%</td><td>47</td><td>Montana</td><td>353</td><td>0.0%</td></tr>
<tr><td>40</td><td>West Virginia</td><td>1,375</td><td>0.2%</td><td>48</td><td>South Dakota</td><td>226</td><td>0.0%</td></tr>
<tr><td>31</td><td>Wisconsin</td><td>4,217</td><td>0.5%</td><td>49</td><td>Wyoming</td><td>220</td><td>0.0%</td></tr>
<tr><td>49</td><td>Wyoming</td><td>220</td><td>0.0%</td><td>50</td><td>North Dakota</td><td>131</td><td>0.0%</td></tr>
<tr><td></td><td></td><td></td><td></td><td></td><td>District of Columbia</td><td>16,259</td><td>1.8%</td></tr>
</table>

Source: U.S. Department of Health and Human Services, Centers for Disease Control and Prevention
   "HIV/AIDS Surveillance Report, 2004" (Vol. 16)
*Cumulative through December 2004. AIDS is Acquired Immunodeficiency Syndrome. It is a specific group of diseases or conditions which are indicative of severe immunosuppression related to infection with the Human Immunodeficiency Virus (HIV). National total does not include 28,202 cases in Puerto Rico, 601 cases in the Virgin Islands and 73 cases in other U.S. territories.

AIDS Cases in Children 12 Years and Younger Through December 2004

National Total = 8,964 Juvenile AIDS Cases*

ALPHA ORDER

RANK	STATE	CASES	% of USA	RANK	STATE	CASES	% of USA
18	Alabama	75	0.8%	1	New York	2,356	26.3%
44	Alaska	7	0.1%	2	Florida	1,504	16.8%
23	Arizona	44	0.5%	3	New Jersey	765	8.5%
24	Arkansas	36	0.4%	4	California	648	7.2%
4	California	648	7.2%	5	Texas	390	4.4%
26	Colorado	31	0.3%	6	Pennsylvania	352	3.9%
11	Connecticut	179	2.0%	7	Maryland	314	3.5%
32	Delaware	25	0.3%	8	Illinois	281	3.1%
2	Florida	1,504	16.8%	9	Georgia	222	2.5%
9	Georgia	222	2.5%	10	Massachusetts	210	2.3%
36	Hawaii	17	0.2%	11	Connecticut	179	2.0%
48	Idaho	2	0.0%	12	Virginia	175	2.0%
8	Illinois	281	3.1%	13	Ohio	134	1.5%
22	Indiana	53	0.6%	14	Louisiana	132	1.5%
38	Iowa	12	0.1%	15	North Carolina	120	1.3%
37	Kansas	13	0.1%	16	Michigan	110	1.2%
28	Kentucky	29	0.3%	17	South Carolina	100	1.1%
14	Louisiana	132	1.5%	18	Alabama	75	0.8%
42	Maine	9	0.1%	19	Missouri	60	0.7%
7	Maryland	314	3.5%	20	Mississippi	56	0.6%
10	Massachusetts	210	2.3%	21	Tennessee	55	0.6%
16	Michigan	110	1.2%	22	Indiana	53	0.6%
30	Minnesota	27	0.3%	23	Arizona	44	0.5%
20	Mississippi	56	0.6%	24	Arkansas	36	0.4%
19	Missouri	60	0.7%	25	Washington	34	0.4%
47	Montana	3	0.0%	26	Colorado	31	0.3%
39	Nebraska	11	0.1%	26	Wisconsin	31	0.3%
29	Nevada	28	0.3%	28	Kentucky	29	0.3%
41	New Hampshire	10	0.1%	29	Nevada	28	0.3%
3	New Jersey	765	8.5%	30	Minnesota	27	0.3%
43	New Mexico	8	0.1%	30	Rhode Island	27	0.3%
1	New York	2,356	26.3%	32	Delaware	25	0.3%
15	North Carolina	120	1.3%	32	Oklahoma	25	0.3%
50	North Dakota	1	0.0%	34	Utah	20	0.2%
13	Ohio	134	1.5%	35	Oregon	19	0.2%
32	Oklahoma	25	0.3%	36	Hawaii	17	0.2%
35	Oregon	19	0.2%	37	Kansas	13	0.1%
6	Pennsylvania	352	3.9%	38	Iowa	12	0.1%
30	Rhode Island	27	0.3%	39	Nebraska	11	0.1%
17	South Carolina	100	1.1%	39	West Virginia	11	0.1%
46	South Dakota	5	0.1%	41	New Hampshire	10	0.1%
21	Tennessee	55	0.6%	42	Maine	9	0.1%
5	Texas	390	4.4%	43	New Mexico	8	0.1%
34	Utah	20	0.2%	44	Alaska	7	0.1%
45	Vermont	6	0.1%	45	Vermont	6	0.1%
12	Virginia	175	2.0%	46	South Dakota	5	0.1%
25	Washington	34	0.4%	47	Montana	3	0.0%
39	West Virginia	11	0.1%	48	Idaho	2	0.0%
26	Wisconsin	31	0.3%	48	Wyoming	2	0.0%
48	Wyoming	2	0.0%	50	North Dakota	1	0.0%
					District of Columbia	180	2.0%

Source: U.S. Department of Health and Human Services, Centers for Disease Control and Prevention "HIV/AIDS Surveillance Report, 2004" (Vol. 16)

Cumulative through December 2004. AIDS is Acquired Immunodeficiency Syndrome. It is a specific group of diseases or conditions which are indicative of severe immunosuppression related to infection with the Human Immunodeficiency Virus (HIV). National total does not include 397 cases in Puerto Rico, 17 cases in the Virgin Islands and one case in Guam.

Chickenpox (Varicella) Cases Reported in 2005

National Total = 26,532 Cases*

ALPHA ORDER

RANK	STATE	CASES	% of USA
25	Alabama	0	0.0%
25	Alaska	0	0.0%
25	Arizona	0	0.0%
23	Arkansas	38	0.1%
25	California	0	0.0%
4	Colorado	1,776	6.7%
NA	Connecticut**	NA	NA
24	Delaware	31	0.1%
25	Florida	0	0.0%
25	Georgia	0	0.0%
25	Hawaii	0	0.0%
25	Idaho	0	0.0%
20	Illinois	82	0.3%
9	Indiana	597	2.3%
NA	Iowa**	NA	NA
25	Kansas	0	0.0%
NA	Kentucky**	NA	NA
19	Louisiana	120	0.5%
15	Maine	213	0.8%
25	Maryland	0	0.0%
11	Massachusetts	543	2.0%
3	Michigan	4,087	15.4%
25	Minnesota	0	0.0%
25	Mississippi	0	0.0%
13	Missouri	488	1.8%
25	Montana	0	0.0%
25	Nebraska	0	0.0%
25	Nevada	0	0.0%
6	New Hampshire	1,418	5.3%
25	New Jersey	0	0.0%
16	New Mexico	174	0.7%
25	New York	0	0.0%
25	North Carolina	0	0.0%
21	North Dakota	55	0.2%
5	Ohio	1,742	6.6%
25	Oklahoma	0	0.0%
25	Oregon	0	0.0%
2	Pennsylvania	4,881	18.4%
25	Rhode Island	0	0.0%
10	South Carolina	544	2.1%
17	South Dakota	128	0.5%
25	Tennessee	0	0.0%
1	Texas	6,310	23.8%
12	Utah	531	2.0%
17	Vermont	128	0.5%
8	Virginia	999	3.8%
NA	Washington**	NA	NA
7	West Virginia	1,120	4.2%
14	Wisconsin	433	1.6%
22	Wyoming	53	0.2%

RANK ORDER

RANK	STATE	CASES	% of USA
1	Texas	6,310	23.8%
2	Pennsylvania	4,881	18.4%
3	Michigan	4,087	15.4%
4	Colorado	1,776	6.7%
5	Ohio	1,742	6.6%
6	New Hampshire	1,418	5.3%
7	West Virginia	1,120	4.2%
8	Virginia	999	3.8%
9	Indiana	597	2.3%
10	South Carolina	544	2.1%
11	Massachusetts	543	2.0%
12	Utah	531	2.0%
13	Missouri	488	1.8%
14	Wisconsin	433	1.6%
15	Maine	213	0.8%
16	New Mexico	174	0.7%
17	South Dakota	128	0.5%
17	Vermont	128	0.5%
19	Louisiana	120	0.5%
20	Illinois	82	0.3%
21	North Dakota	55	0.2%
22	Wyoming	53	0.2%
23	Arkansas	38	0.1%
24	Delaware	31	0.1%
25	Alabama	0	0.0%
25	Alaska	0	0.0%
25	Arizona	0	0.0%
25	California	0	0.0%
25	Florida	0	0.0%
25	Georgia	0	0.0%
25	Hawaii	0	0.0%
25	Idaho	0	0.0%
25	Kansas	0	0.0%
25	Maryland	0	0.0%
25	Minnesota	0	0.0%
25	Mississippi	0	0.0%
25	Montana	0	0.0%
25	Nebraska	0	0.0%
25	Nevada	0	0.0%
25	New Jersey	0	0.0%
25	New York	0	0.0%
25	North Carolina	0	0.0%
25	Oklahoma	0	0.0%
25	Oregon	0	0.0%
25	Rhode Island	0	0.0%
25	Tennessee	0	0.0%
NA	Connecticut**	NA	NA
NA	Iowa**	NA	NA
NA	Kentucky**	NA	NA
NA	Washington**	NA	NA
	District of Columbia	41	0.2%

Source: U.S. Department of Health and Human Services, National Center for Health Statistics
    "Morbidity and Mortality Weekly Report" (January 6, 2006, Vol. 54, Nos. 51 & 52)
*Provisional data. An illness with acute onset of generalized maculo-papulovesicular rash without other apparent cause.
**Not notifiable except Connecticut which is listed as unavailable.

Chickenpox (Varicella) Rate in 2005

National Rate = 9.0 Cases per 100,000 Population*

ALPHA ORDER

RANK	STATE	RATE
25	Alabama	0.0
25	Alaska	0.0
25	Arizona	0.0
23	Arkansas	1.4
25	California	0.0
5	Colorado	38.1
NA	Connecticut**	NA
21	Delaware	3.7
25	Florida	0.0
25	Georgia	0.0
25	Hawaii	0.0
25	Idaho	0.0
24	Illinois	0.6
15	Indiana	9.5
NA	Iowa**	NA
25	Kansas	0.0
NA	Kentucky**	NA
22	Louisiana	2.7
10	Maine	16.1
25	Maryland	0.0
18	Massachusetts	8.5
3	Michigan	40.4
25	Minnesota	0.0
25	Mississippi	0.0
19	Missouri	8.4
25	Montana	0.0
25	Nebraska	0.0
25	Nevada	0.0
1	New Hampshire	108.2
25	New Jersey	0.0
16	New Mexico	9.0
25	New York	0.0
25	North Carolina	0.0
17	North Dakota	8.6
11	Ohio	15.2
25	Oklahoma	0.0
25	Oregon	0.0
4	Pennsylvania	39.3
25	Rhode Island	0.0
13	South Carolina	12.8
9	South Dakota	16.5
25	Tennessee	0.0
6	Texas	27.6
7	Utah	21.5
8	Vermont	20.5
12	Virginia	13.2
NA	Washington**	NA
2	West Virginia	61.6
20	Wisconsin	7.8
14	Wyoming	10.4

RANK ORDER

RANK	STATE	RATE
1	New Hampshire	108.2
2	West Virginia	61.6
3	Michigan	40.4
4	Pennsylvania	39.3
5	Colorado	38.1
6	Texas	27.6
7	Utah	21.5
8	Vermont	20.5
9	South Dakota	16.5
10	Maine	16.1
11	Ohio	15.2
12	Virginia	13.2
13	South Carolina	12.8
14	Wyoming	10.4
15	Indiana	9.5
16	New Mexico	9.0
17	North Dakota	8.6
18	Massachusetts	8.5
19	Missouri	8.4
20	Wisconsin	7.8
21	Delaware	3.7
22	Louisiana	2.7
23	Arkansas	1.4
24	Illinois	0.6
25	Alabama	0.0
25	Alaska	0.0
25	Arizona	0.0
25	California	0.0
25	Florida	0.0
25	Georgia	0.0
25	Hawaii	0.0
25	Idaho	0.0
25	Kansas	0.0
25	Maryland	0.0
25	Minnesota	0.0
25	Mississippi	0.0
25	Montana	0.0
25	Nebraska	0.0
25	Nevada	0.0
25	New Jersey	0.0
25	New York	0.0
25	North Carolina	0.0
25	Oklahoma	0.0
25	Oregon	0.0
25	Rhode Island	0.0
25	Tennessee	0.0
NA	Connecticut**	NA
NA	Iowa**	NA
NA	Kentucky**	NA
NA	Washington**	NA

District of Columbia   7.4

Source: Morgan Quitno Press using data from U.S. Dept. of Health & Human Serv's, National Center for Health Statistics
"Morbidity and Mortality Weekly Report" (January 6, 2006, Vol. 54, Nos. 51 & 52)
*Provisional data. An illness with acute onset of generalized maculo-papulovesicular rash without other apparent cause.
**Not notifiable except Connecticut which is listed as unavailable.

E-Coli Cases Reported in 2005

National Total = 3,135 Cases*

ALPHA ORDER

RANK	STATE	CASES	% of USA
30	Alabama	30	1.0%
42	Alaska	12	0.4%
29	Arizona	33	1.1%
44	Arkansas	10	0.3%
5	California	157	5.0%
18	Colorado	72	2.3%
23	Connecticut	58	1.9%
46	Delaware	9	0.3%
7	Florida	142	4.5%
27	Georgia	47	1.5%
41	Hawaii	13	0.4%
26	Idaho	49	1.6%
24	Illinois	54	1.7%
17	Indiana	73	2.3%
13	Iowa	96	3.1%
25	Kansas	53	1.7%
15	Kentucky	77	2.5%
37	Louisiana	18	0.6%
33	Maine	27	0.9%
16	Maryland	75	2.4%
10	Massachusetts	103	3.3%
14	Michigan	93	3.0%
1	Minnesota	195	6.2%
47	Mississippi	8	0.3%
12	Missouri	99	3.2%
38	Montana	16	0.5%
28	Nebraska	37	1.2%
40	Nevada	14	0.4%
38	New Hampshire	16	0.5%
19	New Jersey	69	2.2%
34	New Mexico	23	0.7%
2	New York	188	6.0%
21	North Carolina	64	2.0%
47	North Dakota	8	0.3%
3	Ohio	170	5.4%
32	Oklahoma	28	0.9%
4	Oregon	162	5.2%
8	Pennsylvania	128	4.1%
49	Rhode Island	7	0.2%
43	South Carolina	11	0.4%
31	South Dakota	29	0.9%
22	Tennessee	60	1.9%
35	Texas	20	0.6%
20	Utah	66	2.1%
35	Vermont	20	0.6%
11	Virginia	101	3.2%
9	Washington	126	4.0%
50	West Virginia	5	0.2%
6	Wisconsin	152	4.8%
44	Wyoming	10	0.3%

RANK ORDER

RANK	STATE	CASES	% of USA
1	Minnesota	195	6.2%
2	New York	188	6.0%
3	Ohio	170	5.4%
4	Oregon	162	5.2%
5	California	157	5.0%
6	Wisconsin	152	4.8%
7	Florida	142	4.5%
8	Pennsylvania	128	4.1%
9	Washington	126	4.0%
10	Massachusetts	103	3.3%
11	Virginia	101	3.2%
12	Missouri	99	3.2%
13	Iowa	96	3.1%
14	Michigan	93	3.0%
15	Kentucky	77	2.5%
16	Maryland	75	2.4%
17	Indiana	73	2.3%
18	Colorado	72	2.3%
19	New Jersey	69	2.2%
20	Utah	66	2.1%
21	North Carolina	64	2.0%
22	Tennessee	60	1.9%
23	Connecticut	58	1.9%
24	Illinois	54	1.7%
25	Kansas	53	1.7%
26	Idaho	49	1.6%
27	Georgia	47	1.5%
28	Nebraska	37	1.2%
29	Arizona	33	1.1%
30	Alabama	30	1.0%
31	South Dakota	29	0.9%
32	Oklahoma	28	0.9%
33	Maine	27	0.9%
34	New Mexico	23	0.7%
35	Texas	20	0.6%
35	Vermont	20	0.6%
37	Louisiana	18	0.6%
38	Montana	16	0.5%
38	New Hampshire	16	0.5%
40	Nevada	14	0.4%
41	Hawaii	13	0.4%
42	Alaska	12	0.4%
43	South Carolina	11	0.4%
44	Arkansas	10	0.3%
44	Wyoming	10	0.3%
46	Delaware	9	0.3%
47	Mississippi	8	0.3%
47	North Dakota	8	0.3%
49	Rhode Island	7	0.2%
50	West Virginia	5	0.2%
	District of Columbia	2	0.1%

Source: U.S. Department of Health and Human Services, National Center for Health Statistics
     "Morbidity and Mortality Weekly Report" (January 6, 2006, Vol. 54, Nos. 51 & 52)
*Escherichia Coli is a common bacterium that normally inhabits the intestinal tracts of humans and animals but can cause infection in other parts of the body, especially the urinary tract. One strain, sometimes transmitted in hamburger meat, can cause serious infection resulting in sickness and death.

E-Coli Rate in 2005

National Rate = 1.1 Cases per 100,000 Population*

ALPHA ORDER

RANK	STATE	RATE
37	Alabama	0.7
14	Alaska	1.8
40	Arizona	0.6
43	Arkansas	0.4
43	California	0.4
20	Colorado	1.5
16	Connecticut	1.7
28	Delaware	1.1
34	Florida	0.8
42	Georgia	0.5
29	Hawaii	1.0
4	Idaho	3.4
43	Illinois	0.4
25	Indiana	1.2
5	Iowa	3.2
13	Kansas	1.9
14	Kentucky	1.8
43	Louisiana	0.4
10	Maine	2.0
22	Maryland	1.3
19	Massachusetts	1.6
33	Michigan	0.9
2	Minnesota	3.8
47	Mississippi	0.3
16	Missouri	1.7
16	Montana	1.7
9	Nebraska	2.1
40	Nevada	0.6
25	New Hampshire	1.2
34	New Jersey	0.8
25	New Mexico	1.2
29	New York	1.0
37	North Carolina	0.7
22	North Dakota	1.3
20	Ohio	1.5
34	Oklahoma	0.8
1	Oregon	4.4
29	Pennsylvania	1.0
37	Rhode Island	0.7
47	South Carolina	0.3
3	South Dakota	3.7
29	Tennessee	1.0
50	Texas	0.1
7	Utah	2.7
5	Vermont	3.2
22	Virginia	1.3
10	Washington	2.0
47	West Virginia	0.3
7	Wisconsin	2.7
10	Wyoming	2.0

RANK ORDER

RANK	STATE	RATE
1	Oregon	4.4
2	Minnesota	3.8
3	South Dakota	3.7
4	Idaho	3.4
5	Iowa	3.2
5	Vermont	3.2
7	Utah	2.7
7	Wisconsin	2.7
9	Nebraska	2.1
10	Maine	2.0
10	Washington	2.0
10	Wyoming	2.0
13	Kansas	1.9
14	Alaska	1.8
14	Kentucky	1.8
16	Connecticut	1.7
16	Missouri	1.7
16	Montana	1.7
19	Massachusetts	1.6
20	Colorado	1.5
20	Ohio	1.5
22	Maryland	1.3
22	North Dakota	1.3
22	Virginia	1.3
25	Indiana	1.2
25	New Hampshire	1.2
25	New Mexico	1.2
28	Delaware	1.1
29	Hawaii	1.0
29	New York	1.0
29	Pennsylvania	1.0
29	Tennessee	1.0
33	Michigan	0.9
34	Florida	0.8
34	New Jersey	0.8
34	Oklahoma	0.8
37	Alabama	0.7
37	North Carolina	0.7
37	Rhode Island	0.7
40	Arizona	0.6
40	Nevada	0.6
42	Georgia	0.5
43	Arkansas	0.4
43	California	0.4
43	Illinois	0.4
43	Louisiana	0.4
47	Mississippi	0.3
47	South Carolina	0.3
47	West Virginia	0.3
50	Texas	0.1
	District of Columbia	0.4

Source: Morgan Quitno Press using data from U.S. Dept. of Health & Human Serv's, National Center for Health Statistics "Morbidity and Mortality Weekly Report" (January 6, 2006, Vol. 54, Nos. 51 & 52)
*Escherichia Coli is a common bacterium that normally inhabits the intestinal tracts of humans and animals but can cause infection in other parts of the body, especially the urinary tract. One strain, sometimes transmitted in hamburger meat, can cause serious infection resulting in sickness and death.

Hepatitis A and B Cases Reported in 2005

National Total = 9,781 Cases*

ALPHA ORDER

RANK	STATE	CASES	% of USA
21	Alabama	122	1.2%
46	Alaska	11	0.1%
4	Arizona	621	6.3%
31	Arkansas	67	0.7%
1	California	1,270	13.0%
24	Colorado	108	1.1%
28	Connecticut	78	0.8%
34	Delaware	53	0.5%
3	Florida	805	8.2%
11	Georgia	258	2.6%
41	Hawaii	29	0.3%
40	Idaho	36	0.4%
14	Illinois	224	2.3%
23	Indiana	111	1.1%
35	Iowa	50	0.5%
36	Kansas	48	0.5%
26	Kentucky	86	0.9%
20	Louisiana	139	1.4%
43	Maine	18	0.2%
13	Maryland	242	2.5%
6	Massachusetts	565	5.8%
8	Michigan	322	3.3%
32	Minnesota	63	0.6%
27	Mississippi	79	0.8%
16	Missouri	190	1.9%
45	Montana	13	0.1%
41	Nebraska	29	0.3%
38	Nevada	38	0.4%
25	New Hampshire	106	1.1%
2	New Jersey	819	8.4%
39	New Mexico	37	0.4%
5	New York	618	6.3%
12	North Carolina	251	2.6%
50	North Dakota	0	0.0%
17	Ohio	187	1.9%
36	Oklahoma	48	0.5%
19	Oregon	147	1.5%
9	Pennsylvania	316	3.2%
43	Rhode Island	18	0.2%
18	South Carolina	174	1.8%
48	South Dakota	5	0.1%
10	Tennessee	278	2.8%
7	Texas	545	5.6%
30	Utah	68	0.7%
46	Vermont	11	0.1%
15	Virginia	210	2.1%
22	Washington	119	1.2%
33	West Virginia	57	0.6%
29	Wisconsin	71	0.7%
49	Wyoming	3	0.0%

RANK ORDER

RANK	STATE	CASES	% of USA
1	California	1,270	13.0%
2	New Jersey	819	8.4%
3	Florida	805	8.2%
4	Arizona	621	6.3%
5	New York	618	6.3%
6	Massachusetts	565	5.8%
7	Texas	545	5.6%
8	Michigan	322	3.3%
9	Pennsylvania	316	3.2%
10	Tennessee	278	2.8%
11	Georgia	258	2.6%
12	North Carolina	251	2.6%
13	Maryland	242	2.5%
14	Illinois	224	2.3%
15	Virginia	210	2.1%
16	Missouri	190	1.9%
17	Ohio	187	1.9%
18	South Carolina	174	1.8%
19	Oregon	147	1.5%
20	Louisiana	139	1.4%
21	Alabama	122	1.2%
22	Washington	119	1.2%
23	Indiana	111	1.1%
24	Colorado	108	1.1%
25	New Hampshire	106	1.1%
26	Kentucky	86	0.9%
27	Mississippi	79	0.8%
28	Connecticut	78	0.8%
29	Wisconsin	71	0.7%
30	Utah	68	0.7%
31	Arkansas	67	0.7%
32	Minnesota	63	0.6%
33	West Virginia	57	0.6%
34	Delaware	53	0.5%
35	Iowa	50	0.5%
36	Kansas	48	0.5%
36	Oklahoma	48	0.5%
38	Nevada	38	0.4%
39	New Mexico	37	0.4%
40	Idaho	36	0.4%
41	Hawaii	29	0.3%
41	Nebraska	29	0.3%
43	Maine	18	0.2%
43	Rhode Island	18	0.2%
45	Montana	13	0.1%
46	Alaska	11	0.1%
46	Vermont	11	0.1%
48	South Dakota	5	0.1%
49	Wyoming	3	0.0%
50	North Dakota	0	0.0%
	District of Columbia	18	0.2%

Source: U.S. Department of Health and Human Services, National Center for Health Statistics
"Morbidity and Mortality Weekly Report" (January 6, 2006, Vol. 54, Nos. 51 & 52)
Provisional data. An inflammation of the liver.

Hepatitis A and B Rate in 2005

National Rate = 3.3 Cases per 100,000 Population*

ALPHA ORDER				RANK ORDER		
RANK	STATE	RATE		RANK	STATE	RATE
21	Alabama	2.7		1	Arizona	10.5
36	Alaska	1.7		2	New Jersey	9.4
1	Arizona	10.5		3	Massachusetts	8.8
25	Arkansas	2.4		4	New Hampshire	8.1
11	California	3.5		5	Delaware	6.3
27	Colorado	2.3		6	Tennessee	4.7
29	Connecticut	2.2		7	Florida	4.5
5	Delaware	6.3		8	Maryland	4.3
7	Florida	4.5		9	South Carolina	4.1
18	Georgia	2.8		10	Oregon	4.0
27	Hawaii	2.3		11	California	3.5
23	Idaho	2.5		12	Missouri	3.3
33	Illinois	1.8		13	Michigan	3.2
33	Indiana	1.8		13	New York	3.2
36	Iowa	1.7		15	Louisiana	3.1
36	Kansas	1.7		15	West Virginia	3.1
30	Kentucky	2.1		17	North Carolina	2.9
15	Louisiana	3.1		18	Georgia	2.8
43	Maine	1.4		18	Utah	2.8
8	Maryland	4.3		18	Virginia	2.8
3	Massachusetts	8.8		21	Alabama	2.7
13	Michigan	3.2		21	Mississippi	2.7
47	Minnesota	1.2		23	Idaho	2.5
21	Mississippi	2.7		23	Pennsylvania	2.5
12	Missouri	3.3		25	Arkansas	2.4
43	Montana	1.4		25	Texas	2.4
40	Nebraska	1.6		27	Colorado	2.3
40	Nevada	1.6		27	Hawaii	2.3
4	New Hampshire	8.1		29	Connecticut	2.2
2	New Jersey	9.4		30	Kentucky	2.1
31	New Mexico	1.9		31	New Mexico	1.9
13	New York	3.2		31	Washington	1.9
17	North Carolina	2.9		33	Illinois	1.8
50	North Dakota	0.0		33	Indiana	1.8
40	Ohio	1.6		33	Vermont	1.8
43	Oklahoma	1.4		36	Alaska	1.7
10	Oregon	4.0		36	Iowa	1.7
23	Pennsylvania	2.5		36	Kansas	1.7
36	Rhode Island	1.7		36	Rhode Island	1.7
9	South Carolina	4.1		40	Nebraska	1.6
48	South Dakota	0.6		40	Nevada	1.6
6	Tennessee	4.7		40	Ohio	1.6
25	Texas	2.4		43	Maine	1.4
18	Utah	2.8		43	Montana	1.4
33	Vermont	1.8		43	Oklahoma	1.4
18	Virginia	2.8		46	Wisconsin	1.3
31	Washington	1.9		47	Minnesota	1.2
15	West Virginia	3.1		48	South Dakota	0.6
46	Wisconsin	1.3		48	Wyoming	0.6
48	Wyoming	0.6		50	North Dakota	0.0

District of Columbia   3.3

Source: Morgan Quitno Press using data from U.S. Dept. of Health & Human Serv's, National Center for Health Statistics
"Morbidity and Mortality Weekly Report" (January 6, 2006, Vol. 54, Nos. 51 & 52)
*Provisional data. An inflammation of the liver.

Hepatitis C Cases Reported in 2005

National Total = 708 Cases*

ALPHA ORDER

RANK	STATE	CASES	% of USA
18	Alabama	14	2.0%
39	Alaska	0	0.0%
39	Arizona	0	0.0%
30	Arkansas	1	0.1%
7	California	26	3.7%
8	Colorado	25	3.5%
28	Connecticut	6	0.8%
26	Delaware	7	1.0%
4	Florida	49	6.9%
21	Georgia	9	1.3%
30	Hawaii	1	0.1%
30	Idaho	1	0.1%
39	Illinois	0	0.0%
9	Indiana	24	3.4%
39	Iowa	0	0.0%
39	Kansas	0	0.0%
16	Kentucky	15	2.1%
14	Louisiana	17	2.4%
39	Maine	0	0.0%
10	Maryland	22	3.1%
30	Massachusetts	1	0.1%
1	Michigan	110	15.5%
25	Minnesota	8	1.1%
5	Mississippi	35	4.9%
20	Missouri	10	1.4%
30	Montana	1	0.1%
30	Nebraska	1	0.1%
21	Nevada	9	1.3%
39	New Hampshire	0	0.0%
39	New Jersey	0	0.0%
30	New Mexico	1	0.1%
10	New York	22	3.1%
12	North Carolina	21	3.0%
30	North Dakota	1	0.1%
21	Ohio	9	1.3%
26	Oklahoma	7	1.0%
13	Oregon	18	2.5%
2	Pennsylvania	82	11.6%
39	Rhode Island	0	0.0%
29	South Carolina	4	0.6%
39	South Dakota	0	0.0%
14	Tennessee	17	2.4%
3	Texas	68	9.6%
21	Utah	9	1.3%
16	Vermont	15	2.1%
19	Virginia	13	1.8%
NA	Washington**	NA	NA
6	West Virginia	28	4.0%
39	Wisconsin	0	0.0%
30	Wyoming	1	0.1%

RANK ORDER

RANK	STATE	CASES	% of USA
1	Michigan	110	15.5%
2	Pennsylvania	82	11.6%
3	Texas	68	9.6%
4	Florida	49	6.9%
5	Mississippi	35	4.9%
6	West Virginia	28	4.0%
7	California	26	3.7%
8	Colorado	25	3.5%
9	Indiana	24	3.4%
10	Maryland	22	3.1%
10	New York	22	3.1%
12	North Carolina	21	3.0%
13	Oregon	18	2.5%
14	Louisiana	17	2.4%
14	Tennessee	17	2.4%
16	Kentucky	15	2.1%
16	Vermont	15	2.1%
18	Alabama	14	2.0%
19	Virginia	13	1.8%
20	Missouri	10	1.4%
21	Georgia	9	1.3%
21	Nevada	9	1.3%
21	Ohio	9	1.3%
21	Utah	9	1.3%
25	Minnesota	8	1.1%
26	Delaware	7	1.0%
26	Oklahoma	7	1.0%
28	Connecticut	6	0.8%
29	South Carolina	4	0.6%
30	Arkansas	1	0.1%
30	Hawaii	1	0.1%
30	Idaho	1	0.1%
30	Massachusetts	1	0.1%
30	Montana	1	0.1%
30	Nebraska	1	0.1%
30	New Mexico	1	0.1%
30	North Dakota	1	0.1%
30	Wyoming	1	0.1%
39	Alaska	0	0.0%
39	Arizona	0	0.0%
39	Illinois	0	0.0%
39	Iowa	0	0.0%
39	Kansas	0	0.0%
39	Maine	0	0.0%
39	New Hampshire	0	0.0%
39	New Jersey	0	0.0%
39	Rhode Island	0	0.0%
39	South Dakota	0	0.0%
39	Wisconsin	0	0.0%
NA	Washington**	NA	NA
	District of Columbia	0	0.0%

Source: U.S. Department of Health and Human Services, National Center for Health Statistics
"Morbidity and Mortality Weekly Report" (January 6, 2006, Vol. 54, Nos. 51 & 52)
*Provisional data. An inflammation of the liver. It is the leading cause for liver transplantation and is transmitted by blood-to-blood contact. Most new cases of C are caused by high-risk drug behaviors.
**Not available.

Hepatitis C Rate in 2005

National Rate = 0.2 Cases per 100,000 Population*

ALPHA ORDER

RANK	STATE	RATE
15	Alabama	0.3
37	Alaska	0.0
37	Arizona	0.0
37	Arkansas	0.0
27	California	0.1
7	Colorado	0.5
19	Connecticut	0.2
5	Delaware	0.8
15	Florida	0.3
27	Georgia	0.1
27	Hawaii	0.1
27	Idaho	0.1
37	Illinois	0.0
9	Indiana	0.4
37	Iowa	0.0
37	Kansas	0.0
9	Kentucky	0.4
9	Louisiana	0.4
37	Maine	0.0
9	Maryland	0.4
37	Massachusetts	0.0
4	Michigan	1.1
19	Minnesota	0.2
3	Mississippi	1.2
19	Missouri	0.2
27	Montana	0.1
27	Nebraska	0.1
9	Nevada	0.4
37	New Hampshire	0.0
37	New Jersey	0.0
27	New Mexico	0.1
27	New York	0.1
19	North Carolina	0.2
19	North Dakota	0.2
27	Ohio	0.1
19	Oklahoma	0.2
7	Oregon	0.5
6	Pennsylvania	0.7
37	Rhode Island	0.0
27	South Carolina	0.1
37	South Dakota	0.0
15	Tennessee	0.3
15	Texas	0.3
9	Utah	0.4
1	Vermont	2.4
19	Virginia	0.2
NA	Washington**	NA
2	West Virginia	1.5
37	Wisconsin	0.0
19	Wyoming	0.2

RANK ORDER

RANK	STATE	RATE
1	Vermont	2.4
2	West Virginia	1.5
3	Mississippi	1.2
4	Michigan	1.1
5	Delaware	0.8
6	Pennsylvania	0.7
7	Colorado	0.5
7	Oregon	0.5
9	Indiana	0.4
9	Kentucky	0.4
9	Louisiana	0.4
9	Maryland	0.4
9	Nevada	0.4
9	Utah	0.4
15	Alabama	0.3
15	Florida	0.3
15	Tennessee	0.3
15	Texas	0.3
19	Connecticut	0.2
19	Minnesota	0.2
19	Missouri	0.2
19	North Carolina	0.2
19	North Dakota	0.2
19	Oklahoma	0.2
19	Virginia	0.2
19	Wyoming	0.2
27	California	0.1
27	Georgia	0.1
27	Hawaii	0.1
27	Idaho	0.1
27	Montana	0.1
27	Nebraska	0.1
27	New Mexico	0.1
27	New York	0.1
27	Ohio	0.1
27	South Carolina	0.1
37	Alaska	0.0
37	Arizona	0.0
37	Arkansas	0.0
37	Illinois	0.0
37	Iowa	0.0
37	Kansas	0.0
37	Maine	0.0
37	Massachusetts	0.0
37	New Hampshire	0.0
37	New Jersey	0.0
37	Rhode Island	0.0
37	South Dakota	0.0
37	Wisconsin	0.0
NA	Washington**	NA

District of Columbia   0.0

Source: Morgan Quitno Press using data from U.S. Dept. of Health & Human Serv's, National Center for Health Statistics "Morbidity and Mortality Weekly Report" (January 6, 2006, Vol. 54, Nos. 51 & 52)
Provisional data. An inflammation of the liver. It is the leading cause for liver transplantation and is transmitted by blood-to-blood contact. Most new cases of C are caused by high-risk drug behaviors.
**Not available.*

Legionellosis Cases Reported in 2005

National Total = 2,050 Cases*

ALPHA ORDER

RANK	STATE	CASES	% of USA
29	Alabama	13	0.6%
48	Alaska	1	0.0%
18	Arizona	27	1.3%
38	Arkansas	4	0.2%
8	California	85	4.1%
22	Colorado	22	1.1%
12	Connecticut	35	1.7%
24	Delaware	19	0.9%
4	Florida	122	6.0%
15	Georgia	31	1.5%
40	Hawaii	3	0.1%
40	Idaho	3	0.1%
27	Illinois	15	0.7%
18	Indiana	27	1.3%
35	Iowa	6	0.3%
45	Kansas	2	0.1%
15	Kentucky	31	1.5%
45	Louisiana	2	0.1%
35	Maine	6	0.3%
7	Maryland	111	5.4%
9	Massachusetts	46	2.2%
5	Michigan	118	5.8%
17	Minnesota	30	1.5%
40	Mississippi	3	0.1%
12	Missouri	35	1.7%
35	Montana	6	0.3%
40	Nebraska	3	0.1%
32	Nevada	8	0.4%
32	New Hampshire	8	0.4%
6	New Jersey	112	5.5%
40	New Mexico	3	0.1%
1	New York	321	15.7%
11	North Carolina	36	1.8%
45	North Dakota	2	0.1%
3	Ohio	206	10.0%
34	Oklahoma	7	0.3%
NA	Oregon**	NA	NA
2	Pennsylvania	298	14.5%
24	Rhode Island	19	0.9%
28	South Carolina	14	0.7%
23	South Dakota	21	1.0%
14	Tennessee	34	1.7%
30	Texas	12	0.6%
26	Utah	17	0.8%
31	Vermont	11	0.5%
9	Virginia	46	2.2%
49	Washington	0	0.0%
21	West Virginia	24	1.2%
18	Wisconsin	27	1.3%
38	Wyoming	4	0.2%

RANK ORDER

RANK	STATE	CASES	% of USA
1	New York	321	15.7%
2	Pennsylvania	298	14.5%
3	Ohio	206	10.0%
4	Florida	122	6.0%
5	Michigan	118	5.8%
6	New Jersey	112	5.5%
7	Maryland	111	5.4%
8	California	85	4.1%
9	Massachusetts	46	2.2%
9	Virginia	46	2.2%
11	North Carolina	36	1.8%
12	Connecticut	35	1.7%
12	Missouri	35	1.7%
14	Tennessee	34	1.7%
15	Georgia	31	1.5%
15	Kentucky	31	1.5%
17	Minnesota	30	1.5%
18	Arizona	27	1.3%
18	Indiana	27	1.3%
18	Wisconsin	27	1.3%
21	West Virginia	24	1.2%
22	Colorado	22	1.1%
23	South Dakota	21	1.0%
24	Delaware	19	0.9%
24	Rhode Island	19	0.9%
26	Utah	17	0.8%
27	Illinois	15	0.7%
28	South Carolina	14	0.7%
29	Alabama	13	0.6%
30	Texas	12	0.6%
31	Vermont	11	0.5%
32	Nevada	8	0.4%
32	New Hampshire	8	0.4%
34	Oklahoma	7	0.3%
35	Iowa	6	0.3%
35	Maine	6	0.3%
35	Montana	6	0.3%
38	Arkansas	4	0.2%
38	Wyoming	4	0.2%
40	Hawaii	3	0.1%
40	Idaho	3	0.1%
40	Mississippi	3	0.1%
40	Nebraska	3	0.1%
40	New Mexico	3	0.1%
45	Kansas	2	0.1%
45	Louisiana	2	0.1%
45	North Dakota	2	0.1%
48	Alaska	1	0.0%
49	Washington	0	0.0%
NA	Oregon**	NA	NA
	District of Columbia	14	0.7%

Source: U.S. Department of Health and Human Services, National Center for Health Statistics
    "Morbidity and Mortality Weekly Report" (January 6, 2006, Vol. 54, Nos. 51 & 52)
*Provisional data. A pneumonia-like disease (Legionnaire's Disease).
**Not notifiable.

Legionellosis Rate in 2005

National Rate = 0.7 Cases per 100,000 Population*

RANK	STATE	RATE
30	Alabama	0.3
35	Alaska	0.2
24	Arizona	0.5
43	Arkansas	0.1
35	California	0.2
24	Colorado	0.5
12	Connecticut	1.0
3	Delaware	2.3
14	Florida	0.7
30	Georgia	0.3
35	Hawaii	0.2
35	Idaho	0.2
43	Illinois	0.1
28	Indiana	0.4
35	Iowa	0.2
43	Kansas	0.1
14	Kentucky	0.7
48	Louisiana	0.0
24	Maine	0.5
4	Maryland	2.0
14	Massachusetts	0.7
11	Michigan	1.2
18	Minnesota	0.6
43	Mississippi	0.1
18	Missouri	0.6
18	Montana	0.6
35	Nebraska	0.2
30	Nevada	0.3
18	New Hampshire	0.6
9	New Jersey	1.3
35	New Mexico	0.2
8	New York	1.7
28	North Carolina	0.4
30	North Dakota	0.3
5	Ohio	1.8
35	Oklahoma	0.2
NA	Oregon**	NA
2	Pennsylvania	2.4
5	Rhode Island	1.8
30	South Carolina	0.3
1	South Dakota	2.7
18	Tennessee	0.6
43	Texas	0.1
14	Utah	0.7
5	Vermont	1.8
18	Virginia	0.6
48	Washington	0.0
9	West Virginia	1.3
24	Wisconsin	0.5
13	Wyoming	0.8

RANK	STATE	RATE
1	South Dakota	2.7
2	Pennsylvania	2.4
3	Delaware	2.3
4	Maryland	2.0
5	Ohio	1.8
5	Rhode Island	1.8
5	Vermont	1.8
8	New York	1.7
9	New Jersey	1.3
9	West Virginia	1.3
11	Michigan	1.2
12	Connecticut	1.0
13	Wyoming	0.8
14	Florida	0.7
14	Kentucky	0.7
14	Massachusetts	0.7
14	Utah	0.7
18	Minnesota	0.6
18	Missouri	0.6
18	Montana	0.6
18	New Hampshire	0.6
18	Tennessee	0.6
18	Virginia	0.6
24	Arizona	0.5
24	Colorado	0.5
24	Maine	0.5
24	Wisconsin	0.5
28	Indiana	0.4
28	North Carolina	0.4
30	Alabama	0.3
30	Georgia	0.3
30	Nevada	0.3
30	North Dakota	0.3
30	South Carolina	0.3
35	Alaska	0.2
35	California	0.2
35	Hawaii	0.2
35	Idaho	0.2
35	Iowa	0.2
35	Nebraska	0.2
35	New Mexico	0.2
35	Oklahoma	0.2
43	Arkansas	0.1
43	Illinois	0.1
43	Kansas	0.1
43	Mississippi	0.1
43	Texas	0.1
48	Louisiana	0.0
48	Washington	0.0
NA	Oregon**	NA

District of Columbia 2.5

Source: Morgan Quitno Press using data from U.S. Dept. of Health & Human Serv's, National Center for Health Statistics "Morbidity and Mortality Weekly Report" (January 6, 2006, Vol. 54, Nos. 51 & 52)
Provisional data. A pneumonia-like disease (Legionnaire's Disease).
**Not notifiable.*

Lyme Disease Cases in 2005

National Total = 21,304 Cases*

ALPHA ORDER					RANK ORDER			
RANK	STATE		CASES	% of USA	RANK	STATE	CASES	% of USA
38	Alabama		2	0.0%	1	Pennsylvania	5,510	25.9%
35	Alaska		3	0.0%	2	New York	4,181	19.6%
30	Arizona		8	0.0%	3	New Jersey	3,661	17.2%
33	Arkansas		5	0.0%	4	Wisconsin	1,363	6.4%
13	California		149	0.7%	5	Massachusetts	1,232	5.8%
35	Colorado		3	0.0%	6	Maryland	1,211	5.7%
7	Connecticut		1,137	5.3%	7	Connecticut	1,137	5.3%
9	Delaware		626	2.9%	8	Minnesota	851	4.0%
15	Florida		81	0.4%	9	Delaware	626	2.9%
32	Georgia		6	0.0%	10	Virginia	241	1.1%
NA	Hawaii**		NA	NA	11	Maine	228	1.1%
38	Idaho		2	0.0%	12	New Hampshire	220	1.0%
45	Illinois		0	0.0%	13	California	149	0.7%
21	Indiana		33	0.2%	14	Iowa	90	0.4%
14	Iowa		90	0.4%	15	Florida	81	0.4%
29	Kansas		10	0.0%	16	Michigan	63	0.3%
33	Kentucky		5	0.0%	17	Ohio	60	0.3%
30	Louisiana		8	0.0%	18	North Carolina	49	0.2%
11	Maine		228	1.1%	18	Vermont	49	0.2%
6	Maryland		1,211	5.7%	20	Texas	48	0.2%
5	Massachusetts		1,232	5.8%	21	Indiana	33	0.2%
16	Michigan		63	0.3%	22	Rhode Island	32	0.2%
8	Minnesota		851	4.0%	23	Tennessee	29	0.1%
45	Mississippi		0	0.0%	24	South Carolina	21	0.1%
25	Missouri		20	0.1%	25	Missouri	20	0.1%
45	Montana		0	0.0%	26	Oregon	19	0.1%
38	Nebraska		2	0.0%	27	West Virginia	17	0.1%
38	Nevada		2	0.0%	28	Washington	11	0.1%
12	New Hampshire		220	1.0%	29	Kansas	10	0.0%
3	New Jersey		3,661	17.2%	30	Arizona	8	0.0%
44	New Mexico		1	0.0%	30	Louisiana	8	0.0%
2	New York		4,181	19.6%	32	Georgia	6	0.0%
18	North Carolina		49	0.2%	33	Arkansas	5	0.0%
45	North Dakota		0	0.0%	33	Kentucky	5	0.0%
17	Ohio		60	0.3%	35	Alaska	3	0.0%
45	Oklahoma		0	0.0%	35	Colorado	3	0.0%
26	Oregon		19	0.1%	35	Wyoming	3	0.0%
1	Pennsylvania		5,510	25.9%	38	Alabama	2	0.0%
22	Rhode Island		32	0.2%	38	Idaho	2	0.0%
24	South Carolina		21	0.1%	38	Nebraska	2	0.0%
38	South Dakota		2	0.0%	38	Nevada	2	0.0%
23	Tennessee		29	0.1%	38	South Dakota	2	0.0%
20	Texas		48	0.2%	38	Utah	2	0.0%
38	Utah		2	0.0%	44	New Mexico	1	0.0%
18	Vermont		49	0.2%	45	Illinois	0	0.0%
10	Virginia		241	1.1%	45	Mississippi	0	0.0%
28	Washington		11	0.1%	45	Montana	0	0.0%
27	West Virginia		17	0.1%	45	North Dakota	0	0.0%
4	Wisconsin		1,363	6.4%	45	Oklahoma	0	0.0%
35	Wyoming		3	0.0%	NA	Hawaii**	NA	NA
						District of Columbia	8	0.0%

Source: U.S. Department of Health and Human Services, National Center for Health Statistics
    "Morbidity and Mortality Weekly Report" (January 6, 2006, Vol. 54, Nos. 51 & 52)

*Provisional data. Caused by ticks-lesions, followed by arthritis of large joints, myalgia, malaise and neurologic
and cardiac manifestations. Named after Old Lyme, CT, where the disease was first reported.
**Not notifiable.

Lyme Disease Rate in 2005

National Rate = 7.2 Cases per 100,000 Population*

ALPHA ORDER

RANK	STATE	RATE
44	Alabama	0.0
20	Alaska	0.5
35	Arizona	0.1
31	Arkansas	0.2
27	California	0.4
35	Colorado	0.1
4	Connecticut	32.4
1	Delaware	74.2
20	Florida	0.5
35	Georgia	0.1
NA	Hawaii**	NA
35	Idaho	0.1
44	Illinois	0.0
20	Indiana	0.5
14	Iowa	3.0
27	Kansas	0.4
35	Kentucky	0.1
31	Louisiana	0.2
9	Maine	17.3
7	Maryland	21.6
8	Massachusetts	19.3
17	Michigan	0.6
11	Minnesota	16.6
44	Mississippi	0.0
29	Missouri	0.3
44	Montana	0.0
35	Nebraska	0.1
35	Nevada	0.1
10	New Hampshire	16.8
3	New Jersey	42.0
35	New Mexico	0.1
6	New York	21.7
17	North Carolina	0.6
44	North Dakota	0.0
20	Ohio	0.5
44	Oklahoma	0.0
20	Oregon	0.5
2	Pennsylvania	44.3
14	Rhode Island	3.0
20	South Carolina	0.5
29	South Dakota	0.3
20	Tennessee	0.5
31	Texas	0.2
35	Utah	0.1
12	Vermont	7.9
13	Virginia	3.2
31	Washington	0.2
16	West Virginia	0.9
5	Wisconsin	24.6
17	Wyoming	0.6

RANK ORDER

RANK	STATE	RATE
1	Delaware	74.2
2	Pennsylvania	44.3
3	New Jersey	42.0
4	Connecticut	32.4
5	Wisconsin	24.6
6	New York	21.7
7	Maryland	21.6
8	Massachusetts	19.3
9	Maine	17.3
10	New Hampshire	16.8
11	Minnesota	16.6
12	Vermont	7.9
13	Virginia	3.2
14	Iowa	3.0
14	Rhode Island	3.0
16	West Virginia	0.9
17	Michigan	0.6
17	North Carolina	0.6
17	Wyoming	0.6
20	Alaska	0.5
20	Florida	0.5
20	Indiana	0.5
20	Ohio	0.5
20	Oregon	0.5
20	South Carolina	0.5
20	Tennessee	0.5
27	California	0.4
27	Kansas	0.4
29	Missouri	0.3
29	South Dakota	0.3
31	Arkansas	0.2
31	Louisiana	0.2
31	Texas	0.2
31	Washington	0.2
35	Arizona	0.1
35	Colorado	0.1
35	Georgia	0.1
35	Idaho	0.1
35	Kentucky	0.1
35	Nebraska	0.1
35	Nevada	0.1
35	New Mexico	0.1
35	Utah	0.1
44	Alabama	0.0
44	Illinois	0.0
44	Mississippi	0.0
44	Montana	0.0
44	North Dakota	0.0
44	Oklahoma	0.0
NA	Hawaii**	NA

District of Columbia 1.5

Source: Morgan Quitno Press using data from U.S. Dept. of Health & Human Serv's, National Center for Health Statistics "Morbidity and Mortality Weekly Report" (January 6, 2006, Vol. 54, Nos. 51 & 52)
Provisional data. Caused by ticks-lesions, followed by arthritis of large joints, myalgia, malaise and neurologic and cardiac manifestations. Named after Old Lyme, CT, where the disease was first reported.
***Not notifiable.*

Malaria Cases Reported in 2005

National Total = 1,252 Cases*

ALPHA ORDER

RANK	STATE	CASES	% of USA
30	Alabama	6	0.5%
30	Alaska	6	0.5%
21	Arizona	14	1.1%
30	Arkansas	6	0.5%
2	California	172	13.7%
14	Colorado	24	1.9%
16	Connecticut	21	1.7%
37	Delaware	3	0.2%
5	Florida	69	5.5%
7	Georgia	42	3.4%
18	Hawaii	17	1.4%
46	Idaho	0	0.0%
11	Illinois	33	2.6%
33	Indiana	5	0.4%
27	Iowa	9	0.7%
33	Kansas	5	0.4%
27	Kentucky	9	0.7%
37	Louisiana	3	0.2%
33	Maine	5	0.4%
3	Maryland	100	8.0%
9	Massachusetts	35	2.8%
15	Michigan	23	1.8%
24	Minnesota	11	0.9%
46	Mississippi	0	0.0%
17	Missouri	18	1.4%
46	Montana	0	0.0%
37	Nebraska	3	0.2%
42	Nevada	2	0.2%
33	New Hampshire	5	0.4%
4	New Jersey	74	5.9%
42	New Mexico	2	0.2%
1	New York	224	17.9%
8	North Carolina	40	3.2%
46	North Dakota	0	0.0%
13	Ohio	30	2.4%
24	Oklahoma	11	0.9%
23	Oregon	12	1.0%
9	Pennsylvania	35	2.8%
42	Rhode Island	2	0.2%
24	South Carolina	11	0.9%
46	South Dakota	0	0.0%
22	Tennessee	13	1.0%
6	Texas	61	4.9%
27	Utah	9	0.7%
37	Vermont	3	0.2%
12	Virginia	32	2.6%
19	Washington	16	1.3%
37	West Virginia	3	0.2%
20	Wisconsin	15	1.2%
42	Wyoming	2	0.2%

RANK ORDER

RANK	STATE	CASES	% of USA
1	New York	224	17.9%
2	California	172	13.7%
3	Maryland	100	8.0%
4	New Jersey	74	5.9%
5	Florida	69	5.5%
6	Texas	61	4.9%
7	Georgia	42	3.4%
8	North Carolina	40	3.2%
9	Massachusetts	35	2.8%
9	Pennsylvania	35	2.8%
11	Illinois	33	2.6%
12	Virginia	32	2.6%
13	Ohio	30	2.4%
14	Colorado	24	1.9%
15	Michigan	23	1.8%
16	Connecticut	21	1.7%
17	Missouri	18	1.4%
18	Hawaii	17	1.4%
19	Washington	16	1.3%
20	Wisconsin	15	1.2%
21	Arizona	14	1.1%
22	Tennessee	13	1.0%
23	Oregon	12	1.0%
24	Minnesota	11	0.9%
24	Oklahoma	11	0.9%
24	South Carolina	11	0.9%
27	Iowa	9	0.7%
27	Kentucky	9	0.7%
27	Utah	9	0.7%
30	Alabama	6	0.5%
30	Alaska	6	0.5%
30	Arkansas	6	0.5%
33	Indiana	5	0.4%
33	Kansas	5	0.4%
33	Maine	5	0.4%
33	New Hampshire	5	0.4%
37	Delaware	3	0.2%
37	Louisiana	3	0.2%
37	Nebraska	3	0.2%
37	Vermont	3	0.2%
37	West Virginia	3	0.2%
42	Nevada	2	0.2%
42	New Mexico	2	0.2%
42	Rhode Island	2	0.2%
42	Wyoming	2	0.2%
46	Idaho	0	0.0%
46	Mississippi	0	0.0%
46	Montana	0	0.0%
46	North Dakota	0	0.0%
46	South Dakota	0	0.0%
	District of Columbia	11	0.9%

Source: U.S. Department of Health and Human Services, National Center for Health Statistics
    "Morbidity and Mortality Weekly Report" (January 6, 2006, Vol. 54, Nos. 51 & 52)
*Provisional data. Infectious disease usually transmitted by bites of infected mosquitoes. Symptoms include high fever, shaking chills, sweating and anemia.

Malaria Rate in 2005

National Rate = 0.4 Cases per 100,000 Population*

ALPHA ORDER

RANK ORDER

RANK	STATE	RATE		RANK	STATE	RATE
41	Alabama	0.1		1	Maryland	1.8
4	Alaska	0.9		2	Hawaii	1.3
31	Arizona	0.2		3	New York	1.2
31	Arkansas	0.2		4	Alaska	0.9
7	California	0.5		5	New Jersey	0.8
7	Colorado	0.5		6	Connecticut	0.6
6	Connecticut	0.6		7	California	0.5
13	Delaware	0.4		7	Colorado	0.5
13	Florida	0.4		7	Georgia	0.5
7	Georgia	0.5		7	Massachusetts	0.5
2	Hawaii	1.3		7	North Carolina	0.5
46	Idaho	0.0		7	Vermont	0.5
20	Illinois	0.3		13	Delaware	0.4
41	Indiana	0.1		13	Florida	0.4
20	Iowa	0.3		13	Maine	0.4
31	Kansas	0.2		13	New Hampshire	0.4
31	Kentucky	0.2		13	Utah	0.4
41	Louisiana	0.1		13	Virginia	0.4
13	Maine	0.4		13	Wyoming	0.4
1	Maryland	1.8		20	Illinois	0.3
7	Massachusetts	0.5		20	Iowa	0.3
31	Michigan	0.2		20	Missouri	0.3
31	Minnesota	0.2		20	Ohio	0.3
46	Mississippi	0.0		20	Oklahoma	0.3
20	Missouri	0.3		20	Oregon	0.3
46	Montana	0.0		20	Pennsylvania	0.3
31	Nebraska	0.2		20	South Carolina	0.3
41	Nevada	0.1		20	Texas	0.3
13	New Hampshire	0.4		20	Washington	0.3
5	New Jersey	0.8		20	Wisconsin	0.3
41	New Mexico	0.1		31	Arizona	0.2
3	New York	1.2		31	Arkansas	0.2
7	North Carolina	0.5		31	Kansas	0.2
46	North Dakota	0.0		31	Kentucky	0.2
20	Ohio	0.3		31	Michigan	0.2
20	Oklahoma	0.3		31	Minnesota	0.2
20	Oregon	0.3		31	Nebraska	0.2
20	Pennsylvania	0.3		31	Rhode Island	0.2
31	Rhode Island	0.2		31	Tennessee	0.2
20	South Carolina	0.3		31	West Virginia	0.2
46	South Dakota	0.0		41	Alabama	0.1
31	Tennessee	0.2		41	Indiana	0.1
20	Texas	0.3		41	Louisiana	0.1
13	Utah	0.4		41	Nevada	0.1
7	Vermont	0.5		41	New Mexico	0.1
13	Virginia	0.4		46	Idaho	0.0
20	Washington	0.3		46	Mississippi	0.0
31	West Virginia	0.2		46	Montana	0.0
20	Wisconsin	0.3		46	North Dakota	0.0
13	Wyoming	0.4		46	South Dakota	0.0

District of Columbia 2.0

Source: Morgan Quitno Press using data from U.S. Dept. of Health & Human Serv's, National Center for Health Statistics "Morbidity and Mortality Weekly Report" (January 6, 2006, Vol. 54, Nos. 51 & 52)

Provisional data. Infectious disease usually transmitted by bites of infected mosquitoes. Symptoms include high fever, shaking chills, sweating and anemia.

Meningococcal Infections Reported in 2005

National Total = 1,111 Cases*

ALPHA ORDER

RANK	STATE	CASES	% of USA
36	Alabama	7	0.6%
40	Alaska	5	0.5%
7	Arizona	39	3.5%
26	Arkansas	15	1.4%
1	California	144	13.0%
20	Colorado	17	1.5%
26	Connecticut	15	1.4%
43	Delaware	4	0.4%
2	Florida	85	7.7%
20	Georgia	17	1.5%
30	Hawaii	13	1.2%
39	Idaho	6	0.5%
26	Illinois	15	1.4%
19	Indiana	19	1.7%
20	Iowa	17	1.5%
34	Kansas	8	0.7%
20	Kentucky	17	1.5%
14	Louisiana	28	2.5%
47	Maine	2	0.2%
18	Maryland	21	1.9%
9	Massachusetts	34	3.1%
9	Michigan	34	3.1%
24	Minnesota	16	1.4%
36	Mississippi	7	0.6%
16	Missouri	27	2.4%
49	Montana	0	0.0%
40	Nebraska	5	0.5%
34	Nevada	8	0.7%
31	New Hampshire	12	1.1%
9	New Jersey	34	3.1%
46	New Mexico	3	0.3%
3	New York	65	5.9%
12	North Carolina	32	2.9%
48	North Dakota	1	0.1%
6	Ohio	45	4.1%
24	Oklahoma	16	1.4%
14	Oregon	28	2.5%
4	Pennsylvania	56	5.0%
43	Rhode Island	4	0.4%
26	South Carolina	15	1.4%
43	South Dakota	4	0.4%
17	Tennessee	24	2.2%
8	Texas	35	3.2%
32	Utah	11	1.0%
40	Vermont	5	0.5%
13	Virginia	31	2.8%
5	Washington	48	4.3%
36	West Virginia	7	0.6%
33	Wisconsin	10	0.9%
49	Wyoming	0	0.0%

RANK ORDER

RANK	STATE	CASES	% of USA
1	California	144	13.0%
2	Florida	85	7.7%
3	New York	65	5.9%
4	Pennsylvania	56	5.0%
5	Washington	48	4.3%
6	Ohio	45	4.1%
7	Arizona	39	3.5%
8	Texas	35	3.2%
9	Massachusetts	34	3.1%
9	Michigan	34	3.1%
9	New Jersey	34	3.1%
12	North Carolina	32	2.9%
13	Virginia	31	2.8%
14	Louisiana	28	2.5%
14	Oregon	28	2.5%
16	Missouri	27	2.4%
17	Tennessee	24	2.2%
18	Maryland	21	1.9%
19	Indiana	19	1.7%
20	Colorado	17	1.5%
20	Georgia	17	1.5%
20	Iowa	17	1.5%
20	Kentucky	17	1.5%
24	Minnesota	16	1.4%
24	Oklahoma	16	1.4%
26	Arkansas	15	1.4%
26	Connecticut	15	1.4%
26	Illinois	15	1.4%
26	South Carolina	15	1.4%
30	Hawaii	13	1.2%
31	New Hampshire	12	1.1%
32	Utah	11	1.0%
33	Wisconsin	10	0.9%
34	Kansas	8	0.7%
34	Nevada	8	0.7%
36	Alabama	7	0.6%
36	Mississippi	7	0.6%
36	West Virginia	7	0.6%
39	Idaho	6	0.5%
40	Alaska	5	0.5%
40	Nebraska	5	0.5%
40	Vermont	5	0.5%
43	Delaware	4	0.4%
43	Rhode Island	4	0.4%
43	South Dakota	4	0.4%
46	New Mexico	3	0.3%
47	Maine	2	0.2%
48	North Dakota	1	0.1%
49	Montana	0	0.0%
49	Wyoming	0	0.0%
	District of Columbia	0	0.0%

Source: U.S. Department of Health and Human Services, National Center for Health Statistics
"Morbidity and Mortality Weekly Report" (January 6, 2006, Vol. 54, Nos. 51 & 52)
*Provisional data. A bacterium (Neisseria meningitidis) that causes cerebrospinal meningitis.

Meningococcal Infection Rate in 2005

National Rate = 0.4 Cases per 100,000 Population*

ALPHA ORDER

RANK	STATE	RATE
40	Alabama	0.2
3	Alaska	0.8
7	Arizona	0.7
10	Arkansas	0.5
18	California	0.4
18	Colorado	0.4
18	Connecticut	0.4
10	Delaware	0.5
10	Florida	0.5
40	Georgia	0.2
1	Hawaii	1.0
18	Idaho	0.4
48	Illinois	0.1
33	Indiana	0.3
8	Iowa	0.6
33	Kansas	0.3
18	Kentucky	0.4
8	Louisiana	0.6
40	Maine	0.2
18	Maryland	0.4
10	Massachusetts	0.5
33	Michigan	0.3
33	Minnesota	0.3
40	Mississippi	0.2
10	Missouri	0.5
49	Montana	0.0
33	Nebraska	0.3
33	Nevada	0.3
2	New Hampshire	0.9
18	New Jersey	0.4
40	New Mexico	0.2
33	New York	0.3
18	North Carolina	0.4
40	North Dakota	0.2
18	Ohio	0.4
10	Oklahoma	0.5
3	Oregon	0.8
10	Pennsylvania	0.5
18	Rhode Island	0.4
18	South Carolina	0.4
10	South Dakota	0.5
18	Tennessee	0.4
40	Texas	0.2
18	Utah	0.4
3	Vermont	0.8
18	Virginia	0.4
3	Washington	0.8
18	West Virginia	0.4
40	Wisconsin	0.2
49	Wyoming	0.0

RANK ORDER

RANK	STATE	RATE
1	Hawaii	1.0
2	New Hampshire	0.9
3	Alaska	0.8
3	Oregon	0.8
3	Vermont	0.8
3	Washington	0.8
7	Arizona	0.7
8	Iowa	0.6
8	Louisiana	0.6
10	Arkansas	0.5
10	Delaware	0.5
10	Florida	0.5
10	Massachusetts	0.5
10	Missouri	0.5
10	Oklahoma	0.5
10	Pennsylvania	0.5
10	South Dakota	0.5
18	California	0.4
18	Colorado	0.4
18	Connecticut	0.4
18	Idaho	0.4
18	Kentucky	0.4
18	Maryland	0.4
18	New Jersey	0.4
18	North Carolina	0.4
18	Ohio	0.4
18	Rhode Island	0.4
18	South Carolina	0.4
18	Tennessee	0.4
18	Utah	0.4
18	Virginia	0.4
18	West Virginia	0.4
33	Indiana	0.3
33	Kansas	0.3
33	Michigan	0.3
33	Minnesota	0.3
33	Nebraska	0.3
33	Nevada	0.3
33	New York	0.3
40	Alabama	0.2
40	Georgia	0.2
40	Maine	0.2
40	Mississippi	0.2
40	New Mexico	0.2
40	North Dakota	0.2
40	Texas	0.2
40	Wisconsin	0.2
48	Illinois	0.1
49	Montana	0.0
49	Wyoming	0.0
	District of Columbia	0.0

Source: Morgan Quitno Press using data from U.S. Dept. of Health & Human Serv's, National Center for Health Statistics
"Morbidity and Mortality Weekly Report" (January 6, 2006, Vol. 54, Nos. 51 & 52)
*Provisional data. A bacterium (Neisseria meningitidis) that causes cerebrospinal meningitis.

Rabies (Animal) Cases Reported in 2005

National Total = 5,277 Cases*

RANK	STATE	CASES	% of USA
15	Alabama	74	1.4%
44	Alaska	1	0.0%
11	Arizona	140	2.7%
26	Arkansas	33	0.6%
10	California	175	3.3%
32	Colorado	16	0.3%
9	Connecticut	206	3.9%
45	Delaware	0	0.0%
42	Florida	4	0.1%
8	Georgia	248	4.7%
45	Hawaii	0	0.0%
37	Idaho	12	0.2%
23	Illinois	50	0.9%
37	Indiana	12	0.2%
12	Iowa	108	2.0%
15	Kansas	74	1.4%
30	Kentucky	17	0.3%
45	Louisiana	0	0.0%
21	Maine	57	1.1%
7	Maryland	320	6.1%
6	Massachusetts	329	6.2%
25	Michigan	39	0.7%
18	Minnesota	70	1.3%
43	Mississippi	2	0.0%
13	Missouri	79	1.5%
33	Montana	15	0.3%
45	Nebraska	0	0.0%
35	Nevada	13	0.2%
35	New Hampshire	13	0.2%
NA	New Jersey**	NA	NA
39	New Mexico	10	0.2%
2	New York	581	11.0%
4	North Carolina	455	8.6%
29	North Dakota	25	0.5%
18	Ohio	70	1.3%
14	Oklahoma	76	1.4%
40	Oregon	7	0.1%
5	Pennsylvania	380	7.2%
28	Rhode Island	26	0.5%
41	South Carolina	5	0.1%
20	South Dakota	64	1.2%
24	Tennessee	46	0.9%
1	Texas	734	13.9%
33	Utah	15	0.3%
22	Vermont	55	1.0%
3	Virginia	504	9.6%
NA	Washington**	NA	NA
17	West Virginia	71	1.3%
27	Wisconsin	29	0.5%
30	Wyoming	17	0.3%

RANK	STATE	CASES	% of USA
1	Texas	734	13.9%
2	New York	581	11.0%
3	Virginia	504	9.6%
4	North Carolina	455	8.6%
5	Pennsylvania	380	7.2%
6	Massachusetts	329	6.2%
7	Maryland	320	6.1%
8	Georgia	248	4.7%
9	Connecticut	206	3.9%
10	California	175	3.3%
11	Arizona	140	2.7%
12	Iowa	108	2.0%
13	Missouri	79	1.5%
14	Oklahoma	76	1.4%
15	Alabama	74	1.4%
15	Kansas	74	1.4%
17	West Virginia	71	1.3%
18	Minnesota	70	1.3%
18	Ohio	70	1.3%
20	South Dakota	64	1.2%
21	Maine	57	1.1%
22	Vermont	55	1.0%
23	Illinois	50	0.9%
24	Tennessee	46	0.9%
25	Michigan	39	0.7%
26	Arkansas	33	0.6%
27	Wisconsin	29	0.5%
28	Rhode Island	26	0.5%
29	North Dakota	25	0.5%
30	Kentucky	17	0.3%
30	Wyoming	17	0.3%
32	Colorado	16	0.3%
33	Montana	15	0.3%
33	Utah	15	0.3%
35	Nevada	13	0.2%
35	New Hampshire	13	0.2%
37	Idaho	12	0.2%
37	Indiana	12	0.2%
39	New Mexico	10	0.2%
40	Oregon	7	0.1%
41	South Carolina	5	0.1%
42	Florida	4	0.1%
43	Mississippi	2	0.0%
44	Alaska	1	0.0%
45	Delaware	0	0.0%
45	Hawaii	0	0.0%
45	Louisiana	0	0.0%
45	Nebraska	0	0.0%
NA	New Jersey**	NA	NA
NA	Washington**	NA	NA
	District of Columbia	0	0.0%

Source: U.S. Department of Health and Human Services, National Center for Health Statistics
    "Morbidity and Mortality Weekly Report" (January 6, 2006, Vol. 54, Nos. 51 & 52)
*Provisional data. An acute, infectious, often fatal viral disease of most warm-blooded animals, especially wolves, cats, and dogs, that attacks the central nervous system and is transmitted by the bite of infected animals.
**Not available.

Rabies (Animal) Rate in 2005

National Rate = 1.8 Cases per 100,000 Human Population*

ALPHA ORDER				RANK ORDER			
RANK	STATE	RATE	% of USA	RANK	STATE	RATE	% of USA
21	Alabama	1.6	0.0%	1	Vermont	8.8	0.0%
39	Alaska	0.2	0.0%	2	South Dakota	8.2	0.0%
18	Arizona	2.4	0.0%	3	Virginia	6.7	0.0%
25	Arkansas	1.2	0.0%	4	Connecticut	5.9	0.0%
31	California	0.5	0.0%	5	Maryland	5.7	0.0%
38	Colorado	0.3	0.0%	6	North Carolina	5.2	0.0%
4	Connecticut	5.9	0.0%	7	Massachusetts	5.1	0.0%
44	Delaware	0.0	0.0%	8	Maine	4.3	0.0%
44	Florida	0.0	0.0%	9	North Dakota	3.9	0.0%
16	Georgia	2.7	0.0%	9	West Virginia	3.9	0.0%
44	Hawaii	0.0	0.0%	11	Iowa	3.6	0.0%
27	Idaho	0.8	0.0%	12	Wyoming	3.3	0.0%
35	Illinois	0.4	0.0%	13	Texas	3.2	0.0%
39	Indiana	0.2	0.0%	14	Pennsylvania	3.1	0.0%
11	Iowa	3.6	0.0%	15	New York	3.0	0.0%
16	Kansas	2.7	0.0%	16	Georgia	2.7	0.0%
35	Kentucky	0.4	0.0%	16	Kansas	2.7	0.0%
44	Louisiana	0.0	0.0%	18	Arizona	2.4	0.0%
8	Maine	4.3	0.0%	18	Rhode Island	2.4	0.0%
5	Maryland	5.7	0.0%	20	Oklahoma	2.1	0.0%
7	Massachusetts	5.1	0.0%	21	Alabama	1.6	0.0%
35	Michigan	0.4	0.0%	21	Montana	1.6	0.0%
23	Minnesota	1.4	0.0%	23	Minnesota	1.4	0.0%
42	Mississippi	0.1	0.0%	23	Missouri	1.4	0.0%
23	Missouri	1.4	0.0%	25	Arkansas	1.2	0.0%
21	Montana	1.6	0.0%	26	New Hampshire	1.0	0.0%
44	Nebraska	0.0	0.0%	27	Idaho	0.8	0.0%
31	Nevada	0.5	0.0%	27	Tennessee	0.8	0.0%
26	New Hampshire	1.0	0.0%	29	Ohio	0.6	0.0%
NA	New Jersey**	NA	0.0%	29	Utah	0.6	0.0%
31	New Mexico	0.5	0.0%	31	California	0.5	0.0%
15	New York	3.0	0.0%	31	Nevada	0.5	0.0%
6	North Carolina	5.2	0.0%	31	New Mexico	0.5	0.0%
9	North Dakota	3.9	0.0%	31	Wisconsin	0.5	0.0%
29	Ohio	0.6	0.0%	35	Illinois	0.4	0.0%
20	Oklahoma	2.1	0.0%	35	Kentucky	0.4	0.0%
39	Oregon	0.2	0.0%	35	Michigan	0.4	0.0%
14	Pennsylvania	3.1	0.0%	38	Colorado	0.3	0.0%
18	Rhode Island	2.4	0.0%	39	Alaska	0.2	0.0%
42	South Carolina	0.1	0.0%	39	Indiana	0.2	0.0%
2	South Dakota	8.2	0.0%	39	Oregon	0.2	0.0%
27	Tennessee	0.8	0.0%	42	Mississippi	0.1	0.0%
13	Texas	3.2	0.0%	42	South Carolina	0.1	0.0%
29	Utah	0.6	0.0%	44	Delaware	0.0	0.0%
1	Vermont	8.8	0.0%	44	Florida	0.0	0.0%
3	Virginia	6.7	0.0%	44	Hawaii	0.0	0.0%
NA	Washington**	NA	0.0%	44	Louisiana	0.0	0.0%
9	West Virginia	3.9	0.0%	44	Nebraska	0.0	0.0%
31	Wisconsin	0.5	0.0%	NA	New Jersey**	NA	0.0%
12	Wyoming	3.3	0.0%	NA	Washington**	NA	0.0%
					District of Columbia	0.0	0.0%

Source: Morgan Quitno Press using data from U.S. Dept. of Health & Human Serv's, National Center for Health Statistics
"Morbidity and Mortality Weekly Report" (January 6, 2006, Vol. 54, Nos. 51 & 52)
*Provisional data. An acute, infectious, often fatal viral disease of most warm-blooded animals, especially wolves, cats, and dogs, that attacks the central nervous system and is transmitted by the bite of infected animals.
**Not available.

Rocky Mountain Spotted Fever Cases Reported in 2005

National Total = 1,843 Cases*

ALPHA ORDER

RANK	STATE	CASES	% of USA
9	Alabama	66	3.6%
43	Alaska	0	0.0%
14	Arizona	21	1.1%
4	Arkansas	130	7.1%
21	California	8	0.4%
25	Colorado	5	0.3%
43	Connecticut	0	0.0%
19	Delaware	9	0.5%
16	Florida	19	1.0%
7	Georgia	68	3.7%
43	Hawaii	0	0.0%
30	Idaho	3	0.2%
38	Illinois	1	0.1%
30	Indiana	3	0.2%
22	Iowa	7	0.4%
17	Kansas	14	0.8%
30	Kentucky	3	0.2%
24	Louisiana	6	0.3%
NA	Maine**	NA	NA
6	Maryland	96	5.2%
38	Massachusetts	1	0.1%
22	Michigan	7	0.4%
34	Minnesota	2	0.1%
27	Mississippi	4	0.2%
3	Missouri	133	7.2%
38	Montana	1	0.1%
27	Nebraska	4	0.2%
43	Nevada	0	0.0%
38	New Hampshire	1	0.1%
12	New Jersey	35	1.9%
30	New Mexico	3	0.2%
17	New York	14	0.8%
1	North Carolina	625	33.9%
43	North Dakota	0	0.0%
13	Ohio	22	1.2%
11	Oklahoma	52	2.8%
34	Oregon	2	0.1%
10	Pennsylvania	60	3.3%
38	Rhode Island	1	0.1%
8	South Carolina	67	3.6%
25	South Dakota	5	0.3%
2	Tennessee	198	10.7%
15	Texas	20	1.1%
27	Utah	4	0.2%
43	Vermont	0	0.0%
5	Virginia	108	5.9%
43	Washington	0	0.0%
19	West Virginia	9	0.5%
34	Wisconsin	2	0.1%
34	Wyoming	2	0.1%

RANK ORDER

RANK	STATE	CASES	% of USA
1	North Carolina	625	33.9%
2	Tennessee	198	10.7%
3	Missouri	133	7.2%
4	Arkansas	130	7.1%
5	Virginia	108	5.9%
6	Maryland	96	5.2%
7	Georgia	68	3.7%
8	South Carolina	67	3.6%
9	Alabama	66	3.6%
10	Pennsylvania	60	3.3%
11	Oklahoma	52	2.8%
12	New Jersey	35	1.9%
13	Ohio	22	1.2%
14	Arizona	21	1.1%
15	Texas	20	1.1%
16	Florida	19	1.0%
17	Kansas	14	0.8%
17	New York	14	0.8%
19	Delaware	9	0.5%
19	West Virginia	9	0.5%
21	California	8	0.4%
22	Iowa	7	0.4%
22	Michigan	7	0.4%
24	Louisiana	6	0.3%
25	Colorado	5	0.3%
25	South Dakota	5	0.3%
27	Mississippi	4	0.2%
27	Nebraska	4	0.2%
27	Utah	4	0.2%
30	Idaho	3	0.2%
30	Indiana	3	0.2%
30	Kentucky	3	0.2%
30	New Mexico	3	0.2%
34	Minnesota	2	0.1%
34	Oregon	2	0.1%
34	Wisconsin	2	0.1%
34	Wyoming	2	0.1%
38	Illinois	1	0.1%
38	Massachusetts	1	0.1%
38	Montana	1	0.1%
38	New Hampshire	1	0.1%
38	Rhode Island	1	0.1%
43	Alaska	0	0.0%
43	Connecticut	0	0.0%
43	Hawaii	0	0.0%
43	Nevada	0	0.0%
43	North Dakota	0	0.0%
43	Vermont	0	0.0%
43	Washington	0	0.0%
NA	Maine**	NA	NA
	District of Columbia	2	0.1%

Source: U.S. Department of Health and Human Services, National Center for Health Statistics
   "Morbidity and Mortality Weekly Report" (January 6, 2006, Vol. 54, Nos. 51 & 52)
*Provisional data. An illness caused by Rickettsia rickettsii, a bacterial pathogen transmitted to humans through contact with ticks. Characterized by acute onset of fever, and may be accompanied by headache, malaise, myalgia, nausea/vomiting, or neurologic signs. A rash is often present on the palms and soles.
**Not available.

Rocky Mountain Spotted Fever Rate in 2005

National Rate = 0.6 Cases per 100,000 Population*

ALPHA ORDER				RANK ORDER		
RANK	STATE	RATE		RANK	STATE	RATE
8	Alabama	1.4		1	North Carolina	7.2
37	Alaska	0.0		2	Arkansas	4.7
16	Arizona	0.4		3	Tennessee	3.3
2	Arkansas	4.7		4	Missouri	2.3
37	California	0.0		5	Maryland	1.7
25	Colorado	0.1		6	South Carolina	1.6
37	Connecticut	0.0		7	Oklahoma	1.5
10	Delaware	1.1		8	Alabama	1.4
25	Florida	0.1		8	Virginia	1.4
11	Georgia	0.7		10	Delaware	1.1
37	Hawaii	0.0		11	Georgia	0.7
19	Idaho	0.2		12	South Dakota	0.6
37	Illinois	0.0		13	Kansas	0.5
37	Indiana	0.0		13	Pennsylvania	0.5
19	Iowa	0.2		13	West Virginia	0.5
13	Kansas	0.5		16	Arizona	0.4
25	Kentucky	0.1		16	New Jersey	0.4
25	Louisiana	0.1		16	Wyoming	0.4
NA	Maine**	NA		19	Idaho	0.2
5	Maryland	1.7		19	Iowa	0.2
37	Massachusetts	0.0		19	Nebraska	0.2
25	Michigan	0.1		19	New Mexico	0.2
37	Minnesota	0.0		19	Ohio	0.2
25	Mississippi	0.1		19	Utah	0.2
4	Missouri	2.3		25	Colorado	0.1
25	Montana	0.1		25	Florida	0.1
19	Nebraska	0.2		25	Kentucky	0.1
37	Nevada	0.0		25	Louisiana	0.1
25	New Hampshire	0.1		25	Michigan	0.1
16	New Jersey	0.4		25	Mississippi	0.1
19	New Mexico	0.2		25	Montana	0.1
25	New York	0.1		25	New Hampshire	0.1
1	North Carolina	7.2		25	New York	0.1
37	North Dakota	0.0		25	Oregon	0.1
19	Ohio	0.2		25	Rhode Island	0.1
7	Oklahoma	1.5		25	Texas	0.1
25	Oregon	0.1		37	Alaska	0.0
13	Pennsylvania	0.5		37	California	0.0
25	Rhode Island	0.1		37	Connecticut	0.0
6	South Carolina	1.6		37	Hawaii	0.0
12	South Dakota	0.6		37	Illinois	0.0
3	Tennessee	3.3		37	Indiana	0.0
25	Texas	0.1		37	Massachusetts	0.0
19	Utah	0.2		37	Minnesota	0.0
37	Vermont	0.0		37	Nevada	0.0
8	Virginia	1.4		37	North Dakota	0.0
37	Washington	0.0		37	Vermont	0.0
13	West Virginia	0.5		37	Washington	0.0
37	Wisconsin	0.0		37	Wisconsin	0.0
16	Wyoming	0.4		NA	Maine**	NA

District of Columbia   0.4

Source: Morgan Quitno Press using data from U.S. Dept. of Health & Human Serv's, National Center for Health Statistics "Morbidity and Mortality Weekly Report" (January 6, 2006, Vol. 54, Nos. 51 & 52)
*Provisional data. An illness caused by Rickettsia rickettsii, a bacterial pathogen transmitted to humans through contact with ticks. Characterized by acute onset of fever, and may be accompanied by headache, malaise, myalgia, nausea/vomiting, or neurologic signs. A rash is often present on the palms and soles.
**Not available.

Salmonellosis Cases Reported in 2005

National Total = 41,820 Cases*

ALPHA ORDER

RANK	STATE	CASES	% of USA
20	Alabama	780	1.9%
49	Alaska	58	0.1%
23	Arizona	701	1.7%
22	Arkansas	723	1.7%
2	California	4,246	10.2%
25	Colorado	581	1.4%
29	Connecticut	457	1.1%
43	Delaware	124	0.3%
1	Florida	5,555	13.3%
4	Georgia	1,900	4.5%
35	Hawaii	294	0.7%
41	Idaho	147	0.4%
7	Illinois	1,555	3.7%
24	Indiana	640	1.5%
30	Iowa	417	1.0%
33	Kansas	362	0.9%
28	Kentucky	478	1.1%
17	Louisiana	839	2.0%
39	Maine	153	0.4%
18	Maryland	820	2.0%
11	Massachusetts	1,103	2.6%
13	Michigan	919	2.2%
26	Minnesota	576	1.4%
14	Mississippi	909	2.2%
19	Missouri	807	1.9%
40	Montana	148	0.4%
44	Nebraska	121	0.3%
47	Nevada	86	0.2%
38	New Hampshire	164	0.4%
16	New Jersey	866	2.1%
36	New Mexico	228	0.5%
3	New York	2,459	5.9%
5	North Carolina	1,701	4.1%
50	North Dakota	39	0.1%
9	Ohio	1,340	3.2%
31	Oklahoma	401	1.0%
32	Oregon	378	0.9%
6	Pennsylvania	1,664	4.0%
46	Rhode Island	87	0.2%
10	South Carolina	1,322	3.2%
42	South Dakota	143	0.3%
21	Tennessee	744	1.8%
8	Texas	1,481	3.5%
34	Utah	329	0.8%
45	Vermont	94	0.2%
11	Virginia	1,103	2.6%
27	Washington	532	1.3%
37	West Virginia	196	0.5%
15	Wisconsin	905	2.2%
48	Wyoming	85	0.2%

RANK ORDER

RANK	STATE	CASES	% of USA
1	Florida	5,555	13.3%
2	California	4,246	10.2%
3	New York	2,459	5.9%
4	Georgia	1,900	4.5%
5	North Carolina	1,701	4.1%
6	Pennsylvania	1,664	4.0%
7	Illinois	1,555	3.7%
8	Texas	1,481	3.5%
9	Ohio	1,340	3.2%
10	South Carolina	1,322	3.2%
11	Massachusetts	1,103	2.6%
11	Virginia	1,103	2.6%
13	Michigan	919	2.2%
14	Mississippi	909	2.2%
15	Wisconsin	905	2.2%
16	New Jersey	866	2.1%
17	Louisiana	839	2.0%
18	Maryland	820	2.0%
19	Missouri	807	1.9%
20	Alabama	780	1.9%
21	Tennessee	744	1.8%
22	Arkansas	723	1.7%
23	Arizona	701	1.7%
24	Indiana	640	1.5%
25	Colorado	581	1.4%
26	Minnesota	576	1.4%
27	Washington	532	1.3%
28	Kentucky	478	1.1%
29	Connecticut	457	1.1%
30	Iowa	417	1.0%
31	Oklahoma	401	1.0%
32	Oregon	378	0.9%
33	Kansas	362	0.9%
34	Utah	329	0.8%
35	Hawaii	294	0.7%
36	New Mexico	228	0.5%
37	West Virginia	196	0.5%
38	New Hampshire	164	0.4%
39	Maine	153	0.4%
40	Montana	148	0.4%
41	Idaho	147	0.4%
42	South Dakota	143	0.3%
43	Delaware	124	0.3%
44	Nebraska	121	0.3%
45	Vermont	94	0.2%
46	Rhode Island	87	0.2%
47	Nevada	86	0.2%
48	Wyoming	85	0.2%
49	Alaska	58	0.1%
50	North Dakota	39	0.1%
	District of Columbia	60	0.1%

Source: U.S. Department of Health and Human Services, National Center for Health Statistics
"Morbidity and Mortality Weekly Report" (January 6, 2006, Vol. 54, Nos. 51 & 52)
*Provisional data. Any disease caused by a salmonella infection, which may be manifested as food poisoning with acute gastroenteritis, vomiting and diarrhea.

Salmonellosis Rate in 2005

National Rate = 14.1 Cases per 100,000 Population*

ALPHA ORDER

RANK ORDER

RANK	STATE	RATE		RANK	STATE	RATE
11	Alabama	17.1		1	Florida	31.2
44	Alaska	8.7		2	Mississippi	31.1
30	Arizona	11.8		2	South Carolina	31.1
4	Arkansas	26.0		4	Arkansas	26.0
30	California	11.8		5	Hawaii	23.1
26	Colorado	12.5		6	Georgia	20.9
24	Connecticut	13.0		7	North Carolina	19.6
16	Delaware	14.7		8	Louisiana	18.5
1	Florida	31.2		9	South Dakota	18.4
6	Georgia	20.9		10	Massachusetts	17.2
5	Hawaii	23.1		11	Alabama	17.1
40	Idaho	10.3		12	Wyoming	16.7
29	Illinois	12.2		13	Wisconsin	16.3
41	Indiana	10.2		14	Montana	15.8
19	Iowa	14.1		15	Vermont	15.1
23	Kansas	13.2		16	Delaware	14.7
35	Kentucky	11.5		17	Maryland	14.6
8	Louisiana	18.5		17	Virginia	14.6
34	Maine	11.6		19	Iowa	14.1
17	Maryland	14.6		20	Missouri	13.9
10	Massachusetts	17.2		21	Pennsylvania	13.4
43	Michigan	9.1		22	Utah	13.3
37	Minnesota	11.2		23	Kansas	13.2
2	Mississippi	31.1		24	Connecticut	13.0
20	Missouri	13.9		25	New York	12.8
14	Montana	15.8		26	Colorado	12.5
47	Nebraska	6.9		26	New Hampshire	12.5
50	Nevada	3.6		26	Tennessee	12.5
26	New Hampshire	12.5		29	Illinois	12.2
42	New Jersey	9.9		30	Arizona	11.8
30	New Mexico	11.8		30	California	11.8
25	New York	12.8		30	New Mexico	11.8
7	North Carolina	19.6		33	Ohio	11.7
49	North Dakota	6.1		34	Maine	11.6
33	Ohio	11.7		35	Kentucky	11.5
36	Oklahoma	11.3		36	Oklahoma	11.3
39	Oregon	10.4		37	Minnesota	11.2
21	Pennsylvania	13.4		38	West Virginia	10.8
46	Rhode Island	8.1		39	Oregon	10.4
2	South Carolina	31.1		40	Idaho	10.3
9	South Dakota	18.4		41	Indiana	10.2
26	Tennessee	12.5		42	New Jersey	9.9
48	Texas	6.5		43	Michigan	9.1
22	Utah	13.3		44	Alaska	8.7
15	Vermont	15.1		45	Washington	8.5
17	Virginia	14.6		46	Rhode Island	8.1
45	Washington	8.5		47	Nebraska	6.9
38	West Virginia	10.8		48	Texas	6.5
13	Wisconsin	16.3		49	North Dakota	6.1
12	Wyoming	16.7		50	Nevada	3.6

District of Columbia   10.9

Source: Morgan Quitno Press using data from U.S. Dept. of Health & Human Serv's, National Center for Health Statistics "Morbidity and Mortality Weekly Report" (January 6, 2006, Vol. 54, Nos. 51 & 52)
*Provisional data. Any disease caused by a salmonella infection, which may be manifested as food poisoning with acute gastroenteritis, vomiting and diarrhea.

Shigellosis Cases Reported in 2005

National Total = 13,749 Cases*

ALPHA ORDER

RANK	STATE	CASES	% of USA
16	Alabama	231	1.7%
46	Alaska	7	0.1%
8	Arizona	532	3.9%
35	Arkansas	64	0.5%
1	California	2,088	15.2%
20	Colorado	166	1.2%
36	Connecticut	55	0.4%
44	Delaware	11	0.1%
3	Florida	1,271	9.2%
7	Georgia	624	4.5%
38	Hawaii	35	0.3%
40	Idaho	17	0.1%
11	Illinois	306	2.2%
19	Indiana	176	1.3%
30	Iowa	105	0.8%
13	Kansas	268	1.9%
10	Kentucky	327	2.4%
24	Louisiana	136	1.0%
45	Maine	10	0.1%
28	Maryland	107	0.8%
18	Massachusetts	186	1.4%
15	Michigan	233	1.7%
33	Minnesota	96	0.7%
31	Mississippi	104	0.8%
4	Missouri	1,009	7.3%
47	Montana	5	0.0%
34	Nebraska	82	0.6%
39	Nevada	28	0.2%
42	New Hampshire	14	0.1%
12	New Jersey	297	2.2%
25	New Mexico	130	0.9%
5	New York	678	4.9%
17	North Carolina	202	1.5%
49	North Dakota	4	0.0%
23	Ohio	139	1.0%
6	Oklahoma	652	4.7%
26	Oregon	125	0.9%
14	Pennsylvania	235	1.7%
42	Rhode Island	14	0.1%
32	South Carolina	99	0.7%
29	South Dakota	106	0.8%
9	Tennessee	510	3.7%
2	Texas	1,750	12.7%
37	Utah	48	0.3%
40	Vermont	17	0.1%
27	Virginia	124	0.9%
22	Washington	149	1.1%
50	West Virginia	2	0.0%
21	Wisconsin	155	1.1%
47	Wyoming	5	0.0%

RANK ORDER

RANK	STATE	CASES	% of USA
1	California	2,088	15.2%
2	Texas	1,750	12.7%
3	Florida	1,271	9.2%
4	Missouri	1,009	7.3%
5	New York	678	4.9%
6	Oklahoma	652	4.7%
7	Georgia	624	4.5%
8	Arizona	532	3.9%
9	Tennessee	510	3.7%
10	Kentucky	327	2.4%
11	Illinois	306	2.2%
12	New Jersey	297	2.2%
13	Kansas	268	1.9%
14	Pennsylvania	235	1.7%
15	Michigan	233	1.7%
16	Alabama	231	1.7%
17	North Carolina	202	1.5%
18	Massachusetts	186	1.4%
19	Indiana	176	1.3%
20	Colorado	166	1.2%
21	Wisconsin	155	1.1%
22	Washington	149	1.1%
23	Ohio	139	1.0%
24	Louisiana	136	1.0%
25	New Mexico	130	0.9%
26	Oregon	125	0.9%
27	Virginia	124	0.9%
28	Maryland	107	0.8%
29	South Dakota	106	0.8%
30	Iowa	105	0.8%
31	Mississippi	104	0.8%
32	South Carolina	99	0.7%
33	Minnesota	96	0.7%
34	Nebraska	82	0.6%
35	Arkansas	64	0.5%
36	Connecticut	55	0.4%
37	Utah	48	0.3%
38	Hawaii	35	0.3%
39	Nevada	28	0.2%
40	Idaho	17	0.1%
40	Vermont	17	0.1%
42	New Hampshire	14	0.1%
42	Rhode Island	14	0.1%
44	Delaware	11	0.1%
45	Maine	10	0.1%
46	Alaska	7	0.1%
47	Montana	5	0.0%
47	Wyoming	5	0.0%
49	North Dakota	4	0.0%
50	West Virginia	2	0.0%
	District of Columbia	15	0.1%

Source: U.S. Department of Health and Human Services, National Center for Health Statistics
"Morbidity and Mortality Weekly Report" (January 6, 2006, Vol. 54, Nos. 51 & 52)
*Provisional data. Dysentery caused by any of various species of shigellae, occurring most frequently in areas where poor sanitation and malnutrition are prevalent and commonly affecting children and infants.

Shigellosis Rate in 2005

National Rate = 4.6 Cases per 100,000 Population*

ALPHA ORDER

RANK	STATE	RATE
13	Alabama	5.1
44	Alaska	1.1
5	Arizona	9.0
29	Arkansas	2.3
12	California	5.8
15	Colorado	3.6
37	Connecticut	1.6
39	Delaware	1.3
9	Florida	7.1
10	Georgia	6.9
25	Hawaii	2.7
41	Idaho	1.2
27	Illinois	2.4
23	Indiana	2.8
17	Iowa	3.5
4	Kansas	9.8
7	Kentucky	7.8
21	Louisiana	3.0
47	Maine	0.8
33	Maryland	1.9
22	Massachusetts	2.9
29	Michigan	2.3
33	Minnesota	1.9
15	Mississippi	3.6
2	Missouri	17.4
49	Montana	0.5
14	Nebraska	4.7
41	Nevada	1.2
44	New Hampshire	1.1
19	New Jersey	3.4
11	New Mexico	6.7
17	New York	3.5
29	North Carolina	2.3
48	North Dakota	0.6
41	Ohio	1.2
1	Oklahoma	18.4
19	Oregon	3.4
33	Pennsylvania	1.9
39	Rhode Island	1.3
29	South Carolina	2.3
3	South Dakota	13.7
6	Tennessee	8.6
8	Texas	7.7
33	Utah	1.9
25	Vermont	2.7
37	Virginia	1.6
27	Washington	2.4
50	West Virginia	0.1
23	Wisconsin	2.8
46	Wyoming	1.0

RANK ORDER

RANK	STATE	RATE
1	Oklahoma	18.4
2	Missouri	17.4
3	South Dakota	13.7
4	Kansas	9.8
5	Arizona	9.0
6	Tennessee	8.6
7	Kentucky	7.8
8	Texas	7.7
9	Florida	7.1
10	Georgia	6.9
11	New Mexico	6.7
12	California	5.8
13	Alabama	5.1
14	Nebraska	4.7
15	Colorado	3.6
15	Mississippi	3.6
17	Iowa	3.5
17	New York	3.5
19	New Jersey	3.4
19	Oregon	3.4
21	Louisiana	3.0
22	Massachusetts	2.9
23	Indiana	2.8
23	Wisconsin	2.8
25	Hawaii	2.7
25	Vermont	2.7
27	Illinois	2.4
27	Washington	2.4
29	Arkansas	2.3
29	Michigan	2.3
29	North Carolina	2.3
29	South Carolina	2.3
33	Maryland	1.9
33	Minnesota	1.9
33	Pennsylvania	1.9
33	Utah	1.9
37	Connecticut	1.6
37	Virginia	1.6
39	Delaware	1.3
39	Rhode Island	1.3
41	Idaho	1.2
41	Nevada	1.2
41	Ohio	1.2
44	Alaska	1.1
44	New Hampshire	1.1
46	Wyoming	1.0
47	Maine	0.8
48	North Dakota	0.6
49	Montana	0.5
50	West Virginia	0.1

	District of Columbia	2.7

Source: Morgan Quitno Press using data from U.S. Dept. of Health & Human Serv's, National Center for Health Statistics
"Morbidity and Mortality Weekly Report" (January 6, 2006, Vol. 54, Nos. 51 & 52)
*Provisional data. Dysentery caused by any of various species of shigellae, occurring most frequently in areas
where poor sanitation and malnutrition are prevalent and commonly affecting children and infants.

Tuberculosis Cases Reported in 2005

National Total = 11,547 Cases*

ALPHA ORDER

RANK	STATE	CASES	% of USA
19	Alabama	185	1.6%
33	Alaska	44	0.4%
16	Arizona	221	1.9%
24	Arkansas	113	1.0%
1	California	2,034	17.6%
29	Colorado	62	0.5%
27	Connecticut	85	0.7%
40	Delaware	20	0.2%
4	Florida	932	8.1%
7	Georgia	385	3.3%
24	Hawaii	113	1.0%
47	Idaho	0	0.0%
5	Illinois	570	4.9%
22	Indiana	127	1.1%
32	Iowa	47	0.4%
30	Kansas	57	0.5%
23	Kentucky	114	1.0%
47	Louisiana	0	0.0%
41	Maine	17	0.1%
13	Maryland	252	2.2%
12	Massachusetts	256	2.2%
17	Michigan	209	1.8%
20	Minnesota	181	1.6%
47	Mississippi	0	0.0%
26	Missouri	99	0.9%
43	Montana	8	0.1%
37	Nebraska	29	0.3%
36	Nevada	31	0.3%
45	New Hampshire	6	0.1%
6	New Jersey	462	4.0%
35	New Mexico	35	0.3%
3	New York	1,263	10.9%
9	North Carolina	315	2.7%
46	North Dakota	2	0.0%
11	Ohio	259	2.2%
21	Oklahoma	141	1.2%
31	Oregon	54	0.5%
8	Pennsylvania	325	2.8%
34	Rhode Island	37	0.3%
17	South Carolina	209	1.8%
42	South Dakota	15	0.1%
14	Tennessee	250	2.2%
2	Texas	1,270	11.0%
38	Utah	27	0.2%
44	Vermont	7	0.1%
10	Virginia	281	2.4%
15	Washington	243	2.1%
39	West Virginia	26	0.2%
28	Wisconsin	77	0.7%
47	Wyoming	0	0.0%

RANK ORDER

RANK	STATE	CASES	% of USA
1	California	2,034	17.6%
2	Texas	1,270	11.0%
3	New York	1,263	10.9%
4	Florida	932	8.1%
5	Illinois	570	4.9%
6	New Jersey	462	4.0%
7	Georgia	385	3.3%
8	Pennsylvania	325	2.8%
9	North Carolina	315	2.7%
10	Virginia	281	2.4%
11	Ohio	259	2.2%
12	Massachusetts	256	2.2%
13	Maryland	252	2.2%
14	Tennessee	250	2.2%
15	Washington	243	2.1%
16	Arizona	221	1.9%
17	Michigan	209	1.8%
17	South Carolina	209	1.8%
19	Alabama	185	1.6%
20	Minnesota	181	1.6%
21	Oklahoma	141	1.2%
22	Indiana	127	1.1%
23	Kentucky	114	1.0%
24	Arkansas	113	1.0%
24	Hawaii	113	1.0%
26	Missouri	99	0.9%
27	Connecticut	85	0.7%
28	Wisconsin	77	0.7%
29	Colorado	62	0.5%
30	Kansas	57	0.5%
31	Oregon	54	0.5%
32	Iowa	47	0.4%
33	Alaska	44	0.4%
34	Rhode Island	37	0.3%
35	New Mexico	35	0.3%
36	Nevada	31	0.3%
37	Nebraska	29	0.3%
38	Utah	27	0.2%
39	West Virginia	26	0.2%
40	Delaware	20	0.2%
41	Maine	17	0.1%
42	South Dakota	15	0.1%
43	Montana	8	0.1%
44	Vermont	7	0.1%
45	New Hampshire	6	0.1%
46	North Dakota	2	0.0%
47	Idaho	0	0.0%
47	Louisiana	0	0.0%
47	Mississippi	0	0.0%
47	Wyoming	0	0.0%
	District of Columbia	52	0.5%

Source: U.S. Department of Health and Human Services, National Center for Health Statistics
"Morbidity and Mortality Weekly Report" (January 6, 2006, Vol. 54, Nos. 51 & 52)

*Provisional data. An infectious disease caused by the tubercle bacillus and causing the formation of tubercles on the lungs and other tissues of the body, often developing long after the initial infection. Characterized by the coughing up of mucus and sputum, fever, weight loss, and chest pain.

Tuberculosis Rate in 2005

National Rate = 3.9 Cases per 100,000 Population*

ALPHA ORDER

RANK ORDER

RANK	STATE	RATE		RANK	STATE	RATE
13	Alabama	4.1		1	Hawaii	8.9
2	Alaska	6.6		2	Alaska	6.6
18	Arizona	3.7		2	New York	6.6
13	Arkansas	4.1		4	California	5.6
4	California	5.6		4	Texas	5.6
39	Colorado	1.3		6	New Jersey	5.3
25	Connecticut	2.4		7	Florida	5.2
25	Delaware	2.4		8	South Carolina	4.9
7	Florida	5.2		9	Illinois	4.5
11	Georgia	4.2		9	Maryland	4.5
1	Hawaii	8.9		11	Georgia	4.2
47	Idaho	0.0		11	Tennessee	4.2
9	Illinois	4.5		13	Alabama	4.1
30	Indiana	2.0		13	Arkansas	4.1
34	Iowa	1.6		15	Massachusetts	4.0
28	Kansas	2.1		15	Oklahoma	4.0
23	Kentucky	2.7		17	Washington	3.9
47	Louisiana	0.0		18	Arizona	3.7
39	Maine	1.3		18	Virginia	3.7
9	Maryland	4.5		20	North Carolina	3.6
15	Massachusetts	4.0		21	Minnesota	3.5
28	Michigan	2.1		22	Rhode Island	3.4
21	Minnesota	3.5		23	Kentucky	2.7
47	Mississippi	0.0		24	Pennsylvania	2.6
33	Missouri	1.7		25	Connecticut	2.4
44	Montana	0.9		25	Delaware	2.4
34	Nebraska	1.6		27	Ohio	2.3
39	Nevada	1.3		28	Kansas	2.1
45	New Hampshire	0.5		28	Michigan	2.1
6	New Jersey	5.3		30	Indiana	2.0
32	New Mexico	1.8		31	South Dakota	1.9
2	New York	6.6		32	New Mexico	1.8
20	North Carolina	3.6		33	Missouri	1.7
46	North Dakota	0.3		34	Iowa	1.6
27	Ohio	2.3		34	Nebraska	1.6
15	Oklahoma	4.0		36	Oregon	1.5
36	Oregon	1.5		37	West Virginia	1.4
24	Pennsylvania	2.6		37	Wisconsin	1.4
22	Rhode Island	3.4		39	Colorado	1.3
8	South Carolina	4.9		39	Maine	1.3
31	South Dakota	1.9		39	Nevada	1.3
11	Tennessee	4.2		42	Utah	1.1
4	Texas	5.6		42	Vermont	1.1
42	Utah	1.1		44	Montana	0.9
42	Vermont	1.1		45	New Hampshire	0.5
18	Virginia	3.7		46	North Dakota	0.3
17	Washington	3.9		47	Idaho	0.0
37	West Virginia	1.4		47	Louisiana	0.0
37	Wisconsin	1.4		47	Mississippi	0.0
47	Wyoming	0.0		47	Wyoming	0.0
					District of Columbia	9.4

Source: Morgan Quitno Press using data from U.S. Dept. of Health & Human Serv's, National Center for Health Statistics "Morbidity and Mortality Weekly Report" (January 6, 2006, Vol. 54, Nos. 51 & 52)
*Provisional data. An infectious disease caused by the tubercle bacillus and causing the formation of tubercles on the lungs and other tissues of the body, often developing long after the initial infection. Characterized by the coughing up of mucus and sputum, fever, weight loss, and chest pain.

West Nile Virus Disease Cases Reported in 2005

National Total = 2,675 Cases*

ALPHA ORDER

RANK	STATE	CASES	% of USA
32	Alabama	10	0.4%
43	Alaska	0	0.0%
7	Arizona	104	3.9%
20	Arkansas	26	1.0%
1	California	796	29.8%
8	Colorado	101	3.8%
34	Connecticut	6	0.2%
41	Delaware	1	0.0%
23	Florida	21	0.8%
27	Georgia	16	0.6%
43	Hawaii	0	0.0%
29	Idaho	13	0.5%
3	Illinois	220	8.2%
30	Indiana	12	0.4%
15	Iowa	35	1.3%
23	Kansas	21	0.8%
37	Kentucky	5	0.2%
5	Louisiana	138	5.2%
43	Maine	0	0.0%
37	Maryland	5	0.2%
34	Massachusetts	6	0.2%
13	Michigan	47	1.8%
14	Minnesota	44	1.6%
10	Mississippi	70	2.6%
17	Missouri	31	1.2%
21	Montana	25	0.9%
6	Nebraska	133	5.0%
19	Nevada	29	1.1%
43	New Hampshire	0	0.0%
34	New Jersey	6	0.2%
16	New Mexico	33	1.2%
28	New York	14	0.5%
40	North Carolina	4	0.1%
9	North Dakota	86	3.2%
11	Ohio	61	2.3%
18	Oklahoma	30	1.1%
33	Oregon	7	0.3%
21	Pennsylvania	25	0.9%
41	Rhode Island	1	0.0%
37	South Carolina	5	0.2%
2	South Dakota	227	8.5%
25	Tennessee	17	0.6%
4	Texas	163	6.1%
12	Utah	52	1.9%
43	Vermont	0	0.0%
43	Virginia	0	0.0%
43	Washington	0	0.0%
43	West Virginia	0	0.0%
25	Wisconsin	17	0.6%
30	Wyoming	12	0.4%

RANK ORDER

RANK	STATE	CASES	% of USA
1	California	796	29.8%
2	South Dakota	227	8.5%
3	Illinois	220	8.2%
4	Texas	163	6.1%
5	Louisiana	138	5.2%
6	Nebraska	133	5.0%
7	Arizona	104	3.9%
8	Colorado	101	3.8%
9	North Dakota	86	3.2%
10	Mississippi	70	2.6%
11	Ohio	61	2.3%
12	Utah	52	1.9%
13	Michigan	47	1.8%
14	Minnesota	44	1.6%
15	Iowa	35	1.3%
16	New Mexico	33	1.2%
17	Missouri	31	1.2%
18	Oklahoma	30	1.1%
19	Nevada	29	1.1%
20	Arkansas	26	1.0%
21	Montana	25	0.9%
21	Pennsylvania	25	0.9%
23	Florida	21	0.8%
23	Kansas	21	0.8%
25	Tennessee	17	0.6%
25	Wisconsin	17	0.6%
27	Georgia	16	0.6%
28	New York	14	0.5%
29	Idaho	13	0.5%
30	Indiana	12	0.4%
30	Wyoming	12	0.4%
32	Alabama	10	0.4%
33	Oregon	7	0.3%
34	Connecticut	6	0.2%
34	Massachusetts	6	0.2%
34	New Jersey	6	0.2%
37	Kentucky	5	0.2%
37	Maryland	5	0.2%
37	South Carolina	5	0.2%
40	North Carolina	4	0.1%
41	Delaware	1	0.0%
41	Rhode Island	1	0.0%
43	Alaska	0	0.0%
43	Hawaii	0	0.0%
43	Maine	0	0.0%
43	New Hampshire	0	0.0%
43	Vermont	0	0.0%
43	Virginia	0	0.0%
43	Washington	0	0.0%
43	West Virginia	0	0.0%
	District of Columbia	0	0.0%

Source: U.S. Department of Health and Human Services, National Center for Health Statistics "Morbidity and Mortality Weekly Report" (January 6, 2006, Vol. 54, Nos. 51 & 52)

*Provisional data as of 12/28/04. A flavivirus typically carried by mosquitoes. Figures do not include 1,101 West Nile Fever cases caused by the West Nile virus that result in mild, flu-like symptoms. Encephalitis refers to an inflammation of the brain, meningitis is an inflammation of the membrane around the brain and the spinal cord, and meningoencephalitis refers to inflammation of the brain and the membrane surrounding it.

West Nile Disease Rate in 2005

National Rate = 0.9 Cases per 100,000 Population

RANK	STATE	RATE		RANK	STATE	RATE
27	Alabama	0.2		1	South Dakota	29.3
42	Alaska	0.0		2	North Dakota	13.5
11	Arizona	1.8		3	Nebraska	7.6
16	Arkansas	0.9		4	Louisiana	3.1
8	California	2.2		5	Montana	2.7
8	Colorado	2.2		6	Mississippi	2.4
27	Connecticut	0.2		6	Wyoming	2.4
33	Delaware	0.1		8	California	2.2
33	Florida	0.1		8	Colorado	2.2
27	Georgia	0.2		10	Utah	2.1
42	Hawaii	0.0		11	Arizona	1.8
16	Idaho	0.9		12	Illinois	1.7
12	Illinois	1.7		12	New Mexico	1.7
27	Indiana	0.2		14	Iowa	1.2
14	Iowa	1.2		14	Nevada	1.2
19	Kansas	0.8		16	Arkansas	0.9
33	Kentucky	0.1		16	Idaho	0.9
4	Louisiana	3.1		16	Minnesota	0.9
42	Maine	0.0		19	Kansas	0.8
33	Maryland	0.1		19	Oklahoma	0.8
33	Massachusetts	0.1		21	Texas	0.7
22	Michigan	0.5		22	Michigan	0.5
16	Minnesota	0.9		22	Missouri	0.5
6	Mississippi	2.4		22	Ohio	0.5
22	Missouri	0.5		25	Tennessee	0.3
5	Montana	2.7		25	Wisconsin	0.3
3	Nebraska	7.6		27	Alabama	0.2
14	Nevada	1.2		27	Connecticut	0.2
42	New Hampshire	0.0		27	Georgia	0.2
33	New Jersey	0.1		27	Indiana	0.2
12	New Mexico	1.7		27	Oregon	0.2
33	New York	0.1		27	Pennsylvania	0.2
42	North Carolina	0.0		33	Delaware	0.1
2	North Dakota	13.5		33	Florida	0.1
22	Ohio	0.5		33	Kentucky	0.1
19	Oklahoma	0.8		33	Maryland	0.1
27	Oregon	0.2		33	Massachusetts	0.1
27	Pennsylvania	0.2		33	New Jersey	0.1
33	Rhode Island	0.1		33	New York	0.1
33	South Carolina	0.1		33	Rhode Island	0.1
1	South Dakota	29.3		33	South Carolina	0.1
25	Tennessee	0.3		42	Alaska	0.0
21	Texas	0.7		42	Hawaii	0.0
10	Utah	2.1		42	Maine	0.0
42	Vermont	0.0		42	New Hampshire	0.0
42	Virginia	0.0		42	North Carolina	0.0
42	Washington	0.0		42	Vermont	0.0
42	West Virginia	0.0		42	Virginia	0.0
25	Wisconsin	0.3		42	Washington	0.0
6	Wyoming	2.4		42	West Virginia	0.0

	District of Columbia	0.0

Source: Morgan Quitno Press using data from U.S. Dept. of Health & Human Serv's, National Center for Health Statistics "Morbidity and Mortality Weekly Report" (January 6, 2006, Vol. 54, Nos. 51 & 52)
*Provisional data as of 12/28/04. A flavivirus typically carried by mosquitoes. Figures do not include 1,101 West Nile Fever cases caused by the West Nile virus that result in mild, flu-like symptoms. Encephalitis refers to an inflammation of the brain, meningitis is an inflammation of the membrane around the brain and the spinal cord, and meningoencephalitis refers to inflammation of the brain and the membrane surrounding it.

Whooping Cough (Pertussis) Cases Reported in 2005

National Total = 21,003 Cases*

ALPHA ORDER

RANK	STATE	CASES	% of USA
39	Alabama	84	0.4%
36	Alaska	125	0.6%
8	Arizona	959	4.6%
23	Arkansas	292	1.4%
1	California	1,622	7.7%
3	Colorado	1,373	6.5%
40	Connecticut	53	0.3%
49	Delaware	15	0.1%
26	Florida	209	1.0%
44	Georgia	42	0.2%
32	Hawaii	154	0.7%
24	Idaho	231	1.1%
11	Illinois	698	3.3%
20	Indiana	335	1.6%
9	Iowa	896	4.3%
17	Kansas	550	2.6%
33	Kentucky	145	0.7%
45	Louisiana	39	0.2%
46	Maine	37	0.2%
27	Maryland	199	0.9%
7	Massachusetts	996	4.7%
22	Michigan	304	1.4%
6	Minnesota	1,086	5.2%
41	Mississippi	52	0.2%
14	Missouri	606	2.9%
16	Montana	570	2.7%
29	Nebraska	177	0.8%
48	Nevada	32	0.2%
37	New Hampshire	119	0.6%
25	New Jersey	228	1.1%
31	New Mexico	159	0.8%
12	New York	653	3.1%
35	North Carolina	127	0.6%
34	North Dakota	139	0.7%
4	Ohio	1,185	5.6%
50	Oklahoma	0	0.0%
15	Oregon	575	2.7%
18	Pennsylvania	443	2.1%
47	Rhode Island	34	0.2%
19	South Carolina	378	1.8%
30	South Dakota	161	0.8%
28	Tennessee	196	0.9%
2	Texas	1,602	7.6%
13	Utah	643	3.1%
38	Vermont	86	0.4%
20	Virginia	335	1.6%
10	Washington	835	4.0%
43	West Virginia	47	0.2%
5	Wisconsin	1,117	5.3%
42	Wyoming	49	0.2%

RANK ORDER

RANK	STATE	CASES	% of USA
1	California	1,622	7.7%
2	Texas	1,602	7.6%
3	Colorado	1,373	6.5%
4	Ohio	1,185	5.6%
5	Wisconsin	1,117	5.3%
6	Minnesota	1,086	5.2%
7	Massachusetts	996	4.7%
8	Arizona	959	4.6%
9	Iowa	896	4.3%
10	Washington	835	4.0%
11	Illinois	698	3.3%
12	New York	653	3.1%
13	Utah	643	3.1%
14	Missouri	606	2.9%
15	Oregon	575	2.7%
16	Montana	570	2.7%
17	Kansas	550	2.6%
18	Pennsylvania	443	2.1%
19	South Carolina	378	1.8%
20	Indiana	335	1.6%
20	Virginia	335	1.6%
22	Michigan	304	1.4%
23	Arkansas	292	1.4%
24	Idaho	231	1.1%
25	New Jersey	228	1.1%
26	Florida	209	1.0%
27	Maryland	199	0.9%
28	Tennessee	196	0.9%
29	Nebraska	177	0.8%
30	South Dakota	161	0.8%
31	New Mexico	159	0.8%
32	Hawaii	154	0.7%
33	Kentucky	145	0.7%
34	North Dakota	139	0.7%
35	North Carolina	127	0.6%
36	Alaska	125	0.6%
37	New Hampshire	119	0.6%
38	Vermont	86	0.4%
39	Alabama	84	0.4%
40	Connecticut	53	0.3%
41	Mississippi	52	0.2%
42	Wyoming	49	0.2%
43	West Virginia	47	0.2%
44	Georgia	42	0.2%
45	Louisiana	39	0.2%
46	Maine	37	0.2%
47	Rhode Island	34	0.2%
48	Nevada	32	0.2%
49	Delaware	15	0.1%
50	Oklahoma	0	0.0%
	District of Columbia	11	0.1%

Source: U.S. Department of Health and Human Services, National Center for Health Statistics
"Morbidity and Mortality Weekly Report" (January 6, 2006, Vol. 54, Nos. 51 & 52)
*Provisional data. Acute, highly contagious infection of respiratory tract.

Whooping Cough (Pertussis) Rate in 2005

National Rate = 7.1 Cases per 100,000 Population*

ALPHA ORDER

RANK	STATE	RATE
41	Alabama	1.8
10	Alaska	18.8
12	Arizona	16.1
18	Arkansas	10.5
29	California	4.5
3	Colorado	29.4
44	Connecticut	1.5
41	Delaware	1.8
47	Florida	1.2
49	Georgia	0.5
17	Hawaii	12.1
11	Idaho	16.2
27	Illinois	5.5
28	Indiana	5.3
2	Iowa	30.2
9	Kansas	20.0
33	Kentucky	3.5
48	Louisiana	0.9
38	Maine	2.8
31	Maryland	3.6
14	Massachusetts	15.6
37	Michigan	3.0
6	Minnesota	21.2
41	Mississippi	1.8
19	Missouri	10.4
1	Montana	60.9
21	Nebraska	10.1
46	Nevada	1.3
23	New Hampshire	9.1
39	New Jersey	2.6
25	New Mexico	8.2
34	New York	3.4
44	North Carolina	1.5
5	North Dakota	21.8
20	Ohio	10.3
50	Oklahoma	0.0
13	Oregon	15.8
31	Pennsylvania	3.6
36	Rhode Island	3.2
24	South Carolina	8.9
7	South Dakota	20.7
35	Tennessee	3.3
26	Texas	7.0
4	Utah	26.0
15	Vermont	13.8
30	Virginia	4.4
16	Washington	13.3
39	West Virginia	2.6
8	Wisconsin	20.2
22	Wyoming	9.6

RANK ORDER

RANK	STATE	RATE
1	Montana	60.9
2	Iowa	30.2
3	Colorado	29.4
4	Utah	26.0
5	North Dakota	21.8
6	Minnesota	21.2
7	South Dakota	20.7
8	Wisconsin	20.2
9	Kansas	20.0
10	Alaska	18.8
11	Idaho	16.2
12	Arizona	16.1
13	Oregon	15.8
14	Massachusetts	15.6
15	Vermont	13.8
16	Washington	13.3
17	Hawaii	12.1
18	Arkansas	10.5
19	Missouri	10.4
20	Ohio	10.3
21	Nebraska	10.1
22	Wyoming	9.6
23	New Hampshire	9.1
24	South Carolina	8.9
25	New Mexico	8.2
26	Texas	7.0
27	Illinois	5.5
28	Indiana	5.3
29	California	4.5
30	Virginia	4.4
31	Maryland	3.6
31	Pennsylvania	3.6
33	Kentucky	3.5
34	New York	3.4
35	Tennessee	3.3
36	Rhode Island	3.2
37	Michigan	3.0
38	Maine	2.8
39	New Jersey	2.6
39	West Virginia	2.6
41	Alabama	1.8
41	Delaware	1.8
41	Mississippi	1.8
44	Connecticut	1.5
44	North Carolina	1.5
46	Nevada	1.3
47	Florida	1.2
48	Louisiana	0.9
49	Georgia	0.5
50	Oklahoma	0.0

	District of Columbia	2.0

Source: Morgan Quitno Press using data from U.S. Dept. of Health & Human Serv's, National Center for Health Statistics
"Morbidity and Mortality Weekly Report" (January 6, 2006, Vol. 54, Nos. 51 & 52)
*Provisional data. Acute, highly contagious infection of respiratory tract.

Percent of Children Aged 19 to 35 Months Immunized in 2004

National Percent = 82.5%*

ALPHA ORDER				RANK ORDER		
RANK	STATE	PERCENT		RANK	STATE	PERCENT
27	Alabama	83.0		1	Massachusetts	90.9
46	Alaska	76.1		2	Florida	89.7
41	Arizona	81.0		3	New Hampshire	89.0
18	Arkansas	84.9		4	Vermont	88.8
26	California	83.1		5	Connecticut	88.7
43	Colorado	80.1		6	Rhode Island	88.2
5	Connecticut	88.7		7	South Dakota	88.0
10	Delaware	86.4		8	West Virginia	87.7
2	Florida	89.7		9	Pennsylvania	87.1
15	Georgia	85.5		10	Delaware	86.4
30	Hawaii	82.6		11	Iowa	86.1
30	Idaho	82.6		12	Missouri	86.0
22	Illinois	83.7		13	Mississippi	85.8
36	Indiana	81.3		14	Minnesota	85.7
11	Iowa	86.1		15	Georgia	85.5
44	Kansas	79.5		16	Wisconsin	85.1
42	Kentucky	80.4		17	Maine	85.0
45	Louisiana	76.3		18	Arkansas	84.9
17	Maine	85.0		19	New Mexico	84.8
36	Maryland	81.3		20	Wyoming	84.1
1	Massachusetts	90.9		21	North Dakota	84.0
36	Michigan	81.3		22	Illinois	83.7
14	Minnesota	85.7		23	Virginia	83.4
13	Mississippi	85.8		24	New Jersey	83.3
12	Missouri	86.0		25	Tennessee	83.2
35	Montana	81.6		26	California	83.1
27	Nebraska	83.0		27	Alabama	83.0
50	Nevada	70.6		27	Nebraska	83.0
3	New Hampshire	89.0		29	New York	82.8
24	New Jersey	83.3		30	Hawaii	82.6
19	New Mexico	84.8		30	Idaho	82.6
29	New York	82.8		32	North Carolina	82.3
32	North Carolina	82.3		33	Ohio	82.2
21	North Dakota	84.0		33	South Carolina	82.2
33	Ohio	82.2		35	Montana	81.6
49	Oklahoma	72.6		36	Indiana	81.3
40	Oregon	81.1		36	Maryland	81.3
9	Pennsylvania	87.1		36	Michigan	81.3
6	Rhode Island	88.2		39	Washington	81.2
33	South Carolina	82.2		40	Oregon	81.1
7	South Dakota	88.0		41	Arizona	81.0
25	Tennessee	83.2		42	Kentucky	80.4
48	Texas	74.4		43	Colorado	80.1
47	Utah	75.2		44	Kansas	79.5
4	Vermont	88.8		45	Louisiana	76.3
23	Virginia	83.4		46	Alaska	76.1
39	Washington	81.2		47	Utah	75.2
8	West Virginia	87.7		48	Texas	74.4
16	Wisconsin	85.1		49	Oklahoma	72.6
20	Wyoming	84.1		50	Nevada	70.6
					District of Columbia	86.0

Source: U.S. Department of Health and Human Services, Centers for Disease Control and Prevention
    "State Vaccination Coverage Levels" (Morbidity and Mortality Weekly Report, Vol. 54, No. 29, July 29, 2005)
*This table is consistent with previous tables showing "fully" immunized children. Figures here are for the 4:3:1:3
series. Children received four doses of DTP/DT/DTaP (Diphtheria, Tetanus, Pertussis (Whooping Cough), Acellular
Pertussis), three doses of OPV (Oral Poliovirus Vaccine), one dose of MCV (Measles-Containing Vaccine) and three
doses of Hib (Haemophilus influenzae type b). Hepatitis B and Varicella vaccines are not included in this series.

Percent of Children Aged 19 to 35 Months Fully Immunized in 2004

National Percent = 76.0%*

ALPHA ORDER			RANK ORDER		
RANK	STATE	PERCENT	RANK	STATE	PERCENT
9	Alabama	80.1	1	Connecticut	84.8
46	Alaska	66.4	2	Florida	84.7
34	Arizona	73.0	3	Massachusetts	84.0
7	Arkansas	80.6	4	Georgia	82.0
15	California	78.6	5	Pennsylvania	81.8
32	Colorado	73.4	6	Rhode Island	81.5
1	Connecticut	84.8	7	Arkansas	80.6
10	Delaware	79.9	8	Mississippi	80.4
2	Florida	84.7	9	Alabama	80.1
4	Georgia	82.0	10	Delaware	79.9
11	Hawaii	79.8	11	Hawaii	79.8
39	Idaho	70.4	12	Michigan	79.2
31	Illinois	73.7	13	Tennessee	79.1
42	Indiana	68.2	14	New Mexico	79.0
23	Iowa	76.1	15	California	78.6
47	Kansas	65.8	16	New Hampshire	78.4
22	Kentucky	77.1	17	New York	78.0
40	Louisiana	70.1	17	Wisconsin	78.0
29	Maine	73.8	19	North Carolina	77.8
24	Maryland	76.0	20	Minnesota	77.7
3	Massachusetts	84.0	21	South Carolina	77.2
12	Michigan	79.2	22	Kentucky	77.1
20	Minnesota	77.7	23	Iowa	76.1
8	Mississippi	80.4	24	Maryland	76.0
26	Missouri	75.2	24	West Virginia	76.0
49	Montana	64.5	26	Missouri	75.2
35	Nebraska	72.6	27	New Jersey	74.4
48	Nevada	65.1	28	Virginia	73.9
16	New Hampshire	78.4	29	Maine	73.8
27	New Jersey	74.4	29	Oregon	73.8
14	New Mexico	79.0	31	Illinois	73.7
17	New York	78.0	32	Colorado	73.4
19	North Carolina	77.8	33	South Dakota	73.3
37	North Dakota	71.0	34	Arizona	73.0
38	Ohio	70.6	35	Nebraska	72.6
36	Oklahoma	71.4	36	Oklahoma	71.4
29	Oregon	73.8	37	North Dakota	71.0
5	Pennsylvania	81.8	38	Ohio	70.6
6	Rhode Island	81.5	39	Idaho	70.4
21	South Carolina	77.2	40	Louisiana	70.1
33	South Dakota	73.3	41	Texas	69.3
13	Tennessee	79.1	42	Indiana	68.2
41	Texas	69.3	43	Utah	67.8
43	Utah	67.8	44	Vermont	66.6
44	Vermont	66.6	45	Washington	66.5
28	Virginia	73.9	46	Alaska	66.4
45	Washington	66.5	47	Kansas	65.8
24	West Virginia	76.0	48	Nevada	65.1
17	Wisconsin	78.0	49	Montana	64.5
50	Wyoming	64.1	50	Wyoming	64.1
				District of Columbia	79.5

Source: U.S. Department of Health and Human Services, Centers for Disease Control and Prevention
   "State Vaccination Coverage Levels" (Morbidity and Mortality Weekly Report, Vol. 54, No. 29, July 29, 2005)
   *Fully immunized (4:3:1:3:3:1 series) children received four doses of DTP/DT/DTaP (Diphtheria, Tetanus, Pertussis (Whooping Cough), Acellular Pertussis), three doses of OPV (Oral Poliovirus Vaccine), one dose of MCV (Measles-Containing Vaccine), three doses of Hib (Haemophilus influenzae type b), three doses of Hepatitis B vaccine and one dose of Varicella (chickenpox) vaccine. This differs from previous "fully" immunized tables.

Percent of Adults Aged 65 Years and Older Who Received Flu Shots in 2004

National Median = 67.8%*

<table>
<thead>
<tr><th colspan="3">ALPHA ORDER</th><th colspan="3">RANK ORDER</th></tr>
<tr><th>RANK</th><th>STATE</th><th>PERCENT</th><th>RANK</th><th>STATE</th><th>PERCENT</th></tr>
</thead>
<tbody>
<tr><td>36</td><td>Alabama</td><td>66.1</td><td>1</td><td>Colorado</td><td>78.8</td></tr>
<tr><td>47</td><td>Alaska</td><td>64.1</td><td>2</td><td>Minnesota</td><td>78.2</td></tr>
<tr><td>36</td><td>Arizona</td><td>66.1</td><td>3</td><td>South Dakota</td><td>76.8</td></tr>
<tr><td>22</td><td>Arkansas</td><td>68.7</td><td>4</td><td>Nebraska</td><td>75.8</td></tr>
<tr><td>17</td><td>California</td><td>70.9</td><td>5</td><td>Utah</td><td>75.4</td></tr>
<tr><td>1</td><td>Colorado</td><td>78.8</td><td>6</td><td>Oklahoma</td><td>74.9</td></tr>
<tr><td>11</td><td>Connecticut</td><td>73.0</td><td>7</td><td>North Dakota</td><td>74.2</td></tr>
<tr><td>20</td><td>Delaware</td><td>69.2</td><td>7</td><td>Wisconsin</td><td>74.2</td></tr>
<tr><td>42</td><td>Florida</td><td>65.1</td><td>9</td><td>Iowa</td><td>74.0</td></tr>
<tr><td>44</td><td>Georgia</td><td>64.4</td><td>10</td><td>Wyoming</td><td>73.8</td></tr>
<tr><td>NA</td><td>Hawaii**</td><td>NA</td><td>11</td><td>Connecticut</td><td>73.0</td></tr>
<tr><td>36</td><td>Idaho</td><td>66.1</td><td>11</td><td>Rhode Island</td><td>73.0</td></tr>
<tr><td>41</td><td>Illinois</td><td>65.3</td><td>13</td><td>New Mexico</td><td>72.3</td></tr>
<tr><td>45</td><td>Indiana</td><td>64.2</td><td>14</td><td>Maine</td><td>72.1</td></tr>
<tr><td>9</td><td>Iowa</td><td>74.0</td><td>14</td><td>Montana</td><td>72.1</td></tr>
<tr><td>25</td><td>Kansas</td><td>68.1</td><td>16</td><td>Oregon</td><td>71.0</td></tr>
<tr><td>45</td><td>Kentucky</td><td>64.2</td><td>17</td><td>California</td><td>70.9</td></tr>
<tr><td>23</td><td>Louisiana</td><td>68.6</td><td>18</td><td>New Hampshire</td><td>70.7</td></tr>
<tr><td>14</td><td>Maine</td><td>72.1</td><td>19</td><td>Massachusetts</td><td>70.5</td></tr>
<tr><td>43</td><td>Maryland</td><td>64.6</td><td>20</td><td>Delaware</td><td>69.2</td></tr>
<tr><td>19</td><td>Massachusetts</td><td>70.5</td><td>21</td><td>Missouri</td><td>69.1</td></tr>
<tr><td>31</td><td>Michigan</td><td>66.9</td><td>22</td><td>Arkansas</td><td>68.7</td></tr>
<tr><td>2</td><td>Minnesota</td><td>78.2</td><td>23</td><td>Louisiana</td><td>68.6</td></tr>
<tr><td>33</td><td>Mississippi</td><td>66.8</td><td>23</td><td>Virginia</td><td>68.6</td></tr>
<tr><td>21</td><td>Missouri</td><td>69.1</td><td>25</td><td>Kansas</td><td>68.1</td></tr>
<tr><td>14</td><td>Montana</td><td>72.1</td><td>26</td><td>Washington</td><td>67.9</td></tr>
<tr><td>4</td><td>Nebraska</td><td>75.8</td><td>27</td><td>West Virginia</td><td>67.8</td></tr>
<tr><td>49</td><td>Nevada</td><td>59.0</td><td>28</td><td>New Jersey</td><td>67.5</td></tr>
<tr><td>18</td><td>New Hampshire</td><td>70.7</td><td>28</td><td>Ohio</td><td>67.5</td></tr>
<tr><td>28</td><td>New Jersey</td><td>67.5</td><td>30</td><td>Texas</td><td>67.0</td></tr>
<tr><td>13</td><td>New Mexico</td><td>72.3</td><td>31</td><td>Michigan</td><td>66.9</td></tr>
<tr><td>40</td><td>New York</td><td>65.9</td><td>31</td><td>North Carolina</td><td>66.9</td></tr>
<tr><td>31</td><td>North Carolina</td><td>66.9</td><td>33</td><td>Mississippi</td><td>66.8</td></tr>
<tr><td>7</td><td>North Dakota</td><td>74.2</td><td>34</td><td>Vermont</td><td>66.6</td></tr>
<tr><td>28</td><td>Ohio</td><td>67.5</td><td>35</td><td>Tennessee</td><td>66.3</td></tr>
<tr><td>6</td><td>Oklahoma</td><td>74.9</td><td>36</td><td>Alabama</td><td>66.1</td></tr>
<tr><td>16</td><td>Oregon</td><td>71.0</td><td>36</td><td>Arizona</td><td>66.1</td></tr>
<tr><td>48</td><td>Pennsylvania</td><td>63.8</td><td>36</td><td>Idaho</td><td>66.1</td></tr>
<tr><td>11</td><td>Rhode Island</td><td>73.0</td><td>39</td><td>South Carolina</td><td>66.0</td></tr>
<tr><td>39</td><td>South Carolina</td><td>66.0</td><td>40</td><td>New York</td><td>65.9</td></tr>
<tr><td>3</td><td>South Dakota</td><td>76.8</td><td>41</td><td>Illinois</td><td>65.3</td></tr>
<tr><td>35</td><td>Tennessee</td><td>66.3</td><td>42</td><td>Florida</td><td>65.1</td></tr>
<tr><td>30</td><td>Texas</td><td>67.0</td><td>43</td><td>Maryland</td><td>64.6</td></tr>
<tr><td>5</td><td>Utah</td><td>75.4</td><td>44</td><td>Georgia</td><td>64.4</td></tr>
<tr><td>34</td><td>Vermont</td><td>66.6</td><td>45</td><td>Indiana</td><td>64.2</td></tr>
<tr><td>23</td><td>Virginia</td><td>68.6</td><td>45</td><td>Kentucky</td><td>64.2</td></tr>
<tr><td>26</td><td>Washington</td><td>67.9</td><td>47</td><td>Alaska</td><td>64.1</td></tr>
<tr><td>27</td><td>West Virginia</td><td>67.8</td><td>48</td><td>Pennsylvania</td><td>63.8</td></tr>
<tr><td>7</td><td>Wisconsin</td><td>74.2</td><td>49</td><td>Nevada</td><td>59.0</td></tr>
<tr><td>10</td><td>Wyoming</td><td>73.8</td><td>NA</td><td>Hawaii**</td><td>NA</td></tr>
<tr><td></td><td></td><td></td><td></td><td>District of Columbia</td><td>54.8</td></tr>
</tbody>
</table>

Source: U.S. Department of Health and Human Services, Centers for Disease Control and Prevention
   "2004 Behavioral Risk Factor Surveillance Summary Prevalence Data" (http://apps.nccd.cdc.gov/brfss/)
Percent of adults 65 years old and older who reported receiving influenza vaccine during the preceding 12 months.
**Not available.*

Sexually Transmitted Diseases in 2004

National Total = 1,267,604 Cases*

ALPHA ORDER				RANK ORDER			
RANK	STATE	CASES	% of USA	RANK	STATE	CASES	% of USA
21	Alabama	21,685	1.7%	1	California	153,709	12.1%
38	Alaska	4,529	0.4%	2	Texas	95,433	7.5%
22	Arizona	21,010	1.7%	3	New York	78,565	6.2%
29	Arkansas	12,048	1.0%	4	Illinois	68,168	5.4%
1	California	153,709	12.1%	5	Florida	61,863	4.9%
24	Colorado	17,268	1.4%	6	Ohio	60,083	4.7%
28	Connecticut	12,459	1.0%	7	Michigan	58,816	4.6%
41	Delaware	3,857	0.3%	8	Georgia	50,612	4.0%
5	Florida	61,863	4.9%	9	Pennsylvania	49,380	3.9%
8	Georgia	50,612	4.0%	10	North Carolina	44,354	3.5%
36	Hawaii	6,508	0.5%	11	Louisiana	32,709	2.6%
43	Idaho	2,913	0.2%	12	Tennessee	31,121	2.5%
4	Illinois	68,168	5.4%	13	Missouri	30,631	2.4%
18	Indiana	25,351	2.0%	14	Virginia	30,316	2.4%
35	Iowa	8,210	0.6%	15	Maryland	28,629	2.3%
31	Kansas	10,059	0.8%	16	South Carolina	27,714	2.2%
34	Kentucky	9,275	0.7%	17	Mississippi	26,085	2.1%
11	Louisiana	32,709	2.6%	18	Indiana	25,351	2.0%
46	Maine	2,325	0.2%	19	Wisconsin	24,299	1.9%
15	Maryland	28,629	2.3%	20	New Jersey	24,294	1.9%
25	Massachusetts	16,416	1.3%	21	Alabama	21,685	1.7%
7	Michigan	58,816	4.6%	22	Arizona	21,010	1.7%
27	Minnesota	14,586	1.2%	23	Washington	20,595	1.6%
17	Mississippi	26,085	2.1%	24	Colorado	17,268	1.4%
13	Missouri	30,631	2.4%	25	Massachusetts	16,416	1.3%
45	Montana	2,700	0.2%	26	Oklahoma	14,844	1.2%
37	Nebraska	6,392	0.5%	27	Minnesota	14,586	1.2%
33	Nevada	9,809	0.8%	28	Connecticut	12,459	1.0%
48	New Hampshire	1,874	0.1%	29	Arkansas	12,048	1.0%
20	New Jersey	24,294	1.9%	30	New Mexico	10,423	0.8%
30	New Mexico	10,423	0.8%	31	Kansas	10,059	0.8%
3	New York	78,565	6.2%	32	Oregon	10,022	0.8%
10	North Carolina	44,354	3.5%	33	Nevada	9,809	0.8%
47	North Dakota	1,920	0.2%	34	Kentucky	9,275	0.7%
6	Ohio	60,083	4.7%	35	Iowa	8,210	0.6%
26	Oklahoma	14,844	1.2%	36	Hawaii	6,508	0.5%
32	Oregon	10,022	0.8%	37	Nebraska	6,392	0.5%
9	Pennsylvania	49,380	3.9%	38	Alaska	4,529	0.4%
40	Rhode Island	4,284	0.3%	39	Utah	4,474	0.4%
16	South Carolina	27,714	2.2%	40	Rhode Island	4,284	0.3%
44	South Dakota	2,836	0.2%	41	Delaware	3,857	0.3%
12	Tennessee	31,121	2.5%	42	West Virginia	3,653	0.3%
2	Texas	95,433	7.5%	43	Idaho	2,913	0.2%
39	Utah	4,474	0.4%	44	South Dakota	2,836	0.2%
49	Vermont	1,224	0.1%	45	Montana	2,700	0.2%
14	Virginia	30,316	2.4%	46	Maine	2,325	0.2%
23	Washington	20,595	1.6%	47	North Dakota	1,920	0.2%
42	West Virginia	3,653	0.3%	48	New Hampshire	1,874	0.1%
19	Wisconsin	24,299	1.9%	49	Vermont	1,224	0.1%
50	Wyoming	1,144	0.1%	50	Wyoming	1,144	0.1%
					District of Columbia	6,130	0.5%

Source: Morgan Quitno Press using data from U.S. Dept. of Health and Human Services, Nat'l Center for Health Statistics "Sexually Transmitted Disease Surveillance 2004" (http://www.cdc.gov/std/stats/TOC2004.htm)
*Includes chancroid, chlamydia, gonorrhea and primary and secondary syphilis.

Sexually Transmitted Disease Rate in 2004

National Rate = 435.8 Cases per 100,000 Population*

ALPHA ORDER

RANK	STATE	RATE
15	Alabama	481.8
3	Alaska	698.0
29	Arizona	376.4
18	Arkansas	442.0
20	California	433.2
28	Colorado	379.5
34	Connecticut	357.7
16	Delaware	471.8
33	Florida	363.5
6	Georgia	582.7
14	Hawaii	517.5
45	Idaho	213.2
8	Illinois	538.8
25	Indiana	409.2
41	Iowa	278.9
31	Kansas	369.3
44	Kentucky	225.2
2	Louisiana	727.5
49	Maine	178.1
13	Maryland	519.7
42	Massachusetts	255.1
5	Michigan	583.5
38	Minnesota	288.2
1	Mississippi	905.3
9	Missouri	536.9
37	Montana	294.2
32	Nebraska	367.5
19	Nevada	437.6
50	New Hampshire	145.5
40	New Jersey	281.2
7	New Mexico	556.1
24	New York	409.4
11	North Carolina	527.5
36	North Dakota	303.0
12	Ohio	525.4
22	Oklahoma	422.7
39	Oregon	281.5
26	Pennsylvania	399.4
27	Rhode Island	398.0
4	South Carolina	668.2
30	South Dakota	371.1
10	Tennessee	532.7
21	Texas	431.4
48	Utah	190.2
47	Vermont	197.7
23	Virginia	410.5
35	Washington	335.8
46	West Virginia	201.8
17	Wisconsin	444.0
43	Wyoming	228.3

RANK ORDER

RANK	STATE	RATE
1	Mississippi	905.3
2	Louisiana	727.5
3	Alaska	698.0
4	South Carolina	668.2
5	Michigan	583.5
6	Georgia	582.7
7	New Mexico	556.1
8	Illinois	538.8
9	Missouri	536.9
10	Tennessee	532.7
11	North Carolina	527.5
12	Ohio	525.4
13	Maryland	519.7
14	Hawaii	517.5
15	Alabama	481.8
16	Delaware	471.8
17	Wisconsin	444.0
18	Arkansas	442.0
19	Nevada	437.6
20	California	433.2
21	Texas	431.4
22	Oklahoma	422.7
23	Virginia	410.5
24	New York	409.4
25	Indiana	409.2
26	Pennsylvania	399.4
27	Rhode Island	398.0
28	Colorado	379.5
29	Arizona	376.4
30	South Dakota	371.1
31	Kansas	369.3
32	Nebraska	367.5
33	Florida	363.5
34	Connecticut	357.7
35	Washington	335.8
36	North Dakota	303.0
37	Montana	294.2
38	Minnesota	288.2
39	Oregon	281.5
40	New Jersey	281.2
41	Iowa	278.9
42	Massachusetts	255.1
43	Wyoming	228.3
44	Kentucky	225.2
45	Idaho	213.2
46	West Virginia	201.8
47	Vermont	197.7
48	Utah	190.2
49	Maine	178.1
50	New Hampshire	145.5

District of Columbia 1,105.9

Source: Morgan Quitno Press using data from U.S. Dept. of Health and Human Services, Nat'l Center for Health Statistics
"Sexually Transmitted Disease Surveillance 2004" (http://www.cdc.gov/std/stats/TOC2004.htm)
*Includes chancroid, chlamydia, gonorrhea and primary and secondary syphilis.

Chlamydia Cases Reported in 2004

National Total = 929,462 Cases*

ALPHA ORDER

RANK	STATE	CASES	% of USA
24	Alabama	13,314	1.4%
38	Alaska	3,954	0.4%
22	Arizona	16,786	1.8%
31	Arkansas	7,864	0.8%
1	California	122,197	13.1%
23	Colorado	14,151	1.5%
28	Connecticut	9,552	1.0%
41	Delaware	2,954	0.3%
5	Florida	42,554	4.6%
9	Georgia	34,280	3.7%
36	Hawaii	5,307	0.6%
42	Idaho	2,784	0.3%
4	Illinois	47,185	5.1%
18	Indiana	18,440	2.0%
33	Iowa	6,956	0.7%
32	Kansas	7,493	0.8%
35	Kentucky	6,470	0.7%
12	Louisiana	21,837	2.3%
46	Maine	2,113	0.2%
15	Maryland	19,952	2.1%
25	Massachusetts	13,242	1.4%
6	Michigan	41,246	4.4%
26	Minnesota	11,602	1.2%
17	Mississippi	18,863	2.0%
14	Missouri	21,319	2.3%
44	Montana	2,608	0.3%
37	Nebraska	5,238	0.6%
34	Nevada	6,690	0.7%
48	New Hampshire	1,736	0.2%
21	New Jersey	17,448	1.9%
29	New Mexico	9,035	1.0%
3	New York	59,097	6.4%
10	North Carolina	28,967	3.1%
47	North Dakota	1,810	0.2%
7	Ohio	39,379	4.2%
27	Oklahoma	10,366	1.1%
30	Oregon	8,690	0.9%
8	Pennsylvania	38,025	4.1%
40	Rhode Island	3,442	0.4%
19	South Carolina	18,423	2.0%
45	South Dakota	2,532	0.3%
11	Tennessee	22,515	2.4%
2	Texas	70,232	7.6%
39	Utah	3,857	0.4%
49	Vermont	1,137	0.1%
13	Virginia	21,635	2.3%
20	Washington	17,635	1.9%
43	West Virginia	2,758	0.3%
16	Wisconsin	19,217	2.1%
50	Wyoming	1,082	0.1%

RANK ORDER

RANK	STATE	CASES	% of USA
1	California	122,197	13.1%
2	Texas	70,232	7.6%
3	New York	59,097	6.4%
4	Illinois	47,185	5.1%
5	Florida	42,554	4.6%
6	Michigan	41,246	4.4%
7	Ohio	39,379	4.2%
8	Pennsylvania	38,025	4.1%
9	Georgia	34,280	3.7%
10	North Carolina	28,967	3.1%
11	Tennessee	22,515	2.4%
12	Louisiana	21,837	2.3%
13	Virginia	21,635	2.3%
14	Missouri	21,319	2.3%
15	Maryland	19,952	2.1%
16	Wisconsin	19,217	2.1%
17	Mississippi	18,863	2.0%
18	Indiana	18,440	2.0%
19	South Carolina	18,423	2.0%
20	Washington	17,635	1.9%
21	New Jersey	17,448	1.9%
22	Arizona	16,786	1.8%
23	Colorado	14,151	1.5%
24	Alabama	13,314	1.4%
25	Massachusetts	13,242	1.4%
26	Minnesota	11,602	1.2%
27	Oklahoma	10,366	1.1%
28	Connecticut	9,552	1.0%
29	New Mexico	9,035	1.0%
30	Oregon	8,690	0.9%
31	Arkansas	7,864	0.8%
32	Kansas	7,493	0.8%
33	Iowa	6,956	0.7%
34	Nevada	6,690	0.7%
35	Kentucky	6,470	0.7%
36	Hawaii	5,307	0.6%
37	Nebraska	5,238	0.6%
38	Alaska	3,954	0.4%
39	Utah	3,857	0.4%
40	Rhode Island	3,442	0.4%
41	Delaware	2,954	0.3%
42	Idaho	2,784	0.3%
43	West Virginia	2,758	0.3%
44	Montana	2,608	0.3%
45	South Dakota	2,532	0.3%
46	Maine	2,113	0.2%
47	North Dakota	1,810	0.2%
48	New Hampshire	1,736	0.2%
49	Vermont	1,137	0.1%
50	Wyoming	1,082	0.1%
	District of Columbia	3,493	0.4%

Source: U.S. Department of Health and Human Services, National Center for Health Statistics
"Sexually Transmitted Disease Surveillance 2004" (http://www.cdc.gov/std/stats/TOC2004.htm)
*Any of several common, often asymptomatic, sexually transmitted diseases caused by the microorganism Chlamydia trachomatis, including nonspecific urethritis in men.

Chlamydia Rate in 2004

National Rate = 319.6 Cases per 100,000 Population*

ALPHA ORDER

RANK	STATE	RATE
28	Alabama	295.8
2	Alaska	609.4
25	Arizona	300.8
31	Arkansas	288.5
16	California	344.4
21	Colorado	311.0
36	Connecticut	274.2
13	Delaware	361.3
37	Florida	250.0
8	Georgia	394.7
6	Hawaii	422.0
43	Idaho	203.8
11	Illinois	372.9
27	Indiana	297.6
39	Iowa	236.3
35	Kansas	275.1
48	Kentucky	157.1
3	Louisiana	485.7
47	Maine	161.8
12	Maryland	362.2
42	Massachusetts	205.8
7	Michigan	409.2
40	Minnesota	229.3
1	Mississippi	654.7
10	Missouri	373.7
34	Montana	284.2
24	Nebraska	301.2
26	Nevada	298.5
50	New Hampshire	134.8
44	New Jersey	202.0
4	New Mexico	482.0
22	New York	308.0
15	North Carolina	344.5
33	North Dakota	285.6
17	Ohio	344.3
29	Oklahoma	295.2
38	Oregon	244.1
23	Pennsylvania	307.5
19	Rhode Island	319.8
5	South Carolina	444.2
18	South Dakota	331.3
9	Tennessee	385.4
20	Texas	317.5
46	Utah	164.0
45	Vermont	183.6
30	Virginia	292.9
32	Washington	287.6
49	West Virginia	152.3
14	Wisconsin	351.2
41	Wyoming	215.9

RANK ORDER

RANK	STATE	RATE
1	Mississippi	654.7
2	Alaska	609.4
3	Louisiana	485.7
4	New Mexico	482.0
5	South Carolina	444.2
6	Hawaii	422.0
7	Michigan	409.2
8	Georgia	394.7
9	Tennessee	385.4
10	Missouri	373.7
11	Illinois	372.9
12	Maryland	362.2
13	Delaware	361.3
14	Wisconsin	351.2
15	North Carolina	344.5
16	California	344.4
17	Ohio	344.3
18	South Dakota	331.3
19	Rhode Island	319.8
20	Texas	317.5
21	Colorado	311.0
22	New York	308.0
23	Pennsylvania	307.5
24	Nebraska	301.2
25	Arizona	300.8
26	Nevada	298.5
27	Indiana	297.6
28	Alabama	295.8
29	Oklahoma	295.2
30	Virginia	292.9
31	Arkansas	288.5
32	Washington	287.6
33	North Dakota	285.6
34	Montana	284.2
35	Kansas	275.1
36	Connecticut	274.2
37	Florida	250.0
38	Oregon	244.1
39	Iowa	236.3
40	Minnesota	229.3
41	Wyoming	215.9
42	Massachusetts	205.8
43	Idaho	203.8
44	New Jersey	202.0
45	Vermont	183.6
46	Utah	164.0
47	Maine	161.8
48	Kentucky	157.1
49	West Virginia	152.3
50	New Hampshire	134.8
	District of Columbia	630.2

Source: U.S. Department of Health and Human Services, National Center for Health Statistics
    "Sexually Transmitted Disease Surveillance 2004" (http://www.cdc.gov/std/stats/TOC2004.htm)
*Any of several common, often asymptomatic, sexually transmitted diseases caused by the microorganism Chlamydia trachomatis, including nonspecific urethritis in men.

Gonorrhea Cases Reported in 2004

National Total = 330,132 Cases*

ALPHA ORDER

RANK	STATE	CASES	% of USA
17	Alabama	8,206	2.5%
42	Alaska	567	0.2%
24	Arizona	4,065	1.2%
23	Arkansas	4,137	1.3%
1	California	30,155	9.1%
27	Colorado	3,054	0.9%
29	Connecticut	2,862	0.9%
38	Delaware	894	0.3%
6	Florida	18,580	5.6%
8	Georgia	15,783	4.8%
36	Hawaii	1,193	0.4%
47	Idaho	103	0.0%
3	Illinois	20,597	6.2%
19	Indiana	6,851	2.1%
35	Iowa	1,249	0.4%
32	Kansas	2,542	0.8%
31	Kentucky	2,758	0.8%
11	Louisiana	10,538	3.2%
44	Maine	210	0.1%
16	Maryland	8,297	2.5%
26	Massachusetts	3,057	0.9%
7	Michigan	17,376	5.3%
28	Minnesota	2,957	0.9%
18	Mississippi	7,163	2.2%
12	Missouri	9,218	2.8%
48	Montana	88	0.0%
37	Nebraska	1,147	0.3%
25	Nevada	3,078	0.9%
45	New Hampshire	133	0.0%
20	New Jersey	6,696	2.0%
33	New Mexico	1,306	0.4%
5	New York	18,737	5.7%
9	North Carolina	15,194	4.6%
46	North Dakota	110	0.0%
4	Ohio	20,467	6.2%
22	Oklahoma	4,453	1.3%
34	Oregon	1,302	0.4%
10	Pennsylvania	11,236	3.4%
40	Rhode Island	816	0.2%
13	South Carolina	9,171	2.8%
43	South Dakota	304	0.1%
15	Tennessee	8,475	2.6%
2	Texas	24,371	7.4%
41	Utah	603	0.2%
49	Vermont	86	0.0%
14	Virginia	8,565	2.6%
30	Washington	2,810	0.9%
39	West Virginia	892	0.3%
21	Wisconsin	5,053	1.5%
50	Wyoming	59	0.0%

RANK ORDER

RANK	STATE	CASES	% of USA
1	California	30,155	9.1%
2	Texas	24,371	7.4%
3	Illinois	20,597	6.2%
4	Ohio	20,467	6.2%
5	New York	18,737	5.7%
6	Florida	18,580	5.6%
7	Michigan	17,376	5.3%
8	Georgia	15,783	4.8%
9	North Carolina	15,194	4.6%
10	Pennsylvania	11,236	3.4%
11	Louisiana	10,538	3.2%
12	Missouri	9,218	2.8%
13	South Carolina	9,171	2.8%
14	Virginia	8,565	2.6%
15	Tennessee	8,475	2.6%
16	Maryland	8,297	2.5%
17	Alabama	8,206	2.5%
18	Mississippi	7,163	2.2%
19	Indiana	6,851	2.1%
20	New Jersey	6,696	2.0%
21	Wisconsin	5,053	1.5%
22	Oklahoma	4,453	1.3%
23	Arkansas	4,137	1.3%
24	Arizona	4,065	1.2%
25	Nevada	3,078	0.9%
26	Massachusetts	3,057	0.9%
27	Colorado	3,054	0.9%
28	Minnesota	2,957	0.9%
29	Connecticut	2,862	0.9%
30	Washington	2,810	0.9%
31	Kentucky	2,758	0.8%
32	Kansas	2,542	0.8%
33	New Mexico	1,306	0.4%
34	Oregon	1,302	0.4%
35	Iowa	1,249	0.4%
36	Hawaii	1,193	0.4%
37	Nebraska	1,147	0.3%
38	Delaware	894	0.3%
39	West Virginia	892	0.3%
40	Rhode Island	816	0.2%
41	Utah	603	0.2%
42	Alaska	567	0.2%
43	South Dakota	304	0.1%
44	Maine	210	0.1%
45	New Hampshire	133	0.0%
46	North Dakota	110	0.0%
47	Idaho	103	0.0%
48	Montana	88	0.0%
49	Vermont	86	0.0%
50	Wyoming	59	0.0%
	District of Columbia	2,568	0.8%

Source: U.S. Department of Health and Human Services, National Center for Health Statistics
"Sexually Transmitted Disease Surveillance 2004" (http://www.cdc.gov/std/stats/TOC2004.htm)
*Gonorrhea is a sexually transmitted disease caused by gonococcal bacteria that affects the mucous membrane chiefly of the genital and urinary tracts and is characterized by an acute purulent discharge and painful or difficult urination, though women often have no symptoms.

Gonorrhea Rate in 2004

National Rate = 113.5 Cases per 100,000 Population*

ALPHA ORDER

RANK	STATE	RATE
4	Alabama	182.3
26	Alaska	87.4
31	Arizona	72.8
11	Arkansas	151.8
27	California	85.0
33	Colorado	67.1
28	Connecticut	82.2
19	Delaware	109.4
20	Florida	109.2
5	Georgia	181.7
22	Hawaii	94.9
50	Idaho	7.5
9	Illinois	162.8
17	Indiana	110.6
40	Iowa	42.4
23	Kansas	93.3
34	Kentucky	67.0
2	Louisiana	234.4
45	Maine	16.1
12	Maryland	150.6
38	Massachusetts	47.5
8	Michigan	172.4
36	Minnesota	58.4
1	Mississippi	248.6
10	Missouri	161.6
49	Montana	9.6
35	Nebraska	65.9
14	Nevada	137.3
48	New Hampshire	10.3
29	New Jersey	77.5
32	New Mexico	69.7
21	New York	97.6
6	North Carolina	180.7
44	North Dakota	17.4
7	Ohio	179.0
15	Oklahoma	126.8
42	Oregon	36.6
25	Pennsylvania	90.9
30	Rhode Island	75.8
3	South Carolina	221.1
41	South Dakota	39.8
13	Tennessee	145.1
18	Texas	110.2
43	Utah	25.6
46	Vermont	13.9
16	Virginia	116.0
39	Washington	45.8
37	West Virginia	49.3
24	Wisconsin	92.3
47	Wyoming	11.8

RANK ORDER

RANK	STATE	RATE
1	Mississippi	248.6
2	Louisiana	234.4
3	South Carolina	221.1
4	Alabama	182.3
5	Georgia	181.7
6	North Carolina	180.7
7	Ohio	179.0
8	Michigan	172.4
9	Illinois	162.8
10	Missouri	161.6
11	Arkansas	151.8
12	Maryland	150.6
13	Tennessee	145.1
14	Nevada	137.3
15	Oklahoma	126.8
16	Virginia	116.0
17	Indiana	110.6
18	Texas	110.2
19	Delaware	109.4
20	Florida	109.2
21	New York	97.6
22	Hawaii	94.9
23	Kansas	93.3
24	Wisconsin	92.3
25	Pennsylvania	90.9
26	Alaska	87.4
27	California	85.0
28	Connecticut	82.2
29	New Jersey	77.5
30	Rhode Island	75.8
31	Arizona	72.8
32	New Mexico	69.7
33	Colorado	67.1
34	Kentucky	67.0
35	Nebraska	65.9
36	Minnesota	58.4
37	West Virginia	49.3
38	Massachusetts	47.5
39	Washington	45.8
40	Iowa	42.4
41	South Dakota	39.8
42	Oregon	36.6
43	Utah	25.6
44	North Dakota	17.4
45	Maine	16.1
46	Vermont	13.9
47	Wyoming	11.8
48	New Hampshire	10.3
49	Montana	9.6
50	Idaho	7.5

District of Columbia   463.3

Source: U.S. Department of Health and Human Services, National Center for Health Statistics
"Sexually Transmitted Disease Surveillance 2004" (http://www.cdc.gov/std/stats/TOC2004.htm)
*Gonorrhea is a sexually transmitted disease caused by gonococcal bacteria that affects the mucous membrane chiefly of the genital and urinary tracts and is characterized by an acute purulent discharge and painful or difficult urination, though women often have no symptoms.

Syphilis Cases Reported in 2004

National Total = 7,980 Cases*

RANK	STATE	CASES	% of USA
12	Alabama	165	2.1%
39	Alaska	8	0.1%
13	Arizona	157	2.0%
26	Arkansas	47	0.6%
1	California	1,356	17.0%
23	Colorado	63	0.8%
28	Connecticut	45	0.6%
38	Delaware	9	0.1%
3	Florida	728	9.1%
5	Georgia	549	6.9%
39	Hawaii	8	0.1%
35	Idaho	24	0.3%
6	Illinois	386	4.8%
24	Indiana	60	0.8%
42	Iowa	5	0.1%
35	Kansas	24	0.3%
26	Kentucky	47	0.6%
8	Louisiana	332	4.2%
47	Maine	2	0.0%
7	Maryland	380	4.8%
20	Massachusetts	114	1.4%
10	Michigan	192	2.4%
32	Minnesota	27	0.3%
25	Mississippi	59	0.7%
21	Missouri	94	1.2%
44	Montana	4	0.1%
41	Nebraska	7	0.1%
29	Nevada	40	0.5%
42	New Hampshire	5	0.1%
14	New Jersey	150	1.9%
22	New Mexico	82	1.0%
4	New York	727	9.1%
10	North Carolina	192	2.4%
49	North Dakota	0	0.0%
9	Ohio	237	3.0%
34	Oklahoma	25	0.3%
30	Oregon	29	0.4%
17	Pennsylvania	118	1.5%
33	Rhode Island	26	0.3%
18	South Carolina	116	1.5%
49	South Dakota	0	0.0%
16	Tennessee	130	1.6%
2	Texas	827	10.4%
37	Utah	13	0.2%
48	Vermont	1	0.0%
18	Virginia	116	1.5%
14	Washington	150	1.9%
45	West Virginia	3	0.0%
30	Wisconsin	29	0.4%
45	Wyoming	3	0.0%

ALPHA ORDER

RANK ORDER

RANK	STATE	CASES	% of USA
1	California	1,356	17.0%
2	Texas	827	10.4%
3	Florida	728	9.1%
4	New York	727	9.1%
5	Georgia	549	6.9%
6	Illinois	386	4.8%
7	Maryland	380	4.8%
8	Louisiana	332	4.2%
9	Ohio	237	3.0%
10	Michigan	192	2.4%
10	North Carolina	192	2.4%
12	Alabama	165	2.1%
13	Arizona	157	2.0%
14	New Jersey	150	1.9%
14	Washington	150	1.9%
16	Tennessee	130	1.6%
17	Pennsylvania	118	1.5%
18	South Carolina	116	1.5%
18	Virginia	116	1.5%
20	Massachusetts	114	1.4%
21	Missouri	94	1.2%
22	New Mexico	82	1.0%
23	Colorado	63	0.8%
24	Indiana	60	0.8%
25	Mississippi	59	0.7%
26	Arkansas	47	0.6%
26	Kentucky	47	0.6%
28	Connecticut	45	0.6%
29	Nevada	40	0.5%
30	Oregon	29	0.4%
30	Wisconsin	29	0.4%
32	Minnesota	27	0.3%
33	Rhode Island	26	0.3%
34	Oklahoma	25	0.3%
35	Idaho	24	0.3%
35	Kansas	24	0.3%
37	Utah	13	0.2%
38	Delaware	9	0.1%
39	Alaska	8	0.1%
39	Hawaii	8	0.1%
41	Nebraska	7	0.1%
42	Iowa	5	0.1%
42	New Hampshire	5	0.1%
44	Montana	4	0.1%
45	West Virginia	3	0.0%
45	Wyoming	3	0.0%
47	Maine	2	0.0%
48	Vermont	1	0.0%
49	North Dakota	0	0.0%
49	South Dakota	0	0.0%
	District of Columbia	69	0.9%

Source: U.S. Department of Health and Human Services, National Center for Health Statistics
"Sexually Transmitted Disease Surveillance 2004" (http://www.cdc.gov/std/stats/TOC2004.htm)
*Includes only primary and secondary cases. Does not include 25,421 cases in other stages. A chronic infectious disease caused by a spirochete (Treponema pallidum), either transmitted by direct contact, usually in sexual intercourse, or passed from mother to child in utero, and progressing through three stages characterized respectively by local formation of chancres, ulcerous skin eruptions, and systemic infection leading to general paresis.

Syphilis Rate in 2004

National Rate = 2.7 Cases per 100,000 Population*

ALPHA ORDER

RANK	STATE	RATE
8	Alabama	3.7
29	Alaska	1.2
11	Arizona	2.8
23	Arkansas	1.7
6	California	3.8
27	Colorado	1.4
28	Connecticut	1.3
30	Delaware	1.1
5	Florida	4.3
3	Georgia	6.3
37	Hawaii	0.6
20	Idaho	1.8
10	Illinois	3.1
32	Indiana	1.0
45	Iowa	0.2
34	Kansas	0.9
30	Kentucky	1.1
1	Louisiana	7.4
45	Maine	0.2
2	Maryland	6.9
20	Massachusetts	1.8
19	Michigan	1.9
40	Minnesota	0.5
18	Mississippi	2.0
25	Missouri	1.6
42	Montana	0.4
42	Nebraska	0.4
20	Nevada	1.8
42	New Hampshire	0.4
23	New Jersey	1.7
4	New Mexico	4.4
6	New York	3.8
15	North Carolina	2.3
49	North Dakota	0.0
17	Ohio	2.1
36	Oklahoma	0.7
35	Oregon	0.8
32	Pennsylvania	1.0
13	Rhode Island	2.4
11	South Carolina	2.8
49	South Dakota	0.0
16	Tennessee	2.2
8	Texas	3.7
37	Utah	0.6
45	Vermont	0.2
25	Virginia	1.6
13	Washington	2.4
45	West Virginia	0.2
40	Wisconsin	0.5
37	Wyoming	0.6

RANK ORDER

RANK	STATE	RATE
1	Louisiana	7.4
2	Maryland	6.9
3	Georgia	6.3
4	New Mexico	4.4
5	Florida	4.3
6	California	3.8
6	New York	3.8
8	Alabama	3.7
8	Texas	3.7
10	Illinois	3.1
11	Arizona	2.8
11	South Carolina	2.8
13	Rhode Island	2.4
13	Washington	2.4
15	North Carolina	2.3
16	Tennessee	2.2
17	Ohio	2.1
18	Mississippi	2.0
19	Michigan	1.9
20	Idaho	1.8
20	Massachusetts	1.8
20	Nevada	1.8
23	Arkansas	1.7
23	New Jersey	1.7
25	Missouri	1.6
25	Virginia	1.6
27	Colorado	1.4
28	Connecticut	1.3
29	Alaska	1.2
30	Delaware	1.1
30	Kentucky	1.1
32	Indiana	1.0
32	Pennsylvania	1.0
34	Kansas	0.9
35	Oregon	0.8
36	Oklahoma	0.7
37	Hawaii	0.6
37	Utah	0.6
37	Wyoming	0.6
40	Minnesota	0.5
40	Wisconsin	0.5
42	Montana	0.4
42	Nebraska	0.4
42	New Hampshire	0.4
45	Iowa	0.2
45	Maine	0.2
45	Vermont	0.2
45	West Virginia	0.2
49	North Dakota	0.0
49	South Dakota	0.0

	District of Columbia	12.4

Source: U.S. Department of Health and Human Services, National Center for Health Statistics
"Sexually Transmitted Disease Surveillance 2004" (http://www.cdc.gov/std/stats/TOC2004.htm)
*Includes only primary and secondary cases. Does not include 25,421 cases in other stages. A chronic infectious disease caused by a spirochete (Treponema pallidum), either transmitted by direct contact, usually in sexual intercourse, or passed from mother to child in utero, and progressing through three stages characterized respectively by local formation of chancres, ulcerous skin eruptions, and systemic infection leading to general paresis.

Percent of Adults Who Have Asthma: 2004

National Median = 8.2% of Adults*

<table>
<tr><td colspan="3">ALPHA ORDER</td><td colspan="3">RANK ORDER</td></tr>
<tr><td>RANK</td><td>STATE</td><td>PERCENT</td><td>RANK</td><td>STATE</td><td>PERCENT</td></tr>
<tr><td>17</td><td>Alabama</td><td>8.6</td><td>1</td><td>New Hampshire</td><td>10.2</td></tr>
<tr><td>12</td><td>Alaska</td><td>9.0</td><td>2</td><td>West Virginia</td><td>10.1</td></tr>
<tr><td>42</td><td>Arizona</td><td>7.1</td><td>3</td><td>Delaware</td><td>9.9</td></tr>
<tr><td>39</td><td>Arkansas</td><td>7.3</td><td>4</td><td>Connecticut</td><td>9.7</td></tr>
<tr><td>32</td><td>California</td><td>7.6</td><td>5</td><td>Maine</td><td>9.6</td></tr>
<tr><td>16</td><td>Colorado</td><td>8.7</td><td>5</td><td>Massachusetts</td><td>9.6</td></tr>
<tr><td>4</td><td>Connecticut</td><td>9.7</td><td>5</td><td>Oregon</td><td>9.6</td></tr>
<tr><td>3</td><td>Delaware</td><td>9.9</td><td>5</td><td>Rhode Island</td><td>9.6</td></tr>
<tr><td>41</td><td>Florida</td><td>7.2</td><td>9</td><td>New Mexico</td><td>9.2</td></tr>
<tr><td>36</td><td>Georgia</td><td>7.4</td><td>10</td><td>Missouri</td><td>9.1</td></tr>
<tr><td>NA</td><td>Hawaii**</td><td>NA</td><td>10</td><td>Washington</td><td>9.1</td></tr>
<tr><td>29</td><td>Idaho</td><td>7.9</td><td>12</td><td>Alaska</td><td>9.0</td></tr>
<tr><td>23</td><td>Illinois</td><td>8.4</td><td>13</td><td>Tennessee</td><td>8.9</td></tr>
<tr><td>23</td><td>Indiana</td><td>8.4</td><td>14</td><td>New York</td><td>8.8</td></tr>
<tr><td>47</td><td>Iowa</td><td>6.6</td><td>14</td><td>Pennsylvania</td><td>8.8</td></tr>
<tr><td>36</td><td>Kansas</td><td>7.4</td><td>16</td><td>Colorado</td><td>8.7</td></tr>
<tr><td>25</td><td>Kentucky</td><td>8.2</td><td>17</td><td>Alabama</td><td>8.6</td></tr>
<tr><td>49</td><td>Louisiana</td><td>6.1</td><td>17</td><td>Montana</td><td>8.6</td></tr>
<tr><td>5</td><td>Maine</td><td>9.6</td><td>17</td><td>New Jersey</td><td>8.6</td></tr>
<tr><td>30</td><td>Maryland</td><td>7.8</td><td>20</td><td>Ohio</td><td>8.5</td></tr>
<tr><td>5</td><td>Massachusetts</td><td>9.6</td><td>20</td><td>Vermont</td><td>8.5</td></tr>
<tr><td>25</td><td>Michigan</td><td>8.2</td><td>20</td><td>Wisconsin</td><td>8.5</td></tr>
<tr><td>36</td><td>Minnesota</td><td>7.4</td><td>23</td><td>Illinois</td><td>8.4</td></tr>
<tr><td>45</td><td>Mississippi</td><td>7.0</td><td>23</td><td>Indiana</td><td>8.4</td></tr>
<tr><td>10</td><td>Missouri</td><td>9.1</td><td>25</td><td>Kentucky</td><td>8.2</td></tr>
<tr><td>17</td><td>Montana</td><td>8.6</td><td>25</td><td>Michigan</td><td>8.2</td></tr>
<tr><td>46</td><td>Nebraska</td><td>6.9</td><td>25</td><td>Oklahoma</td><td>8.2</td></tr>
<tr><td>42</td><td>Nevada</td><td>7.1</td><td>28</td><td>Utah</td><td>8.0</td></tr>
<tr><td>1</td><td>New Hampshire</td><td>10.2</td><td>29</td><td>Idaho</td><td>7.9</td></tr>
<tr><td>17</td><td>New Jersey</td><td>8.6</td><td>30</td><td>Maryland</td><td>7.8</td></tr>
<tr><td>9</td><td>New Mexico</td><td>9.2</td><td>31</td><td>North Dakota</td><td>7.7</td></tr>
<tr><td>14</td><td>New York</td><td>8.8</td><td>32</td><td>California</td><td>7.6</td></tr>
<tr><td>35</td><td>North Carolina</td><td>7.5</td><td>32</td><td>South Carolina</td><td>7.6</td></tr>
<tr><td>31</td><td>North Dakota</td><td>7.7</td><td>32</td><td>Wyoming</td><td>7.6</td></tr>
<tr><td>20</td><td>Ohio</td><td>8.5</td><td>35</td><td>North Carolina</td><td>7.5</td></tr>
<tr><td>25</td><td>Oklahoma</td><td>8.2</td><td>36</td><td>Georgia</td><td>7.4</td></tr>
<tr><td>5</td><td>Oregon</td><td>9.6</td><td>36</td><td>Kansas</td><td>7.4</td></tr>
<tr><td>14</td><td>Pennsylvania</td><td>8.8</td><td>36</td><td>Minnesota</td><td>7.4</td></tr>
<tr><td>5</td><td>Rhode Island</td><td>9.6</td><td>39</td><td>Arkansas</td><td>7.3</td></tr>
<tr><td>32</td><td>South Carolina</td><td>7.6</td><td>39</td><td>Virginia</td><td>7.3</td></tr>
<tr><td>47</td><td>South Dakota</td><td>6.6</td><td>41</td><td>Florida</td><td>7.2</td></tr>
<tr><td>13</td><td>Tennessee</td><td>8.9</td><td>42</td><td>Arizona</td><td>7.1</td></tr>
<tr><td>42</td><td>Texas</td><td>7.1</td><td>42</td><td>Nevada</td><td>7.1</td></tr>
<tr><td>28</td><td>Utah</td><td>8.0</td><td>42</td><td>Texas</td><td>7.1</td></tr>
<tr><td>20</td><td>Vermont</td><td>8.5</td><td>45</td><td>Mississippi</td><td>7.0</td></tr>
<tr><td>39</td><td>Virginia</td><td>7.3</td><td>46</td><td>Nebraska</td><td>6.9</td></tr>
<tr><td>10</td><td>Washington</td><td>9.1</td><td>47</td><td>Iowa</td><td>6.6</td></tr>
<tr><td>2</td><td>West Virginia</td><td>10.1</td><td>47</td><td>South Dakota</td><td>6.6</td></tr>
<tr><td>20</td><td>Wisconsin</td><td>8.5</td><td>49</td><td>Louisiana</td><td>6.1</td></tr>
<tr><td>32</td><td>Wyoming</td><td>7.6</td><td>NA</td><td>Hawaii**</td><td>NA</td></tr>
<tr><td></td><td></td><td></td><td></td><td>District of Columbia</td><td>9.2</td></tr>
</table>

Source: U.S. Department of Health and Human Services, Centers for Disease Control and Prevention
    "2004 Behavioral Risk Factor Surveillance Summary Prevalence Data" (http://apps.nccd.cdc.gov/brfss/)
*Percent of adults who answered yes to the questions "Have you ever been told by a doctor, nurse or other health professional that you had asthma?" and "Do you still have asthma?"
**Not available.

Percent of Adults Who Have Been Told They Have Diabetes: 2004

National Median = 7.0% of Adults*

<table>
<tr><td colspan="3">ALPHA ORDER</td><td colspan="3">RANK ORDER</td></tr>
<tr><td>RANK</td><td>STATE</td><td>PERCENT</td><td>RANK</td><td>STATE</td><td>PERCENT</td></tr>
<tr><td>7</td><td>Alabama</td><td>8.1</td><td>1</td><td>West Virginia</td><td>10.9</td></tr>
<tr><td>49</td><td>Alaska</td><td>4.1</td><td>2</td><td>Mississippi</td><td>9.5</td></tr>
<tr><td>27</td><td>Arizona</td><td>6.6</td><td>3</td><td>North Carolina</td><td>8.4</td></tr>
<tr><td>22</td><td>Arkansas</td><td>7.0</td><td>3</td><td>Tennessee</td><td>8.4</td></tr>
<tr><td>22</td><td>California</td><td>7.0</td><td>5</td><td>Louisiana</td><td>8.2</td></tr>
<tr><td>48</td><td>Colorado</td><td>4.3</td><td>5</td><td>South Carolina</td><td>8.2</td></tr>
<tr><td>38</td><td>Connecticut</td><td>6.0</td><td>7</td><td>Alabama</td><td>8.1</td></tr>
<tr><td>22</td><td>Delaware</td><td>7.0</td><td>8</td><td>Oklahoma</td><td>8.0</td></tr>
<tr><td>11</td><td>Florida</td><td>7.7</td><td>9</td><td>Ohio</td><td>7.8</td></tr>
<tr><td>18</td><td>Georgia</td><td>7.3</td><td>9</td><td>Pennsylvania</td><td>7.8</td></tr>
<tr><td>NA</td><td>Hawaii**</td><td>NA</td><td>11</td><td>Florida</td><td>7.7</td></tr>
<tr><td>37</td><td>Idaho</td><td>6.1</td><td>11</td><td>Indiana</td><td>7.7</td></tr>
<tr><td>38</td><td>Illinois</td><td>6.0</td><td>13</td><td>Michigan</td><td>7.6</td></tr>
<tr><td>11</td><td>Indiana</td><td>7.7</td><td>13</td><td>Texas</td><td>7.6</td></tr>
<tr><td>32</td><td>Iowa</td><td>6.4</td><td>15</td><td>Kentucky</td><td>7.5</td></tr>
<tr><td>32</td><td>Kansas</td><td>6.4</td><td>15</td><td>New York</td><td>7.5</td></tr>
<tr><td>15</td><td>Kentucky</td><td>7.5</td><td>17</td><td>Maine</td><td>7.4</td></tr>
<tr><td>5</td><td>Louisiana</td><td>8.2</td><td>18</td><td>Georgia</td><td>7.3</td></tr>
<tr><td>17</td><td>Maine</td><td>7.4</td><td>19</td><td>Missouri</td><td>7.2</td></tr>
<tr><td>20</td><td>Maryland</td><td>7.1</td><td>20</td><td>Maryland</td><td>7.1</td></tr>
<tr><td>43</td><td>Massachusetts</td><td>5.6</td><td>20</td><td>Rhode Island</td><td>7.1</td></tr>
<tr><td>13</td><td>Michigan</td><td>7.6</td><td>22</td><td>Arkansas</td><td>7.0</td></tr>
<tr><td>46</td><td>Minnesota</td><td>5.0</td><td>22</td><td>California</td><td>7.0</td></tr>
<tr><td>2</td><td>Mississippi</td><td>9.5</td><td>22</td><td>Delaware</td><td>7.0</td></tr>
<tr><td>19</td><td>Missouri</td><td>7.2</td><td>22</td><td>Virginia</td><td>7.0</td></tr>
<tr><td>40</td><td>Montana</td><td>5.9</td><td>26</td><td>New Jersey</td><td>6.7</td></tr>
<tr><td>36</td><td>Nebraska</td><td>6.2</td><td>27</td><td>Arizona</td><td>6.6</td></tr>
<tr><td>32</td><td>Nevada</td><td>6.4</td><td>28</td><td>New Hampshire</td><td>6.5</td></tr>
<tr><td>28</td><td>New Hampshire</td><td>6.5</td><td>28</td><td>New Mexico</td><td>6.5</td></tr>
<tr><td>26</td><td>New Jersey</td><td>6.7</td><td>28</td><td>Oregon</td><td>6.5</td></tr>
<tr><td>28</td><td>New Mexico</td><td>6.5</td><td>28</td><td>South Dakota</td><td>6.5</td></tr>
<tr><td>15</td><td>New York</td><td>7.5</td><td>32</td><td>Iowa</td><td>6.4</td></tr>
<tr><td>3</td><td>North Carolina</td><td>8.4</td><td>32</td><td>Kansas</td><td>6.4</td></tr>
<tr><td>42</td><td>North Dakota</td><td>5.8</td><td>32</td><td>Nevada</td><td>6.4</td></tr>
<tr><td>9</td><td>Ohio</td><td>7.8</td><td>35</td><td>Washington</td><td>6.3</td></tr>
<tr><td>8</td><td>Oklahoma</td><td>8.0</td><td>36</td><td>Nebraska</td><td>6.2</td></tr>
<tr><td>28</td><td>Oregon</td><td>6.5</td><td>37</td><td>Idaho</td><td>6.1</td></tr>
<tr><td>9</td><td>Pennsylvania</td><td>7.8</td><td>38</td><td>Connecticut</td><td>6.0</td></tr>
<tr><td>20</td><td>Rhode Island</td><td>7.1</td><td>38</td><td>Illinois</td><td>6.0</td></tr>
<tr><td>5</td><td>South Carolina</td><td>8.2</td><td>40</td><td>Montana</td><td>5.9</td></tr>
<tr><td>28</td><td>South Dakota</td><td>6.5</td><td>40</td><td>Wyoming</td><td>5.9</td></tr>
<tr><td>3</td><td>Tennessee</td><td>8.4</td><td>42</td><td>North Dakota</td><td>5.8</td></tr>
<tr><td>13</td><td>Texas</td><td>7.6</td><td>43</td><td>Massachusetts</td><td>5.6</td></tr>
<tr><td>46</td><td>Utah</td><td>5.0</td><td>43</td><td>Wisconsin</td><td>5.6</td></tr>
<tr><td>45</td><td>Vermont</td><td>5.3</td><td>45</td><td>Vermont</td><td>5.3</td></tr>
<tr><td>22</td><td>Virginia</td><td>7.0</td><td>46</td><td>Minnesota</td><td>5.0</td></tr>
<tr><td>35</td><td>Washington</td><td>6.3</td><td>46</td><td>Utah</td><td>5.0</td></tr>
<tr><td>1</td><td>West Virginia</td><td>10.9</td><td>48</td><td>Colorado</td><td>4.3</td></tr>
<tr><td>43</td><td>Wisconsin</td><td>5.6</td><td>49</td><td>Alaska</td><td>4.1</td></tr>
<tr><td>40</td><td>Wyoming</td><td>5.9</td><td>NA</td><td>Hawaii**</td><td>NA</td></tr>
<tr><td></td><td></td><td></td><td></td><td>District of Columbia</td><td>8.2</td></tr>
</table>

Source: U.S. Department of Health and Human Services, Centers for Disease Control and Prevention
    "2004 Behavioral Risk Factor Surveillance Summary Prevalence Data" (http://apps.nccd.cdc.gov/brfss/)
*Of population 18 years old and older. Does not include pregnancy-related diabetes.
**Not available.

Percent of Population Reporting Serious Mental Illness: 2003

National Percent = 8.8% of Population*

ALPHA ORDER

RANK	STATE	PERCENT
16	Alabama	9.6
37	Alaska	8.5
17	Arizona	9.5
8	Arkansas	10.0
40	California	8.2
31	Colorado	8.7
41	Connecticut	8.1
28	Delaware	8.9
45	Florida	7.9
10	Georgia	9.8
50	Hawaii	7.2
4	Idaho	10.5
46	Illinois	7.8
21	Indiana	9.1
43	Iowa	8.0
21	Kansas	9.1
8	Kentucky	10.0
26	Louisiana	9.0
10	Maine	9.8
43	Maryland	8.0
31	Massachusetts	8.7
38	Michigan	8.4
29	Minnesota	8.8
31	Mississippi	8.7
6	Missouri	10.4
10	Montana	9.8
46	Nebraska	7.8
10	Nevada	9.8
29	New Hampshire	8.8
49	New Jersey	7.4
15	New Mexico	9.7
21	New York	9.1
17	North Carolina	9.5
26	North Dakota	9.0
19	Ohio	9.3
3	Oklahoma	10.9
10	Oregon	9.8
48	Pennsylvania	7.6
1	Rhode Island	11.0
21	South Carolina	9.1
35	South Dakota	8.6
21	Tennessee	9.1
38	Texas	8.4
1	Utah	11.0
35	Vermont	8.6
41	Virginia	8.1
4	Washington	10.5
7	West Virginia	10.3
31	Wisconsin	8.7
19	Wyoming	9.3

RANK ORDER

RANK	STATE	PERCENT
1	Rhode Island	11.0
1	Utah	11.0
3	Oklahoma	10.9
4	Idaho	10.5
4	Washington	10.5
6	Missouri	10.4
7	West Virginia	10.3
8	Arkansas	10.0
8	Kentucky	10.0
10	Georgia	9.8
10	Maine	9.8
10	Montana	9.8
10	Nevada	9.8
10	Oregon	9.8
15	New Mexico	9.7
16	Alabama	9.6
17	Arizona	9.5
17	North Carolina	9.5
19	Ohio	9.3
19	Wyoming	9.3
21	Indiana	9.1
21	Kansas	9.1
21	New York	9.1
21	South Carolina	9.1
21	Tennessee	9.1
26	Louisiana	9.0
26	North Dakota	9.0
28	Delaware	8.9
29	Minnesota	8.8
29	New Hampshire	8.8
31	Colorado	8.7
31	Massachusetts	8.7
31	Mississippi	8.7
31	Wisconsin	8.7
35	South Dakota	8.6
35	Vermont	8.6
37	Alaska	8.5
38	Michigan	8.4
38	Texas	8.4
40	California	8.2
41	Connecticut	8.1
41	Virginia	8.1
43	Iowa	8.0
43	Maryland	8.0
45	Florida	7.9
46	Illinois	7.8
46	Nebraska	7.8
48	Pennsylvania	7.6
49	New Jersey	7.4
50	Hawaii	7.2

District of Columbia 8.6

Source: U.S. Department of Health and Human Services, Substance Abuse and Mental Health Services Administration
      "2002-2003 National Surveys on Drug Use and Health" (January 2005)
*Population 12 years and older. Serious mental illness is defined as having a diagnosable mental, behavioral
or emotional disorder that resulted in functional impairment that substantially interfered with or limited one or more
major life activities.

VI. PROVIDERS

VI. PROVIDERS (continued)

Health Care Practitioners and Technicians in 2004

National Total = 6,360,520 Practitioners and Technicians*

ALPHA ORDER

RANK	STATE	PRACTITIONERS	% of USA
22	Alabama	102,720	1.6%
49	Alaska	11,880	0.2%
23	Arizona	98,260	1.5%
33	Arkansas	62,030	1.0%
1	California	581,330	9.1%
25	Colorado	91,740	1.4%
27	Connecticut	86,970	1.4%
46	Delaware	19,740	0.3%
4	Florida	377,840	5.9%
12	Georgia	173,880	2.7%
43	Hawaii	22,380	0.4%
42	Idaho	26,000	0.4%
7	Illinois	280,670	4.4%
14	Indiana	148,680	2.3%
29	Iowa	70,510	1.1%
31	Kansas	66,390	1.0%
24	Kentucky	95,340	1.5%
21	Louisiana	107,160	1.7%
39	Maine	33,530	0.5%
19	Maryland	128,950	2.0%
10	Massachusetts	186,370	2.9%
8	Michigan	222,550	3.5%
17	Minnesota	134,350	2.1%
32	Mississippi	63,100	1.0%
16	Missouri	147,230	2.3%
45	Montana	20,380	0.3%
35	Nebraska	47,660	0.7%
37	Nevada	36,400	0.6%
40	New Hampshire	29,890	0.5%
9	New Jersey	189,200	3.0%
38	New Mexico	35,980	0.6%
2	New York	432,490	6.8%
11	North Carolina	184,710	2.9%
47	North Dakota	17,940	0.3%
6	Ohio	289,360	4.5%
28	Oklahoma	76,370	1.2%
30	Oregon	67,490	1.1%
5	Pennsylvania	325,230	5.1%
41	Rhode Island	27,340	0.4%
26	South Carolina	89,550	1.4%
44	South Dakota	21,800	0.3%
15	Tennessee	147,570	2.3%
3	Texas	430,920	6.8%
34	Utah	48,070	0.8%
48	Vermont	14,900	0.2%
13	Virginia	152,390	2.4%
20	Washington	121,350	1.9%
36	West Virginia	44,500	0.7%
18	Wisconsin	131,120	2.1%
50	Wyoming	10,100	0.2%

RANK ORDER

RANK	STATE	PRACTITIONERS	% of USA
1	California	581,330	9.1%
2	New York	432,490	6.8%
3	Texas	430,920	6.8%
4	Florida	377,840	5.9%
5	Pennsylvania	325,230	5.1%
6	Ohio	289,360	4.5%
7	Illinois	280,670	4.4%
8	Michigan	222,550	3.5%
9	New Jersey	189,200	3.0%
10	Massachusetts	186,370	2.9%
11	North Carolina	184,710	2.9%
12	Georgia	173,880	2.7%
13	Virginia	152,390	2.4%
14	Indiana	148,680	2.3%
15	Tennessee	147,570	2.3%
16	Missouri	147,230	2.3%
17	Minnesota	134,350	2.1%
18	Wisconsin	131,120	2.1%
19	Maryland	128,950	2.0%
20	Washington	121,350	1.9%
21	Louisiana	107,160	1.7%
22	Alabama	102,720	1.6%
23	Arizona	98,260	1.5%
24	Kentucky	95,340	1.5%
25	Colorado	91,740	1.4%
26	South Carolina	89,550	1.4%
27	Connecticut	86,970	1.4%
28	Oklahoma	76,370	1.2%
29	Iowa	70,510	1.1%
30	Oregon	67,490	1.1%
31	Kansas	66,390	1.0%
32	Mississippi	63,100	1.0%
33	Arkansas	62,030	1.0%
34	Utah	48,070	0.8%
35	Nebraska	47,660	0.7%
36	West Virginia	44,500	0.7%
37	Nevada	36,400	0.6%
38	New Mexico	35,980	0.6%
39	Maine	33,530	0.5%
40	New Hampshire	29,890	0.5%
41	Rhode Island	27,340	0.4%
42	Idaho	26,000	0.4%
43	Hawaii	22,380	0.4%
44	South Dakota	21,800	0.3%
45	Montana	20,380	0.3%
46	Delaware	19,740	0.3%
47	North Dakota	17,940	0.3%
48	Vermont	14,900	0.2%
49	Alaska	11,880	0.2%
50	Wyoming	10,100	0.2%
	District of Columbia	28,480	0.4%

Source: U.S. Department of Labor, Bureau of Labor Statistics
    "Occupational Employment and Wages, 2004" (http://www.bls.gov/oes/)
*Does not include self-employed. Includes various doctors, dentists, nurses, therapists, optometrists, paramedics
and technicians. Does not include assistants and aides listed under health care support occupations.
Veterinarians and veterinarian technicians have been subtracted from the totals.

Rate of Health Care Practitioners and Technicians in 2004

National Rate = 2,166 Practitioners and Technicians per 100,000 Population*

ALPHA ORDER

RANK	STATE	RATE
24	Alabama	2,270
46	Alaska	1,806
48	Arizona	1,712
25	Arkansas	2,256
49	California	1,622
38	Colorado	1,994
12	Connecticut	2,486
19	Delaware	2,378
32	Florida	2,173
41	Georgia	1,950
47	Hawaii	1,773
45	Idaho	1,864
27	Illinois	2,208
16	Indiana	2,388
16	Iowa	2,388
14	Kansas	2,429
22	Kentucky	2,302
19	Louisiana	2,378
8	Maine	2,550
21	Maryland	2,319
1	Massachusetts	2,909
28	Michigan	2,203
5	Minnesota	2,636
31	Mississippi	2,175
7	Missouri	2,556
29	Montana	2,199
4	Nebraska	2,727
50	Nevada	1,560
23	New Hampshire	2,301
30	New Jersey	2,178
43	New Mexico	1,891
26	New York	2,243
34	North Carolina	2,163
3	North Dakota	2,819
10	Ohio	2,527
33	Oklahoma	2,167
44	Oregon	1,879
6	Pennsylvania	2,624
9	Rhode Island	2,532
35	South Carolina	2,133
2	South Dakota	2,829
11	Tennessee	2,504
42	Texas	1,918
39	Utah	1,986
15	Vermont	2,398
36	Virginia	2,037
40	Washington	1,955
13	West Virginia	2,455
18	Wisconsin	2,382
37	Wyoming	1,996

RANK ORDER

RANK	STATE	RATE
1	Massachusetts	2,909
2	South Dakota	2,829
3	North Dakota	2,819
4	Nebraska	2,727
5	Minnesota	2,636
6	Pennsylvania	2,624
7	Missouri	2,556
8	Maine	2,550
9	Rhode Island	2,532
10	Ohio	2,527
11	Tennessee	2,504
12	Connecticut	2,486
13	West Virginia	2,455
14	Kansas	2,429
15	Vermont	2,398
16	Indiana	2,388
16	Iowa	2,388
18	Wisconsin	2,382
19	Delaware	2,378
19	Louisiana	2,378
21	Maryland	2,319
22	Kentucky	2,302
23	New Hampshire	2,301
24	Alabama	2,270
25	Arkansas	2,256
26	New York	2,243
27	Illinois	2,208
28	Michigan	2,203
29	Montana	2,199
30	New Jersey	2,178
31	Mississippi	2,175
32	Florida	2,173
33	Oklahoma	2,167
34	North Carolina	2,163
35	South Carolina	2,133
36	Virginia	2,037
37	Wyoming	1,996
38	Colorado	1,994
39	Utah	1,986
40	Washington	1,955
41	Georgia	1,950
42	Texas	1,918
43	New Mexico	1,891
44	Oregon	1,879
45	Idaho	1,864
46	Alaska	1,806
47	Hawaii	1,773
48	Arizona	1,712
49	California	1,622
50	Nevada	1,560

	District of Columbia	5,139

Source: Morgan Quitno Press using data from U.S. Department of Labor, Bureau of Labor Statistics
    "Occupational Employment and Wages, 2004" (http://www.bls.gov/oes/)
*Does not include self-employed. Includes various doctors, dentists, nurses, therapists, optometrists, paramedics and technicians. Does not include assistants and aides listed under health care support occupations. Veterinarians and veterinarian technicians have been subtracted from the totals.

Average Annual Wages of Health Care Practitioners and Technicians in 2004

National Average = $58,310*

ALPHA ORDER

RANK	STATE	WAGES
46	Alabama	$48,590
5	Alaska	65,900
19	Arizona	58,770
47	Arkansas	48,540
1	California	68,640
15	Colorado	61,480
7	Connecticut	65,350
13	Delaware	62,160
25	Florida	56,980
31	Georgia	53,900
4	Hawaii	66,160
39	Idaho	51,140
37	Illinois	51,650
36	Indiana	52,270
45	Iowa	49,510
40	Kansas	51,110
42	Kentucky	49,760
43	Louisiana	49,720
21	Maine	58,370
3	Maryland	66,510
9	Massachusetts	63,130
12	Michigan	62,190
11	Minnesota	62,240
48	Mississippi	48,160
34	Missouri	52,740
49	Montana	47,360
35	Nebraska	52,610
5	Nevada	65,900
16	New Hampshire	60,100
2	New Jersey	67,900
27	New Mexico	56,540
8	New York	65,070
28	North Carolina	55,530
41	North Dakota	50,220
20	Ohio	58,600
50	Oklahoma	46,890
10	Oregon	62,710
29	Pennsylvania	54,060
17	Rhode Island	60,080
32	South Carolina	53,640
38	South Dakota	51,540
44	Tennessee	49,620
26	Texas	56,580
22	Utah	57,490
18	Vermont	59,470
23	Virginia	57,400
14	Washington	61,760
33	West Virginia	52,770
24	Wisconsin	57,220
30	Wyoming	53,960

RANK ORDER

RANK	STATE	WAGES
1	California	$68,640
2	New Jersey	67,900
3	Maryland	66,510
4	Hawaii	66,160
5	Alaska	65,900
5	Nevada	65,900
7	Connecticut	65,350
8	New York	65,070
9	Massachusetts	63,130
10	Oregon	62,710
11	Minnesota	62,240
12	Michigan	62,190
13	Delaware	62,160
14	Washington	61,760
15	Colorado	61,480
16	New Hampshire	60,100
17	Rhode Island	60,080
18	Vermont	59,470
19	Arizona	58,770
20	Ohio	58,600
21	Maine	58,370
22	Utah	57,490
23	Virginia	57,400
24	Wisconsin	57,220
25	Florida	56,980
26	Texas	56,580
27	New Mexico	56,540
28	North Carolina	55,530
29	Pennsylvania	54,060
30	Wyoming	53,960
31	Georgia	53,900
32	South Carolina	53,640
33	West Virginia	52,770
34	Missouri	52,740
35	Nebraska	52,610
36	Indiana	52,270
37	Illinois	51,650
38	South Dakota	51,540
39	Idaho	51,140
40	Kansas	51,110
41	North Dakota	50,220
42	Kentucky	49,760
43	Louisiana	49,720
44	Tennessee	49,620
45	Iowa	49,510
46	Alabama	48,590
47	Arkansas	48,540
48	Mississippi	48,160
49	Montana	47,360
50	Oklahoma	46,890
	District of Columbia	64,590

Source: U.S. Department of Labor, Bureau of Labor Statistics
"Occupational Employment and Wages, 2004" (http://www.bls.gov/oes/)
*Does not include self-employed. Includes various doctors, dentists, nurses, therapists, optometrists, paramedics and technicians. Does not include assistants and aides listed under health care support occupations.

Physicians in 2004

National Total = 872,267 Physicians*

ALPHA ORDER

RANK	STATE	PHYSICIANS	% of USA
27	Alabama	10,564	1.2%
49	Alaska	1,580	0.2%
22	Arizona	14,012	1.6%
32	Arkansas	6,202	0.7%
1	California	105,766	12.1%
23	Colorado	13,455	1.5%
21	Connecticut	14,044	1.6%
46	Delaware	2,325	0.3%
4	Florida	51,025	5.8%
14	Georgia	21,639	2.5%
39	Hawaii	4,433	0.5%
43	Idaho	2,693	0.3%
6	Illinois	37,908	4.3%
20	Indiana	14,696	1.7%
31	Iowa	6,288	0.7%
29	Kansas	6,870	0.8%
28	Kentucky	10,464	1.2%
24	Louisiana	12,999	1.5%
41	Maine	4,052	0.5%
11	Maryland	25,098	2.9%
8	Massachusetts	31,216	3.6%
10	Michigan	26,999	3.1%
17	Minnesota	15,952	1.8%
33	Mississippi	5,872	0.7%
19	Missouri	15,026	1.7%
45	Montana	2,425	0.3%
37	Nebraska	4,672	0.5%
36	Nevada	4,934	0.6%
42	New Hampshire	3,884	0.4%
9	New Jersey	29,248	3.4%
35	New Mexico	5,169	0.6%
2	New York	81,716	9.4%
12	North Carolina	24,087	2.8%
48	North Dakota	1,716	0.2%
7	Ohio	33,103	3.8%
30	Oklahoma	6,846	0.8%
25	Oregon	10,957	1.3%
5	Pennsylvania	40,832	4.7%
40	Rhode Island	4,141	0.5%
26	South Carolina	10,762	1.2%
47	South Dakota	1,904	0.2%
16	Tennessee	16,863	1.9%
3	Texas	52,060	6.0%
34	Utah	5,643	0.6%
44	Vermont	2,589	0.3%
13	Virginia	22,587	2.6%
15	Washington	18,894	2.2%
38	West Virginia	4,613	0.5%
18	Wisconsin	15,625	1.8%
50	Wyoming	1,094	0.1%

RANK ORDER

RANK	STATE	PHYSICIANS	% of USA
1	California	105,766	12.1%
2	New York	81,716	9.4%
3	Texas	52,060	6.0%
4	Florida	51,025	5.8%
5	Pennsylvania	40,832	4.7%
6	Illinois	37,908	4.3%
7	Ohio	33,103	3.8%
8	Massachusetts	31,216	3.6%
9	New Jersey	29,248	3.4%
10	Michigan	26,999	3.1%
11	Maryland	25,098	2.9%
12	North Carolina	24,087	2.8%
13	Virginia	22,587	2.6%
14	Georgia	21,639	2.5%
15	Washington	18,894	2.2%
16	Tennessee	16,863	1.9%
17	Minnesota	15,952	1.8%
18	Wisconsin	15,625	1.8%
19	Missouri	15,026	1.7%
20	Indiana	14,696	1.7%
21	Connecticut	14,044	1.6%
22	Arizona	14,012	1.6%
23	Colorado	13,455	1.5%
24	Louisiana	12,999	1.5%
25	Oregon	10,957	1.3%
26	South Carolina	10,762	1.2%
27	Alabama	10,564	1.2%
28	Kentucky	10,464	1.2%
29	Kansas	6,870	0.8%
30	Oklahoma	6,846	0.8%
31	Iowa	6,288	0.7%
32	Arkansas	6,202	0.7%
33	Mississippi	5,872	0.7%
34	Utah	5,643	0.6%
35	New Mexico	5,169	0.6%
36	Nevada	4,934	0.6%
37	Nebraska	4,672	0.5%
38	West Virginia	4,613	0.5%
39	Hawaii	4,433	0.5%
40	Rhode Island	4,141	0.5%
41	Maine	4,052	0.5%
42	New Hampshire	3,884	0.4%
43	Idaho	2,693	0.3%
44	Vermont	2,589	0.3%
45	Montana	2,425	0.3%
46	Delaware	2,325	0.3%
47	South Dakota	1,904	0.2%
48	North Dakota	1,716	0.2%
49	Alaska	1,580	0.2%
50	Wyoming	1,094	0.1%
	District of Columbia	4,725	0.5%

Source: American Medical Association (Chicago, Illinois)
   "Physician Characteristics and Distribution in the U.S." (2006 Edition)
As of December 31, 2004. Total does not include 12,707 physicians in the U.S. territories and possessions, at APO's and FPO's and whose addresses are unknown.

Rate of Physicians in 2004

National Rate = 297 Physicians per 100,000 Population*

<table>
<tr><td colspan="3">ALPHA ORDER</td><td colspan="3">RANK ORDER</td></tr>
<tr><th>RANK</th><th>STATE</th><th>RATE</th><th>RANK</th><th>STATE</th><th>RATE</th></tr>
<tr><td>42</td><td>Alabama</td><td>233</td><td>1</td><td>Massachusetts</td><td>486</td></tr>
<tr><td>39</td><td>Alaska</td><td>241</td><td>2</td><td>Maryland</td><td>452</td></tr>
<tr><td>38</td><td>Arizona</td><td>244</td><td>3</td><td>New York</td><td>425</td></tr>
<tr><td>44</td><td>Arkansas</td><td>225</td><td>4</td><td>Vermont</td><td>417</td></tr>
<tr><td>17</td><td>California</td><td>295</td><td>5</td><td>Connecticut</td><td>401</td></tr>
<tr><td>19</td><td>Colorado</td><td>292</td><td>6</td><td>Rhode Island</td><td>383</td></tr>
<tr><td>5</td><td>Connecticut</td><td>401</td><td>7</td><td>Hawaii</td><td>351</td></tr>
<tr><td>25</td><td>Delaware</td><td>280</td><td>8</td><td>New Jersey</td><td>336</td></tr>
<tr><td>18</td><td>Florida</td><td>293</td><td>9</td><td>Pennsylvania</td><td>329</td></tr>
<tr><td>37</td><td>Georgia</td><td>245</td><td>10</td><td>Minnesota</td><td>313</td></tr>
<tr><td>7</td><td>Hawaii</td><td>351</td><td>11</td><td>Maine</td><td>308</td></tr>
<tr><td>50</td><td>Idaho</td><td>193</td><td>12</td><td>Oregon</td><td>305</td></tr>
<tr><td>16</td><td>Illinois</td><td>298</td><td>12</td><td>Washington</td><td>305</td></tr>
<tr><td>40</td><td>Indiana</td><td>236</td><td>14</td><td>Virginia</td><td>303</td></tr>
<tr><td>46</td><td>Iowa</td><td>213</td><td>15</td><td>New Hampshire</td><td>299</td></tr>
<tr><td>35</td><td>Kansas</td><td>251</td><td>16</td><td>Illinois</td><td>298</td></tr>
<tr><td>34</td><td>Kentucky</td><td>252</td><td>17</td><td>California</td><td>295</td></tr>
<tr><td>21</td><td>Louisiana</td><td>288</td><td>18</td><td>Florida</td><td>293</td></tr>
<tr><td>11</td><td>Maine</td><td>308</td><td>19</td><td>Colorado</td><td>292</td></tr>
<tr><td>2</td><td>Maryland</td><td>452</td><td>20</td><td>Ohio</td><td>289</td></tr>
<tr><td>1</td><td>Massachusetts</td><td>486</td><td>21</td><td>Louisiana</td><td>288</td></tr>
<tr><td>28</td><td>Michigan</td><td>267</td><td>22</td><td>Tennessee</td><td>286</td></tr>
<tr><td>10</td><td>Minnesota</td><td>313</td><td>23</td><td>Wisconsin</td><td>284</td></tr>
<tr><td>48</td><td>Mississippi</td><td>202</td><td>24</td><td>North Carolina</td><td>282</td></tr>
<tr><td>31</td><td>Missouri</td><td>261</td><td>25</td><td>Delaware</td><td>280</td></tr>
<tr><td>30</td><td>Montana</td><td>262</td><td>26</td><td>New Mexico</td><td>272</td></tr>
<tr><td>28</td><td>Nebraska</td><td>267</td><td>27</td><td>North Dakota</td><td>271</td></tr>
<tr><td>47</td><td>Nevada</td><td>211</td><td>28</td><td>Michigan</td><td>267</td></tr>
<tr><td>15</td><td>New Hampshire</td><td>299</td><td>28</td><td>Nebraska</td><td>267</td></tr>
<tr><td>8</td><td>New Jersey</td><td>336</td><td>30</td><td>Montana</td><td>262</td></tr>
<tr><td>26</td><td>New Mexico</td><td>272</td><td>31</td><td>Missouri</td><td>261</td></tr>
<tr><td>3</td><td>New York</td><td>425</td><td>32</td><td>South Carolina</td><td>256</td></tr>
<tr><td>24</td><td>North Carolina</td><td>282</td><td>33</td><td>West Virginia</td><td>254</td></tr>
<tr><td>27</td><td>North Dakota</td><td>271</td><td>34</td><td>Kentucky</td><td>252</td></tr>
<tr><td>20</td><td>Ohio</td><td>289</td><td>35</td><td>Kansas</td><td>251</td></tr>
<tr><td>49</td><td>Oklahoma</td><td>194</td><td>36</td><td>South Dakota</td><td>247</td></tr>
<tr><td>12</td><td>Oregon</td><td>305</td><td>37</td><td>Georgia</td><td>245</td></tr>
<tr><td>9</td><td>Pennsylvania</td><td>329</td><td>38</td><td>Arizona</td><td>244</td></tr>
<tr><td>6</td><td>Rhode Island</td><td>383</td><td>39</td><td>Alaska</td><td>241</td></tr>
<tr><td>32</td><td>South Carolina</td><td>256</td><td>40</td><td>Indiana</td><td>236</td></tr>
<tr><td>36</td><td>South Dakota</td><td>247</td><td>40</td><td>Utah</td><td>236</td></tr>
<tr><td>22</td><td>Tennessee</td><td>286</td><td>42</td><td>Alabama</td><td>233</td></tr>
<tr><td>43</td><td>Texas</td><td>231</td><td>43</td><td>Texas</td><td>231</td></tr>
<tr><td>40</td><td>Utah</td><td>236</td><td>44</td><td>Arkansas</td><td>225</td></tr>
<tr><td>4</td><td>Vermont</td><td>417</td><td>45</td><td>Wyoming</td><td>216</td></tr>
<tr><td>14</td><td>Virginia</td><td>303</td><td>46</td><td>Iowa</td><td>213</td></tr>
<tr><td>12</td><td>Washington</td><td>305</td><td>47</td><td>Nevada</td><td>211</td></tr>
<tr><td>33</td><td>West Virginia</td><td>254</td><td>48</td><td>Mississippi</td><td>202</td></tr>
<tr><td>23</td><td>Wisconsin</td><td>284</td><td>49</td><td>Oklahoma</td><td>194</td></tr>
<tr><td>45</td><td>Wyoming</td><td>216</td><td>50</td><td>Idaho</td><td>193</td></tr>
<tr><td></td><td></td><td></td><td></td><td>District of Columbia</td><td>854</td></tr>
</table>

Source: Morgan Quitno Press using data from American Medical Association (Chicago, Illinois)
"Physician Characteristics and Distribution in the U.S." (2006 Edition)
*As of December 31, 2004. National rate does not include physicians in the U.S. territories and possessions, at APO's and FPO's and whose addresses are unknown.

Percent of Physicians Who Are Female: 2004

National Percent = 26.6% of Physicians*

RANK	STATE	PERCENT	RANK	STATE	PERCENT
41	Alabama	20.9	1	Massachusetts	32.7
8	Alaska	28.8	2	Maryland	31.1
30	Arizona	23.9	3	New York	30.8
42	Arkansas	20.7	4	Illinois	30.5
17	California	26.9	5	New Jersey	30.2
13	Colorado	27.7	5	Rhode Island	30.2
11	Connecticut	27.9	7	New Mexico	29.4
8	Delaware	28.8	8	Alaska	28.8
45	Florida	20.6	8	Delaware	28.8
26	Georgia	25.3	10	Vermont	28.7
21	Hawaii	26.3	11	Connecticut	27.9
50	Idaho	17.0	11	Michigan	27.9
4	Illinois	30.5	13	Colorado	27.7
31	Indiana	23.7	14	Virginia	27.6
35	Iowa	21.9	15	Minnesota	27.3
29	Kansas	24.0	16	Pennsylvania	27.1
31	Kentucky	23.7	17	California	26.9
33	Louisiana	23.5	18	Ohio	26.8
22	Maine	25.7	18	Washington	26.8
2	Maryland	31.1	20	Oregon	26.4
1	Massachusetts	32.7	21	Hawaii	26.3
11	Michigan	27.9	22	Maine	25.7
15	Minnesota	27.3	23	North Carolina	25.6
46	Mississippi	19.4	24	Missouri	25.5
24	Missouri	25.5	25	Texas	25.4
46	Montana	19.4	26	Georgia	25.3
34	Nebraska	23.2	26	New Hampshire	25.3
39	Nevada	21.3	26	Wisconsin	25.3
26	New Hampshire	25.3	29	Kansas	24.0
5	New Jersey	30.2	30	Arizona	23.9
7	New Mexico	29.4	31	Indiana	23.7
3	New York	30.8	31	Kentucky	23.7
23	North Carolina	25.6	33	Louisiana	23.5
42	North Dakota	20.7	34	Nebraska	23.2
18	Ohio	26.8	35	Iowa	21.9
40	Oklahoma	21.0	36	Tennessee	21.6
20	Oregon	26.4	37	West Virginia	21.5
16	Pennsylvania	27.1	38	South Carolina	21.4
5	Rhode Island	30.2	39	Nevada	21.3
38	South Carolina	21.4	40	Oklahoma	21.0
42	South Dakota	20.7	41	Alabama	20.9
36	Tennessee	21.6	42	Arkansas	20.7
25	Texas	25.4	42	North Dakota	20.7
48	Utah	19.3	42	South Dakota	20.7
10	Vermont	28.7	45	Florida	20.6
14	Virginia	27.6	46	Mississippi	19.4
18	Washington	26.8	46	Montana	19.4
37	West Virginia	21.5	48	Utah	19.3
26	Wisconsin	25.3	49	Wyoming	18.5
49	Wyoming	18.5	50	Idaho	17.0

| | | | | District of Columbia | 34.1 |

*Source: Morgan Quitno Press using data from American Medical Association (Chicago, Illinois)
"Physician Characteristics and Distribution in the U.S." (2006 Edition)*
As of December 31, 2004. National percent does not include physicians in the U.S. territories and possessions, at APO's and FPO's and whose addresses are unknown.

Percent of Physicians Under 35 Years Old in 2004

National Percent = 16.1% of Physicians*

ALPHA ORDER

RANK	STATE	PERCENT
22	Alabama	15.5
47	Alaska	8.6
40	Arizona	11.8
16	Arkansas	16.2
32	California	13.8
35	Colorado	13.4
15	Connecticut	16.3
24	Delaware	15.4
45	Florida	10.0
30	Georgia	14.7
37	Hawaii	13.0
48	Idaho	6.7
1	Illinois	20.9
24	Indiana	15.4
14	Iowa	16.9
28	Kansas	14.9
21	Kentucky	15.6
8	Louisiana	19.0
46	Maine	9.6
16	Maryland	16.2
2	Massachusetts	20.2
6	Michigan	19.6
11	Minnesota	17.3
31	Mississippi	14.3
6	Missouri	19.6
50	Montana	4.8
9	Nebraska	18.5
43	Nevada	10.5
42	New Hampshire	10.8
32	New Jersey	13.8
36	New Mexico	13.1
3	New York	20.0
12	North Carolina	17.2
38	North Dakota	12.7
4	Ohio	19.9
32	Oklahoma	13.8
41	Oregon	11.5
10	Pennsylvania	17.7
5	Rhode Island	19.7
16	South Carolina	16.2
43	South Dakota	10.5
22	Tennessee	15.5
12	Texas	17.2
26	Utah	15.2
27	Vermont	15.1
19	Virginia	16.1
39	Washington	11.9
20	West Virginia	15.8
29	Wisconsin	14.8
49	Wyoming	6.0

RANK ORDER

RANK	STATE	PERCENT
1	Illinois	20.9
2	Massachusetts	20.2
3	New York	20.0
4	Ohio	19.9
5	Rhode Island	19.7
6	Michigan	19.6
6	Missouri	19.6
8	Louisiana	19.0
9	Nebraska	18.5
10	Pennsylvania	17.7
11	Minnesota	17.3
12	North Carolina	17.2
12	Texas	17.2
14	Iowa	16.9
15	Connecticut	16.3
16	Arkansas	16.2
16	Maryland	16.2
16	South Carolina	16.2
19	Virginia	16.1
20	West Virginia	15.8
21	Kentucky	15.6
22	Alabama	15.5
22	Tennessee	15.5
24	Delaware	15.4
24	Indiana	15.4
26	Utah	15.2
27	Vermont	15.1
28	Kansas	14.9
29	Wisconsin	14.8
30	Georgia	14.7
31	Mississippi	14.3
32	California	13.8
32	New Jersey	13.8
32	Oklahoma	13.8
35	Colorado	13.4
36	New Mexico	13.1
37	Hawaii	13.0
38	North Dakota	12.7
39	Washington	11.9
40	Arizona	11.8
41	Oregon	11.5
42	New Hampshire	10.8
43	Nevada	10.5
43	South Dakota	10.5
45	Florida	10.0
46	Maine	9.6
47	Alaska	8.6
48	Idaho	6.7
49	Wyoming	6.0
50	Montana	4.8

	District of Columbia	23.8

Source: Morgan Quitno Press using data from American Medical Association (Chicago, Illinois)
   "Physician Characteristics and Distribution in the U.S." (2006 Edition)
*As of December 31, 2004. National percent does not include physicians in the U.S. territories and possessions, at APO's and FPO's and whose addresses are unknown.

Percent of Physicians 65 Years Old and Older in 2004

National Percent = 18.3% of Physicians*

RANK	STATE	PERCENT	RANK	STATE	PERCENT
46	Alabama	15.5	1	Florida	25.5
50	Alaska	13.3	2	Montana	21.8
3	Arizona	21.7	3	Arizona	21.7
31	Arkansas	16.8	3	California	21.7
3	California	21.7	5	Maine	21.2
26	Colorado	17.7	6	Nevada	20.4
17	Connecticut	18.7	7	Idaho	20.1
14	Delaware	19.2	7	Wyoming	20.1
1	Florida	25.5	9	New Hampshire	20.0
45	Georgia	15.6	10	Vermont	19.8
12	Hawaii	19.3	11	Oregon	19.5
7	Idaho	20.1	12	Hawaii	19.3
46	Illinois	15.5	12	Oklahoma	19.3
35	Indiana	16.2	14	Delaware	19.2
31	Iowa	16.8	15	Washington	18.9
16	Kansas	18.8	16	Kansas	18.8
43	Kentucky	15.7	17	Connecticut	18.7
33	Louisiana	16.6	18	New York	18.6
5	Maine	21.2	19	New Jersey	18.3
25	Maryland	17.9	19	Pennsylvania	18.3
36	Massachusetts	16.0	21	Virginia	18.2
28	Michigan	17.2	21	West Virginia	18.2
46	Minnesota	15.5	23	Mississippi	18.1
23	Mississippi	18.1	24	Rhode Island	18.0
49	Missouri	15.2	25	Maryland	17.9
2	Montana	21.8	26	Colorado	17.7
39	Nebraska	15.8	27	New Mexico	17.3
6	Nevada	20.4	28	Michigan	17.2
9	New Hampshire	20.0	29	South Carolina	17.0
19	New Jersey	18.3	30	Ohio	16.9
27	New Mexico	17.3	31	Arkansas	16.8
18	New York	18.6	31	Iowa	16.8
38	North Carolina	15.9	33	Louisiana	16.6
39	North Dakota	15.8	34	Wisconsin	16.3
30	Ohio	16.9	35	Indiana	16.2
12	Oklahoma	19.3	36	Massachusetts	16.0
11	Oregon	19.5	36	South Dakota	16.0
19	Pennsylvania	18.3	38	North Carolina	15.9
24	Rhode Island	18.0	39	Nebraska	15.8
29	South Carolina	17.0	39	North Dakota	15.8
36	South Dakota	16.0	39	Tennessee	15.8
39	Tennessee	15.8	39	Utah	15.8
43	Texas	15.7	43	Kentucky	15.7
39	Utah	15.8	43	Texas	15.7
10	Vermont	19.8	45	Georgia	15.6
21	Virginia	18.2	46	Alabama	15.5
15	Washington	18.9	46	Illinois	15.5
21	West Virginia	18.2	46	Minnesota	15.5
34	Wisconsin	16.3	49	Missouri	15.2
7	Wyoming	20.1	50	Alaska	13.3

District of Columbia   18.7

Source: Morgan Quitno Press using data from American Medical Association (Chicago, Illinois)
"Physician Characteristics and Distribution in the U.S." (2006 Edition)
*As of December 31, 2004. National percent does not include physicians in the U.S. territories and possessions, at APO's and FPO's and whose addresses are unknown.

Physicians in Patient Care in 2004

National Total = 691,251 Physicians*

ALPHA ORDER

RANK	STATE	PHYSICIANS	% of USA
25	Alabama	8,833	1.3%
49	Alaska	1,347	0.2%
22	Arizona	10,856	1.6%
31	Arkansas	5,214	0.8%
1	California	82,143	11.9%
24	Colorado	10,732	1.6%
21	Connecticut	10,970	1.6%
46	Delaware	1,847	0.3%
4	Florida	38,675	5.6%
14	Georgia	17,700	2.6%
39	Hawaii	3,552	0.5%
43	Idaho	2,239	0.3%
6	Illinois	30,696	4.4%
20	Indiana	12,223	1.8%
32	Iowa	4,915	0.7%
30	Kansas	5,491	0.8%
27	Kentucky	8,712	1.3%
23	Louisiana	10,809	1.6%
41	Maine	3,157	0.5%
12	Maryland	18,827	2.7%
8	Massachusetts	24,000	3.5%
10	Michigan	21,588	3.1%
17	Minnesota	12,925	1.9%
33	Mississippi	4,873	0.7%
19	Missouri	12,317	1.8%
45	Montana	1,938	0.3%
37	Nebraska	3,779	0.5%
36	Nevada	4,011	0.6%
42	New Hampshire	3,075	0.4%
9	New Jersey	23,287	3.4%
35	New Mexico	4,044	0.6%
2	New York	63,517	9.2%
11	North Carolina	19,272	2.8%
48	North Dakota	1,400	0.2%
7	Ohio	26,376	3.8%
29	Oklahoma	5,509	0.8%
28	Oregon	8,510	1.2%
5	Pennsylvania	31,741	4.6%
40	Rhode Island	3,323	0.5%
26	South Carolina	8,816	1.3%
47	South Dakota	1,568	0.2%
16	Tennessee	13,839	2.0%
3	Texas	42,506	6.1%
34	Utah	4,539	0.7%
44	Vermont	1,978	0.3%
13	Virginia	18,065	2.6%
15	Washington	14,630	2.1%
38	West Virginia	3,706	0.5%
18	Wisconsin	12,721	1.8%
50	Wyoming	895	0.1%

RANK ORDER

RANK	STATE	PHYSICIANS	% of USA
1	California	82,143	11.9%
2	New York	63,517	9.2%
3	Texas	42,506	6.1%
4	Florida	38,675	5.6%
5	Pennsylvania	31,741	4.6%
6	Illinois	30,696	4.4%
7	Ohio	26,376	3.8%
8	Massachusetts	24,000	3.5%
9	New Jersey	23,287	3.4%
10	Michigan	21,588	3.1%
11	North Carolina	19,272	2.8%
12	Maryland	18,827	2.7%
13	Virginia	18,065	2.6%
14	Georgia	17,700	2.6%
15	Washington	14,630	2.1%
16	Tennessee	13,839	2.0%
17	Minnesota	12,925	1.9%
18	Wisconsin	12,721	1.8%
19	Missouri	12,317	1.8%
20	Indiana	12,223	1.8%
21	Connecticut	10,970	1.6%
22	Arizona	10,856	1.6%
23	Louisiana	10,809	1.6%
24	Colorado	10,732	1.6%
25	Alabama	8,833	1.3%
26	South Carolina	8,816	1.3%
27	Kentucky	8,712	1.3%
28	Oregon	8,510	1.2%
29	Oklahoma	5,509	0.8%
30	Kansas	5,491	0.8%
31	Arkansas	5,214	0.8%
32	Iowa	4,915	0.7%
33	Mississippi	4,873	0.7%
34	Utah	4,539	0.7%
35	New Mexico	4,044	0.6%
36	Nevada	4,011	0.6%
37	Nebraska	3,779	0.5%
38	West Virginia	3,706	0.5%
39	Hawaii	3,552	0.5%
40	Rhode Island	3,323	0.5%
41	Maine	3,157	0.5%
42	New Hampshire	3,075	0.4%
43	Idaho	2,239	0.3%
44	Vermont	1,978	0.3%
45	Montana	1,938	0.3%
46	Delaware	1,847	0.3%
47	South Dakota	1,568	0.2%
48	North Dakota	1,400	0.2%
49	Alaska	1,347	0.2%
50	Wyoming	895	0.1%
	District of Columbia	3,565	0.5%

Source: American Medical Association (Chicago, Illinois)
   "Physician Characteristics and Distribution in the U.S." (2006 Edition)
*As of December 31, 2004. Total does not include 9,036 physicians in U.S. territories and possessions.

Rate of Physicians in Patient Care in 2004

National Rate = 235 Physicians per 100,000 Population*

ALPHA ORDER

RANK	STATE	RATE
40	Alabama	195
34	Alaska	206
42	Arizona	189
42	Arkansas	189
22	California	229
19	Colorado	233
5	Connecticut	313
24	Delaware	222
24	Florida	222
38	Georgia	200
7	Hawaii	281
49	Idaho	161
12	Illinois	241
39	Indiana	196
48	Iowa	166
37	Kansas	201
31	Kentucky	210
14	Louisiana	239
13	Maine	240
2	Maryland	339
1	Massachusetts	374
29	Michigan	213
10	Minnesota	253
47	Mississippi	168
28	Missouri	214
33	Montana	209
27	Nebraska	216
46	Nevada	172
15	New Hampshire	237
8	New Jersey	268
30	New Mexico	212
3	New York	330
23	North Carolina	226
26	North Dakota	221
21	Ohio	230
50	Oklahoma	156
15	Oregon	237
9	Pennsylvania	256
6	Rhode Island	308
31	South Carolina	210
36	South Dakota	203
18	Tennessee	235
42	Texas	189
41	Utah	190
4	Vermont	318
11	Virginia	242
17	Washington	236
35	West Virginia	204
20	Wisconsin	231
45	Wyoming	177

RANK ORDER

RANK	STATE	RATE
1	Massachusetts	374
2	Maryland	339
3	New York	330
4	Vermont	318
5	Connecticut	313
6	Rhode Island	308
7	Hawaii	281
8	New Jersey	268
9	Pennsylvania	256
10	Minnesota	253
11	Virginia	242
12	Illinois	241
13	Maine	240
14	Louisiana	239
15	New Hampshire	237
15	Oregon	237
17	Washington	236
18	Tennessee	235
19	Colorado	233
20	Wisconsin	231
21	Ohio	230
22	California	229
23	North Carolina	226
24	Delaware	222
24	Florida	222
26	North Dakota	221
27	Nebraska	216
28	Missouri	214
29	Michigan	213
30	New Mexico	212
31	Kentucky	210
31	South Carolina	210
33	Montana	209
34	Alaska	206
35	West Virginia	204
36	South Dakota	203
37	Kansas	201
38	Georgia	200
39	Indiana	196
40	Alabama	195
41	Utah	190
42	Arizona	189
42	Arkansas	189
42	Texas	189
45	Wyoming	177
46	Nevada	172
47	Mississippi	168
48	Iowa	166
49	Idaho	161
50	Oklahoma	156

	District of Columbia	644

Source: Morgan Quitno Press using data from American Medical Association (Chicago, Illinois)
    "Physician Characteristics and Distribution in the U.S." (2006 Edition)
*As of December 31, 2004. National rate does not include physicians in U.S. territories and possessions.

Physicians in Primary Care in 2004

National Total = 291,621 Physicians*

ALPHA ORDER

RANK	STATE	PHYSICIANS	% of USA
25	Alabama	3,832	1.3%
49	Alaska	674	0.2%
23	Arizona	4,418	1.5%
31	Arkansas	2,261	0.8%
1	California	35,280	12.1%
21	Colorado	4,532	1.6%
22	Connecticut	4,473	1.5%
46	Delaware	733	0.3%
4	Florida	15,238	5.2%
12	Georgia	7,810	2.7%
38	Hawaii	1,615	0.6%
43	Idaho	977	0.3%
5	Illinois	13,753	4.7%
19	Indiana	5,191	1.8%
32	Iowa	2,115	0.7%
30	Kansas	2,349	0.8%
28	Kentucky	3,620	1.2%
24	Louisiana	4,313	1.5%
40	Maine	1,391	0.5%
14	Maryland	7,704	2.6%
9	Massachusetts	9,366	3.2%
10	Michigan	9,358	3.2%
16	Minnesota	5,840	2.0%
33	Mississippi	2,047	0.7%
20	Missouri	4,976	1.7%
45	Montana	835	0.3%
36	Nebraska	1,733	0.6%
37	Nevada	1,718	0.6%
42	New Hampshire	1,324	0.5%
8	New Jersey	9,835	3.4%
35	New Mexico	1,831	0.6%
2	New York	26,741	9.2%
11	North Carolina	8,082	2.8%
48	North Dakota	677	0.2%
7	Ohio	11,097	3.8%
29	Oklahoma	2,388	0.8%
27	Oregon	3,753	1.3%
6	Pennsylvania	12,568	4.3%
41	Rhode Island	1,371	0.5%
26	South Carolina	3,821	1.3%
47	South Dakota	730	0.3%
17	Tennessee	5,763	2.0%
3	Texas	17,493	6.0%
34	Utah	1,850	0.6%
44	Vermont	914	0.3%
13	Virginia	7,805	2.7%
15	Washington	6,434	2.2%
39	West Virginia	1,608	0.6%
18	Wisconsin	5,521	1.9%
50	Wyoming	433	0.1%

RANK ORDER

RANK	STATE	PHYSICIANS	% of USA
1	California	35,280	12.1%
2	New York	26,741	9.2%
3	Texas	17,493	6.0%
4	Florida	15,238	5.2%
5	Illinois	13,753	4.7%
6	Pennsylvania	12,568	4.3%
7	Ohio	11,097	3.8%
8	New Jersey	9,835	3.4%
9	Massachusetts	9,366	3.2%
10	Michigan	9,358	3.2%
11	North Carolina	8,082	2.8%
12	Georgia	7,810	2.7%
13	Virginia	7,805	2.7%
14	Maryland	7,704	2.6%
15	Washington	6,434	2.2%
16	Minnesota	5,840	2.0%
17	Tennessee	5,763	2.0%
18	Wisconsin	5,521	1.9%
19	Indiana	5,191	1.8%
20	Missouri	4,976	1.7%
21	Colorado	4,532	1.6%
22	Connecticut	4,473	1.5%
23	Arizona	4,418	1.5%
24	Louisiana	4,313	1.5%
25	Alabama	3,832	1.3%
26	South Carolina	3,821	1.3%
27	Oregon	3,753	1.3%
28	Kentucky	3,620	1.2%
29	Oklahoma	2,388	0.8%
30	Kansas	2,349	0.8%
31	Arkansas	2,261	0.8%
32	Iowa	2,115	0.7%
33	Mississippi	2,047	0.7%
34	Utah	1,850	0.6%
35	New Mexico	1,831	0.6%
36	Nebraska	1,733	0.6%
37	Nevada	1,718	0.6%
38	Hawaii	1,615	0.6%
39	West Virginia	1,608	0.6%
40	Maine	1,391	0.5%
41	Rhode Island	1,371	0.5%
42	New Hampshire	1,324	0.5%
43	Idaho	977	0.3%
44	Vermont	914	0.3%
45	Montana	835	0.3%
46	Delaware	733	0.3%
47	South Dakota	730	0.3%
48	North Dakota	677	0.2%
49	Alaska	674	0.2%
50	Wyoming	433	0.1%
	District of Columbia	1,430	0.5%

Source: American Medical Association (Chicago, Illinois)
    "Physician Characteristics and Distribution in the U.S." (2006 Edition)
*As of December 31, 2004. National total does not include 4,874 physicians in U.S. territories and possessions.
Primary Care Specialties include Family Practice, General Practice, Internal Medicine, Obstetrics/Gynecology and
Pediatrics excluding subspecialties within each category.

Rate of Physicians in Primary Care in 2004

National Rate = 99 Physicians per 100,000 Population*

ALPHA ORDER

RANK	STATE	RATE
39	Alabama	85
16	Alaska	103
44	Arizona	77
42	Arkansas	82
21	California	98
21	Colorado	98
5	Connecticut	128
33	Delaware	88
33	Florida	88
33	Georgia	88
5	Hawaii	128
49	Idaho	70
10	Illinois	108
41	Indiana	83
47	Iowa	72
37	Kansas	86
36	Kentucky	87
25	Louisiana	96
12	Maine	106
3	Maryland	139
2	Massachusetts	146
29	Michigan	93
8	Minnesota	114
48	Mississippi	71
37	Missouri	86
31	Montana	90
20	Nebraska	99
46	Nevada	74
17	New Hampshire	102
9	New Jersey	113
25	New Mexico	96
3	New York	139
27	North Carolina	95
11	North Dakota	107
24	Ohio	97
50	Oklahoma	68
14	Oregon	104
18	Pennsylvania	101
7	Rhode Island	127
30	South Carolina	91
27	South Dakota	95
21	Tennessee	98
43	Texas	78
44	Utah	77
1	Vermont	147
13	Virginia	105
14	Washington	104
32	West Virginia	89
19	Wisconsin	100
39	Wyoming	85

RANK ORDER

RANK	STATE	RATE
1	Vermont	147
2	Massachusetts	146
3	Maryland	139
3	New York	139
5	Connecticut	128
5	Hawaii	128
7	Rhode Island	127
8	Minnesota	114
9	New Jersey	113
10	Illinois	108
11	North Dakota	107
12	Maine	106
13	Virginia	105
14	Oregon	104
14	Washington	104
16	Alaska	103
17	New Hampshire	102
18	Pennsylvania	101
19	Wisconsin	100
20	Nebraska	99
21	California	98
21	Colorado	98
21	Tennessee	98
24	Ohio	97
25	Louisiana	96
25	New Mexico	96
27	North Carolina	95
27	South Dakota	95
29	Michigan	93
30	South Carolina	91
31	Montana	90
32	West Virginia	89
33	Delaware	88
33	Florida	88
33	Georgia	88
36	Kentucky	87
37	Kansas	86
37	Missouri	86
39	Alabama	85
39	Wyoming	85
41	Indiana	83
42	Arkansas	82
43	Texas	78
44	Arizona	77
44	Utah	77
46	Nevada	74
47	Iowa	72
48	Mississippi	71
49	Idaho	70
50	Oklahoma	68

	District of Columbia	258

Source: Morgan Quitno Press using data from American Medical Association (Chicago, Illinois)
"Physician Characteristics and Distribution in the U.S." (2006 Edition)
*As of December 31, 2004. National rate does not include physicians in U.S. territories and possessions. Primary Care Specialties include Family Practice, General Practice, Internal Medicine, Obstetrics/Gynecology and Pediatrics excluding subspecialties within each category.

Percent of Physicians in Primary Care in 2004

National Percent = 33.4% of Physicians*

<table>
<tr><td colspan="3">ALPHA ORDER</td><td colspan="3">RANK ORDER</td></tr>
<tr><td>RANK</td><td>STATE</td><td>PERCENT</td><td>RANK</td><td>STATE</td><td>PERCENT</td></tr>
<tr><td>9</td><td>Alabama</td><td>36.3</td><td>1</td><td>Alaska</td><td>42.7</td></tr>
<tr><td>1</td><td>Alaska</td><td>42.7</td><td>2</td><td>Wyoming</td><td>39.6</td></tr>
<tr><td>45</td><td>Arizona</td><td>31.5</td><td>3</td><td>North Dakota</td><td>39.5</td></tr>
<tr><td>7</td><td>Arkansas</td><td>36.5</td><td>4</td><td>South Dakota</td><td>38.3</td></tr>
<tr><td>38</td><td>California</td><td>33.4</td><td>5</td><td>Nebraska</td><td>37.1</td></tr>
<tr><td>32</td><td>Colorado</td><td>33.7</td><td>6</td><td>Minnesota</td><td>36.6</td></tr>
<tr><td>44</td><td>Connecticut</td><td>31.8</td><td>7</td><td>Arkansas</td><td>36.5</td></tr>
<tr><td>45</td><td>Delaware</td><td>31.5</td><td>8</td><td>Hawaii</td><td>36.4</td></tr>
<tr><td>50</td><td>Florida</td><td>29.9</td><td>9</td><td>Alabama</td><td>36.3</td></tr>
<tr><td>12</td><td>Georgia</td><td>36.1</td><td>9</td><td>Idaho</td><td>36.3</td></tr>
<tr><td>8</td><td>Hawaii</td><td>36.4</td><td>9</td><td>Illinois</td><td>36.3</td></tr>
<tr><td>9</td><td>Idaho</td><td>36.3</td><td>12</td><td>Georgia</td><td>36.1</td></tr>
<tr><td>9</td><td>Illinois</td><td>36.3</td><td>13</td><td>South Carolina</td><td>35.5</td></tr>
<tr><td>15</td><td>Indiana</td><td>35.3</td><td>14</td><td>New Mexico</td><td>35.4</td></tr>
<tr><td>33</td><td>Iowa</td><td>33.6</td><td>15</td><td>Indiana</td><td>35.3</td></tr>
<tr><td>28</td><td>Kansas</td><td>34.2</td><td>15</td><td>Vermont</td><td>35.3</td></tr>
<tr><td>23</td><td>Kentucky</td><td>34.6</td><td>15</td><td>Wisconsin</td><td>35.3</td></tr>
<tr><td>39</td><td>Louisiana</td><td>33.2</td><td>18</td><td>Mississippi</td><td>34.9</td></tr>
<tr><td>26</td><td>Maine</td><td>34.3</td><td>18</td><td>Oklahoma</td><td>34.9</td></tr>
<tr><td>48</td><td>Maryland</td><td>30.7</td><td>18</td><td>West Virginia</td><td>34.9</td></tr>
<tr><td>49</td><td>Massachusetts</td><td>30.0</td><td>21</td><td>Nevada</td><td>34.8</td></tr>
<tr><td>22</td><td>Michigan</td><td>34.7</td><td>22</td><td>Michigan</td><td>34.7</td></tr>
<tr><td>6</td><td>Minnesota</td><td>36.6</td><td>23</td><td>Kentucky</td><td>34.6</td></tr>
<tr><td>18</td><td>Mississippi</td><td>34.9</td><td>23</td><td>Virginia</td><td>34.6</td></tr>
<tr><td>40</td><td>Missouri</td><td>33.1</td><td>25</td><td>Montana</td><td>34.4</td></tr>
<tr><td>25</td><td>Montana</td><td>34.4</td><td>26</td><td>Maine</td><td>34.3</td></tr>
<tr><td>5</td><td>Nebraska</td><td>37.1</td><td>26</td><td>Oregon</td><td>34.3</td></tr>
<tr><td>21</td><td>Nevada</td><td>34.8</td><td>28</td><td>Kansas</td><td>34.2</td></tr>
<tr><td>30</td><td>New Hampshire</td><td>34.1</td><td>28</td><td>Tennessee</td><td>34.2</td></tr>
<tr><td>33</td><td>New Jersey</td><td>33.6</td><td>30</td><td>New Hampshire</td><td>34.1</td></tr>
<tr><td>14</td><td>New Mexico</td><td>35.4</td><td>30</td><td>Washington</td><td>34.1</td></tr>
<tr><td>43</td><td>New York</td><td>32.7</td><td>32</td><td>Colorado</td><td>33.7</td></tr>
<tr><td>33</td><td>North Carolina</td><td>33.6</td><td>33</td><td>Iowa</td><td>33.6</td></tr>
<tr><td>3</td><td>North Dakota</td><td>39.5</td><td>33</td><td>New Jersey</td><td>33.6</td></tr>
<tr><td>37</td><td>Ohio</td><td>33.5</td><td>33</td><td>North Carolina</td><td>33.6</td></tr>
<tr><td>18</td><td>Oklahoma</td><td>34.9</td><td>33</td><td>Texas</td><td>33.6</td></tr>
<tr><td>26</td><td>Oregon</td><td>34.3</td><td>37</td><td>Ohio</td><td>33.5</td></tr>
<tr><td>47</td><td>Pennsylvania</td><td>30.8</td><td>38</td><td>California</td><td>33.4</td></tr>
<tr><td>40</td><td>Rhode Island</td><td>33.1</td><td>39</td><td>Louisiana</td><td>33.2</td></tr>
<tr><td>13</td><td>South Carolina</td><td>35.5</td><td>40</td><td>Missouri</td><td>33.1</td></tr>
<tr><td>4</td><td>South Dakota</td><td>38.3</td><td>40</td><td>Rhode Island</td><td>33.1</td></tr>
<tr><td>28</td><td>Tennessee</td><td>34.2</td><td>42</td><td>Utah</td><td>32.8</td></tr>
<tr><td>33</td><td>Texas</td><td>33.6</td><td>43</td><td>New York</td><td>32.7</td></tr>
<tr><td>42</td><td>Utah</td><td>32.8</td><td>44</td><td>Connecticut</td><td>31.8</td></tr>
<tr><td>15</td><td>Vermont</td><td>35.3</td><td>45</td><td>Arizona</td><td>31.5</td></tr>
<tr><td>23</td><td>Virginia</td><td>34.6</td><td>45</td><td>Delaware</td><td>31.5</td></tr>
<tr><td>30</td><td>Washington</td><td>34.1</td><td>47</td><td>Pennsylvania</td><td>30.8</td></tr>
<tr><td>18</td><td>West Virginia</td><td>34.9</td><td>48</td><td>Maryland</td><td>30.7</td></tr>
<tr><td>15</td><td>Wisconsin</td><td>35.3</td><td>49</td><td>Massachusetts</td><td>30.0</td></tr>
<tr><td>2</td><td>Wyoming</td><td>39.6</td><td>50</td><td>Florida</td><td>29.9</td></tr>
</table>

District of Columbia   30.3

Source: Morgan Quitno Press using data from American Medical Association (Chicago, Illinois)
   "Physician Characteristics and Distribution in the U.S." (2006 Edition)
*As of December 31, 2004. National percent does not include physicians in U.S. territories and possessions.
Primary Care Specialties include Family Practice, General Practice, Internal Medicine, Obstetrics/Gynecology and
Pediatrics excluding subspecialties within each category.

Percent of Population Lacking Access to Primary Care in 2005

National Percent = 11.5% of Population*

ALPHA ORDER

RANK	STATE	PERCENT
3	Alabama	24.6
16	Alaska	14.0
20	Arizona	13.4
31	Arkansas	10.0
30	California	10.1
28	Colorado	10.3
43	Connecticut	6.3
35	Delaware	7.9
11	Florida	15.7
12	Georgia	15.6
48	Hawaii	4.4
10	Idaho	17.9
20	Illinois	13.4
33	Indiana	8.8
32	Iowa	9.7
13	Kansas	15.4
18	Kentucky	13.8
7	Louisiana	21.6
39	Maine	7.3
44	Maryland	6.2
47	Massachusetts	5.1
25	Michigan	11.0
40	Minnesota	7.0
1	Mississippi	30.1
5	Missouri	22.9
9	Montana	20.4
46	Nebraska	5.7
19	Nevada	13.5
45	New Hampshire	5.9
50	New Jersey	2.8
2	New Mexico	28.2
26	New York	10.8
35	North Carolina	7.9
8	North Dakota	20.9
38	Ohio	7.5
14	Oklahoma	15.3
41	Oregon	6.6
42	Pennsylvania	6.4
34	Rhode Island	8.0
15	South Carolina	15.2
4	South Dakota	24.1
24	Tennessee	11.3
22	Texas	12.7
23	Utah	12.6
49	Vermont	3.6
37	Virginia	7.7
27	Washington	10.4
17	West Virginia	13.9
29	Wisconsin	10.2
6	Wyoming	22.5

RANK ORDER

RANK	STATE	PERCENT
1	Mississippi	30.1
2	New Mexico	28.2
3	Alabama	24.6
4	South Dakota	24.1
5	Missouri	22.9
6	Wyoming	22.5
7	Louisiana	21.6
8	North Dakota	20.9
9	Montana	20.4
10	Idaho	17.9
11	Florida	15.7
12	Georgia	15.6
13	Kansas	15.4
14	Oklahoma	15.3
15	South Carolina	15.2
16	Alaska	14.0
17	West Virginia	13.9
18	Kentucky	13.8
19	Nevada	13.5
20	Arizona	13.4
20	Illinois	13.4
22	Texas	12.7
23	Utah	12.6
24	Tennessee	11.3
25	Michigan	11.0
26	New York	10.8
27	Washington	10.4
28	Colorado	10.3
29	Wisconsin	10.2
30	California	10.1
31	Arkansas	10.0
32	Iowa	9.7
33	Indiana	8.8
34	Rhode Island	8.0
35	Delaware	7.9
35	North Carolina	7.9
37	Virginia	7.7
38	Ohio	7.5
39	Maine	7.3
40	Minnesota	7.0
41	Oregon	6.6
42	Pennsylvania	6.4
43	Connecticut	6.3
44	Maryland	6.2
45	New Hampshire	5.9
46	Nebraska	5.7
47	Massachusetts	5.1
48	Hawaii	4.4
49	Vermont	3.6
50	New Jersey	2.8

District of Columbia   27.0

Source: Morgan Quitno Press using data from U.S. Dept. of Health and Human Services, Div. of Shortage Designation "Selected Statistics on Health Professional Shortage Areas" (as of September 30, 2005)

*Percent of population considered under-served by primary medical practitioners (Family & General Practice doctors, Internists, Ob/Gyns and Pediatricians). An under-served population does not have primary medical care within reasonable economic and geographic bounds.

Physicians in General/Family Practice in 2004

National Total = 89,719 Physicians*

ALPHA ORDER

RANK	STATE	PHYSICIANS	% of USA
26	Alabama	1,312	1.5%
45	Alaska	376	0.4%
20	Arizona	1,465	1.6%
28	Arkansas	1,207	1.3%
1	California	10,705	11.9%
17	Colorado	1,787	2.0%
37	Connecticut	609	0.7%
50	Delaware	237	0.3%
3	Florida	4,857	5.4%
15	Georgia	2,280	2.5%
43	Hawaii	427	0.5%
40	Idaho	546	0.6%
4	Illinois	3,842	4.3%
13	Indiana	2,414	2.7%
29	Iowa	1,157	1.3%
30	Kansas	1,114	1.2%
22	Kentucky	1,369	1.5%
24	Louisiana	1,347	1.5%
38	Maine	590	0.7%
23	Maryland	1,367	1.5%
27	Massachusetts	1,270	1.4%
11	Michigan	2,780	3.1%
10	Minnesota	2,800	3.1%
33	Mississippi	810	0.9%
21	Missouri	1,382	1.5%
42	Montana	430	0.5%
32	Nebraska	886	1.0%
39	Nevada	548	0.6%
41	New Hampshire	472	0.5%
18	New Jersey	1,583	1.8%
34	New Mexico	766	0.9%
5	New York	3,831	4.3%
9	North Carolina	2,831	3.2%
46	North Dakota	372	0.4%
7	Ohio	3,460	3.9%
31	Oklahoma	1,039	1.2%
25	Oregon	1,320	1.5%
6	Pennsylvania	3,791	4.2%
49	Rhode Island	241	0.3%
19	South Carolina	1,560	1.7%
44	South Dakota	381	0.4%
16	Tennessee	1,879	2.1%
2	Texas	6,251	7.0%
35	Utah	696	0.8%
47	Vermont	322	0.4%
12	Virginia	2,627	2.9%
8	Washington	2,890	3.2%
36	West Virginia	666	0.7%
14	Wisconsin	2,372	2.6%
48	Wyoming	242	0.3%

RANK ORDER

RANK	STATE	PHYSICIANS	% of USA
1	California	10,705	11.9%
2	Texas	6,251	7.0%
3	Florida	4,857	5.4%
4	Illinois	3,842	4.3%
5	New York	3,831	4.3%
6	Pennsylvania	3,791	4.2%
7	Ohio	3,460	3.9%
8	Washington	2,890	3.2%
9	North Carolina	2,831	3.2%
10	Minnesota	2,800	3.1%
11	Michigan	2,780	3.1%
12	Virginia	2,627	2.9%
13	Indiana	2,414	2.7%
14	Wisconsin	2,372	2.6%
15	Georgia	2,280	2.5%
16	Tennessee	1,879	2.1%
17	Colorado	1,787	2.0%
18	New Jersey	1,583	1.8%
19	South Carolina	1,560	1.7%
20	Arizona	1,465	1.6%
21	Missouri	1,382	1.5%
22	Kentucky	1,369	1.5%
23	Maryland	1,367	1.5%
24	Louisiana	1,347	1.5%
25	Oregon	1,320	1.5%
26	Alabama	1,312	1.5%
27	Massachusetts	1,270	1.4%
28	Arkansas	1,207	1.3%
29	Iowa	1,157	1.3%
30	Kansas	1,114	1.2%
31	Oklahoma	1,039	1.2%
32	Nebraska	886	1.0%
33	Mississippi	810	0.9%
34	New Mexico	766	0.9%
35	Utah	696	0.8%
36	West Virginia	666	0.7%
37	Connecticut	609	0.7%
38	Maine	590	0.7%
39	Nevada	548	0.6%
40	Idaho	546	0.6%
41	New Hampshire	472	0.5%
42	Montana	430	0.5%
43	Hawaii	427	0.5%
44	South Dakota	381	0.4%
45	Alaska	376	0.4%
46	North Dakota	372	0.4%
47	Vermont	322	0.4%
48	Wyoming	242	0.3%
49	Rhode Island	241	0.3%
50	Delaware	237	0.3%
	District of Columbia	213	0.2%

Source: American Medical Association (Chicago, Illinois)
    "Physician Characteristics and Distribution in the U.S." (2006 Edition)
*As of December 31, 2004. Total does not include 2,272 physicians in U.S. territories and possessions.

Rate of Physicians in General/Family Practice in 2004

National Rate = 31 Physicians per 100,000 Population*

ALPHA ORDER				RANK ORDER		
RANK	STATE	RATE		RANK	STATE	RATE
33	Alabama	29		1	North Dakota	59
2	Alaska	57		2	Alaska	57
41	Arizona	26		3	Minnesota	55
11	Arkansas	44		4	Vermont	52
29	California	30		5	Nebraska	51
15	Colorado	39		6	South Dakota	49
50	Connecticut	17		7	Wyoming	48
33	Delaware	29		8	Washington	47
37	Florida	28		9	Montana	46
41	Georgia	26		10	Maine	45
24	Hawaii	34		11	Arkansas	44
15	Idaho	39		12	Wisconsin	43
29	Illinois	30		13	Kansas	41
15	Indiana	39		14	New Mexico	40
15	Iowa	39		15	Colorado	39
13	Kansas	41		15	Idaho	39
25	Kentucky	33		15	Indiana	39
29	Louisiana	30		15	Iowa	39
10	Maine	45		19	Oregon	37
43	Maryland	25		19	South Carolina	37
47	Massachusetts	20		19	West Virginia	37
40	Michigan	27		22	New Hampshire	36
3	Minnesota	55		23	Virginia	35
37	Mississippi	28		24	Hawaii	34
44	Missouri	24		25	Kentucky	33
9	Montana	46		25	North Carolina	33
5	Nebraska	51		27	Tennessee	32
45	Nevada	23		28	Pennsylvania	31
22	New Hampshire	36		29	California	30
49	New Jersey	18		29	Illinois	30
14	New Mexico	40		29	Louisiana	30
47	New York	20		29	Ohio	30
25	North Carolina	33		33	Alabama	29
1	North Dakota	59		33	Delaware	29
29	Ohio	30		33	Oklahoma	29
33	Oklahoma	29		33	Utah	29
19	Oregon	37		37	Florida	28
28	Pennsylvania	31		37	Mississippi	28
46	Rhode Island	22		37	Texas	28
19	South Carolina	37		40	Michigan	27
6	South Dakota	49		41	Arizona	26
27	Tennessee	32		41	Georgia	26
37	Texas	28		43	Maryland	25
33	Utah	29		44	Missouri	24
4	Vermont	52		45	Nevada	23
23	Virginia	35		46	Rhode Island	22
8	Washington	47		47	Massachusetts	20
19	West Virginia	37		47	New York	20
12	Wisconsin	43		49	New Jersey	18
7	Wyoming	48		50	Connecticut	17

District of Columbia   38

Source: Morgan Quitno Press using data from American Medical Association (Chicago, Illinois)
"Physician Characteristics and Distribution in the U.S." (2006 Edition)
As of December 31, 2004. National rate does not include physicians in U.S. territories and possessions.

Average Annual Wages of Family and General Practitioners in 2004

National Average = $137,980*

ALPHA ORDER

RANK	STATE	WAGES
23	Alabama	$146,360
46	Alaska	118,930
11	Arizona	157,700
19	Arkansas	148,700
44	California	122,740
37	Colorado	128,890
25	Connecticut	144,730
41	Delaware	125,500
13	Florida	154,690
39	Georgia	128,510
35	Hawaii	130,410
7	Idaho	159,300
43	Illinois	123,240
20	Indiana	148,040
18	Iowa	150,910
4	Kansas	163,400
29	Kentucky	137,360
5	Louisiana	161,170
42	Maine	125,370
2	Maryland	173,020
14	Massachusetts	153,520
45	Michigan	122,230
21	Minnesota	147,120
16	Mississippi	151,200
26	Missouri	143,200
47	Montana	115,780
6	Nebraska	159,690
1	Nevada	173,660
9	New Hampshire	158,800
38	New Jersey	128,540
15	New Mexico	152,280
24	New York	145,940
22	North Carolina	147,100
3	North Dakota	169,420
27	Ohio	142,340
17	Oklahoma	151,030
NA	Oregon**	NA
33	Pennsylvania	131,850
8	Rhode Island	159,070
31	South Carolina	133,830
30	South Dakota	135,300
49	Tennessee	81,460
40	Texas	127,820
28	Utah	141,570
36	Vermont	129,680
48	Virginia	114,010
32	Washington	133,550
10	West Virginia	158,540
12	Wisconsin	157,180
34	Wyoming	131,840

RANK ORDER

RANK	STATE	WAGES
1	Nevada	$173,660
2	Maryland	173,020
3	North Dakota	169,420
4	Kansas	163,400
5	Louisiana	161,170
6	Nebraska	159,690
7	Idaho	159,300
8	Rhode Island	159,070
9	New Hampshire	158,800
10	West Virginia	158,540
11	Arizona	157,700
12	Wisconsin	157,180
13	Florida	154,690
14	Massachusetts	153,520
15	New Mexico	152,280
16	Mississippi	151,200
17	Oklahoma	151,030
18	Iowa	150,910
19	Arkansas	148,700
20	Indiana	148,040
21	Minnesota	147,120
22	North Carolina	147,100
23	Alabama	146,360
24	New York	145,940
25	Connecticut	144,730
26	Missouri	143,200
27	Ohio	142,340
28	Utah	141,570
29	Kentucky	137,360
30	South Dakota	135,300
31	South Carolina	133,830
32	Washington	133,550
33	Pennsylvania	131,850
34	Wyoming	131,840
35	Hawaii	130,410
36	Vermont	129,680
37	Colorado	128,890
38	New Jersey	128,540
39	Georgia	128,510
40	Texas	127,820
41	Delaware	125,500
42	Maine	125,370
43	Illinois	123,240
44	California	122,740
45	Michigan	122,230
46	Alaska	118,930
47	Montana	115,780
48	Virginia	114,010
49	Tennessee	81,460
NA	Oregon**	NA
	District of Columbia	76,870

Source: U.S. Department of Labor, Bureau of Labor Statistics
     "Occupational Employment and Wages, 2004" (http://www.bls.gov/oes/)
*Does not include self-employed.
**Not available.

Percent of Physicians Who Are Specialists in 2004

National Percent = 73.9% of Physicians*

ALPHA ORDER

RANK	STATE	PERCENT
13	Alabama	75.1
44	Alaska	65.8
27	Arizona	71.3
40	Arkansas	68.1
24	California	72.6
26	Colorado	71.8
1	Connecticut	80.5
18	Delaware	73.5
34	Florida	69.8
9	Georgia	76.1
11	Hawaii	75.2
45	Idaho	65.3
10	Illinois	75.4
30	Indiana	70.9
48	Iowa	64.6
41	Kansas	67.8
17	Kentucky	73.8
8	Louisiana	76.6
38	Maine	68.3
4	Maryland	79.3
2	Massachusetts	80.1
14	Michigan	74.3
38	Minnesota	68.3
25	Mississippi	72.5
7	Missouri	77.8
47	Montana	64.7
43	Nebraska	66.4
22	Nevada	73.0
28	New Hampshire	71.1
4	New Jersey	79.3
37	New Mexico	68.8
6	New York	78.6
20	North Carolina	73.2
49	North Dakota	63.4
19	Ohio	73.4
36	Oklahoma	69.3
32	Oregon	70.1
14	Pennsylvania	74.3
3	Rhode Island	79.8
28	South Carolina	71.1
46	South Dakota	65.2
11	Tennessee	75.2
16	Texas	73.9
20	Utah	73.2
34	Vermont	69.8
23	Virginia	72.9
42	Washington	67.7
33	West Virginia	70.0
31	Wisconsin	70.5
50	Wyoming	62.7

RANK ORDER

RANK	STATE	PERCENT
1	Connecticut	80.5
2	Massachusetts	80.1
3	Rhode Island	79.8
4	Maryland	79.3
4	New Jersey	79.3
6	New York	78.6
7	Missouri	77.8
8	Louisiana	76.6
9	Georgia	76.1
10	Illinois	75.4
11	Hawaii	75.2
11	Tennessee	75.2
13	Alabama	75.1
14	Michigan	74.3
14	Pennsylvania	74.3
16	Texas	73.9
17	Kentucky	73.8
18	Delaware	73.5
19	Ohio	73.4
20	North Carolina	73.2
20	Utah	73.2
22	Nevada	73.0
23	Virginia	72.9
24	California	72.6
25	Mississippi	72.5
26	Colorado	71.8
27	Arizona	71.3
28	New Hampshire	71.1
28	South Carolina	71.1
30	Indiana	70.9
31	Wisconsin	70.5
32	Oregon	70.1
33	West Virginia	70.0
34	Florida	69.8
34	Vermont	69.8
36	Oklahoma	69.3
37	New Mexico	68.8
38	Maine	68.3
38	Minnesota	68.3
40	Arkansas	68.1
41	Kansas	67.8
42	Washington	67.7
43	Nebraska	66.4
44	Alaska	65.8
45	Idaho	65.3
46	South Dakota	65.2
47	Montana	64.7
48	Iowa	64.6
49	North Dakota	63.4
50	Wyoming	62.7

District of Columbia   81.6

Source: Morgan Quitno Press using data from American Medical Association (Chicago, Illinois)
    "Physician Characteristics and Distribution in the U.S." (2006 Edition)
As of December 31, 2004. National percent does not include physicians in U.S. territories and possessions.
Includes physicians in medical, surgical and other specialties.

Physicians in Medical Specialties in 2004

National Total = 277,943 Physicians*

ALPHA ORDER

RANK	STATE	PHYSICIANS	% of USA
25	Alabama	3,341	1.2%
49	Alaska	334	0.1%
22	Arizona	4,070	1.5%
32	Arkansas	1,632	0.6%
1	California	32,541	11.7%
24	Colorado	3,763	1.4%
16	Connecticut	5,266	1.9%
44	Delaware	739	0.3%
4	Florida	15,386	5.5%
13	Georgia	6,888	2.5%
38	Hawaii	1,426	0.5%
45	Idaho	570	0.2%
6	Illinois	12,992	4.7%
23	Indiana	4,037	1.5%
35	Iowa	1,504	0.5%
30	Kansas	1,739	0.6%
26	Kentucky	3,122	1.1%
21	Louisiana	4,108	1.5%
42	Maine	1,051	0.4%
10	Maryland	9,107	3.3%
7	Massachusetts	11,800	4.2%
11	Michigan	8,744	3.1%
19	Minnesota	4,666	1.7%
31	Mississippi	1,639	0.6%
17	Missouri	5,206	1.9%
46	Montana	533	0.2%
40	Nebraska	1,197	0.4%
36	Nevada	1,500	0.5%
41	New Hampshire	1,120	0.4%
8	New Jersey	11,260	4.1%
37	New Mexico	1,462	0.5%
2	New York	30,688	11.0%
12	North Carolina	7,367	2.7%
48	North Dakota	424	0.2%
9	Ohio	10,617	3.8%
29	Oklahoma	1,906	0.7%
27	Oregon	3,078	1.1%
5	Pennsylvania	13,117	4.7%
33	Rhode Island	1,602	0.6%
28	South Carolina	2,969	1.1%
47	South Dakota	475	0.2%
15	Tennessee	5,462	2.0%
3	Texas	15,652	5.6%
34	Utah	1,587	0.6%
43	Vermont	740	0.3%
14	Virginia	6,772	2.4%
18	Washington	5,034	1.8%
39	West Virginia	1,299	0.5%
20	Wisconsin	4,459	1.6%
50	Wyoming	211	0.1%

RANK ORDER

RANK	STATE	PHYSICIANS	% of USA
1	California	32,541	11.7%
2	New York	30,688	11.0%
3	Texas	15,652	5.6%
4	Florida	15,386	5.5%
5	Pennsylvania	13,117	4.7%
6	Illinois	12,992	4.7%
7	Massachusetts	11,800	4.2%
8	New Jersey	11,260	4.1%
9	Ohio	10,617	3.8%
10	Maryland	9,107	3.3%
11	Michigan	8,744	3.1%
12	North Carolina	7,367	2.7%
13	Georgia	6,888	2.5%
14	Virginia	6,772	2.4%
15	Tennessee	5,462	2.0%
16	Connecticut	5,266	1.9%
17	Missouri	5,206	1.9%
18	Washington	5,034	1.8%
19	Minnesota	4,666	1.7%
20	Wisconsin	4,459	1.6%
21	Louisiana	4,108	1.5%
22	Arizona	4,070	1.5%
23	Indiana	4,037	1.5%
24	Colorado	3,763	1.4%
25	Alabama	3,341	1.2%
26	Kentucky	3,122	1.1%
27	Oregon	3,078	1.1%
28	South Carolina	2,969	1.1%
29	Oklahoma	1,906	0.7%
30	Kansas	1,739	0.6%
31	Mississippi	1,639	0.6%
32	Arkansas	1,632	0.6%
33	Rhode Island	1,602	0.6%
34	Utah	1,587	0.6%
35	Iowa	1,504	0.5%
36	Nevada	1,500	0.5%
37	New Mexico	1,462	0.5%
38	Hawaii	1,426	0.5%
39	West Virginia	1,299	0.5%
40	Nebraska	1,197	0.4%
41	New Hampshire	1,120	0.4%
42	Maine	1,051	0.4%
43	Vermont	740	0.3%
44	Delaware	739	0.3%
45	Idaho	570	0.2%
46	Montana	533	0.2%
47	South Dakota	475	0.2%
48	North Dakota	424	0.2%
49	Alaska	334	0.1%
50	Wyoming	211	0.1%
	District of Columbia	1,741	0.6%

Source: American Medical Association (Chicago, Illinois)
     "Physician Characteristics and Distribution in the U.S." (2006 Edition)
*As of December 31, 2004. Total does not include 3,093 physicians in U.S. territories and possessions. Medical Specialties are Allergy/Immunology, Cardiovascular Diseases, Dermatology, Gastroenterology, Internal Medicine, Pediatrics, Pediatric Cardiology and Pulmonary Diseases.

Rate of Nonfederal Physicians in Medical Specialties in 2004

National Rate = 95 Physicians per 100,000 Population*

ALPHA ORDER

RANK	STATE	RATE
31	Alabama	74
47	Alaska	51
33	Arizona	71
43	Arkansas	59
13	California	91
24	Colorado	82
4	Connecticut	150
18	Delaware	89
19	Florida	88
28	Georgia	78
8	Hawaii	113
50	Idaho	41
10	Illinois	102
39	Indiana	65
47	Iowa	51
40	Kansas	64
30	Kentucky	75
13	Louisiana	91
27	Maine	80
2	Maryland	164
1	Massachusetts	184
20	Michigan	86
13	Minnesota	91
45	Mississippi	56
17	Missouri	90
44	Montana	58
36	Nebraska	69
40	Nevada	64
20	New Hampshire	86
6	New Jersey	129
29	New Mexico	77
3	New York	160
20	North Carolina	86
37	North Dakota	67
11	Ohio	93
46	Oklahoma	54
20	Oregon	86
9	Pennsylvania	106
5	Rhode Island	148
33	South Carolina	71
42	South Dakota	62
11	Tennessee	93
35	Texas	70
38	Utah	66
7	Vermont	119
13	Virginia	91
25	Washington	81
32	West Virginia	72
25	Wisconsin	81
49	Wyoming	42

RANK ORDER

RANK	STATE	RATE
1	Massachusetts	184
2	Maryland	164
3	New York	160
4	Connecticut	150
5	Rhode Island	148
6	New Jersey	129
7	Vermont	119
8	Hawaii	113
9	Pennsylvania	106
10	Illinois	102
11	Ohio	93
11	Tennessee	93
13	California	91
13	Louisiana	91
13	Minnesota	91
13	Virginia	91
17	Missouri	90
18	Delaware	89
19	Florida	88
20	Michigan	86
20	New Hampshire	86
20	North Carolina	86
20	Oregon	86
24	Colorado	82
25	Washington	81
25	Wisconsin	81
27	Maine	80
28	Georgia	78
29	New Mexico	77
30	Kentucky	75
31	Alabama	74
32	West Virginia	72
33	Arizona	71
33	South Carolina	71
35	Texas	70
36	Nebraska	69
37	North Dakota	67
38	Utah	66
39	Indiana	65
40	Kansas	64
40	Nevada	64
42	South Dakota	62
43	Arkansas	59
44	Montana	58
45	Mississippi	56
46	Oklahoma	54
47	Alaska	51
47	Iowa	51
49	Wyoming	42
50	Idaho	41

District of Columbia	315

Source: Morgan Quitno Press using data from American Medical Association (Chicago, Illinois)
"Physician Characteristics and Distribution in the U.S." (2006 Edition)
*As of December 31, 2004. National rate does not include physicians in U.S. territories and possessions. Medical Specialties are Allergy/Immunology, Cardiovascular Diseases, Dermatology, Gastroenterology, Internal Medicine, Pediatrics, Pediatric Cardiology and Pulmonary Diseases.

Physicians in Internal Medicine in 2004

National Total = 149,462 Physicians*

ALPHA ORDER					RANK ORDER			

RANK	STATE	PHYSICIANS	% of USA		RANK	STATE	PHYSICIANS	% of USA
26	Alabama	1,795	1.2%		1	New York	17,712	11.9%
49	Alaska	161	0.1%		2	California	17,358	11.6%
21	Arizona	2,082	1.4%		3	Florida	7,732	5.2%
36	Arkansas	755	0.5%		4	Texas	7,603	5.1%
2	California	17,358	11.6%		5	Illinois	7,483	5.0%
24	Colorado	1,949	1.3%		6	Pennsylvania	7,197	4.8%
15	Connecticut	3,099	2.1%		7	Massachusetts	6,927	4.6%
44	Delaware	350	0.2%		8	New Jersey	6,069	4.1%
3	Florida	7,732	5.2%		9	Ohio	5,450	3.6%
13	Georgia	3,640	2.4%		10	Maryland	5,095	3.4%
35	Hawaii	802	0.5%		11	Michigan	4,930	3.3%
46	Idaho	289	0.2%		12	North Carolina	3,760	2.5%
5	Illinois	7,483	5.0%		13	Georgia	3,640	2.4%
23	Indiana	2,042	1.4%		14	Virginia	3,556	2.4%
37	Iowa	715	0.5%		15	Connecticut	3,099	2.1%
30	Kansas	878	0.6%		16	Tennessee	2,844	1.9%
27	Kentucky	1,557	1.0%		17	Missouri	2,795	1.9%
22	Louisiana	2,044	1.4%		18	Washington	2,687	1.8%
42	Maine	568	0.4%		19	Minnesota	2,520	1.7%
10	Maryland	5,095	3.4%		20	Wisconsin	2,400	1.6%
7	Massachusetts	6,927	4.6%		21	Arizona	2,082	1.4%
11	Michigan	4,930	3.3%		22	Louisiana	2,044	1.4%
19	Minnesota	2,520	1.7%		23	Indiana	2,042	1.4%
33	Mississippi	835	0.6%		24	Colorado	1,949	1.3%
17	Missouri	2,795	1.9%		25	Oregon	1,828	1.2%
45	Montana	294	0.2%		26	Alabama	1,795	1.2%
40	Nebraska	606	0.4%		27	Kentucky	1,557	1.0%
32	Nevada	858	0.6%		28	South Carolina	1,464	1.0%
41	New Hampshire	598	0.4%		29	Oklahoma	976	0.7%
8	New Jersey	6,069	4.1%		30	Kansas	878	0.6%
34	New Mexico	825	0.6%		31	Rhode Island	876	0.6%
1	New York	17,712	11.9%		32	Nevada	858	0.6%
12	North Carolina	3,760	2.5%		33	Mississippi	835	0.6%
48	North Dakota	263	0.2%		34	New Mexico	825	0.6%
9	Ohio	5,450	3.6%		35	Hawaii	802	0.5%
29	Oklahoma	976	0.7%		36	Arkansas	755	0.5%
25	Oregon	1,828	1.2%		37	Iowa	715	0.5%
6	Pennsylvania	7,197	4.8%		38	Utah	700	0.5%
31	Rhode Island	876	0.6%		39	West Virginia	699	0.5%
28	South Carolina	1,464	1.0%		40	Nebraska	606	0.4%
47	South Dakota	283	0.2%		41	New Hampshire	598	0.4%
16	Tennessee	2,844	1.9%		42	Maine	568	0.4%
4	Texas	7,603	5.1%		43	Vermont	436	0.3%
38	Utah	700	0.5%		44	Delaware	350	0.2%
43	Vermont	436	0.3%		45	Montana	294	0.2%
14	Virginia	3,556	2.4%		46	Idaho	289	0.2%
18	Washington	2,687	1.8%		47	South Dakota	283	0.2%
39	West Virginia	699	0.5%		48	North Dakota	263	0.2%
20	Wisconsin	2,400	1.6%		49	Alaska	161	0.1%
50	Wyoming	116	0.1%		50	Wyoming	116	0.1%
						District of Columbia	961	0.6%

Source: American Medical Association (Chicago, Illinois)
       "Physician Characteristics and Distribution in the U.S." (2006 Edition)
As of December 31, 2004. Total does not include 1,471 physicians in U.S. territories and possessions. Internal Medicine includes Diabetes, Endocrinology, Geriatrics, Hematology, Infectious Diseases, Nephrology, Nutrition, Medical Oncology and Rheumatology.

Rate of Physicians in Internal Medicine in 2004

National Rate = 51 Physicians per 100,000 Population*

ALPHA ORDER

RANK	STATE	RATE
31	Alabama	40
47	Alaska	25
36	Arizona	36
46	Arkansas	27
15	California	48
27	Colorado	42
4	Connecticut	88
27	Delaware	42
21	Florida	44
29	Georgia	41
8	Hawaii	64
50	Idaho	21
9	Illinois	59
40	Indiana	33
48	Iowa	24
41	Kansas	32
33	Kentucky	38
20	Louisiana	45
24	Maine	43
2	Maryland	92
1	Massachusetts	108
12	Michigan	49
12	Minnesota	49
43	Mississippi	29
12	Missouri	49
41	Montana	32
37	Nebraska	35
34	Nevada	37
19	New Hampshire	46
6	New Jersey	70
24	New Mexico	43
2	New York	92
21	North Carolina	44
29	North Dakota	41
15	Ohio	48
45	Oklahoma	28
11	Oregon	51
10	Pennsylvania	58
5	Rhode Island	81
37	South Carolina	35
34	South Dakota	37
15	Tennessee	48
39	Texas	34
43	Utah	29
6	Vermont	70
15	Virginia	48
24	Washington	43
32	West Virginia	39
21	Wisconsin	44
49	Wyoming	23

RANK ORDER

RANK	STATE	RATE
1	Massachusetts	108
2	Maryland	92
2	New York	92
4	Connecticut	88
5	Rhode Island	81
6	New Jersey	70
6	Vermont	70
8	Hawaii	64
9	Illinois	59
10	Pennsylvania	58
11	Oregon	51
12	Michigan	49
12	Minnesota	49
12	Missouri	49
15	California	48
15	Ohio	48
15	Tennessee	48
15	Virginia	48
19	New Hampshire	46
20	Louisiana	45
21	Florida	44
21	North Carolina	44
21	Wisconsin	44
24	Maine	43
24	New Mexico	43
24	Washington	43
27	Colorado	42
27	Delaware	42
29	Georgia	41
29	North Dakota	41
31	Alabama	40
32	West Virginia	39
33	Kentucky	38
34	Nevada	37
34	South Dakota	37
36	Arizona	36
37	Nebraska	35
37	South Carolina	35
39	Texas	34
40	Indiana	33
41	Kansas	32
41	Montana	32
43	Mississippi	29
43	Utah	29
45	Oklahoma	28
46	Arkansas	27
47	Alaska	25
48	Iowa	24
49	Wyoming	23
50	Idaho	21

District of Columbia   174

Source: Morgan Quitno Press using data from American Medical Association (Chicago, Illinois)
    "Physician Characteristics and Distribution in the U.S." (2006 Edition)
*As of December 31, 2004. National rate does not include physicians in U.S. territories and possessions. Internal Medicine includes Diabetes, Endocrinology, Geriatrics, Hematology, Infectious Diseases, Nephrology, Nutrition, Medical Oncology and Rheumatology.

Physicians in Pediatrics in 2004

National Total = 69,083 Physicians*

ALPHA ORDER

RANK	STATE	PHYSICIANS	% of USA
26	Alabama	815	1.2%
46	Alaska	116	0.2%
23	Arizona	1,023	1.5%
30	Arkansas	468	0.7%
1	California	8,337	12.1%
24	Colorado	972	1.4%
19	Connecticut	1,099	1.6%
43	Delaware	235	0.3%
4	Florida	3,618	5.2%
13	Georgia	1,820	2.6%
34	Hawaii	403	0.6%
45	Idaho	120	0.2%
5	Illinois	3,051	4.4%
22	Indiana	1,046	1.5%
36	Iowa	361	0.5%
32	Kansas	460	0.7%
25	Kentucky	855	1.2%
18	Louisiana	1,102	1.6%
42	Maine	262	0.4%
10	Maryland	2,216	3.2%
9	Massachusetts	2,607	3.8%
11	Michigan	2,147	3.1%
21	Minnesota	1,083	1.6%
33	Mississippi	405	0.6%
16	Missouri	1,281	1.9%
47	Montana	110	0.2%
39	Nebraska	314	0.5%
38	Nevada	320	0.5%
41	New Hampshire	272	0.4%
7	New Jersey	2,855	4.1%
37	New Mexico	356	0.5%
2	New York	7,263	10.5%
12	North Carolina	1,911	2.8%
49	North Dakota	87	0.1%
6	Ohio	2,985	4.3%
31	Oklahoma	466	0.7%
28	Oregon	664	1.0%
8	Pennsylvania	2,834	4.1%
35	Rhode Island	392	0.6%
27	South Carolina	808	1.2%
48	South Dakota	88	0.1%
15	Tennessee	1,418	2.1%
3	Texas	4,391	6.4%
29	Utah	509	0.7%
44	Vermont	182	0.3%
14	Virginia	1,802	2.6%
17	Washington	1,255	1.8%
40	West Virginia	307	0.4%
20	Wisconsin	1,089	1.6%
50	Wyoming	51	0.1%

RANK ORDER

RANK	STATE	PHYSICIANS	% of USA
1	California	8,337	12.1%
2	New York	7,263	10.5%
3	Texas	4,391	6.4%
4	Florida	3,618	5.2%
5	Illinois	3,051	4.4%
6	Ohio	2,985	4.3%
7	New Jersey	2,855	4.1%
8	Pennsylvania	2,834	4.1%
9	Massachusetts	2,607	3.8%
10	Maryland	2,216	3.2%
11	Michigan	2,147	3.1%
12	North Carolina	1,911	2.8%
13	Georgia	1,820	2.6%
14	Virginia	1,802	2.6%
15	Tennessee	1,418	2.1%
16	Missouri	1,281	1.9%
17	Washington	1,255	1.8%
18	Louisiana	1,102	1.6%
19	Connecticut	1,099	1.6%
20	Wisconsin	1,089	1.6%
21	Minnesota	1,083	1.6%
22	Indiana	1,046	1.5%
23	Arizona	1,023	1.5%
24	Colorado	972	1.4%
25	Kentucky	855	1.2%
26	Alabama	815	1.2%
27	South Carolina	808	1.2%
28	Oregon	664	1.0%
29	Utah	509	0.7%
30	Arkansas	468	0.7%
31	Oklahoma	466	0.7%
32	Kansas	460	0.7%
33	Mississippi	405	0.6%
34	Hawaii	403	0.6%
35	Rhode Island	392	0.6%
36	Iowa	361	0.5%
37	New Mexico	356	0.5%
38	Nevada	320	0.5%
39	Nebraska	314	0.5%
40	West Virginia	307	0.4%
41	New Hampshire	272	0.4%
42	Maine	262	0.4%
43	Delaware	235	0.3%
44	Vermont	182	0.3%
45	Idaho	120	0.2%
46	Alaska	116	0.2%
47	Montana	110	0.2%
48	South Dakota	88	0.1%
49	North Dakota	87	0.1%
50	Wyoming	51	0.1%
	District of Columbia	452	0.7%

Source: American Medical Association (Chicago, Illinois)
   "Physician Characteristics and Distribution in the U.S." (2006 Edition)
As of December 31, 2004. Total does not include 1,068 physicians in U.S. territories and possessions. Pediatrics includes Adolescent Medicine, Neonatal-Perinatal, Pediatric Allergy, Pediatric Endocrinology, Pediatric Pulmonology, Pediatric Hematology-Oncology and Pediatric Nephrology.

Rate of Physicians in Pediatrics in 2004

National Rate = 94 Physicians per 100,000 Population 17 Years and Younger*

ALPHA ORDER

RANK ORDER

RANK	STATE	RATE		RANK	STATE	RATE
32	Alabama	74		1	Massachusetts	178
42	Alaska	62		2	Rhode Island	161
39	Arizona	66		3	Maryland	159
36	Arkansas	69		3	New York	159
21	California	87		5	Hawaii	135
27	Colorado	82		5	Vermont	135
8	Connecticut	131		7	New Jersey	132
9	Delaware	121		8	Connecticut	131
18	Florida	90		9	Delaware	121
30	Georgia	78		10	Ohio	107
5	Hawaii	135		11	Tennessee	102
50	Idaho	32		12	Pennsylvania	100
15	Illinois	94		12	Virginia	100
40	Indiana	65		14	Louisiana	95
45	Iowa	53		15	Illinois	94
38	Kansas	67		16	Maine	93
21	Kentucky	87		16	Missouri	93
14	Louisiana	95		18	Florida	90
16	Maine	93		18	North Carolina	90
3	Maryland	159		20	New Hampshire	89
1	Massachusetts	178		21	California	87
24	Michigan	85		21	Kentucky	87
21	Minnesota	87		21	Minnesota	87
43	Mississippi	54		24	Michigan	85
16	Missouri	93		25	Washington	84
45	Montana	53		26	Wisconsin	83
33	Nebraska	72		27	Colorado	82
45	Nevada	53		28	West Virginia	80
20	New Hampshire	89		29	South Carolina	79
7	New Jersey	132		30	Georgia	78
33	New Mexico	72		30	Oregon	78
3	New York	159		32	Alabama	74
18	North Carolina	90		33	Nebraska	72
41	North Dakota	63		33	New Mexico	72
10	Ohio	107		35	Texas	70
43	Oklahoma	54		36	Arkansas	69
30	Oregon	78		36	Utah	69
12	Pennsylvania	100		38	Kansas	67
2	Rhode Island	161		39	Arizona	66
29	South Carolina	79		40	Indiana	65
48	South Dakota	46		41	North Dakota	63
11	Tennessee	102		42	Alaska	62
35	Texas	70		43	Mississippi	54
36	Utah	69		43	Oklahoma	54
5	Vermont	135		45	Iowa	53
12	Virginia	100		45	Montana	53
25	Washington	84		45	Nevada	53
28	West Virginia	80		48	South Dakota	46
26	Wisconsin	83		49	Wyoming	44
49	Wyoming	44		50	Idaho	32

District of Columbia		413

Source: Morgan Quitno Press using data from American Medical Association (Chicago, Illinois)
"Physician Characteristics and Distribution in the U.S." (2006 Edition)

*As of December 31, 2004. National rate does not include physicians in U.S. territories and possessions. Pediatrics includes Adolescent Medicine, Neonatal-Perinatal, Pediatric Allergy, Pediatric Endocrinology, Pediatric Pulmonology, Pediatric Hematology-Oncology and Pediatric Nephrology.

Physicians in Surgical Specialties in 2004

National Total = 159,129 Physicians*

<table>
<tr><td colspan="4">ALPHA ORDER</td><td colspan="4">RANK ORDER</td></tr>
<tr><th>RANK</th><th>STATE</th><th>PHYSICIANS</th><th>% of USA</th><th>RANK</th><th>STATE</th><th>PHYSICIANS</th><th>% of USA</th></tr>
<tr><td>25</td><td>Alabama</td><td>2,281</td><td>1.4%</td><td>1</td><td>California</td><td>18,569</td><td>11.7%</td></tr>
<tr><td>48</td><td>Alaska</td><td>322</td><td>0.2%</td><td>2</td><td>New York</td><td>13,896</td><td>8.7%</td></tr>
<tr><td>24</td><td>Arizona</td><td>2,484</td><td>1.6%</td><td>3</td><td>Texas</td><td>10,302</td><td>6.5%</td></tr>
<tr><td>32</td><td>Arkansas</td><td>1,152</td><td>0.7%</td><td>4</td><td>Florida</td><td>9,160</td><td>5.8%</td></tr>
<tr><td>1</td><td>California</td><td>18,569</td><td>11.7%</td><td>5</td><td>Pennsylvania</td><td>7,276</td><td>4.6%</td></tr>
<tr><td>23</td><td>Colorado</td><td>2,489</td><td>1.6%</td><td>6</td><td>Illinois</td><td>6,609</td><td>4.2%</td></tr>
<tr><td>22</td><td>Connecticut</td><td>2,530</td><td>1.6%</td><td>7</td><td>Ohio</td><td>6,085</td><td>3.8%</td></tr>
<tr><td>46</td><td>Delaware</td><td>418</td><td>0.3%</td><td>8</td><td>New Jersey</td><td>5,303</td><td>3.3%</td></tr>
<tr><td>4</td><td>Florida</td><td>9,160</td><td>5.8%</td><td>9</td><td>Michigan</td><td>4,956</td><td>3.1%</td></tr>
<tr><td>12</td><td>Georgia</td><td>4,452</td><td>2.8%</td><td>10</td><td>Massachusetts</td><td>4,780</td><td>3.0%</td></tr>
<tr><td>39</td><td>Hawaii</td><td>811</td><td>0.5%</td><td>11</td><td>North Carolina</td><td>4,635</td><td>2.9%</td></tr>
<tr><td>43</td><td>Idaho</td><td>596</td><td>0.4%</td><td>12</td><td>Georgia</td><td>4,452</td><td>2.8%</td></tr>
<tr><td>6</td><td>Illinois</td><td>6,609</td><td>4.2%</td><td>13</td><td>Virginia</td><td>4,275</td><td>2.7%</td></tr>
<tr><td>20</td><td>Indiana</td><td>2,745</td><td>1.7%</td><td>14</td><td>Maryland</td><td>4,261</td><td>2.7%</td></tr>
<tr><td>33</td><td>Iowa</td><td>1,144</td><td>0.7%</td><td>15</td><td>Tennessee</td><td>3,487</td><td>2.2%</td></tr>
<tr><td>31</td><td>Kansas</td><td>1,281</td><td>0.8%</td><td>16</td><td>Washington</td><td>3,169</td><td>2.0%</td></tr>
<tr><td>27</td><td>Kentucky</td><td>2,093</td><td>1.3%</td><td>17</td><td>Missouri</td><td>2,924</td><td>1.8%</td></tr>
<tr><td>18</td><td>Louisiana</td><td>2,877</td><td>1.8%</td><td>18</td><td>Louisiana</td><td>2,877</td><td>1.8%</td></tr>
<tr><td>42</td><td>Maine</td><td>700</td><td>0.4%</td><td>19</td><td>Wisconsin</td><td>2,753</td><td>1.7%</td></tr>
<tr><td>14</td><td>Maryland</td><td>4,261</td><td>2.7%</td><td>20</td><td>Indiana</td><td>2,745</td><td>1.7%</td></tr>
<tr><td>10</td><td>Massachusetts</td><td>4,780</td><td>3.0%</td><td>21</td><td>Minnesota</td><td>2,651</td><td>1.7%</td></tr>
<tr><td>9</td><td>Michigan</td><td>4,956</td><td>3.1%</td><td>22</td><td>Connecticut</td><td>2,530</td><td>1.6%</td></tr>
<tr><td>21</td><td>Minnesota</td><td>2,651</td><td>1.7%</td><td>23</td><td>Colorado</td><td>2,489</td><td>1.6%</td></tr>
<tr><td>29</td><td>Mississippi</td><td>1,336</td><td>0.8%</td><td>24</td><td>Arizona</td><td>2,484</td><td>1.6%</td></tr>
<tr><td>17</td><td>Missouri</td><td>2,924</td><td>1.8%</td><td>25</td><td>Alabama</td><td>2,281</td><td>1.4%</td></tr>
<tr><td>44</td><td>Montana</td><td>488</td><td>0.3%</td><td>26</td><td>South Carolina</td><td>2,222</td><td>1.4%</td></tr>
<tr><td>35</td><td>Nebraska</td><td>915</td><td>0.6%</td><td>27</td><td>Kentucky</td><td>2,093</td><td>1.3%</td></tr>
<tr><td>37</td><td>Nevada</td><td>900</td><td>0.6%</td><td>28</td><td>Oregon</td><td>1,974</td><td>1.2%</td></tr>
<tr><td>41</td><td>New Hampshire</td><td>719</td><td>0.5%</td><td>29</td><td>Mississippi</td><td>1,336</td><td>0.8%</td></tr>
<tr><td>8</td><td>New Jersey</td><td>5,303</td><td>3.3%</td><td>30</td><td>Oklahoma</td><td>1,325</td><td>0.8%</td></tr>
<tr><td>38</td><td>New Mexico</td><td>830</td><td>0.5%</td><td>31</td><td>Kansas</td><td>1,281</td><td>0.8%</td></tr>
<tr><td>2</td><td>New York</td><td>13,896</td><td>8.7%</td><td>32</td><td>Arkansas</td><td>1,152</td><td>0.7%</td></tr>
<tr><td>11</td><td>North Carolina</td><td>4,635</td><td>2.9%</td><td>33</td><td>Iowa</td><td>1,144</td><td>0.7%</td></tr>
<tr><td>49</td><td>North Dakota</td><td>294</td><td>0.2%</td><td>34</td><td>Utah</td><td>1,095</td><td>0.7%</td></tr>
<tr><td>7</td><td>Ohio</td><td>6,085</td><td>3.8%</td><td>35</td><td>Nebraska</td><td>915</td><td>0.6%</td></tr>
<tr><td>30</td><td>Oklahoma</td><td>1,325</td><td>0.8%</td><td>36</td><td>West Virginia</td><td>904</td><td>0.6%</td></tr>
<tr><td>28</td><td>Oregon</td><td>1,974</td><td>1.2%</td><td>37</td><td>Nevada</td><td>900</td><td>0.6%</td></tr>
<tr><td>5</td><td>Pennsylvania</td><td>7,276</td><td>4.6%</td><td>38</td><td>New Mexico</td><td>830</td><td>0.5%</td></tr>
<tr><td>40</td><td>Rhode Island</td><td>749</td><td>0.5%</td><td>39</td><td>Hawaii</td><td>811</td><td>0.5%</td></tr>
<tr><td>26</td><td>South Carolina</td><td>2,222</td><td>1.4%</td><td>40</td><td>Rhode Island</td><td>749</td><td>0.5%</td></tr>
<tr><td>47</td><td>South Dakota</td><td>380</td><td>0.2%</td><td>41</td><td>New Hampshire</td><td>719</td><td>0.5%</td></tr>
<tr><td>15</td><td>Tennessee</td><td>3,487</td><td>2.2%</td><td>42</td><td>Maine</td><td>700</td><td>0.4%</td></tr>
<tr><td>3</td><td>Texas</td><td>10,302</td><td>6.5%</td><td>43</td><td>Idaho</td><td>596</td><td>0.4%</td></tr>
<tr><td>34</td><td>Utah</td><td>1,095</td><td>0.7%</td><td>44</td><td>Montana</td><td>488</td><td>0.3%</td></tr>
<tr><td>45</td><td>Vermont</td><td>440</td><td>0.3%</td><td>45</td><td>Vermont</td><td>440</td><td>0.3%</td></tr>
<tr><td>13</td><td>Virginia</td><td>4,275</td><td>2.7%</td><td>46</td><td>Delaware</td><td>418</td><td>0.3%</td></tr>
<tr><td>16</td><td>Washington</td><td>3,169</td><td>2.0%</td><td>47</td><td>South Dakota</td><td>380</td><td>0.2%</td></tr>
<tr><td>36</td><td>West Virginia</td><td>904</td><td>0.6%</td><td>48</td><td>Alaska</td><td>322</td><td>0.2%</td></tr>
<tr><td>19</td><td>Wisconsin</td><td>2,753</td><td>1.7%</td><td>49</td><td>North Dakota</td><td>294</td><td>0.2%</td></tr>
<tr><td>50</td><td>Wyoming</td><td>231</td><td>0.1%</td><td>50</td><td>Wyoming</td><td>231</td><td>0.1%</td></tr>
<tr><td></td><td></td><td></td><td></td><td></td><td>District of Columbia</td><td>861</td><td>0.5%</td></tr>
</table>

Source: American Medical Association (Chicago, Illinois)
   "Physician Characteristics and Distribution in the U.S." (2006 Edition)
As of December 31, 2004. Total does not include 1,684 physicians in U.S. territories and possessions. Surgical Specialties include Colon and Rectal, General, Neurological, Obstetrics & Gynecology, Ophthalmology, Orthopedic, Otolaryngology, Plastic, Thoracic and Urological Surgeries.

Rate of Physicians in Surgical Specialties in 2004

National Rate = 54 Physicians per 100,000 Population*

ALPHA ORDER

RANK	STATE	RATE
28	Alabama	50
34	Alaska	49
45	Arizona	43
47	Arkansas	42
22	California	52
15	Colorado	54
3	Connecticut	72
28	Delaware	50
17	Florida	53
28	Georgia	50
7	Hawaii	64
45	Idaho	43
22	Illinois	52
43	Indiana	44
48	Iowa	39
37	Kansas	47
28	Kentucky	50
7	Louisiana	64
17	Maine	53
1	Maryland	77
2	Massachusetts	74
34	Michigan	49
22	Minnesota	52
38	Mississippi	46
26	Missouri	51
17	Montana	53
22	Nebraska	52
48	Nevada	39
13	New Hampshire	55
9	New Jersey	61
43	New Mexico	44
3	New York	72
15	North Carolina	54
38	North Dakota	46
17	Ohio	53
50	Oklahoma	38
13	Oregon	55
10	Pennsylvania	59
6	Rhode Island	69
17	South Carolina	53
34	South Dakota	49
10	Tennessee	59
38	Texas	46
38	Utah	46
5	Vermont	71
12	Virginia	57
26	Washington	51
28	West Virginia	50
28	Wisconsin	50
38	Wyoming	46

RANK ORDER

RANK	STATE	RATE
1	Maryland	77
2	Massachusetts	74
3	Connecticut	72
3	New York	72
5	Vermont	71
6	Rhode Island	69
7	Hawaii	64
7	Louisiana	64
9	New Jersey	61
10	Pennsylvania	59
10	Tennessee	59
12	Virginia	57
13	New Hampshire	55
13	Oregon	55
15	Colorado	54
15	North Carolina	54
17	Florida	53
17	Maine	53
17	Montana	53
17	Ohio	53
17	South Carolina	53
22	California	52
22	Illinois	52
22	Minnesota	52
22	Nebraska	52
26	Missouri	51
26	Washington	51
28	Alabama	50
28	Delaware	50
28	Georgia	50
28	Kentucky	50
28	West Virginia	50
28	Wisconsin	50
34	Alaska	49
34	Michigan	49
34	South Dakota	49
37	Kansas	47
38	Mississippi	46
38	North Dakota	46
38	Texas	46
38	Utah	46
38	Wyoming	46
43	Indiana	44
43	New Mexico	44
45	Arizona	43
45	Idaho	43
47	Arkansas	42
48	Iowa	39
48	Nevada	39
50	Oklahoma	38

District of Columbia	156

Source: Morgan Quitno Press using data from American Medical Association (Chicago, Illinois)
  "Physician Characteristics and Distribution in the U.S." (2006 Edition)
*As of December 31, 2004. National rate does not include physicians in U.S. territories and possessions. Surgical Specialties include Colon and Rectal, General, Neurological, Obstetrics & Gynecology, Ophthalmology, Orthopedic, Otolaryngology, Plastic, Thoracic and Urological Surgeries.

Average Annual Wages of Surgeons in 2004

National Average = $181,850*

ALPHA ORDER

RANK	STATE	WAGES
33	Alabama	$180,860
NA	Alaska**	NA
41	Arizona	170,960
34	Arkansas	180,400
45	California	164,290
8	Colorado	193,570
43	Connecticut	168,250
42	Delaware	168,380
36	Florida	177,600
20	Georgia	189,010
NA	Hawaii**	NA
35	Idaho	179,900
44	Illinois	165,450
10	Indiana	193,370
39	Iowa	175,550
4	Kansas	194,770
6	Kentucky	194,290
32	Louisiana	182,880
1	Maine	196,960
28	Maryland	184,380
30	Massachusetts	183,410
11	Michigan	191,630
13	Minnesota	191,030
7	Mississippi	193,590
15	Missouri	190,420
23	Montana	187,260
29	Nebraska	184,160
9	Nevada	193,390
2	New Hampshire	196,240
5	New Jersey	194,580
25	New Mexico	186,620
38	New York	176,560
24	North Carolina	187,250
47	North Dakota	153,150
17	Ohio	190,190
14	Oklahoma	190,450
NA	Oregon**	NA
46	Pennsylvania	160,460
37	Rhode Island	176,980
16	South Carolina	190,300
26	South Dakota	186,430
27	Tennessee	186,140
19	Texas	189,420
21	Utah	188,320
40	Vermont	173,560
3	Virginia	195,850
22	Washington	188,240
18	West Virginia	189,600
31	Wisconsin	183,400
12	Wyoming	191,570

RANK ORDER

RANK	STATE	WAGES
1	Maine	$196,960
2	New Hampshire	196,240
3	Virginia	195,850
4	Kansas	194,770
5	New Jersey	194,580
6	Kentucky	194,290
7	Mississippi	193,590
8	Colorado	193,570
9	Nevada	193,390
10	Indiana	193,370
11	Michigan	191,630
12	Wyoming	191,570
13	Minnesota	191,030
14	Oklahoma	190,450
15	Missouri	190,420
16	South Carolina	190,300
17	Ohio	190,190
18	West Virginia	189,600
19	Texas	189,420
20	Georgia	189,010
21	Utah	188,320
22	Washington	188,240
23	Montana	187,260
24	North Carolina	187,250
25	New Mexico	186,620
26	South Dakota	186,430
27	Tennessee	186,140
28	Maryland	184,380
29	Nebraska	184,160
30	Massachusetts	183,410
31	Wisconsin	183,400
32	Louisiana	182,880
33	Alabama	180,860
34	Arkansas	180,400
35	Idaho	179,900
36	Florida	177,600
37	Rhode Island	176,980
38	New York	176,560
39	Iowa	175,550
40	Vermont	173,560
41	Arizona	170,960
42	Delaware	168,380
43	Connecticut	168,250
44	Illinois	165,450
45	California	164,290
46	Pennsylvania	160,460
47	North Dakota	153,150
NA	Alaska**	NA
NA	Hawaii**	NA
NA	Oregon**	NA
	District of Columbia	124,510

Source: U.S. Department of Labor, Bureau of Labor Statistics
   "Occupational Employment and Wages, 2004" (http://www.bls.gov/oes/)
*Does not include self-employed.
**Not available.

Physicians in General Surgery in 2004

National Total = 37,063 Physicians*

ALPHA ORDER

RANK	STATE	PHYSICIANS	% of USA
25	Alabama	541	1.5%
49	Alaska	73	0.2%
23	Arizona	576	1.6%
33	Arkansas	270	0.7%
1	California	3,958	10.7%
24	Colorado	545	1.5%
21	Connecticut	591	1.6%
45	Delaware	104	0.3%
5	Florida	1,860	5.0%
12	Georgia	1,001	2.7%
41	Hawaii	178	0.5%
43	Idaho	139	0.4%
6	Illinois	1,549	4.2%
22	Indiana	585	1.6%
32	Iowa	297	0.8%
29	Kansas	314	0.8%
27	Kentucky	536	1.4%
18	Louisiana	658	1.8%
39	Maine	195	0.5%
14	Maryland	959	2.6%
8	Massachusetts	1,284	3.5%
9	Michigan	1,277	3.4%
20	Minnesota	604	1.6%
31	Mississippi	301	0.8%
17	Missouri	666	1.8%
46	Montana	103	0.3%
34	Nebraska	249	0.7%
38	Nevada	200	0.5%
42	New Hampshire	171	0.5%
10	New Jersey	1,209	3.3%
37	New Mexico	207	0.6%
2	New York	3,409	9.2%
11	North Carolina	1,066	2.9%
48	North Dakota	88	0.2%
7	Ohio	1,530	4.1%
30	Oklahoma	303	0.8%
28	Oregon	451	1.2%
4	Pennsylvania	1,869	5.0%
40	Rhode Island	190	0.5%
25	South Carolina	541	1.5%
47	South Dakota	99	0.3%
15	Tennessee	877	2.4%
3	Texas	2,229	6.0%
36	Utah	216	0.6%
44	Vermont	129	0.3%
13	Virginia	973	2.6%
16	Washington	717	1.9%
35	West Virginia	242	0.7%
19	Wisconsin	635	1.7%
50	Wyoming	51	0.1%

RANK ORDER

RANK	STATE	PHYSICIANS	% of USA
1	California	3,958	10.7%
2	New York	3,409	9.2%
3	Texas	2,229	6.0%
4	Pennsylvania	1,869	5.0%
5	Florida	1,860	5.0%
6	Illinois	1,549	4.2%
7	Ohio	1,530	4.1%
8	Massachusetts	1,284	3.5%
9	Michigan	1,277	3.4%
10	New Jersey	1,209	3.3%
11	North Carolina	1,066	2.9%
12	Georgia	1,001	2.7%
13	Virginia	973	2.6%
14	Maryland	959	2.6%
15	Tennessee	877	2.4%
16	Washington	717	1.9%
17	Missouri	666	1.8%
18	Louisiana	658	1.8%
19	Wisconsin	635	1.7%
20	Minnesota	604	1.6%
21	Connecticut	591	1.6%
22	Indiana	585	1.6%
23	Arizona	576	1.6%
24	Colorado	545	1.5%
25	Alabama	541	1.5%
25	South Carolina	541	1.5%
27	Kentucky	536	1.4%
28	Oregon	451	1.2%
29	Kansas	314	0.8%
30	Oklahoma	303	0.8%
31	Mississippi	301	0.8%
32	Iowa	297	0.8%
33	Arkansas	270	0.7%
34	Nebraska	249	0.7%
35	West Virginia	242	0.7%
36	Utah	216	0.6%
37	New Mexico	207	0.6%
38	Nevada	200	0.5%
39	Maine	195	0.5%
40	Rhode Island	190	0.5%
41	Hawaii	178	0.5%
42	New Hampshire	171	0.5%
43	Idaho	139	0.4%
44	Vermont	129	0.3%
45	Delaware	104	0.3%
46	Montana	103	0.3%
47	South Dakota	99	0.3%
48	North Dakota	88	0.2%
49	Alaska	73	0.2%
50	Wyoming	51	0.1%
	District of Columbia	248	0.7%

Source: American Medical Association (Chicago, Illinois)
      "Physician Characteristics and Distribution in the U.S." (2006 Edition)
*As of December 31, 2004. Total does not include 439 physicians in U.S. territories and possessions. General Surgery includes Abdominal, Cardiovascular, Hand, Head and Neck, Pediatric, Traumatic and Vascular Surgeries.

Rate of Physicians in General Surgery in 2004

National Rate = 13 Physicians per 100,000 Population*

ALPHA ORDER

RANK	STATE	RATE
25	Alabama	12
33	Alaska	11
40	Arizona	10
40	Arkansas	10
33	California	11
25	Colorado	12
5	Connecticut	17
15	Delaware	13
33	Florida	11
33	Georgia	11
11	Hawaii	14
40	Idaho	10
25	Illinois	12
47	Indiana	9
40	Iowa	10
33	Kansas	11
15	Kentucky	13
7	Louisiana	15
7	Maine	15
5	Maryland	17
2	Massachusetts	20
15	Michigan	13
25	Minnesota	12
40	Mississippi	10
25	Missouri	12
33	Montana	11
11	Nebraska	14
47	Nevada	9
15	New Hampshire	13
11	New Jersey	14
33	New Mexico	11
3	New York	18
25	North Carolina	12
11	North Dakota	14
15	Ohio	13
47	Oklahoma	9
15	Oregon	13
7	Pennsylvania	15
3	Rhode Island	18
15	South Carolina	13
15	South Dakota	13
7	Tennessee	15
40	Texas	10
47	Utah	9
1	Vermont	21
15	Virginia	13
25	Washington	12
15	West Virginia	13
25	Wisconsin	12
40	Wyoming	10

RANK ORDER

RANK	STATE	RATE
1	Vermont	21
2	Massachusetts	20
3	New York	18
3	Rhode Island	18
5	Connecticut	17
5	Maryland	17
7	Louisiana	15
7	Maine	15
7	Pennsylvania	15
7	Tennessee	15
11	Hawaii	14
11	Nebraska	14
11	New Jersey	14
11	North Dakota	14
15	Delaware	13
15	Kentucky	13
15	Michigan	13
15	New Hampshire	13
15	Ohio	13
15	Oregon	13
15	South Carolina	13
15	South Dakota	13
15	Virginia	13
15	West Virginia	13
25	Alabama	12
25	Colorado	12
25	Illinois	12
25	Minnesota	12
25	Missouri	12
25	North Carolina	12
25	Washington	12
25	Wisconsin	12
33	Alaska	11
33	California	11
33	Florida	11
33	Georgia	11
33	Kansas	11
33	Montana	11
33	New Mexico	11
40	Arizona	10
40	Arkansas	10
40	Idaho	10
40	Iowa	10
40	Mississippi	10
40	Texas	10
40	Wyoming	10
47	Indiana	9
47	Nevada	9
47	Oklahoma	9
47	Utah	9
	District of Columbia	45

Source: Morgan Quitno Press using data from American Medical Association (Chicago, Illinois)
"Physician Characteristics and Distribution in the U.S." (2006 Edition)
*As of December 31, 2004. National rate does not include physicians in U.S. territories and possessions. General Surgery includes Abdominal, Cardiovascular, Hand, Head and Neck, Pediatric, Traumatic and Vascular Surgeries.

Physicians in Obstetrics and Gynecology in 2004

National Total = 41,468 Physicians*

ALPHA ORDER

RANK	STATE	PHYSICIANS	% of USA
26	Alabama	576	1.4%
47	Alaska	79	0.2%
21	Arizona	662	1.6%
34	Arkansas	261	0.6%
1	California	4,921	11.9%
22	Colorado	657	1.6%
20	Connecticut	710	1.7%
45	Delaware	106	0.3%
4	Florida	2,217	5.3%
9	Georgia	1,380	3.3%
35	Hawaii	251	0.6%
43	Idaho	132	0.3%
5	Illinois	1,874	4.5%
19	Indiana	723	1.7%
36	Iowa	217	0.5%
31	Kansas	284	0.7%
28	Kentucky	505	1.2%
17	Louisiana	729	1.8%
42	Maine	159	0.4%
13	Maryland	1,152	2.8%
13	Massachusetts	1,152	2.8%
10	Michigan	1,370	3.3%
24	Minnesota	590	1.4%
29	Mississippi	350	0.8%
18	Missouri	725	1.7%
46	Montana	104	0.3%
41	Nebraska	191	0.5%
33	Nevada	264	0.6%
39	New Hampshire	197	0.5%
8	New Jersey	1,537	3.7%
38	New Mexico	203	0.5%
2	New York	3,756	9.1%
11	North Carolina	1,303	3.1%
50	North Dakota	50	0.1%
7	Ohio	1,545	3.7%
30	Oklahoma	317	0.8%
27	Oregon	508	1.2%
6	Pennsylvania	1,694	4.1%
40	Rhode Island	194	0.5%
25	South Carolina	588	1.4%
48	South Dakota	74	0.2%
15	Tennessee	862	2.1%
3	Texas	2,862	6.9%
32	Utah	275	0.7%
44	Vermont	113	0.3%
12	Virginia	1,203	2.9%
16	Washington	746	1.8%
37	West Virginia	212	0.5%
23	Wisconsin	613	1.5%
49	Wyoming	52	0.1%

RANK ORDER

RANK	STATE	PHYSICIANS	% of USA
1	California	4,921	11.9%
2	New York	3,756	9.1%
3	Texas	2,862	6.9%
4	Florida	2,217	5.3%
5	Illinois	1,874	4.5%
6	Pennsylvania	1,694	4.1%
7	Ohio	1,545	3.7%
8	New Jersey	1,537	3.7%
9	Georgia	1,380	3.3%
10	Michigan	1,370	3.3%
11	North Carolina	1,303	3.1%
12	Virginia	1,203	2.9%
13	Maryland	1,152	2.8%
13	Massachusetts	1,152	2.8%
15	Tennessee	862	2.1%
16	Washington	746	1.8%
17	Louisiana	729	1.8%
18	Missouri	725	1.7%
19	Indiana	723	1.7%
20	Connecticut	710	1.7%
21	Arizona	662	1.6%
22	Colorado	657	1.6%
23	Wisconsin	613	1.5%
24	Minnesota	590	1.4%
25	South Carolina	588	1.4%
26	Alabama	576	1.4%
27	Oregon	508	1.2%
28	Kentucky	505	1.2%
29	Mississippi	350	0.8%
30	Oklahoma	317	0.8%
31	Kansas	284	0.7%
32	Utah	275	0.7%
33	Nevada	264	0.6%
34	Arkansas	261	0.6%
35	Hawaii	251	0.6%
36	Iowa	217	0.5%
37	West Virginia	212	0.5%
38	New Mexico	203	0.5%
39	New Hampshire	197	0.5%
40	Rhode Island	194	0.5%
41	Nebraska	191	0.5%
42	Maine	159	0.4%
43	Idaho	132	0.3%
44	Vermont	113	0.3%
45	Delaware	106	0.3%
46	Montana	104	0.3%
47	Alaska	79	0.2%
48	South Dakota	74	0.2%
49	Wyoming	52	0.1%
50	North Dakota	50	0.1%
	District of Columbia	223	0.5%

Source: American Medical Association (Chicago, Illinois)
   "Physician Characteristics and Distribution in the U.S." (2006 Edition)
*As of December 31, 2004. Total does not include 591 physicians in U.S. territories and possessions. Obstetrics and Gynecology includes Gynecology and Oncology, Maternal and Fetal Medicine and Reproductive Endocrinology.

Rate of Physicians in Obstetrics and Gynecology in 2004

National Rate = 28 Physicians per 100,000 Female Population*

ALPHA ORDER

RANK	STATE	RATE
23	Alabama	25
23	Alaska	25
32	Arizona	23
45	Arkansas	19
18	California	27
14	Colorado	29
3	Connecticut	39
23	Delaware	25
23	Florida	25
10	Georgia	31
1	Hawaii	40
45	Idaho	19
14	Illinois	29
32	Indiana	23
50	Iowa	14
42	Kansas	21
29	Kentucky	24
10	Louisiana	31
29	Maine	24
1	Maryland	40
6	Massachusetts	35
18	Michigan	27
32	Minnesota	23
32	Mississippi	23
23	Missouri	25
39	Montana	22
39	Nebraska	22
32	Nevada	23
12	New Hampshire	30
8	New Jersey	34
42	New Mexico	21
4	New York	38
12	North Carolina	30
49	North Dakota	16
21	Ohio	26
48	Oklahoma	18
17	Oregon	28
21	Pennsylvania	26
6	Rhode Island	35
18	South Carolina	27
45	South Dakota	19
14	Tennessee	29
23	Texas	25
32	Utah	23
5	Vermont	36
9	Virginia	32
29	Washington	24
32	West Virginia	23
39	Wisconsin	22
42	Wyoming	21

RANK ORDER

RANK	STATE	RATE
1	Hawaii	40
1	Maryland	40
3	Connecticut	39
4	New York	38
5	Vermont	36
6	Massachusetts	35
6	Rhode Island	35
8	New Jersey	34
9	Virginia	32
10	Georgia	31
10	Louisiana	31
12	New Hampshire	30
12	North Carolina	30
14	Colorado	29
14	Illinois	29
14	Tennessee	29
17	Oregon	28
18	California	27
18	Michigan	27
18	South Carolina	27
21	Ohio	26
21	Pennsylvania	26
23	Alabama	25
23	Alaska	25
23	Delaware	25
23	Florida	25
23	Missouri	25
23	Texas	25
29	Kentucky	24
29	Maine	24
29	Washington	24
32	Arizona	23
32	Indiana	23
32	Minnesota	23
32	Mississippi	23
32	Nevada	23
32	Utah	23
32	West Virginia	23
39	Montana	22
39	Nebraska	22
39	Wisconsin	22
42	Kansas	21
42	New Mexico	21
42	Wyoming	21
45	Arkansas	19
45	Idaho	19
45	South Dakota	19
48	Oklahoma	18
49	North Dakota	16
50	Iowa	14

District of Columbia   76

Source: Morgan Quitno Press using data from American Medical Association (Chicago, Illinois)
    "Physician Characteristics and Distribution in the U.S." (2006 Edition)
*As of December 31, 2004. National rate does not include physicians in U.S. territories and possessions. Obstetrics and Gynecology includes Gynecology and Oncology, Maternal and Fetal Medicine and Reproductive Endocrinology.

Physicians in Ophthalmology in 2004

National Total = 18,525 Physicians*

ALPHA ORDER					RANK ORDER			
RANK	STATE	PHYSICIANS	% of USA		RANK	STATE	PHYSICIANS	% of USA
27	Alabama	222	1.2%		1	California	2,295	12.4%
49	Alaska	29	0.2%		2	New York	1,786	9.6%
23	Arizona	294	1.6%		3	Florida	1,230	6.6%
33	Arkansas	135	0.7%		4	Texas	1,116	6.0%
1	California	2,295	12.4%		5	Pennsylvania	891	4.8%
24	Colorado	280	1.5%		6	Illinois	736	4.0%
21	Connecticut	312	1.7%		7	Ohio	649	3.5%
47	Delaware	38	0.2%		8	New Jersey	638	3.4%
3	Florida	1,230	6.6%		9	Michigan	570	3.1%
14	Georgia	437	2.4%		10	Maryland	568	3.1%
38	Hawaii	92	0.5%		11	Massachusetts	554	3.0%
43	Idaho	62	0.3%		12	Virginia	474	2.6%
6	Illinois	736	4.0%		13	North Carolina	452	2.4%
22	Indiana	295	1.6%		14	Georgia	437	2.4%
30	Iowa	159	0.9%		15	Washington	377	2.0%
29	Kansas	162	0.9%		16	Tennessee	360	1.9%
28	Kentucky	204	1.1%		17	Missouri	343	1.9%
19	Louisiana	329	1.8%		18	Wisconsin	341	1.8%
41	Maine	78	0.4%		19	Louisiana	329	1.8%
10	Maryland	568	3.1%		20	Minnesota	318	1.7%
11	Massachusetts	554	3.0%		21	Connecticut	312	1.7%
9	Michigan	570	3.1%		22	Indiana	295	1.6%
20	Minnesota	318	1.7%		23	Arizona	294	1.6%
32	Mississippi	144	0.8%		24	Colorado	280	1.5%
17	Missouri	343	1.9%		25	South Carolina	238	1.3%
44	Montana	54	0.3%		26	Oregon	230	1.2%
37	Nebraska	94	0.5%		27	Alabama	222	1.2%
35	Nevada	100	0.5%		28	Kentucky	204	1.1%
42	New Hampshire	70	0.4%		29	Kansas	162	0.9%
8	New Jersey	638	3.4%		30	Iowa	159	0.9%
40	New Mexico	83	0.4%		31	Oklahoma	145	0.8%
2	New York	1,786	9.6%		32	Mississippi	144	0.8%
13	North Carolina	452	2.4%		33	Arkansas	135	0.7%
48	North Dakota	35	0.2%		34	Utah	123	0.7%
7	Ohio	649	3.5%		35	Nevada	100	0.5%
31	Oklahoma	145	0.8%		36	West Virginia	99	0.5%
26	Oregon	230	1.2%		37	Nebraska	94	0.5%
5	Pennsylvania	891	4.8%		38	Hawaii	92	0.5%
39	Rhode Island	85	0.5%		39	Rhode Island	85	0.5%
25	South Carolina	238	1.3%		40	New Mexico	83	0.4%
46	South Dakota	42	0.2%		41	Maine	78	0.4%
16	Tennessee	360	1.9%		42	New Hampshire	70	0.4%
4	Texas	1,116	6.0%		43	Idaho	62	0.3%
34	Utah	123	0.7%		44	Montana	54	0.3%
45	Vermont	47	0.3%		45	Vermont	47	0.3%
12	Virginia	474	2.6%		46	South Dakota	42	0.2%
15	Washington	377	2.0%		47	Delaware	38	0.2%
36	West Virginia	99	0.5%		48	North Dakota	35	0.2%
18	Wisconsin	341	1.8%		49	Alaska	29	0.2%
50	Wyoming	18	0.1%		50	Wyoming	18	0.1%
						District of Columbia	92	0.5%

Source: American Medical Association (Chicago, Illinois)
    "Physician Characteristics and Distribution in the U.S." (2006 Edition)
*As of December 31, 2004. Total does not include 181 physicians in U.S. territories and possessions.
Ophthalmology is the branch of medicine dealing with the anatomy, functions and diseases of the eye.

Rate of Physicians in Ophthalmology in 2004

National Rate = 6 Physicians per 100,000 Population*

ALPHA ORDER

RANK	STATE	RATE
29	Alabama	5
45	Alaska	4
29	Arizona	5
29	Arkansas	5
12	California	6
12	Colorado	6
2	Connecticut	9
29	Delaware	5
7	Florida	7
29	Georgia	5
7	Hawaii	7
45	Idaho	4
12	Illinois	6
29	Indiana	5
29	Iowa	5
12	Kansas	6
29	Kentucky	5
7	Louisiana	7
12	Maine	6
1	Maryland	10
2	Massachusetts	9
12	Michigan	6
12	Minnesota	6
29	Mississippi	5
12	Missouri	6
12	Montana	6
29	Nebraska	5
45	Nevada	4
29	New Hampshire	5
7	New Jersey	7
45	New Mexico	4
2	New York	9
29	North Carolina	5
12	North Dakota	6
12	Ohio	6
45	Oklahoma	4
12	Oregon	6
7	Pennsylvania	7
5	Rhode Island	8
12	South Carolina	6
29	South Dakota	5
12	Tennessee	6
29	Texas	5
29	Utah	5
5	Vermont	8
12	Virginia	6
12	Washington	6
29	West Virginia	5
12	Wisconsin	6
45	Wyoming	4

RANK ORDER

RANK	STATE	RATE
1	Maryland	10
2	Connecticut	9
2	Massachusetts	9
2	New York	9
5	Rhode Island	8
5	Vermont	8
7	Florida	7
7	Hawaii	7
7	Louisiana	7
7	New Jersey	7
7	Pennsylvania	7
12	California	6
12	Colorado	6
12	Illinois	6
12	Kansas	6
12	Maine	6
12	Michigan	6
12	Minnesota	6
12	Missouri	6
12	Montana	6
12	North Dakota	6
12	Ohio	6
12	Oregon	6
12	South Carolina	6
12	Tennessee	6
12	Virginia	6
12	Washington	6
12	Wisconsin	6
29	Alabama	5
29	Arizona	5
29	Arkansas	5
29	Delaware	5
29	Georgia	5
29	Indiana	5
29	Iowa	5
29	Kentucky	5
29	Mississippi	5
29	Nebraska	5
29	New Hampshire	5
29	North Carolina	5
29	South Dakota	5
29	Texas	5
29	Utah	5
29	West Virginia	5
45	Alaska	4
45	Idaho	4
45	Nevada	4
45	New Mexico	4
45	Oklahoma	4
45	Wyoming	4

District of Columbia 17

Source: Morgan Quitno Press using data from American Medical Association (Chicago, Illinois)
"Physician Characteristics and Distribution in the U.S." (2006 Edition)
*As of December 31, 2004. National rate does not include physicians in U.S. territories and possessions.
Ophthalmology is the branch of medicine dealing with the anatomy, functions and diseases of the eye.

Physicians in Orthopedic Surgery in 2004

National Total = 23,633 Physicians*

ALPHA ORDER

RANK	STATE	PHYSICIANS	% of USA
25	Alabama	356	1.5%
47	Alaska	69	0.3%
24	Arizona	358	1.5%
32	Arkansas	184	0.8%
1	California	2,876	12.2%
20	Colorado	438	1.9%
23	Connecticut	365	1.5%
48	Delaware	67	0.3%
4	Florida	1,301	5.5%
13	Georgia	617	2.6%
42	Hawaii	115	0.5%
40	Idaho	126	0.5%
6	Illinois	912	3.9%
19	Indiana	451	1.9%
31	Iowa	190	0.8%
29	Kansas	217	0.9%
28	Kentucky	304	1.3%
22	Louisiana	418	1.8%
37	Maine	128	0.5%
14	Maryland	594	2.5%
8	Massachusetts	730	3.1%
11	Michigan	629	2.7%
17	Minnesota	478	2.0%
34	Mississippi	181	0.8%
21	Missouri	433	1.8%
44	Montana	110	0.5%
35	Nebraska	165	0.7%
37	Nevada	128	0.5%
39	New Hampshire	127	0.5%
9	New Jersey	712	3.0%
36	New Mexico	153	0.6%
2	New York	1,788	7.6%
10	North Carolina	675	2.9%
50	North Dakota	43	0.2%
7	Ohio	872	3.7%
30	Oklahoma	215	0.9%
27	Oregon	321	1.4%
5	Pennsylvania	1,069	4.5%
42	Rhode Island	115	0.5%
25	South Carolina	356	1.5%
46	South Dakota	71	0.3%
15	Tennessee	534	2.3%
3	Texas	1,472	6.2%
33	Utah	183	0.8%
45	Vermont	75	0.3%
12	Virginia	619	2.6%
16	Washington	529	2.2%
41	West Virginia	118	0.5%
18	Wisconsin	472	2.0%
49	Wyoming	64	0.3%

RANK ORDER

RANK	STATE	PHYSICIANS	% of USA
1	California	2,876	12.2%
2	New York	1,788	7.6%
3	Texas	1,472	6.2%
4	Florida	1,301	5.5%
5	Pennsylvania	1,069	4.5%
6	Illinois	912	3.9%
7	Ohio	872	3.7%
8	Massachusetts	730	3.1%
9	New Jersey	712	3.0%
10	North Carolina	675	2.9%
11	Michigan	629	2.7%
12	Virginia	619	2.6%
13	Georgia	617	2.6%
14	Maryland	594	2.5%
15	Tennessee	534	2.3%
16	Washington	529	2.2%
17	Minnesota	478	2.0%
18	Wisconsin	472	2.0%
19	Indiana	451	1.9%
20	Colorado	438	1.9%
21	Missouri	433	1.8%
22	Louisiana	418	1.8%
23	Connecticut	365	1.5%
24	Arizona	358	1.5%
25	Alabama	356	1.5%
25	South Carolina	356	1.5%
27	Oregon	321	1.4%
28	Kentucky	304	1.3%
29	Kansas	217	0.9%
30	Oklahoma	215	0.9%
31	Iowa	190	0.8%
32	Arkansas	184	0.8%
33	Utah	183	0.8%
34	Mississippi	181	0.8%
35	Nebraska	165	0.7%
36	New Mexico	153	0.6%
37	Maine	128	0.5%
37	Nevada	128	0.5%
39	New Hampshire	127	0.5%
40	Idaho	126	0.5%
41	West Virginia	118	0.5%
42	Hawaii	115	0.5%
42	Rhode Island	115	0.5%
44	Montana	110	0.5%
45	Vermont	75	0.3%
46	South Dakota	71	0.3%
47	Alaska	69	0.3%
48	Delaware	67	0.3%
49	Wyoming	64	0.3%
50	North Dakota	43	0.2%
	District of Columbia	110	0.5%

Source: American Medical Association (Chicago, Illinois)
   "Physician Characteristics and Distribution in the U.S." (2006 Edition)
*As of December 31, 2004. Total does not include 163 physicians in U.S. territories and possessions.
Orthopedics is the branch of medicine dealing with the skeletal system.

Rate of Physicians in Orthopedic Surgery in 2004

National Rate = 8 Physicians per 100,000 Population*

ALPHA ORDER

RANK ORDER

RANK	STATE	RATE		RANK	STATE	RATE
24	Alabama	8		1	Wyoming	13
4	Alaska	11		2	Montana	12
45	Arizona	6		2	Vermont	12
36	Arkansas	7		4	Alaska	11
24	California	8		4	Maryland	11
8	Colorado	10		4	Massachusetts	11
8	Connecticut	10		4	Rhode Island	11
24	Delaware	8		8	Colorado	10
36	Florida	7		8	Connecticut	10
36	Georgia	7		8	Maine	10
12	Hawaii	9		8	New Hampshire	10
12	Idaho	9		12	Hawaii	9
36	Illinois	7		12	Idaho	9
36	Indiana	7		12	Louisiana	9
45	Iowa	6		12	Minnesota	9
24	Kansas	8		12	Nebraska	9
36	Kentucky	7		12	New York	9
12	Louisiana	9		12	Oregon	9
8	Maine	10		12	Pennsylvania	9
4	Maryland	11		12	South Dakota	9
4	Massachusetts	11		12	Tennessee	9
45	Michigan	6		12	Washington	9
12	Minnesota	9		12	Wisconsin	9
45	Mississippi	6		24	Alabama	8
24	Missouri	8		24	California	8
2	Montana	12		24	Delaware	8
12	Nebraska	9		24	Kansas	8
50	Nevada	5		24	Missouri	8
8	New Hampshire	10		24	New Jersey	8
24	New Jersey	8		24	New Mexico	8
24	New Mexico	8		24	North Carolina	8
12	New York	9		24	Ohio	8
24	North Carolina	8		24	South Carolina	8
36	North Dakota	7		24	Utah	8
24	Ohio	8		24	Virginia	8
45	Oklahoma	6		36	Arkansas	7
12	Oregon	9		36	Florida	7
12	Pennsylvania	9		36	Georgia	7
4	Rhode Island	11		36	Illinois	7
24	South Carolina	8		36	Indiana	7
12	South Dakota	9		36	Kentucky	7
12	Tennessee	9		36	North Dakota	7
36	Texas	7		36	Texas	7
24	Utah	8		36	West Virginia	7
2	Vermont	12		45	Arizona	6
24	Virginia	8		45	Iowa	6
12	Washington	9		45	Michigan	6
36	West Virginia	7		45	Mississippi	6
12	Wisconsin	9		45	Oklahoma	6
1	Wyoming	13		50	Nevada	5

District of Columbia   20

*Source: Morgan Quitno Press using data from American Medical Association (Chicago, Illinois)
    "Physician Characteristics and Distribution in the U.S." (2006 Edition)*
*As of December 31, 2004. National rate does not include physicians in U.S. territories and possessions.
Orthopedics is the branch of medicine dealing with the skeletal system.

Physicians in Plastic Surgery in 2004

National Total = 6,814 Physicians*

ALPHA ORDER

RANK	STATE	PHYSICIANS	% of USA
26	Alabama	78	1.1%
49	Alaska	7	0.1%
18	Arizona	125	1.8%
34	Arkansas	35	0.5%
1	California	1,029	15.1%
19	Colorado	106	1.6%
24	Connecticut	90	1.3%
41	Delaware	22	0.3%
3	Florida	550	8.1%
12	Georgia	178	2.6%
35	Hawaii	34	0.5%
43	Idaho	20	0.3%
6	Illinois	251	3.7%
20	Indiana	96	1.4%
40	Iowa	26	0.4%
30	Kansas	62	0.9%
22	Kentucky	93	1.4%
23	Louisiana	92	1.4%
45	Maine	11	0.2%
14	Maryland	167	2.5%
10	Massachusetts	197	2.9%
9	Michigan	198	2.9%
21	Minnesota	95	1.4%
31	Mississippi	41	0.6%
17	Missouri	131	1.9%
44	Montana	15	0.2%
39	Nebraska	27	0.4%
31	Nevada	41	0.6%
41	New Hampshire	22	0.3%
7	New Jersey	222	3.3%
36	New Mexico	30	0.4%
2	New York	620	9.1%
11	North Carolina	180	2.6%
46	North Dakota	10	0.1%
8	Ohio	209	3.1%
31	Oklahoma	41	0.6%
29	Oregon	69	1.0%
5	Pennsylvania	264	3.9%
37	Rhode Island	28	0.4%
27	South Carolina	77	1.1%
46	South Dakota	10	0.1%
15	Tennessee	145	2.1%
4	Texas	531	7.8%
28	Utah	71	1.0%
48	Vermont	9	0.1%
13	Virginia	174	2.6%
16	Washington	132	1.9%
37	West Virginia	28	0.4%
25	Wisconsin	88	1.3%
50	Wyoming	3	0.0%

RANK ORDER

RANK	STATE	PHYSICIANS	% of USA
1	California	1,029	15.1%
2	New York	620	9.1%
3	Florida	550	8.1%
4	Texas	531	7.8%
5	Pennsylvania	264	3.9%
6	Illinois	251	3.7%
7	New Jersey	222	3.3%
8	Ohio	209	3.1%
9	Michigan	198	2.9%
10	Massachusetts	197	2.9%
11	North Carolina	180	2.6%
12	Georgia	178	2.6%
13	Virginia	174	2.6%
14	Maryland	167	2.5%
15	Tennessee	145	2.1%
16	Washington	132	1.9%
17	Missouri	131	1.9%
18	Arizona	125	1.8%
19	Colorado	106	1.6%
20	Indiana	96	1.4%
21	Minnesota	95	1.4%
22	Kentucky	93	1.4%
23	Louisiana	92	1.4%
24	Connecticut	90	1.3%
25	Wisconsin	88	1.3%
26	Alabama	78	1.1%
27	South Carolina	77	1.1%
28	Utah	71	1.0%
29	Oregon	69	1.0%
30	Kansas	62	0.9%
31	Mississippi	41	0.6%
31	Nevada	41	0.6%
31	Oklahoma	41	0.6%
34	Arkansas	35	0.5%
35	Hawaii	34	0.5%
36	New Mexico	30	0.4%
37	Rhode Island	28	0.4%
37	West Virginia	28	0.4%
39	Nebraska	27	0.4%
40	Iowa	26	0.4%
41	Delaware	22	0.3%
41	New Hampshire	22	0.3%
43	Idaho	20	0.3%
44	Montana	15	0.2%
45	Maine	11	0.2%
46	North Dakota	10	0.1%
46	South Dakota	10	0.1%
48	Vermont	9	0.1%
49	Alaska	7	0.1%
50	Wyoming	3	0.0%
	District of Columbia	34	0.5%

Source: American Medical Association (Chicago, Illinois)
    "Physician Characteristics and Distribution in the U.S." (2006 Edition)
*As of December 31, 2004. Total does not include 38 physicians in U.S. territories and possessions.

Rate of Physicians in Plastic Surgery in 2004

National Rate = 2 Physicians per 100,000 Population*

ALPHA ORDER				RANK ORDER		
RANK	STATE	RATE		RANK	STATE	RATE
12	Alabama	2		1	California	3
41	Alaska	1		1	Connecticut	3
12	Arizona	2		1	Delaware	3
41	Arkansas	1		1	Florida	3
1	California	3		1	Hawaii	3
12	Colorado	2		1	Maryland	3
1	Connecticut	3		1	Massachusetts	3
1	Delaware	3		1	New Jersey	3
1	Florida	3		1	New York	3
12	Georgia	2		1	Rhode Island	3
1	Hawaii	3		1	Utah	3
41	Idaho	1		12	Alabama	2
12	Illinois	2		12	Arizona	2
12	Indiana	2		12	Colorado	2
41	Iowa	1		12	Georgia	2
12	Kansas	2		12	Illinois	2
12	Kentucky	2		12	Indiana	2
12	Louisiana	2		12	Kansas	2
41	Maine	1		12	Kentucky	2
1	Maryland	3		12	Louisiana	2
1	Massachusetts	3		12	Michigan	2
12	Michigan	2		12	Minnesota	2
12	Minnesota	2		12	Missouri	2
41	Mississippi	1		12	Montana	2
12	Missouri	2		12	Nebraska	2
12	Montana	2		12	Nevada	2
12	Nebraska	2		12	New Hampshire	2
12	Nevada	2		12	New Mexico	2
12	New Hampshire	2		12	North Carolina	2
1	New Jersey	3		12	North Dakota	2
12	New Mexico	2		12	Ohio	2
1	New York	3		12	Oregon	2
12	North Carolina	2		12	Pennsylvania	2
12	North Dakota	2		12	South Carolina	2
12	Ohio	2		12	Tennessee	2
41	Oklahoma	1		12	Texas	2
12	Oregon	2		12	Virginia	2
12	Pennsylvania	2		12	Washington	2
1	Rhode Island	3		12	West Virginia	2
12	South Carolina	2		12	Wisconsin	2
41	South Dakota	1		41	Alaska	1
12	Tennessee	2		41	Arkansas	1
12	Texas	2		41	Idaho	1
1	Utah	3		41	Iowa	1
41	Vermont	1		41	Maine	1
12	Virginia	2		41	Mississippi	1
12	Washington	2		41	Oklahoma	1
12	West Virginia	2		41	South Dakota	1
12	Wisconsin	2		41	Vermont	1
41	Wyoming	1		41	Wyoming	1
					District of Columbia	6

Source: Morgan Quitno Press using data from American Medical Association (Chicago, Illinois)
    "Physician Characteristics and Distribution in the U.S." (2006 Edition)
*As of December 31, 2004. National rate does not include physicians in U.S. territories and possessions.

Physicians in Other Specialties in 2004

National Total = 207,855 Physicians*

ALPHA ORDER

RANK	STATE	PHYSICIANS	% of USA
28	Alabama	2,309	1.1%
48	Alaska	384	0.2%
22	Arizona	3,439	1.7%
32	Arkansas	1,440	0.7%
1	California	25,640	12.3%
23	Colorado	3,407	1.6%
21	Connecticut	3,509	1.7%
45	Delaware	553	0.3%
4	Florida	11,068	5.3%
14	Georgia	5,136	2.5%
37	Hawaii	1,097	0.5%
44	Idaho	593	0.3%
6	Illinois	8,974	4.3%
18	Indiana	3,634	1.7%
33	Iowa	1,417	0.7%
29	Kansas	1,635	0.8%
26	Kentucky	2,506	1.2%
24	Louisiana	2,970	1.4%
39	Maine	1,016	0.5%
10	Maryland	6,539	3.1%
7	Massachusetts	8,414	4.0%
11	Michigan	6,373	3.1%
19	Minnesota	3,572	1.7%
34	Mississippi	1,284	0.6%
20	Missouri	3,558	1.7%
46	Montana	549	0.3%
40	Nebraska	988	0.5%
36	Nevada	1,200	0.6%
42	New Hampshire	921	0.4%
9	New Jersey	6,639	3.2%
35	New Mexico	1,265	0.6%
2	New York	19,671	9.5%
12	North Carolina	5,641	2.7%
49	North Dakota	370	0.2%
8	Ohio	7,585	3.6%
30	Oklahoma	1,516	0.7%
25	Oregon	2,627	1.3%
5	Pennsylvania	9,947	4.8%
41	Rhode Island	954	0.5%
27	South Carolina	2,465	1.2%
47	South Dakota	387	0.2%
17	Tennessee	3,735	1.8%
3	Texas	12,518	6.0%
31	Utah	1,450	0.7%
43	Vermont	627	0.3%
13	Virginia	5,415	2.6%
15	Washington	4,583	2.2%
38	West Virginia	1,026	0.5%
16	Wisconsin	3,810	1.8%
50	Wyoming	244	0.1%

RANK ORDER

RANK	STATE	PHYSICIANS	% of USA
1	California	25,640	12.3%
2	New York	19,671	9.5%
3	Texas	12,518	6.0%
4	Florida	11,068	5.3%
5	Pennsylvania	9,947	4.8%
6	Illinois	8,974	4.3%
7	Massachusetts	8,414	4.0%
8	Ohio	7,585	3.6%
9	New Jersey	6,639	3.2%
10	Maryland	6,539	3.1%
11	Michigan	6,373	3.1%
12	North Carolina	5,641	2.7%
13	Virginia	5,415	2.6%
14	Georgia	5,136	2.5%
15	Washington	4,583	2.2%
16	Wisconsin	3,810	1.8%
17	Tennessee	3,735	1.8%
18	Indiana	3,634	1.7%
19	Minnesota	3,572	1.7%
20	Missouri	3,558	1.7%
21	Connecticut	3,509	1.7%
22	Arizona	3,439	1.7%
23	Colorado	3,407	1.6%
24	Louisiana	2,970	1.4%
25	Oregon	2,627	1.3%
26	Kentucky	2,506	1.2%
27	South Carolina	2,465	1.2%
28	Alabama	2,309	1.1%
29	Kansas	1,635	0.8%
30	Oklahoma	1,516	0.7%
31	Utah	1,450	0.7%
32	Arkansas	1,440	0.7%
33	Iowa	1,417	0.7%
34	Mississippi	1,284	0.6%
35	New Mexico	1,265	0.6%
36	Nevada	1,200	0.6%
37	Hawaii	1,097	0.5%
38	West Virginia	1,026	0.5%
39	Maine	1,016	0.5%
40	Nebraska	988	0.5%
41	Rhode Island	954	0.5%
42	New Hampshire	921	0.4%
43	Vermont	627	0.3%
44	Idaho	593	0.3%
45	Delaware	553	0.3%
46	Montana	549	0.3%
47	South Dakota	387	0.2%
48	Alaska	384	0.2%
49	North Dakota	370	0.2%
50	Wyoming	244	0.1%
	District of Columbia	1,255	0.6%

Source: American Medical Association (Chicago, Illinois)
    "Physician Characteristics and Distribution in the U.S." (2006 Edition)
*As of December 31, 2004. Total does not include 2,448 physicians in U.S. territories and possessions. Other Specialties include Aerospace Medicine, Anesthesiology, Child Psychiatry, Diagnostic Radiology, Emergency Medicine, Forensic Pathology, Nuclear Medicine, Occupational Medicine, Neurology, Psychiatry, Public Health, Anatomic/Clinical Pathology, Radiology, Radiation Oncology and other specialties.

Rate of Physicians in Other Specialties in 2004

National Rate = 71 Physicians per 100,000 Population*

RANK	STATE	RATE
43	Alabama	51
33	Alaska	59
30	Arizona	60
42	Arkansas	52
15	California	71
11	Colorado	74
5	Connecticut	100
20	Delaware	67
25	Florida	64
36	Georgia	58
7	Hawaii	87
49	Idaho	43
15	Illinois	71
36	Indiana	58
46	Iowa	48
30	Kansas	60
30	Kentucky	60
21	Louisiana	66
9	Maine	77
2	Maryland	118
1	Massachusetts	131
26	Michigan	63
18	Minnesota	70
48	Mississippi	44
28	Missouri	62
33	Montana	59
39	Nebraska	57
43	Nevada	51
15	New Hampshire	71
10	New Jersey	76
21	New Mexico	66
3	New York	102
21	North Carolina	66
36	North Dakota	58
21	Ohio	66
49	Oklahoma	43
13	Oregon	73
8	Pennsylvania	80
6	Rhode Island	88
33	South Carolina	59
45	South Dakota	50
26	Tennessee	63
41	Texas	56
29	Utah	61
4	Vermont	101
13	Virginia	73
11	Washington	74
39	West Virginia	57
19	Wisconsin	69
46	Wyoming	48

RANK	STATE	RATE
1	Massachusetts	131
2	Maryland	118
3	New York	102
4	Vermont	101
5	Connecticut	100
6	Rhode Island	88
7	Hawaii	87
8	Pennsylvania	80
9	Maine	77
10	New Jersey	76
11	Colorado	74
11	Washington	74
13	Oregon	73
13	Virginia	73
15	California	71
15	Illinois	71
15	New Hampshire	71
18	Minnesota	70
19	Wisconsin	69
20	Delaware	67
21	Louisiana	66
21	New Mexico	66
21	North Carolina	66
21	Ohio	66
25	Florida	64
26	Michigan	63
26	Tennessee	63
28	Missouri	62
29	Utah	61
30	Arizona	60
30	Kansas	60
30	Kentucky	60
33	Alaska	59
33	Montana	59
33	South Carolina	59
36	Georgia	58
36	Indiana	58
36	North Dakota	58
39	Nebraska	57
39	West Virginia	57
41	Texas	56
42	Arkansas	52
43	Alabama	51
43	Nevada	51
45	South Dakota	50
46	Iowa	48
46	Wyoming	48
48	Mississippi	44
49	Idaho	43
49	Oklahoma	43

	District of Columbia	227

Source: Morgan Quitno Press using data from American Medical Association (Chicago, Illinois)
"Physician Characteristics and Distribution in the U.S." (2006 Edition)

*As of December 31, 2004. National rate does not include physicians in U.S. territories and possessions. Other Specialties include Aerospace Medicine, Anesthesiology, Child Psychiatry, Diagnostic Radiology, Emergency Medicine, Forensic Pathology, Nuclear Medicine, Occupational Medicine, Neurology, Psychiatry, Public Health, Anatomic/Clinical Pathology, Radiology, Radiation Oncology and other specialties.

Physicians in Anesthesiology in 2004

National Total = 38,585 Physicians*

ALPHA ORDER

RANK	STATE	PHYSICIANS	% of USA
28	Alabama	451	1.2%
47	Alaska	75	0.2%
18	Arizona	791	2.1%
34	Arkansas	293	0.8%
1	California	4,755	12.3%
20	Colorado	675	1.7%
26	Connecticut	509	1.3%
46	Delaware	86	0.2%
4	Florida	2,400	6.2%
15	Georgia	890	2.3%
41	Hawaii	147	0.4%
44	Idaho	106	0.3%
5	Illinois	1,774	4.6%
16	Indiana	876	2.3%
33	Iowa	314	0.8%
30	Kansas	333	0.9%
23	Kentucky	532	1.4%
24	Louisiana	526	1.4%
40	Maine	165	0.4%
10	Maryland	994	2.6%
9	Massachusetts	1,336	3.5%
12	Michigan	922	2.4%
22	Minnesota	558	1.4%
35	Mississippi	244	0.6%
21	Missouri	646	1.7%
42	Montana	119	0.3%
37	Nebraska	215	0.6%
32	Nevada	317	0.8%
39	New Hampshire	167	0.4%
8	New Jersey	1,419	3.7%
36	New Mexico	216	0.6%
2	New York	3,150	8.2%
11	North Carolina	940	2.4%
49	North Dakota	55	0.1%
7	Ohio	1,434	3.7%
31	Oklahoma	330	0.9%
25	Oregon	524	1.4%
6	Pennsylvania	1,606	4.2%
43	Rhode Island	107	0.3%
27	South Carolina	456	1.2%
48	South Dakota	62	0.2%
19	Tennessee	740	1.9%
3	Texas	2,913	7.5%
29	Utah	339	0.9%
45	Vermont	100	0.3%
14	Virginia	918	2.4%
13	Washington	921	2.4%
38	West Virginia	174	0.5%
17	Wisconsin	795	2.1%
50	Wyoming	49	0.1%

RANK ORDER

RANK	STATE	PHYSICIANS	% of USA
1	California	4,755	12.3%
2	New York	3,150	8.2%
3	Texas	2,913	7.5%
4	Florida	2,400	6.2%
5	Illinois	1,774	4.6%
6	Pennsylvania	1,606	4.2%
7	Ohio	1,434	3.7%
8	New Jersey	1,419	3.7%
9	Massachusetts	1,336	3.5%
10	Maryland	994	2.6%
11	North Carolina	940	2.4%
12	Michigan	922	2.4%
13	Washington	921	2.4%
14	Virginia	918	2.4%
15	Georgia	890	2.3%
16	Indiana	876	2.3%
17	Wisconsin	795	2.1%
18	Arizona	791	2.1%
19	Tennessee	740	1.9%
20	Colorado	675	1.7%
21	Missouri	646	1.7%
22	Minnesota	558	1.4%
23	Kentucky	532	1.4%
24	Louisiana	526	1.4%
25	Oregon	524	1.4%
26	Connecticut	509	1.3%
27	South Carolina	456	1.2%
28	Alabama	451	1.2%
29	Utah	339	0.9%
30	Kansas	333	0.9%
31	Oklahoma	330	0.9%
32	Nevada	317	0.8%
33	Iowa	314	0.8%
34	Arkansas	293	0.8%
35	Mississippi	244	0.6%
36	New Mexico	216	0.6%
37	Nebraska	215	0.6%
38	West Virginia	174	0.5%
39	New Hampshire	167	0.4%
40	Maine	165	0.4%
41	Hawaii	147	0.4%
42	Montana	119	0.3%
43	Rhode Island	107	0.3%
44	Idaho	106	0.3%
45	Vermont	100	0.3%
46	Delaware	86	0.2%
47	Alaska	75	0.2%
48	South Dakota	62	0.2%
49	North Dakota	55	0.1%
50	Wyoming	49	0.1%
	District of Columbia	121	0.3%

Source: American Medical Association (Chicago, Illinois)
   "Physician Characteristics and Distribution in the U.S." (2006 Edition)
*As of December 31, 2004. Total does not include 237 physicians in U.S. territories and possessions.

Rate of Physicians in Anesthesiology in 2004

National Rate = 13 Physicians per 100,000 Population*

ALPHA ORDER				RANK ORDER		
RANK	STATE	RATE		RANK	STATE	RATE
39	Alabama	10		1	Massachusetts	21
31	Alaska	11		2	Maryland	18
10	Arizona	14		3	New Jersey	16
31	Arkansas	11		3	New York	16
17	California	13		3	Vermont	16
6	Colorado	15		6	Colorado	15
6	Connecticut	15		6	Connecticut	15
39	Delaware	10		6	Oregon	15
10	Florida	14		6	Washington	15
39	Georgia	10		10	Arizona	14
26	Hawaii	12		10	Florida	14
48	Idaho	8		10	Illinois	14
10	Illinois	14		10	Indiana	14
10	Indiana	14		10	Nevada	14
31	Iowa	11		10	Utah	14
26	Kansas	12		10	Wisconsin	14
17	Kentucky	13		17	California	13
26	Louisiana	12		17	Kentucky	13
17	Maine	13		17	Maine	13
2	Maryland	18		17	Montana	13
1	Massachusetts	21		17	New Hampshire	13
45	Michigan	9		17	Ohio	13
31	Minnesota	11		17	Pennsylvania	13
48	Mississippi	8		17	Tennessee	13
31	Missouri	11		17	Texas	13
17	Montana	13		26	Hawaii	12
26	Nebraska	12		26	Kansas	12
10	Nevada	14		26	Louisiana	12
17	New Hampshire	13		26	Nebraska	12
3	New Jersey	16		26	Virginia	12
31	New Mexico	11		31	Alaska	11
3	New York	16		31	Arkansas	11
31	North Carolina	11		31	Iowa	11
45	North Dakota	9		31	Minnesota	11
17	Ohio	13		31	Missouri	11
45	Oklahoma	9		31	New Mexico	11
6	Oregon	15		31	North Carolina	11
17	Pennsylvania	13		31	South Carolina	11
39	Rhode Island	10		39	Alabama	10
31	South Carolina	11		39	Delaware	10
48	South Dakota	8		39	Georgia	10
17	Tennessee	13		39	Rhode Island	10
17	Texas	13		39	West Virginia	10
10	Utah	14		39	Wyoming	10
3	Vermont	16		45	Michigan	9
26	Virginia	12		45	North Dakota	9
6	Washington	15		45	Oklahoma	9
39	West Virginia	10		48	Idaho	8
10	Wisconsin	14		48	Mississippi	8
39	Wyoming	10		48	South Dakota	8
					District of Columbia	22

Source: Morgan Quitno Press using data from American Medical Association (Chicago, Illinois)
    "Physician Characteristics and Distribution in the U.S." (2006 Edition)
*As of December 31, 2004. National rate does not include physicians in U.S. territories and possessions.

Physicians in Psychiatry in 2004

National Total = 39,860 Physicians*

ALPHA ORDER

RANK ORDER

RANK	STATE	PHYSICIANS	% of USA		RANK	STATE	PHYSICIANS	% of USA
28	Alabama	330	0.8%		1	California	5,503	13.8%
47	Alaska	74	0.2%		2	New York	5,491	13.8%
19	Arizona	571	1.4%		3	Massachusetts	2,148	5.4%
35	Arkansas	220	0.6%		4	Pennsylvania	1,925	4.8%
1	California	5,503	13.8%		5	Texas	1,781	4.5%
18	Colorado	584	1.5%		6	Florida	1,685	4.2%
14	Connecticut	926	2.3%		7	Illinois	1,554	3.9%
44	Delaware	87	0.2%		8	New Jersey	1,402	3.5%
6	Florida	1,685	4.2%		9	Maryland	1,339	3.4%
15	Georgia	869	2.2%		10	Ohio	1,207	3.0%
34	Hawaii	230	0.6%		11	Michigan	1,076	2.7%
47	Idaho	74	0.2%		12	Virginia	1,043	2.6%
7	Illinois	1,554	3.9%		13	North Carolina	1,022	2.6%
24	Indiana	479	1.2%		14	Connecticut	926	2.3%
37	Iowa	208	0.5%		15	Georgia	869	2.2%
29	Kansas	304	0.8%		16	Washington	779	2.0%
27	Kentucky	404	1.0%		17	Wisconsin	597	1.5%
23	Louisiana	527	1.3%		18	Colorado	584	1.5%
33	Maine	242	0.6%		19	Arizona	571	1.4%
9	Maryland	1,339	3.4%		20	Missouri	568	1.4%
3	Massachusetts	2,148	5.4%		21	Tennessee	553	1.4%
11	Michigan	1,076	2.7%		22	Minnesota	542	1.4%
22	Minnesota	542	1.4%		23	Louisiana	527	1.3%
36	Mississippi	214	0.5%		24	Indiana	479	1.2%
20	Missouri	568	1.4%		25	South Carolina	457	1.1%
45	Montana	78	0.2%		26	Oregon	438	1.1%
42	Nebraska	161	0.4%		27	Kentucky	404	1.0%
43	Nevada	158	0.4%		28	Alabama	330	0.8%
39	New Hampshire	192	0.5%		29	Kansas	304	0.8%
8	New Jersey	1,402	3.5%		30	Oklahoma	270	0.7%
31	New Mexico	250	0.6%		31	New Mexico	250	0.6%
2	New York	5,491	13.8%		32	Rhode Island	247	0.6%
13	North Carolina	1,022	2.6%		33	Maine	242	0.6%
46	North Dakota	76	0.2%		34	Hawaii	230	0.6%
10	Ohio	1,207	3.0%		35	Arkansas	220	0.6%
30	Oklahoma	270	0.7%		36	Mississippi	214	0.5%
26	Oregon	438	1.1%		37	Iowa	208	0.5%
4	Pennsylvania	1,925	4.8%		38	Utah	194	0.5%
32	Rhode Island	247	0.6%		39	New Hampshire	192	0.5%
25	South Carolina	457	1.1%		40	West Virginia	166	0.4%
49	South Dakota	69	0.2%		41	Vermont	163	0.4%
21	Tennessee	553	1.4%		42	Nebraska	161	0.4%
5	Texas	1,781	4.5%		43	Nevada	158	0.4%
38	Utah	194	0.5%		44	Delaware	87	0.2%
41	Vermont	163	0.4%		45	Montana	78	0.2%
12	Virginia	1,043	2.6%		46	North Dakota	76	0.2%
16	Washington	779	2.0%		47	Alaska	74	0.2%
40	West Virginia	166	0.4%		47	Idaho	74	0.2%
17	Wisconsin	597	1.5%		49	South Dakota	69	0.2%
50	Wyoming	35	0.1%		50	Wyoming	35	0.1%
						District of Columbia	348	0.9%

Source: American Medical Association (Chicago, Illinois)
   "Physician Characteristics and Distribution in the U.S." (2006 Edition)
*As of December 31, 2004. Total does not include 432 physicians in U.S. territories and possessions. Psychiatry includes psychoanalysis.

Rate of Physicians in Psychiatry in 2004

National Rate = 14 Physicians per 100,000 Population*

<table>
<tr><td colspan="3">ALPHA ORDER</td><td colspan="3">RANK ORDER</td></tr>
<tr><th>RANK</th><th>STATE</th><th>RATE</th><th>RANK</th><th>STATE</th><th>RATE</th></tr>
<tr><td>45</td><td>Alabama</td><td>7</td><td>1</td><td>Massachusetts</td><td>33</td></tr>
<tr><td>22</td><td>Alaska</td><td>11</td><td>2</td><td>New York</td><td>29</td></tr>
<tr><td>29</td><td>Arizona</td><td>10</td><td>3</td><td>Connecticut</td><td>26</td></tr>
<tr><td>39</td><td>Arkansas</td><td>8</td><td>3</td><td>Vermont</td><td>26</td></tr>
<tr><td>11</td><td>California</td><td>15</td><td>5</td><td>Maryland</td><td>24</td></tr>
<tr><td>14</td><td>Colorado</td><td>13</td><td>6</td><td>Rhode Island</td><td>23</td></tr>
<tr><td>3</td><td>Connecticut</td><td>26</td><td>7</td><td>Hawaii</td><td>18</td></tr>
<tr><td>29</td><td>Delaware</td><td>10</td><td>7</td><td>Maine</td><td>18</td></tr>
<tr><td>29</td><td>Florida</td><td>10</td><td>9</td><td>New Jersey</td><td>16</td></tr>
<tr><td>29</td><td>Georgia</td><td>10</td><td>9</td><td>Pennsylvania</td><td>16</td></tr>
<tr><td>7</td><td>Hawaii</td><td>18</td><td>11</td><td>California</td><td>15</td></tr>
<tr><td>50</td><td>Idaho</td><td>5</td><td>11</td><td>New Hampshire</td><td>15</td></tr>
<tr><td>17</td><td>Illinois</td><td>12</td><td>13</td><td>Virginia</td><td>14</td></tr>
<tr><td>39</td><td>Indiana</td><td>8</td><td>14</td><td>Colorado</td><td>13</td></tr>
<tr><td>45</td><td>Iowa</td><td>7</td><td>14</td><td>New Mexico</td><td>13</td></tr>
<tr><td>22</td><td>Kansas</td><td>11</td><td>14</td><td>Washington</td><td>13</td></tr>
<tr><td>29</td><td>Kentucky</td><td>10</td><td>17</td><td>Illinois</td><td>12</td></tr>
<tr><td>17</td><td>Louisiana</td><td>12</td><td>17</td><td>Louisiana</td><td>12</td></tr>
<tr><td>7</td><td>Maine</td><td>18</td><td>17</td><td>North Carolina</td><td>12</td></tr>
<tr><td>5</td><td>Maryland</td><td>24</td><td>17</td><td>North Dakota</td><td>12</td></tr>
<tr><td>1</td><td>Massachusetts</td><td>33</td><td>17</td><td>Oregon</td><td>12</td></tr>
<tr><td>22</td><td>Michigan</td><td>11</td><td>22</td><td>Alaska</td><td>11</td></tr>
<tr><td>22</td><td>Minnesota</td><td>11</td><td>22</td><td>Kansas</td><td>11</td></tr>
<tr><td>45</td><td>Mississippi</td><td>7</td><td>22</td><td>Michigan</td><td>11</td></tr>
<tr><td>29</td><td>Missouri</td><td>10</td><td>22</td><td>Minnesota</td><td>11</td></tr>
<tr><td>39</td><td>Montana</td><td>8</td><td>22</td><td>Ohio</td><td>11</td></tr>
<tr><td>35</td><td>Nebraska</td><td>9</td><td>22</td><td>South Carolina</td><td>11</td></tr>
<tr><td>45</td><td>Nevada</td><td>7</td><td>22</td><td>Wisconsin</td><td>11</td></tr>
<tr><td>11</td><td>New Hampshire</td><td>15</td><td>29</td><td>Arizona</td><td>10</td></tr>
<tr><td>9</td><td>New Jersey</td><td>16</td><td>29</td><td>Delaware</td><td>10</td></tr>
<tr><td>14</td><td>New Mexico</td><td>13</td><td>29</td><td>Florida</td><td>10</td></tr>
<tr><td>2</td><td>New York</td><td>29</td><td>29</td><td>Georgia</td><td>10</td></tr>
<tr><td>17</td><td>North Carolina</td><td>12</td><td>29</td><td>Kentucky</td><td>10</td></tr>
<tr><td>17</td><td>North Dakota</td><td>12</td><td>29</td><td>Missouri</td><td>10</td></tr>
<tr><td>22</td><td>Ohio</td><td>11</td><td>35</td><td>Nebraska</td><td>9</td></tr>
<tr><td>39</td><td>Oklahoma</td><td>8</td><td>35</td><td>South Dakota</td><td>9</td></tr>
<tr><td>17</td><td>Oregon</td><td>12</td><td>35</td><td>Tennessee</td><td>9</td></tr>
<tr><td>9</td><td>Pennsylvania</td><td>16</td><td>35</td><td>West Virginia</td><td>9</td></tr>
<tr><td>6</td><td>Rhode Island</td><td>23</td><td>39</td><td>Arkansas</td><td>8</td></tr>
<tr><td>22</td><td>South Carolina</td><td>11</td><td>39</td><td>Indiana</td><td>8</td></tr>
<tr><td>35</td><td>South Dakota</td><td>9</td><td>39</td><td>Montana</td><td>8</td></tr>
<tr><td>35</td><td>Tennessee</td><td>9</td><td>39</td><td>Oklahoma</td><td>8</td></tr>
<tr><td>39</td><td>Texas</td><td>8</td><td>39</td><td>Texas</td><td>8</td></tr>
<tr><td>39</td><td>Utah</td><td>8</td><td>39</td><td>Utah</td><td>8</td></tr>
<tr><td>3</td><td>Vermont</td><td>26</td><td>45</td><td>Alabama</td><td>7</td></tr>
<tr><td>13</td><td>Virginia</td><td>14</td><td>45</td><td>Iowa</td><td>7</td></tr>
<tr><td>14</td><td>Washington</td><td>13</td><td>45</td><td>Mississippi</td><td>7</td></tr>
<tr><td>35</td><td>West Virginia</td><td>9</td><td>45</td><td>Nevada</td><td>7</td></tr>
<tr><td>22</td><td>Wisconsin</td><td>11</td><td>45</td><td>Wyoming</td><td>7</td></tr>
<tr><td>45</td><td>Wyoming</td><td>7</td><td>50</td><td>Idaho</td><td>5</td></tr>
<tr><td></td><td></td><td></td><td></td><td>District of Columbia</td><td>63</td></tr>
</table>

Source: Morgan Quitno Press using data from American Medical Association (Chicago, Illinois)
    "Physician Characteristics and Distribution in the U.S." (2006 Edition)
*As of December 31, 2004. National rate does not include physicians in U.S. territories and possessions.
Psychiatry includes psychoanalysis.

Percent of Population Lacking Access to Mental Health Care in 2005

National Percent = 16.0% of Population*

<table>
<tr><td colspan="3">ALPHA ORDER</td><td colspan="3">RANK ORDER</td></tr>
<tr><th>RANK</th><th>STATE</th><th>PERCENT</th><th>RANK</th><th>STATE</th><th>PERCENT</th></tr>
<tr><td>3</td><td>Alabama</td><td>49.2</td><td>1</td><td>Wyoming</td><td>73.9</td></tr>
<tr><td>15</td><td>Alaska</td><td>33.3</td><td>2</td><td>Idaho</td><td>61.8</td></tr>
<tr><td>33</td><td>Arizona</td><td>9.6</td><td>3</td><td>Alabama</td><td>49.2</td></tr>
<tr><td>7</td><td>Arkansas</td><td>42.6</td><td>4</td><td>New Mexico</td><td>46.7</td></tr>
<tr><td>36</td><td>California</td><td>8.1</td><td>5</td><td>South Dakota</td><td>45.2</td></tr>
<tr><td>38</td><td>Colorado</td><td>7.9</td><td>6</td><td>Nebraska</td><td>44.4</td></tr>
<tr><td>48</td><td>Connecticut</td><td>1.6</td><td>7</td><td>Arkansas</td><td>42.6</td></tr>
<tr><td>50</td><td>Delaware</td><td>0.0</td><td>8</td><td>Mississippi</td><td>41.8</td></tr>
<tr><td>41</td><td>Florida</td><td>7.2</td><td>9</td><td>Montana</td><td>41.5</td></tr>
<tr><td>19</td><td>Georgia</td><td>26.5</td><td>10</td><td>Kentucky</td><td>40.3</td></tr>
<tr><td>38</td><td>Hawaii</td><td>7.9</td><td>11</td><td>Iowa</td><td>37.8</td></tr>
<tr><td>2</td><td>Idaho</td><td>61.8</td><td>12</td><td>North Dakota</td><td>36.2</td></tr>
<tr><td>27</td><td>Illinois</td><td>17.9</td><td>13</td><td>Oklahoma</td><td>35.6</td></tr>
<tr><td>43</td><td>Indiana</td><td>6.0</td><td>14</td><td>Tennessee</td><td>34.3</td></tr>
<tr><td>11</td><td>Iowa</td><td>37.8</td><td>15</td><td>Alaska</td><td>33.3</td></tr>
<tr><td>18</td><td>Kansas</td><td>31.5</td><td>15</td><td>Utah</td><td>33.3</td></tr>
<tr><td>10</td><td>Kentucky</td><td>40.3</td><td>17</td><td>South Carolina</td><td>33.2</td></tr>
<tr><td>47</td><td>Louisiana</td><td>4.3</td><td>18</td><td>Kansas</td><td>31.5</td></tr>
<tr><td>30</td><td>Maine</td><td>12.7</td><td>19</td><td>Georgia</td><td>26.5</td></tr>
<tr><td>44</td><td>Maryland</td><td>5.0</td><td>20</td><td>Texas</td><td>24.7</td></tr>
<tr><td>49</td><td>Massachusetts</td><td>1.2</td><td>21</td><td>Rhode Island</td><td>21.5</td></tr>
<tr><td>28</td><td>Michigan</td><td>17.0</td><td>22</td><td>Wisconsin</td><td>20.7</td></tr>
<tr><td>24</td><td>Minnesota</td><td>18.9</td><td>23</td><td>Missouri</td><td>19.3</td></tr>
<tr><td>8</td><td>Mississippi</td><td>41.8</td><td>24</td><td>Minnesota</td><td>18.9</td></tr>
<tr><td>23</td><td>Missouri</td><td>19.3</td><td>25</td><td>West Virginia</td><td>18.5</td></tr>
<tr><td>9</td><td>Montana</td><td>41.5</td><td>26</td><td>Oregon</td><td>18.0</td></tr>
<tr><td>6</td><td>Nebraska</td><td>44.4</td><td>27</td><td>Illinois</td><td>17.9</td></tr>
<tr><td>35</td><td>Nevada</td><td>8.2</td><td>28</td><td>Michigan</td><td>17.0</td></tr>
<tr><td>46</td><td>New Hampshire</td><td>4.4</td><td>29</td><td>Washington</td><td>16.9</td></tr>
<tr><td>45</td><td>New Jersey</td><td>4.6</td><td>30</td><td>Maine</td><td>12.7</td></tr>
<tr><td>4</td><td>New Mexico</td><td>46.7</td><td>31</td><td>Vermont</td><td>12.4</td></tr>
<tr><td>42</td><td>New York</td><td>6.6</td><td>32</td><td>Pennsylvania</td><td>9.9</td></tr>
<tr><td>34</td><td>North Carolina</td><td>8.7</td><td>33</td><td>Arizona</td><td>9.6</td></tr>
<tr><td>12</td><td>North Dakota</td><td>36.2</td><td>34</td><td>North Carolina</td><td>8.7</td></tr>
<tr><td>36</td><td>Ohio</td><td>8.1</td><td>35</td><td>Nevada</td><td>8.2</td></tr>
<tr><td>13</td><td>Oklahoma</td><td>35.6</td><td>36</td><td>California</td><td>8.1</td></tr>
<tr><td>26</td><td>Oregon</td><td>18.0</td><td>36</td><td>Ohio</td><td>8.1</td></tr>
<tr><td>32</td><td>Pennsylvania</td><td>9.9</td><td>38</td><td>Colorado</td><td>7.9</td></tr>
<tr><td>21</td><td>Rhode Island</td><td>21.5</td><td>38</td><td>Hawaii</td><td>7.9</td></tr>
<tr><td>17</td><td>South Carolina</td><td>33.2</td><td>38</td><td>Virginia</td><td>7.9</td></tr>
<tr><td>5</td><td>South Dakota</td><td>45.2</td><td>41</td><td>Florida</td><td>7.2</td></tr>
<tr><td>14</td><td>Tennessee</td><td>34.3</td><td>42</td><td>New York</td><td>6.6</td></tr>
<tr><td>20</td><td>Texas</td><td>24.7</td><td>43</td><td>Indiana</td><td>6.0</td></tr>
<tr><td>15</td><td>Utah</td><td>33.3</td><td>44</td><td>Maryland</td><td>5.0</td></tr>
<tr><td>31</td><td>Vermont</td><td>12.4</td><td>45</td><td>New Jersey</td><td>4.6</td></tr>
<tr><td>38</td><td>Virginia</td><td>7.9</td><td>46</td><td>New Hampshire</td><td>4.4</td></tr>
<tr><td>29</td><td>Washington</td><td>16.9</td><td>47</td><td>Louisiana</td><td>4.3</td></tr>
<tr><td>25</td><td>West Virginia</td><td>18.5</td><td>48</td><td>Connecticut</td><td>1.6</td></tr>
<tr><td>22</td><td>Wisconsin</td><td>20.7</td><td>49</td><td>Massachusetts</td><td>1.2</td></tr>
<tr><td>1</td><td>Wyoming</td><td>73.9</td><td>50</td><td>Delaware</td><td>0.0</td></tr>
<tr><td></td><td></td><td></td><td></td><td>District of Columbia</td><td>0.7</td></tr>
</table>

Source: Morgan Quitno Press using data from U.S. Dept. of Health and Human Services, Div. of Shortage Designation "Selected Statistics on Health Professional Shortage Areas" (as of September 30, 2005)
*Percent of population considered under-served by mental health practitioners. An under-served population does not have primary medical care within reasonable economic and geographic bounds.

442

International Medical School Graduates in 2004

National Total = 217,901 Nonfederal Physicians*

ALPHA ORDER

RANK ORDER

RANK	STATE	PHYSICIANS	% of USA		RANK	STATE	PHYSICIANS	% of USA
26	Alabama	1,684	0.8%		1	New York	34,550	15.9%
48	Alaska	106	0.0%		2	California	23,877	11.0%
19	Arizona	2,762	1.3%		3	Florida	18,239	8.4%
33	Arkansas	941	0.4%		4	New Jersey	13,140	6.0%
2	California	23,877	11.0%		5	Illinois	13,049	6.0%
34	Colorado	935	0.4%		6	Texas	12,304	5.6%
14	Connecticut	4,029	1.8%		7	Pennsylvania	10,386	4.8%
38	Delaware	694	0.3%		8	Ohio	9,500	4.4%
3	Florida	18,239	8.4%		9	Michigan	9,062	4.2%
13	Georgia	4,042	1.9%		10	Maryland	6,792	3.1%
39	Hawaii	685	0.3%		11	Massachusetts	6,649	3.1%
50	Idaho	84	0.0%		12	Virginia	4,651	2.1%
5	Illinois	13,049	6.0%		13	Georgia	4,042	1.9%
16	Indiana	3,000	1.4%		14	Connecticut	4,029	1.8%
31	Iowa	1,213	0.6%		15	Missouri	3,321	1.5%
29	Kansas	1,282	0.6%		16	Indiana	3,000	1.4%
23	Kentucky	2,246	1.0%		17	North Carolina	2,923	1.3%
21	Louisiana	2,289	1.1%		18	Wisconsin	2,809	1.3%
41	Maine	543	0.2%		19	Arizona	2,762	1.3%
10	Maryland	6,792	3.1%		20	Tennessee	2,685	1.2%
11	Massachusetts	6,649	3.1%		21	Louisiana	2,289	1.1%
9	Michigan	9,062	4.2%		22	Minnesota	2,251	1.0%
22	Minnesota	2,251	1.0%		23	Kentucky	2,246	1.0%
37	Mississippi	739	0.3%		24	Washington	2,177	1.0%
15	Missouri	3,321	1.5%		25	West Virginia	1,712	0.8%
47	Montana	109	0.1%		26	Alabama	1,684	0.8%
40	Nebraska	643	0.3%		27	Nevada	1,367	0.6%
27	Nevada	1,367	0.6%		28	South Carolina	1,329	0.6%
42	New Hampshire	523	0.2%		29	Kansas	1,282	0.6%
4	New Jersey	13,140	6.0%		30	Oklahoma	1,257	0.6%
36	New Mexico	836	0.4%		31	Iowa	1,213	0.6%
1	New York	34,550	15.9%		32	Rhode Island	1,115	0.5%
17	North Carolina	2,923	1.3%		33	Arkansas	941	0.4%
43	North Dakota	446	0.2%		34	Colorado	935	0.4%
8	Ohio	9,500	4.4%		35	Oregon	910	0.4%
30	Oklahoma	1,257	0.6%		36	New Mexico	836	0.4%
35	Oregon	910	0.4%		37	Mississippi	739	0.3%
7	Pennsylvania	10,386	4.8%		38	Delaware	694	0.3%
32	Rhode Island	1,115	0.5%		39	Hawaii	685	0.3%
28	South Carolina	1,329	0.6%		40	Nebraska	643	0.3%
45	South Dakota	269	0.1%		41	Maine	543	0.2%
20	Tennessee	2,685	1.2%		42	New Hampshire	523	0.2%
6	Texas	12,304	5.6%		43	North Dakota	446	0.2%
44	Utah	437	0.2%		44	Utah	437	0.2%
46	Vermont	218	0.1%		45	South Dakota	269	0.1%
12	Virginia	4,651	2.1%		46	Vermont	218	0.1%
24	Washington	2,177	1.0%		47	Montana	109	0.1%
25	West Virginia	1,712	0.8%		48	Alaska	106	0.0%
18	Wisconsin	2,809	1.3%		49	Wyoming	98	0.0%
49	Wyoming	98	0.0%		50	Idaho	84	0.0%
						District of Columbia	993	0.5%

Source: American Medical Association (Chicago, Illinois)
"Physician Characteristics and Distribution in the U.S." (2006 Edition)
*As of December 31, 2004. Total does not include 6,142 physicians in U.S. territories and possessions.

International Medical School Graduates as a Percent of Physicians in 2004

National Percent = 25.0% of Physicians*

ALPHA ORDER

RANK	STATE	PERCENT
30	Alabama	15.9
48	Alaska	6.7
22	Arizona	19.7
33	Arkansas	15.2
16	California	22.6
47	Colorado	6.9
8	Connecticut	28.7
7	Delaware	29.8
4	Florida	35.7
24	Georgia	18.7
32	Hawaii	15.5
50	Idaho	3.1
5	Illinois	34.4
21	Indiana	20.4
23	Iowa	19.3
24	Kansas	18.7
18	Kentucky	21.5
28	Louisiana	17.6
38	Maine	13.4
11	Maryland	27.1
19	Massachusetts	21.3
6	Michigan	33.6
34	Minnesota	14.1
39	Mississippi	12.6
17	Missouri	22.1
49	Montana	4.5
36	Nebraska	13.8
10	Nevada	27.7
37	New Hampshire	13.5
1	New Jersey	44.9
29	New Mexico	16.2
2	New York	42.3
41	North Carolina	12.1
13	North Dakota	26.0
8	Ohio	28.7
26	Oklahoma	18.4
45	Oregon	8.3
14	Pennsylvania	25.4
12	Rhode Island	26.9
40	South Carolina	12.3
34	South Dakota	14.1
30	Tennessee	15.9
15	Texas	23.6
46	Utah	7.7
44	Vermont	8.4
20	Virginia	20.6
42	Washington	11.5
3	West Virginia	37.1
27	Wisconsin	18.0
43	Wyoming	9.0

RANK ORDER

RANK	STATE	PERCENT
1	New Jersey	44.9
2	New York	42.3
3	West Virginia	37.1
4	Florida	35.7
5	Illinois	34.4
6	Michigan	33.6
7	Delaware	29.8
8	Connecticut	28.7
8	Ohio	28.7
10	Nevada	27.7
11	Maryland	27.1
12	Rhode Island	26.9
13	North Dakota	26.0
14	Pennsylvania	25.4
15	Texas	23.6
16	California	22.6
17	Missouri	22.1
18	Kentucky	21.5
19	Massachusetts	21.3
20	Virginia	20.6
21	Indiana	20.4
22	Arizona	19.7
23	Iowa	19.3
24	Georgia	18.7
24	Kansas	18.7
26	Oklahoma	18.4
27	Wisconsin	18.0
28	Louisiana	17.6
29	New Mexico	16.2
30	Alabama	15.9
30	Tennessee	15.9
32	Hawaii	15.5
33	Arkansas	15.2
34	Minnesota	14.1
34	South Dakota	14.1
36	Nebraska	13.8
37	New Hampshire	13.5
38	Maine	13.4
39	Mississippi	12.6
40	South Carolina	12.3
41	North Carolina	12.1
42	Washington	11.5
43	Wyoming	9.0
44	Vermont	8.4
45	Oregon	8.3
46	Utah	7.7
47	Colorado	6.9
48	Alaska	6.7
49	Montana	4.5
50	Idaho	3.1

	District of Columbia	21.0

Source: Morgan Quitno Press using data from American Medical Association (Chicago, Illinois)
    "Physician Characteristics and Distribution in the U.S." (2006 Edition)
*As of December 31, 2004. National percent does not include physicians in U.S. territories and possessions.

Osteopathic Physicians in 2005

National Total = 50,292 Osteopathic Physicians*

ALPHA ORDER

RANK	STATE	OSTEOPATHS	% of USA
30	Alabama	353	0.7%
45	Alaska	111	0.2%
12	Arizona	1,387	2.8%
37	Arkansas	208	0.4%
6	California	3,236	6.4%
14	Colorado	811	1.6%
31	Connecticut	351	0.7%
36	Delaware	211	0.4%
5	Florida	3,400	6.8%
17	Georgia	664	1.3%
42	Hawaii	167	0.3%
41	Idaho	170	0.3%
9	Illinois	2,234	4.4%
16	Indiana	703	1.4%
13	Iowa	1,032	2.1%
19	Kansas	610	1.2%
32	Kentucky	350	0.7%
44	Louisiana	114	0.2%
23	Maine	563	1.1%
21	Maryland	591	1.2%
25	Massachusetts	522	1.0%
2	Michigan	4,672	9.3%
28	Minnesota	370	0.7%
34	Mississippi	287	0.6%
10	Missouri	1,766	3.5%
46	Montana	104	0.2%
43	Nebraska	133	0.3%
29	Nevada	362	0.7%
40	New Hampshire	185	0.4%
8	New Jersey	2,790	5.5%
39	New Mexico	190	0.4%
4	New York	3,404	6.8%
24	North Carolina	558	1.1%
48	North Dakota	55	0.1%
3	Ohio	3,519	7.0%
11	Oklahoma	1,409	2.8%
26	Oregon	471	0.9%
1	Pennsylvania	5,302	10.5%
38	Rhode Island	202	0.4%
33	South Carolina	301	0.6%
47	South Dakota	79	0.2%
27	Tennessee	447	0.9%
7	Texas	3,013	6.0%
35	Utah	221	0.4%
49	Vermont	53	0.1%
15	Virginia	709	1.4%
18	Washington	631	1.3%
20	West Virginia	600	1.2%
22	Wisconsin	580	1.2%
50	Wyoming	49	0.1%

RANK ORDER

RANK	STATE	OSTEOPATHS	% of USA
1	Pennsylvania	5,302	10.5%
2	Michigan	4,672	9.3%
3	Ohio	3,519	7.0%
4	New York	3,404	6.8%
5	Florida	3,400	6.8%
6	California	3,236	6.4%
7	Texas	3,013	6.0%
8	New Jersey	2,790	5.5%
9	Illinois	2,234	4.4%
10	Missouri	1,766	3.5%
11	Oklahoma	1,409	2.8%
12	Arizona	1,387	2.8%
13	Iowa	1,032	2.1%
14	Colorado	811	1.6%
15	Virginia	709	1.4%
16	Indiana	703	1.4%
17	Georgia	664	1.3%
18	Washington	631	1.3%
19	Kansas	610	1.2%
20	West Virginia	600	1.2%
21	Maryland	591	1.2%
22	Wisconsin	580	1.2%
23	Maine	563	1.1%
24	North Carolina	558	1.1%
25	Massachusetts	522	1.0%
26	Oregon	471	0.9%
27	Tennessee	447	0.9%
28	Minnesota	370	0.7%
29	Nevada	362	0.7%
30	Alabama	353	0.7%
31	Connecticut	351	0.7%
32	Kentucky	350	0.7%
33	South Carolina	301	0.6%
34	Mississippi	287	0.6%
35	Utah	221	0.4%
36	Delaware	211	0.4%
37	Arkansas	208	0.4%
38	Rhode Island	202	0.4%
39	New Mexico	190	0.4%
40	New Hampshire	185	0.4%
41	Idaho	170	0.3%
42	Hawaii	167	0.3%
43	Nebraska	133	0.3%
44	Louisiana	114	0.2%
45	Alaska	111	0.2%
46	Montana	104	0.2%
47	South Dakota	79	0.2%
48	North Dakota	55	0.1%
49	Vermont	53	0.1%
50	Wyoming	49	0.1%
	District of Columbia	42	0.1%

Source: American Osteopathic Association
    "Fact Sheet 2005" (http://www.do-online.osteotech.org/pdf/ost_factsheet.pdf)

*Active osteopaths under age 65 as of June 1, 2005. National total does not include 240 osteopaths not shown by state. Osteopaths practice a system of medicine based on the theory that disturbances in the musculoskeletal system affect other body parts, causing many disorders that can be corrected by various manipulative techniques in conjunction with conventional medical, surgical, pharmacological, and other therapeutic procedures.

Rate of Osteopathic Physicians in 2005

National Rate = 17 Osteopaths per 100,000 Population*

ALPHA ORDER					RANK ORDER		
RANK	STATE	RATE			RANK	STATE	RATE
40	Alabama	8			1	Michigan	46
17	Alaska	17			2	Maine	43
11	Arizona	23			2	Pennsylvania	43
44	Arkansas	7			4	Oklahoma	40
35	California	9			5	Iowa	35
17	Colorado	17			6	West Virginia	33
28	Connecticut	10			7	New Jersey	32
10	Delaware	25			8	Ohio	31
13	Florida	19			9	Missouri	30
44	Georgia	7			10	Delaware	25
21	Hawaii	13			11	Arizona	23
24	Idaho	12			12	Kansas	22
15	Illinois	18			13	Florida	19
25	Indiana	11			13	Rhode Island	19
5	Iowa	35			15	Illinois	18
12	Kansas	22			15	New York	18
40	Kentucky	8			17	Alaska	17
50	Louisiana	3			17	Colorado	17
2	Maine	43			19	Nevada	15
25	Maryland	11			20	New Hampshire	14
40	Massachusetts	8			21	Hawaii	13
1	Michigan	46			21	Oregon	13
44	Minnesota	7			21	Texas	13
28	Mississippi	10			24	Idaho	12
9	Missouri	30			25	Indiana	11
25	Montana	11			25	Maryland	11
40	Nebraska	8			25	Montana	11
19	Nevada	15			28	Connecticut	10
20	New Hampshire	14			28	Mississippi	10
7	New Jersey	32			28	New Mexico	10
28	New Mexico	10			28	South Dakota	10
15	New York	18			28	Washington	10
49	North Carolina	6			28	Wisconsin	10
35	North Dakota	9			28	Wyoming	10
8	Ohio	31			35	California	9
4	Oklahoma	40			35	North Dakota	9
21	Oregon	13			35	Utah	9
2	Pennsylvania	43			35	Vermont	9
13	Rhode Island	19			35	Virginia	9
44	South Carolina	7			40	Alabama	8
28	South Dakota	10			40	Kentucky	8
44	Tennessee	7			40	Massachusetts	8
21	Texas	13			40	Nebraska	8
35	Utah	9			44	Arkansas	7
35	Vermont	9			44	Georgia	7
35	Virginia	9			44	Minnesota	7
28	Washington	10			44	South Carolina	7
6	West Virginia	33			44	Tennessee	7
28	Wisconsin	10			49	North Carolina	6
28	Wyoming	10			50	Louisiana	3

	District of Columbia	8

Source: Morgan Quitno Press using data from American Osteopathic Association
"Fact Sheet 2005" (http://www.do-online.osteotech.org/pdf/ost_factsheet.pdf)
*Active osteopaths under age 65 as of June 1, 2005. National rate does not include osteopaths not shown by state. Osteopaths practice a system of medicine based on the theory that disturbances in the musculoskeletal system affect other body parts, causing many disorders that can be corrected by various manipulative techniques in conjunction with conventional medical, surgical, pharmacological, and other therapeutic procedures.

Podiatrists in 2004

National Total = 6,940 Podiatrists*

ALPHA ORDER

RANK	STATE	PODIATRISTS	% of USA
NA	Alabama**	NA	NA
NA	Alaska**	NA	NA
10	Arizona	240	3.5%
NA	Arkansas**	NA	NA
3	California	500	7.2%
NA	Colorado**	NA	NA
20	Connecticut	100	1.4%
NA	Delaware**	NA	NA
2	Florida	520	7.5%
18	Georgia	120	1.7%
NA	Hawaii**	NA	NA
NA	Idaho**	NA	NA
9	Illinois	300	4.3%
19	Indiana	110	1.6%
23	Iowa	70	1.0%
26	Kansas	40	0.6%
26	Kentucky	40	0.6%
NA	Louisiana**	NA	NA
26	Maine	40	0.6%
11	Maryland	180	2.6%
17	Massachusetts	130	1.9%
8	Michigan	310	4.5%
11	Minnesota	180	2.6%
NA	Mississippi**	NA	NA
20	Missouri	100	1.4%
26	Montana	40	0.6%
NA	Nebraska**	NA	NA
25	Nevada	50	0.7%
NA	New Hampshire**	NA	NA
6	New Jersey	340	4.9%
NA	New Mexico**	NA	NA
1	New York	760	11.0%
15	North Carolina	160	2.3%
NA	North Dakota**	NA	NA
4	Ohio	450	6.5%
NA	Oklahoma**	NA	NA
NA	Oregon**	NA	NA
5	Pennsylvania	430	6.2%
30	Rhode Island	30	0.4%
22	South Carolina	80	1.2%
NA	South Dakota**	NA	NA
23	Tennessee	70	1.0%
7	Texas	320	4.6%
NA	Utah**	NA	NA
NA	Vermont**	NA	NA
13	Virginia	170	2.4%
13	Washington	170	2.4%
NA	West Virginia**	NA	NA
16	Wisconsin	140	2.0%
NA	Wyoming**	NA	NA

RANK ORDER

RANK	STATE	PODIATRISTS	% of USA
1	New York	760	11.0%
2	Florida	520	7.5%
3	California	500	7.2%
4	Ohio	450	6.5%
5	Pennsylvania	430	6.2%
6	New Jersey	340	4.9%
7	Texas	320	4.6%
8	Michigan	310	4.5%
9	Illinois	300	4.3%
10	Arizona	240	3.5%
11	Maryland	180	2.6%
11	Minnesota	180	2.6%
13	Virginia	170	2.4%
13	Washington	170	2.4%
15	North Carolina	160	2.3%
16	Wisconsin	140	2.0%
17	Massachusetts	130	1.9%
18	Georgia	120	1.7%
19	Indiana	110	1.6%
20	Connecticut	100	1.4%
20	Missouri	100	1.4%
22	South Carolina	80	1.2%
23	Iowa	70	1.0%
23	Tennessee	70	1.0%
25	Nevada	50	0.7%
26	Kansas	40	0.6%
26	Kentucky	40	0.6%
26	Maine	40	0.6%
26	Montana	40	0.6%
30	Rhode Island	30	0.4%
NA	Alabama**	NA	NA
NA	Alaska**	NA	NA
NA	Arkansas**	NA	NA
NA	Colorado**	NA	NA
NA	Delaware**	NA	NA
NA	Hawaii**	NA	NA
NA	Idaho**	NA	NA
NA	Louisiana**	NA	NA
NA	Mississippi**	NA	NA
NA	Nebraska**	NA	NA
NA	New Hampshire**	NA	NA
NA	New Mexico**	NA	NA
NA	North Dakota**	NA	NA
NA	Oklahoma**	NA	NA
NA	Oregon**	NA	NA
NA	South Dakota**	NA	NA
NA	Utah**	NA	NA
NA	Vermont**	NA	NA
NA	West Virginia**	NA	NA
NA	Wyoming**	NA	NA
	District of Columbia	30	0.4%

Source: U.S. Department of Labor, Bureau of Labor Statistics
   "Occupational Employment and Wages, 2004" (http://www.bls.gov/oes/)
*Does not include self-employed.
**Not available.

447

Rate of Podiatrists in 2004

National Rate = 2 Podiatrists per 100,000 Population*

ALPHA ORDER

RANK	STATE	RATE
NA	Alabama**	NA
NA	Alaska**	NA
1	Arizona	4
NA	Arkansas**	NA
25	California	1
NA	Colorado**	NA
7	Connecticut	3
NA	Delaware**	NA
7	Florida	3
25	Georgia	1
NA	Hawaii**	NA
NA	Idaho**	NA
16	Illinois	2
16	Indiana	2
16	Iowa	2
25	Kansas	1
25	Kentucky	1
NA	Louisiana**	NA
7	Maine	3
7	Maryland	3
16	Massachusetts	2
7	Michigan	3
1	Minnesota	4
NA	Mississippi**	NA
16	Missouri	2
1	Montana	4
NA	Nebraska**	NA
16	Nevada	2
NA	New Hampshire**	NA
1	New Jersey	4
NA	New Mexico**	NA
1	New York	4
16	North Carolina	2
NA	North Dakota**	NA
1	Ohio	4
NA	Oklahoma**	NA
NA	Oregon**	NA
7	Pennsylvania	3
7	Rhode Island	3
16	South Carolina	2
NA	South Dakota**	NA
25	Tennessee	1
25	Texas	1
NA	Utah**	NA
NA	Vermont**	NA
16	Virginia	2
7	Washington	3
NA	West Virginia**	NA
7	Wisconsin	3
NA	Wyoming**	NA

RANK ORDER

RANK	STATE	RATE
1	Arizona	4
1	Minnesota	4
1	Montana	4
1	New Jersey	4
1	New York	4
1	Ohio	4
7	Connecticut	3
7	Florida	3
7	Maine	3
7	Maryland	3
7	Michigan	3
7	Pennsylvania	3
7	Rhode Island	3
7	Washington	3
7	Wisconsin	3
16	Illinois	2
16	Indiana	2
16	Iowa	2
16	Massachusetts	2
16	Missouri	2
16	Nevada	2
16	North Carolina	2
16	South Carolina	2
16	Virginia	2
25	California	1
25	Georgia	1
25	Kansas	1
25	Kentucky	1
25	Tennessee	1
25	Texas	1
NA	Alabama**	NA
NA	Alaska**	NA
NA	Arkansas**	NA
NA	Colorado**	NA
NA	Delaware**	NA
NA	Hawaii**	NA
NA	Idaho**	NA
NA	Louisiana**	NA
NA	Mississippi**	NA
NA	Nebraska**	NA
NA	New Hampshire**	NA
NA	New Mexico**	NA
NA	North Dakota**	NA
NA	Oklahoma**	NA
NA	Oregon**	NA
NA	South Dakota**	NA
NA	Utah**	NA
NA	Vermont**	NA
NA	West Virginia**	NA
NA	Wyoming**	NA

District of Columbia 5

Source: Morgan Quitno Press using data from U.S. Department of Labor, Bureau of Labor Statistics
    "Occupational Employment and Wages, 2004" (http://www.bls.gov/oes/)
*Does not include self-employed.
**Not available.

Average Annual Wages of Podiatrists in 2004

National Average = $111,130*

ALPHA ORDER

RANK	STATE	WAGES
5	Alabama	$142,670
NA	Alaska**	NA
28	Arizona	89,370
NA	Arkansas**	NA
25	California	92,820
19	Colorado	111,080
17	Connecticut	112,940
NA	Delaware**	NA
15	Florida	115,280
4	Georgia	144,130
NA	Hawaii**	NA
NA	Idaho**	NA
20	Illinois	110,420
11	Indiana	121,140
14	Iowa	117,060
29	Kansas	88,210
1	Kentucky	170,740
NA	Louisiana**	NA
31	Maine	81,100
6	Maryland	138,710
13	Massachusetts	120,030
7	Michigan	137,560
10	Minnesota	125,060
NA	Mississippi**	NA
16	Missouri	113,020
23	Montana	105,960
NA	Nebraska**	NA
2	Nevada	162,240
NA	New Hampshire**	NA
22	New Jersey	106,510
NA	New Mexico**	NA
12	New York	120,880
3	North Carolina	154,380
NA	North Dakota**	NA
24	Ohio	104,740
NA	Oklahoma**	NA
NA	Oregon**	NA
27	Pennsylvania	89,900
NA	Rhode Island**	NA
8	South Carolina	137,180
NA	South Dakota**	NA
21	Tennessee	109,350
26	Texas	90,350
NA	Utah**	NA
NA	Vermont**	NA
9	Virginia	133,250
30	Washington	87,230
NA	West Virginia**	NA
18	Wisconsin	111,520
NA	Wyoming**	NA

RANK ORDER

RANK	STATE	WAGES
1	Kentucky	$170,740
2	Nevada	162,240
3	North Carolina	154,380
4	Georgia	144,130
5	Alabama	142,670
6	Maryland	138,710
7	Michigan	137,560
8	South Carolina	137,180
9	Virginia	133,250
10	Minnesota	125,060
11	Indiana	121,140
12	New York	120,880
13	Massachusetts	120,030
14	Iowa	117,060
15	Florida	115,280
16	Missouri	113,020
17	Connecticut	112,940
18	Wisconsin	111,520
19	Colorado	111,080
20	Illinois	110,420
21	Tennessee	109,350
22	New Jersey	106,510
23	Montana	105,960
24	Ohio	104,740
25	California	92,820
26	Texas	90,350
27	Pennsylvania	89,900
28	Arizona	89,370
29	Kansas	88,210
30	Washington	87,230
31	Maine	81,100
NA	Alaska**	NA
NA	Arkansas**	NA
NA	Delaware**	NA
NA	Hawaii**	NA
NA	Idaho**	NA
NA	Louisiana**	NA
NA	Mississippi**	NA
NA	Nebraska**	NA
NA	New Hampshire**	NA
NA	New Mexico**	NA
NA	North Dakota**	NA
NA	Oklahoma**	NA
NA	Oregon**	NA
NA	Rhode Island**	NA
NA	South Dakota**	NA
NA	Utah**	NA
NA	Vermont**	NA
NA	West Virginia**	NA
NA	Wyoming**	NA

District of Columbia 79,840

Source: U.S. Department of Labor, Bureau of Labor Statistics
"Occupational Employment and Wages, 2004" (http://www.bls.gov/oes/)
Does not include self-employed.
**Not available.*

Doctors of Chiropractic in 2003

National Total = 83,690 Chiropractors*

RANK	STATE	CHIROPRACTORS	% of USA		RANK	STATE	CHIROPRACTORS	% of USA
30	Alabama	749	0.9%		1	California	13,421	16.0%
48	Alaska	204	0.2%		2	New York	6,240	7.5%
10	Arizona	2,394	2.9%		3	Florida	4,687	5.6%
33	Arkansas	557	0.7%		4	Texas	4,190	5.0%
1	California	13,421	16.0%		5	Pennsylvania	4,000	4.8%
11	Colorado	2,258	2.7%		6	Illinois	3,623	4.3%
27	Connecticut	982	1.2%		7	New Jersey	3,294	3.9%
44	Delaware	268	0.3%		8	Georgia	3,126	3.7%
3	Florida	4,687	5.6%		9	Michigan	2,815	3.4%
8	Georgia	3,126	3.7%		10	Arizona	2,394	2.9%
NA	Hawaii**	NA	NA		11	Colorado	2,258	2.7%
37	Idaho	414	0.5%		12	Minnesota	2,233	2.7%
6	Illinois	3,623	4.3%		13	Ohio	2,194	2.6%
24	Indiana	1,043	1.2%		14	Washington	2,131	2.5%
21	Iowa	1,411	1.7%		15	Missouri	1,948	2.3%
26	Kansas	1,009	1.2%		16	Tennessee	1,775	2.1%
23	Kentucky	1,065	1.3%		17	Massachusetts	1,768	2.1%
32	Louisiana	567	0.7%		18	North Carolina	1,729	2.1%
39	Maine	357	0.4%		19	South Carolina	1,455	1.7%
31	Maryland	658	0.8%		20	Virginia	1,414	1.7%
17	Massachusetts	1,768	2.1%		21	Iowa	1,411	1.7%
9	Michigan	2,815	3.4%		22	Oregon	1,091	1.3%
12	Minnesota	2,233	2.7%		23	Kentucky	1,065	1.3%
41	Mississippi	331	0.4%		24	Indiana	1,043	1.2%
15	Missouri	1,948	2.3%		25	Wisconsin	1,029	1.2%
40	Montana	339	0.4%		26	Kansas	1,009	1.2%
38	Nebraska	369	0.4%		27	Connecticut	982	1.2%
34	Nevada	549	0.7%		28	Utah	809	1.0%
36	New Hampshire	431	0.5%		29	Oklahoma	768	0.9%
7	New Jersey	3,294	3.9%		30	Alabama	749	0.9%
35	New Mexico	471	0.6%		31	Maryland	658	0.8%
2	New York	6,240	7.5%		32	Louisiana	567	0.7%
18	North Carolina	1,729	2.1%		33	Arkansas	557	0.7%
46	North Dakota	248	0.3%		34	Nevada	549	0.7%
13	Ohio	2,194	2.6%		35	New Mexico	471	0.6%
29	Oklahoma	768	0.9%		36	New Hampshire	431	0.5%
22	Oregon	1,091	1.3%		37	Idaho	414	0.5%
5	Pennsylvania	4,000	4.8%		38	Nebraska	369	0.4%
45	Rhode Island	263	0.3%		39	Maine	357	0.4%
19	South Carolina	1,455	1.7%		40	Montana	339	0.4%
43	South Dakota	280	0.3%		41	Mississippi	331	0.4%
16	Tennessee	1,775	2.1%		42	West Virginia	299	0.4%
4	Texas	4,190	5.0%		43	South Dakota	280	0.3%
28	Utah	809	1.0%		44	Delaware	268	0.3%
47	Vermont	242	0.3%		45	Rhode Island	263	0.3%
20	Virginia	1,414	1.7%		46	North Dakota	248	0.3%
14	Washington	2,131	2.5%		47	Vermont	242	0.3%
42	West Virginia	299	0.4%		48	Alaska	204	0.2%
25	Wisconsin	1,029	1.2%		49	Wyoming	192	0.2%
49	Wyoming	192	0.2%		NA	Hawaii**	NA	NA
					District of Columbia**		NA	NA

Source: Federation of Chiropractic Licensing Boards
   "Official Directory" (http://www.fclb.org/directory/index.htm)
*As of December 2003. Licensed active doctors. There is some duplication as some doctors are licensed in more than one state.
**Not available.

Rate of Doctors of Chiropractic in 2003

National Rate = 29 Chiropractors per 100,000 Population*

ALPHA ORDER				RANK ORDER		
RANK	STATE	RATE		RANK	STATE	RATE
44	Alabama	17		1	Colorado	50
22	Alaska	31		2	Iowa	48
4	Arizona	43		3	Minnesota	44
39	Arkansas	20		4	Arizona	43
7	California	38		5	North Dakota	39
1	Colorado	50		5	Vermont	39
27	Connecticut	28		7	California	38
18	Delaware	33		7	New Jersey	38
27	Florida	28		7	Wyoming	38
13	Georgia	36		10	Kansas	37
NA	Hawaii**	NA		10	Montana	37
24	Idaho	30		10	South Dakota	37
26	Illinois	29		13	Georgia	36
44	Indiana	17		14	South Carolina	35
2	Iowa	48		14	Washington	35
10	Kansas	37		16	Missouri	34
32	Kentucky	26		16	Utah	34
47	Louisiana	13		18	Delaware	33
31	Maine	27		18	New Hampshire	33
48	Maryland	12		20	New York	32
27	Massachusetts	28		20	Pennsylvania	32
27	Michigan	28		22	Alaska	31
3	Minnesota	44		22	Oregon	31
49	Mississippi	11		24	Idaho	30
16	Missouri	34		24	Tennessee	30
10	Montana	37		26	Illinois	29
37	Nebraska	21		27	Connecticut	28
34	Nevada	24		27	Florida	28
18	New Hampshire	33		27	Massachusetts	28
7	New Jersey	38		27	Michigan	28
33	New Mexico	25		31	Maine	27
20	New York	32		32	Kentucky	26
37	North Carolina	21		33	New Mexico	25
5	North Dakota	39		34	Nevada	24
40	Ohio	19		34	Rhode Island	24
36	Oklahoma	22		36	Oklahoma	22
22	Oregon	31		37	Nebraska	21
20	Pennsylvania	32		37	North Carolina	21
34	Rhode Island	24		39	Arkansas	20
14	South Carolina	35		40	Ohio	19
10	South Dakota	37		40	Texas	19
24	Tennessee	30		40	Virginia	19
40	Texas	19		40	Wisconsin	19
16	Utah	34		44	Alabama	17
5	Vermont	39		44	Indiana	17
40	Virginia	19		44	West Virginia	17
14	Washington	35		47	Louisiana	13
44	West Virginia	17		48	Maryland	12
40	Wisconsin	19		49	Mississippi	11
7	Wyoming	38		NA	Hawaii**	NA
					District of Columbia**	NA

Source: Morgan Quitno Press using data from Federation of Chiropractic Licensing Boards
    "Official Directory" (http://www.fclb.org/directory/index.htm)
*As of December 2003. Licensed active doctors. There is some duplication as some doctors are licensed in more than one state.
**Not available.

Average Annual Wages of Chiropractors in 2004

National Average = $84,020*

ALPHA ORDER				RANK ORDER		
RANK	STATE	WAGES		RANK	STATE	WAGES
23	Alabama	$82,520		1	Alaska	$138,010
1	Alaska	138,010		2	Nevada	123,890
17	Arizona	93,870		3	New Jersey	117,530
4	Arkansas	116,980		4	Arkansas	116,980
29	California	78,820		5	Tennessee	114,330
38	Colorado	65,290		6	New Hampshire	114,130
7	Connecticut	112,120		7	Connecticut	112,120
8	Delaware	110,890		8	Delaware	110,890
33	Florida	75,510		9	Virginia	105,540
39	Georgia	63,420		10	Wisconsin	104,870
42	Hawaii	61,230		11	Oklahoma	103,240
49	Idaho	37,120		12	Washington	100,340
14	Illinois	99,760		13	Ohio	99,900
20	Indiana	89,310		14	Illinois	99,760
48	Iowa	52,640		15	South Carolina	96,960
32	Kansas	75,600		16	Maryland	96,450
35	Kentucky	74,070		17	Arizona	93,870
28	Louisiana	80,040		18	Massachusetts	91,720
43	Maine	60,050		19	West Virginia	89,460
16	Maryland	96,450		20	Indiana	89,310
18	Massachusetts	91,720		21	South Dakota	88,360
26	Michigan	81,670		22	North Carolina	88,160
31	Minnesota	76,320		23	Alabama	82,520
44	Mississippi	59,630		24	Missouri	82,090
24	Missouri	82,090		25	New York	81,820
46	Montana	54,660		26	Michigan	81,670
37	Nebraska	65,970		27	Wyoming	80,090
2	Nevada	123,890		28	Louisiana	80,040
6	New Hampshire	114,130		29	California	78,820
3	New Jersey	117,530		30	Texas	78,540
36	New Mexico	72,930		31	Minnesota	76,320
25	New York	81,820		32	Kansas	75,600
22	North Carolina	88,160		33	Florida	75,510
40	North Dakota	63,050		34	Pennsylvania	74,460
13	Ohio	99,900		35	Kentucky	74,070
11	Oklahoma	103,240		36	New Mexico	72,930
47	Oregon	52,760		37	Nebraska	65,970
34	Pennsylvania	74,460		38	Colorado	65,290
45	Rhode Island	58,330		39	Georgia	63,420
15	South Carolina	96,960		40	North Dakota	63,050
21	South Dakota	88,360		40	Utah	63,050
5	Tennessee	114,330		42	Hawaii	61,230
30	Texas	78,540		43	Maine	60,050
40	Utah	63,050		44	Mississippi	59,630
NA	Vermont**	NA		45	Rhode Island	58,330
9	Virginia	105,540		46	Montana	54,660
12	Washington	100,340		47	Oregon	52,760
19	West Virginia	89,460		48	Iowa	52,640
10	Wisconsin	104,870		49	Idaho	37,120
27	Wyoming	80,090		NA	Vermont**	NA
					District of Columbia**	NA

Source: U.S. Department of Labor, Bureau of Labor Statistics
  "Occupational Employment and Wages, 2004" (http://www.bls.gov/oes/)
*Does not include self-employed.
**Not available.

Physician Assistants in Clinical Practice in 2006

National Total = 58,412 Physician Assistants*

ALPHA ORDER

RANK	STATE	PAs	% of USA
41	Alabama	311	0.5%
39	Alaska	329	0.6%
15	Arizona	1,319	2.3%
50	Arkansas	73	0.1%
2	California	5,790	9.9%
13	Colorado	1,397	2.4%
18	Connecticut	1,140	2.0%
46	Delaware	190	0.3%
4	Florida	3,498	6.0%
8	Georgia	1,883	3.2%
48	Hawaii	149	0.3%
36	Idaho	377	0.6%
12	Illinois	1,463	2.5%
31	Indiana	496	0.8%
24	Iowa	658	1.1%
25	Kansas	640	1.1%
23	Kentucky	694	1.2%
35	Louisiana	410	0.7%
33	Maine	450	0.8%
11	Maryland	1,551	2.7%
14	Massachusetts	1,334	2.3%
7	Michigan	2,501	4.3%
20	Minnesota	918	1.6%
49	Mississippi	74	0.1%
32	Missouri	491	0.8%
42	Montana	296	0.5%
28	Nebraska	584	1.0%
37	Nevada	373	0.6%
40	New Hampshire	313	0.5%
19	New Jersey	1,028	1.8%
34	New Mexico	428	0.7%
1	New York	6,610	11.3%
6	North Carolina	2,839	4.9%
43	North Dakota	216	0.4%
10	Ohio	1,617	2.8%
21	Oklahoma	794	1.4%
27	Oregon	603	1.0%
5	Pennsylvania	3,319	5.7%
44	Rhode Island	214	0.4%
29	South Carolina	531	0.9%
38	South Dakota	344	0.6%
22	Tennessee	780	1.3%
3	Texas	3,660	6.3%
30	Utah	523	0.9%
45	Vermont	199	0.3%
17	Virginia	1,179	2.0%
9	Washington	1,625	2.8%
26	West Virginia	630	1.1%
16	Wisconsin	1,240	2.1%
47	Wyoming	157	0.3%

RANK ORDER

RANK	STATE	PAs	% of USA
1	New York	6,610	11.3%
2	California	5,790	9.9%
3	Texas	3,660	6.3%
4	Florida	3,498	6.0%
5	Pennsylvania	3,319	5.7%
6	North Carolina	2,839	4.9%
7	Michigan	2,501	4.3%
8	Georgia	1,883	3.2%
9	Washington	1,625	2.8%
10	Ohio	1,617	2.8%
11	Maryland	1,551	2.7%
12	Illinois	1,463	2.5%
13	Colorado	1,397	2.4%
14	Massachusetts	1,334	2.3%
15	Arizona	1,319	2.3%
16	Wisconsin	1,240	2.1%
17	Virginia	1,179	2.0%
18	Connecticut	1,140	2.0%
19	New Jersey	1,028	1.8%
20	Minnesota	918	1.6%
21	Oklahoma	794	1.4%
22	Tennessee	780	1.3%
23	Kentucky	694	1.2%
24	Iowa	658	1.1%
25	Kansas	640	1.1%
26	West Virginia	630	1.1%
27	Oregon	603	1.0%
28	Nebraska	584	1.0%
29	South Carolina	531	0.9%
30	Utah	523	0.9%
31	Indiana	496	0.8%
32	Missouri	491	0.8%
33	Maine	450	0.8%
34	New Mexico	428	0.7%
35	Louisiana	410	0.7%
36	Idaho	377	0.6%
37	Nevada	373	0.6%
38	South Dakota	344	0.6%
39	Alaska	329	0.6%
40	New Hampshire	313	0.5%
41	Alabama	311	0.5%
42	Montana	296	0.5%
43	North Dakota	216	0.4%
44	Rhode Island	214	0.4%
45	Vermont	199	0.3%
46	Delaware	190	0.3%
47	Wyoming	157	0.3%
48	Hawaii	149	0.3%
49	Mississippi	74	0.1%
50	Arkansas	73	0.1%
	District of Columbia	174	0.3%

Source: The American Academy of Physician Assistants
"Projected Number of People in Clinical Practice as PAs as of January 1, 2006"
(http://www.aapa.org/research/05number-clinpractice06.pdf)
*Projected. National total does not include 253 physician assistants who work outside the United States or whose location is unknown.

Rate of Physician Assistants in Clinical Practice in 2006

National Rate = 20 PAs per 100,000 Population*

ALPHA ORDER

RANK ORDER

RANK	STATE	RATE		RANK	STATE	RATE
48	Alabama	7		1	Alaska	50
1	Alaska	50		2	South Dakota	44
22	Arizona	22		3	West Virginia	35
49	Arkansas	3		4	Maine	34
35	California	16		4	New York	34
13	Colorado	30		4	North Dakota	34
9	Connecticut	32		7	Nebraska	33
20	Delaware	23		7	North Carolina	33
30	Florida	20		9	Connecticut	32
27	Georgia	21		9	Montana	32
41	Hawaii	12		9	Vermont	32
16	Idaho	26		12	Wyoming	31
44	Illinois	11		13	Colorado	30
46	Indiana	8		14	Maryland	28
22	Iowa	22		15	Pennsylvania	27
20	Kansas	23		16	Idaho	26
33	Kentucky	17		16	Washington	26
45	Louisiana	9		18	Michigan	25
4	Maine	34		19	New Hampshire	24
14	Maryland	28		20	Delaware	23
27	Massachusetts	21		20	Kansas	23
18	Michigan	25		22	Arizona	22
32	Minnesota	18		22	Iowa	22
49	Mississippi	3		22	New Mexico	22
46	Missouri	8		22	Oklahoma	22
9	Montana	32		22	Wisconsin	22
7	Nebraska	33		27	Georgia	21
38	Nevada	15		27	Massachusetts	21
19	New Hampshire	24		27	Utah	21
41	New Jersey	12		30	Florida	20
22	New Mexico	22		30	Rhode Island	20
4	New York	34		32	Minnesota	18
7	North Carolina	33		33	Kentucky	17
4	North Dakota	34		33	Oregon	17
39	Ohio	14		35	California	16
22	Oklahoma	22		35	Texas	16
33	Oregon	17		35	Virginia	16
15	Pennsylvania	27		38	Nevada	15
30	Rhode Island	20		39	Ohio	14
41	South Carolina	12		40	Tennessee	13
2	South Dakota	44		41	Hawaii	12
40	Tennessee	13		41	New Jersey	12
35	Texas	16		41	South Carolina	12
27	Utah	21		44	Illinois	11
9	Vermont	32		45	Louisiana	9
35	Virginia	16		46	Indiana	8
16	Washington	26		46	Missouri	8
3	West Virginia	35		48	Alabama	7
22	Wisconsin	22		49	Arkansas	3
12	Wyoming	31		49	Mississippi	3
					District of Columbia	32

Source: Morgan Quitno Press using data from The American Academy of Physician Assistants
"Projected Number of People in Clinical Practice as PAs as of January 1, 2006"
(http://www.aapa.org/research/05number-clinpractice06.pdf)
*Projected. Rates calculated using 2005 Census population figures.

Average Annual Wages of Physician Assistants in 2004

National Average = $68,500*

ALPHA ORDER

RANK	STATE	WAGES
44	Alabama	$50,800
1	Alaska	89,870
35	Arizona	62,110
42	Arkansas	55,350
3	California	79,480
30	Colorado	65,610
4	Connecticut	78,050
36	Delaware	61,310
12	Florida	72,970
32	Georgia	63,500
48	Hawaii	44,520
28	Idaho	66,100
46	Illinois	49,330
33	Indiana	62,810
13	Iowa	72,860
16	Kansas	72,040
31	Kentucky	63,720
47	Louisiana	47,980
8	Maine	75,180
6	Maryland	76,050
20	Massachusetts	70,230
10	Michigan	74,610
11	Minnesota	73,730
49	Mississippi	42,320
39	Missouri	58,140
34	Montana	62,560
14	Nebraska	72,800
43	Nevada	51,930
25	New Hampshire	67,420
21	New Jersey	69,110
45	New Mexico	49,380
15	New York	72,590
17	North Carolina	71,900
37	North Dakota	60,330
18	Ohio	71,150
NA	Oklahoma**	NA
7	Oregon	75,760
40	Pennsylvania	57,060
26	Rhode Island	67,030
41	South Carolina	55,520
23	South Dakota	68,280
29	Tennessee	65,740
2	Texas	80,460
5	Utah	76,400
22	Vermont	68,960
27	Virginia	66,210
9	Washington	74,830
19	West Virginia	70,380
24	Wisconsin	67,540
38	Wyoming	58,980

RANK ORDER

RANK	STATE	WAGES
1	Alaska	$89,870
2	Texas	80,460
3	California	79,480
4	Connecticut	78,050
5	Utah	76,400
6	Maryland	76,050
7	Oregon	75,760
8	Maine	75,180
9	Washington	74,830
10	Michigan	74,610
11	Minnesota	73,730
12	Florida	72,970
13	Iowa	72,860
14	Nebraska	72,800
15	New York	72,590
16	Kansas	72,040
17	North Carolina	71,900
18	Ohio	71,150
19	West Virginia	70,380
20	Massachusetts	70,230
21	New Jersey	69,110
22	Vermont	68,960
23	South Dakota	68,280
24	Wisconsin	67,540
25	New Hampshire	67,420
26	Rhode Island	67,030
27	Virginia	66,210
28	Idaho	66,100
29	Tennessee	65,740
30	Colorado	65,610
31	Kentucky	63,720
32	Georgia	63,500
33	Indiana	62,810
34	Montana	62,560
35	Arizona	62,110
36	Delaware	61,310
37	North Dakota	60,330
38	Wyoming	58,980
39	Missouri	58,140
40	Pennsylvania	57,060
41	South Carolina	55,520
42	Arkansas	55,350
43	Nevada	51,930
44	Alabama	50,800
45	New Mexico	49,380
46	Illinois	49,330
47	Louisiana	47,980
48	Hawaii	44,520
49	Mississippi	42,320
NA	Oklahoma**	NA
	District of Columbia	55,560

Source: U.S. Department of Labor, Bureau of Labor Statistics
    "Occupational Employment and Wages, 2004" (http://www.bls.gov/oes/)
*Does not include self-employed.
**Not available.

Registered Nurses in 2004

National Total = 2,338,530 Registered Nurses*

ALPHA ORDER

RANK	STATE	NURSES	% of USA
22	Alabama	37,470	1.6%
49	Alaska	5,000	0.2%
26	Arizona	31,710	1.4%
33	Arkansas	19,700	0.8%
1	California	227,350	9.7%
25	Colorado	32,070	1.4%
24	Connecticut	33,800	1.4%
46	Delaware	7,400	0.3%
4	Florida	133,300	5.7%
12	Georgia	59,880	2.6%
44	Hawaii	8,390	0.4%
42	Idaho	9,680	0.4%
7	Illinois	98,000	4.2%
17	Indiana	51,600	2.2%
28	Iowa	30,240	1.3%
30	Kansas	25,820	1.1%
23	Kentucky	36,530	1.6%
21	Louisiana	39,460	1.7%
37	Maine	13,540	0.6%
14	Maryland	52,790	2.3%
10	Massachusetts	75,780	3.2%
8	Michigan	81,960	3.5%
18	Minnesota	47,980	2.1%
31	Mississippi	25,210	1.1%
16	Missouri	52,410	2.2%
45	Montana	7,920	0.3%
34	Nebraska	16,910	0.7%
38	Nevada	13,460	0.6%
39	New Hampshire	11,790	0.5%
9	New Jersey	77,960	3.3%
40	New Mexico	10,690	0.5%
2	New York	165,210	7.1%
11	North Carolina	70,340	3.0%
47	North Dakota	6,740	0.3%
6	Ohio	106,130	4.5%
32	Oklahoma	23,550	1.0%
29	Oregon	26,900	1.2%
5	Pennsylvania	120,180	5.1%
41	Rhode Island	10,250	0.4%
27	South Carolina	31,200	1.3%
43	South Dakota	9,050	0.4%
15	Tennessee	52,680	2.3%
3	Texas	146,170	6.3%
36	Utah	15,440	0.7%
48	Vermont	5,500	0.2%
13	Virginia	53,880	2.3%
20	Washington	45,680	2.0%
35	West Virginia	15,620	0.7%
19	Wisconsin	46,660	2.0%
50	Wyoming	3,680	0.2%

RANK ORDER

RANK	STATE	NURSES	% of USA
1	California	227,350	9.7%
2	New York	165,210	7.1%
3	Texas	146,170	6.3%
4	Florida	133,300	5.7%
5	Pennsylvania	120,180	5.1%
6	Ohio	106,130	4.5%
7	Illinois	98,000	4.2%
8	Michigan	81,960	3.5%
9	New Jersey	77,960	3.3%
10	Massachusetts	75,780	3.2%
11	North Carolina	70,340	3.0%
12	Georgia	59,880	2.6%
13	Virginia	53,880	2.3%
14	Maryland	52,790	2.3%
15	Tennessee	52,680	2.3%
16	Missouri	52,410	2.2%
17	Indiana	51,600	2.2%
18	Minnesota	47,980	2.1%
19	Wisconsin	46,660	2.0%
20	Washington	45,680	2.0%
21	Louisiana	39,460	1.7%
22	Alabama	37,470	1.6%
23	Kentucky	36,530	1.6%
24	Connecticut	33,800	1.4%
25	Colorado	32,070	1.4%
26	Arizona	31,710	1.4%
27	South Carolina	31,200	1.3%
28	Iowa	30,240	1.3%
29	Oregon	26,900	1.2%
30	Kansas	25,820	1.1%
31	Mississippi	25,210	1.1%
32	Oklahoma	23,550	1.0%
33	Arkansas	19,700	0.8%
34	Nebraska	16,910	0.7%
35	West Virginia	15,620	0.7%
36	Utah	15,440	0.7%
37	Maine	13,540	0.6%
38	Nevada	13,460	0.6%
39	New Hampshire	11,790	0.5%
40	New Mexico	10,690	0.5%
41	Rhode Island	10,250	0.4%
42	Idaho	9,680	0.4%
43	South Dakota	9,050	0.4%
44	Hawaii	8,390	0.4%
45	Montana	7,920	0.3%
46	Delaware	7,400	0.3%
47	North Dakota	6,740	0.3%
48	Vermont	5,500	0.2%
49	Alaska	5,000	0.2%
50	Wyoming	3,680	0.2%
	District of Columbia	7,880	0.3%

Source: U.S. Department of Labor, Bureau of Labor Statistics
    "Occupational Employment and Wages, 2004" (http://www.bls.gov/oes/)
*Does not include self-employed.

Rate of Registered Nurses in 2004

National Rate = 796 Nurses per 100,000 Population*

ALPHA ORDER

RANK	STATE	RATE
28	Alabama	828
33	Alaska	760
50	Arizona	552
39	Arkansas	716
47	California	634
40	Colorado	697
8	Connecticut	966
18	Delaware	891
32	Florida	767
42	Georgia	671
44	Hawaii	665
41	Idaho	694
31	Illinois	771
27	Indiana	829
5	Iowa	1,024
11	Kansas	945
20	Kentucky	882
21	Louisiana	876
4	Maine	1,030
9	Maryland	949
1	Massachusetts	1,183
30	Michigan	811
12	Minnesota	941
22	Mississippi	869
14	Missouri	910
25	Montana	854
7	Nebraska	968
48	Nevada	577
15	New Hampshire	908
16	New Jersey	898
49	New Mexico	562
24	New York	857
29	North Carolina	824
3	North Dakota	1,059
13	Ohio	927
43	Oklahoma	668
34	Oregon	749
6	Pennsylvania	970
9	Rhode Island	949
35	South Carolina	743
2	South Dakota	1,174
17	Tennessee	894
45	Texas	650
46	Utah	638
19	Vermont	885
38	Virginia	720
36	Washington	736
23	West Virginia	862
26	Wisconsin	848
37	Wyoming	727

RANK ORDER

RANK	STATE	RATE
1	Massachusetts	1,183
2	South Dakota	1,174
3	North Dakota	1,059
4	Maine	1,030
5	Iowa	1,024
6	Pennsylvania	970
7	Nebraska	968
8	Connecticut	966
9	Maryland	949
9	Rhode Island	949
11	Kansas	945
12	Minnesota	941
13	Ohio	927
14	Missouri	910
15	New Hampshire	908
16	New Jersey	898
17	Tennessee	894
18	Delaware	891
19	Vermont	885
20	Kentucky	882
21	Louisiana	876
22	Mississippi	869
23	West Virginia	862
24	New York	857
25	Montana	854
26	Wisconsin	848
27	Indiana	829
28	Alabama	828
29	North Carolina	824
30	Michigan	811
31	Illinois	771
32	Florida	767
33	Alaska	760
34	Oregon	749
35	South Carolina	743
36	Washington	736
37	Wyoming	727
38	Virginia	720
39	Arkansas	716
40	Colorado	697
41	Idaho	694
42	Georgia	671
43	Oklahoma	668
44	Hawaii	665
45	Texas	650
46	Utah	638
47	California	634
48	Nevada	577
49	New Mexico	562
50	Arizona	552
	District of Columbia	1,422

Source: Morgan Quitno Press using data from U.S. Department of Labor, Bureau of Labor Statistics
"Occupational Employment and Wages, 2004" (http://www.bls.gov/oes/)
*Does not include self-employed.

Average Annual Wages of Registered Nurses in 2004

National Average = $55,680*

ALPHA ORDER

RANK	STATE	WAGES
43	Alabama	$47,170
8	Alaska	60,420
17	Arizona	54,940
40	Arkansas	47,990
1	California	69,140
16	Colorado	55,010
7	Connecticut	61,450
13	Delaware	57,470
23	Florida	52,150
32	Georgia	50,330
3	Hawaii	64,320
39	Idaho	48,000
26	Illinois	51,600
36	Indiana	49,100
50	Iowa	44,000
45	Kansas	46,910
37	Kentucky	48,980
30	Louisiana	50,560
24	Maine	51,930
2	Maryland	65,750
4	Massachusetts	64,120
15	Michigan	55,380
10	Minnesota	58,980
42	Mississippi	47,220
34	Missouri	49,690
44	Montana	47,040
35	Nebraska	49,350
11	Nevada	58,630
28	New Hampshire	51,030
6	New Jersey	61,790
22	New Mexico	52,620
5	New York	62,140
31	North Carolina	50,450
48	North Dakota	46,480
25	Ohio	51,840
47	Oklahoma	46,660
12	Oregon	58,380
20	Pennsylvania	53,670
14	Rhode Island	56,910
29	South Carolina	50,950
46	South Dakota	46,830
33	Tennessee	49,890
18	Texas	53,940
27	Utah	51,590
38	Vermont	48,770
21	Virginia	53,330
9	Washington	59,650
41	West Virginia	47,780
19	Wisconsin	53,700
49	Wyoming	46,200

RANK ORDER

RANK	STATE	WAGES
1	California	$69,140
2	Maryland	65,750
3	Hawaii	64,320
4	Massachusetts	64,120
5	New York	62,140
6	New Jersey	61,790
7	Connecticut	61,450
8	Alaska	60,420
9	Washington	59,650
10	Minnesota	58,980
11	Nevada	58,630
12	Oregon	58,380
13	Delaware	57,470
14	Rhode Island	56,910
15	Michigan	55,380
16	Colorado	55,010
17	Arizona	54,940
18	Texas	53,940
19	Wisconsin	53,700
20	Pennsylvania	53,670
21	Virginia	53,330
22	New Mexico	52,620
23	Florida	52,150
24	Maine	51,930
25	Ohio	51,840
26	Illinois	51,600
27	Utah	51,590
28	New Hampshire	51,030
29	South Carolina	50,950
30	Louisiana	50,560
31	North Carolina	50,450
32	Georgia	50,330
33	Tennessee	49,890
34	Missouri	49,690
35	Nebraska	49,350
36	Indiana	49,100
37	Kentucky	48,980
38	Vermont	48,770
39	Idaho	48,000
40	Arkansas	47,990
41	West Virginia	47,780
42	Mississippi	47,220
43	Alabama	47,170
44	Montana	47,040
45	Kansas	46,910
46	South Dakota	46,830
47	Oklahoma	46,660
48	North Dakota	46,480
49	Wyoming	46,200
50	Iowa	44,000
	District of Columbia	58,330

Source: U.S. Department of Labor, Bureau of Labor Statistics
    "Occupational Employment and Wages, 2004" (http://www.bls.gov/oes/)
*Does not include self-employed.

Licensed Practical and Licensed Vocational Nurses in 2004

National Total = 706,360 LPN/LVNs*

ALPHA ORDER

RANK	STATE	NURSES	% of USA
19	Alabama	15,460	2.2%
50	Alaska	550	0.1%
27	Arizona	9,000	1.3%
21	Arkansas	12,370	1.8%
2	California	52,880	7.5%
33	Colorado	6,800	1.0%
29	Connecticut	7,820	1.1%
47	Delaware	1,690	0.2%
4	Florida	49,250	7.0%
7	Georgia	23,910	3.4%
45	Hawaii	1,880	0.3%
36	Idaho	3,130	0.4%
8	Illinois	22,760	3.2%
11	Indiana	18,750	2.7%
31	Iowa	6,960	1.0%
32	Kansas	6,920	1.0%
22	Kentucky	11,530	1.6%
10	Louisiana	19,250	2.7%
44	Maine	1,950	0.3%
28	Maryland	8,720	1.2%
15	Massachusetts	17,130	2.4%
17	Michigan	16,610	2.4%
14	Minnesota	17,890	2.5%
26	Mississippi	9,390	1.3%
16	Missouri	16,940	2.4%
39	Montana	2,690	0.4%
34	Nebraska	5,850	0.8%
41	Nevada	2,560	0.4%
42	New Hampshire	2,130	0.3%
13	New Jersey	17,950	2.5%
35	New Mexico	4,260	0.6%
3	New York	50,060	7.1%
18	North Carolina	16,490	2.3%
40	North Dakota	2,680	0.4%
5	Ohio	37,150	5.3%
20	Oklahoma	13,260	1.9%
38	Oregon	2,940	0.4%
6	Pennsylvania	34,930	4.9%
46	Rhode Island	1,780	0.3%
23	South Carolina	10,890	1.5%
43	South Dakota	2,030	0.3%
9	Tennessee	22,460	3.2%
1	Texas	63,080	8.9%
37	Utah	2,980	0.4%
48	Vermont	1,450	0.2%
12	Virginia	18,410	2.6%
25	Washington	10,390	1.5%
30	West Virginia	6,990	1.0%
24	Wisconsin	10,510	1.5%
49	Wyoming	800	0.1%

RANK ORDER

RANK	STATE	NURSES	% of USA
1	Texas	63,080	8.9%
2	California	52,880	7.5%
3	New York	50,060	7.1%
4	Florida	49,250	7.0%
5	Ohio	37,150	5.3%
6	Pennsylvania	34,930	4.9%
7	Georgia	23,910	3.4%
8	Illinois	22,760	3.2%
9	Tennessee	22,460	3.2%
10	Louisiana	19,250	2.7%
11	Indiana	18,750	2.7%
12	Virginia	18,410	2.6%
13	New Jersey	17,950	2.5%
14	Minnesota	17,890	2.5%
15	Massachusetts	17,130	2.4%
16	Missouri	16,940	2.4%
17	Michigan	16,610	2.4%
18	North Carolina	16,490	2.3%
19	Alabama	15,460	2.2%
20	Oklahoma	13,260	1.9%
21	Arkansas	12,370	1.8%
22	Kentucky	11,530	1.6%
23	South Carolina	10,890	1.5%
24	Wisconsin	10,510	1.5%
25	Washington	10,390	1.5%
26	Mississippi	9,390	1.3%
27	Arizona	9,000	1.3%
28	Maryland	8,720	1.2%
29	Connecticut	7,820	1.1%
30	West Virginia	6,990	1.0%
31	Iowa	6,960	1.0%
32	Kansas	6,920	1.0%
33	Colorado	6,800	1.0%
34	Nebraska	5,850	0.8%
35	New Mexico	4,260	0.6%
36	Idaho	3,130	0.4%
37	Utah	2,980	0.4%
38	Oregon	2,940	0.4%
39	Montana	2,690	0.4%
40	North Dakota	2,680	0.4%
41	Nevada	2,560	0.4%
42	New Hampshire	2,130	0.3%
43	South Dakota	2,030	0.3%
44	Maine	1,950	0.3%
45	Hawaii	1,880	0.3%
46	Rhode Island	1,780	0.3%
47	Delaware	1,690	0.2%
48	Vermont	1,450	0.2%
49	Wyoming	800	0.1%
50	Alaska	550	0.1%
	District of Columbia	2,080	0.3%

Source: U.S. Department of Labor, Bureau of Labor Statistics
"Occupational Employment and Wages, 2004" (http://www.bls.gov/oes/)
Does not include self-employed.

Rate of Licensed Practical and Licensed Vocational Nurses in 2004

National Rate = 241 LPN/LVNs per 100,000 Population*

ALPHA ORDER			RANK ORDER		
RANK	STATE	RATE	RANK	STATE	RATE
8	Alabama	342	1	Arkansas	450
49	Alaska	84	2	Louisiana	427
41	Arizona	157	3	North Dakota	421
1	Arkansas	450	4	West Virginia	386
44	California	148	5	Tennessee	381
44	Colorado	148	6	Oklahoma	376
30	Connecticut	223	7	Minnesota	351
32	Delaware	204	8	Alabama	342
15	Florida	283	9	Nebraska	335
19	Georgia	268	10	Mississippi	324
43	Hawaii	149	10	Ohio	324
28	Idaho	224	12	Indiana	301
35	Illinois	179	13	Missouri	294
12	Indiana	301	14	Montana	290
26	Iowa	236	15	Florida	283
24	Kansas	253	16	Pennsylvania	282
18	Kentucky	278	17	Texas	281
2	Louisiana	427	18	Kentucky	278
44	Maine	148	19	Georgia	268
41	Maryland	157	20	Massachusetts	267
20	Massachusetts	267	21	South Dakota	263
38	Michigan	164	22	New York	260
7	Minnesota	351	23	South Carolina	259
10	Mississippi	324	24	Kansas	253
13	Missouri	294	25	Virginia	246
14	Montana	290	26	Iowa	236
9	Nebraska	335	27	Vermont	233
48	Nevada	110	28	Idaho	224
38	New Hampshire	164	28	New Mexico	224
31	New Jersey	207	30	Connecticut	223
28	New Mexico	224	31	New Jersey	207
22	New York	260	32	Delaware	204
33	North Carolina	193	33	North Carolina	193
3	North Dakota	421	34	Wisconsin	191
10	Ohio	324	35	Illinois	179
6	Oklahoma	376	36	Washington	167
50	Oregon	82	37	Rhode Island	165
16	Pennsylvania	282	38	Michigan	164
37	Rhode Island	165	38	New Hampshire	164
23	South Carolina	259	40	Wyoming	158
21	South Dakota	263	41	Arizona	157
5	Tennessee	381	41	Maryland	157
17	Texas	281	43	Hawaii	149
47	Utah	123	44	California	148
27	Vermont	233	44	Colorado	148
25	Virginia	246	44	Maine	148
36	Washington	167	47	Utah	123
4	West Virginia	386	48	Nevada	110
34	Wisconsin	191	49	Alaska	84
40	Wyoming	158	50	Oregon	82
				District of Columbia	375

Source: Morgan Quitno Press using data from U.S. Department of Labor, Bureau of Labor Statistics
    "Occupational Employment and Wages, 2004" (http://www.bls.gov/oes/)
*Does not include self-employed.

Average Annual Wages of Licensed Practical and Licensed Vocational Nurses in 2004
National Average = $35,580*

ALPHA ORDER

RANK	STATE	WAGES
48	Alabama	$28,680
8	Alaska	40,150
19	Arizona	36,780
45	Arkansas	29,370
6	California	41,920
14	Colorado	37,410
1	Connecticut	47,860
7	Delaware	41,720
22	Florida	35,250
40	Georgia	30,920
13	Hawaii	37,730
34	Idaho	32,020
23	Illinois	34,980
27	Indiana	34,440
37	Iowa	31,480
36	Kansas	31,710
33	Kentucky	32,210
42	Louisiana	30,360
31	Maine	33,140
4	Maryland	44,110
3	Massachusetts	44,910
18	Michigan	36,920
26	Minnesota	34,660
50	Mississippi	27,500
41	Missouri	30,910
46	Montana	29,300
35	Nebraska	31,860
9	Nevada	38,820
15	New Hampshire	37,400
2	New Jersey	46,010
12	New Mexico	38,030
17	New York	36,970
25	North Carolina	34,710
43	North Dakota	30,220
21	Ohio	36,040
44	Oklahoma	29,980
10	Oregon	38,730
16	Pennsylvania	37,040
5	Rhode Island	42,730
24	South Carolina	34,960
47	South Dakota	28,720
39	Tennessee	30,940
29	Texas	34,260
32	Utah	32,710
30	Vermont	33,410
28	Virginia	34,430
11	Washington	38,700
49	West Virginia	28,420
20	Wisconsin	36,210
38	Wyoming	31,390

RANK ORDER

RANK	STATE	WAGES
1	Connecticut	$47,860
2	New Jersey	46,010
3	Massachusetts	44,910
4	Maryland	44,110
5	Rhode Island	42,730
6	California	41,920
7	Delaware	41,720
8	Alaska	40,150
9	Nevada	38,820
10	Oregon	38,730
11	Washington	38,700
12	New Mexico	38,030
13	Hawaii	37,730
14	Colorado	37,410
15	New Hampshire	37,400
16	Pennsylvania	37,040
17	New York	36,970
18	Michigan	36,920
19	Arizona	36,780
20	Wisconsin	36,210
21	Ohio	36,040
22	Florida	35,250
23	Illinois	34,980
24	South Carolina	34,960
25	North Carolina	34,710
26	Minnesota	34,660
27	Indiana	34,440
28	Virginia	34,430
29	Texas	34,260
30	Vermont	33,410
31	Maine	33,140
32	Utah	32,710
33	Kentucky	32,210
34	Idaho	32,020
35	Nebraska	31,860
36	Kansas	31,710
37	Iowa	31,480
38	Wyoming	31,390
39	Tennessee	30,940
40	Georgia	30,920
41	Missouri	30,910
42	Louisiana	30,360
43	North Dakota	30,220
44	Oklahoma	29,980
45	Arkansas	29,370
46	Montana	29,300
47	South Dakota	28,720
48	Alabama	28,680
49	West Virginia	28,420
50	Mississippi	27,500
	District of Columbia	48,370

Source: U.S. Department of Labor, Bureau of Labor Statistics
    "Occupational Employment and Wages, 2004" (http://www.bls.gov/oes/)
*Does not include self-employed.

Physical Therapists in 2004

National Total = 145,210 Physical Therapists*

ALPHA ORDER

RANK	STATE	THERAPISTS	% of USA
28	Alabama	1,570	1.1%
48	Alaska	410	0.3%
23	Arizona	2,390	1.6%
34	Arkansas	1,100	0.8%
1	California	12,610	8.7%
20	Colorado	3,020	2.1%
21	Connecticut	2,760	1.9%
46	Delaware	460	0.3%
4	Florida	8,210	5.7%
14	Georgia	3,340	2.3%
46	Hawaii	460	0.3%
43	Idaho	560	0.4%
6	Illinois	6,410	4.4%
15	Indiana	3,280	2.3%
30	Iowa	1,330	0.9%
32	Kansas	1,190	0.8%
25	Kentucky	1,950	1.3%
24	Louisiana	1,970	1.4%
37	Maine	990	0.7%
19	Maryland	3,130	2.2%
7	Massachusetts	5,590	3.8%
10	Michigan	4,990	3.4%
11	Minnesota	3,630	2.5%
31	Mississippi	1,270	0.9%
13	Missouri	3,490	2.4%
42	Montana	650	0.4%
38	Nebraska	980	0.7%
36	Nevada	1,060	0.7%
39	New Hampshire	920	0.6%
9	New Jersey	5,040	3.5%
40	New Mexico	850	0.6%
2	New York	11,940	8.2%
12	North Carolina	3,610	2.5%
49	North Dakota	360	0.2%
8	Ohio	5,520	3.8%
27	Oklahoma	1,670	1.2%
29	Oregon	1,530	1.1%
5	Pennsylvania	7,870	5.4%
41	Rhode Island	800	0.6%
26	South Carolina	1,780	1.2%
44	South Dakota	530	0.4%
18	Tennessee	3,230	2.2%
3	Texas	8,340	5.7%
35	Utah	1,070	0.7%
45	Vermont	500	0.3%
16	Virginia	3,270	2.3%
22	Washington	2,670	1.8%
33	West Virginia	1,110	0.8%
16	Wisconsin	3,270	2.3%
50	Wyoming	270	0.2%

RANK ORDER

RANK	STATE	THERAPISTS	% of USA
1	California	12,610	8.7%
2	New York	11,940	8.2%
3	Texas	8,340	5.7%
4	Florida	8,210	5.7%
5	Pennsylvania	7,870	5.4%
6	Illinois	6,410	4.4%
7	Massachusetts	5,590	3.8%
8	Ohio	5,520	3.8%
9	New Jersey	5,040	3.5%
10	Michigan	4,990	3.4%
11	Minnesota	3,630	2.5%
12	North Carolina	3,610	2.5%
13	Missouri	3,490	2.4%
14	Georgia	3,340	2.3%
15	Indiana	3,280	2.3%
16	Virginia	3,270	2.3%
16	Wisconsin	3,270	2.3%
18	Tennessee	3,230	2.2%
19	Maryland	3,130	2.2%
20	Colorado	3,020	2.1%
21	Connecticut	2,760	1.9%
22	Washington	2,670	1.8%
23	Arizona	2,390	1.6%
24	Louisiana	1,970	1.4%
25	Kentucky	1,950	1.3%
26	South Carolina	1,780	1.2%
27	Oklahoma	1,670	1.2%
28	Alabama	1,570	1.1%
29	Oregon	1,530	1.1%
30	Iowa	1,330	0.9%
31	Mississippi	1,270	0.9%
32	Kansas	1,190	0.8%
33	West Virginia	1,110	0.8%
34	Arkansas	1,100	0.8%
35	Utah	1,070	0.7%
36	Nevada	1,060	0.7%
37	Maine	990	0.7%
38	Nebraska	980	0.7%
39	New Hampshire	920	0.6%
40	New Mexico	850	0.6%
41	Rhode Island	800	0.6%
42	Montana	650	0.4%
43	Idaho	560	0.4%
44	South Dakota	530	0.4%
45	Vermont	500	0.3%
46	Delaware	460	0.3%
46	Hawaii	460	0.3%
48	Alaska	410	0.3%
49	North Dakota	360	0.2%
50	Wyoming	270	0.2%
	District of Columbia	260	0.2%

Source: U.S. Department of Labor, Bureau of Labor Statistics
   "Occupational Employment and Wages, 2004" (http://www.bls.gov/oes/)
*Does not include self-employed.

Rate of Physical Therapists in 2004

National Rate = 49 Physical Therapists per 100,000 Population*

RANK	STATE	RATE
49	Alabama	35
12	Alaska	62
41	Arizona	42
44	Arkansas	40
49	California	35
10	Colorado	66
3	Connecticut	79
21	Delaware	55
28	Florida	47
46	Georgia	37
48	Hawaii	36
44	Idaho	40
25	Illinois	50
23	Indiana	53
31	Iowa	45
34	Kansas	44
28	Kentucky	47
34	Louisiana	44
4	Maine	75
19	Maryland	56
1	Massachusetts	87
26	Michigan	49
6	Minnesota	71
34	Mississippi	44
14	Missouri	61
8	Montana	70
19	Nebraska	56
31	Nevada	45
6	New Hampshire	71
17	New Jersey	58
31	New Mexico	45
12	New York	62
41	North Carolina	42
18	North Dakota	57
27	Ohio	48
28	Oklahoma	47
39	Oregon	43
11	Pennsylvania	63
5	Rhode Island	74
41	South Carolina	42
9	South Dakota	69
21	Tennessee	55
46	Texas	37
34	Utah	44
2	Vermont	80
34	Virginia	44
39	Washington	43
14	West Virginia	61
16	Wisconsin	59
23	Wyoming	53

RANK	STATE	RATE
1	Massachusetts	87
2	Vermont	80
3	Connecticut	79
4	Maine	75
5	Rhode Island	74
6	Minnesota	71
6	New Hampshire	71
8	Montana	70
9	South Dakota	69
10	Colorado	66
11	Pennsylvania	63
12	Alaska	62
12	New York	62
14	Missouri	61
14	West Virginia	61
16	Wisconsin	59
17	New Jersey	58
18	North Dakota	57
19	Maryland	56
19	Nebraska	56
21	Delaware	55
21	Tennessee	55
23	Indiana	53
23	Wyoming	53
25	Illinois	50
26	Michigan	49
27	Ohio	48
28	Florida	47
28	Kentucky	47
28	Oklahoma	47
31	Iowa	45
31	Nevada	45
31	New Mexico	45
34	Kansas	44
34	Louisiana	44
34	Mississippi	44
34	Utah	44
34	Virginia	44
39	Oregon	43
39	Washington	43
41	Arizona	42
41	North Carolina	42
41	South Carolina	42
44	Arkansas	40
44	Idaho	40
46	Georgia	37
46	Texas	37
48	Hawaii	36
49	Alabama	35
49	California	35
	District of Columbia	47

Source: Morgan Quitno Press using data from U.S. Department of Labor, Bureau of Labor Statistics
"Occupational Employment and Wages, 2004" (http://www.bls.gov/oes/)
*Does not include self-employed.

Average Annual Wages of Physical Therapists in 2004

National Average = $63,690*

RANK	STATE	WAGES
29	Alabama	$61,700
1	Alaska	78,090
21	Arizona	62,950
26	Arkansas	62,000
5	California	69,570
50	Colorado	54,420
6	Connecticut	68,260
11	Delaware	63,940
20	Florida	63,030
28	Georgia	61,780
37	Hawaii	59,550
33	Idaho	60,250
27	Illinois	61,840
31	Indiana	60,640
41	Iowa	58,250
44	Kansas	57,630
25	Kentucky	62,230
4	Louisiana	69,740
46	Maine	56,540
13	Maryland	63,800
32	Massachusetts	60,530
9	Michigan	65,360
47	Minnesota	56,080
17	Mississippi	63,340
45	Missouri	56,580
34	Montana	59,920
36	Nebraska	59,810
7	Nevada	68,190
42	New Hampshire	58,130
2	New Jersey	73,070
39	New Mexico	58,990
10	New York	64,910
23	North Carolina	62,370
49	North Dakota	54,480
24	Ohio	62,270
15	Oklahoma	63,620
35	Oregon	59,880
14	Pennsylvania	63,760
22	Rhode Island	62,590
40	South Carolina	58,780
43	South Dakota	57,720
18	Tennessee	63,170
3	Texas	69,770
19	Utah	63,140
48	Vermont	55,630
11	Virginia	63,940
16	Washington	63,370
8	West Virginia	67,140
30	Wisconsin	61,030
38	Wyoming	59,530

RANK	STATE	WAGES
1	Alaska	$78,090
2	New Jersey	73,070
3	Texas	69,770
4	Louisiana	69,740
5	California	69,570
6	Connecticut	68,260
7	Nevada	68,190
8	West Virginia	67,140
9	Michigan	65,360
10	New York	64,910
11	Delaware	63,940
11	Virginia	63,940
13	Maryland	63,800
14	Pennsylvania	63,760
15	Oklahoma	63,620
16	Washington	63,370
17	Mississippi	63,340
18	Tennessee	63,170
19	Utah	63,140
20	Florida	63,030
21	Arizona	62,950
22	Rhode Island	62,590
23	North Carolina	62,370
24	Ohio	62,270
25	Kentucky	62,230
26	Arkansas	62,000
27	Illinois	61,840
28	Georgia	61,780
29	Alabama	61,700
30	Wisconsin	61,030
31	Indiana	60,640
32	Massachusetts	60,530
33	Idaho	60,250
34	Montana	59,920
35	Oregon	59,880
36	Nebraska	59,810
37	Hawaii	59,550
38	Wyoming	59,530
39	New Mexico	58,990
40	South Carolina	58,780
41	Iowa	58,250
42	New Hampshire	58,130
43	South Dakota	57,720
44	Kansas	57,630
45	Missouri	56,580
46	Maine	56,540
47	Minnesota	56,080
48	Vermont	55,630
49	North Dakota	54,480
50	Colorado	54,420
	District of Columbia	59,430

Source: U.S. Department of Labor, Bureau of Labor Statistics
   "Occupational Employment and Wages, 2004" (http://www.bls.gov/oes/)
Does not include self-employed.

Dentists in 2002

National Total = 169,894 Dentists*

RANK	STATE	DENTISTS	% of USA
27	Alabama	1,928	1.1%
45	Alaska	463	0.3%
23	Arizona	2,486	1.5%
35	Arkansas	1,088	0.6%
1	California	23,981	14.1%
20	Colorado	2,864	1.7%
22	Connecticut	2,658	1.6%
47	Delaware	362	0.2%
4	Florida	8,584	5.1%
14	Georgia	3,755	2.2%
36	Hawaii	1,008	0.6%
41	Idaho	724	0.4%
5	Illinois	8,133	4.8%
19	Indiana	2,950	1.7%
30	Iowa	1,561	0.9%
32	Kansas	1,379	0.8%
25	Kentucky	2,242	1.3%
26	Louisiana	2,080	1.2%
42	Maine	599	0.4%
12	Maryland	4,079	2.4%
10	Massachusetts	5,229	3.1%
9	Michigan	5,995	3.5%
18	Minnesota	2,969	1.7%
33	Mississippi	1,134	0.7%
21	Missouri	2,744	1.6%
44	Montana	509	0.3%
34	Nebraska	1,095	0.6%
37	Nevada	861	0.5%
40	New Hampshire	745	0.4%
7	New Jersey	6,738	4.0%
39	New Mexico	816	0.5%
2	New York	15,162	8.9%
15	North Carolina	3,553	2.1%
49	North Dakota	302	0.2%
8	Ohio	6,068	3.6%
29	Oklahoma	1,702	1.0%
24	Oregon	2,339	1.4%
6	Pennsylvania	7,964	4.7%
43	Rhode Island	594	0.3%
28	South Carolina	1,879	1.1%
48	South Dakota	358	0.2%
17	Tennessee	2,982	1.8%
3	Texas	10,121	6.0%
31	Utah	1,465	0.9%
46	Vermont	365	0.2%
11	Virginia	4,217	2.5%
13	Washington	4,061	2.4%
38	West Virginia	836	0.5%
16	Wisconsin	3,120	1.8%
50	Wyoming	254	0.1%

RANK	STATE	DENTISTS	% of USA
1	California	23,981	14.1%
2	New York	15,162	8.9%
3	Texas	10,121	6.0%
4	Florida	8,584	5.1%
5	Illinois	8,133	4.8%
6	Pennsylvania	7,964	4.7%
7	New Jersey	6,738	4.0%
8	Ohio	6,068	3.6%
9	Michigan	5,995	3.5%
10	Massachusetts	5,229	3.1%
11	Virginia	4,217	2.5%
12	Maryland	4,079	2.4%
13	Washington	4,061	2.4%
14	Georgia	3,755	2.2%
15	North Carolina	3,553	2.1%
16	Wisconsin	3,120	1.8%
17	Tennessee	2,982	1.8%
18	Minnesota	2,969	1.7%
19	Indiana	2,950	1.7%
20	Colorado	2,864	1.7%
21	Missouri	2,744	1.6%
22	Connecticut	2,658	1.6%
23	Arizona	2,486	1.5%
24	Oregon	2,339	1.4%
25	Kentucky	2,242	1.3%
26	Louisiana	2,080	1.2%
27	Alabama	1,928	1.1%
28	South Carolina	1,879	1.1%
29	Oklahoma	1,702	1.0%
30	Iowa	1,561	0.9%
31	Utah	1,465	0.9%
32	Kansas	1,379	0.8%
33	Mississippi	1,134	0.7%
34	Nebraska	1,095	0.6%
35	Arkansas	1,088	0.6%
36	Hawaii	1,008	0.6%
37	Nevada	861	0.5%
38	West Virginia	836	0.5%
39	New Mexico	816	0.5%
40	New Hampshire	745	0.4%
41	Idaho	724	0.4%
42	Maine	599	0.4%
43	Rhode Island	594	0.3%
44	Montana	509	0.3%
45	Alaska	463	0.3%
46	Vermont	365	0.2%
47	Delaware	362	0.2%
48	South Dakota	358	0.2%
49	North Dakota	302	0.2%
50	Wyoming	254	0.1%
	District of Columbia	670	0.4%

Source: American Dental Association
   "Distribution of Dentists, by Region and State, 2002"
*Professionally active dentists. Total includes 123 dentists for whom state is not known. Total does not include 2,197 dentists in territories nor dentists in the Armed Forces stationed overseas.

Rate of Dentists in 2002

National Rate = 59 Dentists per 100,000 Population*

ALPHA ORDER			RANK ORDER		
RANK	**STATE**	**RATE**	**RANK**	**STATE**	**RATE**
46	Alabama	43	1	Hawaii	82
7	Alaska	72	1	Massachusetts	82
38	Arizona	46	3	New Jersey	79
48	Arkansas	40	3	New York	79
8	California	69	5	Connecticut	77
13	Colorado	64	6	Maryland	75
5	Connecticut	77	7	Alaska	72
43	Delaware	45	8	California	69
28	Florida	51	9	Washington	67
44	Georgia	44	10	Oregon	66
1	Hawaii	82	11	Illinois	65
25	Idaho	54	11	Pennsylvania	65
11	Illinois	65	13	Colorado	64
33	Indiana	48	14	Nebraska	63
26	Iowa	53	14	Utah	63
28	Kansas	51	16	Michigan	60
24	Kentucky	55	17	Minnesota	59
38	Louisiana	46	17	Vermont	59
38	Maine	46	19	New Hampshire	58
6	Maryland	75	19	Virginia	58
1	Massachusetts	82	21	Wisconsin	57
16	Michigan	60	22	Montana	56
17	Minnesota	59	22	Rhode Island	56
48	Mississippi	40	24	Kentucky	55
33	Missouri	48	25	Idaho	54
22	Montana	56	26	Iowa	53
14	Nebraska	63	26	Ohio	53
48	Nevada	40	28	Florida	51
19	New Hampshire	58	28	Kansas	51
3	New Jersey	79	28	Tennessee	51
44	New Mexico	44	28	Wyoming	51
3	New York	79	32	Oklahoma	49
46	North Carolina	43	33	Indiana	48
33	North Dakota	48	33	Missouri	48
26	Ohio	53	33	North Dakota	48
32	Oklahoma	49	36	South Dakota	47
10	Oregon	66	36	Texas	47
11	Pennsylvania	65	38	Arizona	46
22	Rhode Island	56	38	Louisiana	46
38	South Carolina	46	38	Maine	46
36	South Dakota	47	38	South Carolina	46
28	Tennessee	51	38	West Virginia	46
36	Texas	47	43	Delaware	45
14	Utah	63	44	Georgia	44
17	Vermont	59	44	New Mexico	44
19	Virginia	58	46	Alabama	43
9	Washington	67	46	North Carolina	43
38	West Virginia	46	48	Arkansas	40
21	Wisconsin	57	48	Mississippi	40
28	Wyoming	51	48	Nevada	40

	District of Columbia	119

Source: Morgan Quitno Press using data from American Dental Association
    "Distribution of Dentists, by Region and State, 2002"
*Professionally active dentists. National rate includes dentists for whom state is not known. National rate does not include dentists in territories nor dentists in the Armed Forces stationed overseas.

Average Annual Wages of Dentists in 2004

National Average = $132,850*

RANK	STATE	WAGES
26	Alabama	$134,410
1	Alaska	184,460
31	Arizona	132,340
47	Arkansas	86,450
22	California	138,580
10	Colorado	152,450
6	Connecticut	161,830
11	Delaware	151,100
37	Florida	126,000
9	Georgia	152,980
15	Hawaii	149,540
44	Idaho	107,330
46	Illinois	87,680
19	Indiana	141,880
21	Iowa	139,280
42	Kansas	115,610
39	Kentucky	121,260
NA	Louisiana**	NA
34	Maine	129,370
35	Maryland	127,510
23	Massachusetts	135,270
28	Michigan	134,250
16	Minnesota	145,200
41	Mississippi	115,810
25	Missouri	134,600
48	Montana	73,330
14	Nebraska	150,550
29	Nevada	133,150
3	New Hampshire	167,800
17	New Jersey	142,650
36	New Mexico	127,330
24	New York	134,780
5	North Carolina	163,740
2	North Dakota	179,200
7	Ohio	161,050
40	Oklahoma	116,020
NA	Oregon**	NA
43	Pennsylvania	114,990
12	Rhode Island	150,920
32	South Carolina	131,750
13	South Dakota	150,870
33	Tennessee	131,610
30	Texas	132,470
8	Utah	153,990
4	Vermont	165,720
20	Virginia	140,730
18	Washington	142,380
38	West Virginia	121,980
27	Wisconsin	134,260
45	Wyoming	95,350

RANK	STATE	WAGES
1	Alaska	$184,460
2	North Dakota	179,200
3	New Hampshire	167,800
4	Vermont	165,720
5	North Carolina	163,740
6	Connecticut	161,830
7	Ohio	161,050
8	Utah	153,990
9	Georgia	152,980
10	Colorado	152,450
11	Delaware	151,100
12	Rhode Island	150,920
13	South Dakota	150,870
14	Nebraska	150,550
15	Hawaii	149,540
16	Minnesota	145,200
17	New Jersey	142,650
18	Washington	142,380
19	Indiana	141,880
20	Virginia	140,730
21	Iowa	139,280
22	California	138,580
23	Massachusetts	135,270
24	New York	134,780
25	Missouri	134,600
26	Alabama	134,410
27	Wisconsin	134,260
28	Michigan	134,250
29	Nevada	133,150
30	Texas	132,470
31	Arizona	132,340
32	South Carolina	131,750
33	Tennessee	131,610
34	Maine	129,370
35	Maryland	127,510
36	New Mexico	127,330
37	Florida	126,000
38	West Virginia	121,980
39	Kentucky	121,260
40	Oklahoma	116,020
41	Mississippi	115,810
42	Kansas	115,610
43	Pennsylvania	114,990
44	Idaho	107,330
45	Wyoming	95,350
46	Illinois	87,680
47	Arkansas	86,450
48	Montana	73,330
NA	Louisiana**	NA
NA	Oregon**	NA
	District of Columbia	98,650

Source: U.S. Department of Labor, Bureau of Labor Statistics
"Occupational Employment and Wages, 2004" (http://www.bls.gov/oes/)
General dentists. Does not include self-employed.
**Not available.*

Percent of Population Lacking Access to Dental Care in 2005

National Percent = 9.4% of Population*

ALPHA ORDER			RANK ORDER		
RANK	STATE	PERCENT	RANK	STATE	PERCENT
1	Alabama	32.1	1	Alabama	32.1
15	Alaska	13.5	2	New Mexico	26.7
32	Arizona	8.0	3	South Carolina	25.7
42	Arkansas	5.1	4	Montana	23.4
47	California	3.3	5	Idaho	21.5
44	Colorado	4.7	6	Missouri	21.4
39	Connecticut	5.4	7	Maine	19.7
12	Delaware	15.5	8	Kansas	19.2
16	Florida	12.8	9	Tennessee	16.9
27	Georgia	9.1	10	Iowa	16.8
28	Hawaii	8.6	11	Utah	16.5
5	Idaho	21.5	12	Delaware	15.5
29	Illinois	8.4	13	Mississippi	14.6
46	Indiana	4.0	14	Nevada	13.6
10	Iowa	16.8	15	Alaska	13.5
8	Kansas	19.2	16	Florida	12.8
36	Kentucky	6.2	17	North Carolina	12.3
26	Louisiana	9.2	18	Oregon	12.1
7	Maine	19.7	19	Wyoming	11.7
38	Maryland	5.6	20	Michigan	11.2
37	Massachusetts	5.7	21	Texas	11.1
20	Michigan	11.2	22	Wisconsin	10.8
44	Minnesota	4.7	23	South Dakota	10.6
13	Mississippi	14.6	24	Pennsylvania	10.4
6	Missouri	21.4	25	Rhode Island	9.6
4	Montana	23.4	26	Louisiana	9.2
50	Nebraska	1.2	27	Georgia	9.1
14	Nevada	13.6	28	Hawaii	8.6
42	New Hampshire	5.1	29	Illinois	8.4
49	New Jersey	1.7	29	Washington	8.4
2	New Mexico	26.7	31	West Virginia	8.1
41	New York	5.2	32	Arizona	8.0
17	North Carolina	12.3	33	Ohio	7.2
34	North Dakota	7.1	34	North Dakota	7.1
33	Ohio	7.2	35	Virginia	6.4
39	Oklahoma	5.4	36	Kentucky	6.2
18	Oregon	12.1	37	Massachusetts	5.7
24	Pennsylvania	10.4	38	Maryland	5.6
25	Rhode Island	9.6	39	Connecticut	5.4
3	South Carolina	25.7	39	Oklahoma	5.4
23	South Dakota	10.6	41	New York	5.2
9	Tennessee	16.9	42	Arkansas	5.1
21	Texas	11.1	42	New Hampshire	5.1
11	Utah	16.5	44	Colorado	4.7
47	Vermont	3.3	44	Minnesota	4.7
35	Virginia	6.4	46	Indiana	4.0
29	Washington	8.4	47	California	3.3
31	West Virginia	8.1	47	Vermont	3.3
22	Wisconsin	10.8	49	New Jersey	1.7
19	Wyoming	11.7	50	Nebraska	1.2

	District of Columbia	10.7

Source: Morgan Quitno Press using data from U.S. Dept. of Health and Human Services, Div. of Shortage Designation "Selected Statistics on Health Professional Shortage Areas" (as of September 30, 2005)

*Percent of population considered under-served by dental practitioners. An under-served population does not have primary medical care within reasonable economic and geographic bounds.

Pharmacists in 2004

National Total = 226,200 Pharmacists*

ALPHA ORDER

RANK	STATE	PHARMACISTS	% of USA
19	Alabama	4,300	1.9%
50	Alaska	360	0.2%
23	Arizona	3,830	1.7%
29	Arkansas	2,510	1.1%
1	California	23,240	10.3%
24	Colorado	3,530	1.6%
30	Connecticut	2,470	1.1%
47	Delaware	520	0.2%
3	Florida	13,900	6.1%
10	Georgia	6,760	3.0%
40	Hawaii	1,020	0.5%
39	Idaho	1,040	0.5%
7	Illinois	9,510	4.2%
12	Indiana	5,460	2.4%
30	Iowa	2,470	1.1%
32	Kansas	2,390	1.1%
25	Kentucky	3,300	1.5%
20	Louisiana	4,170	1.8%
41	Maine	960	0.4%
21	Maryland	4,000	1.8%
15	Massachusetts	4,850	2.1%
8	Michigan	8,150	3.6%
22	Minnesota	3,990	1.8%
33	Mississippi	2,240	1.0%
17	Missouri	4,730	2.1%
43	Montana	860	0.4%
35	Nebraska	1,830	0.8%
36	Nevada	1,800	0.8%
41	New Hampshire	960	0.4%
9	New Jersey	7,380	3.3%
38	New Mexico	1,280	0.6%
4	New York	13,010	5.8%
11	North Carolina	6,310	2.8%
46	North Dakota	620	0.3%
6	Ohio	9,780	4.3%
27	Oklahoma	2,990	1.3%
28	Oregon	2,900	1.3%
5	Pennsylvania	11,300	5.0%
45	Rhode Island	660	0.3%
26	South Carolina	3,290	1.5%
44	South Dakota	780	0.3%
13	Tennessee	5,270	2.3%
2	Texas	16,010	7.1%
34	Utah	1,900	0.8%
49	Vermont	430	0.2%
14	Virginia	5,250	2.3%
16	Washington	4,800	2.1%
37	West Virginia	1,670	0.7%
18	Wisconsin	4,490	2.0%
48	Wyoming	460	0.2%

RANK ORDER

RANK	STATE	PHARMACISTS	% of USA
1	California	23,240	10.3%
2	Texas	16,010	7.1%
3	Florida	13,900	6.1%
4	New York	13,010	5.8%
5	Pennsylvania	11,300	5.0%
6	Ohio	9,780	4.3%
7	Illinois	9,510	4.2%
8	Michigan	8,150	3.6%
9	New Jersey	7,380	3.3%
10	Georgia	6,760	3.0%
11	North Carolina	6,310	2.8%
12	Indiana	5,460	2.4%
13	Tennessee	5,270	2.3%
14	Virginia	5,250	2.3%
15	Massachusetts	4,850	2.1%
16	Washington	4,800	2.1%
17	Missouri	4,730	2.1%
18	Wisconsin	4,490	2.0%
19	Alabama	4,300	1.9%
20	Louisiana	4,170	1.8%
21	Maryland	4,000	1.8%
22	Minnesota	3,990	1.8%
23	Arizona	3,830	1.7%
24	Colorado	3,530	1.6%
25	Kentucky	3,300	1.5%
26	South Carolina	3,290	1.5%
27	Oklahoma	2,990	1.3%
28	Oregon	2,900	1.3%
29	Arkansas	2,510	1.1%
30	Connecticut	2,470	1.1%
30	Iowa	2,470	1.1%
32	Kansas	2,390	1.1%
33	Mississippi	2,240	1.0%
34	Utah	1,900	0.8%
35	Nebraska	1,830	0.8%
36	Nevada	1,800	0.8%
37	West Virginia	1,670	0.7%
38	New Mexico	1,280	0.6%
39	Idaho	1,040	0.5%
40	Hawaii	1,020	0.5%
41	Maine	960	0.4%
41	New Hampshire	960	0.4%
43	Montana	860	0.4%
44	South Dakota	780	0.3%
45	Rhode Island	660	0.3%
46	North Dakota	620	0.3%
47	Delaware	520	0.2%
48	Wyoming	460	0.2%
49	Vermont	430	0.2%
50	Alaska	360	0.2%
	District of Columbia	430	0.2%

Source: U.S. Department of Labor, Bureau of Labor Statistics
   "Occupational Employment and Wages, 2004" (http://www.bls.gov/oes/)
*Does not include self-employed.

Rate of Pharmacists in 2004

National Rate = 77 Pharmacists per 100,000 Population*

ALPHA ORDER			RANK ORDER		
RANK	STATE	RATE	RANK	STATE	RATE
4	Alabama	95	1	Nebraska	105
50	Alaska	55	2	South Dakota	101
44	Arizona	67	3	North Dakota	97
8	Arkansas	91	4	Alabama	95
47	California	65	5	Louisiana	93
28	Colorado	77	5	Montana	93
40	Connecticut	71	7	West Virginia	92
48	Delaware	63	8	Arkansas	91
23	Florida	80	8	Pennsylvania	91
32	Georgia	76	8	Wyoming	91
20	Hawaii	81	11	Tennessee	89
34	Idaho	75	12	Indiana	88
34	Illinois	75	13	Kansas	87
12	Indiana	88	14	New Jersey	85
17	Iowa	84	14	Ohio	85
13	Kansas	87	14	Oklahoma	85
23	Kentucky	80	17	Iowa	84
5	Louisiana	93	18	Missouri	82
38	Maine	73	18	Wisconsin	82
39	Maryland	72	20	Hawaii	81
32	Massachusetts	76	20	Michigan	81
20	Michigan	81	20	Oregon	81
25	Minnesota	78	23	Florida	80
28	Mississippi	77	23	Kentucky	80
18	Missouri	82	25	Minnesota	78
5	Montana	93	25	South Carolina	78
1	Nebraska	105	25	Utah	78
28	Nevada	77	28	Colorado	77
36	New Hampshire	74	28	Mississippi	77
14	New Jersey	85	28	Nevada	77
44	New Mexico	67	28	Washington	77
44	New York	67	32	Georgia	76
36	North Carolina	74	32	Massachusetts	76
3	North Dakota	97	34	Idaho	75
14	Ohio	85	34	Illinois	75
14	Oklahoma	85	36	New Hampshire	74
20	Oregon	81	36	North Carolina	74
8	Pennsylvania	91	38	Maine	73
49	Rhode Island	61	39	Maryland	72
25	South Carolina	78	40	Connecticut	71
2	South Dakota	101	40	Texas	71
11	Tennessee	89	42	Virginia	70
40	Texas	71	43	Vermont	69
25	Utah	78	44	Arizona	67
43	Vermont	69	44	New Mexico	67
42	Virginia	70	44	New York	67
28	Washington	77	47	California	65
7	West Virginia	92	48	Delaware	63
18	Wisconsin	82	49	Rhode Island	61
8	Wyoming	91	50	Alaska	55
				District of Columbia	78

Source: Morgan Quitno Press using data from U.S. Department of Labor, Bureau of Labor Statistics
    "Occupational Employment and Wages, 2004" (http://www.bls.gov/oes/)
*Does not include self-employed.

Average Annual Wages of Pharmacists in 2004

National Average = $86,910*

ALPHA ORDER				RANK ORDER		
RANK	STATE	WAGES		RANK	STATE	WAGES
34	Alabama	$83,080		1	California	$99,580
3	Alaska	93,530		2	Maine	94,210
26	Arizona	85,620		3	Alaska	93,530
5	Arkansas	91,430		4	Vermont	93,510
1	California	99,580		5	Arkansas	91,430
15	Colorado	87,270		6	Minnesota	91,380
16	Connecticut	87,110		7	Nevada	90,350
12	Delaware	88,480		8	Wisconsin	90,200
19	Florida	86,440		9	Texas	89,410
29	Georgia	84,560		10	New York	89,360
38	Hawaii	80,870		11	Tennessee	89,270
43	Idaho	79,020		12	Delaware	88,480
14	Illinois	87,280		13	Missouri	87,310
36	Indiana	81,330		14	Illinois	87,280
35	Iowa	81,990		15	Colorado	87,270
47	Kansas	76,970		16	Connecticut	87,110
17	Kentucky	86,960		17	Kentucky	86,960
44	Louisiana	78,950		18	North Carolina	86,570
2	Maine	94,210		19	Florida	86,440
20	Maryland	86,340		20	Maryland	86,340
37	Massachusetts	80,930		21	Michigan	86,080
21	Michigan	86,080		22	Ohio	86,040
6	Minnesota	91,380		23	Utah	86,000
39	Mississippi	80,460		24	West Virginia	85,970
13	Missouri	87,310		25	New Jersey	85,680
48	Montana	76,920		26	Arizona	85,620
46	Nebraska	77,780		27	Oregon	85,370
7	Nevada	90,350		28	New Hampshire	84,980
28	New Hampshire	84,980		29	Georgia	84,560
25	New Jersey	85,680		30	Rhode Island	84,470
41	New Mexico	79,970		30	Virginia	84,470
10	New York	89,360		32	South Carolina	84,200
18	North Carolina	86,570		33	Washington	83,260
50	North Dakota	74,160		34	Alabama	83,080
22	Ohio	86,040		35	Iowa	81,990
49	Oklahoma	75,830		36	Indiana	81,330
27	Oregon	85,370		37	Massachusetts	80,930
40	Pennsylvania	80,130		38	Hawaii	80,870
30	Rhode Island	84,470		39	Mississippi	80,460
32	South Carolina	84,200		40	Pennsylvania	80,130
42	South Dakota	79,710		41	New Mexico	79,970
11	Tennessee	89,270		42	South Dakota	79,710
9	Texas	89,410		43	Idaho	79,020
23	Utah	86,000		44	Louisiana	78,950
4	Vermont	93,510		45	Wyoming	78,770
30	Virginia	84,470		46	Nebraska	77,780
33	Washington	83,260		47	Kansas	76,970
24	West Virginia	85,970		48	Montana	76,920
8	Wisconsin	90,200		49	Oklahoma	75,830
45	Wyoming	78,770		50	North Dakota	74,160
					District of Columbia	68,550

Source: U.S. Department of Labor, Bureau of Labor Statistics
"Occupational Employment and Wages, 2004" (http://www.bls.gov/oes/)
*Does not include self-employed.

Optometrists in 2004

National Total = 22,730 Optometrists*

ALPHA ORDER

RANK	STATE	OPTOMETRISTS	% of USA
29	Alabama	270	1.2%
48	Alaska	50	0.2%
20	Arizona	380	1.7%
24	Arkansas	340	1.5%
1	California	1,930	8.5%
23	Colorado	350	1.5%
19	Connecticut	420	1.8%
NA	Delaware**	NA	NA
8	Florida	1,000	4.4%
20	Georgia	380	1.7%
41	Hawaii	110	0.5%
36	Idaho	170	0.7%
4	Illinois	1,300	5.7%
10	Indiana	770	3.4%
25	Iowa	330	1.5%
27	Kansas	310	1.4%
26	Kentucky	320	1.4%
32	Louisiana	200	0.9%
46	Maine	80	0.4%
22	Maryland	360	1.6%
14	Massachusetts	460	2.0%
6	Michigan	1,030	4.5%
11	Minnesota	700	3.1%
41	Mississippi	110	0.5%
15	Missouri	450	2.0%
44	Montana	90	0.4%
31	Nebraska	240	1.1%
37	Nevada	160	0.7%
32	New Hampshire	200	0.9%
9	New Jersey	810	3.6%
38	New Mexico	150	0.7%
2	New York	1,840	8.1%
12	North Carolina	610	2.7%
39	North Dakota	120	0.5%
6	Ohio	1,030	4.5%
30	Oklahoma	260	1.1%
28	Oregon	300	1.3%
5	Pennsylvania	1,220	5.4%
NA	Rhode Island**	NA	NA
34	South Carolina	190	0.8%
44	South Dakota	90	0.4%
15	Tennessee	450	2.0%
3	Texas	1,340	5.9%
34	Utah	190	0.8%
47	Vermont	60	0.3%
15	Virginia	450	2.0%
13	Washington	490	2.2%
41	West Virginia	110	0.5%
15	Wisconsin	450	2.0%
39	Wyoming	120	0.5%

RANK ORDER

RANK	STATE	OPTOMETRISTS	% of USA
1	California	1,930	8.5%
2	New York	1,840	8.1%
3	Texas	1,340	5.9%
4	Illinois	1,300	5.7%
5	Pennsylvania	1,220	5.4%
6	Michigan	1,030	4.5%
6	Ohio	1,030	4.5%
8	Florida	1,000	4.4%
9	New Jersey	810	3.6%
10	Indiana	770	3.4%
11	Minnesota	700	3.1%
12	North Carolina	610	2.7%
13	Washington	490	2.2%
14	Massachusetts	460	2.0%
15	Missouri	450	2.0%
15	Tennessee	450	2.0%
15	Virginia	450	2.0%
15	Wisconsin	450	2.0%
19	Connecticut	420	1.8%
20	Arizona	380	1.7%
20	Georgia	380	1.7%
22	Maryland	360	1.6%
23	Colorado	350	1.5%
24	Arkansas	340	1.5%
25	Iowa	330	1.5%
26	Kentucky	320	1.4%
27	Kansas	310	1.4%
28	Oregon	300	1.3%
29	Alabama	270	1.2%
30	Oklahoma	260	1.1%
31	Nebraska	240	1.1%
32	Louisiana	200	0.9%
32	New Hampshire	200	0.9%
34	South Carolina	190	0.8%
34	Utah	190	0.8%
36	Idaho	170	0.7%
37	Nevada	160	0.7%
38	New Mexico	150	0.7%
39	North Dakota	120	0.5%
39	Wyoming	120	0.5%
41	Hawaii	110	0.5%
41	Mississippi	110	0.5%
41	West Virginia	110	0.5%
44	Montana	90	0.4%
44	South Dakota	90	0.4%
46	Maine	80	0.4%
47	Vermont	60	0.3%
48	Alaska	50	0.2%
NA	Delaware**	NA	NA
NA	Rhode Island**	NA	NA
	District of Columbia	190	0.8%

Source: U.S. Department of Labor, Bureau of Labor Statistics
    "Occupational Employment and Wages, 2004" (http://www.bls.gov/oes/)
*Does not include self-employed.
**Not available.

Rate of Optometrists in 2004

National Rate = 8 Optometrists per 100,000 Population*

ALPHA ORDER

RANK	STATE	RATE
37	Alabama	6
22	Alaska	8
32	Arizona	7
6	Arkansas	12
44	California	5
22	Colorado	8
6	Connecticut	12
NA	Delaware**	NA
37	Florida	6
46	Georgia	4
19	Hawaii	9
6	Idaho	12
13	Illinois	10
6	Indiana	12
11	Iowa	11
11	Kansas	11
22	Kentucky	8
46	Louisiana	4
37	Maine	6
37	Maryland	6
32	Massachusetts	7
13	Michigan	10
4	Minnesota	14
46	Mississippi	4
22	Missouri	8
13	Montana	10
4	Nebraska	14
32	Nevada	7
3	New Hampshire	15
19	New Jersey	9
22	New Mexico	8
13	New York	10
32	North Carolina	7
2	North Dakota	19
19	Ohio	9
32	Oklahoma	7
22	Oregon	8
13	Pennsylvania	10
NA	Rhode Island**	NA
44	South Carolina	5
6	South Dakota	12
22	Tennessee	8
37	Texas	6
22	Utah	8
13	Vermont	10
37	Virginia	6
22	Washington	8
37	West Virginia	6
22	Wisconsin	8
1	Wyoming	24

RANK ORDER

RANK	STATE	RATE
1	Wyoming	24
2	North Dakota	19
3	New Hampshire	15
4	Minnesota	14
4	Nebraska	14
6	Arkansas	12
6	Connecticut	12
6	Idaho	12
6	Indiana	12
6	South Dakota	12
11	Iowa	11
11	Kansas	11
13	Illinois	10
13	Michigan	10
13	Montana	10
13	New York	10
13	Pennsylvania	10
13	Vermont	10
19	Hawaii	9
19	New Jersey	9
19	Ohio	9
22	Alaska	8
22	Colorado	8
22	Kentucky	8
22	Missouri	8
22	New Mexico	8
22	Oregon	8
22	Tennessee	8
22	Utah	8
22	Washington	8
22	Wisconsin	8
32	Arizona	7
32	Massachusetts	7
32	Nevada	7
32	North Carolina	7
32	Oklahoma	7
37	Alabama	6
37	Florida	6
37	Maine	6
37	Maryland	6
37	Texas	6
37	Virginia	6
37	West Virginia	6
44	California	5
44	South Carolina	5
46	Georgia	4
46	Louisiana	4
46	Mississippi	4
NA	Delaware**	NA
NA	Rhode Island**	NA

District of Columbia   34

Source: Morgan Quitno Press using data from U.S. Department of Labor, Bureau of Labor Statistics
    "Occupational Employment and Wages, 2004" (http://www.bls.gov/oes/)
*Does not include self-employed.
**Not available.

473

Average Annual Wages of Optometrists in 2004

National Average = $96,290*

ALPHA ORDER				RANK ORDER		
RANK	**STATE**	**WAGES**		**RANK**	**STATE**	**WAGES**
39	Alabama	$81,810		1	New Hampshire	$147,740
2	Alaska	133,030		2	Alaska	133,030
45	Arizona	75,330		3	North Carolina	118,580
22	Arkansas	97,510		4	Maine	117,190
19	California	99,260		5	Minnesota	116,070
35	Colorado	86,850		6	Washington	113,780
18	Connecticut	100,200		7	Mississippi	113,720
NA	Delaware**	NA		8	Ohio	113,190
20	Florida	98,310		9	Virginia	112,420
14	Georgia	104,550		10	Nebraska	110,470
43	Hawaii	79,890		11	North Dakota	109,630
46	Idaho	72,230		12	South Dakota	107,250
38	Illinois	83,860		13	New Jersey	105,520
17	Indiana	101,000		14	Georgia	104,550
30	Iowa	92,270		15	Vermont	103,950
40	Kansas	81,750		16	Nevada	102,890
36	Kentucky	85,700		17	Indiana	101,000
31	Louisiana	88,920		18	Connecticut	100,200
4	Maine	117,190		19	California	99,260
33	Maryland	88,500		20	Florida	98,310
44	Massachusetts	79,080		21	Michigan	98,180
21	Michigan	98,180		22	Arkansas	97,510
5	Minnesota	116,070		23	Rhode Island	97,450
7	Mississippi	113,720		24	Wyoming	97,180
25	Missouri	96,600		25	Missouri	96,600
48	Montana	70,470		26	West Virginia	96,310
10	Nebraska	110,470		27	Pennsylvania	93,400
16	Nevada	102,890		28	Tennessee	93,230
1	New Hampshire	147,740		29	Wisconsin	93,050
13	New Jersey	105,520		30	Iowa	92,270
49	New Mexico	58,210		31	Louisiana	88,920
34	New York	88,370		31	Texas	88,920
3	North Carolina	118,580		33	Maryland	88,500
11	North Dakota	109,630		34	New York	88,370
8	Ohio	113,190		35	Colorado	86,850
37	Oklahoma	84,760		36	Kentucky	85,700
41	Oregon	81,410		37	Oklahoma	84,760
27	Pennsylvania	93,400		38	Illinois	83,860
23	Rhode Island	97,450		39	Alabama	81,810
42	South Carolina	81,040		40	Kansas	81,750
12	South Dakota	107,250		41	Oregon	81,410
28	Tennessee	93,230		42	South Carolina	81,040
31	Texas	88,920		43	Hawaii	79,890
47	Utah	70,480		44	Massachusetts	79,080
15	Vermont	103,950		45	Arizona	75,330
9	Virginia	112,420		46	Idaho	72,230
6	Washington	113,780		47	Utah	70,480
26	West Virginia	96,310		48	Montana	70,470
29	Wisconsin	93,050		49	New Mexico	58,210
24	Wyoming	97,180		NA	Delaware**	NA
					District of Columbia	71,970

Source: U.S. Department of Labor, Bureau of Labor Statistics
   "Occupational Employment and Wages, 2004" (http://www.bls.gov/oes/)
*Does not include self-employed.
**Not available.

Emergency Medical Technicians and Paramedics in 2004

National Total = 191,070 Technicians and Paramedics*

<table>
<tr><td colspan="4">ALPHA ORDER</td><td colspan="4">RANK ORDER</td></tr>
<tr><td>RANK</td><td>STATE</td><td>PARAMEDICS</td><td>% of USA</td><td>RANK</td><td>STATE</td><td>PARAMEDICS</td><td>% of USA</td></tr>
<tr><td>25</td><td>Alabama</td><td>2,830</td><td>1.5%</td><td>1</td><td>Texas</td><td>13,310</td><td>7.0%</td></tr>
<tr><td>50</td><td>Alaska</td><td>210</td><td>0.1%</td><td>2</td><td>Pennsylvania</td><td>12,110</td><td>6.3%</td></tr>
<tr><td>30</td><td>Arizona</td><td>2,190</td><td>1.1%</td><td>3</td><td>California</td><td>11,670</td><td>6.1%</td></tr>
<tr><td>28</td><td>Arkansas</td><td>2,450</td><td>1.3%</td><td>4</td><td>New York</td><td>10,820</td><td>5.7%</td></tr>
<tr><td>3</td><td>California</td><td>11,670</td><td>6.1%</td><td>5</td><td>Illinois</td><td>10,810</td><td>5.7%</td></tr>
<tr><td>23</td><td>Colorado</td><td>2,990</td><td>1.6%</td><td>6</td><td>Ohio</td><td>10,100</td><td>5.3%</td></tr>
<tr><td>29</td><td>Connecticut</td><td>2,440</td><td>1.3%</td><td>7</td><td>Georgia</td><td>7,740</td><td>4.1%</td></tr>
<tr><td>46</td><td>Delaware</td><td>460</td><td>0.2%</td><td>8</td><td>Florida</td><td>7,650</td><td>4.0%</td></tr>
<tr><td>8</td><td>Florida</td><td>7,650</td><td>4.0%</td><td>9</td><td>Wisconsin</td><td>7,390</td><td>3.9%</td></tr>
<tr><td>7</td><td>Georgia</td><td>7,740</td><td>4.1%</td><td>10</td><td>North Carolina</td><td>7,050</td><td>3.7%</td></tr>
<tr><td>43</td><td>Hawaii</td><td>580</td><td>0.3%</td><td>11</td><td>Tennessee</td><td>6,140</td><td>3.2%</td></tr>
<tr><td>44</td><td>Idaho</td><td>570</td><td>0.3%</td><td>12</td><td>Michigan</td><td>5,440</td><td>2.8%</td></tr>
<tr><td>5</td><td>Illinois</td><td>10,810</td><td>5.7%</td><td>13</td><td>Massachusetts</td><td>4,970</td><td>2.6%</td></tr>
<tr><td>14</td><td>Indiana</td><td>4,900</td><td>2.6%</td><td>14</td><td>Indiana</td><td>4,900</td><td>2.6%</td></tr>
<tr><td>31</td><td>Iowa</td><td>2,070</td><td>1.1%</td><td>15</td><td>New Jersey</td><td>4,640</td><td>2.4%</td></tr>
<tr><td>27</td><td>Kansas</td><td>2,650</td><td>1.4%</td><td>16</td><td>Maryland</td><td>4,170</td><td>2.2%</td></tr>
<tr><td>18</td><td>Kentucky</td><td>4,140</td><td>2.2%</td><td>17</td><td>Missouri</td><td>4,160</td><td>2.2%</td></tr>
<tr><td>26</td><td>Louisiana</td><td>2,820</td><td>1.5%</td><td>18</td><td>Kentucky</td><td>4,140</td><td>2.2%</td></tr>
<tr><td>33</td><td>Maine</td><td>1,550</td><td>0.8%</td><td>19</td><td>Minnesota</td><td>3,980</td><td>2.1%</td></tr>
<tr><td>16</td><td>Maryland</td><td>4,170</td><td>2.2%</td><td>20</td><td>South Carolina</td><td>3,810</td><td>2.0%</td></tr>
<tr><td>13</td><td>Massachusetts</td><td>4,970</td><td>2.6%</td><td>21</td><td>Oklahoma</td><td>3,270</td><td>1.7%</td></tr>
<tr><td>12</td><td>Michigan</td><td>5,440</td><td>2.8%</td><td>22</td><td>Virginia</td><td>3,080</td><td>1.6%</td></tr>
<tr><td>19</td><td>Minnesota</td><td>3,980</td><td>2.1%</td><td>23</td><td>Colorado</td><td>2,990</td><td>1.6%</td></tr>
<tr><td>34</td><td>Mississippi</td><td>1,540</td><td>0.8%</td><td>24</td><td>Washington</td><td>2,890</td><td>1.5%</td></tr>
<tr><td>17</td><td>Missouri</td><td>4,160</td><td>2.2%</td><td>25</td><td>Alabama</td><td>2,830</td><td>1.5%</td></tr>
<tr><td>42</td><td>Montana</td><td>590</td><td>0.3%</td><td>26</td><td>Louisiana</td><td>2,820</td><td>1.5%</td></tr>
<tr><td>45</td><td>Nebraska</td><td>470</td><td>0.2%</td><td>27</td><td>Kansas</td><td>2,650</td><td>1.4%</td></tr>
<tr><td>40</td><td>Nevada</td><td>860</td><td>0.5%</td><td>28</td><td>Arkansas</td><td>2,450</td><td>1.3%</td></tr>
<tr><td>37</td><td>New Hampshire</td><td>940</td><td>0.5%</td><td>29</td><td>Connecticut</td><td>2,440</td><td>1.3%</td></tr>
<tr><td>15</td><td>New Jersey</td><td>4,640</td><td>2.4%</td><td>30</td><td>Arizona</td><td>2,190</td><td>1.1%</td></tr>
<tr><td>38</td><td>New Mexico</td><td>920</td><td>0.5%</td><td>31</td><td>Iowa</td><td>2,070</td><td>1.1%</td></tr>
<tr><td>4</td><td>New York</td><td>10,820</td><td>5.7%</td><td>32</td><td>Utah</td><td>1,630</td><td>0.9%</td></tr>
<tr><td>10</td><td>North Carolina</td><td>7,050</td><td>3.7%</td><td>33</td><td>Maine</td><td>1,550</td><td>0.8%</td></tr>
<tr><td>47</td><td>North Dakota</td><td>400</td><td>0.2%</td><td>34</td><td>Mississippi</td><td>1,540</td><td>0.8%</td></tr>
<tr><td>6</td><td>Ohio</td><td>10,100</td><td>5.3%</td><td>35</td><td>West Virginia</td><td>1,370</td><td>0.7%</td></tr>
<tr><td>21</td><td>Oklahoma</td><td>3,270</td><td>1.7%</td><td>36</td><td>Oregon</td><td>1,160</td><td>0.6%</td></tr>
<tr><td>36</td><td>Oregon</td><td>1,160</td><td>0.6%</td><td>37</td><td>New Hampshire</td><td>940</td><td>0.5%</td></tr>
<tr><td>2</td><td>Pennsylvania</td><td>12,110</td><td>6.3%</td><td>38</td><td>New Mexico</td><td>920</td><td>0.5%</td></tr>
<tr><td>39</td><td>Rhode Island</td><td>880</td><td>0.5%</td><td>39</td><td>Rhode Island</td><td>880</td><td>0.5%</td></tr>
<tr><td>20</td><td>South Carolina</td><td>3,810</td><td>2.0%</td><td>40</td><td>Nevada</td><td>860</td><td>0.5%</td></tr>
<tr><td>41</td><td>South Dakota</td><td>670</td><td>0.4%</td><td>41</td><td>South Dakota</td><td>670</td><td>0.4%</td></tr>
<tr><td>11</td><td>Tennessee</td><td>6,140</td><td>3.2%</td><td>42</td><td>Montana</td><td>590</td><td>0.3%</td></tr>
<tr><td>1</td><td>Texas</td><td>13,310</td><td>7.0%</td><td>43</td><td>Hawaii</td><td>580</td><td>0.3%</td></tr>
<tr><td>32</td><td>Utah</td><td>1,630</td><td>0.9%</td><td>44</td><td>Idaho</td><td>570</td><td>0.3%</td></tr>
<tr><td>49</td><td>Vermont</td><td>350</td><td>0.2%</td><td>45</td><td>Nebraska</td><td>470</td><td>0.2%</td></tr>
<tr><td>22</td><td>Virginia</td><td>3,080</td><td>1.6%</td><td>46</td><td>Delaware</td><td>460</td><td>0.2%</td></tr>
<tr><td>24</td><td>Washington</td><td>2,890</td><td>1.5%</td><td>47</td><td>North Dakota</td><td>400</td><td>0.2%</td></tr>
<tr><td>35</td><td>West Virginia</td><td>1,370</td><td>0.7%</td><td>48</td><td>Wyoming</td><td>370</td><td>0.2%</td></tr>
<tr><td>9</td><td>Wisconsin</td><td>7,390</td><td>3.9%</td><td>49</td><td>Vermont</td><td>350</td><td>0.2%</td></tr>
<tr><td>48</td><td>Wyoming</td><td>370</td><td>0.2%</td><td>50</td><td>Alaska</td><td>210</td><td>0.1%</td></tr>
<tr><td></td><td></td><td></td><td></td><td></td><td>District of Columbia</td><td>860</td><td>0.5%</td></tr>
</table>

Source: U.S. Department of Labor, Bureau of Labor Statistics
    "Occupational Employment and Wages, 2004" (http://www.bls.gov/oes/)
*Does not include self-employed. National total includes EMTs and Paramedics in U.S. territories.

Rate of Emergency Medical Technicians and Paramedics in 2004

National Rate = 65 Technicians and Paramedics per 100,000 Population*

ALPHA ORDER				RANK ORDER		
RANK	STATE	RATE		RANK	STATE	RATE
29	Alabama	63		1	Wisconsin	134
48	Alaska	32		2	Maine	118
45	Arizona	38		3	Tennessee	104
9	Arkansas	89		4	Kentucky	100
47	California	33		5	Pennsylvania	98
27	Colorado	65		6	Kansas	97
24	Connecticut	70		7	Oklahoma	93
35	Delaware	55		8	South Carolina	91
42	Florida	44		9	Arkansas	89
11	Georgia	87		10	Ohio	88
41	Hawaii	46		11	Georgia	87
43	Idaho	41		11	South Dakota	87
13	Illinois	85		13	Illinois	85
16	Indiana	79		14	North Carolina	83
24	Iowa	70		15	Rhode Island	81
6	Kansas	97		16	Indiana	79
4	Kentucky	100		17	Massachusetts	78
29	Louisiana	63		17	Minnesota	78
2	Maine	118		19	West Virginia	76
20	Maryland	75		20	Maryland	75
17	Massachusetts	78		21	Wyoming	73
36	Michigan	54		22	Missouri	72
17	Minnesota	78		22	New Hampshire	72
37	Mississippi	53		24	Connecticut	70
22	Missouri	72		24	Iowa	70
28	Montana	64		26	Utah	67
50	Nebraska	27		27	Colorado	65
46	Nevada	37		28	Montana	64
22	New Hampshire	72		29	Alabama	63
37	New Jersey	53		29	Louisiana	63
39	New Mexico	48		29	North Dakota	63
33	New York	56		32	Texas	59
14	North Carolina	83		33	New York	56
29	North Dakota	63		33	Vermont	56
10	Ohio	88		35	Delaware	55
7	Oklahoma	93		36	Michigan	54
48	Oregon	32		37	Mississippi	53
5	Pennsylvania	98		37	New Jersey	53
15	Rhode Island	81		39	New Mexico	48
8	South Carolina	91		40	Washington	47
11	South Dakota	87		41	Hawaii	46
3	Tennessee	104		42	Florida	44
32	Texas	59		43	Idaho	41
26	Utah	67		43	Virginia	41
33	Vermont	56		45	Arizona	38
43	Virginia	41		46	Nevada	37
40	Washington	47		47	California	33
19	West Virginia	76		48	Alaska	32
1	Wisconsin	134		48	Oregon	32
21	Wyoming	73		50	Nebraska	27

District of Columbia   155

Source: Morgan Quitno Press using data from U.S. Department of Labor, Bureau of Labor Statistics
    "Occupational Employment and Wages, 2004" (http://www.bls.gov/oes/)
*Does not include self-employed.

Average Annual Wages of
Emergency Medical Technicians and Paramedics in 2004
National Average = $27,940*

ALPHA ORDER

RANK	STATE	WAGES
46	Alabama	$21,150
1	Alaska	39,020
27	Arizona	26,610
41	Arkansas	24,350
21	California	27,460
9	Colorado	31,970
8	Connecticut	32,030
13	Delaware	30,150
20	Florida	28,220
31	Georgia	26,470
4	Hawaii	35,960
12	Idaho	30,160
16	Illinois	29,500
30	Indiana	26,490
38	Iowa	24,680
45	Kansas	21,590
43	Kentucky	22,820
24	Louisiana	27,120
39	Maine	24,650
2	Maryland	37,260
5	Massachusetts	34,810
18	Michigan	29,010
14	Minnesota	29,670
34	Mississippi	25,320
11	Missouri	31,250
47	Montana	21,000
28	Nebraska	26,570
NA	Nevada**	NA
19	New Hampshire	28,360
10	New Jersey	31,650
15	New Mexico	29,610
6	New York	34,560
23	North Carolina	27,390
26	North Dakota	26,960
22	Ohio	27,410
NA	Oklahoma**	NA
17	Oregon	29,260
35	Pennsylvania	25,300
7	Rhode Island	33,290
25	South Carolina	26,980
42	South Dakota	23,210
37	Tennessee	25,030
33	Texas	26,040
32	Utah	26,180
40	Vermont	24,590
29	Virginia	26,550
3	Washington	36,410
48	West Virginia	19,650
44	Wisconsin	22,380
36	Wyoming	25,060

RANK ORDER

RANK	STATE	WAGES
1	Alaska	$39,020
2	Maryland	37,260
3	Washington	36,410
4	Hawaii	35,960
5	Massachusetts	34,810
6	New York	34,560
7	Rhode Island	33,290
8	Connecticut	32,030
9	Colorado	31,970
10	New Jersey	31,650
11	Missouri	31,250
12	Idaho	30,160
13	Delaware	30,150
14	Minnesota	29,670
15	New Mexico	29,610
16	Illinois	29,500
17	Oregon	29,260
18	Michigan	29,010
19	New Hampshire	28,360
20	Florida	28,220
21	California	27,460
22	Ohio	27,410
23	North Carolina	27,390
24	Louisiana	27,120
25	South Carolina	26,980
26	North Dakota	26,960
27	Arizona	26,610
28	Nebraska	26,570
29	Virginia	26,550
30	Indiana	26,490
31	Georgia	26,470
32	Utah	26,180
33	Texas	26,040
34	Mississippi	25,320
35	Pennsylvania	25,300
36	Wyoming	25,060
37	Tennessee	25,030
38	Iowa	24,680
39	Maine	24,650
40	Vermont	24,590
41	Arkansas	24,350
42	South Dakota	23,210
43	Kentucky	22,820
44	Wisconsin	22,380
45	Kansas	21,590
46	Alabama	21,150
47	Montana	21,000
48	West Virginia	19,650
NA	Nevada**	NA
NA	Oklahoma**	NA
	District of Columbia	40,800

Source: U.S. Department of Labor, Bureau of Labor Statistics
    "Occupational Employment and Wages, 2004" (http://www.bls.gov/oes/)
*Does not include self-employed.
**Not available.

Employment in Health Care Support Industries in 2004

National Total = 3,307,150 Aides and Assistants*

ALPHA ORDER

RANK	STATE	EMPLOYEES	% of USA
25	Alabama	45,040	1.4%
49	Alaska	6,670	0.2%
22	Arizona	52,680	1.6%
33	Arkansas	30,160	0.9%
1	California	310,520	9.4%
30	Colorado	39,580	1.2%
23	Connecticut	49,790	1.5%
47	Delaware	9,120	0.3%
4	Florida	184,740	5.6%
13	Georgia	77,660	2.3%
43	Hawaii	11,950	0.4%
41	Idaho	15,750	0.5%
7	Illinois	125,850	3.8%
18	Indiana	64,510	2.0%
27	Iowa	42,380	1.3%
29	Kansas	41,240	1.2%
24	Kentucky	48,200	1.5%
21	Louisiana	53,060	1.6%
38	Maine	18,540	0.6%
20	Maryland	56,010	1.7%
11	Massachusetts	91,850	2.8%
8	Michigan	120,750	3.7%
14	Minnesota	74,930	2.3%
32	Mississippi	30,480	0.9%
15	Missouri	73,780	2.2%
44	Montana	11,370	0.3%
34	Nebraska	24,390	0.7%
39	Nevada	18,040	0.5%
42	New Hampshire	13,850	0.4%
10	New Jersey	100,540	3.0%
37	New Mexico	20,310	0.6%
2	New York	278,490	8.4%
9	North Carolina	112,830	3.4%
45	North Dakota	10,920	0.3%
5	Ohio	164,290	5.0%
26	Oklahoma	44,530	1.3%
31	Oregon	36,810	1.1%
6	Pennsylvania	160,900	4.9%
40	Rhode Island	16,440	0.5%
28	South Carolina	41,760	1.3%
46	South Dakota	10,480	0.3%
19	Tennessee	61,840	1.9%
3	Texas	224,150	6.8%
35	Utah	23,240	0.7%
48	Vermont	8,390	0.3%
16	Virginia	69,160	2.1%
17	Washington	64,780	2.0%
36	West Virginia	22,650	0.7%
12	Wisconsin	77,870	2.4%
50	Wyoming	6,140	0.2%

RANK ORDER

RANK	STATE	EMPLOYEES	% of USA
1	California	310,520	9.4%
2	New York	278,490	8.4%
3	Texas	224,150	6.8%
4	Florida	184,740	5.6%
5	Ohio	164,290	5.0%
6	Pennsylvania	160,900	4.9%
7	Illinois	125,850	3.8%
8	Michigan	120,750	3.7%
9	North Carolina	112,830	3.4%
10	New Jersey	100,540	3.0%
11	Massachusetts	91,850	2.8%
12	Wisconsin	77,870	2.4%
13	Georgia	77,660	2.3%
14	Minnesota	74,930	2.3%
15	Missouri	73,780	2.2%
16	Virginia	69,160	2.1%
17	Washington	64,780	2.0%
18	Indiana	64,510	2.0%
19	Tennessee	61,840	1.9%
20	Maryland	56,010	1.7%
21	Louisiana	53,060	1.6%
22	Arizona	52,680	1.6%
23	Connecticut	49,790	1.5%
24	Kentucky	48,200	1.5%
25	Alabama	45,040	1.4%
26	Oklahoma	44,530	1.3%
27	Iowa	42,380	1.3%
28	South Carolina	41,760	1.3%
29	Kansas	41,240	1.2%
30	Colorado	39,580	1.2%
31	Oregon	36,810	1.1%
32	Mississippi	30,480	0.9%
33	Arkansas	30,160	0.9%
34	Nebraska	24,390	0.7%
35	Utah	23,240	0.7%
36	West Virginia	22,650	0.7%
37	New Mexico	20,310	0.6%
38	Maine	18,540	0.6%
39	Nevada	18,040	0.5%
40	Rhode Island	16,440	0.5%
41	Idaho	15,750	0.5%
42	New Hampshire	13,850	0.4%
43	Hawaii	11,950	0.4%
44	Montana	11,370	0.3%
45	North Dakota	10,920	0.3%
46	South Dakota	10,480	0.3%
47	Delaware	9,120	0.3%
48	Vermont	8,390	0.3%
49	Alaska	6,670	0.2%
50	Wyoming	6,140	0.2%
	District of Columbia	7,770	0.2%

Source: U.S. Department of Labor, Bureau of Labor Statistics
    "Occupational Employment and Wages, 2004" (http://www.bls.gov/oes/)
*Does not include self-employed. Includes various health care assistants and aides not included in the category of health care practitioners and technicians. Among the included occupations are home health aides, nursing aides, psychiatric aides, dental assistants and pharmacy aides.

Rate of Employees in Health Care Support Industries in 2004

National Rate = 1,126 Aides and Assistants per 100,000 Population*

ALPHA ORDER

RANK	STATE	RATE
40	Alabama	995
37	Alaska	1,014
46	Arizona	918
28	Arkansas	1,097
48	California	866
49	Colorado	860
9	Connecticut	1,423
27	Delaware	1,099
31	Florida	1,063
47	Georgia	871
44	Hawaii	947
26	Idaho	1,129
42	Illinois	990
35	Indiana	1,036
6	Iowa	1,435
3	Kansas	1,509
24	Kentucky	1,164
23	Louisiana	1,177
11	Maine	1,410
38	Maryland	1,007
8	Massachusetts	1,434
22	Michigan	1,195
4	Minnesota	1,470
32	Mississippi	1,051
17	Missouri	1,281
20	Montana	1,227
12	Nebraska	1,396
50	Nevada	773
30	New Hampshire	1,066
25	New Jersey	1,158
29	New Mexico	1,067
5	New York	1,444
15	North Carolina	1,321
1	North Dakota	1,716
6	Ohio	1,435
18	Oklahoma	1,264
36	Oregon	1,025
16	Pennsylvania	1,298
2	Rhode Island	1,522
40	South Carolina	995
13	South Dakota	1,360
33	Tennessee	1,049
39	Texas	997
43	Utah	960
14	Vermont	1,351
45	Virginia	924
34	Washington	1,044
19	West Virginia	1,250
10	Wisconsin	1,415
21	Wyoming	1,214

RANK ORDER

RANK	STATE	RATE
1	North Dakota	1,716
2	Rhode Island	1,522
3	Kansas	1,509
4	Minnesota	1,470
5	New York	1,444
6	Iowa	1,435
6	Ohio	1,435
8	Massachusetts	1,434
9	Connecticut	1,423
10	Wisconsin	1,415
11	Maine	1,410
12	Nebraska	1,396
13	South Dakota	1,360
14	Vermont	1,351
15	North Carolina	1,321
16	Pennsylvania	1,298
17	Missouri	1,281
18	Oklahoma	1,264
19	West Virginia	1,250
20	Montana	1,227
21	Wyoming	1,214
22	Michigan	1,195
23	Louisiana	1,177
24	Kentucky	1,164
25	New Jersey	1,158
26	Idaho	1,129
27	Delaware	1,099
28	Arkansas	1,097
29	New Mexico	1,067
30	New Hampshire	1,066
31	Florida	1,063
32	Mississippi	1,051
33	Tennessee	1,049
34	Washington	1,044
35	Indiana	1,036
36	Oregon	1,025
37	Alaska	1,014
38	Maryland	1,007
39	Texas	997
40	Alabama	995
40	South Carolina	995
42	Illinois	990
43	Utah	960
44	Hawaii	947
45	Virginia	924
46	Arizona	918
47	Georgia	871
48	California	866
49	Colorado	860
50	Nevada	773

District of Columbia 1,402

Source: Morgan Quitno Press using data from U.S. Department of Labor, Bureau of Labor Statistics
   "Occupational Employment and Wages, 2004" (http://www.bls.gov/oes/)
*Does not include self-employed. Includes various health care assistants and aides not included in the category of health care practitioners and technicians. Among the included occupations are home health aides, nursing aides, psychiatric aides, dental assistants and pharmacy aides.

Average Annual Wages of Employees in Health Care Support Industries in 2004

National Average = $23,510*

ALPHA ORDER				RANK ORDER		
RANK	STATE	WAGES		RANK	STATE	WAGES
47	Alabama	$19,220		1	Alaska	$29,950
1	Alaska	29,950		2	Connecticut	28,000
19	Arizona	23,860		3	Massachusetts	27,670
46	Arkansas	19,330		4	Washington	27,070
7	California	26,660		5	Nevada	26,860
8	Colorado	26,180		6	Hawaii	26,780
2	Connecticut	28,000		7	California	26,660
11	Delaware	25,760		8	Colorado	26,180
27	Florida	22,400		9	New Hampshire	26,080
36	Georgia	21,470		10	Rhode Island	25,940
6	Hawaii	26,780		11	Delaware	25,760
30	Idaho	22,220		12	New Jersey	25,720
20	Illinois	23,330		13	Maryland	25,580
21	Indiana	23,310		14	Minnesota	25,420
28	Iowa	22,290		15	New York	25,220
33	Kansas	21,840		16	Oregon	24,960
34	Kentucky	21,730		17	Michigan	24,190
49	Louisiana	18,110		18	Wisconsin	24,150
26	Maine	22,660		19	Arizona	23,860
13	Maryland	25,580		20	Illinois	23,330
3	Massachusetts	27,670		21	Indiana	23,310
17	Michigan	24,190		22	Pennsylvania	23,270
14	Minnesota	25,420		23	Ohio	23,140
50	Mississippi	18,070		24	Virginia	23,020
39	Missouri	21,160		25	Vermont	22,780
43	Montana	20,380		26	Maine	22,660
29	Nebraska	22,230		27	Florida	22,400
5	Nevada	26,860		28	Iowa	22,290
9	New Hampshire	26,080		29	Nebraska	22,230
12	New Jersey	25,720		30	Idaho	22,220
38	New Mexico	21,340		31	Tennessee	22,020
15	New York	25,220		32	Wyoming	21,900
37	North Carolina	21,400		33	Kansas	21,840
40	North Dakota	20,900		34	Kentucky	21,730
23	Ohio	23,140		35	Utah	21,650
44	Oklahoma	20,360		36	Georgia	21,470
16	Oregon	24,960		37	North Carolina	21,400
22	Pennsylvania	23,270		38	New Mexico	21,340
10	Rhode Island	25,940		39	Missouri	21,160
42	South Carolina	20,760		40	North Dakota	20,900
41	South Dakota	20,810		41	South Dakota	20,810
31	Tennessee	22,020		42	South Carolina	20,760
45	Texas	20,240		43	Montana	20,380
35	Utah	21,650		44	Oklahoma	20,360
25	Vermont	22,780		45	Texas	20,240
24	Virginia	23,020		46	Arkansas	19,330
4	Washington	27,070		47	Alabama	19,220
48	West Virginia	19,200		48	West Virginia	19,200
18	Wisconsin	24,150		49	Louisiana	18,110
32	Wyoming	21,900		50	Mississippi	18,070
					District of Columbia	26,800

Source: U.S. Department of Labor, Bureau of Labor Statistics
   "Occupational Employment and Wages, 2004" (http://www.bls.gov/oes/)
*Does not include self-employed. Includes various health care assistants and aides not included in the category of health care practitioners and technicians. Among the included occupations are home health aides, nursing aides, psychiatric aides, dental assistants and pharmacy aides.

VII. PHYSICAL FITNESS

Users of Exercise Equipment in 2004

National Total = 52,169,000 Users

RANK	STATE	USERS	% of USA
19	Alabama	979,000	1.9%
NA	Alaska*	NA	NA
14	Arizona	1,235,000	2.3%
36	Arkansas	301,000	0.6%
1	California	6,501,000	12.4%
15	Colorado	1,081,000	2.1%
27	Connecticut	608,000	1.2%
42	Delaware	220,000	0.4%
3	Florida	3,464,000	6.6%
9	Georgia	1,750,000	3.3%
NA	Hawaii*	NA	NA
39	Idaho	248,000	0.5%
5	Illinois	2,446,000	4.6%
19	Indiana	979,000	1.9%
30	Iowa	479,000	0.9%
31	Kansas	401,000	0.8%
24	Kentucky	788,000	1.5%
23	Louisiana	843,000	1.6%
41	Maine	242,000	0.5%
22	Maryland	902,000	1.7%
13	Massachusetts	1,309,000	2.5%
7	Michigan	2,146,000	4.1%
21	Minnesota	953,000	1.8%
37	Mississippi	284,000	0.5%
17	Missouri	1,032,000	2.0%
40	Montana	247,000	0.5%
38	Nebraska	259,000	0.5%
43	Nevada	206,000	0.4%
46	New Hampshire	77,000	0.1%
10	New Jersey	1,685,000	3.2%
28	New Mexico	545,000	1.0%
4	New York	3,382,000	6.4%
11	North Carolina	1,484,000	2.8%
47	North Dakota	66,000	0.1%
6	Ohio	2,166,000	4.1%
32	Oklahoma	381,000	0.7%
26	Oregon	707,000	1.3%
8	Pennsylvania	1,956,000	3.7%
45	Rhode Island	81,000	0.2%
29	South Carolina	535,000	1.0%
35	South Dakota	306,000	0.6%
25	Tennessee	773,000	1.5%
2	Texas	3,865,000	7.3%
34	Utah	316,000	0.6%
48	Vermont	51,000	0.1%
12	Virginia	1,328,000	2.5%
16	Washington	1,066,000	2.0%
33	West Virginia	363,000	0.7%
18	Wisconsin	983,000	1.9%
44	Wyoming	85,000	0.2%

RANK	STATE	USERS	% of USA
1	California	6,501,000	12.4%
2	Texas	3,865,000	7.3%
3	Florida	3,464,000	6.6%
4	New York	3,382,000	6.4%
5	Illinois	2,446,000	4.6%
6	Ohio	2,166,000	4.1%
7	Michigan	2,146,000	4.1%
8	Pennsylvania	1,956,000	3.7%
9	Georgia	1,750,000	3.3%
10	New Jersey	1,685,000	3.2%
11	North Carolina	1,484,000	2.8%
12	Virginia	1,328,000	2.5%
13	Massachusetts	1,309,000	2.5%
14	Arizona	1,235,000	2.3%
15	Colorado	1,081,000	2.1%
16	Washington	1,066,000	2.0%
17	Missouri	1,032,000	2.0%
18	Wisconsin	983,000	1.9%
19	Alabama	979,000	1.9%
19	Indiana	979,000	1.9%
21	Minnesota	953,000	1.8%
22	Maryland	902,000	1.7%
23	Louisiana	843,000	1.6%
24	Kentucky	788,000	1.5%
25	Tennessee	773,000	1.5%
26	Oregon	707,000	1.3%
27	Connecticut	608,000	1.2%
28	New Mexico	545,000	1.0%
29	South Carolina	535,000	1.0%
30	Iowa	479,000	0.9%
31	Kansas	401,000	0.8%
32	Oklahoma	381,000	0.7%
33	West Virginia	363,000	0.7%
34	Utah	316,000	0.6%
35	South Dakota	306,000	0.6%
36	Arkansas	301,000	0.6%
37	Mississippi	284,000	0.5%
38	Nebraska	259,000	0.5%
39	Idaho	248,000	0.5%
40	Montana	247,000	0.5%
41	Maine	242,000	0.5%
42	Delaware	220,000	0.4%
43	Nevada	206,000	0.4%
44	Wyoming	85,000	0.2%
45	Rhode Island	81,000	0.2%
46	New Hampshire	77,000	0.1%
47	North Dakota	66,000	0.1%
48	Vermont	51,000	0.1%
NA	Alaska*	NA	NA
NA	Hawaii*	NA	NA
	District of Columbia*	NA	NA

Source: The National Sporting Goods Association
"NSGA Sports Participation Survey, January-December 2004 (Copyright 2005, reprinted with permission)
*Not available.

Participants in Golf in 2004

National Total = 24,479,000 Golfers

ALPHA ORDER

RANK	STATE	GOLFERS	% of USA
23	Alabama	347,000	1.4%
NA	Alaska*	NA	NA
14	Arizona	678,000	2.8%
28	Arkansas	268,000	1.1%
1	California	2,243,000	9.2%
9	Colorado	925,000	3.8%
27	Connecticut	274,000	1.1%
45	Delaware	65,000	0.3%
3	Florida	1,401,000	5.7%
13	Georgia	692,000	2.8%
NA	Hawaii*	NA	NA
37	Idaho	154,000	0.6%
5	Illinois	1,301,000	5.3%
19	Indiana	480,000	2.0%
30	Iowa	241,000	1.0%
31	Kansas	231,000	0.9%
24	Kentucky	325,000	1.3%
32	Louisiana	229,000	0.9%
42	Maine	76,000	0.3%
25	Maryland	319,000	1.3%
17	Massachusetts	609,000	2.5%
4	Michigan	1,377,000	5.6%
16	Minnesota	652,000	2.7%
38	Mississippi	132,000	0.5%
21	Missouri	394,000	1.6%
41	Montana	93,000	0.4%
36	Nebraska	172,000	0.7%
32	Nevada	229,000	0.9%
43	New Hampshire	75,000	0.3%
11	New Jersey	739,000	3.0%
29	New Mexico	244,000	1.0%
2	New York	1,711,000	7.0%
12	North Carolina	708,000	2.9%
47	North Dakota	25,000	0.1%
6	Ohio	1,206,000	4.9%
35	Oklahoma	192,000	0.8%
26	Oregon	278,000	1.1%
8	Pennsylvania	934,000	3.8%
46	Rhode Island	30,000	0.1%
18	South Carolina	492,000	2.0%
39	South Dakota	123,000	0.5%
22	Tennessee	351,000	1.4%
7	Texas	1,179,000	4.8%
34	Utah	221,000	0.9%
44	Vermont	74,000	0.3%
15	Virginia	653,000	2.7%
20	Washington	416,000	1.7%
40	West Virginia	100,000	0.4%
10	Wisconsin	769,000	3.1%
48	Wyoming	22,000	0.1%

RANK ORDER

RANK	STATE	GOLFERS	% of USA
1	California	2,243,000	9.2%
2	New York	1,711,000	7.0%
3	Florida	1,401,000	5.7%
4	Michigan	1,377,000	5.6%
5	Illinois	1,301,000	5.3%
6	Ohio	1,206,000	4.9%
7	Texas	1,179,000	4.8%
8	Pennsylvania	934,000	3.8%
9	Colorado	925,000	3.8%
10	Wisconsin	769,000	3.1%
11	New Jersey	739,000	3.0%
12	North Carolina	708,000	2.9%
13	Georgia	692,000	2.8%
14	Arizona	678,000	2.8%
15	Virginia	653,000	2.7%
16	Minnesota	652,000	2.7%
17	Massachusetts	609,000	2.5%
18	South Carolina	492,000	2.0%
19	Indiana	480,000	2.0%
20	Washington	416,000	1.7%
21	Missouri	394,000	1.6%
22	Tennessee	351,000	1.4%
23	Alabama	347,000	1.4%
24	Kentucky	325,000	1.3%
25	Maryland	319,000	1.3%
26	Oregon	278,000	1.1%
27	Connecticut	274,000	1.1%
28	Arkansas	268,000	1.1%
29	New Mexico	244,000	1.0%
30	Iowa	241,000	1.0%
31	Kansas	231,000	0.9%
32	Louisiana	229,000	0.9%
32	Nevada	229,000	0.9%
34	Utah	221,000	0.9%
35	Oklahoma	192,000	0.8%
36	Nebraska	172,000	0.7%
37	Idaho	154,000	0.6%
38	Mississippi	132,000	0.5%
39	South Dakota	123,000	0.5%
40	West Virginia	100,000	0.4%
41	Montana	93,000	0.4%
42	Maine	76,000	0.3%
43	New Hampshire	75,000	0.3%
44	Vermont	74,000	0.3%
45	Delaware	65,000	0.3%
46	Rhode Island	30,000	0.1%
47	North Dakota	25,000	0.1%
48	Wyoming	22,000	0.1%
NA	Alaska*	NA	NA
NA	Hawaii*	NA	NA
	District of Columbia*	NA	NA

Source: The National Sporting Goods Association
   "NSGA Sports Participation Survey, January-December 2004 (Copyright 2005, reprinted with permission)
*Not available.

Participants in Running/Jogging in 2004

National Total = 24,665,000 Runners/Joggers

ALPHA ORDER

RANK	STATE	RUNNERS	% of USA
18	Alabama	462,000	1.9%
NA	Alaska*	NA	NA
15	Arizona	626,000	2.5%
25	Arkansas	361,000	1.5%
1	California	3,544,000	14.4%
14	Colorado	642,000	2.6%
35	Connecticut	165,000	0.7%
46	Delaware	42,000	0.2%
4	Florida	1,353,000	5.5%
7	Georgia	798,000	3.2%
NA	Hawaii*	NA	NA
38	Idaho	108,000	0.4%
5	Illinois	1,060,000	4.3%
20	Indiana	429,000	1.7%
31	Iowa	239,000	1.0%
33	Kansas	206,000	0.8%
24	Kentucky	362,000	1.5%
21	Louisiana	417,000	1.7%
32	Maine	235,000	1.0%
23	Maryland	382,000	1.5%
16	Massachusetts	564,000	2.3%
8	Michigan	779,000	3.2%
17	Minnesota	480,000	1.9%
28	Mississippi	331,000	1.3%
12	Missouri	651,000	2.6%
39	Montana	105,000	0.4%
37	Nebraska	118,000	0.5%
45	Nevada	56,000	0.2%
NA	New Hampshire*	NA	NA
9	New Jersey	742,000	3.0%
27	New Mexico	340,000	1.4%
3	New York	1,445,000	5.9%
13	North Carolina	650,000	2.6%
47	North Dakota	23,000	0.1%
6	Ohio	1,057,000	4.3%
41	Oklahoma	67,000	0.3%
30	Oregon	250,000	1.0%
11	Pennsylvania	710,000	2.9%
42	Rhode Island	64,000	0.3%
19	South Carolina	443,000	1.8%
36	South Dakota	162,000	0.7%
22	Tennessee	398,000	1.6%
2	Texas	1,960,000	7.9%
34	Utah	194,000	0.8%
43	Vermont	61,000	0.2%
10	Virginia	715,000	2.9%
26	Washington	357,000	1.4%
40	West Virginia	79,000	0.3%
29	Wisconsin	319,000	1.3%
44	Wyoming	59,000	0.2%

RANK ORDER

RANK	STATE	RUNNERS	% of USA
1	California	3,544,000	14.4%
2	Texas	1,960,000	7.9%
3	New York	1,445,000	5.9%
4	Florida	1,353,000	5.5%
5	Illinois	1,060,000	4.3%
6	Ohio	1,057,000	4.3%
7	Georgia	798,000	3.2%
8	Michigan	779,000	3.2%
9	New Jersey	742,000	3.0%
10	Virginia	715,000	2.9%
11	Pennsylvania	710,000	2.9%
12	Missouri	651,000	2.6%
13	North Carolina	650,000	2.6%
14	Colorado	642,000	2.6%
15	Arizona	626,000	2.5%
16	Massachusetts	564,000	2.3%
17	Minnesota	480,000	1.9%
18	Alabama	462,000	1.9%
19	South Carolina	443,000	1.8%
20	Indiana	429,000	1.7%
21	Louisiana	417,000	1.7%
22	Tennessee	398,000	1.6%
23	Maryland	382,000	1.5%
24	Kentucky	362,000	1.5%
25	Arkansas	361,000	1.5%
26	Washington	357,000	1.4%
27	New Mexico	340,000	1.4%
28	Mississippi	331,000	1.3%
29	Wisconsin	319,000	1.3%
30	Oregon	250,000	1.0%
31	Iowa	239,000	1.0%
32	Maine	235,000	1.0%
33	Kansas	206,000	0.8%
34	Utah	194,000	0.8%
35	Connecticut	165,000	0.7%
36	South Dakota	162,000	0.7%
37	Nebraska	118,000	0.5%
38	Idaho	108,000	0.4%
39	Montana	105,000	0.4%
40	West Virginia	79,000	0.3%
41	Oklahoma	67,000	0.3%
42	Rhode Island	64,000	0.3%
43	Vermont	61,000	0.2%
44	Wyoming	59,000	0.2%
45	Nevada	56,000	0.2%
46	Delaware	42,000	0.2%
47	North Dakota	23,000	0.1%
NA	Alaska*	NA	NA
NA	Hawaii*	NA	NA
NA	New Hampshire*	NA	NA
	District of Columbia*	NA	NA

Source: The National Sporting Goods Association
"NSGA Sports Participation Survey, January-December 2004 (Copyright 2005, reprinted with permission)
*Not available.

Participants in Swimming in 2004

National Total = 53,449,000 Swimmers

ALPHA ORDER

RANK	STATE	SWIMMERS	% of USA
19	Alabama	658,000	1.2%
NA	Alaska*	NA	NA
5	Arizona	1,976,000	3.7%
20	Arkansas	597,000	1.1%
1	California	6,594,000	12.3%
10	Colorado	1,184,000	2.2%
13	Connecticut	1,030,000	1.9%
35	Delaware	263,000	0.5%
2	Florida	4,033,000	7.5%
11	Georgia	1,149,000	2.1%
NA	Hawaii*	NA	NA
24	Idaho	472,000	0.9%
4	Illinois	2,601,000	4.9%
14	Indiana	910,000	1.7%
26	Iowa	446,000	0.8%
26	Kansas	446,000	0.8%
17	Kentucky	824,000	1.5%
33	Louisiana	310,000	0.6%
34	Maine	278,000	0.5%
15	Maryland	879,000	1.6%
9	Massachusetts	1,245,000	2.3%
8	Michigan	1,701,000	3.2%
18	Minnesota	768,000	1.4%
29	Mississippi	417,000	0.8%
12	Missouri	1,142,000	2.1%
39	Montana	208,000	0.4%
30	Nebraska	352,000	0.7%
21	Nevada	540,000	1.0%
42	New Hampshire	135,000	0.3%
7	New Jersey	1,790,000	3.3%
22	New Mexico	493,000	0.9%
3	New York	3,183,000	6.0%
6	North Carolina	1,934,000	3.6%
28	North Dakota	444,000	0.8%
25	Ohio	467,000	0.9%
31	Oklahoma	335,000	0.6%
44	Oregon	81,000	0.2%
23	Pennsylvania	490,000	0.9%
47	Rhode Island	38,000	0.1%
32	South Carolina	315,000	0.6%
46	South Dakota	52,000	0.1%
38	Tennessee	210,000	0.4%
16	Texas	825,000	1.5%
41	Utah	138,000	0.3%
43	Vermont	108,000	0.2%
40	Virginia	142,000	0.3%
36	Washington	262,000	0.5%
45	West Virginia	57,000	0.1%
37	Wisconsin	221,000	0.4%
NA	Wyoming*	NA	NA

RANK ORDER

RANK	STATE	SWIMMERS	% of USA
1	California	6,594,000	12.3%
2	Florida	4,033,000	7.5%
3	New York	3,183,000	6.0%
4	Illinois	2,601,000	4.9%
5	Arizona	1,976,000	3.7%
6	North Carolina	1,934,000	3.6%
7	New Jersey	1,790,000	3.3%
8	Michigan	1,701,000	3.2%
9	Massachusetts	1,245,000	2.3%
10	Colorado	1,184,000	2.2%
11	Georgia	1,149,000	2.1%
12	Missouri	1,142,000	2.1%
13	Connecticut	1,030,000	1.9%
14	Indiana	910,000	1.7%
15	Maryland	879,000	1.6%
16	Texas	825,000	1.5%
17	Kentucky	824,000	1.5%
18	Minnesota	768,000	1.4%
19	Alabama	658,000	1.2%
20	Arkansas	597,000	1.1%
21	Nevada	540,000	1.0%
22	New Mexico	493,000	0.9%
23	Pennsylvania	490,000	0.9%
24	Idaho	472,000	0.9%
25	Ohio	467,000	0.9%
26	Iowa	446,000	0.8%
26	Kansas	446,000	0.8%
28	North Dakota	444,000	0.8%
29	Mississippi	417,000	0.8%
30	Nebraska	352,000	0.7%
31	Oklahoma	335,000	0.6%
32	South Carolina	315,000	0.6%
33	Louisiana	310,000	0.6%
34	Maine	278,000	0.5%
35	Delaware	263,000	0.5%
36	Washington	262,000	0.5%
37	Wisconsin	221,000	0.4%
38	Tennessee	210,000	0.4%
39	Montana	208,000	0.4%
40	Virginia	142,000	0.3%
41	Utah	138,000	0.3%
42	New Hampshire	135,000	0.3%
43	Vermont	108,000	0.2%
44	Oregon	81,000	0.2%
45	West Virginia	57,000	0.1%
46	South Dakota	52,000	0.1%
47	Rhode Island	38,000	0.1%
NA	Alaska*	NA	NA
NA	Hawaii*	NA	NA
NA	Wyoming*	NA	NA
	District of Columbia*	NA	NA

Source: The National Sporting Goods Association
  "NSGA Sports Participation Survey, January-December 2004 (Copyright 2005, reprinted with permission)
*Not available.

Participants in Tennis in 2004

National Total = 9,619,000 Tennis Players

ALPHA ORDER

RANK	STATE	PLAYERS	% of USA
31	Alabama	67,000	0.7%
NA	Alaska*	NA	NA
14	Arizona	298,000	3.1%
42	Arkansas	16,000	0.2%
1	California	1,197,000	12.4%
19	Colorado	185,000	1.9%
23	Connecticut	140,000	1.5%
37	Delaware	45,000	0.5%
4	Florida	432,000	4.5%
7	Georgia	388,000	4.0%
NA	Hawaii*	NA	NA
43	Idaho	15,000	0.2%
5	Illinois	420,000	4.4%
29	Indiana	81,000	0.8%
35	Iowa	56,000	0.6%
20	Kansas	176,000	1.8%
28	Kentucky	86,000	0.9%
22	Louisiana	144,000	1.5%
27	Maine	98,000	1.0%
17	Maryland	201,000	2.1%
9	Massachusetts	374,000	3.9%
7	Michigan	388,000	4.0%
11	Minnesota	333,000	3.5%
41	Mississippi	29,000	0.3%
13	Missouri	301,000	3.1%
33	Montana	65,000	0.7%
NA	Nebraska*	NA	NA
30	Nevada	79,000	0.8%
39	New Hampshire	42,000	0.4%
12	New Jersey	330,000	3.4%
24	New Mexico	134,000	1.4%
3	New York	626,000	6.5%
18	North Carolina	200,000	2.1%
NA	North Dakota*	NA	NA
10	Ohio	356,000	3.7%
36	Oklahoma	51,000	0.5%
NA	Oregon*	NA	NA
6	Pennsylvania	407,000	4.2%
26	Rhode Island	108,000	1.1%
16	South Carolina	252,000	2.6%
NA	South Dakota*	NA	NA
38	Tennessee	43,000	0.4%
2	Texas	661,000	6.9%
34	Utah	62,000	0.6%
32	Vermont	66,000	0.7%
14	Virginia	298,000	3.1%
25	Washington	122,000	1.3%
39	West Virginia	42,000	0.4%
21	Wisconsin	154,000	1.6%
NA	Wyoming*	NA	NA

RANK ORDER

RANK	STATE	PLAYERS	% of USA
1	California	1,197,000	12.4%
2	Texas	661,000	6.9%
3	New York	626,000	6.5%
4	Florida	432,000	4.5%
5	Illinois	420,000	4.4%
6	Pennsylvania	407,000	4.2%
7	Georgia	388,000	4.0%
7	Michigan	388,000	4.0%
9	Massachusetts	374,000	3.9%
10	Ohio	356,000	3.7%
11	Minnesota	333,000	3.5%
12	New Jersey	330,000	3.4%
13	Missouri	301,000	3.1%
14	Arizona	298,000	3.1%
14	Virginia	298,000	3.1%
16	South Carolina	252,000	2.6%
17	Maryland	201,000	2.1%
18	North Carolina	200,000	2.1%
19	Colorado	185,000	1.9%
20	Kansas	176,000	1.8%
21	Wisconsin	154,000	1.6%
22	Louisiana	144,000	1.5%
23	Connecticut	140,000	1.5%
24	New Mexico	134,000	1.4%
25	Washington	122,000	1.3%
26	Rhode Island	108,000	1.1%
27	Maine	98,000	1.0%
28	Kentucky	86,000	0.9%
29	Indiana	81,000	0.8%
30	Nevada	79,000	0.8%
31	Alabama	67,000	0.7%
32	Vermont	66,000	0.7%
33	Montana	65,000	0.7%
34	Utah	62,000	0.6%
35	Iowa	56,000	0.6%
36	Oklahoma	51,000	0.5%
37	Delaware	45,000	0.5%
38	Tennessee	43,000	0.4%
39	New Hampshire	42,000	0.4%
39	West Virginia	42,000	0.4%
41	Mississippi	29,000	0.3%
42	Arkansas	16,000	0.2%
43	Idaho	15,000	0.2%
NA	Alaska*	NA	NA
NA	Hawaii*	NA	NA
NA	Nebraska*	NA	NA
NA	North Dakota*	NA	NA
NA	Oregon*	NA	NA
NA	South Dakota*	NA	NA
NA	Wyoming*	NA	NA
	District of Columbia*	NA	NA

Source: The National Sporting Goods Association
  "NSGA Sports Participation Survey, January-December 2004 (Copyright 2005, reprinted with permission)
Not available.

Alcohol Consumption in 2003

National Total = 521,101,000 Gallons*

RANK	STATE	GALLONS	% of USA
25	Alabama	6,917,000	1.3%
49	Alaska	1,228,000	0.2%
16	Arizona	10,882,000	2.1%
35	Arkansas	3,889,000	0.7%
1	California	62,218,000	11.9%
20	Colorado	9,481,000	1.8%
28	Connecticut	6,312,000	1.2%
44	Delaware	2,076,000	0.4%
3	Florida	36,718,000	7.0%
10	Georgia	14,521,000	2.8%
41	Hawaii	2,430,000	0.5%
40	Idaho	2,513,000	0.5%
5	Illinois	23,679,000	4.5%
19	Indiana	9,740,000	1.9%
31	Iowa	4,951,000	1.0%
34	Kansas	4,116,000	0.8%
29	Kentucky	5,836,000	1.1%
23	Louisiana	8,597,000	1.6%
39	Maine	2,592,000	0.5%
21	Maryland	9,403,000	1.8%
12	Massachusetts	13,119,000	2.5%
8	Michigan	17,279,000	3.3%
18	Minnesota	9,904,000	1.9%
32	Mississippi	4,916,000	0.9%
17	Missouri	10,521,000	2.0%
45	Montana	1,971,000	0.4%
37	Nebraska	3,129,000	0.6%
27	Nevada	6,458,000	1.2%
33	New Hampshire	4,268,000	0.8%
9	New Jersey	15,606,000	3.0%
36	New Mexico	3,594,000	0.7%
4	New York	30,330,000	5.8%
11	North Carolina	13,582,000	2.6%
47	North Dakota	1,347,000	0.3%
7	Ohio	18,803,000	3.6%
30	Oklahoma	5,466,000	1.0%
26	Oregon	6,829,000	1.3%
6	Pennsylvania	22,489,000	4.3%
43	Rhode Island	2,153,000	0.4%
24	South Carolina	7,893,000	1.5%
46	South Dakota	1,484,000	0.3%
22	Tennessee	9,319,000	1.8%
2	Texas	37,794,000	7.3%
42	Utah	2,307,000	0.4%
48	Vermont	1,279,000	0.2%
14	Virginia	12,151,000	2.3%
15	Washington	10,890,000	2.1%
38	West Virginia	2,598,000	0.5%
13	Wisconsin	12,557,000	2.4%
50	Wyoming	1,164,000	0.2%

RANK	STATE	GALLONS	% of USA
1	California	62,218,000	11.9%
2	Texas	37,794,000	7.3%
3	Florida	36,718,000	7.0%
4	New York	30,330,000	5.8%
5	Illinois	23,679,000	4.5%
6	Pennsylvania	22,489,000	4.3%
7	Ohio	18,803,000	3.6%
8	Michigan	17,279,000	3.3%
9	New Jersey	15,606,000	3.0%
10	Georgia	14,521,000	2.8%
11	North Carolina	13,582,000	2.6%
12	Massachusetts	13,119,000	2.5%
13	Wisconsin	12,557,000	2.4%
14	Virginia	12,151,000	2.3%
15	Washington	10,890,000	2.1%
16	Arizona	10,882,000	2.1%
17	Missouri	10,521,000	2.0%
18	Minnesota	9,904,000	1.9%
19	Indiana	9,740,000	1.9%
20	Colorado	9,481,000	1.8%
21	Maryland	9,403,000	1.8%
22	Tennessee	9,319,000	1.8%
23	Louisiana	8,597,000	1.6%
24	South Carolina	7,893,000	1.5%
25	Alabama	6,917,000	1.3%
26	Oregon	6,829,000	1.3%
27	Nevada	6,458,000	1.2%
28	Connecticut	6,312,000	1.2%
29	Kentucky	5,836,000	1.1%
30	Oklahoma	5,466,000	1.0%
31	Iowa	4,951,000	1.0%
32	Mississippi	4,916,000	0.9%
33	New Hampshire	4,268,000	0.8%
34	Kansas	4,116,000	0.8%
35	Arkansas	3,889,000	0.7%
36	New Mexico	3,594,000	0.7%
37	Nebraska	3,129,000	0.6%
38	West Virginia	2,598,000	0.5%
39	Maine	2,592,000	0.5%
40	Idaho	2,513,000	0.5%
41	Hawaii	2,430,000	0.5%
42	Utah	2,307,000	0.4%
43	Rhode Island	2,153,000	0.4%
44	Delaware	2,076,000	0.4%
45	Montana	1,971,000	0.4%
46	South Dakota	1,484,000	0.3%
47	North Dakota	1,347,000	0.3%
48	Vermont	1,279,000	0.2%
49	Alaska	1,228,000	0.2%
50	Wyoming	1,164,000	0.2%
	District of Columbia	1,800,000	0.3%

Source: U.S. Department of Health and Human Services, National Institute on Alcohol Abuse and Alcoholism
"Volume Beverage and Ethanol Consumption for States" (http://www.niaaa.nih.gov/Resources/)

This is apparent consumption of actual alcohol, not entire volume of an alcoholic beverage (e.g. wine is roughly 11% absolute alcohol content). Apparent consumption is based on several sources which together approximate sales but do not actually measure consumption. Accordingly, figures for some states may be skewed by purchases by nonresidents.

Adult Per Capita Alcohol Consumption in 2003

National Per Capita = 2.5 Gallons Consumed per Adult 21 Years and Older*

ALPHA ORDER

RANK	STATE	PER CAPITA
41	Alabama	2.2
9	Alaska	2.9
11	Arizona	2.8
47	Arkansas	2.0
27	California	2.5
6	Colorado	3.0
27	Connecticut	2.5
3	Delaware	3.5
6	Florida	3.0
34	Georgia	2.4
18	Hawaii	2.7
18	Idaho	2.7
18	Illinois	2.7
41	Indiana	2.2
37	Iowa	2.3
41	Kansas	2.2
47	Kentucky	2.0
11	Louisiana	2.8
18	Maine	2.7
34	Maryland	2.4
11	Massachusetts	2.8
34	Michigan	2.4
11	Minnesota	2.8
27	Mississippi	2.5
25	Missouri	2.6
6	Montana	3.0
25	Nebraska	2.6
2	Nevada	4.1
1	New Hampshire	4.6
27	New Jersey	2.5
11	New Mexico	2.8
41	New York	2.2
37	North Carolina	2.3
9	North Dakota	2.9
37	Ohio	2.3
41	Oklahoma	2.2
18	Oregon	2.7
27	Pennsylvania	2.5
18	Rhode Island	2.7
18	South Carolina	2.7
11	South Dakota	2.8
41	Tennessee	2.2
27	Texas	2.5
50	Utah	1.6
11	Vermont	2.8
37	Virginia	2.3
27	Washington	2.5
49	West Virginia	1.9
5	Wisconsin	3.2
4	Wyoming	3.3

RANK ORDER

RANK	STATE	PER CAPITA
1	New Hampshire	4.6
2	Nevada	4.1
3	Delaware	3.5
4	Wyoming	3.3
5	Wisconsin	3.2
6	Colorado	3.0
6	Florida	3.0
6	Montana	3.0
9	Alaska	2.9
9	North Dakota	2.9
11	Arizona	2.8
11	Louisiana	2.8
11	Massachusetts	2.8
11	Minnesota	2.8
11	New Mexico	2.8
11	South Dakota	2.8
11	Vermont	2.8
18	Hawaii	2.7
18	Idaho	2.7
18	Illinois	2.7
18	Maine	2.7
18	Oregon	2.7
18	Rhode Island	2.7
18	South Carolina	2.7
25	Missouri	2.6
25	Nebraska	2.6
27	California	2.5
27	Connecticut	2.5
27	Mississippi	2.5
27	New Jersey	2.5
27	Pennsylvania	2.5
27	Texas	2.5
27	Washington	2.5
34	Georgia	2.4
34	Maryland	2.4
34	Michigan	2.4
37	Iowa	2.3
37	North Carolina	2.3
37	Ohio	2.3
37	Virginia	2.3
41	Alabama	2.2
41	Indiana	2.2
41	Kansas	2.2
41	New York	2.2
41	Oklahoma	2.2
41	Tennessee	2.2
47	Arkansas	2.0
47	Kentucky	2.0
49	West Virginia	1.9
50	Utah	1.6

| | District of Columbia | 4.2 |

Source: Morgan Quitno Press using data from U.S. Dept. of HHS, National Institute on Alcohol Abuse and Alcoholism
"Volume Beverage and Ethanol Consumption for States" (http://www.niaaa.nih.gov/Resources/)
*This is apparent consumption of actual alcohol, not entire volume of an alcoholic beverage (e.g. wine is roughly
11% absolute alcohol content). Apparent consumption is based on several sources which together approximate
sales but do not actually measure consumption. Accordingly, figures for some states may be skewed by purchases
by nonresidents.

Apparent Beer Consumption in 2003

National Total = 6,338,388,000 Gallons of Beer Consumed*

ALPHA ORDER

RANK	STATE	GALLONS	% of USA
25	Alabama	96,188,000	1.5%
50	Alaska	14,256,000	0.2%
14	Arizona	137,187,000	2.2%
34	Arkansas	52,045,000	0.8%
1	California	663,750,000	10.5%
22	Colorado	108,026,000	1.7%
32	Connecticut	58,534,000	0.9%
46	Delaware	20,390,000	0.3%
3	Florida	410,967,000	6.5%
10	Georgia	181,575,000	2.9%
41	Hawaii	29,494,000	0.5%
42	Idaho	27,427,000	0.4%
6	Illinois	282,370,000	4.5%
18	Indiana	122,606,000	1.9%
28	Iowa	73,463,000	1.2%
33	Kansas	56,111,000	0.9%
27	Kentucky	76,440,000	1.2%
20	Louisiana	112,891,000	1.8%
39	Maine	30,150,000	0.5%
24	Maryland	101,107,000	1.6%
17	Massachusetts	129,179,000	2.0%
8	Michigan	210,882,000	3.3%
21	Minnesota	110,741,000	1.7%
29	Mississippi	71,325,000	1.1%
15	Missouri	137,037,000	2.2%
43	Montana	26,100,000	0.4%
36	Nebraska	44,219,000	0.7%
30	Nevada	69,712,000	1.1%
38	New Hampshire	40,500,000	0.6%
13	New Jersey	146,835,000	2.3%
35	New Mexico	50,655,000	0.8%
5	New York	322,431,000	5.1%
9	North Carolina	182,250,000	2.9%
47	North Dakota	17,920,000	0.3%
7	Ohio	273,375,000	4.3%
31	Oklahoma	66,861,000	1.1%
26	Oregon	77,369,000	1.2%
4	Pennsylvania	331,190,000	5.2%
44	Rhode Island	22,204,000	0.4%
23	South Carolina	103,058,000	1.6%
45	South Dakota	20,700,000	0.3%
16	Tennessee	133,923,000	2.1%
2	Texas	558,837,000	8.8%
39	Utah	30,150,000	0.5%
49	Vermont	15,188,000	0.2%
11	Virginia	151,706,000	2.4%
19	Washington	116,550,000	1.8%
37	West Virginia	41,400,000	0.7%
12	Wisconsin	151,000,000	2.4%
48	Wyoming	15,535,000	0.2%

RANK ORDER

RANK	STATE	GALLONS	% of USA
1	California	663,750,000	10.5%
2	Texas	558,837,000	8.8%
3	Florida	410,967,000	6.5%
4	Pennsylvania	331,190,000	5.2%
5	New York	322,431,000	5.1%
6	Illinois	282,370,000	4.5%
7	Ohio	273,375,000	4.3%
8	Michigan	210,882,000	3.3%
9	North Carolina	182,250,000	2.9%
10	Georgia	181,575,000	2.9%
11	Virginia	151,706,000	2.4%
12	Wisconsin	151,000,000	2.4%
13	New Jersey	146,835,000	2.3%
14	Arizona	137,187,000	2.2%
15	Missouri	137,037,000	2.2%
16	Tennessee	133,923,000	2.1%
17	Massachusetts	129,179,000	2.0%
18	Indiana	122,606,000	1.9%
19	Washington	116,550,000	1.8%
20	Louisiana	112,891,000	1.8%
21	Minnesota	110,741,000	1.7%
22	Colorado	108,026,000	1.7%
23	South Carolina	103,058,000	1.6%
24	Maryland	101,107,000	1.6%
25	Alabama	96,188,000	1.5%
26	Oregon	77,369,000	1.2%
27	Kentucky	76,440,000	1.2%
28	Iowa	73,463,000	1.2%
29	Mississippi	71,325,000	1.1%
30	Nevada	69,712,000	1.1%
31	Oklahoma	66,861,000	1.1%
32	Connecticut	58,534,000	0.9%
33	Kansas	56,111,000	0.9%
34	Arkansas	52,045,000	0.8%
35	New Mexico	50,655,000	0.8%
36	Nebraska	44,219,000	0.7%
37	West Virginia	41,400,000	0.7%
38	New Hampshire	40,500,000	0.6%
39	Maine	30,150,000	0.5%
39	Utah	30,150,000	0.5%
41	Hawaii	29,494,000	0.5%
42	Idaho	27,427,000	0.4%
43	Montana	26,100,000	0.4%
44	Rhode Island	22,204,000	0.4%
45	South Dakota	20,700,000	0.3%
46	Delaware	20,390,000	0.3%
47	North Dakota	17,920,000	0.3%
48	Wyoming	15,535,000	0.2%
49	Vermont	15,188,000	0.2%
50	Alaska	14,256,000	0.2%
	District of Columbia	14,580,000	0.2%

Source: U.S. Department of Health and Human Services, National Institute on Alcohol Abuse and Alcoholism
"Volume Beverage and Ethanol Consumption for States" (http://www.niaaa.nih.gov/Resources/)
This is apparent consumption and is based on several sources which together approximate sales but do not actually measure consumption. Reported state volumes reflect only in-state purchases. Accordingly, figures for some states may be skewed by purchases by nonresidents.

Adult Per Capita Beer Consumption in 2003

National Per Capita = 30.9 Gallons Consumed per Adult 21 Years and Older*

ALPHA ORDER				RANK ORDER		
RANK	STATE	PER CAPITA		RANK	STATE	PER CAPITA
33	Alabama	30.0		1	Nevada	44.3
20	Alaska	33.6		2	New Hampshire	43.6
14	Arizona	35.7		3	Wyoming	43.5
42	Arkansas	27.0		4	Montana	39.5
41	California	27.1		5	New Mexico	39.3
18	Colorado	33.8		6	North Dakota	39.1
48	Connecticut	23.3		7	South Dakota	38.8
17	Delaware	34.5		8	Wisconsin	38.7
23	Florida	33.1		9	Texas	37.5
31	Georgia	30.2		10	Pennsylvania	36.7
24	Hawaii	32.9		11	Louisiana	36.4
35	Idaho	29.6		12	Nebraska	36.3
25	Illinois	31.8		13	Mississippi	35.8
38	Indiana	28.3		14	Arizona	35.7
16	Iowa	34.7		15	South Carolina	34.9
36	Kansas	29.4		16	Iowa	34.7
46	Kentucky	25.8		17	Delaware	34.5
11	Louisiana	36.4		18	Colorado	33.8
27	Maine	31.2		19	Missouri	33.7
45	Maryland	25.9		20	Alaska	33.6
40	Massachusetts	27.5		21	Ohio	33.5
34	Michigan	29.7		22	Vermont	33.4
28	Minnesota	30.9		23	Florida	33.1
13	Mississippi	35.8		24	Hawaii	32.9
19	Missouri	33.7		25	Illinois	31.8
4	Montana	39.5		25	Tennessee	31.8
12	Nebraska	36.3		27	Maine	31.2
1	Nevada	44.3		28	Minnesota	30.9
2	New Hampshire	43.6		29	West Virginia	30.7
47	New Jersey	23.8		30	North Carolina	30.4
5	New Mexico	39.3		31	Georgia	30.2
49	New York	23.2		31	Oregon	30.2
30	North Carolina	30.4		33	Alabama	30.0
6	North Dakota	39.1		34	Michigan	29.7
21	Ohio	33.5		35	Idaho	29.6
42	Oklahoma	27.0		36	Kansas	29.4
31	Oregon	30.2		37	Virginia	28.8
10	Pennsylvania	36.7		38	Indiana	28.3
39	Rhode Island	28.1		39	Rhode Island	28.1
15	South Carolina	34.9		40	Massachusetts	27.5
7	South Dakota	38.8		41	California	27.1
25	Tennessee	31.8		42	Arkansas	27.0
9	Texas	37.5		42	Oklahoma	27.0
50	Utah	20.3		44	Washington	26.7
22	Vermont	33.4		45	Maryland	25.9
37	Virginia	28.8		46	Kentucky	25.8
44	Washington	26.7		47	New Jersey	23.8
29	West Virginia	30.7		48	Connecticut	23.3
8	Wisconsin	38.7		49	New York	23.2
3	Wyoming	43.5		50	Utah	20.3

District of Columbia 33.8

Source: Morgan Quitno Press using data from U.S. Dept. of HHS, National Institute on Alcohol Abuse and Alcoholism "Volume Beverage and Ethanol Consumption for States" (http://www.niaaa.nih.gov/Resources/)
This is apparent consumption and is based on several sources which together approximate sales but do not actually measure consumption. Reported state volumes reflect only in-state purchases. Accordingly, figures for some states may be skewed by purchases by nonresidents.

Wine Consumption in 2003

National Total = 614,318,000 Gallons of Wine Consumed*

ALPHA ORDER

RANK	STATE	GALLONS	% of USA
29	Alabama	5,416,000	0.9%
46	Alaska	1,465,000	0.2%
15	Arizona	12,440,000	2.0%
40	Arkansas	2,426,000	0.4%
1	California	109,525,000	17.8%
17	Colorado	11,170,000	1.8%
16	Connecticut	11,483,000	1.9%
36	Delaware	2,920,000	0.5%
3	Florida	47,892,000	7.8%
14	Georgia	14,004,000	2.3%
34	Hawaii	3,297,000	0.5%
30	Idaho	5,373,000	0.9%
5	Illinois	27,183,000	4.4%
24	Indiana	8,193,000	1.3%
39	Iowa	2,768,000	0.5%
38	Kansas	2,818,000	0.5%
31	Kentucky	3,914,000	0.6%
25	Louisiana	6,990,000	1.1%
33	Maine	3,353,000	0.5%
18	Maryland	11,040,000	1.8%
7	Massachusetts	22,984,000	3.7%
11	Michigan	16,239,000	2.6%
21	Minnesota	9,307,000	1.5%
41	Mississippi	2,113,000	0.3%
22	Missouri	9,188,000	1.5%
45	Montana	1,955,000	0.3%
44	Nebraska	2,007,000	0.3%
23	Nevada	8,538,000	1.4%
28	New Hampshire	5,728,000	0.9%
6	New Jersey	26,853,000	4.4%
35	New Mexico	3,102,000	0.5%
2	New York	48,741,000	7.9%
13	North Carolina	14,454,000	2.4%
50	North Dakota	703,000	0.1%
12	Ohio	15,819,000	2.6%
37	Oklahoma	2,912,000	0.5%
19	Oregon	10,558,000	1.7%
8	Pennsylvania	18,241,000	3.0%
32	Rhode Island	3,512,000	0.6%
27	South Carolina	6,039,000	1.0%
48	South Dakota	768,000	0.1%
26	Tennessee	6,486,000	1.1%
4	Texas	30,475,000	5.0%
43	Utah	2,014,000	0.3%
42	Vermont	2,053,000	0.3%
10	Virginia	16,722,000	2.7%
9	Washington	17,821,000	2.9%
47	West Virginia	1,208,000	0.2%
20	Wisconsin	10,122,000	1.6%
49	Wyoming	721,000	0.1%

RANK ORDER

RANK	STATE	GALLONS	% of USA
1	California	109,525,000	17.8%
2	New York	48,741,000	7.9%
3	Florida	47,892,000	7.8%
4	Texas	30,475,000	5.0%
5	Illinois	27,183,000	4.4%
6	New Jersey	26,853,000	4.4%
7	Massachusetts	22,984,000	3.7%
8	Pennsylvania	18,241,000	3.0%
9	Washington	17,821,000	2.9%
10	Virginia	16,722,000	2.7%
11	Michigan	16,239,000	2.6%
12	Ohio	15,819,000	2.6%
13	North Carolina	14,454,000	2.4%
14	Georgia	14,004,000	2.3%
15	Arizona	12,440,000	2.0%
16	Connecticut	11,483,000	1.9%
17	Colorado	11,170,000	1.8%
18	Maryland	11,040,000	1.8%
19	Oregon	10,558,000	1.7%
20	Wisconsin	10,122,000	1.6%
21	Minnesota	9,307,000	1.5%
22	Missouri	9,188,000	1.5%
23	Nevada	8,538,000	1.4%
24	Indiana	8,193,000	1.3%
25	Louisiana	6,990,000	1.1%
26	Tennessee	6,486,000	1.1%
27	South Carolina	6,039,000	1.0%
28	New Hampshire	5,728,000	0.9%
29	Alabama	5,416,000	0.9%
30	Idaho	5,373,000	0.9%
31	Kentucky	3,914,000	0.6%
32	Rhode Island	3,512,000	0.6%
33	Maine	3,353,000	0.5%
34	Hawaii	3,297,000	0.5%
35	New Mexico	3,102,000	0.5%
36	Delaware	2,920,000	0.5%
37	Oklahoma	2,912,000	0.5%
38	Kansas	2,818,000	0.5%
39	Iowa	2,768,000	0.5%
40	Arkansas	2,426,000	0.4%
41	Mississippi	2,113,000	0.3%
42	Vermont	2,053,000	0.3%
43	Utah	2,014,000	0.3%
44	Nebraska	2,007,000	0.3%
45	Montana	1,955,000	0.3%
46	Alaska	1,465,000	0.2%
47	West Virginia	1,208,000	0.2%
48	South Dakota	768,000	0.1%
49	Wyoming	721,000	0.1%
50	North Dakota	703,000	0.1%
	District of Columbia	3,263,000	0.5%

Source: U.S. Department of Health and Human Services, National Institute on Alcohol Abuse and Alcoholism "Volume Beverage and Ethanol Consumption for States" (http://www.niaaa.nih.gov/Resources/)
*This is apparent consumption and is based on several sources which together approximate sales but do not actually measure consumption. Reported state volumes reflect only in-state purchases. Accordingly, figures for some states may be skewed by purchases by nonresidents.

Adult Per Capita Wine Consumption in 2003

National Per Capita = 3.0 Gallons Consumed per Adult 21 Years and Older

ALPHA ORDER

RANK	STATE	PER CAPITA
38	Alabama	1.7
15	Alaska	3.5
19	Arizona	3.2
45	Arkansas	1.3
7	California	4.5
15	Colorado	3.5
6	Connecticut	4.6
4	Delaware	4.9
13	Florida	3.9
28	Georgia	2.3
14	Hawaii	3.7
2	Idaho	5.8
21	Illinois	3.1
36	Indiana	1.9
45	Iowa	1.3
40	Kansas	1.5
45	Kentucky	1.3
28	Louisiana	2.3
15	Maine	3.5
23	Maryland	2.8
4	Massachusetts	4.9
28	Michigan	2.3
24	Minnesota	2.6
49	Mississippi	1.1
28	Missouri	2.3
22	Montana	3.0
39	Nebraska	1.6
3	Nevada	5.4
1	New Hampshire	6.2
10	New Jersey	4.3
26	New Mexico	2.4
15	New York	3.5
26	North Carolina	2.4
40	North Dakota	1.5
36	Ohio	1.9
48	Oklahoma	1.2
11	Oregon	4.1
32	Pennsylvania	2.0
9	Rhode Island	4.4
32	South Carolina	2.0
43	South Dakota	1.4
40	Tennessee	1.5
32	Texas	2.0
43	Utah	1.4
7	Vermont	4.5
19	Virginia	3.2
11	Washington	4.1
50	West Virginia	0.9
24	Wisconsin	2.6
32	Wyoming	2.0

RANK ORDER

RANK	STATE	PER CAPITA
1	New Hampshire	6.2
2	Idaho	5.8
3	Nevada	5.4
4	Delaware	4.9
4	Massachusetts	4.9
6	Connecticut	4.6
7	California	4.5
7	Vermont	4.5
9	Rhode Island	4.4
10	New Jersey	4.3
11	Oregon	4.1
11	Washington	4.1
13	Florida	3.9
14	Hawaii	3.7
15	Alaska	3.5
15	Colorado	3.5
15	Maine	3.5
15	New York	3.5
19	Arizona	3.2
19	Virginia	3.2
21	Illinois	3.1
22	Montana	3.0
23	Maryland	2.8
24	Minnesota	2.6
24	Wisconsin	2.6
26	New Mexico	2.4
26	North Carolina	2.4
28	Georgia	2.3
28	Louisiana	2.3
28	Michigan	2.3
28	Missouri	2.3
32	Pennsylvania	2.0
32	South Carolina	2.0
32	Texas	2.0
32	Wyoming	2.0
36	Indiana	1.9
36	Ohio	1.9
38	Alabama	1.7
39	Nebraska	1.6
40	Kansas	1.5
40	North Dakota	1.5
40	Tennessee	1.5
43	South Dakota	1.4
43	Utah	1.4
45	Arkansas	1.3
45	Iowa	1.3
45	Kentucky	1.3
48	Oklahoma	1.2
49	Mississippi	1.1
50	West Virginia	0.9

District of Columbia	7.6

Source: Morgan Quitno Press using data from U.S. Dept. of HHS, National Institute on Alcohol Abuse and Alcoholism
"Volume Beverage and Ethanol Consumption for States" (http://www.niaaa.nih.gov/Resources/)
*This is apparent consumption and is based on several sources which together approximate sales but do not actually measure consumption. Reported state volumes reflect only in-state purchases. Accordingly, figures for some states may be skewed by purchases by nonresidents.

Distilled Spirits Consumption in 2003

National Total = 381,087,000 Gallons of Distilled Spirits Consumed*

ALPHA ORDER

RANK	STATE	GALLONS	% of USA
30	Alabama	4,599,000	1.2%
48	Alaska	968,000	0.3%
21	Arizona	7,551,000	2.0%
34	Arkansas	3,002,000	0.8%
1	California	44,332,000	11.6%
17	Colorado	7,734,000	2.0%
26	Connecticut	5,344,000	1.4%
39	Delaware	1,903,000	0.5%
2	Florida	29,311,000	7.7%
9	Georgia	11,055,000	2.9%
42	Hawaii	1,647,000	0.4%
43	Idaho	1,424,000	0.4%
5	Illinois	18,164,000	4.8%
20	Indiana	7,702,000	2.0%
33	Iowa	3,134,000	0.8%
35	Kansas	2,987,000	0.8%
29	Kentucky	4,602,000	1.2%
22	Louisiana	6,363,000	1.7%
38	Maine	1,952,000	0.5%
15	Maryland	8,344,000	2.2%
12	Massachusetts	10,562,000	2.8%
6	Michigan	13,856,000	3.6%
13	Minnesota	9,050,000	2.4%
32	Mississippi	3,489,000	0.9%
18	Missouri	7,712,000	2.0%
45	Montana	1,324,000	0.3%
37	Nebraska	2,143,000	0.6%
25	Nevada	5,400,000	1.4%
31	New Hampshire	4,153,000	1.1%
7	New Jersey	13,466,000	3.5%
36	New Mexico	2,225,000	0.6%
3	New York	23,196,000	6.1%
14	North Carolina	8,554,000	2.2%
47	North Dakota	1,095,000	0.3%
10	Ohio	10,853,000	2.8%
27	Oklahoma	5,066,000	1.3%
28	Oregon	4,832,000	1.3%
8	Pennsylvania	12,730,000	3.3%
40	Rhode Island	1,706,000	0.4%
23	South Carolina	6,026,000	1.6%
46	South Dakota	1,102,000	0.3%
24	Tennessee	5,975,000	1.6%
4	Texas	21,205,000	5.6%
41	Utah	1,679,000	0.4%
50	Vermont	804,000	0.2%
19	Virginia	7,706,000	2.0%
16	Washington	8,141,000	2.1%
44	West Virginia	1,410,000	0.4%
11	Wisconsin	10,843,000	2.8%
49	Wyoming	904,000	0.2%

RANK ORDER

RANK	STATE	GALLONS	% of USA
1	California	44,332,000	11.6%
2	Florida	29,311,000	7.7%
3	New York	23,196,000	6.1%
4	Texas	21,205,000	5.6%
5	Illinois	18,164,000	4.8%
6	Michigan	13,856,000	3.6%
7	New Jersey	13,466,000	3.5%
8	Pennsylvania	12,730,000	3.3%
9	Georgia	11,055,000	2.9%
10	Ohio	10,853,000	2.8%
11	Wisconsin	10,843,000	2.8%
12	Massachusetts	10,562,000	2.8%
13	Minnesota	9,050,000	2.4%
14	North Carolina	8,554,000	2.2%
15	Maryland	8,344,000	2.2%
16	Washington	8,141,000	2.1%
17	Colorado	7,734,000	2.0%
18	Missouri	7,712,000	2.0%
19	Virginia	7,706,000	2.0%
20	Indiana	7,702,000	2.0%
21	Arizona	7,551,000	2.0%
22	Louisiana	6,363,000	1.7%
23	South Carolina	6,026,000	1.6%
24	Tennessee	5,975,000	1.6%
25	Nevada	5,400,000	1.4%
26	Connecticut	5,344,000	1.4%
27	Oklahoma	5,066,000	1.3%
28	Oregon	4,832,000	1.3%
29	Kentucky	4,602,000	1.2%
30	Alabama	4,599,000	1.2%
31	New Hampshire	4,153,000	1.1%
32	Mississippi	3,489,000	0.9%
33	Iowa	3,134,000	0.8%
34	Arkansas	3,002,000	0.8%
35	Kansas	2,987,000	0.8%
36	New Mexico	2,225,000	0.6%
37	Nebraska	2,143,000	0.6%
38	Maine	1,952,000	0.5%
39	Delaware	1,903,000	0.5%
40	Rhode Island	1,706,000	0.4%
41	Utah	1,679,000	0.4%
42	Hawaii	1,647,000	0.4%
43	Idaho	1,424,000	0.4%
44	West Virginia	1,410,000	0.4%
45	Montana	1,324,000	0.3%
46	South Dakota	1,102,000	0.3%
47	North Dakota	1,095,000	0.3%
48	Alaska	968,000	0.3%
49	Wyoming	904,000	0.2%
50	Vermont	804,000	0.2%
	District of Columbia	1,760,000	0.5%

Source: U.S. Department of Health and Human Services, National Institute on Alcohol Abuse and Alcoholism "Volume Beverage and Ethanol Consumption for States" (http://www.niaaa.nih.gov/Resources/)
This is apparent consumption and is based on several sources which together approximate sales but do not actually measure consumption. Reported state volumes reflect only in-state purchases. Accordingly, figures for some states may be skewed by purchases by nonresidents.

Adult Per Capita Distilled Spirits Consumption in 2003

National Per Capita = 1.9 Gallons Consumed per Adult 21 Years and Older*

ALPHA ORDER

RANK	STATE	PER CAPITA
43	Alabama	1.4
10	Alaska	2.3
18	Arizona	2.0
37	Arkansas	1.6
28	California	1.8
7	Colorado	2.4
14	Connecticut	2.1
3	Delaware	3.2
7	Florida	2.4
28	Georgia	1.8
28	Hawaii	1.8
40	Idaho	1.5
18	Illinois	2.0
28	Indiana	1.8
40	Iowa	1.5
37	Kansas	1.6
37	Kentucky	1.6
14	Louisiana	2.1
18	Maine	2.0
14	Maryland	2.1
11	Massachusetts	2.2
24	Michigan	1.9
5	Minnesota	2.5
28	Mississippi	1.8
24	Missouri	1.9
18	Montana	2.0
28	Nebraska	1.8
2	Nevada	3.4
1	New Hampshire	4.5
11	New Jersey	2.2
35	New Mexico	1.7
35	New York	1.7
43	North Carolina	1.4
7	North Dakota	2.4
48	Ohio	1.3
18	Oklahoma	2.0
24	Oregon	1.9
43	Pennsylvania	1.4
11	Rhode Island	2.2
18	South Carolina	2.0
14	South Dakota	2.1
43	Tennessee	1.4
43	Texas	1.4
49	Utah	1.1
28	Vermont	1.8
40	Virginia	1.5
24	Washington	1.9
50	West Virginia	1.0
4	Wisconsin	2.8
5	Wyoming	2.5

RANK ORDER

RANK	STATE	PER CAPITA
1	New Hampshire	4.5
2	Nevada	3.4
3	Delaware	3.2
4	Wisconsin	2.8
5	Minnesota	2.5
5	Wyoming	2.5
7	Colorado	2.4
7	Florida	2.4
7	North Dakota	2.4
10	Alaska	2.3
11	Massachusetts	2.2
11	New Jersey	2.2
11	Rhode Island	2.2
14	Connecticut	2.1
14	Louisiana	2.1
14	Maryland	2.1
14	South Dakota	2.1
18	Arizona	2.0
18	Illinois	2.0
18	Maine	2.0
18	Montana	2.0
18	Oklahoma	2.0
18	South Carolina	2.0
24	Michigan	1.9
24	Missouri	1.9
24	Oregon	1.9
24	Washington	1.9
28	California	1.8
28	Georgia	1.8
28	Hawaii	1.8
28	Indiana	1.8
28	Mississippi	1.8
28	Nebraska	1.8
28	Vermont	1.8
35	New Mexico	1.7
35	New York	1.7
37	Arkansas	1.6
37	Kansas	1.6
37	Kentucky	1.6
40	Idaho	1.5
40	Iowa	1.5
40	Virginia	1.5
43	Alabama	1.4
43	North Carolina	1.4
43	Pennsylvania	1.4
43	Tennessee	1.4
43	Texas	1.4
48	Ohio	1.3
49	Utah	1.1
50	West Virginia	1.0

| | District of Columbia | 4.1 |

Source: Morgan Quitno Press using data from U.S. Dept. of HHS, National Institute on Alcohol Abuse and Alcoholism
"Volume Beverage and Ethanol Consumption for States" (http://www.niaaa.nih.gov/Resources/)
*This is apparent consumption and is based on several sources which together approximate sales but do not actually measure consumption. Reported state volumes reflect only in-state purchases. Accordingly, figures for some states may be skewed by purchases by nonresidents.

Percent of Adults Who Do Not Drink Alcohol: 2004

National Median = 43.1% of Adults*

ALPHA ORDER			RANK ORDER		
RANK	STATE	PERCENT	RANK	STATE	PERCENT
6	Alabama	59.7	1	Utah	71.2
28	Alaska	42.1	2	West Virginia	69.7
20	Arizona	43.7	3	Kentucky	68.2
7	Arkansas	58.4	4	Tennessee	66.3
20	California	43.7	5	Mississippi	62.3
41	Colorado	37.8	6	Alabama	59.7
43	Connecticut	34.6	7	Arkansas	58.4
36	Delaware	40.3	8	North Carolina	58.0
22	Florida	43.6	9	Oklahoma	56.9
11	Georgia	53.1	10	Louisiana	54.9
NA	Hawaii**	NA	11	Georgia	53.1
13	Idaho	51.9	12	South Carolina	52.4
29	Illinois	41.9	13	Idaho	51.9
15	Indiana	50.0	14	Kansas	50.7
25	Iowa	43.1	15	Indiana	50.0
14	Kansas	50.7	16	Texas	48.2
3	Kentucky	68.2	17	Missouri	48.1
10	Louisiana	54.9	18	Virginia	45.9
34	Maine	40.7	19	New Mexico	44.3
32	Maryland	40.8	20	Arizona	43.7
48	Massachusetts	32.5	20	California	43.7
38	Michigan	40.1	22	Florida	43.6
46	Minnesota	33.7	22	Oregon	43.6
5	Mississippi	62.3	24	Ohio	43.2
17	Missouri	48.1	25	Iowa	43.1
40	Montana	39.3	26	Wyoming	42.8
35	Nebraska	40.5	27	Pennsylvania	42.6
31	Nevada	41.0	28	Alaska	42.1
45	New Hampshire	33.8	29	Illinois	41.9
37	New Jersey	40.2	30	South Dakota	41.6
19	New Mexico	44.3	31	Nevada	41.0
32	New York	40.8	32	Maryland	40.8
8	North Carolina	58.0	32	New York	40.8
42	North Dakota	37.4	34	Maine	40.7
24	Ohio	43.2	35	Nebraska	40.5
9	Oklahoma	56.9	36	Delaware	40.3
22	Oregon	43.6	37	New Jersey	40.2
27	Pennsylvania	42.6	38	Michigan	40.1
47	Rhode Island	33.6	39	Washington	39.4
12	South Carolina	52.4	40	Montana	39.3
30	South Dakota	41.6	41	Colorado	37.8
4	Tennessee	66.3	42	North Dakota	37.4
16	Texas	48.2	43	Connecticut	34.6
1	Utah	71.2	44	Vermont	34.4
44	Vermont	34.4	45	New Hampshire	33.8
18	Virginia	45.9	46	Minnesota	33.7
39	Washington	39.4	47	Rhode Island	33.6
2	West Virginia	69.7	48	Massachusetts	32.5
49	Wisconsin	32.1	49	Wisconsin	32.1
26	Wyoming	42.8	NA	Hawaii**	NA
				District of Columbia	38.5

Source: U.S. Department of Health and Human Services, Centers for Disease Control and Prevention
"2004 Behavioral Risk Factor Surveillance Summary Prevalence Data" (http://apps.nccd.cdc.gov/brfss/)
*Persons 18 and older reporting not having at least one drink of alcohol in the past 30 days.
**Not available.

Percent of Adults Who Are Binge Drinkers: 2004

National Median = 14.9% of Adults*

ALPHA ORDER

RANK	STATE	PERCENT
39	Alabama	12.7
16	Alaska	16.3
23	Arizona	15.5
43	Arkansas	11.2
27	California	14.7
11	Colorado	17.2
26	Connecticut	14.8
10	Delaware	17.4
41	Florida	12.4
42	Georgia	12.1
NA	Hawaii**	NA
40	Idaho	12.6
9	Illinois	17.5
28	Indiana	14.4
4	Iowa	18.9
37	Kansas	12.8
46	Kentucky	9.6
30	Louisiana	14.2
25	Maine	14.9
37	Maryland	12.8
13	Massachusetts	16.9
18	Michigan	16.1
3	Minnesota	19.8
44	Mississippi	10.4
17	Missouri	16.2
12	Montana	17.0
7	Nebraska	17.6
6	Nevada	18.0
21	New Hampshire	16.0
28	New Jersey	14.4
35	New Mexico	13.0
24	New York	15.2
47	North Carolina	9.5
2	North Dakota	20.4
13	Ohio	16.9
35	Oklahoma	13.0
34	Oregon	13.1
7	Pennsylvania	17.6
5	Rhode Island	18.2
33	South Carolina	13.5
13	South Dakota	16.9
49	Tennessee	8.2
22	Texas	15.6
48	Utah	9.2
18	Vermont	16.1
32	Virginia	13.7
30	Washington	14.2
45	West Virginia	9.7
1	Wisconsin	21.8
18	Wyoming	16.1

RANK ORDER

RANK	STATE	PERCENT
1	Wisconsin	21.8
2	North Dakota	20.4
3	Minnesota	19.8
4	Iowa	18.9
5	Rhode Island	18.2
6	Nevada	18.0
7	Nebraska	17.6
7	Pennsylvania	17.6
9	Illinois	17.5
10	Delaware	17.4
11	Colorado	17.2
12	Montana	17.0
13	Massachusetts	16.9
13	Ohio	16.9
13	South Dakota	16.9
16	Alaska	16.3
17	Missouri	16.2
18	Michigan	16.1
18	Vermont	16.1
18	Wyoming	16.1
21	New Hampshire	16.0
22	Texas	15.6
23	Arizona	15.5
24	New York	15.2
25	Maine	14.9
26	Connecticut	14.8
27	California	14.7
28	Indiana	14.4
28	New Jersey	14.4
30	Louisiana	14.2
30	Washington	14.2
32	Virginia	13.7
33	South Carolina	13.5
34	Oregon	13.1
35	New Mexico	13.0
35	Oklahoma	13.0
37	Kansas	12.8
37	Maryland	12.8
39	Alabama	12.7
40	Idaho	12.6
41	Florida	12.4
42	Georgia	12.1
43	Arkansas	11.2
44	Mississippi	10.4
45	West Virginia	9.7
46	Kentucky	9.6
47	North Carolina	9.5
48	Utah	9.2
49	Tennessee	8.2
NA	Hawaii**	NA

District of Columbia 16.6

Source: U.S. Department of Health and Human Services, Centers for Disease Control and Prevention
"2004 Behavioral Risk Factor Surveillance Summary Prevalence Data" (http://apps.nccd.cdc.gov/brfss/)
*Persons 18 and older reporting consumption of five or more alcoholic drinks on one or more occasions during the previous month.
**Not available.

Percent of Adults Who Smoke: 2004

National Median = 20.8% of Adults*

<table>
<tr><td colspan="3">ALPHA ORDER</td><td colspan="3">RANK ORDER</td></tr>
<tr><td>RANK</td><td>STATE</td><td>PERCENT</td><td>RANK</td><td>STATE</td><td>PERCENT</td></tr>
<tr><td>7</td><td>Alabama</td><td>24.8</td><td>1</td><td>Kentucky</td><td>27.5</td></tr>
<tr><td>7</td><td>Alaska</td><td>24.8</td><td>2</td><td>West Virginia</td><td>26.8</td></tr>
<tr><td>44</td><td>Arizona</td><td>18.5</td><td>3</td><td>Tennessee</td><td>26.1</td></tr>
<tr><td>6</td><td>Arkansas</td><td>25.5</td><td>4</td><td>Oklahoma</td><td>26.0</td></tr>
<tr><td>48</td><td>California</td><td>14.7</td><td>5</td><td>Ohio</td><td>25.8</td></tr>
<tr><td>34</td><td>Colorado</td><td>20.0</td><td>6</td><td>Arkansas</td><td>25.5</td></tr>
<tr><td>46</td><td>Connecticut</td><td>18.0</td><td>7</td><td>Alabama</td><td>24.8</td></tr>
<tr><td>11</td><td>Delaware</td><td>24.3</td><td>7</td><td>Alaska</td><td>24.8</td></tr>
<tr><td>32</td><td>Florida</td><td>20.2</td><td>7</td><td>Indiana</td><td>24.8</td></tr>
<tr><td>36</td><td>Georgia</td><td>19.9</td><td>10</td><td>Mississippi</td><td>24.5</td></tr>
<tr><td>NA</td><td>Hawaii**</td><td>NA</td><td>11</td><td>Delaware</td><td>24.3</td></tr>
<tr><td>47</td><td>Idaho</td><td>17.4</td><td>11</td><td>South Carolina</td><td>24.3</td></tr>
<tr><td>19</td><td>Illinois</td><td>22.2</td><td>13</td><td>Missouri</td><td>24.0</td></tr>
<tr><td>7</td><td>Indiana</td><td>24.8</td><td>14</td><td>Louisiana</td><td>23.5</td></tr>
<tr><td>25</td><td>Iowa</td><td>20.8</td><td>15</td><td>Michigan</td><td>23.2</td></tr>
<tr><td>39</td><td>Kansas</td><td>19.8</td><td>15</td><td>Nevada</td><td>23.2</td></tr>
<tr><td>1</td><td>Kentucky</td><td>27.5</td><td>17</td><td>North Carolina</td><td>23.1</td></tr>
<tr><td>14</td><td>Louisiana</td><td>23.5</td><td>18</td><td>Pennsylvania</td><td>22.7</td></tr>
<tr><td>24</td><td>Maine</td><td>20.9</td><td>19</td><td>Illinois</td><td>22.2</td></tr>
<tr><td>41</td><td>Maryland</td><td>19.5</td><td>20</td><td>Wisconsin</td><td>21.9</td></tr>
<tr><td>45</td><td>Massachusetts</td><td>18.4</td><td>21</td><td>Wyoming</td><td>21.7</td></tr>
<tr><td>15</td><td>Michigan</td><td>23.2</td><td>22</td><td>New Hampshire</td><td>21.6</td></tr>
<tr><td>27</td><td>Minnesota</td><td>20.7</td><td>23</td><td>Rhode Island</td><td>21.3</td></tr>
<tr><td>10</td><td>Mississippi</td><td>24.5</td><td>24</td><td>Maine</td><td>20.9</td></tr>
<tr><td>13</td><td>Missouri</td><td>24.0</td><td>25</td><td>Iowa</td><td>20.8</td></tr>
<tr><td>28</td><td>Montana</td><td>20.4</td><td>25</td><td>Virginia</td><td>20.8</td></tr>
<tr><td>32</td><td>Nebraska</td><td>20.2</td><td>27</td><td>Minnesota</td><td>20.7</td></tr>
<tr><td>15</td><td>Nevada</td><td>23.2</td><td>28</td><td>Montana</td><td>20.4</td></tr>
<tr><td>22</td><td>New Hampshire</td><td>21.6</td><td>28</td><td>Texas</td><td>20.4</td></tr>
<tr><td>43</td><td>New Jersey</td><td>18.8</td><td>30</td><td>New Mexico</td><td>20.3</td></tr>
<tr><td>30</td><td>New Mexico</td><td>20.3</td><td>30</td><td>South Dakota</td><td>20.3</td></tr>
<tr><td>36</td><td>New York</td><td>19.9</td><td>32</td><td>Florida</td><td>20.2</td></tr>
<tr><td>17</td><td>North Carolina</td><td>23.1</td><td>32</td><td>Nebraska</td><td>20.2</td></tr>
<tr><td>39</td><td>North Dakota</td><td>19.8</td><td>34</td><td>Colorado</td><td>20.0</td></tr>
<tr><td>5</td><td>Ohio</td><td>25.8</td><td>34</td><td>Oregon</td><td>20.0</td></tr>
<tr><td>4</td><td>Oklahoma</td><td>26.0</td><td>36</td><td>Georgia</td><td>19.9</td></tr>
<tr><td>34</td><td>Oregon</td><td>20.0</td><td>36</td><td>New York</td><td>19.9</td></tr>
<tr><td>18</td><td>Pennsylvania</td><td>22.7</td><td>36</td><td>Vermont</td><td>19.9</td></tr>
<tr><td>23</td><td>Rhode Island</td><td>21.3</td><td>39</td><td>Kansas</td><td>19.8</td></tr>
<tr><td>11</td><td>South Carolina</td><td>24.3</td><td>39</td><td>North Dakota</td><td>19.8</td></tr>
<tr><td>30</td><td>South Dakota</td><td>20.3</td><td>41</td><td>Maryland</td><td>19.5</td></tr>
<tr><td>3</td><td>Tennessee</td><td>26.1</td><td>42</td><td>Washington</td><td>19.2</td></tr>
<tr><td>28</td><td>Texas</td><td>20.4</td><td>43</td><td>New Jersey</td><td>18.8</td></tr>
<tr><td>49</td><td>Utah</td><td>10.4</td><td>44</td><td>Arizona</td><td>18.5</td></tr>
<tr><td>36</td><td>Vermont</td><td>19.9</td><td>45</td><td>Massachusetts</td><td>18.4</td></tr>
<tr><td>25</td><td>Virginia</td><td>20.8</td><td>46</td><td>Connecticut</td><td>18.0</td></tr>
<tr><td>42</td><td>Washington</td><td>19.2</td><td>47</td><td>Idaho</td><td>17.4</td></tr>
<tr><td>2</td><td>West Virginia</td><td>26.8</td><td>48</td><td>California</td><td>14.7</td></tr>
<tr><td>20</td><td>Wisconsin</td><td>21.9</td><td>49</td><td>Utah</td><td>10.4</td></tr>
<tr><td>21</td><td>Wyoming</td><td>21.7</td><td>NA</td><td>Hawaii**</td><td>NA</td></tr>
</table>

District of Columbia   20.8

Source: U.S. Department of Health and Human Services, Centers for Disease Control and Prevention
"2004 Behavioral Risk Factor Surveillance Summary Prevalence Data" (http://apps.nccd.cdc.gov/brfss/)
*Persons 18 and older who have smoked more than 100 cigarettes during their lifetime and who currently smoke everyday or some days.
**Not available.

Percent of Men Who Smoke: 2004

National Median = 23.0% of Men*

ALPHA ORDER

RANK	STATE	PERCENT
3	Alabama	28.9
14	Alaska	26.2
45	Arizona	19.6
5	Arkansas	28.1
48	California	18.4
33	Colorado	22.2
42	Connecticut	20.1
4	Delaware	28.3
24	Florida	23.1
31	Georgia	22.3
NA	Hawaii**	NA
47	Idaho	19.1
15	Illinois	26.0
11	Indiana	26.8
28	Iowa	22.7
34	Kansas	22.1
1	Kentucky	29.3
11	Louisiana	26.8
29	Maine	22.6
30	Maryland	22.5
45	Massachusetts	19.6
17	Michigan	24.9
35	Minnesota	21.9
2	Mississippi	29.1
15	Missouri	26.0
41	Montana	20.6
25	Nebraska	23.0
19	Nevada	24.6
21	New Hampshire	23.8
42	New Jersey	20.1
27	New Mexico	22.8
40	New York	21.0
13	North Carolina	26.5
20	North Dakota	24.0
9	Ohio	27.2
5	Oklahoma	28.1
35	Oregon	21.9
25	Pennsylvania	23.0
22	Rhode Island	23.7
7	South Carolina	28.0
35	South Dakota	21.9
10	Tennessee	27.1
23	Texas	23.6
49	Utah	11.6
38	Vermont	21.7
31	Virginia	22.3
44	Washington	20.0
8	West Virginia	27.4
17	Wisconsin	24.9
39	Wyoming	21.5

RANK ORDER

RANK	STATE	PERCENT
1	Kentucky	29.3
2	Mississippi	29.1
3	Alabama	28.9
4	Delaware	28.3
5	Arkansas	28.1
5	Oklahoma	28.1
7	South Carolina	28.0
8	West Virginia	27.4
9	Ohio	27.2
10	Tennessee	27.1
11	Indiana	26.8
11	Louisiana	26.8
13	North Carolina	26.5
14	Alaska	26.2
15	Illinois	26.0
15	Missouri	26.0
17	Michigan	24.9
17	Wisconsin	24.9
19	Nevada	24.6
20	North Dakota	24.0
21	New Hampshire	23.8
22	Rhode Island	23.7
23	Texas	23.6
24	Florida	23.1
25	Nebraska	23.0
25	Pennsylvania	23.0
27	New Mexico	22.8
28	Iowa	22.7
29	Maine	22.6
30	Maryland	22.5
31	Georgia	22.3
31	Virginia	22.3
33	Colorado	22.2
34	Kansas	22.1
35	Minnesota	21.9
35	Oregon	21.9
35	South Dakota	21.9
38	Vermont	21.7
39	Wyoming	21.5
40	New York	21.0
41	Montana	20.6
42	Connecticut	20.1
42	New Jersey	20.1
44	Washington	20.0
45	Arizona	19.6
45	Massachusetts	19.6
47	Idaho	19.1
48	California	18.4
49	Utah	11.6
NA	Hawaii**	NA

	District of Columbia	25.2

Source: U.S. Department of Health and Human Services, Centers for Disease Control and Prevention
"2004 Behavioral Risk Factor Surveillance System" (http://apps.nccd.cdc.gov/brfss/)
*Males age 18 and older who have smoked more than 100 cigarettes during their lifetime and who currently smoke everyday or some days.
**Not available.

Percent of Women Who Smoke: 2004

National Median = 19.0% of Women*

ALPHA ORDER				RANK ORDER		
RANK	STATE	PERCENT		RANK	STATE	PERCENT
14	Alabama	21.2		1	West Virginia	26.3
6	Alaska	23.3		2	Kentucky	25.8
41	Arizona	17.4		3	Tennessee	25.1
7	Arkansas	23.2		4	Ohio	24.6
48	California	11.1		5	Oklahoma	24.1
35	Colorado	17.7		6	Alaska	23.3
45	Connecticut	16.1		7	Arkansas	23.2
16	Delaware	20.7		8	Indiana	23.0
39	Florida	17.5		9	Pennsylvania	22.4
35	Georgia	17.7		10	Missouri	22.2
NA	Hawaii**	NA		11	Wyoming	21.8
47	Idaho	15.7		12	Michigan	21.7
30	Illinois	18.6		12	Nevada	21.7
8	Indiana	23.0		14	Alabama	21.2
26	Iowa	19.0		15	South Carolina	20.9
39	Kansas	17.5		16	Delaware	20.7
2	Kentucky	25.8		17	Louisiana	20.4
17	Louisiana	20.4		18	Mississippi	20.3
24	Maine	19.3		19	Montana	20.1
44	Maryland	16.7		20	North Carolina	19.9
43	Massachusetts	17.3		21	New Hampshire	19.6
12	Michigan	21.7		22	Minnesota	19.5
22	Minnesota	19.5		23	Virginia	19.4
18	Mississippi	20.3		24	Maine	19.3
10	Missouri	22.2		25	Rhode Island	19.1
19	Montana	20.1		26	Iowa	19.0
37	Nebraska	17.6		27	New York	18.9
12	Nevada	21.7		27	Wisconsin	18.9
21	New Hampshire	19.6		29	South Dakota	18.7
37	New Jersey	17.6		30	Illinois	18.6
34	New Mexico	17.8		31	Washington	18.3
27	New York	18.9		32	Vermont	18.2
20	North Carolina	19.9		33	Oregon	18.1
46	North Dakota	15.8		34	New Mexico	17.8
4	Ohio	24.6		35	Colorado	17.7
5	Oklahoma	24.1		35	Georgia	17.7
33	Oregon	18.1		37	Nebraska	17.6
9	Pennsylvania	22.4		37	New Jersey	17.6
25	Rhode Island	19.1		39	Florida	17.5
15	South Carolina	20.9		39	Kansas	17.5
29	South Dakota	18.7		41	Arizona	17.4
3	Tennessee	25.1		41	Texas	17.4
41	Texas	17.4		43	Massachusetts	17.3
49	Utah	9.3		44	Maryland	16.7
32	Vermont	18.2		45	Connecticut	16.1
23	Virginia	19.4		46	North Dakota	15.8
31	Washington	18.3		47	Idaho	15.7
1	West Virginia	26.3		48	California	11.1
27	Wisconsin	18.9		49	Utah	9.3
11	Wyoming	21.8		NA	Hawaii**	NA
					District of Columbia	17.1

Source: U.S. Department of Health and Human Services, Centers for Disease Control and Prevention
  "2004 Behavioral Risk Factor Surveillance System" (http://apps.nccd.cdc.gov/brfss/)
Females age 18 and older who have smoked more than 100 cigarettes during their lifetime and who currently smoke everyday or some days.
**Not available.*

Percent of Adults Who are Former Smokers: 2004

National Median = 23.9% of Adults*

ALPHA ORDER

RANK	STATE	PERCENT
44	Alabama	20.8
26	Alaska	23.9
17	Arizona	24.4
16	Arkansas	24.6
22	California	24.1
20	Colorado	24.3
3	Connecticut	30.0
10	Delaware	25.1
8	Florida	25.8
43	Georgia	20.9
NA	Hawaii**	NA
30	Idaho	23.3
39	Illinois	21.5
33	Indiana	22.6
40	Iowa	21.3
38	Kansas	21.6
45	Kentucky	20.3
47	Louisiana	19.9
1	Maine	31.2
32	Maryland	22.9
6	Massachusetts	26.9
10	Michigan	25.1
7	Minnesota	26.7
48	Mississippi	19.2
22	Missouri	24.1
13	Montana	25.0
42	Nebraska	21.1
17	Nevada	24.4
5	New Hampshire	28.5
17	New Jersey	24.4
22	New Mexico	24.1
22	New York	24.1
41	North Carolina	21.2
28	North Dakota	23.6
35	Ohio	22.1
34	Oklahoma	22.5
15	Oregon	24.7
27	Pennsylvania	23.8
4	Rhode Island	28.7
37	South Carolina	21.8
28	South Dakota	23.6
35	Tennessee	22.1
46	Texas	20.2
49	Utah	15.7
2	Vermont	30.5
30	Virginia	23.3
9	Washington	25.3
10	West Virginia	25.1
21	Wisconsin	24.2
14	Wyoming	24.8

RANK ORDER

RANK	STATE	PERCENT
1	Maine	31.2
2	Vermont	30.5
3	Connecticut	30.0
4	Rhode Island	28.7
5	New Hampshire	28.5
6	Massachusetts	26.9
7	Minnesota	26.7
8	Florida	25.8
9	Washington	25.3
10	Delaware	25.1
10	Michigan	25.1
10	West Virginia	25.1
13	Montana	25.0
14	Wyoming	24.8
15	Oregon	24.7
16	Arkansas	24.6
17	Arizona	24.4
17	Nevada	24.4
17	New Jersey	24.4
20	Colorado	24.3
21	Wisconsin	24.2
22	California	24.1
22	Missouri	24.1
22	New Mexico	24.1
22	New York	24.1
26	Alaska	23.9
27	Pennsylvania	23.8
28	North Dakota	23.6
28	South Dakota	23.6
30	Idaho	23.3
30	Virginia	23.3
32	Maryland	22.9
33	Indiana	22.6
34	Oklahoma	22.5
35	Ohio	22.1
35	Tennessee	22.1
37	South Carolina	21.8
38	Kansas	21.6
39	Illinois	21.5
40	Iowa	21.3
41	North Carolina	21.2
42	Nebraska	21.1
43	Georgia	20.9
44	Alabama	20.8
45	Kentucky	20.3
46	Texas	20.2
47	Louisiana	19.9
48	Mississippi	19.2
49	Utah	15.7
NA	Hawaii**	NA

District of Columbia 19.1

Source: U.S. Department of Health and Human Services, Centers for Disease Control and Prevention
"2004 Behavioral Risk Factor Surveillance Summary Prevalence Data" (http://apps.nccd.cdc.gov/brfss/)
*Persons 18 and older who have smoked more than 100 cigarettes during their lifetime and who currently do not smoke.
**Not available.

Percent of Adults Who Have Never Smoked: 2004

National Median = 54.9% of Adults*

ALPHA ORDER				RANK ORDER		
RANK	STATE	PERCENT		RANK	STATE	PERCENT
26	Alabama	54.2		1	Utah	73.7
42	Alaska	51.1		2	California	61.0
10	Arizona	56.9		3	Texas	59.2
45	Arkansas	49.7		4	Georgia	59.1
2	California	61.0		4	Idaho	59.1
20	Colorado	55.5		6	Nebraska	58.5
37	Connecticut	51.9		7	Kansas	58.4
43	Delaware	50.4		8	Iowa	57.7
27	Florida	53.9		9	Maryland	57.4
4	Georgia	59.1		10	Arizona	56.9
NA	Hawaii**	NA		11	New Jersey	56.7
4	Idaho	59.1		12	Louisiana	56.4
14	Illinois	56.2		12	North Dakota	56.4
32	Indiana	52.5		14	Illinois	56.2
8	Iowa	57.7		15	Mississippi	56.1
7	Kansas	58.4		16	South Dakota	56.0
35	Kentucky	52.1		17	New York	55.8
12	Louisiana	56.4		17	Virginia	55.8
49	Maine	47.7		19	North Carolina	55.6
9	Maryland	57.4		20	Colorado	55.5
24	Massachusetts	54.5		20	New Mexico	55.5
40	Michigan	51.5		22	Washington	55.4
32	Minnesota	52.5		23	Oregon	55.2
15	Mississippi	56.1		24	Massachusetts	54.5
38	Missouri	51.7		24	Montana	54.5
24	Montana	54.5		26	Alabama	54.2
6	Nebraska	58.5		27	Florida	53.9
34	Nevada	52.3		28	Wisconsin	53.8
45	New Hampshire	49.7		29	South Carolina	53.7
11	New Jersey	56.7		30	Wyoming	53.4
20	New Mexico	55.5		31	Pennsylvania	53.3
17	New York	55.8		32	Indiana	52.5
19	North Carolina	55.6		32	Minnesota	52.5
12	North Dakota	56.4		34	Nevada	52.3
36	Ohio	52.0		35	Kentucky	52.1
41	Oklahoma	51.3		36	Ohio	52.0
23	Oregon	55.2		37	Connecticut	51.9
31	Pennsylvania	53.3		38	Missouri	51.7
44	Rhode Island	49.8		39	Tennessee	51.6
29	South Carolina	53.7		40	Michigan	51.5
16	South Dakota	56.0		41	Oklahoma	51.3
39	Tennessee	51.6		42	Alaska	51.1
3	Texas	59.2		43	Delaware	50.4
1	Utah	73.7		44	Rhode Island	49.8
47	Vermont	49.4		45	Arkansas	49.7
17	Virginia	55.8		45	New Hampshire	49.7
22	Washington	55.4		47	Vermont	49.4
48	West Virginia	48.0		48	West Virginia	48.0
28	Wisconsin	53.8		49	Maine	47.7
30	Wyoming	53.4		NA	Hawaii**	NA

District of Columbia   59.9

Source: U.S. Department of Health and Human Services, Centers for Disease Control and Prevention
"2004 Behavioral Risk Factor Surveillance Summary Prevalence Data" (http://apps.nccd.cdc.gov/brfss/)
*Persons 18 and older who have not smoked more than 100 cigarettes during their lifetime.
**Not available.

Percent of Population Who are Illicit Drug Users: 2003

National Percent = 8.3% of Population*

ALPHA ORDER

RANK	STATE	PERCENT
46	Alabama	6.6
1	Alaska	12.0
16	Arizona	8.9
28	Arkansas	7.8
15	California	9.0
3	Colorado	11.1
19	Connecticut	8.8
20	Delaware	8.7
20	Florida	8.7
33	Georgia	7.5
16	Hawaii	8.9
38	Idaho	7.2
33	Illinois	7.5
24	Indiana	8.1
49	Iowa	6.5
44	Kansas	6.7
23	Kentucky	8.3
24	Louisiana	8.1
11	Maine	9.3
31	Maryland	7.6
11	Massachusetts	9.3
14	Michigan	9.1
31	Minnesota	7.6
46	Mississippi	6.6
13	Missouri	9.2
7	Montana	10.6
29	Nebraska	7.7
8	Nevada	10.3
2	New Hampshire	11.2
42	New Jersey	7.0
9	New Mexico	10.0
16	New York	8.9
27	North Carolina	7.9
38	North Dakota	7.2
26	Ohio	8.0
22	Oklahoma	8.6
6	Oregon	10.8
33	Pennsylvania	7.5
4	Rhode Island	11.0
38	South Carolina	7.2
38	South Dakota	7.2
44	Tennessee	6.7
42	Texas	7.0
50	Utah	6.3
4	Vermont	11.0
29	Virginia	7.7
9	Washington	10.0
46	West Virginia	6.6
33	Wisconsin	7.5
33	Wyoming	7.5

RANK ORDER

RANK	STATE	PERCENT
1	Alaska	12.0
2	New Hampshire	11.2
3	Colorado	11.1
4	Rhode Island	11.0
4	Vermont	11.0
6	Oregon	10.8
7	Montana	10.6
8	Nevada	10.3
9	New Mexico	10.0
9	Washington	10.0
11	Maine	9.3
11	Massachusetts	9.3
13	Missouri	9.2
14	Michigan	9.1
15	California	9.0
16	Arizona	8.9
16	Hawaii	8.9
16	New York	8.9
19	Connecticut	8.8
20	Delaware	8.7
20	Florida	8.7
22	Oklahoma	8.6
23	Kentucky	8.3
24	Indiana	8.1
24	Louisiana	8.1
26	Ohio	8.0
27	North Carolina	7.9
28	Arkansas	7.8
29	Nebraska	7.7
29	Virginia	7.7
31	Maryland	7.6
31	Minnesota	7.6
33	Georgia	7.5
33	Illinois	7.5
33	Pennsylvania	7.5
33	Wisconsin	7.5
33	Wyoming	7.5
38	Idaho	7.2
38	North Dakota	7.2
38	South Carolina	7.2
38	South Dakota	7.2
42	New Jersey	7.0
42	Texas	7.0
44	Kansas	6.7
44	Tennessee	6.7
46	Alabama	6.6
46	Mississippi	6.6
46	West Virginia	6.6
49	Iowa	6.5
50	Utah	6.3

District of Columbia	11.6

Source: U.S. Department of Health and Human Services, Substance Abuse and Mental Health Services Administration
"2002/2003 National Survey on Drug Use and Health" (January 2005)
*Population 12 years and older who used any illicit drug at least once within month of survey.

Percent of Adults Obese: 2004

National Median = 23.1% of Adults*

<table>
<tr><td colspan="3">ALPHA ORDER</td><td colspan="3">RANK ORDER</td></tr>
<tr><td>RANK</td><td>STATE</td><td>PERCENT</td><td>RANK</td><td>STATE</td><td>PERCENT</td></tr>
<tr><td>2</td><td>Alabama</td><td>28.8</td><td>1</td><td>Mississippi</td><td>29.4</td></tr>
<tr><td>21</td><td>Alaska</td><td>23.6</td><td>2</td><td>Alabama</td><td>28.8</td></tr>
<tr><td>38</td><td>Arizona</td><td>21.1</td><td>3</td><td>West Virginia</td><td>27.6</td></tr>
<tr><td>6</td><td>Arkansas</td><td>26.0</td><td>4</td><td>Tennessee</td><td>27.1</td></tr>
<tr><td>31</td><td>California</td><td>22.2</td><td>5</td><td>Louisiana</td><td>26.9</td></tr>
<tr><td>49</td><td>Colorado</td><td>16.7</td><td>6</td><td>Arkansas</td><td>26.0</td></tr>
<tr><td>45</td><td>Connecticut</td><td>19.6</td><td>7</td><td>Kentucky</td><td>25.8</td></tr>
<tr><td>39</td><td>Delaware</td><td>21.0</td><td>8</td><td>Texas</td><td>25.7</td></tr>
<tr><td>29</td><td>Florida</td><td>22.8</td><td>9</td><td>Indiana</td><td>25.5</td></tr>
<tr><td>15</td><td>Georgia</td><td>24.7</td><td>10</td><td>Michigan</td><td>25.4</td></tr>
<tr><td>NA</td><td>Hawaii**</td><td>NA</td><td>11</td><td>Ohio</td><td>25.2</td></tr>
<tr><td>41</td><td>Idaho</td><td>20.8</td><td>12</td><td>South Carolina</td><td>25.0</td></tr>
<tr><td>28</td><td>Illinois</td><td>22.9</td><td>13</td><td>Missouri</td><td>24.9</td></tr>
<tr><td>9</td><td>Indiana</td><td>25.5</td><td>14</td><td>Oklahoma</td><td>24.8</td></tr>
<tr><td>22</td><td>Iowa</td><td>23.5</td><td>15</td><td>Georgia</td><td>24.7</td></tr>
<tr><td>25</td><td>Kansas</td><td>23.1</td><td>16</td><td>North Dakota</td><td>24.5</td></tr>
<tr><td>7</td><td>Kentucky</td><td>25.8</td><td>17</td><td>North Carolina</td><td>24.2</td></tr>
<tr><td>5</td><td>Louisiana</td><td>26.9</td><td>17</td><td>Pennsylvania</td><td>24.2</td></tr>
<tr><td>23</td><td>Maine</td><td>23.3</td><td>19</td><td>Maryland</td><td>23.9</td></tr>
<tr><td>19</td><td>Maryland</td><td>23.9</td><td>20</td><td>South Dakota</td><td>23.8</td></tr>
<tr><td>48</td><td>Massachusetts</td><td>18.3</td><td>21</td><td>Alaska</td><td>23.6</td></tr>
<tr><td>10</td><td>Michigan</td><td>25.4</td><td>22</td><td>Iowa</td><td>23.5</td></tr>
<tr><td>30</td><td>Minnesota</td><td>22.6</td><td>23</td><td>Maine</td><td>23.3</td></tr>
<tr><td>1</td><td>Mississippi</td><td>29.4</td><td>24</td><td>Wisconsin</td><td>23.2</td></tr>
<tr><td>13</td><td>Missouri</td><td>24.9</td><td>25</td><td>Kansas</td><td>23.1</td></tr>
<tr><td>44</td><td>Montana</td><td>19.7</td><td>25</td><td>Nebraska</td><td>23.1</td></tr>
<tr><td>25</td><td>Nebraska</td><td>23.1</td><td>27</td><td>Virginia</td><td>23.0</td></tr>
<tr><td>39</td><td>Nevada</td><td>21.0</td><td>28</td><td>Illinois</td><td>22.9</td></tr>
<tr><td>35</td><td>New Hampshire</td><td>21.5</td><td>29</td><td>Florida</td><td>22.8</td></tr>
<tr><td>34</td><td>New Jersey</td><td>21.9</td><td>30</td><td>Minnesota</td><td>22.6</td></tr>
<tr><td>36</td><td>New Mexico</td><td>21.4</td><td>31</td><td>California</td><td>22.2</td></tr>
<tr><td>33</td><td>New York</td><td>22.0</td><td>32</td><td>Washington</td><td>22.1</td></tr>
<tr><td>17</td><td>North Carolina</td><td>24.2</td><td>33</td><td>New York</td><td>22.0</td></tr>
<tr><td>16</td><td>North Dakota</td><td>24.5</td><td>34</td><td>New Jersey</td><td>21.9</td></tr>
<tr><td>11</td><td>Ohio</td><td>25.2</td><td>35</td><td>New Hampshire</td><td>21.5</td></tr>
<tr><td>14</td><td>Oklahoma</td><td>24.8</td><td>36</td><td>New Mexico</td><td>21.4</td></tr>
<tr><td>37</td><td>Oregon</td><td>21.2</td><td>37</td><td>Oregon</td><td>21.2</td></tr>
<tr><td>17</td><td>Pennsylvania</td><td>24.2</td><td>38</td><td>Arizona</td><td>21.1</td></tr>
<tr><td>46</td><td>Rhode Island</td><td>18.9</td><td>39</td><td>Delaware</td><td>21.0</td></tr>
<tr><td>12</td><td>South Carolina</td><td>25.0</td><td>39</td><td>Nevada</td><td>21.0</td></tr>
<tr><td>20</td><td>South Dakota</td><td>23.8</td><td>41</td><td>Idaho</td><td>20.8</td></tr>
<tr><td>4</td><td>Tennessee</td><td>27.1</td><td>42</td><td>Wyoming</td><td>20.7</td></tr>
<tr><td>8</td><td>Texas</td><td>25.7</td><td>43</td><td>Utah</td><td>20.3</td></tr>
<tr><td>43</td><td>Utah</td><td>20.3</td><td>44</td><td>Montana</td><td>19.7</td></tr>
<tr><td>47</td><td>Vermont</td><td>18.6</td><td>45</td><td>Connecticut</td><td>19.6</td></tr>
<tr><td>27</td><td>Virginia</td><td>23.0</td><td>46</td><td>Rhode Island</td><td>18.9</td></tr>
<tr><td>32</td><td>Washington</td><td>22.1</td><td>47</td><td>Vermont</td><td>18.6</td></tr>
<tr><td>3</td><td>West Virginia</td><td>27.6</td><td>48</td><td>Massachusetts</td><td>18.3</td></tr>
<tr><td>24</td><td>Wisconsin</td><td>23.2</td><td>49</td><td>Colorado</td><td>16.7</td></tr>
<tr><td>42</td><td>Wyoming</td><td>20.7</td><td>NA</td><td>Hawaii**</td><td>NA</td></tr>
<tr><td></td><td></td><td></td><td></td><td>District of Columbia</td><td>22.5</td></tr>
</table>

Source: U.S. Department of Health and Human Services, Centers for Disease Control and Prevention
"2004 Behavioral Risk Factor Surveillance Summary Prevalence Data" (http://apps.nccd.cdc.gov/brfss/)
Persons 18 and older. Obese is defined as a Body Mass Index (BMI) of 30.0 or more regardless of sex. BMI is a ratio of height to weight. As an example, a person 5' 8" and weighing 197 pounds has a BMI of 30.
See http://www.cdc.gov/nccdphp/dnpa/bmi/bmi-adult.htm.
**Not available.*

Percent of Adults Overweight: 2004

National Median = 36.8% of Adults*

ALPHA ORDER

RANK	STATE	PERCENT
41	Alabama	35.8
1	Alaska	38.8
47	Arizona	34.9
32	Arkansas	36.3
6	California	37.9
33	Colorado	36.2
29	Connecticut	36.4
3	Delaware	38.6
23	Florida	36.8
48	Georgia	34.7
NA	Hawaii**	NA
14	Idaho	37.3
28	Illinois	36.5
27	Indiana	36.6
14	Iowa	37.3
11	Kansas	37.5
11	Kentucky	37.5
43	Louisiana	35.6
11	Maine	37.5
49	Maryland	34.6
35	Massachusetts	36.1
46	Michigan	35.4
10	Minnesota	37.6
39	Mississippi	36.0
23	Missouri	36.8
14	Montana	37.3
4	Nebraska	38.5
1	Nevada	38.8
35	New Hampshire	36.1
8	New Jersey	37.7
29	New Mexico	36.4
43	New York	35.6
18	North Carolina	37.1
5	North Dakota	38.3
41	Ohio	35.8
35	Oklahoma	36.1
8	Oregon	37.7
23	Pennsylvania	36.8
20	Rhode Island	37.0
35	South Carolina	36.1
6	South Dakota	37.9
21	Tennessee	36.9
18	Texas	37.1
39	Utah	36.0
43	Vermont	35.6
23	Virginia	36.8
33	Washington	36.2
29	West Virginia	36.4
17	Wisconsin	37.2
21	Wyoming	36.9

RANK ORDER

RANK	STATE	PERCENT
1	Alaska	38.8
1	Nevada	38.8
3	Delaware	38.6
4	Nebraska	38.5
5	North Dakota	38.3
6	California	37.9
6	South Dakota	37.9
8	New Jersey	37.7
8	Oregon	37.7
10	Minnesota	37.6
11	Kansas	37.5
11	Kentucky	37.5
11	Maine	37.5
14	Idaho	37.3
14	Iowa	37.3
14	Montana	37.3
17	Wisconsin	37.2
18	North Carolina	37.1
18	Texas	37.1
20	Rhode Island	37.0
21	Tennessee	36.9
21	Wyoming	36.9
23	Florida	36.8
23	Missouri	36.8
23	Pennsylvania	36.8
23	Virginia	36.8
27	Indiana	36.6
28	Illinois	36.5
29	Connecticut	36.4
29	New Mexico	36.4
29	West Virginia	36.4
32	Arkansas	36.3
33	Colorado	36.2
33	Washington	36.2
35	Massachusetts	36.1
35	New Hampshire	36.1
35	Oklahoma	36.1
35	South Carolina	36.1
39	Mississippi	36.0
39	Utah	36.0
41	Alabama	35.8
41	Ohio	35.8
43	Louisiana	35.6
43	New York	35.6
43	Vermont	35.6
46	Michigan	35.4
47	Arizona	34.9
48	Georgia	34.7
49	Maryland	34.6
NA	Hawaii**	NA

District of Columbia	33.0

Source: U.S. Department of Health and Human Services, Centers for Disease Control and Prevention
"2004 Behavioral Risk Factor Surveillance Summary Prevalence Data" (http://apps.nccd.cdc.gov/brfss/)
*Persons 18 and older. Does not include obese adults. Overweight is defined as a Body Mass Index (BMI) of 25.0 to 29.9 regardless of sex. BMI is a ratio of height to weight. As an example, a person 5' 8" and weighing 171 pounds has a BMI of 26. See http://www.cdc.gov/nccdphp/dnpa/bmi/bmi-adult.htm.

Percent of Adults at Risk for Health Problems
Because of Being Overweight: 2003
National Median = 60.1% of Adults*

RANK	STATE	PERCENT
2	Alabama	63.2
17	Alaska	60.7
38	Arizona	57.1
5	Arkansas	62.0
27	California	59.3
49	Colorado	51.4
46	Connecticut	54.8
22	Delaware	60.2
31	Florida	58.6
18	Georgia	60.6
50	Hawaii	50.0
29	Idaho	59.0
11	Illinois	61.1
7	Indiana	61.7
9	Iowa	61.6
19	Kansas	60.5
3	Kentucky	63.1
11	Louisiana	61.1
35	Maine	58.2
29	Maryland	59.0
48	Massachusetts	53.0
6	Michigan	61.8
14	Minnesota	60.9
1	Mississippi	64.9
28	Missouri	59.2
41	Montana	56.9
14	Nebraska	60.9
32	Nevada	58.5
40	New Hampshire	57.0
37	New Jersey	57.2
43	New Mexico	56.6
44	New York	56.3
13	North Carolina	61.0
4	North Dakota	63.0
14	Ohio	60.9
19	Oklahoma	60.5
34	Oregon	58.3
22	Pennsylvania	60.2
41	Rhode Island	56.9
22	South Carolina	60.2
25	South Dakota	60.1
21	Tennessee	60.4
10	Texas	61.5
47	Utah	54.7
45	Vermont	55.5
36	Virginia	57.7
32	Washington	58.5
7	West Virginia	61.7
26	Wisconsin	60.0
38	Wyoming	57.1

RANK	STATE	PERCENT
1	Mississippi	64.9
2	Alabama	63.2
3	Kentucky	63.1
4	North Dakota	63.0
5	Arkansas	62.0
6	Michigan	61.8
7	Indiana	61.7
7	West Virginia	61.7
9	Iowa	61.6
10	Texas	61.5
11	Illinois	61.1
11	Louisiana	61.1
13	North Carolina	61.0
14	Minnesota	60.9
14	Nebraska	60.9
14	Ohio	60.9
17	Alaska	60.7
18	Georgia	60.6
19	Kansas	60.5
19	Oklahoma	60.5
21	Tennessee	60.4
22	Delaware	60.2
22	Pennsylvania	60.2
22	South Carolina	60.2
25	South Dakota	60.1
26	Wisconsin	60.0
27	California	59.3
28	Missouri	59.2
29	Idaho	59.0
29	Maryland	59.0
31	Florida	58.6
32	Nevada	58.5
32	Washington	58.5
34	Oregon	58.3
35	Maine	58.2
36	Virginia	57.7
37	New Jersey	57.2
38	Arizona	57.1
38	Wyoming	57.1
40	New Hampshire	57.0
41	Montana	56.9
41	Rhode Island	56.9
43	New Mexico	56.6
44	New York	56.3
45	Vermont	55.5
46	Connecticut	54.8
47	Utah	54.7
48	Massachusetts	53.0
49	Colorado	51.4
50	Hawaii	50.0

	District of Columbia	52.1

Source: U.S. Department of Health and Human Services, Centers for Disease Control and Prevention
"2003 Behavioral Risk Factor Surveillance Summary Prevalence Data" (http://apps.nccd.cdc.gov/brfss/)
*Persons 18 and older. "At risk for health problems" is defined according to the NHANES II definition of a Body
Mass Index (BMI) of 27.8 for men and 27.3 for women. BMI is a ratio of height to weight. As an example, a person
5' 8" and weighing 197 pounds has a BMI of 30. See http://www.cdc.gov/nccdphp/dnpa/bmi/bmi-adult.htm.

Percent of Adults Who Do Not Exercise: 2004

National Median = 22.8% of Adults*

ALPHA ORDER

RANK ORDER

RANK	STATE	PERCENT
4	Alabama	29.6
35	Alaska	20.5
18	Arizona	24.2
7	Arkansas	26.5
25	California	22.7
42	Colorado	18.7
40	Connecticut	18.8
28	Delaware	21.8
22	Florida	23.6
10	Georgia	25.7
NA	Hawaii**	NA
38	Idaho	19.0
13	Illinois	24.8
12	Indiana	25.3
32	Iowa	21.3
23	Kansas	23.2
2	Kentucky	29.8
3	Louisiana	29.7
30	Maine	21.5
28	Maryland	21.8
37	Massachusetts	19.9
26	Michigan	22.1
49	Minnesota	15.8
1	Mississippi	31.3
13	Missouri	24.8
40	Montana	18.8
30	Nebraska	21.5
18	Nevada	24.2
43	New Hampshire	18.5
11	New Jersey	25.6
34	New Mexico	21.1
7	New York	26.5
15	North Carolina	24.7
32	North Dakota	21.3
24	Ohio	22.9
6	Oklahoma	27.7
47	Oregon	17.1
17	Pennsylvania	24.3
18	Rhode Island	24.2
21	South Carolina	23.8
39	South Dakota	18.9
4	Tennessee	29.6
9	Texas	26.1
48	Utah	16.8
45	Vermont	18.1
27	Virginia	21.9
46	Washington	17.2
16	West Virginia	24.5
44	Wisconsin	18.4
36	Wyoming	20.1

RANK	STATE	PERCENT
1	Mississippi	31.3
2	Kentucky	29.8
3	Louisiana	29.7
4	Alabama	29.6
4	Tennessee	29.6
6	Oklahoma	27.7
7	Arkansas	26.5
7	New York	26.5
9	Texas	26.1
10	Georgia	25.7
11	New Jersey	25.6
12	Indiana	25.3
13	Illinois	24.8
13	Missouri	24.8
15	North Carolina	24.7
16	West Virginia	24.5
17	Pennsylvania	24.3
18	Arizona	24.2
18	Nevada	24.2
18	Rhode Island	24.2
21	South Carolina	23.8
22	Florida	23.6
23	Kansas	23.2
24	Ohio	22.9
25	California	22.7
26	Michigan	22.1
27	Virginia	21.9
28	Delaware	21.8
28	Maryland	21.8
30	Maine	21.5
30	Nebraska	21.5
32	Iowa	21.3
32	North Dakota	21.3
34	New Mexico	21.1
35	Alaska	20.5
36	Wyoming	20.1
37	Massachusetts	19.9
38	Idaho	19.0
39	South Dakota	18.9
40	Connecticut	18.8
40	Montana	18.8
42	Colorado	18.7
43	New Hampshire	18.5
44	Wisconsin	18.4
45	Vermont	18.1
46	Washington	17.2
47	Oregon	17.1
48	Utah	16.8
49	Minnesota	15.8
NA	Hawaii**	NA

District of Columbia   22.2

Source: U.S. Department of Health and Human Services, Centers for Disease Control and Prevention
"2004 Behavioral Risk Factor Surveillance Summary Prevalence Data" (http://apps.nccd.cdc.gov/brfss/)
*Persons 18 and older who, in the previous month, did not participate in any physical activities.
**Not available.

Percent of Adults Who Exercise Vigorously: 2003

National Median = 26.3% of Adults*

ALPHA ORDER

RANK	STATE	PERCENT
43	Alabama	21.3
2	Alaska	34.6
16	Arizona	29.1
36	Arkansas	23.3
19	California	28.6
4	Colorado	32.9
11	Connecticut	30.6
35	Delaware	23.4
42	Florida	21.4
32	Georgia	24.9
25	Hawaii	26.3
7	Idaho	31.8
34	Illinois	23.5
31	Indiana	25.3
44	Iowa	20.9
37	Kansas	22.8
50	Kentucky	16.3
41	Louisiana	21.5
16	Maine	29.1
18	Maryland	28.8
9	Massachusetts	31.1
23	Michigan	26.6
24	Minnesota	26.4
45	Mississippi	20.2
38	Missouri	22.5
3	Montana	33.2
40	Nebraska	21.6
13	Nevada	30.3
10	New Hampshire	31.0
30	New Jersey	25.4
19	New Mexico	28.6
33	New York	24.5
48	North Carolina	19.3
22	North Dakota	26.7
27	Ohio	26.1
47	Oklahoma	19.5
12	Oregon	30.4
25	Pennsylvania	26.3
15	Rhode Island	29.5
29	South Carolina	25.9
39	South Dakota	22.0
46	Tennessee	20.0
27	Texas	26.1
1	Utah	35.5
5	Vermont	32.3
21	Virginia	28.1
8	Washington	31.3
49	West Virginia	19.1
14	Wisconsin	30.2
6	Wyoming	32.1

RANK ORDER

RANK	STATE	PERCENT
1	Utah	35.5
2	Alaska	34.6
3	Montana	33.2
4	Colorado	32.9
5	Vermont	32.3
6	Wyoming	32.1
7	Idaho	31.8
8	Washington	31.3
9	Massachusetts	31.1
10	New Hampshire	31.0
11	Connecticut	30.6
12	Oregon	30.4
13	Nevada	30.3
14	Wisconsin	30.2
15	Rhode Island	29.5
16	Arizona	29.1
16	Maine	29.1
18	Maryland	28.8
19	California	28.6
19	New Mexico	28.6
21	Virginia	28.1
22	North Dakota	26.7
23	Michigan	26.6
24	Minnesota	26.4
25	Hawaii	26.3
25	Pennsylvania	26.3
27	Ohio	26.1
27	Texas	26.1
29	South Carolina	25.9
30	New Jersey	25.4
31	Indiana	25.3
32	Georgia	24.9
33	New York	24.5
34	Illinois	23.5
35	Delaware	23.4
36	Arkansas	23.3
37	Kansas	22.8
38	Missouri	22.5
39	South Dakota	22.0
40	Nebraska	21.6
41	Louisiana	21.5
42	Florida	21.4
43	Alabama	21.3
44	Iowa	20.9
45	Mississippi	20.2
46	Tennessee	20.0
47	Oklahoma	19.5
48	North Carolina	19.3
49	West Virginia	19.1
50	Kentucky	16.3

| | District of Columbia | 32.9 |

Source: U.S. Department of Health and Human Services, Centers for Disease Control and Prevention
"2003 Behavioral Risk Factor Surveillance Summary Prevalence Data" (http://apps.nccd.cdc.gov/brfss/)
*Persons 18 and older. Activity that caused large increases in breathing or heart rate at least 20 minutes three or more times per week (such as running, aerobics or heavy yard work).

Percent of Adults with High Blood Pressure: 2003

National Median = 24.8% of Adults*

ALPHA ORDER

RANK	STATE	PERCENT
3	Alabama	33.1
48	Alaska	20.8
43	Arizona	22.7
4	Arkansas	30.5
37	California	23.4
49	Colorado	19.8
29	Connecticut	24.2
14	Delaware	27.7
7	Florida	29.3
12	Georgia	28.0
39	Hawaii	23.2
40	Idaho	23.1
30	Illinois	24.1
16	Indiana	27.0
23	Iowa	25.1
38	Kansas	23.3
6	Kentucky	29.8
8	Louisiana	29.0
20	Maine	26.0
24	Maryland	25.0
40	Massachusetts	23.1
17	Michigan	26.8
45	Minnesota	22.2
2	Mississippi	33.4
15	Missouri	27.5
46	Montana	21.3
36	Nebraska	23.5
35	Nevada	23.6
44	New Hampshire	22.5
21	New Jersey	25.6
47	New Mexico	21.1
22	New York	25.3
11	North Carolina	28.6
31	North Dakota	24.0
19	Ohio	26.3
12	Oklahoma	28.0
31	Oregon	24.0
18	Pennsylvania	26.5
9	Rhode Island	28.9
10	South Carolina	28.8
25	South Dakota	24.8
5	Tennessee	30.3
26	Texas	24.6
50	Utah	18.8
40	Vermont	23.1
27	Virginia	24.4
33	Washington	23.8
1	West Virginia	33.6
28	Wisconsin	24.3
33	Wyoming	23.8

RANK ORDER

RANK	STATE	PERCENT
1	West Virginia	33.6
2	Mississippi	33.4
3	Alabama	33.1
4	Arkansas	30.5
5	Tennessee	30.3
6	Kentucky	29.8
7	Florida	29.3
8	Louisiana	29.0
9	Rhode Island	28.9
10	South Carolina	28.8
11	North Carolina	28.6
12	Georgia	28.0
12	Oklahoma	28.0
14	Delaware	27.7
15	Missouri	27.5
16	Indiana	27.0
17	Michigan	26.8
18	Pennsylvania	26.5
19	Ohio	26.3
20	Maine	26.0
21	New Jersey	25.6
22	New York	25.3
23	Iowa	25.1
24	Maryland	25.0
25	South Dakota	24.8
26	Texas	24.6
27	Virginia	24.4
28	Wisconsin	24.3
29	Connecticut	24.2
30	Illinois	24.1
31	North Dakota	24.0
31	Oregon	24.0
33	Washington	23.8
33	Wyoming	23.8
35	Nevada	23.6
36	Nebraska	23.5
37	California	23.4
38	Kansas	23.3
39	Hawaii	23.2
40	Idaho	23.1
40	Massachusetts	23.1
40	Vermont	23.1
43	Arizona	22.7
44	New Hampshire	22.5
45	Minnesota	22.2
46	Montana	21.3
47	New Mexico	21.1
48	Alaska	20.8
49	Colorado	19.8
50	Utah	18.8

District of Columbia	25.2

Source: U.S. Department of Health and Human Services, Centers for Disease Control and Prevention
    "2003 Behavioral Risk Factor Surveillance Summary Prevalence Data" (http://apps.nccd.cdc.gov/brfss/)
*Persons 18 and older who have been told by a doctor, nurse or other health professional that they have high blood pressure.

Percent of Adults with High Cholesterol: 2003

National Median = 33.1% of Adults*

<table>
<tr><td colspan="3">ALPHA ORDER</td><td colspan="3">RANK ORDER</td></tr>
<tr><td>RANK</td><td>STATE</td><td>PERCENT</td><td>RANK</td><td>STATE</td><td>PERCENT</td></tr>
<tr><td>4</td><td>Alabama</td><td>36.0</td><td>1</td><td>Michigan</td><td>38.2</td></tr>
<tr><td>48</td><td>Alaska</td><td>27.6</td><td>2</td><td>West Virginia</td><td>38.1</td></tr>
<tr><td>13</td><td>Arizona</td><td>34.6</td><td>3</td><td>Nevada</td><td>36.8</td></tr>
<tr><td>11</td><td>Arkansas</td><td>34.8</td><td>4</td><td>Alabama</td><td>36.0</td></tr>
<tr><td>31</td><td>California</td><td>32.7</td><td>5</td><td>Kentucky</td><td>35.5</td></tr>
<tr><td>35</td><td>Colorado</td><td>31.9</td><td>6</td><td>Pennsylvania</td><td>35.2</td></tr>
<tr><td>40</td><td>Connecticut</td><td>30.8</td><td>7</td><td>Florida</td><td>35.1</td></tr>
<tr><td>12</td><td>Delaware</td><td>34.7</td><td>7</td><td>Indiana</td><td>35.1</td></tr>
<tr><td>7</td><td>Florida</td><td>35.1</td><td>9</td><td>New York</td><td>34.9</td></tr>
<tr><td>26</td><td>Georgia</td><td>33.2</td><td>9</td><td>Wyoming</td><td>34.9</td></tr>
<tr><td>50</td><td>Hawaii</td><td>27.0</td><td>11</td><td>Arkansas</td><td>34.8</td></tr>
<tr><td>38</td><td>Idaho</td><td>31.1</td><td>12</td><td>Delaware</td><td>34.7</td></tr>
<tr><td>20</td><td>Illinois</td><td>33.6</td><td>13</td><td>Arizona</td><td>34.6</td></tr>
<tr><td>7</td><td>Indiana</td><td>35.1</td><td>14</td><td>Texas</td><td>34.3</td></tr>
<tr><td>36</td><td>Iowa</td><td>31.7</td><td>15</td><td>Oregon</td><td>34.1</td></tr>
<tr><td>46</td><td>Kansas</td><td>29.4</td><td>16</td><td>North Carolina</td><td>34.0</td></tr>
<tr><td>5</td><td>Kentucky</td><td>35.5</td><td>17</td><td>Maryland</td><td>33.9</td></tr>
<tr><td>40</td><td>Louisiana</td><td>30.8</td><td>17</td><td>Ohio</td><td>33.9</td></tr>
<tr><td>20</td><td>Maine</td><td>33.6</td><td>19</td><td>New Jersey</td><td>33.8</td></tr>
<tr><td>17</td><td>Maryland</td><td>33.9</td><td>20</td><td>Illinois</td><td>33.6</td></tr>
<tr><td>33</td><td>Massachusetts</td><td>32.4</td><td>20</td><td>Maine</td><td>33.6</td></tr>
<tr><td>1</td><td>Michigan</td><td>38.2</td><td>20</td><td>Missouri</td><td>33.6</td></tr>
<tr><td>40</td><td>Minnesota</td><td>30.8</td><td>23</td><td>New Hampshire</td><td>33.4</td></tr>
<tr><td>27</td><td>Mississippi</td><td>33.1</td><td>23</td><td>South Carolina</td><td>33.4</td></tr>
<tr><td>20</td><td>Missouri</td><td>33.6</td><td>25</td><td>Washington</td><td>33.3</td></tr>
<tr><td>45</td><td>Montana</td><td>29.8</td><td>26</td><td>Georgia</td><td>33.2</td></tr>
<tr><td>43</td><td>Nebraska</td><td>30.5</td><td>27</td><td>Mississippi</td><td>33.1</td></tr>
<tr><td>3</td><td>Nevada</td><td>36.8</td><td>27</td><td>Rhode Island</td><td>33.1</td></tr>
<tr><td>23</td><td>New Hampshire</td><td>33.4</td><td>29</td><td>Virginia</td><td>32.9</td></tr>
<tr><td>19</td><td>New Jersey</td><td>33.8</td><td>30</td><td>Wisconsin</td><td>32.8</td></tr>
<tr><td>49</td><td>New Mexico</td><td>27.2</td><td>31</td><td>California</td><td>32.7</td></tr>
<tr><td>9</td><td>New York</td><td>34.9</td><td>32</td><td>North Dakota</td><td>32.6</td></tr>
<tr><td>16</td><td>North Carolina</td><td>34.0</td><td>33</td><td>Massachusetts</td><td>32.4</td></tr>
<tr><td>32</td><td>North Dakota</td><td>32.6</td><td>34</td><td>Oklahoma</td><td>32.0</td></tr>
<tr><td>17</td><td>Ohio</td><td>33.9</td><td>35</td><td>Colorado</td><td>31.9</td></tr>
<tr><td>34</td><td>Oklahoma</td><td>32.0</td><td>36</td><td>Iowa</td><td>31.7</td></tr>
<tr><td>15</td><td>Oregon</td><td>34.1</td><td>37</td><td>South Dakota</td><td>31.2</td></tr>
<tr><td>6</td><td>Pennsylvania</td><td>35.2</td><td>38</td><td>Idaho</td><td>31.1</td></tr>
<tr><td>27</td><td>Rhode Island</td><td>33.1</td><td>39</td><td>Vermont</td><td>30.9</td></tr>
<tr><td>23</td><td>South Carolina</td><td>33.4</td><td>40</td><td>Connecticut</td><td>30.8</td></tr>
<tr><td>37</td><td>South Dakota</td><td>31.2</td><td>40</td><td>Louisiana</td><td>30.8</td></tr>
<tr><td>44</td><td>Tennessee</td><td>30.1</td><td>40</td><td>Minnesota</td><td>30.8</td></tr>
<tr><td>14</td><td>Texas</td><td>34.3</td><td>43</td><td>Nebraska</td><td>30.5</td></tr>
<tr><td>47</td><td>Utah</td><td>27.8</td><td>44</td><td>Tennessee</td><td>30.1</td></tr>
<tr><td>39</td><td>Vermont</td><td>30.9</td><td>45</td><td>Montana</td><td>29.8</td></tr>
<tr><td>29</td><td>Virginia</td><td>32.9</td><td>46</td><td>Kansas</td><td>29.4</td></tr>
<tr><td>25</td><td>Washington</td><td>33.3</td><td>47</td><td>Utah</td><td>27.8</td></tr>
<tr><td>2</td><td>West Virginia</td><td>38.1</td><td>48</td><td>Alaska</td><td>27.6</td></tr>
<tr><td>30</td><td>Wisconsin</td><td>32.8</td><td>49</td><td>New Mexico</td><td>27.2</td></tr>
<tr><td>9</td><td>Wyoming</td><td>34.9</td><td>50</td><td>Hawaii</td><td>27.0</td></tr>
<tr><td></td><td></td><td></td><td></td><td>District of Columbia</td><td>29.2</td></tr>
</table>

*Source: U.S. Department of Health and Human Services, Centers for Disease Control and Prevention
"2003 Behavioral Risk Factor Surveillance Summary Prevalence Data" (http://apps.nccd.cdc.gov/brfss/)
Persons 18 and older who have had their cholesterol checked and have been told that they have high blood cholesterol.

Percent of Adults Who Have Visited a Dentist or Dental Clinic: 2004

National Median = 70.2%*

ALPHA ORDER

RANK	STATE	PERCENT
31	Alabama	69.2
27	Alaska	69.6
33	Arizona	68.5
48	Arkansas	60.8
25	California	70.4
18	Colorado	72.2
1	Connecticut	80.6
7	Delaware	77.1
35	Florida	68.2
37	Georgia	68.1
NA	Hawaii**	NA
40	Idaho	67.7
16	Illinois	72.6
41	Indiana	66.5
12	Iowa	75.0
13	Kansas	74.5
23	Kentucky	71.2
35	Louisiana	68.2
28	Maine	69.5
9	Maryland	75.8
3	Massachusetts	79.4
8	Michigan	76.8
2	Minnesota	79.7
49	Mississippi	59.4
44	Missouri	63.9
42	Montana	65.8
11	Nebraska	75.2
43	Nevada	64.4
5	New Hampshire	77.5
10	New Jersey	75.7
39	New Mexico	67.9
21	New York	71.7
30	North Carolina	69.4
28	North Dakota	69.5
19	Ohio	72.1
46	Oklahoma	61.3
33	Oregon	68.5
26	Pennsylvania	69.8
4	Rhode Island	78.5
32	South Carolina	68.6
20	South Dakota	72.0
22	Tennessee	71.5
47	Texas	61.2
17	Utah	72.3
14	Vermont	74.2
15	Virginia	73.5
24	Washington	71.0
45	West Virginia	62.5
5	Wisconsin	77.5
37	Wyoming	68.1

RANK ORDER

RANK	STATE	PERCENT
1	Connecticut	80.6
2	Minnesota	79.7
3	Massachusetts	79.4
4	Rhode Island	78.5
5	New Hampshire	77.5
5	Wisconsin	77.5
7	Delaware	77.1
8	Michigan	76.8
9	Maryland	75.8
10	New Jersey	75.7
11	Nebraska	75.2
12	Iowa	75.0
13	Kansas	74.5
14	Vermont	74.2
15	Virginia	73.5
16	Illinois	72.6
17	Utah	72.3
18	Colorado	72.2
19	Ohio	72.1
20	South Dakota	72.0
21	New York	71.7
22	Tennessee	71.5
23	Kentucky	71.2
24	Washington	71.0
25	California	70.4
26	Pennsylvania	69.8
27	Alaska	69.6
28	Maine	69.5
28	North Dakota	69.5
30	North Carolina	69.4
31	Alabama	69.2
32	South Carolina	68.6
33	Arizona	68.5
33	Oregon	68.5
35	Florida	68.2
35	Louisiana	68.2
37	Georgia	68.1
37	Wyoming	68.1
39	New Mexico	67.9
40	Idaho	67.7
41	Indiana	66.5
42	Montana	65.8
43	Nevada	64.4
44	Missouri	63.9
45	West Virginia	62.5
46	Oklahoma	61.3
47	Texas	61.2
48	Arkansas	60.8
49	Mississippi	59.4
NA	Hawaii**	NA
	District of Columbia	72.1

Source: U.S. Department of Health and Human Services, Centers for Disease Control and Prevention
   "2004 Behavioral Risk Factor Surveillance Summary Prevalence Data" (http://apps.nccd.cdc.gov/brfss/)
*Persons 18 and older who have visited a dentist within the past year for any reason.
**Not available.

Percent of Adults 65 Years Old and Older
Who Have Lost All Their Natural Teeth: 2004
National Median = 21.2%*

ALPHA ORDER

RANK	STATE	PERCENT
4	Alabama	31.9
20	Alaska	23.0
45	Arizona	14.9
15	Arkansas	24.6
47	California	13.7
35	Colorado	18.0
49	Connecticut	12.4
26	Delaware	21.1
32	Florida	18.7
9	Georgia	28.2
NA	Hawaii**	NA
21	Idaho	22.4
32	Illinois	18.7
11	Indiana	27.3
18	Iowa	23.2
10	Kansas	27.8
2	Kentucky	38.1
5	Louisiana	31.3
16	Maine	24.2
41	Maryland	16.6
43	Massachusetts	16.4
37	Michigan	17.1
46	Minnesota	14.3
7	Mississippi	29.5
13	Missouri	25.2
29	Montana	19.6
19	Nebraska	23.1
42	Nevada	16.5
27	New Hampshire	21.0
38	New Jersey	16.9
22	New Mexico	21.8
39	New York	16.8
8	North Carolina	28.3
14	North Dakota	24.9
28	Ohio	20.4
6	Oklahoma	31.1
36	Oregon	17.7
17	Pennsylvania	23.7
34	Rhode Island	18.4
22	South Carolina	21.8
12	South Dakota	26.1
3	Tennessee	32.2
39	Texas	16.8
48	Utah	13.5
25	Vermont	21.2
31	Virginia	19.3
44	Washington	16.1
1	West Virginia	42.8
29	Wisconsin	19.6
22	Wyoming	21.8

RANK ORDER

RANK	STATE	PERCENT
1	West Virginia	42.8
2	Kentucky	38.1
3	Tennessee	32.2
4	Alabama	31.9
5	Louisiana	31.3
6	Oklahoma	31.1
7	Mississippi	29.5
8	North Carolina	28.3
9	Georgia	28.2
10	Kansas	27.8
11	Indiana	27.3
12	South Dakota	26.1
13	Missouri	25.2
14	North Dakota	24.9
15	Arkansas	24.6
16	Maine	24.2
17	Pennsylvania	23.7
18	Iowa	23.2
19	Nebraska	23.1
20	Alaska	23.0
21	Idaho	22.4
22	New Mexico	21.8
22	South Carolina	21.8
22	Wyoming	21.8
25	Vermont	21.2
26	Delaware	21.1
27	New Hampshire	21.0
28	Ohio	20.4
29	Montana	19.6
29	Wisconsin	19.6
31	Virginia	19.3
32	Florida	18.7
32	Illinois	18.7
34	Rhode Island	18.4
35	Colorado	18.0
36	Oregon	17.7
37	Michigan	17.1
38	New Jersey	16.9
39	New York	16.8
39	Texas	16.8
41	Maryland	16.6
42	Nevada	16.5
43	Massachusetts	16.4
44	Washington	16.1
45	Arizona	14.9
46	Minnesota	14.3
47	California	13.7
48	Utah	13.5
49	Connecticut	12.4
NA	Hawaii**	NA
	District of Columbia	19.3

Source: U.S. Department of Health and Human Services, Centers for Disease Control and Prevention
"2004 Behavioral Risk Factor Surveillance Summary Prevalence Data" (http://apps.nccd.cdc.gov/brfss/)
*Those who have had all their natural teeth extracted.
**Not available.

Percent of Adults Who Average Five or More Servings of Fruits and Vegetables Each Day: 2003
National Median = 22.6%*

ALPHA ORDER

RANK	STATE	PERCENT
24	Alabama	22.6
24	Alaska	22.6
22	Arizona	22.9
36	Arkansas	20.8
9	California	26.9
14	Colorado	24.2
2	Connecticut	29.8
31	Delaware	22.0
17	Florida	23.6
21	Georgia	23.0
6	Hawaii	27.6
37	Idaho	20.4
19	Illinois	23.1
31	Indiana	22.0
48	Iowa	17.1
43	Kansas	18.8
45	Kentucky	18.2
49	Louisiana	16.4
8	Maine	27.0
4	Maryland	28.9
3	Massachusetts	29.0
40	Michigan	20.1
14	Minnesota	24.2
46	Mississippi	17.9
39	Missouri	20.2
33	Montana	21.9
47	Nebraska	17.8
37	Nevada	20.4
5	New Hampshire	28.5
10	New Jersey	26.6
27	New Mexico	22.4
11	New York	25.8
19	North Carolina	23.1
34	North Dakota	21.5
23	Ohio	22.7
50	Oklahoma	15.4
16	Oregon	24.1
13	Pennsylvania	24.7
7	Rhode Island	27.1
28	South Carolina	22.3
42	South Dakota	19.0
29	Tennessee	22.2
26	Texas	22.5
41	Utah	19.5
1	Vermont	32.5
11	Virginia	25.8
18	Washington	23.3
44	West Virginia	18.7
34	Wisconsin	21.5
30	Wyoming	22.1

RANK ORDER

RANK	STATE	PERCENT
1	Vermont	32.5
2	Connecticut	29.8
3	Massachusetts	29.0
4	Maryland	28.9
5	New Hampshire	28.5
6	Hawaii	27.6
7	Rhode Island	27.1
8	Maine	27.0
9	California	26.9
10	New Jersey	26.6
11	New York	25.8
11	Virginia	25.8
13	Pennsylvania	24.7
14	Colorado	24.2
14	Minnesota	24.2
16	Oregon	24.1
17	Florida	23.6
18	Washington	23.3
19	Illinois	23.1
19	North Carolina	23.1
21	Georgia	23.0
22	Arizona	22.9
23	Ohio	22.7
24	Alabama	22.6
24	Alaska	22.6
26	Texas	22.5
27	New Mexico	22.4
28	South Carolina	22.3
29	Tennessee	22.2
30	Wyoming	22.1
31	Delaware	22.0
31	Indiana	22.0
33	Montana	21.9
34	North Dakota	21.5
34	Wisconsin	21.5
36	Arkansas	20.8
37	Idaho	20.4
37	Nevada	20.4
39	Missouri	20.2
40	Michigan	20.1
41	Utah	19.5
42	South Dakota	19.0
43	Kansas	18.8
44	West Virginia	18.7
45	Kentucky	18.2
46	Mississippi	17.9
47	Nebraska	17.8
48	Iowa	17.1
49	Louisiana	16.4
50	Oklahoma	15.4

	District of Columbia	29.6

Source: U.S. Department of Health and Human Services, Centers for Disease Control and Prevention
  "2003 Behavioral Risk Factor Surveillance Summary Prevalence Data" (http://apps.nccd.cdc.gov/brfss/)
*Persons 18 and older.

Percent of Adults Rating Their Health as Fair or Poor in 2004

National Median = 15.1% of Adults*

RANK	STATE	PERCENT	RANK	STATE	PERCENT
5	Alabama	20.1	1	West Virginia	23.5
38	Alaska	12.2	2	Mississippi	22.9
25	Arizona	14.8	3	Kentucky	21.9
6	Arkansas	19.8	4	Texas	20.4
14	California	17.5	5	Alabama	20.1
46	Colorado	11.6	6	Arkansas	19.8
47	Connecticut	11.4	7	Oklahoma	19.6
29	Delaware	13.6	8	Tennessee	19.4
17	Florida	16.5	9	Louisiana	18.8
24	Georgia	15.3	10	New Mexico	18.6
NA	Hawaii**	NA	11	Nevada	18.1
35	Idaho	12.5	12	North Carolina	18.0
22	Illinois	15.5	13	South Carolina	17.7
16	Indiana	17.4	14	California	17.5
37	Iowa	12.4	14	New York	17.5
30	Kansas	13.0	16	Indiana	17.4
3	Kentucky	21.9	17	Florida	16.5
9	Louisiana	18.8	18	Pennsylvania	15.9
19	Maine	15.8	19	Maine	15.8
45	Maryland	11.8	20	Missouri	15.7
42	Massachusetts	12.0	20	New Jersey	15.7
28	Michigan	14.1	22	Illinois	15.5
49	Minnesota	10.0	22	Oregon	15.5
2	Mississippi	22.9	24	Georgia	15.3
20	Missouri	15.7	25	Arizona	14.8
32	Montana	12.8	25	Rhode Island	14.8
38	Nebraska	12.2	27	Ohio	14.5
11	Nevada	18.1	28	Michigan	14.1
48	New Hampshire	11.0	29	Delaware	13.6
20	New Jersey	15.7	30	Kansas	13.0
10	New Mexico	18.6	30	Washington	13.0
14	New York	17.5	32	Montana	12.8
12	North Carolina	18.0	33	South Dakota	12.6
40	North Dakota	12.1	33	Virginia	12.6
27	Ohio	14.5	35	Idaho	12.5
7	Oklahoma	19.6	35	Utah	12.5
22	Oregon	15.5	37	Iowa	12.4
18	Pennsylvania	15.9	38	Alaska	12.2
25	Rhode Island	14.8	38	Nebraska	12.2
13	South Carolina	17.7	40	North Dakota	12.1
33	South Dakota	12.6	40	Wyoming	12.1
8	Tennessee	19.4	42	Massachusetts	12.0
4	Texas	20.4	42	Vermont	12.0
35	Utah	12.5	44	Wisconsin	11.9
42	Vermont	12.0	45	Maryland	11.8
33	Virginia	12.6	46	Colorado	11.6
30	Washington	13.0	47	Connecticut	11.4
1	West Virginia	23.5	48	New Hampshire	11.0
44	Wisconsin	11.9	49	Minnesota	10.0
40	Wyoming	12.1	NA	Hawaii**	NA

| | | | | District of Columbia | 11.1 |

Source: U.S. Department of Health and Human Services, Centers for Disease Control and Prevention
   "2004 Behavioral Risk Factor Surveillance Summary Prevalence Data" (http://apps.nccd.cdc.gov/brfss/)
*Persons 18 and older.
**Not available.

Safety Belt Usage Rate in 2005

National Rate = 82.0% Use Safety Belts*

<table>
<tr><td colspan="3">ALPHA ORDER</td><td colspan="3">RANK ORDER</td></tr>
<tr><th>RANK</th><th>STATE</th><th>PERCENT</th><th>RANK</th><th>STATE</th><th>PERCENT</th></tr>
<tr><td>23</td><td>Alabama</td><td>81.8</td><td>1</td><td>Hawaii</td><td>95.3</td></tr>
<tr><td>32</td><td>Alaska</td><td>78.4</td><td>2</td><td>Washington</td><td>95.2</td></tr>
<tr><td>4</td><td>Arizona</td><td>94.2</td><td>3</td><td>Nevada</td><td>94.8</td></tr>
<tr><td>45</td><td>Arkansas</td><td>68.3</td><td>4</td><td>Arizona</td><td>94.2</td></tr>
<tr><td>7</td><td>California</td><td>92.5</td><td>5</td><td>Oregon</td><td>93.3</td></tr>
<tr><td>29</td><td>Colorado</td><td>79.2</td><td>6</td><td>Michigan</td><td>92.9</td></tr>
<tr><td>24</td><td>Connecticut</td><td>81.6</td><td>7</td><td>California</td><td>92.5</td></tr>
<tr><td>19</td><td>Delaware</td><td>83.8</td><td>8</td><td>Maryland</td><td>91.1</td></tr>
<tr><td>40</td><td>Florida</td><td>73.9</td><td>9</td><td>Texas</td><td>89.9</td></tr>
<tr><td>24</td><td>Georgia</td><td>81.6</td><td>10</td><td>New Mexico</td><td>89.5</td></tr>
<tr><td>1</td><td>Hawaii</td><td>95.3</td><td>11</td><td>Utah</td><td>86.9</td></tr>
<tr><td>36</td><td>Idaho</td><td>76.0</td><td>12</td><td>North Carolina</td><td>86.7</td></tr>
<tr><td>13</td><td>Illinois</td><td>86.0</td><td>13</td><td>Illinois</td><td>86.0</td></tr>
<tr><td>26</td><td>Indiana</td><td>81.2</td><td>13</td><td>New Jersey</td><td>86.0</td></tr>
<tr><td>15</td><td>Iowa</td><td>85.9</td><td>15</td><td>Iowa</td><td>85.9</td></tr>
<tr><td>43</td><td>Kansas</td><td>69.0</td><td>16</td><td>New York</td><td>85.0</td></tr>
<tr><td>46</td><td>Kentucky</td><td>66.7</td><td>17</td><td>West Virginia</td><td>84.9</td></tr>
<tr><td>33</td><td>Louisiana</td><td>77.7</td><td>18</td><td>Vermont</td><td>84.7</td></tr>
<tr><td>37</td><td>Maine</td><td>75.8</td><td>19</td><td>Delaware</td><td>83.8</td></tr>
<tr><td>8</td><td>Maryland</td><td>91.1</td><td>20</td><td>Pennsylvania</td><td>83.3</td></tr>
<tr><td>47</td><td>Massachusetts</td><td>64.8</td><td>21</td><td>Oklahoma</td><td>83.1</td></tr>
<tr><td>6</td><td>Michigan</td><td>92.9</td><td>22</td><td>Minnesota</td><td>82.6</td></tr>
<tr><td>22</td><td>Minnesota</td><td>82.6</td><td>23</td><td>Alabama</td><td>81.8</td></tr>
<tr><td>48</td><td>Mississippi</td><td>60.8</td><td>24</td><td>Connecticut</td><td>81.6</td></tr>
<tr><td>34</td><td>Missouri</td><td>77.4</td><td>24</td><td>Georgia</td><td>81.6</td></tr>
<tr><td>28</td><td>Montana</td><td>80.0</td><td>26</td><td>Indiana</td><td>81.2</td></tr>
<tr><td>29</td><td>Nebraska</td><td>79.2</td><td>27</td><td>Virginia</td><td>80.4</td></tr>
<tr><td>3</td><td>Nevada</td><td>94.8</td><td>28</td><td>Montana</td><td>80.0</td></tr>
<tr><td>NA</td><td>New Hampshire**</td><td>NA</td><td>29</td><td>Colorado</td><td>79.2</td></tr>
<tr><td>13</td><td>New Jersey</td><td>86.0</td><td>29</td><td>Nebraska</td><td>79.2</td></tr>
<tr><td>10</td><td>New Mexico</td><td>89.5</td><td>31</td><td>Ohio</td><td>78.7</td></tr>
<tr><td>16</td><td>New York</td><td>85.0</td><td>32</td><td>Alaska</td><td>78.4</td></tr>
<tr><td>12</td><td>North Carolina</td><td>86.7</td><td>33</td><td>Louisiana</td><td>77.7</td></tr>
<tr><td>35</td><td>North Dakota</td><td>76.3</td><td>34</td><td>Missouri</td><td>77.4</td></tr>
<tr><td>31</td><td>Ohio</td><td>78.7</td><td>35</td><td>North Dakota</td><td>76.3</td></tr>
<tr><td>21</td><td>Oklahoma</td><td>83.1</td><td>36</td><td>Idaho</td><td>76.0</td></tr>
<tr><td>5</td><td>Oregon</td><td>93.3</td><td>37</td><td>Maine</td><td>75.8</td></tr>
<tr><td>20</td><td>Pennsylvania</td><td>83.3</td><td>38</td><td>Rhode Island</td><td>74.7</td></tr>
<tr><td>38</td><td>Rhode Island</td><td>74.7</td><td>39</td><td>Tennessee</td><td>74.4</td></tr>
<tr><td>42</td><td>South Carolina</td><td>69.7</td><td>40</td><td>Florida</td><td>73.9</td></tr>
<tr><td>44</td><td>South Dakota</td><td>68.8</td><td>41</td><td>Wisconsin</td><td>73.3</td></tr>
<tr><td>39</td><td>Tennessee</td><td>74.4</td><td>42</td><td>South Carolina</td><td>69.7</td></tr>
<tr><td>9</td><td>Texas</td><td>89.9</td><td>43</td><td>Kansas</td><td>69.0</td></tr>
<tr><td>11</td><td>Utah</td><td>86.9</td><td>44</td><td>South Dakota</td><td>68.8</td></tr>
<tr><td>18</td><td>Vermont</td><td>84.7</td><td>45</td><td>Arkansas</td><td>68.3</td></tr>
<tr><td>27</td><td>Virginia</td><td>80.4</td><td>46</td><td>Kentucky</td><td>66.7</td></tr>
<tr><td>2</td><td>Washington</td><td>95.2</td><td>47</td><td>Massachusetts</td><td>64.8</td></tr>
<tr><td>17</td><td>West Virginia</td><td>84.9</td><td>48</td><td>Mississippi</td><td>60.8</td></tr>
<tr><td>41</td><td>Wisconsin</td><td>73.3</td><td>NA</td><td>New Hampshire**</td><td>NA</td></tr>
<tr><td>NA</td><td>Wyoming**</td><td>NA</td><td>NA</td><td>Wyoming**</td><td>NA</td></tr>
</table>

District of Columbia 88.8

Source: U.S. Department of Transportation, National Highway Traffic Safety Administration
    "Safety Belt Use in 2005" (http://www-nrd.nhtsa.dot.gov/pdf/nrd-30/NCSA/RNotes/2005/809932.pdf)
*National estimate is from the National Occupant Protection Use Survey (NOPUS) using a different methodology.
**Not available.

VIII. APPENDIX

Population Charts

Population in 2005

National Total = 296,410,404*

ALPHA ORDER

RANK	STATE	POPULATION	% of USA
23	Alabama	4,557,808	1.5%
47	Alaska	663,661	0.2%
17	Arizona	5,939,292	2.0%
32	Arkansas	2,779,154	0.9%
1	California	36,132,147	12.2%
22	Colorado	4,665,177	1.6%
29	Connecticut	3,510,297	1.2%
45	Delaware	843,524	0.3%
4	Florida	17,789,864	6.0%
9	Georgia	9,072,576	3.1%
42	Hawaii	1,275,194	0.4%
39	Idaho	1,429,096	0.5%
5	Illinois	12,763,371	4.3%
15	Indiana	6,271,973	2.1%
30	Iowa	2,966,334	1.0%
33	Kansas	2,744,687	0.9%
26	Kentucky	4,173,405	1.4%
24	Louisiana	4,523,628	1.5%
40	Maine	1,321,505	0.4%
19	Maryland	5,600,388	1.9%
13	Massachusetts	6,398,743	2.2%
8	Michigan	10,120,860	3.4%
21	Minnesota	5,132,799	1.7%
31	Mississippi	2,921,088	1.0%
18	Missouri	5,800,310	2.0%
44	Montana	935,670	0.3%
38	Nebraska	1,758,787	0.6%
35	Nevada	2,414,807	0.8%
41	New Hampshire	1,309,940	0.4%
10	New Jersey	8,717,925	2.9%
36	New Mexico	1,928,384	0.7%
3	New York	19,254,630	6.5%
11	North Carolina	8,683,242	2.9%
48	North Dakota	636,677	0.2%
7	Ohio	11,464,042	3.9%
28	Oklahoma	3,547,884	1.2%
27	Oregon	3,641,056	1.2%
6	Pennsylvania	12,429,616	4.2%
43	Rhode Island	1,076,189	0.4%
25	South Carolina	4,255,083	1.4%
46	South Dakota	775,933	0.3%
16	Tennessee	5,962,959	2.0%
2	Texas	22,859,968	7.7%
34	Utah	2,469,585	0.8%
49	Vermont	623,050	0.2%
12	Virginia	7,567,465	2.6%
14	Washington	6,287,759	2.1%
37	West Virginia	1,816,856	0.6%
20	Wisconsin	5,536,201	1.9%
50	Wyoming	509,294	0.2%

RANK ORDER

RANK	STATE	POPULATION	% of USA
1	California	36,132,147	12.2%
2	Texas	22,859,968	7.7%
3	New York	19,254,630	6.5%
4	Florida	17,789,864	6.0%
5	Illinois	12,763,371	4.3%
6	Pennsylvania	12,429,616	4.2%
7	Ohio	11,464,042	3.9%
8	Michigan	10,120,860	3.4%
9	Georgia	9,072,576	3.1%
10	New Jersey	8,717,925	2.9%
11	North Carolina	8,683,242	2.9%
12	Virginia	7,567,465	2.6%
13	Massachusetts	6,398,743	2.2%
14	Washington	6,287,759	2.1%
15	Indiana	6,271,973	2.1%
16	Tennessee	5,962,959	2.0%
17	Arizona	5,939,292	2.0%
18	Missouri	5,800,310	2.0%
19	Maryland	5,600,388	1.9%
20	Wisconsin	5,536,201	1.9%
21	Minnesota	5,132,799	1.7%
22	Colorado	4,665,177	1.6%
23	Alabama	4,557,808	1.5%
24	Louisiana	4,523,628	1.5%
25	South Carolina	4,255,083	1.4%
26	Kentucky	4,173,405	1.4%
27	Oregon	3,641,056	1.2%
28	Oklahoma	3,547,884	1.2%
29	Connecticut	3,510,297	1.2%
30	Iowa	2,966,334	1.0%
31	Mississippi	2,921,088	1.0%
32	Arkansas	2,779,154	0.9%
33	Kansas	2,744,687	0.9%
34	Utah	2,469,585	0.8%
35	Nevada	2,414,807	0.8%
36	New Mexico	1,928,384	0.7%
37	West Virginia	1,816,856	0.6%
38	Nebraska	1,758,787	0.6%
39	Idaho	1,429,096	0.5%
40	Maine	1,321,505	0.4%
41	New Hampshire	1,309,940	0.4%
42	Hawaii	1,275,194	0.4%
43	Rhode Island	1,076,189	0.4%
44	Montana	935,670	0.3%
45	Delaware	843,524	0.3%
46	South Dakota	775,933	0.3%
47	Alaska	663,661	0.2%
48	North Dakota	636,677	0.2%
49	Vermont	623,050	0.2%
50	Wyoming	509,294	0.2%
	District of Columbia	550,521	0.2%

Source: U.S. Bureau of the Census
   "Population Estimates" (December 22, 2005, http://www.census.gov/popest/estimates.php)
*Resident population.

Population in 2004

National Total = 293,656,842*

ALPHA ORDER

RANK	STATE	POPULATION	% of USA
23	Alabama	4,525,375	1.5%
47	Alaska	657,755	0.2%
18	Arizona	5,739,879	2.0%
32	Arkansas	2,750,000	0.9%
1	California	35,842,038	12.2%
22	Colorado	4,601,821	1.6%
29	Connecticut	3,498,966	1.2%
45	Delaware	830,069	0.3%
4	Florida	17,385,430	5.9%
9	Georgia	8,918,129	3.0%
42	Hawaii	1,262,124	0.4%
39	Idaho	1,395,140	0.5%
5	Illinois	12,712,016	4.3%
14	Indiana	6,226,537	2.1%
30	Iowa	2,952,904	1.0%
33	Kansas	2,733,697	0.9%
26	Kentucky	4,141,835	1.4%
24	Louisiana	4,506,685	1.5%
40	Maine	1,314,985	0.4%
19	Maryland	5,561,332	1.9%
13	Massachusetts	6,407,382	2.2%
8	Michigan	10,104,206	3.4%
21	Minnesota	5,096,546	1.7%
31	Mississippi	2,900,768	1.0%
17	Missouri	5,759,532	2.0%
44	Montana	926,920	0.3%
38	Nebraska	1,747,704	0.6%
35	Nevada	2,332,898	0.8%
41	New Hampshire	1,299,169	0.4%
10	New Jersey	8,685,166	3.0%
36	New Mexico	1,903,006	0.6%
3	New York	19,280,727	6.6%
11	North Carolina	8,540,468	2.9%
48	North Dakota	636,308	0.2%
7	Ohio	11,450,143	3.9%
28	Oklahoma	3,523,546	1.2%
27	Oregon	3,591,363	1.2%
6	Pennsylvania	12,394,471	4.2%
43	Rhode Island	1,079,916	0.4%
25	South Carolina	4,197,892	1.4%
46	South Dakota	770,621	0.3%
16	Tennessee	5,893,298	2.0%
2	Texas	22,471,549	7.7%
34	Utah	2,420,708	0.8%
49	Vermont	621,233	0.2%
12	Virginia	7,481,332	2.5%
15	Washington	6,207,046	2.1%
37	West Virginia	1,812,548	0.6%
20	Wisconsin	5,503,533	1.9%
50	Wyoming	505,887	0.2%

RANK ORDER

RANK	STATE	POPULATION	% of USA
1	California	35,842,038	12.2%
2	Texas	22,471,549	7.7%
3	New York	19,280,727	6.6%
4	Florida	17,385,430	5.9%
5	Illinois	12,712,016	4.3%
6	Pennsylvania	12,394,471	4.2%
7	Ohio	11,450,143	3.9%
8	Michigan	10,104,206	3.4%
9	Georgia	8,918,129	3.0%
10	New Jersey	8,685,166	3.0%
11	North Carolina	8,540,468	2.9%
12	Virginia	7,481,332	2.5%
13	Massachusetts	6,407,382	2.2%
14	Indiana	6,226,537	2.1%
15	Washington	6,207,046	2.1%
16	Tennessee	5,893,298	2.0%
17	Missouri	5,759,532	2.0%
18	Arizona	5,739,879	2.0%
19	Maryland	5,561,332	1.9%
20	Wisconsin	5,503,533	1.9%
21	Minnesota	5,096,546	1.7%
22	Colorado	4,601,821	1.6%
23	Alabama	4,525,375	1.5%
24	Louisiana	4,506,685	1.5%
25	South Carolina	4,197,892	1.4%
26	Kentucky	4,141,835	1.4%
27	Oregon	3,591,363	1.2%
28	Oklahoma	3,523,546	1.2%
29	Connecticut	3,498,966	1.2%
30	Iowa	2,952,904	1.0%
31	Mississippi	2,900,768	1.0%
32	Arkansas	2,750,000	0.9%
33	Kansas	2,733,697	0.9%
34	Utah	2,420,708	0.8%
35	Nevada	2,332,898	0.8%
36	New Mexico	1,903,006	0.6%
37	West Virginia	1,812,548	0.6%
38	Nebraska	1,747,704	0.6%
39	Idaho	1,395,140	0.5%
40	Maine	1,314,985	0.4%
41	New Hampshire	1,299,169	0.4%
42	Hawaii	1,262,124	0.4%
43	Rhode Island	1,079,916	0.4%
44	Montana	926,920	0.3%
45	Delaware	830,069	0.3%
46	South Dakota	770,621	0.3%
47	Alaska	657,755	0.2%
48	North Dakota	636,308	0.2%
49	Vermont	621,233	0.2%
50	Wyoming	505,887	0.2%
	District of Columbia	554,239	0.2%

Source: U.S. Bureau of the Census
"Population Estimates" (December 22, 2005, http://www.census.gov/popest/estimates.php)
*Resident population. Revised estimates.

Male Population in 2004

National Total = 144,537,408 Males

ALPHA ORDER					RANK ORDER			
RANK	STATE	MALES	% of USA		RANK	STATE	MALES	% of USA
23	Alabama	2,196,208	1.5%		1	California	17,913,717	12.4%
47	Alaska	338,910	0.2%		2	Texas	11,201,268	7.7%
17	Arizona	2,873,663	2.0%		3	New York	9,304,581	6.4%
33	Arkansas	1,348,719	0.9%		4	Florida	8,524,398	5.9%
1	California	17,913,717	12.4%		5	Illinois	6,243,216	4.3%
22	Colorado	2,321,504	1.6%		6	Pennsylvania	6,013,662	4.2%
29	Connecticut	1,700,186	1.2%		7	Ohio	5,580,635	3.9%
45	Delaware	404,676	0.3%		8	Michigan	4,968,663	3.4%
4	Florida	8,524,398	5.9%		9	Georgia	4,365,423	3.0%
9	Georgia	4,365,423	3.0%		10	New Jersey	4,235,853	2.9%
42	Hawaii	630,025	0.4%		11	North Carolina	4,198,851	2.9%
39	Idaho	698,624	0.5%		12	Virginia	3,671,433	2.5%
5	Illinois	6,243,216	4.3%		13	Massachusetts	3,106,345	2.1%
15	Indiana	3,068,975	2.1%		14	Washington	3,094,471	2.1%
30	Iowa	1,454,107	1.0%		15	Indiana	3,068,975	2.1%
32	Kansas	1,358,381	0.9%		16	Tennessee	2,886,284	2.0%
26	Kentucky	2,033,894	1.4%		17	Arizona	2,873,663	2.0%
24	Louisiana	2,193,983	1.5%		18	Missouri	2,810,852	1.9%
40	Maine	643,143	0.4%		19	Wisconsin	2,726,992	1.9%
20	Maryland	2,690,901	1.9%		20	Maryland	2,690,901	1.9%
13	Massachusetts	3,106,345	2.1%		21	Minnesota	2,531,918	1.8%
8	Michigan	4,968,663	3.4%		22	Colorado	2,321,504	1.6%
21	Minnesota	2,531,918	1.8%		23	Alabama	2,196,208	1.5%
31	Mississippi	1,408,733	1.0%		24	Louisiana	2,193,983	1.5%
18	Missouri	2,810,852	1.9%		25	South Carolina	2,045,177	1.4%
44	Montana	462,265	0.3%		26	Kentucky	2,033,894	1.4%
38	Nebraska	863,628	0.6%		27	Oregon	1,786,769	1.2%
35	Nevada	1,188,803	0.8%		28	Oklahoma	1,740,265	1.2%
41	New Hampshire	640,940	0.4%		29	Connecticut	1,700,186	1.2%
10	New Jersey	4,235,853	2.9%		30	Iowa	1,454,107	1.0%
36	New Mexico	936,067	0.6%		31	Mississippi	1,408,733	1.0%
3	New York	9,304,581	6.4%		32	Kansas	1,358,381	0.9%
11	North Carolina	4,198,851	2.9%		33	Arkansas	1,348,719	0.9%
48	North Dakota	316,631	0.2%		34	Utah	1,199,315	0.8%
7	Ohio	5,580,635	3.9%		35	Nevada	1,188,803	0.8%
28	Oklahoma	1,740,265	1.2%		36	New Mexico	936,067	0.6%
27	Oregon	1,786,769	1.2%		37	West Virginia	887,302	0.6%
6	Pennsylvania	6,013,662	4.2%		38	Nebraska	863,628	0.6%
43	Rhode Island	521,215	0.4%		39	Idaho	698,624	0.5%
25	South Carolina	2,045,177	1.4%		40	Maine	643,143	0.4%
46	South Dakota	383,249	0.3%		41	New Hampshire	640,940	0.4%
16	Tennessee	2,886,284	2.0%		42	Hawaii	630,025	0.4%
2	Texas	11,201,268	7.7%		43	Rhode Island	521,215	0.4%
34	Utah	1,199,315	0.8%		44	Montana	462,265	0.3%
49	Vermont	305,802	0.2%		45	Delaware	404,676	0.3%
12	Virginia	3,671,433	2.5%		46	South Dakota	383,249	0.3%
14	Washington	3,094,471	2.1%		47	Alaska	338,910	0.2%
37	West Virginia	887,302	0.6%		48	North Dakota	316,631	0.2%
19	Wisconsin	2,726,992	1.9%		49	Vermont	305,802	0.2%
50	Wyoming	255,056	0.2%		50	Wyoming	255,056	0.2%
						District of Columbia	261,730	0.2%

Source: Morgan Quitno Press using data from U.S. Bureau of the Census
"SC-EST2004-AGESEX_RES - State Characteristic Estimates"
(http://www.census.gov/popest/datasets.html)

Female Population in 2004

National Total = 149,117,996 Females

ALPHA ORDER

RANK	STATE	FEMALES	% of USA
22	Alabama	2,333,974	1.6%
48	Alaska	316,525	0.2%
18	Arizona	2,870,171	1.9%
32	Arkansas	1,403,910	0.9%
1	California	17,980,082	12.1%
24	Colorado	2,279,899	1.5%
28	Connecticut	1,803,418	1.2%
45	Delaware	425,688	0.3%
4	Florida	8,872,763	6.0%
9	Georgia	4,463,960	3.0%
42	Hawaii	632,815	0.4%
39	Idaho	694,638	0.5%
5	Illinois	6,470,418	4.3%
14	Indiana	3,168,594	2.1%
30	Iowa	1,500,344	1.0%
33	Kansas	1,377,121	0.9%
26	Kentucky	2,112,028	1.4%
23	Louisiana	2,321,787	1.6%
40	Maine	674,110	0.5%
19	Maryland	2,867,157	1.9%
13	Massachusetts	3,310,160	2.2%
8	Michigan	5,143,957	3.4%
21	Minnesota	2,569,040	1.7%
31	Mississippi	1,494,233	1.0%
17	Missouri	2,943,766	2.0%
44	Montana	464,600	0.3%
38	Nebraska	883,586	0.6%
35	Nevada	1,145,968	0.8%
41	New Hampshire	658,560	0.4%
10	New Jersey	4,463,026	3.0%
36	New Mexico	967,222	0.6%
3	New York	9,922,507	6.7%
11	North Carolina	4,342,370	2.9%
47	North Dakota	317,735	0.2%
7	Ohio	5,878,376	3.9%
29	Oklahoma	1,783,288	1.2%
27	Oregon	1,807,817	1.2%
6	Pennsylvania	6,392,630	4.3%
43	Rhode Island	559,417	0.4%
25	South Carolina	2,152,891	1.4%
46	South Dakota	387,634	0.3%
16	Tennessee	3,014,678	2.0%
2	Texas	11,288,754	7.6%
34	Utah	1,189,724	0.8%
49	Vermont	315,592	0.2%
12	Virginia	3,788,394	2.5%
15	Washington	3,109,317	2.1%
37	West Virginia	928,052	0.6%
20	Wisconsin	2,782,034	1.9%
50	Wyoming	251,473	0.2%

RANK ORDER

RANK	STATE	FEMALES	% of USA
1	California	17,980,082	12.1%
2	Texas	11,288,754	7.6%
3	New York	9,922,507	6.7%
4	Florida	8,872,763	6.0%
5	Illinois	6,470,418	4.3%
6	Pennsylvania	6,392,630	4.3%
7	Ohio	5,878,376	3.9%
8	Michigan	5,143,957	3.4%
9	Georgia	4,463,960	3.0%
10	New Jersey	4,463,026	3.0%
11	North Carolina	4,342,370	2.9%
12	Virginia	3,788,394	2.5%
13	Massachusetts	3,310,160	2.2%
14	Indiana	3,168,594	2.1%
15	Washington	3,109,317	2.1%
16	Tennessee	3,014,678	2.0%
17	Missouri	2,943,766	2.0%
18	Arizona	2,870,171	1.9%
19	Maryland	2,867,157	1.9%
20	Wisconsin	2,782,034	1.9%
21	Minnesota	2,569,040	1.7%
22	Alabama	2,333,974	1.6%
23	Louisiana	2,321,787	1.6%
24	Colorado	2,279,899	1.5%
25	South Carolina	2,152,891	1.4%
26	Kentucky	2,112,028	1.4%
27	Oregon	1,807,817	1.2%
28	Connecticut	1,803,418	1.2%
29	Oklahoma	1,783,288	1.2%
30	Iowa	1,500,344	1.0%
31	Mississippi	1,494,233	1.0%
32	Arkansas	1,403,910	0.9%
33	Kansas	1,377,121	0.9%
34	Utah	1,189,724	0.8%
35	Nevada	1,145,968	0.8%
36	New Mexico	967,222	0.6%
37	West Virginia	928,052	0.6%
38	Nebraska	883,586	0.6%
39	Idaho	694,638	0.5%
40	Maine	674,110	0.5%
41	New Hampshire	658,560	0.4%
42	Hawaii	632,815	0.4%
43	Rhode Island	559,417	0.4%
44	Montana	464,600	0.3%
45	Delaware	425,688	0.3%
46	South Dakota	387,634	0.3%
47	North Dakota	317,735	0.2%
48	Alaska	316,525	0.2%
49	Vermont	315,592	0.2%
50	Wyoming	251,473	0.2%
	District of Columbia	291,793	0.2%

Source: Morgan Quitno Press using data from U.S. Bureau of the Census
"SC-EST2004-AGESEX_RES - State Characteristic Estimates"
(http://www.census.gov/popest/datasets.html)

IX. SOURCES

American Academy of Physicians Assistants
950 North Washington Street
Alexandria, VA 22314-1552
703-836-2272
www.aapa.org

American Cancer Society, Inc.
1599 Clifton Road, NE.
Atlanta, GA   30329-4251
800-227-2345
www.cancer.org

American Dental Association
211 E. Chicago Ave.
Chicago, IL   60611-2678
312-440-2500
www.ada.org

American Hospital Association
One North Franklin
Chicago, IL   60606-3421
312-422-3000
www.aha.org

American Medical Association
515 North State Street
Chicago, IL   60610
800-621-8335
www.ama-assn.org

American Osteopathic Association
142 East Ontario Street
Chicago, IL   60611
800-621-1773
www.osteopathic.org

Bureau of Labor Statistics
2 Massachusetts Ave., NE
Washington, DC 20212-0001
202-691-5200
www.bls.gov/iif/

Census Bureau
4700 Silver Hill Road
Washington, DC   20233-0001
301-457-2800
www.census.gov

Centers for Disease Control and Prevention
1600 Clifton Road, NE.
Atlanta, GA   30333
800-311-3435
www.cdc.gov

Centers for Medicare and Medicaid Services
7500 Security Boulevard
Baltimore, MD   21244-1850
877-267-2323
www.cms.hhs.gov

Federation of Chiropractic Licensing Boards
5401 W 10th Street, Ste 101
Greeley, CO   80634-4400
970-356-3500
www.fclb.org

Health Resources and Services Admin
Division of Practitioner Data Banks
7519 Standish Place, Ste 300
Rockville MD   20857
800-767-6732
www.npdb-hipdb.com

HealthLeaders/InterStudy
210 12th Avenue South
Nashville TN   37203
888-293-9675
www.hmodata.com

Medical Expenditure Panel Survey
Agency for Healthcare Research and Quality
540 Gaither Road
Rockville MD   20850
301-427-1656
www.meps.ahrq.gov

National Association of State Budget Officers
444 N Capitol Street, NW
Washington DC   20001-1551
202-624-5382
www.nasbo.org

National Center for Health Statistics
U.S. Department of Health and Human Services
3311 Toledo Road
Hyattsville, MD   20782
866-441-NCHS
www.cdc.gov/nchs/

**National Institute on Alcohol Abuse
and Alcoholism**
National Institutes of Health
5635 Fishers Lane, MSC 9304
Bethesda, MD   20892-9304
301-443-9970
www.niaaa.nih.gov/

National Highway Traffic Safety Admin.
400 Seventh Street, SW
Washington, DC   20590
888-327-4236
www.nhtsa.dot.gov

National Sporting Goods Association
1601 Feehanville Drive, Ste 300
Mt. Prospect, IL   60056
847-296-6742
www.nsga.org

Smoking and Health Office
Centers for Disease Control and Prevention
4770 Buford Hwy, NE., Mail Stop K-50
Atlanta, GA   30341-3717
770-488-5705
www.cdc.gov/tobacco/

Substance Abuse and Mental Health Services Admin.
1 Choke Cherry Road, Room 8-1036
Rockville MD   20857
240-276-2130
www.samhsa.gov

X. INDEX

X. INDEX (continued)

X. INDEX (continued)

CHAPTER INDEX

HOW TO USE THIS INDEX

Place left thumb on the outer edge of this page. To locate the desired entry, fold back the remaining page edges and align the index edge mark with the appropriate page edge mark.

Other books by Morgan Quitno Press:

- *State Statistical Trends*
- *State Rankings*
- *Crime State Rankings*
- *City Crime Rankings*
- *Education State Rankings*

Call toll free: 1-800-457-0742 or
visit us at www.statestats.com